平 成 28 年

人 口 動 態 統 計

VITAL STATISTICS OF JAPAN
2016

上 巻
Volume 1

厚生労働省政策統括官（統計・情報政策担当）編
DIRECTOR-GENERAL FOR STATISTICS AND
INFORMATION POLICY,
MINISTRY OF HEALTH, LABOUR AND WELFARE

一般財団法人厚生労働統計協会
HEALTH, LABOUR AND WELFARE STATISTICS ASSOCIATION

編　集　内　容

　平成28年における「人口動態統計」は、上・中・下巻の3分冊にして編集した。

　上巻は、人口動態調査の概要及び解析を収録している。

　中巻は、出生・死亡（死因を除く。）・死産（死産原因を除く。）・婚姻及び離婚に関する統計表を収録している。

　下巻は、死因に関する統計表を収録している。

　用語、比率の解説…上巻第2章を参照されたい。

　死因分類について…上巻第2章及び下巻死因統計分類の分類体系並びに分類表を参照されたい。

　また、都道府県（21大都市再掲）に関する統計表で「外国」とあるのは、日本において発生した事件で、住所が外国のものを表している。

担　当
人口動態・保健社会統計室
ＴＥＬ　03（5253）1111
（死亡・死産）
年報第一係　内線　7490
（出生・婚姻・離婚）
年報第二係　内線　7491

ま　え　が　き

　この報告書は、平成28年の人口動態統計についてとりまとめたものです。

　人口動態統計は、出生、死亡、婚姻、離婚及び死産の５種類の「人口動態事象」について、その実態を明らかにするため、各種届書等から移記することによって調査されており、人口に関する基礎資料として活用されております。この人口動態調査は、「戸籍法」制定の翌年の明治32年から現在の近代的な人口動態統計制度として行われるようになりました。

　現在、人口動態統計の公表資料として主なものは「人口動態統計（月報）」と、この「人口動態統計（年報）」があります。

　「人口動態統計（年報）」は、昭和54年から、上巻・中巻・下巻の３分冊として編集し、上巻には、人口動態調査の概要及び結果の解析を、中巻には、出生、死亡（死因を除く。）、死産（死産原因を除く。）、婚姻及び離婚の統計表を、下巻には、主として死因に関する統計表をそれぞれ収録しております。

　この報告書を刊行するに当たり、調査にひとかたならぬ御協力をいただいた市区町村、保健所、都道府県の方々をはじめ、関係各位に厚く御礼を申し上げますとともに、この報告書が厚生労働行政施策はじめ広範な分野に活用されることを願っております。

　平成30年３月

厚生労働省政策統括官（統計・情報政策担当）

酒　光　一　章

平 成 28 年

人口動態統計　上巻
目　次

まえがき
Ⅰ　人口動態調査の概要
　第1章　調査の概要
　　1　調査の概要 ……………………………………………………………………… 46
　　2　調査票及び届書 ………………………………………………………………… 48
　　3　観察対象の範囲 ………………………………………………………………… 58
　第2章　調査結果の利用上の解説
　　1　平成7年調査からの主な改正点 ……………………………………………… 60
　　2　昭和22年以降の年次推移についての注意 …………………………………… 62
　　3　用語の解説 ……………………………………………………………………… 64
　　4　比率の解説 ……………………………………………………………………… 67
　　5　死因分類の解説 ………………………………………………………………… 70
Ⅱ　人口動態調査結果の概要
　　　平成28年の概況
　　　　出生 ………………………………………………………………………………… 76
　　　　死亡 ………………………………………………………………………………… 78
　　　　乳児死亡 …………………………………………………………………………… 81
　　　　自然増減 …………………………………………………………………………… 82
　　　　死産 ………………………………………………………………………………… 82
　　　　周産期死亡 ………………………………………………………………………… 83
　　　　婚姻 ………………………………………………………………………………… 84
　　　　離婚 ………………………………………………………………………………… 85
　第3章　総　覧
　　　表 3. 1　人口動態の年間発生件数・率・平均発生間隔－前年との比較－ ………… 87
　　　表 3. 2　年次別にみた人口動態総覧 …………………………………………………… 88
　　　表 3. 3　都道府県（21大都市再掲）別にみた人口動態総覧 ………………………… 96
　　　表 3. 4　世界各国における人口動態 …………………………………………………… 100
　第4章　出　生
　　〔出生の年次推移〕
　　　表 4. 1　年次別にみた出生数・率（人口千対）・出生性比及び合計特殊出生率 ……… 102
　　〔月別にみた出生〕
　　　表 4. 2　月別にみた年次別出生数及び率（人口千対） ……………………………… 104
　　〔地域別にみた出生〕
　　　表 4. 3　都道府県別にみた年次別出生数 …………………………………………… 106
　　　表 4. 4　都道府県別にみた年次別出生率（人口千対） ……………………………… 108
　　　表 4. 5　都道府県別にみた年次別合計特殊出生率 ………………………………… 110
　　〔母の年齢（5歳階級）別にみた出生〕
　　　表 4. 6　母の年齢別にみた年次別出生数・百分率及び出生率（女性人口千対） …… 112
　　〔出生の場所別にみた出生〕
　　　表 4. 7　市部－郡部・出生の場所別にみた年次別出生数 ………………………… 114
　　　表 4. 8　市部－郡部・出生の場所別にみた年次別出生数百分率 ………………… 115
　　　表 4. 9　都道府県（21大都市再掲）・出生の場所別にみた出生数 ………………… 116
　　　表 4.10　都道府県（21大都市再掲）・出生の場所別にみた出生数百分率 ………… 117

〔出産順位及び出生順位別にみた出生〕
表 4.11	出産順位別にみた年次別出生数及び百分率	118
表 4.12	出生順位別にみた年次別出生数及び百分率	119
表 4.13	都道府県（21大都市再掲）・出産順位別にみた出生数	120
表 4.14	都道府県（21大都市再掲）・出産順位別にみた出生数百分率	121
表 4.15	出生順位別にみた母の年齢別出生数及び百分率	122
表 4.16	出産順位別にみた母の年齢別出生数及び百分率	122
表 4.17	出生順位別にみた年次別母の年齢別出生数	124
表 4.18	出生順位別にみた年次別母の年齢別出生率	126
表 4.19	出生順位別にみた年次別母の平均年齢	128
表 4.20	出生順位別にみた年次別父の平均年齢	128
表 4.21	出生順位・都道府県（21大都市再掲）別にみた父・母の平均年齢	129
表 4.22	父母が結婚生活に入ってから出生順位第1子出生までの期間別にみた年次別嫡出出生数百分率及び平均期間	130
表 4.23	世帯の主な仕事別にみた出生順位別出生数及び百分率	130

〔妊娠期間別にみた出生〕
表 4.24	妊娠期間別にみた年次別出生数及び百分率	131

〔出生時の体重別にみた出生〕
表 4.25	性・出生時の体重別にみた年次別出生数・百分率及び平均体重	132
表 4.26	都道府県（21大都市再掲）・性別にみた出生時の平均体重及び2,500ｇ未満の出生数及び割合	136
表 4.27	単産－複産・性別にみた出生時の体重別出生数・百分率及び平均体重	137
表 4.28	母の年齢・単産－複産・性別にみた2,500ｇ未満の出生数及び割合	138

〔嫡出子－嫡出でない子別にみた出生〕
表 4.29	嫡出子－嫡出でない子別にみた年次別出生数及び百分率	139
表 4.30	性・年次別にみた嫡出でない子の出生数及び割合	139
表 4.31	母の年齢・年次別にみた嫡出でない子の出生数及び割合	140

〔父母の国籍別にみた出生〕
表 4.32	父母の国籍別にみた年次別出生数及び百分率	142
表 4.33	父母の国籍別にみた都道府県（21大都市再掲）別出生数	144
表 4.34	父母の国籍別にみた都道府県（21大都市再掲）別出生数百分率	146

〔出生時の身長別にみた出生〕
表 4.35	性・出生時の身長別にみた年次別出生数・百分率及び平均身長	148

〔単産－複産の種類別にみた分娩件数〕
表 4.36	単産－複産（複産の種類・出生－死産の組合せ）別にみた年次別分娩件数	150
表 4.37	都道府県別にみた単産－複産（複産の種類）別分娩件数	152
表 4.38	都道府県別にみた複産の種類別分娩件数百分率	153

第5章 死　亡

〔死亡の年次推移〕
表 5. 1	年次別にみた性別死亡数・率（人口千対）及び死亡性比	154
表 5. 2	年次別にみた性別粗死亡率及び年齢調整死亡率（人口千対）	156
表 5. 3	世界各国における粗死亡率及び年齢調整死亡率（人口10万対）	157

〔月別にみた死亡〕
表 5. 4	月別にみた年次別死亡数及び率（人口千対）	158

〔死亡の場所別にみた死亡〕
表 5. 5	死亡の場所別にみた年次別死亡数	160
表 5. 6	死亡の場所別にみた年次別死亡数百分率	162
表 5. 7	死亡の場所別にみた都道府県（21大都市再掲）別死亡数	164
表 5. 8	死亡の場所別にみた都道府県（21大都市再掲）別死亡数百分率	165

〔地域別にみた死亡〕

　　表 5. 9　　都道府県別にみた年次別死亡数　　　　　　　　　　　　　　　　　166

　　表 5.10　　都道府県別にみた年次別死亡率（人口千対）　　　　　　　　　　　168

〔死亡原因の年次推移〕

　　表 5.11　　年次別にみた死因順位　　　　　　　　　　　　　　　　　　　　170

　　表 5.12　　死因年次推移分類別にみた性別死亡数及び率（人口10万対）　　　　178

　　表 5.13　　年次別にみた死因簡単分類・性別死亡数及び率（人口10万対）　　　202

　　表 5.14　　死因年次推移分類別にみた性別年齢調整死亡率（人口10万対）　　　226

〔性・年齢（5歳階級）別にみた死因〕

　　表 5.15　　性・年齢別にみた死因年次推移分類別死亡数及び率（人口10万対）　228

　　表 5.16　　性・年齢別にみた死因簡単分類別死亡率（人口10万対）　　　　　　296

　　表 5.17　　性・年齢別にみた死因順位　　　　　　　　　　　　　　　　　　　310

〔月別にみた死因〕

　　表 5.18　　月別にみた死因簡単分類別死亡率（人口10万対）　　　　　　　　　322

〔地域別にみた死因〕

　　表 5.19　　都道府県（21大都市再掲）別にみた死因簡単分類別死亡率（人口10万対）　326

　　表 5.20　　都道府県（21大都市再掲）別にみた死因順位　　　　　　　　　　　338

〔死亡の場所別にみた死因〕

　　表 5.21　　死亡の場所別にみた主な死因の性・年次別死亡数及び百分率　　　　340

　　表 5.22　　死亡の場所別にみた主な死因の性・年齢別死亡数及び百分率　　　　346

〔世帯の主な仕事別にみた死因〕

　　表 5.23　　世帯の主な仕事別にみた選択死因分類別死亡数及び百分率　　　　　352

〔主な死因〕

　悪性新生物

　　表 5.24　　悪性新生物の主な部位別にみた性・年次別死亡数及び率（人口10万対）　356

　　表 5.25　　悪性新生物の主な部位別にみた性・年齢・年次別死亡率（人口10万対）　362

　　表 5.26　　悪性新生物の主な部位別にみた性・年次別年齢調整死亡率（人口10万対）　370

　脳血管疾患

　　表 5.27　　脳血管疾患の病類別にみた性・年次別死亡数・百分率・粗死亡率及び年齢調整死亡率（人口10万対）　372

　心疾患（高血圧性を除く）

　　表 5.28　　心疾患の病類別にみた性・年次別死亡数・百分率・粗死亡率及び年齢調整死亡率（人口10万対）　374

　感染症

　　表 5.29　　感染症分類別にみた年次別死亡数及び率（人口10万対）　　　　　　378

　不慮の事故

　　表 5.30　　不慮の事故の種類別にみた年次別死亡数及び率（人口10万対）　　　382

　　表 5.31　　不慮の事故の種類別にみた年齢別死亡数　　　　　　　　　　　　　384

　　表 5.32　　不慮の事故の種類別にみた年齢別死亡数百分率　　　　　　　　　　385

　　表 5.33　　交通事故の種類別にみた年次別死亡数及び百分率　　　　　　　　　386

　　表 5.34　　交通事故以外の不慮の事故の傷害発生の場所別にみた年齢別死亡数及び百分率　　388

　　表 5.35　　家庭における主な不慮の事故の種類別にみた年齢別死亡数及び百分率　　389

　自殺

　　表 5.36　　自殺の手段別にみた性・年次別死亡数及び百分率　　　　　　　　　390

　妊産婦死亡

　　表 5.37　　妊産婦死亡の死因別にみた年次別死亡数及び率（出産10万対）　　　394

　　表 5.38　　後発妊産婦死亡の死因別にみた年次別死亡数及び率（出産10万対）　　395

　　表 5.39　　都道府県別にみた年次別妊産婦死亡数及び率（出産10万対）　　　　396

第6章　乳児死亡

〔乳児死亡の年次推移〕

表 6. 1　年次別にみた乳児死亡数・率（出生千対）・乳児死亡性比及び総死亡中
乳児死亡の占める割合 ･･･ 398

表 6. 2　年次別にみた新生児死亡数・率（出生千対）・新生児死亡性比及び乳児死亡中
新生児死亡の占める割合 ･････････････････････････････････････ 400

〔生存期間別にみた乳児死亡〕

表 6. 3　生存期間別にみた性別乳児死亡率（出生10万対）・乳児死亡率性比及び百分率 ･･････････ 402

表 6. 4　生存期間別にみた性・年次別乳児死亡率（出生10万対） ････････････････････ 404

〔月別にみた乳児死亡〕

表 6. 5　月別にみた年次別乳児死亡数及び率（出生千対） ････････････････････････ 406

表 6. 6　出生年月別にみた出生数・乳児死亡数及び率（出生千対） ･･･････････････････ 408

〔死亡の場所別にみた乳児死亡〕

表 6. 7　死亡の場所別にみた年次別乳児死亡数及び百分率 ･･･････････････････････ 409

表 6. 8　死亡の場所別にみた都道府県（21大都市再掲）別乳児死亡数百分率 ･･･････････････ 410

〔世帯の主な仕事別にみた乳児死亡〕

表 6. 9　世帯の主な仕事別にみた生存期間別乳児死亡数・率（世帯の主な仕事別出生千対）及び百分率 ･･･････ 411

〔地域別にみた乳児死亡〕

表 6.10　都道府県別にみた年次別乳児死亡数 ･･････････････････････････････ 412

表 6.11　都道府県別にみた年次別乳児死亡率（出生千対） ････････････････････････ 414

表 6.12　都道府県（21大都市再掲）別にみた生存期間別乳児死亡率（出生10万対）及び
乳児死亡中新生児死亡・早期新生児死亡の占める割合 ････････････････････ 416

〔乳児死亡の原因〕

表 6.13　年次別にみた乳児死因簡単分類別乳児死亡数及び率（出生10万対） ･････････････ 418

表 6.14　生存期間別にみた乳児死因簡単分類別乳児死亡数及び率（出生10万対） ･･･････････ 420

表 6.15　生存期間別にみた乳児死因簡単分類別乳児死亡数百分率及び乳児死因簡単分類別に
みた生存期間別乳児死亡数百分率 ･･･････････････････････････ 422

表 6.16　年次別にみた乳児・新生児の死因順位 ･･･････････････････････････ 424

表 6.17　都道府県（21大都市再掲）別にみた乳児死因簡単分類別乳児死亡率（出生10万対） ･･････････ 432

〔病死の乳児死亡〕

表 6.18　体重別にみた乳児死因簡単分類別病死による乳児死亡数及び率（出生10万対） ･･･････････ 436

表 6.19　体重別にみた乳児死因簡単分類別病死による新生児死亡数及び率（出生10万対） ･･･････････ 440

第7章　死　産

〔死産の年次推移〕

表 7. 1　年次別にみた死産数・率（出産千対）及び死産性比 ･･････････････････････ 444

表 7. 2　年次別にみた市部－郡部・自然－人工別死産数 ････････････････････････ 446

表 7. 3　年次別にみた市部－郡部・自然－人工別死産率（出産千対）及び全死産中
人工死産の占める割合 ･･･････････････････････････････････ 447

表 7. 4　年次別にみた自然－人工別妊娠満22週以後の死産数・妊娠満22週以後の死産率
（出産千対）及び全死産中妊娠満22週以後の死産の占める割合 ････････････････ 448

〔妊娠期間別にみた死産〕

表 7. 5　妊娠期間別にみた自然－人工・年次別死産数及び百分率 ･･････････････････ 450

〔月別にみた死産〕

表 7. 6　月別にみた自然－人工・年次別死産数及び死産率（出産千対） ･･････････････ 452

〔出産の場所別にみた死産〕

表 7. 7　出産の場所別にみた自然－人工・年次別死産数及び百分率 ･･･････････････ 456

〔母の年齢（5歳階級）別にみた死産〕

表 7. 8　母の年齢・世帯の主な仕事別にみた自然－人工別死産率（出産千対） ････････････ 458

〔嫡出子－嫡出でない子別にみた死産〕

表 7. 9　嫡出子－嫡出でない子・自然－人工別にみた妊娠期間別死産数及び百分率 ･･･････････････ 460

表 7.10　嫡出子－嫡出でない子別にみた年次別妊娠満22週以後の死産数及び百分率 ･････････ 461

〔地域別にみた死産〕

表 7.11　都道府県（21大都市再掲）別にみた出産の場所別死産数及び百分率 ･････････ 462

表 7.12　都道府県別にみた年次別死産数 ･･･････････････････････ 464

表 7.13　都道府県別にみた年次別死産率（出産千対） ･･･････････････ 466

表 7.14　都道府県別にみた年次別自然死産数 ･････････････････ 468

表 7.15　都道府県別にみた年次別自然死産率（出産千対） ･･････････････ 470

表 7.16　都道府県別にみた年次別人工死産数 ･････････････････ 472

表 7.17　都道府県別にみた年次別人工死産率（出産千対） ･･････････････ 474

〔死産の原因〕

表 7.18　死産原因別にみた死産数及び百分率 ･･･････････････････ 476

表 7.19　死因・母側病態－児側病態別にみた自然死産数及び百分率 ･････････ 480

第8章　周産期死亡

〔周産期死亡の年次推移〕

表 8. 1　年次別にみた性・妊娠満22週以後の死産－早期新生児死亡別周産期死亡数 ･････････ 484

表 8. 2　年次別にみた性・妊娠満22週以後の死産－早期新生児死亡別周産期死亡率 ･････････ 485

〔月別にみた周産期死亡〕

表 8. 3　月別にみた年次別妊娠満22週以後の死産－早期新生児死亡別周産期死亡数及び率 ･･････････ 486

〔出産時の体重別にみた周産期死亡〕

表 8. 4　体重別にみた年次別妊娠満22週以後の死産－早期新生児死亡別周産期死亡数及び百分率 ･･････ 488

表 8. 5　体重別にみた性別妊娠満22週以後の死産－早期新生児死亡別周産期死亡数・率及び百分率 ･････ 489

〔母の年齢（5歳階級）別にみた周産期死亡〕

表 8. 6　母の年齢別にみた年次別妊娠満22週以後の死産－早期新生児死亡別周産期死亡数及び率 ･･････ 490

表 8. 7　母の年齢別にみた世帯の主な仕事別妊娠満22週以後の死産－早期新生児死亡別
周産期死亡数 ･･･････････････････････ 491

表 8. 8　母の年齢別にみた世帯の主な仕事別妊娠満22週以後の死産－早期新生児死亡別
周産期死亡率 ･････････････････････ 492

表 8. 9　母の年齢別にみた性別妊娠満22週以後の死産－早期新生児死亡別周産期死亡数及び率 ･･･････ 493

〔単産－複産・出産順位別にみた周産期死亡〕

表 8.10　単産－複産・出産順位別にみた妊娠満22週以後の死産－早期新生児死亡別周産期
死亡数及び率 ･････････････････････ 494

〔地域別にみた周産期死亡〕

表 8.11　都道府県（21大都市再掲）別にみた妊娠満22週以後の死産－早期新生児死亡別周産期死亡数・率
及び周産期死亡中妊娠満22週以後の死産の占める割合 ･････････ 495

表 8.12　都道府県別にみた年次別妊娠満22週以後の死産－早期新生児死亡別周産期死亡数 ････････ 496

表 8.13　都道府県別にみた年次別妊娠満22週以後の死産－早期新生児死亡別周産期死亡率 ･･････････ 500

〔周産期死亡の原因〕

表 8.14　死因・母側病態－児側病態別にみた妊娠満22週以後の死産－早期新生児死亡別
周産期死亡数及び百分率 ･･･････････････ 504

第9章　婚　姻

〔地域別にみた婚姻〕

表 9. 1　都道府県別にみた年次別婚姻件数 ･･･････････････････ 512

表 9. 2　都道府県別にみた年次別婚姻率（人口千対） ･････････････ 514

〔月別にみた婚姻〕

表 9. 3　届出月別にみた年次別婚姻件数及び百分率 ･･･････････････ 516

〔初婚と再婚別にみた婚姻〕

表 9. 4 初婚－再婚別にみた年次別婚姻件数及び総数に対する再婚の割合－夫・妻－ ……………………… 518

表 9. 5 夫妻の初婚－再婚の組合せ別にみた年次別婚姻件数及び百分率 ……………………… 520

表 9. 6 前婚解消後から再婚までの期間別にみた年次別再婚件数百分率－夫・妻－

（各届出年に結婚生活に入り届け出たもの） ……………………… 522

〔結婚生活に入ったときの年齢別にみた婚姻〕

表 9. 7 結婚生活に入ったときの年齢別にみた年次別婚姻件数－初婚の夫・妻及び再婚の夫・妻－

（各届出年に結婚生活に入り届け出たもの） ……………………… 524

表 9. 8 結婚生活に入ったときの年齢別にみた年次別初婚率・再婚率（人口千対）－夫・妻－

（各届出年に結婚生活に入り届け出たもの） ……………………… 528

表 9. 9 結婚生活に入ったときの年齢別にみた夫妻の初婚－再婚別件数及び百分率

（平成28年に結婚生活に入り届け出たもの） ……………………… 530

表 9.10 結婚生活に入ったときの年齢別にみた夫・妻の初婚－再婚別件数百分率

（平成28年に結婚生活に入り届け出たもの） ……………………… 532

表 9.11 年次別平均婚姻年齢及び夫妻の年齢差 ……………………… 534

表 9.12 都道府県別にみた年次別平均婚姻年齢－初婚の夫・初婚の妻－

（各届出年に結婚生活に入り届け出たもの） ……………………… 536

表 9.13 結婚生活に入ったときの初婚夫妻の年齢別にみた婚姻件数及び百分率

（平成28年に結婚生活に入り届け出たもの） ……………………… 540

表 9.14 初婚夫妻の年齢差別にみた年次別婚姻件数及び百分率

（各届出年に結婚生活に入り届け出たもの） ……………………… 542

〔夫妻の結婚生活に入る前の世帯の主な仕事別にみた婚姻〕

表 9.15 夫の結婚生活に入る前の世帯の主な仕事別にみた妻の結婚生活に入る前の世帯の主な仕事別

初婚夫妻の婚姻件数及び百分率（平成28年に結婚生活に入り届け出たもの） ……………………… 543

〔結婚生活に入ったときから婚姻届出までの期間別にみた婚姻〕

表 9.16 結婚生活に入ったときから婚姻届出までの期間別にみた年次別婚姻件数百分率 ……………………… 544

表 9.17 結婚生活に入ったときから婚姻届出までの期間別にみた年次別婚姻件数累積百分率 ……………………… 545

〔夫妻の国籍別にみた婚姻〕

表 9.18 夫妻の国籍別にみた年次別婚姻件数 ……………………… 546

表 9.19 夫妻の国籍別にみた年次別婚姻件数百分率 ……………………… 548

表 9.20 夫妻の国籍別にみた都道府県（21大都市再掲）別婚姻件数 ……………………… 550

表 9.21 夫妻の国籍別にみた都道府県（21大都市再掲）別婚姻件数百分率 ……………………… 552

第10章 **離　婚**

〔地域別にみた離婚〕

表10. 1 都道府県別にみた年次別離婚件数 ……………………… 554

表10. 2 都道府県別にみた年次別離婚率（人口千対） ……………………… 556

〔月別にみた離婚〕

表10. 3 届出月別にみた年次別離婚件数及び百分率 ……………………… 558

〔種類別にみた離婚〕

表10. 4 離婚の種類別にみた年次別離婚件数及び百分率 ……………………… 560

〔夫妻の同居期間・同居をやめたときの年齢別にみた離婚〕

表10. 5 結婚生活に入ってから同居をやめたときまでの期間別にみた年次別離婚件数・

百分率及び平均同居期間 ……………………… 562

表10. 6 同居をやめたときの年齢別にみた年次別離婚件数－夫・妻－

（各届出年に同居をやめ届け出たもの） ……………………… 564

表10. 7 同居をやめたときの年齢別にみた年次別離婚率（人口千対）－夫・妻－

（各届出年に同居をやめ届け出たもの） ……………………… 566

表10. 8 同居をやめたときの夫妻の年齢別にみた離婚件数及び百分率

（平成28年に同居をやめ届け出たもの） ……………………… 568

〔親権を行わなければならない子の数別にみた離婚〕

表10. 9 夫妻が親権を行わなければならない子の数別にみた年次別離婚件数及び百分率 ･････････････ 570

表10.10 親権を行わなければならない子をもつ夫妻別にみた年次別離婚件数及び百分率 ････････････ 571

表10.11 親権を行わなければならない子の数別にみた年次別離婚件数及び百分率 ････････････････ 572

〔同居をやめた当時の世帯の主な仕事別にみた離婚〕

表10.12 同居をやめた当時の世帯の主な仕事別にみた同居期間別離婚件数及び百分率 ･･･････････ 573

〔夫妻の国籍別にみた離婚〕

表10.13 夫妻の国籍別にみた年次別離婚件数及び百分率 ･････････････････････････････････ 574

表10.14 夫妻の国籍別にみた都道府県（21大都市再掲）別離婚件数 ･･････････････････････････ 576

表10.15 夫妻の国籍別にみた都道府県（21大都市再掲）別離婚件数百分率 ･･････････････････････ 578

付録

基礎人口

表 1 年次・性別人口 ･･･ 580

表 2 月別推計人口（各月 1 日現在） ･･･ 582

表 3 年次・性・年齢別人口 ･･･ 583

表 4 年次・都道府県・性別人口 ･･･ 586

表 5 21大都市・性別人口 ･･ 592

参考表

1 各種分類表

表 1 死因簡単分類と死因基本分類との対照表 ･･････････････････････････････････ 595

表 2 選択死因分類と死因簡単分類及び死因基本分類との対照表 ･･･････････････････ 596

表 3 死因年次推移分類と死因簡単分類及び死因基本分類との対照表 ･･･････････････ 597

表 4 乳児死因簡単分類と死因基本分類及び死因簡単分類との対照表 ･･･････････････ 598

表 5 - 1 感染症分類と死因基本分類との対照表（平成28年） ･･････････････････････ 599

表 5 - 2 感染症分類と死因基本分類との対照表（平成27年） ･･････････････････････ 600

表 5 - 3 感染症分類と死因基本分類との対照表（平成25年から26年まで） ･･･････････ 601

表 5 - 4 感染症分類と死因基本分類との対照表（平成24年） ･･････････････････････ 602

表 5 - 5 感染症分類と死因基本分類との対照表（平成20年から23年まで） ･･･････････ 603

表 5 - 6 感染症分類と死因基本分類との対照表（平成19年） ･･････････････････････ 604

表 5 - 7 感染症分類と死因基本分類との対照表（平成18年） ･･････････････････････ 605

表 5 - 8 感染症分類と死因基本分類との対照表（平成15年から17年まで） ･･･････････ 606

表 5 - 9 感染症分類と死因基本分類との対照表（平成11年から14年まで） ･･･････････ 607

表 6 - 1 死因順位及び乳児死因順位に用いる分類項目（平成 7 年以降） ･････････････ 608

表 6 - 2 死因順位及び乳児死因順位に用いる分類項目（昭和54年から平成 6 年まで） ････ 609

2 年次推移

表 1 - 1 死因簡単分類別にみた平成18年と17年の性別死亡数及び率（人口10万対） ････････････ 610

表 1 - 2 死因簡単分類別にみた平成 7 年と 6 年の性別死亡数及び率（人口10万対） ････････････ 614

表 1 - 3 死因簡単分類別にみた昭和55・60・平成 2 ・ 4 ～ 6 年の性別死亡数及び率（人口10万対） ･････ 618

表 2 - 1 乳児死因簡単分類別にみた平成 7 年と 6 年の乳児死亡数及び率（出生10万対） ･････････ 630

表 2 - 2 乳児死因簡単分類別にみた昭和55・60・平成 2 ・ 4 ～ 6 年の乳児死亡数及び率
（出生10万対） ･･ 632

表 3 - 1 感染症分類（平成27年改正）別にみた年次別死亡数及び率（人口10万対）（平成27年） ････････ 634

表 3 - 2 感染症分類（平成25年改正）別にみた年次別死亡数及び率（人口10万対）（平成25年・26年） ･･･ 638

表 3 - 3 感染症分類（平成24年改正）別にみた年次別死亡数及び率（人口10万対）（平成24年） ････････ 642

表 3 - 4 感染症分類（平成20年改正）別にみた年次別死亡数及び率（人口10万対）（平成20～23年） ･････ 646

表 3 - 5 感染症分類（平成19年改正）別にみた年次別死亡数及び率（人口10万対）（平成19年） ････････ 650

表 3 - 6 感染症分類（平成18年改正）別にみた年次別死亡数及び率（人口10万対）（平成18年） ････････ 654

表 3 - 7 感染症分類（平成15年改正）別にみた年次別死亡数及び率（人口10万対）（平成15～17年） ････ 656

表 3 - 8 感染症分類（平成11年改正）別にみた年次別死亡数及び率（人口10万対）（平成11～14年） ････ 658

表 4 年次別にみた性・妊娠満28週以後の死産－早期新生児死亡別周産期死亡数 ･････ 660

表 5 年次別にみた自然－人工別妊娠満28週以後の死産数・妊娠満28週以後の死産比
（出生千対）及び全死産中妊娠満28週以後の死産の占める割合 ･････････････････ 662

表 6 合計特殊出生率 ･･ 664

11

中 巻 内 容

統 計 表

統 計 表 一 覧

総 覧
第1表　人口動態総覧，都道府県（21大都市再掲）別
第2表　人口動態総覧，都道府県；保健所・市区町村別

出 生
第1表　出生数，出生の場所・都道府県・市部－郡部（21大都市再掲）別
第2表　出生数，性・出生月・市部－郡部（全国）・都道府県（21大都市再掲）別
第3表　出生数，性・出産順位・都道府県（21大都市再掲）別
第4表　出生数，性・出生月・出生順位・母の年齢（5歳階級）別
第5表　出生数，性・母の年齢（5歳階級）・都道府県（21大都市再掲）別
第6表　出生数，性・母の年齢（5歳階級）・出産順位別
第7表　出生数，性・母の年齢（各歳）・出生順位・嫡出子－嫡出でない子別
第8表　嫡出出生数，父の年齢（各歳）・母の年齢（各歳）・出生順位別
第9表　嫡出出生数，結婚生活に入った年・母の年齢（各歳）・出生順位別
第10表　出生数，母の年齢（5歳階級）・出生順位・出生当時の世帯の主な仕事別
第11表　出生数，出生時の体重；出生時の平均体重，性・単産－複産・都道府県（21大都市再掲）別
第12表　出生数，出生時の体重；出生時の平均体重，性・単産－複産・母の年齢（5歳階級）別
第13表　出生数，出生時の体重；出生時の平均体重，性・単産－複産・出産順位別
第14表　出生数，出生時の体重；出生時の平均体重，性・単産－複産・妊娠期間（4週区分・早期－正期－過期再掲）別
第15表　出生数，出生時の体重；出生時の平均体重，性・嫡出子－嫡出でない子・母の年齢（5歳階級）別
第16表　出生数，出生時の身長；出生時の平均身長，性・都道府県（21大都市再掲）別
第17表　嫡出出生数，結婚期間・母の年齢（各歳）・出生順位別
第18表　出生数，性・母の年齢（5歳階級）・市部－郡部・嫡出子－嫡出でない子別

死 亡
第1表　死亡数・乳児（1歳未満）死亡数・新生児（生後4週未満）死亡数・早期新生児（生後1週未満）死亡数，死亡の場所・都道府県・市部－郡部（21大都市再掲）別
第2表　死亡数，性・死亡月・市部－郡部（全国）・都道府県（21大都市再掲）別
第3表　死亡数，性・年齢（5歳階級）・都道府県（21大都市再掲）別
第4表　死亡数，性・年齢（各歳）・都道府県（21大都市再掲）別
第5表　死亡数，性・死亡月・生年年齢別
第6表　死亡数，性・年齢（5歳階級）・死亡当時の世帯の主な仕事別
第7表　15歳以上の死亡数，性・年齢（5歳階級）・配偶関係別
第8表　死亡数，性・死亡の場所・年齢（5歳階級）別

乳児死亡
第1表　乳児（1歳未満）死亡数・新生児（生後4週未満）死亡数，性・死亡月・市部－郡部（全国）・都道府県（21大都市再掲）別
第2表　乳児（1歳未満）死亡数，性・生存期間・市部－郡部（全国）・都道府県（21大都市再掲）別
第3表　乳児（1歳未満）死亡数，性・生存期間・死亡当時の世帯の主な仕事別
第4表　乳児（1歳未満）死亡数，死亡月・出生年月別
第5表　病死による乳児（1歳未満）死亡数，出生時の体重；出生時の平均体重，性・単産－複産・母の年齢（5歳階級）別
第6表　病死による乳児（1歳未満）死亡数，出生時の体重；出生時の平均体重，性・単産－複産・出産順位別
第7表　病死による乳児（1歳未満）死亡数，出生時の体重；出生時の平均体重，性・妊娠期間（4週区分・早期－正期－過期再掲）別

死　産

第1表　死産数，出産の場所・都道府県・市部－郡部（21大都市再掲）別

第2表　死産数，自然－人工・出産の場所・市部－郡部（全国）・都道府県（21大都市再掲）別

第3表　死産数，自然－人工・死産月・市部－郡部（全国）・都道府県（21大都市再掲）別

第4表－1　死産数，自然－人工・妊娠期間（4週区分）・都道府県・市部－郡部（21大都市再掲）別

第4表－2　死産数，自然－人工・妊娠期間（早期－正期－過期）・都道府県・市部－郡部（21大都市再掲）別

第5表－1　死産数，自然－人工・性・妊娠期間（4週区分）・嫡出子－嫡出でない子別

第5表－2　死産数，自然－人工・性・妊娠期間（早期－正期－過期）・嫡出子－嫡出でない子別

第6表　死産数，自然－人工・母の年齢（5歳階級）・死産当時の世帯の主な仕事別

第7表　妊娠満22週以後の死産数，性・母の年齢（5歳階級）・都道府県（21大都市再掲）別

第8表　妊娠満22週以後の死産数，自然－人工・出産の場所・胎児死亡の時期・市部－郡部（全国）・都道府県（21大都市再掲）別

第9表　妊娠満22週以後の死産数，自然－人工・性・母の年齢（5歳階級）・出産順位別

周産期死亡

第1表　周産期死亡数，妊娠満22週以後の死産－早期新生児死亡・性・死亡月・市部－郡部（全国）・都道府県（21大都市再掲）別

第2表　周産期死亡数，出産時の体重；出産時の平均体重，妊娠満22週以後の死産－早期新生児死亡・性・都道府県（21大都市再掲）別

第3表　周産期死亡数，出産時の体重；出産時の平均体重，妊娠満22週以後の死産－早期新生児死亡・性・単産－複産・母の年齢（5歳階級）別

第4表　周産期死亡数，出産時の体重；出産時の平均体重，妊娠満22週以後の死産－早期新生児死亡・性・単産－複産・出産順位別

第5表　周産期死亡数，出産時の体重；出産時の平均体重，妊娠満22週以後の死産－早期新生児死亡・性・単産－複産・妊娠期間（4週区分・早期－正期－過期再掲）別

婚　姻

第1表　婚姻件数，届出月・都道府県（21大都市再掲）別

第2表　婚姻件数，届出月・結婚生活に入った年月別－全国・21大都市の計（再掲）－

第3表　婚姻件数（平成28年に結婚生活に入り届け出たもの），届出月・結婚生活に入ったときの年齢（5歳階級）・初婚－再婚別

第4表　婚姻件数，夫の初婚－再婚（死別－離別）・妻の初婚－再婚（死別－離別）・都道府県（21大都市再掲）別

第5表　婚姻件数（平成28年に結婚生活に入り届け出たもの），夫の同居時の年齢（各歳）・妻の同居時の年齢（各歳）・夫の初婚－再婚・妻の初婚－再婚別

第6表　平均婚姻年齢；初婚者数・再婚者数（平成28年に結婚生活に入り届け出た夫・妻別），夫－妻の同居時の年齢（各歳）・都道府県（21大都市再掲）別

第7表　再婚者数，夫－妻・死別－離別・前婚解消の年・前婚解消時の年齢（各歳）別

第8表　婚姻件数，夫の国籍・妻の国籍・夫の初婚－再婚・妻の初婚－再婚別

離　婚

第1表　離婚件数，届出月・都道府県（21大都市再掲）別

第2表　離婚件数，届出月・同居をやめた年月別

第3表　離婚件数（平成28年に同居をやめ届け出たもの），夫の別居時の年齢（各歳）・妻の別居時の年齢（各歳）別

第4表　離婚件数，種類・都道府県（21大都市再掲）別

第5表　離婚件数，種類・同居期間・同居をやめた当時の世帯の主な仕事別

第6表　離婚件数（平成28年に同居をやめ届け出たもの），夫－妻の別居時の年齢（5歳階級）・同居期間・夫－妻別

第7表　離婚件数，夫妻が親権を行わなければならない子の数・妻が親権を行う子の数別－平成28年に同居をやめ届け出たもの（再掲）－

第8表　離婚件数，同居期間・夫妻が親権を行わなければならない子の数別－平成28年に同居をやめ届け出たもの（再掲）－

【前年以前の日本における日本人】

出　生
第1表　届出遅れ出生数，性・出生の年・届出地による都道府県（21大都市再掲）別

死　亡
第1表　届出遅れ死亡数，性・死亡の年・届出地による都道府県（21大都市再掲）別

【日本における外国人】

出　生
第1表　嫡出出生数，父の国籍・母の国籍別

第2表　出生数，性・出生月・母の国籍別

第3表　嫡出出生数，父の国籍・都道府県（21大都市再掲）別

第4表　出生数，母の国籍・都道府県（21大都市再掲）別

第5表　出生数，母の平均年齢；母の国籍・母の年齢（5歳階級）別

死　亡
第1表　死亡数，性・死亡月・国籍別

第2表　死亡数，性・死亡の場所・国籍別

第3表　死亡数，国籍・都道府県（21大都市再掲）別

第4表　死亡数，性・年齢（5歳階級）・国籍別

乳児死亡
第1表　乳児（1歳未満）死亡数，性・死亡月・国籍別

死　産
第1表　死産数，性・死産月・母の国籍別

第2表　死産数，自然－人工・母の年齢（5歳階級）・妊娠期間（早期－正期－過期）別

婚姻・離婚
第1表　婚姻件数，夫の国籍・妻の国籍別

第2表　平均婚姻年齢；初婚・再婚者数，夫－妻別（平成28年に結婚生活に入り届け出たもの）

第3表　離婚件数，種類別

第4表　離婚件数，夫の国籍・妻の国籍別

【外国における日本人】
第1表　出生数・死亡数・乳児（1歳未満）死亡数，性・月別

第2表　平均婚姻年齢；初婚・再婚者数，夫－妻別（平成28年に結婚生活に入り届け出たもの）

第3表　離婚件数，種類別

第4表　死亡数，性・年齢（5歳階級）別

【前年以前の日本における外国人】
第1表　出生数・死亡数・乳児（1歳未満）死亡数・死産数，性・年・国籍別

【前年以前の外国における日本人】
第1表　出生数・死亡数・乳児（1歳未満）死亡数，性・年別

下　巻　内　容

死因統計分類の分類体系並びに分類表
　疾病、傷害および死因統計分類の分類体系
　疾病、傷害および死因の統計分類
　　1　死因基本分類表
　　2　死因簡単分類表
　　3　選択死因分類表
　　4　乳児死因簡単分類表
　　5　感染症分類表
　統計表一覧

死　因　（死産原因を含む）
（死　亡）
第1表－1　死亡数，性・年齢（5歳階級）・死因（三桁基本分類）別
第1表－2　死亡数，性・死因（死因基本分類）別
第2表　死亡数，性・年齢（5歳階級）・死因（死因簡単分類）別
第3表　死亡数，性・死亡月・死因（死因簡単分類）別
第4表　死亡数，性・死因（死因簡単分類）・都道府県（21大都市再掲）別
第5表　死亡数，性・死亡の場所・死因（死因簡単分類）別
第6表　死亡数，性・年齢（特定階級）・死因（選択死因分類）・死亡当時の世帯の主な仕事別
第7表　15歳以上の死亡数，性・年齢（特定階級）・配偶関係・死因（選択死因分類）別
第8表　感染症による死亡数，死因（感染症分類）・都道府県（21大都市再掲）別
第9表　交通事故以外の不慮の事故（W00－X59）死亡数，年齢（特定階級）・発生場所・外因（三桁基本分類）別
第10表　外因による死亡数，性・年齢（特定階級）・外因（死因簡単分類）・外因の影響別
第11表　路上交通事故死亡数，性・年齢（特定階級）・傷害発生地による都道府県（21大都市再掲）別
（乳児死亡）
第1表　乳児（1歳未満）死亡数，性・生存期間・死因（乳児死因簡単分類）別
第2表　乳児（1歳未満）死亡数・新生児（生後4週未満）死亡数，性・死因（乳児死因簡単分類）・都道府県（21大都市再掲）別
第3表　乳児（1歳未満）死亡数・新生児（生後4週未満）死亡数，性・死亡月・死因（乳児死因簡単分類）別
第4表　病死による乳児（1歳未満）死亡数・新生児（生後4週未満）死亡数・早期新生児（生後1週未満）死亡数，性・死因（乳児死因簡単分類）・出生時の体重別
第5表　病死による乳児（1歳未満）死亡数・新生児（生後4週未満）死亡数・早期新生児（生後1週未満）死亡数，性・死因（乳児死因簡単分類）・妊娠期間（早期－正期－過期）別
（死　産）
第1表　死産数，母の年齢（5歳階級）・死産原因（三桁基本分類；自然－人工）別
第2表　死産数，妊娠期間（早期－正期－過期）・死産原因（三桁基本分類；自然－人工）別
第3表　妊娠満22週以後の死産数，出産時の体重・死産原因（三桁基本分類；自然－人工）別
（周産期死亡）
第1表　周産期死亡数，妊娠満22週以後の死産－早期新生児死亡・児側病態（三桁基本分類）・母側病態（三桁基本分類）別
【日本における外国人】
【外国における日本人】
第1表　死亡数（日本における外国人－国籍別，外国における日本人），性・死因（死因簡単分類）別
第2表　乳児死亡数（日本における外国人－国籍別，外国における日本人），性・死因（乳児死因簡単分類）別

　上・中・下巻の統計表は、「政府統計の総合窓口（e-Stat）」にも掲載している。

保 管 統 計 表（報告書非掲載）一 覧

（出　　生）

第 1 表	出生数，出生の場所・出生時の立会者・都道府県・市部－郡部（21大都市再掲）別
第 2 表	出生数（複産のみ），性・複産の種類・複産の順位別
第 3 表	出生数（複産のみ），複産の種類・都道府県（21大都市再掲）別
第 4 表	出生数，性・出生時の体重（100 g 階級）・妊娠期間（各週）・単産－複産別
第 5 表	出生数，出生時の体重；出生時の平均体重，性・母の年齢（5 歳階級）・出産順位別
第 6 表	出生数，出生時の体重；出生時の平均体重，性・母の年齢（5 歳階級）・出生順位別
第 7 表	出生数，出生年月日時・出生の場所別
第 8 表	出生数，出生月・母の生年年齢別
第 9 表	出生数，性・出生順位・出産順位・母の年齢（5 歳階級）別
第10表	出生数，性・出生順位・都道府県（21大都市再掲）別
第11表	嫡出出生数，父の年齢（5 歳階級）・出生当時の世帯の主な仕事別
第12表	出生数，出生時の体重；出生時の平均体重，性・単産－複産・母の年齢（5 歳階級）・出生当時の世帯の主な仕事別
第13表	出生数，出生時の身長；出生時の平均身長，性・単産－複産・妊娠期間（4 週区分・早期－正期－過期再掲）別
第14表	出生数，性・出生時の身長・妊娠期間（各週）別
第15表	出生数，性・出生時の身長・出生時の体重（100 g 階級）別
第16表	日本における父外国人・母日本人の嫡出出生数，性・父の国籍・都道府県（21大都市再掲）別
第17表	日本における父外国人・母日本人の嫡出出生数，性・出生月・父の国籍別
第18表	日本における父外国人・母日本人の嫡出出生数，父の年齢（各歳）・母の年齢（各歳）別
第19表	日本における父日本人・母外国人の嫡出出生数，性・母の国籍・都道府県（21大都市再掲）別
第20表	日本における父日本人・母外国人の嫡出出生数，性・出生月・母の国籍別
第21表	日本における父日本人・母外国人の嫡出出生数，父の年齢（各歳）・母の年齢（各歳）別

（死　　亡）

第 1 表	15歳以上有配偶死亡数，性・年齢（5 歳階級）・配偶者の年齢（5 歳階級）別

（乳児死亡）

第 1 表	病死による乳児（1 歳未満）死亡数，出生時の体重；出生時の平均体重，性・単産－複産・都道府県（21大都市再掲）別

（死　　産）

第 1 表	死産数，出産時の体重・性・単産－複産・自然－人工・妊娠期間（4 週区分）別
第 2 表	死産数，出産時の体重・性・単産－複産・自然－人工・妊娠期間（早期－正期－過期）別
第 3 表	死産数，出産時の体重（100 g 階級）・単産－複産・自然－人工・妊娠期間（各週）別
第 4 表	死産数，出産時の身長（1 cm 階級）・単産－複産・自然－人工・妊娠期間（各週）別
第 5 表	妊娠満22週以後の死産数，性・出産時の体重（100 g 階級）・出産時の身長（1 cm 階級）別
第 6 表	自然死産数（妊娠満22週以後），胎児死亡の時期・妊娠期間（4 週区分）・出産の場所別
第 7 表	自然死産数（妊娠満22週以後），胎児死亡の時期・妊娠期間（早期－正期－過期）・出産の場所別
第 8 表	人工死産数，妊娠期間（4 週区分）・法による－法によらないもの・都道府県（21大都市再掲）別
第 9 表	死産数（複産のみ），性・複産の種類・都道府県（21大都市再掲）別
第10表	死産数（複産のみ），性・複産の種類・複産の順位別
第11表	日本における父外国人－母日本人の死産数，性・自然－人工・国籍別
第12表	日本における父日本人－母外国人の死産数，性・自然－人工・国籍別
第13表	死産数，出産の場所・出産時の立会者・都道府県・市部－郡部（21大都市再掲）別
第14表	妊娠満22週以後の死産数，自然－人工・出産の場所・出産時の立会者・胎児死亡の時期・市部－郡部（全国）・都道府県（21大都市再掲）別

（周産期死亡）
第1表　周産期死亡数，妊娠満22週以後の死産－早期新生児死亡・出産時の体重（100ｇ階級）・単産－複産・妊娠期間（各週）別

第2表　周産期死亡数，妊娠満22週以後の死産－早期新生児死亡・母の年齢（5歳階級）・出産当時の世帯の主な仕事別

第3表　周産期死亡数（複産のみ），妊娠満22週以後の死産－早期新生児死亡・性・複産の種類－複産の順位別

（婚　　姻）
第1表　婚姻件数，夫の初婚－再婚・妻の初婚－再婚・届出時の年齢（各歳）別
第2表　婚姻件数，届出月・夫－妻の届出時の生年年齢別
第3表　婚姻件数，夫の氏・妻の氏・都道府県（21大都市再掲）別－平成28年に結婚生活に入り届け出たもの（再掲）－
第4表　婚姻件数（平成24年～28年までに結婚生活に入ったもの），結婚生活に入った年・夫の初婚－再婚・妻の初婚－再婚・同居時の年齢（各歳）別
第5表　初婚者数（平成28年に結婚生活に入り届け出たもの），夫－妻の結婚生活に入る前の世帯の主な仕事・同居時の年齢（各歳）別
第6表　平均初婚年齢；初婚者数（平成28年に結婚生活に入り届け出た夫－妻別再掲），夫－妻の届出時の年齢（5歳階級）・都道府県（21大都市再掲）別
第7表　日本における夫外国人・妻日本人の婚姻件数，夫の届出時の年齢（各歳）・妻の届出時の年齢（各歳）別
第8表　日本における夫日本人・妻外国人の婚姻件数，夫の届出時の年齢（各歳）・妻の届出時の年齢（各歳）別

（離　　婚）
第1表　離婚件数，夫－妻の届出時の年齢（各歳）・都道府県（21大都市再掲）別
第2表　離婚件数，届出月・夫－妻の届出時の生年年齢別
第3表　離婚件数，同居を始めた年・同居をやめた年別
第4表　離婚件数，（平成24年～28年までに同居をやめたもの），同居をやめた年・夫－妻の別居時の年齢（各歳）別
第5表　離婚件数，夫妻が親権を行わなければならない子の数・同居をやめた当時の世帯の主な仕事別
第6表　離婚件数，同居期間・夫妻が親権を行わなければならない子の数・種類別
第7表　離婚件数（平成28年に同居をやめ届け出たもの），夫の別居時の年齢（各歳）・妻の別居時の年齢（各歳）・同居をやめた当時の世帯の主な仕事別
第8表　日本における夫外国人・妻日本人の離婚件数，夫の届出時の年齢（各歳）・妻の届出時の年齢（各歳）別
第9表　日本における夫日本人・妻外国人の離婚件数，夫の届出時の年齢（各歳）・妻の届出時の年齢（各歳）別

（死　　因）
（死　　亡）
第1表　死亡数，性・年齢（5歳階級）・死因（死因基本分類）別
第2表　死亡数，性・年齢（5歳階級）・死因（死因簡単分類）・死亡の場所別
第3表　死亡数，性・年齢（各歳）・小学生－中学生（再掲）・死因（死因簡単分類）別
第4表　死亡数，性・年齢（5歳階級）・死亡の場所・死因（悪性新生物・心疾患・脳血管疾患）・都道府県（21大都市再掲）別
第5表　15歳以上の死亡数，性・年齢（5歳階級）・死因（選択死因分類）・配偶関係別
第6表　100歳以上の死亡数，性・年齢（各歳）・死因（死因基本分類）別
第7表　感染症による死亡数，性・死亡月・死因（感染症分類）別
第8表　感染症による死亡数，死亡月・死因（感染症分類）・都道府県（21大都市再掲）別
第9表　感染症による死亡数，性・年齢（5歳階級）・死因（感染症分類）別
第10表　交通事故以外の不慮の事故（W00～X59）の死亡数，性・年齢（特定階級）・外因（三桁基本分類）・発生場所別
第11表　路上交通事故死亡数，性・年齢（特定階級）・受傷者の種類・外因の影響別
第12表　手術有りの死亡数（乳児死亡再掲），死亡の場所・市部－郡部・都道府県（21大都市再掲）別
第13表　手術有りの死亡数，性・死因（死因簡単分類）・都道府県（21大都市再掲）別
第14表　手術有りの死亡数，性・年齢（5歳階級）・死因（死因簡単分類）別

第15表	解剖有りの死亡数（乳児死亡再掲），死亡の場所・市部－郡部・都道府県（21大都市再掲）別
第16表	解剖有りの死亡数，性・死因（死因簡単分類）・都道府県（21大都市再掲）別
第17表	解剖有りの死亡数，性・年齢（5歳階級）・死因（死因簡単分類）別

（乳児死亡）

第1表	乳児（1歳未満）死亡数，性・生存期間・死因（死因基本分類）別
第2表	病死による乳児（1歳未満）死亡数，妊娠期間・母側病態（三桁基本分類）・死因（乳児死因簡単分類）別
第3表	病死による乳児（1歳未満）死亡数，母の年齢（5歳階級）・死因（乳児死因簡単分類）別

（死　産）

第1表	死産数，自然－人工・性・出産時の立会者・児側病態（三桁基本分類）・母側病態（三桁基本分類）別
第2表	死産数，自然－人工・児側病態・母側病態（死因基本分類）別
第3表	死産数，自然－人工・児側病態（死因基本分類）・母側病態（死因基本分類）別
第4表	死産数，自然－人工・妊娠期間（3区分）・母側病態（三桁基本分類）・児側病態（三桁基本分類）別
第5表	死産数，自然－人工・妊娠期間（早期－正期－過期）・児側病態（三桁基本分類）・母側病態（三桁基本分類）別
第6表	死産数，手術の有無・自然－人工・妊娠期間（妊娠満22週未満－妊娠満22週以後）・児側病態（死因基本分類）別
第7表	死産数，解剖の有無・自然－人工・妊娠期間（妊娠満22週未満－妊娠満22週以後）・児側病態（死因基本分類）別

（周産期死亡）

第1表	周産期死亡数，妊娠満22週以後の死産－早期新生児死亡・児側病態（三桁基本分類）・母側病態（死因基本分類）別
第2表	周産期死亡数，妊娠満22週以後の死産－早期新生児死亡・児側病態（死因基本分類）・母側病態（死因基本分類）別
第3表	周産期死亡数，妊娠満22週以後の死産－早期新生児死亡・妊娠期間（4週区分）・児側病態（三桁基本分類）・母側病態（三桁基本分類）別
第4表	周産期死亡数，妊娠満22週以後の死産（自然－人工）－早期新生児死亡・児側病態（三桁基本分類）・母側病態（三桁基本分類）・出産時の体重；平均体重別
第5表	周産期死亡数，解剖の有無・妊娠満22週以後の死産（胎児死亡の時期別）－早期新生児死亡・児側病態（三桁基本分類）別

（都 道 府 県 編）

（出　生）

第1表	出生数，出生の場所・出生時の立会者・都道府県・保健所・市区町村別
第2表	出生数，性・出生月・都道府県・保健所別
第3表	出生数，出生当時の世帯の主な仕事・都道府県（21大都市再掲）別
第4表	出生数，2,500g未満出生数（再掲），性・母の年齢（各歳）・出生順位・都道府県（21大都市再掲）別
第5表	出生数，性・母の年齢（5歳階級）・都道府県・保健所・市区町村別

（死亡・乳児死亡）

第1表	死亡数，性・年齢（5歳階級）・都道府県・保健所・市区町村別
第2表	死亡数，性・死亡月・都道府県・保健所別
第3表	死亡数，乳児（1歳未満）死亡数，新生児（生後4週未満）死亡数，早期新生児（生後1週未満）死亡数，死亡当時の世帯の主な仕事・都道府県（21大都市再掲）別

（死　産）

第1表	死産数，自然－人工・性・妊娠期間（4週区分・早期－正期－過期再掲）・都道府県・保健所別
第2表	死産数，自然－人工・妊娠期間（4週区分・早期－正期－過期再掲）・母の年齢（5歳階級）・都道府県（21大都市再掲）別

（婚　　姻）

第1表　　平均初婚年齢；初婚者数（平成28年に結婚生活に入り届け出た夫－妻別再掲），夫－妻の同居時の年齢（5歳階級）・結婚生活に入る前の世帯の主な仕事・都道府県（21大都市再掲）別

第2表　　平均初婚年齢；初婚者数（平成28年に結婚生活に入り届け出た夫－妻別再掲），夫－妻の届出時の年齢（5歳階級）・結婚生活に入る前の世帯の主な仕事・都道府県（21大都市再掲）別

（離　　婚）

第1表　　離婚件数，同居期間・夫妻が親権を行わなければならない子の数・種類・都道府県（21大都市再掲）別

（死　　因）

第1表　　死亡数，性・死因（死因基本分類）・都道府県（21大都市再掲）別

第2表　　死亡数，死亡月・性・年齢（5歳階級）・死因（死因簡単分類）・都道府県（21大都市再掲）別

第3表　　死亡数，性・死亡月・死因（死因簡単分類）・都道府県（21大都市再掲）別

第4表　　死亡数，性・死因（死因簡単分類）・都道府県・保健所別

第5表　　乳児（1歳未満）死亡数・新生児（生後4週未満）死亡数，性・死亡月・死因（乳児死因簡単分類）・都道府県（21大都市再掲）別

第6表　　死亡数，性・死因（選択死因分類）・都道府県・市区町村別

【日本における外国人】

（出　　生）

第1表　　出生数，出生の場所・母の国籍別

第2表　　出生数；出生時の平均体重，母の国籍別

第3表　　出生数，父の年齢（各歳）・母の年齢（各歳）・嫡出子－嫡出でない子別

（婚　　姻）

第1表　　婚姻件数，夫の国籍・都道府県（21大都市再掲）別

第2表　　婚姻件数，妻の国籍・都道府県（21大都市再掲）別

第3表　　婚姻件数，夫の届出時の年齢（各歳）・妻の届出時の年齢（各歳）別

（離　　婚）

第1表　　離婚件数，夫の届出時の年齢（各歳）・妻の届出時の年齢（各歳）別

（死　　因）

（死　　亡）

第1表　　死亡数，性・年齢（特定階級）・死因（選択死因分類）・国籍別

【外国における日本人】

第1表　　外国における父日本人・母日本人の出生数，性・出生月別

第2表　　外国における父外国人・母日本人の出生数，性・出生月・父の国籍別

第3表　　外国における父日本人・母外国人の出生数，性・出生月・母の国籍別

第4表　　前年以前の外国における父日本人・母日本人の出生数，性・出生月別

第5表　　外国における日本人の婚姻件数，夫妻の国籍別

保管統計表（報告書非掲載）は、「政府統計の総合窓口（e-Stat）」に掲載している。

VITAL STATISTICS OF JAPAN, 2016, VOLUME 1
CONTENTS

Preface

Part I Outline of Vital Statistics

Part II Summary of Vital Statistics

Brief Summary, 2016

Natality $\cdots\cdots$ 76

General mortality $\cdots\cdots$ 78

Infant mortality $\cdots\cdots$ 81

Natural change $\cdots\cdots$ 82

Foetal mortality $\cdots\cdots$ 82

Perinatal mortality $\cdots\cdots$ 83

Marriages $\cdots\cdots$ 84

Divorces $\cdots\cdots$ 85

Chapter 3 Summary

Table 3. 1 Summary of vital statistics (number, rates, interval of occurrence), 2016 and 2015 $\cdots\cdots$ 87

Table 3. 2 Trends in indices of vital statistics : Japan $\cdots\cdots$ 88

Table 3. 3 Summary tables of vital statistics : Japan, each prefecture and 21 major cities, 2016 $\cdots\cdots$ 96

Table 3. 4 International comparison of vital statistics $\cdots\cdots$ 100

Chapter 4 Natality

[Trends in live births]

Table 4. 1 Trends in live births, live birth rates (per 1,000 population), total fertility rates and sex ratio of live births : Japan $\cdots\cdots$ 102

[Live births by month]

Table 4. 2 Trends in live births and live birth rates (per 1,000 population) by month : Japan $\cdots\cdots$ 104

[Live births by prefecture]

Table 4. 3 Trends in live births by each prefecture : Japan $\cdots\cdots$ 106

Table 4. 4 Trends in live birth rates by each prefecture (per 1,000 population) : Japan $\cdots\cdots$ 108

Table 4. 5 Trends in total fertility rates by each prefecture : Japan $\cdots\cdots$ 110

[Live births by age of mother (5-year age groups)]

Table 4. 6 Trends in live births, percent distribution and rates (per 1,000 females) by age of mother : Japan $\cdots\cdots$ 112

[Live births by place of delivery]

Table 4. 7 Trends in live births by place of delivery : Japan, urban/rural residence $\cdots\cdots$ 114

Table 4. 8 Trends in percent distribution of live births by place of delivery : Japan, urban/rural residence $\cdots\cdots$ 115

Table 4. 9 Live births by place of delivery : Japan, each prefecture and 21 major cities, 2016 $\cdots\cdots$ 116

Table 4.10 Percent distribution of live births by place of delivery : Japan, each prefecture and 21 major cities, 2016 $\cdots\cdots$ 117

[Live births by birth order and live birth order]

Table	4.11	Trends in live births and percent distribution by birth order : Japan	118
Table	4.12	Trends in live births and percent distribution by live birth order : Japan	119
Table	4.13	Live births by birth order : Japan, each prefecture and 21 major cities, 2016	120
Table	4.14	Percent distribution of live births by birth order : Japan, each prefecture and 21 major cities, 2016	121
Table	4.15	Live births and percent distribution by live birth order and age of mother : Japan, 2016	122
Table	4.16	Live births and percent distribution by birth order and age of mother : Japan, 2016	122
Table	4.17	Trends in live births by age of mother, by live birth order : Japan	124
Table	4.18	Trends in live birth rates by age of mother, by live birth order : Japan	126
Table	4.19	Trends in mean age of mother by live birth order : Japan	128
Table	4.20	Trends in mean age of father by live birth order : Japan	128
Table	4.21	Mean age of father and mother by live birth order : Japan, each prefecture and 21 major cities, 2016	129
Table	4.22	Trends in percent distribution of duration and mean duration from marriage performed to the first bearing (for live births born in wedlock only) : Japan	130
Table	4.23	Live births and percent distribution by live birth order and type of occupation of household : Japan, 2016	130

[Live births by period of gestation]

| Table | 4.24 | Trends in live births and percent distribution by period of gestation : Japan | 131 |

[Live births by birth weight]

Table	4.25	Trends in live births and percent distribution by sex and birth weight : Japan	132
Table	4.26	Mean birth weight, number and percent distribution of live births under 2,500g by sex : Japan, each prefecture and 21 major cities, 2016	136
Table	4.27	Live births and percent distribution by sex, birth weight and plurality of birth : Japan, 2016	137
Table	4.28	Live births and percent distribution under 2,500g by sex, age of mother and plurality of birth : Japan, 2016	138

[Live births by legitimacy status]

Table	4.29	Trends in live births and percent distribution by legitimacy status : Japan	139
Table	4.30	Trends in live births born out of wedlock and proportion by sex : Japan	139
Table	4.31	Trends in live births born out of wedlock and proportion by age of mother : Japan	140

[Live births by nationality of father and mother]

Table	4.32	Trends in live births and percent distribution by nationality of father and mother : Japan	142
Table	4.33	Live births by nationality of father and mother : Japan, each prefecture and 21 major cities, 2016	144
Table	4.34	Percent distribution of live births by nationality of father and mother : Japan, each prefecture and 21 major cities, 2016	146

[Live births by birth length]

| Table | 4.35 | Live births and percent distribution by sex and birth length and mean birth length : Japan | 148 |

[Deliveries by plurality of birth]
Table　4.36　Trends in deliveries by plurality of birth (type of plurality, combination of live birth and foetal death) : Japan　……………………………………………… 150
Table　4.37　Deliveries by plurality of birth (type of plurality) : Japan, each prefecture, 2016　…………………………………………… 152
Table　4.38　Percent distribution of plural deliveries by type of plurality : Japan, each prefecture, 2016　…………………………… 153

Chapter 5　General mortality
[Trends in deaths]
Table　5. 1　Trends in deaths, death rates (per 1,000 population) by sex and sex ratio : Japan　……………………………………………………… 154
Table　5. 2　Trends in crude death rates and age-adjusted death rates (per 1,000 population) by sex : Japan　……………………………… 156
Table　5. 3　International comparison of crude death rates and age-standardized death rates (per 100,000 population)　………………………… 157
[Deaths by month]
Table　5. 4　Trends in deaths and death rates (per 1,000 population) by month : Japan　………………………………………………………… 158
[Deaths by place of occurrence]
Table　5. 5　Trends in deaths by place of occurrence : Japan　……………………… 160
Table　5. 6　Trends in percent distribution of deaths by place of occurrence : Japan　………… 162
Table　5. 7　Deaths by place of occurrence : Japan, each prefecture and 21 major cities, 2016　……………………………………………… 164
Table　5. 8　Percent distribution of deaths by place of occurrence : Japan, each prefecture and 21 major cities, 2016　………………………………… 165
[Deaths by prefecture]
Table　5. 9　Trends in deaths by each prefecture : Japan　………………………… 166
Table　5.10　Trends in death rates (per 1,000 population) by each prefecture : Japan　………… 168
[Trends in causes of death]
Table　5.11　Trends in leading causes of death : Japan　………………………… 170
Table　5.12　Trends in deaths and death rates (per 100,000 population) by sex and causes of death : Japan　……………………………………… 178
Table　5.13　Trends in deaths and death rates (per 100,000 population) by sex and causes (the condensed list of causes of death for Japan) : Japan　………………… 202
Table　5.14　Trends in age-adjusted death rates (per 100,000 population) by sex and causes of death : Japan　……………………………………… 226
[Causes of death by sex and age (5-year age groups)]
Table　5.15　Trends in deaths and death rates (per 100,000 population) by sex, age and causes of death : Japan　…………………………………… 228
Table　5.16　Death rates (per 100,000 population) by sex, age and causes (the condensed list of causes of death for Japan) : Japan, 2016　……………………… 296
Table　5.17　Leading causes of death by sex and age : Japan, 2016　……………………… 310
[Causes of death by month]
Table　5.18　Death rates (per 100,000 population) by causes (the condensed list of causes of death for Japan) by month : Japan, 2016　……………………… 322

[Causes of death by prefecture]

Table 5.19 Death rates (per 100,000 population) by causes (the condensed list of causes of death for Japan) : Japan, each prefecture and 21 major cities, 2016 326

Table 5.20 Leading causes of death : Japan, each prefecture and 21 major cities, 2016 338

[Causes of death by place of occurrence]

Table 5.21 Trends in deaths and percent distribution from leading causes of death by sex and place of occurrence : Japan 340

Table 5.22 Deaths and percent distribution from leading causes of death by sex, age and place of occurrence : Japan, 2016 346

[Causes of death by type of occupation of household]

Table 5.23 Deaths and percent distribution by causes (the selected list of causes of death for Japan) and type of occupation of household : Japan, 2016 352

[Selected causes of death]

Table 5.24 Trends in deaths and death rates (per 100,000 population) from malignant neoplasms by sex and site : Japan 356

Table 5.25 Trends in death rates (per 100,000 population) from malignant neoplasms by sex, age and site : Japan 362

Table 5.26 Trends in age-adjusted death rates (per 100,000 population) from malignant neoplasms by sex and site : Japan 370

Table 5.27 Trends in deaths, percent distribution, crude death rates and age-adjusted death rates (per 100,000 population) from cerebrovascular diseases by sex and disease type : Japan 372

Table 5.28 Trends in deaths, percent distribution, crude death rates and age-adjusted death rates (per 100,000 population) from heart diseases by sex and disease type : Japan 374

Table 5.29 Trends in deaths and death rates (per 100,000 population) by causes (the list of infectious diseases) : Japan 378

Table 5.30 Trends in deaths and death rates (per 100,000 population) from accidents by external causes : Japan 382

Table 5.31 Deaths from accidents by age and external causes : Japan, 2016 384

Table 5.32 Percent distribution of deaths from accidents by age and external causes : Japan, 2016 385

Table 5.33 Trends in deaths and percent distribution from transportation accidents by external causes : Japan 386

Table 5.34 Deaths and percent distribution from nontransportation accidents by age and place of occurrence : Japan, 2016 388

Table 5.35 Deaths and percent distribution from accidents at home by age and external causes : Japan, 2016 389

Table 5.36 Trends in deaths and percent distribution from suicide by sex and external causes : Japan 390

Table 5.37 Trends in maternal deaths and maternal mortality rates (per 100,000 total births) by causes of death : Japan 394

Table 5.38 Trends in late maternal deaths and late maternal mortality rates (per 100,000 total births) by causes of death : Japan 395

Table 5.39 Trends in maternal deaths and maternal mortality rates (per 100,000 total births) by each prefecture : Japan 396

Chapter 6　Infant mortality

[Trends in infant deaths]

Table　6.　1　Trends in infant deaths, infant mortality rates (per 1,000 live births), sex ratio and proportion of infant deaths to total deaths : Japan ·················· 398

Table　6.　2　Trends in neonatal deaths, neonatal mortality rates (per 1,000 live births), sex ratio and proportion of neonatal deaths to infant deaths : Japan ·············· 400

[Infant deaths by age]

Table　6.　3　Infant mortality rates (per 100,000 live births) and percent distribution by sex and age (days, weeks and months) : Japan, 2016 ·············· 402

Table　6.　4　Trends in infant mortality rates (per 100,000 live births) by sex and age (days, weeks and months) : Japan ···················· 404

[Infant deaths by month]

Table　6.　5　Trends in infant deaths and infant mortality rates (per 1,000 live births) by month : Japan ························· 406

Table　6.　6　Live births, infant deaths and infant mortality rates (per 1,000 live births) by months of birth : Japan ··················· 408

[Infant deaths by place of occurrence]

Table　6.　7　Trends in infant deaths and percent distribution by place of occurrence : Japan ···················· 409

Table　6.　8　Percent distribution of infant deaths by place of occurrence : Japan, each prefecture and 21 major cities, 2016 ··················· 410

[Infant deaths by type of occupation of household]

Table　6.　9　Infant deaths, infant mortality rates (per 1,000 live births) and percent distribution by type of occupation of household : Japan, 2016 ··················· 411

[Infant deaths by prefecture]

Table　6.10　Trends in infant deaths by each prefecture : Japan ··················· 412

Table　6.11　Trends in infant mortality rates (per 1,000 live births) by each prefecture : Japan ··················· 414

Table　6.12　Infant mortality rates (per 100,000 live births) by age and proportion of neonatal deaths : Japan, each prefecture and 21 major cities, 2016 ··················· 416

[Causes of infant death]

Table　6.13　Trends in infant deaths and infant mortality rates (per 100,000 live births) by causes (the list of causes of infant death) : Japan ··················· 418

Table　6.14　Infant deaths and infant mortality rates (per 100,000 live births) by age and causes (the list of causes of infant death) : Japan, 2016 ··················· 420

Table　6.15　Percent distribution of infant deaths by age and causes (the list of causes of infant death) : Japan, 2016 ··················· 422

Table　6.16　Trends in leading causes of neonatal and infant death : Japan ··················· 424

Table　6.17　Infant mortality rates (per 100,000 live births) by causes (the list of causes of infant death) : Japan, each prefecture and 21 major cities, 2016 ·········· 432

[Infant deaths by diseases]

Table　6.18　Infant deaths and infant mortality rates (per 100,000 live births) by diseases, causes (the list of causes of infant death) and birth weight : Japan, 2016 ··········· 436

Table　6.19　Neonatal deaths and neonatal mortality rates (per 100,000 live births) by diseases, causes (the list of causes of infant death) and birth weight : Japan, 2016 ··················· 440

Chapter 7　Foetal mortality

[Trends in foetal death]

Table　7. 1　Trends in foetal deaths, foetal death rates （per 1,000 total births） and sex ratio : Japan ⋯⋯⋯⋯⋯⋯⋯⋯⋯⋯⋯⋯⋯ 444

Table　7. 2　Trends in foetal deaths by type of extraction : Japan, urban／rural residence ⋯⋯⋯⋯⋯⋯⋯⋯⋯⋯⋯⋯⋯⋯ 446

Table　7. 3　Trends in foetal death rates （per 1,000 total births） by type of extraction and proportion of artificial intervention : Japan, urban／rural residence ⋯⋯⋯ 447

Table　7. 4　Trends in foetal deaths, foetal death rates at 22 completed weeks and over of gestation and proportion by type of extraction : Japan ⋯⋯⋯⋯⋯⋯ 448

[Foetal deaths by period of gestation]

Table　7. 5　Trends in foetal deaths and percent distribution by period of gestation and type of extraction : Japan ⋯⋯⋯⋯⋯⋯⋯⋯⋯⋯⋯ 450

[Foetal deaths by month]

Table　7. 6　Trends in foetal deaths and foetal death rates （per 1,000 total births） by type of extraction by month : Japan ⋯⋯⋯⋯⋯⋯⋯⋯⋯ 452

[Foetal deaths by place of delivery]

Table　7. 7　Trends in foetal deaths and percent distribution by place of delivery and type of extraction : Japan ⋯⋯⋯⋯⋯⋯⋯⋯⋯⋯⋯ 456

[Foetal deaths by age of mother （5-year age groups）]

Table　7. 8　Foetal death rates （per 1,000 total births） by age of mother, type of extraction and type of occupation of household : Japan, 2016 ⋯⋯⋯⋯⋯⋯⋯⋯ 458

[Foetal deaths by legitimacy status]

Table　7. 9　Foetal deaths and percent distribution by legitimacy status, type of extraction and period of gestation : Japan, 2016 ⋯⋯⋯⋯⋯⋯⋯⋯⋯ 460

Table　7. 10　Trends in foetal deaths at 22 completed weeks and over of gestation and percent distribution by legitimacy status : Japan ⋯⋯⋯⋯⋯⋯⋯⋯ 461

[Foetal deaths by prefecture]

Table　7. 11　Foetal deaths and percent distribution by place of delivery : Japan, urban／rural residence, each prefecture and 21 major cities, 2016 ⋯⋯⋯⋯ 462

Table　7. 12　Trends in foetal deaths by each prefecture : Japan ⋯⋯⋯⋯⋯⋯⋯ 464

Table　7. 13　Trends in foetal death rates （per 1,000 total births） by each prefecture : Japan ⋯⋯⋯⋯⋯⋯⋯⋯⋯⋯⋯⋯⋯⋯ 466

Table　7. 14　Trends in spontaneous foetal deaths by each prefecture : Japan ⋯⋯⋯⋯ 468

Table　7. 15　Trends in spontaneous foetal death rates （per 1,000 total births） by each prefecture : Japan ⋯⋯⋯⋯⋯⋯⋯⋯⋯⋯⋯ 470

Table　7. 16　Trends in artificial foetal deaths by each prefecture : Japan ⋯⋯⋯⋯⋯ 472

Table　7. 17　Trends in artificial foetal death rates （per 1,000 total births） by each prefecture : Japan ⋯⋯⋯⋯⋯⋯⋯⋯⋯⋯⋯⋯ 474

[Causes of foetal death]

Table　7. 18　Foetal deaths and percent distribution by causes : Japan, 2016 ⋯⋯⋯⋯ 476

Table　7. 19　Foetal deaths and percent distribution of spontaneous by causes on child and maternal condition : Japan, 2016 ⋯⋯⋯⋯⋯⋯⋯⋯⋯ 480

Chapter 8　Perinatal mortality

[Trends in perinatal deaths]

Table　8. 1　Trends in perinatal deaths by sex : Japan ⋯⋯⋯⋯⋯⋯⋯⋯⋯⋯⋯ 484

Table 8. 2 Trends in perinatal death rates by sex : Japan ……………………………………… 485

[Perinatal deaths by month]

Table 8. 3 Trends in perinatal deaths and perinatal death rates by month : Japan ………… 486

[Perinatal deaths by birth weight]

Table 8. 4 Trends in perinatal deaths and percent distribution by birth weight : Japan ……………………………………………………………………… 488

Table 8. 5 Perinatal deaths, perinatal death rates and percent distribution by sex and birth weight : Japan, 2016 ……………………………………………… 489

[Perinatal deaths by age of mother (5-year age groups)]

Table 8. 6 Trends in perinatal deaths and perinatal death rates by age of mother : Japan ……………………………………………………………………… 490

Table 8. 7 Perinatal deaths by age of mother and type of occupation of household : Japan, 2016 ………………………………………………………………… 491

Table 8. 8 Perinatal death rates by age of mother and type of occupation of household : Japan, 2016 ………………………………………………………………… 492

Table 8. 9 Perinatal deaths and perinatal death rates by sex and age of mother : Japan, 2016 ………………………………………………………………… 493

[Perinatal deaths by plurality of birth and birth order]

Table 8.10 Perinatal deaths and perinatal death rates by plurality of birth and birth order : Japan, 2016 …………………………………………………… 494

[Perinatal deaths by prefecture]

Table 8.11 Perinatal deaths, perinatal death rates and proportion of foetal deaths at 22 completed weeks and over of gestation : Japan, each prefecture and 21 major cities, 2016 …………………………………………………… 495

Table 8.12 Trends in perinatal deaths by each prefecture : Japan ………………………… 496

Table 8.13 Trends in perinatal death rates by each prefecture : Japan …………………… 500

[Causes of perinatal death]

Table 8.14 Perinatal deaths and percent distribution by maternal condition and causes on child (the list of three-character categories) : Japan, 2016 ……………… 504

Chapter 9 Marriages

[Marriages by prefecture]

Table 9. 1 Trends in marriages by each prefecture : Japan ………………………………… 512

Table 9. 2 Trends in marriage rates (per 1,000 population) by each prefecture : Japan ……………………………………………………………………… 514

[Marriages by month of registration]

Table 9. 3 Trends in number and percent distribution of marriages by month of registration : Japan ……………………………………………………… 516

[Marriages by previous marital status of bride and groom]

Table 9. 4 Trends in marriages by previous marital status of bride and groom, and percentage of remarriages : Japan ……………………………………… 518

Table 9. 5 Trends in number and percent distribution of marriages by number of marriages of bride and groom : Japan ……………………………………… 520

Table 9. 6 Trends in percent distribution of remarriages by period between termination of the last marriage and remarriage (for marriages performed and registered each year) : Japan ……………………………………………………… 522

[Marriages by age]

Table 9. 7 Trends in marriages by age for first married and remarried (for marriages performed and registered each year) : Japan 524

Table 9. 8 Trends in first married rates and remarried rates (per 1,000 population) of marriages by age (for marriages performed and registered each year) : Japan 528

Table 9. 9 Marriages and percent distribution by marriage order and age at marriage (for marriages performed and registered in 2016) : Japan, 2016 530

Table 9. 10 Percent distribution of marriages by marriage order and age at marriage (for marriages performed and registered in 2016) : Japan, 2016 532

Table 9. 11 Trends in mean age of bride and groom at marriage and difference in mean age between bride and groom : Japan 534

Table 9. 12 Trends in mean age of bride and groom at marriage (for first marriage) by each prefecture (for marriages performed and registered each year) : Japan 536

Table 9. 13 First marriages and percent distribution by age of bride and groom (for marriages performed and registered in 2016) : Japan, 2016 540

Table 9. 14 Trends in first marriages and percent distribution by difference in age between bride and groom (for marriages performed and registered each year) : Japan 542

[Marriages by type of occupation of household before marriage]

Table 9. 15 First marriages and percent distribution by type of occupation of household before marriage (for marriages performed and registered in 2016) : Japan, 2016 543

[Marriages by period between marriage and registration]

Table 9. 16 Percentage of marriages by period between marriage and registration : Japan 544

Table 9. 17 Cumulative percentage of marriages by period between marriage and registration : Japan 545

[Marriages by nationality of bride and groom]

Table 9. 18 Trends in marriages by nationality of bride and groom : Japan 546

Table 9. 19 Trends in percent distribution of marriages by nationality of bride and groom : Japan 548

Table 9. 20 Marriages by nationality of bride and groom : Japan, each prefecture and 21 major cities, 2016 550

Table 9. 21 Percent distribution of marriages by nationality of bride and groom : Japan, each prefecture and 21 major cities, 2016 552

Chapter 10 Divorces

[Divorces by prefecture]

Table 10. 1 Trends in divorces by each prefecture : Japan 554

Table 10. 2 Trends in divorce rates (per 1,000 population) by each prefecture : Japan 556

[Divorces by month of registration]

Table 10. 3 Trends in divorces and percent distribution by month of registration : Japan 558

[Divorces by legal type]

Table 10. 4 Trends in divorces and percent distribution by legal type : Japan 560

[Divorces by duration of cohabitation and age of wife and husband at end of cohabitation]

Table 10. 5 　Trends in divorces and percent distribution by duration of cohabitation, and mean duration of cohabitation : Japan ⋯⋯⋯⋯ 562

Table 10. 6 　Trends in divorces by age of wife and husband at time of decree (for divorces separated and registered each year) : Japan ⋯⋯⋯⋯ 564

Table 10. 7 　Trends in divorce rates (per 1,000 population) by age of wife and husband at time of decree (for divorces separated and registered each year) : Japan ⋯⋯⋯⋯ 566

Table 10. 8 　Divorces and percent distribution by age of wife and husband at time of decree (for divorces separated and registered in 2016) : Japan, 2016 ⋯⋯⋯⋯ 568

[Divorces by number of children involved in divorce]

Table 10. 9 　Trends in divorces and percent distribution by number of children involved in divorce : Japan ⋯⋯⋯⋯ 570

Table 10.10 　Trends in divorces and percent distribution by wife and husband who have children involved in divorce : Japan ⋯⋯⋯⋯ 571

Table 10.11 　Trends in divorces and percent distribution by number of children and custody of wife and husband : Japan ⋯⋯⋯⋯ 572

[Divorces by type of occupation of household at time of decree]

Table 10.12 　Divorces and percent distribution by duration of cohabitation, by type of occupation of household : Japan, 2016 ⋯⋯⋯⋯ 573

[Divorces by nationality of wife and husband]

Table 10.13 　Trends in divorces and percent distribution by nationality of wife and husband : Japan ⋯⋯⋯⋯ 574

Table 10.14 　Divorces by nationality of wife and husband : Japan, each prefecture and 21 major cities, 2016 ⋯⋯⋯⋯ 576

Table 10.15 　Percent distribution of divorces by nationality of wife and husband : Japan, each prefecture and 21 major cities, 2016 ⋯⋯⋯⋯ 578

Appendix Population Table

Table 1 　Population by sex : Japan ⋯⋯⋯⋯ 580

Table 2 　Estimated population by month (as of first day of each month) : Japan ⋯⋯⋯⋯ 582

Table 3 　Trends in population by sex and age : Japan ⋯⋯⋯⋯ 583

Table 4 　Trends in population by sex : Japan, each prefecture ⋯⋯⋯⋯ 586

Table 5 　Total population by sex : 21 major cities ⋯⋯⋯⋯ 592

Reference Table

1　List of death

Table 1 　Condensed list of causes of death for Japan ⋯⋯⋯⋯ 595

Table 2 　Selected list of causes of death for Japan ⋯⋯⋯⋯ 596

Table 3 　List for trends in causes of death ⋯⋯⋯⋯ 597

Table 4 　List of causes of infant death ⋯⋯⋯⋯ 598

Table 5-1 　List of infectious diseases (2016) ⋯⋯⋯⋯ 599

Table 5-2 　List of infectious diseases (2015) ⋯⋯⋯⋯ 600

Table 5-3 　List of infectious diseases (2013-2014) ⋯⋯⋯⋯ 601

Table 5-4 　List of infectious diseases (2012) ⋯⋯⋯⋯ 602

Table 5-5 　List of infectious diseases (2008-2011) ⋯⋯⋯⋯ 603

Table 5-6 　List of infectious diseases (2007) ⋯⋯⋯⋯ 604

Table 5-7 　List of infectious diseases (2006) ⋯⋯⋯⋯ 605

Table 5-8 　List of infectious diseases (2003-2005) ⋯⋯⋯⋯ 606

Table	5-9	List of infectious diseases (1999-2002)	607
Table	6-1	Categories for ranking of causes of death (since 1995)	608
Table	6-2	Categories for ranking of causes of death (1979-1994)	609

2　Trends in death and birth

Table	1-1	Deaths and death rates (per 100,000 population) by sex and causes of death : Japan, 2006 and 2005	610
Table	1-2	Deaths and death rates (per 100,000 population) by sex and causes of death : Japan, 1995 and 1994	614
Table	1-3	Deaths and death rates (per 100,000 population) by sex and causes of death (the 117 rubrics list) : Japan, 1980, 1985, 1990, 1992-1994	618
Table	2-1	Infant deaths and infant mortality rates (per 100,000 live births) by causes of death : Japan, 1995 and 1994	630
Table	2-2	Infant deaths and infant mortality rates (per 100,000 live births) by causes of death (the 54 rubrics list) : Japan, 1980, 1985, 1990, 1992-1994	632
Table	3-1	Trends in deaths and death rates (per 100,000 population) by causes of death (the list of infectious diseases revised in 2015) : Japan, 2015	634
Table	3-2	Trends in deaths and death rates (per 100,000 population) by causes of death (the list of infectious diseases revised in 2013) : Japan, 2013 and 2014	638
Table	3-3	Trends in deaths and death rates (per 100,000 population) by causes of death (the list of infectious diseases revised in 2012) : Japan, 2012	642
Table	3-4	Trends in deaths and death rates (per 100,000 population) by causes of death (the list of infectious diseases revised in 2008) : Japan, 2008-2011	646
Table	3-5	Trends in deaths and death rates (per 100,000 population) by causes of death (the list of infectious diseases revised in 2007) : Japan, 2007	650
Table	3-6	Trends in deaths and death rates (per 100,000 population) by causes of death (the list of infectious diseases revised in 2006) : Japan, 2006	654
Table	3-7	Trends in deaths and death rates (per 100,000 population) by causes of death (the list of infectious diseases revised in 2003) : Japan, 2003-2005	656
Table	3-8	Trends in deaths and death rates (per 100,000 population) by causes of death (the list of infectious diseases revised in 1999) : Japan, 1999-2002	658
Table	4	Trends in perinatal deaths by sex : Japan	660
Table	5	Trends in foetal deaths, foetal death ratio at 28 completed weeks and over of gestation (per 1,000 live births) and proportion by type of extraction : Japan	662
Table	6	Total fertility rates : Japan	664

VITAL STATISTICS OF JAPAN, 2016, VOLUME 2
CONTENTS

Statistical Tables
Summary
Table 1. Summary tables of vital statistics : Japan, each prefecture and 21 major cities*

Table 2. Summary tables of vital statistics : each prefecture, each health center and each municipality (city, town, village)*

Natality
Table 1. Live births by place of delivery, for urban/rural residence : Japan, each prefecture and 21 major cities*

Table 2. Live births by sex and month : Japan, urban/rural residence, each prefecture and 21 major cities*

Table 3. Live births by sex and birth order : Japan, each prefecture and 21 major cities*

Table 4. Live births by sex, month of birth, age of mother and live birth order : Japan

Table 5. Live births by sex and age of mother : Japan, each prefecture and 21 major cities*

Table 6. Live births by sex, age of mother and birth order : Japan

Table 7. Live births by sex, single years of age of mother, live birth order and legitimacy status : Japan

Table 8. Live births born in wedlock by single years of age of father and mother, and live birth order : Japan

Table 9. Live births born in wedlock by year marriage performed, single years of age of mother and live birth order : Japan

Table 10. Live births by age of mother, live birth order and type of occupation of household : Japan

Table 11. Live births distributed according to birth weight and mean birth weight, by sex and plurality of birth : Japan, each prefecture and 21 major cities*

Table 12. Live births distributed according to birth weight and mean birth weight, by sex, age of mother and plurality of birth : Japan

Table 13. Live births distributed according to birth weight and mean birth weight, by sex, birth order and plurality of birth : Japan

Table 14. Live births distributed according to birth weight and mean birth weight, by sex, period of gestation and plurality of birth : Japan

Table 15. Live births distributed according to birth weight and mean birth weight, by sex, legitimacy status and age of mother : Japan

Table 16. Live births distributed according to birth length and mean birth length by sex : Japan, each prefecture and 21 major cities*

Table 17. Live births born in wedlock by duration of marriage, single years of age of mother and live birth order : Japan

Table 18. Live births by legitimacy status, sex and age of mother : Japan and urban/rural residence

General mortality
Table 1. Deaths, infant deaths (under 1 year), neonatal deaths (under 4 weeks) and early neonatal deaths (under 1 week), by place of occurrence, for urban/rural residence : Japan, each prefecture and 21 major cities*

Table 2. Deaths by sex and month of occurrence : Japan, urban/rural residence, each prefecture and 21 major cities*

Table 3. Deaths by sex and age : Japan, each prefecture and 21 major cities*

Table 4. Deaths by sex and single years of age : Japan, each prefecture and 21 major cities*

Table 5. Deaths by sex, month of occurrence, birth year and age of decedent (single years of age) : Japan

Table 6. Deaths by sex, age and type of occupation of household : Japan

Table 7. Deaths 15 years and over by sex, age and marital status : Japan

Table 8. Deaths by sex, place of occurrence and age : Japan

Infant mortality

Table 1. Infant deaths (under 1 year), neonatal deaths (under 4 weeks) by sex and month of occurrence : Japan, urban/rural residence, each prefecture and 21 major cities*

Table 2. Infant deaths (under 1 year) by age and sex : Japan, urban/rural residence, each prefecture and 21 major cities*

Table 3. Infant deaths (under 1 year) by age, sex and type of occupation of household : Japan

Table 4. Infant deaths (under 1 year) by month of occurrence and date of birth : Japan

Table 5. Infant deaths (under 1 year) from diseases, birth weight and mean birth weight by sex, plurality of birth and age of mother : Japan

Table 6. Infant deaths (under 1 year) from diseases, birth weight and mean birth weight by sex, plurality of birth and birth order : Japan

Table 7. Infant deaths (under 1 year) from diseases, birth weight and mean birth weight by sex and period of gestation : Japan

Foetal mortality

Table 1. Foetal deaths by place of delivery for urban/rural residence : Japan, each prefecture and 21 major cities*

Table 2. Foetal deaths by type of extraction and place of delivery : Japan, urban/rural residence, each prefecture and 21 major cities*

Table 3. Foetal deaths by type of extraction and month of occurrence : Japan, urban/rural residence, each prefecture and 21 major cities*

Table 4−1. Foetal deaths by type of extraction and period of gestation (by every 4 weeks) for urban/rural residence : Japan, each prefecture and 21 major cities*

Table 4−2. Foetal deaths by type of extraction and specified period of gestation for urban/rural residence : Japan, each prefecture and 21 major cities*

Table 5−1. Foetal deaths by sex, period of gestation (by every 4 weeks), type of extraction and legitimacy status : Japan

Table 5−2. Foetal deaths by sex, specified period of gestation, type of extraction and legitimacy status : Japan

Table 6. Foetal deaths by type of extraction, age of mother and type of occupation of household : Japan

Table 7. Foetal deaths at 22 completed weeks and over of gestation by sex and age of mother : Japan, each prefecture and 21 major cities*

Table 8. Foetal deaths at 22 completed weeks and over of gestation by type of extraction, place of delivery and time of foetal deaths : Japan, urban/rural residence, each prefecture and 21 major cities*

Table 9. Foetal deaths at 22 completed weeks and over of gestation by type of extraction, sex, age of mother and birth order : Japan

Perinatal mortality

Table 1. Perinatal deaths (foetal deaths at 22 completed weeks and over of gestation, early neonatal deaths) by sex and month of occurrence : Japan, urban/rural residence, each prefecture and 21 major cities*

Table 2. Perinatal deaths (foetal deaths at 22 completed weeks and over of gestation, early neonatal deaths) by sex, birth weight and mean birth weight : Japan, each prefecture and 21 major cities*

Table 3. Perinatal deaths (foetal deaths at 22 completed weeks and over of gestation, early neonatal deaths), birth weight and mean birth weight by sex, plurality of birth and age of mother : Japan

Table 4. Perinatal deaths (foetal deaths at 22 completed weeks and over of gestation, early neonatal deaths), birth weight and mean birth weight by sex, plurality of birth and birth order : Japan

Table 5. Perinatal deaths (foetal deaths at 22 completed weeks and over of gestation, early neonatal deaths), birth weight and mean birth weight by sex, plurality of birth and period of gestation : Japan

Marriages

Table 1. Marriages by month of registration : Japan, each prefecture and 21 major cities*

Table 2. Marriages by month of registration by month and year marriage performed : Japan and total of 21 major cities*

Table 3. Marriages (performed and registered in 2016) by month of registration, age of bride and groom at marriage performed, by marriage order : Japan

Table 4. Marriages by previous marital status of bride and groom : Japan, each prefecture and 21 major cities*

Table 5. Marriages by single years of age of bride and groom, by marriage order of bride and groom (for marriages performed and registered in 2016) : Japan

Table 6. Mean age of bride and groom at marriage and marriages by single years of age of bride and groom, by marriage order (for marriages performed and registered in 2016) : Japan, each prefecture and 21 major cities*

Table 7. Remarriages of bride and groom, by previous marital status, by year of termination of last marriage, and single years of age at termination of last marriage : Japan

Table 8. Marriages by marriage order and nationality of bride and groom : Japan

Divorces

Table 1. Divorces by month of registration : Japan, each prefecture and 21 major cities*

Table 2. Divorces by month of registration by month and year cohabitation terminated : Japan

Table 3. Divorces by single years of age of husband and wife (for divorces separated and registered in 2016) : Japan

Table 4. Divorces by legal type : Japan, each prefecture and 21 major cities*

Table 5. Divorces by legal type, duration of marriage and type of occupation of household : Japan

Table 6. Divorces by age of husband and wife and duration of marriage (for divorces separated and registered in 2016) : Japan

Table 7. Divorces by number of children involved in divorce and number of children who are to be in wife's custody (all divorces and divorces separated and registered in 2016) : Japan

Table 8. Divorces by duration of marriage and number of children involved in divorce (all divorces and divorces separated and registered in 2016) : Japan

【Delayed registrations for Japanese in Japan】
Natality
    Table 1.   Delayed registrations of live births, by sex and year of birth : Japan, each prefecture and 21 major cities**

General mortality
    Table 1.   Delayed registrations of deaths, by sex and year of death : Japan, each prefecture and 21 major cities**

【Foreigners in Japan】
Natality
    Table 1.   Live births born in wedlock by nationality of father and mother
    Table 2.   Live births by sex, month of occurrence and nationality of mother
    Table 3.   Live births born in wedlock by nationality of father, each prefecture and 21 major cities*
    Table 4.   Live births by nationality of mother, each prefecture and 21 major cities*
    Table 5.   Live births, mean age of mother, by nationality and age of mother

General mortality
    Table 1.   Deaths by sex, month of occurrence and nationality
    Table 2.   Deaths by sex, place of occurrence and nationality
    Table 3.   Deaths by nationality, each prefecture and 21 major cities*
    Table 4.   Deaths by sex, age and nationality

Infant mortality
    Table 1.   Infant deaths (under 1 year) by sex, month of occurrence and nationality

Foetal motality
    Table 1.   Foetal deaths by month of occurrence, sex and nationality of mother
    Table 2.   Foetal deaths by type of extraction, age of mother and specified period of gestation

Marriages and Divorces
    Table 1.   Marriages by nationality of bride and groom
    Table 2.   Mean ages, marriages and their percent distribution, of bride and groom (for first marriages and remarriages performed and registered in 2016)
    Table 3.   Divorces and their percent distribution, by legal type
    Table 4.   Divorces by nationality of wife and husband

【Japanese in foreign countries】
Natality, General mortality, Infant mortality, Marriages and Divorces
    Table 1.   Live births, deaths and infant deaths (under 1 year), by sex and month of occurrence
    Table 2.   Mean ages, marriages and their percent distribution, of bride and groom (for first marriages and remarriages performed and registered in 2016)
    Table 3.   Divorces and their percent distribution, by legal type
    Table 4.   Deaths by sex and age

【Delayed registrations for foreigners in Japan】
Natality, General mortality, Infant mortality and Foetal mortality
    Table 1.   Live births, deaths, infant deaths (under 1 year) and foetal deaths, by sex, year of occurrence and nationality

【Delayed registrations for Japanese in foreign countries】
Natality, General mortality and Infant mortality
    Table 1.   Live births, deaths and infant deaths (under 1 year), by sex and year of occurrence
        *   Reported as place of residence.
        **   Reported as place of registration.

VITAL STATISTICS OF JAPAN, 2016, VOLUME 3
CONTENTS

Explanation of structure and list of statistical classification of causes of death in Japan
Structure of the international statistical classification of diseases, injuries and causes of death
List of statistical classification of diseases, injuries and causes of death for Japan

1. The detailed list of statistical classification of diseases, injuries and causes of death
   (ICD－10　adapted for use in Japan)
2. Condensed list of causes of death for Japan
3. Selected list of causes of death for Japan
4. List of causes of infant death
5. List of infectious diseases

Causes of death

(General mortality)

Table 1－1.　Deaths by causes (the list of three-character categories), sex and age：Japan

Table 1－2.　Deaths by causes (the list of four-character categories) and sex：Japan

Table 2.　　Deaths by causes (the condensed list of causes of death for Japan), sex and age：Japan

Table 3.　　Deaths by causes (the condensed list of causes of death for Japan), sex and month of occurrence：Japan

Table 4.　　Deaths by causes (the condensed list of causes of death for Japan) and sex：Japan, each prefecture and 21 major cities*

Table 5.　　Deaths by causes (the condensed list of causes of death for Japan), sex and place of occurrence：Japan

Table 6.　　Deaths by causes (the selected list of causes of death for Japan), sex for specified age groups and type of occupation of household：Japan

Table 7.　　Deaths 15 years and over by causes (the selected list of causes of death for Japan), sex for specified age groups and marital status：Japan

Table 8.　　Deaths by causes (the list of infectious diseases)：Japan, each prefecture and 21 major cities*

Table 9.　　Deaths from nontransportation accidents for specified age groups by place of occurrence and causes of death (W00－X59, the list of three-character categories)：Japan

Table 10.　 Deaths from external causes by external factors and sex for specified age groups：Japan

Table 11.　 Deaths from traffic accidents by age and sex for place of accidents：Japan, each prefecture and 21 major cities**

(Infant mortality)

Table 1.　　Infant deaths (under 1 year) by causes (the list of causes of infant death), sex and age：Japan

Table 2.　　Infant deaths (under 1 year) and neonatal deaths (under 4 weeks) by causes (the list of causes of infant death) and sex：Japan, each prefecture and 21 major cities*

Table 3.　　Infant deaths (under 1 year) and neonatal deaths (under 4 weeks) by causes (the list of causes of infant death), sex and month of occurrence：Japan

Table 4. Infant deaths (under 1 year), neonatal deaths (under 4 weeks) and early neonatal deaths (under 1 week) from diseases by causes (the list of causes of infant death), sex and birth weight : Japan

Table 5. Infant deaths (under 1 year), neonatal deaths (under 4 weeks) and early neonatal deaths (under 1 week) from diseases by causes (the list of causes of infant death), sex and specified period of gestation : Japan

(Foetal mortality)

Table 1. Foetal deaths by causes (the list of three-character categories), age of mother : Japan

Table 2. Foetal deaths by causes (the list of three-character categories), specified period of gestation : Japan

Table 3. Foetal deaths at 22 completed weeks and over of gestation by causes (the list of three-character categories) and birth weight : Japan

(Perinatal mortality)

Table 1. Perinatal deaths (foetal deaths at 22 completed weeks and over of gestation, early neonatal deaths) by maternal condition and causes on child (the list of three-character categories) : Japan

【Foreigners in Japan】
【Japanese in foreign countries】

Table 1. Deaths of foreigners in Japan, nationality and of Japanese in foreign countries, by sex and causes (the condensed list of causes of death for Japan)

Table 2. Infant deaths (under 1 year) of foreigners in Japan, nationality and of Japanese in foreign countries, by sex and causes (the list of causes of infant death)

     *   Reported as place of residence.
     * * Reported as place of occurrence.

The tables shown in Vital Statistics Vol.1,2,3 are also available online at the Portal Site of Official Statistics of Japan "e-Stat".

Preserved Statistic tables (Not included in "Vital Statistics")

(Natality)

Table 1. Live births by place of delivery and person present at delivery : Japan, urban/rural residence, each prefecture and 21 major cities

Table 2. Live births (plural birth only) by sex, type of plurality and plurality order : Japan

Table 3. Live births (plural birth only) by type of plurality : Japan, each prefecture and 21 major cities

Table 4. Live births by sex, birth weight (100g groups), period of gestation (by week) and plurality of birth : Japan

Table 5. Live births distributed according to birth weight and mean birth weight by sex, age of mother and birth order : Japan

Table 6. Live births distributed according to birth weight and mean birth weight by sex, age of mother and live birth order : Japan

Table 7. Live births by year, month, date and hour of birth and place of delivery : Japan

Table 8. Live births by month and birth year and age of mother : Japan

Table 9. Live births by sex, live birth order, birth order and age of mother : Japan

Table 10. Live births by sex and live birth order : Japan, each prefecture and 21 major cities

Table 11. Live births born in wedlock by age of father and type of occupation of household : Japan

Table 12. Live births distributed according to birth weight and mean birth weight by sex, plurality of birth, age of mother and type of occupation of household : Japan

Table 13. Live births distributed according to birth length and mean birth length by sex, plurality of birth and period of gestation : Japan

Table 14. Live births by sex, birth length and period of gestation (by week) : Japan

Table 15. Live births by sex, birth length and birth weight (100g groups) : Japan

Table 16. Live births born in wedlock (non-Japanese father, Japanese mother) by sex and nationality of father : Japan, each prefecture and 21 major cities

Table 17. Live births born in wedlock (non-Japanese father, Japanese mother) by sex, month, and nationality of father : Japan

Table 18. Live births born in wedlock (non-Japanese father, Japanese mother) by single years of age of father and mother : Japan

Table 19. Live births born in wedlock (Japanese father, non-Japanese mother) by sex and nationality of mother : Japan, each prefecture and 21 major cities

Table 20. Live births born in wedlock (Japanese father, non-Japanese mother) by sex, month and nationality of mother : Japan

Table 21. Live births born in wedlock (Japanese father, non-Japanese mother) by single years of age of father and mother : Japan

(General mortality)

Table 1.   Deaths 15 years with spouse and over by sex, age and age of spouse : Japan

(Infant mortality)

Table 1.   Infant deaths (under 1 year) from diseases, birth weight and mean birth weight by sex and plurality of birth : Japan, each prefecture and 21 major cities

(Foetal mortality)

Table 1.   Foetal deaths by birth weight, sex, plurality of birth, type of extraction and period of gestation (by every 4 weeks) : Japan

Table 2.   Foetal deaths by birth weight, sex, plurality of birth, type of extraction and specified period of gestation : Japan

Table 3.   Foetal deaths by birth weight (100g groups), plurality of birth, type of extraction and period of gestation (by week) : Japan

Table 4.   Foetal deaths by birth length (1cm groups), plurality of birth, type of extraction and period of gestation (by week) : Japan

Table 5.   Foetal deaths at 22 completed weeks and over of gestation by sex, birth weight (100g groups) and birth length (1cm groups) : Japan

Table 6.   Spontaneous foetal deaths (at 22 completed weeks and over) by time of foetal deaths, period of gestation (by every 4 weeks) and place of delivery : Japan

Table 7.   Spontaneous foetal deaths (at 22 completed weeks and over) by time of foetal deaths, specified period of gestation and place of delivery : Japan

Table 8.   Artificial foetal deaths by period of gestation (by every 4 weeks) and legitimacy status : Japan, each prefecture and 21 major cities

Table 9.   Foetal deaths (plural birth only) by sex and type of plural birth : Japan, each prefecture and 21 major cities

Table 10.   Foetal deaths (plural birth only) by sex, type of plural birth and birth order : Japan

Table 11.   Foetal deaths (non-Japanese father, Japanese mother) by sex, type of extraction and nationality of father : Japan

Table 12.   Foetal deaths (Japanese father, non-Japanese mother) by sex, type of extraction and nationality of mother : Japan

Table 13.   Foetal deaths by place of delivery and attendant at delivery : Japan, urban/rural residence, each prefecture and 21 major cities

Table 14.   Foetal deaths at 22 completed weeks and over of gestation by type of extraction, place of delivery, attendant at delivery and time of foetal deaths : Japan, urban/rural residence, each prefecture and 21 major cities

(Perinatal mortality)

Table 1. Perinatal deaths (foetal deaths at 22 completed weeks and over of gestation, early neonatal deaths) by birth weight (100g groups), plurality of birth and period of gestation (by week) : Japan

Table 2. Perinatal deaths (foetal deaths at 22 completed weeks and over of gestation, early neonatal deaths) by age of mother and type of occupation of household : Japan

Table 3. Perinatal deaths (foetal deaths at 22 completed weeks and over of gestation, early neonatal deaths) (plural birth only) by sex, type of plural birth and birth order : Japan

(Marriages)

Table 1. Marriages by previous marital status of bride and groom and single years of age at registration : Japan

Table 2. Marriages by month of registration, birth year and age of bride and groom

Table 3. Marriages by choice of surname : Japan, each prefecture and 21 major cities － Marriage performed and registered in 2016 (regrouped) －

Table 4. Marriages (performed between 2012 and 2016) by year marriage performed, previous marital status of bride and groom, and single years of age at cohabitation : Japan

Table 5. First marriage (performed and registered in 2016) by type of occupation of household and single years of age of bride and groom at cohabitation : Japan

Table 6. Mean age of first marriage by first marriage (for marriage performed and registered in 2016 (regrouped)) and age of bride and groom at registration : Japan, each prefecture and 21 major cities

Table 7. International marriage between non-Japanese groom and Japanese bride by single years of age of bride and groom at registration : Japan

Table 8. International marriage between Japanese groom and non-Japanese bride by single years of age of bride and groom at registration : Japan

(Divorce)

Table 1. Divorce by single years of age of wife and husband at registration : Japan, each prefecture and 21 major cities

Table 2. Divorce by month of registration and birth year and age of wife and husband : Japan

Table 3. Divorce by month and year of cohabitation and separation : Japan

Table 4. Divorce (separated between 2012 and 2016) by year of separation and single years of age of wife and husband at separation : Japan

Table 5. Divorce by number of children and type of occupation of household at time of separation : Japan

Table 6. Divorce by duration of cohabitation, number of children and type of divorce : Japan

Table 7. Divorce (separated and registered in 2016) by single years of age of wife and husband at separation and type of occupation of household at time of separation : Japan

Table 8. International divorce between non-Japanese husband and Japanese wife by single years of age of wife and husband at registration : Japan

Table 9. International divorce between Japanese husband and non-Japanese wife by single years of age of wife and husband at registration : Japan

(Causes of death)

(General mortality)

Table 1. Deaths by causes (the list of four-character categories), sex and age : Japan

Table 2. Deaths by causes (the condensed list of causes of death for Japan), sex, age and place of occurrence : Japan

Table 3. Deaths by causes (the condensed list of causes of death for Japan), sex, single years of age and enrollment (elementary school, junior high school regrouped) : Japan

Table 4. Deaths by causes (malignant neoplasms, heart diseases, cerebrovascular diseases), sex, age and place of occurrence : Japan, each prefecture and 21 major cities

Table 5. Deaths 15 years and over by causes (the selected list of causes of death for Japan), sex, age and marital status : Japan

Table 6. Deaths 100 years and over by causes (the list of four-character categories), sex and single years of age : Japan

Table 7. Deaths by causes (the list of infectious diseases), sex and month of occurrence : Japan

Table 8. Deaths by causes (the list of infectious diseases) and month of occurrence : Japan, each prefecture and 21 major cities

Table 9. Deaths by causes (the list of infectious diseases), sex and age : Japan

Table 10. Deaths from nontransportation accidents by causes (W00-X59, the list of three-character categories), sex, specified age groups and place of occurrence : Japan

Table 11. Deaths from traffic accidents by external factors, sex, specified age and mode of transport : Japan

Table 12. Deaths with surgery (infant deaths regrouped) by place of occurrence : Japan, urban/rural residence, each prefecture and 21 major cities

Table 13. Deaths with surgery by causes (the condensed list of causes of death for Japan) and sex : Japan, each prefecture and 21 major cities

Table 14. Deaths with surgery by causes (the condensed list of causes of death for Japan), sex and age : Japan

Table 15. Deaths with autopsy (infant deaths regrouped) by place of occurrence : Japan, urban/rural residence, each prefecture and 21 major cities

Table 16. Deaths with autopsy by causes (the condensed list of causes of death for Japan) and sex : Japan, each prefecture and 21 major cities

Table 17. Deaths with autopsy by causes (the condensed list of causes of death for Japan), sex and age : Japan

(**Infant mortality**)

Table 1. Infant deaths (under 1 year) by causes (the list of four-character categories), sex and age : Japan

Table 2. Infant deaths (under 1 year) from diseases by causes (the list of causes of infant death), specified period of gestation, maternal condition (the list of three-character categories) : Japan

Table 3. Infant deaths (under 1 year) from diseases by causes (the list of causes of infant death) and age of mother : Japan

(**Foetal mortality**)

Table 1. Foetal deaths by causes on child and maternal condition (the list of three-character categories), type of extraction, sex and attendant at delivery : Japan

Table 2. Foetal deaths by causes on child (the list of four-character categories), maternal condition and type of extraction : Japan

Table 3. Foetal deaths by causes on child and maternal condition (the list of four-character categories) and type of extraction : Japan

Table 4. Foetal deaths by maternal condition and causes on child (the list of three-character categories), type of extraction and specified period of gestation : Japan

Table 5. Foetal deaths by causes on child and maternal condition (the list of three-character categories), type of extraction and specified period of gestation : Japan

Table 6. Foetal deaths by causes on child (the list of four-character categories), usage of surgery, type of extraction and specified period of gestation : Japan

Table 7. Foetal deaths by causes on child (the list of four-character categories), usage of autopsy, type of extraction and specified period of gestation : Japan

(**Perinatal mortality**)

Table 1. Perinatal deaths (foetal deaths at 22 completed weeks and over of gestation, early neonatal deaths) by causes on child (the list of three-character categories) and maternal condition (the list of four-character categories) : Japan

Table 2. Perinatal deaths (foetal deaths at 22 completed weeks and over of gestation, early neonatal deaths) by causes on child and maternal condition (the list of four-character categories) : Japan

Table 3. Perinatal deaths (foetal deaths at 22 completed weeks and over of gestation, early neonatal deaths) by causes on child and maternal condition (the list of three-character categories) and period of gestation (by every 4 weeks) : Japan

Table 4. Perinatal deaths (foetal deaths at 22 completed weeks and over of gestation (by type of extraction), early neonatal deaths) by causes on child and maternal condition (the list of three-character categories), birth weight and mean birth weight : Japan

Table 5. Perinatal deaths (foetal deaths at 22 completed weeks and over of gestation (by time of foetal deaths), early neonatal deaths) by causes on child (the list of three-character categories) and usage of autopsy : Japan

Preserved Statistic tables by each prefecture

(Natality)

Table 1. Live births by place of delivery and person present at delivery : each prefecture, each health center and each municipality

Table 2. Live births by sex and month of birth : each prefecture and each health center

Table 3. Live births by type of occupation of household : each prefecture and 21 major cities

Table 4. Live births by live birth under 2,500g, sex, single years of age of mother and live birth order : each prefecture and 21 major cities

Table 5. Live births by sex and age of mother : each prefecture, each health center and each municipality

(General mortality・Infant mortality)

Table 1. Deaths by sex and age : each prefecture, each health center and each municipality (city, town, village)

Table 2. Deaths by sex and month of occurrence : each prefecture and each health center

Table 3. Deaths, infant deaths (under 1 year), neonatal deaths (under 4 weeks) and early neonatal deaths (under 1 week) by type of occupation of household : each prefecture and 21 major cities

(Foetal mortality)

Table 1. Foetal deaths by type of extraction, sex and period of gestation : each prefecture and each health center

Table 2. Foetal deaths by type of extraction, period of gestation and age of mother : each prefecture and 21 major cities

(Marriages)

Table 1. Mean age of first marriage by first marriage (for marriage performed and registered in 2016 (regrouped)) and age of bride and groom at cohabitation, and type of occupation of household before marriage : each prefecture and 21 major cities

Table 2. Mean age of first marriage by first marriage (for marriage performed and registered in 2016 (regrouped)) and age of bride and groom at registration, and type of occupation of household before marriage : each prefecture and 21 major cities

(Divorce)

Table 1. Divorce by duration of cohabitation, number of children and type of divorce : each prefecture and 21 major cities

(Causes of death)

Table 1. Deaths by causes (the list of four-character categories) and sex : each prefecture and 21 major cities

Table 2. Deaths by causes (the condensed list of causes of death for Japan), month of occurrence, sex and age : each prefecture and 21 major cities

Table 3. Deaths by causes (the condensed list of causes of death for Japan), sex and month of occurrence : each prefecture and 21 major cities

Table 4. Deaths by causes (the condensed list of causes of death for Japan) and sex : each prefecture and each health center

Table 5. Infant deaths (under 1 year) and neonatal deaths (under 4 weeks) by causes (the list of causes of infant death), sex and month of occurrence : each prefecture and 21 major cities

Table 6. Deaths by causes (the selected list of causes of death for Japan) and sex : each prefecture and each municipality

【Foreigners in Japan】

(Natality)

Table 1. Live births by place of delivery and nationality of mother

Table 2. Live births by mean birth weight and nationality of mother

Table 3. Live births by single years of age of mother and father, and legitimacy status

(Marriage)

Table 1. Marriage by nationality of groom : each prefecture and 21 major cities

Table 2. Marriage by nationality of bride : each prefecture and 21 major cities

Table 3. Marriage by single years of age of bride and groom at registration

(Divorce)

Table 1. Divorce by single years of age of wife and husband at registration

(Causes of death)

(General mortality)

Table 1. Deaths by causes (the selected list of causes of death for Japan), sex, specified age and nationality

42

【Japanese in foreign countries】

Table 1.   Live births in foreign countries (Japanese father and Japanese mother) by sex and month of birth

Table 2.   Live births in foreign countries (non-Japanese father and Japanese mother) by sex, month of birth and nationality of father

Table 3.   Live births in foreign countries (Japanese father and non-Japanese mother) by sex, month of birth and nationality of mother

Table 4.   Delayed registrations of live births in foreign countries (Japanese father and Japanese mother) by sex and month of birth

Table 5.   Marriage of Japanese in foreign countries by nationality of bride and groom

Each prefecture is denoted by the serial number given here. Prefecture is an administrative area over cities, towns and villages.

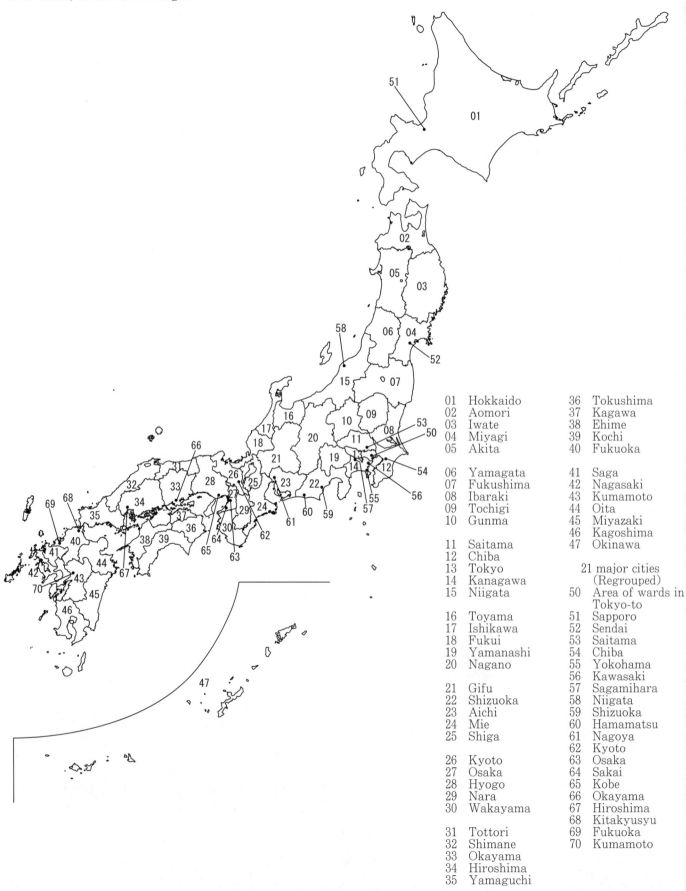

記　　　　　述

DESCRIPTION

(1) 表章記号の規約

Symbols used in tables

－	計数のない場合 Magnitude zero	
…	計数不明の場合 Data not available	
・	統計項目のあり得ない場合 Category not applicable	
0.0, 0.00, 0.0000	比率が微小（0.05未満，0.005未満，0.00005未満）の場合 Figure less than 0.05, less than 0.005, less than 0.00005	
△	減少数（率）の場合 Negative	

(2) 利用上の注意

　　掲載の数値は四捨五入してあるので、内訳の合計が「総数」に合わない場合がある。

Note

　　The figures indicated are rounded off.　Thus, the total may not equal to the "total number".

I 人口動態調査の概要

Part I Outline of Vital Statistics

第1章 調査の概要

1 調査の概要

我が国の人口動態統計は、市区町村長が作成する人口動態調査票に基づいて表章される。すなわち、出生・死亡・婚姻及び離婚については戸籍法（昭和22年法律第224号）による届書等から、死産については死産の届出に関する規程（昭和21年厚生省令第42号）による届書等から人口動態調査票が作成され、これを収集し集計した統計が人口動態統計である。

1）調査の目的

我が国の人口動態事象を把握し、人口及び厚生労働行政施策の基礎資料を得ることを目的とする。

2）調査の沿革

人口動態調査は、明治31年「戸籍法」が制定され登録制度が法体系的にも整備されたのを機会に、同32年から人口動態調査票は1件につき1枚の個別票を作成し、中央集計をする近代的な人口動態統計制度が確立した。

その後、昭和22年6月に「統計法」に基づき「指定統計第5号」として指定され、その事務の所管は同年9月1日に総理庁から厚生省に移管された。さらに、平成21年4月からは、新統計法（平成19年法律第53号）に基づく基幹統計調査となった。

3）調査の対象

人口動態調査は、出生・死亡・婚姻・離婚及び死産の全数を対象としているが、本報告書は、日本において発生した日本人に関して集計したものである。日本人の外国における事象及び外国人の日本における事象については、中巻及び下巻にそれぞれ掲載している。

4）調査の期間

調査該当年の1月1日から同年12月31日までに発生したものであって、調査該当翌年の1月14日までに市区町村長に届け出られたものである。

なお、婚姻や協議離婚は、届書が市区町村長に受理されたことによって発生する。したがって、届出遅れの問題はないが、出生・死亡・死産や調停・審判・和解・請求の認諾・判決による離婚は、発生から届出までに相当の遅れのある場合がある。前年以前に発生した出生・死亡については、中巻に掲載している。

5）調査票の種類及び調査の項目

調査票は、次の5種類である。その様式及び各届書は、別掲（48～57ページ）のとおりである。

人口動態調査出生票　　　人口動態調査死亡票　　　人口動態調査死産票
人口動態調査婚姻票　　　人口動態調査離婚票

調査の項目は、前記5種類の調査票を参照されたい。ただし、職業及び産業の項目については、国勢調査実施年の4月1日から翌年3月31日までについてのみ調査を行う。

6〕調査の方法及び報告の系統

届書の届出義務者及び届出期間は、次のとおりである。

種　別	届　出　義　務　者	届　出　先	届出期間[1]
出　生	1 父又は母　2 同居者　3 出産に立ち会った医師、助産師又はその他の者	市区町村長	14 日
死　亡	1 同居の親族　2 その他の同居者　3 家主、地主又は家屋もしくは土地の管理人　4 同居の親族以外の親族、後見人、保佐人、補助人及び任意後見人		7 日
死　産	1 父又は母　2 同居人　3 死産に立ち会った医師　4 死産に立ち会った助産師　5 その他の立会者		7 日
婚　姻	夫　妻	夫又は妻の本籍地もしくは所在地の市区町村長	規定なし
離　婚	夫　妻		協議離婚は規定なし　調停・審判・和解・請求の認諾・判決離婚は10日

注：1）　出生・死亡及び裁判による離婚は届出事件発生の日から、死産はその日の翌日から起算。

　市区町村長は、出生・死亡・死産・婚姻・離婚の届出を受けたときは、その届書等に基づいて人口動態調査票を作成し、これを保健所の管轄区域によって当該保健所長に送付する。

　保健所長は、市区町村長から提出された調査票を取りまとめ、毎月、都道府県知事に送付する。

　この場合、保健所を設置する市の保健所長は、当該市の市長を経由する。

　都道府県知事は、保健所長から提出された調査票の内容を審査し、厚生労働大臣に送付する。

注：保健所を設置する市とは、地域保健法施行令（昭和23年4月2日政令第77号）第1条に規定する市をいう。

7〕集計及び結果の公表

　集計は厚生労働省政策統括官（統計・情報政策担当）が行い、調査結果は、人口動態統計（速報）、人口動態統計月報（概数）、人口動態統計年報（確定数）として速やかに公表する。

8〕関係法規

　人口動態調査令（昭和21年9月30日勅令第447号）

　人口動態調査令施行細則（昭和23年2月24日厚生省令第6号）

　戸籍法（昭和22年12月22日法律第224号）

　戸籍法施行規則（昭和22年12月29日司法省令第94号）

　出生証明書の様式等を定める省令（昭和27年11月17日法務・厚生省令第1号）

　国籍法（昭和25年5月4日法律第147号）

　死産の届出に関する規程（昭和21年9月30日厚生省令第42号）

　　　ポツダム宣言の受諾に伴い発する命令に関する件に基づく厚生省関係諸命令の措置に関する法律（昭和27年4月28日法律第120号）第3条により法律としての効力を有する。

　死産届書、死産証書及び死胎検案書に関する省令（昭和27年4月28日厚生省令第12号）

2 調査票及び届書

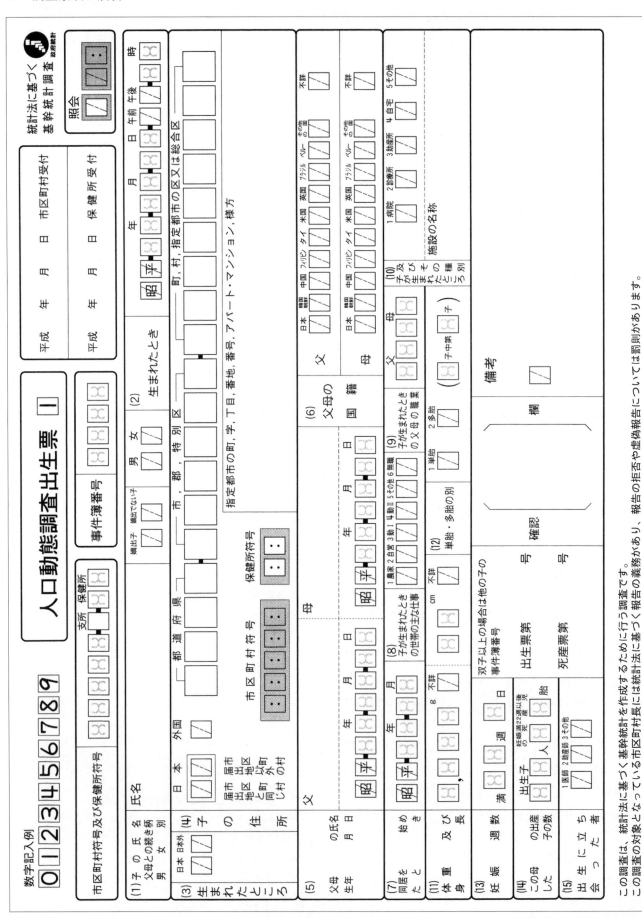

数字記入例 ０１２３４５６７８９

人口動態調査死亡票 ②

平成　年　月　日　市区町村受付
平成　年　月　日　保健所受付

統計法に基づく基幹統計調査　政府統計

照会

市区町村符号及び保健所符号　　　支所　保健所
事件簿番号

(1) 氏　名	(3)	生　年　月　日	(4)	死　亡　し　た　と　き

明大昭平　年　月　日　午前午後　時　分　生年月日不詳
昭平　年　月　日　午前午後　時　分　死亡したとき不詳

(2) 男女別　男　女
(6) 死亡した人の住所　日本　外国　不詳　——都道府県——　市，郡，特別区　　町，村，指定都市の区又は総合区

(5) 死亡したところ　日本　日本外
届出地区町村　届出地区以外の市区町村

市区町村符号　　保健所符号　　指定都市の町，字，丁目，番地，番号，アパート・マンション，様方

(7) 死亡した人の国籍　日本　韓国朝鮮　中国　フィリピン　タイ　米国　英国　ブラジル　ペルー　その他の国　不詳

(8)(9) 死亡した人の夫または妻　いる　満　　　歳　いない（未婚　死別　離別）　不詳

(10) 死亡したときの世帯の主な仕事　1農家　2自営　3勤I　4勤II　5その他　6無職
(11) 死亡したときの職業・産業　職業　産業
(12)(13) 死亡したところの種別　1病院　2診療所　3老人ホーム保健施設　4助産所　5ホーム　6自宅　7その他　施設の名称

原死因符号　　外因の状況符号　　発生したところ符号　　傷害発生したところ符号　　母側符号

(14) 死亡の原因

I
(ア) 直接死因
▼枠内に記入しきれない分は下欄に記入してください。

(イ)（ア）の原因
▼枠内に記入しきれない分は下欄に記入してください。

(ウ)（イ）の原因
▼枠内に記入しきれない分は下欄に記入してください。

(エ)（ウ）の原因
▼枠内に記入しきれない分は下欄に記入してください。

II　Iぼした欄に影響を及ぼした傷病名等
▼枠内に記入しきれない分は下欄に記入してください。

発病（発症）又は受傷から死亡までの期間

手術　1無　2有　部位及び主要所見　手術年月日　平成昭和　年　月　日
解剖　1無　2有　主要所見

(15) 死因の種類
1病死・自然死　——不慮の外因死——　2交通　3転倒　4溺水　5火災　6窒息　7中毒　8その他　——その他及び不詳の外因死——　9自殺　10他殺　11その他の外因死　12不詳の死

(17) 生後1年未満で病死した場合の追加事項
出生時体重　ｇ　不詳
単胎・多胎の別　1単胎　2多胎　（　子中第　子）
妊娠週数　満　　週　不詳

(16) 外因死の追加事項
傷害が発生したとき　平成・昭和　年　月　日　午前・午後　時　分
傷害が発生したところの種別　1住居　2工場及び建築現場　3道路　4その他（　）
傷害が発生したところ　都道府県　市郡　区町村
手段及び状況

妊娠・分娩時における母体の病態又は異状　1無　2有　3不詳
母の生年月日　昭平　年　月　日　前回までの妊娠の結果　出生児　人　妊娠満22週以後の死産児　胎

(18)その他特に付言すべきことがら

(19) 施設の所在地又は医師の住所及び氏名
住所　　　丁目　番地　番　号
氏名
確認欄
備考欄

この調査は、統計法に基づく基幹統計を作成するために行う調査です。
この調査の対象となっている市区町村長には統計法に基づく報告の義務があり、報告の拒否や虚偽報告については罰則があります。

数字記入例 **0 1 2 3 4 5 6 7 8 9**

人口動態調査死産票 3

平成　年　月　日　市区町村受付

平成　年　月　日　保健所受付

統計法に基づく基幹統計調査

照会

市区町村符号及び保健所符号　　　　支所　保健所　　事件簿番号

(1) 父母の国籍	父	日本 韓国朝鮮 中国 フィリピン タイ 米国 英国 ブラジル ペルー その他の国 不詳
	母	日本 韓国朝鮮 中国 フィリピン タイ 米国 英国 ブラジル ペルー その他の国 不詳

(2) 父母の氏名及び年齢　父　　母　　満　　歳　　満　　歳

(3) 死産児の男女別及び嫡出子か否かの別　男 女 不詳　嫡出子 嫡出でない子　(4) 死産があったとき　昭 平　年　月　日　午前 午後　時

(5) 死産があったときの母の住所　日本 外国 不詳　都道府県　市,郡,特別区　町,村,指定都市の区又は総合区

届出地区町村と同じ　届出地区町村以外の村　市区町村符号　保健所符号　指定都市の町,字,丁目,番地,番号,アパート・マンション,様方

(6) 死産があったときの世帯の主な仕事　1農家 2自営 3勤I 4勤II 5その他 6無職

(7) 死産があったときの父母の職業　父　母

(8) この母の出産した子の数　出生子　人　妊娠満22週以後の死産児　胎　妊娠満21週以前の死産児　胎

(9) 妊娠週数　満　週　日

(10) 死産児の体重及び身長　, g 不詳　cm 不詳

(11) 胎児死亡の時期（妊娠満22週以後の自然死産）　1分娩前 2分娩中 3不詳

(12) 死産があったところの種別　1病院 2診療所 3助産所 4自宅 5その他

(13) 単胎・多胎の別　1単胎 2多胎（ 子中第 子） 3不詳

(14) 死産の自然人工別　1自然 2法による人工死産 3法によらない人工死産 4不明

(15) 自然死産の原因若しくは理由又は人工死産の理由

		胎児の側	母の側
I	(ア) 直接又は原因	▼枠内に記入しきれない分は下欄に記入してください。	▼枠内に記入しきれない分は下欄に記入してください。
	(イ)(ア)の原因	▼枠内に記入しきれない分は下欄に記入してください。	▼枠内に記入しきれない分は下欄に記入してください。
	(ウ)(イ)の原因	▼枠内に記入しきれない分は下欄に記入してください。	▼枠内に記入しきれない分は下欄に記入してください。
	(エ)(ウ)の原因	▼枠内に記入しきれない分は下欄に記入してください。	▼枠内に記入しきれない分は下欄に記入してください。
II	Iぼした傷病名等に影響を及	▼枠内に記入しきれない分は下欄に記入してください。	▼枠内に記入しきれない分は下欄に記入してください。

母体保護法による場合　1母体側の疾患　2その他　疾患名又は理由　▼枠内に記入しきれない分は下欄に記入してください。

母体保護法によらない場合　1母体側の疾患　2その他　疾患名又は理由　▼枠内に記入しきれない分は下欄に記入してください。

(16) 胎児手術の有無　1無 2有　部位及び主要所見

(17) 死胎解剖の有無　1無 2有　主要所見

(18) 死産に立ち会った者　1医師 2助産師 3その他

双子以上の場合は他の子の事件簿番号　出生票第　号　死産票第　号　確認（　）欄　備考

この調査は、統計法に基づく基幹統計を作成するために行う調査です。
この調査の対象となっている市区町村長には統計法に基づく報告の義務があり、報告の拒否や虚偽報告については罰則があります。

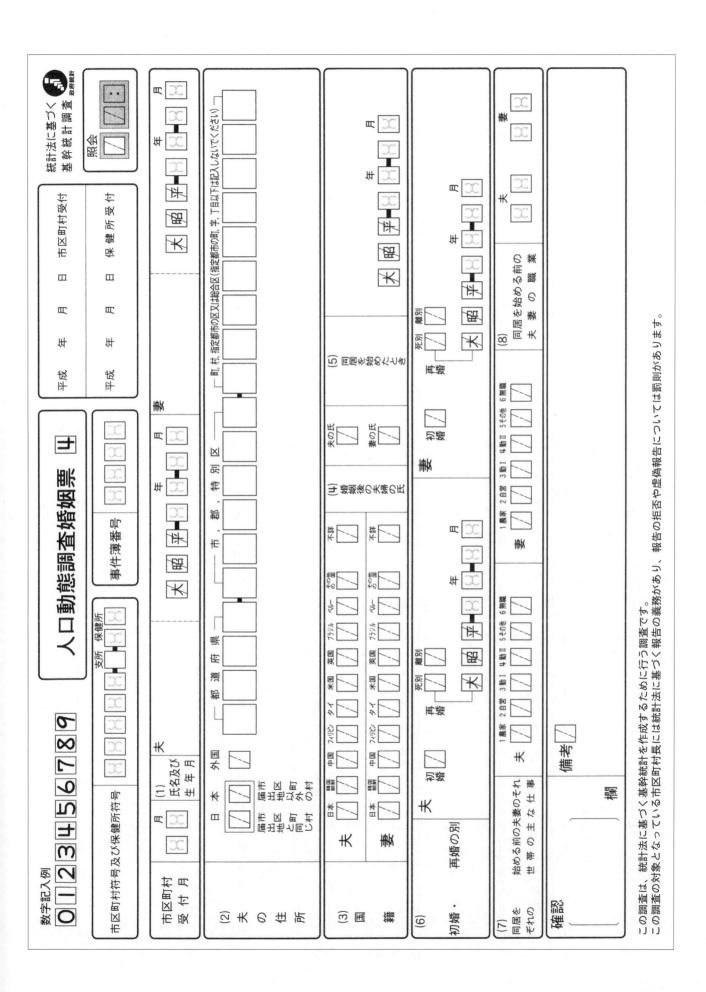

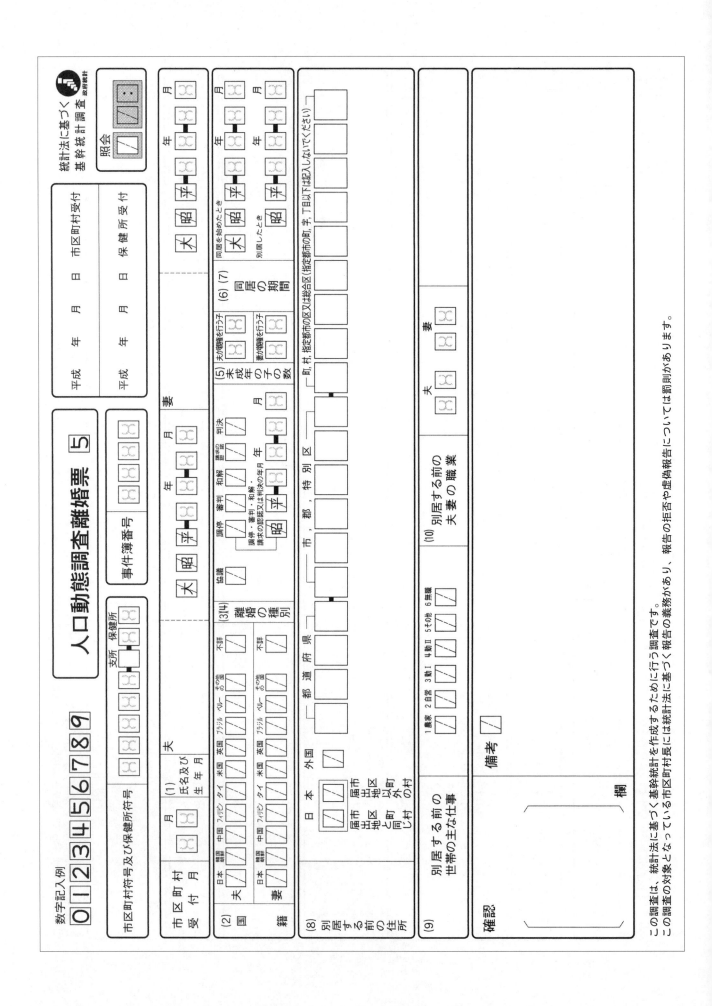

出 生 届

平成　　　年　　月　　日届出

　　　　　　　　　長　殿

受理 平成	年	月	日	発送 平成	年	月	日
	第		号			第	号		長印
送付 平成	年	月	日				
事項調査	戸籍記載	記載調査	調査票	附票	住民票	通知

(1) 生まれた子の氏名 （よみかた） （外国人のときはローマ字を付記してください。）	子 の 氏 名	氏　　　　　名
	父母との続き柄	□嫡出子　　□男 □嫡出でない子（　）□女
(2) 生まれたとき	生まれたとき	平成　年　月　日　□午前 時　分 　　　　　　　　　　　　□午後
(3) 生まれたところ	生まれたところ	番地 　　　　　　　　　　番
(4) 住所 （住民登録をするところ）	住　　所	番地 　　　　　　　　　　番
	世帯主の氏名	世帯主との続き柄
(5) 父母の氏名 生年月日 （子が生まれたときの年齢）	父	母
	年　月　日（満　歳）	年　月　日（満　歳）
(6) 本籍 （外国人のときは国籍だけを書いてください）	本　籍	番地 　　　　　　　　番
	筆頭者の氏名	
(7) 同居を始めたとき		年　月（結婚式をあげたとき、または、同居を始めたときのうち早いほうを書いてください）
(8) 子が生まれたときの世帯のおもな仕事と	□1. 農業だけまたは農業とその他の仕事を持っている世帯 □2. 自由業・商工業・サービス業等を個人で経営している世帯 □3. 企業・個人商店等（官公庁は除く）の常用勤労者世帯で勤め先の従業者数が1人から99人までの世帯（日々または1年未満の契約の雇用者は5） □4. 3にあてはまらない常用勤労者世帯及び会社団体の役員の世帯（日々または1年未満の契約の雇用者は5） □5. 1から4にあてはまらないその他の仕事をしている者のいる世帯 □6. 仕事をしている者のいない世帯
(9) 父母の職業 （国勢調査の年…　年…4月1日から翌年3月31日までに子が生まれたときだけ書いてください）	父の職業 母の職業
その他	

届出人	□1.父　□2.法定代理人（　　）□3.同居者　□4.医師　□5.助産師　□6.その他の立会者 □7.公設所の長
	住所　　　　　　　　　　番地 　　　　　　　　　　　　番
	本籍　　　　　　　　　番地　　筆頭者の氏名 　　　　　　　　　　　番
	署名　　　　　　　　印　　　年　　月　　日生

事件簿番号

記入の注意

鉛筆や消えやすいインキで書かないでください。

子が生まれた日からかぞえて14日以内に出してください。

子の本籍地でない役場に出すときは、2通出してください（役場が相当と認めたときは1通で足りることもあります。2通の場合でも、出生証明書は、原本1通を写し1通としてさしつかえありません。

子の名は、常用漢字、人名用漢字、かたかな、ひらがなで書いてください。子が外国人のときは、原則かたかなで書くとともに、住民票の処理上必要ですから、ローマ字を付記してください。

よみかたは、戸籍には記載されません。住民票の処理上必要ですから書いてください。

□には、あてはまるものに□のように、しるしをつけてください。

筆頭者の氏名には、戸籍のはじめに記載されている人の氏名を書いてください。

子の父または母が、まだ戸籍の筆頭者となっていない場合は、新しい戸籍がつくられますので、この欄に希望する本籍を書いてください。

届け出られた事項は、人口動態調査（統計法に基づく基幹統計調査、厚生労働省所管）にも用いられます。

出 生 証 明 書

(1) 子 の 氏 名	子の氏名		男女の別	1男　2女
(2) 生まれたとき	生まれたとき	平成　年　月　日　午前 時　分 　　　　　　　　　　　午後	
(3) 出生したところの種別	出生したところの種別	1病院　2診療所　3助産所 4自宅　5その他	
(10) 出生したところ及びその種別	出生したところ	番地 　　　　　　　　　　番　　　　号	
	施設の名称		
(11) 体重及び身長	体重	グラム　　身長 センチメートル	
(12) 単胎・多胎の別	単胎・多胎の別	1単胎　2多胎（子中第　子）	
(13) 母の氏名	母の氏名		妊娠週数	満　　週
(14) この母の出産した子の数	この母の出産した子（この出生子及び出生後に死亡した子を含む）	出生子（この出生子及び出生後に死亡した子を含む）人 死産児（妊娠満22週以後）胎	
(15)	上記のとおり証明する。　　平成　年　月　日		
	1医師　2助産師　3その他	（住所）　　　　　　　番地 　　　　　　　　　　　番　　号	
		（氏名）　　　　　　　印	

記入の注意

夜の12時は「午前0時」、昼の12時は「午後0時」と書いてください。

体重及び身長は、立会者が医師又は助産師以外の者で、わからないときは書かなくてもさしつかえありません。

この母の出産した子の数は、当該母又は本人などから聞いて書いてください。

この出生証明書の作成者が医師、助産師、又はその他の立会者が立ち会った場合には医師、助産師、その他の立会者の順に1、2、3の順で書いてください。

死亡届

平成　年　月　日届出

長殿

受理　平成　年　月　日 第　号	発送　平成　年　月　日
送付　平成　年　月　日 第　号	長印

書類調査	戸籍記載	記載調査	調査票	附票	住民票	通知

(1)	（よみかた）	
(2)	氏名	氏　名　□男　□女
(3)	生年月日	年　月　日（生まれてから30日以内に死亡したときは生まれた時刻も書いてください）□午前 □午後　時　分
(4)	死亡したとき	平成　年　月　日　□午前 □午後　時　分
(5)	死亡したところ	番地 番　号
(6)	住所（住民登録をしているところ）	番地 番　号 世帯主の氏名
(7)	本籍（外国人のときは国籍だけを書いてください）	番地 番 筆頭者の氏名
(8)(9)	死亡した人の夫または妻	□いる（満　歳）　いない（□未婚　□死別　□離別）
(10)	死亡したときの世帯のおもな仕事と	□1. 農業だけまたは農業とその他の仕事を持っている世帯 □2. 自由業・商工業・サービス業等を個人で経営している世帯 □3. 企業・個人商店等（官公庁は除く）の常用勤労者世帯で勤め先の従業者数が1人から99人までの世帯（日々または1年未満の契約の雇用者は5） □4. 3にあてはまらない常用勤労者世帯及び会社団体の役員の世帯（日々または1年未満の契約の雇用者は5） □5. 1から4にあてはまらないその他の仕事をしている者のいる世帯 □6. 仕事をしている者のいない世帯
(11)	死亡した人の職業・産業	（国勢調査の年…　年…の4月1日から翌年3月31日までに死亡したときだけ書いてください） 職業　産業
	その他	
	届出人	□1. 同居の親族 □2. 同居していない親族 □3. 同居者 □4. 家主 □5. 地主 □6. 家屋管理人 □7. 土地管理人 □8. 公設所の長 □9. 後見人 □10. 保佐人 □11. 補助人 □12. 任意後見人 住所　番地 番　号 本籍　番地 番　筆頭者の氏名 署名　印　年　月　日生
	事件簿番号	

記入の注意

鉛筆や消えやすいインキで書かないでください。

死亡したことを知った日からかぞえて7日以内に出してください。

死亡者の本籍地でない役場に出すときは、2通出してください（役場が相当と認めたときは、1通で足りることもあります。）。2通の場合でも、死亡診断書は、原本1通と写し1通でさしつかえありません。

→「筆頭者の氏名」には、戸籍のはじめに記載されている人の氏名を書いてください。

→内縁のものはふくまれません。

□には、あてはまるものに☑のようにしるしをつけてください。

→死亡者について書いてください。

届け出られた事項は、人口動態調査（統計法に基づく基幹統計調査、厚生労働省所管）、がん登録等の推進に関する法律に基づく全国がん登録（厚生労働省所管）にも用いられます。

死亡診断書（死体検案書）

この死亡診断書（死体検案書）は、我が国の死因統計作成の資料としても用いられます。かい書で、できるだけ詳しく書いてください。

	氏名	1男 2女　生年月日　明治 昭和 大正 平成　年　月　日（生まれてから30日以内に死亡したときは生まれた時刻も書いてください）午前・午後　時　分
	死亡したとき	平成　年　月　日　午前・午後　時　分
(12)(13)	死亡したところ及びその種別	死亡したところの種別　1病院 2診療所 3介護老人保健施設 4助産所 5老人ホーム 6自宅 7その他 死亡したところ　番地 番　号 （死亡したところの種別1～5）施設の名称
(14)	死亡の原因 ◆I欄、II欄ともに疾患の終末期の状態としての心不全、呼吸不全等は書かないでください ◆I欄では、最も死亡に影響を与えた傷病名を医学的因果関係の順番で書いてください ◆I欄の傷病名の記載は各欄一つにしてください ただし、欄が不足する場合は(エ)欄に残りを医学的因果関係の順番で書いてください	I　(ア)直接死因／(イ)(ア)の原因／(ウ)(イ)の原因／(エ)(ウ)の原因 II　直接には死因に関係しないがI欄の傷病経過に影響を及ぼした傷病名等 発病（発症）又は受傷から死亡までの期間　◆年、月、日等の単位で書いてください　ただし、1日未満の場合は、時、分等の単位で書いてください（例：1年3か月、5時間20分） 手術　1無 2有｛部位及び主要所見｝　手術年月日　平成 昭和　年　月　日 解剖　1無 2有｛主要所見｝
(15)	死因の種類	1病死及び自然死 外因死　不慮の外因死｛2交通事故 3転倒・転落 4溺水 5煙、火災及び火焔による傷害 6窒息 7中毒 8その他｝ その他及び不詳の外因死｛9自殺 10他殺 11その他及び不詳の外因｝ 12不詳の死
(16)	外因死の追加事項 ◆伝聞又は推定情報の場合でも書いてください	傷害が発生したとき　平成・昭和　年　月　日　午前・午後　時　分 傷害が発生したところ　都道府県　市 区 郡 町村 傷害が発生したところの種別　1住居 2工場及び建築現場 3道路 4その他（　） 手段及び状況
(17)	生後1年未満で病死した場合の追加事項	出生時体重　グラム　単胎・多胎の別　1単胎 2多胎（　子中第　子）　妊娠週数　満　週 妊娠・分娩時における母体の病態又は異状　1無 2有［　］3不詳　母の生年月日　昭和 平成　年　月　日 前回までの妊娠の結果　出生児　人　死産児　胎（妊娠満22週以後に限る）
(18)	その他特に付言すべきことがら	
(19)	上記のとおり診断（検案）する	診断（検案）年月日　平成　年　月　日 本診断書（検案書）発行年月日　平成　年　月　日 （病院、診療所若しくは介護老人保健施設等の名称及び所在地又は医師の住所）　番地 番　号 （氏名）　医師　印

記入の注意

←生年月日が不詳の場合は、推定年齢をカッコを付して書いてください。

夜の12時は「午前0時」、昼の12時は「午後0時」と書いてください。

←「老人ホーム」は、養護老人ホーム、特別養護老人ホーム、軽費老人ホーム及び有料老人ホームをいいます。

傷病名等は、日本語で書いてください。
I欄では、各傷病について発病の型（例：急性）、病因（例：病原体名）、部位（例：胃噴門部がん）、性状（例：病理組織型）等もできるだけ書いてください。

妊娠中の死亡の場合は「妊娠満何週」、また、分娩中の死亡の場合は「妊娠満何週の分娩中」と書いてください。

産後42日未満の死亡の場合は「妊娠満何週産後満何日」と書いてください。

←I欄及びII欄に関係した手術について、術式又はその診断名と関連のある所見等を書いてください。紹介状や伝聞等による情報についてもカッコを付して書いてください。

←「2交通事故」は、事故発生からの期間にかかわらず、その事故による死亡が該当します。
「5煙、火災及び火焔による傷害」は、火災による一酸化炭素中毒、窒息等も含まれます。

←「1住居」とは、住宅、庭等をいい、老人ホーム等の居住施設は含まれません。

←傷害がどういう状況で起こったかを具体的に書いてください。

←妊娠週数は、最終月経、基礎体温、超音波計測等により推定し、できるだけ正確に書いてください。
母子健康手帳等を参考に書いてください。

死産証書（死胎検査書）

この死産証書（死胎検査書）は、我が国の死産統計作成の資料として用いられますから、かん書で、できるだけ詳しく書いてください。

| (9) | 死産児の男女別 | 1 男　2 女　3 不詳 |
| | 母の氏名 | |

(10)	死産があったとき	平成　年　月　日　午前・午後　時　分
(11)	死産児の体重及び身長	体重　グラム　身長　センチメートル　妊娠週数 満　週 日（妊娠満22週以後の自然死産に限る）
(12)	胎児死亡の時期（自然死産に限る）	1 分娩前　2 分娩中　3 分娩後
	死産があったところ及びその種別	1 病院　2 診療所　3 助産所　4 自宅　5 その他
	死産があったところの施設の名称	番地　番　号
(13)	単胎・多胎の別	1 単胎　2 多胎（　子中第　子）
(14)	自然死産 人工死産の別	1 自然死産　2 母体保護法による人工死産　3 母体保護法によらない人工死産　4 不明

	自然死産の場合		人工死産の場合	
	胎児側	母の側	胎児側	母の側
I	ア 直接原因又は理由			1 母体側の身体保護法による場合 2 その他 理由
	イ（アの原因）			
	ウ（イの原因）			
	エ（ウの原因）		1 母体側の身体保護法によらない場合 2 その他 疾患名 理由	
II	直接死産又は死産に影響を及ぼした傷病名等			

(16)	胎児手術の有無	1 無　2 有
(17)	死胎解剖の有無	1 無　2 有
(18)		上記のとおり証明（検案）する　平成　年　月　日　証明（検案）年月日 平成　年　月　日　本証明書（検案書）発行年月日
	1 医　師	病院、診療所若しくは助産所の名称及び所在地又は医師若しくは助産師の住所 番地 番 号
	2 助　産　師	（氏　名）　印

記入の注意

妊娠週数は、最終月経、基礎体温、超音波計測等により測定し、医師が判断できるだけ正確に書いてください。

夜の12時は、「午前0時」、昼の12時は、「午後0時」と書いてください。

I欄及びII欄に関連した手術について、術式又はその診断名と関連のある所見等を中心に書いてください。

死　産　届

平成　年　月　日　届出

　　　　　　　　長殿

| | | 受付　年　月　日　平成　年　月　日 調査票作成 |
| | | 事件簿番号　死産第　号 |

(1)	父母の本籍（外国人のときは国籍を書いてください）	父 都道府県名 母 都道府県名
(2)	氏名 生年月日（死産があったときの年齢）	父 年 月 日（満 歳） 母 年 月 日（満 歳）
(3)	死産児の男女別	□男　□女　□不詳
	及び嫡出子か嫡出でない子かの別	□嫡出子　□嫡出でない子
(4)	死産があったとき	平成　年　月　日　午前・午後　時　分
(5)	死産があったところ	番地 番 号
	死産があったときの母の住所（住民登録をしているところを書いてください）	番地 番 号
(6)	死産があったときの世帯のおもな仕事と	□1.農業だけまたは農業とその他の仕事を持っている世帯 □2.自由業・商工業・サービス業等を個人で経営している世帯 □3.企業・個人商店等（官公庁を除く）の常用勤労者世帯で勤め先の従業者数が1人から99人までの世帯（日々または1年未満の契約の雇用者は5） □4.3にあてはまらない常用勤労者世帯及び会社団体の役員の世帯（日々または1年未満の契約の雇用者は5） □5.1から4にあてはまらないその他の仕事をしている者のいる世帯 □6.仕事をしている者のいない世帯
(7)	父母の職業（国勢調査の年…　年…の4月1日から翌年3月31日までに死産があったときだけ書いてください）	父の職業 母の職業
(8)	この母の出産した子の数	出生子（出生後死亡した子を含む）　人 妊娠満22週以後の死産児（この死産児を含む）　胎 妊娠満22週以前の死産児又は流産死胎（この死産胎を含む）　胎
届 出 人		□父 □母 □同居者 □医師 □助産師 □その他の立会者 住所 番地 番 号 氏名 印

記入の注意

鉛筆や消えやすいインキで書かないでください。

この届は妊娠満12週（満12週を含む）以後の死産について、死産後7日以内に役場に出してください。

□にあてはまるものに□のように記入をつけてください。

この死産証書又は死胎検査書の作成者は医師又は助産師ですが、医師・助産師ともに死産に立ち会う場合には医師が書いてください。

医師又は助産師の死産証書又は死胎検査書が得られないときは届出人はその理由を余白に書き死産の事実を証明しうる者の死産証書又は死胎検査書の次に「死産（事実）証書」という文字を書いて「死産（事実）証書」としてください。

(11)胎児死亡の時期について「分娩前」とは陣痛開始前、「分娩中」とは陣痛開始から胎児が娩出に終るまでの間、「陣痛開始後」は陣痛開始から胎児の娩出の切開分娩の場合は、陣痛開始後分娩出までで「分娩中」とします。

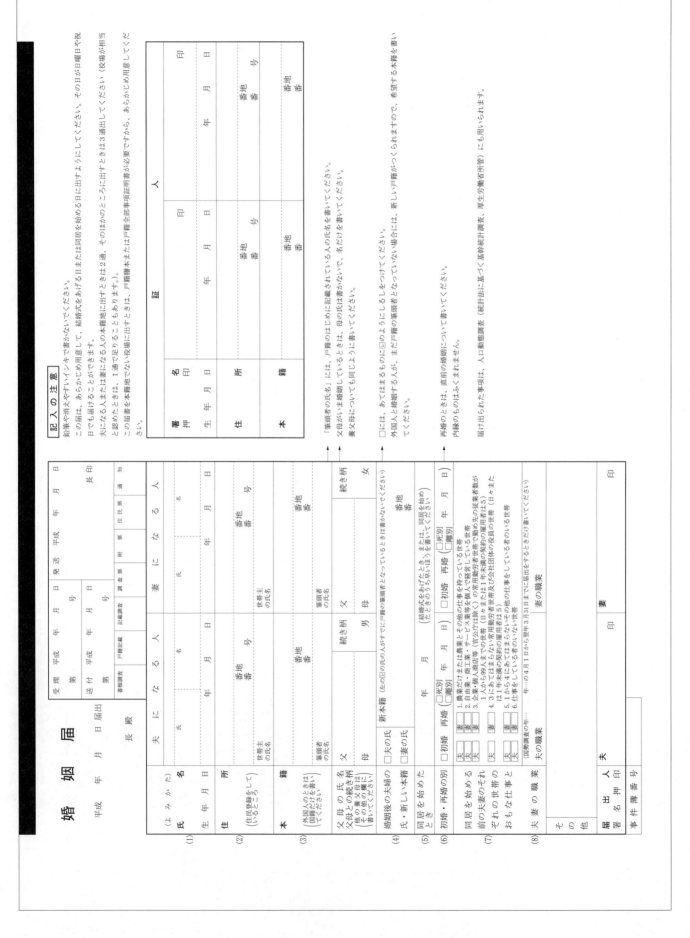

離婚届

平成　年　月　日届出　　　　　　　長　殿

受理　平成　年　月　日　第　　号	発送　平成　年　月　日
送付　平成　年　月　日　第　　号	長　印
書類調査　戸籍記載　記載調査　調査票　附票　住民票	通知

	夫	妻
(1) 氏名（よみかた）	氏　名	氏　名
生年月日	年　月　日	年　月　日
住所（住民登録をしているところ）	番地　番　号　世帯主の氏名	番地　番　号　世帯主の氏名
本籍（外国人のときは国籍だけを書いてください）	番地　番　筆頭者の氏名	番地　番　筆頭者の氏名

(2) 父母の氏名　父母との続き柄（その他の欄は養父母など書いてください）
夫の父　　　　　母　　　続き柄　男　　妻の父　　　　母　　　続き柄　女

(3) 離婚の種別
□協議離婚　□調停　年月日成立　□審判　年月日確定　□和解　□請求の認諾　□判決　年月日確定

(4) 婚姻前の氏にもどる者の本籍
□夫　□妻　は　□もとの戸籍にもどる　□新しい戸籍をつくる　番地　番　筆頭者の氏名

(5) 未成年の子の名
夫が親権を行う子　　　　　　妻が親権を行う子

(6)(7) 同居の期間（同居を始めたとき）年　月から（別居したとき）年　月まで

(8) 別居する前の住所　番地　番　号

(9) 別居する前の世帯のおもな仕事と
□1.農業だけまたは農業とその他の仕事を持っている世帯
□2.自由業・商工業・サービス業等を個人で経営している世帯
□3.企業・個人商店等（官公庁は除く）の常用勤労者世帯で勤め先の従業者数が1人から99人までの世帯（日々または1年未満の契約の雇用者は5）
□4.3にあてはまらない常用勤労者世帯及び会社団体の役員の世帯（日々または1年未満の契約の雇用者は5）
□5.1から4にあてはまらないその他の仕事をしている者のいる世帯
□6.仕事をしている者のいない世帯

(10) 夫妻の職業（国勢調査の年…　年…の4月1日から翌年3月31日までに届出をするときだけ書いてください）
夫の職業　　　　　　　妻の職業

その他

届出人署名押印	夫　　　　　　印	妻　　　　　　印

事件簿番号

記入の注意

鉛筆や消えやすいインキで書かないでください。

筆頭者の氏名欄には、戸籍のはじめに記載されている人の氏名を書いてください。

本籍地でない役場に出すときは、2通または3通出してください（役場が相当と認めたときは、1通で足りることもあります）。また、その際に戸籍謄本も必要です。

その他必要なもの
　調停離婚のとき－調停調書の謄本
　審判離婚のとき－審判書の謄本と確定証明書
　和解離婚のとき－和解調書の謄本
　認諾離婚のとき－認諾調書の謄本と確定証明書
　判決離婚のとき－判決書の謄本と確定証明書

証人（協議離婚のときだけ必要です）

署名押印	印	印
生年月日	年　月　日	年　月　日
住所	番地　番　号	番地　番　号
本籍	番地　番	番地　番

父母がいま婚姻しているときは、母の氏は書かないで、名だけを書いてください。
養父母については、その他の欄に養父母と書き、名だけを書いてください。
□には、あてはまるものに☑のようにしるしをつけてください。

今後も離婚の際に称していた氏を称する場合には、左の欄には何も記載しないでください（この場合にはこの離婚届と同時に別の届書を提出する必要があります）。

同居を始めたときは、結婚式をあげた年月または同居を始めた年月のうち早いほうを書いてください。

届け出られた事項は、人口動態調査（統計法に基づく基幹統計調査、厚生労働省所管）にも用いられます。

未成年の子がいる場合は、次の□のあてはまるものにしるしをつけてください。
（面会交流）
□取決めをしている。
□まだ決めていない。
（養育費の分担）
□取決めをしている。
□まだ決めていない。

未成年の子がいる場合は父母が離婚をするときは、面会交流や養育費の分担など子の監護に必要な事項についても父母の協議で定めることとされています。この場合には、子の利益を最も優先して考えなければならないこととされています。

3 観察対象の範囲

本報告書の観察対象は、次の表に示す範囲である。

		出　　　　生	死　　　　亡
地域範囲	昭和18年以前	沖縄を含む旧内地（樺太を除く）	
	昭和22〜25年	北海道、本州、四国、九州に属する地域のうち、北海道根室支庁の一部、東京都小笠原支庁、島根県竹	
	昭和26〜47年	昭和26年12月5日以降：鹿児島県大島郡十島村北緯29度〜30度（吐喝喇列島）を含む 昭和28年12月25日以降：同村北緯29度以南（奄美群島）を含む 昭和43年6月26日以降：東京都小笠原村を含む	
	昭和48年以降	沖縄を含む。したがって、北海道、本州、四国、九州に属する地域のうち、北海道根室支庁の一部、島根	
観察対象の地域的属性	昭和18年以前	出生の場所が前掲の地域にあるもの	死亡の場所が前掲の地域にあるもの
	昭和22〜24年		
	昭和25、26年		
	昭和27年以降		
観察対象の人的範囲	昭和18年以前	出生児の本籍が沖縄、樺太を含む旧内地にあるもの	死亡者の本籍が沖縄、樺太を含む旧内地にあるもの
	昭和22〜57年	出生児の本籍が北海道（根室支庁の一部を除く）、本州、四国、九州及び沖縄にあるもの （昭和54年から、出生子と表現を変えた）	死亡者の本籍が北海道（根室支庁の一部を除く）、本州、四国、九州及び沖縄にあるもの
	昭和58〜平成6年	出生子の本籍が北海道（昭和58年3月以前は根室支庁の一部を除く）、本州、四国、九州及び沖縄にあるもの	死亡者の本籍が北海道（昭和58年3月以前は根室支庁の一部を除く）、本州、四国、九州及び沖縄にあるもの
	平成7年以降		
観察期間	大正11年以前	各年1月1日から翌年3月31日までに届け出られたもののうち1月1日〜同年12月31日までの期間に事	
	大正12〜昭和18年	各年1月1日から翌年1月31日までに届け出られたもののうち1月1日〜同年12月31日までの期間に事	
	昭和22年	同年1月1日から12月31日までに届け出られたもののうち同年中に事件発生のもの	
	昭和23、24年	各年1月1日から翌年4月14日までに届け出られたもののうち1月1日〜同年12月31日までの期間に事	
	昭和25〜42年		
	昭和43〜45年	各年1月1日から翌年2月14日までに届け出られたもののうち1月1日〜同年12月31日までの期間に事	
	昭和46年以降	各年1月1日から翌年1月14日までに届け出られたもののうち1月1日〜同年12月31日までの期間に事	
都道府県・市部−郡部等の分類の基準	昭和18年以前	発生地に基づき各年1月1日現在の行政区画によって分類	
	昭和22〜24年		
	昭和25、26年	出生当時の母親の住所に基づき事件発生当時の行政区画によって分類	死亡当時の住所に基づき事件発生当時の行政区画によって分類
	昭和27〜42年	出生当時の子の住所に基づき事件発生当時の行政区画によって分類	
	昭和43〜46年		
	昭和47年以降	出生当時の子の住所に基づき届出当時の行政区画によって分類	死亡当時の住所に基づき届出当時の行政区画によって分類
	昭和54年以降	出生当時の子の住所に基づき事件発生当時の行政区画によって分類	死亡当時の住所に基づき事件発生当時の行政区画によって分類

死　　　　　産	婚　　　姻	離　　　婚

島、鹿児島県大島郡十島村北緯30度以南、沖縄全県を除く地域

県竹島を除く地域

死　産	婚　姻	離　婚
分娩の場所が前掲の地域にあるもの	届出当時の夫の住所。なお、婿養子縁組・入婚のときは届出当時の妻の住所。裁判上の離婚は訴訟提起者の住所が前掲の地域にあるもの	
	結婚式をあげた場所が前掲の地域にあるもの	離婚当時の夫の住所が前掲の地域にあるもの
	結婚式直前の夫の住所が前掲の地域にあるもの	
	届出当時の夫の住所が前掲の地域にあるもの	
母親の本籍が沖縄、樺太を含む旧内地にあるもの	夫妻双方又は夫妻のいずれか一方の本籍が沖縄、樺太を含む旧内地にあるもの	
母親の本籍が北海道（根室支庁の一部を除く）、本州、四国、九州及び沖縄にあるもの	夫妻双方又は夫妻のいずれか一方の本籍が北海道（根室支庁の一部を除く）、本州、四国、九州及び沖縄にあるもの	
母親の本籍が北海道（昭和58年3月以前は根室支庁の一部を除く）、本州、四国、九州及び沖縄にあるもの	夫妻双方又は夫妻のいずれか一方の本籍が北海道（昭和58年3月以前は根室支庁の一部を除く）、本州、四国、九州及び沖縄にあるもの	
父親又は母親の本籍が北海道、本州、四国、九州及び沖縄にあるもの		
件発生のもの	各年1月1日から12月31日までの間に届け出られたもの	
件発生のもの		
件発生のもの		
		各年1月1日から12月31日までの間に届け出られたもの。ただし、調停、審判、判決による離婚は、各年1月1日から翌年4月14日までに届け出られたもののうち、各年1月1日から12月31日までの間に成立又は確定があったもの
件発生のもの		各年1月1日から12月31日までの間に届け出られたもの。ただし、調停、審判、判決による離婚は、各年1月1日から翌年2月14日までに届け出られたもののうち、各年1月1日から12月31日までの間に成立又は確定があったもの
件発生のもの		各年1月1日から12月31日までの間に届け出られたもの。ただし、調停、審判、和解、請求の認諾（平成16年3月以前は和解、請求の認諾を除く）、判決による離婚は、各年1月1日から翌年1月14日までに届け出られたもののうち、各年1月1日から12月31日までの間に成立又は確定があったもの
	前掲の観察対象の地域的属性による夫又は妻の住所に基づき各年1月1日現在の行政区画によって分類	
	前掲の観察対象の地域的属性による挙式の場所に基づき各年1月1日現在の行政区画によって分類	
分娩当時の母親の住所に基づき事件発生当時の行政区画によって分類	前掲の観察対象の地域的属性による夫又は妻の住所により届出当時の行政区画によって分類	
	前掲の観察対象の地域的属性による夫の住所により届出当時の行政区画によって分類	前掲の観察対象の地域的属性による夫妻の別居する前の住所により届出当時の行政区画によって分類
分娩当時の母親の住所に基づき届出当時の行政区画によって分類		
分娩当時の母親の住所に基づき事件発生当時の行政区画によって分類		

第2章　調査結果の利用上の解説

1　平成7年調査からの主な改正点

第10回改訂国際疾病傷害死因分類（ICD−10）の勧告を契機として、平成7年調査で人口動態調査票及び死亡診断書等の改正を行い、報告書においても一部統計表の変更を行った。

以下は平成7年調査以降の主な改正点である。なお、平成7年に適用した「ICD−10（初版）準拠」及び、平成18年から適用したICD−10の一部改正である「ICD−10（2003年版）準拠」については、死因分類の解説（70ページ）を参照されたい。

1）　出生票の主な改正点

体重及び身長 （事項の新設）	「子の体重」欄を「体重及び身長」欄とした。
この母の出産した子の数 （事項の変更）	死産児数を「妊娠満20週以後」から「妊娠満22週以後」に変更した。

2）　死亡票の主な改正点

死亡したところ及びその種別 （種別の追加等）	種別の選択肢の中に「老人ホーム」を追加した。
死亡の原因 （Ⅰ欄の増設）	3欄から4欄に増設した。
死因の種類 （外因死の選択肢の充実）	外因死を「不慮の外因死」と「その他及び不詳の外因死」に分割するとともに、外因の選択肢を大幅に充実した。
生後1年未満で病死した場合の追加事項 （対象の拡大）	対象を早期新生児死亡から乳児死亡（病死）に拡大し、事項を明確化した。
外因死の追加事項 （従業中か否かを判断する事項の削除）	「1従業中　2従業中でない時」は削除した。

注：　死亡診断書（死体検案書）の「死亡の原因」欄に「疾患の終末期の状態としての心不全、呼吸不全等は書かないでください」という注意書きを追加した。

3）　死産票の主な改正点

父母の国籍 （父の国籍の追加）	「母の国籍」欄を「父母の国籍」欄とした。
死産児の体重及び身長 （事項の新設）	「死産児の体重」欄を「死産児の体重及び身長」欄とした。
自然死産の原因若しくは理由又は人工死産の理由 （Ⅰ欄の削減）	5欄から4欄に削減した。
胎児手術の有無 （項目の新設）	有無及び「有」の場合の「部位及び主要所見」欄を新設した。
母体保護法による場合 （項目の削除）	「父・近親者の疾患」を削除した。 「優生保護法」の法律改正に伴い「母体保護法」に改めた。 （平成8年9月26日から）

4） 離婚票の主な改正点

離婚の種別	種別の選択肢の中に「和解」、「請求の認諾」を追加した。 人事訴訟法の施行に伴う戸籍法施行規則改正により、離婚届書の変更。 （平成16年4月1日から）

5） 各調査票共通の主な改正点

世帯の主な仕事 （項目の変更）	「専業農家世帯」と「兼業農家世帯」を併せ「農家世帯」とした。 「常用勤労者世帯」を、企業規模による区分とした。 「その他の世帯」を「その他の世帯」と「無職の世帯」とに区分した。 （詳細は66ページを参照）

6） ＩＣＤ－10（2003年版）、ＩＣＤ－10（初版）と ＩＣＤ－9での各種分類表及び項目数の比較

ＩＣＤ－10	2003年版の 項目数	初版の 項目数	ＩＣＤ－9	項目数
疾病、傷害及び死因の統計 分類基本分類	14,258	14,195	疾病、傷害及び死因の統計 分類基本分類	7,129
死因簡単分類	132	130	死因簡単分類	117
選択死因分類	34	34	特定死因	32
死因年次推移分類	16	16	主要死因	17
乳児死因簡単分類	56	56	乳児死因簡単分類	54
感染症分類	88	83	——	—
死因順位（乳児を除く死亡）	40	40	死因順位（乳児を除く死亡）	55
乳児死因順位（乳児死亡）	28	28	乳児死因順位（乳児死亡）	30

注：1） 各分類の正式名称及び詳細については、「5　死因分類の解説　3）分類表」を参照されたい。
　　2） 感染症分類は、平成7年に新たに作成した分類であり、初版の欄に記載している83は15年からの項目数である。

7） ＩＣＤ－10の採用による定義等の改正

周産期死亡の定義	「妊娠満28週以後の死産に早期新生児死亡を加えたもの」から「妊娠満22週以後の死産に早期新生児死亡を加えたもの」に変更した。
後発妊産婦死亡	新たに後発妊産婦死亡（妊娠終了後満42日以後1年未満における死亡）が定義された。（詳細は65ページを参照）

8）「ＩＣＤ－10（2003年版）準拠」の適用に伴う主な改正点（平成18年１月１日から）

WHO勧告に基づく改正		
	分類項目の新設 　特殊目的用コード（U） 　（第XXII章）	・原因不明の新たな疾患の暫定分類 　　重症急性呼吸器症候群＜SARS＞ ・抗生物質に耐性の細菌性病原体 　　（MRSA肺炎等の把握や、感染症分類表でのメチシリン耐性黄色ブドウ球 　　菌感染症等の表章が可能となった。）
	Uコード以外	ハンタ〈Hanta〉ウイルス(心)肺症候群（B33.4）等
	分類項目の廃止	硬口蓋裂，両側性（Q35.0）等
	分類項目の移動	大腸〈結腸〉のポリープ　　新生物（D12.6）から消化器系の疾患（K63.5）へ移動。 C型肝炎　　　　　　　　　急性と明示されない、期間不明又は期間が６ヵ月以上の 　　　　　　　　　　　　　　C型肝炎は、急性（B17.1）から慢性（B18.2）へ移動。
	死亡統計における原死因 選択ルール等の変更	原死因選択ルールの一部変更及び適用例が具体的に示される等の変更が行われた。 巻末　参考表　２　年次推移　表１－１「死因簡単分類別にみた平成18年と17年の 性別死亡数及び率（人口10万対）」の脚注及び「疾病、傷害および死因統計分類提 要ＩＣＤ－10（2003年版）準拠」の第１巻、第２巻を参照のこと。
法令の改正等に基づく名称の変更		精神分裂病　　→　　統合失調症 痴呆　　　　　→　　認知症
医学の進歩等に対応した名称の変更		慢性関節リウマチ　　→　　関節リウマチ 妊娠中毒症　　　　　→　　妊娠高血圧症候群 尿路性器系　　　　　→　　腎尿路生殖器系

2　昭和22年以降の年次推移についての注意

１）出生

　(1) 月別出生率　　　　　　昭和30年の報告書から表章しており、昭和22年から41年は、各年10月１日現在の人口で算出した。昭和42年以降は、各月の月初人口で算出している。

　(2) 都道府県別出生数　　　平成４年から「外国」を表章している。

　(3) 父母の平均年齢　　　　昭和62年の報告書から表章した。昭和25年から45年までの５年毎の年次については母の平均年齢のみ、昭和50年以降は父母の平均年齢を算出している。

　　　　　　　　　　　　　　昭和25年から平成３年までは、満年齢の算術平均値に0.5歳を加えた。

　　　　　　　　　　　　　　平成４年に調査票を改正し、以後は日齢の算術平均値から算出している。

　(4) 父母の国籍　　　　　　昭和22年から61年までは表章していない。ただし、昭和60年、61年は、日本における父外国人・母日本人の出生については父の国籍が表章された保管表がある。

　　　　　　　　　　　　　　昭和62年から平成３年までは、日本、韓国・朝鮮、中国、米国、その他、の区分で表章した。

　　　　　　　　　　　　　　平成４年に調査票を改正し、上記のほかフィリピン、タイ、英国、ブラジル、ペルーを追加した。

　(5) 出生時の体重　　　　　昭和25、26、30、35年は、「人口動態特殊報告　出生時の体重に関する統計（昭和38年刊）」による。昭和43年以降は毎年集計している。

　　　　　　　　　　　　　　平成３年までは、100グラム単位で把握したため、平均体重は算術平均値に0.05キログラムを加えた。平成４年に調査票を改正し、以後はグラム単位で把握している。

2）死亡

月別 死亡率 昭和30年の報告書から表章しており、昭和22年から41年は、各年10月1日現在の人口で算出した。昭和42年以降は、各月の月初人口で算出している。

3）死産

死産数 昭和23、24年は概数である。

4）婚姻

　(1) 年齢 昭和22年以降、各年に同居し、届け出たものについて集計している。

昭和22年から42年は、結婚式をあげたとき（結婚式をあげないときは、結婚生活に入ったとき）の年齢である。

昭和43年以降は、結婚式をあげたとき、または、同居したときのうち早いほうの年齢である。

平均年齢は、平成3年までは出生年月及び同居年月による年齢の算術平均値に0.46歳を加えた。

平成4年に調査票を改正し、以後は月齢の算術平均値から算出している。

　(2) 夫妻の国籍 昭和22年から39年は、国籍別の表章を行っていない。

昭和40年から42年の調査区分は、日本、朝鮮、中国、ヨーロッパ諸国、アメリカ、その他の外国、である。

昭和43年から61年の調査区分は、日本、朝鮮、中国、アメリカ（又は米国）、その他、である。

昭和62年から平成3年の調査区分は、日本、韓国・朝鮮、中国、米国、その他、である。

平成4年に調査票を改正し、上記のほかフィリピン、タイ、英国、ブラジル、ペルーを追加した。

5）離婚

　(1) 都道府県別及び
　　 市部・郡部別離婚数 昭和22年は、協議離婚は夫の離婚当時の住所地、裁判離婚は訴訟提起者（夫又は妻）の離婚当時の住所地による。

昭和23年から42年は離婚当時の夫の住所による。

昭和43年以降は別居する前の住所による。

　(2) 離婚の種類 昭和22年は協議上の離婚、裁判上の離婚の2種である。また裁判上の離婚の事由を表章した。

昭和23年に家事審判法が施行されて協議離婚、調停離婚、審判離婚、判決離婚の4種となり、以後平成15年までは同様である。裁判上の離婚の事由は昭和23年の民法改正により変更され、昭和26年まで表章された。

平成16年4月に人事訴訟法により和解離婚、認諾離婚の2種が追加された。

　(3) 平均同居期間 昭和22年から昭和47年までの数値は、1年未満の月数を0.5年等として（ただし20年以上は22.5年として）年単位で算定したもの。

昭和48年以降の数値は、月数の算術平均から算出したもの。ただし、昭和48年から平成3年までの数値は、平成4年にこの方法で再計算した。

　(4) 夫妻の国籍 平成4年に調査票を改正して夫妻の国籍を調査するようになり、以後日本、韓国・朝鮮、中国、フィリピン、タイ、米国、英国、ブラジル、ペルー、その他、の区分で表章している。

3 用語の解説

自 然 増 減 　出生数から死亡数を減じたものをいう。

乳 児 死 亡 　生後1年未満の死亡をいう。

新 生 児 死 亡 　生後4週未満の死亡をいう。

早期新生児死亡 　生後1週未満の死亡をいう。

妊 娠 期 間 　出生、死産及び周産期死亡の妊娠期間は満週数による。（昭和53年までは、数えによる妊娠月数）

　　　　　　　早期：妊娠満37週未満（259日未満）

　　　　　　　正期：妊娠満37週から満42週未満（259日から293日）

　　　　　　　過期：妊娠満42週以上（294日以上）

死 　 産 　妊娠満12週（妊娠第4月）以後の死児の出産をいい、死児とは、出産後において心臓膊動、随意筋の運動及び呼吸のいずれも認めないものをいう。

自然死産と人工死産 　人工死産とは、胎児の母体内生存が確実であるときに、人工的処置（胎児又は付属物に対する措置及び陣痛促進剤の使用）を加えたことにより死産に至った場合をいい、それ以外はすべて自然死産とする。

　　　　　　　なお、人工的処置を加えた場合でも、次のものは自然死産とする。

　　　　　　　(1)　胎児を出生させることを目的とした場合

　　　　　　　(2)　母体内の胎児が生死不明か、又は死亡している場合

（参　考）

死産統計を観察する場合、次の沿革を考慮する必要がある。

昭和23年以降：優生保護法の施行（7月）により、人工妊娠中絶の中の、妊娠第4月以降のものも人工死産に含むことになった。

昭和24年以降：優生保護法の改正（6月）により、人工妊娠中絶の理由に「経済的理由により母体の健康を著しく害するおそれのあるもの」も含むことになった。

昭和27年以降：優生保護法の改正（5月）により、優生保護審査会の審査を廃止するなど、その手続が簡素適正化され、優生保護法による指定医師は本人及び配偶者の同意を得て、要件に該当する者に対し、人工妊娠中絶を行うことができるようになった。

昭和43年以降：胎児を出生させる目的で人工的処置を加えたにもかかわらず死産をした場合、従来は人工死産であったが、自然死産として取り扱うこととなった。

昭和51年以降：優生保護法による人工妊娠中絶を実施することができる時期の基準を、従来の「通常妊娠8月未満」から「通常妊娠第7月未満」に改めた。

　　　　　　（昭和51年1月20日付け厚生省発衛第15号厚生事務次官通知）

昭和54年以降：優生保護法による人工妊娠中絶を実施することのできる時期の基準を、従来の「通常妊娠第7月未満」から「通常妊娠満23週以前」に表現を改めた。（昭和53年11月21日付け厚生省発衛第252号厚生事務次官通知）

平成3年以降：優生保護法による人工妊娠中絶を実施することのできる時期の基準を、従来の「通常妊娠満23週以前」から「通常妊娠満22週未満」に改めた。（平成2年3月20日付け厚生省発健医第55号厚生事務次官通知）

周 産 期 死 亡　　　妊娠満22週（154日）以後の死産に早期新生児死亡を加えたものをいう。

妊 産 婦 死 亡　　　妊娠中又は妊娠終了後満42日未満[1]の女性の死亡で、妊娠の期間及び部位には関係しない
　　　　　　　　　が、妊娠もしくはその管理に関連した又はそれらによって悪化したすべての原因によるもの
　　　　　　　　　をいう。ただし、不慮又は偶発の原因によるものを除く。
　　　　　　　　　　　その範囲は、直接産科的死亡（O00〜O92）及び間接産科的死亡（O98〜O99）に原因不
　　　　　　　　　明の産科的死亡（O95）、産科的破傷風（A34）及びヒト免疫不全ウイルス［HIV］病
　　　　　　　　　（B20〜B24）を加えたものである[2]。
　　　　　　　　　　　直接産科的死亡：妊娠時における産科的合併症が原因で死亡したもの
　　　　　　　　　　　間接産科的死亡：妊娠前から存在した疾患又は妊娠中に発症した疾患により死亡したもの
　　　　　　　　　　　　　　　　　　をいい、これらの疾患は、直接産科的原因によるものではないが、妊娠の
　　　　　　　　　　　　　　　　　　生理的作用によって悪化したものである。
　　　　注：1）昭和53年までは「産後90日以内」とし、昭和54年から平成6年までは「分娩後42日以内」としている。
　　　　　　2）昭和53年までの範囲は、基本分類表「XI　妊娠、分娩および産褥の合併症」には「間接産科的死亡」
　　　　　　は含まれないので、「直接産科的死亡」がほぼ該当する。また、昭和54年から平成6年までは、基本分類
　　　　　　表「XI　妊娠、分娩及び産じょく〈褥〉の合併症」（630〜676）が該当する。

後発妊産婦死亡　　　妊娠終了後満42日以後1年未満における直接又は間接産科的原因による女性の死亡をいい、
　　　　　　　　　その範囲は、あらゆる産科的原因による母体死亡（O96）、産科的破傷風（A34）及びヒト
　　　　　　　　　免疫不全ウイルス［HIV］病（B20〜B24）であり、ICD−10で新たに定義されたもの
　　　　　　　　　である。

施設の種類

　病　　　院　　　医師又は歯科医師が、公衆又は特定多数人のため医業又は歯科医業を行う場所であって、20
　　　　　　　　　人以上の患者を入院させるための施設を有するものをいう。

　診　療　所　　　医師又は歯科医師が、公衆又は特定多数人のため医業又は歯科医業を行う場所であって、患
　　　　　　　　　者を入院させるための施設を有しないもの又は19人以下の患者を入院させるための施設を有す
　　　　　　　　　るものをいう。

　介 護 老 人　　　要介護者に対し、看護、医学的管理の下における介護及び機能訓練その他必要な医療並びに
　保 健 施 設　　　日常生活上の世話を行うことを目的とした施設で、介護保険法（平成9年法律第123号。平成
　　　　　　　　　12年4月1日施行）による都道府県知事の許可を受けたものをいう。
　　　　　　　　　（参考）介護保険法施行前は老人保健法（昭和57年法律第80号）による老人保健施設である。

　助 産 所　　　　助産師が公衆又は特定多数人のためその業務（病院又は診療所において行うものを除く。）
　　　　　　　　　を行う場所をいう。

　老人ホーム　　　養護老人ホーム、特別養護老人ホーム、軽費老人ホーム及び有料老人ホームをいう。

　自　　　宅　　　自宅の他、グループホーム、サービス付き高齢者向け住宅を含む。

世帯の主な仕事

農 家 世 帯　最多所得者が農業だけ又は農業とその他の仕事を持っている世帯

自 営 業 者 世 帯　最多所得者が自由業・商工業・サービス業等を個人で経営している世帯

常用勤労者世帯（Ⅰ）　最多所得者が企業・個人商店等（官公庁は除く）の常用勤労者世帯で勤め先の従事者
　　　　　　　　　　数が１人から99人までの世帯（日々または１年未満の契約の雇用者はその他の世帯）

常用勤労者世帯（Ⅱ）　最多所得者が常用勤労者世帯（Ⅰ）にあてはまらない常用勤労者世帯及び会社団体の役
　　　　　　　　　　員の世帯（日々または１年未満の契約の雇用者はその他の世帯）

そ の 他 の 世 帯　最多所得者が上記にあてはまらないその他の仕事をしている世帯

無 職 の 世 帯　仕事をしている者のいない世帯（年金・利子等の収入で生活している世帯を含む）

（参　　考）

平成７年からの区分	昭和43年から平成６年までの区分
農　家　世　帯	専 業 農 家 世 帯　農業だけをしている世帯 兼 業 農 家 世 帯　農業とその他の仕事を持っている世帯
自 営 業 者 世 帯	自 営 業 者 世 帯　店や事務所を持って自由業・商工業・サービス業などを個人 　　　　　　　　　　で経営している世帯
常用勤労者世帯（Ⅰ） 常用勤労者世帯（Ⅱ）	常用勤労者世帯（Ⅰ）　管理・事務・教員・販売・外交・医療保健技術者・旧専門学 　　　　　　　　　　校卒業以上の技術者などの勤労者世帯（日々又は１年未満の契 　　　　　　　　　　約の雇用者はその他の世帯） 常用勤労者世帯（Ⅱ）　常用勤労者世帯（Ⅰ）にあてはまらない勤労者世帯 　　　　　　　　　　（日々又は１年未満の契約の雇用者はその他の世帯）
そ の 他 の 世 帯 無　職　の　世　帯	そ の 他 の 世 帯　上記以外の世帯

離婚の種類

協議離婚　戸籍法上の届出によって成立する（民763・764・739）が、これが有効に成立するためには、夫
　　　　婦間に離婚についての意思の合致がなければならない。離婚意思の合致のない離婚は無効である。

裁判離婚　裁判所が関与して成立する離婚であって、調停離婚、審判離婚、和解離婚、認諾離婚及び判決離
　　　　婚の５種があり、調停が成立したとき、和解が成立したとき、請求の認諾をしたとき、又は審判若
　　　　しくは判決が確定したときに離婚の効果が生ずる。

調停離婚　当事者の申立て又は家庭裁判所の調停に付する処置により調停が開始される（家257Ⅰ・Ⅱ・274
　　　　Ⅰ）。調停において当事者間に離婚の合意が成立し、これを調書に記載したときは、調停が成立
　　　　したものとし、その記載は、確定判決と同一の効力を有する（家268Ⅰ）。

審判離婚　調停が成立しない場合に、家庭裁判所は、調停に代わる審判をすることができる（家284Ⅰ）。
　　　　当事者から適法な異議の申立てがあったときは、審判はその効力を失うが、異議がなければ、審
　　　　判は確定判決と同一の効力を有する（家286Ⅰ・Ⅴ・287）。

和解離婚　離婚訴訟上において和解ができる（人訴37Ⅰ）。和解が成立し、それが調書に記載されたとき
　　　　は、その記載は、確定判決と同一の効力を有する（民訴267）。

認諾離婚　離婚訴訟上において請求の認諾ができる（人訴37Ⅰ）。請求の認諾があり、それが調書に記載
　　　　されたときは、その記載は、確定判決と同一の効力を有する（民訴267）。

判決離婚　調停が成立せず、審判も確定しない場合に、法定の離婚原因があるときは、当事者の訴えの提
　　　　起により離婚の判決がなされる（民770、人訴2・4以下）。

　　（引用の条文 民＝民法、家＝家事事件手続法、民訴＝民事訴訟法、人訴＝人事訴訟法、条数は1,2、項数はⅠ,Ⅱ）

　　注：平成25年1月1日、従前の家事審判法が廃止され、新たに家事事件手続法が施行された。

4 比率の解説

本報告書で用いている比率の算出方法は以下のとおりである。

年次推移の表の昭和45年、50年及び55年については、10月1日現在日本人人口を国勢調査の確定数を用いて再計算したので、昭和45年、50年及び55年の報告書の数値と異なる場合がある。なお、比率の算出に用いた分母人口は巻末の付録を参照されたい。

1）総　覧

$$出　生　率 = \frac{年間出生数}{10月1日現在日本人人口} \times 1,000$$

$$死　亡　率 = \frac{年間死亡数}{10月1日現在日本人人口} \times 1,000$$

$$乳児死亡率 = \frac{年間乳児死亡数}{年間出生数} \times 1,000$$

$$新生児死亡率 = \frac{年間新生児死亡数}{年間出生数} \times 1,000$$

$$自然増減率 = \frac{年間自然増減数（年間出生数－年間死亡数）}{10月1日現在日本人人口} \times 1,000$$

$$死　産　率 = \frac{年間死産数（妊娠満12週以後の死児の出産）}{年間出産数（年間出生数＋年間死産数）} \times 1,000$$

$$自然死産率 = \frac{年間自然死産数}{年間出産数（年間出生数＋年間死産数）} \times 1,000$$

$$人工死産率 = \frac{年間人工死産数}{年間出産数（年間出生数＋年間死産数）} \times 1,000$$

$$周産期死亡率 = \frac{年間周産期死亡数}{年間出生数＋年間の妊娠満22週以後の死産数} \times 1,000$$

妊娠満22週以後の死産率（総数・自然・人工）

$$= \frac{年間の妊娠満22週以後の死産数（総数・自然・人工）}{年間出生数＋年間の妊娠満22週以後の死産数} \times 1,000$$

$$早期新生児死亡率 = \frac{年間早期新生児死亡数（生後1週（7日）未満の死亡数）}{年間出生数} \times 1,000$$

$$婚　姻　率 = \frac{年間婚姻届出件数}{10月1日現在日本人人口} \times 1,000$$

$$離　婚　率 = \frac{年間離婚届出件数}{10月1日現在日本人人口} \times 1,000$$

2）出　生

$$出　生　性　比 = \frac{年間の男子出生数}{年間の女子出生数} \times 100$$

母の年齢（年齢階級）別出生率

$$= \frac{ある年齢（年齢階級）の母が1年間に生んだ子の数}{10月1日現在における日本人女性のある年齢（年齢階級）の人口} \times 1,000$$

$$月間出生率（年換算率） = \frac{月間出生数}{月初人口×年換算係数} \times 1,000$$

（注）$年換算係数 = \dfrac{月間日数（30, 31, 28又は29）}{年間日数（365又は366）}$

すなわち1年の長さを1とした場合の各月の長さをいう。

$$合計特殊出生率 = \left\{ \frac{年間の母の年齢別出生数}{10月1日現在年齢別女性人口} \right\} 15歳から49歳までの合計$$

（都道府県及び21大都市は5歳階級で算出し、5倍したものを合計している。
ただし、平成27年以降の国勢調査が実施された年は各歳の合計。）

　合計特殊出生率は「15歳から49歳までの女性の年齢別出生率を合計したもの」で、1人の女性がその年齢別出生率で一生の間に生むとしたときの子ども数に相当する。

　なお、算出に用いた出生数の15歳及び49歳にはそれぞれ14歳以下、50歳以上を含んでいる。

（参　　考）
　合計特殊出生率には次の2つの種類がある。
　期間合計特殊出生率：　　ある期間（1年間）の出生状況に着目したもので、その年における各年齢（15〜49歳）の女性の出生率を合計したもの。女性人口の年齢構成の違いを除いた「その年の合計特殊出生率」として、年次比較、国際比較、地域比較に用いられている。人口動態統計では上記計算式に基づき、期間合計特殊出生率を算出している。
　コーホート合計特殊出生率：ある世代の出生状況に着目したもので、同一世代生まれ（コーホート）の女性の各年齢（15〜49歳）の出生率を過去から積み上げたもの。「その世代の合計特殊出生率」である。

　実際に「1人の女性が一生の間に生む子どもの数」はコーホート合計特殊出生率であるが、この値はその世代が50歳に到達するまで得られないため、それに相当するものとして期間合計特殊出生率が一般に用いられている。なお、各年齢の出生率が世代（コーホート）によらず同じであれば、この二つの「合計特殊出生率」は同じ値になる。
　ただし、晩婚化・晩産化が進行している状況等、各世代の結婚や出産の行動に違いがあり、各年齢の出生率が世代により異なる場合には、別々の世代の年齢別出生率の合計である期間合計特殊出生率は同一世代のコーホート合計特殊出生率の値と異なることに注意が必要である。
　コーホート合計特殊出生率については、巻末の参考表「2　年次推移」の「表6」を参照されたい。

3）死　　　亡

$$死　亡　性　比 = \frac{年間の男子死亡数}{年間の女子死亡数} \times 100$$

年齢（年齢階級）別死亡率（総数・男・女）

$$= \frac{年間のある年齢（年齢階級）の死亡数（総数・男・女）}{10月1日現在における日本人（総数・男・女）のある年齢（年齢階級）の人口} \times 1,000$$

$$月間死亡率（年換算率） = \frac{月間死亡数}{月初人口 \times 年換算係数} \times 1,000$$

$$（注）年換算係数 = \frac{月間日数（30, 31, 28又は29）}{年間日数（365又は366）}$$

　　　すなわち1年の長さを1とした場合の各月の長さをいう。

$$死因別死亡率（年間） = \frac{年間の死因別死亡数}{10月1日現在日本人人口} \times 100,000$$

$$年齢調整死亡率 = \frac{\left\{ \left[\begin{array}{c} 観察集団の各年齢 \\ （年齢階級）の死亡率 \end{array} \right] \times \left[\begin{array}{c} 基準人口集団のその年齢 \\ （年齢階級）の人口 \end{array} \right] \right\} \begin{array}{c} の各年齢（年齢 \\ 階級）の総和 \end{array}}{基準人口集団の総数}$$

（参　　考）
　死亡率は年齢によって異なるので、国際比較や年次推移の観察には、人口の年齢構成の差異を取り除いて観察するために、年齢調整死亡率を使用することが有用である。
　年齢調整死亡率の基準人口については、平成元年までは昭和10年の性別総人口（都道府県は昭和35年総人口）を使用してきたが、現実の人口構成からかけ離れてきたため、平成2年からは昭和60年モデル人口（昭和60年国勢調査日本人人口をもとに、ベビーブーム等の極端な増減を補正し1,000人単位で作成したもの）を使用している。
　なお、計算式中の「観察集団の各年齢（年齢階級）の死亡率」は、1,000倍（死因別の場合は100,000倍）されたものである。

基準人口—昭和60年モデル人口—

年齢	基準人口	年齢	基準人口
0〜4歳	8 180 000	50〜54	7 616 000
5〜9	8 338 000	55〜59	6 581 000
10〜14	8 497 000	60〜64	5 546 000
15〜19	8 655 000	65〜69	4 511 000
20〜24	8 814 000	70〜74	3 476 000
25〜29	8 972 000	75〜79	2 441 000
30〜34	9 130 000	80〜84	1 406 000
35〜39	9 289 000	85歳以上	784 000
40〜44	9 400 000		
45〜49	8 651 000	総　数	120 287 000

4） 乳 児 死 亡

乳 児 死 亡 性 比 ＝ $\dfrac{\text{年間の男子乳児死亡数}}{\text{年間の女子乳児死亡数}} \times 100$

新生児死亡性比 ＝ $\dfrac{\text{年間の男子新生児死亡数}}{\text{年間の女子新生児死亡数}} \times 100$

日齢（月齢）別乳児死亡率性比 ＝ $\dfrac{\text{ある日齢（月齢）の男子乳児死亡率}}{\text{ある日齢（月齢）の女子乳児死亡率}} \times 100$

月間乳児死亡率（年換算率）
（平成 6 年以前）

$$= \dfrac{\text{その月の月間乳児死亡数}}{\text{その月を含む過去1年間の出生数} \times \dfrac{\text{その月の月間日数}}{\text{その月を含む過去1年間の日数}}} \times 1,000$$

月間乳児死亡率（年換算率）
（平成 7 年以降） ＝ $\dfrac{\text{月間乳児死亡数}}{\text{年間出生数} \times \text{年換算係数}} \times 1,000$

（注）年換算係数 ＝ $\dfrac{\text{月間日数（30, 31, 28又は29）}}{\text{年間日数（365又は366）}}$

すなわち 1 年の長さを 1 とした場合の各月の長さをいう。

死因別乳児死亡率
又は生存期間別乳児死亡率 ＝ $\dfrac{\text{年間の死因別乳児死亡数（又は生存期間別乳児死亡数）}}{\text{年間出生数}} \times 100,000$

死因別新生児死亡率 ＝ $\dfrac{\text{年間の死因別新生児死亡数}}{\text{年間出生数}} \times 100,000$

5） 死 　 産

死 　 産 　 性 　 比 ＝ $\dfrac{\text{年間の男子死産数}}{\text{年間の女子死産数}} \times 100$

月間死産率（総数・自然・人工） ＝ $\dfrac{\text{月間死産数（総数・自然・人工）}}{\text{月間出産数（月間出生数＋月間死産数）}} \times 1,000$

月間の妊娠満22週以後の死産率（総数・自然・人工）

$$= \dfrac{\text{月間の妊娠満22週以後の死産数（総数・自然・人工）}}{\text{月間出生数＋月間の妊娠満22週以後の死産数}} \times 1,000$$

6） 周産期死亡

月間周産期死亡率 ＝ $\dfrac{\text{月間周産期死亡数}}{\text{月間出生数＋月間の妊娠満22週以後の死産数}} \times 1,000$

7） 妊産婦死亡

妊 産 婦 死 亡 率 ＝ $\dfrac{\text{年間の妊産婦死亡数}}{\text{年間出産数（年間出生数＋年間死産数）（又は年間出生数）}} \times 100,000$

後発妊産婦死亡率 ＝ $\dfrac{\text{年間の後発妊産婦死亡数}}{\text{年間出産数（年間出生数＋年間死産数）}} \times 100,000$

注：妊産婦死亡については65ページを参照されたい。

5　死因分類の解説

1）沿革

　我が国の死因分類の歴史は長く、明治8年（1875年）には解剖学的な11項目の分類である日本最初の死因分類が制定されている。国際的には、明治26年(1893年)に国際統計協会の会議で採択された国際死因リストについて、明治33年（1900年）に国際死因リストの改訂に関する第1回国際会議が開催され、ここで第1回改訂国際疾病分類（ICD）が採択されて10年周期の改訂が望ましいことが確認された。我が国は同年、この第1回改訂のICDを採用し、以来、日本の死因統計について国際的な分類を尊重しながら適切な適用に努めてきている。

　戸籍法の制定により人口動態統計が整備された明治32年以降の死因分類の推移を示すと、次表のとおりである。

（参　　考）　　　　　　　　　　　国際疾病傷害死因分類の推移

国際疾病,死因分類改訂国際会議	所　轄　機　関		我が国の適用対象となった年次
	国　　際	日　　本	
第1回 1900年	国　際　統　計　協　会	内　閣　統　計　局	明治32年～　　41年（1899年～1908年）
2　1909	国　際　統　計　協　会	内　閣　統　計　局	明治42年～大正11年（1909年～1922年）
3　1920	国　際　統　計　協　会	内　閣　統　計　局	大正12年～昭和7年（1923年～1932年）
4　1929	国　際　統　計　協　会 国　際　連　盟	内　閣　統　計　局	昭和8年～　　18年（1933年～1943年）
5　1938	国　際　統　計　協　会 国　際　連　盟	厚生省予防局衛生統計部	昭和21年～　　24年（1946年～1949年）
6　1948	世界保健機関（WHO）	厚　生　省　統　計　調　査　部	昭和25年～　　32年（1950年～1957年）
7　1955	世界保健機関（WHO）	厚　生　省　統　計　調　査　部	昭和33年～　　42年（1958年～1967年）
8　1965	世界保健機関（WHO）	厚　生　省　統　計　調　査　部	昭和43年～　　53年（1968年～1978年）
9　1975	世界保健機関（WHO）	厚　生　省　統　計　情　報　部	昭和54年～平成6年（1979年～1994年）
10　1989	世界保健機関（WHO）	厚　生　省　統　計　情　報　部	平成7年～　　17年（1995年～2005年）
10　2003	世界保健機関（WHO）	厚生労働省統計情報部	平成18年～　　（2006年～

　平成7年（1995年）から我が国が適用した死因分類は、平成2年（1990年）に世界保健機関（以下「WHO」という。）の第43回世界保健総会において採択され、平成5年（1993年）からの使用を加盟各国に勧告された「疾病及び関連保健問題の国際統計分類第10回改訂」（ICD－10）に準拠した「疾病、傷害及び死因の統計基本分類表」（以下「日本分類」という。）及び日本分類を集約した「死因分類表」（平成6年10月12日総務庁告示第75号）を使用していたが、平成18年（2006年）から、平成2年（1990年）以降15年（2003年）までの一部改正を集積した「ICD－10（2003年版）」に準拠した日本分類及び死因分類表（平成17年10月7日総務省告示第1147号）を使用している。

2）「原死因」と死因の選択

　死因統計は死亡診断書に基づき作成するが、死亡に関与した全ての事項が死亡診断書に記載されるように、昭和42年（1967年）の第20回世界保健総会において、死亡診断書に記載する死因は「死亡を引き起こしたか、その一因となった全ての疾病、病態または損傷、及びこれらの損傷を引き起こした事故または暴力の状況」と定義された。これに先立ち昭和23年（1948年）の第6回改訂会議においては、一次製表のための死因は原死因とするべきであるということが合意されている。

　WHOは、「死亡の防止という観点からは、病的事象の連鎖をある時点で切るか、ある時点で疾病を治すことが重要である。また、最も効果的な公衆衛生の目的は、その活動によって原因を防止することである。」として、この目的のために原死因を次のように定義した。

①直接に死亡を引き起こした一連の事象の起因となった疾病若しくは損傷

　　②致命傷を負わせた事故若しくは暴力の状況

　また、原死因を選択するために、WHOは死亡診断書の国際様式及び原死因選択手順を定め加盟各国に勧告しており、我が国もこれを基本としている。

　原死因選択手順には原死因選択のための複雑なルールが規定されているが、我が国は医師の作成した一枚一枚の死亡診断書の記載状況に従ってこの原死因選択手順を適用して、最終的に統計として表章する原死因を選択し決定している。

　死亡診断書の様式においては、死亡の原因を記載する欄がⅠ欄とⅡ欄に分かれており、Ⅰ欄には直接死因のみならず、その原因となった一連の病態についても記載し、Ⅱ欄には、死亡に寄与したその他の重要な病態を記載することとなっている。

　死亡診断書に死因となる傷病名が一つだけ記載されている場合には、その傷病名の属する分類が原死因となりうるが、同じ傷病名が記載されていても年齢や性別、先天性か否かなど多くの条件や手術・解剖欄などの記載状況によって属する分類が変化するため、死亡診断書全体の記載状況を把握して原死因を決定する。

　死亡診断書に二つ以上の傷病名が記載されている場合には、統計表章のためにただ一つの原死因を選択しなければならない。死亡診断書のⅠ欄の一番上に直接死因の傷病名が記載され、その下欄に原因となった傷病名が因果関係の順番に正しく記載されている場合は、Ⅰ欄の最下欄に記載された疾病または損傷の属する分類が原死因と考えられる。しかし死亡の状況は死亡者によって異なるため、診断書の記載状況は多様であり、原死因の選択にあたっては、傷病名の組み合わせ、記載された位置や欄、合併症や手術・解剖の記載及び死亡の場所や死亡の状況等の全ての記載事項を確認した上で、それぞれの状況に該当する原死因選択手順を判断・適用し、最終的な原死因を決定している。

　WHOは、周産期死亡についても用語の定義、死亡診断書の様式、原死因選択基準を定めるほか、児側病態・母側病態の主要な疾病または病態の解析のためのクロス表の作成を勧告しており、我が国はWHOの勧告する周産期死亡診断書の様式は採用していないものの、この様式に盛り込まれた項目の多くを死亡診断書及び死産証書の様式に加えることにより、勧告されたクロス表を作成している。

　死産の原因については、ICD－10採用時から児側病態と母側病態を一体としてとらえて原死因を選択することとした。また、児側病態、母側病態からそれぞれ原死因を選び両者のクロス表を作成している。

　原死因の選択及び死因分類等の詳細については、「疾病、傷害および死因統計分類提要ICD－10（2003年版）準拠」の第1巻、第2巻、第3巻を参照されたい。

３）分類表

　本報告書の死因統計に使用している分類表は、次のとおりである。

(1)　人口動態死因統計分類基本分類表（「死因基本分類表」という。）

　人口動態統計で使用する死因基本分類表は、日本分類に更に人口動態統計用としての細分類項目を加えたものである。

　日本分類として国際分類に追加した細分類項目は、５桁目にアルファベットの小文字で表示し、人口動態統計用として追加した細分類項目は、４桁目は数字で、５桁目はアルファベットの大文字で表示することとしている。

　詳細については、本報告書の下巻を参照されたい。

(2)　死因分類表（「死因簡単分類表」という。）

　我が国の死因構造を全体的に概観することを目的とし、死因基本分類表をもとに、ＷＨＯの死亡製表用リストを参考にして作成した分類表である。

　分類項目は、死亡数が一定数以上認められるもの、死亡数は少ないが国民、研究者等にとって関心の高いものを、これまでとの連続性等も考慮しつつ選定した。分類項目には５桁の分類番号を設定し、最初の２桁をＩＣＤ－10の章構成に合わせ、３桁目をいくつかの項目を統合した中間分類とし、最後の２桁は整理番号とした。

(3)　選択死因分類表

　社会的に関心の強い死因について、死因簡単分類表から選択したものであり、ＩＣＤ－９との連続性についても配慮した。

　分類項目の選定は、死因簡単分類表で死亡数の多い上位15の疾病を参考とし、更に、悪性新生物、心疾患、脳血管疾患及び不慮の事故については社会的重要性から細分化している。細分化の基準としては、悪性新生物では、部位別死亡順位の上位10程度の部位と健康増進事業において「がん検診」が実施されている部位、心疾患、脳血管疾患及び不慮の事故では死亡数が一定数以上の疾病、事故を選定した。

　また、結核は社会的に関心が高いので加えることとした。

(4)　死因年次推移分類表

　年次ごとの死因の動向を観察することを主目的とした分類表であり、明治32年以降の主要な死因の動向を踏まえ、ＩＣＤ－９の主要死因について一部見直しを行った。

(5)　乳児死因分類表（「乳児死因簡単分類表」という。）

　ＷＨＯの勧告では、５歳までの小児死因分類表の作成が勧告されている。我が国では、５歳までの死亡に占める乳児死亡の割合が高く、医学的・行政的にも乳児死亡への対策が重視されているので、乳児死亡のみを対象とした分類表とした。

　分類項目の選定は、死因簡単分類表と同様の考え方で行ったが、乳児死亡の特徴も考慮し、「悪性新生物」等を簡略化し、「周産期に発生した病態」及び「先天奇形、変形および染色体異常」を詳細に分類し、更に喘息や乳幼児突然死症候群を加えた。

(6)　感染症分類表

　感染症による死亡数の割合が少ない状況が続いたため、時代に適合するよう、平成７年に適用した「ＩＣＤ－10（初版）準拠」では死因簡単分類表から感染症の分類項目を一部を除き削除したが、感染症に関する状況を把握しておく必要があったことから、同年、新たに作成した分類である。

　分類項目の選定に当たっては、法的に届出等が義務づけられていること、保健衛生面において対応が必要

な疾病の動向を把握すること、国際比較を容易にすること等に配慮した。

　なお、平成11年以降の分類名は「感染症の予防及び感染症の患者に対する医療に関する法律」（平成10年法律第114号。以下「感染症法」という。）、感染症法施行令（平成10年政令第420号）及び感染症法施行規則（平成10年厚生省令第99号）並びに「結核予防法」（昭和26年法律第96号）に規定された疾病名であるため、必ずしもＩＣＤ－10とは一致していない。

　また、平成11、15、19、20、24、25、27、28年に感染症法等の改正に伴い分類を変更、平成18年に「ＩＣＤ－10（2003年版）準拠」の適用に伴い分類を変更した。

(7)　死因順位及び乳児死因順位に用いる分類項目

　死因簡単分類表及び乳児死因簡単分類表から主要な死因を選択した。

　これらの分類表のうち、(1)人口動態死因統計分類基本分類表、(2)死因分類表、(6)感染症分類表については、平成18年1月1日から「ＩＣＤ－10（2003年版）準拠」の適用に伴い、分類の追加、削除、変更及び原死因選択ルールの変更が行われている。

　(2)死因分類表、(6)感染症分類表の詳細については、巻末「参考表　年次推移」の各表脚注を参照されたい。

4）死因年次推移分類の変遷

本報告書の記述に、結核、悪性新生物、脳血管疾患などを主要死因として解析しているが、その場合の主要死因を、それぞれの年次の死因分類番号で示すと、次のとおりである。

表 2.1 死 因 年 次 推 移

	Hi01 結核 小分類	Hi01 結核 中分類	Hi02 悪性新生物 小分類	Hi02 悪性新生物 中分類	Hi03 糖尿病 小分類	Hi03 糖尿病 中分類	Hi04 高血圧性疾患 小分類	Hi04 高血圧性疾患 中分類	Hi05 心疾患（高血圧性を除く）小分類	Hi05 心疾患（高血圧性を除く）中分類	Hi06 脳血管疾患 小分類	Hi06 脳血管疾患 中分類	Hi07 肺炎 小分類	Hi07 肺炎 中分類	Hi08 慢性気管支炎及び肺気腫 小分類	Hi08 慢性気管支炎及び肺気腫 中分類
（第1回）明治32〜39年（1899〜1906）	・	12-15 *44	・	17-18 *44	・	・	・	・	・	24 *44	・	21	・	27	・	・
明治40〜41年（1907〜1908）	・	13-16 *51	・	20-21 *51	・	・	・	・	・	29 *51	・	26	・	32	・	・
（第2回）明治42〜大正11年（1909〜1922）	25-32	13-16	40-48 58	21-22 *26	55	25	・	・	83-85 86	33 *34	71-73	30 *32	97-98	37	・	・
（第3回）大正12〜昭和7年（1923〜1932）	31-37	13-15	43-49 65	16 *37	57	37の再掲	・	・	87-90	19 *37	74-75 83	18 *37	100-101	22	99（ロ）106	*21 *23
（第4回）昭和8〜18年（1933〜1943）	23-32	11-12	45-53 72	18 *27	59	22	・	・	90-95	38-43	82	32	107-109	48	106（ロ）113	*47 *50
（第5回）昭和21〜24年（1946〜1949）	13-22	・	45-55 74	・	61	・	・	・	90-95	・	83	・	107-109	・	106.b 113	・
（第6回）昭和25〜32年（1950〜1957）	001-019	B1-B2	140-205	B18	260	B20	440-447	B28-B29	410-434	B25-B27	330-334	B22	490-493 763	B31 B43.a	502	**527
（第7回）昭和33〜42年（1958〜1967）	001-019	B1-B2	140-205	B18	260	B20	440-447	B28-B29	410-434	B25-B27	330-334	B22	490-493 763	B31 B43.a	502	**527
（第8回）昭和43〜53年（1968〜1978）	001-019	B5-B6	140-209	B19	250	B21	400-404	B27	393-398 410-429	B26 B28-B29	430-438	B30	480-486	B32	491-492	*B33.a B33.b
（第9回）昭和54〜平成6年（1979〜1994）	010-018	5-6	140-208	28-37	250	39	401-405	48-49	393-398 410-429	46 51-52 54-56	430-438	58-60	480-486	63	491-492	*66-67
（第10回）平成7年〜（1995〜）	A15-A19	01200	C00-C97	02100	E10-E14	04100	I10-I13	09100	I01-I02.0 I05-I09 I20-I25 I27 I30-I51	09200	I60-I69	09300	J12-J18	10200	J41-J43	*10400

注： 1 死因名は第10回分類による。なお、表頭の分類の名称、小分類、中分類は、第10回分類の死因基本分類表、死因簡単分類表に対応する。

2 ＊印はこの番号の一部であることを示す。このため変遷を観察する場合は数字を計上していない。

3 ＊＊印はこの番号の大部分であることを示す。このため変遷を観察する場合は数字を計上した。

4 ・印は分類は存在するが、死因統計には用いていない。

5 明治32〜39年及び明治40〜41年は同じ分類を使用しているが、分類番号が異なるのは、再掲を組み入れて通し番号にしたためである。

6 結核について
(1) 明治41年以前は、る̇い̇れ̇き̇を含まない。
(2) 昭和54年以降は、後遺症及び原因の記載のない滲出性胸膜炎を含まない。
(3) 平成7年以降は、結核を伴うじん肺（J65）を含まない。

7 悪性新生物について
(1) 明治41年以前は、白血病及び仮性白血病を含まない。

8 心疾患について
(1) 明治41年以前は、狭心症を含まない。
(2) 昭和54年以降は、心臓麻痺、心臓衰弱を含む。

分　類　の　変　遷

Hi09 喘息		Hi10 胃潰瘍及び十二指腸潰瘍		Hi11 肝疾患		Hi12 腎不全		Hi13 老衰		Hi14 不慮の事故		Hi15（再掲）交通事故		Hi16 自殺	
小分類	中分類	小分類	中分類	小分類	中分類	小分類	中分類	小分類	中分類	小分類	中分類	小分類	中分類	小分類	中分類
·	·	·	·	·	·			·	39	·	40 ＊＊42 43	·	·	·	41
·	·	·	·	·	·			·	46	·	47 ＊＊49 50	·	·	·	48
102	＊38	108	＊39	118,120	45, ＊46			161	56	64-66,160 170-179 180-197	＊27 ＊55 58	·	·	162-169	57
105	＊23	111	＊24	120-122 124	28, ＊37			164	34	67-68,163 175-189 192-196	＊37 ＊33 ＊＊35	·	·	165-174	36
112	＊50	117	51	124-125	56-57			162（再掲を除く）	＊＊78	76-77 176-195	29 81-82	·	·	163-171	79
112	·	117	·	124-125	·			162.b	·	78-79 169-195	·	169-173		163-164	·
241	·	540-541	B33	580-583	B37 ＊B46.e			794	B45.a	E800-E965	BE47-BE48	E800-E802 E810-E835 E840-E866	BE47 BE48.a	E970-E979	BE49
241	·	540-541	B33	580-583	B37 ＊B46.e			794	B45.a	E800-E962	BE47-BE48	E800-E802 E810-E835 E840-E866	BE47 BE48.a	E963 E970-E979	BE49
493	B33.c	531-533	B34	570-573	B37 B46.f			794	B45.a	E800-E949	BE47-BE48	E800-E807 E810-E823 E825-E845	BE47 BE48.a	E950-E959	BE49
493	68	531-533	69	570-573	73-74	584-586	·	797	88	E800-E949	E104-E114	E800-E807 E810-E848	E104-E105	E950-E959	E115
J45-J46	10500	K25-K27	11100	K70-K76	11300	N17-N19	14200	R54	18100	V01-X59	20100	V01-V98	20101	X60-X84	20200

　(3)　平成７年以降は、心臓併発症を伴うリウマチ熱（Ⅰ01）・心臓併発症を伴うリウマチ性舞踏病（Ⅰ02.0）を含み、肺塞栓症（Ⅰ26）・その他の肺血管の疾患（Ⅰ28）を含まない。

　9　脳血管疾患について

　(1)　昭和25年は、B22にB46.b（352の一部、すなわちB22の後遺症及び１年以上経過したもの）を含めること。

　(2)　平成７年以降は、脳動静脈奇形の破裂（Ⅰ60.8の一部）を含み、一過性脳虚血（G45）を含まない。

　10　腎不全について

　(1)　平成７年以降は、先天性腎不全（P96.0）を含まない。

　11　老衰について

　(1)　昭和７年以前は、老衰性痴呆を含む。

　12　不慮の事故について

　(1)　昭和24年以前は、アルコール中毒を含まない。

　(2)　平成７年以降は、後遺症（Y86）を含まない。

　13　自殺について

　(1)　平成７年以降は、後遺症（Y87.0）を含まない。

Ⅱ 人口動態調査結果の概要

Part Ⅱ Summary of Vital Statistics

平成28年の概況

出　　　生（第4章の統計表参照）

　平成28年の出生数は976,978人で、前年の1,005,677人より28,699人減少し、出生率（人口千対）は7.8で前年より低下した。合計特殊出生率は1.44で前年の1.45より低下した。出生数を性別にみると男501,880人、女475,098人で、女を100とする出生性比は男105.6であり、昭和50年代後半からおおむね105台で推移している。

　出生数と合計特殊出生率の年次推移をみると、第2次世界大戦前は戦争のあった時を除いて出生数はおおむね増加していた。戦後は、昭和22～24年の第1次ベビーブーム期には出生数は260万人台、合計特殊出生率は4を超えていたが、25年以降、数・率ともに急激に減少かつ低下した。その後、ひのえうま前後の特殊な動きを除けば、出生数は緩やかな増加傾向となり、昭和46～49年の第2次ベビーブーム期に200万人を超え、合計特殊出生率は2以上で推移していた。昭和50年以降、出生数は減少を続け、平成3年からは増減を繰り返していたが、13年以降は5年連続で減少した。平成18年からは再び増減を繰り返し、23年以降は減少していたが、27年は5年ぶりに増加し、28年は再び減少した。合計特殊出生率は昭和50年に2を下回ってからは50年代後半を除いて平成17年まで低下傾向が続き、18年以降は緩やかな上昇傾向が続いていたが、28年は低下した。（図1）

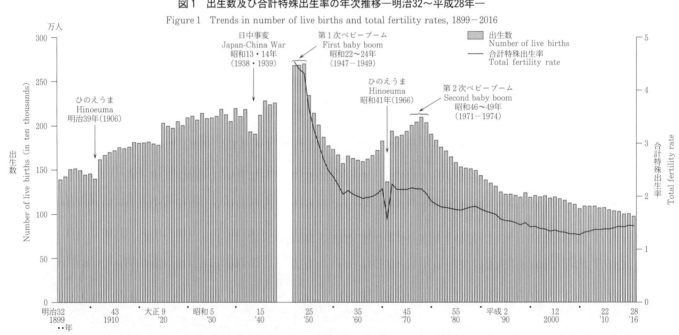

図1　出生数及び合計特殊出生率の年次推移―明治32～平成28年―
Figure 1　Trends in number of live births and total fertility rates, 1899－2016

　出生数を母の年齢（5歳階級）別にみると、15～39歳の各階級及び50歳以上では前年より減少したが、14歳以下及び40～49歳の各階級では増加した。

　合計特殊出生率の内訳を母の年齢（5歳階級）別にみると、34歳以下の各階級では前年より低下したが、35歳以上の各階級では上昇した。なお、30～34歳の階級が最も高くなった。（図2）

図2　母の年齢階級別出生率の年次推移―昭和22～平成28年―
Figure 2　Trends in live birth rates by age of mother, 1947-2016

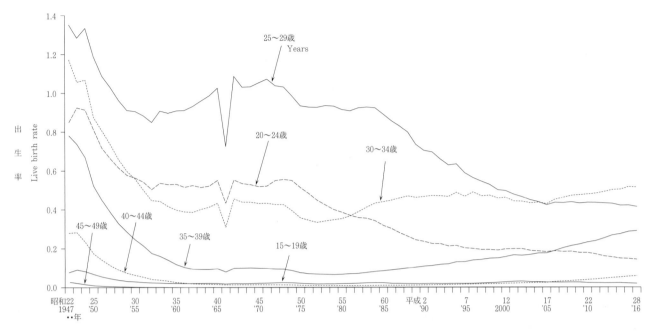

注：母の各歳別出生率を足し上げたもので、各階級の合計が合計特殊出生率である。

　出生数を出生順位別にみると、第1子は459,751人、第2子355,784人、第3子以上は161,443人で、いずれの出生順位についても前年より減少した。また、出生順位別の母の平均年齢は第1子30.7歳、第2子32.6歳、第3子33.6歳であり、前年と比較すると、第1子は同年齢、第2子及び第3子では0.1歳高くなった。
　合計特殊出生率の内訳を出生順位別にみると、第1子は前年より低下したが、第2子及び第3子以上は前年より上昇した。
　合計特殊出生率を都道府県別にみると、最も高いのは沖縄県1.95、次いで島根県1.75、宮崎県・長崎県1.71であった。一方で最も低いのは東京都1.24、次いで北海道1.29、宮城県・京都府1.34であり、おおむね大都市を有する都道府県で低い傾向がみられた。
　結婚生活に入ってから第1子出生までの平均期間は2.42年で、前年より0.01年長くなった。
　妊娠期間別出生数は正期（満37～41週）920,299人（妊娠期間不詳を除く出生数の94.2%）、早期（満37週未満）54,594人（同5.6%）、過期（満42週以上）1,885人（同0.2%）であった。割合でみると、早期は増加傾向から、近年は横ばいとなっており、過期は減少傾向から、近年は横ばいとなっている。
　出生時の平均体重は男3.05kg、女2.96kgであった。2,500g未満の出生数は男41,688人（体重不詳を除く男の出生数の8.3%）、女50,394人（体重不詳を除く女の出生数の10.6%）で近年は男女とも出生に占める割合は横ばいとなっている。
　出生時の平均身長は、前年と同じ男49.2cm、女48.6cmであった。
　父母の一方が外国人の出生数は19,118人（全出生数の2.0%）で、前年の19,079人（同1.9%）より39人増加した。全出生数に対する割合はゆるやかに増加を続けていたが、近年は横ばいとなっている。また、その内訳をみると「父日本・母外国」は9,371人で、そのうち母の国籍で最も多いのは中国3,671人、次いでフィリピン、韓国・朝鮮であり、一方、「母日本・父外国」は9,747人で、そのうち父の国籍で最も多いのは韓国・朝鮮2,250人、次いで米国、中国であった。

死　　　亡（第5章の統計表参照）

　平成28年の死亡数は1,307,748人で、前年の1,290,444人より17,304人増加し、死亡率（人口千対）は10.5で前年の10.3より上昇した。また、男の死亡数は674,733人、死亡率は11.1で、女の死亡数は633,015人、死亡率は9.9であった。

　死亡数及び死亡率の年次推移をみると、第2次世界大戦前は、インフルエンザの流行や関東大震災を除くと、死亡数は90万～120万人台、死亡率は16～20台前半で推移してきた。昭和20年代後半からは、死亡の状況は急速に改善され、41年には67万人と最少の死亡数、54年には6.0と最低の死亡率を記録した。昭和50年代後半からは、人口の高齢化を反映して死亡数は増加傾向に転じ、平成15年に100万人を超え、死亡率も上昇傾向にある。（図3）

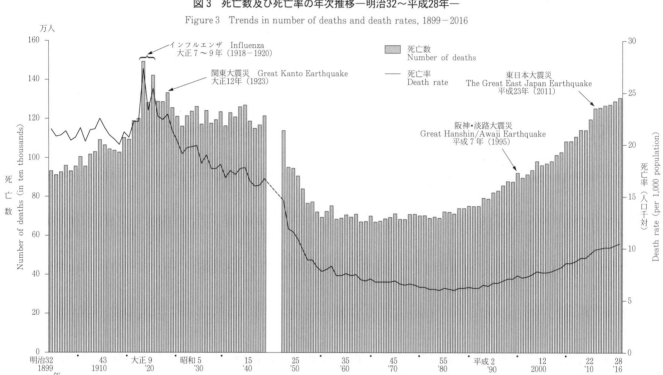

　死亡の状況はその集団における人口の年齢構成に影響されるので、年齢構成の差を取り除いて比較するための年齢調整死亡率を年次推移でみると、近年は緩やかな低下傾向にある。平成28年の年齢調整死亡率（人口千対）は、男4.8、女2.5で、男は前年の4.9より低下したが、女は前年と同率となった。

　主な死因別に死亡率の年次推移をみると、明治・大正・昭和初期は感染症の値が高く、昭和33年以降は悪性新生物、心疾患、脳血管疾患が死因順位の第1位から第3位を占めていたが、平成23年からは肺炎が脳血管疾患を上回り第3位に、脳血管疾患は第4位となっている。

　昭和22年以降の悪性新生物、心疾患、肺炎、脳血管疾患の死亡率（人口10万対）の推移をみると、悪性新生物は一貫して上昇を続け、56年に死因順位の第1位となり、その後も上昇傾向は続き、平成28年は298.3（死亡数372,986人、死因順位第1位）であった。心疾患は昭和60年に第2位となり、その後も上昇傾向は続き、平成6年から低下したが、9年には再び上昇傾向に転じ、28年は158.4（198,006人、第2位）であった。肺炎は、昭和50年から第4位が続いたが、この間おおむね上昇傾向が続き、平成23年に脳血管疾患を抜いて第3位となり、28年は95.4（119,300人、第3位）であった。脳血管疾患は昭和45年をピークに低下、平成3年以降は横ばいで推移し、7年に上昇したものの、8年以降低下傾向にあり、28年は87.4（109,320人、第4位）であった。

　自殺の死亡率は、平成28年は16.8で前年の18.5より低下し、第8位であった。（図4）

図4　主要死因別死亡率の年次推移―明治32～平成28年―
Figure 4　Trends in death rates from leading causes of death, 1899－2016

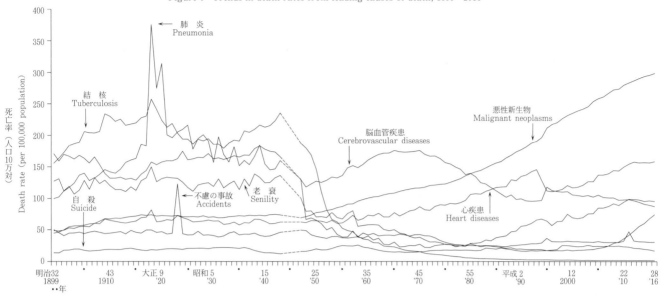

　死因順位第1位である悪性新生物の主な部位別死亡率の年次推移を性別にみると、男は、「肺」が一貫して上昇を続け、平成5年には「胃」を上回って第1位となり、引き続き上昇していたが、28年は低下した。「胃」は昭和43年以降緩やかな低下傾向が続いたものの、平成6年からは上昇傾向となっていたが、平成20年以降低下傾向となっている。「大腸」は上昇傾向にあり、平成19年から「肝」を上回って第3位となっている。上昇傾向にあった「肝」は近年低下傾向で推移している。

　女は、「大腸」が上昇を続け、平成15年からは「胃」を上回って第1位となり、19年には「肺」も「胃」を上回って第2位となり、引き続き上昇している。「膵」は上昇傾向にあり、平成28年には「胃」を上回って第3位となった。「胃」は低下傾向となっている。「乳房」は上昇傾向で、低下傾向だった「子宮」は、平成6年からは緩やかな上昇傾向にある。（図5）

図5　悪性新生物の主な部位別死亡率の年次推移―昭和25～平成28年―
Figure 5　Trends in death rates from malignant neoplasms by site, 1950－2016

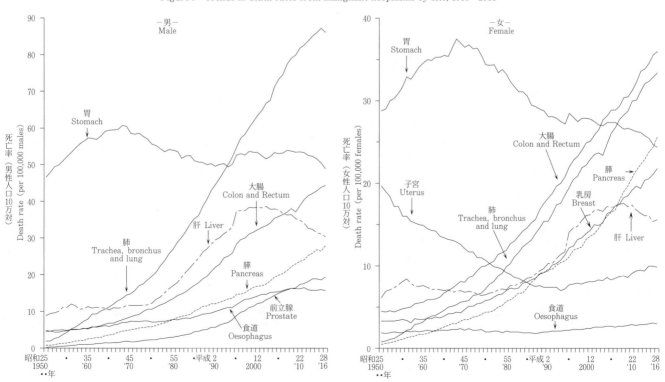

悪性新生物の主な部位別にみた年齢調整死亡率の年次推移を性別にみると、男女とも「胃」は、戦後上昇傾向にあったが、昭和30年代半ばをピークに低下を続けている。男は「肺」が上昇を続け平成５年に「胃」を上回ったが、９年以降は低下傾向にある。女は「子宮」が平成５年まで低下傾向にあったが、近年は横ばいとなっている。「大腸」は平成８年まで上昇傾向にあったが、近年横ばいに推移している。「乳房」は緩やかな上昇傾向にある。（図６）

図６　悪性新生物の主な部位別にみた年齢調整死亡率の年次推移―昭和22～平成28年―
Figure 6　Trends in age-adjusted death rates from malignant neoplasms by site, 1947－2016

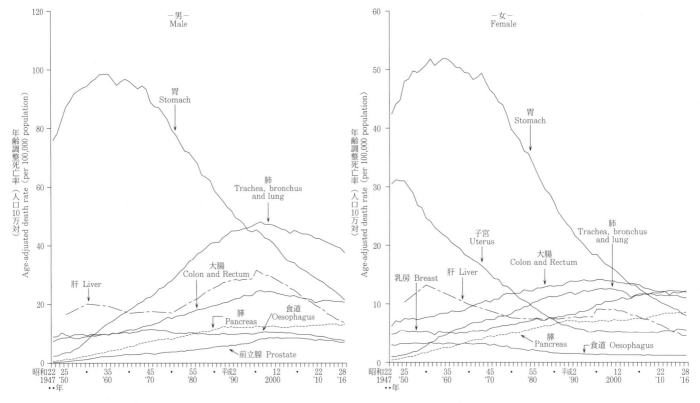

注：男女とも「肝」については、昭和55年以前は5年ごとの数値を用いており、昭和25年、30年の数値は「胆のう及びその他の胆道」を含む。

　平成28年の死因順位を性・年齢（５歳階級）別にみると、男女とも０～４歳は先天奇形，変形及び染色体異常、５～９歳は悪性新生物が第１位となった。
　男では10～14歳は不慮の事故、15～44歳は自殺、45～94歳は悪性新生物、95歳以上は老衰、女では10～14歳は悪性新生物、15～29歳は自殺、30～89歳は悪性新生物、90～94歳は心疾患、95歳以上は老衰が第１位となった。
　平成28年の死亡総数に占める悪性新生物の割合を性・年齢別にみると、男は60歳代で、女は50歳代でピークになるが、以降の年代は徐々に少なくなっている。

乳 児 死 亡（第 6 章の統計表参照）

　平成28年の乳児死亡（生後 1 年未満の死亡）数は1,928人で、前年の1,916人より12人増加し、乳児死亡率（出生千対）は2.0で前年の1.9より上昇した。

　乳児死亡率の年次推移をみると、明治から大正にかけては、大正 7 年のインフルエンザの大流行による高い死亡率を除くと140〜170台で推移していたが、それ以降は低下傾向となり、昭和15年には100を割り、90.0となった。第 2 次世界大戦後からは急速に低下し、昭和51年には10を割り、9.3となった。その後は緩やかな低下傾向にある。

　新生児死亡（生後 4 週未満の死亡）率の年次推移をみると、乳児死亡率と同様に、昭和40年代前半までは急速に低下し、その後は緩やかな低下傾向にある。（図 7 ）

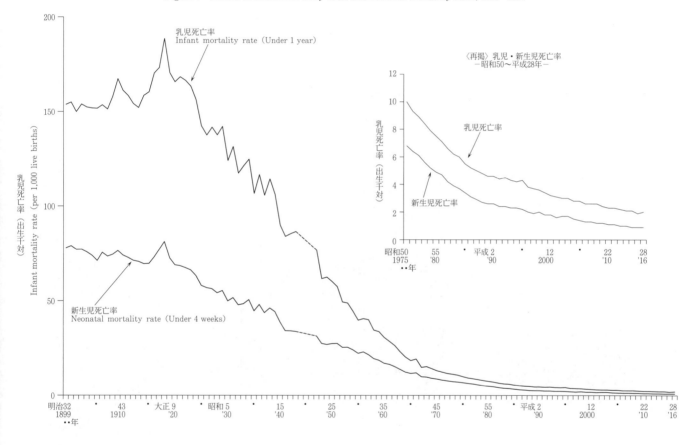

図 7　乳児死亡率及び新生児死亡率の年次推移―明治32〜平成28年―
Figure 7　Trends in infant mortality rates and neonatal mortality rates, 1899－2016

自 然 増 減（第 3 章の統計表参照）

　平成28年の自然増減数（出生数から死亡数を減じたもの）は△330,770人で、前年の△284,767人より46,003人減少し、自然増減率（人口千対）は△2.6で前年の△2.3より低下した。

　自然増減数の年次推移をみると、第 2 次世界大戦前は増加傾向であったが、戦後は第1次ベビーブーム期の昭和24年の175万人をピークに減少した。その後、昭和37年に再び増加に転じ、昭和46～49年の第 2 次ベビーブーム期には130万人を超えていたが、50年以降は出生数の減少により自然増減数も減少し、平成元年に50万人を割った。平成 2 年からは出生数は横ばいであったが、人口の高齢化による死亡数の増加により減少し、11年には20万人を割り、12年に一旦増加したものの、13年以降は出生数の減少と死亡数の増加の双方により減少し、16年には10万人を割った。平成17年には統計の得られていない昭和19年から21年を除き、現在の形式で統計をとり始めた明治32年以降初めて出生数が死亡数を下回りマイナスとなった。平成18年に一旦プラスとなったが、19年からは10年連続でマイナスとなり減少幅も拡大している。（図 8 ）

　都道府県別に自然増減率（人口千対）をみると、最も高いのは沖縄県3.4、次いで東京都・愛知県、滋賀県で、最も低いのは秋田県△9.5、次いで高知県、山形県であった。

　出生数が死亡数を上回った都道府県は、沖縄県のみであった。これ以外は全ての都道府県で出生数が死亡数を下回った。21大都市では、東京都の区部、仙台市、さいたま市、川崎市、広島市、福岡市の 6 都市で出生数が死亡数を上回った。

図 8　自然増減数及び自然増減率の年次推移―明治32～平成28年―

Figure 8　Trends in number of natural changes and natural change rates, 1899－2016

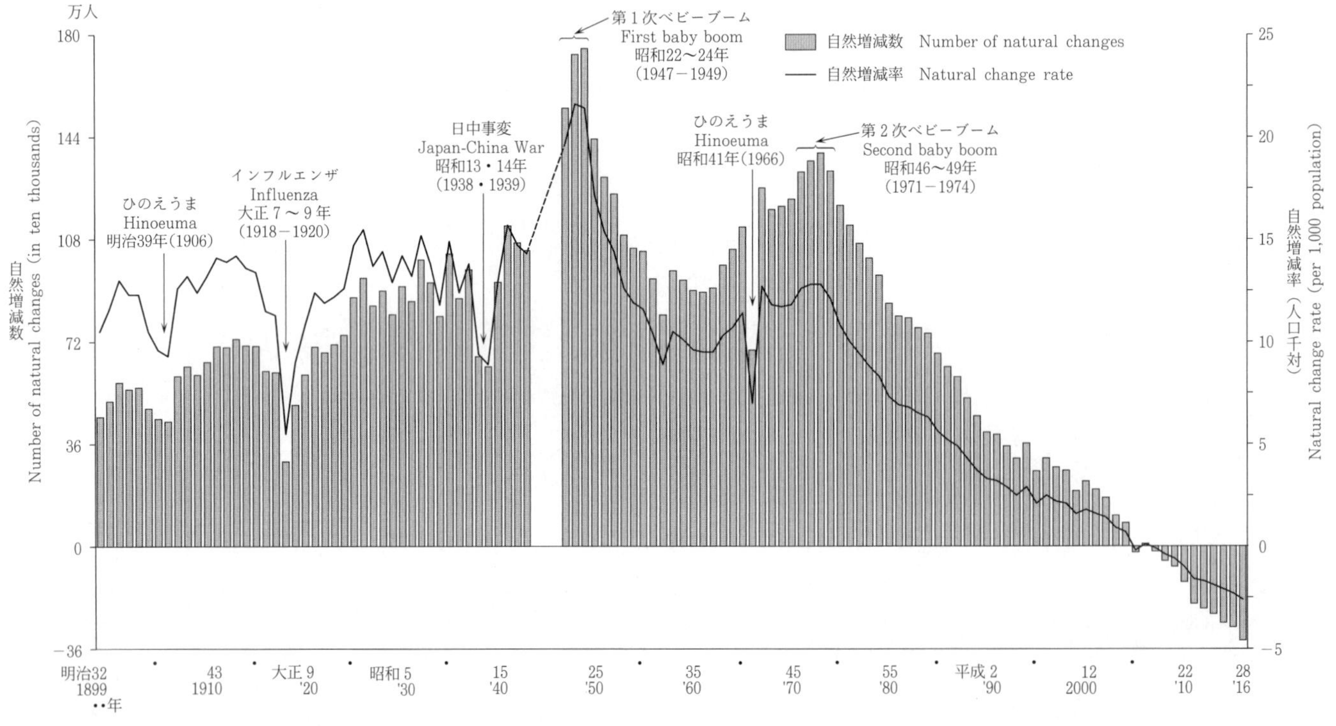

死　　　　産（第 7 章の統計表参照）

　平成28年の死産（妊娠満12週以後の死児の出産）数は20,934胎で、前年の22,617胎より1,683胎減少し、死産率（出産（出生＋死産）千対）は21.0で前年の22.0より低下した。自然死産数は10,067胎、自然死産率10.1、人工死産数は10,867胎、人工死産率10.9であった。

　死産率の年次推移をみると、明治30年代はおおむね90前後で推移していたが、その後低下傾向となり、昭和18年には40を割り、39.6にまで低下した。昭和23年以降は優生保護法（平成 8 年から母体保護法に改めた。）により、妊娠満12週以後の人工死産が含まれたため急激に上昇し、32年から36年にかけて100を超え、37年からは41

年のひのえうまの影響を除き、急激に低下し、50年には50.8となった。その後はおおむね低下し、平成7年からは横ばいで推移していたが、15年以降低下している。

自然死産・人工死産別にみると自然死産率は昭和30年代後半から低下傾向にある。人工死産率は昭和30年代半ばから低下していたが、50年からは上昇傾向に転じ、60年には自然死産率を上回った。昭和63年からは再び低下傾向に転じ、平成6年から14年まではおおむね横ばいとなったが、15年以降低下している。（図9）

図9　死産数及び死産率の年次推移—明治32～平成28年—
Figure 9　Trends in number of foetal deaths and foetal death rates, 1899－2016

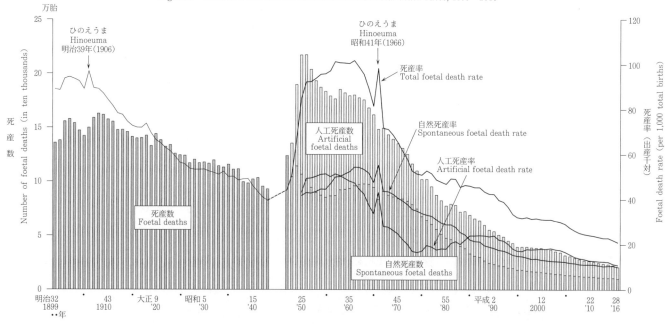

周産期死亡（第8章の統計表参照）

平成28年の周産期死亡（妊娠満22週以後の死産に早期新生児死亡を加えたもの）数は3,516（胎・人）で、前年の3,728（胎・人）より212（胎・人）減少し、周産期死亡率（出産（出生＋妊娠満22週以後の死産）千対）は3.6で前年の3.7より低下した。周産期死亡のうち、妊娠満22週以後の死産数は2,840胎で前年の3,063胎より223胎減少し、妊娠満22週以後の死産率（出産千対）は2.9で前年の3.0より低下した。また、早期新生児死亡数は676人で前年の665人より11人増加し、早期新生児死亡率（出生千対）は0.7で前年と同率であった。

周産期死亡数及び周産期死亡率の年次推移をみると、周産期死亡数は減少傾向にあり、周産期死亡率は近年横ばいとなっている。（図10）

図10　周産期死亡数及び周産期死亡率の年次推移—昭和54～平成28年—
Figure 10　Trends in number of perinatal deaths and perinatal death rates, 1979－2016

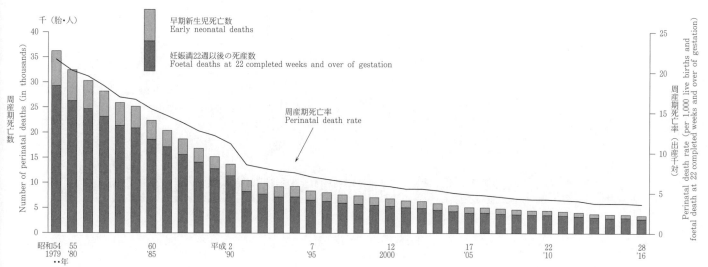

婚　　　姻（第9章の統計表参照）

　平成28年の婚姻件数は620,531組で、前年の635,156組より14,625組減少し、婚姻率（人口千対）は5.0で前年の5.1より低下した。

　婚姻件数の年次推移をみると、第2次世界大戦前は緩やかな増加傾向となっており、終戦直後は、戦争により繰り延べられていた婚姻によって、昭和22、23年の第1次婚姻ブームには急増して90万組を超えたが、24年からは急激に減少し、26年は67万組となった。その後は増加に転じ、昭和45年には第2次婚姻ブームを迎え、47年には110万組となった。昭和48年から53年にかけて再び急激に減少した後は、緩やかな減少傾向となったが、63年から増加に転じた。平成6年以降は増減を繰り返し、14年からは減少し続け、18年以降は再び増減を繰り返した。平成21年以降は減少が続き、24年は一旦増加したが、25年からは4年連続で減少し28年は戦後最少となった。（図11）

　婚姻を初婚－再婚別にみると、初婚の夫は499,233人、妻は516,547人、再婚の夫は121,298人、妻は103,984人であり、全婚姻件数に対する再婚件数の割合は、夫19.5％、妻16.8％であった。再婚の割合は夫・妻とも昭和48年以降増加を続け、平成2年から5年にかけて一旦減少したもののその後は再び増加が続いた。夫は平成20年、妻は21年から22年にかけて再び減少したが、23年からは夫・妻とも増加傾向にあり、28年は夫のみ減少した。

　また、初婚－再婚を夫妻の組合せ別にみると、平成28年は「夫妻とも初婚」は454,750組（全婚姻件数の73.3％）、「夫妻とも再婚又はどちらか一方が再婚」は165,781組（同26.7％）であった。「夫妻とも再婚又はどちらか一方が再婚」の全婚姻件数に占める割合は平成17年に全体の4分の1を超え、その後は増加傾向となっている。婚姻件数をみると、「夫妻とも初婚」は昭和48年以降減少傾向となり、平成2年から5年にかけて一旦増加した後、6年以降は増減を繰り返し、13年からは減少傾向となっている。「夫妻とも再婚又はどちらか一方が再婚」は昭和54年から増加傾向となっていたが、平成21年から減少傾向となっている。

　結婚生活に入ったときの年齢（5歳階級）別に夫・妻の初婚率（人口千対）をみると、25〜29歳が夫・妻ともに最も高く、夫48.02、妻57.99、次いで、30〜34歳が夫29.42、妻28.06、20〜24歳が夫16.58、妻25.55であった。同様に、再婚率（人口千対）をみると、夫は35〜39歳が4.67、次いで30〜34歳が4.15、妻は30〜34歳が4.78、次いで35〜39歳が4.19であった。

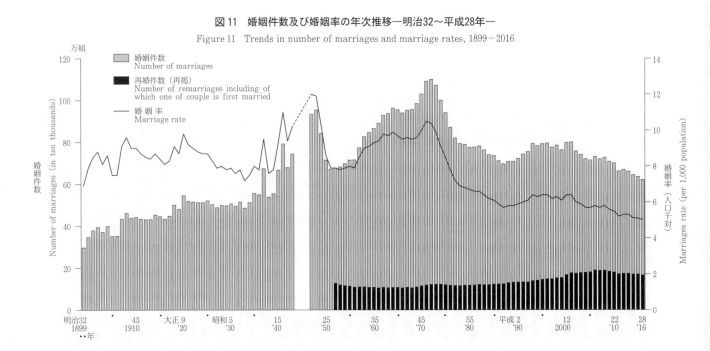

図11　婚姻件数及び婚姻率の年次推移―明治32〜平成28年―
Figure 11　Trends in number of marriages and marriage rates, 1899－2016

妻の年齢別初婚件数を平成 8、18、28年で比較してみると、ピークの年齢は 8 年では25歳であったが、18年、28年では27歳であった。（図12）

　夫・妻の平均初婚年齢をみると、前年と同じ夫31.1歳、妻29.4歳であった。年次推移でみると、夫・妻とも昭和40年代終わりから上昇傾向にあり、夫は昭和50年に27.0歳、57年に28.0歳、平成13年に29.0歳、18年に30.0歳となっており、妻は昭和52年に25.0歳、平成 4 年に26.0歳、12年に27.0歳、17年に28.0歳、23年に29.0歳となった。

　夫妻の一方が外国人の婚姻件数は21,180組（全婚姻件数の3.4％）で、前年の20,976組（同3.3％）より204組増加した。内訳をみると、「夫日本・妻外国」は14,851組（同2.4％）で、そのうち妻の国籍で最も多いのは中国5,526組、次いでフィリピン、韓国・朝鮮であった。一方、「妻日本・夫外国」は6,329組（同1.0％）で、そのうち夫の国籍で最も多いのは韓国・朝鮮1,627組、次いで米国、中国であった。

　夫妻の一方が外国人の婚姻件数の年次推移をみると、昭和60年代から急激に増加し、平成に入ってからも増加傾向が続いていたが、平成19年からは 9 年連続の減少となり、28年は再び増加した。（図13）

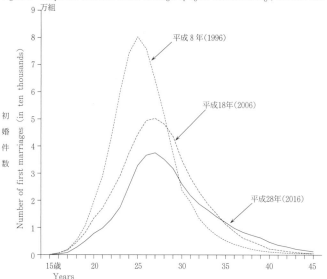

図12　結婚生活に入ったときの妻の年齢（各歳）別初婚件数の年次比較
—平成 8・18・28年—
Figure 12　Comparison of number of first marriages by age of bride at marriage, 1996・2006・2016

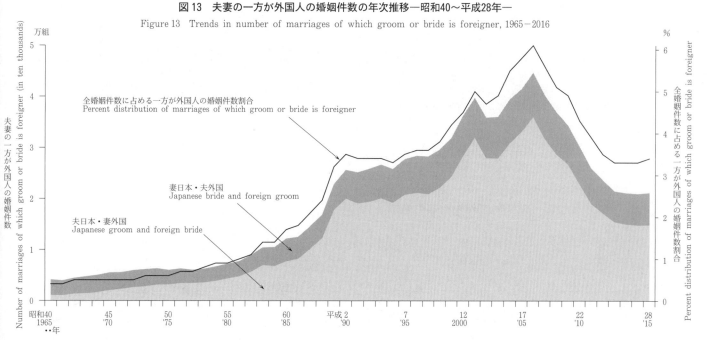

図13　夫妻の一方が外国人の婚姻件数の年次推移—昭和40～平成28年—
Figure 13　Trends in number of marriages of which groom or bride is foreigner, 1965−2016

離　　婚（第10章の統計表参照）

　平成28年の離婚件数は216,798組で、前年の226,215組より9,417組減少し、離婚率（人口千対）は1.73で前年の1.81より低下した。

　離婚件数と離婚率の年次推移をみると、第 2 次世界大戦前は、離婚件数はおおむね横ばい、離婚率は低下傾向にあった。戦後から昭和30年代までは、離婚件数は 7 ～ 8 万組で推移し、離婚率は1.00前後で推移していたが、徐々に低下傾向となった。昭和40年以降は、数・率ともに増加かつ上昇し、58年には 179,150組、1.51となったが、その後減少かつ低下傾向となった。平成 3 年以降再び増加かつ上昇し、14年には289,836組、2.30となり、

統計の得られていない昭和19年から21年を除き、現在の形式で統計をとり始めた明治32年以降最多かつ最高となった。平成15年以降は数・率ともに減少かつ低下傾向が続いている。（図14）

同居をやめたときの年齢（5歳階級）別に離婚率（人口千対）をみると、夫は30〜34歳が7.04で最も高く、次いで35〜39歳が6.53であり、妻は30〜34歳が8.23で最も高く、次いで25〜29歳が7.61であった。

同居期間別離婚件数は、5年未満が68,011組で最も多く、次いで5〜10年未満が44,391組であった。前年と比べると、全ての同居期間で減少した。（図15）

種類別離婚件数は、協議離婚が188,960組で最も多く、次いで調停離婚21,651組、和解離婚3,458組、判決離婚2,166組、審判離婚547組、認諾離婚（請求の認諾）16組であった。

親権を行わなければならない子をもつ夫妻別離婚件数は125,946組（全離婚件数の58.1%）で、前年より6,220組減少した。また、親権を行う者別にみると、「妻が全児の親権を行う」が106,314組（親権を行わなければならない子をもつ夫妻の離婚件数の84.4%）で最も多く、「夫が全児の親権を行う」が15,033組（同11.9%）、「夫と妻がそれぞれ分け合って子どもの親権を行う」が4,599組（同3.7%）であった。

図14　離婚件数及び離婚率の年次推移—明治32〜平成28年—
Figure 14　Trends in number of divorces and divorce rates, 1899－2016

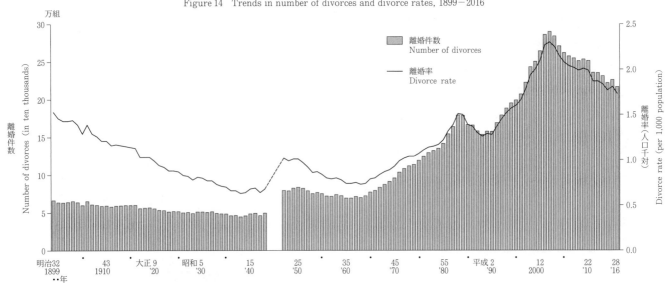

図15　同居期間別離婚件数の年次推移—昭和22〜平成28年—
Figure 15　Trends in number of divorces by duration of cohabitation, 1947－2016

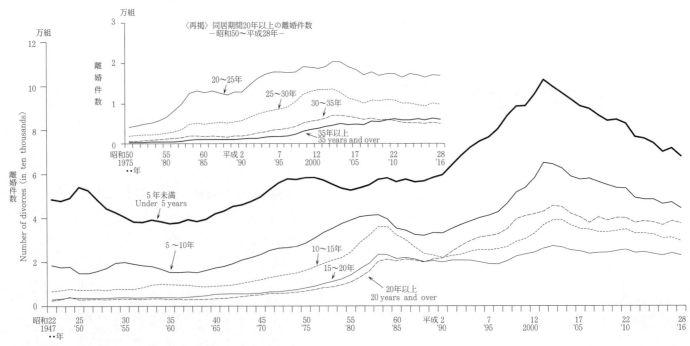

総　覧

第 3 章　総　　覧

Chapter 3 Summary

表 3.1　人口動態の年間発生件数・率・平均発生間隔－前年との比較－

Table 3.1　Summary of vital statistics (number, rates, interval of occurrence), 2016 and 2015

	件　　数 Number			率 Rate		平均発生間隔 Interval of occurrence	
	2016 平成28年	2015 平成27年	対前年増減 change over the year	2016 平成28年	2015 平成27年	2016 平成28年	2015 平成27年
出　　　　　生 Live births	976 978	1 005 677	△　28 699	7.8	8.0	32 s	31 s
男　Male	501 880	515 452	△　13 572	8.2	8.4	1m3 s	1m1 s
女　Female	475 098	490 225	△　15 127	7.4	7.6	1m7 s	1m4 s
死　　　　　亡 Deaths	1 307 748	1 290 444	17 304	10.5	10.3	24 s	24 s
男　Male	674 733	666 707	8 026	11.1	10.9	47 s	47 s
女　Female	633 015	623 737	9 278	9.9	9.7	50 s	51 s
（再掲） Regrouped							
乳　児　死　亡 Infant deaths	1 928	1 916	12	2.0	1.9	4 h 33m22 s	4 h 34m19 s
新　生　児　死　亡 Neonatal deaths	874	902	△　28	0.9	0.9	10 h 3m1 s	9 h 42m42 s
自　然　増　減 Natural change	△ 330 770	△ 284 767	△　46 003	△　2.6	△　2.3	…	…
死　　　　　産 Foetal deaths	20 934	22 617	△　1 683	21.0	22.0	25m11 s	23m14 s
自　然　死　産 Spontaneous	10 067	10 862	△　795	10.1	10.6	52m21 s	48m23 s
人　工　死　産 Artificial	10 867	11 755	△　888	10.9	11.4	48m30 s	44m43 s
周　産　期　死　亡 Perinatal deaths	3 516	3 728	△　212	3.6	3.7	2 h 29m54 s	2 h 20m59 s
妊娠満 22 週以後の死産 Foetal deaths at 22 completed weeks and over of gestation	2 840	3 063	△　223	2.9	3.0	3 h 5m35 s	2 h 51m36 s
早　期　新　生　児　死　亡 Early neonatal deaths	676	665	11	0.7	0.7	12 h 59m39 s	13 h 10m23 s
婚　　　　　姻 Marriages	620 531	635 156	△　14 625	5.0	5.1	51 s	50 s
離　　　　　婚 Divorces	216 798	226 215	△　9 417	1.73	1.81	2m26 s	2m19 s

注：　率の算出方法は、「第 2 章　調査結果の利用上の解説」の「 4．比率の解説（67～69ページ）」を参照されたい。

本報告において別掲とした件数
Number of cases tabulated separately in this report

	日本における日本人 前年以前に事件発生 Japanese in Japan Occured in previous year or before	日本における外国人 Foreigners in Japan		外国における日本人 Japanese in foreign countries	
		本年事件発生 Occured in this year	前年以前に事件発生 Occured in previous year or before	本年事件発生 Occured in this year	前年以前に事件発生 Occured in previous year or before
出　　　　　生 Live births	596	17 039	75	14 445	1 270
死　　　　　亡 Deaths	1 175	6 915	19	1 813	1 360
死　　　　　産 Foetal deaths	6	443	1	・	・
婚　　　　　姻 Marriages	8	4 028	1	11 839	3
離　　　　　婚 Divorces	121	1 278	32	2 077	640

注：　「第 1 章　調査の概要」の「 3）調査の対象」、「 4）調査の期間」（46ページ）を参照されたい。

総　覧

表 3.2　年次別にみた
Table 3.2　Trends in indices of

年次[1]　Year		出　生　数　Live births	死　亡　数　Deaths	（再掲）(Regrouped) 乳児（1歳未満）死亡数　Infant deaths (under 1 year)	新生児（生後4週未満）死亡数[2]　Neonatal deaths (under 4 weeks)	自然増減数　Natural change
1899	明治32年	1 386 981	932 087	213 359	108 077	454 894
1900	33	1 420 534	910 744	220 211	112 259	509 790
01	34	1 501 591	925 810	225 107	115 794	575 781
02	35	1 510 835	959 126	232 652	116 654	551 709
03	36	1 489 816	931 008	226 982	112 909	558 808
04	37	1 440 371	955 400	218 756	106 477	484 971
05	38	1 452 770	1 004 661	220 450	103 382	448 109
06	39	1 394 295	955 256	214 148	105 307	439 039
07	40	1 614 472	1 016 798	244 300	118 617	597 674
08	41	1 662 815	1 029 447	262 801	123 867	633 368
09	42	1 693 850	1 091 264	283 436	129 629	602 586
1910	43	1 712 857	1 064 234	276 136	126 910	648 623
11	44	1 747 803	1 043 906	276 798	127 302	703 897
12	大正元年	1 737 674	1 037 016	268 025	123 902	700 658
13	2	1 757 441	1 027 257	267 281	124 213	730 184
14	3	1 808 402	1 101 815	286 678	125 745	706 587
15	4	1 799 326	1 093 793	288 634	125 337	705 533
16	5	1 804 822	1 187 832	307 283	132 000	616 990
17	6	1 812 413	1 199 669	313 872	139 717	612 744
18	7	1 791 992	1 493 162	337 919	145 710	298 830
19	8	1 778 685	1 281 965	303 202	129 072	496 720
1920	9	2 025 564	1 422 096	335 613	139 681	603 468
21	10	1 990 876	1 288 570	335 143	136 342	702 306
22	11	1 969 314	1 286 941	327 604	132 856	682 373
23	12	2 043 297	1 332 485	333 930	135 504	710 812
24	13	1 998 520	1 254 946	312 267	126 385	743 574
25	14	2 086 091	1 210 706	297 008	121 238	875 385
26	昭和元年	2 104 405	1 160 734	289 275	119 642	943 671
27	2	2 060 737	1 214 323	292 084	116 240	846 414
28	3	2 135 852	1 236 711	293 881	115 682	899 141
29	4	2 077 026	1 261 228	295 178	115 009	815 798
1930	5	2 085 101	1 170 867	258 703	104 101	914 234
31	6	2 102 784	1 240 891	276 584	108 812	861 893
32	7	2 182 742	1 175 344	256 505	104 573	1 007 398
33	8	2 121 253	1 193 987	257 251	102 887	927 266
34	9	2 043 783	1 234 684	255 063	103 408	809 099
35	10	2 190 704	1 161 936	233 706	97 994	1 028 768
36	11	2 101 969	1 230 278	245 357	101 043	871 691
37	12	2 180 734	1 207 899	230 701	95 465	972 835
38	13	1 928 321	1 259 805	220 695	89 159	668 516
39	14	1 901 573	1 268 760	202 018	84 204	632 813
1940	15	2 115 867	1 186 595	190 509	81 869	929 272
41	16	2 277 283	1 149 559	191 420	77 829	1 127 724
42	17	2 233 660	1 166 630	190 897	76 177	1 067 030
43	18	2 253 535	1 213 811	195 219	76 588	1 039 724
47	22	2 678 792	1 138 238	205 360	84 204	1 540 554
48	23	2 681 624	950 610	165 406	73 855	1 731 014
49	24	2 696 638	945 444	168 467	72 432	1 751 194
1950	25	2 337 507	904 876	140 515	64 142	1 432 631
51	26	2 137 689	838 998	122 869	58 686	1 298 691
52	27	2 005 162	765 068	99 114	51 015	1 240 094
53	28	1 868 040	772 547	91 424	47 580	1 095 493
54	29	1 769 580	721 491	78 944	42 726	1 048 089

注：1) 昭和19～21年は資料不備のため省略した。昭和22～47年は沖縄県を含まない。
　　 昭和23・24年の＊印は概数であり、23年には8 637、24年には3 255の自然死産・人工死産の不詳がある。
　2) 新生児死亡の昭和18年以前は1か月未満の死亡である。また、新生児死亡の昭和18年は樺太を含む数字である。

Summary

人 口 動 態 総 覧
vital statistics : Japan

年　　　次[1] Year		出　生　数 Live births	死　亡　数 Deaths	（再　　　　　　　掲）(Regrouped)		自 然 増 減 数 Natural change
				乳　児（１歳未満）死 亡 数 Infant deaths (under 1 year)	新生児（生後４週未満）死 亡 数[2] Neonatal deaths (under 4 weeks)	
1955	昭和30年	1 730 692	693 523	68 801	38 646	1 037 169
56	31	1 665 278	724 460	67 691	38 232	940 818
57	32	1 566 713	752 445	62 678	33 847	814 268
58	33	1 653 469	684 189	57 052	32 237	969 280
59	34	1 626 088	689 959	54 768	30 235	936 129
1960	35	1 606 041	706 599	49 293	27 362	899 442
61	36	1 589 372	695 644	45 465	26 255	893 728
62	37	1 618 616	710 265	42 797	24 777	908 351
63	38	1 659 521	670 770	38 442	22 965	988 751
64	39	1 716 761	673 067	34 967	21 344	1 043 694
65	40	1 823 697	700 438	33 742	21 260	1 123 259
66	41	1 360 974	670 342	26 217	16 296	690 632
67	42	1 935 647	675 006	28 928	19 248	1 260 641
68	43	1 871 839	686 555	28 600	18 326	1 185 284
69	44	1 889 815	693 787	26 874	17 116	1 196 028
1970	45	1 934 239	712 962	25 412	16 742	1 221 277
71	46	2 000 973	684 521	24 805	16 450	1 316 452
72	47	2 038 682	683 751	23 773	15 817	1 354 931
73	48	2 091 983	709 416	23 683	15 473	1 382 567
74	49	2 029 989	710 510	21 888	14 472	1 319 479
75	50	1 901 440	702 275	19 103	12 912	1 199 165
76	51	1 832 617	703 270	17 105	11 638	1 129 347
77	52	1 755 100	690 074	15 666	10 773	1 065 026
78	53	1 708 643	695 821	14 327	9 628	1 012 822
79	54	1 642 580	689 664	12 923	8 590	952 916
1980	55	1 576 889	722 801	11 841	7 796	854 088
81	56	1 529 455	720 262	10 891	7 188	809 193
82	57	1 515 392	711 883	9 969	6 425	803 509
83	58	1 508 687	740 038	9 406	5 894	768 649
84	59	1 489 780	740 247	8 920	5 527	749 533
85	60	1 431 577	752 283	7 899	4 910	679 294
86	61	1 382 946	750 620	7 251	4 296	632 326
87	62	1 346 658	751 172	6 711	3 933	595 486
88	63	1 314 006	793 014	6 265	3 592	520 992
89	平成元年	1 246 802	788 594	5 724	3 214	458 208
1990	2	1 221 585	820 305	5 616	3 179	401 280
91	3	1 223 245	829 797	5 418	2 978	393 448
92	4	1 208 989	856 643	5 477	2 905	352 346
93	5	1 188 282	878 532	5 169	2 765	309 750
94	6	1 238 328	875 933	5 261	2 889	362 395
95	7	1 187 064	922 139	5 054	2 615	264 925
96	8	1 206 555	896 211	4 546	2 438	310 344
97	9	1 191 665	913 402	4 403	2 307	278 263
98	10	1 203 147	936 484	4 380	2 353	266 663
99	11	1 177 669	982 031	4 010	2 137	195 638
2000	12	1 190 547	961 653	3 830	2 106	228 894
01	13	1 170 662	970 331	3 599	1 909	200 331
02	14	1 153 855	982 379	3 497	1 937	171 476
03	15	1 123 610	1 014 951	3 364	1 879	108 659
04	16	1 110 721	1 028 602	3 122	1 622	82 119
05	17	1 062 530	1 083 796	2 958	1 510	△ 21 266
06	18	1 092 674	1 084 450	2 864	1 444	8 224
07	19	1 089 818	1 108 334	2 828	1 434	△ 18 516
08	20	1 091 156	1 142 407	2 798	1 331	△ 51 251
09	21	1 070 035	1 141 865	2 556	1 254	△ 71 830
2010	22	1 071 304	1 197 012	2 450	1 167	△ 125 708
11	23	1 050 806	1 253 066	2 463	1 147	△ 202 260
12	24	1 037 231	1 256 359	2 299	1 065	△ 219 128
13	25	1 029 816	1 268 436	2 185	1 026	△ 238 620
14	26	1 003 539	1 273 004	2 080	952	△ 269 465
15	27	1 005 677	1 290 444	1 916	902	△ 284 767
16	28	976 978	1 307 748	1 928	874	△ 330 770

89

総　覧

表3.2　年　次　別　に　み　た
Table 3.2　Trends in indices of

年　　次 [1] Year		死　産　数 Foetal deaths			周　産　期　死　亡　数 Perinatal deaths			婚　姻　件　数 Marriages	離　婚　件　数 Divorces
		総　数 Total	自然死産 Spontaneous	人工死産 Artificial	総　数 Total	妊娠満22週以後の死産数 Foetal deaths at 22 completed weeks and over of gestation	早期新生児死亡数 Early neonatal deaths		
1899	明治32年	135 727	…	…	…	…	…	297 372	66 545
1900	33	137 987	…	…	…	…	…	346 528	63 828
01	34	155 489	…	…	…	…	…	378 457	63 442
02	35	157 708	…	…	…	…	…	394 165	64 139
03	36	153 920	…	…	…	…	…	370 961	65 392
04	37	147 058	…	…	…	…	…	398 930	63 913
05	38	142 092	…	…	…	…	…	350 898	60 061
06	39	149 731	…	…	…	…	…	352 857	65 398
07	40	158 814	…	…	…	…	…	432 949	61 058
08	41	162 676	…	…	…	…	…	461 254	60 226
09	42	161 576	…	…	…	…	…	437 882	58 936
1910	43	157 392	…	…	…	…	…	441 222	59 432
11	44	155 319	…	…	…	…	…	433 117	58 067
12	大正元年	147 545	…	…	…	…	…	430 422	59 143
13	2	147 769	…	…	…	…	…	431 287	59 536
14	3	145 692	…	…	…	…	…	452 932	59 992
15	4	141 301	…	…	…	…	…	445 210	59 943
16	5	139 998	…	…	…	…	…	433 680	60 254
17	6	140 328	…	…	…	…	…	447 970	55 812
18	7	142 507	…	…	…	…	…	500 580	56 474
19	8	132 939	…	…	…	…	…	480 136	56 812
1920	9	144 038	…	…	…	…	…	546 207	55 511
21	10	138 301	…	…	…	…	…	519 217	53 402
22	11	132 244	…	…	…	…	…	515 916	53 053
23	12	133 863	…	…	…	…	…	512 689	51 212
24	13	125 839	…	…	…	…	…	513 130	51 770
25	14	124 403	…	…	…	…	…	521 438	51 687
26	昭和元年	124 038	…	…	…	…	…	502 847	50 119
27	2	116 922	…	…	…	…	…	487 850	50 626
28	3	120 191	…	…	…	…	…	499 555	49 119
29	4	116 971	…	…	…	…	…	497 410	51 222
1930	5	117 730	…	…	…	…	…	506 674	51 259
31	6	116 509	…	…	…	…	…	496 574	50 609
32	7	119 579	…	…	…	…	…	515 270	51 437
33	8	114 138	…	…	…	…	…	486 058	49 282
34	9	113 043	…	…	…	…	…	512 654	48 610
35	10	115 593	…	…	…	…	…	556 730	48 528
36	11	111 056	…	…	…	…	…	549 116	46 167
37	12	111 485	…	…	…	…	…	674 500	46 500
38	13	99 528	…	…	…	…	…	538 831	44 656
39	14	98 349	…	…	…	…	…	554 321	45 970
1940	15	102 034	…	…	…	…	…	666 575	48 556
41	16	103 400	…	…	…	…	…	791 625	49 424
42	17	95 448	…	…	…	…	…	679 044	46 268
43	18	92 889	…	…	…	…	…	743 842	49 705
47	22	123 837	…	…	…	…	…	934 170	79 551
48	23	143 963	＊104 325	＊31 055	…	…	…	953 999	79 032
49	24	192 677	＊114 161	＊75 585	…	…	…	842 170	82 575
1950	25	216 974	106 594	110 380	…	…	35 184	715 081	83 689
51	26	217 231	101 237	115 994	…	…	32 644	671 905	82 331
52	27	203 824	94 508	109 316	…	…	28 741	676 995	79 021
53	28	193 274	89 751	103 523	…	…	26 737	682 077	75 255
54	29	187 119	87 201	99 918	…	…	24 274	697 809	76 759

Summary

人 口 動 態 総 覧（つづき）
vital statistics : Japan－CON.

年　　次 [1] Year		死　産　数 Foetal deaths			周　産　期　死　亡　数 Perinatal deaths		早期新生児 死亡数 Early neonatal deaths	婚姻件数 Marriages	離婚件数 Divorces
		総　数 Total	自然死産 Spontaneous	人工死産 Artificial	総　数 Total	妊娠満22週 以後の死産数 Foetal deaths at 22 completed weeks and over of gestation			
1955	昭和30年	183 265	85 159	98 106	…	…	22 621	714 861	75 267
56	31	179 007	86 558	92 449	…	…	22 505	715 934	72 040
57	32	176 353	86 895	89 458	…	…	19 608	773 362	71 651
58	33	185 148	92 282	92 866	…	…	19 240	826 902	74 004
59	34	181 893	92 688	89 205	…	…	18 418	847 135	72 455
1960	35	179 281	93 424	85 857	…	…	17 040	866 115	69 410
61	36	179 895	96 032	83 863	…	…	16 879	890 158	69 323
62	37	177 363	97 256	80 107	…	…	16 242	928 341	71 394
63	38	175 424	97 711	77 713	…	…	15 285	937 516	69 996
64	39	168 046	97 357	70 689	…	…	14 676	963 130	72 306
65	40	161 617	94 476	67 141	…	…	14 949	954 852	77 195
66	41	148 248	83 253	64 995	…	…	11 765	940 120	79 432
67	42	149 389	90 938	58 451	…	…	14 108	953 096	83 478
68	43	143 259	87 381	55 878	…	…	13 693	956 312	87 327
69	44	139 211	85 788	53 423	…	…	12 810	984 142	91 280
1970	45	135 095	84 073	51 022	…	…	12 810	1 029 405	95 937
71	46	130 920	83 827	47 093	…	…	12 665	1 091 229	103 595
72	47	125 154	81 741	43 413	…	…	12 425	1 099 984	108 382
73	48	116 171	78 613	37 558	…	…	12 156	1 071 923	111 877
74	49	109 738	74 618	35 120	…	…	11 394	1 000 455	113 622
75	50	101 862	67 643	34 219	…	…	10 245	941 628	119 135
76	51	101 930	64 046	37 884	…	…	9 392	871 543	124 512
77	52	95 247	60 330	34 917	…	…	8 686	821 029	129 485
78	53	87 463	55 818	31 645	…	…	7 701	793 257	132 146
79	54	82 311	51 083	31 228	36 190	29 289	6 901	788 505	135 250
1980	55	77 446	47 651	29 795	32 422	26 268	6 154	774 702	141 689
81	56	79 222	46 296	32 926	30 274	24 672	5 602	776 531	154 221
82	57	78 107	44 135	33 972	28 204	23 137	5 067	781 252	163 980
83	58	71 941	40 108	31 833	25 925	21 354	4 571	762 552	179 150
84	59	72 361	37 976	34 385	25 149	20 875	4 274	739 991	178 746
85	60	69 009	33 114	35 895	22 379	18 642	3 737	735 850	166 640
86	61	65 678	31 050	34 628	20 389	17 143	3 246	710 962	166 054
87	62	63 834	29 956	33 878	18 699	15 634	3 065	696 173	158 227
88	63	59 636	26 804	32 832	16 839	14 090	2 749	707 716	153 600
89	平成元年	55 204	24 558	30 646	15 183	12 797	2 386	708 316	157 811
1990	2	53 892	23 383	30 509	13 704	11 367	2 337	722 138	157 608
91	3	50 510	22 317	28 193	10 426	8 258	2 168	742 264	168 969
92	4	48 896	21 689	27 207	9 888	7 758	2 130	754 441	179 191
93	5	45 090	20 205	24 885	9 226	7 191	2 035	792 658	188 297
94	6	42 962	19 754	23 208	9 286	7 200	2 086	782 738	195 106
95	7	39 403	18 262	21 141	8 412	6 580	1 832	791 888	199 016
96	8	39 536	18 329	21 207	8 080	6 333	1 747	795 080	206 955
97	9	39 546	17 453	22 093	7 624	6 009	1 615	775 651	222 635
98	10	38 988	16 936	22 052	7 447	5 804	1 643	784 595	243 183
99	11	38 452	16 711	21 741	7 102	5 567	1 535	762 028	250 529
2000	12	38 393	16 200	22 193	6 881	5 362	1 519	798 138	264 246
01	13	37 467	15 704	21 763	6 476	5 114	1 362	799 999	285 911
02	14	36 978	15 161	21 817	6 333	4 959	1 374	757 331	289 836
03	15	35 330	14 644	20 686	5 929	4 626	1 303	740 191	283 854
04	16	34 365	14 288	20 077	5 541	4 357	1 184	720 417	270 804
05	17	31 818	13 502	18 316	5 149	4 058	1 091	714 265	261 917
06	18	30 911	13 424	17 487	5 100	4 047	1 053	730 971	257 475
07	19	29 313	13 107	16 206	4 906	3 854	1 052	719 822	254 832
08	20	28 177	12 625	15 552	4 720	3 751	969	726 106	251 136
09	21	27 005	12 214	14 791	4 519	3 645	874	707 734	253 353
2010	22	26 560	12 245	14 315	4 515	3 637	878	700 214	251 378
11	23	25 751	11 940	13 811	4 315	3 491	824	661 895	235 719
12	24	24 800	11 448	13 352	4 133	3 343	790	668 869	235 406
13	25	24 102	10 938	13 164	3 862	3 110	752	660 613	231 383
14	26	23 524	10 905	12 619	3 750	3 039	711	643 749	222 107
15	27	22 617	10 862	11 755	3 728	3 063	665	635 156	226 215
16	28	20 934	10 067	10 867	3 516	2 840	676	620 531	216 798

91

総　覧

表3.2　年　次　別　に　み　た
Table 3.2　Trends in indices of

年　　次[1] Year		出　生　率 （人口千対） Live birth rate [per 1,000 population]	合計特殊出生率 Total fertility rate	死　亡　率 （人口千対） Death rate [per 1,000 population]	乳児死亡率 （出生千対） Infant mortality rate [per 1,000 live births]	新生児死亡率[2] （出生千対） Neonatal mortality rate [per 1,000 live births]	自然増減率 （人口千対） Natural change rate [per 1,000 population]
1899	明治32年	32.0	…	21.5	153.8	77.9	10.5
1900	33	32.4	…	20.8	155.0	79.0	11.6
01	34	33.9	…	20.9	149.9	77.1	13.0
02	35	33.6	…	21.3	154.0	77.2	12.3
03	36	32.7	…	20.4	152.4	75.8	12.3
04	37	31.2	…	20.7	151.9	73.9	10.5
05	38	31.2	…	21.6	151.7	71.2	9.6
06	39	29.6	…	20.3	153.6	75.5	9.3
07	40	34.0	…	21.4	151.3	73.5	12.6
08	41	34.7	…	21.5	158.0	74.5	13.2
09	42	34.9	…	22.5	167.3	76.5	12.4
1910	43	34.8	…	21.6	161.2	74.1	13.2
11	44	35.1	…	20.9	158.4	72.8	14.1
12	大正元年	34.4	…	20.5	154.2	71.3	13.9
13	2	34.3	…	20.0	152.1	70.7	14.2
14	3	34.8	…	21.2	158.5	69.5	13.6
15	4	34.1	…	20.7	160.4	69.7	13.4
16	5	33.7	…	22.2	170.3	73.1	11.5
17	6	33.5	…	22.2	173.2	77.1	11.3
18	7	32.7	…	27.3	188.6	81.3	5.5
19	8	32.3	…	23.3	170.5	72.6	9.0
1920	9	36.2	…	25.4	165.7	69.0	10.8
21	10	35.1	…	22.7	168.3	68.5	12.4
22	11	34.3	…	22.4	166.4	67.5	11.9
23	12	35.2	…	22.9	163.4	66.3	12.2
24	13	33.9	…	21.3	156.2	63.2	12.6
25	14	34.9	…	20.3	142.4	58.1	14.7
26	昭和元年	34.6	…	19.1	137.5	56.9	15.5
27	2	33.4	…	19.7	141.7	56.4	13.7
28	3	34.1	…	19.8	137.6	54.2	14.4
29	4	32.7	…	19.9	142.1	55.4	12.9
1930	5	32.4	…	18.2	124.1	49.9	14.2
31	6	32.1	…	19.0	131.5	51.7	13.2
32	7	32.9	…	17.7	117.5	47.9	15.2
33	8	31.5	…	17.7	121.3	48.5	13.8
34	9	29.9	…	18.1	124.8	50.6	11.8
35	10	31.6	…	16.8	106.7	44.7	14.9
36	11	30.0	…	17.5	116.7	48.1	12.4
37	12	30.9	…	17.1	105.8	43.8	13.8
38	13	27.2	…	17.7	114.4	46.2	9.4
39	14	26.6	…	17.8	106.2	44.3	8.9
1940	15	29.4	…	16.5	90.0	38.7	12.9
41	16	31.8	…	16.0	84.1	34.2	15.7
42	17	30.9	…	16.1	85.5	34.1	14.7
43	18	30.9	…	16.7	86.6	33.8	14.3
47	22	34.3	4.54	14.6	76.7	31.4	19.7
48	23	33.5	4.40	11.9	61.7	27.5	21.6
49	24	33.0	4.32	11.6	62.5	26.9	21.4
1950	25	28.1	3.65	10.9	60.1	27.4	17.2
51	26	25.3	3.26	9.9	57.5	27.5	15.4
52	27	23.4	2.98	8.9	49.4	25.4	14.4
53	28	21.5	2.69	8.9	48.9	25.5	12.6
54	29	20.0	2.48	8.2	44.6	24.1	11.9

注：率の算出方法は、「第2章 調査結果の利用上の解説」の「4．比率の解説（67〜69ページ）」を参照されたい。
　　1）　昭和19〜21年は資料不備のため省略した。昭和22〜47年は沖縄県を含まない。
　　　　昭和23・24年の＊印は概数である。
　　2）　新生児死亡の昭和18年以前は1か月未満の死亡である。

92

Summary

人 口 動 態 総 覧 (つづき)
vital statistics : Japan－CON.

年　　次[1]　　　Year		出　生　率 (人口千対) Live birth rate [per 1,000 population]	合計特殊出生率 Total fertility rate	死　亡　率 (人口千対) Death rate [per 1,000 population]	乳児死亡率 (出生千対) Infant mortality rate [per 1,000 live births]	新生児死亡率[2] (出生千対) Neonatal mortality rate [per 1,000 live births]	自然増減率 (人口千対) Natural change rate [per 1,000 population]
1955	昭和30年	19.4	2.37	7.8	39.8	22.3	11.6
56	31	18.4	2.22	8.0	40.6	23.0	10.4
57	32	17.2	2.04	8.3	40.0	21.6	8.9
58	33	18.0	2.11	7.4	34.5	19.5	10.5
59	34	17.5	2.04	7.4	33.7	18.6	10.1
1960	35	17.2	2.00	7.6	30.7	17.0	9.6
61	36	16.9	1.96	7.4	28.6	16.5	9.5
62	37	17.0	1.98	7.5	26.4	15.3	9.5
63	38	17.3	2.00	7.0	23.2	13.8	10.3
64	39	17.7	2.05	6.9	20.4	12.4	10.7
65	40	18.6	2.14	7.1	18.5	11.7	11.4
66	41	13.7	1.58	6.8	19.3	12.0	7.0
67	42	19.4	2.23	6.8	14.9	9.9	12.7
68	43	18.6	2.13	6.8	15.3	9.8	11.8
69	44	18.5	2.13	6.8	14.2	9.1	11.7
1970	45	18.8	2.13	6.9	13.1	8.7	11.8
71	46	19.2	2.16	6.6	12.4	8.2	12.6
72	47	19.3	2.14	6.5	11.7	7.8	12.8
73	48	19.4	2.14	6.6	11.3	7.4	12.8
74	49	18.6	2.05	6.5	10.8	7.1	12.1
75	50	17.1	1.91	6.3	10.0	6.8	10.8
76	51	16.3	1.85	6.3	9.3	6.4	10.0
77	52	15.5	1.80	6.1	8.9	6.1	9.4
78	53	14.9	1.79	6.1	8.4	5.6	8.8
79	54	14.2	1.77	6.0	7.9	5.2	8.3
1980	55	13.6	1.75	6.2	7.5	4.9	7.3
81	56	13.0	1.74	6.1	7.1	4.7	6.9
82	57	12.8	1.77	6.0	6.6	4.2	6.8
83	58	12.7	1.80	6.2	6.2	3.9	6.5
84	59	12.5	1.81	6.2	6.0	3.7	6.3
85	60	11.9	1.76	6.3	5.5	3.4	5.6
86	61	11.4	1.72	6.2	5.2	3.1	5.2
87	62	11.1	1.69	6.2	5.0	2.9	4.9
88	63	10.8	1.66	6.5	4.8	2.7	4.3
89	平成元年	10.2	1.57	6.4	4.6	2.6	3.7
1990	2	10.0	1.54	6.7	4.6	2.6	3.3
91	3	9.9	1.53	6.7	4.4	2.4	3.2
92	4	9.8	1.50	6.9	4.5	2.4	2.9
93	5	9.6	1.46	7.1	4.3	2.3	2.5
94	6	10.0	1.50	7.1	4.2	2.3	2.9
95	7	9.6	1.42	7.4	4.3	2.2	2.1
96	8	9.7	1.43	7.2	3.8	2.0	2.5
97	9	9.5	1.39	7.3	3.7	1.9	2.2
98	10	9.6	1.38	7.5	3.6	2.0	2.1
99	11	9.4	1.34	7.8	3.4	1.8	1.6
2000	12	9.5	1.36	7.7	3.2	1.8	1.8
01	13	9.3	1.33	7.7	3.1	1.6	1.6
02	14	9.2	1.32	7.8	3.0	1.7	1.4
03	15	8.9	1.29	8.0	3.0	1.7	0.9
04	16	8.8	1.29	8.2	2.8	1.5	0.7
05	17	8.4	1.26	8.6	2.8	1.4	△ 0.2
06	18	8.7	1.32	8.6	2.6	1.3	0.1
07	19	8.6	1.34	8.8	2.6	1.3	△ 0.1
08	20	8.7	1.37	9.1	2.6	1.2	△ 0.4
09	21	8.5	1.37	9.1	2.4	1.2	△ 0.6
2010	22	8.5	1.39	9.5	2.3	1.1	△ 1.0
11	23	8.3	1.39	9.9	2.3	1.1	△ 1.6
12	24	8.2	1.41	10.0	2.2	1.0	△ 1.7
13	25	8.2	1.43	10.1	2.1	1.0	△ 1.9
14	26	8.0	1.42	10.1	2.1	0.9	△ 2.1
15	27	8.0	1.45	10.3	1.9	0.9	△ 2.3
16	**28**	**7.8**	**1.44**	**10.5**	**2.0**	**0.9**	**△ 2.6**

総　覧

表3.2　年　次　別　に　み　た
Table 3.2　Trends in indices of

年　　　次[1] Year		死　産　率 （出産千対） Foetal death rate (per 1,000 total births[a])			周産期死亡率 （出産千対） Perinatal death rate [per 1,000 total births[b]]	妊娠満22週 以後の死産率 （出産千対） Foetal death rate at 22 completed weeks and over of gestation [per 1,000 total births[b]]	早期新生児死亡率 （出生千対） Early neonatal death rate [per 1,000 live births]	婚　姻　率 （人口千対） Marriage rate [per 1,000 population]	離　婚　率 （人口千対） Divorce rate [per 1,000 population]
		総　数 Total	自然死産 Spontaneous	人工死産 Artificial					
1899	明治32年	89.1	…	…	…	…	…	6.9	1.53
1900	33	88.5	…	…	…	…	…	7.9	1.46
01	34	93.8	…	…	…	…	…	8.5	1.43
02	35	94.5	…	…	…	…	…	8.8	1.43
03	36	93.6	…	…	…	…	…	8.1	1.44
04	37	92.6	…	…	…	…	…	8.6	1.39
05	38	89.1	…	…	…	…	…	7.5	1.29
06	39	97.0	…	…	…	…	…	7.5	1.39
07	40	89.6	…	…	…	…	…	9.1	1.29
08	41	89.1	…	…	…	…	…	9.6	1.26
09	42	87.1	…	…	…	…	…	9.0	1.21
1910	43	84.2	…	…	…	…	…	9.0	1.21
11	44	81.6	…	…	…	…	…	8.7	1.16
12	大正元年	78.3	…	…	…	…	…	8.5	1.17
13	2	77.6	…	…	…	…	…	8.4	1.16
14	3	74.6	…	…	…	…	…	8.7	1.15
15	4	72.8	…	…	…	…	…	8.4	1.14
16	5	72.0	…	…	…	…	…	8.1	1.13
17	6	71.9	…	…	…	…	…	8.3	1.03
18	7	73.7	…	…	…	…	…	9.1	1.03
19	8	69.5	…	…	…	…	…	8.7	1.03
1920	9	66.4	…	…	…	…	…	9.8	0.99
21	10	65.0	…	…	…	…	…	9.2	0.94
22	11	62.9	…	…	…	…	…	9.0	0.92
23	12	61.5	…	…	…	…	…	8.8	0.88
24	13	59.2	…	…	…	…	…	8.7	0.88
25	14	56.3	…	…	…	…	…	8.7	0.87
26	昭和元年	55.7	…	…	…	…	…	8.3	0.83
27	2	53.7	…	…	…	…	…	7.9	0.82
28	3	53.3	…	…	…	…	…	8.0	0.78
29	4	53.3	…	…	…	…	…	7.8	0.81
1930	5	53.4	…	…	…	…	…	7.9	0.80
31	6	52.5	…	…	…	…	…	7.6	0.77
32	7	51.9	…	…	…	…	…	7.8	0.77
33	8	51.1	…	…	…	…	…	7.2	0.73
34	9	52.4	…	…	…	…	…	7.5	0.71
35	10	50.1	…	…	…	…	…	8.0	0.70
36	11	50.2	…	…	…	…	…	7.8	0.66
37	12	48.6	…	…	…	…	…	9.5	0.66
38	13	49.1	…	…	…	…	…	7.6	0.63
39	14	49.2	…	…	…	…	…	7.8	0.64
1940	15	46.0	…	…	…	…	…	9.3	0.68
41	16	43.4	…	…	…	…	…	11.0	0.69
42	17	41.0	…	…	…	…	…	9.4	0.64
43	18	39.6	…	…	…	…	…	10.2	0.68
47	22	44.2	…	…	…	…	…	12.0	1.02
48	23	50.9	＊36.9	＊10.9	…	…	…	11.9	0.99
49	24	66.7	＊39.1	＊25.9	…	…	…	10.3	1.01
1950	25	84.9	41.7	43.2	…	…	15.1	8.6	1.01
51	26	92.2	43.0	49.3	…	…	15.3	7.9	0.97
52	27	92.3	42.8	49.5	…	…	14.3	7.9	0.92
53	28	93.8	43.5	50.2	…	…	14.3	7.8	0.86
54	29	95.6	44.6	51.1	…	…	13.7	7.9	0.87

94

Summary

人 口 動 態 総 覧 (つづき)
vital statistics : Japan—CON.

年　次 [1] / Year		死　産　率 (出産千対) Foetal death rate (per 1,000 total births[a])			周産期死亡率 (出産千対) Perinatal death rate [per 1,000 total births[b]]	妊娠満22週以後の死産率 (出産千対) Foetal death rate at 22 completed weeks and over of gestation [per 1,000 total births[b]]	早期新生児死亡率 (出生千対) Early neonatal death rate [per 1,000 live births]	婚　姻　率 (人口千対) Marriage rate [per 1,000 population]	離　婚　率 (人口千対) Divorce rate [per 1,000 population]
		総　数 Total	自然死産 Spontaneous	人工死産 Artificial					
1955	昭和30年	95.8	44.5	51.3	…	…	13.1	8.0	0.84
56	31	97.1	46.9	50.1	…	…	13.5	7.9	0.80
57	32	101.2	49.9	51.3	…	…	12.5	8.5	0.79
58	33	100.7	50.2	50.5	…	…	11.6	9.0	0.80
59	34	100.6	51.3	49.3	…	…	11.3	9.1	0.78
1960	35	100.4	52.3	48.1	…	…	10.6	9.3	0.74
61	36	101.7	54.3	47.4	…	…	10.6	9.4	0.74
62	37	98.8	54.2	44.6	…	…	10.0	9.8	0.75
63	38	95.6	53.3	42.4	…	…	9.2	9.7	0.73
64	39	89.2	51.7	37.5	…	…	8.5	9.9	0.74
65	40	81.4	47.6	33.8	…	…	8.2	9.7	0.79
66	41	98.2	55.2	43.1	…	…	8.6	9.5	0.80
67	42	71.6	43.6	28.0	…	…	7.3	9.6	0.84
68	43	71.1	43.4	27.7	…	…	7.3	9.5	0.87
69	44	68.6	42.3	26.3	…	…	6.8	9.6	0.89
1970	45	65.3	40.6	24.7	…	…	6.6	10.0	0.93
71	46	61.4	39.3	22.1	…	…	6.3	10.5	0.99
72	47	57.8	37.8	20.1	…	…	6.1	10.4	1.02
73	48	52.6	35.6	17.0	…	…	5.8	9.9	1.04
74	49	51.3	34.9	16.4	…	…	5.6	9.1	1.04
75	50	50.8	33.8	17.1	…	…	5.4	8.5	1.07
76	51	52.7	33.1	19.6	…	…	5.1	7.8	1.11
77	52	51.5	32.6	18.9	…	…	4.9	7.2	1.14
78	53	48.7	31.1	17.6	…	…	4.5	6.9	1.15
79	54	47.7	29.6	18.1	21.6	17.5	4.2	6.8	1.17
1980	55	46.8	28.8	18.0	20.2	16.4	3.9	6.7	1.22
81	56	49.2	28.8	20.5	19.5	15.9	3.7	6.6	1.32
82	57	49.0	27.7	21.3	18.3	15.0	3.3	6.6	1.39
83	58	45.5	25.4	20.1	16.9	14.0	3.0	6.4	1.51
84	59	46.3	24.3	22.0	16.6	13.8	2.9	6.2	1.50
85	60	46.0	22.1	23.9	15.4	12.9	2.6	6.1	1.39
86	61	45.3	21.4	23.9	14.6	12.2	2.3	5.9	1.37
87	62	45.3	21.2	24.0	13.7	11.5	2.3	5.7	1.30
88	63	43.4	19.5	23.9	12.7	10.6	2.1	5.8	1.26
89	平成元年	42.4	18.9	23.5	12.1	10.2	1.9	5.8	1.29
1990	2	42.3	18.3	23.9	11.1	9.2	1.9	5.9	1.28
91	3	39.7	17.5	22.1	8.5	6.7	1.8	6.0	1.37
92	4	38.9	17.2	21.6	8.1	6.4	1.8	6.1	1.45
93	5	36.6	16.4	20.2	7.7	6.0	1.7	6.4	1.52
94	6	33.5	15.4	18.1	7.5	5.8	1.7	6.3	1.57
95	7	32.1	14.9	17.2	7.0	5.5	1.5	6.4	1.60
96	8	31.7	14.7	17.0	6.7	5.2	1.4	6.4	1.66
97	9	32.1	14.2	17.9	6.4	5.0	1.4	6.2	1.78
98	10	31.4	13.6	17.8	6.2	4.8	1.4	6.3	1.94
99	11	31.6	13.7	17.9	6.0	4.7	1.3	6.1	2.00
2000	12	31.2	13.2	18.1	5.8	4.5	1.3	6.4	2.10
01	13	31.0	13.0	18.0	5.5	4.3	1.2	6.4	2.27
02	14	31.1	12.7	18.3	5.5	4.3	1.2	6.0	2.30
03	15	30.5	12.6	17.8	5.3	4.1	1.2	5.9	2.25
04	16	30.0	12.5	17.5	5.0	3.9	1.1	5.7	2.15
05	17	29.1	12.3	16.7	4.8	3.8	1.0	5.7	2.08
06	18	27.5	11.9	15.6	4.7	3.7	1.0	5.8	2.04
07	19	26.2	11.7	14.5	4.5	3.5	1.0	5.7	2.02
08	20	25.2	11.3	13.9	4.3	3.4	0.9	5.8	1.99
09	21	24.6	11.1	13.5	4.2	3.4	0.8	5.6	2.01
2010	22	24.2	11.2	13.0	4.2	3.4	0.8	5.5	1.99
11	23	23.9	11.1	12.8	4.1	3.3	0.8	5.2	1.87
12	24	23.4	10.8	12.6	4.0	3.2	0.8	5.3	1.87
13	25	22.9	10.4	12.5	3.7	3.0	0.7	5.3	1.84
14	26	22.9	10.6	12.3	3.7	3.0	0.7	5.1	1.77
15	27	22.0	10.6	11.4	3.7	3.0	0.7	5.1	1.81
16	28	21.0	10.1	10.9	3.6	2.9	0.7	5.0	1.73

Note : a) Per 1,000 live births and foetal deaths at 12 completed weeks and over of gestation.
　　　b) Per 1,000 live births and foetal deaths at 22 completed weeks and over of gestation.

総　覧

表 3.3　都道府県（21大都市再掲）
Table 3.3　Summary tables of vital statistics

都道府県[1] Prefecture	人　口[2] Population	出　生　数 Live births	死　亡　数 Deaths	（再　　掲）(Regrouped) 乳児(1歳未満)死亡数 Infant deaths (under 1 year)	新生児(生後4週未満)死亡数 Neonatal deaths (under 4 weeks)	自然増減数 Natural change	死 総　数 Total
全　国　Total	125 020 252	976 978	1 307 748	1 928	874	△ 330 770	20 934
01[a] 北　海　道	5 327 000	35 125	61 906	76	33	△ 26 781	901
02 青　　森	1 290 000	8 626	17 309	18	8	△ 8 683	183
03 岩　　手	1 263 000	8 341	16 959	17	7	△ 8 618	184
04 宮　　城	2 314 000	17 347	23 426	40	24	△ 6 079	402
05 秋　　田	1 007 000	5 666	15 244	13	6	△ 9 578	133
06 山　　形	1 107 000	7 547	15 181	24	17	△ 7 634	165
07 福　　島	1 891 000	13 744	24 166	27	12	△ 10 422	306
08 茨　　城	2 861 000	20 878	31 414	40	21	△ 10 536	423
09 栃　　木	1 939 000	14 621	21 436	26	12	△ 6 815	321
10 群　　馬	1 926 000	13 661	22 125	22	12	△ 8 464	330
11 埼　　玉	7 169 000	54 447	63 466	118	52	△ 9 019	1 181
12 千　　葉	6 137 000	45 387	56 396	95	45	△ 11 009	1 001
13 東　　京	13 207 000	111 962	113 415	222	97	△ 1 453	2 365
14 神　奈　川	8 986 000	70 648	77 361	147	80	△ 6 713	1 400
15 新　　潟	2 273 000	15 736	28 822	20	9	△ 13 086	320
16 富　　山	1 049 000	7 302	12 864	16	12	△ 5 562	152
17 石　　川	1 140 000	8 927	12 422	19	7	△ 3 495	159
18 福　　井	772 000	6 112	9 228	16	8	△ 3 116	146
19 山　　梨	818 000	5 819	9 565	10	4	△ 3 746	101
20 長　　野	2 060 000	15 169	25 110	29	16	△ 9 941	312
21 岐　　阜	1 985 000	14 831	22 471	35	19	△ 7 640	289
22 静　　岡	3 623 000	27 652	39 294	46	23	△ 11 642	538
23 愛　　知	7 324 000	64 226	65 227	117	57	△ 1 001	1 182
24 三　　重	1 775 000	13 202	19 830	22	12	△ 6 628	272
25 滋　　賀	1 392 000	12 072	12 507	20	10	△ 435	213
26 京　　都	2 559 000	19 327	25 830	41	21	△ 6 503	401
27 大　　阪	8 672 000	68 816	84 390	111	46	△ 15 574	1 480
28 兵　　庫	5 438 000	43 378	55 422	67	18	△ 12 044	856
29 奈　　良	1 347 000	9 430	14 054	30	12	△ 4 624	190
30 和　歌　山	949 000	6 658	12 619	12	3	△ 5 961	155
31 鳥　　取	566 000	4 436	7 357	13	8	△ 2 921	98
32 島　　根	684 000	5 300	9 562	11	4	△ 4 262	136
33 岡　　山	1 896 000	15 477	21 532	30	11	△ 6 055	325
34 広　　島	2 799 000	22 736	29 994	43	19	△ 7 258	501
35 山　　口	1 381 000	9 844	18 366	24	6	△ 8 522	195
36 徳　　島	746 000	5 346	9 855	16	6	△ 4 509	94
37 香　　川	964 000	7 510	11 908	8	4	△ 4 398	144
38 愛　　媛	1 366 000	9 911	17 734	16	2	△ 7 823	245
39 高　　知	718 000	4 779	10 305	9	2	△ 5 526	106
40 福　　岡	5 054 000	44 033	51 006	89	30	△ 6 973	1 018
41 佐　　賀	824 000	6 811	9 725	13	4	△ 2 914	135
42 長　　崎	1 358 000	10 886	17 071	19	12	△ 6 185	247
43 熊　　本	1 765 000	14 894	21 379	29	16	△ 6 485	396
44 大　　分	1 150 000	9 059	14 264	22	11	△ 5 205	221
45 宮　　崎	1 092 000	8 929	13 702	25	11	△ 4 773	240
46 鹿　児　島	1 630 000	13 688	21 610	32	9	△ 7 922	327
47 沖　　縄	1 427 000	16 617	11 706	31	14	4 911	434
外　　国 Foreign countries	·	65	131	2	2	△ 66	10
不　　詳 Place of residence not stated	·	·	1 082	-	-	·	1
21 大 都 市(再掲) 21 major cities (Regrouped)							
50 東 京 都 の 区 部	9 375 000	80 213	76 826	150	68	3 387	1 735
51 札　　幌	1 958 000	14 021	18 504	29	12	△ 4 483	344
52 仙　　台	1 085 000	8 904	8 589	26	15	315	175
53 さ い た ま	1 275 000	10 549	10 177	30	17	372	216
54 千　　葉	974 000	6 927	8 112	15	8	△ 1 185	158
55 横　　浜	3 731 000	28 889	31 414	58	32	△ 2 525	568
56 川　　崎	1 489 000	14 158	10 379	32	16	3 779	255
57 相　模　原	722 000	5 196	5 611	15	8	△ 415	122
58 新　　潟	807 000	5 936	8 590	5	2	△ 2 654	133
59 静　　岡	702 000	5 106	7 745	11	3	△ 2 639	121
60 浜　　松	797 000	6 558	7 852	6	3	△ 1 294	90
61 名　古　屋	2 305 000	19 542	21 221	35	20	△ 1 679	383
62 京　　都	1 475 000	10 921	13 966	22	10	△ 3 045	233
63 大　　阪	2 702 000	22 099	27 815	37	16	△ 5 716	494
64 堺	838 000	6 844	7 951	9	4	△ 1 107	138
65 神　　戸	1 536 000	11 786	15 350	16	4	△ 3 564	254
66 岡　　山	721 000	6 264	6 520	11	5	△ 256	116
67 広　　島	1 196 000	10 559	9 951	20	7	608	234
68 北　九　州	956 000	7 621	10 759	22	9	△ 3 138	181
69 福　　岡	1 554 000	14 488	11 521	24	6	2 967	323
70 熊　　本	740 000	6 797	6 916	11	8	△ 119	184

注：1）都道府県別の表章は出生は子の住所、死亡は死亡者の住所、死産は母の住所、婚姻は夫の住所、離婚は別居する前の住所による。
　　2）都道府県については、総務省統計局「人口推計（平成28年10月1日現在）」の日本人人口、21大都市については、各指定都市及び東京都が推計した平成28年10月1日現在の総人口である。

Summary

別にみた人口動態総覧
: Japan, each prefecture and 21 major cities, 2016

平成28年

産　数 Foetal deaths		周　産　期　死　亡　数 Perinatal deaths			婚 姻 件 数	離 婚 件 数	都 道 府 県 [1]		
自 然 死 産	人 工 死 産	総　数	妊娠満22週以後の死産数	早期新生児死亡数					
Spontaneous	Artificial	Total	Foetal deaths at 22 completed weeks and over of gestation	Early neonatal deaths	Marriages	Divorces	Prefecture		
10 067	10 867	3 516	2 840	676	620 531	216 798	全　国　Total		
345	556	117	89	28	24 636	10 476	01 [a]	北　海	道
81	102	26	20	6	5 135	2 164	02	青	森
95	89	32	28	4	4 872	1 877	03	岩	手
174	228	64	44	20	11 127	3 783	04	宮	城
73	60	26	21	5	3 510	1 393	05	秋	田
83	82	33	24	9	4 284	1 522	06	山	形
170	136	63	56	7	8 682	3 278	07	福	島
208	215	83	70	13	13 201	4 816	08	茨	城
147	174	46	34	12	9 321	3 429	09	栃	木
163	167	48	38	10	8 444	3 241	10	群	馬
575	606	185	145	40	34 199	12 481	11	埼	玉
546	455	188	154	34	29 610	10 612	12	千	葉
1 131	1 234	402	322	80	86 009	23 470	13	東　京	
665	735	258	196	62	46 695	15 673	14	神 奈 川	
175	145	59	54	5	9 311	2 987	15	新	潟
84	68	29	20	9	4 486	1 368	16	富	山
85	74	24	18	6	5 126	1 653	17	石	川
70	76	26	18	8	3 453	1 119	18	福	井
52	49	15	12	3	3 673	1 369	19	山	梨
178	134	56	41	15	8 967	3 180	20	長	野
154	135	55	40	15	8 581	3 058	21	岐	阜
288	250	115	99	16	17 079	6 237	22	静	岡
615	567	237	192	45	40 671	12 464	23	愛	知
143	129	75	67	8	8 174	2 923	24	三	重
101	112	29	21	8	6 822	2 202	25	滋	賀
190	211	70	53	17	12 143	4 222	26	京	都
670	810	239	205	34	46 186	17 279	27	大	阪
414	442	120	104	16	25 808	9 302	28	兵	庫
89	101	35	25	10	5 628	2 183	29	奈	良
64	91	20	18	2	4 061	1 771	30	和　歌	山
46	52	23	17	6	2 444	937	31	鳥	取
78	58	17	15	2	2 753	949	32	島	根
147	178	61	50	11	8 916	3 245	33	岡	山
249	252	84	72	12	13 594	4 691	34	広	島
103	92	43	39	4	5 906	2 149	35	山	口
41	53	18	13	5	3 177	1 184	36	徳	島
74	70	19	16	3	4 593	1 613	37	香	川
102	143	31	30	1	5 861	2 244	38	愛	媛
47	59	14	12	2	2 916	1 228	39	高	知
450	568	149	123	26	26 567	9 772	40	福	岡
51	84	17	14	3	3 726	1 378	41	佐	賀
123	124	46	39	7	6 013	2 169	42	長	崎
176	220	48	38	10	7 976	2 915	43	熊	本
86	135	32	22	10	5 151	1 999	44	大	分
99	141	31	23	8	5 097	2 202	45	宮	崎
149	178	42	35	7	7 483	2 891	46	鹿　児	島
213	221	63	52	11	8 464	3 700	47	沖	縄
4	6	2	1	1	・	・	外　　国 Foreign countries		
1	-	1	1	-	・	・	不　　詳 Place of residence not stated		
							21　大　都　市(再掲) 21 major cities (Regrouped)		
840	895	297	242	55	66 235	16 892	50	東 京 都 の 区 部	
108	236	47	38	9	10 495	4 096	51	札	幌
79	96	33	21	12	6 019	1 752	52	仙	台
122	94	45	34	11	6 682	1 965	53	さ い た ま	
84	74	23	17	6	4 661	1 629	54	千	葉
292	276	121	93	28	19 132	6 386	55	横	浜
104	151	42	32	10	10 008	2 458	56	川	崎
55	67	20	16	4	3 349	1 354	57	相　模	原
77	56	25	23	2	3 590	1 126	58	新	潟
67	54	28	23	3	3 282	1 144	59	静	岡
50	40	18	15	3	3 833	1 230	60	浜	松
194	189	70	56	14	13 735	4 157	61	名　古	屋
115	118	42	33	9	7 511	2 460	62	京	都
212	282	80	67	13	17 757	5 991	63	大	阪
58	80	18	15	3	4 135	1 633	64	堺	
110	144	31	27	4	7 506	2 715	65	神	戸
45	71	28	23	5	3 744	1 270	66	岡	山
110	124	41	36	5	6 288	2 035	67	広	島
76	105	25	19	6	4 907	1 848	68	北 九 州	
140	183	52	47	5	9 805	2 975	69	福	岡
88	96	24	21	3	3 767	1 256	70	熊	本

Note：a) See page 44.

総　覧

表3.3　都道府県（21大都市再掲）
Table 3.3　Summary tables of vital statistics

都道府県 Prefecture	出生率 （人口千対） Live birth rate [per 1,000 population]	死亡率 （人口千対） Death rate [per 1,000 population]	乳児死亡率 （出生千対） Infant mortality rate [per 1,000 live births]	新生児死亡率 （出生千対） Neonatal mortality rate [per 1,000 live births]	自然増減率 （人口千対） Natural change rate [per 1,000 population]	死産（出産千対） Foetal death rate (per 1,000 total births[a]) 総数 Total	自然死産 Spontaneous
全　国　Total	7.8	10.5	2.0	0.9	△ 2.6	21.0	10.1
01[c] 北海道	6.6	11.6	2.2	0.9	△ 5.0	25.0	9.6
02 青森	6.7	13.4	2.1	0.9	△ 6.7	20.8	9.2
03 岩手	6.6	13.4	2.0	0.8	△ 6.8	21.6	11.1
04 宮城	7.5	10.1	2.3	1.4	△ 2.6	22.6	9.8
05 秋田	5.6	15.1	2.3	1.1	△ 9.5	22.9	12.6
06 山形	6.8	13.7	3.2	2.3	△ 6.9	21.4	10.8
07 福島	7.3	12.8	2.0	0.9	△ 5.5	21.8	12.1
08 茨城	7.3	11.0	1.9	1.0	△ 3.7	19.9	9.8
09 栃木	7.5	11.1	1.8	0.8	△ 3.5	21.5	9.8
10 群馬	7.1	11.5	1.6	0.9	△ 4.4	23.6	11.7
11 埼玉	7.6	8.9	2.2	1.0	△ 1.3	21.2	10.3
12 千葉	7.4	9.2	2.1	1.0	△ 1.8	21.6	11.8
13 東京	8.5	8.6	2.0	0.9	△ 0.1	20.7	9.9
14 神奈川	7.9	8.6	2.1	1.1	△ 0.7	19.4	9.2
15 新潟	6.9	12.7	1.3	0.6	△ 5.8	19.9	10.9
16 富山	7.0	12.3	2.2	1.6	△ 5.3	20.4	11.3
17 石川	7.8	10.9	2.1	0.8	△ 3.1	17.5	9.4
18 福井	7.9	12.0	2.6	1.3	△ 4.0	23.3	11.2
19 山梨	7.1	11.7	1.7	0.7	△ 4.6	17.1	8.8
20 長野	7.4	12.2	1.9	1.1	△ 4.8	20.2	11.5
21 岐阜	7.5	11.3	2.4	1.3	△ 3.8	19.1	10.2
22 静岡	7.6	10.8	1.7	0.8	△ 3.2	19.1	10.2
23 愛知	8.8	8.9	1.8	0.9	△ 0.1	18.1	9.4
24 三重	7.4	11.2	1.7	0.9	△ 3.7	20.2	10.6
25 滋賀	8.7	9.0	1.7	0.8	△ 0.3	17.3	8.2
26 京都	7.6	10.1	2.1	1.1	△ 2.5	20.3	9.6
27 大阪	7.9	9.7	1.6	0.7	△ 1.8	21.1	9.5
28 兵庫	8.0	10.2	1.5	0.4	△ 2.2	19.4	9.4
29 奈良	7.0	10.4	3.2	1.3	△ 3.4	19.8	9.3
30 和歌山	7.0	13.3	1.8	0.5	△ 6.3	22.8	9.4
31 鳥取	7.8	13.0	2.9	1.8	△ 5.2	21.6	10.1
32 島根	7.7	14.0	2.1	0.8	△ 6.2	25.0	14.3
33 岡山	8.2	11.4	1.9	0.7	△ 3.2	20.6	9.3
34 広島	8.1	10.7	1.9	0.8	△ 2.6	21.6	10.7
35 山口	7.1	13.3	2.4	0.6	△ 6.2	19.4	10.3
36 徳島	7.2	13.2	3.0	1.1	△ 6.0	17.3	7.5
37 香川	7.8	12.4	1.1	0.5	△ 4.6	18.8	9.7
38 愛媛	7.3	13.0	1.6	0.2	△ 5.7	24.1	10.0
39 高知	6.7	14.4	1.9	0.4	△ 7.7	21.7	9.6
40 福岡	8.7	10.1	2.0	0.7	△ 1.4	22.6	10.0
41 佐賀	8.3	11.8	1.9	0.6	△ 3.5	19.4	7.3
42 長崎	8.0	12.6	1.7	1.1	△ 4.6	22.2	11.0
43 熊本	8.4	12.1	1.9	1.1	△ 3.7	25.9	11.5
44 大分	7.9	12.4	2.4	1.2	△ 4.5	23.8	9.3
45 宮崎	8.2	12.5	2.8	1.2	△ 4.4	26.2	10.8
46 鹿児島	8.4	13.3	2.3	0.7	△ 4.9	23.3	10.6
47 沖縄	11.6	8.2	1.9	0.8	3.4	25.5	12.5
21 大都市（再掲） 21 major cities (Regrouped)							
50 東京都の区部	8.6	8.2	1.9	0.8	0.4	21.2	10.3
51 札幌	7.2	9.5	2.1	0.9	△ 2.3	23.9	7.5
52 仙台	8.2	7.9	2.9	1.7	0.3	19.3	8.7
53 さいたま	8.3	8.0	2.8	1.6	0.3	20.1	11.3
54 千葉	7.1	8.3	2.2	1.2	△ 1.2	22.3	11.9
55 横浜	7.7	8.4	2.0	1.1	△ 0.7	19.3	9.9
56 川崎	9.5	7.0	2.3	1.1	2.5	17.7	7.2
57 相模原	7.2	7.8	2.9	1.5	△ 0.6	22.9	10.3
58 新潟	7.4	10.6	0.8	0.3	△ 3.3	21.9	12.7
59 静岡	7.3	11.0	2.2	0.6	△ 3.8	23.1	12.8
60 浜松	8.2	9.9	0.9	0.5	△ 1.6	13.5	7.5
61 名古屋	8.5	9.2	1.8	1.0	△ 0.7	19.2	9.7
62 京都	7.4	9.5	2.0	0.9	△ 2.1	20.9	10.3
63 大阪	8.2	10.3	1.7	0.7	△ 2.1	21.9	9.4
64 堺	8.2	9.5	1.3	0.6	△ 1.3	19.8	8.3
65 神戸	7.7	10.0	1.4	0.3	△ 2.3	21.1	9.1
66 岡山	8.7	9.0	0.8	0.6	△ 0.4	18.2	7.1
67 広島	8.8	8.3	1.9	0.7	0.5	21.7	10.2
68 北九州	8.0	11.3	2.9	1.2	△ 3.3	23.2	9.7
69 福岡	9.3	7.4	1.7	0.4	1.9	21.8	9.5
70 熊本	9.2	9.3	1.6	1.2	△ 0.2	26.4	12.6

注：率の算出方法は、「第2章　調査結果の利用上の解説」の「4．比率の解説（67～69ページ）」を参照されたい。

Summary

別にみた人口動態総覧（つづき）
: Japan, each prefecture and 21 major cities, 2016－CON.

平成28年

率 人工死産 Artificial	周産期死亡率（出産千対）Perinatal death rate [per 1,000 total births b)]	妊娠満22週以後の死産率（出産千対）Foetal death rate at 22 completed weeks and over of gestation [per 1,000 total births b)]	早期新生児死亡率（出生千対）Early neonatal death rate [per 1,000 live births]	婚姻率（人口千対）Marriage rate [per 1,000 population]	離婚率（人口千対）Divorce rate [per 1,000 population]	合計特殊出生率 Total fertility rate	都道府県 Prefecture
10.9	3.6	2.9	0.7	5.0	1.73	1.44	全 国 Total
15.4	3.3	2.5	0.8	4.6	1.97	1.29	01 c) 北海道
11.6	3.0	2.3	0.7	4.0	1.68	1.48	02 青森
10.4	3.8	3.3	0.5	3.9	1.49	1.45	03 岩手
12.8	3.7	2.5	1.2	4.8	1.63	1.34	04 宮城
10.3	4.6	3.7	0.9	3.5	1.38	1.39	05 秋田
10.6	4.4	3.2	1.2	3.9	1.37	1.47	06 山形
9.7	4.6	4.1	0.5	4.6	1.73	1.59	07 福島
10.1	4.0	3.3	0.6	4.6	1.68	1.47	08 茨城
11.6	3.1	2.3	0.8	4.8	1.77	1.46	09 栃木
11.9	3.5	2.8	0.7	4.4	1.68	1.48	10 群馬
10.9	3.4	2.7	0.7	4.8	1.74	1.37	11 埼玉
9.8	4.1	3.4	0.7	4.8	1.73	1.35	12 千葉
10.8	3.6	2.9	0.7	6.5	1.78	1.24	13 東京
10.2	3.6	2.8	0.9	5.2	1.74	1.36	14 神奈川
9.0	3.7	3.4	0.3	4.1	1.31	1.43	15 新潟
9.1	4.0	2.7	1.2	4.3	1.30	1.50	16 富山
8.1	2.7	2.0	0.7	4.5	1.45	1.53	17 石川
12.1	4.2	2.9	1.3	4.5	1.45	1.65	18 福井
8.3	2.6	2.1	0.5	4.5	1.67	1.51	19 山梨
8.7	3.7	2.7	1.0	4.4	1.54	1.59	20 長野
8.9	3.7	2.7	1.0	4.3	1.54	1.54	21 岐阜
8.9	4.1	3.6	0.6	4.7	1.72	1.55	22 静岡
8.7	3.7	3.0	0.7	5.6	1.70	1.56	23 愛知
9.6	5.7	5.0	0.7	4.6	1.65	1.51	24 三重
9.1	2.4	1.7	0.7	4.9	1.58	1.56	25 滋賀
10.7	3.6	2.7	0.9	4.7	1.65	1.34	26 京都
11.5	3.5	3.0	0.5	5.3	1.99	1.37	27 大阪
10.0	2.8	2.4	0.4	4.7	1.71	1.49	28 兵庫
10.5	3.7	2.6	1.1	4.2	1.62	1.36	29 奈良
13.4	3.0	2.7	0.3	4.3	1.87	1.50	30 和歌山
11.5	5.2	3.8	1.4	4.3	1.66	1.60	31 鳥取
10.7	3.2	2.8	0.4	4.0	1.39	1.75	32 島根
11.3	3.9	3.2	0.7	4.7	1.71	1.56	33 岡山
10.8	3.7	3.2	0.5	4.9	1.68	1.57	34 広島
9.2	4.4	3.9	0.4	4.3	1.56	1.58	35 山口
9.7	3.4	2.4	0.9	4.3	1.59	1.51	36 徳島
9.1	2.5	2.1	0.4	4.8	1.67	1.64	37 香川
14.1	3.1	3.0	0.1	4.3	1.64	1.54	38 愛媛
12.1	2.9	2.5	0.4	4.1	1.71	1.47	39 高知
12.6	3.4	2.8	0.6	5.3	1.93	1.50	40 福岡
12.1	2.5	2.1	0.4	4.5	1.67	1.63	41 佐賀
11.1	4.2	3.6	0.6	4.4	1.60	1.71	42 長崎
14.4	3.2	2.5	0.7	4.5	1.65	1.66	43 熊本
14.5	3.5	2.4	1.1	4.5	1.74	1.65	44 大分
15.4	3.5	2.6	0.9	4.7	2.02	1.71	45 宮崎
12.7	3.1	2.6	0.5	4.6	1.77	1.68	46 鹿児島
13.0	3.8	3.1	0.7	5.9	2.59	1.95	47 沖縄
							21 大都市（再掲）21 major cities (Regrouped)
10.9	3.7	3.0	0.7	7.1	1.80	…	50 東京都の区部
16.4	3.3	2.7	0.6	5.4	2.09	…	51 札幌
10.6	3.7	2.4	1.3	5.5	1.61	…	52 仙台
8.7	4.3	3.2	1.0	5.2	1.54	…	53 さいたま
10.4	3.3	2.4	0.9	4.8	1.67	…	54 千葉
9.4	4.2	3.2	1.0	5.1	1.71	…	55 横浜
10.5	3.0	2.3	0.7	6.7	1.65	…	56 川崎
12.6	3.8	3.1	0.8	4.6	1.88	…	57 相模原
9.2	4.2	3.9	0.3	4.4	1.40	…	58 新潟
10.3	5.5	4.9	0.6	4.7	1.63	…	59 静岡
6.0	2.7	2.3	0.5	4.8	1.54	…	60 浜松
9.5	3.6	2.9	0.7	6.0	1.80	…	61 名古屋
10.6	3.8	3.0	0.8	5.1	1.67	…	62 京都
12.5	3.6	3.0	0.6	6.6	2.22	…	63 大阪
11.5	2.6	2.2	0.4	4.9	1.95	…	64 堺
12.0	2.6	2.3	0.3	4.9	1.77	…	65 神戸
11.1	4.5	3.7	0.8	5.2	1.76	…	66 岡山
11.5	3.9	3.4	0.5	5.3	1.70	…	67 広島
13.5	3.3	2.5	0.8	5.1	1.93	…	68 北九州
12.4	3.6	3.2	0.3	6.3	1.91	…	69 福岡
13.8	3.5	3.1	0.4	5.1	1.70	…	70 熊本

Note : a) Per 1,000 live births and foetal deaths at 12 completed weeks and over of gestation.
　　　 b) Per 1,000 live births and foetal deaths at 22 completed weeks and over of gestation.
　　　 c) See page 44.

総　覧

表 3.4　世界各国にお
Table 3.4　International comparison

出生数・出生率（人口千対）　Live births and live birth rates（per 1,000 population）

年次 Year	日本 Japan 数 Number	率 Rate	カナダ Canada 数 Number	率 Rate	アメリカ合衆国 U.S.A. 数 Number	率 Rate	フランス France 数 Number	率 Rate	ドイツ Germany 数 Number	率 Rate	イタリア Italy 数 Number	率 Rate	ロシア Russian Federation 数 Number	率 Rate	イギリス United Kingdom 数 Number	率 Rate
2007	1 089 818	8.6	367 864	11.2	4 316 233	14.3	785 985	12.7	684 862	8.3	563 933	9.5	1 610 122	11.3	772 245	12.7
2008	1 091 156	8.7	377 886	11.3	4 247 694	14.0	796 044	12.8	682 514	8.3	576 659	9.6	1 713 947	12.0	794 383	12.9
2009	1 070 035	8.5	380 863	11.3	4 130 665	13.5	793 420	12.7	665 126	8.1	568 857	9.6	1 761 687	12.3	790 204	12.7
2010	1 071 304	8.5	376 951	11.1	3 999 386	12.9	802 224	12.8	677 947	8.3	561 944	9.5	1 788 948	12.5	807 271	12.9
2011	1 050 806	8.3	377 897	11.0	3 953 590	12.7	792 996	12.5	662 685	8.3	546 585	9.2	1 796 629	12.6	807 776	12.8
2012	1 037 231	8.2	381 869	11.0	3 952 841	12.6	790 290	12.4	673 544	8.4	534 186	9.0	1 902 084	13.3	812 970	12.8
2013	1 029 816	8.2	380 323	11.0	3 932 181	12.4	781 621	12.2	682 069	8.5	514 308	8.5	1 895 822	13.2	778 358	12.1
2014	1 003 539	8.0	388 729*	10.9*	3 988 076	12.5	781 167	12.2	714 927	8.8	502 596	8.3	…	…	775 908	12.0
2015	1 005 677	8.0	…	…	3 978 497	12.4	760 421	11.8	737 575	9.0	485 780	8.0	…	…	776 746	11.9
2016	976 978	7.8	…	…	…	…	745 000*	11.5*	770 000*	9.4*	473 438	7.8	…	…	774 841*	11.9*

合計特殊出生率　Total fertility rates

年次 Year	日本 Japan	カナダ Canada	アメリカ合衆国 U.S.A.	フランス France	ドイツ Germany	イタリア Italy	ロシア Russian Federation	イギリス United Kingdom
2007	1.34	1.66	2.12	1.96	1.37	1.37	1.41	1.90
2008	1.37	1.68	2.09	2.00	1.38	1.41	1.49	1.96
2009	1.37	1.67	2.00	…	…	1.41	1.54	…
2010	1.39	…	1.93	2.02	1.39	1.41	…	…
2011	1.39	…	1.90	2.00	1.36	1.39	…	1.91
2012	1.41	1.61	1.88	1.99	1.41	1.42	…	1.92
2013	1.43	1.59	1.86	1.97	1.42	1.39	…	1.83
2014	1.42	…	1.86	1.97*	1.47	1.37	…	1.82
2015	1.45	…	1.84	1.92*	1.50	1.35	…	…
2016	1.44	…	…	1.89*	…	…	…	…

死亡数・死亡率（人口千対）　Deaths and death rates（per 1,000 population）

年次 Year	日本 Japan 数 Number	率 Rate	カナダ Canada 数 Number	率 Rate	アメリカ合衆国 U.S.A. 数 Number	率 Rate	フランス France 数 Number	率 Rate	ドイツ Germany 数 Number	率 Rate	イタリア Italy 数 Number	率 Rate	ロシア Russian Federation 数 Number	率 Rate	イギリス United Kingdom 数 Number	率 Rate
2007	1 108 334	8.8	235 217	7.1	2 423 712	8.0	521 016	8.4	827 155	10.1	572 881	9.6	2 080 445	14.6	574 687	9.4
2008	1 142 407	9.1	238 617	7.2	2 471 984	8.1	532 131	8.5	844 439	10.3	578 192	9.7	2 075 954	14.5	579 697	9.4
2009	1 141 865	9.1	238 418	7.1	2 437 163	7.9	538 116	8.6	854 544	10.4	585 182	9.9	2 010 543	14.1	559 617	9.0
2010	1 197 012	9.5	244 968	7.2	2 468 435	8.0	540 469	8.6	858 768	10.5	587 488	9.9	2 028 516	14.2	561 666	8.9
2011	1 253 066	9.9	243 651	7.1	2 515 458	8.1	534 795	8.5	852 328	10.6	593 402	10.0	1 925 720	13.5	552 232	8.7
2012	1 256 359	10.0	246 596	7.1	2 543 279	8.1	559 227	8.8	869 582	10.8	612 883	10.3	1 906 335	13.3	569 024	8.9
2013	1 268 436	10.1	252 338	7.2	2 596 993	8.2	558 408	8.7	893 825	11.1	600 744	10.0	1 871 809	13.0	574 945	9.0
2014	1 273 004	10.1	268 056*	7.5*	2 626 418	8.2	547 003	8.5	868 356	10.7	598 364	9.8	…	…	568 840	8.8
2015	1 290 444	10.3	…	…	2 712 630	8.5	581 770	9.0	925 200	11.3	647 571	10.7	…	…	601 272	9.2
2016	1 307 748	10.5	…	…	…	…	580 100*	9.0*	920 000*	11.2*	615 261	10.1	…	…	597 208*	9.1*

乳児死亡数・乳児死亡率（出生千対）　Infant deaths and infant mortality rates（per 1,000 live births）

年次 Year	日本 Japan 数 Number	率 Rate	カナダ Canada 数 Number	率 Rate	アメリカ合衆国 U.S.A. 数 Number	率 Rate	フランス France 数 Number	率 Rate	ドイツ Germany 数 Number	率 Rate	イタリア Italy 数 Number	率 Rate	ロシア Russian Federation 数 Number	率 Rate	イギリス United Kingdom 数 Number	率 Rate
2007	2 828	2.6	1 881	5.1	29 138	6.8	2 822	3.6	2 656	3.9	1 959	3.5	14 858	9.2	3 740	4.8
2008	2 798	2.6	1 911	5.1	28 059	6.6	2 856	3.6	2 414	3.5	1 896	3.3	14 436	8.4	3 745	4.7
2009	2 556	2.4	…	…	26 412	6.4	2 903	3.7	2 334	3.5	1 947	3.4	14 271	8.1	3 677	4.7
2010	2 450	2.3	…	…	24 586	6.1	2 785	3.5	2 322	3.4	1 773	3.2	13 405	7.5	3 504	4.3
2011	2 463	2.3	…	…	23 985	6.1	2 604	3.3	2 408	3.6	1 595	2.9	13 168	7.3	3 502	4.3
2012	2 299	2.2	1 818	4.8	23 629	6.0	2 643	3.3	2 202	3.3	1 532	2.9	16 306	8.6	3 347	4.1
2013	2 185	2.1	1 884	5.0	23 440	6.0	2 710	3.5	2 250	3.3	1 493	2.9	…	…	…	…
2014	2 080	2.1	…	…	23 215	5.8	2 598	3.3	2 284	3.2	1 523	3.0	…	…	2 990	3.9
2015	1 916	1.9	…	…	23 455	5.9	2 655	3.5	2 405	3.3	1 398	2.9	…	…	3 005	3.9
2016	1 928	2.0	…	…	…	…	…	…	…	…	…	…	…	…	…	…

注　　＊印は暫定値である。
　　1）諸外国は、妊娠期間不詳の死産を含む。フランスについては、妊娠期間180日以後の死産である。
資料：日本は厚生労働省「人口動態統計」、諸外国はUN, Demographic Yearbook

Summary

けける人口動態
of vital statistics

妊娠満28週以後の死産数・死産比（出生千対）[1]　Foetal deaths and foetal death ratio at 28 completed weeks and over of gestation (per 1,000 live births)

年次 Year	日本 Japan		カナダ Canada		アメリカ合衆国 U.S.A.		フランス France		ドイツ Germany		イタリア Italy		ロシア Russian Federation		イギリス United Kingdom	
	数 Number	死産比 Ratio	数 Number	死産比 Ratio	数 Number	死産比 Ratio	数 Number	死産比 Ratio	数 Number	死産比 Ratio	数 Number	死産比 Ratio	数 Number	死産比 Ratio	数 Number	死産比 Ratio
2007	2 254	2.1	1 172	3.2	...	...	7 246	9.2	2 371	3.5	1 570*	2.8*	8 612	5.3	4 027	5.2
2008	2 209	2.0	1 170	3.1	...	...	8 356	10.5	2 412	3.5	1 568	2.7	8 594	5.0	4 057	5.1
2009	2 222	2.1	1 145	3.0	12 059	2.9	9 377	11.8	2 338	3.5	1 564	2.7	8 380	4.8	4 124	5.2
2010	2 187	2.0	1 084	2.9	11 870	3.0	8 206	10.2	2 466	3.6	1 532	2.7	8 300	4.6	4 110	5.1
2011	2 137	2.0	1 115*	3.0*	11 857	3.0	...	...	2 387	3.6	1 422	2.6	8 109	4.5	4 201	5.2
2012	1 969	1.9	1 102	2.9	11 739	3.0	...	...	2 400	3.6	1 439	2.7	12 142	6.4	3 938	4.8
2013	1 897	1.8	1 077	2.8	11 721	3.0	...	...	2 556	3.7	1 262*	2.5*	...	...	...	...
2014	1 790	1.8	...	...	11 311	2.8	...	...	2 597	3.6	1 364	2.7	...	...	3 563	4.6
2015	1 830	1.8	...	...	11 354	2.9	...	...	2 787	3.8	...	...	...	...	3 434	4.4
2016	1 699	1.7	...	...	...	...	...	...	...	...	...	...	...	...	...	...

婚姻件数・婚姻率（人口千対）　Marriages and marriage rates (per 1,000 population)

年次 Year	日本 Japan		カナダ Canada		アメリカ合衆国 U.S.A.		フランス France		ドイツ Germany		イタリア Italy		ロシア Russian Federation		イギリス United Kingdom	
	数 Number	率 Rate	数 Number	率 Rate	数 Number	率 Rate	数 Number	率 Rate	数 Number	率 Rate	数 Number	率 Rate	数 Number	率 Rate	数 Number	率 Rate
2007	719 822	5.7	151 695*	4.6*	2 197 000	7.3	267 194	4.3	368 922	4.5	250 360	4.2	1 262 500	8.9	273 920	4.5
2008	726 106	5.8	147 288	4.4	2 157 000	7.1	258 739	4.2	376 998	4.6	246 613	4.1	1 179 007	8.3	273 207	4.4
2009	707 734	5.6	...	...	2 077 000	6.8	245 151	3.9	378 439	4.6	230 613	3.9	1 199 446	8.4	267 898	4.3
2010	700 214	5.5	...	...	2 096 000	6.8	245 334	3.9	382 047	4.7	217 700	3.7	1 215 066	8.5	280 444	4.5
2011	661 895	5.2	...	...	2 118 000	6.8	231 100	3.7	377 816	4.7	204 830	3.4	1 316 011	9.2	258 391	4.5
2012	668 869	5.3	...	...	2 131 000	6.8	239 840	3.8	387 423	4.8	207 138	3.5	1 213 598	8.5	...	...
2013	660 613	5.3	...	...	2 081 301	6.6	233 108	3.7	373 655	4.6	194 057	3.2	1 225 501	8.5	...	...
2014	643 749	5.1	...	...	2 140 272	6.7	235 315	3.7	385 952	4.8	189 765	3.1	...	...	...	...
2015	635 156	5.1	...	...	2 221 579	6.9	230 364	3.6	400 115	4.9	194 377	3.2	...	...	...	...
2016	620 531	5.0	...	...	...	...	...	...	...	...	...	...	...	...	...	...

離婚件数・離婚率（人口千対）　Divorces and divorce rates (per 1,000 population)

年次 Year	日本 Japan		カナダ Canada		アメリカ合衆国 U.S.A.		フランス France		ドイツ Germany		イタリア Italy		ロシア Russian Federation		イギリス United Kingdom	
	数 Number	率 Rate	数 Number	率 Rate	数 Number	率 Rate	数 Number	率 Rate	数 Number	率 Rate	数 Number	率 Rate	数 Number	率 Rate	数 Number	率 Rate
2007	254 832	2.02	...	...	...	...	131 316	2.12	187 072	2.27	50 669	0.85	685 910	4.83	143 857	2.36
2008	251 136	1.99	70 226	2.11	844 000	2.77	129 379	2.08	191 948	2.34	54 351	0.91	703 412	4.93	135 942	2.21
2009	253 353	2.01	...	...	840 000	2.74	127 578	2.04	185 817	2.27	54 456	0.92	699 430	4.90	126 520	2.03
2010	251 378	1.99	...	...	872 000	2.82	130 810	2.08	187 027	2.29	54 160	0.91	639 321	4.48	132 338	2.11
2011	235 719	1.87	...	...	877 000	2.81	129 802	2.05	187 640	2.34	53 806	0.91	669 376	4.68	129 764	2.05
2012	235 406	1.87	...	...	851 000	2.71	125 217	1.97	179 147	2.23	51 319	0.86	644 101	4.50	130 469	2.05
2013	231 383	1.84	...	...	832 157	2.63	121 849	1.91	169 833	2.11	52 943	0.88	667 971	4.65	126 716	1.98
2014	222 107	1.77	...	...	813 862	2.55	120 568	1.88	166 199	2.05	52 355	0.86	...	...	122 556	1.90
2015	226 215	1.81	...	...	800 909	2.50	120 731	1.87	163 335	2.00	82 469	1.36	...	...	...	...
2016	216 798	1.73	...	...	...	...	...	...	...	...	...	...	...	...	...	...

第4章 出 生

出 生

〔出生の年次推移〕
〔Trends in live births〕

Chapter 4 Natality

表4.1 年次別にみた出生数
Table 4.1 Trends in live births, and sex ratio of live

年 次 [1] Year		出 生 数 Live births			出 生 率（人口千対）Live birth rate [per 1,000 population]	出 生 性 比 Sex ratio of live births	合計特殊出生率 [3] Total fertility rate
		総 数 [2] Total	男 Male	女 Female			
1899	明治32年	1 386 981	713 442	673 539	32.0	105.9	…
1900	33	1 420 534	727 916	692 618	32.4	105.1	…
01	34	1 501 591	769 494	732 097	33.9	105.1	…
02	35	1 510 835	773 296	737 539	33.6	104.8	…
03	36	1 489 816	763 806	726 010	32.7	105.2	…
04	37	1 440 371	738 230	702 141	31.2	105.1	…
05	38	1 452 770	735 948	716 822	31.2	102.7	…
06	39	1 394 295	726 155	668 140	29.6	108.7	…
07	40	1 614 472	818 114	796 358	34.0	102.7	…
08	41	1 662 815	850 209	812 606	34.7	104.6	…
09	42	1 693 850	863 855	829 995	34.9	104.1	…
1910	43	1 712 857	872 779	840 078	34.8	103.9	…
11	44	1 747 803	891 049	856 754	35.1	104.0	…
12	大正元年	1 737 674	886 449	851 225	34.4	104.1	…
13	2	1 757 441	897 824	859 617	34.3	104.4	…
14	3	1 808 402	925 855	882 547	34.8	104.9	…
15	4	1 799 326	918 296	881 030	34.1	104.2	…
16	5	1 804 822	921 347	883 475	33.7	104.3	…
17	6	1 812 413	924 953	887 460	33.5	104.2	…
18	7	1 791 992	914 685	877 307	32.7	104.3	…
19	8	1 778 685	910 400	868 285	32.3	104.9	…
1920	9	2 025 564	1 035 134	990 430	36.2	104.5	…
21	10	1 990 876	1 017 457	973 419	35.1	104.5	…
22	11	1 969 314	1 004 022	965 292	34.3	104.0	…
23	12	2 043 297	1 043 599	999 698	35.2	104.4	…
24	13	1 998 520	1 019 988	978 532	33.9	104.2	…
25	14	2 086 091	1 060 827	1 025 264	34.9	103.5	…
26	昭和元年	2 104 405	1 081 793	1 022 611	34.6	105.8	…
27	2	2 060 737	1 048 946	1 011 791	33.4	103.7	…
28	3	2 135 852	1 090 702	1 045 150	34.1	104.4	…
29	4	2 077 026	1 058 666	1 018 360	32.7	104.0	…
1930	5	2 085 101	1 069 551	1 015 549	32.4	105.3	…
31	6	2 102 784	1 073 385	1 029 399	32.1	104.3	…
32	7	2 182 742	1 117 954	1 064 788	32.9	105.0	…
33	8	2 121 253	1 087 688	1 033 565	31.5	105.2	…
34	9	2 043 783	1 042 736	1 001 047	29.9	104.2	…
35	10	2 190 704	1 122 867	1 067 836	31.6	105.2	…
36	11	2 101 969	1 076 197	1 025 772	30.0	104.9	…
37	12	2 180 734	1 116 154	1 064 580	30.9	104.8	…
38	13	1 928 321	990 888	937 433	27.2	105.7	…
39	14	1 901 573	973 744	927 829	26.6	104.9	…
1940	15	2 115 867	1 084 282	1 031 585	29.4	105.1	…
41	16	2 277 283	1 165 437	1 111 846	31.8	104.8	…
42	17	2 233 660	1 145 068	1 088 592	30.9	105.2	…
43	18	2 253 535	1 155 983	1 097 552	30.9	105.3	…
47	22	2 678 792	1 376 986	1 301 806	34.3	105.8	4.54
48	23	2 681 624	1 378 564	1 303 060	33.5	105.8	4.40
49	24	2 696 638	1 380 008	1 316 630	33.0	104.8	4.32
1950	25	2 337 507	1 203 111	1 134 396	28.1	106.1	3.65
51	26	2 137 689	1 094 641	1 043 048	25.3	104.9	3.26
52	27	2 005 162	1 028 061	977 101	23.4	105.2	2.98
53	28	1 868 040	957 524	910 516	21.5	105.2	2.69
54	29	1 769 580	911 212	858 368	20.0	106.2	2.48

注：1) 昭和19～21年は資料不備のため省略した。昭和22～47年は沖縄県を含まない。
2) 昭和元年・5年・10年の出生数の総数には、男女不詳が各1含まれている。
3) 率算出に用いた分母人口は日本人人口である。
資料：国立社会保障・人口問題研究所「人口統計資料集」、厚生労働省「人口動態統計」

Natality

・率（人口千対）・出生性比及び合計特殊出生率
live birth rates (per 1,000 population), total fertility rates
births : Japan

年　次 [1] Year		出　　生　　数 Live births			出　生　率 （人口千対） Live birth rate [per 1,000 population]	出　生　性　比 Sex ratio of live births	合計特殊 [3] 出　生　率 Total fertility rate
		総　数 Total	男 Male	女 Female			
1955	昭和30年	1 730 692	889 670	841 022	19.4	105.8	2.37
56	31	1 665 278	856 084	809 194	18.4	105.8	2.22
57	32	1 566 713	805 220	761 493	17.2	105.7	2.04
58	33	1 653 469	848 733	804 736	18.0	105.5	2.11
59	34	1 626 088	835 822	790 266	17.5	105.8	2.04
1960	35	1 606 041	824 761	781 280	17.2	105.6	2.00
61	36	1 589 372	817 599	771 773	16.9	105.9	1.96
62	37	1 618 616	833 269	785 347	17.0	106.1	1.98
63	38	1 659 521	852 561	806 960	17.3	105.7	2.00
64	39	1 716 761	882 924	833 837	17.7	105.9	2.05
65	40	1 823 697	935 366	888 331	18.6	105.3	2.14
66	41	1 360 974	705 463	655 511	13.7	107.6	1.58
67	42	1 935 647	992 778	942 869	19.4	105.3	2.23
68	43	1 871 839	967 996	903 843	18.6	107.1	2.13
69	44	1 889 815	977 687	912 128	18.5	107.2	2.13
1970	45	1 934 239	1 000 403	933 836	18.8	107.1	2.13
71	46	2 000 973	1 032 937	968 036	19.2	106.7	2.16
72	47	2 038 682	1 051 389	987 293	19.3	106.5	2.14
73	48	2 091 983	1 077 517	1 014 466	19.4	106.2	2.14
74	49	2 029 989	1 046 538	983 451	18.6	106.4	2.05
75	50	1 901 440	979 091	922 349	17.1	106.2	1.91
76	51	1 832 617	943 829	888 788	16.3	106.2	1.85
77	52	1 755 100	903 380	851 720	15.5	106.1	1.80
78	53	1 708 643	879 149	829 494	14.9	106.0	1.79
79	54	1 642 580	845 884	796 696	14.2	106.2	1.77
1980	55	1 576 889	811 418	765 471	13.6	106.0	1.75
81	56	1 529 455	786 596	742 859	13.0	105.9	1.74
82	57	1 515 392	777 855	737 537	12.8	105.5	1.77
83	58	1 508 687	775 206	733 481	12.7	105.7	1.80
84	59	1 489 780	764 597	725 183	12.5	105.4	1.81
85	60	1 431 577	735 284	696 293	11.9	105.6	1.76
86	61	1 382 946	711 301	671 645	11.4	105.9	1.72
87	62	1 346 658	692 304	654 354	11.1	105.8	1.69
88	63	1 314 006	674 883	639 123	10.8	105.6	1.66
89	平成元年	1 246 802	640 506	606 296	10.2	105.6	1.57
1990	2	1 221 585	626 971	594 614	10.0	105.4	1.54
91	3	1 223 245	628 615	594 630	9.9	105.7	1.53
92	4	1 208 989	622 136	586 853	9.8	106.0	1.50
93	5	1 188 282	610 244	578 038	9.6	105.6	1.46
94	6	1 238 328	635 915	602 413	10.0	105.6	1.50
95	7	1 187 064	608 547	578 517	9.6	105.2	1.42
96	8	1 206 555	619 793	586 762	9.7	105.6	1.43
97	9	1 191 665	610 905	580 760	9.5	105.2	1.39
98	10	1 203 147	617 414	585 733	9.6	105.4	1.38
99	11	1 177 669	604 769	572 900	9.4	105.6	1.34
2000	12	1 190 547	612 148	578 399	9.5	105.8	1.36
01	13	1 170 662	600 918	569 744	9.3	105.5	1.33
02	14	1 153 855	592 840	561 015	9.2	105.7	1.32
03	15	1 123 610	576 736	546 874	8.9	105.5	1.29
04	16	1 110 721	569 559	541 162	8.8	105.2	1.29
05	17	1 062 530	545 032	517 498	8.4	105.3	1.26
06	18	1 092 674	560 439	532 235	8.7	105.3	1.32
07	19	1 089 818	559 847	529 971	8.6	105.6	1.34
08	20	1 091 156	559 513	531 643	8.7	105.2	1.37
09	21	1 070 035	548 993	521 042	8.5	105.4	1.37
2010	22	1 071 304	550 742	520 562	8.5	105.8	1.39
11	23	1 050 806	538 271	512 535	8.3	105.0	1.39
12	24	1 037 231	531 781	505 450	8.2	105.2	1.41
13	25	1 029 816	527 657	502 159	8.2	105.1	1.43
14	26	1 003 539	515 533	488 006	8.0	105.6	1.42
15	27	1 005 677	515 452	490 225	8.0	105.1	1.45
16	**28**	**976 978**	**501 880**	**475 098**	**7.8**	**105.6**	**1.44**

103

出　生

〔月別にみた出生〕
〔Live births by month〕

表4.2　月別にみた年次別
Table 4.2　Trends in live births and live birth

年　　次 Year		総　　数 Total	1　月 January	2　月 February	3　月 March	4　月 April	5　月 May
						実	数
1947	昭和22年 2)	2 678 792	295 465	226 018	235 891	209 159	195 574
50	25	2 337 507	256 132	219 654	214 964	188 188	170 659
55	30	1 730 692	200 116	157 071	156 751	148 066	132 368
60	35	1 606 041	166 782	142 765	149 415	144 241	126 974
65	40	1 823 697	167 220	151 449	159 421	154 749	140 137
70	45	1 934 239	174 550	154 966	164 241	166 087	160 860
75	50	1 901 440	168 095	152 985	159 750	159 940	161 271
80	55	1 576 889	135 848	125 070	129 692	128 240	134 367
85	60	1 431 577	120 404	110 470	115 172	114 977	120 997
90	平成 2 年	1 221 585	104 065	92 531	101 119	99 284	106 308
95	7	1 187 064	102 692	90 495	98 348	95 520	101 422
2000	12	1 190 547	101 351	93 683	98 985	94 902	100 134
01	13	1 170 662	99 647	88 001	94 653	93 106	99 540
02	14	1 153 855	98 407	88 750	95 563	93 832	98 589
03	15	1 123 610	96 324	84 712	92 321	91 416	95 863
04	16	1 110 721	94 171	87 080	93 251	91 581	91 952
05	17	1 062 530	92 842	80 875	89 541	86 281	87 151
06	18	1 092 674	90 977	82 851	90 903	87 981	92 228
07	19	1 089 818	91 885	81 794	89 701	87 369	91 894
08	20	1 091 156	91 675	85 021	89 185	88 047	91 523
09	21	1 070 035	91 320	80 924	87 865	87 207	87 241
10	22	1 071 304	90 577	81 334	87 853	87 312	86 721
11	23	1 050 806	88 492	79 755	87 512	85 254	86 491
12	24	1 037 231	87 680	81 469	83 749	81 718	85 841
13	25	1 029 816	85 853	77 066	82 997	81 856	85 297
14	26	1 003 539	83 572	73 897	79 340	78 834	83 310
15	27	1 005 677	84 740	75 989	81 942	83 408	83 827
16	**28**	**976 978**	**82 292**	**76 765**	**81 208**	**79 753**	**80 905**
						出　生	率
1947	昭和22年	34.3	44.5	37.7	35.6	32.6	29.5
50	25	28.1	36.2	34.4	30.4	27.5	24.2
55	30	19.4	26.4	22.9	20.7	20.2	17.5
60	35	17.2	21.1	19.3	18.9	18.8	16.0
65	40	18.6	20.0	20.1	19.1	19.2	16.8
70	45	18.8	20.1	19.7	18.9	19.7	18.4
75	50	17.1	18.0	18.2	17.1	17.7	17.2
80	55	13.6	13.9	13.6	13.2	13.5	13.7
85	60	11.9	11.8	12.0	11.3	11.7	11.9
90	平成 2 年	10.0	10.0	9.8	9.7	9.9	10.2
95	7	9.6	9.7	9.5	9.3	9.4	9.6
2000	12	9.5	9.5	9.4	9.3	9.2	9.4
01	13	9.3	9.3	9.1	8.9	9.0	9.3
02	14	9.2	9.2	9.2	8.9	9.1	9.2
03	15	8.9	9.0	8.8	8.6	8.8	8.9
04	16	8.8	8.8	8.7	8.7	8.9	8.6
05	17	8.4	8.7	8.4	8.4	8.3	8.1
06	18	8.7	8.5	8.6	8.5	8.5	8.6
07	19	8.6	8.6	8.5	8.4	8.4	8.6
08	20	8.7	8.6	8.5	8.4	8.5	8.6
09	21	8.5	8.5	8.4	8.2	8.4	8.2
10	22	8.5	8.5	8.4	8.2	8.4	8.1
11	23	8.3	8.2	8.2	8.2	8.2	8.1
12	24	8.2	8.2	8.2	7.8	7.9	8.0
13	25	8.2	8.0	8.0	7.8	7.9	8.0
14	26	8.0	7.8	7.7	7.4	7.6	7.8
15	27	8.0	8.0	7.9	7.7	8.1	7.9
16	**28**	**7.8**	**7.8**	**7.7**	**7.7**	**7.8**	**7.6**

注：1)　各月の率は年率に換算したものである。計算方法は、比率の解説を参照されたい。
　　　　なお、分母に用いた人口は、昭和45年以降は各月の月初人口であるが、40年以前は各年の10月 1 日現在人口である。
　　2)　昭和22年の総数には、月不詳 4 を含む。

104

出生数及び率[1]（人口千対）
rates (per 1,000 population) by month : Japan

6　月 June	7　月 July	8　月 August	9　月 September	10　月 October	11　月 November	12　月 December
Number						
194 633	226 560	236 831	231 874	229 058	210 764	186 961
161 891	185 380	190 724	191 798	187 863	185 213	185 041
118 513	132 759	142 036	138 323	137 054	132 986	134 649
115 415	125 991	129 803	128 977	125 258	123 072	127 348
135 226	151 439	157 205	158 681	159 240	144 084	144 846
153 129	169 825	163 974	157 094	152 911	148 875	167 727
152 785	167 835	164 422	159 301	155 050	142 880	157 126
128 227	138 952	138 266	136 886	133 342	120 455	127 544
116 341	130 375	126 433	122 563	123 053	111 961	118 831
99 869	107 568	106 991	102 113	102 899	97 078	101 760
99 783	105 878	105 391	100 759	96 208	92 999	97 569
95 465	102 806	103 706	103 131	100 752	96 407	99 225
95 160	101 511	102 745	102 619	103 308	94 650	95 722
93 373	102 331	100 775	99 261	97 586	90 400	94 988
91 671	99 235	97 381	95 173	95 853	89 082	94 579
89 451	97 373	94 517	95 947	92 463	90 221	92 714
87 165	90 976	92 455	92 705	90 770	83 990	87 779
89 773	93 813	95 200	93 137	93 524	90 053	92 234
88 833	94 050	94 487	92 946	96 066	89 689	91 104
87 541	94 982	93 720	95 118	94 630	87 388	92 326
87 313	93 968	91 793	92 075	92 997	85 752	91 580
89 532	93 040	92 467	92 104	92 270	88 225	89 869
87 266	91 383	93 066	92 497	89 180	84 667	85 243
83 451	90 537	90 906	89 758	90 438	85 577	86 107
82 397	91 467	92 118	90 618	90 667	83 126	86 354
81 401	89 516	87 732	90 309	88 592	80 993	86 043
83 200	88 612	86 344	86 832	85 825	80 659	84 299
80 546	**85 027**	**84 977**	**84 863**	**83 250**	**77 963**	**79 429**
Live birth rate						
30. 3	34. 2	35. 7	36. 1	34. 5	32. 8	28. 2
23. 7	26. 2	27. 0	28. 0	26. 6	27. 1	26. 2
16. 2	17. 5	18. 7	18. 9	18. 1	18. 1	17. 8
15. 1	15. 9	16. 4	16. 8	15. 8	16. 1	16. 1
16. 7	18. 1	18. 8	19. 6	19. 1	17. 8	17. 4
18. 1	19. 4	18. 7	18. 5	17. 5	17. 6	19. 1
16. 9	17. 9	17. 5	17. 5	16. 5	15. 7	16. 7
13. 5	14. 1	14. 1	14. 4	13. 5	12. 6	12. 9
11. 8	12. 8	12. 4	12. 4	12. 0	11. 3	11. 6
9. 9	10. 3	10. 3	10. 1	9. 9	9. 6	9. 8
9. 8	10. 0	10. 0	9. 9	9. 1	9. 1	9. 2
9. 3	9. 7	9. 8	10. 0	9. 5	9. 4	9. 3
9. 2	9. 5	9. 6	9. 9	9. 7	9. 1	8. 9
9. 0	9. 6	9. 4	9. 6	9. 1	8. 7	8. 9
8. 8	9. 3	9. 1	9. 2	8. 9	8. 6	8. 8
8. 6	9. 1	8. 8	9. 3	8. 7	8. 7	8. 7
8. 4	8. 5	8. 6	8. 9	8. 5	8. 1	8. 2
8. 7	8. 8	8. 9	9. 0	8. 7	8. 7	8. 6
8. 6	8. 8	8. 8	9. 0	9. 0	8. 7	8. 5
8. 5	8. 9	8. 8	9. 2	8. 9	8. 5	8. 7
8. 4	8. 8	8. 6	8. 9	8. 7	8. 3	8. 6
8. 7	8. 7	8. 7	8. 9	8. 6	8. 5	8. 4
8. 4	8. 5	8. 7	8. 9	8. 3	8. 2	8. 0
8. 1	8. 5	8. 5	8. 7	8. 5	8. 3	8. 1
8. 0	8. 6	8. 6	8. 8	8. 5	8. 0	8. 1
7. 9	8. 4	8. 2	8. 8	8. 3	7. 9	8. 1
8. 1	8. 3	8. 1	8. 4	8. 1	7. 8	7. 9
7. 9	**8. 0**	**8. 0**	**8. 3**	**7. 9**	**7. 6**	**7. 5**

出 生

〔地域別にみた出生〕
〔Live births by prefecture〕

表 4.3 都道府県別にみた
Table 4.3 Trends in live births

都道府県[1] Prefecture	1 9 3 5 昭和10年	1 9 4 7 22 年	1 9 5 0 25 年[2]	1 9 5 5 30 年	1 9 6 0 35 年	1 9 6 5 40 年	1 9 7 0 45 年	1 9 7 5 50 年	1 9 8 0 55 年
全 国 Total	2 190 704	2 678 792	2 337 507	1 730 692	1 606 041	1 823 697	1 934 239	1 901 440	1 576 889
01 北 海 道 [a]	109 941	141 577	147 055	103 678	93 852	96 666	91 867	89 631	75 526
02 青　　森	41 046	48 997	46 137	35 219	29 881	28 204	26 369	24 031	21 761
03 岩　　手	40 429	46 083	45 664	34 704	27 827	24 629	22 077	22 182	19 638
04 宮　　城	45 039	55 512	53 224	38 509	31 363	29 240	30 428	32 760	31 129
05 秋　　田	41 722	47 838	42 659	30 401	23 553	19 872	17 754	17 499	16 324
06 山　　形	41 073	43 941	40 694	27 311	22 288	18 864	17 222	17 226	16 871
07 福　　島	56 059	71 232	67 562	48 949	39 239	32 807	29 952	31 287	29 504
08 茨　　城	53 532	69 164	59 723	44 592	35 664	35 460	38 597	40 466	36 369
09 栃　　木	41 799	54 870	46 804	33 428	26 066	25 739	27 535	29 673	25 928
10 群　　馬	42 171	54 605	44 780	32 339	25 510	27 885	29 429	29 616	25 140
11 埼　　玉	53 679	77 234	62 558	47 813	43 421	66 585	91 113	96 033	75 090
12 千　　葉	50 917	73 955	57 451	43 764	39 563	54 170	72 481	77 416	65 554
13 東　　京	175 890	157 306	148 423	127 847	164 826	225 492	229 687	186 701	139 953
14 神 奈 川	55 404	74 699	65 719	51 786	60 704	97 386	123 714	118 656	94 356
15 新　　潟	71 303	86 204	72 013	51 566	41 131	40 261	37 368	37 524	32 812
16 富　　山	27 737	41 428	27 880	18 435	16 126	16 342	17 493	17 305	13 555
17 石　　川	23 958	37 289	26 192	18 021	15 990	16 605	18 125	18 817	15 138
18 福　　井	20 550	25 445	21 209	14 828	12 888	12 736	12 181	12 421	10 724
19 山　　梨	21 594	26 305	21 366	15 659	12 787	12 721	12 269	11 872	10 014
20 長　　野	53 314	61 920	49 989	35 605	30 750	31 532	31 390	31 712	27 187
21 岐　　阜	41 446	51 432	41 465	29 348	28 516	32 112	32 287	31 538	25 834
22 静　　岡	65 427	81 560	70 307	54 455	49 533	55 328	58 139	58 276	47 160
23 愛　　知	89 574	104 377	87 860	65 322	73 237	101 924	116 271	111 528	87 697
24 三　　重	37 796	46 234	37 240	25 456	24 113	27 057	26 154	25 862	21 446
25 滋　　賀	21 305	25 869	21 422	15 053	13 477	14 277	15 593	17 629	15 946
26 京　　都	44 449	53 828	41 236	27 943	29 194	36 703	41 235	39 921	32 139
27 大　　阪	105 202	103 782	93 889	73 374	95 012	147 249	169 880	150 653	111 956
28 兵　　庫	82 133	97 371	81 866	62 404	64 642	82 500	91 169	86 839	68 677
29 奈　　良	18 026	23 989	18 594	13 079	11 994	14 571	17 516	17 983	15 949
30 和 歌 山	24 490	30 803	23 739	17 434	15 905	18 054	17 974	16 340	13 444
31 鳥　　取	14 625	19 348	16 108	11 901	9 575	8 560	7 998	8 755	8 196
32 島　　根	24 019	32 534	25 857	17 162	14 113	11 796	10 539	10 939	9 959
33 岡　　山	38 499	53 528	40 364	28 475	25 315	25 451	28 717	30 102	24 463
34 広　　島	53 426	67 757	52 802	37 643	34 453	38 967	44 532	46 843	37 360
35 山　　口	34 241	49 246	42 761	28 756	24 981	24 537	24 584	23 956	19 798
36 徳　　島	24 382	31 646	25 469	18 042	13 317	12 622	11 852	12 020	10 544
37 香　　川	24 502	34 284	24 633	16 641	13 540	13 721	14 522	15 539	12 993
38 愛　　媛	38 367	52 775	45 549	30 584	25 039	24 424	22 877	23 315	19 721
39 高　　知	20 867	28 656	23 037	16 029	12 663	12 028	11 842	11 773	9 378
40 福　　岡	83 422	108 237	109 156	76 427	67 318	68 854	69 632	71 059	64 404
41 佐　　賀	23 041	31 958	29 996	22 267	17 294	14 443	13 187	13 085	12 466
42 長　　崎	41 373	53 021	54 602	43 131	36 508	30 188	26 720	25 639	22 232
43 熊　　本	43 424	61 213	55 372	42 164	33 005	28 920	25 112	25 596	24 446
44 大　　分	32 262	42 330	36 701	26 429	20 127	18 534	17 579	18 336	16 296
45 宮　　崎	28 450	38 641	35 330	26 740	21 920	18 438	16 986	18 123	16 991
46 鹿 児 島	52 386	58 769	55 038	49 979	37 821	29 243	24 291	24 592	24 540
47 沖　　縄	16 413	…	…	…	…	…	…	22 371	20 281
外　　国 Foreign countries	…	…	…	…	…	…	…	…	…

注：1) 昭和10年・22年は事件発生地により、昭和25年は母の住所地により、昭和30年以降は子の住所地による。
　　2) 昭和25年の全国には、不詳12を含む。

106

年次別出生数
by each prefecture : Japan

1985 60　年	1990 平成 2 年	1995 7　年	2000 12　年	2005 17　年	2010 22　年	2014 26　年	2015 27　年	2016 28　年	都道府県[1] Prefecture
1 431 577	1 221 585	1 187 064	1 190 547	1 062 530	1 071 304	1 003 539	1 005 677	976 978	全国　Total
									a) 01 北 海 道
66 413	54 428	49 950	46 780	41 420	40 158	37 058	36 695	35 125	01 北 海 道
19 095	14 635	13 972	12 920	10 524	9 711	8 853	8 621	8 626	02 青　　森
17 232	14 254	13 021	12 410	10 545	9 745	8 803	8 814	8 341	03 岩　　手
28 025	23 324	22 267	22 154	19 326	19 126	18 069	17 999	17 347	04 宮　　城
13 663	10 992	9 995	9 007	7 697	6 688	5 998	5 861	5 666	05 秋　　田
14 893	12 555	11 507	10 919	9 357	8 651	7 966	7 831	7 547	06 山　　形
27 305	22 721	21 306	20 332	17 538	16 126	14 517	14 195	13 744	07 福　　島
33 479	28 784	28 234	28 220	24 244	23 989	21 873	21 700	20 878	08 茨　　城
23 842	19 995	18 662	18 976	17 363	16 473	15 442	15 306	14 621	09 栃　　木
22 917	19 470	19 431	19 445	17 134	16 023	14 522	14 256	13 661	10 群　　馬
67 260	63 299	67 750	66 376	59 731	59 437	55 765	56 077	54 447	11 埼　　玉
60 719	53 356	54 388	55 318	50 588	51 633	46 749	47 014	45 387	12 千　　葉
126 178	103 983	96 823	100 209	96 542	108 135	110 629	113 194	111 962	13 東　　京
86 101	79 437	80 692	82 906	76 196	78 077	72 996	73 475	70 648	14 神 奈 川
29 200	24 061	22 694	21 886	18 505	18 083	16 480	16 339	15 736	15 新　　潟
11 986	10 050	10 049	10 170	8 973	8 188	7 556	7 567	7 302	16 富　　山
13 256	11 535	11 093	11 467	10 049	9 602	8 961	9 072	8 927	17 石　　川
10 044	8 668	8 244	8 036	7 148	6 874	6 166	6 230	6 112	18 福　　井
9 843	8 582	8 833	8 374	7 149	6 651	6 063	5 987	5 819	19 山　　梨
24 176	21 384	21 187	21 194	18 517	17 233	15 848	15 638	15 169	20 長　　野
23 873	20 292	20 187	20 276	17 706	16 887	15 138	15 464	14 831	21 岐　　阜
43 932	37 045	35 345	35 794	31 908	31 896	28 684	28 352	27 652	22 静　　岡
80 186	70 942	71 899	74 736	67 110	69 872	65 218	65 615	64 226	23 愛　　知
19 745	17 917	17 500	17 726	15 345	15 262	13 727	13 950	13 202	24 三　　重
14 863	13 607	13 320	14 087	12 899	13 363	12 729	12 622	12 072	25 滋　　賀
28 479	24 209	23 219	23 997	21 560	21 234	19 583	19 662	19 327	26 京　　都
100 328	86 840	86 076	88 163	76 111	75 080	69 968	70 596	68 816	27 大　　阪
61 332	53 916	51 947	54 455	47 273	47 834	44 352	44 015	43 378	28 兵　　庫
14 659	13 315	13 337	13 270	11 184	10 694	9 625	9 832	9 430	29 奈　　良
12 086	10 126	9 879	9 566	7 835	7 587	7 140	7 030	6 658	30 和 歌 山
7 508	6 412	5 723	5 645	5 012	4 790	4 527	4 624	4 436	31 鳥　　取
9 051	7 510	6 764	6 522	5 697	5 756	5 359	5 551	5 300	32 島　　根
22 698	19 117	18 622	19 059	16 688	16 759	15 837	15 599	15 477	33 岡　　山
33 501	28 857	27 609	27 384	24 740	25 546	23 775	23 678	22 736	34 広　　島
17 674	13 729	13 240	13 121	11 514	11 551	10 197	10 360	9 844	35 山　　口
9 708	7 943	7 472	7 224	5 913	5 904	5 502	5 586	5 346	36 徳　　島
11 529	9 555	9 301	9 808	8 686	8 397	7 745	7 719	7 510	37 香　　川
17 644	14 612	13 849	13 207	11 528	11 427	10 399	10 146	9 911	38 愛　　媛
9 350	7 182	6 939	6 811	5 916	5 518	5 015	5 052	4 779	39 高　　知
58 837	48 164	46 849	47 290	43 421	46 818	45 203	45 235	44 033	40 福　　岡
11 705	9 555	8 729	8 745	7 508	7 640	7 159	7 064	6 811	41 佐　　賀
20 365	16 517	14 780	14 098	12 148	12 004	11 323	11 020	10 886	42 長　　崎
23 183	18 992	17 895	17 262	15 645	16 246	15 558	15 577	14 894	43 熊　　本
14 420	11 631	11 125	10 910	9 780	10 072	9 279	9 112	9 059	44 大　　分
15 262	12 107	11 693	11 037	9 738	10 217	9 509	9 226	8 929	45 宮　　崎
23 375	18 892	16 649	16 272	14 834	15 124	14 236	14 125	13 688	46 鹿 児 島
20 657	17 088	16 751	16 773	16 115	17 098	16 373	16 941	16 617	47 沖　　縄
…	…	267	210	170	125	65	53	65	外　　国 Foreign countries

Note : a) See page 44.

出 生

表 4.4　都道府県別にみた
Table 4.4　Trends in live birth rates by each

都道府県 [1] Prefecture	1935 昭和10年	1947 22　年	1950 25　年 [2]	1955 30　年	1960 35　年	1965 40　年	1970 45　年	1975 50　年	1980 55　年
全国　Total	31.6	34.3	28.1	19.4	17.2	18.6	18.8	17.1	13.6
01 北 海 道 [a]	35.8	36.7	34.2	21.7	18.6	18.7	17.7	16.8	13.6
02 青　　森	42.4	41.5	36.0	25.5	20.9	19.9	18.5	16.4	14.3
03 岩　　手	38.6	36.5	33.9	24.3	19.2	17.5	16.1	16.0	13.8
04 宮　　城	36.5	35.4	32.0	22.3	18.0	16.7	16.8	16.8	15.0
05 秋　　田	40.2	38.0	32.6	22.5	17.6	15.5	14.3	14.2	13.0
06 山　　形	36.8	32.9	30.0	20.2	16.9	14.9	14.1	14.1	13.5
07 福　　島	35.4	35.8	32.8	23.4	19.1	16.5	15.4	15.9	14.5
08 茨　　城	34.6	34.3	29.3	21.6	17.4	17.2	18.0	17.8	14.2
09 栃　　木	35.0	35.8	30.2	21.6	17.2	16.9	17.4	17.5	14.5
10 群　　馬	33.9	34.7	28.0	20.0	16.2	17.4	17.8	16.9	13.6
11 埼　　玉	35.1	36.8	29.1	21.1	17.9	22.1	23.6	20.0	13.9
12 千　　葉	32.9	35.0	26.9	19.8	17.2	20.0	21.6	18.7	13.9
13 東　　京	27.6	31.5	23.6	15.9	17.0	20.7	20.3	16.1	12.2
14 神 奈 川	30.1	33.7	26.4	17.7	17.6	22.0	22.7	18.7	13.7
15 新　　潟	35.7	35.6	29.3	20.8	16.8	16.8	15.8	15.7	13.4
16 富　　山	34.7	42.3	27.6	18.1	15.6	15.9	17.0	16.2	12.3
17 石　　川	31.2	40.2	27.4	18.7	16.4	16.9	18.1	17.6	13.6
18 福　　井	31.8	35.0	28.2	19.7	17.1	17.0	16.5	16.2	13.6
19 山　　梨	33.4	32.6	26.3	19.4	16.4	16.7	16.1	15.2	12.5
20 長　　野	31.1	30.1	24.3	17.6	15.5	16.1	16.1	15.8	13.1
21 岐　　阜	33.8	34.4	26.8	18.5	17.4	18.9	18.5	17.0	13.2
22 静　　岡	33.7	34.7	28.4	20.5	18.0	19.0	18.9	17.7	13.7
23 愛　　知	31.3	33.4	25.9	17.3	17.4	21.2	21.8	19.0	14.2
24 三　　重	32.2	32.6	25.5	17.1	16.2	17.9	17.0	16.0	12.8
25 滋　　賀	29.9	30.1	24.9	17.6	16.0	16.7	17.6	18.0	14.9
26 京　　都	26.1	31.0	22.5	14.4	14.6	17.5	18.7	16.8	12.9
27 大　　阪	24.5	31.1	24.3	15.9	17.3	22.1	22.8	18.6	13.5
28 兵　　庫	28.1	31.8	24.7	17.2	16.5	19.1	19.8	17.7	13.6
29 奈　　良	29.1	30.8	24.3	16.8	15.4	17.6	18.9	16.8	13.3
30 和 歌 山	28.3	32.1	24.2	17.3	15.9	17.6	17.3	15.3	12.4
31 鳥　　取	29.8	32.9	26.8	19.4	16.0	14.8	14.1	15.1	13.6
32 島　　根	32.1	36.4	28.3	18.5	15.9	14.4	13.7	14.3	12.7
33 岡　　山	28.9	33.0	24.3	16.9	15.2	15.5	16.9	16.7	13.1
34 広　　島	29.6	33.7	25.4	17.5	15.8	17.1	18.4	17.8	13.7
35 山　　口	28.8	33.3	27.8	17.9	15.6	15.9	16.4	15.5	12.6
36 徳　　島	33.5	37.0	29.0	20.5	15.7	15.5	15.0	14.9	12.8
37 香　　川	32.7	37.4	26.0	17.6	14.7	15.2	16.0	16.2	13.0
38 愛　　媛	32.9	36.3	29.9	19.9	16.7	16.9	16.2	15.9	13.1
39 高　　知	29.2	33.8	26.4	18.2	14.8	14.8	15.1	14.6	11.3
40 福　　岡	30.3	34.1	30.9	19.8	16.8	17.4	17.4	16.7	14.2
41 佐　　賀	33.6	34.8	31.7	22.9	18.3	16.6	15.8	15.6	14.4
42 長　　崎	31.9	34.6	33.2	24.7	20.7	18.4	17.1	16.3	14.0
43 熊　　本	31.3	34.7	30.3	22.2	17.8	16.3	14.8	14.9	13.7
44 大　　分	32.9	34.3	29.3	20.7	16.2	15.6	15.3	15.4	13.3
45 宮　　崎	34.5	37.7	32.4	23.5	19.3	17.1	16.2	16.7	14.8
46 鹿 児 島	32.9	33.7	30.5	24.5	19.3	15.8	14.1	14.3	13.8
47 沖　　縄	27.7	…	…	…	…	…	…	21.6	18.4

注：1)　昭和10年・22年は事件発生地により、昭和25年は母の住所地により、昭和30年以降は子の住所地による。
　　2)　昭和25年の全国には不詳を含む。

Natality

年次別出生率（人口千対）
prefecture（per 1,000 population）: Japan

1985 60　年	1990 平成2年	1995 7　年	2000 12　年	2005 17　年	2010 22　年	2014 26　年	2015 27　年	2016 28　年	都道府県[1] Prefecture
11.9	10.0	9.6	9.5	8.4	8.5	8.0	8.0	7.8	全国　Total
11.7	9.7	8.8	8.2	7.4	7.3	6.9	6.8	6.6	01 北 海 道 [a]
12.6	9.9	9.5	8.8	7.3	7.1	6.7	6.6	6.7	02 青 　 森
11.8	10.1	9.2	8.8	7.6	7.4	6.9	6.9	6.6	03 岩 　 手
12.9	10.4	9.6	9.4	8.2	8.2	7.8	7.8	7.5	04 宮 　 城
10.9	9.0	8.2	7.6	6.7	6.2	5.8	5.7	5.6	05 秋 　 田
11.9	10.0	9.2	8.8	7.7	7.4	7.1	7.0	6.8	06 山 　 形
13.3	10.8	10.0	9.6	8.4	8.0	7.5	7.5	7.3	07 福 　 島
12.3	10.2	9.6	9.6	8.3	8.2	7.6	7.5	7.3	08 茨 　 城
12.7	10.4	9.5	9.6	8.7	8.3	7.9	7.9	7.5	09 栃 　 木
12.0	10.0	9.8	9.7	8.6	8.1	7.5	7.4	7.1	10 群 　 馬
11.5	9.9	10.1	9.7	8.6	8.4	7.8	7.8	7.6	11 埼 　 玉
11.7	9.7	9.5	9.4	8.5	8.4	7.6	7.7	7.4	12 千 　 葉
10.7	8.9	8.4	8.5	7.8	8.4	8.5	8.6	8.5	13 東 　 京
11.7	10.0	9.9	9.9	8.8	8.8	8.1	8.2	7.9	14 神 奈 川
11.9	9.7	9.1	8.9	7.6	7.7	7.2	7.1	6.9	15 新 　 潟
10.7	9.0	9.0	9.1	8.1	7.6	7.1	7.2	7.0	16 富 　 山
11.5	9.9	9.4	9.8	8.6	8.3	7.8	7.9	7.8	17 石 　 川
12.2	10.6	10.1	9.8	8.8	8.6	7.9	8.0	7.9	18 福 　 井
12.0	10.1	10.1	9.5	8.2	7.8	7.3	7.3	7.1	19 山 　 梨
11.1	10.0	9.7	9.7	8.6	8.1	7.6	7.5	7.4	20 長 　 野
11.7	9.9	9.7	9.7	8.6	8.3	7.5	7.7	7.5	21 岐 　 阜
12.3	10.1	9.6	9.6	8.6	8.6	7.9	7.8	7.6	22 静 　 岡
12.4	10.7	10.6	10.8	9.4	9.6	8.9	9.0	8.8	23 愛 　 知
11.4	10.1	9.6	9.7	8.4	8.4	7.7	7.8	7.4	24 三 　 重
12.7	11.2	10.5	10.6	9.5	9.6	9.1	9.1	8.7	25 滋 　 賀
11.1	9.5	9.0	9.2	8.3	8.2	7.6	7.7	7.6	26 京 　 都
11.6	10.1	10.0	10.2	8.8	8.6	8.1	8.1	7.9	27 大 　 阪
11.6	10.1	9.8	10.0	8.6	8.7	8.1	8.1	8.0	28 兵 　 庫
11.2	9.7	9.4	9.3	7.9	7.7	7.0	7.3	7.0	29 奈 　 良
11.1	9.5	9.2	9.0	7.6	7.6	7.4	7.3	7.0	30 和 歌 山
12.1	10.4	9.3	9.3	8.3	8.2	7.9	8.1	7.8	31 鳥 　 取
11.3	9.6	8.8	8.6	7.7	8.1	7.7	8.1	7.7	32 島 　 根
11.9	10.0	9.6	9.8	8.6	8.7	8.3	8.2	8.2	33 岡 　 山
11.9	10.2	9.7	9.6	8.7	9.0	8.5	8.4	8.1	34 広 　 島
11.1	8.8	8.6	8.7	7.8	8.0	7.3	7.4	7.1	35 山 　 口
11.7	9.6	9.0	8.8	7.3	7.6	7.2	7.4	7.2	36 徳 　 島
11.1	9.4	9.1	9.6	8.6	8.5	8.0	8.0	7.8	37 香 　 川
11.5	9.7	9.2	8.9	7.9	8.0	7.5	7.4	7.3	38 愛 　 媛
11.1	8.7	8.5	8.4	7.5	7.2	6.8	7.0	6.7	39 高 　 知
12.4	10.1	9.6	9.5	8.7	9.3	9.0	9.0	8.7	40 福 　 岡
13.1	10.9	9.9	10.0	8.7	9.0	8.6	8.5	8.3	41 佐 　 賀
12.7	10.6	9.6	9.3	8.2	8.5	8.2	8.0	8.0	42 長 　 崎
12.6	10.3	9.6	9.3	8.5	9.0	8.7	8.8	8.4	43 熊 　 本
11.6	9.4	9.1	9.0	8.1	8.5	8.0	7.9	7.9	44 大 　 分
12.9	10.4	10.0	9.5	8.5	9.0	8.6	8.4	8.2	45 宮 　 崎
12.7	10.5	9.3	9.1	8.5	8.9	8.6	8.6	8.4	46 鹿 児 島
17.6	14.0	13.2	12.8	11.9	12.3	11.6	11.9	11.6	47 沖 　 縄

Note : a)　See page 44.

出　生

表 4.5　都道府県別にみた
Table 4.5　Trends in total fertility

都道府県 Prefecture	1960 昭和35年	1965 40 年	1970 45 年	1975 50 年	1980 55 年	1985 60 年	1990 平成2年	1995 7 年	2000 12 年	2005 17 年
全国　Total	2.00	2.14	2.13	1.91	1.75	1.76	1.54	1.42	1.36	1.26
01 北 海 道 a)	2.17	2.13	1.93	1.82	1.64	1.61	1.43	1.31	1.23	1.15
02 青　　森	2.48	2.45	2.25	2.00	1.85	1.80	1.56	1.56	1.47	1.29
03 岩　　手	2.30	2.22	2.11	2.14	1.95	1.88	1.72	1.62	1.56	1.41
04 宮　　城	2.13	2.08	2.06	1.96	1.86	1.80	1.57	1.46	1.39	1.24
05 秋　　田	2.09	2.03	1.88	1.86	1.79	1.69	1.57	1.56	1.45	1.34
06 山　　形	2.04	2.04	1.98	1.96	1.93	1.87	1.75	1.69	1.62	1.45
07 福　　島	2.43	2.31	2.16	2.13	1.99	1.98	1.79	1.72	1.65	1.49
08 茨　　城	2.31	2.35	2.30	2.09	1.87	1.86	1.64	1.53	1.47	1.32
09 栃　　木	2.22	2.27	2.21	2.06	1.86	1.90	1.67	1.52	1.48	1.40
10 群　　馬	2.03	2.21	2.16	1.99	1.81	1.85	1.63	1.56	1.51	1.39
11 埼　　玉	2.16	2.40	2.35	2.06	1.73	1.72	1.50	1.41	1.30	1.22
12 千　　葉	2.13	2.31	2.28	2.03	1.74	1.75	1.47	1.36	1.30	1.22
13 東　　京	1.70	2.00	1.96	1.63	1.44	1.44	1.23	1.11	1.07	1.00
14 神 奈 川	1.89	2.22	2.23	1.95	1.70	1.68	1.45	1.34	1.28	1.19
15 新　　潟	2.13	2.24	2.10	2.03	1.88	1.88	1.69	1.59	1.51	1.34
16 富　　山	1.91	1.94	1.94	1.94	1.77	1.79	1.56	1.49	1.45	1.37
17 石　　川	2.05	2.11	2.07	2.08	1.87	1.79	1.60	1.46	1.45	1.35
18 福　　井	2.17	2.25	2.10	2.06	1.93	1.93	1.75	1.67	1.60	1.50
19 山　　梨	2.16	2.30	2.20	1.98	1.76	1.85	1.62	1.60	1.51	1.38
20 長　　野	1.94	2.10	2.09	2.05	1.89	1.85	1.71	1.64	1.59	1.46
21 岐　　阜	2.04	2.22	2.12	2.00	1.80	1.81	1.57	1.49	1.47	1.37
22 静　　岡	2.11	2.21	2.12	2.02	1.80	1.85	1.60	1.48	1.47	1.39
23 愛　　知	1.90	2.23	2.19	2.02	1.81	1.82	1.57	1.47	1.44	1.34
24 三　　重	1.95	2.19	2.04	1.99	1.82	1.80	1.61	1.50	1.48	1.36
25 滋　　賀	2.02	2.19	2.19	2.13	1.96	1.97	1.75	1.58	1.53	1.39
26 京　　都	1.72	2.02	2.02	1.81	1.67	1.68	1.48	1.33	1.28	1.18
27 大　　阪	1.81	2.20	2.17	1.90	1.67	1.69	1.46	1.33	1.31	1.21
28 兵　　庫	1.90	2.15	2.12	1.96	1.76	1.75	1.53	1.41	1.38	1.25
29 奈　　良	1.87	2.09	2.08	1.85	1.70	1.69	1.49	1.36	1.30	1.19
30 和 歌 山	1.95	2.21	2.10	1.95	1.80	1.79	1.55	1.48	1.45	1.32
31 鳥　　取	2.05	2.08	1.96	2.02	1.93	1.93	1.82	1.69	1.62	1.47
32 島　　根	2.13	2.10	2.02	2.10	2.01	2.01	1.85	1.73	1.65	1.50
33 岡　　山	1.89	1.99	2.03	2.05	1.86	1.89	1.66	1.55	1.51	1.37
34 広　　島	1.92	2.07	2.07	2.05	1.84	1.83	1.63	1.48	1.41	1.34
35 山　　口	1.92	2.00	1.98	1.92	1.79	1.82	1.56	1.50	1.47	1.38
36 徳　　島	2.02	2.12	1.97	1.89	1.76	1.80	1.61	1.52	1.45	1.26
37 香　　川	1.84	1.99	1.97	1.96	1.82	1.81	1.60	1.51	1.53	1.43
38 愛　　媛	2.10	2.20	2.02	1.97	1.79	1.78	1.60	1.53	1.45	1.35
39 高　　知	1.94	2.02	1.97	1.91	1.64	1.81	1.54	1.51	1.45	1.32
40 福　　岡	1.92	2.00	1.95	1.83	1.74	1.75	1.52	1.42	1.36	1.26
41 佐　　賀	2.35	2.28	2.13	2.03	1.93	1.95	1.75	1.64	1.67	1.48
42 長　　崎	2.72	2.54	2.33	2.13	1.87	1.87	1.70	1.60	1.57	1.45
43 熊　　本	2.25	2.19	1.98	1.94	1.83	1.85	1.65	1.61	1.56	1.46
44 大　　分	2.05	2.08	1.97	1.93	1.82	1.78	1.58	1.55	1.51	1.40
45 宮　　崎	2.43	2.30	2.15	2.11	1.93	1.90	1.68	1.70	1.62	1.48
46 鹿 児 島	2.66	2.39	2.21	2.11	1.95	1.93	1.73	1.62	1.58	1.49
47 沖　　縄	…	…	…	2.88	2.38	2.31	1.95	1.87	1.82	1.72

注：1）　全国値は母の年齢15～49歳の各歳における出生率の合計である。
　　　　　都道府県の値は平成26年まで及び平成28年は母の年齢5歳階級における出生率5倍の合計、平成27年は母の年齢15～49歳の各歳における出生率の合計である。
　　　　　分母に用いた人口は、全国は各歳別日本人人口、都道府県は平成22年までの国勢調査年次は5歳階級別日本人人口、平成27年の国勢調査年次は各歳別日本人人口、他の年次は平成26年までは5歳階級別総人口、平成28年は5歳階級別日本人人口である。
　　資料：　国立社会保障・人口問題研究所「人口統計資料集」、厚生労働省「人口動態統計」

Natality

年次別合計特殊出生率[1]
rates by each prefecture : Japan

2007 19 年	2008 20 年	2009 21 年	2010 22 年	2011 23 年	2012 24 年	2013 25 年	2014 26 年	2015 27 年	2016 28 年	都道府県 Prefecture
1.34	1.37	1.37	1.39	1.39	1.41	1.43	1.42	1.45	1.44	全 国 Total
1.19	1.20	1.19	1.26	1.25	1.26	1.28	1.27	1.31	1.29	01 北 海 道 a)
1.28	1.30	1.26	1.38	1.38	1.36	1.40	1.42	1.43	1.48	02 青　　森
1.39	1.39	1.37	1.46	1.41	1.44	1.46	1.44	1.49	1.45	03 岩　　手
1.27	1.29	1.25	1.30	1.25	1.30	1.34	1.30	1.36	1.34	04 宮　　城
1.31	1.32	1.29	1.31	1.35	1.37	1.35	1.34	1.35	1.39	05 秋　　田
1.42	1.44	1.39	1.48	1.46	1.44	1.47	1.47	1.48	1.47	06 山　　形
1.49	1.52	1.49	1.52	1.48	1.41	1.53	1.58	1.58	1.59	07 福　　島
1.35	1.37	1.37	1.44	1.39	1.41	1.42	1.43	1.48	1.47	08 茨　　城
1.39	1.42	1.43	1.44	1.38	1.43	1.43	1.46	1.49	1.46	09 栃　　木
1.36	1.40	1.38	1.46	1.41	1.39	1.41	1.44	1.49	1.48	10 群　　馬
1.26	1.28	1.28	1.32	1.28	1.29	1.33	1.31	1.39	1.37	11 埼　　玉
1.25	1.29	1.31	1.34	1.31	1.31	1.33	1.32	1.38	1.35	12 千　　葉
1.05	1.09	1.12	1.12	1.06	1.09	1.13	1.15	1.24	1.24	13 東　　京
1.25	1.27	1.28	1.31	1.27	1.30	1.31	1.31	1.39	1.36	14 神 奈 川
1.37	1.37	1.37	1.43	1.41	1.43	1.44	1.43	1.44	1.43	15 新　　潟
1.34	1.38	1.37	1.42	1.37	1.42	1.43	1.45	1.51	1.50	16 富　　山
1.40	1.41	1.40	1.44	1.43	1.47	1.49	1.45	1.54	1.53	17 石　　川
1.52	1.54	1.55	1.61	1.56	1.60	1.60	1.55	1.63	1.65	18 福　　井
1.35	1.35	1.31	1.46	1.41	1.43	1.44	1.43	1.51	1.51	19 山　　梨
1.47	1.45	1.43	1.53	1.50	1.51	1.54	1.54	1.58	1.59	20 長　　野
1.34	1.35	1.37	1.48	1.44	1.45	1.45	1.42	1.56	1.54	21 岐　　阜
1.44	1.44	1.43	1.54	1.49	1.52	1.53	1.50	1.54	1.55	22 静　　岡
1.38	1.43	1.43	1.52	1.46	1.46	1.47	1.46	1.57	1.56	23 愛　　知
1.37	1.38	1.40	1.51	1.47	1.47	1.49	1.45	1.56	1.51	24 三　　重
1.42	1.45	1.44	1.54	1.51	1.53	1.53	1.53	1.61	1.56	25 滋　　賀
1.18	1.22	1.20	1.28	1.25	1.23	1.26	1.24	1.35	1.34	26 京　　都
1.24	1.28	1.28	1.33	1.30	1.31	1.32	1.31	1.39	1.37	27 大　　阪
1.30	1.34	1.33	1.41	1.40	1.40	1.42	1.41	1.48	1.49	28 兵　　庫
1.22	1.22	1.23	1.29	1.27	1.32	1.31	1.27	1.38	1.36	29 奈　　良
1.34	1.41	1.36	1.47	1.49	1.53	1.52	1.55	1.54	1.50	30 和 歌 山
1.47	1.43	1.46	1.54	1.58	1.57	1.62	1.60	1.65	1.60	31 鳥　　取
1.53	1.51	1.55	1.68	1.61	1.68	1.65	1.66	1.78	1.75	32 島　　根
1.41	1.43	1.39	1.50	1.48	1.47	1.49	1.49	1.54	1.56	33 岡　　山
1.43	1.45	1.47	1.55	1.53	1.54	1.57	1.55	1.60	1.57	34 広　　島
1.42	1.43	1.43	1.56	1.52	1.52	1.56	1.54	1.60	1.58	35 山　　口
1.30	1.30	1.35	1.42	1.43	1.44	1.43	1.46	1.53	1.51	36 徳　　島
1.48	1.47	1.48	1.57	1.56	1.56	1.59	1.57	1.63	1.64	37 香　　川
1.40	1.40	1.41	1.50	1.51	1.52	1.52	1.50	1.53	1.54	38 愛　　媛
1.31	1.36	1.29	1.42	1.39	1.43	1.47	1.45	1.51	1.47	39 高　　知
1.34	1.37	1.37	1.44	1.42	1.43	1.45	1.46	1.52	1.50	40 福　　岡
1.51	1.55	1.49	1.61	1.61	1.61	1.59	1.63	1.64	1.63	41 佐　　賀
1.48	1.50	1.50	1.61	1.60	1.63	1.64	1.66	1.67	1.71	42 長　　崎
1.54	1.58	1.58	1.62	1.62	1.62	1.65	1.64	1.68	1.66	43 熊　　本
1.47	1.53	1.50	1.56	1.55	1.53	1.56	1.57	1.59	1.65	44 大　　分
1.59	1.60	1.61	1.68	1.68	1.67	1.72	1.69	1.71	1.71	45 宮　　崎
1.54	1.59	1.56	1.62	1.64	1.64	1.63	1.62	1.70	1.68	46 鹿 児 島
1.75	1.78	1.79	1.87	1.86	1.90	1.94	1.86	1.96	1.95	47 沖　　縄

Note : a) See page 44.

出 生

〔母の年齢（５歳階級）別にみた出生〕
〔Live births by age of mother (5-year age groups)〕

表 4.6　母の年齢別にみた年次別出生数
Table 4.6　Trends in live births, percent distribution and

母の年齢 Age of mother	1950 昭和25年	1955 30　年	1960 35　年	1965 40　年	1970 45　年	1975 50　年	1980 55　年	1985 60　年	1990 平成２年
					実				
総　数　　Total	2 337 507	1 730 692	1 606 041	1 823 697	1 934 239	1 901 440	1 576 889	1 431 577	1 221 585
〜14歳　Years	49	8	5	7	12	9	14	23	18
15〜19	56 316	25 211	19 734	17 712	20 165	15 990	14 576	17 854	17 478
20〜24	624 797	469 027	447 097	513 645	513 172	479 041	296 854	247 341	191 859
25〜29	794 241	691 349	745 253	854 399	951 246	1 014 624	810 204	682 885	550 994
30〜34	496 240	372 175	300 684	355 269	358 375	320 060	388 935	381 466	356 026
35〜39	278 781	138 158	78 104	72 355	80 581	62 663	59 127	93 501	92 377
40〜44	81 953	33 055	14 217	9 828	9 860	8 727	6 911	8 224	12 587
45〜49	4 213	1 572	864	462	523	312	257	244	224
50〜	311	134	78	18	25	7	1	1	-
不　詳 Not stated	606	3	5	2	280	7	10	38	22
					百		分		
総　数　　Total	100.0	100.0	100.0	100.0	100.0	100.0	100.0	100.0	100.0
〜19歳　Years	2.4	1.5	1.2	1.0	1.0	0.8	0.9	1.2	1.4
20〜24	26.7	27.1	27.8	28.2	26.5	25.2	18.8	17.3	15.7
25〜29	34.0	39.9	46.4	46.8	49.2	53.4	51.4	47.7	45.1
30〜34	21.2	21.5	18.7	19.5	18.5	16.8	24.7	26.6	29.1
35〜39	11.9	8.0	4.9	4.0	4.2	3.3	3.7	6.5	7.6
40〜44	3.5	1.9	0.9	0.5	0.5	0.5	0.4	0.6	1.0
45〜	0.2	0.1	0.1	0.0	0.0	0.0	0.0	0.0	0.0
					出		生		
15〜19歳　Years	13.3	5.9	4.3	3.3	4.5	4.1	3.6	4.1	3.6
20〜24	161.4	112.0	107.2	113.0	96.5	107.0	77.1	61.7	44.8
25〜29	237.7	181.5	181.9	204.2	209.2	190.1	181.5	178.4	139.8
30〜34	175.6	112.8	80.1	86.8	86.0	69.6	73.1	84.9	93.2
35〜39	104.9	49.7	24.0	19.4	19.8	15.0	12.9	17.7	20.8
40〜44	36.1	12.7	5.2	3.1	2.7	2.1	1.7	1.8	2.4
45〜49	2.1	0.7	0.3	0.2	0.2	0.1	0.1	0.1	0.0

注：　1)　年齢不詳を除く出生数に対する百分率である。

Natality

・百分率[1] 及び出生率（女性人口千対）
rates (per 1,000 females) by age of mother : Japan

1995 7 年	2000 12 年	2005 17 年	2010 22 年	2012 24 年	2013 25 年	2014 26 年	2015 27 年	2016 28 年	母の年齢 Age of mother
数　Number									
1 187 064	1 190 547	1 062 530	1 071 304	1 037 231	1 029 816	1 003 539	1 005 677	976 978	総　数　　Total
37	43	42	51	59	51	43	39	46	〜14歳　Years
16 075	19 729	16 531	13 495	12 711	12 913	12 968	11 890	11 049	15〜19
193 514	161 361	128 135	110 956	95 805	91 250	86 590	84 461	82 169	20〜24
492 714	470 833	339 328	306 910	292 464	282 794	267 847	262 256	250 639	25〜29
371 773	396 901	404 700	384 385	367 715	365 404	359 323	364 870	354 911	30〜34
100 053	126 409	153 440	220 101	225 480	229 741	225 889	228 293	223 287	35〜39
12 472	14 848	19 750	34 609	42 031	46 546	49 606	52 558	53 474	40〜44
414	396	564	773	928	1 069	1 214	1 256	1 350	45〜49
-	6	34	19	32	47	58	52	51	50〜
12	21	6	5	6	1	1	2	2	不　詳 Not stated
率　Percentage									
100.0	100.0	100.0	100.0	100.0	100.0	100.0	100.0	100.0	総　数　　Total
1.4	1.7	1.6	1.3	1.2	1.3	1.3	1.2	1.1	〜19歳　Years
16.3	13.6	12.1	10.4	9.2	8.9	8.6	8.4	8.4	20〜24
41.5	39.5	31.9	28.6	28.2	27.5	26.7	26.1	25.7	25〜29
31.3	33.3	38.1	35.9	35.5	35.5	35.8	36.3	36.3	30〜34
8.4	10.6	14.4	20.5	21.7	22.3	22.5	22.7	22.9	35〜39
1.1	1.2	1.9	3.2	4.1	4.5	4.9	5.2	5.5	40〜44
0.0	0.0	0.1	0.1	0.1	0.1	0.1	0.1	0.1	45〜
率（女性人口千対）Live birth rate　（per 1,000 females）									
3.9	5.4	5.2	4.6	4.4	4.4	4.5	4.1	3.8	15〜19歳　Years
40.4	39.9	36.6	36.1	32.4	31.2	29.7	29.4	28.6	20〜24
116.1	99.5	85.3	87.4	87.2	86.7	84.8	85.1	83.5	25〜29
94.5	93.5	85.6	95.3	97.9	100.1	100.5	103.3	102.7	30〜34
26.2	32.1	36.1	46.2	49.5	52.5	54.0	56.4	57.3	35〜39
2.8	3.9	5.0	8.1	9.2	9.9	10.4	11.0	11.4	40〜44
0.1	0.1	0.1	0.2	0.2	0.3	0.3	0.3	0.3	45〜49

出 生

〔出生の場所別にみた出生〕
〔Live births by place of delivery〕

表 4.7　市部－郡部[1]・出生の場所別にみた年次別出生数
Table 4.7　Trends in live births by place of delivery : Japan, urban／rural residence

年　　次 Year		総　　数 Total	施　　設　　内 Hospitalized				自宅・その他 Nonhosp.
			総　　数 Total	病　　院 Hospital	診　療　所 Clinic	助　産　所 Maternity home	
全　　　国[2]　Total							
1947	昭和22年	2 678 792	64 180	...	...	...	2 614 612
50	25	2 337 507	106 826	68 638	25 770	12 418	2 230 681
55	30	1 730 692	305 127	186 509	77 636	40 982	1 425 565
60	35	1 606 041	804 557	386 973	280 292	137 292	801 484
65	40	1 823 697	1 531 812	670 619	625 409	235 784	291 885
70	45	1 934 239	1 858 738	838 078	814 695	205 965	75 501
75	50	1 901 440	1 879 404	901 779	840 741	136 884	22 036
80	55	1 576 889	1 569 643	815 611	694 107	59 925	7 246
85	60	1 431 577	1 428 305	793 902	606 476	27 927	3 272
90	平成 2 年	1 221 585	1 220 138	681 873	525 744	12 521	1 447
95	7	1 187 064	1 185 359	647 430	526 791	11 138	1 705
2000	12	1 190 547	1 188 400	639 067	537 980	11 353	2 147
05	17	1 062 530	1 060 021	545 766	503 579	10 676	2 509
10	22	1 071 304	1 069 067	555 277	504 257	9 533	2 237
11	23	1 050 806	1 048 849	546 361	493 556	8 932	1 957
12	24	1 037 231	1 035 337	546 793	480 262	8 282	1 894
13	25	1 029 816	1 028 122	548 744	471 419	7 959	1 694
14	26	1 003 539	1 001 922	536 279	458 250	7 393	1 617
15	27	1 005 677	1 004 251	539 939	457 427	6 885	1 426
16	**28**	**976 978**	**975 511**	**530 172**	**439 371**	**5 968**	**1 467**
市　　　部[3]　Urban residence							
1947	昭和22年	842 302	55 067	...	...	...	787 235
50	25	794 279	89 490	59 865	19 055	10 570	704 789
55	30	884 206	249 089	153 621	60 277	35 191	635 117
60	35	1 013 741	644 524	313 050	222 491	108 983	369 217
65	40	1 312 974	1 185 559	533 275	489 243	163 041	127 415
70	45	1 476 173	1 440 835	666 122	641 585	133 128	35 338
75	50	1 495 437	1 483 993	726 874	668 571	88 548	11 444
80	55	1 216 194	1 212 117	640 957	533 397	37 763	4 077
85	60	1 107 841	1 105 763	625 176	461 275	19 312	2 078
90	平成 2 年	960 690	959 678	541 787	408 024	9 867	1 012
95	7	948 442	947 100	522 905	414 884	9 311	1 342
2000	12	962 392	960 613	522 451	428 322	9 840	1 779
05	17	917 831	915 668	475 445	430 575	9 648	2 163
10	22	980 669	978 666	508 736	460 927	9 003	2 003
11	23	963 922	962 185	501 700	452 119	8 366	1 737
12	24	953 933	952 258	503 143	441 355	7 760	1 675
13	25	948 589	947 104	505 842	433 792	7 470	1 485
14	26	926 229	924 780	495 067	422 839	6 874	1 449
15	27	928 962	927 698	498 664	422 613	6 421	1 264
16	**28**	**902 855**	**901 555**	**489 461**	**406 553**	**5 541**	**1 300**
郡　　　部[3]　Rural residence							
1947	昭和22年	1 836 490	9 113	...	...	...	1 827 377
50	25	1 543 228	17 336	8 773	6 715	1 848	1 525 892
55	30	846 486	56 038	32 888	17 359	5 791	790 448
60	35	592 300	160 033	73 923	57 801	28 309	432 267
65	40	510 723	346 253	137 344	136 166	72 743	164 470
70	45	458 066	417 903	171 956	173 110	72 837	40 163
75	50	406 003	395 411	174 905	172 170	48 336	10 592
80	55	360 695	357 526	174 654	160 710	22 162	3 169
85	60	323 736	322 542	168 726	145 201	8 615	1 194
90	平成 2 年	260 895	260 460	140 086	117 720	2 654	435
95	7	238 355	237 994	124 353	111 818	1 823	361
2000	12	227 945	227 581	116 476	109 597	1 508	364
05	17	144 529	144 192	70 215	72 950	1 027	337
10	22	90 510	90 290	46 463	43 297	530	220
11	23	86 762	86 558	44 584	41 411	563	204
12	24	83 231	83 019	43 611	38 886	522	212
13	25	81 173	80 969	42 865	37 615	489	204
14	26	77 245	77 078	41 175	35 386	517	167
15	27	76 662	76 500	41 238	34 798	464	162
16	**28**	**74 058**	**73 892**	**40 672**	**32 793**	**427**	**166**

注：1)　昭和22年は事件発生地により、昭和25年は母の住所地により、昭和30年以降は子の住所地による。
　　　2)　全国には住所地外国を含む。
　　　3)　本表においては、平成 7 年からの市部、郡部には、住所地外国を含まない。

Natality

表 4.8 市部−郡部[1]・出生の場所別にみた年次別出生数百分率
Table 4.8 Trends in percent distribution of live births by place of delivery : Japan, urban/rural residence

年　　　次 Year		総　　数 Total	施　設　内 Hospitalized				自宅・その他 Nonhosp.
			総　　数 Total	病　　院 Hospital	診 療 所 Clinic	助 産 所 Maternity home	
全　　国[2]　Total							
1947	昭和22年	100.0	2.4	…	…	…	97.6
50	25	100.0	4.6	2.9	1.1	0.5	95.4
55	30	100.0	17.6	10.8	4.5	2.4	82.4
60	35	100.0	50.1	24.1	17.5	8.5	49.9
65	40	100.0	84.0	36.8	34.3	12.9	16.0
70	45	100.0	96.1	43.3	42.1	10.6	3.9
75	50	100.0	98.8	47.4	44.2	7.2	1.2
80	55	100.0	99.5	51.7	44.0	3.8	0.5
85	60	100.0	99.8	55.5	42.4	2.0	0.2
90	平成2年	100.0	99.9	55.8	43.0	1.0	0.1
95	7	100.0	99.9	54.5	44.4	0.9	0.1
2000	12	100.0	99.8	53.7	45.2	1.0	0.2
05	17	100.0	99.8	51.4	47.4	1.0	0.2
10	22	100.0	99.8	51.8	47.1	0.9	0.2
11	23	100.0	99.8	52.0	47.0	0.9	0.2
12	24	100.0	99.8	52.7	46.3	0.8	0.2
13	25	100.0	99.8	53.3	45.8	0.8	0.2
14	26	100.0	99.8	53.4	45.7	0.7	0.2
15	27	100.0	99.9	53.7	45.5	0.7	0.1
16	**28**	**100.0**	**99.9**	**54.3**	**45.0**	**0.6**	**0.2**
市　　部[3]　Urban residence							
1947	昭和22年	100.0	6.5	…	…	…	93.5
50	25	100.0	11.3	7.5	2.4	1.3	88.7
55	30	100.0	28.2	17.4	6.8	4.0	71.8
60	35	100.0	63.6	30.9	21.9	10.8	36.4
65	40	100.0	90.3	40.6	37.3	12.4	9.7
70	45	100.0	97.6	45.1	43.5	9.0	2.4
75	50	100.0	99.2	48.6	44.7	5.9	0.8
80	55	100.0	99.7	52.7	43.9	3.1	0.3
85	60	100.0	99.8	56.4	41.6	1.7	0.2
90	平成2年	100.0	99.9	56.4	42.5	1.0	0.1
95	7	100.0	99.9	55.1	43.7	1.0	0.1
2000	12	100.0	99.8	54.3	44.5	1.0	0.2
05	17	100.0	99.8	51.8	46.9	1.1	0.2
10	22	100.0	99.8	51.9	47.0	0.9	0.2
11	23	100.0	99.8	52.0	46.9	0.9	0.2
12	24	100.0	99.8	52.7	46.3	0.8	0.2
13	25	100.0	99.8	53.3	45.7	0.8	0.2
14	26	100.0	99.8	53.4	45.7	0.7	0.2
15	27	100.0	99.9	53.7	45.5	0.7	0.1
16	**28**	**100.0**	**99.9**	**54.2**	**45.0**	**0.6**	**0.1**
郡　　部[3]　Rural residence							
1947	昭和22年	100.0	0.5	…	…	…	99.5
50	25	100.0	1.1	0.6	0.4	0.1	98.9
55	30	100.0	6.6	3.9	2.1	0.7	93.4
60	35	100.0	27.0	12.5	9.8	4.8	73.0
65	40	100.0	67.8	26.9	26.7	14.2	32.2
70	45	100.0	91.2	37.5	37.8	15.9	8.8
75	50	100.0	97.4	43.1	42.4	11.9	2.6
80	55	100.0	99.1	48.4	44.6	6.1	0.9
85	60	100.0	99.6	52.1	44.9	2.7	0.4
90	平成2年	100.0	99.8	53.7	45.1	1.0	0.2
95	7	100.0	99.8	52.2	46.9	0.8	0.2
2000	12	100.0	99.8	51.1	48.1	0.7	0.2
05	17	100.0	99.8	48.6	50.5	0.7	0.2
10	22	100.0	99.8	51.3	47.8	0.6	0.2
11	23	100.0	99.8	51.4	47.7	0.6	0.2
12	24	100.0	99.7	52.4	46.7	0.6	0.3
13	25	100.0	99.7	52.8	46.3	0.6	0.2
14	26	100.0	99.8	53.3	45.8	0.7	0.2
15	27	100.0	99.8	53.8	45.4	0.6	0.2
16	**28**	**100.0**	**99.8**	**54.9**	**44.3**	**0.6**	**0.2**

注：1) 昭和22年は事件発生地により、昭和25年は母の住所地により、昭和30年以降は子の住所地による。
　　2) 全国には住所地外国を含む。
　　3) 本表においては、平成7年からの市部、郡部には、住所地外国を含まない。

115

出　生

表 4.9　都道府県（21大都市再掲）・出生の場所別にみた出生数
Table 4.9　Live births by place of delivery : Japan, each prefecture and 21 major cities, 2016

平成28年

都道府県 Prefecture	総数 Total	施設内 Hospitalized				施設外 Nonhosp.		
		総数 Total	病院 Hospital	診療所 Clinic	助産所 Maternity home	総数 Total	自宅 Home	その他 Others
全　国　　Total	976 978	975 511	530 172	439 371	5 968	1 467	1 168	299
a)								
01 北海道	35 125	35 050	24 173	10 788	89	75	62	13
02 青森	8 626	8 620	4 518	4 044	58	6	3	3
03 岩手	8 341	8 333	4 773	3 556	4	8	7	1
04 宮城	17 347	17 336	9 917	7 314	105	11	9	2
05 秋田	5 666	5 662	4 238	1 422	2	4	3	1
06 山形	7 547	7 545	4 635	2 909	1	2	2	-
07 福島	13 744	13 729	7 575	6 135	19	15	8	7
08 茨城	20 878	20 833	12 121	8 662	50	45	34	11
09 栃木	14 621	14 603	5 600	8 965	38	18	12	6
10 群馬	13 661	13 640	6 956	6 669	15	21	13	8
11 埼玉	54 447	54 356	31 578	22 476	302	91	74	17
12 千葉	45 387	45 321	21 766	23 343	212	66	58	8
13 東京	111 962	111 797	76 334	34 676	787	165	148	17
14 神奈川	70 648	70 528	42 811	26 892	825	120	100	20
15 新潟	15 736	15 728	7 876	7 833	19	8	6	2
16 富山	7 302	7 292	4 274	3 016	2	10	9	1
17 石川	8 927	8 920	4 479	4 417	24	7	5	2
18 福井	6 112	6 105	3 298	2 783	24	7	5	2
19 山梨	5 819	5 813	3 677	2 114	22	6	6	-
20 長野	15 169	15 139	10 764	4 201	174	30	26	4
21 岐阜	14 831	14 806	5 926	8 782	98	25	21	4
22 静岡	27 652	27 613	13 429	13 808	376	39	31	8
23 愛知	64 226	64 149	28 015	35 790	344	77	66	11
24 三重	13 202	13 183	5 934	7 014	235	19	14	5
25 滋賀	12 072	12 059	4 712	7 310	37	13	13	-
26 京都	19 327	19 275	11 190	8 014	71	52	44	8
27 大阪	68 816	68 741	42 952	25 232	557	75	59	16
28 兵庫	43 378	43 335	22 389	20 685	261	43	37	6
29 奈良	9 430	9 420	4 644	4 603	173	10	8	2
30 和歌山	6 658	6 648	3 323	3 240	85	10	8	2
31 鳥取	4 436	4 430	1 813	2 614	3	6	6	-
32 島根	5 300	5 294	3 311	1 969	14	6	5	1
33 岡山	15 477	15 458	8 131	7 120	207	19	14	5
34 広島	22 736	22 684	11 943	10 725	16	52	44	8
35 山口	9 844	9 828	5 862	3 939	27	16	14	2
36 徳島	5 346	5 342	3 261	2 079	2	4	4	-
37 香川	7 510	7 499	5 019	2 392	88	11	9	2
38 愛媛	9 911	9 904	4 247	5 590	67	7	7	-
39 高知	4 779	4 773	2 823	1 936	14	6	6	-
40 福岡	44 033	43 901	14 249	29 433	219	132	71	61
41 佐賀	6 811	6 808	1 782	5 019	7	3	2	1
42 長崎	10 886	10 877	3 692	7 173	12	9	4	5
43 熊本	14 894	14 863	7 048	7 802	13	31	24	7
44 大分	9 059	9 045	2 670	6 296	79	14	12	2
45 宮崎	8 929	8 912	3 689	5 144	79	17	13	4
46 鹿児島	13 688	13 660	6 355	7 234	71	28	25	3
47 沖縄	16 617	16 590	10 361	6 188	41	27	17	10
外　国　Foreign countries	65	64	39	25	-	1	-	1
21 大都市（再掲）21 major cities (Regrouped)								
50 東京都の区部	80 213	80 118	56 572	23 173	373	95	81	14
51 札幌	14 021	13 991	8 563	5 403	25	30	27	3
52 仙台	8 904	8 902	5 318	3 506	78	2	2	-
53 さいたま	10 549	10 534	6 259	4 241	34	15	10	5
54 千葉	6 927	6 919	2 483	4 409	27	8	8	-
55 横浜	28 889	28 852	19 446	9 042	364	37	31	6
56 川崎	14 158	14 137	8 806	5 074	257	21	18	3
57 相模原	5 196	5 183	3 820	1 339	24	13	12	1
58 新潟	5 936	5 934	2 348	3 576	10	2	2	-
59 静岡	5 106	5 096	2 418	2 595	83	10	8	2
60 浜松	6 558	6 551	4 419	2 066	66	7	5	2
61 名古屋	19 542	19 512	9 113	10 299	100	30	27	3
62 京都	10 921	10 887	6 776	4 078	33	34	28	6
63 大阪	22 099	22 073	16 325	5 647	101	26	18	8
64 堺	6 844	6 836	4 273	2 517	46	8	7	1
65 神戸	11 786	11 778	6 929	4 696	153	8	7	1
66 岡山	6 264	6 259	2 472	3 763	24	5	4	1
67 広島	10 559	10 531	5 500	5 025	6	28	25	3
68 北九州	7 621	7 580	2 853	4 668	59	41	8	33
69 福岡	14 488	14 457	4 738	9 690	29	31	30	1
70 熊本	6 797	6 789	4 349	2 435	5	8	6	2

Note : a)　See page 44.

Natality

表 4.10 都道府県（21大都市再掲）・出生の場所別にみた出生数百分率
Table 4.10 Percent distribution of live births by place of delivery : Japan, each prefecture and 21 major cities, 2016

平成28年

都道府県 Prefecture	総数 Total	施設内 Hospitalized				施設外 Nonhosp.		
		総数 Total	病院 Hospital	診療所 Clinic	助産所 Maternity home	総数 Total	自宅 Home	その他 Others
全　国　　Total	100.0	99.8	54.3	45.0	0.6	0.2	0.1	0.0
a)								
01 北海道	100.0	99.8	68.8	30.7	0.3	0.2	0.2	0.0
02 青森	100.0	99.9	52.4	46.9	0.7	0.1	0.0	0.0
03 岩手	100.0	99.9	57.2	42.6	0.0	0.1	0.1	0.0
04 宮城	100.0	99.9	57.2	42.2	0.6	0.1	0.1	0.0
05 秋田	100.0	99.9	74.8	25.1	0.0	0.1	0.1	0.0
06 山形	100.0	100.0	61.4	38.5	0.0	0.0	0.0	-
07 福島	100.0	99.9	55.1	44.6	0.1	0.1	0.1	0.1
08 茨城	100.0	99.8	58.1	41.5	0.2	0.2	0.2	0.1
09 栃木	100.0	99.9	38.3	61.3	0.3	0.1	0.1	0.1
10 群馬	100.0	99.8	50.9	48.8	0.1	0.2	0.1	0.1
11 埼玉	100.0	99.8	58.0	41.3	0.6	0.2	0.1	0.0
12 千葉	100.0	99.9	48.0	51.4	0.5	0.1	0.1	0.0
13 東京	100.0	99.9	68.2	31.0	0.7	0.1	0.1	0.0
14 神奈川	100.0	99.8	60.6	38.1	1.2	0.2	0.1	0.0
15 新潟	100.0	99.9	50.1	49.8	0.1	0.1	0.0	0.0
16 富山	100.0	99.9	58.5	41.3	0.0	0.1	0.1	0.0
17 石川	100.0	99.9	50.2	49.5	0.3	0.1	0.1	0.0
18 福井	100.0	99.9	54.0	45.5	0.4	0.1	0.1	0.0
19 山梨	100.0	99.9	63.2	36.3	0.4	0.1	0.1	-
20 長野	100.0	99.8	71.0	27.7	1.1	0.2	0.2	0.0
21 岐阜	100.0	99.8	40.0	59.2	0.7	0.2	0.1	0.0
22 静岡	100.0	99.9	48.6	49.9	1.4	0.1	0.1	0.0
23 愛知	100.0	99.9	43.6	55.7	0.5	0.1	0.1	0.0
24 三重	100.0	99.9	44.9	53.1	1.8	0.1	0.1	0.0
25 滋賀	100.0	99.9	39.0	60.6	0.3	0.1	0.1	-
26 京都	100.0	99.7	57.9	41.5	0.4	0.3	0.2	0.0
27 大阪	100.0	99.9	62.4	36.7	0.8	0.1	0.1	0.0
28 兵庫	100.0	99.9	51.6	47.7	0.6	0.1	0.1	0.0
29 奈良	100.0	99.9	49.2	48.8	1.8	0.1	0.1	0.0
30 和歌山	100.0	99.8	49.9	48.7	1.3	0.2	0.1	-
31 鳥取	100.0	99.9	40.9	58.9	0.1	0.1	0.1	-
32 島根	100.0	99.9	62.5	37.2	0.3	0.1	0.1	0.0
33 岡山	100.0	99.9	52.5	46.0	1.3	0.1	0.1	0.0
34 広島	100.0	99.8	52.5	47.2	0.1	0.2	0.2	0.0
35 山口	100.0	99.8	59.5	40.0	0.3	0.2	0.1	0.0
36 徳島	100.0	99.9	61.0	38.9	0.0	0.1	0.1	-
37 香川	100.0	99.9	66.8	31.9	1.2	0.1	0.1	0.0
38 愛媛	100.0	99.9	42.9	56.4	0.7	0.1	0.1	0.0
39 高知	100.0	99.9	59.1	40.5	0.3	0.1	0.1	-
40 福岡	100.0	99.7	32.4	66.8	0.5	0.3	0.2	0.1
41 佐賀	100.0	100.0	26.2	73.7	0.1	0.0	0.0	0.0
42 長崎	100.0	99.9	33.9	65.9	0.1	0.1	0.0	0.0
43 熊本	100.0	99.8	47.3	52.4	0.1	0.2	0.2	0.0
44 大分	100.0	99.8	29.5	69.5	0.9	0.2	0.1	0.0
45 宮崎	100.0	99.8	41.3	57.6	0.9	0.2	0.1	0.0
46 鹿児島	100.0	99.8	46.4	52.8	0.5	0.2	0.2	0.0
47 沖縄	100.0	99.8	62.4	37.2	0.2	0.2	0.1	0.1
外　国　Foreign countries	100.0	98.5	60.0	38.5	-	1.5	-	1.5
21 大 都 市（再掲） 21 major cities (Regrouped)								
50 東京都の区部	100.0	99.9	70.5	28.9	0.5	0.1	0.1	0.0
51 札幌	100.0	99.8	61.1	38.5	0.2	0.2	0.2	0.0
52 仙台	100.0	100.0	59.7	39.4	0.9	0.0	0.0	-
53 さいたま	100.0	99.9	59.3	40.2	0.3	0.1	0.1	0.0
54 千葉	100.0	99.9	35.8	63.6	0.4	0.1	0.1	-
55 横浜	100.0	99.9	67.3	31.3	1.3	0.1	0.1	0.0
56 川崎	100.0	99.9	62.2	35.8	1.8	0.1	0.1	0.0
57 相模原	100.0	99.7	73.5	25.8	0.5	0.3	0.2	0.0
58 新潟	100.0	100.0	39.6	60.2	0.2	0.0	0.0	-
59 静岡	100.0	99.8	47.4	50.8	1.6	0.2	0.2	0.0
60 浜松	100.0	99.9	67.4	31.5	1.0	0.1	0.1	0.0
61 名古屋	100.0	99.8	46.6	52.7	0.5	0.2	0.1	0.0
62 京都	100.0	99.7	62.0	37.3	0.3	0.3	0.3	0.1
63 大阪	100.0	99.9	73.9	25.6	0.5	0.1	0.1	0.0
64 堺	100.0	99.9	62.4	36.8	0.7	0.1	0.1	0.0
65 神戸	100.0	99.9	58.8	39.8	1.3	0.1	0.1	0.0
66 岡山	100.0	99.9	39.5	60.1	0.4	0.1	0.1	0.0
67 広島	100.0	99.7	52.1	47.6	0.1	0.3	0.2	0.0
68 北九州	100.0	99.5	37.4	61.3	0.8	0.5	0.2	0.4
69 福岡	100.0	99.8	32.7	66.9	0.2	0.2	0.2	0.0
70 熊本	100.0	99.9	64.0	35.8	0.1	0.1	0.1	0.0

Note : a)　See page 44.

出　生

〔出産順位及び出生順位別にみた出生〕
〔Live births by birth order and live birth order〕

表4.11　出産順位[1]別にみた年次別出生数及び百分率[2]
Table 4.11　Trends in live births and percent distribution by birth order : Japan

年　　次		総　　数	第　1　児	第　2　児	第　3　児	第　4　児	第　5　児～	不　　詳
	Year	Total	1st	2nd	3rd	4th	5th and over	Not stated
実　　　数　Number								
1947	昭和22年	2 678 792	765 860	542 269	407 944	305 521	655 881	1 317
55	30	1 730 692	562 317	453 186	331 381	198 287	185 510	11
60	35	1 606 041	699 840	523 126	227 263	84 219	71 576	17
65	40	1 823 697	851 081	683 294	213 248	49 555	26 470	49
70	45	1 934 239	866 014	751 665	253 369	45 456	17 735	-
75	50	1 901 440	851 709	765 763	231 562	37 976	14 430	-
80	55	1 576 889	660 681	639 491	232 710	33 529	10 478	-
85	60	1 431 577	596 902	560 763	228 518	35 463	9 931	-
90	平成2年	1 221 585	528 140	457 890	195 032	32 511	8 012	-
95	7	1 187 064	564 964	427 086	158 440	28 917	7 657	-
2000	12	1 190 547	580 932	433 935	142 656	25 766	7 258	-
01	13	1 170 662	571 866	427 184	139 297	25 146	7 169	-
02	14	1 153 855	569 468	420 221	133 060	23 993	7 113	-
03	15	1 123 610	545 227	418 310	129 396	23 586	7 091	-
04	16	1 110 721	536 062	416 777	127 461	23 388	7 033	-
05	17	1 062 530	510 576	398 588	123 836	22 653	6 877	-
06	18	1 092 674	522 793	407 784	130 796	24 030	7 271	-
07	19	1 089 818	518 091	402 854	136 173	25 043	7 657	-
08	20	1 091 156	516 097	401 386	139 094	26 617	7 962	-
09	21	1 070 035	511 135	389 317	135 313	26 099	8 171	-
10	22	1 071 304	508 216	389 486	137 309	27 673	8 620	-
11	23	1 050 806	493 185	383 020	137 695	28 034	8 872	-
12	24	1 037 231	483 141	381 934	135 244	27 987	8 925	-
13	25	1 029 816	479 984	378 890	134 127	27 864	8 951	-
14	26	1 003 539	472 843	364 180	130 536	27 147	8 833	-
15	27	1 005 677	476 762	362 669	130 532	26 985	8 729	-
16	**28**	**976 978**	**458 448**	**355 311**	**127 283**	**27 124**	**8 812**	**-**
百　分　率　Percentage								
1947	昭和22年	100.0	28.6	20.3	15.2	11.4	24.5	・
55	30	100.0	32.5	26.2	19.1	11.5	10.7	・
60	35	100.0	43.6	32.6	14.2	5.2	4.5	・
65	40	100.0	46.7	37.5	11.7	2.7	1.5	・
70	45	100.0	44.8	38.9	13.1	2.4	0.9	・
75	50	100.0	44.8	40.3	12.2	2.0	0.8	・
80	55	100.0	41.9	40.6	14.8	2.1	0.7	・
85	60	100.0	41.7	39.2	16.0	2.5	0.7	・
90	平成2年	100.0	43.2	37.5	16.0	2.7	0.7	・
95	7	100.0	47.6	36.0	13.3	2.4	0.6	・
2000	12	100.0	48.8	36.4	12.0	2.2	0.6	・
01	13	100.0	48.8	36.5	11.9	2.1	0.6	・
02	14	100.0	49.4	36.4	11.5	2.1	0.6	・
03	15	100.0	48.5	37.2	11.5	2.1	0.6	・
04	16	100.0	48.3	37.5	11.5	2.1	0.6	・
05	17	100.0	48.1	37.5	11.7	2.1	0.6	・
06	18	100.0	47.8	37.3	12.0	2.2	0.7	・
07	19	100.0	47.5	37.0	12.5	2.3	0.7	・
08	20	100.0	47.3	36.8	12.7	2.4	0.7	・
09	21	100.0	47.8	36.4	12.6	2.4	0.8	・
10	22	100.0	47.4	36.4	12.8	2.6	0.8	・
11	23	100.0	46.9	36.5	13.1	2.7	0.8	・
12	24	100.0	46.6	36.8	13.0	2.7	0.9	・
13	25	100.0	46.6	36.8	13.0	2.7	0.9	・
14	26	100.0	47.1	36.3	13.0	2.7	0.9	・
15	27	100.0	47.4	36.1	13.0	2.7	0.9	・
16	**28**	**100.0**	**46.9**	**36.4**	**13.0**	**2.8**	**0.9**	**・**

注：1)　出産順位とは、同じ母親がこれまでに出産した児の総数（平成6年までは妊娠満20週以後、平成7年から妊娠満22週以後の死産胎を含む。）について数えた順序である。
　　2)　各年次における順位不詳を除いた出生数に対する百分率である。

Natality

表 4.12 出生順位[1] 別にみた年次別出生数及び百分率
Table 4.12 Trends in live births and percent distribution by live birth order : Japan

年 次 Year		総 数 Total	第 1 子 1st	第 2 子 2nd	第 3 子 3rd	第 4 子 4th	第 5 子〜 5th and over	不 詳 Not stated
				実 数 Number				
1950	昭和25年	2 337 507	634 324	654 572	384 455	247 790	415 163	1 203
55	30	1 730 692	573 592	455 512	330 192	193 906	177 479	11
60	35	1 606 041	714 827	522 867	221 595	79 718	67 017	17
65	40	1 823 697	866 485	685 027	203 913	44 523	23 700	49
70	45	1 934 239	878 979	753 834	245 824	40 207	15 395	-
75	50	1 901 440	862 356	767 669	224 576	33 994	12 845	-
80	55	1 576 889	667 683	642 573	227 604	29 901	9 128	-
85	60	1 431 577	602 005	562 920	225 304	32 597	8 751	-
90	平成 2 年	1 221 585	531 648	459 569	192 788	30 453	7 127	-
95	7	1 187 064	567 530	428 394	156 586	27 556	6 998	-
2000	12	1 190 547	583 220	434 964	141 011	24 644	6 708	-
01	13	1 170 662	573 918	428 197	137 814	24 058	6 675	-
02	14	1 153 855	571 501	421 042	131 636	23 037	6 639	-
03	15	1 123 610	547 170	419 100	128 083	22 615	6 642	-
04	16	1 110 721	537 913	417 647	126 117	22 458	6 586	-
05	17	1 062 530	512 412	399 307	122 501	21 841	6 469	-
06	18	1 092 674	524 581	408 531	129 555	23 164	6 843	-
07	19	1 089 818	519 767	403 656	134 951	24 203	7 241	-
08	20	1 091 156	517 724	402 152	137 945	25 804	7 531	-
09	21	1 070 035	512 742	390 073	134 171	25 303	7 746	-
10	22	1 071 304	509 736	390 212	136 302	26 885	8 169	-
11	23	1 050 806	494 712	383 666	136 687	27 280	8 461	-
12	24	1 037 231	484 710	382 461	134 339	27 218	8 503	-
13	25	1 029 816	481 418	379 466	133 183	27 193	8 556	-
14	26	1 003 539	474 196	364 763	129 680	26 445	8 455	-
15	27	1 005 677	478 082	363 225	129 704	26 271	8 395	-
16	28	976 978	459 751	355 784	126 533	26 417	8 493	-
				百 分 率 Percentage				
1950	昭和25年	100.0	27.2	28.0	16.5	10.6	17.8	・
55	30	100.0	33.1	26.3	19.1	11.2	10.3	・
60	35	100.0	44.5	32.6	13.8	5.0	4.2	・
65	40	100.0	47.5	37.6	11.2	2.4	1.3	・
70	45	100.0	45.4	39.0	12.7	2.1	0.8	・
75	50	100.0	45.4	40.4	11.8	1.8	0.7	・
80	55	100.0	42.3	40.7	14.4	1.9	0.6	・
85	60	100.0	42.1	39.3	15.7	2.3	0.6	・
90	平成 2 年	100.0	43.5	37.6	15.8	2.5	0.6	・
95	7	100.0	47.8	36.1	13.2	2.3	0.6	・
2000	12	100.0	49.0	36.5	11.8	2.1	0.6	・
01	13	100.0	49.0	36.6	11.8	2.1	0.6	・
02	14	100.0	49.5	36.5	11.4	2.0	0.6	・
03	15	100.0	48.7	37.3	11.4	2.0	0.6	・
04	16	100.0	48.4	37.6	11.4	2.0	0.6	・
05	17	100.0	48.2	37.6	11.5	2.1	0.6	・
06	18	100.0	48.0	37.4	11.9	2.1	0.6	・
07	19	100.0	47.7	37.0	12.4	2.2	0.7	・
08	20	100.0	47.4	36.9	12.6	2.4	0.7	・
09	21	100.0	47.9	36.5	12.5	2.4	0.7	・
10	22	100.0	47.6	36.4	12.7	2.5	0.8	・
11	23	100.0	47.1	36.5	13.0	2.6	0.8	・
12	24	100.0	46.7	36.9	13.0	2.6	0.8	・
13	25	100.0	46.7	36.8	12.9	2.6	0.8	・
14	26	100.0	47.3	36.3	12.9	2.6	0.8	・
15	27	100.0	47.5	36.1	12.9	2.6	0.8	・
16	28	100.0	47.1	36.4	13.0	2.7	0.9	・

注：1）　出生順位とは、同じ母親がこれまでに生んだ出生子の総数について数えた順序である。
　　　2）　各年次における順位不詳を除いた出生数に対する百分率である。

出　生

表 4.13　都道府県（21大都市再掲）・出産順位[1]別にみた出生数
Table 4.13　Live births by birth order : Japan, each prefecture and 21 major cities, 2016

平成28年

都道府県 Prefecture	総数 Total	第1児 1st	第2児 2nd	第3児 3rd	第4児 4th	第5児〜 5th and over
全国　Total	976 978	458 448	355 311	127 283	27 124	8 812
a)						
01 北海道	35 125	16 620	12 493	4 559	1 047	406
02 青森	8 626	3 874	3 113	1 249	296	94
03 岩手	8 341	3 667	2 963	1 283	317	111
04 宮城	17 347	8 062	6 245	2 377	496	167
05 秋田	5 666	2 532	2 183	769	143	39
06 山形	7 547	3 335	2 819	1 121	215	57
07 福島	13 744	6 138	4 880	2 061	491	174
08 茨城	20 878	9 450	7 720	2 930	601	177
09 栃木	14 621	6 804	5 456	1 919	328	114
10 群馬	13 661	6 199	5 167	1 803	380	112
11 埼玉	54 447	25 860	20 379	6 529	1 232	447
12 千葉	45 387	21 762	16 879	5 311	1 091	344
13 東京	111 962	60 842	38 816	10 064	1 740	500
14 神奈川	70 648	35 251	26 069	7 489	1 407	432
15 新潟	15 736	7 294	5 790	2 144	410	98
16 富山	7 302	3 404	2 707	970	169	52
17 石川	8 927	3 999	3 232	1 354	272	70
18 福井	6 112	2 759	2 209	954	155	35
19 山梨	5 819	2 676	2 185	754	148	56
20 長野	15 169	6 895	5 613	2 140	413	108
21 岐阜	14 831	6 658	5 643	2 048	368	114
22 静岡	27 652	12 658	10 515	3 612	668	199
23 愛知	64 226	30 783	23 857	7 637	1 482	467
24 三重	13 202	6 126	4 913	1 711	337	115
25 滋賀	12 072	5 393	4 606	1 700	298	75
26 京都	19 327	9 052	7 106	2 485	538	146
27 大阪	68 816	33 284	24 641	8 416	1 871	604
28 兵庫	43 378	20 007	16 143	5 729	1 139	360
29 奈良	9 430	4 264	3 535	1 288	247	96
30 和歌山	6 658	2 900	2 459	986	233	80
31 鳥取	4 436	1 900	1 565	750	168	53
32 島根	5 300	2 185	1 934	910	211	60
33 岡山	15 477	6 885	5 722	2 226	516	128
34 広島	22 736	10 032	8 362	3 378	737	227
35 山口	9 844	4 224	3 632	1 527	347	114
36 徳島	5 346	2 385	2 023	720	164	54
37 香川	7 510	3 451	2 750	1 012	230	67
38 愛媛	9 911	4 386	3 577	1 511	309	128
39 高知	4 779	2 032	1 744	762	175	66
40 福岡	44 033	19 697	15 663	6 547	1 526	600
41 佐賀	6 811	2 765	2 433	1 195	326	92
42 長崎	10 886	4 388	3 794	2 018	530	156
43 熊本	14 894	6 124	5 293	2 582	683	212
44 大分	9 059	3 831	3 248	1 511	344	125
45 宮崎	8 929	3 632	3 088	1 650	421	138
46 鹿児島	13 688	5 525	4 834	2 468	660	201
47 沖縄	16 617	6 425	5 286	3 120	1 245	541
外国 Foreign countries	65	33	27	4	-	1
21 大都市（再掲） 21 major cities (Regrouped)						
50 東京都の区部	80 213	45 492	26 888	6 508	1 037	288
51 札幌	14 021	7 197	4 927	1 486	292	119
52 仙台	8 904	4 426	3 196	1 043	183	56
53 さいたま	10 549	5 267	3 977	1 070	175	60
54 千葉	6 927	3 353	2 572	826	133	43
55 横浜	28 889	14 666	10 723	2 865	501	134
56 川崎	14 158	7 742	5 007	1 162	188	59
57 相模原	5 196	2 440	1 931	643	136	46
58 新潟	5 936	2 885	2 169	721	123	38
59 静岡	5 106	2 393	1 923	632	120	38
60 浜松	6 558	3 077	2 517	779	155	30
61 名古屋	19 542	10 007	7 039	1 992	379	125
62 京都	10 921	5 426	3 894	1 272	263	66
63 大阪	22 099	11 792	7 241	2 342	533	191
64 堺	6 844	3 215	2 507	868	202	52
65 神戸	11 786	5 701	4 305	1 443	249	88
66 岡山	6 264	3 019	2 262	771	174	38
67 広島	10 559	4 778	3 890	1 509	301	81
68 北九州	7 621	3 469	2 712	1 092	227	121
69 福岡	14 488	7 129	5 038	1 794	413	114
70 熊本	6 797	3 027	2 413	1 052	239	66

注：1）　出産順位とは、同じ母親がこれまでに出産した児の総数（平成6年までは妊娠満20週以後・平成7年から妊娠満22週以後の死産胎を含む。）について数えた順序である。
Note : a)　See page 44.

Natality

表 4.14　都道府県（21大都市再掲）・出産順位[1]別にみた出生数百分率
Table 4.14 Percent distribution of live births by birth order : Japan, each prefecture and 21 major cities, 2016

平成28年

都　道　府　県 Prefecture	総　数 Total	第 1 児 1st	第 2 児 2nd	第 3 児 3rd	第 4 児 4th	第 5 児～ 5th and over
全　国　Total	100.0	46.9	36.4	13.0	2.8	0.9
a)						
01 北海道	100.0	47.3	35.6	13.0	3.0	1.2
02 青森	100.0	44.9	36.1	14.5	3.4	1.1
03 岩手	100.0	44.0	35.5	15.4	3.8	1.3
04 宮城	100.0	46.5	36.0	13.7	2.9	1.0
05 秋田	100.0	44.7	38.5	13.6	2.5	0.7
06 山形	100.0	44.2	37.4	14.9	2.8	0.8
07 福島	100.0	44.7	35.5	15.0	3.6	1.3
08 茨城	100.0	45.3	37.0	14.0	2.9	0.8
09 栃木	100.0	46.5	37.3	13.1	2.2	0.8
10 群馬	100.0	45.4	37.8	13.2	2.8	0.8
11 埼玉	100.0	47.5	37.4	12.0	2.3	0.8
12 千葉	100.0	47.9	37.2	11.7	2.4	0.8
13 東京	100.0	54.3	34.7	9.0	1.6	0.4
14 神奈川	100.0	49.9	36.9	10.6	2.0	0.6
15 新潟	100.0	46.4	36.8	13.6	2.6	0.6
16 富山	100.0	46.6	37.1	13.3	2.3	0.7
17 石川	100.0	44.8	36.2	15.2	3.0	0.8
18 福井	100.0	45.1	36.1	15.6	2.5	0.6
19 山梨	100.0	46.0	37.5	13.0	2.5	1.0
20 長野	100.0	45.5	37.0	14.1	2.7	0.7
21 岐阜	100.0	44.9	38.0	13.8	2.5	0.8
22 静岡	100.0	45.8	38.0	13.1	2.4	0.7
23 愛知	100.0	47.9	37.1	11.9	2.3	0.7
24 三重	100.0	46.4	37.2	13.0	2.6	0.9
25 滋賀	100.0	44.7	38.2	14.1	2.5	0.6
26 京都	100.0	46.8	36.8	12.9	2.8	0.8
27 大阪	100.0	48.4	35.8	12.2	2.7	0.9
28 兵庫	100.0	46.1	37.2	13.2	2.6	0.8
29 奈良	100.0	45.2	37.5	13.7	2.6	1.0
30 和歌山	100.0	43.6	36.9	14.8	3.5	1.2
31 鳥取	100.0	42.8	35.3	16.9	3.8	1.2
32 島根	100.0	41.2	36.5	17.2	4.0	1.1
33 岡山	100.0	44.5	37.0	14.4	3.3	0.8
34 広島	100.0	44.1	36.8	14.9	3.2	1.0
35 山口	100.0	42.9	36.9	15.5	3.5	1.2
36 徳島	100.0	44.6	37.8	13.5	3.1	1.0
37 香川	100.0	46.0	36.6	13.5	3.1	0.9
38 愛媛	100.0	44.3	36.1	15.2	3.1	1.3
39 高知	100.0	42.5	36.5	15.9	3.7	1.4
40 福岡	100.0	44.7	35.6	14.9	3.5	1.4
41 佐賀	100.0	40.6	35.7	17.5	4.8	1.4
42 長崎	100.0	40.3	34.9	18.5	4.9	1.4
43 熊本	100.0	41.1	35.5	17.3	4.7	1.4
44 大分	100.0	42.3	35.9	16.7	3.8	1.4
45 宮崎	100.0	40.7	34.6	18.5	4.7	1.5
46 鹿児島	100.0	40.4	35.3	18.0	4.8	1.5
47 沖縄	100.0	38.7	31.8	18.8	7.5	3.3
外　国 Foreign countries	100.0	50.8	41.5	6.2	-	1.5
21 大 都 市（再掲）21 major cities（Regrouped）						
50 東京都の区部	100.0	56.7	33.5	8.1	1.3	0.4
51 札幌	100.0	51.3	35.1	10.6	2.1	0.8
52 仙台	100.0	49.7	35.9	11.7	2.1	0.6
53 さいたま	100.0	49.9	37.7	10.1	1.7	0.6
54 千葉	100.0	48.4	37.1	11.9	1.9	0.6
55 横浜	100.0	50.8	37.1	9.9	1.7	0.5
56 川崎	100.0	54.7	35.4	8.2	1.3	0.4
57 相模原	100.0	47.0	37.2	12.4	2.6	0.9
58 新潟	100.0	48.6	36.5	12.1	2.1	0.6
59 静岡	100.0	46.9	37.7	12.4	2.4	0.7
60 浜松	100.0	46.9	38.4	11.9	2.4	0.5
61 名古屋	100.0	51.2	36.0	10.2	1.9	0.6
62 京都	100.0	49.7	35.7	11.6	2.4	0.6
63 大阪	100.0	53.4	32.8	10.6	2.4	0.9
64 堺	100.0	47.0	36.6	12.7	3.0	0.8
65 神戸	100.0	48.4	36.5	12.2	2.1	0.7
66 岡山	100.0	48.2	36.1	12.3	2.8	0.6
67 広島	100.0	45.3	36.8	14.3	2.9	0.8
68 北九州	100.0	45.5	35.6	14.3	3.0	1.6
69 福岡	100.0	49.2	34.8	12.4	2.9	0.8
70 熊本	100.0	44.5	35.5	15.5	3.5	1.0

注：1)　出産順位とは、同じ母親がこれまでに出産した児の総数（平成6年までは妊娠満20週以後、平成7年から妊娠満22週以後の死産胎を含む。）について数えた順序である。

Note : a)　See page 44.

出　生

表4.15　出生順位[1]別にみた母の年齢別出生数及び百分率
Table 4.15　Live births and percent distribution by live birth order and age of mother : Japan, 2016

平成28年

母 の 年 齢 Age of mother	実　　数　Number				百 分 率　Percentage			
	総　数[3] Total	第 1 子 1st	第 2 子 2nd	第 3 子 3rd	総　数 Total	第 1 子 1st	第 2 子 2nd	第 3 子 3rd
総　数[2]　Total	976 976	459 749	355 784	126 533	100.0	100.0	100.0	100.0
～19歳　Years	11 095	9 760	1 270	63	1.1	2.1	0.4	0.0
20～24	82 169	55 273	22 324	4 038	8.4	12.0	6.3	3.2
25～29	250 639	146 621	77 795	21 480	25.7	31.9	21.9	17.0
30～34	354 911	148 836	142 033	51 292	36.3	32.4	39.9	40.5
35～39	223 287	78 107	91 489	41 002	22.9	17.0	25.7	32.4
40～44	53 474	20 466	20 476	8 483	5.5	4.5	5.8	6.7
45～	1 401	686	397	175	0.1	0.1	0.1	0.1

注：1)　出生順位とは、同じ母親がこれまでに生んだ出生子の総数について数えた順序である。
　　2)　総数は母の年齢が不詳の出生子を除いた出生数である。
　　3)　総数には、第4子以上が含まれている。

表4.16　出産順位[1]別にみた母の年齢別出生数及び百分率
Table 4.16　Live births and percent distribution by birth order and age of mother : Japan, 2016

平成28年

母 の 年 齢 Age of mother	実　　数　Number				百 分 率　Percentage			
	総　数[3] Total	第 1 児 1st	第 2 児 2nd	第 3 児 3rd	総　数 Total	第 1 児 1st	第 2 児 2nd	第 3 児 3rd
総　数[2]　Total	976 976	458 446	355 311	127 283	100.0	100.0	100.0	100.0
～19歳　Years	11 095	9 747	1 279	67	1.1	2.1	0.4	0.1
20～24	82 169	55 174	22 332	4 098	8.4	12.0	6.3	3.2
25～29	250 639	146 324	77 806	21 616	25.7	31.9	21.9	17.0
30～34	354 911	148 405	141 805	51 572	36.3	32.4	39.9	40.5
35～39	223 287	77 761	91 284	41 176	22.9	17.0	25.7	32.3
40～44	53 474	20 352	20 409	8 576	5.5	4.4	5.7	6.7
45～	1 401	683	396	178	0.1	0.1	0.1	0.1

注：1)　出産順位とは、同じ母親がこれまでに出産した児の総数（平成6年までは妊娠満20週以後、平成7年から妊娠満22週以後の死産胎を含む。）について数えた順序である。
　　2)　総数は母の年齢が不詳の出生子を除いた出生数である。
　　3)　総数には、第4児以上が含まれている。

出　生

表4.17　出生順位[1]別にみた
Table 4.17　Trends in live births by age

母の年齢 Age of mother	1970 昭和45年	1975 50　年	1980 55　年	1985 60　年	1990 平成2年	1995 7　年	2000 12　年	2005 17　年
	総				数			
総　数[2] Total	1 933 959	1 901 433	1 576 879	1 431 539	1 221 563	1 187 052	1 190 526	1 062 524
～19歳Years	20 177	15 999	14 590	17 877	17 496	16 112	19 772	16 573
20～24	513 172	479 041	296 854	247 341	191 859	193 514	161 361	128 135
25～29	951 246	1 014 624	810 204	682 885	550 994	492 714	470 833	339 328
30～34	358 375	320 060	388 935	381 466	356 026	371 773	396 901	404 700
35～39	80 581	62 663	59 127	93 501	92 377	100 053	126 409	153 440
40～44	9 860	8 727	6 911	8 224	12 587	12 472	14 848	19 750
45～	548	319	258	245	224	414	402	598
	第			1			子	
総　数[2] Total	878 829	862 351	667 675	601 969	531 628	567 519	583 200	512 406
～19歳Years	18 606	14 698	13 553	16 413	16 084	14 721	18 169	14 794
20～24	400 628	356 732	225 457	181 779	140 171	140 748	118 064	87 276
25～29	380 658	417 948	336 833	307 508	271 152	271 120	268 923	192 672
30～34	61 081	58 135	77 273	75 676	82 943	114 813	140 709	162 367
35～39	15 416	12 626	12 840	18 593	18 262	23 046	33 122	48 573
40～44	2 317	2 138	1 655	1 952	2 962	2 982	4 097	6 492
45～	123	74	64	48	54	89	116	232
	第			2			子	
総　数[2] Total	753 721	767 667	642 573	562 920	459 567	428 393	434 963	399 307
～19歳Years	1 502	1 229	1 000	1 405	1 363	1 341	1 545	1 699
20～24	102 621	111 393	64 709	59 277	46 094	47 051	38 498	35 529
25～29	453 904	485 530	374 413	297 944	220 801	177 089	162 518	117 269
30～34	164 983	145 740	179 585	168 612	155 905	163 779	177 463	174 733
35～39	28 042	21 506	20 950	33 331	31 549	35 371	50 202	63 206
40～44	2 573	2 219	1 861	2 308	3 807	3 673	4 636	6 709
45～	96	50	55	43	48	89	101	162
	第	3		子	以		上	
総　数[2] Total	301 409	271 415	266 631	266 650	230 368	191 140	172 363	150 811
～19歳Years	69	72	37	59	49	50	58	80
20～24	9 923	10 916	6 688	6 285	5 594	5 715	4 799	5 330
25～29	116 684	111 146	98 958	77 433	59 041	44 505	39 392	29 387
30～34	132 311	116 185	132 077	137 178	117 178	93 181	78 729	67 600
35～39	37 123	28 531	25 337	41 577	42 566	41 636	43 085	41 661
40～44	4 970	4 370	3 395	3 964	5 818	5 817	6 115	6 549
45～	329	195	139	154	122	236	185	204

注：1)　出生順位とは、同じ母親がこれまでに生んだ出生子の総数について数えた順序である。
　　 2)　総数は母の年齢が不詳の出生子を除いた出生数である。

年次別母の年齢別出生数
of mother, by live birth order : Japan

2009 21 年	2010 22 年	2011 23 年	2012 24 年	2013 25 年	2014 26 年	2015 27 年	2016 28 年	母の年齢 Age of mother
			Total					
1 070 029	1 071 299	1 050 803	1 037 225	1 029 815	1 003 538	1 005 675	976 976	総　数2) Total
14 687	13 546	13 318	12 770	12 964	13 011	11 929	11 095	〜19歳Years
116 808	110 956	104 059	95 805	91 250	86 590	84 461	82 169	20〜24
307 765	306 910	300 384	292 464	282 794	267 847	262 256	250 639	25〜29
389 793	384 385	373 490	367 715	365 404	359 323	364 870	354 911	30〜34
209 706	220 101	221 272	225 480	229 741	225 889	228 293	223 287	35〜39
30 566	34 609	37 437	42 031	46 546	49 606	52 558	53 474	40〜44
704	792	843	960	1 116	1 272	1 308	1 401	45〜
			1st					
512 737	509 732	494 709	484 705	481 417	474 195	478 081	459 749	総　数2) Total
13 169	12 102	11 900	11 417	11 660	11 618	10 548	9 760	〜19歳Years
79 224	74 635	69 536	63 625	61 033	58 556	57 000	55 273	20〜24
176 222	174 264	169 533	163 841	158 323	152 493	153 005	146 621	25〜29
163 474	161 537	154 997	153 147	152 245	151 727	155 201	148 836	30〜34
69 866	74 576	74 945	76 849	80 051	80 142	81 256	78 107	35〜39
10 525	12 297	13 451	15 413	17 609	19 084	20 449	20 466	40〜44
257	321	347	413	496	575	622	686	45〜
			2nd					
390 072	390 211	383 666	382 461	379 466	364 763	363 224	355 784	総　数2) Total
1 444	1 388	1 350	1 292	1 240	1 317	1 315	1 270	〜19歳Years
31 812	30 838	29 120	26 981	25 300	23 244	22 815	22 324	20〜24
100 084	99 951	97 665	96 211	92 517	85 469	81 233	77 795	25〜29
159 422	156 033	151 689	149 088	148 301	143 580	144 598	142 033	30〜34
86 138	89 428	89 944	93 047	94 263	92 201	93 249	91 489	35〜39
10 998	12 356	13 671	15 568	17 534	18 602	19 660	20 476	40〜44
174	217	227	274	311	350	354	397	45〜
			3rd and over					
167 220	171 356	172 428	170 059	168 932	164 580	164 370	161 443	総　数2) Total
74	56	68	61	64	76	66	65	〜19歳Years
5 772	5 483	5 403	5 199	4 917	4 790	4 646	4 572	20〜24
31 459	32 695	33 186	32 412	31 954	29 885	28 018	26 223	25〜29
66 897	66 815	66 804	65 480	64 858	64 016	65 071	64 042	30〜34
53 702	56 097	56 383	55 584	55 427	53 546	53 788	53 691	35〜39
9 043	9 956	10 315	11 050	11 403	11 920	12 449	12 532	40〜44
273	254	269	273	309	347	332	318	45〜

出　生

表4.18　出生順位[1]別にみた
Table 4.18　Trends in live birth rates by age

母の年齢[2] Age of mother	1970 昭和45年	1975 50　年	1980 55　年	1985 60　年	1990 平成2年	1995 7　年	2000 12　年	2005 17　年
				総		数		
総　数　Total （合計特殊出生率） (Total fertility rate)	2.1346	1.9094	1.7465	1.7639	1.5426	1.4227	1.3592	1.2601
15～19歳Years	0.0209	0.0205	0.0189	0.0229	0.0180	0.0185	0.0269	0.0253
20～24	0.5184	0.5128	0.3855	0.3173	0.2357	0.2022	0.1965	0.1823
25～29	1.0515	0.9331	0.9140	0.8897	0.7031	0.5880	0.4967	0.4228
30～34	0.4314	0.3569	0.3529	0.4397	0.4663	0.4677	0.4620	0.4285
35～39	0.0984	0.0751	0.0666	0.0846	0.1079	0.1311	0.1572	0.1761
40～44	0.0133	0.0106	0.0083	0.0094	0.0113	0.0148	0.0194	0.0242
45～49	0.0008	0.0004	0.0003	0.0003	0.0003	0.0004	0.0005	0.0008
				第	1	子		
総　数　Total	0.9426	0.8622	0.7853	0.7611	0.6631	0.6607	0.6617	0.6240
15～19歳Years	0.0193	0.0189	0.0175	0.0210	0.0166	0.0169	0.0248	0.0226
20～24	0.3985	0.3841	0.2929	0.2326	0.1710	0.1471	0.1442	0.1243
25～29	0.4292	0.3763	0.3883	0.4006	0.3430	0.3196	0.2838	0.2409
30～34	0.0734	0.0651	0.0701	0.0878	0.1086	0.1433	0.1623	0.1723
35～39	0.0188	0.0151	0.0144	0.0169	0.0212	0.0302	0.0412	0.0557
40～44	0.0031	0.0026	0.0020	0.0022	0.0027	0.0035	0.0054	0.0079
45～49	0.0002	0.0001	0.0001	0.0001	0.0001	0.0001	0.0001	0.0003
				第	2	子		
総　数　Total	0.8436	0.7595	0.6918	0.6950	0.5871	0.5209	0.4949	0.4643
15～19歳Years	0.0015	0.0016	0.0013	0.0019	0.0014	0.0015	0.0021	0.0026
20～24	0.1090	0.1173	0.0839	0.0765	0.0575	0.0492	0.0465	0.0505
25～29	0.4966	0.4485	0.4183	0.3883	0.2836	0.2137	0.1714	0.1456
30～34	0.1987	0.1636	0.1623	0.1955	0.2042	0.2057	0.2065	0.1849
35～39	0.0342	0.0258	0.0237	0.0301	0.0369	0.0463	0.0623	0.0724
40～44	0.0035	0.0027	0.0022	0.0027	0.0034	0.0044	0.0061	0.0082
45～49	0.0001	0.0001	0.0001	0.0001	0.0001	0.0001	0.0001	0.0002
				第	3	子　以　上		
総　数　Total	0.3484	0.2876	0.2694	0.3078	0.2923	0.2410	0.2026	0.1717
15～19歳Years	0.0001	0.0001	0.0000	0.0001	0.0001	0.0001	0.0001	0.0001
20～24	0.0108	0.0114	0.0087	0.0082	0.0072	0.0060	0.0057	0.0076
25～29	0.1257	0.1082	0.1075	0.1008	0.0765	0.0547	0.0415	0.0363
30～34	0.1593	0.1281	0.1204	0.1564	0.1535	0.1186	0.0932	0.0714
35～39	0.0453	0.0342	0.0285	0.0376	0.0497	0.0545	0.0538	0.0480
40～44	0.0067	0.0053	0.0041	0.0045	0.0052	0.0069	0.0080	0.0080
45～49	0.0005	0.0003	0.0002	0.0002	0.0001	0.0002	0.0002	0.0003

注：出生順位別の総数の数値は出生順位ごとに15歳から49歳の母の各歳別出生率を合計したものであり、これを第1子から第3子以上まで合計したものが、合計特殊出生率である。
　1)　出生順位とは、同じ母親がこれまでに生んだ出生子の総数について数えた順序である。
　2)　算出に用いた出生数の15歳及び49歳にはそれぞれ14歳以下、50歳以上を含んでいる。なお年齢不詳は含まない。

Natality

年次別母の年齢別出生率
of mother, by live birth order : Japan

2009 21　年	2010 22　年	2011 23　年	2012 24　年	2013 25　年	2014 26　年	2015 27　年	**2016** **28　年**	母の年齢[2] Age of mother
				Total				
1.3683	1.3873	1.3931	1.4052	1.4265	1.4224	1.4504	**1.4413**	総　数　Total （合計特殊出生率） (Total fertility rate)
0.0249	0.0232	0.0227	0.0219	0.0221	0.0224	0.0206	**0.0190**	15～19歳 Years
0.1779	0.1781	0.1710	0.1607	0.1555	0.1487	0.1475	**0.1433**	20～24
0.4320	0.4356	0.4349	0.4325	0.4298	0.4204	0.4215	**0.4138**	25～29
0.4755	0.4789	0.4836	0.4916	0.5016	0.5033	0.5173	**0.5145**	30～34
0.2217	0.2318	0.2390	0.2525	0.2677	0.2747	0.2864	**0.2906**	35～39
0.0354	0.0387	0.0408	0.0448	0.0486	0.0516	0.0557	**0.0586**	40～44
0.0009	0.0010	0.0011	0.0012	0.0013	0.0014	0.0015	**0.0015**	45～49
				1st				
0.6782	0.6835	0.6786	0.6781	0.6871	0.6914	0.7090	**0.6971**	総　数　Total
0.0223	0.0207	0.0203	0.0195	0.0199	0.0200	0.0182	**0.0167**	15～19歳 Years
0.1211	0.1202	0.1146	0.1069	0.1041	0.1005	0.0995	**0.0963**	20～24
0.2476	0.2475	0.2458	0.2428	0.2412	0.2398	0.2464	**0.2425**	25～29
0.2008	0.2024	0.2018	0.2057	0.2097	0.2130	0.2205	**0.2166**	30～34
0.0738	0.0786	0.0810	0.0861	0.0933	0.0975	0.1020	**0.1017**	35～39
0.0122	0.0138	0.0147	0.0164	0.0184	0.0198	0.0216	**0.0224**	40～44
0.0003	0.0004	0.0005	0.0005	0.0006	0.0007	0.0007	**0.0007**	45～49
				2nd				
0.4889	0.4956	0.4996	0.5095	0.5174	0.5088	0.5154	**0.5168**	総　数　Total
0.0024	0.0024	0.0023	0.0022	0.0021	0.0023	0.0023	**0.0022**	15～19歳 Years
0.0482	0.0493	0.0477	0.0452	0.0431	0.0399	0.0399	**0.0389**	20～24
0.1404	0.1417	0.1412	0.1420	0.1403	0.1338	0.1303	**0.1281**	25～29
0.1940	0.1940	0.1960	0.1990	0.2033	0.2009	0.2048	**0.2056**	30～34
0.0910	0.0942	0.0972	0.1043	0.1099	0.1122	0.1170	**0.1191**	35～39
0.0127	0.0138	0.0149	0.0166	0.0183	0.0193	0.0208	**0.0225**	40～44
0.0002	0.0003	0.0003	0.0003	0.0004	0.0004	0.0004	**0.0004**	45～49
				3rd and over				
0.2013	0.2082	0.2150	0.2176	0.2221	0.2222	0.2260	**0.2275**	総　数　Total
0.0001	0.0001	0.0001	0.0001	0.0001	0.0001	0.0001	**0.0001**	15～19歳 Years
0.0087	0.0087	0.0088	0.0086	0.0083	0.0082	0.0081	**0.0080**	20～24
0.0441	0.0463	0.0479	0.0477	0.0483	0.0467	0.0448	**0.0431**	25～29
0.0807	0.0826	0.0858	0.0870	0.0886	0.0894	0.0920	**0.0923**	30～34
0.0568	0.0590	0.0608	0.0621	0.0644	0.0650	0.0674	**0.0698**	35～39
0.0105	0.0112	0.0112	0.0118	0.0119	0.0124	0.0132	**0.0137**	40～44
0.0003	0.0003	0.0004	0.0003	0.0004	0.0004	0.0004	**0.0003**	45～49

出　生

表 4.19　出生順位[1]別にみた年次別母の平均年齢[2]
Table 4.19　Trends in mean age of mother by live birth order : Japan

年　　次 Year		総　数[3] Total	第 1 子 1st	第 2 子 2nd	第 3 子 3rd
1950	昭和25年	28.7歳Years	24.4歳Years	26.7歳Years	29.4歳Years
55	30	28.2	24.8	27.2	29.5
60	35	27.6	25.4	27.8	29.9
65	40	27.4	25.7	28.3	30.3
70	45	27.5	25.6	28.3	30.6
75	50	27.4	25.7	28.0	30.3
80	55	28.1	26.4	28.7	30.6
85	60	28.6	26.7	29.1	31.4
90	平成 2 年	28.9	27.0	29.5	31.8
95	7	29.1	27.5	29.8	32.0
96	8	29.2	27.6	29.9	32.0
97	9	29.3	27.7	30.0	32.1
98	10	29.4	27.8	30.1	32.1
99	11	29.4	27.9	30.2	32.2
2000	12	29.6	28.0	30.4	32.3
01	13	29.7	28.2	30.4	32.4
02	14	29.8	28.3	30.6	32.5
03	15	30.0	28.6	30.7	32.5
04	16	30.2	28.9	30.9	32.6
05	17	30.4	29.1	31.0	32.6
06	18	30.5	29.2	31.2	32.8
07	19	30.7	29.4	31.4	32.9
08	20	30.9	29.5	31.6	33.0
09	21	31.0	29.7	31.7	33.1
10	22	31.2	29.9	31.8	33.2
11	23	31.3	30.1	32.0	33.2
12	24	31.5	30.3	32.1	33.3
13	25	31.6	30.4	32.3	33.4
14	26	31.7	30.6	32.4	33.4
15	27	31.8	30.7	32.5	33.5
16	**28**	**31.9**	**30.7**	**32.6**	**33.6**

注：1)　出生順位とは、同じ母親がこれまでに生んだ出生子の総数について数えた順序である。
　　2)　平成3年までの母の平均年齢は、満年齢の算術平均値に0.5歳の補正値を加えたものだが、平成4年に調査票を改正し、これ以降は、日齢の算術平均値から算出している。
　　3)　総数は第4子以上が含まれた平均年齢である。

表 4.20　出生順位[1]別にみた年次別父の平均年齢[2]
Table 4.20　Trends in mean age of father by live birth order : Japan

年　　次 Year		総　数[3] Total	第 1 子 1st	第 2 子 2nd	第 3 子 3rd
1975	昭和50年	30.1歳Years	28.3歳Years	30.8歳Years	33.4歳Years
80	55	30.8	29.2	31.4	33.3
85	60	31.4	29.6	32.0	34.2
90	平成 2 年	31.8	29.9	32.4	34.7
95	7	31.7	30.0	32.4	34.8
96	8	31.8	30.1	32.4	34.8
97	9	31.7	30.1	32.5	34.8
98	10	31.7	30.1	32.5	34.7
99	11	31.7	30.1	32.6	34.7
2000	12	31.8	30.2	32.6	34.7
01	13	31.8	30.2	32.6	34.7
02	14	31.9	30.4	32.6	34.7
03	15	32.0	30.6	32.7	34.7
04	16	32.2	30.9	32.8	34.6
05	17	32.3	31.1	32.9	34.6
06	18	32.5	31.3	33.1	34.7
07	19	32.7	31.4	33.3	34.8
08	20	32.8	31.6	33.5	34.8
09	21	33.0	31.8	33.6	34.9
10	22	33.1	32.0	33.7	35.0
11	23	33.3	32.1	33.8	35.0
12	24	33.5	32.3	34.0	35.2
13	25	33.6	32.5	34.2	35.2
14	26	33.7	32.6	34.3	35.3
15	27	33.8	32.7	34.4	35.4
16	**28**	**33.9**	**32.8**	**34.5**	**35.5**

注：1)　出生順位とは、同じ母親がこれまでに生んだ出生子の総数について数えた順序である。
　　2)　平成3年までの父の平均年齢は、満年齢の算術平均値に0.5歳の補正値を加えたものだが、平成4年に調査票を改正し、これ以降は、日齢の算術平均値から算出している。
　　3)　総数は第4子以上が含まれた平均年齢である。

Natality

表 4.21　出生順位[1]・都道府県（21大都市再掲）別にみた父・母の平均年齢
Table 4.21　Mean age of father and mother by live birth order : Japan, each prefecture and 21 major cities, 2016

平成28年

都 道 府 県 Prefecture	父　Father				母　Mother			
	総　数[2] Total	第 1 子 1st	第 2 子 2nd	第 3 子 3rd	総　数[2] Total	第 1 子 1st	第 2 子 2nd	第 3 子 3rd
全　　国　　Total	33.9歳	32.8歳	34.5歳	35.5歳	31.9歳	30.7歳	32.6歳	33.6歳
01 北　海　道	33.5	32.4	34.1	35.2	31.5	30.3	32.2	33.3
02 青　森	33.4	32.1	33.8	35.2	31.3	30.0	31.8	33.2
03 岩　手	33.2	31.8	33.6	34.8	31.2	29.8	31.7	33.0
04 宮　城	33.5	32.3	34.0	35.2	31.6	30.4	32.2	33.6
05 秋　田	33.4	32.2	34.0	35.1	31.6	30.2	32.3	33.6
06 山　形	33.4	32.1	33.9	35.3	31.5	30.0	32.2	33.6
07 福　島	32.9	31.5	33.3	34.6	30.8	29.4	31.3	32.8
08 茨　城	33.4	32.3	34.0	35.3	31.5	30.2	32.1	33.4
09 栃　木	33.5	32.4	34.1	35.3	31.6	30.2	32.3	33.3
10 群　馬	33.6	32.4	34.2	35.4	31.6	30.2	32.3	33.6
11 埼　玉	34.2	33.1	34.8	35.9	32.1	30.9	32.9	33.9
12 千　葉	34.2	33.0	34.9	36.0	32.1	30.9	32.9	34.0
13 東　京	35.3	34.5	36.1	36.9	33.2	32.3	34.1	34.8
14 神奈川	34.7	33.7	35.4	36.3	32.6	31.5	33.4	34.3
15 新　潟	33.5	32.2	34.1	35.5	31.7	30.4	32.4	33.8
16 富　山	33.9	32.5	34.6	35.9	32.0	30.6	32.7	34.1
17 石　川	33.7	32.4	34.3	35.6	31.8	30.4	32.5	33.8
18 福　井	33.4	31.9	34.1	35.5	31.5	30.0	32.1	33.8
19 山　梨	34.0	32.7	34.6	35.5	31.8	30.5	32.5	33.7
20 長　野	34.0	32.8	34.4	35.9	32.0	30.6	32.5	34.0
21 岐　阜	33.6	32.3	34.2	35.5	31.6	30.2	32.2	33.7
22 静　岡	33.8	32.6	34.4	35.5	31.7	30.4	32.5	33.5
23 愛　知	33.8	32.6	34.5	35.5	31.7	30.5	32.5	33.6
24 三　重	33.4	32.2	34.1	35.2	31.4	30.0	32.1	33.3
25 滋　賀	33.9	32.5	34.5	35.7	31.9	30.5	32.6	33.7
26 京　都	34.3	33.2	35.0	35.9	32.3	31.1	33.1	33.9
27 大　阪	33.9	32.8	34.6	35.5	31.8	30.6	32.6	33.6
28 兵　庫	33.9	32.7	34.5	35.4	31.9	30.7	32.6	33.6
29 奈　良	34.1	32.9	34.6	35.8	32.0	30.6	32.7	33.9
30 和歌山	33.3	32.0	33.7	35.1	31.3	29.8	31.8	33.3
31 鳥　取	33.5	32.0	34.0	35.3	31.6	29.9	32.1	33.8
32 島　根	33.5	32.0	34.0	34.8	31.6	30.1	32.1	33.3
33 岡　山	33.2	31.9	33.7	35.0	31.3	29.9	31.9	33.3
34 広　島	33.3	32.1	33.9	34.9	31.4	30.1	32.0	33.2
35 山　口	33.0	31.6	33.5	34.7	31.1	29.5	31.8	33.0
36 徳　島	33.3	31.9	33.8	35.4	31.6	30.2	32.2	33.5
37 香　川	33.4	32.1	34.0	35.0	31.4	30.1	32.1	33.2
38 愛　媛	33.1	31.9	33.5	34.7	31.2	29.8	31.7	33.1
39 高　知	33.6	32.2	34.1	35.3	31.7	30.2	32.2	33.6
40 福　岡	33.5	32.3	34.0	35.1	31.6	30.2	32.2	33.4
41 佐　賀	32.8	31.5	33.1	34.4	31.1	29.7	31.4	32.8
42 長　崎	33.0	31.6	33.3	34.7	31.3	29.7	31.6	33.2
43 熊　本	33.1	31.7	33.4	34.8	31.3	29.8	31.7	33.2
44 大　分	33.2	31.8	33.7	35.0	31.4	29.7	32.0	33.3
45 宮　崎	32.9	31.4	33.4	34.5	31.1	29.3	31.6	33.0
46 鹿児島	33.2	31.9	33.5	34.7	31.4	29.9	31.8	33.1
47 沖　縄	33.3	31.8	33.4	34.6	31.4	29.6	31.6	32.9
外　　国 Foreign countries	36.1	35.5	36.7	34.6	34.3	34.1	34.8	30.7
21 大 都 市（再掲） 21 major cities (Regrouped)								
50 東京都の区部	35.5	34.7	36.4	37.2	33.4	32.5	34.3	35.0
51 札　幌	34.0	33.0	34.6	35.8	32.0	30.9	32.8	34.0
52 仙　台	33.9	32.9	34.5	35.6	32.1	31.0	32.7	33.9
53 さいたま	34.4	33.3	35.2	36.2	32.5	31.4	33.3	34.2
54 千　葉	34.4	33.2	35.1	36.6	32.4	31.1	33.2	34.4
55 横　浜	34.8	33.9	35.6	36.5	32.8	31.7	33.7	34.5
56 川　崎	34.8	33.9	35.7	36.7	32.9	32.0	33.9	34.6
57 相模原	34.2	33.1	34.8	35.8	32.1	30.9	32.9	33.8
58 新　潟	33.8	32.6	34.5	35.6	32.1	30.9	32.8	34.1
59 静　岡	34.2	33.0	34.7	36.1	32.2	30.9	32.9	34.0
60 浜　松	34.0	32.9	34.6	35.3	31.9	30.6	32.7	33.4
61 名古屋	34.2	33.2	35.1	35.8	32.1	31.0	33.0	33.8
62 京　都	34.6	33.5	35.3	36.2	32.5	31.4	33.4	34.1
63 大　阪	34.1	33.2	34.8	35.8	31.9	30.9	32.8	33.6
64 堺	33.6	32.4	34.3	35.4	31.7	30.3	32.5	33.5
65 神　戸	34.4	33.2	35.1	35.8	32.3	31.1	33.2	34.0
66 岡　山	33.6	32.6	34.2	35.3	31.7	30.5	32.2	33.7
67 広　島	33.8	32.6	34.4	35.3	31.8	30.6	32.5	33.5
68 北九州	33.0	31.7	33.6	34.8	31.1	29.7	31.7	33.2
69 福　岡	34.3	33.2	35.0	36.0	32.3	31.1	33.2	34.1
70 熊　本	33.5	32.2	33.9	35.3	31.7	30.3	32.3	33.7

注：1）　出生順位とは、同じ母親がこれまでに生んだ出生子の総数について数えた順序である。
　　2）　総数は第4子以上が含まれた平均年齢である。

Note : a)　See page 44.

出　生

表4.22　父母が結婚生活に入ってから出生順位[1]　第1子出生までの期間別にみた年次別嫡出出生数[2]百分率[3]及び平均期間

Table 4.22 Trends in percent distribution of duration and mean duration from marriage performed to the first bearing (for live births born in wedlock only) : Japan

期　　間 Duration	1974 昭和49年	1975 50年	1980 55年	1985 60年	1990 平成2年	1995 7年	2000 12年	2005 17年	2010 22年	2014 26年	2015 27年	2016 28年
総　数　Total	100.0	100.0	100.0	100.0	100.0	100.0	100.0	100.0	100.0	100.0	100.0	100.0
1年未満　Under 1 year	40.5	39.4	41.1	41.5	41.2	38.5	39.0	37.0	34.1	30.3	28.9	28.9
1年以上2年未満 1 year and over, less than 2 years	40.0	39.9	36.8	35.5	33.8	32.0	28.3	26.5	27.0	27.1	27.4	27.0
2　～　3	10.7	11.2	10.8	11.6	12.2	14.0	13.9	14.1	14.9	16.0	16.8	17.0
3　～　4	4.1	4.5	4.7	5.0	5.4	6.7	7.5	8.1	8.3	9.3	9.4	9.7
4　～　5	1.9	2.1	2.5	2.4	2.8	3.5	4.4	5.0	5.0	5.7	5.9	5.8
5　～　6	1.0	1.1	1.5	1.4	1.6	2.0	2.6	3.2	3.4	3.7	3.7	3.8
6　～　7	0.6	0.6	0.9	0.8	1.0	1.2	1.6	2.0	2.2	2.4	2.4	2.4
7　～　8	0.4	0.4	0.6	0.5	0.6	0.7	1.0	1.3	1.5	1.6	1.7	1.6
8　～　9	0.3	0.3	0.4	0.4	0.4	0.5	0.6	0.9	1.1	1.2	1.1	1.2
9　～　10	0.2	0.2	0.3	0.3	0.3	0.3	0.4	0.6	0.8	0.8	0.8	0.8
10　～　15	0.4	0.4	0.4	0.6	0.6	0.6	0.7	1.1	1.5	1.7	1.6	1.6
15　～　20	0.0	0.0	0.1	0.1	0.1	0.1	0.1	0.1	0.2	0.3	0.2	0.3
20　～　20years and over	0.0	0.0	0.0	0.0	0.0	0.0	0.0	0.0	0.0	0.0	0.0	0.0
平均期間[4](年)Mean duration (years)	1.52	1.55	1.61	1.61	1.66	1.78	1.89	2.09	2.24	2.39	2.41	2.42

注:1)　出生順位とは、同じ母親がこれまでに生んだ出生子の総数について数えた順序である。
　　2)　実数は中巻・出生第17表を参照されたい。
　　3)　期間不詳を除いた百分率である。
　　4)　平均期間算出の計算式を月数の算術平均から算出する方法に改め、昭和49年から再計算をした。

表4.23　世帯の主な仕事別にみた出生順位[1]別出生数及び百分率

Table 4.23　Live births and percent distribution by live birth order and type of occupation of household : Japan, 2016

平成28年

出　生　順　位 Live birth order	総　数[2] Total	農家世帯 Agriculture[a]	自営業者世帯 Self employed	常用勤労者世帯（I） Employee[b]	常用勤労者世帯（II） Employee[c] or director	その他の世帯 Other	無職の世帯 Not working
実　　数　Number							
総　数　Total	976 978	11 953	69 517	319 901	448 242	80 332	16 764
第1子　1st	459 751	4 676	29 069	146 444	219 037	38 077	7 933
2　　2nd	355 784	4 225	24 468	116 631	167 000	28 254	4 548
3　　3rd	126 533	2 282	11 435	44 052	51 763	10 750	2 441
4　　4th	26 417	597	3 315	9 648	8 459	2 367	1 114
5～　5th and over	8 493	173	1 230	3 126	1 983	884	728
百　分　率　Percentage							
総　数　Total	100.0	100.0	100.0	100.0	100.0	100.0	100.0
第1子　1st	47.1	39.1	41.8	45.8	48.9	47.4	47.3
2　　2nd	36.4	35.3	35.2	36.5	37.3	35.2	27.1
3　　3rd	13.0	19.1	16.4	13.8	11.5	13.4	14.6
4　　4th	2.7	5.0	4.8	3.0	1.9	2.9	6.6
5～　5th and over	0.9	1.4	1.8	1.0	0.4	1.1	4.3

注:平成7年から世帯の主な仕事の区分を変更した。
　　1)　出生順位とは、同じ母親がこれまでに生んだ出生子の総数について数えた順序である。
　　2)　総数には、世帯の主な仕事不詳を含む。
Note : a)　Agriculture only or that with other work.
　　　　b)　Employee at office (excluding governmental office) with 1-99 employee (excluding daily or less than one year contracts).
　　　　c)　Employee at office excluding　b)　above.

Natality

〔妊娠期間別にみた出生〕
〔Live births by period of gestation〕

表4.24　妊娠期間別にみた年次別出生数及び百分率[1]
Table 4.24　Trends in live births and percent distribution by period of gestation : Japan

妊　娠　期　間 Period of gestation	1980 昭和55年	1985 60年	1990 平成2年	1995 7年	2000 12年	2005 17年	2010 22年	2014 26年	2015 27年	2016 28年
				実　　数　Number						
総　数　Total	1 576 889	1 431 577	1 221 585	1 187 064	1 190 547	1 062 530	1 071 304	1 003 539	1 005 677	976 978
満22週未満 Under 22 completed weeks	33	37	26	12	5	4	4	6	5	1
満22週～満23週 22－23 completed weeks	106	188	194	277	308	421	442	445	448	444
満24週～満27週 24－27 completed weeks	1 818	2 067	2 092	2 095	2 227	2 242	2 336	2 129	2 091	1 994
満28週～満31週 28－31 completed weeks	5 980	5 520	4 710	5 067	5 837	5 139	5 025	4 693	4 558	4 309
満32週～満35週 32－35 completed weeks	28 418	24 957	21 881	22 762	24 435	22 638	22 735	21 062	20 904	20 241
満36週～満39週 36－39 completed weeks	791 837	758 482	701 683	694 759	708 282	636 063	662 432	631 260	635 644	624 587
満40週以上 40 completed weeks and over	748 270	639 908	490 640	461 637	448 945	395 586	377 956	343 703	341 811	325 202
不　　詳 Not stated	427	418	359	455	508	437	374	241	216	200
（再掲） (Regrouped)										
（早期)満37週未満 (Pre-term)Under 37 completed weeks	64 889	59 795	55 231	58 293	64 006	60 377	61 315	56 906	56 144	54 594
満28週未満 　Under 28 completed weeks	1 957	2 292	2 312	2 384	2 540	2 667	2 782	2 580	2 544	2 439
満28週～満31週 　28－31 completed weeks	5 980	5 520	4 710	5 067	5 837	5 139	5 025	4 693	4 558	4 309
満32週～満36週 　32－36 completed weeks	56 952	51 983	48 209	50 842	55 629	52 571	53 508	49 633	49 042	47 846
（正期)満37週～満41週 (Term)37－41 completed weeks	1 441 700	1 326 256	1 145 520	1 114 271	1 116 195	995 674	1 006 033	943 957	947 146	920 299
（過期)満42週以上 (Post-term)42 completed weeks and over	69 873	45 108	20 475	14 045	9 838	6 042	3 582	2 435	2 171	1 885
				百　分　率　Percentage						
総　数　Total	100.0	100.0	100.0	100.0	100.0	100.0	100.0	100.0	100.0	100.0
満22週未満 Under 22 completed weeks	0.0	0.0	0.0	0.0	0.0	0.0	0.0	0.0	0.0	0.0
満22週～満23週 22－23 completed weeks	0.0	0.0	0.0	0.0	0.0	0.0	0.0	0.0	0.0	0.0
満24週～満27週 24－27 completed weeks	0.1	0.1	0.2	0.2	0.2	0.2	0.2	0.2	0.2	0.2
満28週～満31週 28－31 completed weeks	0.4	0.4	0.4	0.4	0.5	0.5	0.5	0.5	0.5	0.4
満32週～満35週 32－35 completed weeks	1.8	1.7	1.8	1.9	2.1	2.1	2.1	2.1	2.1	2.1
満36週～満39週 36－39 completed weeks	50.2	53.0	57.5	58.5	59.5	59.9	61.9	62.9	63.2	63.9
満40週以上 40 completed weeks and over	47.5	44.7	40.2	38.9	37.7	37.2	35.3	34.3	34.0	33.3
（再掲） (Regrouped)										
（早期)満37週未満 (Pre-term)Under 37 completed weeks	4.1	4.2	4.5	4.9	5.4	5.7	5.7	5.7	5.6	5.6
満28週未満 　Under 28 completed weeks	0.1	0.2	0.2	0.2	0.2	0.3	0.3	0.3	0.3	0.2
満28週～満31週 　28－31 completed weeks	0.4	0.4	0.4	0.4	0.5	0.5	0.5	0.5	0.5	0.4
満32週～満36週 　32－36 completed weeks	3.6	3.6	3.9	4.3	4.7	4.9	5.0	4.9	4.9	4.9
（正期)満37週～満41週 (Term)37－41 completed weeks	91.5	92.7	93.8	93.9	93.8	93.7	93.9	94.1	94.2	94.2
（過期)満42週以上 (Post-term)42 completed weeks and over	4.4	3.2	1.7	1.2	0.8	0.6	0.3	0.2	0.2	0.2

注：1）　妊娠期間不詳を除いた出生数に対する百分率である。

出　生

〔出生時の体重別にみた出生〕
〔Live births by birth weight〕

表 4.25　性・出生時の体重別にみた
Table 4.25　Trends in live births and percent

男
Male

出生時の体重 Birth weight	1951 昭和26年	1955 30年	1960 35年	1970 45年	1975 50年	1980 55年	1985 60年	1990 平成2年	1995 7年	2000 12年
	実　　　　　　数									
総　数　Total	1 094 641	889 670	824 761	1 000 403	979 091	811 418	735 284	626 971	608 547	612 148
1.0kg未満 Under 1.0kg	53	121	207	721	448	678	1 022	1 151	1 311	1 452
1.0kg以上1.5kg未満 1.0kg and over, less than 1.5kg	1 908	1 807	2 211	2 839	2 602	2 269	2 428	2 200	2 400	2 593
1.5～2.0	11 498	9 777	9 474	9 504	7 912	6 338	5 793	5 463	5 880	6 698
2.0～2.5	56 691	46 274	41 665	39 328	35 077	29 438	27 460	27 181	31 413	36 994
2.5～3.0	273 757	215 750	217 187	228 666	214 698	184 080	177 886	172 242	186 552	202 033
3.0～3.5	524 671	424 672	387 494	462 500	456 578	380 149	345 724	293 246	278 617	272 538
3.5～4.0	185 219	154 078	140 205	217 891	222 942	178 570	151 853	110 920	91 705	81 352
4.0～4.5	31 729	26 262	20 938	34 925	35 511	27 348	21 190	13 451	9 817	7 863
4.5kg以上 4.5kg and over	3 512	2 734	1 806	2 967	3 013	2 452	1 768	1 009	693	553
不　詳　Not stated	5 603	8 195	3 574	1 062	310	96	160	108	159	72
（再掲） (Regrouped) 1.0kg以上 1.0kg and over	1 088 985	881 354	820 980	998 620	978 333	810 644	734 102	625 712	607 077	610 624
2.5kg未満 Under 2.5kg	70 150	57 979	53 557	52 392	46 039	38 723	36 703	35 995	41 004	47 737
	百　　分　　率									
総　数　Total	100.0	100.0	100.0	100.0	100.0	100.0	100.0	100.0	100.0	100.0
1.0kg未満 Under 1.0kg	0.0	0.0	0.0	0.1	0.0	0.1	0.1	0.2	0.2	0.2
1.0kg以上1.5kg未満 1.0kg and over, less than 1.5kg	0.2	0.2	0.3	0.3	0.3	0.3	0.3	0.4	0.4	0.4
1.5～2.0	1.1	1.1	1.2	1.0	0.8	0.8	0.8	0.9	1.0	1.1
2.0～2.5	5.2	5.2	5.1	3.9	3.6	3.6	3.7	4.3	5.2	6.0
2.5～3.0	25.1	24.5	26.4	22.9	21.9	22.7	24.2	27.5	30.7	33.0
3.0～3.5	48.2	48.2	47.2	46.3	46.6	46.9	47.0	46.8	45.8	44.5
3.5～4.0	17.0	17.5	17.1	21.8	22.8	22.0	20.7	17.7	15.1	13.3
4.0～4.5	2.9	3.0	2.5	3.5	3.6	3.4	2.9	2.1	1.6	1.3
4.5kg以上 4.5kg and over	0.3	0.3	0.2	0.3	0.3	0.3	0.2	0.2	0.1	0.1
（再掲） (Regrouped) 1.0kg以上 1.0kg and over	99.5	99.1	99.5	99.8	99.9	99.9	99.8	99.8	99.8	99.8
2.5kg未満 Under 2.5kg	6.4	6.5	6.5	5.2	4.7	4.8	5.0	5.7	6.7	7.8
平均体重（kg） Mean weight	3.14	3.15	3.14	3.22	3.24	3.23	3.20	3.16	3.11	3.07

注：1）　出生時の体重不詳を除いた出生数に対する百分率である。
　　　2）　平成3年までの出生時の体重は、100グラム単位で把握したため、算出平均値に0.05kgを加えたが、平成4年に調査票を改正し、これ以降はグラム単位で把握した算術平均値である。
　資　料：昭和26年、30年、35年は、人口動態統計特殊報告「出生時の体重に関する統計」による。

Natality

年次別出生数・百分率[1]及び平均体重[2]
distribution by sex and birth weight : Japan

2005 17年	2008 20年	2009 21年	2010 22年	2011 23年	2012 24年	2013 25年	2014 26年	2015 27年	2016 28年	出生時の体重 Birth weight
				Number						
545 032	559 513	548 993	550 742	538 271	531 781	527 657	515 533	515 452	501 880	総　数 Total
1 536	1 619	1 606	1 673	1 544	1 624	1 527	1 542	1 580	1 424	1.0kg未満 Under 1.0kg
2 591	2 563	2 479	2 525	2 512	2 425	2 399	2 283	2 301	2 168	1.0kg以上1.5kg未満 1.0kg and over, less than 1.5kg
6 613	6 560	6 384	6 384	6 208	6 165	6 162	5 943	5 844	5 694	1.5 ～ 2.0
35 534	36 710	36 173	36 414	35 369	34 846	34 609	33 666	33 418	32 402	2.0 ～ 2.5
187 674	195 406	192 615	194 231	188 316	186 444	184 822	181 376	181 531	175 676	2.5 ～ 3.0
238 515	243 318	238 862	239 004	234 391	232 349	230 061	224 124	224 979	219 626	3.0 ～ 3.5
66 286	66 832	64 877	64 615	64 183	62 174	62 639	61 125	60 420	59 724	3.5 ～ 4.0
5 861	6 055	5 605	5 466	5 361	5 384	5 096	5 115	5 057	4 847	4.0 ～ 4.5
333	339	283	305	271	260	271	275	237	228	4.5kg以上 4.5kg and over
89	111	109	125	116	110	71	84	85	91	不　詳　Not stated
										（再掲） (Regrouped)
543 407	557 783	547 278	548 944	536 611	530 047	526 059	513 907	513 787	500 365	1.0kg以上 1.0kg and over
46 274	47 452	46 642	46 996	45 633	45 060	44 697	43 434	43 143	41 688	2.5kg未満 Under 2.5kg
				Percentage						
100. 0	100. 0	100. 0	100. 0	100. 0	100. 0	100. 0	100. 0	100. 0	100. 0	総　数 Total
0. 3	0. 3	0. 3	0. 3	0. 3	0. 3	0. 3	0. 3	0. 3	0. 3	1.0kg未満 Under 1.0kg
0. 5	0. 5	0. 5	0. 5	0. 5	0. 5	0. 5	0. 4	0. 4	0. 4	1.0kg以上1.5kg未満 1.0kg and over, less than 1.5kg
1. 2	1. 2	1. 2	1. 2	1. 2	1. 2	1. 2	1. 2	1. 1	1. 1	1.5 ～ 2.0
6. 5	6. 6	6. 6	6. 6	6. 6	6. 6	6. 6	6. 5	6. 5	6. 5	2.0 ～ 2.5
34. 4	34. 9	35. 1	35. 3	35. 0	35. 1	35. 0	35. 2	35. 2	35. 0	2.5 ～ 3.0
43. 8	43. 5	43. 5	43. 4	43. 6	43. 7	43. 6	43. 5	43. 7	43. 8	3.0 ～ 3.5
12. 2	11. 9	11. 8	11. 7	11. 9	11. 7	11. 9	11. 9	11. 7	11. 9	3.5 ～ 4.0
1. 1	1. 1	1. 0	1. 0	1. 0	1. 0	1. 0	1. 0	1. 0	1. 0	4.0 ～ 4.5
0. 1	0. 1	0. 1	0. 1	0. 1	0. 0	0. 1	0. 1	0. 0	0. 0	4.5kg以上 4.5kg and over
										（再掲） (Regrouped)
99. 7	99. 7	99. 7	99. 7	99. 7	99. 7	99. 7	99. 7	99. 7	99. 7	1.0kg以上 1.0kg and over
8. 5	8. 5	8. 5	8. 5	8. 5	8. 5	8. 5	8. 4	8. 4	8. 3	2.5kg未満 Under 2.5kg
3. 05	3. 05	3. 04	3. 04	3. 04	3. 04	3. 04	3. 04	3. 04	3. 05	平均体重（kg） Mean weight

出　生

〔出生時の体重別にみた出生〕
〔Live births by birth weight〕

表4.25　性・出生時の体重別にみた
Table 4.25　Trends in live births and percent

女
Female

出生時の体重 Birth weight	1951 昭和26年	1955 30年	1960 35年	1970 45年	1975 50年	1980 55年	1985 60年	1990 平成2年	1995 7年	2000 12年
	実　　　　　　数									
総　数　Total	1 043 048	841 022	781 280	933 836	922 349	765 471	696 293	594 614	578 517	578 399
1.0kg未満　Under 1.0kg	61	163	259	725	592	812	1 132	1 140	1 299	1 414
1.0kg以上1.5kg未満　1.0kg and over, less than 1.5kg	2 313	2 183	2 556	3 039	2 679	2 213	2 217	2 027	2 303	2 441
1.5～2.0	12 581	10 627	10 104	9 239	7 799	6 227	5 663	5 337	5 956	6 601
2.0～2.5	71 943	53 539	47 165	44 331	39 858	33 684	32 459	32 833	38 550	44 695
2.5～3.0	325 317	254 797	253 896	269 576	259 189	222 066	214 681	204 417	218 243	232 699
3.0～3.5	465 282	387 733	353 629	431 912	431 232	356 197	320 444	265 100	245 481	233 908
3.5～4.0	139 177	107 146	97 049	153 222	158 287	126 932	106 079	75 265	60 628	52 093
4.0～4.5	18 953	15 369	12 087	19 346	20 756	15 972	12 443	7 802	5 522	4 215
4.5kg以上　4.5kg and over	1 961	1 499	977	1 490	1 645	1 278	1 047	605	403	246
不　詳　Not stated	5 460	7 966	3 558	956	312	90	128	88	132	87
（再掲）(Regrouped) 1.0kg以上　1.0kg and over	1 037 527	832 893	777 463	932 155	921 445	764 569	695 033	593 386	577 086	576 898
2.5kg未満　Under 2.5kg	86 898	66 512	60 084	57 334	50 928	42 936	41 471	41 337	48 108	55 151
	百　　　分　　　率									
総　数　Total	100.0	100.0	100.0	100.0	100.0	100.0	100.0	100.0	100.0	100.0
1.0kg未満　Under 1.0kg	0.0	0.0	0.0	0.1	0.1	0.1	0.2	0.2	0.2	0.2
1.0kg以上1.5kg未満　1.0kg and over, less than 1.5kg	0.2	0.3	0.3	0.3	0.3	0.3	0.3	0.3	0.4	0.4
1.5～2.0	1.2	1.3	1.3	1.0	0.8	0.8	0.8	0.9	1.0	1.1
2.0～2.5	6.9	6.4	6.1	4.8	4.3	4.4	4.7	5.5	6.7	7.7
2.5～3.0	31.4	30.6	32.6	28.9	28.1	29.0	30.8	34.4	37.7	40.2
3.0～3.5	44.8	46.5	45.5	46.3	46.8	46.5	46.0	44.6	42.4	40.4
3.5～4.0	13.4	12.9	12.5	16.4	17.2	16.6	15.2	12.7	10.5	9.0
4.0～4.5	1.8	1.8	1.6	2.1	2.3	2.1	1.8	1.3	1.0	0.7
4.5kg以上　4.5kg and over	0.2	0.2	0.1	0.2	0.2	0.2	0.2	0.1	0.1	0.0
（再掲）(Regrouped) 1.0kg以上　1.0kg and over	99.5	99.0	99.5	99.8	99.9	99.9	99.8	99.8	99.8	99.8
2.5kg未満　Under 2.5kg	8.3	7.9	7.7	6.1	5.5	5.6	6.0	7.0	8.3	9.5
平均体重（kg）　Mean weight	3.06	3.06	3.06	3.13	3.15	3.14	3.12	3.08	3.03	2.99

注：1）　出生時の体重不詳を除いた出生数に対する百分率である。
　　2）　平成3年までの出生時の体重は、100グラム単位で把握したため、算出平均値に0.05kgを加えたが、平成4年に調査票を改正し、これ以降はグラム単位で把握した算術平均値である。
　資　料：昭和26年、30年、35年は、人口動態統計特殊報告「出生時の体重に関する統計」による。

Natality

年次別出生数・百分率[1]及び平均体重[2]（つづき）
distribution by sex and birth weight : Japan－CON.

2005 17年	2008 20年	2009 21年	2010 22年	2011 23年	2012 24年	2013 25年	2014 26年	2015 27年	2016 28年	出生時の体重 Birth weight
Number										
517 498	531 643	521 042	520 562	512 535	505 450	502 159	488 006	490 225	475 098	総　数 Total
1 579	1 674	1 544	1 559	1 576	1 575	1 572	1 535	1 504	1 467	1.0kg未満 Under 1.0kg
2 491	2 426	2 374	2 329	2 310	2 361	2 390	2 333	2 125	1 956	1.0kg以上1.5kg未満 1.0kg and over, less than 1.5kg
6 918	6 835	6 601	6 610	6 406	6 337	6 328	6 199	6 004	5 928	1.5 ～ 2.0
44 010	46 092	45 510	45 555	44 453	43 978	43 637	42 267	42 430	41 043	2.0 ～ 2.5
215 227	223 733	220 398	221 062	217 398	214 850	213 665	206 467	209 034	201 773	2.5 ～ 3.0
201 613	205 709	200 641	200 325	197 320	194 558	192 800	188 753	188 610	183 682	3.0 ～ 3.5
42 216	41 882	40 793	40 065	40 012	38 944	38 949	37 749	37 767	36 604	3.5 ～ 4.0
3 170	3 028	2 909	2 776	2 814	2 635	2 625	2 527	2 562	2 436	4.0 ～ 4.5
185	151	158	166	132	136	134	114	111	127	4.5kg以上 4.5kg and over
89	113	114	115	114	76	59	62	78	82	不　詳　Not stated
										（再掲） (Regrouped)
515 830	529 856	519 384	518 888	510 845	503 799	500 528	486 409	488 643	473 549	1.0kg以上 1.0kg and over
54 998	57 027	56 029	56 053	54 745	54 251	53 927	52 334	52 063	50 394	2.5kg未満 Under 2.5kg
Percentage										
100.0	100.0	100.0	100.0	100.0	100.0	100.0	100.0	100.0	100.0	総　数 Total
0.3	0.3	0.3	0.3	0.3	0.3	0.3	0.3	0.3	0.3	1.0kg未満 Under 1.0kg
0.5	0.5	0.5	0.4	0.5	0.5	0.5	0.5	0.4	0.4	1.0kg以上1.5kg未満 1.0kg and over, less than 1.5kg
1.3	1.3	1.3	1.3	1.3	1.3	1.3	1.3	1.2	1.2	1.5 ～ 2.0
8.5	8.7	8.7	8.8	8.7	8.7	8.7	8.7	8.7	8.6	2.0 ～ 2.5
41.6	42.1	42.3	42.5	42.4	42.5	42.6	42.3	42.6	42.5	2.5 ～ 3.0
39.0	38.7	38.5	38.5	38.5	38.5	38.4	38.7	38.5	38.7	3.0 ～ 3.5
8.2	7.9	7.8	7.7	7.8	7.7	7.8	7.7	7.7	7.7	3.5 ～ 4.0
0.6	0.6	0.6	0.5	0.5	0.5	0.5	0.5	0.5	0.5	4.0 ～ 4.5
0.0	0.0	0.0	0.0	0.0	0.0	0.0	0.0	0.0	0.0	4.5kg以上 4.5kg and over
										（再掲） (Regrouped)
99.7	99.7	99.7	99.7	99.7	99.7	99.7	99.7	99.7	99.7	1.0kg以上 1.0kg and over
10.6	10.7	10.8	10.8	10.7	10.7	10.7	10.7	10.6	10.6	2.5kg未満 Under 2.5kg
2.96	2.96	2.96	2.96	2.96	2.96	2.96	2.96	2.96	2.96	平均体重（kg） Mean weight

出　生

表4.26　都道府県（21大都市再掲）・性別にみた出生時の平均体重[1]及び 2,500g未満の出生数及び割合[2]

Table 4.26　Mean birth weight, number and percent distribution of live births under 2,500g by sex : Japan, each prefecture and 21 major cities, 2016

平成28年

都道府県 Prefecture	総数 Total 平均体重(kg) Mean weight	2,500g未満出生 Live births weighted under 2,500g 実数 Number	出生数に対する割合(%) Percentage to live births	男 Male 平均体重(kg) Mean weight	2,500g未満出生 Live births weighted under 2,500g 実数 Number	出生数に対する割合(%) Percentage to live births	女 Female 平均体重(kg) Mean weight	2,500g未満出生 Live births weighted under 2,500g 実数 Number	出生数に対する割合(%) Percentage to live births
全国 Total	3.00	92 082	9.4	3.05	41 688	8.3	2.96	50 394	10.6
01 北海道 a)	3.01	3 233	9.2	3.05	1 519	8.5	2.97	1 714	9.9
02 青森	3.02	725	8.4	3.06	316	7.3	2.98	409	9.7
03 岩手	3.01	816	9.8	3.06	366	8.5	2.96	450	11.1
04 宮城	3.01	1 683	9.7	3.05	781	8.8	2.96	902	10.7
05 秋田	2.98	597	10.5	3.03	246	8.7	2.94	351	12.4
06 山形	3.01	705	9.3	3.05	329	8.5	2.96	376	10.3
07 福島	3.00	1 302	9.5	3.05	582	8.3	2.96	720	10.7
08 茨城	3.00	1 955	9.4	3.04	882	8.2	2.96	1 073	10.6
09 栃木	2.99	1 524	10.4	3.03	698	9.2	2.94	826	11.8
10 群馬	3.00	1 234	9.0	3.04	576	8.1	2.96	658	10.1
11 埼玉	3.00	4 988	9.2	3.05	2 246	8.0	2.96	2 742	10.4
12 千葉	3.01	4 194	9.2	3.05	1 833	7.9	2.96	2 361	10.7
13 東京	3.00	10 293	9.2	3.04	4 653	8.1	2.96	5 640	10.3
14 神奈川	2.99	6 694	9.5	3.04	2 984	8.2	2.95	3 710	10.8
15 新潟	3.03	1 418	9.0	3.07	670	8.2	2.99	748	9.8
16 富山	3.00	711	9.7	3.04	342	9.2	2.97	369	10.3
17 石川	3.03	772	8.6	3.08	320	6.9	2.97	452	10.6
18 福井	3.03	535	8.8	3.07	251	7.9	2.99	284	9.7
19 山梨	2.98	595	10.2	3.03	264	9.0	2.93	331	11.5
20 長野	3.00	1 451	9.6	3.04	649	8.3	2.95	802	11.0
21 岐阜	3.01	1 349	9.1	3.05	642	8.5	2.97	707	9.7
22 静岡	2.98	2 798	10.1	3.03	1 265	8.9	2.94	1 533	11.4
23 愛知	3.00	6 261	9.7	3.04	2 795	8.5	2.95	3 466	11.1
24 三重	3.02	1 214	9.2	3.06	542	8.0	2.98	672	10.5
25 滋賀	3.01	1 105	9.2	3.05	482	7.8	2.96	623	10.5
26 京都	3.00	1 858	9.6	3.04	809	8.2	2.96	1 049	11.1
27 大阪	3.01	6 222	9.0	3.06	2 845	8.1	2.97	3 377	10.1
28 兵庫	3.01	4 155	9.6	3.05	1 869	8.4	2.96	2 286	10.9
29 奈良	3.00	891	9.4	3.05	399	8.3	2.96	492	10.6
30 和歌山	2.99	640	9.6	3.03	297	8.6	2.95	343	10.7
31 鳥取	3.00	444	10.0	3.05	194	8.4	2.94	250	11.8
32 島根	2.99	533	10.1	3.02	245	9.0	2.95	288	11.2
33 岡山	3.01	1 338	8.6	3.05	614	7.8	2.97	724	9.6
34 広島	3.00	2 208	9.7	3.04	1 015	8.6	2.95	1 193	10.9
35 山口	3.00	925	9.4	3.04	401	7.9	2.96	524	11.0
36 徳島	3.01	543	10.2	3.05	248	9.1	2.96	295	11.3
37 香川	3.02	683	9.1	3.05	324	8.4	2.98	359	9.9
38 愛媛	3.02	857	8.6	3.07	389	7.6	2.97	468	9.8
39 高知	3.00	429	9.0	3.05	188	7.6	2.95	241	10.5
40 福岡	3.00	4 247	9.6	3.04	1 964	8.6	2.96	2 283	10.7
41 佐賀	3.01	638	9.4	3.06	302	8.6	2.97	336	10.1
42 長崎	3.03	976	9.0	3.06	443	7.9	2.99	533	10.1
43 熊本	3.02	1 300	8.7	3.06	595	7.8	2.97	705	9.7
44 大分	3.02	874	9.6	3.06	382	8.2	2.97	492	11.2
45 宮崎	3.00	883	9.9	3.05	427	9.4	2.96	456	10.4
46 鹿児島	2.99	1 410	10.3	3.03	629	9.0	2.94	781	11.7
47 沖縄	2.97	1 873	11.3	3.01	875	10.3	2.93	998	12.3
外国 Foreign countries	3.07	3	4.8	3.15	1	3.2	2.99	2	6.5
21大都市（再掲） 21 major cities (Regrouped)									
50 東京都の区部	3.00	7 503	9.4	3.04	3 375	8.2	2.96	4 128	10.5
51 札幌	3.01	1 316	9.4	3.04	628	8.8	2.98	688	10.0
52 仙台	3.00	878	9.9	3.04	436	9.4	2.96	442	10.3
53 さいたま	3.00	1 004	9.5	3.05	468	8.3	2.95	536	10.9
54 千葉	3.00	649	9.4	3.05	293	8.1	2.95	356	10.7
55 横浜	2.99	2 731	9.5	3.04	1 204	8.2	2.95	1 527	10.8
56 川崎	3.00	1 295	9.1	3.04	588	8.0	2.96	707	10.3
57 相模原	2.98	518	10.0	3.04	224	8.5	2.93	294	11.5
58 新潟	3.03	521	8.8	3.07	251	8.1	2.99	270	9.5
59 静岡	2.98	507	9.9	3.02	227	8.7	2.93	280	11.2
60 浜松	2.99	622	9.5	3.02	295	8.6	2.95	327	10.5
61 名古屋	2.99	1 944	9.9	3.04	828	8.3	2.94	1 116	11.7
62 京都	3.00	1 039	9.5	3.05	420	7.5	2.95	619	11.6
63 大阪	3.02	2 004	9.1	3.06	925	8.2	2.97	1 079	10.0
64 堺	3.00	659	9.6	3.05	298	8.5	2.96	361	10.8
65 神戸	3.00	1 146	9.7	3.05	491	8.0	2.96	655	11.5
66 岡山	3.01	524	8.4	3.06	242	7.5	2.96	282	9.3
67 広島	3.00	1 034	9.8	3.04	459	8.5	2.96	575	11.1
68 北九州	3.00	764	10.0	3.04	339	8.8	2.96	425	11.3
69 福岡	3.00	1 380	9.5	3.05	625	8.3	2.95	755	10.8
70 熊本	3.01	597	8.8	3.05	281	8.0	2.96	316	9.6

注：1)　平成3年までの出生時の体重は、100グラム単位で把握したため、算出平均値に0.05kgを加えたが、平成4年に調査票を改正し、これ以降はグラム単位で把握した算術平均値である。
　　2)　出生時の体重不詳を除いた出生数に対する割合である。

Note：a)　See page 44.

Natality

表 4.27 単産－複産・性別にみた出生時の体重別出生数・百分率[1] 及び平均体重[2]
Table 4.27　Live births and percent distribution by sex, birth weight and plurality of birth : Japan, 2016

平成28年

出生時の体重 Birth weight	実　数 Number			百　分　率 Percentage		
	総　数 Total	単　産 Single delivery	複　産 Plural delivery	総　数 Total	単　産 Single delivery	複　産 Plural delivery
総　数　Total 総 数 Total	976 978	957 614	19 364	100.0	100.0	100.0
1.0kg未満　Under 1.0kg	2 891	2 352	539	0.3	0.2	2.8
1.0kg以上1.5kg未満 1.0kg and over, less than 1.5kg	4 124	3 146	978	0.4	0.3	5.1
1.5 ～ 2.0	11 622	8 422	3 200	1.2	0.9	16.5
2.0 ～ 2.5	73 445	64 464	8 981	7.5	6.7	46.4
2.5 ～ 3.0	377 449	372 296	5 153	38.6	38.9	26.6
3.0 ～ 3.5	403 308	402 829	479	41.3	42.1	2.5
3.5 ～ 4.0	96 328	96 307	21	9.9	10.1	0.1
4.0 ～ 4.5	7 283	7 283	-	0.7	0.8	-
4.5kg以上 4.5kg and over	355	354	1	0.0	0.0	0.0
不　詳　Not stated	173	161	12	・	・	・
(再掲) (Regrouped)						
1.0kg以上 1.0kg and over	973 914	955 101	18 813	99.7	99.8	97.2
2.5kg未満 Under 2.5kg	92 082	78 384	13 698	9.4	8.2	70.8
平均体重(kg)Mean weight	3.00	3.02	2.23	・	・	・
総　数　Total 男 Male	501 880	492 044	9 836	100.0	100.0	100.0
1.0kg未満　Under 1.0kg	1 424	1 151	273	0.3	0.2	2.8
1.0kg以上1.5kg未満 1.0kg and over, less than 1.5kg	2 168	1 666	502	0.4	0.3	5.1
1.5 ～ 2.0	5 694	4 210	1 484	1.1	0.9	15.1
2.0 ～ 2.5	32 402	28 135	4 267	6.5	5.7	43.4
2.5 ～ 3.0	175 676	172 725	2 951	35.0	35.1	30.0
3.0 ～ 3.5	219 626	219 290	336	43.8	44.6	3.4
3.5 ～ 4.0	59 724	59 708	16	11.9	12.1	0.2
4.0 ～ 4.5	4 847	4 847	-	1.0	1.0	-
4.5kg以上 4.5kg and over	228	228	-	0.0	0.0	-
不　詳　Not stated	91	84	7	・	・	・
(再掲) (Regrouped)						
1.0kg以上 1.0kg and over	500 365	490 809	9 556	99.7	99.8	97.2
2.5kg未満 Under 2.5kg	41 688	35 162	6 526	8.3	7.1	66.4
平均体重(kg)Mean weight	3.05	3.06	2.27	・	・	・
総　数　Total 女 Female	475 098	465 570	9 528	100.0	100.0	100.0
1.0kg未満　Under 1.0kg	1 467	1 201	266	0.3	0.3	2.8
1.0kg以上1.5kg未満 1.0kg and over, less than 1.5kg	1 956	1 480	476	0.4	0.3	5.0
1.5 ～ 2.0	5 928	4 212	1 716	1.2	0.9	18.0
2.0 ～ 2.5	41 043	36 329	4 714	8.6	7.8	49.5
2.5 ～ 3.0	201 773	199 571	2 202	42.5	42.9	23.1
3.0 ～ 3.5	183 682	183 539	143	38.7	39.4	1.5
3.5 ～ 4.0	36 604	36 599	5	7.7	7.9	0.1
4.0 ～ 4.5	2 436	2 436	-	0.5	0.5	-
4.5kg以上 4.5kg and over	127	126	1	0.0	0.0	0.0
不　詳　Not stated	82	77	5	・	・	・
(再掲) (Regrouped)						
1.0kg以上 1.0kg and over	473 549	464 292	9 257	99.7	99.7	97.2
2.5kg未満 Under 2.5kg	50 394	43 222	7 172	10.6	9.3	75.3
平均体重(kg)Mean weight	2.96	2.97	2.20	・	・	・

注：1)　出生時の体重不詳を除く出生数に対する百分率である。
　　2)　平成3年までの出生時の体重は、100グラム単位で把握したため、算出平均値に0.05kgを加えたが、平成4年に調査票を改正し、これ以降はグラム単位で把握した算術平均値である。

出 生

表4.28 母の年齢・単産－複産・性別にみた2,500g未満の出生数及び割合 [1]
Table 4.28 Live births and percent distribution under 2,500g by sex, age of mother and plurality of birth : Japan, 2016

平成28年

母の年齢 Age of mother	総　数 Total			男 Male			女 Female		
	出 生 数 Live births	2,500g未満 出生数 Birth weight under 2,500g	2,500g未満 出生数割合(%) Percentage under 2,500g	出 生 数 Live births	2,500g未満 出生数 Birth weight under 2,500g	2,500g未満 出生数割合(%) Percentage under 2,500g	出 生 数 Live births	2,500g未満 出生数 Birth weight under 2,500g	2,500g未満 出生数割合(%) Percentage under 2,500g
総　数　Total					総　数　Total				
総　数　Total	976 978	92 082	9.4	501 880	41 688	8.3	475 098	50 394	10.6
～19歳Years	11 095	1 116	10.1	5 727	560	9.8	5 368	556	10.4
20～24	82 169	7 228	8.8	42 151	3 305	7.8	40 018	3 923	9.8
25～29	250 639	21 656	8.6	128 804	9 725	7.6	121 835	11 931	9.8
30～34	354 911	32 632	9.2	182 633	14 632	8.0	172 278	18 000	10.4
35～39	223 287	22 686	10.2	114 541	10 406	9.1	108 746	12 280	11.3
40～44	53 474	6 501	12.2	27 296	2 942	10.8	26 178	3 559	13.6
45～	1 401	263	18.8	726	118	16.3	675	145	21.5
不 詳 Not stated	2	-	・	2	-	・	-	-	・
単　産　Single delivery									
総　数　Total	957 614	78 384	8.2	492 044	35 162	7.1	465 570	43 222	9.3
～19歳Years	10 982	1 037	9.4	5 668	521	9.2	5 314	516	9.7
20～24	81 162	6 459	8.0	41 652	2 939	7.1	39 510	3 520	8.9
25～29	246 444	18 609	7.6	126 664	8 260	6.5	119 780	10 349	8.6
30～34	347 774	27 474	7.9	179 039	12 173	6.8	168 735	15 301	9.1
35～39	217 888	19 076	8.8	111 745	8 677	7.8	106 143	10 399	9.8
40～44	52 056	5 535	10.6	26 595	2 505	9.4	25 461	3 030	11.9
45～	1 306	194	14.9	679	87	12.8	627	107	17.1
不 詳 Not stated	2	-	・	2	-	・	-	-	・
複　産　Plural delivery									
総　数　Total	19 364	13 698	70.7	9 836	6 526	66.3	9 528	7 172	75.3
～19歳Years	113	79	69.9	59	39	66.1	54	40	74.1
20～24	1 007	769	76.4	499	366	73.3	508	403	79.3
25～29	4 195	3 047	72.6	2 140	1 465	68.5	2 055	1 582	77.0
30～34	7 137	5 158	72.3	3 594	2 459	68.4	3 543	2 699	76.2
35～39	5 399	3 610	66.9	2 796	1 729	61.8	2 603	1 881	72.3
40～44	1 418	966	68.1	701	437	62.3	717	529	73.8
45～	95	69	72.6	47	31	66.0	48	38	79.2
不 詳 Not stated	-	-	・	-	-	・	-	-	・

注：1）　出生時の体重不詳を含んだ出生数に対する割合である。

Natality

〔嫡出子－嫡出でない子別にみた出生〕
〔Live births by legitimacy status〕

表4.29 嫡出子－嫡出でない子別にみた年次別出生数及び百分率
Table 4.29 Trends in live births and percent distribution by legitimacy status：Japan

年　　　次 Year		出　生　数 Live births			百　分　率 Percent distribution		
		総　数 Total	嫡　出　子 Born in wedlock	嫡出でない子 Born out of wedlock	総　数 Total	嫡　出　子 Born in wedlock	嫡出でない子 Born out of wedlock
1947	昭和22年	2 678 792	2 577 212	101 580	100.0	96.2	3.8
50	25	2 337 507	2 279 718	57 789	100.0	97.5	2.5
55	30	1 730 692	1 701 674	29 018	100.0	98.3	1.7
60	35	1 606 041	1 586 429	19 612	100.0	98.8	1.2
65	40	1 823 697	1 806 245	17 452	100.0	99.0	1.0
70	45	1 934 239	1 916 257	17 982	100.0	99.1	0.9
75	50	1 901 440	1 886 174	15 266	100.0	99.2	0.8
80	55	1 576 889	1 564 341	12 548	100.0	99.2	0.8
85	60	1 431 577	1 417 409	14 168	100.0	99.0	1.0
90	平成2年	1 221 585	1 208 546	13 039	100.0	98.9	1.1
95	7	1 187 064	1 172 346	14 718	100.0	98.8	1.2
2000	12	1 190 547	1 171 111	19 436	100.0	98.4	1.6
01	13	1 170 662	1 150 293	20 369	100.0	98.3	1.7
02	14	1 153 855	1 132 224	21 631	100.0	98.1	1.9
03	15	1 123 610	1 101 976	21 634	100.0	98.1	1.9
04	16	1 110 721	1 088 565	22 156	100.0	98.0	2.0
05	17	1 062 530	1 040 997	21 533	100.0	98.0	2.0
06	18	1 092 674	1 069 649	23 025	100.0	97.9	2.1
07	19	1 089 818	1 067 648	22 170	100.0	98.0	2.0
08	20	1 091 156	1 068 184	22 972	100.0	97.9	2.1
09	21	1 070 035	1 047 175	22 860	100.0	97.9	2.1
10	22	1 071 304	1 048 318	22 986	100.0	97.9	2.1
11	23	1 050 806	1 027 452	23 354	100.0	97.8	2.2
12	24	1 037 231	1 014 093	23 138	100.0	97.8	2.2
13	25	1 029 816	1 007 026	22 790	100.0	97.8	2.2
14	26	1 003 539	980 688	22 851	100.0	97.7	2.3
15	27	1 005 677	982 645	23 032	100.0	97.7	2.3
16	**28**	**976 978**	**954 576**	**22 402**	**100.0**	**97.7**	**2.3**

表4.30 性・年次別にみた嫡出でない子の出生数及び割合[1]
Table 4.30 Trends in live births born out of wedlock and proportion by sex：Japan

年　　　次 Year		総　数 Total		男 Male		女 Female	
		実　数 Number	出生数に対する割合(%) Proportion to live births	実　数 Number	出生数に対する割合(%) Proportion to live births	実　数 Number	出生数に対する割合(%) Proportion to live births
1947	昭和22年	101 580	3.8	51 803	3.8	49 777	3.8
50	25	57 789	2.5	29 369	2.4	28 420	2.5
55	30	29 018	1.7	14 755	1.7	14 263	1.7
60	35	19 612	1.2	9 916	1.2	9 696	1.2
65	40	17 452	1.0	8 927	1.0	8 525	1.0
70	45	17 982	0.9	9 061	0.9	8 921	1.0
75	50	15 266	0.8	7 839	0.8	7 427	0.8
80	55	12 548	0.8	6 433	0.8	6 115	0.8
85	60	14 168	1.0	7 272	1.0	6 896	1.0
90	平成2年	13 039	1.1	6 718	1.1	6 321	1.1
95	7	14 718	1.2	7 416	1.2	7 302	1.3
2000	12	19 436	1.6	9 878	1.6	9 558	1.7
01	13	20 369	1.7	10 362	1.7	10 007	1.8
02	14	21 631	1.9	11 017	1.9	10 614	1.9
03	15	21 634	1.9	11 082	1.9	10 552	1.9
04	16	22 156	2.0	11 380	2.0	10 776	2.0
05	17	21 533	2.0	10 969	2.0	10 564	2.0
06	18	23 025	2.1	11 792	2.1	11 233	2.1
07	19	22 170	2.0	11 369	2.0	10 801	2.0
08	20	22 972	2.1	11 890	2.1	11 082	2.1
09	21	22 860	2.1	11 708	2.1	11 152	2.1
10	22	22 986	2.1	11 787	2.1	11 199	2.2
11	23	23 354	2.2	12 053	2.2	11 301	2.2
12	24	23 138	2.2	11 890	2.2	11 248	2.2
13	25	22 790	2.2	11 720	2.2	11 070	2.2
14	26	22 851	2.3	11 700	2.3	11 151	2.3
15	27	23 032	2.3	11 741	2.3	11 291	2.3
16	**28**	**22 402**	**2.3**	**11 432**	**2.3**	**10 970**	**2.3**

注：1) 出生数の総数・男・女に対する割合である。

出　生

表4.31　母の年齢・年次別にみた嫡出でない子の出生数及び割合[1]
Table 4.31 Trends in live births born out of wedlock and proportion by age of mother：Japan

年　　次 Year		総　数 Total	～19歳 Years	20～24	25～29	30～34	35～39	40～	不　詳 Not stated
		実　　数　　Number							
1947	昭和22年	101 580	7 934	31 677	27 069	18 319	11 527	4 530	524
50	25	57 789	5 079	16 208	15 618	11 432	7 090	2 302	60
55	30	29 018	1 723	7 465	8 524	6 407	3 755	1 141	3
60	35	19 612	1 167	4 821	6 353	4 239	2 391	639	2
65	40	17 452	946	4 555	5 513	3 986	1 948	502	2
70	45	17 982	999	4 849	5 737	3 914	2 013	457	13
75	50	15 266	834	3 273	5 220	3 719	1 758	458	4
80	55	12 548	1 103	2 449	3 340	3 500	1 735	411	10
85	60	14 168	1 604	2 803	3 178	3 252	2 635	658	38
90	平成2年	13 039	1 635	2 800	3 128	2 699	2 034	721	22
95	7	14 718	1 815	3 316	3 804	3 216	1 915	641	11
2000	12	19 436	3 041	3 943	4 804	4 253	2 611	767	17
01	13	20 369	3 372	3 952	4 825	4 605	2 843	758	14
02	14	21 631	3 649	4 222	5 023	4 955	2 936	831	15
03	15	21 634	3 430	4 260	4 854	5 081	3 099	897	13
04	16	22 156	3 458	4 401	4 665	5 289	3 356	977	10
05	17	21 533	3 094	4 558	4 467	5 084	3 349	975	6
06	18	23 025	3 296	4 991	4 689	5 134	3 807	1 100	8
07	19	22 170	3 082	4 794	4 513	4 806	3 797	1 172	6
08	20	22 972	3 370	5 094	4 648	4 876	3 820	1 156	8
09	21	22 860	3 533	4 986	4 731	4 553	3 826	1 227	4
10	22	22 986	3 534	5 099	4 792	4 323	3 908	1 325	5
11	23	23 354	3 687	5 193	4 824	4 398	3 882	1 367	3
12	24	23 138	3 821	5 193	4 689	4 234	3 708	1 488	5
13	25	22 790	3 918	5 222	4 426	4 194	3 560	1 469	1
14	26	22 851	3 995	5 169	4 361	4 173	3 668	1 484	1
15	27	23 032	3 714	5 330	4 434	4 356	3 587	1 609	2
16	**28**	**22 402**	**3 334**	**5 236**	**4 239**	**4 300**	**3 706**	**1 585**	**2**
		出生数に対する割合（％）　Proportion to live births							
1947	昭和22年	3.8	13.0	5.1	3.3	2.8	2.9	3.5	・
50	25	2.5	9.0	2.6	2.0	2.3	2.5	2.7	・
55	30	1.7	6.8	1.6	1.2	1.7	2.7	3.3	・
60	35	1.2	5.9	1.1	0.9	1.4	3.1	4.2	・
65	40	1.0	5.3	0.9	0.6	1.1	2.7	4.9	・
70	45	0.9	5.0	0.9	0.6	1.1	2.5	4.4	・
75	50	0.8	5.2	0.7	0.5	1.2	2.8	5.1	・
80	55	0.8	7.6	0.8	0.4	0.9	2.9	5.7	・
85	60	1.0	9.0	1.1	0.5	0.9	2.8	7.8	・
90	平成2年	1.1	9.3	1.5	0.6	0.8	2.2	5.6	・
95	7	1.2	11.3	1.7	0.8	0.9	1.9	5.0	・
2000	12	1.6	15.4	2.4	1.0	1.1	2.1	5.0	・
01	13	1.7	16.1	2.5	1.1	1.2	2.2	4.9	・
02	14	1.9	17.1	2.8	1.2	1.2	2.2	5.0	・
03	15	1.9	17.5	3.0	1.2	1.2	2.2	5.0	・
04	16	2.0	18.6	3.2	1.3	1.3	2.2	5.1	・
05	17	2.0	18.7	3.6	1.3	1.3	2.2	4.8	・
06	18	2.1	20.6	3.8	1.4	1.2	2.2	5.0	・
07	19	2.0	20.2	3.8	1.4	1.2	2.0	4.7	・
08	20	2.1	21.8	4.1	1.5	1.2	1.9	4.1	・
09	21	2.1	24.1	4.3	1.5	1.2	1.8	3.9	・
10	22	2.1	26.1	4.6	1.6	1.1	1.8	3.7	・
11	23	2.2	27.7	5.0	1.6	1.2	1.8	3.6	・
12	24	2.2	29.9	5.4	1.6	1.2	1.6	3.5	・
13	25	2.2	30.2	5.7	1.6	1.1	1.5	3.1	・
14	26	2.3	30.7	6.0	1.6	1.2	1.6	2.9	・
15	27	2.3	31.1	6.3	1.7	1.2	1.6	3.0	・
16	**28**	**2.3**	**30.0**	**6.4**	**1.7**	**1.2**	**1.7**	**2.9**	**・**

注：1）　母の各年齢階級別出生数に対する割合である。

出　生

〔父母の国籍別にみた出生〕
〔Live births by nationality of father and mother〕

表 4.32　父母の国籍別にみた[1]
Table 4.32　Trends in live births and percent distribution

年　次 Year		総　数 Total	父母とも日本[2] Japanese parents	父母の一方が外国 One parent is foreigner	父日本・母外国 Japanese father and foreign mother	母日本・父外国 Japanese mother and foreign father	父　日　本・母　外　国 Japanese father and foreign mother 総　数 Total	韓国・朝鮮 Korea	中　国 China	フィリピン Philippines	タ　イ Thailand	米　国 U.S.A.	英　国 United Kingdom
						実			数				
1987	昭和62年	1 346 658	1 336 636	10 022	5 538	4 484	5 538	2 850	803	…	…	188	…
90	平成2年	1 221 585	1 207 899	13 686	8 695	4 991	8 695	3 184	1 264	…	…	161	…
95	7	1 187 064	1 166 810	20 254	13 371	6 883	13 371	3 519	2 244	5 488	851	178	55
96	8	1 206 555	1 185 491	21 064	13 752	7 312	13 752	3 550	2 376	5 551	827	202	87
97	9	1 191 665	1 170 140	21 525	13 580	7 945	13 580	3 440	2 667	5 203	859	165	56
98	10	1 203 147	1 181 126	22 021	13 635	8 386	13 635	3 389	2 734	5 137	852	165	73
99	11	1 177 669	1 156 205	21 464	13 004	8 460	13 004	3 208	2 850	4 645	836	150	59
2000	12	1 190 547	1 168 210	22 337	13 396	8 941	13 396	3 345	3 040	4 705	736	142	51
01	13	1 170 662	1 148 486	22 176	13 177	8 999	13 177	3 204	3 056	4 586	742	142	55
02	14	1 153 855	1 131 604	22 251	13 294	8 957	13 294	3 141	3 338	4 539	670	132	62
03	15	1 123 610	1 102 088	21 522	12 690	8 832	12 690	2 911	3 133	4 309	638	146	66
04	16	1 110 721	1 088 548	22 173	13 198	8 975	13 198	2 749	3 510	4 558	579	131	50
05	17	1 062 530	1 040 657	21 873	12 872	9 001	12 872	2 583	3 478	4 441	509	122	47
06	18	1 092 674	1 069 211	23 463	14 040	9 423	14 040	2 593	3 925	4 998	512	130	51
07	19	1 089 818	1 065 641	24 177	14 474	9 703	14 474	2 530	4 271	5 140	507	141	53
08	20	1 091 156	1 067 200	23 956	13 782	10 174	13 782	2 439	4 203	4 623	446	124	62
09	21	1 070 035	1 047 524	22 511	12 707	9 804	12 707	2 285	4 209	3 815	427	116	45
2010	22	1 071 304	1 049 338	21 966	11 990	9 976	11 990	2 129	4 109	3 364	380	135	46
11	23	1 050 806	1 030 495	20 311	10 922	9 389	10 922	2 005	3 796	2 820	394	104	46
12	24	1 037 231	1 016 695	20 536	10 825	9 711	10 825	2 057	4 041	2 474	325	148	46
13	25	1 029 816	1 010 284	19 532	10 019	9 513	10 019	1 850	3 872	2 138	346	130	40
14	26	1 003 539	983 892	19 647	9 845	9 802	9 845	1 819	3 932	1 861	349	133	44
15	27	1 005 677	986 598	19 079	9 459	9 620	9 459	1 823	3 477	1 773	389	146	41
16	**28**	**976 978**	**957 860**	**19 118**	**9 371**	**9 747**	**9 371**	**1 686**	**3 671**	**1 734**	**318**	**132**	**41**
						百		分		率			
1987	昭和62年	100.0	99.3	0.7	0.4	0.3	100.0	51.5	14.5	…	…	3.4	…
90	平成2年	100.0	98.9	1.1	0.7	0.4	100.0	36.6	14.5	…	…	1.9	…
95	7	100.0	98.3	1.7	1.1	0.6	100.0	26.3	16.8	41.0	6.4	1.3	0.4
96	8	100.0	98.3	1.7	1.1	0.6	100.0	25.8	17.3	40.4	6.0	1.5	0.6
97	9	100.0	98.2	1.8	1.1	0.7	100.0	25.3	19.6	38.3	6.3	1.2	0.4
98	10	100.0	98.2	1.8	1.1	0.7	100.0	24.9	20.1	37.7	6.2	1.2	0.5
99	11	100.0	98.2	1.8	1.1	0.7	100.0	24.7	21.9	35.7	6.4	1.2	0.5
2000	12	100.0	98.1	1.9	1.1	0.8	100.0	25.0	22.7	35.1	5.5	1.1	0.4
01	13	100.0	98.1	1.9	1.1	0.8	100.0	24.3	23.2	34.8	5.6	1.1	0.4
02	14	100.0	98.1	1.9	1.2	0.8	100.0	23.6	25.1	34.1	5.0	1.0	0.5
03	15	100.0	98.1	1.9	1.1	0.8	100.0	22.9	24.7	34.0	5.0	1.2	0.5
04	16	100.0	98.0	2.0	1.2	0.8	100.0	20.8	26.6	34.5	4.4	1.0	0.4
05	17	100.0	97.9	2.1	1.2	0.8	100.0	20.1	27.0	34.5	4.0	0.9	0.4
06	18	100.0	97.9	2.1	1.3	0.9	100.0	18.5	28.0	35.6	3.6	0.9	0.4
07	19	100.0	97.8	2.2	1.3	0.9	100.0	17.5	29.5	35.5	3.5	1.0	0.4
08	20	100.0	97.8	2.2	1.3	0.9	100.0	17.7	30.5	33.5	3.2	0.9	0.4
09	21	100.0	97.9	2.1	1.2	0.9	100.0	18.0	33.1	30.0	3.4	0.9	0.4
2010	22	100.0	97.9	2.1	1.1	0.9	100.0	17.8	34.3	28.1	3.2	1.1	0.4
11	23	100.0	98.1	1.9	1.0	0.9	100.0	18.4	34.8	25.8	3.6	1.0	0.4
12	24	100.0	98.0	2.0	1.0	0.9	100.0	19.0	37.3	22.9	3.0	1.4	0.4
13	25	100.0	98.1	1.9	1.0	0.9	100.0	18.5	38.6	21.3	3.5	1.3	0.4
14	26	100.0	98.0	2.0	1.0	1.0	100.0	18.5	39.9	18.9	3.5	1.4	0.4
15	27	100.0	98.1	1.9	0.9	1.0	100.0	19.3	36.8	18.7	4.1	1.5	0.4
16	**28**	**100.0**	**98.0**	**2.0**	**1.0**	**1.0**	**100.0**	**18.0**	**39.2**	**18.5**	**3.4**	**1.4**	**0.4**

注：1）　フィリピン・タイ・英国・ブラジル・ペルーについては平成4年から調査しており、平成3年までは「その他の国」に含まれる。
　　2）　「父母とも日本」の出生数には、母の国籍が日本の嫡出でない子を含む。

年次別出生数及び百分率
by nationality of father and mother : Japan

ブラジル Brazil	ペルー Peru	その他の国 Other foreign countries	母日本・父外国 Japanese mother and foreign father										年次 Year	
			総数 Total	韓国・朝鮮 Korea	中国 China	フィリピン Philippines	タイ Thailand	米国 U.S.A.	英国 United Kingdom	ブラジル Brazil	ペルー Peru	その他の国 Other foreign countries		
Number														
...	...	1 697	4 484	3 039	287	...	...	641	...	...	...	517	1987	昭和62年
...	...	4 086	4 991	3 048	375	...	...	829	...	...	...	739	90	平成2年
406	105	525	6 883	3 281	716	83	22	1 171	183	130	76	1 221	95	7
439	109	611	7 312	3 418	678	88	34	1 212	204	165	64	1 449	96	8
430	111	649	7 945	3 469	772	100	52	1 353	212	207	84	1 696	97	9
429	106	750	8 386	3 529	822	126	58	1 356	204	250	93	1 948	98	10
358	116	782	8 460	3 479	769	138	49	1 361	245	241	140	2 038	99	11
397	85	895	8 941	3 427	913	151	77	1 380	256	305	135	2 297	2000	12
339	112	941	8 999	3 437	820	138	65	1 402	296	294	145	2 402	01	13
309	109	994	8 957	3 177	861	143	82	1 451	273	297	145	2 528	02	14
289	96	1 102	8 832	2 965	833	130	72	1 480	318	305	137	2 592	03	15
290	105	1 226	8 975	2 791	873	143	77	1 559	307	362	160	2 703	04	16
217	92	1 383	9 001	2 604	952	131	89	1 547	340	345	157	2 836	05	17
256	99	1 476	9 423	2 680	949	145	75	1 635	362	334	141	3 102	06	18
268	98	1 466	9 703	2 679	1 140	155	105	1 633	351	389	141	3 110	07	19
249	84	1 552	10 174	2 554	1 221	166	91	1 779	458	402	158	3 345	08	20
235	93	1 482	9 804	2 543	1 120	168	82	1 640	420	374	128	3 329	09	21
230	103	1 494	9 976	2 502	1 225	180	98	1 754	441	362	145	3 269	2010	22
268	101	1 388	9 389	2 391	1 128	161	83	1 598	424	418	131	3 055	11	23
229	103	1 402	9 711	2 467	1 316	169	80	1 618	473	391	146	3 051	12	24
245	107	1 291	9 513	2 384	1 223	227	79	1 583	470	395	120	3 032	13	25
237	94	1 376	9 802	2 343	1 359	205	83	1 635	430	407	151	3 189	14	26
270	100	1 440	9 620	2 387	1 247	234	73	1 480	395	432	172	3 200	15	27
268	**93**	**1 428**	**9 747**	**2 250**	**1 428**	**253**	**76**	**1 558**	**427**	**447**	**143**	**3 165**	**16**	**28**
Percentage														
...	...	30.6	100.0	67.8	6.4	...	...	14.3	...	...	...	11.5	1987	昭和62年
...	...	47.0	100.0	61.1	7.5	...	...	16.6	...	...	...	14.8	90	平成2年
3.0	0.8	3.9	100.0	47.7	10.4	1.2	0.3	17.0	2.7	1.9	1.1	17.7	95	7
3.2	0.8	4.4	100.0	46.7	9.3	1.2	0.5	16.6	2.8	2.3	0.9	19.8	96	8
3.2	0.8	4.8	100.0	43.7	9.7	1.3	0.7	17.0	2.7	2.6	1.1	21.3	97	9
3.1	0.8	5.5	100.0	42.1	9.8	1.5	0.7	16.2	2.4	3.0	1.1	23.2	98	10
2.8	0.9	6.0	100.0	41.1	9.1	1.6	0.6	16.1	2.9	2.8	1.7	24.1	99	11
3.0	0.6	6.7	100.0	38.3	10.2	1.7	0.9	15.4	2.9	3.4	1.5	25.7	2000	12
2.6	0.8	7.1	100.0	38.2	9.1	1.5	0.7	15.6	3.3	3.3	1.6	26.7	01	13
2.3	0.8	7.5	100.0	35.5	9.6	1.6	0.9	16.2	3.0	3.3	1.6	28.2	02	14
2.3	0.8	8.7	100.0	33.6	9.4	1.5	0.8	16.8	3.6	3.5	1.6	29.3	03	15
2.2	0.8	9.3	100.0	31.1	9.7	1.6	0.9	17.4	3.4	4.0	1.8	30.1	04	16
1.7	0.7	10.7	100.0	28.9	10.6	1.5	1.0	17.2	3.8	3.8	1.7	31.5	05	17
1.8	0.7	10.5	100.0	28.4	10.1	1.5	0.8	17.4	3.8	3.5	1.5	32.9	06	18
1.9	0.7	10.1	100.0	27.6	11.7	1.6	1.1	16.8	3.6	4.0	1.5	32.1	07	19
1.8	0.6	11.3	100.0	25.1	12.0	1.6	0.9	17.5	4.5	4.0	1.6	32.9	08	20
1.8	0.7	11.7	100.0	25.9	11.4	1.7	0.8	16.7	4.3	3.8	1.3	34.0	09	21
1.9	0.9	12.5	100.0	25.1	12.3	1.8	1.0	17.6	4.4	3.6	1.5	32.8	2010	22
2.5	0.9	12.7	100.0	25.5	12.0	1.7	0.9	17.0	4.5	4.5	1.4	32.5	11	23
2.1	1.0	13.0	100.0	25.4	13.6	1.7	0.8	16.7	4.9	4.0	1.5	31.4	12	24
2.4	1.1	12.9	100.0	25.1	12.9	2.4	0.8	16.6	4.9	4.2	1.3	31.9	13	25
2.4	1.0	14.0	100.0	23.9	13.9	2.1	0.8	16.7	4.4	4.2	1.5	32.5	14	26
2.9	1.1	15.2	100.0	24.8	13.0	2.4	0.8	15.4	4.1	4.5	1.8	33.3	15	27
2.9	**1.0**	**15.2**	**100.0**	**23.1**	**14.7**	**2.6**	**0.8**	**16.0**	**4.4**	**4.6**	**1.5**	**32.5**	**16**	**28**

出　生

表4.33　父母の国籍別にみた
Table 4.33　Live births by nationality of father and mother

都道府県 Prefecture	総数 Total	父母とも日本 1) Japanese parents	父母の一方が外国 One parent is foreigner	父日本・母外国 Japanese father and foreign mother							
				総数 Total	韓国・朝鮮 Korea	中国 China	フィリピン Philippines	タイ Thailand	米国 U.S.A.	英国 United Kingdom	ブラジル Brazil
全国　Total a)	976 978	957 860	19 118	9 371	1 686	3 671	1 734	318	132	41	268
01 北海道	35 125	34 835	290	105	18	39	11	7	4	1	-
02 青森	8 626	8 569	57	15	2	3	5	1	1	-	-
03 岩手	8 341	8 293	48	31	3	10	7	3	-	-	-
04 宮城	17 347	17 188	159	82	16	39	9	1	2	-	-
05 秋田	5 666	5 637	29	15	3	7	3	-	-	-	1
06 山形	7 547	7 489	58	31	3	17	6	-	-	-	-
07 福島	13 744	13 630	114	73	5	26	25	1	-	-	-
08 茨城	20 878	20 539	339	173	21	54	35	25	2	-	12
09 栃木	14 621	14 393	228	121	6	44	32	9	-	-	17
10 群馬	13 661	13 408	253	143	3	38	57	1	1	-	12
11 埼玉	54 447	53 141	1 306	709	67	348	132	22	5	2	18
12 千葉	45 387	44 263	1 124	574	66	259	120	25	5	1	8
13 東京	111 962	108 155	3 807	1 700	311	775	216	49	42	14	17
14 神奈川	70 648	68 700	1 948	952	116	415	147	28	16	3	26
15 新潟	15 736	15 594	142	72	3	28	23	5	1	-	1
16 富山	7 302	7 177	125	81	7	40	19	2	-	-	4
17 石川	8 927	8 820	107	56	6	28	6	3	2	1	-
18 福井	6 112	6 030	82	53	9	18	13	4	-	-	4
19 山梨	5 819	5 735	84	49	5	18	14	1	1	-	4
20 長野	15 169	14 916	253	153	6	67	33	19	4	-	8
21 岐阜	14 831	14 578	253	145	11	41	72	2	-	-	6
22 静岡	27 652	27 155	497	279	20	82	78	13	4	1	28
23 愛知	64 226	62 635	1 591	904	125	289	284	23	7	1	57
24 三重	13 202	12 979	223	121	13	43	23	7	1	-	12
25 滋賀	12 072	11 903	169	103	15	36	17	3	1	-	9
26 京都	19 327	18 829	498	221	68	78	9	1	4	2	3
27 大阪	68 816	67 000	1 816	848	358	301	53	22	8	1	7
28 兵庫	43 378	42 491	887	434	168	130	41	9	4	1	2
29 奈良	9 430	9 293	137	74	26	31	9	2	1	-	1
30 和歌山	6 658	6 576	82	40	10	12	6	2	1	2	1
31 鳥取	4 436	4 397	39	20	4	6	6	1	-	1	-
32 島根	5 300	5 251	49	27	1	7	11	-	-	1	-
33 岡山	15 477	15 298	179	95	25	33	19	1	1	-	-
34 広島	22 736	22 412	324	177	32	58	35	2	-	1	8
35 山口	9 844	9 730	114	42	14	11	11	-	2	1	-
36 徳島	5 346	5 304	42	24	-	11	11	1	-	1	-
37 香川	7 510	7 419	91	52	8	21	11	1	2	-	1
38 愛媛	9 911	9 831	80	29	6	11	5	1	-	-	1
39 高知	4 779	4 745	34	14	4	3	5	-	-	-	2
40 福岡	44 033	43 496	537	244	67	93	42	6	1	3	2
41 佐賀	6 811	6 758	53	27	1	10	3	7	-	-	-
42 長崎	10 886	10 770	116	36	4	18	7	-	2	-	-
43 熊本	14 894	14 776	118	65	4	23	24	2	2	1	-
44 大分	9 059	8 988	71	34	8	14	8	-	2	-	-
45 宮崎	8 929	8 874	55	20	2	6	6	2	2	-	-
46 鹿児島	13 688	13 600	88	46	4	13	10	3	1	1	-
47 沖縄	16 617	16 203	414	60	12	16	15	1	1	1	1
外国 Foreign countries	65	57	8	2	-	1	-	-	1	-	-
21大都市（再掲）21 major cities(Regrouped)											
50 東京都の区部	80 213	77 170	3 043	1 337	264	619	158	41	30	12	13
51 札幌	14 021	13 868	153	56	14	19	3	3	3	-	-
52 仙台	8 904	8 809	95	42	9	20	4	1	1	-	-
53 さいたま	10 549	10 337	212	118	17	66	8	4	2	-	3
54 千葉	6 927	6 745	182	86	13	42	16	3	-	-	2
55 横浜	28 889	28 075	814	392	53	206	36	14	8	2	12
56 川崎	14 158	13 769	389	212	34	98	37	4	6	-	3
57 相模原	5 196	5 075	121	67	5	20	11	2	1	-	1
58 新潟	5 936	5 881	55	19	1	10	1	4	1	-	-
59 静岡	5 106	5 026	80	44	8	14	4	2	1	1	5
60 浜松	6 558	6 432	126	72	5	26	20	3	2	-	8
61 名古屋	19 542	18 964	578	312	69	115	82	7	4	1	2
62 京都	10 921	10 541	380	170	52	55	6	1	4	2	3
63 大阪	22 099	21 225	874	403	209	125	23	9	4	-	2
64 堺	6 844	6 709	135	66	16	34	6	2	2	-	-
65 神戸	11 786	11 438	348	165	68	46	11	2	3	-	-
66 岡山	6 264	6 181	83	41	9	18	6	-	-	-	-
67 広島	10 559	10 414	145	81	18	28	22	-	-	1	3
68 北九州	7 621	7 541	80	42	20	10	3	2	-	1	1
69 福岡	14 488	14 218	270	114	28	55	12	1	1	2	1
70 熊本	6 797	6 741	56	29	2	10	8	2	1	1	-

注：1)「父母とも日本」の出生数には、母の国籍が日本の嫡出でない子を含む。

Natality

都道府県（21大都市再掲）別出生数
: Japan, each prefecture and 21 major cities, 2016

平成28年

ペルー Peru	その他の国 Other foreign countries	母 日本・父 外国 Japanese mother and foreign father										都道府県 Prefecture
		総数 Total	韓国・朝鮮 Korea	中国 China	フィリピン Philippines	タイ Thailand	米国 U.S.A.	英国 United Kingdom	ブラジル Brazil	ペルー Peru	その他の国 Other foreign countries	
93	1 428	9 747	2 250	1 428	253	76	1 558	427	447	143	3 165	全国 Total a)
1	24	185	41	26	2	1	27	7	2	1	78	01 北海道
-	3	42	2	2	1	-	32	-	-	-	5	02 青森
-	8	17	5	4	1	-	3	-	-	-	4	03 岩手
-	15	77	16	13	2	-	15	4	-	-	27	04 宮城
-	1	14	5	1	-	-	2	-	-	-	6	05 秋田
-	5	27	2	6	-	-	4	1	1	-	13	06 山形
-	16	41	6	6	2	1	7	3	1	1	14	07 福島
5	19	166	21	21	8	12	14	4	14	2	70	08 茨城
4	9	107	17	16	5	-	16	6	12	8	27	09 栃木
6	25	110	12	18	9	1	8	3	18	5	36	10 群馬
8	107	597	116	127	22	5	47	23	26	9	222	11 埼玉
3	87	550	99	120	26	4	61	25	22	10	183	12 千葉
5	271	2 107	430	321	41	5	335	120	21	11	823	13 東京
18	183	996	150	130	27	11	228	45	41	13	351	14 神奈川
-	11	70	19	11	7	1	9	3	2	-	18	15 新潟
-	9	44	5	6	1	1	1	-	6	-	24	16 富山
-	10	51	13	9	1	-	4	2	4	-	18	17 石川
-	5	29	9	4	2	-	-	1	5	1	7	18 福井
-	6	35	5	8	1	-	5	4	2	-	10	19 山梨
1	15	100	12	22	1	2	15	9	12	-	27	20 長野
1	12	108	27	13	6	1	8	7	16	4	26	21 岐阜
9	44	218	30	28	8	4	28	7	47	16	50	22 静岡
16	102	687	180	72	21	3	59	23	98	21	210	23 愛知
4	18	102	22	11	2	-	6	2	22	7	30	24 三重
2	20	66	15	4	-	-	6	4	11	3	23	25 滋賀
-	56	277	75	35	1	1	30	13	3	2	117	26 京都
2	96	968	431	157	14	10	73	32	19	4	228	27 大阪
6	73	453	183	60	5	2	45	16	10	3	129	28 兵庫
-	6	63	16	8	2	1	5	2	2	2	25	29 奈良
-	6	42	10	5	-	1	8	3	2	1	12	30 和歌山
-	2	19	11	-	1	-	2	-	1	-	4	31 鳥取
1	6	22	13	1	-	-	3	1	-	-	4	32 島根
1	16	84	26	9	2	1	6	4	6	3	27	33 岡山
1	40	147	30	27	7	2	14	6	13	5	43	34 広島
-	3	72	18	10	3	1	24	2	1	1	12	35 山口
-	1	18	5	1	1	-	5	1	-	-	5	36 徳島
-	9	39	7	8	2	-	5	2	1	3	11	37 香川
-	5	51	11	3	3	1	8	-	2	1	22	38 愛媛
-	2	20	2	1	1	1	5	1	-	-	9	39 高知
-	30	293	88	46	5	-	39	19	1	1	94	40 福岡
-	6	26	6	5	-	1	4	2	-	-	8	41 佐賀
-	5	80	9	11	-	1	41	3	-	-	15	42 長崎
-	9	53	13	7	1	-	12	7	-	-	13	43 熊本
-	3	37	7	8	1	-	8	-	1	-	12	44 大分
-	2	35	4	4	2	1	5	2	-	-	17	45 宮崎
-	14	42	8	5	1	-	7	3	-	1	17	46 鹿児島
-	13	354	18	18	5	-	264	4	2	4	39	47 沖縄
-	-	6	-	-	-	-	5	1	-	-	-	外国 Foreign countries
												21大都市（再掲） 21 major cities (Regrouped)
3	197	1 706	362	268	27	4	254	101	15	8	667	50 東京都の区部
1	13	97	22	17	1	1	15	3	1	-	37	51 札幌
-	7	53	11	7	1	-	10	3	-	-	21	52 仙台
2	16	94	22	26	-	-	8	7	2	1	28	53 さいたま
1	9	96	15	27	4	-	11	4	7	2	26	54 千葉
5	56	422	63	84	8	6	57	22	24	3	155	55 横浜
-	30	177	39	26	5	1	23	9	2	1	72	56 川崎
1	26	54	10	3	-	1	5	1	3	1	28	57 相模原
-	2	36	11	9	-	1	5	1	1	-	8	58 新潟
-	9	36	8	6	1	-	5	1	3	-	12	59 静岡
2	12	54	11	1	3	1	2	-	21	6	9	60 浜松
3	23	266	79	39	4	1	29	10	16	5	83	61 名古屋
-	47	210	54	28	1	-	20	10	3	1	93	62 京都
-	31	471	230	78	7	1	28	17	10	2	98	63 大阪
1	5	69	26	17	-	-	5	3	1	-	17	64 堺
2	33	183	68	28	2	1	18	11	3	1	51	65 神戸
-	8	42	13	5	2	1	3	2	2	2	14	66 岡山
-	9	64	18	12	2	1	10	4	5	2	10	67 広島
-	5	38	21	3	-	-	3	1	1	-	9	68 北九州
-	15	156	40	32	3	-	23	12	-	1	45	69 福岡
-	5	27	6	4	1	-	7	2	-	-	7	70 熊本

Note：a) See page 44.

出　生

表4.34　父母の国籍別にみた
Table 4.34　Percent distribution of live births by nationality

都道府県 Prefecture	総数 Total	父母とも日本 1) Japanese parents	父母の一方が外国 One parent is foreigner	父日本・母外国 Japanese father and foreign mother	母日本・父外国 Japanese mother and foreign father	父日本・母外国 Japanese father and foreign mother							
						総数 Total	韓国・朝鮮 Korea	中国 China	フィリピン Philippines	タイ Thailand	米国 U.S.A.	英国 United Kingdom	ブラジル Brazil
全国　Total	100.0	98.0	2.0	1.0	1.0	100.0	18.0	39.2	18.5	3.4	1.4	0.4	2.9
a)													
01 北海道	100.0	99.2	0.8	0.3	0.5	100.0	17.1	37.1	10.5	6.7	3.8	1.0	-
02 青森	100.0	99.3	0.7	0.2	0.5	100.0	13.3	20.0	33.3	6.7	6.7	-	-
03 岩手	100.0	99.4	0.6	0.4	0.2	100.0	9.7	32.3	22.6	9.7	-	-	-
04 宮城	100.0	99.1	0.9	0.5	0.4	100.0	19.5	47.6	11.0	1.2	2.4	-	-
05 秋田	100.0	99.5	0.5	0.3	0.2	100.0	20.0	46.7	20.0	-	-	6.7	-
06 山形	100.0	99.2	0.8	0.4	0.4	100.0	9.7	54.8	19.4	-	-	-	-
07 福島	100.0	99.2	0.8	0.5	0.3	100.0	6.8	35.6	34.2	1.4	-	-	-
08 茨城	100.0	98.4	1.6	0.8	0.8	100.0	12.1	31.2	20.2	14.5	1.2	-	6.9
09 栃木	100.0	98.4	1.6	0.8	0.7	100.0	5.0	36.4	26.4	7.4	0.7	-	14.0
10 群馬	100.0	98.1	1.9	1.0	0.8	100.0	2.1	26.6	39.9	0.7	0.7	-	8.4
11 埼玉	100.0	97.6	2.4	1.3	1.1	100.0	9.4	49.1	18.6	3.1	0.7	0.3	2.5
12 千葉	100.0	97.5	2.5	1.3	1.2	100.0	11.5	45.1	20.9	4.4	0.9	0.2	1.4
13 東京	100.0	96.6	3.4	1.5	1.9	100.0	18.3	45.6	12.7	2.9	2.5	0.8	1.0
14 神奈川	100.0	97.2	2.8	1.3	1.4	100.0	12.2	43.6	15.4	2.9	1.7	0.3	2.7
15 新潟	100.0	99.1	0.9	0.5	0.4	100.0	4.2	38.9	31.9	6.9	1.4	-	1.4
16 富山	100.0	98.3	1.7	1.1	0.6	100.0	8.6	49.4	23.5	2.5	-	-	4.9
17 石川	100.0	98.8	1.2	0.6	0.6	100.0	10.7	50.0	10.7	5.4	3.6	1.8	-
18 福井	100.0	98.7	1.3	0.9	0.5	100.0	17.0	34.0	24.5	7.5	-	-	7.5
19 山梨	100.0	98.6	1.4	0.8	0.6	100.0	10.2	36.7	28.6	2.0	2.0	-	8.2
20 長野	100.0	98.3	1.7	1.0	0.7	100.0	3.9	43.8	21.6	12.4	2.6	-	5.2
21 岐阜	100.0	98.3	1.7	1.0	0.7	100.0	7.6	28.3	49.7	1.4	-	-	4.1
22 静岡	100.0	98.2	1.8	1.0	0.8	100.0	7.2	29.4	28.0	4.7	1.4	0.4	10.0
23 愛知	100.0	97.5	2.5	1.4	1.1	100.0	13.8	32.0	31.4	2.5	0.8	0.1	6.3
24 三重	100.0	98.3	1.7	0.9	0.8	100.0	10.7	35.5	19.0	5.8	0.8	-	9.9
25 滋賀	100.0	98.6	1.4	0.9	0.5	100.0	14.6	35.0	16.5	2.9	1.0	-	8.7
26 京都	100.0	97.4	2.6	1.1	1.4	100.0	30.8	35.3	4.1	0.5	1.8	0.9	1.4
27 大阪	100.0	97.4	2.6	1.2	1.4	100.0	42.2	35.5	6.3	2.6	0.9	0.1	0.8
28 兵庫	100.0	98.0	2.0	1.0	1.0	100.0	38.7	30.0	9.4	2.1	0.9	0.2	0.5
29 奈良	100.0	98.5	1.5	0.8	0.7	100.0	35.1	41.9	12.2	2.7	-	-	-
30 和歌山	100.0	98.8	1.2	0.6	0.6	100.0	25.0	30.0	15.0	5.0	2.5	5.0	2.5
31 鳥取	100.0	99.1	0.9	0.5	0.4	100.0	20.0	30.0	30.0	5.0	-	5.0	-
32 島根	100.0	99.1	0.9	0.5	0.4	100.0	3.7	25.9	40.7	-	-	3.7	-
33 岡山	100.0	98.8	1.2	0.6	0.5	100.0	26.3	34.7	20.0	1.1	1.1	-	-
34 広島	100.0	98.6	1.4	0.8	0.6	100.0	18.1	32.8	19.8	1.1	-	0.6	4.5
35 山口	100.0	98.8	1.2	0.4	0.7	100.0	33.3	26.2	26.2	-	4.8	2.4	-
36 徳島	100.0	99.2	0.8	0.4	0.3	100.0	-	45.8	45.8	4.2	-	-	-
37 香川	100.0	98.8	1.2	0.7	0.5	100.0	15.4	40.4	21.2	1.9	3.8	-	-
38 愛媛	100.0	99.2	0.8	0.3	0.5	100.0	20.7	37.9	17.2	3.4	-	-	3.4
39 高知	100.0	99.3	0.7	0.3	0.4	100.0	28.6	21.4	35.7	-	-	-	-
40 福岡	100.0	98.8	1.2	0.6	0.7	100.0	27.5	38.1	17.2	2.5	0.4	1.2	0.8
41 佐賀	100.0	99.2	0.8	0.4	0.4	100.0	3.7	37.0	11.1	25.9	-	-	-
42 長崎	100.0	98.9	1.1	0.3	0.7	100.0	11.1	50.0	19.4	-	5.6	-	-
43 熊本	100.0	99.2	0.8	0.4	0.4	100.0	6.2	35.4	36.9	3.1	3.1	1.5	-
44 大分	100.0	99.2	0.8	0.4	0.4	100.0	23.5	41.2	23.5	-	2.9	-	-
45 宮崎	100.0	99.4	0.6	0.2	0.4	100.0	10.0	30.0	30.0	10.0	10.0	-	-
46 鹿児島	100.0	99.4	0.6	0.3	0.3	100.0	8.7	28.3	21.7	6.5	2.2	2.2	-
47 沖縄	100.0	97.5	2.5	0.4	2.1	100.0	20.0	26.7	25.0	1.7	1.7	1.7	1.7
外国　Foreign countries	100.0	87.7	12.3	3.1	9.2	100.0	-	50.0	-	-	50.0	-	-
21大都市(再掲) 21 major cities(Regrouped)													
50 東京都の区部	100.0	96.2	3.8	1.7	2.1	100.0	19.7	46.3	11.8	3.1	2.2	0.9	1.0
51 札幌	100.0	98.9	1.1	0.4	0.7	100.0	25.0	33.9	5.4	5.4	5.4	-	-
52 仙台	100.0	98.9	1.1	0.5	0.6	100.0	21.4	47.6	9.5	2.4	2.4	-	-
53 さいたま	100.0	98.0	2.0	1.1	0.9	100.0	14.4	55.9	6.8	3.4	1.7	-	2.5
54 千葉	100.0	97.4	2.6	1.2	1.4	100.0	15.1	48.8	18.6	3.5	-	-	2.3
55 横浜	100.0	97.2	2.8	1.4	1.5	100.0	13.5	52.6	9.2	3.6	2.0	0.5	3.1
56 川崎	100.0	97.3	2.7	1.5	1.3	100.0	16.0	46.2	17.5	1.9	2.8	-	1.4
57 相模原	100.0	97.7	2.3	1.3	1.0	100.0	7.5	29.9	16.4	3.0	1.5	-	1.5
58 新潟	100.0	99.1	0.9	0.3	0.6	100.0	5.3	52.6	5.3	21.1	5.3	-	-
59 静岡	100.0	98.4	1.6	0.9	0.7	100.0	18.2	31.8	9.1	4.5	2.3	2.3	11.4
60 浜松	100.0	98.1	1.9	1.1	0.8	100.0	6.9	36.1	27.8	4.2	2.8	-	2.8
61 名古屋	100.0	97.0	3.0	1.6	1.4	100.0	22.1	36.9	26.3	2.2	1.3	0.3	2.6
62 京都	100.0	96.5	3.5	1.6	1.9	100.0	30.6	32.4	3.5	0.6	2.4	1.2	1.8
63 大阪	100.0	96.0	4.0	1.8	2.1	100.0	51.9	31.0	5.7	2.2	1.0	-	0.5
64 堺	100.0	98.0	2.0	1.0	1.0	100.0	24.2	51.5	9.1	3.0	3.0	-	-
65 神戸	100.0	97.0	3.0	1.4	1.6	100.0	41.2	27.9	6.7	1.2	1.8	-	-
66 岡山	100.0	98.7	1.3	0.7	0.7	100.0	22.0	43.9	14.6	-	-	-	-
67 広島	100.0	98.6	1.4	0.8	0.6	100.0	22.2	34.6	27.2	-	-	1.2	3.7
68 北九州	100.0	99.0	1.0	0.6	0.5	100.0	47.6	23.8	7.1	4.8	-	2.4	2.4
69 福岡	100.0	98.1	1.9	0.8	1.1	100.0	24.6	48.2	10.5	0.9	0.9	1.8	-
70 熊本	100.0	99.2	0.8	0.4	0.4	100.0	6.9	34.5	27.6	6.9	3.4	3.4	-

注：1)　「父母とも日本」の出生数には、母の国籍が日本の嫡出でない子を含む。

Natality

都道府県（21大都市再掲）別出生数百分率
of father and mother：Japan, each prefecture and 21 major cities, 2016

平成28年

ペルー Peru	その他の国 Other foreign countries	母日本・父外国 Japanese mother and foreign father 総数 Total	韓国・朝鮮 Korea	中国 China	フィリピン Philippines	タイ Thailand	米国 U.S.A.	英国 United Kingdom	ブラジル Brazil	ペルー Peru	その他の国 Other foreign countries	都道府県 Prefecture
1.0	15.2	100.0	23.1	14.7	2.6	0.8	16.0	4.4	4.6	1.5	32.5	全国 Total a)
1.0	22.9	100.0	22.2	14.1	1.1	0.5	14.6	3.8	1.1	0.5	42.2	01 北海道
-	20.0	100.0	4.8	4.8	2.4	-	76.2	-	-	-	11.9	02 青森
-	25.8	100.0	29.4	23.5	5.9	-	17.6	-	-	-	23.5	03 岩手
-	18.3	100.0	20.8	16.9	2.6	-	19.5	5.2	-	-	35.1	04 宮城
-	6.7	100.0	35.7	7.1	-	-	14.3	-	-	-	42.9	05 秋田
-	16.1	100.0	7.4	22.2	-	-	14.8	3.7	3.7	-	48.1	06 山形
-	21.9	100.0	14.6	14.6	4.9	2.4	17.1	7.3	2.4	2.4	34.1	07 福島
2.9	11.0	100.0	12.7	12.7	4.8	7.2	8.4	2.4	8.4	1.2	42.2	08 茨城
3.3	7.4	100.0	15.9	15.0	4.7	-	15.0	5.6	11.2	7.5	25.2	09 栃木
4.2	17.5	100.0	10.9	16.4	8.2	0.9	7.3	2.7	16.4	4.5	32.7	10 群馬
1.1	15.1	100.0	19.4	21.3	3.7	0.8	7.9	3.9	4.4	1.5	37.2	11 埼玉
0.5	15.2	100.0	18.0	21.8	4.7	0.7	11.1	4.5	4.0	1.8	33.3	12 千葉
0.3	15.9	100.0	20.4	15.2	1.9	0.2	15.9	5.7	1.0	0.5	39.1	13 東京
1.9	19.2	100.0	15.1	13.1	2.7	1.1	22.9	4.5	4.1	1.3	35.2	14 神奈川
-	15.3	100.0	27.1	15.7	10.0	1.4	12.9	4.3	2.9	-	25.7	15 新潟
-	11.1	100.0	11.4	13.6	2.3	2.3	2.3	-	13.6	-	54.5	16 富山
-	17.9	100.0	25.5	17.6	2.0	-	7.8	3.9	7.8	-	35.3	17 石川
-	9.4	100.0	31.0	13.8	6.9	-	-	3.4	17.2	3.4	24.1	18 福井
-	12.2	100.0	14.3	22.9	2.9	-	14.3	11.4	5.7	-	28.6	19 山梨
0.7	9.8	100.0	12.0	22.0	1.0	2.0	15.0	9.0	12.0	-	27.0	20 長野
0.7	8.3	100.0	25.0	12.0	5.6	0.9	7.4	6.5	14.8	3.7	24.1	21 岐阜
3.2	15.8	100.0	13.8	12.8	3.7	1.8	12.8	3.2	21.6	7.3	22.9	22 静岡
1.8	11.3	100.0	26.2	10.5	3.1	0.4	8.6	3.3	14.3	3.1	30.6	23 愛知
3.3	14.9	100.0	21.6	10.8	2.0	-	5.9	2.0	21.6	6.9	29.4	24 三重
1.9	19.4	100.0	22.7	6.1	-	-	9.1	6.1	16.7	4.5	34.8	25 滋賀
-	25.3	100.0	27.1	12.6	0.4	0.4	10.8	4.7	1.1	0.7	42.2	26 京都
0.2	11.3	100.0	44.5	16.2	1.4	1.0	7.5	3.3	2.0	0.4	23.6	27 大阪
1.4	16.8	100.0	40.4	13.2	1.1	0.4	9.9	3.5	2.2	0.7	28.5	28 兵庫
-	8.1	100.0	25.4	12.7	3.2	1.6	7.9	3.2	3.2	3.2	39.7	29 奈良
-	15.0	100.0	23.8	11.9	-	2.4	19.0	7.1	4.8	2.4	28.6	30 和歌山
-	10.0	100.0	57.9	-	5.3	-	10.5	-	5.3	-	21.1	31 鳥取
3.7	22.2	100.0	59.1	4.5	-	-	13.6	4.5	-	-	18.2	32 島根
-	16.8	100.0	31.0	10.7	2.4	1.2	7.1	4.8	7.1	3.6	32.1	33 岡山
0.6	22.6	100.0	20.4	18.4	4.8	1.4	9.5	4.1	8.8	3.4	29.3	34 広島
-	7.1	100.0	25.0	13.9	4.2	1.4	33.3	2.8	1.4	1.4	16.7	35 山口
-	4.2	100.0	27.8	5.6	5.6	-	27.8	5.6	-	-	27.8	36 徳島
-	17.3	100.0	17.9	20.5	5.1	-	12.8	5.1	2.6	7.7	28.2	37 香川
-	17.2	100.0	21.6	5.9	5.9	2.0	15.7	-	3.9	2.0	43.1	38 愛媛
-	14.3	100.0	10.0	5.0	5.0	5.0	25.0	5.0	-	-	45.0	39 高知
-	12.3	100.0	30.0	15.7	1.7	-	13.3	6.5	0.3	0.3	32.1	40 福岡
-	22.2	100.0	23.1	19.2	-	3.8	15.4	7.7	-	-	30.8	41 佐賀
-	13.9	100.0	11.3	13.8	-	1.3	51.3	3.8	-	-	18.8	42 長崎
-	13.8	100.0	24.5	13.2	1.9	-	22.6	13.2	-	-	24.5	43 熊本
-	8.8	100.0	18.9	21.6	2.7	-	21.6	-	2.7	-	32.4	44 大分
-	10.0	100.0	11.4	11.4	5.7	2.9	14.3	5.7	-	-	48.6	45 宮崎
-	30.4	100.0	19.0	11.9	2.4	-	16.7	7.1	-	2.4	40.5	46 鹿児島
-	21.7	100.0	5.1	5.1	1.4	-	74.6	1.1	0.6	1.1	11.0	47 沖縄
-	-	100.0	-	-	-	-	83.3	16.7	-	-	-	外国 Foreign countries
												21大都市(再掲) 21 major cities(Regrouped)
0.2	14.7	100.0	21.2	15.7	1.6	0.2	14.9	5.9	0.9	0.5	39.1	50 東京都の区部
1.8	23.2	100.0	22.7	17.5	1.0	1.0	15.5	3.1	1.0	-	38.1	51 札幌
-	16.7	100.0	20.8	13.2	1.9	-	18.9	5.7	-	-	39.6	52 仙台
1.7	13.6	100.0	23.4	27.7	-	-	8.5	7.4	2.1	1.1	29.8	53 さいたま
1.2	10.5	100.0	15.6	28.1	4.2	-	11.5	4.2	7.3	2.1	27.1	54 千葉
1.3	14.3	100.0	14.9	19.9	1.9	1.4	13.5	5.2	5.7	0.7	36.7	55 横浜
-	14.2	100.0	22.0	14.7	2.8	0.6	13.0	5.1	1.1	-	40.7	56 川崎
1.5	38.8	100.0	18.5	5.6	3.7	1.9	9.3	1.9	5.6	1.9	51.9	57 相模原
-	10.5	100.0	30.6	25.0	-	2.8	13.9	2.8	2.8	-	22.2	58 新潟
-	20.5	100.0	22.2	16.7	2.8	-	13.9	2.8	8.3	-	33.3	59 静岡
2.8	16.7	100.0	20.4	1.9	5.6	1.9	3.7	-	38.9	11.1	16.7	60 浜松
1.0	7.4	100.0	29.7	14.7	1.5	0.4	10.9	3.8	6.0	1.9	31.2	61 名古屋
-	27.6	100.0	25.7	13.3	0.5	-	9.5	4.8	1.4	0.5	44.3	62 京都
-	7.7	100.0	48.8	16.6	1.5	0.2	5.9	3.6	2.1	0.4	20.8	63 大阪
1.5	7.6	100.0	37.7	24.6	-	-	7.2	4.3	1.4	-	24.6	64 堺
1.2	20.0	100.0	37.2	15.3	1.1	0.5	9.8	6.0	1.6	0.5	27.9	65 神戸
-	19.5	100.0	31.0	11.9	2.4	-	7.1	4.8	4.8	4.8	33.3	66 岡山
-	11.1	100.0	28.1	18.8	3.1	1.6	15.6	6.3	7.8	3.1	15.6	67 広島
-	11.9	100.0	55.3	7.9	-	-	7.9	2.6	2.6	-	23.7	68 北九州
-	13.2	100.0	25.6	20.5	1.9	-	14.7	7.7	-	0.6	28.8	69 福岡
-	17.2	100.0	22.2	14.8	3.7	-	25.9	7.4	-	-	25.9	70 熊本

Note：a) See page 44.

出 生

〔出生時の身長別にみた出生〕
〔Live births by birth length〕

表 4.35　性・出生時の身長別にみた
Table 4.35　Live births and percent distribution

身　長 Birth length	1995 平成 7 年		2000 12　年		2005 17　年		2008 20　年		2009 21　年		2010 22　年	
	実　数 Live births	百分率 Percentage	実　数 Live births	百分率 Percentage	実　数 Live births	百分率 Percentage	実　数 Live births	百分率 Percentage	実　数 Live births	百分率 Percentage	実　数 Live births	百分率 Percentage
											男	
総　数　Total	608 547	100.0	612 148	100.0	545 032	100.0	559 513	100.0	548 993	100.0	550 742	100.0
46 cm 以下 　46 cm and under	53 697	8.9	59 590	9.8	56 480	10.4	57 570	10.3	56 176	10.3	56 288	10.2
47 cm	51 398	8.5	54 587	8.9	50 446	9.3	51 609	9.2	50 022	9.1	50 324	9.2
48	82 911	13.8	85 685	14.0	78 257	14.4	80 362	14.4	78 250	14.3	78 579	14.3
49	109 470	18.2	111 573	18.3	99 834	18.4	102 575	18.4	101 283	18.5	101 234	18.4
50	135 163	22.5	132 686	21.7	115 707	21.3	119 361	21.4	117 329	21.4	117 984	21.5
51	89 551	14.9	88 963	14.6	77 493	14.3	80 094	14.3	79 146	14.4	79 548	14.5
52 cm 以上 　52 cm and over	79 131	13.2	77 200	12.6	65 432	12.0	66 679	11.9	65 590	12.0	65 597	11.9
不　詳 　Not stated	7 226	・	1 864	・	1 383	・	1 263	・	1 197	・	1 188	・
平均身長（cm） 　Mean birth length	49.3	・	49.2	・	49.1	・	49.1	・	49.1	・	49.1	・
											女	
総　数　Total	578 517	100.0	578 399	100.0	517 498	100.0	531 643	100.0	521 042	100.0	520 562	100.0
46 cm 以下 　46 cm and under	70 717	12.4	77 227	13.4	75 107	14.5	77 127	14.5	74 850	14.4	74 208	14.3
47 cm	65 467	11.4	68 246	11.8	63 781	12.4	65 119	12.3	63 821	12.3	63 900	12.3
48	96 252	16.8	98 627	17.1	88 891	17.2	91 378	17.2	90 086	17.3	89 321	17.2
49	111 566	19.5	111 827	19.4	99 854	19.3	102 832	19.4	100 886	19.4	101 492	19.5
50	116 736	20.4	114 179	19.8	98 326	19.0	101 694	19.2	99 548	19.1	100 345	19.3
51	65 159	11.4	63 122	10.9	54 535	10.6	56 132	10.6	54 934	10.6	55 259	10.6
52 cm 以上 　52 cm and over	45 905	8.0	43 542	7.5	35 772	6.9	36 283	6.8	35 859	6.9	35 003	6.7
不　詳 　Not stated	6 715	・	1 629	・	1 232	・	1 078	・	1 058	・	1 034	・
平均身長（cm） 　Mean birth length	48.8	・	48.7	・	48.6	・	48.6	・	48.6	・	48.6	・

注：1）　出生時の身長不詳を除いた出生数に対する百分率である。

Natality

年次別出生数・百分率[1]及び平均身長
by sex and birth length and mean birth length：Japan

2011 23 年		2012 24 年		2013 25 年		2014 26 年		2015 27 年		2016 28 年		身 長 Birth length
実 数 Live births	百分率 Percentage	実 数 Live births	百分率 Percentage	実 数 Live births	百分率 Percentage	実 数 Live births	百分率 Percentage	実 数 Live births	百分率 Percentage	実 数 Live births	百分率 Percentage	
						Male						
538 271	100.0	531 781	100.0	527 657	100.0	515 533	100.0	515 452	100.0	501 880	100.0	総 数 Total
54 265	10.1	52 981	10.0	52 144	9.9	50 155	9.8	49 990	9.7	48 070	9.6	46 cm 以下 46 cm and under
48 293	9.0	47 428	8.9	46 730	8.9	45 353	8.8	44 917	8.7	43 804	8.7	47 cm
75 848	14.1	74 773	14.1	73 710	14.0	71 915	14.0	71 730	13.9	69 545	13.9	48
99 147	18.5	98 586	18.6	97 568	18.5	94 971	18.5	95 623	18.6	92 968	18.6	49
115 416	21.5	114 618	21.6	114 386	21.7	113 040	22.0	112 901	22.0	110 910	22.2	50
79 000	14.7	78 129	14.7	77 926	14.8	76 415	14.9	76 997	15.0	74 916	15.0	51
65 027	12.1	64 032	12.1	64 027	12.2	62 524	12.2	62 116	12.1	60 460	12.1	52 cm 以上 52 cm and over
1 275	・	1 234	・	1 166	・	1 160	・	1 178	・	1 207	・	不 詳 Not stated
49.1	・	49.2	・	49.2	・	49.2	・	49.2	・	49.2	・	平均身長（cm） Mean birth length
						Female						
512 535	100.0	505 450	100.0	502 159	100.0	488 006	100.0	490 225	100.0	475 098	100.0	総 数 Total
71 921	14.1	70 785	14.0	69 691	13.9	66 786	13.7	66 888	13.7	64 315	13.6	46 cm 以下 46 cm and under
62 079	12.1	61 224	12.1	60 435	12.1	58 195	11.9	57 987	11.9	56 265	11.9	47 cm
87 855	17.2	86 507	17.2	85 219	17.0	82 488	16.9	83 737	17.1	80 693	17.0	48
99 852	19.5	98 789	19.6	98 161	19.6	96 330	19.8	96 282	19.7	93 878	19.8	49
98 928	19.3	97 361	19.3	98 848	19.7	96 569	19.8	97 551	19.9	94 563	19.9	50
55 266	10.8	55 289	11.0	54 740	10.9	53 474	11.0	53 527	10.9	52 653	11.1	51
35 493	6.9	34 449	6.8	34 072	6.8	33 153	6.8	33 237	6.8	31 695	6.7	52 cm 以上 52 cm and over
1 141	・	1 046	・	993	・	1 011	・	1 016	・	1 036	・	不 詳 Not stated
48.6	・	48.6	・	48.6	・	48.6	・	48.6	・	48.6	・	平均身長（cm） Mean birth length

149

出 生

〔単産－複産の種類別にみた分娩件数〕
〔Deliveries by plurality of birth〕

表 4.36　単産－複産（複産の種類・出生－
Table 4.36　Trends in deliveries by plurality of birth（type

複　産　の　種　類 Type of plurality	分　娩　件　数 Deliveries							
	1 9 9 5 平成7年	2 0 0 0 12　年	2 0 0 3 15　年	2 0 0 4 16　年	2 0 0 5 17　年	2 0 0 6 18　年	2 0 0 7 19　年	2 0 0 8 20　年
総　　数[2)]　　Total	1 215 174	1 216 168	1 145 592	1 131 567	1 081 393	1 110 448	1 106 288	1 107 467
単　産　Single delivery	1 204 082	1 203 627	1 132 508	1 118 308	1 068 633	1 097 536	1 093 632	1 095 749
複　産　Plural deliveries	10 900	12 443	13 045	13 215	12 707	12 883	12 619	11 684
双　子　Twins	10 529	12 107	12 743	12 900	12 455	12 631	12 394	11 496
三つ児　Triplets	337	328	286	307	246	246	219	181
四つ児　Quadruplets	30	8	15	6	5	3	5	6
五つ児　Quintuplets	3	-	-	2	1	2	1	1
六つ児　Sextuplets	-	-	-	-	-	1	-	-
七つ児　Septuplets	1	-	1	-	-	-	-	-
（複産の再掲） （Regrouped plural deliveries） 出生－死産の組合せ別分娩件数 Combination of live birth and foetal death								
双　子　Twins	10 529	12 107	12 743	12 900	12 455	12 631	12 394	11 496
2出生　　　2 live births	9 585	11 211	11 856	12 009	11 614	11 795	11 591	10 814
1出生1死産　1 live birth and 1 foetal death	302	263	278	274	238	264	270	219
1出生1不詳　1 live birth and 1 unknown	3	2	-	1	2	2	1	1
2死産　　　2 foetal deaths	630	618	595	598	592	564	525	452
1死産1不詳　1 foetal death and 1 unknown	9	13	14	18	9	6	7	10
三つ児　Triplets	337	328	286	307	246	246	219	181
3出生　　　3 live births	277	298	240	268	206	217	195	157
2出生1死産　2 live births and 1 foetal death	23	9	19	16	13	8	8	8
1出生2死産　1 live birth and 2 foetal deaths	6	5	3	3	4	4	4	4
3死産　　　3 foetal deaths	28	16	24	19	23	17	12	10
2死産1不詳　2 foetal deaths and 1 unknown	1	-	-	-	-	-	-	1
1死産2不詳　1 foetal death and 2 unknown	2	-	-	1	-	-	-	1
四つ児　Quadruplets	30	8	15	6	5	3	5	6
4出生　　　4 live births	24	4	14	5	3	-	5	2
3出生1死産　3 live births and 1 foetal death	2	-	1	-	-	2	-	-
2出生2死産　2 live births and 2 foetal deaths	-	-	-	-	1	1	-	3
1出生3死産　1 live birth and 3 foetal deaths	-	1	-	-	-	-	-	1
4死産　　　4 foetal deaths	4	3	-	1	1	-	-	-
五つ児　Quintuplets	3	-	-	2	1	2	1	1
5出生　　　5 live births	1	-	-	1	-	-	-	1
3出生2死産　3 live births and 2 foetal deaths	-	-	-	-	-	-	1	-
2出生3死産　2 live births and 3 foetal deaths	-	-	-	-	-	1	-	-
5死産　　　5 foetal deaths	2	-	-	1	1	1	-	-
六つ児　Sextuplets	-	-	-	-	-	1	-	-
2出生4死産　2 live births and 4 foetal deaths	-	-	-	-	-	1	-	-
1出生5死産　1 live birth and 5 foetal deaths	-	-	-	-	-	-	-	-
七つ児　Septuplets	1	-	1	-	-	-	-	-
3出生4死産　3 live births and 4 foetal deaths	1	-	-	-	-	-	-	-
3死産4不詳　3 foetal deaths and 4 unknown	-	-	1	-	-	-	-	-

注：1)　分娩件数とは出産（出生及び死産）をした母の数である。
　　2)　総数には死産の単産・複産の別不詳を含む。

死産の組合せ）別にみた年次別分娩件数 [1]
of plurality, combination of live birth and foetal death）：Japan

| 分　娩　件　数 Deliveries | | | | | | | | 複　産　の　種　類 |
2009 21 年	2010 22 年	2011 23 年	2012 24 年	2013 25 年	2014 26 年	2015 27 年	2016 28 年	Type of plurality
1 085 912	1 087 148	1 066 129	1 051 359	1 043 276	1 016 709	1 017 975	987 654	総　数 [2]　Total
1 074 919	1 076 562	1 055 832	1 040 831	1 032 763	1 006 458	1 007 746	977 513	単 産　Single delivery
10 966	10 558	10 279	10 505	10 489	10 216	10 194	10 129	複 産　Plural deliveries
10 803	10 394	10 124	10 333	10 328	10 073	10 066	9 998	双 子　Twins
157	162	151	168	158	141	122	129	三つ児　Triplets
4	2	3	4	3	2	5	2	四つ児　Quadruplets
1	-	1	-	-	-	1	-	五つ児　Quintuplets
1	-	-	-	-	-	-	-	六つ児　Sextuplets
-	-	-	-	-	-	-	-	七つ児　Septuplets
								（複産の再掲）
								（Regrouped plural deliveries）
								出生－死産の組合せ別分娩件数
								Combination of live birth and foetal death
10 803	10 394	10 124	10 333	10 328	10 073	10 066	9 998	双 子　Twins
10 100	9 763	9 495	9 703	9 688	9 453	9 443	9 398	2 出生　　　　2 live births
231	207	204	205	209	202	249	229	1 出生 1 死産 1 live birth and 1 foetal death
2	2	2	-	1	2	3	1	1 出生 1 不詳 1 live birth and 1 unknown
464	416	415	416	420	411	364	368	2 死産　　　　2 foetal deaths
6	6	8	9	10	5	7	2	1 死産 1 不詳 1 foetal death and 1 unknown
157	162	151	168	158	141	122	129	三つ児　Triplets
144	148	132	141	133	115	96	104	3 出生　　　　3 live births
6	6	7	10	5	10	13	7	2 出生 1 死産 2 live births and 1 foetal death
2	2	3	3	5	5	4	6	1 出生 2 死産 1 live birth and 2 foetal deaths
4	6	8	14	15	11	9	12	3 死産　　　　3 foetal deaths
-	-	1	-	-	-	-	-	2 死産 1 不詳 2 foetal deaths and 1 unknown
1	-	-	-	-	-	-	-	1 死産 2 不詳 1 foetal death and 2 unknown
4	2	3	4	3	2	5	2	四つ児　Quadruplets
3	2	2	2	1	2	2	1	4 出生　　　　4 live births
-	-	-	-	-	-	-	-	3 出生 1 死産 3 live births and 1 foetal death
1	-	-	1	1	-	1	1	2 出生 2 死産 2 live births and 2 foetal deaths
-	-	-	-	-	-	-	-	1 出生 3 死産 1 live birth and 3 foetal deaths
-	-	1	1	1	-	2	-	4 死産　　　　4 foetal deaths
1	-	1	-	-	-	1	-	五つ児　Quintuplets
-	-	-	-	-	-	-	-	5 出生　　　　5 live births
-	-	-	-	-	-	-	-	3 出生 2 死産 3 live births and 2 foetal deaths
-	-	1	-	-	-	-	-	2 出生 3 死産 2 live births and 3 foetal deaths
1	-	-	-	-	-	1	-	5 死産　　　　5 foetal deaths
1	-	-	-	-	-	-	-	六つ児　Sextuplets
-	-	-	-	-	-	-	-	2 出生 4 死産 2 live births and 4 foetal deaths
1	-	-	-	-	-	-	-	1 出生 5 死産 1 live birth and 5 foetal deaths
-	-	-	-	-	-	-	-	七つ児　Septuplets
-	-	-	-	-	-	-	-	3 出生 4 死産 3 live births and 4 foetal deaths
-	-	-	-	-	-	-	-	3 死産 4 不詳 3 foetal deaths and 4 unknown

出 生

表 4.37 都道府県別にみた単産－複産（複産の種類）別分娩件数[1]
Table 4.37 Deliveries by plurality of birth (type of plurality)：Japan, each prefecture, 2016

平成28年

| 都道府県 Prefecture | 単 産 － 複 産 別 分 娩 件 数 Deliveries by plurality | | | | | | |
| | 総　数[2] Total | 単　産 Single delivery | 複　産 Plural deliveries | 複 産 の 種 類 Type of plurality | | | |
				双 子 Twins	三つ児 Triplets	四つ児 Quadruplets	五つ児～ Quintuplets and others
全　国　　Total	987 654	977 513	10 129	9 998	129	2	-
01[a] 北　海　道	35 704	35 388	316	310	6	-	-
02 青　　　森	8 722	8 636	86	85	1	-	-
03 岩　　　手	8 457	8 390	67	66	1	-	-
04 宮　　　城	17 573	17 400	173	170	3	-	-
05 秋　　　田	5 740	5 681	59	59	-	-	-
06 山　　　形	7 638	7 565	73	72	1	-	-
07 福　　　島	13 934	13 819	115	114	1	-	-
08 茨　　　城	21 106	20 913	193	191	2	-	-
09 栃　　　木	14 762	14 583	179	178	1	-	-
10 群　　　馬	13 817	13 644	172	170	2	-	-
11 埼　　　玉	55 096	54 564	530	527	3	-	-
12 千　　　葉	45 932	45 482	448	440	8	-	-
13 東　　　京	113 107	111 903	1 200	1 181	19	-	-
14 神　奈　川	71 326	70 615	711	700	11	-	-
15 新　　　潟	15 828	15 605	223	219	3	1	-
16 富　　　山	7 382	7 312	70	68	2	-	-
17 石　　　川	8 986	8 889	97	94	3	-	-
18 福　　　井	6 202	6 147	55	54	1	-	-
19 山　　　梨	5 849	5 779	70	69	1	-	-
20 長　　　野	15 329	15 182	147	142	5	-	-
21 岐　　　阜	14 977	14 835	142	141	1	-	-
22 静　　　岡	27 905	27 628	277	269	8	-	-
23 愛　　　知	64 649	63 893	756	752	4	-	-
24 三　　　重	13 364	13 254	110	110	-	-	-
25 滋　　　賀	12 149	12 015	134	133	1	-	-
26 京　　　都	19 490	19 254	236	232	4	-	-
27 大　　　阪	69 572	68 855	717	709	8	-	-
28 兵　　　庫	43 729	43 229	500	495	5	-	-
29 奈　　　良	9 496	9 373	123	122	1	-	-
30 和　歌　山	6 748	6 683	65	65	-	-	-
31 鳥　　　取	4 478	4 423	55	54	1	-	-
32 島　　　根	5 367	5 299	68	67	1	-	-
33 岡　　　山	15 646	15 492	154	152	2	-	-
34 広　　　島	23 019	22 801	218	218	-	-	-
35 山　　　口	9 939	9 840	98	96	2	-	-
36 徳　　　島	5 379	5 318	61	61	-	-	-
37 香　　　川	7 580	7 508	72	70	2	-	-
38 愛　　　媛	10 074	9 992	82	82	-	-	-
39 高　　　知	4 833	4 781	52	52	-	-	-
40 福　　　岡	44 575	44 105	470	465	4	1	-
41 佐　　　賀	6 882	6 819	63	62	1	-	-
42 長　　　崎	11 045	10 958	87	86	1	-	-
43 熊　　　本	15 130	14 972	158	156	2	-	-
44 大　　　分	9 200	9 121	79	77	2	-	-
45 宮　　　崎	9 082	8 995	87	87	-	-	-
46 鹿　児　島	13 887	13 759	127	126	1	-	-
47 沖　　　縄	16 894	16 741	153	149	4	-	-
外　　　国 Foreign countries	74	73	1	1	-	-	-
不　　　詳 Place of residence not stated	1	-	-	-	-	-	-

注：1） 分娩件数とは出産（出生及び死産）をした母の数である。
　　2） 総数には死産の単産・複産の別不詳を含む。
Notes：a) See page 44.

表4.38 都道府県別にみた複産の種類別分娩件数[1] 百分率
Table 4.38 Percent distribution of plural deliveries by type of plurality：Japan, each prefecture, 2016

平成28年

都道府県 Prefecture	複 産 Plural deliveries	双 子 Twins	三つ児 Triplets	四つ児 Quadruplets	五つ児～ Quintuplets and others
全 国　Total	100.0	98.7	1.3	0.0	-
01 北 海 道 [a]	100.0	98.1	1.9	-	-
02 青 森	100.0	98.8	1.2	-	-
03 岩 手	100.0	98.5	1.5	-	-
04 宮 城	100.0	98.3	1.7	-	-
05 秋 田	100.0	100.0	-	-	-
06 山 形	100.0	98.6	1.4	-	-
07 福 島	100.0	99.1	0.9	-	-
08 茨 城	100.0	99.0	1.0	-	-
09 栃 木	100.0	99.4	0.6	-	-
10 群 馬	100.0	98.8	1.2	-	-
11 埼 玉	100.0	99.4	0.6	-	-
12 千 葉	100.0	98.2	1.8	-	-
13 東 京	100.0	98.4	1.6	-	-
14 神 奈 川	100.0	98.5	1.5	-	-
15 新 潟	100.0	98.2	1.3	0.4	-
16 富 山	100.0	97.1	2.9	-	-
17 石 川	100.0	96.9	3.1	-	-
18 福 井	100.0	98.2	1.8	-	-
19 山 梨	100.0	98.6	1.4	-	-
20 長 野	100.0	96.6	3.4	-	-
21 岐 阜	100.0	99.3	0.7	-	-
22 静 岡	100.0	97.1	2.9	-	-
23 愛 知	100.0	99.5	0.5	-	-
24 三 重	100.0	100.0	-	-	-
25 滋 賀	100.0	99.3	0.7	-	-
26 京 都	100.0	98.3	1.7	-	-
27 大 阪	100.0	98.9	1.1	-	-
28 兵 庫	100.0	99.0	1.0	-	-
29 奈 良	100.0	99.2	0.8	-	-
30 和 歌 山	100.0	100.0	-	-	-
31 鳥 取	100.0	98.2	1.8	-	-
32 島 根	100.0	98.5	1.5	-	-
33 岡 山	100.0	98.7	1.3	-	-
34 広 島	100.0	100.0	-	-	-
35 山 口	100.0	98.0	2.0	-	-
36 徳 島	100.0	100.0	-	-	-
37 香 川	100.0	97.2	2.8	-	-
38 愛 媛	100.0	100.0	-	-	-
39 高 知	100.0	100.0	-	-	-
40 福 岡	100.0	98.9	0.9	0.2	-
41 佐 賀	100.0	98.4	1.6	-	-
42 長 崎	100.0	98.9	1.1	-	-
43 熊 本	100.0	98.7	1.3	-	-
44 大 分	100.0	97.5	2.5	-	-
45 宮 崎	100.0	100.0	-	-	-
46 鹿 児 島	100.0	99.2	0.8	-	-
47 沖 縄	100.0	97.4	2.6	-	-
外 国 Foreign countries	100.0	100.0	-	-	-
不 詳 Place of residence not stated	-	-	-	-	-

注：1） 分娩件数とは出産（出生及び死産）をした母の数である。

Notes：a) See page 44.

死 亡

〔死亡の年次推移〕
〔Trends in deaths〕

第5章 死　　亡

Chapter 5 General mortality

表5.1　年次別にみた性別死亡数・

Table 5.1　Trends in deaths, death rates

年　次[1] Year		死　亡　数 Deaths				死　亡　率 Death rates			死亡性比 Sex ratio of deaths
		総　数 Total	男 Male	女 Female	不　詳 Not stated	総　数 Total	男 Male	女 Female	
1899	明治32年	932 087	476 249	455 828	10	21.5	21.8	21.1	104.5
1900	33	910 744	464 072	446 664	8	20.8	21.0	20.5	103.9
01	34	925 810	468 524	457 278	8	20.9	21.0	20.7	102.5
02	35	959 126	486 410	472 710	6	21.3	21.5	21.1	102.9
03	36	931 008	472 249	458 755	4	20.4	20.6	20.3	102.9
04	37	955 400	481 445	473 950	5	20.7	20.8	20.7	101.6
05	38	1 004 661	505 290	499 365	6	21.6	21.6	21.5	101.2
06	39	955 256	480 077	475 176	3	20.3	20.3	20.3	101.0
07	40	1 016 798	512 110	504 681	7	21.4	21.5	21.4	101.5
08	41	1 029 447	517 755	511 687	5	21.5	21.5	21.4	101.2
09	42	1 091 264	550 267	540 992	5	22.5	22.6	22.3	101.7
1910	43	1 064 234	535 076	529 156	2	21.6	21.7	21.6	101.1
11	44	1 043 906	526 141	517 762	3	20.9	21.1	20.8	101.6
12	大正元年	1 037 016	523 604	513 410	2	20.5	20.6	20.4	102.0
13	2	1 027 257	521 210	506 042	5	20.0	20.3	19.8	103.0
14	3	1 101 815	559 337	542 473	5	21.2	21.4	20.9	103.1
15	4	1 093 793	556 179	537 610	4	20.7	21.0	20.5	103.5
16	5	1 187 832	604 156	583 674	2	22.2	22.5	21.9	103.5
17	6	1 199 669	609 310	590 359	-	22.2	22.4	21.9	103.2
18	7	1 493 162	753 392	739 770	-	27.3	27.4	27.1	101.8
19	8	1 281 965	648 984	632 981	-	23.3	23.5	23.1	102.5
1920	9	1 422 096	720 655	701 441	-	25.4	25.7	25.1	102.7
21	10	1 288 570	659 328	629 242	-	22.7	23.2	22.3	104.8
22	11	1 286 941	655 740	631 201	-	22.4	22.8	22.1	103.9
23	12	1 332 485	679 072	653 405	8	22.9	23.3	22.6	103.9
24	13	1 254 946	642 969	611 977	-	21.3	21.7	20.9	105.1
25	14	1 210 706	621 357	589 349	-	20.3	20.7	19.8	105.4
26	昭和元年	1 160 734	597 292	563 435	7	19.1	19.6	18.6	106.0
27	2	1 214 323	624 311	590 012	-	19.7	20.2	19.2	105.8
28	3	1 236 711	639 214	597 497	-	19.8	20.3	19.2	107.0
29	4	1 261 228	645 994	615 234	-	19.9	20.3	19.5	105.0
1930	5	1 170 867	603 995	566 871	1	18.2	18.6	17.7	106.5
31	6	1 240 891	642 146	598 745	-	19.0	19.5	18.4	107.2
32	7	1 175 344	607 267	568 077	-	17.7	18.2	17.2	106.9
33	8	1 193 987	618 496	575 491	-	17.7	18.3	17.1	107.5
34	9	1 234 684	639 098	595 507	79	18.1	18.6	17.5	107.3
35	10	1 161 936	603 566	558 367	3	16.8	17.4	16.2	108.1
36	11	1 230 278	637 854	592 421	3	17.5	18.2	16.9	107.7
37	12	1 207 899	625 625	582 274	-	17.1	17.8	16.4	107.4
38	13	1 259 805	652 936	606 869	-	17.7	18.6	16.9	107.6
39	14	1 268 760	658 589	610 171	-	17.8	18.7	16.9	107.9
1940	15	1 186 595	615 311	571 284	-	16.5	17.4	15.6	107.7
41	16	1 149 559	597 373	552 186	-	16.0	17.2	14.9	108.2
42	17	1 166 630	609 038	557 592	-	16.1	17.5	14.9	109.2
43	18	1 219 073	638 135	580 938	-	16.7	18.4	15.2	109.8
47	22	1 138 238	595 670	542 568	-	14.6	15.6	13.6	109.8
48	23	950 610	493 573	457 037	-	11.9	12.6	11.2	108.0
49	24	945 444	489 817	455 627	-	11.6	12.2	10.9	107.5
1950	25	904 876	467 073	437 803	-	10.9	11.4	10.3	106.7
51	26	838 998	432 540	406 458	-	9.9	10.4	9.4	106.4
52	27	765 068	395 205	369 863	-	8.9	9.4	8.5	106.9
53	28	772 547	399 859	372 688	-	8.9	9.4	8.4	107.3
54	29	721 491	379 658	341 833	-	8.2	8.8	7.6	111.1

注：1)　昭和18年のみは樺太を含む数値であり、第3章総覧における死亡数とは一致しない。
　　　　昭和19～21年は資料不備のため省略した。
　　　　昭和22～47年は沖縄県を含まない。

General mortality

率（人口千対）及び死亡性比
(per 1,000 population) by sex and sex ratio : Japan

年　次[1] Year		死　亡　数 Deaths				死　亡　率 Death rates			死亡性比 Sex ratio of deaths
		総　数 Total	男 Male	女 Female	不　詳 Not stated	総　数 Total	男 Male	女 Female	
1955	昭和30年	693 523	365 246	328 277	-	7.8	8.3	7.2	111.3
56	31	724 460	381 395	343 065	-	8.0	8.6	7.5	111.2
57	32	752 445	397 502	354 943	-	8.3	8.9	7.7	112.0
58	33	684 189	363 647	320 542	-	7.4	8.0	6.9	113.4
59	34	689 959	367 562	322 370	27	7.4	8.0	6.8	114.0
1960	35	706 599	377 526	329 073		7.6	8.2	6.9	114.7
61	36	695 644	371 858	323 786		7.4	8.0	6.7	114.8
62	37	710 265	380 826	329 439		7.5	8.1	6.8	115.6
63	38	670 770	361 469	309 301		7.0	7.7	6.3	116.9
64	39	673 067	363 531	309 536		6.9	7.6	6.3	117.4
65	40	700 438	378 716	321 722	-	7.1	7.9	6.4	117.7
66	41	670 342	363 356	306 986	-	6.8	7.5	6.1	118.4
67	42	675 006	366 076	308 930	-	6.8	7.5	6.1	118.5
68	43	686 555	372 931	313 624	-	6.8	7.5	6.1	118.9
69	44	693 787	379 506	314 281	-	6.8	7.6	6.1	120.8
1970	45	712 962	387 880	325 082	-	6.9	7.7	6.2	119.3
71	46	684 521	372 942	311 579	-	6.6	7.3	5.9	119.7
72	47	683 751	372 833	310 918	-	6.5	7.2	5.8	119.9
73	48	709 416	383 592	325 824	-	6.6	7.2	5.9	117.7
74	49	710 510	381 869	328 641	-	6.5	7.1	5.9	116.2
75	50	702 275	377 827	324 448	-	6.3	6.9	5.7	116.5
76	51	703 270	378 630	324 640	-	6.3	6.8	5.7	116.6
77	52	690 074	372 175	317 899	-	6.1	6.7	5.5	117.1
78	53	695 821	375 625	320 196	-	6.1	6.7	5.5	117.3
79	54	689 664	373 183	316 481	-	6.0	6.6	5.4	117.9
1980	55	722 801	390 644	332 157	-	6.2	6.8	5.6	117.6
81	56	720 262	388 575	331 687	-	6.1	6.7	5.6	117.2
82	57	711 883	385 494	326 389	-	6.0	6.6	5.4	118.1
83	58	740 038	401 232	338 806	-	6.2	6.9	5.6	118.4
84	59	740 247	402 220	338 027	-	6.2	6.8	5.6	119.0
85	60	752 283	407 769	344 514	-	6.3	6.9	5.6	118.4
86	61	750 620	406 918	343 702	-	6.2	6.8	5.6	118.4
87	62	751 172	408 094	343 078	-	6.2	6.8	5.6	119.0
88	63	793 014	428 094	364 920	-	6.5	7.1	5.9	117.3
89	平成元年	788 594	427 114	361 480	-	6.4	7.1	5.8	118.2
1990	2	820 305	443 718	376 587	-	6.7	7.4	6.0	117.8
91	3	829 797	450 344	379 453	-	6.7	7.5	6.1	118.7
92	4	856 643	465 544	391 099	-	6.9	7.7	6.2	119.0
93	5	878 532	476 462	402 070	-	7.1	7.8	6.4	118.5
94	6	875 933	476 080	399 853	-	7.1	7.8	6.3	119.1
95	7	922 139	501 276	420 863	-	7.4	8.2	6.6	119.1
96	8	896 211	488 605	407 606	-	7.2	8.0	6.4	119.9
97	9	913 402	497 796	415 606	-	7.3	8.1	6.5	119.8
98	10	936 484	512 128	424 356	-	7.5	8.4	6.6	120.7
99	11	982 031	534 778	447 253	-	7.8	8.7	7.0	119.6
2000	12	961 653	525 903	435 750	-	7.7	8.6	6.8	120.7
01	13	970 331	528 768	441 563	-	7.7	8.6	6.9	119.7
02	14	982 379	535 305	447 074	-	7.8	8.7	6.9	119.7
03	15	1 014 951	551 746	463 205	-	8.0	9.0	7.2	119.1
04	16	1 028 602	557 097	471 505	-	8.2	9.0	7.3	118.2
05	17	1 083 796	584 970	498 826	-	8.6	9.5	7.7	117.3
06	18	1 084 450	581 370	503 080	-	8.6	9.4	7.8	115.6
07	19	1 108 334	592 784	515 550	-	8.8	9.6	8.0	115.0
08	20	1 142 407	608 711	533 696	-	9.1	9.9	8.3	114.1
09	21	1 141 865	609 042	532 823	-	9.1	9.9	8.3	114.3
2010	22	1 197 012	633 700	563 312	-	9.5	10.3	8.7	112.5
11	23	1 253 066	656 540	596 526	-	9.9	10.7	9.2	110.1
12	24	1 256 359	655 526	600 833	-	10.0	10.7	9.3	109.1
13	25	1 268 436	658 684	609 752	-	10.1	10.8	9.5	108.0
14	26	1 273 004	660 334	612 670	-	10.1	10.8	9.5	107.8
15	27	1 290 444	666 707	623 737	-	10.3	10.9	9.7	106.9
16	28	1 307 748	674 733	633 015	-	10.5	11.1	9.9	106.6

155

死　亡

表5.2　年次別にみた性別粗死亡率及び年齢調整死亡率[1]　（人口千対）
Table 5.2　Trends in crude death rates and age-adjusted death rates (per 1,000 population) by sex : Japan

年　　　　次 Year		粗　死　亡　率 Death rates		年　齢　調　整　死　亡　率 Age-adjusted death rates	
		男 Male	女 Female	男 Male	女 Female
1947	昭和22年	15.6	13.6	23.6	18.3
48	23	12.6	11.2	19.3	15.4
49	24	12.2	10.9	18.9	15.0
1950	25	11.4	10.3	18.6	14.6
51	26	10.4	9.4	16.9	13.4
52	27	9.4	8.5	15.7	12.4
53	28	9.4	8.4	16.4	12.6
54	29	8.8	7.6	15.2	11.3
55	30	8.3	7.2	14.8	11.0
56	31	8.6	7.5	15.6	11.5
57	32	8.9	7.7	16.3	11.8
58	33	8.0	6.9	14.4	10.4
59	34	8.0	6.8	14.4	10.2
1960	35	8.2	6.9	14.8	10.4
61	36	8.0	6.7	14.3	10.0
62	37	8.1	6.8	14.6	10.0
63	38	7.7	6.3	13.4	9.3
64	39	7.6	6.3	13.2	9.1
65	40	7.9	6.4	13.7	9.3
66	41	7.5	6.1	12.7	8.7
67	42	7.5	6.1	12.6	8.5
68	43	7.5	6.1	12.5	8.4
69	44	7.6	6.1	12.4	8.2
1970	45	7.7	6.2	12.3	8.2
71	46	7.3	5.9	11.5	7.6
72	47	7.2	5.8	11.2	7.4
73	48	7.2	5.9	11.2	7.4
74	49	7.1	5.9	10.9	7.2
75	50	6.9	5.7	10.4	6.9
76	51	6.8	5.7	10.1	6.6
77	52	6.7	5.5	9.6	6.2
78	53	6.7	5.5	9.4	6.0
79	54	6.6	5.4	9.0	5.7
1980	55	6.8	5.6	9.2	5.8
81	56	6.7	5.6	8.9	5.6
82	57	6.6	5.4	8.5	5.2
83	58	6.9	5.6	8.6	5.2
84	59	6.8	5.6	8.3	5.0
85	60	6.9	5.6	8.1	4.8
86	61	6.8	5.6	7.8	4.6
87	62	6.8	5.6	7.6	4.4
88	63	7.1	5.9	7.7	4.5
89	平成元年	7.1	5.8	7.4	4.2
1990	2	7.4	6.0	7.5	4.2
91	3	7.5	6.1	7.4	4.1
92	4	7.7	6.2	7.4	4.0
93	5	7.8	6.4	7.3	4.0
94	6	7.8	6.3	7.1	3.8
95	7	8.2	6.6	7.2	3.8
96	8	8.0	6.4	6.8	3.6
97	9	8.1	6.5	6.7	3.5
98	10	8.4	6.6	6.6	3.4
99	11	8.7	7.0	6.7	3.4
2000	12	8.6	6.9	6.3	3.2
01	13	8.6	6.9	6.2	3.1
02	14	8.7	6.9	6.0	3.0
03	15	9.0	7.2	6.0	3.0
04	16	9.0	7.3	5.9	3.0
05	17	9.5	7.7	5.9	3.0
06	18	9.4	7.8	5.7	2.9
07	19	9.6	8.0	5.6	2.8
08	20	9.9	8.3	5.6	2.8
09	21	9.9	8.3	5.4	2.7
2010	22	10.3	8.7	5.4	2.7
11	23	10.7	9.2	5.5	2.9
12	24	10.7	9.3	5.2	2.7
13	25	10.8	9.5	5.1	2.7
14	26	10.8	9.5	5.0	2.6
15	27	10.9	9.7	4.9	2.5
16	28	11.1	9.9	4.8	2.5

注：1）　年齢調整死亡率の基準人口は、昭和60年モデル人口である。なお、計算方法は、68ページ　3）死亡を参照されたい。
　　　　粗死亡率は、年齢調整死亡率と並記したので粗死亡率と表現したが、単に死亡率とよんでいるものである。

156

General mortality

表5.3 世界各国における粗死亡率及び年齢調整死亡率（人口10万対）
Table 5.3 International comparison of crude death rates and age-standardized death rates (per 100,000 population)

国名 Country （年次） （Year）	人　口 Population	粗死亡率[1] Death rates	年齢調整死亡率[2] Age-standardized death rates	日本の年齢調整死亡率を100 とした年齢調整死亡率指数[1] Proportion of age-standardized death rates index （Japan＝100）
日本 Japan (2014)	125 432 000	1 014.9	307.8	100.0
カナダ Canada (2012)	34 868 151	707.2	367.3	119.3
アメリカ合衆国 United States of America (2014)	319 448 634	822.2	468.8	152.3
オーストリア Austria (2014)	8 543 932	915.9	386.3	125.5
チェコ共和国 Czech Republic (2014)	10 524 783	1 004.0	496.6	161.3
デンマーク Denmark (2014)	5 639 719	904.2	416.4	135.3
フランス France (2013)	63 781 775	871.8	362.4	117.7
ドイツ Germany (2014)	80 982 500	1 072.3	405.9	131.9
ハンガリー Hungary (2014)	9 866 468	1 280.2	629.7	204.6
イタリア Italy (2012)	59 539 725	1 030.4	364.8	118.5
オランダ Netherlands (2015)	16 939 924	868.6	388.4	126.2
ノルウェー Norway (2014)	5 137 429	785.3	366.9	119.2
ポーランド Poland (2014)	38 006 154	990.5	536.2	174.2
スウェーデン Sweden (2015)	9 696 110	938.5	369.7	120.1
スイス Switzerland (2013)	8 089 346	803.0	340.6	110.7
イギリス United Kingdom (2013)	64 105 654	899.2	407.4	132.4
オーストラリア Australia (2014)	23 460 694	654.6	342.4	111.2
ニュージーランド New Zealand (2012)	4 432 300	683.1	386.8	125.7

注：1）厚生労働省政策統括官付参事官付人口動態・保健社会統計室にて算出
　　2）標準人口はWHOが作成した世界標準人口による。
資料：WHO Mortality Database

WHO 世界標準人口
WHO World Standard Population

All ages	100,000
0	1,822
1〜4	7,033
5〜9	8,687
10〜14	8,597
15〜19	8,474
20〜24	8,222
25〜29	7,928
30〜34	7,605
35〜39	7,145
40〜44	6,590
45〜49	6,038
50〜54	5,371
55〜59	4,547
60〜64	3,723
65〜69	2,955
70〜74	2,210
75〜79	1,515
80〜84	905
85＋	632

死　亡

〔月別にみた死亡〕
〔Deaths by month〕

表5.4　月別にみた年次別
Table 5.4　Trends in deaths and death rates

年　次 Year		総　数 Total	1　月 January	2　月 February	3　月 March	4　月 April	5　月 May
						死	亡
1947	昭和22年	1 138 238	109 940	115 405	116 996	99 403	92 456
50	25	904 876	91 367	81 463	88 905	71 320	68 775
55	30	693 523	72 754	63 206	64 545	58 779	55 939
60	35	706 599	71 233	64 302	72 999	71 747	56 201
65	40	700 438	67 929	64 568	89 876	61 960	54 451
70	45	712 962	89 354	64 394	66 317	56 564	55 707
75	50	702 275	67 682	66 330	70 204	58 657	54 546
80	55	722 801	70 362	66 245	69 135	60 975	58 924
85	60	752 283	71 890	62 025	66 571	60 953	59 890
90	平成2年	820 305	86 321	72 327	72 963	66 321	65 776
95	7	922 139	104 324	86 085	86 986	74 787	72 093
2000	12	961 653	98 264	92 537	88 682	79 799	76 985
05	17	1 083 796	103 215	95 754	108 113	91 577	86 307
06	18	1 084 450	109 342	92 842	95 705	90 660	88 613
07	19	1 108 334	104 985	91 426	101 911	92 130	90 112
08	20	1 142 407	110 384	102 413	102 778	94 055	91 597
09	21	1 141 865	114 307	94 331	100 985	93 694	92 714
10	22	1 197 012	113 091	97 955	103 220	98 875	97 707
11	23	1 253 066	121 775	103 008	130 052	103 701	101 201
12	24	1 256 359	123 101	114 199	111 130	102 562	98 945
13	25	1 268 436	127 352	110 772	111 065	103 570	102 065
14	26	1 273 004	124 705	110 317	113 808	104 420	100 843
15	27	1 290 444	134 256	110 041	113 859	104 885	102 731
16	**28**	**1 307 748**	**124 667**	**114 526**	**116 067**	**105 262**	**103 259**
						死	亡
1947	昭和22年	14.6	16.6	19.3	17.6	15.5	13.9
50	25	10.9	12.9	12.8	12.6	10.4	9.7
55	30	7.8	9.6	9.2	8.5	8.0	7.4
60	35	7.6	9.0	8.7	9.2	9.4	7.1
65	40	7.1	8.1	8.6	10.8	7.7	6.5
70	45	6.9	10.3	8.2	7.6	6.7	6.4
75	50	6.3	7.3	7.9	7.5	6.5	5.8
80	55	6.2	7.2	7.2	7.0	6.4	6.0
85	60	6.3	7.1	6.8	6.5	6.2	5.9
90	平成2年	6.7	8.3	7.7	7.0	6.6	6.3
95	7	7.4	9.9	9.0	8.3	7.3	6.8
2000	12	7.7	9.2	9.3	8.3	7.8	7.2
05	17	8.6	9.6	9.9	10.1	8.8	8.1
06	18	8.6	10.2	9.6	8.9	8.7	8.3
07	19	8.8	9.8	9.4	9.5	8.9	8.4
08	20	9.1	10.3	10.3	9.6	9.1	8.6
09	21	9.1	10.7	9.8	9.4	9.1	8.7
10	22	9.5	10.6	10.2	9.7	9.6	9.1
11	23	9.9	11.3	10.6	12.1	10.0	9.4
12	24	10.0	11.5	11.4	10.4	9.9	9.3
13	25	10.1	11.9	11.5	10.4	10.0	9.6
14	26	10.1	11.7	11.4	10.7	10.1	9.5
15	27	10.3	12.6	11.4	10.7	10.2	9.7
16	**28**	**10.5**	**11.7**	**11.5**	**10.9**	**10.3**	**9.7**

注：1) 各月の率は年率に換算したものである。計算方法は、68ページ　3）死亡を参照されたい。
　　　なお、分母に用いた人口は、昭和45年以降は各月の月初人口であるが、40年以前は各年の10月1日現在人口である。

General mortality

死亡数及び率[1]（人口千対）
(per 1,000 population) by month : Japan

6　月 June	7　月 July	8　月 August	9　月 September	10　月 October	11　月 November	12　月 December	不　詳 Not stated
数　　　Deaths							
84 516	96 451	95 290	79 305	77 592	78 563	92 232	89
66 047	71 707	73 491	66 578	66 830	67 701	90 629	63
51 183	52 319	51 661	50 331	53 397	57 304	62 089	16
49 546	49 126	49 226	47 647	54 242	54 946	65 364	20
48 896	49 342	48 905	46 609	52 993	52 409	62 475	25
50 444	55 325	51 408	48 005	55 087	56 808	63 549	-
50 616	55 014	53 403	49 305	55 598	56 699	64 221	-
52 539	53 571	53 653	52 472	58 267	60 124	66 534	-
55 584	58 231	58 738	54 709	61 804	63 122	78 766	-
61 009	63 735	64 117	60 061	66 399	68 203	73 073	-
65 931	68 778	69 268	65 904	70 587	75 284	82 112	-
69 247	72 554	72 004	69 524	75 892	79 313	86 852	-
78 091	80 430	82 140	78 716	85 391	90 964	103 098	-
81 168	82 915	83 443	80 604	86 512	91 726	100 920	-
82 231	84 523	88 049	82 998	91 459	94 706	103 804	-
84 258	87 663	88 063	85 018	92 765	97 922	105 491	-
84 824	86 861	88 685	87 591	94 708	97 110	106 055	-
90 408	95 164	95 699	91 715	98 355	103 939	110 884	-
94 571	94 281	96 080	92 090	100 419	101 395	114 493	-
90 959	94 741	96 964	92 880	102 648	108 280	119 950	-
92 313	96 883	99 049	96 208	103 060	108 764	117 335	-
92 507	95 994	98 116	97 609	104 329	108 188	122 168	-
94 567	99 445	101 036	98 242	107 927	106 614	116 841	-
95 441	**99 201**	**103 346**	**100 070**	**109 498**	**113 848**	**122 563**	-
率　　　Death rates							
13. 2	14. 5	14. 4	12. 4	11. 7	12. 2	13. 9	…
9. 7	10. 1	10. 4	9. 7	9. 5	9. 9	12. 8	…
7. 0	6. 9	6. 8	6. 9	7. 0	7. 8	8. 2	…
6. 5	6. 2	6. 2	6. 2	6. 9	7. 2	8. 3	…
6. 1	5. 9	5. 9	5. 8	6. 3	6. 5	7. 5	…
6. 0	6. 3	5. 9	5. 7	6. 3	6. 7	7. 2	-
5. 6	5. 9	5. 7	5. 4	5. 9	6. 2	6. 8	-
5. 5	5. 4	5. 5	5. 5	5. 9	6. 3	6. 7	-
5. 6	5. 7	5. 8	5. 5	6. 0	6. 4	7. 7	-
6. 1	6. 1	6. 2	6. 0	6. 4	6. 8	7. 0	-
6. 5	6. 5	6. 6	6. 5	6. 7	7. 3	7. 8	-
6. 7	6. 8	6. 8	6. 8	7. 1	7. 7	8. 2	-
7. 5	7. 5	7. 7	7. 6	8. 0	8. 8	9. 6	-
7. 8	7. 7	7. 8	7. 8	8. 1	8. 8	9. 4	-
7. 9	7. 9	8. 2	8. 0	8. 5	9. 1	9. 7	-
8. 2	8. 2	8. 3	8. 2	8. 7	9. 5	9. 9	-
8. 2	8. 1	8. 3	8. 5	8. 9	9. 4	9. 9	-
8. 7	8. 9	9. 0	8. 9	9. 2	10. 0	10. 3	-
9. 1	8. 8	9. 0	8. 9	9. 4	9. 8	10. 7	-
8. 8	8. 9	9. 1	9. 0	9. 6	10. 5	11. 2	-
8. 9	9. 1	9. 3	9. 3	9. 7	10. 5	11. 0	-
9. 0	9. 0	9. 2	9. 5	9. 8	10. 5	11. 5	-
9. 2	9. 3	9. 5	9. 5	10. 1	10. 4	11. 0	-
9. 3	**9. 4**	**9. 8**	**9. 8**	**10. 3**	**11. 1**	**11. 6**	-

死 亡

〔死亡の場所別にみた死亡〕
〔Deaths by place of occurrence〕

表5.5 死亡の場所別に
Table 5.5 Trends in deaths by

年　　次 Year		総　数 Total	施　　設　　内 Hospitalized						施　　設　　外 Nonhosp.		
			総　数 Total	病　　院 Hospital	診療所 Clinic	介護老人保健施設 HSFE[a]	助産所 Maternity home	老人ホーム[1] Home for the elderly	総　数 Total	自　宅 Home	その他 Others
1951	昭和26年	838 998	97 716	75 944	21 511	・	261	・	741 282	691 901	49 381
52	27	765 068	95 185	74 456	20 503	・	226	・	669 883	622 062	47 821
53	28	772 547	99 430	78 027	21 114	・	289	・	673 117	621 105	52 012
54	29	721 491	104 640	82 588	21 731	・	321	・	616 851	562 995	53 856
55	30	693 523	107 134	85 086	21 646	・	402	・	586 389	533 098	53 291
56	31	724 460	118 080	94 339	23 299	・	442	・	606 380	551 900	54 480
57	32	752 445	130 706	105 744	24 474	・	488	・	621 739	566 302	55 437
58	33	684 189	134 062	109 773	23 633	・	656	・	550 127	496 213	53 914
59	34	689 959	142 790	117 306	24 814	・	670	・	547 169	491 384	55 785
1960	35	706 599	155 038	128 306	25 941	・	791	・	551 561	499 406	52 155
61	36	695 644	162 763	135 041	26 868	・	854	・	532 881	481 616	51 265
62	37	710 265	173 556	145 200	27 430	・	926	・	536 709	488 197	48 512
63	38	670 770	177 249	149 729	26 700	・	820	・	493 521	446 242	47 279
64	39	673 067	190 310	162 520	26 999	・	791	・	482 757	437 287	45 470
65	40	700 438	200 342	172 091	27 477	・	774	・	500 096	455 081	45 015
66	41	670 342	206 183	179 699	25 952	・	532	・	464 159	420 085	44 074
67	42	675 006	221 347	193 234	27 464	・	649	・	453 659	411 175	42 484
68	43	686 555	238 099	207 117	30 417	・	565	・	448 456	407 598	40 858
69	44	693 787	252 734	221 250	30 909	・	575	・	441 053	399 585	41 468
1970	45	712 962	267 292	234 915	31 949	・	428	・	445 670	403 870	41 800
71	46	684 521	271 418	239 148	31 871	・	399	・	413 103	372 794	40 309
72	47	683 751	288 009	254 630	33 013	・	366	・	395 742	355 428	40 314
73	48	709 416	313 408	277 603	35 555	・	250	・	396 008	356 432	39 576
74	49	710 510	322 434	286 813	35 416	・	205	・	388 076	349 399	38 677
75	50	702 275	328 101	293 352	34 556	・	193	・	374 174	334 980	39 194
76	51	703 270	339 816	305 798	33 867	・	151	・	363 454	325 310	38 144
77	52	690 074	349 235	315 398	33 692	・	145	・	340 839	303 416	37 423
78	53	695 821	366 697	332 594	34 006	・	97	・	329 124	292 565	36 559
79	54	689 664	383 399	349 490	33 804	・	105	・	306 265	270 998	35 267
1980	55	722 801	411 970	376 838	35 102	・	30	・	310 831	274 966	35 865
81	56	720 262	430 537	396 074	34 434	・	29	・	289 725	254 789	34 936
82	57	711 883	445 746	411 821	33 909	・	16	・	266 137	232 617	33 520
83	58	740 038	467 122	433 886	33 224	・	12	・	272 916	237 225	35 691
84	59	740 247	481 178	449 066	32 107	・	5	・	259 069	224 463	34 606
85	60	752 283	506 054	473 691	32 353	・	10	・	246 229	212 763	33 466
86	61	750 620	515 437	484 593	30 838	・	6	・	235 183	202 670	32 513
87	62	751 172	530 771	500 874	29 890	・	7	・	220 401	189 520	30 881
88	63	793 014	570 340	540 408	29 929	・	3	・	222 674	191 654	31 020
89	平成元年	788 594	585 257	556 497	28 609	147	4	・	203 337	175 416	27 921

注：1）平成6年までは老人ホームでの死亡は、自宅又はその他に含まれる。
Note：a）Health services facilities for the elderly

160

みた年次別死亡数
place of occurrence : Japan

年　次 Year		総　数 Total	施　設　内 Hospitalized						施　設　外 Nonhosp.		
			総　数 Total	病　院 Hospital	診療所 Clinic	介護老人保健施設 HSFE[a]	助産所 Maternity home	老人ホーム[1] Home for the elderly	総　数 Total	自　宅 Home	その他 Others
1990	平成2年	820 305	615 759	587 438	27 968	351	2	・	204 546	177 657	26 889
91	3	829 797	629 449	600 914	27 902	631	2	・	200 348	173 141	27 207
92	4	856 643	656 535	627 799	27 955	778	3	・	200 108	172 439	27 669
93	5	878 532	676 633	647 621	27 927	1 081	4	・	201 899	173 669	28 230
94	6	875 933	672 908	644 612	26 938	1 355	3	・	203 025	174 682	28 343
95	7	922 139	726 836	682 943	27 555	2 080	2	14 256	195 303	168 756	26 547
96	8	896 211	721 347	678 450	26 139	2 335	1	14 422	174 864	149 925	24 939
97	9	913 402	740 981	696 252	26 493	2 890	-	15 346	172 421	146 736	25 685
98	10	936 484	759 481	713 474	26 642	3 627	2	15 736	177 003	148 779	28 224
99	11	982 031	806 828	757 257	28 476	4 306	1	16 788	175 203	147 103	28 100
2000	12	961 653	801 295	751 581	27 087	4 818	2	17 807	160 358	133 534	26 824
01	13	970 331	812 777	760 681	27 627	5 461	-	19 008	157 554	131 337	26 217
02	14	982 379	824 442	772 638	27 479	5 611	1	18 713	157 937	131 379	26 558
03	15	1 014 951	854 670	801 125	27 898	5 986	2	19 659	160 281	131 991	28 290
04	16	1 028 602	873 978	818 586	27 586	6 490	3	21 313	154 624	127 445	27 179
05	17	1 083 796	923 546	864 338	28 581	7 346	3	23 278	160 250	132 702	27 548
06	18	1 084 450	926 217	864 702	27 881	8 162	-	25 472	158 233	131 854	26 379
07	19	1 108 334	945 677	879 692	28 505	9 232	1	28 247	162 657	136 437	26 220
08	20	1 142 407	970 809	897 814	28 946	10 921	-	33 128	171 598	144 771	26 827
09	21	1 141 865	972 574	895 356	27 802	12 600	2	36 814	169 291	141 955	27 336
2010	22	1 197 012	1 018 525	931 905	28 869	15 651	1	42 099	178 487	150 783	27 704
11	23	1 253 066	1 052 333	954 745	29 203	18 393	1	49 991	200 733	156 491	44 242
12	24	1 256 359	1 067 865	958 991	29 066	21 544	-	58 264	188 494	161 242	27 252
13	25	1 268 436	1 077 685	958 755	27 942	24 069	-	66 919	190 751	163 049	27 702
14	26	1 273 004	1 082 864	956 913	26 574	26 037	2	73 338	190 140	162 599	27 541
15	27	1 290 444	1 098 886	962 597	25 482	29 127	-	81 680	191 558	163 973	27 585
16	28	1 307 748	1 111 421	965 779	24 861	30 713	1	90 067	196 327	169 400	26 927

死　亡

表 5.6　死亡の場所別に
Table 5.6　Trends in percent distribution

年　次 Year		総　数 Total	施　設　内 Hospitalized						施　設　外 Nonhosp.		
			総　数 Total	病　院 Hospital	診療所 Clinic	介護老人保健施設 HSFE[a]	助産所 Maternity home	老人ホーム[1] Home for the elderly	総　数 Total	自　宅 Home	その他 Others
1951	昭和26年	100.0	11.6	9.1	2.6	・	0.0	・	88.4	82.5	5.9
52	27	100.0	12.4	9.7	2.7	・	0.0	・	87.6	81.3	6.3
53	28	100.0	12.9	10.1	2.7	・	0.0	・	87.1	80.4	6.7
54	29	100.0	14.5	11.4	3.0	・	0.0	・	85.5	78.0	7.5
55	30	100.0	15.4	12.3	3.1	・	0.1	・	84.6	76.9	7.7
56	31	100.0	16.3	13.0	3.2	・	0.1	・	83.7	76.2	7.5
57	32	100.0	17.4	14.1	3.3	・	0.1	・	82.6	75.3	7.4
58	33	100.0	19.6	16.0	3.5	・	0.1	・	80.4	72.5	7.9
59	34	100.0	20.7	17.0	3.6	・	0.1	・	79.3	71.2	8.1
1960	35	100.0	21.9	18.2	3.7	・	0.1	・	78.1	70.7	7.4
61	36	100.0	23.4	19.4	3.9	・	0.1	・	76.6	69.2	7.4
62	37	100.0	24.4	20.4	3.9	・	0.1	・	75.6	68.7	6.8
63	38	100.0	26.4	22.3	4.0	・	0.1	・	73.6	66.5	7.0
64	39	100.0	28.3	24.1	4.0	・	0.1	・	71.7	65.0	6.8
65	40	100.0	28.6	24.6	3.9	・	0.1	・	71.4	65.0	6.4
66	41	100.0	30.8	26.8	3.9	・	0.1	・	69.2	62.7	6.6
67	42	100.0	32.8	28.6	4.1	・	0.1	・	67.2	60.9	6.3
68	43	100.0	34.7	30.2	4.4	・	0.1	・	65.3	59.4	6.0
69	44	100.0	36.4	31.9	4.5	・	0.1	・	63.6	57.6	6.0
1970	45	100.0	37.5	32.9	4.5	・	0.1	・	62.5	56.6	5.9
71	46	100.0	39.7	34.9	4.7	・	0.1	・	60.3	54.5	5.9
72	47	100.0	42.1	37.2	4.8	・	0.1	・	57.9	52.0	5.9
73	48	100.0	44.2	39.1	5.0	・	0.0	・	55.8	50.2	5.6
74	49	100.0	45.4	40.4	5.0	・	0.0	・	54.6	49.2	5.4
75	50	100.0	46.7	41.8	4.9	・	0.0	・	53.3	47.7	5.6
76	51	100.0	48.3	43.5	4.8	・	0.0	・	51.7	46.3	5.4
77	52	100.0	50.6	45.7	4.9	・	0.0	・	49.4	44.0	5.4
78	53	100.0	52.7	47.8	4.9	・	0.0	・	47.3	42.0	5.3
79	54	100.0	55.6	50.7	4.9	・	0.0	・	44.4	39.3	5.1
1980	55	100.0	57.0	52.1	4.9	・	0.0	・	43.0	38.0	5.0
81	56	100.0	59.8	55.0	4.8	・	0.0	・	40.2	35.4	4.9
82	57	100.0	62.6	57.8	4.8	・	0.0	・	37.4	32.7	4.7
83	58	100.0	63.1	58.6	4.5	・	0.0	・	36.9	32.1	4.8
84	59	100.0	65.0	60.7	4.3	・	0.0	・	35.0	30.3	4.7
85	60	100.0	67.3	63.0	4.3	・	0.0	・	32.7	28.3	4.4
86	61	100.0	68.7	64.6	4.1	・	0.0	・	31.3	27.0	4.3
87	62	100.0	70.7	66.7	4.0	・	0.0	・	29.3	25.2	4.1
88	63	100.0	71.9	68.1	3.8	・	0.0	・	28.1	24.2	3.9
89	平成元年	100.0	74.2	70.6	3.6	0.0	0.0	・	25.8	22.2	3.5

注：1)　平成6年までは老人ホームでの死亡は、自宅又はその他に含まれる。
Note：a) Health services facilities for the elderly

General mortality

みた年次別死亡数百分率
of deaths by place of occurrence : Japan

年　　次 Year		総　数 Total	施　　設　　内 Hospitalized						施　　設　　外 Nonhosp.		
			総　数 Total	病　院 Hospital	診療所 Clinic	介護老人保健施設 HSFE[a]	助産所 Maternity home	老人ホーム[1] Home for the elderly	総　数 Total	自　宅 Home	その他 Others
1990	平成2年	100.0	75.1	71.6	3.4	0.0	0.0	・	24.9	21.7	3.3
91	3	100.0	75.9	72.4	3.4	0.1	0.0	・	24.1	20.9	3.3
92	4	100.0	76.6	73.3	3.3	0.1	0.0	・	23.4	20.1	3.2
93	5	100.0	77.0	73.7	3.2	0.1	0.0	・	23.0	19.8	3.2
94	6	100.0	76.8	73.6	3.1	0.2	0.0	・	23.2	19.9	3.2
95	7	100.0	78.8	74.1	3.0	0.2	0.0	1.5	21.2	18.3	2.9
96	8	100.0	80.5	75.7	2.9	0.3	0.0	1.6	19.5	16.7	2.8
97	9	100.0	81.1	76.2	2.9	0.3	-	1.7	18.9	16.1	2.8
98	10	100.0	81.1	76.2	2.8	0.4	0.0	1.7	18.9	15.9	3.0
99	11	100.0	82.2	77.1	2.9	0.4	0.0	1.7	17.8	15.0	2.9
2000	12	100.0	83.3	78.2	2.8	0.5	0.0	1.9	16.7	13.9	2.8
01	13	100.0	83.8	78.4	2.8	0.6	-	2.0	16.2	13.5	2.7
02	14	100.0	83.9	78.6	2.8	0.6	0.0	1.9	16.1	13.4	2.7
03	15	100.0	84.2	78.9	2.7	0.6	0.0	1.9	15.8	13.0	2.8
04	16	100.0	85.0	79.6	2.7	0.6	0.0	2.1	15.0	12.4	2.6
05	17	100.0	85.2	79.8	2.6	0.7	0.0	2.1	14.8	12.2	2.5
06	18	100.0	85.4	79.7	2.6	0.8	-	2.3	14.6	12.2	2.4
07	19	100.0	85.3	79.4	2.6	0.8	0.0	2.5	14.7	12.3	2.4
08	20	100.0	85.0	78.6	2.5	1.0	-	2.9	15.0	12.7	2.3
09	21	100.0	85.2	78.4	2.4	1.1	0.0	3.2	14.8	12.4	2.4
2010	22	100.0	85.1	77.9	2.4	1.3	0.0	3.5	14.9	12.6	2.3
11	23	100.0	84.0	76.2	2.3	1.5	0.0	4.0	16.0	12.5	3.5
12	24	100.0	85.0	76.3	2.3	1.7	-	4.6	15.0	12.8	2.2
13	25	100.0	85.0	75.6	2.2	1.9	-	5.3	15.0	12.9	2.2
14	26	100.0	85.1	75.2	2.1	2.0	0.0	5.8	14.9	12.8	2.2
15	27	100.0	85.2	74.6	2.0	2.3	-	6.3	14.8	12.7	2.1
16	28	100.0	85.0	73.9	1.9	2.3	0.0	6.9	15.0	13.0	2.1

死　亡

表5.7　死亡の場所別にみた都道府県（21大都市再掲）別死亡数
Table 5.7　Deaths by place of occurrence : Japan, each prefecture and 21 major cities, 2016

平成28年

都道府県 Prefecture	総数 Total	施設内 Hospitalized 総数 Total	病院 Hospital	診療所 Clinic	介護老人保健施設 HSFE b)	助産所 Maternity home	老人ホーム Home for the elderly	施設外 Nonhosp. 総数 Total	自宅 Home	その他 Others
全国　Total	1 307 748	1 111 421	965 779	24 861	30 713	1	90 067	196 327	169 400	26 927
市部　Total for urban residence	1 162 734	984 973	856 990	21 156	27 061	1	79 765	177 761	154 230	23 531
郡部　Total for rural residence	143 801	125 839	108 204	3 697	3 647	-	10 291	17 962	15 170	2 792
01 北海道	61 906	54 919	50 552	1 424	974	-	1 969	6 987	5 874	1 113
02 青森	17 309	15 088	12 224	899	585	-	1 380	2 221	1 851	370
03 岩手	16 959	14 706	12 700	267	600	-	1 139	2 253	1 968	285
04 宮城	23 426	19 449	16 763	518	860	-	1 308	3 977	3 460	517
05 秋田	15 244	13 303	11 596	230	588	-	889	1 941	1 406	535
06 山形	15 181	13 265	11 144	206	390	-	1 525	1 916	1 645	271
07 福島	24 166	20 467	17 915	263	829	-	1 460	3 699	3 185	514
08 茨城	31 414	27 381	24 159	915	814	-	1 493	4 033	3 465	568
09 栃木	21 436	18 138	15 295	540	668	-	1 635	3 298	2 837	461
10 群馬	22 125	19 270	16 402	300	645	-	1 923	2 855	2 338	517
11 埼玉	63 466	54 519	49 020	1 073	978	-	3 448	8 947	7 912	1 035
12 千葉	56 396	46 779	41 810	893	1 122	-	2 954	9 617	8 534	1 083
13 東京	113 415	91 786	80 851	1 323	1 447	-	8 165	21 629	19 840	1 789
14 神奈川	77 361	62 903	54 381	630	1 213	-	6 679	14 458	12 855	1 603
15 新潟	28 822	25 363	21 822	46	784	-	2 711	3 459	2 986	473
16 富山	12 864	11 272	9 982	88	416	-	786	1 592	1 361	231
17 石川	12 422	11 049	9 454	137	492	-	966	1 373	1 163	210
18 福井	9 228	7 981	6 715	268	328	-	670	1 247	1 061	186
19 山梨	9 565	8 160	6 907	229	312	-	712	1 405	1 220	185
20 長野	25 110	21 599	17 795	316	813	1	2 674	3 511	3 067	444
21 岐阜	22 471	19 098	16 123	482	768	-	1 725	3 373	2 808	565
22 静岡	39 294	33 335	27 503	495	1 692	-	3 645	5 959	5 295	664
23 愛知	65 227	55 691	48 131	892	1 633	-	5 035	9 536	8 506	1 030
24 三重	19 830	16 847	14 033	329	809	-	1 676	2 983	2 477	506
25 滋賀	12 507	10 506	9 563	41	178	-	724	2 001	1 750	251
26 京都	25 830	21 590	19 392	90	383	-	1 725	4 240	3 837	403
27 大阪	84 390	69 505	62 939	467	1 138	-	4 961	14 885	12 970	1 915
28 兵庫	55 422	45 320	39 154	914	1 164	-	4 088	10 102	8 766	1 336
29 奈良	14 054	11 405	10 141	58	278	-	928	2 649	2 247	402
30 和歌山	12 619	10 787	8 966	365	410	-	1 046	1 832	1 554	278
31 鳥取	7 357	6 309	5 016	173	425	-	695	1 048	841	207
32 島根	9 562	8 445	7 048	62	307	-	1 028	1 117	908	209
33 岡山	21 532	18 584	15 466	793	671	-	1 654	2 948	2 458	490
34 広島	29 994	25 322	21 691	748	633	-	2 250	4 672	3 816	856
35 山口	18 366	16 102	14 218	419	284	-	1 181	2 264	1 881	383
36 徳島	9 855	8 622	7 117	504	428	-	573	1 233	992	241
37 香川	11 908	9 945	7 877	590	369	-	1 109	1 963	1 625	338
38 愛媛	17 734	14 889	12 779	642	434	-	1 034	2 845	2 240	605
39 高知	10 305	9 030	8 366	120	175	-	369	1 275	1 053	222
40 福岡	51 006	44 983	41 186	733	715	-	2 349	6 023	5 081	942
41 佐賀	9 725	8 643	7 497	372	244	-	530	1 082	883	199
42 長崎	17 071	15 010	12 690	849	448	-	1 023	2 061	1 708	353
43 熊本	21 379	19 070	16 164	873	479	-	1 554	2 309	1 927	382
44 大分	14 264	12 938	10 136	803	674	-	1 325	1 326	1 133	193
45 宮崎	13 702	12 308	9 967	735	284	-	1 322	1 394	1 172	222
46 鹿児島	21 610	19 254	15 762	1 542	543	-	1 407	2 356	1 938	418
47 沖縄	11 706	9 877	8 782	197	284	-	614	1 829	1 506	323
外国　Foreign countries	131	63	60	1	-	-	2	68	-	68
不詳　Place of residence not stated	1 082	546	525	7	5	-	9	536	-	536
21 大都市（再掲）21 major cities (Regrouped)										
50 東京都の区部	76 826	61 181	54 221	890	903	-	5 167	15 645	14 290	1 355
51 札幌	18 504	16 083	15 105	267	201	-	510	2 421	2 053	368
52 仙台	8 589	6 859	5 527	273	406	-	653	1 730	1 524	206
53 さいたま	10 177	8 701	7 846	40	112	-	703	1 476	1 301	175
54 千葉	8 112	6 715	5 996	176	135	-	408	1 397	1 247	150
55 横浜	31 414	25 176	21 471	242	676	-	2 787	6 238	5 525	713
56 川崎	10 379	8 420	7 367	69	128	-	856	1 959	1 744	215
57 相模原	5 611	4 781	4 389	20	49	-	323	830	750	80
58 新潟	8 590	7 683	6 867	9	209	-	598	907	763	144
59 静岡	7 745	6 496	5 548	4	268	-	676	1 249	1 098	151
60 浜松	7 852	6 738	5 162	144	502	-	930	1 114	976	138
61 名古屋	21 221	17 909	15 260	233	512	-	1 904	3 312	3 051	261
62 京都	13 966	11 580	10 469	22	221	-	868	2 386	2 165	221
63 大阪	27 815	22 382	20 522	125	346	-	1 389	5 433	4 712	721
64 堺	7 951	6 565	5 998	17	148	-	402	1 386	1 214	172
65 神戸	15 350	12 355	10 407	401	425	-	1 122	2 995	2 612	383
66 岡山	6 520	5 473	4 378	350	186	-	559	1 047	847	200
67 広島	9 951	8 173	7 041	238	135	-	759	1 778	1 474	304
68 北九州	10 759	9 562	8 836	113	115	-	498	1 197	1 025	172
69 福岡	11 521	9 891	9 113	121	139	-	518	1 630	1 378	252
70 熊本	6 916	6 018	5 253	173	155	-	437	898	732	166

注：市部・郡部の計には住所地外国・不詳を含まない。
Note : a) See page 44.
　　　b) Health services facilities for the elderly

General mortality

表5.8　死亡の場所別にみた都道府県（21大都市再掲）別死亡数百分率
Table 5.8　Percent distribution of deaths by place of occurrence : Japan, each prefecture and 21 major cities, 2016

平成28年

都道府県 Prefecture	総数 Total	施設内 Hospitalized						施設外 Nonhosp.		
		総数 Total	病院 Hospital	診療所 Clinic	介護老人保健施設 HSFE b)	助産所 Maternity home	老人ホーム Home for the elderly	総数 Total	自宅 Home	その他 Others
全国　Total	100.0	85.0	73.9	1.9	2.3	0.0	6.9	15.0	13.0	2.1
市部　Total for urban residence	100.0	84.7	73.7	1.8	2.3	0.0	6.9	15.3	13.3	2.0
郡部　Total for rural residence	100.0	87.5	75.2	2.6	2.5	-	7.2	12.5	10.5	1.9
a)										
01 北海道	100.0	88.7	81.7	2.3	1.6	-	3.2	11.3	9.5	1.8
02 青森	100.0	87.2	70.6	5.2	3.4	-	8.0	12.8	10.7	2.1
03 岩手	100.0	86.7	74.9	1.6	3.5	-	6.7	13.3	11.6	1.7
04 宮城	100.0	83.0	71.6	2.2	3.7	-	5.6	17.0	14.8	2.2
05 秋田	100.0	87.3	76.1	1.5	3.9	-	5.8	12.7	9.2	3.5
06 山形	100.0	87.4	73.4	1.4	2.6	-	10.0	12.6	10.8	1.8
07 福島	100.0	84.7	74.1	1.1	3.4	-	6.0	15.3	13.2	2.1
08 茨城	100.0	87.2	76.9	2.9	2.6	-	4.8	12.8	11.0	1.8
09 栃木	100.0	84.6	71.4	2.5	3.1	-	7.6	15.4	13.2	2.2
10 群馬	100.0	87.1	74.1	1.4	2.9	-	8.7	12.9	10.6	2.3
11 埼玉	100.0	85.9	77.2	1.7	1.5	-	5.4	14.1	12.5	1.6
12 千葉	100.0	82.9	74.1	1.6	2.0	-	5.2	17.1	15.1	1.9
13 東京	100.0	80.9	71.3	1.2	1.3	-	7.2	19.1	17.5	1.6
14 神奈川	100.0	81.3	70.3	0.8	1.6	-	8.6	18.7	16.6	2.1
15 新潟	100.0	88.0	75.7	0.2	2.7	-	9.4	12.0	10.4	1.6
16 富山	100.0	87.6	77.6	0.7	3.2	-	6.1	12.4	10.6	1.8
17 石川	100.0	88.9	76.1	1.1	4.0	-	7.8	11.1	9.4	1.7
18 福井	100.0	86.5	72.8	2.9	3.6	-	7.3	13.5	11.5	2.0
19 山梨	100.0	85.3	72.2	2.4	3.3	-	7.4	14.7	12.8	1.9
20 長野	100.0	86.0	70.9	1.3	3.2	0.0	10.6	14.0	12.2	1.8
21 岐阜	100.0	85.0	71.8	2.1	3.4	-	7.7	15.0	12.5	2.5
22 静岡	100.0	84.8	70.0	1.3	4.3	-	9.3	15.2	13.5	1.7
23 愛知	100.0	85.4	73.8	1.4	2.5	-	7.7	14.6	13.0	1.6
24 三重	100.0	85.0	70.8	1.7	4.1	-	8.5	15.0	12.5	2.6
25 滋賀	100.0	84.0	76.5	0.3	1.4	-	5.8	16.0	14.0	2.0
26 京都	100.0	83.6	75.1	0.3	1.5	-	6.7	16.4	14.9	1.6
27 大阪	100.0	82.4	74.6	0.6	1.3	-	5.9	17.6	15.4	2.3
28 兵庫	100.0	81.8	70.6	1.6	2.1	-	7.4	18.2	15.8	2.4
29 奈良	100.0	81.2	72.2	0.4	2.0	-	6.6	18.8	16.0	2.9
30 和歌山	100.0	85.5	71.1	2.9	3.2	-	8.3	14.5	12.3	2.2
31 鳥取	100.0	85.8	68.2	2.4	5.8	-	9.4	14.2	11.4	2.8
32 島根	100.0	88.3	73.7	0.6	3.2	-	10.8	11.7	9.5	2.2
33 岡山	100.0	86.3	71.8	3.7	3.1	-	7.7	13.7	11.4	2.3
34 広島	100.0	84.4	72.3	2.5	2.1	-	7.5	15.6	12.7	2.9
35 山口	100.0	87.7	77.4	2.3	1.5	-	6.4	12.3	10.2	2.1
36 徳島	100.0	87.5	72.2	5.1	4.3	-	5.8	12.5	10.1	2.4
37 香川	100.0	83.5	66.1	5.0	3.1	-	9.3	16.5	13.6	2.8
38 愛媛	100.0	84.0	72.1	3.6	2.4	-	5.8	16.0	12.6	3.4
39 高知	100.0	87.6	81.2	1.2	1.7	-	3.6	12.4	10.2	2.2
40 福岡	100.0	88.2	80.7	1.4	1.4	-	4.6	11.8	10.0	1.8
41 佐賀	100.0	88.9	77.1	3.8	2.5	-	5.4	11.1	9.1	2.0
42 長崎	100.0	87.9	74.3	5.0	2.6	-	6.0	12.1	10.0	2.1
43 熊本	100.0	89.2	75.6	4.1	2.2	-	7.3	10.8	9.0	1.8
44 大分	100.0	90.7	71.1	5.6	4.7	-	9.3	9.3	7.9	1.4
45 宮崎	100.0	89.8	72.7	5.4	2.1	-	9.6	10.2	8.6	1.6
46 鹿児島	100.0	89.1	72.9	7.1	2.5	-	6.5	10.9	9.0	1.9
47 沖縄	100.0	84.4	75.0	1.7	2.4	-	5.2	15.6	12.9	2.8
外国　Foreign countries	100.0	48.1	45.8	0.8	-	-	1.5	51.9	-	51.9
不詳　Place of residence not stated	100.0	50.5	48.5	0.6	0.5	-	0.8	49.5	-	49.5
21 大都市（再掲）21 major cities (Regrouped)										
50 東京都の区部	100.0	79.6	70.6	1.2	1.2	-	6.7	20.4	18.6	1.8
51 札幌	100.0	86.9	81.6	1.4	1.1	-	2.8	13.1	11.1	2.0
52 仙台	100.0	79.9	64.3	3.2	4.7	-	7.6	20.1	17.7	2.4
53 さいたま	100.0	85.5	77.1	0.4	1.1	-	6.9	14.5	12.8	1.7
54 千葉	100.0	82.8	73.9	2.2	1.7	-	5.0	17.2	15.4	1.8
55 横浜	100.0	80.1	68.3	0.8	2.2	-	8.9	19.9	17.6	2.3
56 川崎	100.0	81.1	71.0	0.7	1.2	-	8.2	18.9	16.8	2.1
57 相模原	100.0	85.2	78.2	0.4	0.9	-	5.8	14.8	13.4	1.4
58 新潟	100.0	89.4	79.9	0.1	2.4	-	7.0	10.6	8.9	1.7
59 静岡	100.0	83.9	71.6	0.1	3.5	-	8.7	16.1	14.2	1.9
60 浜松	100.0	85.8	65.7	1.8	6.4	-	11.8	14.2	12.4	1.8
61 名古屋	100.0	84.4	71.9	1.1	2.4	-	9.0	15.6	14.4	1.2
62 京都	100.0	82.9	75.0	0.2	1.6	-	6.2	17.1	15.5	1.6
63 大阪	100.0	80.5	73.8	0.4	1.2	-	5.0	19.5	16.9	2.6
64 堺	100.0	82.6	75.4	0.2	1.9	-	5.1	17.4	15.3	2.2
65 神戸	100.0	80.5	67.8	2.6	2.8	-	7.3	19.5	17.0	2.5
66 岡山	100.0	83.9	67.1	5.4	2.9	-	8.6	16.1	13.0	3.1
67 広島	100.0	82.1	70.8	2.4	1.4	-	7.6	17.9	14.8	3.1
68 北九州	100.0	88.9	82.1	1.1	1.1	-	4.6	11.1	9.5	1.6
69 福岡	100.0	85.9	79.1	1.1	1.2	-	4.5	14.1	12.0	2.2
70 熊本	100.0	87.0	76.0	2.5	2.2	-	6.3	13.0	10.6	2.4

Note : a) See page 44.

b) Health services facilities for the elderly

死　亡

〔地域別にみた死亡〕
〔Deaths by prefecture〕

表5.9　都　道　府　県　別　に
Table 5.9　Trends in deaths by

都道府県[1] Prefecture	1947 昭和22年	1950 25　年	1955 30　年	1960 35　年	1965 40　年	1970 45　年	1975 50　年	1980 55　年	1985 60　年
全国　Total	1 138 238	904 876	693 523	706 599	700 438	712 962	702 275	722 801	752 283
01[a] 北　海　道	51 472	42 745	32 729	31 509	31 779	31 884	31 037	32 434	34 314
02　青　　　森	18 092	16 707	11 094	10 742	9 805	9 669	9 546	10 052	10 547
03　岩　　　手	19 619	17 575	12 461	11 586	10 799	10 546	9 943	9 892	10 073
04　宮　　　城	20 703	17 373	12 646	12 301	12 437	12 390	12 152	12 651	12 828
05　秋　　　田	19 952	15 968	11 358	10 348	9 807	9 574	9 110	9 279	9 412
06　山　　　形	20 871	15 502	11 691	10 986	10 698	10 299	9 585	9 955	9 800
07　福　　　島	28 345	23 619	18 287	17 044	16 109	15 672	14 801	14 869	14 967
08　茨　　　城	28 475	24 867	18 732	17 709	17 042	17 395	16 773	16 858	17 261
09　栃　　　木	21 329	18 432	13 067	12 505	12 405	12 672	12 112	12 109	12 349
10　群　　　馬	21 908	17 390	12 821	12 827	12 775	12 979	12 344	12 290	12 790
11　埼　　　玉	30 268	26 258	19 238	19 089	20 117	21 836	22 688	24 129	26 417
12　千　　　葉	30 780	25 777	19 293	19 209	19 739	21 051	21 768	22 965	24 891
13　東　　　京	58 723	51 790	44 718	50 048	51 644	56 183	55 323	58 258	62 499
14　神　奈　川	26 826	22 047	18 614	20 564	22 751	25 814	27 319	29 923	33 809
15　新　　　潟	36 442	28 963	21 282	19 775	20 507	19 163	17 768	17 719	18 085
16　富　　　山	16 259	12 760	8 539	8 711	8 514	8 179	7 770	7 923	8 275
17　石　　　川	15 185	12 630	8 713	8 698	8 445	7 776	7 706	7 681	7 657
18　福　　　井	11 965	9 405	6 755	6 738	6 511	6 036	5 887	5 892	6 003
19　山　　　梨	10 970	8 419	6 332	6 488	6 396	6 470	6 003	6 143	6 213
20　長　　　野	27 744	21 442	16 993	17 202	17 476	16 535	15 685	15 703	15 975
21　岐　　　阜	22 199	17 297	12 749	13 013	12 782	13 008	12 908	13 011	13 240
22　静　　　岡	30 574	24 530	19 741	19 935	19 966	20 302	19 788	20 550	21 415
23　愛　　　知	42 987	34 433	26 873	28 829	28 897	30 681	30 993	31 734	33 357
24　三　　　重	22 210	16 210	12 190	12 981	12 551	12 679	12 240	12 154	12 724
25　滋　　　賀	14 675	10 031	7 552	7 892	7 643	7 484	7 307	7 276	7 255
26　京　　　都	25 686	17 850	13 797	15 265	15 109	15 577	15 460	16 059	16 942
27　大　　　阪	48 379	35 797	30 518	35 253	36 860	40 464	41 299	44 272	48 152
28　兵　　　庫	44 814	33 340	26 690	29 350	29 489	30 259	30 466	32 275	33 952
29　奈　　　良	12 200	8 571	6 697	6 952	6 701	6 843	7 055	7 623	8 295
30　和　歌　山	13 804	10 449	8 266	8 703	8 651	8 805	8 423	8 721	8 921
31　鳥　　　取	9 149	6 654	5 106	5 473	5 322	5 210	4 901	4 970	4 851
32　島　　　根	14 768	11 704	8 397	8 434	8 176	7 789	7 197	7 105	6 633
33　岡　　　山	25 683	18 734	13 783	14 916	14 139	13 875	13 865	14 019	14 358
34　広　　　島	30 212	22 240	17 560	18 584	17 969	18 404	18 057	18 235	19 129
35　山　　　口	23 869	17 259	13 428	13 621	13 000	12 695	11 937	12 347	12 278
36　徳　　　島	14 628	11 674	8 185	7 960	7 902	7 508	7 012	7 003	6 656
37　香　　　川	13 986	10 959	8 086	8 185	7 797	7 656	7 312	7 418	7 516
38　愛　　　媛	22 153	16 743	12 655	12 821	12 402	12 285	11 651	11 319	11 547
39　高　　　知	12 988	10 485	7 955	8 255	7 988	8 499	7 806	7 435	7 311
40　福　　　岡	48 082	36 874	29 078	28 770	28 124	28 056	27 576	29 517	30 888
41　佐　　　賀	15 546	11 322	8 515	8 060	7 267	7 141	6 728	6 873	6 811
42　長　　　崎	24 003	19 512	14 401	14 202	13 289	13 183	11 897	11 886	11 918
43　熊　　　本	26 498	20 963	15 721	16 023	15 280	14 902	13 868	13 594	13 683
44　大　　　分	21 120	15 875	11 359	11 273	10 587	10 418	9 859	9 744	9 736
45　宮　　　崎	15 376	12 570	9 351	8 772	8 752	8 676	8 266	8 382	8 355
46　鹿　児　島	26 721	21 223	17 335	16 876	16 237	16 293	15 404	15 497	15 519
47　沖　　　縄	…	…	…	…	…	…	5 667	5 348	5 283
外　　　　　国 Foreign countries	…	…	…	…	…	…	…	…	…
不　　　　　詳 Place of residence not stated	-	1 908	2 172	2 122	1 802	2 147	2 013	1 709	1 393

注：1)　昭和22年は事件発生地により、25年以降は住所地により表章している。

General mortality

みた年次別死亡数
each prefecture : Japan

1990 平成 2 年	1995 7 年	2000 12 年	2005 17 年	2010 22 年	2014 26 年	2015 27 年	2016 28 年	都道府県[1)] Prefecture
820 305	922 139	961 653	1 083 796	1 197 012	1 273 004	1 290 444	1 307 748	全国　Total
36 720	40 678	43 407	49 982	55 404	60 018	60 667	61 906	01[a)] 北 海 道
10 812	12 496	13 147	14 882	16 030	17 042	17 148	17 309	02 青　　森
10 882	12 043	12 517	14 638	15 756	16 274	16 502	16 959	03 岩　　手
13 982	15 980	17 127	19 765	21 932	22 854	23 070	23 426	04 宮　　城
10 005	10 931	12 026	13 061	14 288	15 096	14 794	15 244	05 秋　　田
10 423	11 259	11 842	13 255	14 084	15 032	14 960	15 181	06 山　　形
15 746	17 743	18 642	20 981	22 747	23 495	24 205	24 166	07 福　　島
18 962	21 621	22 877	25 839	28 615	30 341	31 025	31 414	08 茨　　城
13 608	14 672	15 613	18 091	19 712	20 755	20 519	21 436	09 栃　　木
13 607	15 428	16 144	18 546	20 385	21 441	21 519	22 125	10 群　　馬
31 222	36 799	40 486	48 095	55 487	61 269	62 565	63 466	11 埼　　玉
28 857	34 317	37 238	44 021	50 014	53 975	56 079	56 396	12 千　　葉
70 370	78 651	83 849	93 599	104 238	111 023	111 673	113 415	13 東　　京
39 543	46 507	50 539	58 801	67 760	74 387	75 762	77 361	14 神 奈 川
18 735	21 222	21 835	24 396	26 618	28 316	28 297	28 822	15 新　　潟
8 641	9 552	9 734	10 861	11 875	12 584	12 731	12 864	16 富　　山
8 231	9 174	9 391	10 376	11 607	12 190	12 280	12 422	17 石　　川
6 220	6 782	6 931	7 772	8 417	8 817	8 971	9 228	18 福　　井
6 606	7 168	7 297	8 291	9 268	9 755	9 636	9 565	19 山　　梨
16 646	18 052	19 320	21 369	23 133	24 751	24 536	25 110	20 長　　野
14 055	15 811	16 577	18 511	20 220	21 658	21 996	22 471	21 岐　　阜
23 543	26 666	28 323	31 747	36 420	38 342	39 518	39 294	22 静　　岡
37 435	42 944	45 810	52 536	58 477	62 426	64 060	65 227	23 愛　　知
13 630	15 072	15 292	17 154	18 691	19 525	20 139	19 830	24 三　　重
7 961	8 958	9 232	10 419	11 602	12 266	12 507	12 507	25 滋　　賀
18 031	19 321	20 233	22 134	23 714	25 507	25 495	25 830	26 京　　都
52 844	58 255	61 315	68 648	76 556	81 653	83 577	84 390	27 大　　阪
36 787	47 044	41 724	46 657	51 568	54 147	55 391	55 422	28 兵　　庫
8 958	10 106	10 362	11 880	13 036	13 835	13 920	14 054	29 奈　　良
9 281	10 064	10 225	11 251	12 049	12 609	12 549	12 619	30 和 歌 山
5 224	5 789	5 935	6 303	6 947	7 076	7 271	7 357	31 鳥　　取
7 078	7 687	7 700	8 557	9 109	9 369	9 604	9 562	32 島　　根
15 343	16 543	16 907	18 428	20 248	21 051	21 525	21 532	33 岡　　山
20 468	22 650	23 188	25 579	27 561	29 463	29 879	29 994	34 広　　島
13 265	14 484	15 126	16 522	17 646	17 910	18 211	18 366	35 山　　口
7 268	7 641	7 940	8 609	9 307	9 853	9 847	9 855	36 徳　　島
8 339	8 863	9 433	10 265	11 064	11 503	11 593	11 908	37 香　　川
12 458	13 509	13 757	15 469	16 344	17 529	17 585	17 734	38 愛　　媛
7 684	8 093	8 306	9 119	9 769	9 984	10 020	10 305	39 高　　知
33 595	37 158	38 505	42 675	46 996	49 317	50 259	51 006	40 福　　岡
7 260	7 947	7 899	8 546	9 212	9 732	9 702	9 725	41 佐　　賀
12 475	13 605	13 519	14 866	16 303	17 091	16 855	17 071	42 長　　崎
14 536	15 389	15 973	17 906	19 217	20 461	20 692	21 379	43 熊　　本
10 224	10 937	11 289	12 160	12 988	14 065	13 958	14 264	44 大　　分
8 867	9 846	9 906	11 167	12 334	13 110	13 494	13 702	45 宮　　崎
15 850	17 272	16 993	18 980	20 294	21 413	21 354	21 610	46 鹿 児 島
6 469	7 283	7 946	9 021	10 156	11 361	11 326	11 706	47 沖　　縄
…	49	89	191	176	163	143	131	外　　国 Foreign countries
1 559	2 078	2 187	1 875	1 638	1 170	1 035	1 082	不　　詳 Place of residence not stated

Note : a) See page 44.

死　亡

表5.10　都道府県別にみた
Table 5.10　Trends in death rates (per

都道府県[1] Prefecture	1947 昭和22年	1950 25　年	1955 30　年	1960 35　年	1965 40　年	1970 45　年	1975 50　年	1980 55　年	1985 60　年
全国　Total	14.6	10.9	7.8	7.6	7.1	6.9	6.3	6.2	6.3
01[a] 北 海 道	13.4	10.0	6.9	6.3	6.1	6.2	5.8	5.8	6.0
02 青　　森	15.3	13.0	8.0	7.5	6.9	6.8	6.5	6.6	6.9
03 岩　　手	15.5	13.1	8.7	8.0	7.7	7.7	7.2	7.0	6.9
04 宮　　城	13.2	10.4	7.3	7.1	7.1	6.8	6.2	6.1	5.9
05 秋　　田	15.9	12.2	8.4	7.7	7.7	7.7	7.4	7.4	7.5
06 山　　形	15.6	11.4	8.6	8.3	8.5	8.4	7.9	8.0	7.8
07 福　　島	14.2	11.5	8.7	8.3	8.1	8.1	7.5	7.3	7.3
08 茨　　城	14.1	12.2	9.1	8.7	8.3	8.1	7.2	6.6	6.4
09 栃　　木	13.9	11.9	8.4	8.3	8.2	8.0	7.1	6.8	6.6
10 群　　馬	13.9	10.9	7.9	8.1	8.0	7.8	7.0	6.7	6.7
11 埼　　玉	14.4	12.2	8.5	7.9	6.7	5.7	4.7	4.5	4.5
12 千　　葉	14.6	12.1	8.7	8.3	7.3	6.3	5.3	4.9	4.8
13 東　　京	11.7	8.3	5.6	5.2	4.8	5.0	4.8	5.1	5.3
14 神 奈 川	12.1	8.9	6.4	6.0	5.1	4.7	4.3	4.3	4.6
15 新　　潟	15.1	11.8	8.6	8.1	8.5	8.1	7.4	7.2	7.4
16 富　　山	16.6	12.6	8.4	8.4	8.3	8.0	7.3	7.2	7.4
17 石　　川	16.4	13.2	9.0	8.9	8.6	7.8	7.2	6.9	6.6
18 福　　井	16.5	12.5	9.0	9.0	8.7	8.2	7.7	7.5	7.3
19 山　　梨	13.6	10.4	7.8	8.3	8.4	8.5	7.7	7.7	7.5
20 長　　野	13.5	10.4	8.4	8.7	8.9	8.5	7.8	7.6	7.4
21 岐　　阜	14.9	11.2	8.1	7.9	7.5	7.4	6.9	6.7	6.5
22 静　　岡	13.0	9.9	7.4	7.2	6.9	6.6	6.0	6.0	6.0
23 愛　　知	13.8	10.2	7.1	6.9	6.0	5.7	5.3	5.1	5.1
24 三　　重	15.7	11.1	8.2	8.7	8.3	8.3	7.6	7.2	7.3
25 滋　　賀	17.1	11.6	8.8	9.4	9.0	8.5	7.5	6.8	6.2
26 京　　都	14.8	9.7	7.1	7.7	7.2	7.0	6.5	6.5	6.6
27 大　　阪	14.5	9.3	6.6	6.4	5.5	5.4	5.1	5.3	5.6
28 兵　　庫	14.7	10.1	7.4	7.5	6.8	6.6	6.2	6.4	6.4
29 奈　　良	15.6	11.2	8.6	8.9	8.1	7.4	6.6	6.3	6.4
30 和 歌 山	14.4	10.6	8.2	8.7	8.4	8.5	7.9	8.1	8.2
31 鳥　　取	15.6	11.1	8.3	9.1	9.2	9.2	8.5	8.3	7.8
32 島　　根	16.5	12.8	9.0	9.5	10.0	10.1	9.4	9.1	8.3
33 岡　　山	15.9	11.3	8.2	8.9	8.6	8.2	7.7	7.5	7.5
34 広　　島	15.0	10.7	8.2	8.5	7.9	7.6	6.9	6.7	6.8
35 山　　口	16.1	11.2	8.3	8.5	8.4	8.5	7.7	7.9	7.7
36 徳　　島	17.1	13.3	9.3	9.4	9.7	9.5	8.7	8.5	8.0
37 香　　川	15.2	11.6	8.6	8.9	8.7	8.4	7.6	7.4	7.3
38 愛　　媛	15.2	11.0	8.2	8.5	8.6	8.7	8.0	7.5	7.5
39 高　　知	15.3	12.0	9.0	9.7	9.8	10.8	9.7	9.0	8.7
40 福　　岡	15.1	10.4	7.5	7.2	7.1	7.0	6.5	6.5	6.5
41 佐　　賀	16.9	12.0	8.7	8.5	8.3	8.5	8.0	8.0	7.6
42 長　　崎	15.7	11.9	8.2	8.1	8.1	8.4	7.6	7.5	7.5
43 熊　　本	15.0	11.5	8.3	8.6	8.6	8.8	8.1	7.6	7.5
44 大　　分	17.1	12.7	8.9	9.1	8.9	9.0	8.3	8.0	7.8
45 宮　　崎	15.0	11.5	8.2	7.7	8.1	8.3	7.6	7.3	7.1
46 鹿 児 島	15.3	11.8	8.5	8.6	8.8	9.4	8.9	8.7	8.5
47 沖　　縄	…	…	…	…	…	…	5.5	4.9	4.5

注：1)　昭和22年は事件発生地により、25年以降は住所地により表章している。

168

年次別死亡率（人口千対）
1,000 population) by each prefecture : Japan

1990 平成2年	1995 7 年	2000 12 年	2005 17 年	2010 22 年	2014 26 年	2015 27 年	2016 28 年	都道府県[1] Prefecture
6.7	7.4	7.7	8.6	9.5	10.1	10.3	10.5	全国　Total
6.5	7.2	7.7	8.9	10.1	11.2	11.3	11.6	01[a] 北 海 道
7.3	8.5	8.9	10.4	11.7	12.9	13.1	13.4	02 青　　森
7.7	8.5	8.9	10.6	11.9	12.7	12.9	13.4	03 岩　　手
6.2	6.9	7.3	8.4	9.4	9.9	9.9	10.1	04 宮　　城
8.2	9.0	10.1	11.4	13.2	14.6	14.5	15.1	05 秋　　田
8.3	9.0	9.6	11.0	12.1	13.4	13.4	13.7	06 山　　形
7.5	8.3	8.8	10.1	11.3	12.2	12.7	12.8	07 福　　島
6.7	7.4	7.7	8.8	9.8	10.5	10.8	11.0	08 茨　　城
7.1	7.5	7.9	9.1	10.0	10.6	10.5	11.1	09 栃　　木
7.0	7.8	8.1	9.3	10.3	11.0	11.1	11.5	10 群　　馬
4.9	5.5	5.9	6.9	7.8	8.6	8.7	8.9	11 埼　　玉
5.2	6.0	6.3	7.4	8.2	8.8	9.1	9.2	12 千　　葉
6.0	6.8	7.1	7.6	8.1	8.5	8.5	8.6	13 東　　京
5.0	5.7	6.0	6.8	7.6	8.3	8.4	8.6	14 神 奈 川
7.6	8.6	8.9	10.1	11.3	12.3	12.3	12.7	15 新　　潟
7.7	8.5	8.7	9.9	11.0	11.9	12.1	12.3	16 富　　山
7.1	7.8	8.0	8.9	10.0	10.6	10.7	10.9	17 石　　川
7.6	8.3	8.5	9.6	10.6	11.3	11.5	12.0	18 福　　井
7.8	8.2	8.3	9.5	10.9	11.8	11.7	11.7	19 山　　梨
7.7	8.3	8.9	9.9	10.9	11.9	11.8	12.2	20 長　　野
6.8	7.6	8.0	8.9	9.9	10.8	11.0	11.3	21 岐　　阜
6.4	7.2	7.6	8.5	9.8	10.5	10.9	10.8	22 静　　岡
5.7	6.3	6.6	7.4	8.1	8.6	8.8	8.9	23 愛　　知
7.6	8.3	8.3	9.4	10.3	10.9	11.3	11.2	24 三　　重
6.6	7.0	7.0	7.7	8.4	8.8	9.0	9.0	25 滋　　賀
7.1	7.5	7.8	8.5	9.1	9.9	9.9	10.1	26 京　　都
6.2	6.8	7.1	7.9	8.8	9.4	9.6	9.7	27 大　　阪
6.9	8.8	7.6	8.5	9.4	9.9	10.2	10.2	28 兵　　庫
6.5	7.1	7.2	8.4	9.4	10.1	10.3	10.4	29 奈　　良
8.7	9.4	9.6	10.9	12.1	13.0	13.1	13.3	30 和 歌 山
8.5	9.4	9.7	10.5	11.9	12.4	12.8	13.0	31 鳥　　取
9.1	10.0	10.2	11.6	12.8	13.5	13.9	14.0	32 島　　根
8.0	8.5	8.7	9.5	10.5	11.0	11.3	11.4	33 岡　　山
7.2	7.9	8.1	9.0	9.7	10.5	10.6	10.7	34 広　　島
8.5	9.4	10.0	11.2	12.3	12.8	13.1	13.3	35 山　　口
8.7	9.2	9.7	10.7	11.9	13.0	13.1	13.2	36 徳　　島
8.2	8.7	9.3	10.2	11.2	11.8	12.0	12.4	37 香　　川
8.2	9.0	9.2	10.6	11.5	12.6	12.8	13.0	38 愛　　媛
9.3	9.9	10.2	11.5	12.8	13.6	13.8	14.4	39 高　　知
7.0	7.6	7.7	8.5	9.3	9.8	9.9	10.1	40 福　　岡
8.3	9.0	9.0	9.9	10.9	11.7	11.7	11.8	41 佐　　賀
8.0	8.8	8.9	10.1	11.5	12.4	12.3	12.6	42 長　　崎
7.9	8.3	8.6	9.8	10.6	11.5	11.6	12.1	43 熊　　本
8.3	8.9	9.3	10.1	10.9	12.1	12.1	12.4	44 大　　分
7.6	8.4	8.5	9.7	10.9	11.8	12.3	12.5	45 宮　　崎
8.8	9.6	9.5	10.9	11.9	12.9	13.0	13.3	46 鹿 児 島
5.3	5.8	6.1	6.7	7.3	8.1	8.0	8.2	47 沖　　縄

Note : a) See page 44.

死亡

〔死亡原因の年次推移〕

表5.11 年次別にみた

死亡率（人口10万対）

年次[2]	第1位 死因	死亡率	第2位 死因	死亡率	第3位 死因	死亡率	第4位 死因	死亡率	第5位 死因	死亡率
明治32年	肺炎及び気管支炎	206.1	脳血管疾患	170.5	全結核	155.7	胃腸炎	149.7	老衰	127.2
33	肺炎及び気管支炎	226.1	全結核	163.7	脳血管疾患	159.2	胃腸炎	133.8	老衰	131.0
38	肺炎及び気管支炎	247.4	全結核	206.0	脳血管疾患	163.4	老衰	139.9	胃腸炎	137.2
43	肺炎及び気管支炎	262.0	全結核	230.2	胃腸炎	213.4	脳血管疾患	131.9	老衰	120.2
大正4年	肺炎及び気管支炎	261.1	胃腸炎	223.7	全結核	219.7	脳血管疾患	128.8	老衰	112.5
9	肺炎及び気管支炎	408.0	胃腸炎	254.2	全結核	223.7	インフルエンザ	193.7	脳血管疾患	157.6
14	肺炎及び気管支炎	275.6	胃腸炎	238.2	全結核	194.1	脳血管疾患	161.2	老衰	117.3
昭和5年	胃腸炎	221.4	肺炎及び気管支炎	200.1	全結核	185.6	脳血管疾患	162.8	老衰	118.8
10	全結核	190.8	肺炎及び気管支炎	186.7	胃腸炎	173.2	脳血管疾患	165.4	老衰	114.0
15	全結核	212.9	肺炎及び気管支炎	185.8	脳血管疾患	177.7	胃腸炎	159.2	老衰	124.5
22	全結核	187.2	肺炎及び気管支炎	174.8	胃腸炎	136.8	脳血管疾患	129.4	老衰	100.3
23	全結核	179.9	脳血管疾患	117.9	胃腸炎	109.9	肺炎及び気管支炎	98.6	老衰	79.5
24	全結核	168.9	脳血管疾患	122.6	肺炎及び気管支炎	100.0	胃腸炎	92.6	老衰	80.2
25	全結核	146.4	脳血管疾患	127.1	肺炎及び気管支炎	93.2	胃腸炎	82.4	悪性新生物	77.4
26	脳血管疾患	125.2	全結核	110.3	肺炎及び気管支炎	82.2	悪性新生物	78.5	老衰	70.7
27	脳血管疾患	128.5	全結核	82.2	悪性新生物	80.9	老衰	69.3	肺炎及び気管支炎	67.1
28	脳血管疾患	133.7	悪性新生物	82.2	老衰	77.6	肺炎及び気管支炎	71.3	全結核	66.5
29	脳血管疾患	132.4	悪性新生物	85.3	老衰	69.5	全結核	62.4	心疾患	60.2
30	脳血管疾患	136.1	悪性新生物	87.1	老衰	67.1	心疾患	60.9	全結核	52.3
31	脳血管疾患	148.4	悪性新生物	90.7	老衰	75.8	心疾患	66.0	全結核	48.6
32	脳血管疾患	151.7	悪性新生物	91.3	老衰	80.5	心疾患	73.1	肺炎及び気管支炎	59.2
33	脳血管疾患	148.6	悪性新生物	95.5	心疾患	64.8	老衰	55.5	肺炎及び気管支炎	47.6
34	脳血管疾患	153.7	悪性新生物	98.2	心疾患	67.7	老衰	56.7	肺炎及び気管支炎	45.2
35	脳血管疾患	160.7	悪性新生物	100.4	心疾患	73.2	老衰	58.0	肺炎及び気管支炎	49.3
36	脳血管疾患	165.5	悪性新生物	102.3	心疾患	72.1	老衰	58.2	不慮の事故	44.1
37	脳血管疾患	169.4	悪性新生物	103.2	心疾患	76.2	老衰	57.5	肺炎及び気管支炎	45.0
38	脳血管疾患	171.4	悪性新生物	105.5	心疾患	70.4	老衰	50.4	不慮の事故	41.3
39	脳血管疾患	171.7	悪性新生物	107.3	心疾患	70.3	老衰	48.4	不慮の事故	41.6
40	脳血管疾患	175.8	悪性新生物	108.4	心疾患	77.0	老衰	50.0	不慮の事故	40.9
41	脳血管疾患	173.8	悪性新生物	110.9	心疾患	71.9	老衰	44.6	不慮の事故	43.0
42	脳血管疾患	173.1	悪性新生物	113.0	心疾患	75.7	老衰	43.3	不慮の事故	41.9
43	脳血管疾患	173.5	悪性新生物	114.6	心疾患	80.2	不慮の事故	40.2	老衰	39.4
44	脳血管疾患	174.4	悪性新生物	116.2	心疾患	81.7	不慮の事故	42.2	老衰	37.1
45	脳血管疾患	175.8	悪性新生物	116.3	心疾患	86.7	不慮の事故	42.5	老衰	38.1
46	脳血管疾患	169.6	悪性新生物	117.7	心疾患	82.0	不慮の事故	40.7	老衰	34.0

注：1) 死因順位の選び方については、巻末の参考表「1 各種分類表」の平成7年以降は「表6−1(1)」、平成6年以前は「表6−2(1)」を参照されたい。
　　2) 昭和22〜47年は沖縄県を含まない。昭和24年以前は25年以降と大きく死因分類が変わっているので5位まで掲載した。
　　　昭和42年以前の「その他の新生児固有の疾患」は、「その他の新生児固有の疾患及び性質不明の未熟児」である。
　　　平成6年までの「老衰」は、「精神病の記載のない老衰」である。平成7年以降の「心疾患」は、「心疾患（高血圧性を除く）」である。

死因順位[1]

General mortality

第 6 位		第 7 位		第 8 位		第 9 位		第 10 位	
死　因	死亡率	死　因	死亡率	死　因	死亡率	死　因	死亡率	死　因	死亡率
老　　衰	70.2	心　疾　患	64.2	その他の新生児固有の疾患	62.2	不慮の事故	39.5	腎炎及びネフローゼ	32.4
胃　腸　炎	67.7	心　疾　患	63.6	その他の新生児固有の疾患	56.0	不慮の事故	37.8	腎炎及びネフローゼ	29.2
心　疾　患	61.3	胃　腸　炎	53.1	その他の新生児固有の疾患	47.3	不慮の事故	36.4	腎炎及びネフローゼ	25.8
心　疾　患	64.9	胃　腸　炎	46.1	その他の新生児固有の疾患	42.1	不慮の事故	39.3	腎炎及びネフローゼ	23.2
肺炎及び気管支炎	54.7	不慮の事故	39.4	胃　腸　炎	39.0	その他の新生児固有の疾患	36.2	自　　殺	23.4
肺炎及び気管支炎	48.3	不慮の事故	37.3	胃　腸　炎	31.7	その他の新生児固有の疾患	31.4	自　　殺	25.2
肺炎及び気管支炎	48.4	不慮の事故	36.8	その他の新生児固有の疾患	30.5	胃　腸　炎	30.0	自　　殺	24.5
全　結　核	46.9	不慮の事故	37.9	その他の新生児固有の疾患	26.4	胃　腸　炎	25.7	自　　殺	24.3
全　結　核	39.4	不慮の事故	38.9	自　　殺	25.7	胃　腸　炎	25.1	その他の新生児固有の疾患	23.4
不慮の事故	44.8	全　結　核	35.5	胃　腸　炎	23.3	自　　殺	22.7	その他の新生児固有の疾患	21.0
不慮の事故	41.7	全　結　核	34.2	自　　殺	21.6	胃　腸　炎	21.2	その他の新生児固有の疾患	18.5
肺炎及び気管支炎	41.6	全　結　核	29.6	自　　殺	19.6	胃　腸　炎	19.5	その他の新生児固有の疾患	17.4
不慮の事故	40.3	全　結　核	29.3	高血圧性疾患	18.4	胃　腸　炎	18.0	自　　殺	17.6
肺炎及び気管支炎	33.2	全　結　核	24.2	高血圧性疾患	18.2	自　　殺	16.1	胃　腸　炎	16.1
肺炎及び気管支炎	32.1	全　結　核	23.6	高血圧性疾患	18.7	自　　殺	15.1	胃　腸　炎	14.6
肺炎及び気管支炎	37.3	全　結　核	22.8	高血圧性疾患	19.3	自　　殺	14.7	胃　腸　炎	12.9
肺炎及び気管支炎	28.2	全　結　核	20.3	高血圧性疾患	18.6	自　　殺	15.2	胃　腸　炎	11.3
肺炎及び気管支炎	28.7	高血圧性疾患	18.3	全　結　核	17.8	自　　殺	14.2	その他の新生児固有の疾患	11.4
肺炎及び気管支炎	31.8	高血圧性疾患	17.9	全　結　核	16.8	自　　殺	14.5	肝　硬　変	11.2
肺炎及び気管支炎	31.6	高血圧性疾患	17.0	全　結　核	16.1	自　　殺	14.5	肝　硬　変	11.8
肺炎及び気管支炎	34.1	高血圧性疾患	17.7	全　結　核	15.4	自　　殺	15.3	肝　硬　変	12.5
肺炎及び気管支炎	28.4	高血圧性疾患	16.7	自　　殺	15.6	全　結　核	13.0	肝　硬　変	12.5

死　亡

表5.11　年　次　別　に　み　た

死亡率（人口10万対）

年　次[2]	第　1　位		第　2　位		第　3　位		第　4　位		第　5　位	
	死　　因	死亡率	死　　因	死亡率	死　　因	死亡率	死　　因	死亡率	死　　因	死亡率
昭和47年	脳血管疾患	166.7	悪性新生物	120.4	心　疾　患	81.2	不慮の事故	40.1	老　　　衰	30.8
48	脳血管疾患	166.9	悪性新生物	121.2	心　疾　患	87.3	不慮の事故	37.2	肺炎及び気管支炎	31.3
49	脳血管疾患	163.0	悪性新生物	122.2	心　疾　患	89.8	不慮の事故	33.0	肺炎及び気管支炎	32.6
50	脳血管疾患	156.7	悪性新生物	122.6	心　疾　患	89.2	肺炎及び気管支炎	33.7	不慮の事故	30.3
51	脳血管疾患	154.5	悪性新生物	125.3	心　疾　患	92.2	肺炎及び気管支炎	32.6	不慮の事故	28.0
52	脳血管疾患	149.8	悪性新生物	128.4	心　疾　患	91.2	肺炎及び気管支炎	28.6	不慮の事故	26.7
53	脳血管疾患	146.2	悪性新生物	131.3	心　疾　患	93.3	肺炎及び気管支炎	30.3	不慮の事故	26.2
54	脳血管疾患	137.7	悪性新生物	135.7	心　疾　患	96.9	肺炎及び気管支炎	28.5	老　　　衰	25.5
55	脳血管疾患	139.5	悪性新生物	139.1	心　疾　患	106.2	肺炎及び気管支炎	33.7	老　　　衰	27.6
56	悪性新生物	142.0	脳血管疾患	134.3	心　疾　患	107.5	肺炎及び気管支炎	33.7	老　　　衰	25.5
57	悪性新生物	144.2	脳血管疾患	125.0	心　疾　患	106.7	肺炎及び気管支炎	35.0	不慮の事故	24.7
58	悪性新生物	148.3	脳血管疾患	122.8	心　疾　患	111.3	肺炎及び気管支炎	39.3	不慮の事故	25.0
59	悪性新生物	152.5	脳血管疾患	117.2	心　疾　患	113.9	肺炎及び気管支炎	37.6	不慮の事故	24.6
60	悪性新生物	156.1	心　疾　患	117.3	脳血管疾患	112.2	肺炎及び気管支炎	42.7	不慮の事故	24.6
61	悪性新生物	158.5	心　疾　患	117.9	脳血管疾患	106.9	肺炎及び気管支炎	43.9	不慮の事故	23.7
62	悪性新生物	164.2	心　疾　患	118.4	脳血管疾患	101.7	肺炎及び気管支炎	44.9	不慮の事故	23.2
63	悪性新生物	168.4	心　疾　患	129.4	脳血管疾患	105.5	肺炎及び気管支炎	51.6	不慮の事故	24.8
平成元年	悪性新生物	173.6	心　疾　患	128.1	脳血管疾患	98.5	肺炎及び気管支炎	52.7	不慮の事故	25.4
2	悪性新生物	177.2	心　疾　患	134.8	脳血管疾患	99.4	肺炎及び気管支炎	60.7	不慮の事故	26.2
3	悪性新生物	181.7	心　疾　患	137.2	脳血管疾患	96.2	肺炎及び気管支炎	62.0	不慮の事故	26.9
4	悪性新生物	187.8	心　疾　患	142.2	脳血管疾患	95.6	肺炎及び気管支炎	65.0	不慮の事故	28.1
5	悪性新生物	190.4	心　疾　患	145.6	脳血管疾患	96.0	肺炎及び気管支炎	70.6	不慮の事故	28.0
6	悪性新生物	196.4	心　疾　患	128.6	脳血管疾患	96.9	肺炎及び気管支炎	72.4	不慮の事故	29.1
7	悪性新生物	211.6	脳血管疾患	117.9	心　疾　患	112.0	肺　　　炎	64.1	不慮の事故	36.5
8	悪性新生物	217.5	脳血管疾患	112.6	心　疾　患	110.8	肺　　　炎	56.9	不慮の事故	31.4
9	悪性新生物	220.4	心　疾　患	112.2	脳血管疾患	111.0	肺　　　炎	63.1	不慮の事故	31.1
10	悪性新生物	226.7	心　疾　患	114.3	脳血管疾患	110.0	肺　　　炎	63.8	不慮の事故	31.1
11	悪性新生物	231.6	心　疾　患	120.4	脳血管疾患	110.8	肺　　　炎	74.9	不慮の事故	32.0
12	悪性新生物	235.2	心　疾　患	116.8	脳血管疾患	105.5	肺　　　炎	69.2	不慮の事故	31.4
13	悪性新生物	238.8	心　疾　患	117.8	脳血管疾患	104.7	肺　　　炎	67.8	不慮の事故	31.4
14	悪性新生物	241.7	心　疾　患	121.0	脳血管疾患	103.4	肺　　　炎	69.4	不慮の事故	30.7
15	悪性新生物	245.4	心　疾　患	126.5	脳血管疾患	104.7	肺　　　炎	75.3	不慮の事故	30.7
16	悪性新生物	253.9	心　疾　患	126.5	脳血管疾患	102.3	肺　　　炎	75.7	不慮の事故	30.3
17	悪性新生物	258.3	心　疾　患	137.2	脳血管疾患	105.3	肺　　　炎	85.0	不慮の事故	31.6
18	悪性新生物	261.0	心　疾　患	137.2	脳血管疾患	101.7	肺　　　炎	85.0	不慮の事故	30.3
19	悪性新生物	266.9	心　疾　患	139.2	脳血管疾患	100.8	肺　　　炎	87.4	不慮の事故	30.1
20	悪性新生物	272.3	心　疾　患	144.4	脳血管疾患	100.9	肺　　　炎	91.6	不慮の事故	30.3
21	悪性新生物	273.5	心　疾　患	143.7	脳血管疾患	97.2	肺　　　炎	89.0	老　　　衰	30.7
22	悪性新生物	279.7	心　疾　患	149.8	脳血管疾患	97.7	肺　　　炎	94.1	老　　　衰	35.9
23	悪性新生物	283.2	心　疾　患	154.5	肺　　　炎	98.9	脳血管疾患	98.2	不慮の事故	47.1
24	悪性新生物	286.6	心　疾　患	157.9	肺　　　炎	98.4	脳血管疾患	96.5	老　　　衰	48.2
25	悪性新生物	290.3	心　疾　患	156.5	肺　　　炎	97.8	脳血管疾患	94.1	老　　　衰	55.5
26	悪性新生物	293.5	心　疾　患	157.0	肺　　　炎	95.4	脳血管疾患	91.1	老　　　衰	60.1
27	悪性新生物	295.5	心　疾　患	156.5	肺　　　炎	96.5	脳血管疾患	89.4	老　　　衰	67.7
28	悪性新生物	298.3	心　疾　患	158.4	肺　　　炎	95.4	脳血管疾患	87.4	老　　　衰	74.2

死 因 順 位 [1]（つづき）

第 6 位		第 7 位		第 8 位		第 9 位		第 10 位	
死 因	死亡率	死 因	死亡率	死 因	死亡率	死 因	死亡率	死 因	死亡率
肺炎及び気管支炎	28.1	自殺	17.0	高血圧性疾患	16.5	肝硬変	12.8	全結核	11.9
老衰	30.9	高血圧性疾患	17.5	自殺	17.4	肝硬変	13.2	全結核	11.1
老衰	29.7	高血圧性疾患	18.4	自殺	17.5	肝硬変	13.4	全結核	10.4
老衰	26.9	自殺	18.0	高血圧性疾患	17.8	肝硬変	13.6	全結核	9.5
老衰	26.4	高血圧性疾患	17.6	自殺	17.6	肝硬変	13.8	全結核	8.5
老衰	25.0	自殺	17.9	高血圧性疾患	17.0	肝硬変	13.6	糖尿病	8.4
老衰	24.4	自殺	17.6	高血圧性疾患	16.4	肝硬変	14.0	糖尿病	8.5
不慮の事故及び有害作用	25.3	自殺	18.0	慢性肝疾患及び肝硬変	14.2	高血圧性疾患	14.0	腎炎及びネフローゼ症候群	8.0
不慮の事故及び有害作用	25.1	自殺	17.7	慢性肝疾患及び肝硬変	14.2	高血圧性疾患	13.7	腎炎及びネフローゼ症候群	8.8
不慮の事故及び有害作用	24.8	自殺	17.1	慢性肝疾患及び肝硬変	14.2	高血圧性疾患	13.0	腎炎及びネフローゼ症候群	9.1
老衰	23.3	自殺	17.5	慢性肝疾患及び肝硬変	14.0	高血圧性疾患	11.7	腎炎及びネフローゼ症候群	9.7
老衰	24.7	自殺	21.0	慢性肝疾患及び肝硬変	14.1	高血圧性疾患	11.3	腎炎及びネフローゼ症候群	10.3
老衰	24.1	自殺	20.4	慢性肝疾患及び肝硬変	14.2	高血圧性疾患	10.9	腎炎及びネフローゼ症候群	10.6
老衰	23.1	自殺	19.4	慢性肝疾患及び肝硬変	14.3	腎炎及びネフローゼ症候群	11.2	高血圧性疾患	10.6
老衰	22.2	自殺	21.2	慢性肝疾患及び肝硬変	14.0	腎炎及びネフローゼ症候群	11.6	高血圧性疾患	9.7
老衰	20.8	自殺	19.6	慢性肝疾患及び肝硬変	13.7	腎炎及びネフローゼ症候群	11.8	高血圧性疾患	8.8
老衰	21.6	自殺	18.7	慢性肝疾患及び肝硬変	13.9	腎炎及びネフローゼ症候群	13.0	高血圧性疾患	8.4
老衰	19.4	自殺	17.3	慢性肝疾患及び肝硬変	13.6	腎炎及びネフローゼ症候群	13.4	高血圧性疾患	7.6
老衰	19.7	自殺	16.4	腎炎及びネフローゼ症候群	14.0	慢性肝疾患及び肝硬変	13.7	糖尿病	7.7
老衰	18.8	自殺	16.1	腎炎及びネフローゼ症候群	13.8	慢性肝疾患及び肝硬変	13.7	糖尿病	7.8
老衰	18.9	自殺	16.9	腎炎及びネフローゼ症候群	14.8	慢性肝疾患及び肝硬変	13.8	糖尿病	8.0
老衰	18.7	自殺	16.6	腎炎及びネフローゼ症候群	14.9	慢性肝疾患及び肝硬変	13.6	糖尿病	8.3
老衰	18.9	自殺	16.9	腎炎及びネフローゼ症候群	15.1	慢性肝疾患及び肝硬変	13.3	糖尿病	8.8
老衰	17.3	自殺	17.2	肝疾患	13.7	腎不全	13.0	糖尿病	11.4
自殺	17.8	老衰	16.7	肝疾患	13.2	腎不全	13.0	糖尿病	10.3
自殺	18.8	老衰	17.2	腎不全	13.3	肝疾患	13.3	糖尿病	9.9
自殺	25.4	老衰	17.1	腎不全	13.3	肝疾患	12.9	糖尿病	10.0
自殺	25.0	老衰	18.2	腎不全	14.1	肝疾患	13.2	慢性閉塞性肺疾患	10.4
自殺	24.1	老衰	16.9	腎不全	13.7	肝疾患	12.8	慢性閉塞性肺疾患	10.2
自殺	23.3	老衰	17.6	腎不全	14.0	肝疾患	12.6	慢性閉塞性肺疾患	10.4
自殺	23.8	老衰	18.0	腎不全	14.4	肝疾患	12.3	慢性閉塞性肺疾患	10.3
自殺	25.5	老衰	18.6	腎不全	14.9	肝疾患	12.5	慢性閉塞性肺疾患	10.8
自殺	24.0	老衰	19.1	腎不全	15.2	肝疾患	12.6	慢性閉塞性肺疾患	10.7
自殺	24.2	老衰	20.9	腎不全	16.3	肝疾患	13.0	慢性閉塞性肺疾患	11.4
自殺	23.7	老衰	22.0	腎不全	16.8	肝疾患	12.9	慢性閉塞性肺疾患	11.4
自殺	24.4	老衰	24.4	腎不全	17.2	肝疾患	12.8	慢性閉塞性肺疾患	11.8
老衰	28.6	自殺	24.0	腎不全	17.9	肝疾患	12.9	慢性閉塞性肺疾患	12.3
不慮の事故	30.0	自殺	24.4	腎不全	18.1	肝疾患	12.7	慢性閉塞性肺疾患	12.2
不慮の事故	32.2	自殺	23.4	腎不全	18.8	慢性閉塞性肺疾患	12.9	肝疾患	12.8
老衰	41.4	自殺	22.9	腎不全	19.4	慢性閉塞性肺疾患	13.2	肝疾患	13.0
不慮の事故	32.6	自殺	21.0	腎不全	19.9	慢性閉塞性肺疾患	13.0	肝疾患	12.7
不慮の事故	31.5	自殺	20.7	腎不全	20.0	慢性閉塞性肺疾患	13.1	大動脈瘤及び解離	12.8
不慮の事故	31.1	腎不全	19.8	自殺	19.5	大動脈瘤及び解離	13.1	慢性閉塞性肺疾患	12.9
不慮の事故	30.6	腎不全	19.6	自殺	18.5	大動脈瘤及び解離	13.5	慢性閉塞性肺疾患	12.6
不慮の事故	**30.6**	**腎不全**	**19.7**	**自殺**	**16.8**	**大動脈瘤及び解離**	**14.5**	**肝疾患**	**12.6**

死 亡

〔Trends in causes of death〕

Table 5.11 Trends in leading

Death rates (per 100,000 population)

Year	1		2		3		4		5	
	Causes of death	Rates	Causes of death	Rates	Causes of death	Rates	Causes of death	Rates	Causes of death	Rates
1899	Pneu. & Bronch.	206.1	C. V. D.	170.5	Tuberculosis	155.7	Gastroenteritis	149.7	Senility	127.2
1900	Pneu. & Bronch.	226.1	Tuberculosis	163.7	C. V. D.	159.2	Gastroenteritis	133.8	Senility	131.0
05	Pneu. & Bronch.	247.4	Tuberculosis	206.0	C. V. D.	163.4	Senility	139.9	Gastroenteritis	137.2
10	Pneu. & Bronch.	262.0	Tuberculosis	230.2	Gastroenteritis	213.4	C. V. D.	131.9	Senility	120.2
1915	Pneu. & Bronch.	261.1	Gastroenteritis	223.7	Tuberculosis	219.7	C. V. D.	128.8	Senility	112.5
20	Pneu. & Bronch.	408.0	Gastroenteritis	254.2	Tuberculosis	223.7	Influenza	193.7	C. V. D.	157.6
25	Pneu. & Bronch.	275.6	Gastroenteritis	238.2	Tuberculosis	194.1	C. V. D.	161.2	Senility	117.3
1930	Gastroenteritis	221.4	Pneu. & Bronch.	200.1	Tuberculosis	185.6	C. V. D.	162.8	Senility	118.8
35	Tuberculosis	190.8	Pneu. & Bronch.	186.7	Gastroenteritis	173.2	C. V. D.	165.4	Senility	114.0
40	Tuberculosis	212.9	Pneu. & Bronch.	185.8	C. V. D.	177.7	Gastroenteritis	159.2	Senility	124.5
1947	Tuberculosis	187.2	Pneu. & Bronch.	174.8	Gastroenteritis	136.8	C. V. D.	129.4	Senility	100.3
48	Tuberculosis	179.9	C. V. D.	117.9	Gastroenteritis	109.9	Pneu. & Bronch.	98.6	Senility	79.5
49	Tuberculosis	168.9	C. V. D.	122.6	Pneu. & Bronch.	100.0	Gastroenteritis	92.6	Senility	80.2
1950	Tuberculosis	146.4	C. V. D.	127.1	Pneu. & Bronch.	93.2	Gastroenteritis	82.4	Malignant neoplasms	77.4
51	C. V. D.	125.2	Tuberculosis	110.3	Pneu. & Bronch.	82.2	Malignant neoplasms	78.5	Senility	70.7
52	C. V. D.	128.5	Tuberculosis	82.2	Malignant neoplasms	80.9	Senility	69.3	Pneu. & Bronch.	67.1
53	C. V. D.	133.7	Malignant neoplasms	82.2	Senility	77.6	Pneu. & Bronch.	71.3	Tuberculosis	66.5
54	C. V. D.	132.4	Malignant neoplasms	85.3	Senility	69.5	Tuberculosis	62.4	Heart dis.	60.2
55	C. V. D.	136.1	Malignant neoplasms	87.1	Senility	67.1	Heart dis.	60.9	Tuberculosis	52.3
56	C. V. D.	148.4	Malignant neoplasms	90.7	Senility	75.8	Heart dis.	66.0	Tuberculosis	48.6
57	C. V. D.	151.7	Malignant neoplasms	91.3	Senility	80.5	Heart dis.	73.1	Pneu. & Bronch.	59.2
58	C. V. D.	148.6	Malignant neoplasms	95.5	Heart dis.	64.8	Senility	55.5	Pneu. & Bronch.	47.6
59	C. V. D.	153.7	Malignant neoplasms	98.2	Heart dis.	67.7	Senility	56.7	Pneu. & Bronch.	45.2
1960	C. V. D.	160.7	Malignant neoplasms	100.4	Heart dis.	73.2	Senility	58.0	Pneu. & Bronch.	49.3
61	C. V. D.	165.4	Malignant neoplasms	102.3	Heart dis.	72.1	Senility	58.2	Accidents	44.1
62	C. V. D.	169.4	Malignant neoplasms	103.2	Heart dis.	76.2	Senility	57.5	Pneu. & Bronch.	45.0
63	C. V. D.	171.4	Malignant neoplasms	105.5	Heart dis.	70.4	Senility	50.4	Accidents	41.3
64	C. V. D.	171.7	Malignant neoplasms	107.3	Heart dis.	70.3	Senility	48.4	Accidents	41.6
65	C. V. D.	175.8	Malignant neoplasms	108.4	Heart dis.	77.0	Senility	50.0	Accidents	40.9
66	C. V. D.	173.8	Malignant neoplasms	110.9	Heart dis.	71.9	Senility	44.6	Accidents	43.0
67	C. V. D.	173.1	Malignant neoplasms	113.0	Heart dis.	75.7	Senility	43.3	Accidents	41.9
68	C. V. D.	173.5	Malignant neoplasms	114.6	Heart dis.	80.2	Accidents	40.2	Senility	39.4
69	C. V. D.	174.4	Malignant neoplasms	116.2	Heart dis.	81.7	Accidents	42.2	Senility	37.1
70	C. V. D.	175.8	Malignant neoplasms	116.3	Heart dis.	86.7	Accidents	42.5	Senility	38.1
71	C. V. D.	169.6	Malignant neoplasms	117.7	Heart dis.	82.0	Accidents	40.7	Senility	34.0

Note : C. V. D. ← Cerebrovascular diseases   Nephritis ← Nephritis, nephrotic syndroms and nephrosis   Heart dis. ← Heart diseases (excluding
Pneu. & Bronch. ← Pneumonia & Bronchitis   D.M. ← Diabetes mellitus   hypertensive heart diseases)
Accidents ← −1994, Accidents and adverse effects   Senility ← −1994, Senility without mention of psychosis
1995−, Accidents   1995−, Senility
Liver cirrhosis ← Chronic liver dis. and cirrhosis   Aortic aneurysm ← Aortic aneurysm and dissection

General mortality

causes of death : Japan

6		7		8		9		10	
Causes of death	Rates	Causes of death	Rates	Causes of death	Rates	Causes of death	Rates	Causes of death	Rates
Senility	70. 2	Heart dis.	64. 2	Dis. of infancy	62. 2	Accidents	39. 5	Nephritis	32. 4
Gastroenteritis	67. 7	Heart dis.	63. 6	Dis. of infancy	56. 0	Accidents	37. 8	Nephritis	29. 2
Heart dis.	61. 3	Gastroenteritis	53. 1	Dis. of infancy	47. 3	Accidents	36. 4	Nephritis	25. 8
Heart dis.	64. 9	Gastroenteritis	46. 1	Dis. of infancy	42. 1	Accidents	39. 3	Nephritis	23. 2
Pneu. & Bronch.	54. 7	Accidents	39. 4	Gastroenteritis	39. 0	Dis. of infancy	36. 2	Suicide	23. 4
Pneu. & Bronch.	48. 3	Accidents	37. 3	Gastroenteritis	31. 7	Dis. of infancy	31. 4	Suicide	25. 2
Pneu. & Bronch.	48. 4	Accidents	36. 8	Dis. of infancy	30. 5	Gastroenteritis	30. 0	Suicide	24. 5
Tuberculosis	46. 9	Accidents	37. 9	Dis. of infancy	26. 4	Gastroenteritis	25. 7	Suicide	24. 3
Tuberculosis	39. 4	Accidents	38. 9	Suicide	25. 7	Gastroenteritis	25. 1	Dis. of infancy	23. 4
Accidents	44. 8	Tuberculosis	35. 5	Gastroenteritis	23. 3	Suicide	22. 7	Dis. of infancy	21. 0
Accidents	41. 7	Tuberculosis	34. 2	Suicide	21. 6	Gastroenteritis	21. 2	Dis. of infancy	18. 5
Pneu. & Bronch.	41. 6	Tuberculosis	29. 6	Suicide	19. 6	Gastroenteritis	19. 5	Dis. of infancy	17. 4
Accidents	40. 3	Tuberculosis	29. 3	Hypertensive dis.	18. 4	Gastroenteritis	18. 0	Suicide	17. 6
Pneu. & Bronch.	33. 2	Tuberculosis	24. 2	Hypertensive dis.	18. 2	Suicide	16. 1	Gastroenteritis	16. 1
Pneu. & Bronch.	32. 1	Tuberculosis	23. 6	Hypertensive dis.	18. 7	Suicide	15. 1	Gastroenteritis	14. 6
Pneu. & Bronch.	37. 3	Tuberculosis	22. 8	Hypertensive dis.	19. 3	Suicide	14. 7	Gastroenteritis	12. 9
Pneu. & Bronch.	28. 2	Tuberculosis	20. 3	Hypertensive dis.	18. 6	Suicide	15. 2	Gastroenteritis	11. 3
Pneu. & Bronch.	28. 7	Hypertensive dis.	18. 3	Tuberculosis	17. 8	Suicide	14. 2	Dis. of infancy	11. 4
Pneu. & Bronch.	31. 8	Hypertensive dis.	17. 9	Tuberculosis	16. 8	Suicide	14. 5	Liver cirrhosis	11. 2
Pneu. & Bronch.	31. 6	Hypertensive dis.	17. 0	Tuberculosis	16. 1	Suicide	14. 5	Liver cirrhosis	11. 8
Pneu. & Bronch.	34. 1	Hypertensive dis.	17. 7	Tuberculosis	15. 4	Suicide	15. 3	Liver cirrhosis	12. 5
Pneu. & Bronch.	28. 4	Hypertensive dis.	16. 7	Suicide	15. 6	Tuberculosis	13. 0	Liver cirrhosis	12. 5

175

死 亡

Table 5.11 Trends in leading

Death rates (per 100,000 population)

Year	1		2		3		4		5	
	Causes of death	Rates	Causes of death	Rates	Causes of death	Rates	Causes of death	Rates	Causes of death	Rates
1972	C. V. D.	166. 7	Malignant neoplasms	120. 4	Heart dis.	81. 2	Accidents	40. 1	Senility	30. 8
73	C. V. D.	166. 9	Malignant neoplasms	121. 2	Heart dis.	87. 3	Accidents	37. 2	Pneu. & Bronch.	31. 3
74	C. V. D.	163. 0	Malignant neoplasms	122. 2	Heart dis.	89. 8	Accidents	33. 0	Pneu. & Bronch.	32. 6
75	C. V. D.	156. 7	Malignant neoplasms	122. 6	Heart dis.	89. 2	Pneu. & Bronch.	33. 7	Accidents	30. 3
76	C. V. D.	154. 5	Malignant neoplasms	125. 3	Heart dis.	92. 2	Pneu. & Bronch.	32. 6	Accidents	28. 0
77	C. V. D.	149. 8	Malignant neoplasms	128. 4	Heart dis.	91. 2	Pneu. & Bronch.	28. 6	Accidents	26. 7
78	C. V. D.	146. 2	Malignant neoplasms	131. 3	Heart dis.	93. 3	Pneu. & Bronch.	30. 3	Accidents	26. 2
79	C. V. D.	137. 7	Malignant neoplasms	135. 7	Heart dis.	96. 9	Pneu. & Bronch.	28. 5	Senility	25. 5
1980	C. V. D.	139. 5	Malignant neoplasms	139. 1	Heart dis.	106. 2	Pneu. & Bronch.	33. 7	Senility	27. 6
81	Malignant neoplasms	142. 0	C. V. D.	134. 3	Heart dis.	107. 5	Pneu. & Bronch.	33. 7	Senility	25. 5
82	Malignant neoplasms	144. 2	C. V. D.	125. 0	Heart dis.	106. 7	Pneu. & Bronch.	35. 0	Accidents	24. 7
83	Malignant neoplasms	148. 3	C. V. D.	122. 8	Heart dis.	111. 3	Pneu. & Bronch.	39. 3	Accidents	25. 0
84	Malignant neoplasms	152. 5	C. V. D.	117. 2	Heart dis.	113. 9	Pneu. & Bronch.	37. 6	Accidents	24. 6
85	Malignant neoplasms	156. 1	Heart dis.	117. 3	C. V. D.	112. 2	Pneu. & Bronch.	42. 7	Accidents	24. 6
86	Malignant neoplasms	158. 5	Heart dis.	117. 9	C. V. D.	106. 9	Pneu. & Bronch.	43. 9	Accidents	23. 7
87	Malignant neoplasms	164. 2	Heart dis.	118. 4	C. V. D.	101. 7	Pneu. & Bronch.	44. 9	Accidents	23. 2
88	Malignant neoplasms	168. 4	Heart dis.	129. 4	C. V. D.	105. 5	Pneu. & Bronch.	51. 6	Accidents	24. 8
89	Malignant neoplasms	173. 6	Heart dis.	128. 1	C. V. D.	98. 5	Pneu. & Bronch.	52. 7	Accidents	25. 4
1990	Malignant neoplasms	177. 2	Heart dis.	134. 8	C. V. D.	99. 4	Pneu. & Bronch.	60. 7	Accidents	26. 2
91	Malignant neoplasms	181. 7	Heart dis.	137. 2	C. V. D.	96. 2	Pneu. & Bronch.	62. 0	Accidents	26. 9
92	Malignant neoplasms	187. 8	Heart dis.	142. 2	C. V. D.	95. 6	Pneu. & Bronch.	65. 0	Accidents	28. 1
93	Malignant neoplasms	190. 4	Heart dis.	145. 6	C. V. D.	96. 0	Pneu. & Bronch.	70. 6	Accidents	28. 0
94	Malignant neoplasms	196. 4	Heart dis.	128. 6	C. V. D.	96. 9	Pneu. & Bronch.	72. 4	Accidents	29. 1
95	Malignant neoplasms	211. 6	C. V. D.	117. 9	Heart dis.	112. 0	Pneumonia	64. 1	Accidents	36. 5
96	Malignant neoplasms	217. 5	C. V. D.	112. 6	Heart dis.	110. 8	Pneumonia	56. 9	Accidents	31. 4
97	Malignant neoplasms	220. 4	Heart dis.	112. 2	C. V. D.	111. 0	Pneumonia	63. 1	Accidents	31. 1
98	Malignant neoplasms	226. 7	Heart dis.	114. 3	C. V. D.	110. 0	Pneumonia	63. 8	Accidents	31. 1
99	Malignant neoplasms	231. 6	Heart dis.	120. 4	C. V. D.	110. 8	Pneumonia	74. 9	Accidents	32. 0
2000	Malignant neoplasms	235. 2	Heart dis.	116. 8	C. V. D.	105. 5	Pneumonia	69. 2	Accidents	31. 4
01	Malignant neoplasms	238. 8	Heart dis.	117. 8	C. V. D.	104. 7	Pneumonia	67. 8	Accidents	31. 4
02	Malignant neoplasms	241. 7	Heart dis.	121. 0	C. V. D.	103. 4	Pneumonia	69. 4	Accidents	30. 7
03	Malignant neoplasms	245. 4	Heart dis.	126. 5	C. V. D.	104. 7	Pneumonia	75. 3	Accidents	30. 7
04	Malignant neoplasms	253. 9	Heart dis.	126. 5	C. V. D.	102. 3	Pneumonia	75. 7	Accidents	30. 3
05	Malignant neoplasms	258. 3	Heart dis.	137. 2	C. V. D.	105. 3	Pneumonia	85. 0	Accidents	31. 6
06	Malignant neoplasms	261. 0	Heart dis.	137. 2	C. V. D.	101. 7	Pneumonia	85. 0	Accidents	30. 3
07	Malignant neoplasms	266. 9	Heart dis.	139. 2	C. V. D.	100. 8	Pneumonia	87. 4	Accidents	30. 1
08	Malignant neoplasms	272. 3	Heart dis.	144. 4	C. V. D.	100. 9	Pneumonia	91. 6	Accidents	30. 3
09	Malignant neoplasms	273. 5	Heart dis.	143. 7	C. V. D.	97. 2	Pneumonia	89. 0	Senility	30. 7
2010	Malignant neoplasms	279. 7	Heart dis.	149. 8	C. V. D.	97. 7	Pneumonia	94. 1	Senility	35. 9
11	Malignant neoplasms	283. 2	Heart dis.	154. 5	Pneumonia	98. 9	C. V. D.	98. 2	Accidents	47. 1
12	Malignant neoplasms	286. 6	Heart dis.	157. 9	Pneumonia	98. 4	C. V. D.	96. 5	Senility	48. 2
13	Malignant neoplasms	290. 3	Heart dis.	156. 5	Pneumonia	97. 8	C. V. D.	94. 1	Senility	55. 5
14	Malignant neoplasms	293. 5	Heart dis.	157. 0	Pneumonia	95. 4	C. V. D.	91. 1	Senility	60. 1
15	Malignant neoplasms	295. 5	Heart dis.	156. 5	Pneumonia	96. 5	C. V. D.	89. 4	Senility	67. 7
16	Malignant neoplasms	298. 3	Heart dis.	158. 4	Pneumonia	95. 4	C. V. D.	87. 4	Senility	74. 2

causes of death : Japan－CON.

General mortality

6		7		8		9		10	
Causes of death	Rates	Causes of death	Rates	Causes of death	Rates	Causes of death	Rates	Causes of death	Rates
Pneu. & Bronch.	28.1	Suicide	17.0	Hypertensive dis.	16.5	Liver cirrhosis	12.8	Tuberculosis	11.9
Senility	30.9	Hypertensive dis.	17.5	Suicide	17.4	Liver cirrhosis	13.2	Tuberculosis	11.1
Senility	29.7	Hypertensive dis.	18.4	Suicide	17.5	Liver cirrhosis	13.4	Tuberculosis	10.4
Senility	26.9	Suicide	18.0	Hypertensive dis.	17.8	Liver cirrhosis	13.6	Tuberculosis	9.5
Senility	26.4	Hypertensive dis.	17.6	Suicide	17.6	Liver cirrhosis	13.8	Tuberculosis	8.5
Senility	25.0	Suicide	17.9	Hypertensive dis.	17.0	Liver cirrhosis	13.6	D.M.	8.4
Senility	24.4	Suicide	17.6	Hypertensive dis.	16.4	Liver cirrhosis	14.0	D.M.	8.5
Accidents	25.3	Suicide	18.0	Liver cirrhosis	14.2	Hypertensive dis.	14.0	Nephritis	8.0
Accidents	25.1	Suicide	17.7	Liver cirrhosis	14.2	Hypertensive dis.	13.7	Nephritis	8.8
Accidents	24.8	Suicide	17.1	Liver cirrhosis	14.2	Hypertensive dis.	13.0	Nephritis	9.1
Senility	23.3	Suicide	17.5	Liver cirrhosis	14.0	Hypertensive dis.	11.7	Nephritis	9.7
Senility	24.7	Suicide	21.0	Liver cirrhosis	14.1	Hypertensive dis.	11.3	Nephritis	10.3
Senility	24.1	Suicide	20.4	Liver cirrhosis	14.2	Hypertensive dis.	10.9	Nephritis	10.6
Senility	23.1	Suicide	19.4	Liver cirrhosis	14.3	Nephritis	11.2	Hypertensive dis.	10.6
Senility	22.2	Suicide	21.2	Liver cirrhosis	14.0	Nephritis	11.6	Hypertensive dis.	9.7
Senility	20.8	Suicide	19.6	Liver cirrhosis	13.7	Nephritis	11.8	Hypertensive dis.	8.8
Senility	21.6	Suicide	18.7	Liver cirrhosis	13.9	Nephritis	13.0	Hypertensive dis.	8.4
Senility	19.4	Suicide	17.3	Liver cirrhosis	13.6	Nephritis	13.4	Hypertensive dis.	7.6
Senility	19.7	Suicide	16.4	Nephritis	14.0	Liver cirrhosis	13.7	D.M.	7.7
Senility	18.8	Suicide	16.1	Nephritis	13.8	Liver cirrhosis	13.7	D.M.	7.8
Senility	18.9	Suicide	16.9	Nephritis	14.8	Liver cirrhosis	13.8	D.M.	8.0
Senility	18.7	Suicide	16.6	Nephritis	14.9	Liver cirrhosis	13.6	D.M.	8.3
Senility	18.9	Suicide	16.9	Nephritis	15.1	Liver cirrhosis	13.3	D.M.	8.8
Senility	17.3	Suicide	17.2	Dis. of liver	13.7	Renal failure	13.0	D.M.	11.4
Suicide	17.8	Senility	16.7	Dis. of liver	13.2	Renal failure	13.0	D.M.	10.3
Suicide	18.8	Senility	17.2	Renal failure	13.3	Dis. of liver	13.3	D.M.	9.9
Suicide	25.4	Senility	17.1	Renal failure	13.3	Dis. of liver	12.9	D.M.	10.0
Suicide	25.0	Senility	18.2	Renal failure	14.1	Dis. of liver	13.2	Chronic obstructive pulmonary dis.	10.4
Suicide	24.1	Senility	16.9	Renal failure	13.7	Dis. of liver	12.8	Chronic obstructive pulmonary dis.	10.2
Suicide	23.3	Senility	17.6	Renal failure	14.0	Dis. of liver	12.6	Chronic obstructive pulmonary dis.	10.4
Suicide	23.8	Senility	18.0	Renal failure	14.4	Dis. of liver	12.3	Chronic obstructive pulmonary dis.	10.3
Suicide	25.5	Senility	18.6	Renal failure	14.9	Dis. of liver	12.5	Chronic obstructive pulmonary dis.	10.8
Suicide	24.0	Senility	19.1	Renal failure	15.2	Dis. of liver	12.6	Chronic obstructive pulmonary dis.	10.7
Suicide	24.2	Senility	20.9	Renal failure	16.3	Dis. of liver	13.0	Chronic obstructive pulmonary dis.	11.4
Suicide	23.7	Senility	22.0	Renal failure	16.8	Dis. of liver	12.9	Chronic obstructive pulmonary dis.	11.4
Suicide	24.4	Senility	24.4	Renal failure	17.2	Dis. of liver	12.8	Chronic obstructive pulmonary dis.	11.8
Senility	28.6	Suicide	24.0	Renal failure	17.9	Dis. of liver	12.9	Chronic obstructive pulmonary dis.	12.3
Accidents	30.0	Suicide	24.4	Renal failure	18.1	Dis. of liver	12.7	Chronic obstructive pulmonary dis.	12.2
Accidents	32.2	Suicide	23.4	Renal failure	18.8	Chronic obstructive pulmonary dis.	12.9	Dis. of liver	12.8
Senility	41.4	Suicide	22.9	Renal failure	19.4	Chronic obstructive pulmonary dis.	13.2	Dis. of liver	13.0
Accidents	32.6	Suicide	21.0	Renal failure	19.9	Chronic obstructive pulmonary dis.	13.0	Dis. of liver	12.7
Accidents	31.5	Suicide	20.7	Renal failure	20.0	Chronic obstructive pulmonary dis.	13.1	Aortic aneurysm	12.8
Accidents	31.1	Renal failure	19.8	Suicide	19.5	Aortic aneurysm	13.1	Chronic obstructive pulmonary dis.	12.9
Accidents	30.6	Renal failure	19.6	Suicide	18.5	Aortic aneurysm	13.5	Chronic obstructive pulmonary dis.	12.6
Accidents	30.6	Renal failure	19.7	Suicide	16.8	Aortic aneurysm	14.5	Dis. of liver	12.6

死　亡

表5.12　死因年次推移分類[1]別にみた
Table 5.12　Trends in deaths and death rates (per 100,000

総　数[4]
Total

年　次[2] Year	死亡総数[3] 死亡数 Deaths	死亡率 Death rates	Hi 01 結　核 死亡数 Deaths	死亡率 Death rates	Hi 02 悪性新生物 死亡数 Deaths	死亡率 Death rates	Hi 03 糖尿病 死亡数 Deaths	死亡率 Death rates	Hi 04 高血圧性疾患 死亡数 Deaths	死亡率 Death rates
1899 明治32年	932 087	2 147.5	67 599	155.7	19 382	44.7	…	…	…	…
1900　33	910 744	2 077.1	71 771	163.7	20 334	46.4	…	…	…	…
01　34	925 810	2 087.1	76 614	172.7	22 149	49.9	…	…	…	…
02　35	959 126	2 133.1	82 559	183.6	24 598	54.7	…	…	…	…
03　36	931 008	2 044.1	85 132	186.9	25 550	56.1	…	…	…	…
04　37	955 400	2 070.9	87 260	189.1	25 993	56.3	…	…	…	…
05　38	1 004 661	2 155.0	96 030	206.0	26 668	57.2	…	…	…	…
06　39	955 256	2 030.8	96 069	204.2	27 863	59.2	…	…	…	…
07　40	1 016 798	2 144.4	96 584	203.7	28 451	60.0	…	…	…	…
08　41	1 029 447	2 146.2	98 871	206.1	30 440	63.5	…	…	…	…
09　42	1 091 264	2 247.5	113 622	234.0	32 797	67.5	1 057	2.2	…	…
1910　43	1 064 234	2 163.8	113 203	230.2	32 998	67.1	1 089	2.2	…	…
11　44	1 043 906	2 094.0	110 722	222.1	34 219	68.6	1 212	2.4	…	…
12 大正元年	1 037 016	2 050.4	114 197	225.8	34 444	68.1	1 331	2.6	…	…
13　2	1 027 257	2 002.3	110 753	215.9	35 712	69.6	1 373	2.7	…	…
14　3	1 101 815	2 117.3	113 341	217.8	36 931	71.0	1 467	2.8	…	…
15　4	1 093 793	2 073.5	115 913	219.7	37 789	71.6	1 609	3.1	…	…
16　5	1 187 832	2 220.4	121 810	227.7	39 410	73.7	1 737	3.2	…	…
17　6	1 199 669	2 216.1	124 787	230.5	39 365	72.7	1 801	3.3	…	…
18　7	1 493 162	2 727.8	140 747	257.1	40 281	73.6	1 995	3.6	…	…
19　8	1 281 965	2 329.4	132 565	240.9	39 438	71.7	1 625	3.0	…	…
1920　9	1 422 096	2 541.1	125 165	223.7	40 648	72.6	1 725	3.1	…	…
21　10	1 288 570	2 274.0	120 719	213.0	40 877	72.1	1 890	3.3	…	…
22　11	1 286 941	2 242.4	125 506	218.7	41 116	71.6	1 904	3.3	…	…
23　12	1 332 485	2 292.7	118 216	203.4	42 231	72.7	1 873	3.2	…	…
24　13	1 254 946	2 131.5	114 229	194.0	41 671	70.8	1 963	3.3	…	…
25　14	1 210 706	2 026.7	115 956	194.1	42 177	70.6	1 979	3.3	…	…
26 昭和元年	1 160 734	1 911.0	113 045	186.1	43 119	71.0	2 045	3.4	…	…
27　2	1 214 323	1 969.4	119 439	193.7	43 351	70.3	2 173	3.5	…	…
28　3	1 236 711	1 975.7	119 632	191.1	45 086	72.0	2 171	3.5	…	…
29　4	1 261 228	1 987.4	123 490	194.6	44 299	69.8	2 300	3.6	…	…
1930　5	1 170 867	1 816.7	119 635	185.6	45 488	70.6	2 247	3.5	…	…
31　6	1 240 891	1 895.7	121 875	186.2	45 164	69.0	2 209	3.4	…	…
32　7	1 175 344	1 769.2	119 196	179.4	45 883	69.1	2 331	3.5	…	…
33　8	1 193 987	1 770.7	126 703	187.9	47 705	70.7	2 589	3.8	…	…
34　9	1 234 684	1 807.5	131 525	192.5	48 822	71.5	2 718	4.0	…	…
35　10	1 161 936	1 677.8	132 151	190.8	50 080	72.3	2 527	3.6	…	…
36　11	1 230 278	1 754.7	145 160	207.0	50 203	71.6	2 629	3.7	…	…
37　12	1 207 899	1 710.2	144 620	204.8	51 578	73.0	2 812	4.0	…	…
38　13	1 259 805	1 774.1	148 827	209.6	51 358	72.3	3 043	4.3	…	…
39　14	1 268 760	1 777.5	154 371	216.3	52 059	72.9	2 795	3.9	…	…
1940　15	1 186 595	1 649.6	153 154	212.9	51 879	72.1	2 762	3.8	…	…
41　16	1 149 559	1 603.7	154 344	215.3	52 949	73.9	2 657	3.7	…	…
42　17	1 166 630	1 611.7	161 484	223.1	53 897	74.5	2 619	3.6	…	…
43　18	1 219 073	1 672.6	171 473	235.3	53 580	73.5	2 477	3.4	…	…
47　22	1 138 238	1 457.4	146 241	187.2	53 886	69.0	1 827	2.3	…	…
48　23	950 610	1 188.2	143 909	179.9	56 633	70.8	1 789	2.2	…	…
49　24	945 444	1 156.2	138 113	168.9	59 889	73.2	1 876	2.3	…	…
1950　25	904 876	1 087.6	121 769	146.4	64 428	77.4	2 034	2.4	9 935	11.9
51　26	838 998	992.0	93 307	110.3	66 354	78.5	2 058	2.4	8 865	10.5
52　27	765 068	891.1	70 558	82.2	69 488	80.9	1 993	2.3	8 950	10.4
53　28	772 547	887.6	57 849	66.5	71 578	82.2	2 119	2.4	9 343	10.7
54　29	721 491	817.2	55 124	62.4	75 309	85.3	2 040	2.3	9 100	10.3

注：1) 死因分類の改正により、年次別比較には完全な内容の一致をみることはできない。死因内容の変遷は74ページの表2.1を参照されたい。
　　昭和25年の脳血管疾患には、B46.b（352の一部、B22の後遺症及び1年以上経過したもの）を含むため、昭和25年報告書とは一致しない。
　　平成6年の心疾患の減少は、新しい死亡診断書（死体検案書）（平成7年1月施行）における「死亡の原因欄には、疾患の終末期の状態としての心不全、呼吸不全等は書かないでください。」という注意書きの、事前周知の影響によるものと考えられる。
　　表頭の死因名等はICD-10の死因年次推移分類による。
　　2) 昭和18年のみは樺太を含む数値であり、第3章総覧における死亡数とは一致しない。
　　昭和19～21年は資料不備のため省略した。
　　昭和22～47年は沖縄県を含まない。
　　3) 死亡総数には死因年次推移分類以外の死因を含む。
　　4) 昭和34年以前は男女不詳を含む。

178

General mortality

性別死亡数及び率（人口10万対）
population) by sex and causes of death : Japan

総数[4]
Total

Hi 05 心疾患（高血圧性を除く）		Hi 06 脳血管疾患		Hi 07 肺炎		Hi 08 慢性気管支炎及び肺気腫		年次[2] Year	
死亡数 Deaths	死亡率 Death rates	死亡数 Deaths	死亡率 Death rates	死亡数 Deaths	死亡率 Death rates	死亡数 Deaths	死亡率 Death rates		
21 113	48.6	73 989	170.5	43 313	99.8	...	...	1899	明治32年
21 107	48.1	69 799	159.2	44 853	102.3	...	...	1900	33
21 869	49.3	75 250	169.6	49 614	111.8	...	...	01	34
23 837	53.0	74 935	166.7	53 502	119.0	...	...	02	35
23 665	52.0	73 939	162.3	48 578	106.7	...	...	03	36
25 435	55.1	77 588	168.2	52 152	113.0	...	...	04	37
25 888	55.5	76 169	163.4	59 877	128.4	...	...	05	38
25 792	54.8	73 449	156.1	53 778	114.3	...	...	06	39
28 645	60.4	78 580	165.7	62 575	132.0	...	...	07	40
28 575	59.6	73 760	153.8	66 260	138.1	...	...	08	41
32 580	67.1	67 788	139.6	70 676	145.6	...	...	09	42
31 976	65.0	64 888	131.9	69 888	142.1	...	...	1910	43
31 555	63.3	65 731	131.9	69 621	139.7	...	...	11	44
31 223	61.7	67 489	133.4	73 902	146.1	...	...	12	大正元年
31 092	60.6	66 771	130.1	80 548	157.0	...	...	13	2
32 476	62.4	68 571	131.8	83 646	160.7	...	...	14	3
33 586	63.7	67 921	128.8	86 014	163.1	...	...	15	4
37 022	69.2	73 912	138.2	99 489	186.0	...	...	16	5
37 862	69.9	77 999	144.1	99 236	183.3	...	...	17	6
44 760	81.8	86 262	157.6	205 533	375.5	...	...	18	7
34 426	62.6	84 382	153.3	151 063	274.5	...	...	19	8
35 540	63.5	88 186	157.6	175 674	313.9	...	...	1920	9
37 420	66.0	90 523	159.7	113 709	200.7	...	...	21	10
37 312	65.0	91 433	159.3	112 642	196.3	...	...	22	11
42 184	72.6	94 615	162.8	119 263	205.2	16 151	27.8	23	12
40 676	69.1	102 810	174.6	123 403	209.6	16 580	28.2	24	13
39 895	66.8	96 293	161.2	129 129	216.2	17 134	28.7	25	14
37 949	62.5	98 688	162.5	108 106	178.0	14 778	24.3	26	昭和元年
38 971	63.2	101 705	164.9	119 960	194.6	15 380	24.9	27	2
39 908	63.8	102 985	164.5	125 787	201.0	15 073	24.1	28	3
41 532	65.4	108 439	170.9	121 181	191.0	15 264	24.1	29	4
41 138	63.8	104 942	162.8	101 046	156.8	13 529	21.0	1930	5
41 867	64.0	107 352	164.0	129 380	197.7	14 752	22.5	31	6
38 973	58.7	107 378	161.6	112 681	169.6	13 174	19.8	32	7
40 111	59.5	110 719	164.2	106 247	157.6	11 958	17.7	33	8
42 519	62.2	114 447	167.5	124 117	181.7	12 749	18.7	34	9
39 902	57.6	114 554	165.4	105 078	151.7	11 780	17.0	35	10
42 910	61.2	118 152	168.5	112 204	160.0	12 539	17.9	36	11
42 822	60.6	118 761	168.1	108 256	153.3	11 237	15.9	37	12
47 461	66.8	126 861	178.6	118 153	166.4	12 668	17.8	38	13
47 442	66.5	130 826	183.3	131 542	184.3	12 123	17.0	39	14
45 542	63.3	127 847	177.7	111 077	154.4	10 667	14.8	1940	15
42 543	59.4	125 124	174.6	104 073	145.2	9 948	13.9	41	16
43 487	60.1	125 349	173.2	106 022	146.5	10 125	14.0	42	17
45 428	62.3	120 985	166.0	116 494	159.8	10 036	13.8	43	18
48 575	62.2	101 095	129.4	101 601	130.1	9 960	12.8	47	22
49 046	61.3	94 329	117.9	52 979	66.2	8 385	10.5	48	23
52 763	64.5	100 278	122.6	56 213	68.7	7 654	9.4	49	24
53 377	64.2	105 728	127.1	54 169	65.1	7 055	8.5	1950	25
53 750	63.6	105 858	125.2	50 612	59.8	5 804	6.9	51	26
52 603	61.3	110 359	128.5	42 880	49.9	4 923	5.7	52	27
56 477	64.9	116 351	133.7	46 703	53.7	4 829	5.5	53	28
53 128	60.2	116 925	132.4	37 719	42.7	3 768	4.3	54	29

Note : List for trends in causes of death see page 74.

死　亡

表 5.12　死因年次推移分類[1]別にみた
Table 5.12　Trends in deaths and death rates (per 100,000

総　数[4]
Total

年　次[2] Year		死亡総数[3]		Hi 0 1 結　　核		Hi 0 2 悪 性 新 生 物		Hi 0 3 糖 尿 病		Hi 0 4 高血圧性疾患	
		死亡数 Deaths	死亡率 Death rates	死亡数 Deaths	死亡率 Death rates	死亡数 Deaths	死亡率 Death rates	死亡数 Deaths	死亡率 Death rates	死亡数 Deaths	死亡率 Death rates
1955	昭和30年	693 523	776.8	46 735	52.3	77 721	87.1	2 191	2.5	9 073	10.2
56	31	724 460	802.6	43 874	48.6	81 879	90.7	2 556	2.8	10 371	11.5
57	32	752 445	826.1	42 718	46.9	83 155	91.3	2 712	3.0	11 158	12.2
58	33	684 189	743.6	36 274	39.4	87 895	95.5	2 664	2.9	12 565	13.7
59	34	689 959	742.1	32 992	35.5	91 286	98.2	2 794	3.0	13 503	14.5
1960	35	706 599	756.4	31 959	34.2	93 773	100.4	3 195	3.4	15 115	16.2
61	36	695 644	737.8	27 916	29.6	96 442	102.3	3 453	3.7	16 083	17.1
62	37	710 265	746.2	27 852	29.3	98 224	103.2	3 823	4.0	17 547	18.4
63	38	670 770	697.6	23 302	24.2	101 426	105.5	3 980	4.1	17 469	18.2
64	39	673 067	692.6	22 929	23.6	104 324	107.3	4 610	4.7	18 207	18.7
65	40	700 438	712.7	22 366	22.8	106 536	108.4	5 115	5.2	18 987	19.3
66	41	670 342	676.7	20 064	20.3	109 805	110.9	5 750	5.8	18 405	18.6
67	42	675 006	677.5	17 708	17.8	112 593	113.0	6 132	6.2	18 211	18.3
68	43	686 555	681.1	16 922	16.8	115 462	114.6	6 403	6.4	18 046	17.9
69	44	693 787	680.0	16 392	16.1	118 559	116.2	7 079	6.9	17 374	17.0
1970	45	712 962	691.4	15 899	15.4	119 977	116.3	7 642	7.4	18 303	17.7
71	46	684 521	656.0	13 608	13.0	122 850	117.7	7 647	7.3	17 386	16.7
72	47	683 751	646.6	12 565	11.9	127 299	120.4	7 875	7.4	17 421	16.5
73	48	709 416	656.4	11 965	11.1	130 964	121.2	8 344	7.7	18 891	17.5
74	49	710 510	649.4	11 418	10.4	133 751	122.2	8 954	8.2	20 117	18.4
75	50	702 275	631.2	10 567	9.5	136 383	122.6	9 032	8.1	19 831	17.8
76	51	703 270	625.6	9 578	8.5	140 893	125.3	9 183	8.2	19 829	17.6
77	52	690 074	608.0	8 803	7.8	145 772	128.4	9 509	8.4	19 333	17.0
78	53	695 821	607.6	8 261	7.2	150 336	131.3	9 685	8.5	18 779	16.4
79	54	689 664	597.3	6 738	5.8	156 661	135.7	8 044	7.0	16 143	14.0
1980	55	722 801	621.4	6 439	5.5	161 764	139.1	8 504	7.3	15 911	13.7
81	56	720 262	614.5	5 698	4.9	166 399	142.0	8 418	7.2	15 289	13.0
82	57	711 883	603.2	5 343	4.5	170 130	144.2	8 687	7.4	13 771	11.7
83	58	740 038	623.0	5 329	4.5	176 206	148.3	8 892	7.5	13 482	11.3
84	59	740 247	619.3	4 950	4.1	182 280	152.5	9 470	7.9	13 073	10.9
85	60	752 283	625.5	4 692	3.9	187 714	156.1	9 244	7.7	12 700	10.6
86	61	750 620	620.6	4 170	3.4	191 654	158.5	9 144	7.6	11 689	9.7
87	62	751 172	618.1	4 022	3.3	199 563	164.2	9 134	7.5	10 734	8.8
88	63	793 014	649.9	3 872	3.2	205 470	168.4	9 647	7.9	10 258	8.4
89	平成元年	788 594	644.0	3 527	2.9	212 625	173.6	9 211	7.5	9 271	7.6
1990	2	820 305	668.4	3 664	3.0	217 413	177.2	9 470	7.7	9 246	7.5
91	3	829 797	674.1	3 325	2.7	223 727	181.7	9 634	7.8	9 083	7.4
92	4	856 643	693.8	3 347	2.7	231 917	187.8	9 823	8.0	8 688	7.0
93	5	878 532	709.7	3 249	2.6	235 707	190.4	10 239	8.3	8 360	6.8
94	6	875 933	706.0	3 094	2.5	243 670	196.4	10 872	8.8	7 938	6.4
95	7	922 139	741.9	3 178	2.6	263 022	211.6	14 225	11.4	8 222	6.6
96	8	896 211	718.6	2 858	2.3	271 183	217.5	12 838	10.3	7 245	5.8
97	9	913 402	730.9	2 742	2.2	275 413	220.4	12 370	9.9	6 884	5.5
98	10	936 484	747.7	2 795	2.2	283 921	226.7	12 537	10.0	6 716	5.4
99	11	982 031	782.9	2 935	2.3	290 556	231.6	12 814	10.2	6 650	5.3
2000	12	961 653	765.6	2 656	2.1	295 484	235.2	12 303	9.8	6 063	4.8
01	13	970 331	770.7	2 491	2.0	300 658	238.8	12 147	9.6	5 857	4.7
02	14	982 379	779.6	2 317	1.8	304 568	241.7	12 635	10.0	5 621	4.5
03	15	1 014 951	804.6	2 337	1.9	309 543	245.4	12 879	10.2	5 597	4.4
04	16	1 028 602	815.2	2 330	1.8	320 358	253.9	12 637	10.0	5 706	4.5
05	17	1 083 796	858.8	2 296	1.8	325 941	258.3	13 621	10.8	5 835	4.6
06	18	1 084 450	859.6	2 269	1.8	329 314	261.0	13 650	10.8	5 810	4.6
07	19	1 108 334	879.0	2 194	1.7	336 468	266.9	13 999	11.1	6 144	4.9
08	20	1 142 407	907.1	2 220	1.8	342 963	272.3	14 462	11.5	6 264	5.0
09	21	1 141 865	907.5	2 159	1.7	344 105	273.5	13 987	11.1	6 223	4.9
2010	22	1 197 012	947.1	2 129	1.7	353 499	279.7	14 422	11.4	6 760	5.3
11	23	1 253 066	993.1	2 166	1.7	357 305	283.2	14 664	11.6	7 023	5.6
12	24	1 256 359	997.5	2 110	1.7	360 963	286.6	14 486	11.5	7 261	5.8
13	25	1 268 436	1 009.1	2 087	1.7	364 872	290.3	13 812	11.0	7 165	5.7
14	26	1 273 004	1 014.9	2 100	1.7	368 103	293.5	13 669	10.9	6 932	5.5
15	27	1 290 444	1 029.7	1 956	1.6	370 346	295.5	13 327	10.6	6 726	5.4
16	28	1 307 748	1 046.0	1 892	1.5	372 986	298.3	13 480	10.8	6 841	5.5

180

General mortality

性別死亡数及び率（人口10万対）（つづき）
population) by sex and causes of death : Japan－CON.

総　数[4]
Total

Hi　05 心疾患（高血圧性を除く）		Hi　06 脳血管疾患		Hi　07 肺　炎		Hi　08 慢性気管支炎及び肺気腫		年　次[2] Year
死亡数 Deaths	死亡率 Death rates	死亡数 Deaths	死亡率 Death rates	死亡数 Deaths	死亡率 Death rates	死亡数 Deaths	死亡率 Death rates	
54 351	60.9	121 504	136.1	34 309	38.4	3 446	3.9	1955 昭和30年
59 543	66.0	133 931	148.4	34 870	38.6	3 304	3.7	56 31
66 571	73.1	138 181	151.7	43 754	48.0	3 340	3.7	57 32
59 603	64.8	136 767	148.6	35 252	38.3	2 813	3.1	58 33
62 954	67.7	142 858	153.7	34 229	36.8	2 517	2.7	59 34
68 400	73.2	150 109	160.7	37 534	40.2	2 664	2.9	1960 35
68 017	72.1	155 966	165.4	31 839	33.8	2 539	2.7	61 36
72 493	76.2	161 228	169.4	34 839	36.6	3 034	3.2	62 37
67 672	70.4	164 818	171.4	26 109	27.2	2 620	2.7	63 38
68 328	70.3	166 901	171.7	25 547	26.3	2 822	2.9	64 39
75 672	77.0	172 773	175.8	29 868	30.4	3 016	3.1	65 40
71 188	71.9	172 186	173.8	22 654	22.9	2 576	2.6	66 41
75 424	75.7	172 464	173.1	23 451	23.5	2 741	2.8	67 42
80 866	80.2	174 905	173.5	25 188	25.0	3 715	3.7	68 43
83 357	81.7	177 894	174.4	25 408	24.9	3 814	3.7	69 44
89 411	86.7	181 315	175.8	27 929	27.1	3 970	3.8	1970 45
85 529	82.0	176 952	169.6	23 102	22.1	3 847	3.7	71 46
85 885	81.2	176 228	166.7	23 204	21.9	3 957	3.7	72 47
94 324	87.3	180 332	166.9	26 996	25.0	4 115	3.8	73 48
98 251	89.8	178 365	163.0	28 557	26.1	4 432	4.1	74 49
99 226	89.2	174 367	156.7	30 441	27.4	4 392	3.9	75 50
103 638	92.2	173 745	154.5	29 913	26.6	4 427	3.9	76 51
103 564	91.2	170 029	149.8	26 440	23.3	4 442	3.9	77 52
106 786	93.3	167 452	146.2	28 241	24.7	4 834	4.2	78 53
111 938	96.9	158 974	137.7	27 330	23.7	4 464	3.9	79 54
123 505	106.2	162 317	139.5	33 051	28.4	5 100	4.4	1980 55
126 012	107.5	157 351	134.3	33 590	28.7	5 291	4.5	81 56
125 905	106.7	147 537	125.0	35 338	29.9	5 662	4.8	82 57
132 244	111.3	145 880	122.8	40 237	33.9	5 989	5.0	83 58
136 162	113.9	140 093	117.2	38 895	32.5	6 280	5.3	84 59
141 097	117.3	134 994	112.2	45 075	37.5	6 953	5.8	85 60
142 581	117.9	129 289	106.9	47 256	39.1	6 733	5.6	86 61
143 909	118.4	123 626	101.7	49 013	40.3	6 614	5.4	87 62
157 920	129.4	128 695	105.5	57 055	46.8	7 217	5.9	88 63
156 831	128.1	120 652	98.5	58 963	48.1	7 231	5.9	89 平成元年
165 478	134.8	121 944	99.4	68 194	55.6	7 834	6.4	1990 2
168 878	137.2	118 448	96.2	70 057	56.9	8 182	6.6	91 3
175 546	142.2	118 058	95.6	74 274	60.2	8 172	6.6	92 4
180 297	145.6	118 794	96.0	81 138	65.5	8 540	6.9	93 5
159 579	128.6	120 239	96.9	83 354	67.2	9 212	7.4	94 6
139 206	112.0	146 552	117.9	79 629	64.1	10 977	8.8	95 7
138 229	110.8	140 366	112.6	70 971	56.9	9 923	8.0	96 8
140 174	112.2	138 697	111.0	78 904	63.1	10 197	8.2	97 9
143 120	114.3	137 819	110.0	79 952	63.8	10 155	8.1	98 10
151 079	120.4	138 989	110.8	93 994	74.9	11 197	8.9	99 11
146 741	116.8	132 529	105.5	86 938	69.2	10 877	8.7	2000 12
148 292	117.8	131 856	104.7	85 305	67.8	10 944	8.7	01 13
152 518	121.0	130 257	103.4	87 421	69.4	10 833	8.6	02 14
159 545	126.5	132 067	104.7	94 942	75.3	11 233	8.9	03 15
159 625	126.5	129 055	102.3	95 534	75.7	10 613	8.4	04 16
173 125	137.2	132 847	105.3	107 241	85.0	10 985	8.7	05 17
173 024	137.2	128 268	101.7	107 242	85.0	10 548	8.4	06 18
175 539	139.2	127 041	100.8	110 159	87.4	10 566	8.4	07 19
181 928	144.4	127 023	100.9	115 317	91.6	10 371	8.2	08 20
180 745	143.7	122 350	97.2	112 004	89.0	9 923	7.9	09 21
189 360	149.8	123 461	97.7	118 888	94.1	9 929	7.9	2010 22
194 926	154.5	123 867	98.2	124 749	98.9	9 598	7.6	11 23
198 836	157.9	121 602	96.5	123 925	98.4	9 276	7.4	12 24
196 723	156.5	118 347	94.1	122 969	97.8	8 621	6.9	13 25
196 925	157.0	114 207	91.1	119 650	95.4	7 988	6.4	14 26
196 113	156.5	111 973	89.4	120 953	96.5	7 580	6.0	15 27
198 006	**158.4**	**109 320**	**87.4**	**119 300**	**95.4**	**7 105**	**5.7**	**16 28**

181

死　亡

表 5.12　死因年次推移分類[1]別にみた
Table 5.12　Trends in deaths and death rates（per 100,000

総　数[4]
Total

年　次[2] Year		Hi　0 9 喘　　息		Hi　1 0 胃潰瘍及び十二指腸潰瘍		Hi　1 1 肝　疾　患		Hi　1 2 腎　不　全	
		死亡数 Deaths	死亡率 Death rates	死亡数 Deaths	死亡率 Death rates	死亡数 Deaths	死亡率 Death rates	死亡数 Deaths	死亡率 Death rates
1899	明治32年	…	…	…	…	…	…	…	…
1900	33	…	…	…	…	…	…	…	…
01	34	…	…	…	…	…	…	…	…
02	35	…	…	…	…	…	…	…	…
03	36	…	…	…	…	…	…	…	…
04	37	…	…	…	…	…	…	…	…
05	38	…	…	…	…	…	…	…	…
06	39	…	…	…	…	…	…	…	…
07	40	…	…	…	…	…	…	…	…
08	41	…	…	…	…	…	…	…	…
09	42	6 786	14.0	4 960	10.2	8 684	17.9	…	…
1910	43	6 880	14.0	5 079	10.3	8 481	17.2	…	…
11	44	6 115	12.3	4 884	9.8	9 833	19.7	…	…
12	大正元年	6 427	12.7	5 117	10.1	10 133	20.0	…	…
13	2	6 704	13.1	5 131	10.0	9 755	19.0	…	…
14	3	6 501	12.5	5 410	10.4	10 589	20.3	…	…
15	4	6 329	12.0	5 218	9.9	10 386	19.7	…	…
16	5	7 624	14.3	5 721	10.7	10 937	20.4	…	…
17	6	7 370	13.6	6 121	11.3	10 724	19.8	…	…
18	7	9 515	17.4	6 126	11.2	10 822	19.8	…	…
19	8	6 623	12.0	5 783	10.5	9 931	18.0	…	…
1920	9	7 933	14.2	6 245	11.2	11 279	20.2	…	…
21	10	7 137	12.6	6 704	11.8	11 444	20.2	…	…
22	11	8 068	14.1	6 386	11.1	11 311	19.7	…	…
23	12	6 452	11.1	7 142	12.3	10 457	18.0	…	…
24	13	6 714	11.4	7 391	12.6	10 122	17.2	…	…
25	14	7 421	12.4	7 769	13.0	9 667	16.2	…	…
26	昭和元年	6 160	10.1	7 837	12.9	9 478	15.6	…	…
27	2	6 701	10.9	8 030	13.0	10 002	16.2	…	…
28	3	6 884	11.0	8 610	13.8	10 026	16.0	…	…
29	4	7 043	11.1	8 689	13.7	10 181	16.0	…	…
1930	5	6 651	10.3	9 190	14.3	10 469	16.2	…	…
31	6	7 994	12.2	9 701	14.8	10 045	15.3	…	…
32	7	6 849	10.3	10 056	15.1	10 214	15.4	…	…
33	8	7 422	11.0	10 524	15.6	8 375	12.4	…	…
34	9	8 647	12.7	11 329	16.6	8 270	12.1	…	…
35	10	7 679	11.1	11 276	16.3	8 074	11.7	…	…
36	11	9 485	13.5	11 977	17.1	8 446	12.0	…	…
37	12	8 000	11.3	12 322	17.4	8 680	12.3	…	…
38	13	9 648	13.6	13 279	18.7	8 680	12.2	…	…
39	14	10 321	14.5	13 222	18.5	8 650	12.1	…	…
1940	15	9 172	12.8	12 923	18.0	8 824	12.3	…	…
41	16	9 123	12.7	12 900	18.0	8 679	12.1	…	…
42	17	9 660	13.3	14 911	20.6	8 970	12.4	…	…
43	18	10 960	15.0	17 106	23.5	8 981	12.3	…	…
47	22	14 234	18.2	25 908	33.2	8 762	11.2	…	…
48	23	11 525	14.4	20 705	25.9	9 032	11.3	…	…
49	24	12 002	14.7	19 409	23.7	9 576	11.7	…	…
1950	25	16 233	19.5	19 323	23.2	8 630	10.4	…	…
51	26	14 867	17.6	18 297	21.6	8 929	10.6	…	…
52	27	12 837	15.0	16 991	19.8	10 048	11.7	…	…
53	28	15 776	18.1	16 230	18.6	10 960	12.6	…	…
54	29	11 321	12.8	14 320	16.2	11 657	13.2	…	…

General mortality

性別死亡数及び率（人口10万対）（つづき）
population) by sex and causes of death : Japan－CON.

総数[4]
Total

Hi 13 老衰		Hi 14 不慮の事故		（再掲）Hi 15 交通事故		Hi 16 自殺		年次[2] Year	
死亡数 Deaths	死亡率 Death rates	死亡数 Deaths	死亡率 Death rates	死亡数 Deaths	死亡率 Death rates	死亡数 Deaths	死亡率 Death rates		
55 189	127.2	21 767	50.1	…	…	5 932	13.7	1899	明治32年
57 442	131.0	19 874	45.3	…	…	5 863	13.4	1900	33
49 412	111.4	17 993	40.6	…	…	7 847	17.7	01	34
52 786	117.4	20 035	44.6	…	…	8 059	17.9	02	35
56 490	124.0	20 472	44.9	…	…	8 814	19.4	03	36
63 123	136.8	21 327	46.2	…	…	8 966	19.4	04	37
65 233	139.9	20 469	43.9	…	…	8 089	17.4	05	38
60 199	128.0	21 720	46.2	…	…	7 657	16.3	06	39
62 991	132.8	22 713	47.9	…	…	7 999	16.9	07	40
59 197	123.4	22 084	46.0	…	…	8 324	17.4	08	41
62 487	128.7	21 328	43.9	…	…	9 141	18.8	09	42
59 117	120.2	22 009	44.7	…	…	9 372	19.1	1910	43
56 792	113.9	22 781	45.7	…	…	9 373	18.8	11	44
57 765	114.2	23 877	47.2	…	…	9 475	18.7	12	大正元年
56 791	110.7	22 333	43.5	…	…	10 367	20.2	13	2
61 574	118.3	25 524	49.0	…	…	10 902	20.9	14	3
59 346	112.5	24 321	46.1	…	…	10 153	19.2	15	4
68 370	127.8	23 914	44.7	…	…	9 599	17.9	16	5
71 628	132.3	26 892	49.7	…	…	9 254	17.1	17	6
82 073	149.9	27 160	49.6	…	…	10 101	18.5	18	7
69 431	126.2	25 165	45.7	…	…	9 924	18.0	19	8
73 468	131.3	26 198	46.8	…	…	10 630	19.0	1920	9
75 654	133.5	24 558	43.3	…	…	11 358	20.0	21	10
75 957	132.4	25 500	44.4	…	…	11 546	20.1	22	11
76 579	131.8	71 322	122.7	…	…	11 488	19.8	23	12
74 003	125.7	25 739	43.7	…	…	11 261	19.1	24	13
70 065	117.3	24 982	41.8	…	…	12 249	20.5	25	14
67 576	111.3	25 627	42.2	…	…	12 484	20.6	26	昭和元年
74 664	121.1	29 327	47.6	…	…	12 845	20.8	27	2
77 251	123.4	26 040	41.6	…	…	13 032	20.8	28	3
79 181	124.8	26 634	42.0	…	…	12 740	20.1	29	4
76 591	118.8	26 295	40.8	…	…	13 942	21.6	1930	5
85 650	130.8	25 270	38.6	…	…	14 353	21.9	31	6
77 529	116.7	26 734	40.2	…	…	14 746	22.2	32	7
82 932	123.0	30 220	44.8	…	…	14 805	22.0	33	8
87 045	127.4	32 029	46.9	…	…	14 554	21.3	34	9
78 972	114.0	29 023	41.9	…	…	14 172	20.5	35	10
91 672	130.7	30 193	43.1	…	…	15 423	22.0	36	11
84 478	119.6	30 205	42.8	…	…	14 295	20.2	37	12
98 451	138.6	31 700	44.6	…	…	12 223	17.2	38	13
95 173	133.3	29 328	41.1	…	…	10 785	15.1	39	14
89 540	124.5	28 408	39.5	…	…	9 877	13.7	1940	15
89 673	125.1	28 808	40.2	…	…	9 713	13.6	41	16
95 998	132.6	31 134	43.0	…	…	9 393	13.0	42	17
99 162	136.1	33 519	46.0	…	…	8 784	12.1	43	18
78 342	100.3	38 533	49.3	4 922	6.3	12 262	15.7	47	22
63 639	79.5	38 975	48.7	6 197	7.7	12 753	15.9	48	23
65 574	80.2	34 277	41.9	5 861	7.2	14 201	17.4	49	24
58 412	70.2	32 850	39.5	7 542	9.1	16 311	19.6	1950	25
59 796	70.7	31 968	37.8	7 861	9.3	15 415	18.2	51	26
59 514	69.3	31 215	36.4	8 158	9.5	15 776	18.4	52	27
67 514	77.6	34 236	39.3	9 238	10.6	17 731	20.4	53	28
61 334	69.5	34 812	39.4	11 731	13.3	20 635	23.4	54	29

183

死　亡

表 5.12　死因年次推移分類[1]別にみた
Table 5.12　Trends in deaths and death rates (per 100,000

総　数[4]
Total

年　次[2] Year		Hi　09 喘　　息		Hi　10 胃潰瘍及び十二指腸潰瘍		Hi　11 肝　疾　患		Hi　12 腎　不　全	
		死亡数 Deaths	死亡率 Death rates	死亡数 Deaths	死亡率 Death rates	死亡数 Deaths	死亡率 Death rates	死亡数 Deaths	死亡率 Death rates
1955	昭和30年	11 309	12. 7	13 387	15. 0	11 827	13. 2	…	…
56	31	12 047	13. 3	13 241	14. 7	12 599	14. 0	…	…
57	32	14 248	15. 6	12 888	14. 1	12 674	13. 9	…	…
58	33	10 164	11. 0	11 889	12. 9	12 463	13. 5	…	…
59	34	9 777	10. 5	11 325	12. 2	12 836	13. 8	…	…
1960	35	11 221	12. 0	11 057	11. 8	13 389	14. 3	…	…
61	36	9 627	10. 2	10 336	11. 0	13 633	14. 5	…	…
62	37	11 513	12. 1	10 097	10. 6	13 549	14. 2	…	…
63	38	8 889	9. 2	9 600	10. 0	13 944	14. 5	…	…
64	39	9 096	9. 4	9 332	9. 6	13 945	14. 3	…	…
65	40	10 812	11. 0	9 165	9. 3	13 663	13. 9	…	…
66	41	9 113	9. 2	8 816	8. 9	13 853	14. 0	…	…
67	42	9 224	9. 3	8 739	8. 8	14 395	14. 4	…	…
68	43	9 395	9. 3	8 759	8. 7	15 470	15. 3	…	…
69	44	8 662	8. 5	8 439	8. 3	16 348	16. 0	…	…
1970	45	9 113	8. 8	7 997	7. 8	17 097	16. 6	…	…
71	46	7 925	7. 6	7 388	7. 1	16 815	16. 1	…	…
72	47	7 353	7. 0	7 377	7. 0	16 911	16. 0	…	…
73	48	7 198	6. 7	7 207	6. 7	17 573	16. 3	…	…
74	49	7 347	6. 7	7 138	6. 5	18 039	16. 5	…	…
75	50	6 928	6. 2	6 865	6. 2	18 101	16. 3	…	…
76	51	6 948	6. 2	6 311	5. 6	18 280	16. 3	…	…
77	52	6 161	5. 4	5 924	5. 2	18 173	16. 0	…	…
78	53	5 768	5. 0	5 810	5. 1	18 789	16. 4	…	…
79	54	5 999	5. 2	5 502	4. 8	18 754	16. 2	6 047	5. 2
1980	55	6 370	5. 5	5 530	4. 8	18 978	16. 3	7 048	6. 1
81	56	6 291	5. 4	5 446	4. 6	19 101	16. 3	7 811	6. 7
82	57	6 050	5. 1	4 778	4. 0	18 958	16. 1	8 866	7. 5
83	58	6 593	5. 6	4 859	4. 1	19 324	16. 3	9 892	8. 3
84	59	6 117	5. 1	4 606	3. 9	19 433	16. 3	10 457	8. 7
85	60	6 340	5. 3	4 493	3. 7	19 803	16. 5	11 508	9. 6
86	61	6 358	5. 3	4 227	3. 5	19 532	16. 1	12 057	10. 0
87	62	6 037	5. 0	3 874	3. 2	19 286	15. 9	12 627	10. 4
88	63	6 157	5. 0	3 688	3. 0	19 781	16. 2	14 224	11. 7
89	平成元年	5 808	4. 7	3 665	3. 0	19 719	16. 1	14 853	12. 1
1990	2	5 947	4. 8	3 615	2. 9	19 700	16. 1	15 575	12. 7
91	3	5 941	4. 8	3 687	3. 0	19 817	16. 1	15 560	12. 6
92	4	5 929	4. 8	3 581	2. 9	20 162	16. 3	16 945	13. 7
93	5	6 210	5. 0	3 680	3. 0	19 923	16. 1	17 157	13. 9
94	6	5 855	4. 7	3 678	3. 0	19 372	15. 6	17 376	14. 0
95	7	7 253	5. 8	4 314	3. 5	17 018	13. 7	16 187	13. 0
96	8	5 995	4. 8	3 918	3. 1	16 517	13. 2	16 196	13. 0
97	9	5 661	4. 5	3 876	3. 1	16 599	13. 3	16 615	13. 3
98	10	5 148	4. 1	3 871	3. 1	16 133	12. 9	16 638	13. 3
99	11	5 401	4. 3	4 053	3. 2	16 585	13. 2	17 704	14. 1
2000	12	4 473	3. 6	3 869	3. 1	16 079	12. 8	17 260	13. 7
01	13	4 014	3. 2	3 886	3. 1	15 848	12. 6	17 690	14. 0
02	14	3 771	3. 0	3 740	3. 0	15 490	12. 3	18 185	14. 4
03	15	3 701	2. 9	3 719	2. 9	15 737	12. 5	18 821	14. 9
04	16	3 283	2. 6	3 409	2. 7	15 885	12. 6	19 117	15. 2
05	17	3 198	2. 5	3 490	2. 8	16 430	13. 0	20 528	16. 3
06	18	2 778	2. 2	3 403	2. 7	16 267	12. 9	21 158	16. 8
07	19	2 540	2. 0	3 274	2. 6	16 195	12. 8	21 632	17. 2
08	20	2 348	1. 9	3 283	2. 6	16 268	12. 9	22 517	17. 9
09	21	2 139	1. 7	3 166	2. 5	15 969	12. 7	22 743	18. 1
2010	22	2 065	1. 6	3 233	2. 6	16 216	12. 8	23 725	18. 8
11	23	2 060	1. 6	3 110	2. 5	16 390	13. 0	24 526	19. 4
12	24	1 874	1. 5	3 132	2. 5	15 980	12. 7	25 107	19. 9
13	25	1 728	1. 4	2 828	2. 2	15 930	12. 7	25 101	20. 0
14	26	1 550	1. 2	2 795	2. 2	15 692	12. 5	24 776	19. 8
15	27	1 511	1. 2	2 666	2. 1	15 659	12. 5	24 560	19. 6
16	28	1 454	1. 2	2 657	2. 1	15 773	12. 6	24 612	19. 7

General mortality

性別死亡数及び率（人口10万対）（つづき）
population）by sex and causes of death : Japan－CON.

総数[4]
Total

Hi 13 老衰 死亡数 Deaths	死亡率 Death rates	Hi 14 不慮の事故 死亡数 Deaths	死亡率 Death rates	（再掲）Hi 15 交通事故 死亡数 Deaths	死亡率 Death rates	Hi 16 自殺 死亡数 Deaths	死亡率 Death rates	年次[2] Year	
59 932	67.1	33 265	37.3	10 500	11.8	22 477	25.2	1955	昭和30年
68 414	75.8	33 258	36.8	11 032	12.2	22 107	24.5	56	31
73 283	80.5	34 528	37.9	12 256	13.5	22 136	24.3	57	32
51 046	55.5	35 785	38.9	13 440	14.6	23 641	25.7	58	33
52 687	56.7	41 662	44.8	15 442	16.6	21 090	22.7	59	34
54 139	58.0	38 964	41.7	17 757	19.0	20 143	21.6	1960	35
54 880	58.2	41 614	44.1	19 056	20.2	18 446	19.6	61	36
54 738	57.5	38 393	40.3	17 796	18.7	16 724	17.6	62	37
48 466	50.4	39 698	41.3	19 071	19.8	15 490	16.1	63	38
46 995	48.4	40 437	41.6	20 257	20.8	14 707	15.1	64	39
49 092	50.0	40 188	40.9	19 516	19.9	14 444	14.7	65	40
44 209	44.6	42 547	43.0	21 385	21.6	15 050	15.2	66	41
43 129	43.3	41 769	41.9	20 535	20.6	14 121	14.2	67	42
39 750	39.4	40 564	40.2	21 193	21.0	14 601	14.5	68	43
37 817	37.1	43 011	42.2	23 336	22.9	14 844	14.5	69	44
39 277	38.1	43 802	42.5	24 096	23.4	15 728	15.3	1970	45
35 457	34.0	42 433	40.7	23 763	22.8	16 239	15.6	71	46
32 520	30.8	42 431	40.1	22 975	21.7	18 015	17.0	72	47
33 415	30.9	40 244	37.2	21 283	19.7	18 859	17.4	73	48
32 486	29.7	36 085	33.0	17 576	16.1	19 105	17.5	74	49
29 916	26.9	33 710	30.3	16 191	14.6	19 975	18.0	75	50
29 659	26.4	31 489	28.0	14 787	13.2	19 786	17.6	76	51
28 381	25.0	30 352	26.7	13 859	12.2	20 269	17.9	77	52
27 976	24.4	30 017	26.2	13 686	12.0	20 199	17.6	78	53
29 419	25.5	29 227	25.3	13 362	11.6	20 823	18.0	79	54
32 154	27.6	29 217	25.1	13 302	11.4	20 542	17.7	1980	55
29 873	25.5	29 089	24.8	13 416	11.4	20 096	17.1	81	56
27 501	23.3	29 197	24.7	13 749	11.7	20 668	17.5	82	57
29 391	24.7	29 668	25.0	14 253	12.0	24 985	21.0	83	58
28 805	24.1	29 344	24.6	13 622	11.4	24 344	20.4	84	59
27 804	23.1	29 597	24.6	14 401	12.0	23 383	19.4	85	60
26 810	22.2	28 610	23.7	13 588	11.2	25 667	21.2	86	61
25 274	20.8	28 255	23.2	13 762	11.3	23 831	19.6	87	62
26 400	21.6	30 212	24.8	14 758	12.1	22 795	18.7	88	63
23 781	19.4	31 049	25.4	15 629	12.8	21 125	17.3	89	平成元年
24 187	19.7	32 122	26.2	15 828	12.9	20 088	16.4	1990	2
23 200	18.8	33 155	26.9	15 754	12.8	19 875	16.1	91	3
23 361	18.9	34 677	28.1	15 828	12.8	20 893	16.9	92	4
23 115	18.7	34 717	28.0	15 193	12.3	20 516	16.6	93	5
23 464	18.9	36 115	29.1	14 869	12.0	20 923	16.9	94	6
21 493	17.3	45 323	36.5	15 147	12.2	21 420	17.2	95	7
20 878	16.7	39 184	31.4	14 343	11.5	22 138	17.8	96	8
21 434	17.2	38 886	31.1	13 981	11.2	23 494	18.8	97	9
21 374	17.1	38 925	31.1	13 464	10.7	31 755	25.4	98	10
22 829	18.2	40 079	32.0	13 111	10.5	31 413	25.0	99	11
21 213	16.9	39 484	31.4	12 857	10.2	30 251	24.1	2000	12
22 145	17.6	39 496	31.4	12 378	9.8	29 375	23.3	01	13
22 682	18.0	38 643	30.7	11 743	9.3	29 949	23.8	02	14
23 449	18.6	38 714	30.7	10 913	8.7	32 109	25.5	03	15
24 126	19.1	38 193	30.3	10 551	8.4	30 247	24.0	04	16
26 360	20.9	39 863	31.6	10 028	7.9	30 553	24.2	05	17
27 764	22.0	38 270	30.3	9 048	7.2	29 921	23.7	06	18
30 734	24.4	37 966	30.1	8 268	6.6	30 827	24.4	07	19
35 975	28.6	38 153	30.3	7 499	6.0	30 229	24.0	08	20
38 670	30.7	37 756	30.0	7 309	5.8	30 707	24.4	09	21
45 342	35.9	40 732	32.2	7 222	5.7	29 554	23.4	2010	22
52 242	41.4	59 416	47.1	6 741	5.3	28 896	22.9	11	23
60 719	48.2	41 031	32.6	6 414	5.1	26 433	21.0	12	24
69 720	55.5	39 574	31.5	6 060	4.8	26 063	20.7	13	25
75 389	60.1	39 029	31.1	5 717	4.6	24 417	19.5	14	26
84 810	67.7	38 306	30.6	5 646	4.5	23 152	18.5	15	27
92 806	**74.2**	**38 306**	**30.6**	**5 278**	**4.2**	**21 017**	**16.8**	**16**	**28**

死 亡

表5.12 死因年次推移分類[1]別にみた
Table 5.12 Trends in deaths and death rates (per 100,000

男
Male

年　　　次[2] Year		死 亡 総 数[3]		Hi　0 1 結　　　核		Hi　0 2 悪 性 新 生 物		Hi　0 3 糖 尿 病		Hi　0 4 高血圧性疾患	
		死亡数 Deaths	死亡率 Death rates	死亡数 Deaths	死亡率 Death rates	死亡数 Deaths	死亡率 Death rates	死亡数 Deaths	死亡率 Death rates	死亡数 Deaths	死亡率 Death rates
1899	明治32年	476 249	2 181.0	33 816	154.9	9 780	44.8	…	…	…	…
1900	33	464 072	2 104.5	35 713	162.0	10 250	46.5	…	…	…	…
01	34	468 524	2 101.2	37 577	168.5	11 050	49.6	…	…	…	…
02	35	486 410	2 151.7	39 300	173.8	12 304	54.4	…	…	…	…
03	36	472 249	2 062.1	40 354	176.2	12 972	56.6	…	…	…	…
04	37	481 445	2 075.6	41 643	179.5	13 177	56.8	…	…	…	…
05	38	505 290	2 157.4	45 167	192.8	13 564	57.9	…	…	…	…
06	39	480 077	2 034.3	44 737	189.6	14 261	60.4	…	…	…	…
07	40	512 110	2 153.0	45 152	189.8	14 411	60.6	…	…	…	…
08	41	517 755	2 153.6	46 116	191.8	15 352	63.9	…	…	…	…
09	42	550 267	2 262.1	53 098	218.3	16 726	68.8	598	2.5	…	…
1910	43	535 076	2 170.7	52 774	214.1	16 754	68.0	631	2.6	…	…
11	44	526 141	2 105.2	51 663	206.7	17 356	69.4	653	2.6	…	…
12	大正元年	523 604	2 064.3	53 663	211.6	17 540	69.2	757	3.0	…	…
13	2	521 210	2 025.1	52 329	203.3	18 414	71.5	744	2.9	…	…
14	3	559 337	2 142.6	53 233	203.9	18 895	72.4	781	3.0	…	…
15	4	556 179	2 101.6	54 740	206.8	19 384	73.2	912	3.4	…	…
16	5	604 156	2 250.9	56 791	211.6	20 152	75.1	976	3.6	…	…
17	6	609 310	2 243.6	57 592	212.1	20 144	74.2	974	3.6	…	…
18	7	753 392	2 744.3	64 239	234.0	20 184	73.5	1 080	3.9	…	…
19	8	648 984	2 351.2	61 246	221.9	19 935	72.2	890	3.2	…	…
1920	9	720 655	2 569.7	58 557	208.8	20 779	74.1	908	3.2	…	…
21	10	659 328	2 320.6	57 176	201.2	20 732	73.0	1 056	3.7	…	…
22	11	655 740	2 276.9	59 096	205.2	21 019	73.0	1 013	3.5	…	…
23	12	679 072	2 327.4	55 497	190.2	21 506	73.7	986	3.4	…	…
24	13	642 969	2 174.5	54 429	184.1	21 071	71.3	1 048	3.5	…	…
25	14	621 357	2 070.3	55 546	185.1	21 405	71.3	1 055	3.5	…	…
26	昭和元年	597 292	1 957.0	54 503	178.6	21 947	71.9	1 060	3.5	…	…
27	2	624 311	2 015.1	58 316	188.2	21 775	70.3	1 123	3.6	…	…
28	3	639 214	2 032.5	58 397	185.7	22 832	72.6	1 121	3.6	…	…
29	4	645 994	2 025.7	60 168	188.7	22 251	69.8	1 168	3.7	…	…
1930	5	603 995	1 864.7	59 148	182.6	22 908	70.7	1 143	3.5	…	…
31	6	642 146	1 951.9	61 197	186.0	22 920	69.7	1 165	3.5	…	…
32	7	607 267	1 820.6	60 751	182.1	23 067	69.2	1 200	3.6	…	…
33	8	618 496	1 827.5	64 603	190.9	24 150	71.4	1 392	4.1	…	…
34	9	639 098	1 863.6	66 823	194.9	24 378	71.1	1 350	3.9	…	…
35	10	603 566	1 737.7	67 238	193.6	25 328	72.9	1 288	3.7	…	…
36	11	637 854	1 817.1	73 495	209.4	25 443	72.5	1 379	3.9	…	…
37	12	625 625	1 781.0	73 040	207.9	26 340	75.0	1 460	4.2	…	…
38	13	652 936	1 858.9	75 361	214.6	26 029	74.1	1 541	4.4	…	…
39	14	658 589	1 869.6	79 336	225.2	26 340	74.8	1 427	4.1	…	…
1940	15	615 311	1 738.8	80 599	227.8	26 617	75.2	1 426	4.0	…	…
41	16	597 373	1 721.2	83 395	240.3	27 074	78.0	1 325	3.8	…	…
42	17	609 038	1 746.4	88 131	252.7	27 670	79.3	1 318	3.8	…	…
43	18	638 135	1 835.5	94 623	272.2	27 468	79.0	1 342	3.9	…	…
47	22	595 670	1 562.2	79 640	208.9	26 645	69.9	1 010	2.6	…	…
48	23	493 573	1 261.4	77 705	198.6	28 023	71.6	964	2.5	…	…
49	24	489 817	1 222.6	74 267	185.4	30 256	75.5	977	2.4	…	…
1950	25	467 073	1 144.5	65 089	159.5	32 670	80.1	1 005	2.5	4 639	11.4
51	26	432 540	1 042.4	50 224	121.0	33 872	81.6	1 003	2.4	4 091	9.9
52	27	395 205	937.7	38 433	91.2	35 845	85.0	939	2.2	4 223	10.0
53	28	399 859	935.4	31 901	74.6	37 386	87.5	1 006	2.4	4 433	10.4
54	29	379 658	875.2	31 239	72.0	39 703	91.5	952	2.2	4 381	10.1

General mortality

性別死亡数及び率（人口10万対）（つづき）
population）by sex and causes of death : Japan－CON.

男
Male

Hi 05 心疾患（高血圧性を除く）		Hi 06 脳血管疾患		Hi 07 肺炎		Hi 08 慢性気管支炎及び肺気腫		年次 [2] Year	
死亡数 Deaths	死亡率 Death rates	死亡数 Deaths	死亡率 Death rates	死亡数 Deaths	死亡率 Death rates	死亡数 Deaths	死亡率 Death rates		
10 533	48.2	39 959	183.0	23 379	107.1	…	…	1899	明治32年
10 351	46.9	37 857	171.7	24 292	110.2	…	…	1900	33
10 597	47.5	40 470	181.5	26 593	119.3	…	…	01	34
11 733	51.9	40 444	178.9	28 434	125.8	…	…	02	35
11 576	50.5	39 957	174.5	25 938	113.3	…	…	03	36
12 051	52.0	41 844	180.4	27 578	118.9	…	…	04	37
12 460	53.2	41 131	175.6	31 323	133.7	…	…	05	38
12 004	50.9	39 979	169.4	28 072	119.0	…	…	06	39
13 456	56.6	42 610	179.1	33 149	139.4	…	…	07	40
13 476	56.1	40 168	167.1	35 010	145.6	…	…	08	41
15 747	64.7	36 713	150.9	37 166	152.8	…	…	09	42
15 100	61.3	35 578	144.3	36 643	148.7	…	…	1910	43
14 926	59.7	35 859	143.5	36 379	145.6	…	…	11	44
14 776	58.3	36 787	145.0	38 694	152.5	…	…	12	大正元年
14 682	57.0	36 644	142.4	42 456	165.0	…	…	13	2
15 558	59.6	37 202	142.5	44 320	169.8	…	…	14	3
15 991	60.4	37 357	141.2	45 127	170.5	…	…	15	4
17 867	66.6	40 458	150.7	52 429	195.3	…	…	16	5
18 405	67.8	42 809	157.6	52 727	194.1	…	…	17	6
21 104	76.9	47 370	172.5	105 507	384.3	…	…	18	7
16 396	59.4	46 415	168.2	76 970	278.9	…	…	19	8
16 775	59.8	49 181	175.4	88 551	315.8	…	…	1920	9
18 299	64.4	51 024	179.6	58 694	206.6	…	…	21	10
17 777	61.7	51 183	177.7	59 137	205.3	…	…	22	11
20 807	71.3	53 372	182.9	62 488	214.2	8 849	30.3	23	12
19 524	66.0	57 851	195.6	65 224	220.6	8 977	30.4	24	13
19 485	64.9	54 767	182.5	67 662	225.4	9 307	31.0	25	14
18 267	59.9	55 732	182.6	57 045	186.9	8 019	26.3	26	昭和元年
18 717	60.4	57 186	184.6	63 366	204.5	8 359	27.0	27	2
19 751	62.8	58 087	184.7	66 558	211.6	8 211	26.1	28	3
20 508	64.3	60 242	188.9	64 241	201.4	8 198	25.7	29	4
20 190	62.3	58 276	179.9	53 976	166.6	7 405	22.9	1930	5
20 666	62.8	59 760	181.6	69 464	211.1	8 054	24.5	31	6
18 932	56.8	59 299	177.8	60 071	180.1	7 280	21.8	32	7
19 662	58.1	61 114	180.6	56 907	168.1	6 634	19.6	33	8
21 067	61.4	63 333	184.7	67 045	195.5	7 019	20.5	34	9
19 936	57.4	62 983	181.3	56 677	163.2	6 484	18.7	35	10
21 468	61.2	65 323	186.1	60 030	171.0	7 017	20.0	36	11
21 480	61.1	65 097	185.3	58 066	165.3	6 175	17.6	37	12
23 998	68.3	69 991	199.3	64 435	183.4	7 009	20.0	38	13
23 783	67.5	71 912	204.1	72 245	205.1	6 740	19.1	39	14
22 507	63.6	70 075	198.0	61 393	173.5	5 894	16.7	1940	15
20 974	60.4	67 357	194.1	55 891	161.0	5 611	16.2	41	16
21 265	61.0	67 144	192.5	57 871	165.9	5 608	16.1	42	17
21 894	63.0	64 538	185.6	64 047	184.2	5 690	16.4	43	18
23 618	61.9	51 841	136.0	55 703	146.1	5 652	14.8	47	22
23 927	61.1	46 779	119.5	28 499	72.8	4 724	12.1	48	23
25 624	64.0	49 172	122.7	29 682	74.1	4 301	10.7	49	24
26 108	64.0	52 188	127.9	28 090	68.8	4 042	9.9	1950	25
26 116	62.9	52 388	126.3	26 705	64.4	3 293	7.9	51	26
25 825	61.3	55 011	130.5	22 628	53.7	2 797	6.6	52	27
28 339	66.3	58 421	136.7	24 450	57.2	2 763	6.5	53	28
26 729	61.6	59 940	138.2	19 740	45.5	2 212	5.1	54	29

Note : See page 74.

死　亡

表5.12　死因年次推移分類[1]別にみた
Table 5.12　Trends in deaths and death rates (per 100,000

男
Male

年　次[2] Year		死亡総数[3]		Hi　0　1 結　　核		Hi　0　2 悪性新生物		Hi　0　3 糖　尿　病		Hi　0　4 高血圧性疾患	
		死亡数 Deaths	死亡率 Death rates	死亡数 Deaths	死亡率 Death rates	死亡数 Deaths	死亡率 Death rates	死亡数 Deaths	死亡率 Death rates	死亡数 Deaths	死亡率 Death rates
1955	昭和30年	365 246	832.7	26 601	60.6	41 223	94.0	1 020	2.3	4 385	10.0
56	31	381 395	859.9	25 513	57.5	43 628	98.4	1 173	2.6	4 935	11.1
57	32	397 502	887.9	25 175	56.2	44 777	100.0	1 293	2.9	5 376	12.0
58	33	363 647	804.0	21 744	48.1	47 237	104.4	1 222	2.7	6 143	13.6
59	34	367 562	804.2	20 042	43.8	49 215	107.7	1 293	2.8	6 692	14.6
1960	35	377 526	822.9	19 769	43.1	50 898	110.9	1 482	3.2	7 360	16.0
61	36	371 858	803.1	17 512	37.8	52 254	112.8	1 549	3.3	7 774	16.8
62	37	380 826	814.7	17 705	37.9	53 499	114.5	1 757	3.8	8 561	18.3
63	38	361 469	765.3	14 957	31.7	55 567	117.7	1 814	3.8	8 500	18.0
64	39	363 531	761.4	14 842	31.1	57 705	120.9	2 133	4.5	8 711	18.2
65	40	378 716	785.0	14 781	30.6	58 899	122.1	2 463	5.1	9 176	19.0
66	41	363 356	747.2	13 204	27.2	60 803	125.0	2 735	5.6	8 812	18.1
67	42	366 076	748.6	11 773	24.1	62 308	127.4	2 970	6.1	8 691	17.8
68	43	372 931	753.7	11 374	23.0	64 244	129.8	3 100	6.3	8 578	17.3
69	44	379 506	757.5	11 086	22.1	66 270	132.3	3 432	6.8	8 134	16.2
1970	45	387 880	766.6	10 914	21.6	67 074	132.6	3 753	7.4	8 423	16.6
71	46	372 942	728.0	9 470	18.5	68 399	133.5	3 704	7.2	7 866	15.4
72	47	372 833	719.1	8 702	16.8	71 298	137.5	3 821	7.4	7 877	15.2
73	48	383 592	723.7	8 448	15.9	73 401	138.5	4 074	7.7	8 352	15.8
74	49	381 869	711.4	7 998	14.9	75 456	140.6	4 415	8.2	8 716	16.2
75	50	377 827	690.4	7 406	13.5	76 922	140.6	4 377	8.0	8 683	15.9
76	51	378 630	684.3	6 835	12.4	79 995	144.6	4 347	7.9	8 620	15.6
77	52	372 175	666.3	6 309	11.3	83 088	148.7	4 550	8.1	8 255	14.8
78	53	375 625	666.5	5 949	10.6	85 630	151.9	4 632	8.2	8 062	14.3
79	54	373 183	656.6	4 896	8.6	90 136	158.6	3 839	6.8	6 861	12.1
1980	55	390 644	682.9	4 715	8.2	93 501	163.5	4 055	7.1	6 654	11.6
81	56	388 575	674.0	4 245	7.4	96 524	167.4	3 879	6.7	6 288	10.9
82	57	385 494	664.0	3 930	6.8	99 114	170.7	4 121	7.1	5 556	9.6
83	58	401 232	686.6	3 866	6.6	103 330	176.8	4 194	7.2	5 400	9.2
84	59	402 220	684.1	3 685	6.3	107 175	182.3	4 443	7.6	5 163	8.8
85	60	407 769	690.6	3 442	5.8	110 660	187.4	4 322	7.3	4 991	8.5
86	61	406 918	684.6	3 112	5.2	113 589	191.1	4 335	7.3	4 555	7.7
87	62	408 094	683.3	2 959	5.0	119 161	199.5	4 261	7.1	4 090	6.8
88	63	428 094	713.9	2 954	4.9	122 015	203.5	4 569	7.6	3 892	6.5
89	平成元年	427 114	709.8	2 676	4.4	127 211	211.4	4 399	7.3	3 486	5.8
1990	2	443 718	736.5	2 745	4.6	130 395	216.4	4 491	7.5	3 399	5.6
91	3	450 344	745.3	2 449	4.1	134 475	222.5	4 633	7.7	3 410	5.6
92	4	465 544	768.3	2 514	4.1	139 674	230.5	4 758	7.9	3 174	5.2
93	5	476 462	784.6	2 424	4.0	142 222	234.2	4 972	8.2	3 117	5.1
94	6	476 080	782.5	2 290	3.8	146 896	241.5	5 276	8.7	2 824	4.6
95	7	501 276	822.9	2 267	3.7	159 623	262.0	7 107	11.7	3 027	5.0
96	8	488 605	799.5	2 064	3.4	164 824	269.7	6 394	10.5	2 613	4.3
97	9	497 796	813.3	1 955	3.2	167 076	273.0	6 295	10.3	2 537	4.1
98	10	512 128	835.3	1 977	3.2	172 306	281.0	6 424	10.5	2 360	3.8
99	11	534 778	871.6	2 114	3.4	175 817	286.5	6 527	10.6	2 376	3.9
2000	12	525 903	855.3	1 876	3.1	179 140	291.3	6 489	10.6	2 163	3.5
01	13	528 768	858.5	1 715	2.8	181 393	294.5	6 368	10.3	2 102	3.4
02	14	535 305	869.1	1 584	2.6	184 033	298.8	6 631	10.8	2 108	3.4
03	15	551 746	895.4	1 615	2.6	186 912	303.3	6 709	10.9	2 016	3.3
04	16	557 097	904.4	1 555	2.5	193 096	313.5	6 694	10.9	2 066	3.4
05	17	584 970	949.4	1 579	2.6	196 603	319.1	7 131	11.6	2 145	3.5
06	18	581 370	944.3	1 517	2.5	198 052	321.7	7 268	11.8	2 095	3.4
07	19	592 784	963.7	1 458	2.4	202 743	329.6	7 395	12.0	2 323	3.8
08	20	608 711	991.0	1 467	2.4	206 354	336.0	7 618	12.4	2 354	3.8
09	21	609 042	992.9	1 357	2.2	206 352	336.4	7 399	12.1	2 266	3.7
2010	22	633 700	1 029.2	1 338	2.2	211 435	343.4	7 620	12.4	2 517	4.1
11	23	656 540	1 068.4	1 349	2.2	213 190	346.9	7 738	12.6	2 616	4.3
12	24	655 526	1 068.9	1 279	2.1	215 110	350.8	7 639	12.5	2 738	4.5
13	25	658 684	1 076.5	1 246	2.0	216 975	354.6	7 294	11.9	2 657	4.3
14	26	660 334	1 081.8	1 251	2.0	218 397	357.8	7 265	11.9	2 637	4.3
15	27	666 707	1 092.6	1 169	1.9	219 508	359.7	7 125	11.7	2 605	4.3
16	28	674 733	1 108.5	1 133	1.9	219 785	361.1	7 243	11.9	2 720	4.5

General mortality

性別死亡数及び率（人口10万対）（つづき）
population) by sex and causes of death : Japan－CON.

男
Male

Hi 05 心疾患（高血圧性を除く）		Hi 06 脳血管疾患		Hi 07 肺炎		Hi 08 慢性気管支炎及び肺気腫		年次[2] Year	
死亡数 Deaths	死亡率 Death rates	死亡数 Deaths	死亡率 Death rates	死亡数 Deaths	死亡率 Death rates	死亡数 Deaths	死亡率 Death rates		
27 282	62.2	62 737	143.0	17 965	41.0	2 075	4.7	1955	昭和30年
29 993	67.6	69 427	156.5	18 524	41.8	1 944	4.4	56	31
34 030	76.0	72 802	162.6	23 318	52.1	1 969	4.4	57	32
30 358	67.1	71 642	158.4	18 661	41.3	1 616	3.6	58	33
32 135	70.3	75 169	164.5	18 304	40.0	1 528	3.3	59	34
34 755	75.8	78 965	172.1	20 152	43.9	1 538	3.4	1960	35
34 324	74.1	82 817	178.9	16 791	36.3	1 550	3.3	61	36
37 230	79.6	85 877	183.7	18 547	39.7	1 785	3.8	62	37
34 605	73.3	87 943	186.2	14 010	29.7	1 592	3.4	63	38
34 986	73.3	89 040	186.5	13 556	28.4	1 735	3.6	64	39
38 827	80.5	92 723	192.2	15 962	33.1	1 811	3.8	65	40
36 607	75.3	92 066	189.3	12 186	25.1	1 620	3.3	66	41
38 900	79.6	92 024	188.2	12 507	25.6	1 735	3.5	67	42
41 766	84.4	93 773	189.5	13 309	26.9	2 370	4.8	68	43
43 305	86.4	95 622	190.9	13 647	27.2	2 575	5.1	69	44
45 988	90.9	96 910	191.5	15 030	29.7	2 607	5.2	1970	45
44 380	86.6	94 404	184.3	12 442	24.3	2 554	5.0	71	46
44 192	85.2	93 290	179.9	12 462	24.0	2 626	5.1	72	47
48 300	91.1	94 323	178.0	14 287	27.0	2 816	5.3	73	48
49 655	92.5	92 620	172.5	15 404	28.7	2 913	5.4	74	49
50 395	92.1	89 924	164.3	16 371	29.9	2 972	5.4	75	50
52 673	95.2	89 189	161.2	16 234	29.3	3 038	5.5	76	51
53 079	95.0	86 807	155.4	14 341	25.7	3 076	5.5	77	52
54 643	97.0	85 308	151.4	15 653	27.8	3 361	6.0	78	53
58 065	102.2	80 134	141.0	15 233	26.8	3 103	5.5	79	54
64 103	112.1	81 650	142.7	18 633	32.6	3 550	6.2	1980	55
64 281	111.5	78 510	136.2	18 853	32.7	3 710	6.4	81	56
64 578	111.2	73 192	126.1	19 988	34.4	4 019	6.9	82	57
67 412	115.4	71 631	122.6	22 795	39.0	4 266	7.3	83	58
69 582	118.4	68 262	116.1	22 327	38.0	4 469	7.6	84	59
71 766	121.5	65 287	110.6	25 520	43.2	4 973	8.4	85	60
72 072	121.3	61 832	104.0	26 739	45.0	4 825	8.1	86	61
72 566	121.5	58 744	98.4	27 930	46.8	4 741	7.9	87	62
78 640	131.1	60 832	101.4	32 485	54.2	5 230	8.7	88	63
77 901	129.5	56 938	94.6	33 470	55.6	5 277	8.8	89	平成元年
81 774	135.7	57 627	95.6	38 596	64.1	5 664	9.4	1990	2
83 646	138.4	55 740	92.2	39 843	65.9	5 955	9.9	91	3
86 384	142.6	55 431	91.5	42 328	69.9	5 952	9.8	92	4
88 309	145.4	55 279	91.0	45 797	75.4	6 241	10.3	93	5
78 868	129.6	55 510	91.2	46 939	77.2	6 777	11.1	94	6
69 718	114.4	69 587	114.2	42 419	69.6	8 018	13.2	95	7
68 977	112.9	66 479	108.8	38 472	63.0	7 195	11.8	96	8
69 776	114.0	65 790	107.5	42 314	69.1	7 497	12.2	97	9
71 134	116.0	65 529	106.9	42 663	69.6	7 471	12.2	98	10
73 979	120.6	66 452	108.3	49 903	81.3	8 451	13.8	99	11
72 156	117.3	63 127	102.7	46 722	76.0	8 237	13.4	2000	12
72 727	118.1	63 146	102.5	45 756	74.3	8 244	13.4	01	13
74 986	121.7	62 229	101.0	47 033	76.4	8 289	13.5	02	14
77 989	126.6	63 274	102.7	50 614	82.1	8 657	14.0	03	15
77 465	125.8	61 547	99.9	51 306	83.3	8 164	13.3	04	16
83 979	136.3	63 657	103.3	57 310	93.0	8 525	13.8	05	17
82 811	134.5	61 348	99.6	56 572	91.9	8 093	13.1	06	18
83 090	135.1	60 992	99.2	58 575	95.2	8 177	13.3	07	19
86 139	140.2	61 121	99.5	61 343	99.9	8 044	13.1	08	20
85 543	139.5	59 293	96.7	59 889	97.6	7 685	12.5	09	21
88 803	144.2	60 186	97.7	63 569	103.2	7 711	12.5	2010	22
91 298	148.6	59 616	97.0	66 601	108.4	7 473	12.2	11	23
92 976	151.6	58 625	95.6	66 386	108.2	7 205	11.7	12	24
91 445	149.5	56 718	92.7	66 362	108.5	6 758	11.0	13	25
92 278	151.2	54 995	90.1	64 780	106.1	6 321	10.4	14	26
92 142	151.0	53 576	87.8	65 609	107.5	5 949	9.7	15	27
93 419	**153.5**	**52 706**	**86.6**	**65 636**	**107.8**	**5 594**	**9.2**	**16**	**28**

死 亡

表 5.12 死因年次推移分類[1] 別にみた
Table 5.12 Trends in deaths and death rates (per 100,000

男
Male

年 次[2] Year		Hi 09 喘 息		Hi 10 胃潰瘍及び十二指腸潰瘍		Hi 11 肝 疾 患		Hi 12 腎 不 全	
		死亡数 Deaths	死亡率 Death rates	死亡数 Deaths	死亡率 Death rates	死亡数 Deaths	死亡率 Death rates	死亡数 Deaths	死亡率 Death rates
1899	明治32年	…	…	…	…	…	…	…	…
1900	33	…	…	…	…	…	…	…	…
01	34	…	…	…	…	…	…	…	…
02	35	…	…	…	…	…	…	…	…
03	36	…	…	…	…	…	…	…	…
04	37	…	…	…	…	…	…	…	…
05	38	…	…	…	…	…	…	…	…
06	39	…	…	…	…	…	…	…	…
07	40	…	…	…	…	…	…	…	…
08	41	…	…	…	…	…	…	…	…
09	42	3 577	14.7	3 037	12.5	5 188	21.3	…	…
1910	43	3 654	14.8	3 107	12.6	5 150	20.9	…	…
11	44	3 301	13.2	2 949	11.8	6 002	24.0	…	…
12	大正元年	3 537	13.9	3 140	12.4	6 011	23.7	…	…
13	2	3 727	14.5	3 171	12.3	5 796	22.5	…	…
14	3	3 569	13.7	3 310	12.7	6 325	24.2	…	…
15	4	3 534	13.4	3 202	12.1	6 153	23.2	…	…
16	5	4 274	15.9	3 531	13.2	6 687	24.9	…	…
17	6	4 147	15.3	3 883	14.3	6 387	23.5	…	…
18	7	5 329	19.4	3 789	13.8	6 523	23.8	…	…
19	8	3 744	13.6	3 704	13.4	6 093	22.1	…	…
1920	9	4 559	16.3	4 068	14.5	6 870	24.5	…	…
21	10	4 008	14.1	4 177	14.7	6 960	24.5	…	…
22	11	4 588	15.9	4 022	14.0	6 881	23.9	…	…
23	12	3 640	12.5	4 487	15.4	6 247	21.4	…	…
24	13	3 841	13.0	4 689	15.9	5 974	20.2	…	…
25	14	4 265	14.2	5 038	16.8	5 757	19.2	…	…
26	昭和元年	3 563	11.7	5 209	17.1	5 606	18.4	…	…
27	2	3 856	12.4	5 282	17.0	5 937	19.2	…	…
28	3	4 082	13.0	5 659	18.0	6 009	19.1	…	…
29	4	4 063	12.7	5 687	17.8	5 952	18.7	…	…
1930	5	3 927	12.1	6 171	19.1	6 090	18.8	…	…
31	6	4 621	14.0	6 410	19.5	5 902	17.9	…	…
32	7	4 044	12.1	6 817	20.4	5 962	17.9	…	…
33	8	4 430	13.1	7 140	21.1	5 029	14.9	…	…
34	9	5 046	14.7	7 714	22.5	4 976	14.5	…	…
35	10	4 557	13.1	7 710	22.2	4 808	13.8	…	…
36	11	5 618	16.0	8 258	23.5	5 077	14.5	…	…
37	12	4 713	13.4	8 591	24.5	5 261	15.0	…	…
38	13	5 744	16.4	9 218	26.2	5 245	14.9	…	…
39	14	6 063	17.2	9 198	26.1	5 059	14.4	…	…
1940	15	5 466	15.4	9 129	25.8	5 176	14.6	…	…
41	16	5 410	15.6	9 152	26.4	5 121	14.8	…	…
42	17	5 739	16.5	10 784	30.9	5 299	15.2	…	…
43	18	6 556	18.9	12 505	36.0	5 264	15.1	…	…
47	22	8 506	22.3	18 950	49.7	5 054	13.3	…	…
48	23	6 756	17.3	14 886	38.0	5 079	13.0	…	…
49	24	7 167	17.9	13 906	34.7	5 365	13.4	…	…
1950	25	9 461	23.2	13 656	33.5	4 887	12.0	…	…
51	26	8 888	21.4	12 998	31.3	5 078	12.2	…	…
52	27	7 706	18.3	11 997	28.5	5 688	13.5	…	…
53	28	9 446	22.1	11 444	26.8	6 230	14.6	…	…
54	29	6 960	16.0	10 028	23.1	6 660	15.4	…	…

190

General mortality

性別死亡数及び率（人口10万対）（つづき）
population) by sex and causes of death : Japan−CON.

男
Male

Hi 13 老衰		Hi 14 不慮の事故		（再掲）Hi 15 交通事故		Hi 16 自殺		年次[2]	
死亡数 Deaths	死亡率 Death rates	死亡数 Deaths	死亡率 Death rates	死亡数 Deaths	死亡率 Death rates	死亡数 Deaths	死亡率 Death rates	Year	
22 759	104.2	13 947	63.9	…	…	3 699	16.9	1899	明治32年
23 971	108.7	12 919	58.6	…	…	3 716	16.9	1900	33
20 098	90.1	11 734	52.6	…	…	4 872	21.8	01	34
21 727	96.1	13 109	58.0	…	…	4 986	22.1	02	35
23 400	102.2	13 339	58.2	…	…	5 547	24.2	03	36
25 610	110.4	13 985	60.3	…	…	5 585	24.1	04	37
26 449	112.9	13 424	57.3	…	…	5 020	21.4	05	38
24 923	105.6	14 606	61.9	…	…	4 665	19.8	06	39
25 821	108.6	14 819	62.3	…	…	4 836	20.3	07	40
23 998	99.8	14 571	60.6	…	…	5 100	21.2	08	41
25 514	104.9	13 642	56.1	…	…	5 735	23.6	09	42
24 134	97.9	14 018	56.9	…	…	5 928	24.0	1910	43
23 489	94.0	14 947	59.8	…	…	5 847	23.4	11	44
23 779	93.7	15 757	62.1	…	…	5 955	23.5	12	大正元年
23 816	92.5	14 519	56.4	…	…	6 474	25.2	13	2
25 375	97.2	17 001	65.1	…	…	6 894	26.4	14	3
24 616	93.0	15 850	59.9	…	…	6 503	24.6	15	4
28 254	105.3	15 740	58.6	…	…	6 065	22.6	16	5
29 322	108.0	17 688	65.1	…	…	5 724	21.1	17	6
33 256	121.1	18 214	66.3	…	…	6 147	22.4	18	7
28 276	102.4	17 106	62.0	…	…	6 158	22.3	19	8
30 668	109.4	17 605	62.8	…	…	6 521	23.3	1920	9
31 324	110.3	16 339	57.5	…	…	6 923	24.4	21	10
31 368	108.9	17 210	59.8	…	…	6 984	24.3	22	11
31 679	108.6	38 353	131.4	…	…	7 065	24.2	23	12
30 486	103.1	17 417	58.9	…	…	6 958	23.5	24	13
29 149	97.1	16 638	55.4	…	…	7 521	25.1	25	14
27 806	91.1	17 349	56.8	…	…	7 675	25.1	26	昭和元年
30 681	99.0	19 038	61.4	…	…	7 912	25.5	27	2
32 388	103.0	17 826	56.7	…	…	7 984	25.4	28	3
32 189	100.9	18 249	57.2	…	…	7 915	24.8	29	4
31 535	97.4	17 969	55.5	…	…	8 810	27.2	1930	5
35 237	107.1	17 091	52.0	…	…	9 102	27.7	31	6
31 607	94.8	18 144	54.4	…	…	9 272	27.8	32	7
33 797	99.9	20 618	60.9	…	…	9 110	26.9	33	8
34 922	101.8	21 755	63.4	…	…	9 065	26.4	34	9
31 918	91.9	20 641	59.4	…	…	8 733	25.1	35	10
37 074	105.6	21 506	61.3	…	…	9 766	27.8	36	11
34 142	97.2	21 640	61.6	…	…	8 923	25.4	37	12
39 995	113.9	22 659	64.5	…	…	7 585	21.6	38	13
38 419	109.1	21 393	60.7	…	…	6 502	18.5	39	14
35 575	100.5	20 429	57.7	…	…	5 841	16.5	1940	15
36 251	104.5	20 666	59.5	…	…	5 667	16.3	41	16
38 846	111.4	21 936	62.9	…	…	5 498	15.8	42	17
39 694	114.2	23 079	66.4	…	…	5 115	14.7	43	18
32 164	84.4	26 538	69.6	3 569	9.4	7 108	18.6	47	22
25 796	65.9	26 272	67.1	4 537	11.6	7 331	18.7	48	23
26 656	66.5	24 500	61.2	4 413	11.0	8 391	20.9	49	24
23 474	57.5	23 783	58.3	5 795	14.2	9 820	24.1	1950	25
23 618	56.9	23 199	55.9	6 074	14.6	9 035	21.8	51	26
23 468	55.7	22 902	54.3	6 375	15.1	9 171	21.8	52	27
26 725	62.5	24 862	58.2	7 237	16.9	10 450	24.4	53	28
24 358	56.2	26 144	60.3	9 234	21.3	12 641	29.1	54	29

死　亡

表 5.12　死因年次推移分類[1]別にみた
Table 5.12　Trends in deaths and death rates (per 100,000

男
Male

年　次[2] Year		Hi　0 9 喘　　息		Hi　1 0 胃潰瘍及び十二指腸潰瘍		Hi　1 1 肝　疾　患		Hi　1 2 腎　不　全	
		死亡数 Deaths	死亡率 Death rates	死亡数 Deaths	死亡率 Death rates	死亡数 Deaths	死亡率 Death rates	死亡数 Deaths	死亡率 Death rates
1955	昭和30年	6 737	15.4	9 422	21.5	6 749	15.4	…	…
56	31	7 201	16.2	9 369	21.1	7 351	16.6	…	…
57	32	8 553	19.1	8 906	19.9	7 450	16.6	…	…
58	33	6 094	13.5	8 218	18.2	7 367	16.3	…	…
59	34	5 850	12.8	7 729	16.9	7 552	16.5	…	…
1960	35	6 756	14.7	7 640	16.7	8 013	17.5	…	…
61	36	5 721	12.4	7 142	15.4	8 068	17.4	…	…
62	37	6 963	14.9	6 967	14.9	8 230	17.6	…	…
63	38	5 327	11.3	6 678	14.1	8 473	17.9	…	…
64	39	5 467	11.5	6 487	13.6	8 586	18.0	…	…
65	40	6 591	13.7	6 367	13.2	8 582	17.8	…	…
66	41	5 512	11.3	6 151	12.6	8 699	17.9	…	…
67	42	5 597	11.4	5 985	12.2	9 305	19.0	…	…
68	43	5 612	11.3	5 937	12.0	9 831	19.9	…	…
69	44	5 273	10.5	5 757	11.5	10 432	20.8	…	…
1970	45	5 528	10.9	5 419	10.7	11 047	21.8	…	…
71	46	4 788	9.3	4 864	9.5	11 136	21.7	…	…
72	47	4 400	8.5	4 900	9.5	11 472	22.1	…	…
73	48	4 366	8.2	4 697	8.9	11 908	22.5	…	…
74	49	4 423	8.2	4 598	8.6	12 414	23.1	…	…
75	50	4 107	7.5	4 472	8.2	12 461	22.8	…	…
76	51	4 171	7.5	3 969	7.2	12 919	23.3	…	…
77	52	3 740	6.7	3 777	6.8	12 708	22.7	…	…
78	53	3 448	6.1	3 641	6.5	13 171	23.4	…	…
79	54	3 661	6.4	3 382	6.0	13 311	23.4	3 129	5.5
1980	55	3 870	6.8	3 349	5.9	13 348	23.3	3 611	6.3
81	56	3 745	6.5	3 261	5.7	13 293	23.1	4 069	7.1
82	57	3 624	6.2	2 758	4.8	13 197	22.7	4 532	7.8
83	58	3 938	6.7	2 686	4.6	13 409	22.9	5 009	8.6
84	59	3 608	6.1	2 520	4.3	13 484	22.9	5 288	9.0
85	60	3 776	6.4	2 428	4.1	13 591	23.0	5 809	9.8
86	61	3 658	6.2	2 297	3.9	13 282	22.3	6 099	10.3
87	62	3 485	5.8	2 067	3.5	13 053	21.9	6 239	10.4
88	63	3 596	6.0	1 992	3.3	13 320	22.2	6 983	11.6
89	平成元年	3 302	5.5	1 995	3.3	13 138	21.8	7 324	12.2
1990	2	3 412	5.7	1 933	3.2	13 256	22.0	7 632	12.7
91	3	3 382	5.6	1 970	3.3	13 113	21.7	7 641	12.6
92	4	3 308	5.5	1 917	3.2	13 394	22.1	8 123	13.4
93	5	3 463	5.7	1 965	3.2	13 279	21.9	8 425	13.9
94	6	3 310	5.4	1 956	3.2	12 962	21.3	8 374	13.8
95	7	4 052	6.7	2 274	3.7	11 576	19.0	7 800	12.8
96	8	3 308	5.4	2 087	3.4	11 198	18.3	7 488	12.3
97	9	3 027	4.9	2 127	3.5	11 377	18.6	7 714	12.6
98	10	2 748	4.5	2 131	3.5	11 167	18.2	7 731	12.6
99	11	2 842	4.6	2 250	3.7	11 454	18.7	8 309	13.5
2000	12	2 300	3.7	2 161	3.5	11 068	18.0	8 029	13.1
01	13	2 086	3.4	2 121	3.4	10 911	17.7	8 202	13.3
02	14	1 872	3.0	2 089	3.4	10 532	17.1	8 428	13.7
03	15	1 846	3.0	2 104	3.4	10 703	17.4	8 686	14.1
04	16	1 576	2.6	1 920	3.1	10 705	17.4	8 806	14.3
05	17	1 565	2.5	1 897	3.1	11 007	17.9	9 463	15.4
06	18	1 290	2.1	1 924	3.1	10 909	17.7	9 714	15.8
07	19	1 135	1.8	1 849	3.0	10 708	17.4	9 928	16.1
08	20	1 085	1.8	1 787	2.9	10 615	17.3	10 429	17.0
09	21	934	1.5	1 779	2.9	10 463	17.1	10 716	17.5
2010	22	898	1.5	1 835	3.0	10 619	17.2	11 035	17.9
11	23	845	1.4	1 750	2.8	10 644	17.3	11 587	18.9
12	24	769	1.3	1 697	2.8	10 441	17.0	11 835	19.3
13	25	694	1.1	1 588	2.6	10 360	16.9	12 003	19.6
14	26	590	1.0	1 609	2.6	10 031	16.4	11 935	19.6
15	27	573	0.9	1 511	2.5	10 016	16.4	11 908	19.5
16	28	567	0.9	1 527	2.5	10 112	16.6	12 231	20.1

192

General mortality

性別死亡数及び率（人口10万対）（つづき）
population）by sex and causes of death : Japan−CON.

男
Male

Hi 13 老衰		Hi 14 不慮の事故		（再掲）Hi 15 交通事故		Hi 16 自殺		年次[2] Year	
死亡数 Deaths	死亡率 Death rates	死亡数 Deaths	死亡率 Death rates	死亡数 Deaths	死亡率 Death rates	死亡数 Deaths	死亡率 Death rates		
23 581	53.8	24 908	56.8	8 244	18.8	13 836	31.5	1955	昭和30年
27 069	61.0	25 107	56.6	8 821	19.9	13 222	29.8	56	31
28 427	63.5	25 988	58.0	9 702	21.7	13 276	29.7	57	32
19 479	43.1	26 751	59.1	10 734	23.7	13 895	30.7	58	33
19 991	43.7	30 203	66.1	12 320	27.0	12 179	26.6	59	34
20 547	44.8	29 787	64.9	14 170	30.9	11 506	25.1	1960	35
20 294	43.8	32 089	69.3	15 251	32.9	10 333	22.3	61	36
20 335	43.5	29 520	63.2	14 358	30.7	9 541	20.4	62	37
17 533	37.1	30 700	65.0	15 306	32.4	8 923	18.9	63	38
16 738	35.1	31 286	65.5	16 280	34.1	8 336	17.5	64	39
17 504	36.3	30 674	63.6	15 499	32.1	8 330	17.3	65	40
15 531	31.9	32 530	66.9	17 074	35.1	8 450	17.4	66	41
15 345	31.4	31 742	64.9	16 206	33.1	7 940	16.2	67	42
14 035	28.4	30 795	62.2	16 437	33.2	8 174	16.5	68	43
13 396	26.7	32 620	65.1	18 198	36.3	8 241	16.4	69	44
13 580	26.8	33 112	65.4	18 629	36.8	8 761	17.3	1970	45
12 370	24.1	31 757	62.0	18 234	35.6	9 157	17.9	71	46
11 367	21.9	31 689	61.1	17 728	34.2	10 231	19.7	72	47
11 776	22.2	29 998	56.6	16 345	30.8	10 730	20.2	73	48
11 012	20.5	26 824	50.0	13 593	25.3	10 723	20.0	74	49
10 287	18.8	24 865	45.4	12 466	22.8	11 744	21.5	75	50
10 301	18.6	23 236	42.0	11 389	20.6	11 744	21.2	76	51
9 831	17.6	22 407	40.1	10 675	19.1	12 299	22.0	77	52
9 907	17.6	22 049	39.1	10 478	18.6	12 409	22.0	78	53
10 271	18.1	21 337	37.5	10 132	17.8	12 851	22.6	79	54
11 244	19.7	21 153	37.0	10 111	17.7	12 769	22.3	1980	55
10 552	18.3	21 147	36.7	10 166	17.6	12 708	22.0	81	56
9 567	16.5	21 046	36.3	10 444	18.0	13 203	22.7	82	57
10 225	17.5	21 261	36.4	10 699	18.3	16 876	28.9	83	58
10 149	17.3	21 223	36.1	10 329	17.6	16 251	27.6	84	59
9 669	16.4	21 318	36.1	10 832	18.3	15 356	26.0	85	60
9 129	15.4	20 480	34.5	10 196	17.2	16 499	27.8	86	61
8 658	14.5	20 124	33.7	10 225	17.1	15 281	25.6	87	62
8 910	14.9	21 358	35.6	10 927	18.2	14 290	23.8	88	63
7 877	13.1	21 848	36.3	11 464	19.1	12 939	21.5	89	平成元年
8 054	13.4	22 199	36.8	11 481	19.1	12 316	20.4	1990	2
7 676	12.7	22 879	37.9	11 409	18.9	12 477	20.6	91	3
7 613	12.6	23 606	39.0	11 435	18.9	13 516	22.3	92	4
7 324	12.1	23 397	38.5	10 920	18.0	13 540	22.3	93	5
7 333	12.1	24 082	39.6	10 593	17.4	14 058	23.1	94	6
6 684	11.0	28 229	46.3	10 772	17.7	14 231	23.4	95	7
6 372	10.4	25 485	41.7	10 170	16.6	14 853	24.3	96	8
6 384	10.4	25 157	41.1	9 824	16.0	15 901	26.0	97	9
6 293	10.3	24 984	40.7	9 552	15.6	22 349	36.5	98	10
6 600	10.8	25 551	41.6	9 189	15.0	22 402	36.5	99	11
6 017	9.8	25 162	40.9	9 072	14.8	21 656	35.2	2000	12
6 094	9.9	24 993	40.6	8 698	14.1	21 085	34.2	01	13
6 209	10.1	24 283	39.4	8 171	13.3	21 677	35.2	02	14
6 288	10.2	23 969	38.9	7 565	12.3	23 396	38.0	03	15
6 172	10.0	23 667	38.4	7 355	11.9	21 955	35.6	04	16
6 683	10.8	24 591	39.9	7 015	11.4	22 236	36.1	05	17
6 872	11.2	23 329	37.9	6 258	10.2	21 419	34.8	06	18
7 493	12.2	22 666	36.8	5 559	9.0	22 007	35.8	07	19
8 751	14.2	22 801	37.1	5 191	8.5	21 546	35.1	08	20
9 301	15.2	22 588	36.8	5 010	8.2	22 189	36.2	09	21
10 787	17.5	23 975	38.9	4 871	7.9	21 028	34.2	2010	22
12 525	20.4	32 483	52.9	4 578	7.4	19 904	32.4	11	23
14 737	24.0	23 714	38.7	4 294	7.0	18 485	30.1	12	24
16 821	27.5	23 043	37.7	4 119	6.7	18 158	29.7	13	25
18 316	30.0	22 562	37.0	3 923	6.4	16 875	27.6	14	26
20 894	34.2	22 121	36.3	3 886	6.4	16 202	26.6	15	27
23 077	**37.9**	**22 066**	**36.3**	**3 665**	**6.0**	**14 639**	**24.1**	**16**	**28**

193

死　亡

表 5.12　死因年次推移分類[1]別にみた
Table 5.12　Trends in deaths and death rates (per 100,000

女
Female

年　次[2] Year		死亡総数[3]		Hi　0 1 結　　核		Hi　0 2 悪 性 新 生 物		Hi　0 3 糖 尿 病		Hi　0 4 高血圧性疾患	
		死亡数 Deaths	死亡率 Death rates	死亡数 Deaths	死亡率 Death rates	死亡数 Deaths	死亡率 Death rates	死亡数 Deaths	死亡率 Death rates	死亡数 Deaths	死亡率 Death rates
1899	明治32年	455 828	2 113.4	33 783	156.6	9 602	44.5	…	…	…	…
1900	33	446 664	2 049.3	36 058	165.4	10 084	46.3	…	…	…	…
01	34	457 278	2 072.8	39 037	177.0	11 099	50.3	…	…	…	…
02	35	472 710	2 114.3	43 259	193.5	12 294	55.0	…	…	…	…
03	36	458 755	2 025.9	44 778	197.7	12 578	55.5	…	…	…	…
04	37	473 950	2 066.0	45 617	198.9	12 816	55.9	…	…	…	…
05	38	499 365	2 152.5	50 863	219.2	13 104	56.5	…	…	…	…
06	39	475 176	2 027.3	51 332	219.0	13 602	58.0	…	…	…	…
07	40	504 681	2 135.8	51 432	217.7	14 040	59.4	…	…	…	…
08	41	511 687	2 138.8	52 755	220.5	15 088	63.1	…	…	…	…
09	42	540 992	2 232.9	60 524	249.8	16 071	66.3	459	1.9	…	…
1910	43	529 156	2 156.8	60 429	246.3	16 244	66.2	458	1.9	…	…
11	44	517 762	2 082.8	59 059	237.6	16 863	67.8	559	2.2	…	…
12	大正元年	513 410	2 036.4	60 534	240.1	16 904	67.0	574	2.3	…	…
13	2	506 042	1 979.2	58 424	228.5	17 298	67.7	629	2.5	…	…
14	3	542 473	2 091.7	60 108	231.8	18 036	69.5	686	2.6	…	…
15	4	537 610	2 045.2	61 173	232.7	18 405	70.0	697	2.7	…	…
16	5	583 674	2 189.7	65 019	243.9	19 258	72.2	761	2.9	…	…
17	6	590 359	2 188.5	67 195	249.1	19 221	71.3	827	3.1	…	…
18	7	739 770	2 711.2	76 508	280.4	20 097	73.7	915	3.4	…	…
19	8	632 981	2 307.5	71 319	260.0	19 503	71.1	735	2.7	…	…
1920	9	701 441	2 512.4	66 608	238.6	19 869	71.2	817	2.9	…	…
21	10	629 242	2 227.1	63 543	224.9	20 145	71.3	834	3.0	…	…
22	11	631 201	2 207.7	66 410	232.3	20 097	70.3	891	3.1	…	…
23	12	653 405	2 257.6	62 719	216.7	20 725	71.6	887	3.1	…	…
24	13	611 977	2 088.2	59 800	204.0	20 600	70.3	915	3.1	…	…
25	14	589 349	1 982.8	60 410	203.2	20 772	69.9	924	3.1	…	…
26	昭和元年	563 435	1 864.5	58 542	193.7	21 172	70.1	985	3.3	…	…
27	2	590 012	1 923.3	61 123	199.2	21 576	70.3	1 050	3.4	…	…
28	3	597 497	1 918.4	61 235	196.6	22 254	71.5	1 050	3.4	…	…
29	4	615 234	1 948.8	63 322	200.6	22 048	69.8	1 132	3.6	…	…
1930	5	566 871	1 768.2	60 487	188.7	22 580	70.4	1 104	3.4	…	…
31	6	598 745	1 839.0	60 678	186.4	22 244	68.3	1 044	3.2	…	…
32	7	568 077	1 717.3	58 445	176.7	22 816	69.0	1 131	3.4	…	…
33	8	575 491	1 713.4	62 100	184.9	23 555	70.1	1 197	3.6	…	…
34	9	595 507	1 750.7	64 701	190.2	24 444	71.9	1 368	4.0	…	…
35	10	558 367	1 617.5	64 913	188.0	24 752	71.7	1 239	3.6	…	…
36	11	592 421	1 692.1	71 665	204.7	24 760	70.7	1 250	3.6	…	…
37	12	582 274	1 640.1	71 580	201.6	25 238	71.1	1 352	3.8	…	…
38	13	606 869	1 691.0	73 466	204.7	25 329	70.6	1 502	4.2	…	…
39	14	610 171	1 687.7	75 035	207.5	25 719	71.1	1 368	3.8	…	…
1940	15	571 284	1 563.2	72 555	198.5	25 262	69.1	1 336	3.7	…	…
41	16	552 186	1 493.4	70 949	191.9	25 875	70.0	1 332	3.6	…	…
42	17	557 592	1 486.5	73 353	195.6	26 227	69.9	1 301	3.5	…	…
43	18	580 938	1 524.1	76 850	201.6	26 112	68.5	1 135	3.0	…	…
47	22	542 568	1 357.4	66 601	166.6	27 241	68.2	817	2.0	…	…
48	23	457 037	1 118.2	66 204	162.0	28 610	70.0	825	2.0	…	…
49	24	455 627	1 092.4	63 846	153.1	29 633	71.0	899	2.2	…	…
1950	25	437 803	1 032.8	56 680	133.7	31 758	74.9	1 029	2.4	5 296	12.5
51	26	406 458	943.5	43 083	100.0	32 482	75.4	1 055	2.4	4 774	11.1
52	27	369 863	846.3	32 125	73.5	33 643	77.0	1 054	2.4	4 727	10.8
53	28	372 688	841.6	25 948	58.6	34 192	77.2	1 113	2.5	4 910	11.1
54	29	341 833	761.1	23 885	53.2	35 606	79.3	1 088	2.4	4 719	10.5

194

General mortality

性別死亡数及び率（人口10万対）（つづき）
population) by sex and causes of death : Japan－CON.

女
Female

Hi 05 心疾患（高血圧性を除く）		Hi 06 脳血管疾患		Hi 07 肺炎		Hi 08 慢性気管支炎及び肺気腫		年次[2) Year	
死亡数 Deaths	死亡率 Death rates	死亡数 Deaths	死亡率 Death rates	死亡数 Deaths	死亡率 Death rates	死亡数 Deaths	死亡率 Death rates		
10 580	49.1	34 030	157.8	19 934	92.4	…	…	1899	明治32年
10 756	49.3	31 942	146.5	20 561	94.3	…	…	1900	33
11 272	51.1	34 780	157.7	23 021	104.4	…	…	01	34
12 104	54.1	34 491	154.3	25 068	112.1	…	…	02	35
12 089	53.4	33 982	150.1	22 640	100.0	…	…	03	36
13 384	58.3	35 744	155.8	24 574	107.1	…	…	04	37
13 428	57.9	35 038	151.0	28 554	123.1	…	…	05	38
13 788	58.8	33 470	142.8	25 706	109.7	…	…	06	39
15 189	64.3	35 970	152.2	29 426	124.5	…	…	07	40
15 099	63.1	33 592	140.4	31 250	130.6	…	…	08	41
16 833	69.5	31 075	128.3	33 510	138.3	…	…	09	42
16 876	68.8	29 310	119.5	33 245	135.5	…	…	1910	43
16 629	66.9	29 872	120.2	33 242	133.7	…	…	11	44
16 447	65.2	30 702	121.8	35 208	139.6	…	…	12	大正元年
16 410	64.2	30 127	117.8	38 092	149.0	…	…	13	2
16 918	65.2	31 369	121.0	39 326	151.6	…	…	14	3
17 595	66.9	30 564	116.3	40 887	155.5	…	…	15	4
19 155	71.9	33 454	125.5	47 060	176.6	…	…	16	5
19 457	72.1	35 190	130.4	46 509	172.4	…	…	17	6
23 656	86.7	38 892	142.5	100 026	366.6	…	…	18	7
18 030	65.7	37 967	138.4	74 093	270.1	…	…	19	8
18 765	67.2	39 005	139.7	87 123	312.1	…	…	1920	9
19 121	67.7	39 499	139.8	55 015	194.7	…	…	21	10
19 535	68.3	40 250	140.8	53 505	187.1	…	…	22	11
21 377	73.9	41 243	142.5	56 775	196.2	7 302	25.2	23	12
21 152	72.2	44 959	153.4	58 179	198.5	7 603	25.9	24	13
20 410	68.7	41 526	139.7	61 467	206.8	7 827	26.3	25	14
19 682	65.1	42 956	142.1	51 061	169.0	6 759	22.4	26	昭和元年
20 254	66.0	44 519	145.1	56 594	184.5	7 021	22.9	27	2
20 157	64.7	44 898	144.2	59 229	190.2	6 862	22.0	28	3
21 024	66.6	48 197	152.7	56 940	180.4	7 066	22.4	29	4
20 948	65.3	46 666	145.6	47 070	146.8	6 124	19.1	1930	5
21 201	65.1	47 592	146.2	59 916	184.0	6 698	20.6	31	6
20 041	60.6	48 079	145.3	52 610	159.0	5 894	17.8	32	7
20 449	60.9	49 605	147.7	49 340	146.9	5 324	15.9	33	8
21 452	63.1	51 114	150.3	57 072	167.8	5 730	16.8	34	9
19 966	57.8	51 571	149.4	48 401	140.2	5 296	15.3	35	10
21 442	61.2	52 829	150.9	52 174	149.0	5 522	15.8	36	11
21 342	60.1	53 664	151.2	50 190	141.4	5 062	14.3	37	12
23 463	65.4	56 870	158.5	53 718	149.7	5 659	15.8	38	13
23 659	65.4	58 914	163.0	59 297	164.0	5 383	14.9	39	14
23 035	63.0	57 772	158.1	49 684	136.0	4 773	13.1	1940	15
21 569	58.3	57 767	156.2	48 182	130.3	4 337	11.7	41	16
22 222	59.2	58 205	155.2	48 151	128.4	4 517	12.0	42	17
23 534	61.7	56 447	148.1	52 447	137.6	4 346	11.4	43	18
24 957	62.4	49 254	123.2	45 898	114.8	4 308	10.8	47	22
25 119	61.5	47 550	116.3	24 480	59.9	3 661	9.0	48	23
27 139	65.1	51 106	122.5	26 531	63.6	3 353	8.0	49	24
27 269	64.3	53 540	126.3	26 079	61.5	3 013	7.1	1950	25
27 634	64.1	53 470	124.1	23 907	55.5	2 511	5.8	51	26
26 778	61.3	55 348	126.6	20 252	46.3	2 126	4.9	52	27
28 138	63.5	57 930	130.8	22 253	50.3	2 066	4.7	53	28
26 399	58.8	56 985	126.9	17 979	40.0	1 556	3.5	54	29

Note : See page 74.

死　亡

表 5.12　死因年次推移分類[1]　別にみた
Table 5.12　Trends in deaths and death rates (per 100,000

女
Female

年　次[2] Year		死亡総数[3]		Hi　0 1 結　核		Hi　0 2 悪 性 新 生 物		Hi　0 3 糖 尿 病		Hi　0 4 高血圧性疾患	
		死亡数 Deaths	死亡率 Death rates	死亡数 Deaths	死亡率 Death rates	死亡数 Deaths	死亡率 Death rates	死亡数 Deaths	死亡率 Death rates	死亡数 Deaths	死亡率 Death rates
1955	昭和30年	328 277	722.8	20 134	44.3	36 498	80.4	1 171	2.6	4 688	10.3
56	31	343 065	747.4	18 361	40.0	38 251	83.3	1 383	3.0	5 436	11.8
57	32	354 943	766.3	17 543	37.9	38 378	82.9	1 419	3.1	5 782	12.5
58	33	320 542	685.2	14 530	31.1	40 658	86.9	1 442	3.1	6 422	13.7
59	34	322 370	682.1	12 950	27.4	42 071	89.0	1 501	3.2	6 811	14.4
1960	35	329 073	692.2	12 190	25.6	42 875	90.2	1 713	3.6	7 755	16.3
61	36	323 786	674.8	10 404	21.7	44 188	92.1	1 904	4.0	8 309	17.3
62	37	329 439	680.2	10 147	21.0	44 725	92.3	2 066	4.3	8 986	18.6
63	38	309 301	632.2	8 345	17.1	45 859	93.7	2 166	4.4	8 969	18.3
64	39	309 536	626.0	8 087	16.4	46 619	94.3	2 477	5.0	9 496	19.2
65	40	321 722	643.1	7 585	15.2	47 637	95.2	2 652	5.3	9 811	19.6
66	41	306 986	608.7	6 860	13.6	49 002	97.2	3 015	6.0	9 593	19.0
67	42	308 930	608.9	5 935	11.7	50 285	99.1	3 162	6.2	9 520	18.8
68	43	313 624	611.2	5 548	10.8	51 218	99.8	3 303	6.4	9 468	18.5
69	44	314 281	605.3	5 306	10.2	52 289	100.7	3 647	7.0	9 240	17.8
1970	45	325 082	619.0	4 985	9.5	52 903	100.7	3 889	7.4	9 880	18.8
71	46	311 579	586.6	4 138	7.8	54 451	102.5	3 943	7.4	9 520	17.9
72	47	310 918	576.9	3 863	7.2	56 001	103.9	4 054	7.5	9 544	17.7
73	48	325 824	591.6	3 517	6.4	57 563	104.5	4 270	7.8	10 539	19.1
74	49	328 641	589.7	3 420	6.1	58 295	104.6	4 539	8.1	11 401	20.5
75	50	324 448	574.0	3 161	5.6	59 461	105.2	4 655	8.2	11 148	19.7
76	51	324 640	568.7	2 743	4.8	60 898	106.7	4 836	8.5	11 209	19.6
77	52	317 899	551.5	2 494	4.3	62 684	108.8	4 959	8.6	11 078	19.2
78	53	320 196	550.6	2 312	4.0	64 706	111.3	5 053	8.7	10 717	18.4
79	54	316 481	539.8	1 842	3.1	66 525	113.5	4 205	7.2	9 282	15.8
1980	55	332 157	561.8	1 724	2.9	68 263	115.5	4 449	7.5	9 257	15.7
81	56	331 687	557.0	1 453	2.4	69 875	117.3	4 539	7.6	9 001	15.1
82	57	326 389	544.4	1 413	2.4	71 016	118.4	4 566	7.6	8 215	13.7
83	58	338 806	561.4	1 463	2.4	72 876	120.8	4 698	7.8	8 082	13.4
84	59	338 027	556.6	1 265	2.1	75 105	123.7	5 027	8.3	7 910	13.0
85	60	344 514	562.7	1 250	2.0	77 054	125.9	4 922	8.0	7 709	12.6
86	61	343 702	558.8	1 058	1.7	78 065	126.9	4 809	7.8	7 134	11.6
87	62	343 078	555.0	1 063	1.7	80 402	130.1	4 873	7.9	6 644	10.7
88	63	364 920	588.0	918	1.5	83 455	134.5	5 078	8.2	6 366	10.3
89	平成元年	361 480	580.3	851	1.4	85 414	137.1	4 812	7.7	5 785	9.3
1990	2	376 587	602.8	919	1.5	87 018	139.3	4 979	8.0	5 847	9.4
91	3	379 453	605.4	876	1.4	89 252	142.4	5 001	8.0	5 673	9.1
92	4	391 099	622.0	833	1.3	92 243	146.7	5 065	8.1	5 514	8.8
93	5	402 070	637.6	825	1.3	93 485	148.3	5 267	8.4	5 243	8.3
94	6	399 853	632.4	804	1.3	96 774	153.1	5 596	8.9	5 114	8.1
95	7	420 863	664.0	911	1.4	103 399	163.1	7 118	11.2	5 195	8.2
96	8	407 606	641.0	794	1.2	106 359	167.2	6 444	10.1	4 632	7.3
97	9	415 606	651.9	787	1.2	108 337	169.9	6 075	9.5	4 347	6.8
98	10	424 356	663.7	818	1.3	111 615	174.6	6 113	9.6	4 356	6.8
99	11	447 253	698.0	821	1.3	114 739	179.1	6 287	9.8	4 274	6.7
2000	12	435 750	679.5	780	1.2	116 344	181.4	5 814	9.1	3 900	6.1
01	13	441 563	686.6	776	1.2	119 265	185.4	5 779	9.0	3 755	5.8
02	14	447 074	694.0	733	1.1	120 535	187.1	6 004	9.3	3 513	5.5
03	15	463 205	717.9	722	1.1	122 631	190.1	6 170	9.6	3 581	5.6
04	16	471 505	730.1	775	1.2	127 262	197.1	5 943	9.2	3 640	5.6
05	17	498 826	772.3	717	1.1	129 338	200.3	6 490	10.0	3 690	5.7
06	18	503 080	778.9	752	1.2	131 262	203.2	6 382	9.9	3 715	5.8
07	19	515 550	798.4	736	1.1	133 725	207.1	6 604	10.2	3 821	5.9
08	20	533 696	827.1	753	1.2	136 609	211.7	6 844	10.6	3 910	6.1
09	21	532 823	826.3	802	1.2	137 753	213.6	6 588	10.2	3 957	6.1
2010	22	563 312	869.2	791	1.2	142 064	219.2	6 802	10.5	4 243	6.5
11	23	596 526	921.6	817	1.3	144 115	222.7	6 926	10.7	4 407	6.8
12	24	600 833	929.7	831	1.3	145 853	225.7	6 847	10.6	4 523	7.0
13	25	609 752	945.1	841	1.3	147 897	229.2	6 518	10.1	4 508	7.0
14	26	612 670	951.5	849	1.3	149 706	232.5	6 404	9.9	4 295	6.7
15	27	623 737	970.1	787	1.2	150 838	234.6	6 202	9.6	4 121	6.4
16	28	633 015	986.7	759	1.2	153 201	238.8	6 237	9.7	4 121	6.4

196

General mortality

性別死亡数及び率（人口10万対）（つづき）
population）by sex and causes of death : Japan−CON.

女
Female

Hi 05 心疾患（高血圧性を除く）		Hi 06 脳血管疾患		Hi 07 肺炎		Hi 08 慢性気管支炎及び肺気腫		年次[2] Year	
死亡数 Deaths	死亡率 Death rates	死亡数 Deaths	死亡率 Death rates	死亡数 Deaths	死亡率 Death rates	死亡数 Deaths	死亡率 Death rates		
27 069	59.6	58 767	129.4	16 344	36.0	1 371	3.0	1955	昭和30年
29 550	64.4	64 504	140.5	16 346	35.6	1 360	3.0	56	31
32 541	70.3	65 379	141.2	20 436	44.1	1 371	3.0	57	32
29 245	62.5	65 125	139.2	16 591	35.5	1 197	2.6	58	33
30 819	65.2	67 689	143.2	15 925	33.7	989	2.1	59	34
33 645	70.8	71 144	149.6	17 382	36.6	1 126	2.4	1960	35
33 693	70.2	73 149	152.5	15 048	31.4	989	2.1	61	36
35 263	72.8	75 351	155.6	16 292	33.6	1 249	2.6	62	37
33 067	67.6	76 875	157.1	12 099	24.7	1 028	2.1	63	38
33 342	67.4	77 861	157.5	11 991	24.3	1 087	2.2	64	39
36 845	73.6	80 050	160.0	13 906	27.8	1 205	2.4	65	40
34 581	68.6	80 120	158.9	10 468	20.8	956	1.9	66	41
36 524	72.0	80 440	158.5	10 944	21.6	1 006	2.0	67	42
39 100	76.2	81 132	158.1	11 879	23.1	1 345	2.6	68	43
40 052	77.1	82 272	158.5	11 761	22.7	1 239	2.4	69	44
43 423	82.7	84 405	160.7	12 899	24.6	1 363	2.6	1970	45
41 149	77.5	82 548	155.4	10 660	20.1	1 293	2.4	71	46
41 693	77.4	82 938	153.9	10 742	19.9	1 331	2.5	72	47
46 024	83.6	86 009	156.2	12 709	23.1	1 299	2.4	73	48
48 596	87.2	85 745	153.9	13 153	23.6	1 519	2.7	74	49
48 831	86.4	84 443	149.4	14 070	24.9	1 420	2.5	75	50
50 965	89.3	84 556	148.1	13 679	24.0	1 389	2.4	76	51
50 485	87.6	83 222	144.4	12 099	21.0	1 366	2.4	77	52
52 143	89.7	82 144	141.3	12 588	21.6	1 473	2.5	78	53
53 873	91.9	78 840	134.5	12 097	20.6	1 361	2.3	79	54
59 402	100.5	80 667	136.4	14 418	24.4	1 550	2.6	1980	55
61 731	103.7	78 841	132.4	14 737	24.7	1 581	2.7	81	56
61 327	102.3	74 345	124.0	15 350	25.6	1 643	2.7	82	57
64 832	107.4	74 249	123.0	17 442	28.9	1 723	2.9	83	58
66 580	109.6	71 831	118.3	16 568	27.3	1 811	3.0	84	59
69 331	113.2	69 707	113.9	19 555	31.9	1 980	3.2	85	60
70 509	114.6	67 457	109.7	20 517	33.4	1 908	3.1	86	61
71 343	115.4	64 882	105.0	21 083	34.1	1 873	3.0	87	62
79 280	127.7	67 863	109.3	24 570	39.6	1 987	3.2	88	63
78 930	126.7	63 714	102.3	25 493	40.9	1 954	3.1	89	平成元年
83 704	134.0	64 317	103.0	29 598	47.4	2 170	3.5	1990	2
85 232	136.0	62 708	100.0	30 214	48.2	2 227	3.6	91	3
89 162	141.8	62 627	99.6	31 946	50.8	2 220	3.5	92	4
91 988	145.9	63 515	100.7	35 341	56.0	2 299	3.6	93	5
80 711	127.6	64 729	102.4	36 415	57.6	2 435	3.9	94	6
69 488	109.6	76 965	121.4	37 210	58.7	2 959	4.7	95	7
69 252	108.9	73 887	116.2	32 499	51.1	2 728	4.3	96	8
70 398	110.4	72 907	114.4	36 590	57.4	2 700	4.2	97	9
71 986	112.6	72 290	113.1	37 289	58.3	2 684	4.2	98	10
77 100	120.3	72 537	113.2	44 091	68.8	2 746	4.3	99	11
74 585	116.3	69 402	108.2	40 216	62.7	2 640	4.1	2000	12
75 565	117.5	68 710	106.8	39 549	61.5	2 700	4.2	01	13
77 532	120.4	68 028	105.6	40 388	62.7	2 544	3.9	02	14
81 556	126.4	68 793	106.6	44 328	68.7	2 576	4.0	03	15
82 160	127.2	67 508	104.5	44 228	68.5	2 449	3.8	04	16
89 146	138.0	69 190	107.1	49 931	77.3	2 460	3.8	05	17
90 213	139.7	66 920	103.6	50 670	78.5	2 455	3.8	06	18
92 449	143.2	66 049	102.3	51 584	79.9	2 389	3.7	07	19
95 789	148.5	65 902	102.1	53 974	83.7	2 327	3.6	08	20
95 202	147.6	63 057	97.8	52 115	80.8	2 238	3.5	09	21
100 557	155.2	63 275	97.6	55 319	85.4	2 218	3.4	2010	22
103 628	160.1	64 251	99.3	58 148	89.8	2 125	3.3	11	23
105 860	163.8	62 977	97.4	57 539	89.0	2 071	3.2	12	24
105 278	163.2	61 629	95.5	56 607	87.7	1 863	2.9	13	25
104 647	162.5	59 212	92.0	54 870	85.2	1 667	2.6	14	26
103 971	161.7	58 397	90.8	55 344	86.1	1 631	2.5	15	27
104 587	**163.0**	**56 614**	**88.2**	**53 664**	**83.6**	**1 511**	**2.4**	**16**	**28**

197

死　亡

表5.12　死因年次推移分類[1]別にみた
Table 5.12　Trends in deaths and death rates (per 100,000

女
Female

年　　次[2] Year		Hi　09 喘　　　息		Hi　10 胃潰瘍及び十二指腸潰瘍		Hi　11 肝　疾　患		Hi　12 腎　不　全	
		死亡数 Deaths	死亡率 Death rates	死亡数 Deaths	死亡率 Death rates	死亡数 Deaths	死亡率 Death rates	死亡数 Deaths	死亡率 Death rates
1899	明治32年	…	…	…	…	…	…	…	…
1900	33	…	…	…	…	…	…	…	…
01	34	…	…	…	…	…	…	…	…
02	35	…	…	…	…	…	…	…	…
03	36	…	…	…	…	…	…	…	…
04	37	…	…	…	…	…	…	…	…
05	38	…	…	…	…	…	…	…	…
06	39	…	…	…	…	…	…	…	…
07	40	…	…	…	…	…	…	…	…
08	41	…	…	…	…	…	…	…	…
09	42	3 209	13.2	1 923	7.9	3 496	14.4	…	…
1910	43	3 226	13.1	1 972	8.0	3 331	13.6	…	…
11	44	2 814	11.3	1 935	7.8	3 831	15.4	…	…
12	大正元年	2 890	11.5	1 977	7.8	4 122	16.3	…	…
13	2	2 977	11.6	1 960	7.7	3 959	15.5	…	…
14	3	2 932	11.3	2 100	8.1	4 264	16.4	…	…
15	4	2 795	10.6	2 016	7.7	4 233	16.1	…	…
16	5	3 350	12.6	2 190	8.2	4 250	15.9	…	…
17	6	3 223	11.9	2 238	8.3	4 337	16.1	…	…
18	7	4 186	15.3	2 337	8.6	4 299	15.8	…	…
19	8	2 879	10.5	2 079	7.6	3 838	14.0	…	…
1920	9	3 374	12.1	2 177	7.8	4 409	15.8	…	…
21	10	3 129	11.1	2 527	8.9	4 484	15.9	…	…
22	11	3 480	12.2	2 364	8.3	4 430	15.5	…	…
23	12	2 812	9.7	2 655	9.2	4 210	14.5	…	…
24	13	2 873	9.8	2 702	9.2	4 148	14.2	…	…
25	14	3 156	10.6	2 731	9.2	3 910	13.2	…	…
26	昭和元年	2 597	8.6	2 628	8.7	3 872	12.8	…	…
27	2	2 845	9.3	2 748	9.0	4 065	13.3	…	…
28	3	2 802	9.0	2 951	9.5	4 017	12.9	…	…
29	4	2 980	9.4	3 002	9.5	4 229	13.4	…	…
1930	5	2 724	8.5	3 019	9.4	4 379	13.7	…	…
31	6	3 373	10.4	3 291	10.1	4 143	12.7	…	…
32	7	2 805	8.5	3 239	9.8	4 252	12.9	…	…
33	8	2 992	8.9	3 384	10.1	3 346	10.0	…	…
34	9	3 601	10.6	3 615	10.6	3 294	9.7	…	…
35	10	3 122	9.0	3 566	10.3	3 266	9.5	…	…
36	11	3 867	11.0	3 719	10.6	3 369	9.6	…	…
37	12	3 287	9.3	3 731	10.5	3 419	9.6	…	…
38	13	3 904	10.9	4 061	11.3	3 435	9.6	…	…
39	14	4 258	11.8	4 024	11.1	3 591	9.9	…	…
1940	15	3 706	10.1	3 794	10.4	3 648	10.0	…	…
41	16	3 713	10.0	3 748	10.1	3 558	9.6	…	…
42	17	3 921	10.5	4 127	11.0	3 671	9.8	…	…
43	18	4 404	11.6	4 601	12.1	3 717	9.8	…	…
47	22	5 728	14.3	6 958	17.4	3 708	9.3	…	…
48	23	4 769	11.7	5 819	14.2	3 953	9.7	…	…
49	24	4 835	11.6	5 503	13.2	4 211	10.1	…	…
1950	25	6 772	16.0	5 667	13.4	3 743	8.8	…	…
51	26	5 979	13.9	5 299	12.3	3 851	8.9	…	…
52	27	5 131	11.7	4 994	11.4	4 360	10.0	…	…
53	28	6 330	14.3	4 786	10.8	4 730	10.7	…	…
54	29	4 361	9.7	4 292	9.6	4 997	11.1	…	…

General mortality

性別死亡数及び率（人口10万対）（つづき）
population) by sex and causes of death : Japan－CON.

女
Female

Hi 13 老衰 死亡数 Deaths	Hi 13 老衰 死亡率 Death rates	Hi 14 不慮の事故 死亡数 Deaths	Hi 14 不慮の事故 死亡率 Death rates	（再掲） Hi 15 交通事故 死亡数 Deaths	（再掲） Hi 15 交通事故 死亡率 Death rates	Hi 16 自殺 死亡数 Deaths	Hi 16 自殺 死亡率 Death rates	年次 Year	
32 430	150.4	7 815	36.2	...	...	2 233	10.4	1899	明治32年
33 471	153.6	6 952	31.9	...	...	2 147	9.9	1900	33
29 314	132.9	6 257	28.4	...	...	2 974	13.5	01	34
31 059	138.9	6 922	31.0	...	...	3 073	13.7	02	35
33 090	146.1	7 130	31.5	...	...	3 267	14.4	03	36
37 513	163.5	7 340	32.0	...	...	3 381	14.7	04	37
38 784	167.2	7 042	30.4	...	...	3 069	13.2	05	38
35 276	150.5	7 114	30.4	...	...	2 992	12.8	06	39
37 170	157.3	7 890	33.4	...	...	3 163	13.4	07	40
35 199	147.1	7 509	31.4	...	...	3 224	13.5	08	41
36 973	152.6	7 685	31.7	...	...	3 405	14.1	09	42
34 983	142.6	7 991	32.6	...	...	3 444	14.0	1910	43
33 303	134.0	7 834	31.5	...	...	3 526	14.2	11	44
33 986	134.8	8 120	32.2	...	...	3 520	14.0	12	大正元年
32 975	129.0	7 812	30.6	...	...	3 893	15.2	13	2
36 199	139.6	8 520	32.9	...	...	4 008	15.5	14	3
34 730	132.1	8 467	32.2	...	...	3 650	13.9	15	4
40 116	150.5	8 173	30.7	...	...	3 534	13.3	16	5
42 306	156.8	9 204	34.1	...	...	3 530	13.1	17	6
48 817	178.9	8 946	32.8	...	...	3 954	14.5	18	7
41 155	150.0	8 059	29.4	...	...	3 766	13.7	19	8
42 800	153.3	8 593	30.8	...	...	4 109	14.7	1920	9
44 330	156.9	8 219	29.1	...	...	4 435	15.7	21	10
44 589	156.0	8 290	29.0	...	...	4 562	16.0	22	11
44 900	155.1	32 969	113.9	...	...	4 423	15.3	23	12
43 517	148.5	8 322	28.4	...	...	4 303	14.7	24	13
40 916	137.7	8 344	28.1	...	...	4 728	15.9	25	14
39 770	131.6	8 277	27.4	...	...	4 805	15.9	26	昭和元年
43 983	143.4	10 289	33.5	...	...	4 933	16.1	27	2
44 863	144.0	8 214	26.4	...	...	5 048	16.2	28	3
46 992	148.9	8 385	26.6	...	...	4 825	15.3	29	4
45 056	140.5	8 326	26.0	...	...	5 132	16.0	1930	5
50 413	154.8	8 179	25.1	...	...	5 251	16.1	31	6
45 922	138.8	8 590	26.0	...	...	5 474	16.5	32	7
49 135	146.3	9 602	28.6	...	...	5 695	17.0	33	8
52 123	153.2	10 197	30.0	...	...	5 489	16.1	34	9
47 054	136.3	8 381	24.3	...	...	5 438	15.8	35	10
54 598	155.9	8 685	24.8	...	...	5 657	16.2	36	11
50 336	141.8	8 565	24.1	...	...	5 372	15.1	37	12
58 456	162.9	9 041	25.2	...	...	4 638	12.9	38	13
56 754	157.0	7 935	21.9	...	...	4 283	11.8	39	14
53 965	147.7	7 979	21.8	...	...	4 036	11.0	1940	15
53 422	144.5	8 142	22.0	...	...	4 046	10.9	41	16
57 152	152.4	9 198	24.5	...	...	3 895	10.4	42	17
59 468	156.0	10 440	27.4	...	...	3 669	9.6	43	18
46 178	115.5	11 995	30.0	1 353	3.4	5 154	12.9	47	22
37 843	92.6	12 703	31.1	1 660	4.1	5 422	13.3	48	23
38 918	93.3	9 777	23.4	1 448	3.5	5 810	13.9	49	24
34 938	82.4	9 067	21.4	1 747	4.1	6 491	15.3	1950	25
36 178	84.0	8 769	20.4	1 787	4.1	6 380	14.8	51	26
36 046	82.5	8 313	19.0	1 783	4.1	6 605	15.1	52	27
40 789	92.1	9 374	21.2	2 001	4.5	7 281	16.4	53	28
36 976	82.3	8 668	19.3	2 497	5.6	7 994	17.8	54	29

死 亡

表5.12 死因年次推移分類[1]別にみた
Table 5.12 Trends in deaths and death rates (per 100,000

女
Female

年　　次[2] Year		Hi 0 9 喘　　息		Hi 1 0 胃潰瘍及び十二指腸潰瘍		Hi 1 1 肝　疾　患		Hi 1 2 腎　不　全	
		死亡数 Deaths	死亡率 Death rates	死亡数 Deaths	死亡率 Death rates	死亡数 Deaths	死亡率 Death rates	死亡数 Deaths	死亡率 Death rates
1955	昭和30年	4 572	10.1	3 965	8.7	5 078	11.2	…	…
56	31	4 846	10.6	3 872	8.4	5 248	11.4	…	…
57	32	5 695	12.3	3 982	8.6	5 224	11.3	…	…
58	33	4 070	8.7	3 671	7.8	5 096	10.9	…	…
59	34	3 927	8.3	3 596	7.6	5 284	11.2	…	…
1960	35	4 465	9.4	3 417	7.2	5 376	11.3	…	…
61	36	3 906	8.1	3 194	6.7	5 565	11.6	…	…
62	37	4 550	9.4	3 130	6.5	5 319	11.0	…	…
63	38	3 562	7.3	2 922	6.0	5 471	11.2	…	…
64	39	3 629	7.3	2 845	5.8	5 359	10.8	…	…
65	40	4 221	8.4	2 798	5.6	5 081	10.2	…	…
66	41	3 601	7.1	2 665	5.3	5 154	10.2	…	…
67	42	3 627	7.1	2 754	5.4	5 090	10.0	…	…
68	43	3 783	7.4	2 822	5.5	5 639	11.0	…	…
69	44	3 389	6.5	2 682	5.2	5 916	11.4	…	…
1970	45	3 585	6.8	2 578	4.9	6 050	11.5	…	…
71	46	3 137	5.9	2 524	4.8	5 679	10.7	…	…
72	47	2 953	5.5	2 477	4.6	5 439	10.1	…	…
73	48	2 832	5.1	2 510	4.6	5 665	10.3	…	…
74	49	2 924	5.2	2 540	4.6	5 625	10.1	…	…
75	50	2 821	5.0	2 393	4.2	5 640	10.0	…	…
76	51	2 777	4.9	2 342	4.1	5 361	9.4	…	…
77	52	2 421	4.2	2 147	3.7	5 465	9.5	…	…
78	53	2 320	4.0	2 169	3.7	5 618	9.7	…	…
79	54	2 338	4.0	2 120	3.6	5 443	9.3	2 918	5.0
1980	55	2 500	4.2	2 181	3.7	5 630	9.5	3 437	5.8
81	56	2 546	4.3	2 185	3.7	5 808	9.8	3 742	6.3
82	57	2 426	4.0	2 020	3.4	5 761	9.6	4 334	7.2
83	58	2 655	4.4	2 173	3.6	5 915	9.8	4 883	8.1
84	59	2 509	4.1	2 086	3.4	5 949	9.8	5 169	8.5
85	60	2 564	4.2	2 065	3.4	6 212	10.1	5 699	9.3
86	61	2 700	4.4	1 930	3.1	6 250	10.2	5 958	9.7
87	62	2 552	4.1	1 807	2.9	6 233	10.1	6 388	10.3
88	63	2 561	4.1	1 696	2.7	6 461	10.4	7 241	11.7
89	平成元年	2 506	4.0	1 670	2.7	6 581	10.6	7 529	12.1
1990	2	2 535	4.1	1 682	2.7	6 444	10.3	7 943	12.7
91	3	2 559	4.1	1 717	2.7	6 704	10.7	7 919	12.6
92	4	2 621	4.2	1 664	2.6	6 768	10.8	8 822	14.0
93	5	2 747	4.4	1 715	2.7	6 644	10.5	8 732	13.8
94	6	2 545	4.0	1 722	2.7	6 410	10.1	9 002	14.2
95	7	3 201	5.1	2 040	3.2	5 442	8.6	8 387	13.2
96	8	2 687	4.2	1 831	2.9	5 319	8.4	8 708	13.7
97	9	2 634	4.1	1 749	2.7	5 222	8.2	8 901	14.0
98	10	2 400	3.8	1 740	2.7	4 966	7.8	8 907	13.9
99	11	2 559	4.0	1 803	2.8	5 131	8.0	9 395	14.7
2000	12	2 173	3.4	1 708	2.7	5 011	7.8	9 231	14.4
01	13	1 928	3.0	1 765	2.7	4 937	7.7	9 488	14.8
02	14	1 899	2.9	1 651	2.6	4 958	7.7	9 757	15.1
03	15	1 855	2.9	1 615	2.5	5 034	7.8	10 135	15.7
04	16	1 707	2.6	1 489	2.3	5 180	8.0	10 311	16.0
05	17	1 633	2.5	1 593	2.5	5 423	8.4	11 065	17.1
06	18	1 488	2.3	1 479	2.3	5 358	8.3	11 444	17.7
07	19	1 405	2.2	1 425	2.2	5 487	8.5	11 704	18.1
08	20	1 263	2.0	1 496	2.3	5 653	8.8	12 088	18.7
09	21	1 205	1.9	1 387	2.2	5 506	8.5	12 027	18.7
2010	22	1 167	1.8	1 398	2.2	5 597	8.6	12 690	19.6
11	23	1 215	1.9	1 360	2.1	5 746	8.9	12 939	20.0
12	24	1 105	1.7	1 435	2.2	5 539	8.6	13 272	20.5
13	25	1 034	1.6	1 240	1.9	5 570	8.6	13 098	20.3
14	26	960	1.5	1 186	1.8	5 661	8.8	12 841	19.9
15	27	938	1.5	1 155	1.8	5 643	8.8	12 652	19.7
16	28	887	1.4	1 130	1.8	5 661	8.8	12 381	19.3

General mortality

性別死亡数及び率（人口10万対）（つづき）
population) by sex and causes of death : Japan−CON.

女
Female

Hi 1 3 老　　衰		Hi 1 4 不 慮 の 事 故		（再　　掲） Hi 1 5 交 通 事 故		Hi 1 6 自　　殺		年　　次 [2] Year	
死亡数 Deaths	死亡率 Death rates	死亡数 Deaths	死亡率 Death rates	死亡数 Deaths	死亡率 Death rates	死亡数 Deaths	死亡率 Death rates		
36 351	80. 0	8 357	18. 4	2 256	5. 0	8 641	19. 0	1955	昭和30年
41 345	90. 1	8 151	17. 8	2 211	4. 8	8 885	19. 4	56	31
44 856	96. 8	8 540	18. 4	2 554	5. 5	8 860	19. 1	57	32
31 567	67. 5	9 034	19. 3	2 706	5. 8	9 746	20. 8	58	33
32 696	69. 2	11 432	24. 2	3 122	6. 6	8 911	18. 9	59	34
33 592	70. 7	9 177	19. 3	3 587	7. 5	8 637	18. 2	1960	35
34 586	72. 1	9 525	19. 9	3 805	7. 9	8 113	16. 9	61	36
34 403	71. 0	8 873	18. 3	3 438	7. 1	7 183	14. 8	62	37
30 933	63. 2	8 998	18. 4	3 765	7. 7	6 567	13. 4	63	38
30 257	61. 2	9 151	18. 5	3 977	8. 0	6 371	12. 9	64	39
31 588	63. 1	9 514	19. 0	4 017	8. 0	6 114	12. 2	65	40
28 678	56. 9	10 017	19. 9	4 311	8. 5	6 600	13. 1	66	41
27 784	54. 8	10 027	19. 8	4 329	8. 5	6 181	12. 2	67	42
25 715	50. 1	9 769	19. 0	4 756	9. 3	6 427	12. 5	68	43
24 421	47. 0	10 391	20. 0	5 138	9. 9	6 603	12. 7	69	44
25 697	48. 9	10 690	20. 4	5 467	10. 4	6 967	13. 3	1970	45
23 087	43. 5	10 676	20. 1	5 529	10. 4	7 082	13. 3	71	46
21 153	39. 2	10 742	19. 9	5 247	9. 7	7 784	14. 4	72	47
21 639	39. 3	10 246	18. 6	4 938	9. 0	8 129	14. 8	73	48
21 474	38. 5	9 261	16. 6	3 983	7. 1	8 382	15. 0	74	49
19 629	34. 7	8 845	15. 6	3 725	6. 6	8 231	14. 6	75	50
19 358	33. 9	8 253	14. 5	3 398	6. 0	8 042	14. 1	76	51
18 550	32. 2	7 945	13. 8	3 184	5. 5	7 970	13. 8	77	52
18 069	31. 1	7 968	13. 7	3 208	5. 5	7 790	13. 4	78	53
19 148	32. 7	7 890	13. 5	3 230	5. 5	7 972	13. 6	79	54
20 910	35. 4	8 064	13. 6	3 191	5. 4	7 773	13. 1	1980	55
19 321	32. 4	7 942	13. 3	3 250	5. 5	7 388	12. 4	81	56
17 934	29. 9	8 151	13. 6	3 305	5. 5	7 465	12. 5	82	57
19 166	31. 8	8 407	13. 9	3 554	5. 9	8 109	13. 4	83	58
18 656	30. 7	8 121	13. 4	3 293	5. 4	8 093	13. 3	84	59
18 135	29. 6	8 279	13. 5	3 569	5. 8	8 027	13. 1	85	60
17 681	28. 7	8 130	13. 2	3 392	5. 5	9 168	14. 9	86	61
16 616	26. 9	8 131	13. 2	3 537	5. 7	8 550	13. 8	87	62
17 490	28. 2	8 854	14. 3	3 831	6. 2	8 505	13. 7	88	63
15 904	25. 5	9 201	14. 8	4 165	6. 7	8 186	13. 1	89	平成元年
16 133	25. 8	9 923	15. 9	4 347	7. 0	7 772	12. 4	1990	2
15 524	24. 8	10 276	16. 4	4 345	6. 9	7 398	11. 8	91	3
15 748	25. 0	11 071	17. 6	4 393	7. 0	7 377	11. 7	92	4
15 791	25. 0	11 320	18. 0	4 273	6. 8	6 976	11. 1	93	5
16 131	25. 5	12 033	19. 0	4 276	6. 8	6 865	10. 9	94	6
14 809	23. 4	17 094	27. 0	4 375	6. 9	7 189	11. 3	95	7
14 506	22. 8	13 699	21. 5	4 173	6. 6	7 285	11. 5	96	8
15 050	23. 6	13 729	21. 5	4 157	6. 5	7 593	11. 9	97	9
15 081	23. 6	13 941	21. 8	3 912	6. 1	9 406	14. 7	98	10
16 229	25. 3	14 528	22. 7	3 922	6. 1	9 011	14. 1	99	11
15 196	23. 7	14 322	22. 3	3 785	5. 9	8 595	13. 4	2000	12
16 051	25. 0	14 503	22. 6	3 680	5. 7	8 290	12. 9	01	13
16 473	25. 6	14 360	22. 3	3 572	5. 5	8 272	12. 8	02	14
17 161	26. 6	14 745	22. 9	3 348	5. 2	8 713	13. 5	03	15
17 954	27. 8	14 526	22. 5	3 196	4. 9	8 292	12. 8	04	16
19 677	30. 5	15 272	23. 6	3 013	4. 7	8 317	12. 9	05	17
20 892	32. 3	14 941	23. 1	2 790	4. 3	8 502	13. 2	06	18
23 241	36. 0	15 300	23. 7	2 709	4. 2	8 820	13. 7	07	19
27 224	42. 2	15 352	23. 8	2 308	3. 6	8 683	13. 5	08	20
29 369	45. 5	15 168	23. 5	2 299	3. 6	8 518	13. 2	09	21
34 555	53. 3	16 757	25. 9	2 351	3. 6	8 526	13. 2	2010	22
39 717	61. 4	26 933	41. 6	2 163	3. 3	8 992	13. 9	11	23
45 982	71. 1	17 317	26. 8	2 120	3. 3	7 948	12. 3	12	24
52 899	82. 0	16 531	25. 6	1 941	3. 0	7 905	12. 3	13	25
57 073	88. 6	16 467	25. 6	1 794	2. 8	7 542	11. 7	14	26
63 916	99. 4	16 185	25. 2	1 760	2. 7	6 950	10. 8	15	27
69 729	**108. 7**	**16 240**	**25. 3**	**1 613**	**2. 5**	**6 378**	**9. 9**	**16**	**28**

201

死　亡

表 5.13　年次別にみた死因簡単分類・
Table 5.13　Trends in deaths and death rates（per 100,000 population）

総　数
Total

死因簡単分類コード Code[a]	死　因 Causes of death	死　亡　数 Deaths						
		1995 平成7年	2000 12年	2005 17年	2010 22年	2014 26年	2015 27年	2016 28年
	死　亡　総　数 Deaths Total	922 139	961 653	1 083 796	1 197 012	1 273 004	1 290 444	1 307 748
01000	感染症及び寄生虫症	18 925	19 858	23 538	25 863	25 569	25 240	25 099
01100	腸管感染症	1 097	1 212	1 752	2 313	2 417	2 332	2 551
01200	結　核	3 178	2 656	2 296	2 129	2 100	1 956	1 892
01201	呼吸器結核	2 986	2 461	2 086	1 880	1 836	1 723	1 662
01202	その他の結核	192	195	210	249	264	233	230
01300	敗　血　症	4 905	6 216	8 504	10 676	11 279	11 357	11 510
01400	ウイルス肝炎	5 029	5 121	6 042	5 614	4 747	4 514	3 848
01401	B型ウイルス肝炎	880	885	786	539	482	407	407
01402	C型ウイルス肝炎	3 542	3 756	4 855	4 754	4 033	3 881	3 256
01403	その他のウイルス肝炎	607	480	401	321	232	226	185
01500	ヒト免疫不全ウイルス［HIV］病	56	50	69	61	45	56	66
01600	その他の感染症及び寄生虫症	4 660	4 603	4 875	5 070	4 981	5 025	5 232
02000	新　生　物	270 293	304 489	335 870	363 641	379 109	381 664	384 460
02100	悪性新生物	263 022	295 484	325 941	353 499	368 103	370 346	372 986
02101	口唇, 口腔及び咽頭の悪性新生物	4 099	5 066	5 679	6 802	7 415	7 380	7 675
02102	食道の悪性新生物	8 638	10 256	11 182	11 867	11 576	11 739	11 483
02103	胃の悪性新生物	50 076	50 650	50 311	50 136	47 903	46 679	45 531
02104	結腸の悪性新生物	20 286	23 637	27 121	30 040	33 297	34 338	34 521
02105	直腸S状結腸移行部及び直腸の悪性新生物	10 988	12 311	13 709	14 198	15 188	15 361	15 578
02106	肝及び肝内胆管の悪性新生物	31 707	33 981	34 268	32 765	29 543	28 889	28 528
02107	胆のう及びその他の胆道の悪性新生物	13 746	15 153	16 586	17 585	18 117	18 152	17 965
02108	膵の悪性新生物	16 019	19 094	22 927	28 017	31 716	31 866	33 475
02109	喉頭の悪性新生物	959	1 046	1 090	1 002	978	971	944
02110	気管, 気管支及び肺の悪性新生物	45 745	53 724	62 063	69 813	73 396	74 378	73 838
02111	皮膚の悪性新生物	869	986	1 207	1 404	1 657	1 505	1 553
02112	乳房の悪性新生物	7 819	9 248	10 808	12 545	13 323	13 705	14 132
02113	子宮の悪性新生物[1]	4 865	5 202	5 381	5 930	6 429	6 429	6 345
02114	卵巣の悪性新生物[1]	3 892	3 993	4 467	4 654	4 840	4 676	4 758
02115	前立腺の悪性新生物[2]	5 399	7 514	9 265	10 722	11 507	11 326	11 803
02116	膀胱の悪性新生物	3 931	4 680	6 029	6 804	7 760	8 130	8 432
02117	中枢神経系の悪性新生物	1 574	1 574	1 681	1 959	2 326	2 445	2 650

注：1)　率については、女性人口10万対である。
　　2)　率については、男性人口10万対である。

General mortality

性別死亡数及び率（人口10万対）
by sex and causes（the condensed list of causes of death for Japan）：Japan

総　数
Total

死　亡　率 Death rates							死因簡単分類コード Code[a]	死　因 Causes of death
1995 平成7年	2000 12年	2005 17年	2010 22年	2014 26年	2015 27年	2016 28年		
741.9	765.6	858.8	947.1	1 014.9	1 029.7	1 046.0		死亡総数 Deaths Total
15.2	15.8	18.7	20.5	20.4	20.1	20.1	01000	感染症及び寄生虫症
0.9	1.0	1.4	1.8	1.9	1.9	2.0	01100	腸管感染症
2.6	2.1	1.8	1.7	1.7	1.6	1.5	01200	結　核
2.4	2.0	1.7	1.5	1.5	1.4	1.3	01201	呼吸器結核
0.2	0.2	0.2	0.2	0.2	0.2	0.2	01202	その他の結核
3.9	4.9	6.7	8.4	9.0	9.1	9.2	01300	敗　血　症
4.0	4.1	4.8	4.4	3.8	3.6	3.1	01400	ウイルス肝炎
0.7	0.7	0.6	0.4	0.4	0.3	0.3	01401	B型ウイルス肝炎
2.8	3.0	3.8	3.8	3.2	3.1	2.6	01402	C型ウイルス肝炎
0.5	0.4	0.3	0.3	0.2	0.2	0.1	01403	その他のウイルス肝炎
0.0	0.0	0.1	0.0	0.0	0.0	0.1	01500	ヒト免疫不全ウイルス［HIV］病
3.7	3.7	3.9	4.0	4.0	4.0	4.2	01600	その他の感染症及び寄生虫症
217.5	242.4	266.1	287.7	302.2	304.6	307.5	02000	新　生　物
211.6	235.2	258.3	279.7	293.5	295.5	298.3	02100	悪性新生物
3.3	4.0	4.5	5.4	5.9	5.9	6.1	02101	口唇，口腔及び咽頭の悪性新生物
6.9	8.2	8.9	9.4	9.2	9.4	9.2	02102	食道の悪性新生物
40.3	40.3	39.9	39.7	38.2	37.2	36.4	02103	胃の悪性新生物
16.3	18.8	21.5	23.8	26.5	27.4	27.6	02104	結腸の悪性新生物
8.8	9.8	10.9	11.2	12.1	12.3	12.5	02105	直腸S状結腸移行部及び直腸の悪性新生物
25.5	27.1	27.2	25.9	23.6	23.1	22.8	02106	肝及び肝内胆管の悪性新生物
11.1	12.1	13.1	13.9	14.4	14.5	14.4	02107	胆のう及びその他の胆道の悪性新生物
12.9	15.2	18.2	22.2	25.3	25.4	26.8	02108	膵の悪性新生物
0.8	0.8	0.9	0.8	0.8	0.8	0.8	02109	喉頭の悪性新生物
36.8	42.8	49.2	55.2	58.5	59.4	59.1	02110	気管，気管支及び肺の悪性新生物
0.7	0.8	1.0	1.1	1.3	1.2	1.2	02111	皮膚の悪性新生物
6.3	7.4	8.6	9.9	10.6	10.9	11.3	02112	乳房の悪性新生物
7.7	8.1	8.3	9.1	10.0	10.0	9.9	02113	子宮の悪性新生物[1]
6.1	6.2	6.9	7.2	7.5	7.3	7.4	02114	卵巣の悪性新生物[1]
8.9	12.2	15.0	17.4	18.9	18.6	19.4	02115	前立腺の悪性新生物[2]
3.2	3.7	4.8	5.4	6.2	6.5	6.7	02116	膀胱の悪性新生物
1.3	1.3	1.3	1.6	1.9	2.0	2.1	02117	中枢神経系の悪性新生物

Note : a) Code see page 595.

死　亡

表5.13　年次別にみた死因簡単分類・
Table 5.13　Trends in deaths and death rates（per 100,000 population）

総　数
Total

死因簡単分類コード Code[a]	死因 Causes of death	死亡数 Deaths						
		1995 平成7年	2000 12年	2005 17年	2010 22年	2014 26年	2015 27年	2016 28年
02118	悪性リンパ腫	6 342	7 918	8 537	10 172	11 480	11 829	12 325
02119	白血病	6 129	6 766	7 283	8 078	8 196	8 631	8 801
02120	その他のリンパ組織，造血組織及び関連組織の悪性新生物	3 008	3 425	3 932	4 287	4 237	4 174	4 443
02121	その他の悪性新生物	16 931	19 260	22 415	24 719	27 219	27 743	28 206
02200	その他の新生物	7 271	9 005	9 929	10 142	11 006	11 318	11 474
02201	中枢神経系のその他の新生物	2 295	2 653	2 864	2 589	2 581	2 491	2 471
02202	中枢神経系を除くその他の新生物	4 976	6 352	7 065	7 553	8 425	8 827	9 003
03000	血液及び造血器の疾患並びに免疫機構の障害	4 106	4 057	4 173	4 336	4 313	4 342	4 541
03100	貧血	1 652	1 707	1 668	1 812	1 926	1 994	2 117
03200	その他の血液及び造血器の疾患並びに免疫機構の障害	2 454	2 350	2 505	2 524	2 387	2 348	2 424
04000	内分泌，栄養及び代謝疾患	19 360	17 110	19 726	21 684	21 065	20 943	21 331
04100	糖尿病	14 225	12 303	13 621	14 422	13 669	13 327	13 480
04200	その他の内分泌，栄養及び代謝疾患	5 135	4 807	6 105	7 262	7 396	7 616	7 851
05000	精神及び行動の障害	3 762	3 920	4 602	8 049	12 684	13 190	14 181
05100	血管性及び詳細不明の認知症	2 697	2 891	3 334	6 451	10 587	11 118	11 894
05200	その他の精神及び行動の障害	1 065	1 029	1 268	1 598	2 097	2 072	2 287
06000	神経系の疾患	8 625	9 567	13 004	19 429	28 384	30 911	33 357
06100	髄膜炎	405	327	378	339	304	293	288
06200	脊髄性筋萎縮症及び関連症候群	1 249	1 371	1 730	2 007	2 314	2 266	2 664
06300	パーキンソン病	2 427	2 805	3 634	5 136	6 578	7 159	7 543
06400	アルツハイマー病	511	835	1 814	4 166	9 453	10 544	11 969
06500	その他の神経系の疾患	4 033	4 229	5 448	7 781	9 735	10 649	10 893
07000	眼及び付属器の疾患	1	12	3	5	3	4	7
08000	耳及び乳様突起の疾患	20	19	14	19	12	14	15
09000	循環器系の疾患	304 824	298 338	329 475	341 882	341 795	339 134	339 847
09100	高血圧性疾患	8 222	6 063	5 835	6 760	6 932	6 726	6 841
09101	高血圧性心疾患及び心腎疾患	5 068	3 748	3 470	3 601	3 394	3 213	3 097
09102	その他の高血圧性疾患	3 154	2 315	2 365	3 159	3 538	3 513	3 744
09200	心疾患（高血圧性を除く）	139 206	146 741	173 125	189 360	196 925	196 113	198 006
09201	慢性リウマチ性心疾患	2 755	2 522	2 520	2 416	2 308	2 313	2 266
09202	急性心筋梗塞	52 533	45 885	47 193	42 629	38 991	37 222	35 926
09203	その他の虚血性心疾患	23 040	24 298	29 310	34 588	34 894	34 451	34 534

General mortality

性別死亡数及び率（人口10万対）（つづき）
by sex and causes（the condensed list of causes of death for Japan）：Japan－CON.

総　数
Total

死　亡　率 Death rates							死因 簡単 分類 コード Code[a]	死　因 Causes of death
1995 平成7年	2000 12年	2005 17年	2010 22年	2014 26年	2015 27年	2016 28年		
5.1	6.3	6.8	8.0	9.2	9.4	9.9	02118	悪性リンパ腫
4.9	5.4	5.8	6.4	6.5	6.9	7.0	02119	白　血　病
2.4	2.7	3.1	3.4	3.4	3.3	3.6	02120	その他のリンパ組織，造血組織及び 関連組織の悪性新生物
13.6	15.3	17.8	19.6	21.7	22.1	22.6	02121	その他の悪性新生物
5.8	7.2	7.9	8.0	8.8	9.0	9.2	02200	その他の新生物
1.8	2.1	2.3	2.0	2.1	2.0	2.0	02201	中枢神経系のその他の新生物
4.0	5.1	5.6	6.0	6.7	7.0	7.2	02202	中枢神経系を除くその他の新生物
3.3	3.2	3.3	3.4	3.4	3.5	3.6	03000	血液及び造血器の疾患並びに免疫機構の障害
1.3	1.4	1.3	1.4	1.5	1.6	1.7	03100	貧　　血
2.0	1.9	2.0	2.0	1.9	1.9	1.9	03200	その他の血液及び造血器の疾患並びに 免疫機構の障害
15.6	13.6	15.6	17.2	16.8	16.7	17.1	04000	内分泌，栄養及び代謝疾患
11.4	9.8	10.8	11.4	10.9	10.6	10.8	04100	糖　尿　病
4.1	3.8	4.8	5.7	5.9	6.1	6.3	04200	その他の内分泌，栄養及び代謝疾患
3.0	3.1	3.6	6.4	10.1	10.5	11.3	05000	精神及び行動の障害
2.2	2.3	2.6	5.1	8.4	8.9	9.5	05100	血管性及び詳細不明の認知症
0.9	0.8	1.0	1.3	1.7	1.7	1.8	05200	その他の精神及び行動の障害
6.9	7.6	10.3	15.4	22.6	24.7	26.7	06000	神経系の疾患
0.3	0.3	0.3	0.3	0.2	0.2	0.2	06100	髄　膜　炎
1.0	1.1	1.4	1.6	1.8	1.8	2.1	06200	脊髄性筋萎縮症及び関連症候群
2.0	2.2	2.9	4.1	5.2	5.7	6.0	06300	パーキンソン病
0.4	0.7	1.4	3.3	7.5	8.4	9.6	06400	アルツハイマー病
3.2	3.4	4.3	6.2	7.8	8.5	8.7	06500	その他の神経系の疾患
0.0	0.0	0.0	0.0	0.0	0.0	0.0	07000	眼及び付属器の疾患
0.0	0.0	0.0	0.0	0.0	0.0	0.0	08000	耳及び乳様突起の疾患
245.2	237.5	261.1	270.5	272.5	270.6	271.8	09000	循環器系の疾患
6.6	4.8	4.6	5.3	5.5	5.4	5.5	09100	高血圧性疾患
4.1	3.0	2.7	2.8	2.7	2.6	2.5	09101	高血圧性心疾患及び心腎疾患
2.5	1.8	1.9	2.5	2.8	2.8	3.0	09102	その他の高血圧性疾患
112.0	116.8	137.2	149.8	157.0	156.5	158.4	09200	心疾患（高血圧性を除く）
2.2	2.0	2.0	1.9	1.8	1.8	1.8	09201	慢性リウマチ性心疾患
42.3	36.5	37.4	33.7	31.1	29.7	28.7	09202	急性心筋梗塞
18.5	19.3	23.2	27.4	27.8	27.5	27.6	09203	その他の虚血性心疾患

死　亡

表 5.13　年次別にみた死因簡単分類・
Table 5.13　Trends in deaths and death rates（per 100,000 population）

総　数
Total

死因簡単分類コード Code[a]	死　因 Causes of death	死　亡　数 Deaths						
		1995 平成7年	2000 12年	2005 17年	2010 22年	2014 26年	2015 27年	2016 28年
09204	慢性非リウマチ性心内膜疾患	5 357	5 995	7 532	9 125	10 217	10 656	11 044
09205	心　筋　症	3 455	3 303	3 625	3 749	3 841	3 831	3 800
09206	不整脈及び伝導障害	12 841	15 097	22 517	25 119	29 739	30 300	31 045
09207	心　不　全	36 179	46 460	56 327	66 858	71 656	71 860	73 545
09208	その他の心疾患	3 046	3 181	4 101	4 876	5 279	5 480	5 846
09300	脳血管疾患	146 552	132 529	132 847	123 461	114 207	111 973	109 320
09301	くも膜下出血	14 424	14 815	14 883	13 591	12 662	12 476	12 318
09302	脳　内　出　血	33 187	31 051	33 362	33 695	32 550	32 113	31 975
09303	脳　梗　塞	89 431	82 651	80 964	72 885	66 058	64 523	62 277
09304	その他の脳血管疾患	9 510	4 012	3 638	3 290	2 937	2 861	2 750
09400	大動脈瘤及び解離	6 214	8 214	11 392	15 209	16 423	16 887	18 145
09500	その他の循環器系の疾患	4 630	4 791	6 276	7 092	7 308	7 435	7 535
10000	呼吸器系の疾患	126 661	134 501	165 999	187 609	202 628	208 400	208 603
10100	インフルエンザ	1 244	575	1 818	161	1 130	2 262	1 463
10200	肺　　炎	79 629	86 938	107 241	118 888	119 650	120 953	119 300
10300	急性気管支炎	1 874	1 393	962	581	505	445	451
10400	慢性閉塞性肺疾患	13 092	12 841	14 416	16 293	16 184	15 756	15 686
10500	喘　　息	7 253	4 473	3 198	2 065	1 550	1 511	1 454
10600	その他の呼吸器系の疾患	23 569	28 281	38 364	49 621	63 609	67 473	70 249
11000	消化器系の疾患	38 726	38 268	41 802	45 503	47 944	48 275	48 737
11100	胃潰瘍及び十二指腸潰瘍	4 314	3 869	3 490	3 233	2 795	2 666	2 657
11200	ヘルニア及び腸閉塞	4 132	4 467	5 260	5 985	6 841	6 919	6 971
11300	肝　疾　患	17 018	16 079	16 430	16 216	15 692	15 659	15 773
11301	肝硬変（アルコール性を除く）	11 301	9 840	9 387	8 597	7 800	7 649	7 702
11302	その他の肝疾患	5 717	6 239	7 043	7 619	7 892	8 010	8 071
11400	その他の消化器系の疾患	13 262	13 853	16 622	20 069	22 616	23 031	23 336
12000	皮膚及び皮下組織の疾患	866	854	969	1 319	1 633	1 648	1 652
13000	筋骨格系及び結合組織の疾患	4 070	4 419	4 603	5 606	5 992	6 100	6 445
14000	腎尿路生殖器系の疾患	21 381	21 977	26 952	32 874	36 757	37 065	38 597
14100	糸球体疾患及び腎尿細管間質性疾患	3 188	2 604	3 028	3 880	4 354	4 489	5 031
14200	腎　不　全	16 187	17 260	20 528	23 725	24 776	24 560	24 612
14201	急性腎不全	4 278	3 963	4 012	4 144	3 687	3 571	3 399

206

General mortality

性別死亡数及び率（人口10万対）（つづき）
by sex and causes（the condensed list of causes of death for Japan）：Japan－CON.

総　数
Total

死　亡　率 Death rates							死因 簡単 分類 コード Code[a]	死　因 Causes of death
1995 平成7年	2000 12年	2005 17年	2010 22年	2014 26年	2015 27年	2016 28年		
4.3	4.8	6.0	7.2	8.1	8.5	8.8	09204	慢性非リウマチ性心内膜疾患
2.8	2.6	2.9	3.0	3.1	3.1	3.0	09205	心　筋　症
10.3	12.0	17.8	19.9	23.7	24.2	24.8	09206	不整脈及び伝導障害
29.1	37.0	44.6	52.9	57.1	57.3	58.8	09207	心　不　全
2.5	2.5	3.2	3.9	4.2	4.4	4.7	09208	その他の心疾患
117.9	105.5	105.3	97.7	91.1	89.4	87.4	09300	脳血管疾患
11.6	11.8	11.8	10.8	10.1	10.0	9.9	09301	くも膜下出血
26.7	24.7	26.4	26.7	26.0	25.6	25.6	09302	脳　内　出　血
71.9	65.8	64.2	57.7	52.7	51.5	49.8	09303	脳　梗　塞
7.7	3.2	2.9	2.6	2.3	2.3	2.2	09304	その他の脳血管疾患
5.0	6.5	9.0	12.0	13.1	13.5	14.5	09400	大動脈瘤及び解離
3.7	3.8	5.0	5.6	5.8	5.9	6.0	09500	その他の循環器系の疾患
101.9	107.1	131.5	148.4	161.5	166.3	166.9	10000	呼吸器系の疾患
1.0	0.5	1.4	0.1	0.9	1.8	1.2	10100	インフルエンザ
64.1	69.2	85.0	94.1	95.4	96.5	95.4	10200	肺　　炎
1.5	1.1	0.8	0.5	0.4	0.4	0.4	10300	急性気管支炎
10.5	10.2	11.4	12.9	12.9	12.6	12.5	10400	慢性閉塞性肺疾患
5.8	3.6	2.5	1.6	1.2	1.2	1.2	10500	喘　　息
19.0	22.5	30.4	39.3	50.7	53.8	56.2	10600	その他の呼吸器系の疾患
31.2	30.5	33.1	36.0	38.2	38.5	39.0	11000	消化器系の疾患
3.5	3.1	2.8	2.6	2.2	2.1	2.1	11100	胃潰瘍及び十二指腸潰瘍
3.3	3.6	4.2	4.7	5.5	5.5	5.6	11200	ヘルニア及び腸閉塞
13.7	12.8	13.0	12.8	12.5	12.5	12.6	11300	肝　疾　患
9.1	7.8	7.4	6.8	6.2	6.1	6.2	11301	肝硬変（アルコール性を除く）
4.6	5.0	5.6	6.0	6.3	6.4	6.5	11302	その他の肝疾患
10.7	11.0	13.2	15.9	18.0	18.4	18.7	11400	その他の消化器系の疾患
0.7	0.7	0.8	1.0	1.3	1.3	1.3	12000	皮膚及び皮下組織の疾患
3.3	3.5	3.6	4.4	4.8	4.9	5.2	13000	筋骨格系及び結合組織の疾患
17.2	17.5	21.4	26.0	29.3	29.6	30.9	14000	腎尿路生殖器系の疾患
2.6	2.1	2.4	3.1	3.5	3.6	4.0	14100	糸球体疾患及び腎尿細管間質性疾患
13.0	13.7	16.3	18.8	19.8	19.6	19.7	14200	腎　不　全
3.4	3.2	3.2	3.3	2.9	2.8	2.7	14201	急性腎不全

207

死　亡

表5.13　年次別にみた死因簡単分類・
Table 5.13　Trends in deaths and death rates（per 100,000 population）

総　数
Total

死因簡単分類コード Code[a]	死　因 Causes of death	死　亡　数 Deaths						
		1995 平成7年	2000 12年	2005 17年	2010 22年	2014 26年	2015 27年	2016 28年
14202	慢性腎不全	7 099	8 688	11 539	14 366	15 717	15 739	15 988
14203	詳細不明の腎不全	4 810	4 609	4 977	5 215	5 372	5 250	5 225
14300	その他の腎尿路生殖器系の疾患	2 006	2 113	3 396	5 269	7 627	8 016	8 954
15000	妊娠，分娩及び産じょく[1]	90	84	66	49	33	44	36
16000	周産期に発生した病態	1 547	1 125	842	639	532	497	526
16100	妊娠期間及び胎児発育に関連する障害	78	74	67	65	59	39	43
16200	出産外傷	30	8	7	2	13	6	3
16300	周産期に特異的な呼吸障害及び心血管障害	786	615	425	349	266	251	288
16400	周産期に特異的な感染症	137	85	64	57	44	35	43
16500	胎児及び新生児の出血性障害及び血液障害	245	208	161	86	64	84	68
16600	その他の周産期に発生した病態	271	135	118	80	86	82	81
17000	先天奇形，変形及び染色体異常	3 285	2 702	2 324	2 194	2 042	2 022	2 020
17100	神経系の先天奇形	171	147	119	105	102	89	85
17200	循環器系の先天奇形	1 843	1 439	1 215	1 128	945	952	911
17201	心臓の先天奇形	1 385	1 121	931	859	659	670	590
17202	その他の循環器系の先天奇形	458	318	284	269	286	282	321
17300	消化器系の先天奇形	135	100	97	97	111	113	101
17400	その他の先天奇形及び変形	819	737	663	563	584	568	585
17500	染色体異常，他に分類されないもの	317	279	230	301	300	300	338
18000	症状，徴候及び異常臨床所見・異常検査所見で他に分類されないもの	25 720	26 548	34 454	60 346	92 960	103 046	112 446
18100	老　衰	21 493	21 213	26 360	45 342	75 389	84 810	92 806
18200	乳幼児突然死症候群	579	363	196	147	145	96	109
18300	その他の症状，徴候及び異常臨床所見・異常検査所見で他に分類されないもの	3 648	4 972	7 898	14 857	17 426	18 140	19 531
20000	傷病及び死亡の外因	69 877	73 805	75 380	75 965	69 549	67 905	65 848
20100	不慮の事故	45 323	39 484	39 863	40 732	39 029	38 306	38 306
20101	交通事故	15 147	12 857	10 028	7 222	5 717	5 646	5 278
20102	転倒・転落	5 911	6 245	6 702	7 517	7 946	7 992	8 030
20103	不慮の溺死及び溺水	5 588	5 978	6 222	6 948	7 508	7 484	7 705
20104	不慮の窒息	7 104	7 794	9 319	9 879	9 806	9 356	9 485
20105	煙，火及び火炎への曝露	1 383	1 416	1 593	1 338	1 086	940	891
20106	有害物質による不慮の中毒及び有害物質への曝露	568	605	891	862	677	612	565
20107	その他の不慮の事故	9 622	4 589	5 108	6 966	6 289	6 276	6 352
20200	自　殺	21 420	30 251	30 553	29 554	24 417	23 152	21 017
20300	他　殺	727	768	600	437	357	314	290
20400	その他の外因	2 407	3 302	4 364	5 242	5 746	6 133	6 235
22000	特殊目的用コード	…	…	…	-	-	-	-
22100	重症急性呼吸器症候群〔SARS〕	…	…	…	-	-	-	-

注：1）　率については、女性人口10万対である。

208

General mortality

性別死亡数及び率（人口10万対）（つづき）
by sex and causes（the condensed list of causes of death for Japan）：Japan－CON.

総 数
Total

死　亡　率 Death rates							死因簡単分類コード Code[a]	死　因 Causes of death
1995 平成7年	2000 12年	2005 17年	2010 22年	2014 26年	2015 27年	2016 28年		
5.7	6.9	9.1	11.4	12.5	12.6	12.8	14202	慢性腎不全
3.9	3.7	3.9	4.1	4.3	4.2	4.2	14203	詳細不明の腎不全
1.6	1.7	2.7	4.2	6.1	6.4	7.2	14300	その他の腎尿路生殖器系の疾患
0.1	0.1	0.1	0.1	0.1	0.1	0.1	15000	妊娠，分娩及び産じょく[1]
1.2	0.9	0.7	0.5	0.4	0.4	0.4	16000	周産期に発生した病態
0.1	0.1	0.1	0.1	0.0	0.0	0.0	16100	妊娠期間及び胎児発育に関連する障害
0.0	0.0	0.0	0.0	0.0	0.0	0.0	16200	出産外傷
0.6	0.5	0.3	0.3	0.2	0.2	0.2	16300	周産期に特異的な呼吸障害及び心血管障害
0.1	0.1	0.1	0.0	0.0	0.0	0.0	16400	周産期に特異的な感染症
0.2	0.2	0.1	0.1	0.1	0.1	0.1	16500	胎児及び新生児の出血性障害及び血液障害
0.2	0.1	0.1	0.1	0.1	0.1	0.1	16600	その他の周産期に発生した病態
2.6	2.2	1.8	1.7	1.6	1.6	1.6	17000	先天奇形，変形及び染色体異常
0.1	0.1	0.1	0.1	0.1	0.1	0.1	17100	神経系の先天奇形
1.5	1.1	1.0	0.9	0.8	0.8	0.7	17200	循環器系の先天奇形
1.1	0.9	0.7	0.7	0.5	0.5	0.5	17201	心臓の先天奇形
0.4	0.3	0.2	0.2	0.2	0.2	0.3	17202	その他の循環器系の先天奇形
0.1	0.1	0.1	0.1	0.1	0.1	0.1	17300	消化器系の先天奇形
0.7	0.6	0.5	0.4	0.5	0.5	0.5	17400	その他の先天奇形及び変形
0.3	0.2	0.2	0.2	0.2	0.2	0.3	17500	染色体異常，他に分類されないもの
20.7	21.1	27.3	47.7	74.1	82.2	89.9	18000	症状，徴候及び異常臨床所見・異常検査所見で他に分類されないもの
17.3	16.9	20.9	35.9	60.1	67.7	74.2	18100	老　衰
0.5	0.3	0.2	0.1	0.1	0.1	0.1	18200	乳幼児突然死症候群
2.9	4.0	6.3	11.8	13.9	14.5	15.6	18300	その他の症状，徴候及び異常臨床所見・異常検査所見で他に分類されないもの
56.2	58.8	59.7	60.1	55.4	54.2	52.7	20000	傷病及び死亡の外因
36.5	31.4	31.6	32.2	31.1	30.6	30.6	20100	不慮の事故
12.2	10.2	7.9	5.7	4.6	4.5	4.2	20101	交通事故
4.8	5.0	5.3	5.9	6.3	6.4	6.4	20102	転倒・転落
4.5	4.8	4.9	5.5	6.0	6.0	6.2	20103	不慮の溺死及び溺水
5.7	6.2	7.4	7.8	7.8	7.5	7.6	20104	不慮の窒息
1.1	1.1	1.3	1.1	0.9	0.8	0.7	20105	煙，火及び火炎への曝露
0.5	0.5	0.7	0.7	0.5	0.5	0.5	20106	有害物質による不慮の中毒及び有害物質への曝露
7.7	3.7	4.0	5.5	5.0	5.0	5.1	20107	その他の不慮の事故
17.2	24.1	24.2	23.4	19.5	18.5	16.8	20200	自　殺
0.6	0.6	0.5	0.3	0.3	0.3	0.2	20300	他　殺
1.9	2.6	3.5	4.1	4.6	4.9	5.0	20400	その他の外因
…	…	…	-	-	-	-	22000	特殊目的用コード
…	…	…	-	-	-	-	22100	重症急性呼吸器症候群〔SARS〕

死　亡

表 5.13　年次別にみた死因簡単分類・
Table 5.13　Trends in deaths and death rates（per 100,000 population）

男
Male

死因簡単分類コード Code[a]	死因 Causes of death	死　亡　数 Deaths						
		1995 平成7年	2000 12年	2005 17年	2010 22年	2014 26年	2015 27年	2016 28年
	死　亡　総　数 Deaths Total	501 276	525 903	584 970	633 700	660 334	666 707	674 733
01000	感染症及び寄生虫症	10 671	10 907	12 211	12 795	12 321	12 307	12 130
01100	腸管感染症	476	524	733	999	1 048	1 036	1 135
01200	結　核	2 267	1 876	1 579	1 338	1 251	1 169	1 133
01201	呼吸器結核	2 163	1 781	1 482	1 234	1 130	1 064	1 034
01202	その他の結核	104	95	97	104	121	105	99
01300	敗　血　症	2 269	2 897	4 045	5 112	5 339	5 485	5 597
01400	ウイルス肝炎	2 899	2 839	3 093	2 641	2 151	2 024	1 677
01401	B型ウイルス肝炎	568	584	524	328	284	234	217
01402	C型ウイルス肝炎	2 006	1 998	2 350	2 145	1 755	1 673	1 360
01403	その他のウイルス肝炎	325	257	219	168	112	117	100
01500	ヒト免疫不全ウイルス［HIV］病	52	47	62	56	40	50	60
01600	その他の感染症及び寄生虫症	2 708	2 724	2 699	2 649	2 492	2 543	2 528
02000	新　生　物	163 649	183 901	201 728	216 614	224 124	225 453	225 782
02100	悪性新生物	159 623	179 140	196 603	211 435	218 397	219 508	219 785
02101	口唇，口腔及び咽頭の悪性新生物	2 980	3 610	4 151	4 840	5 268	5 258	5 396
02102	食道の悪性新生物	7 253	8 706	9 465	9 992	9 629	9 774	9 533
02103	胃の悪性新生物	32 015	32 798	32 643	32 943	31 483	30 809	29 854
02104	結腸の悪性新生物	10 420	12 139	13 436	14 947	16 478	17 063	17 116
02105	直腸S状結腸移行部及び直腸の悪性新生物	6 892	7 729	8 710	8 974	9 699	9 755	9 910
02106	肝及び肝内胆管の悪性新生物	22 773	23 602	23 203	21 510	19 208	19 008	18 510
02107	胆のう及びその他の胆道の悪性新生物	6 189	6 913	7 845	8 440	9 052	9 066	8 970
02108	膵の悪性新生物	8 965	10 380	12 284	14 569	16 411	16 186	17 060
02109	喉頭の悪性新生物	872	958	1 006	916	908	899	856
02110	気管，気管支及び肺の悪性新生物	33 389	39 053	45 189	50 395	52 505	53 208	52 430
02111	皮膚の悪性新生物	451	502	628	666	797	745	754
02112	乳房の悪性新生物	56	77	87	90	83	121	117
02113	子宮の悪性新生物	・	・	・	・	・	・	・
02114	卵巣の悪性新生物	・	・	・	・	・	・	・
02115	前立腺の悪性新生物	5 399	7 514	9 265	10 722	11 507	11 326	11 803
02116	膀胱の悪性新生物	2 700	3 184	4 141	4 719	5 308	5 582	5 792
02117	中枢神経系の悪性新生物	906	869	938	1 127	1 344	1 406	1 483

General mortality

性別死亡数及び率（人口10万対）（つづき）
by sex and causes（the condensed list of causes of death for Japan）：Japan－CON.

男
Male

死　亡　率 Death rates							死因 簡単 分類 コード Code[a)]	死　因 Causes of death
1995 平成7年	2000 12年	2005 17年	2010 22年	2014 26年	2015 27年	2016 28年		
822.9	855.3	949.4	1 029.2	1 081.8	1 092.6	1 108.5		死　亡　総　数 Deaths Total
17.5	17.7	19.8	20.8	20.2	20.2	19.9	01000	感染症及び寄生虫症
0.8	0.9	1.2	1.6	1.7	1.7	1.9	01100	腸管感染症
3.7	3.1	2.6	2.2	2.0	1.9	1.9	01200	結　　核
3.6	2.9	2.4	2.0	1.9	1.7	1.7	01201	呼吸器結核
0.2	0.2	0.2	0.2	0.2	0.2	0.2	01202	その他の結核
3.7	4.7	6.6	8.3	8.7	9.0	9.2	01300	敗　血　症
4.8	4.6	5.0	4.3	3.5	3.3	2.8	01400	ウイルス肝炎
0.9	0.9	0.9	0.5	0.5	0.4	0.4	01401	B型ウイルス肝炎
3.3	3.2	3.8	3.5	2.9	2.7	2.2	01402	C型ウイルス肝炎
0.5	0.4	0.4	0.3	0.2	0.2	0.2	01403	その他のウイルス肝炎
0.1	0.1	0.1	0.1	0.1	0.1	0.1	01500	ヒト免疫不全ウイルス［HIV］病
4.4	4.4	4.4	4.3	4.1	4.2	4.2	01600	その他の感染症及び寄生虫症
268.6	299.1	327.4	351.8	367.2	369.5	370.9	02000	新　生　物
262.0	291.3	319.1	343.4	357.8	359.7	361.1	02100	悪性新生物
4.9	5.9	6.7	7.9	8.6	8.6	8.9	02101	口唇，口腔及び咽頭の悪性新生物
11.9	14.2	15.4	16.2	15.8	16.0	15.7	02102	食道の悪性新生物
52.6	53.3	53.0	53.5	51.6	50.5	49.0	02103	胃の悪性新生物
17.1	19.7	21.8	24.3	27.0	28.0	28.1	02104	結腸の悪性新生物
11.3	12.6	14.1	14.6	15.9	16.0	16.3	02105	直腸S状結腸移行部及び直腸の悪性新生物
37.4	38.4	37.7	34.9	31.5	31.1	30.4	02106	肝及び肝内胆管の悪性新生物
10.2	11.2	12.7	13.7	14.8	14.9	14.7	02107	胆のう及びその他の胆道の悪性新生物
14.7	16.9	19.9	23.7	26.9	26.5	28.0	02108	膵の悪性新生物
1.4	1.6	1.6	1.5	1.5	1.5	1.4	02109	喉頭の悪性新生物
54.8	63.5	73.3	81.8	86.0	87.2	86.1	02110	気管，気管支及び肺の悪性新生物
0.7	0.8	1.0	1.1	1.3	1.2	1.2	02111	皮膚の悪性新生物
0.1	0.1	0.1	0.1	0.1	0.2	0.2	02112	乳房の悪性新生物
・	・	・	・	・	・	・	02113	子宮の悪性新生物
・	・	・	・	・	・	・	02114	卵巣の悪性新生物
8.9	12.2	15.0	17.4	18.9	18.6	19.4	02115	前立腺の悪性新生物
4.4	5.2	6.7	7.7	8.7	9.1	9.5	02116	膀胱の悪性新生物
1.5	1.4	1.5	1.8	2.2	2.3	2.4	02117	中枢神経系の悪性新生物

211

死　亡

表 5.13　年次別にみた死因簡単分類・
Table 5.13　Trends in deaths and death rates（per 100,000 population）

男
Male

死因簡単分類コード Code[1]	死　因 Causes of death	死　亡　数 Deaths						
		1995 平成7年	2000 12年	2005 17年	2010 22年	2014 26年	2015 27年	2016 28年
02118	悪性リンパ腫	3 735	4 578	4 829	5 689	6 427	6 656	6 883
02119	白　血　病	3 645	3 970	4 311	4 860	4 896	5 104	5 398
02120	その他のリンパ組織，造血組織及び関連組織の悪性新生物	1 565	1 774	2 004	2 200	2 233	2 044	2 240
02121	その他の悪性新生物	9 418	10 784	12 468	13 836	15 161	15 498	15 680
02200	その他の新生物	4 026	4 761	5 125	5 179	5 727	5 945	5 997
02201	中枢神経系のその他の新生物	1 160	1 297	1 332	1 252	1 212	1 200	1 133
02202	中枢神経系を除くその他の新生物	2 866	3 464	3 793	3 927	4 515	4 745	4 864
03000	血液及び造血器の疾患並びに免疫機構の障害	1 832	1 789	1 872	1 948	1 862	1 923	2 003
03100	貧　血	666	669	650	694	749	778	842
03200	その他の血液及び造血器の疾患並びに免疫機構の障害	1 166	1 120	1 222	1 254	1 113	1 145	1 161
04000	内分泌，栄養及び代謝疾患	9 487	8 741	9 974	10 862	10 561	10 497	10 734
04100	糖　尿　病	7 107	6 489	7 131	7 620	7 265	7 125	7 243
04200	その他の内分泌，栄養及び代謝疾患	2 380	2 252	2 843	3 242	3 296	3 372	3 491
05000	精神及び行動の障害	1 670	1 555	1 692	2 632	3 979	4 088	4 414
05100	血管性及び詳細不明の認知症	943	909	952	1 788	3 021	3 150	3 377
05200	その他の精神及び行動の障害	727	646	740	844	958	938	1 037
06000	神経系の疾患	4 527	5 023	6 650	9 619	13 032	13 843	14 940
06100	髄　膜　炎	232	179	216	201	178	153	165
06200	脊髄性筋萎縮症及び関連症候群	707	774	1 010	1 170	1 353	1 331	1 507
06300	パーキンソン病	1 099	1 342	1 728	2 445	3 133	3 332	3 686
06400	アルツハイマー病	189	328	648	1 514	3 033	3 315	3 747
06500	その他の神経系の疾患	2 300	2 400	3 048	4 289	5 335	5 712	5 835
07000	眼及び付属器の疾患	1	2	1	2	2	3	4
08000	耳及び乳様突起の疾患	8	6	8	8	8	7	6
09000	循環器系の疾患	148 515	144 629	159 268	163 018	161 823	160 357	161 575
09100	高血圧性疾患	3 027	2 163	2 145	2 517	2 637	2 605	2 720
09101	高血圧性心疾患及び心腎疾患	1 852	1 337	1 256	1 296	1 253	1 176	1 142
09102	その他の高血圧性疾患	1 175	826	889	1 221	1 384	1 429	1 578
09200	心疾患（高血圧性を除く）	69 718	72 156	83 979	88 803	92 278	92 142	93 419
09201	慢性リウマチ性心疾患	858	773	829	743	720	740	741
09202	急性心筋梗塞	28 401	24 960	25 762	23 497	21 801	21 137	20 470
09203	その他の虚血性心疾患	11 659	12 915	16 208	19 253	20 119	19 939	19 959

212

General mortality

性別死亡数及び率（人口10万対）（つづき）
by sex and causes（the condensed list of causes of death for Japan）：Japan－CON.

男
Male

死　亡　率 Death rates							死因簡単分類コード Code[a)]	死　因 Causes of death
1995 平成7年	2000 12年	2005 17年	2010 22年	2014 26年	2015 27年	2016 28年		
6.1	7.4	7.8	9.2	10.5	10.9	11.3	02118	悪性リンパ腫
6.0	6.5	7.0	7.9	8.0	8.4	8.9	02119	白　血　病
2.6	2.9	3.3	3.6	3.7	3.3	3.7	02120	その他のリンパ組織，造血組織及び関連組織の悪性新生物
15.5	17.5	20.2	22.5	24.8	25.4	25.8	02121	その他の悪性新生物
6.6	7.7	8.3	8.4	9.4	9.7	9.9	02200	その他の新生物
1.9	2.1	2.2	2.0	2.0	2.0	1.9	02201	中枢神経系のその他の新生物
4.7	5.6	6.2	6.4	7.4	7.8	8.0	02202	中枢神経系を除くその他の新生物
3.0	2.9	3.0	3.2	3.1	3.2	3.3	03000	血液及び造血器の疾患並びに免疫機構の障害
1.1	1.1	1.1	1.1	1.2	1.3	1.4	03100	貧　血
1.9	1.8	2.0	2.0	1.8	1.9	1.9	03200	その他の血液及び造血器の疾患並びに免疫機構の障害
15.6	14.2	16.2	17.6	17.3	17.2	17.6	04000	内分泌，栄養及び代謝疾患
11.7	10.6	11.6	12.4	11.9	11.7	11.9	04100	糖　尿　病
3.9	3.7	4.6	5.3	5.4	5.5	5.7	04200	その他の内分泌，栄養及び代謝疾患
2.7	2.5	2.7	4.3	6.5	6.7	7.3	05000	精神及び行動の障害
1.5	1.5	1.5	2.9	4.9	5.2	5.5	05100	血管性及び詳細不明の認知症
1.2	1.1	1.2	1.4	1.6	1.5	1.7	05200	その他の精神及び行動の障害
7.4	8.2	10.8	15.6	21.3	22.7	24.5	06000	神経系の疾患
0.4	0.3	0.4	0.3	0.3	0.3	0.3	06100	髄　膜　炎
1.2	1.3	1.6	1.9	2.2	2.2	2.5	06200	脊髄性筋萎縮症及び関連症候群
1.8	2.2	2.8	4.0	5.1	5.5	6.1	06300	パーキンソン病
0.3	0.5	1.1	2.5	5.0	5.4	6.2	06400	アルツハイマー病
3.8	3.9	4.9	7.0	8.7	9.4	9.6	06500	その他の神経系の疾患
0.0	0.0	0.0	0.0	0.0	0.0	0.0	07000	眼及び付属器の疾患
0.0	0.0	0.0	0.0	0.0	0.0	0.0	08000	耳及び乳様突起の疾患
243.8	235.2	258.5	264.8	265.1	262.8	265.5	09000	循環器系の疾患
5.0	3.5	3.5	4.1	4.3	4.3	4.5	09100	高血圧性疾患
3.0	2.2	2.0	2.1	2.1	1.9	1.9	09101	高血圧性心疾患及び心腎疾患
1.9	1.3	1.4	2.0	2.3	2.3	2.6	09102	その他の高血圧性疾患
114.4	117.3	136.3	144.2	151.2	151.0	153.5	09200	心疾患（高血圧性を除く）
1.4	1.3	1.3	1.2	1.2	1.2	1.2	09201	慢性リウマチ性心疾患
46.6	40.6	41.8	38.2	35.7	34.6	33.6	09202	急性心筋梗塞
19.1	21.0	26.3	31.3	33.0	32.7	32.8	09203	その他の虚血性心疾患

213

死　亡

表5.13　年次別にみた死因簡単分類・
Table 5.13　Trends in deaths and death rates（per 100,000 population）

男
Male

死因簡単分類コード Code[a]	死　因 Causes of death	死　亡　数 Deaths						
		1995 平成7年	2000 12年	2005 17年	2010 22年	2014 26年	2015 27年	2016 28年
09204	慢性非リウマチ性心内膜疾患	2 055	2 106	2 483	2 916	3 264	3 528	3 493
09205	心筋症	2 188	2 174	2 266	2 226	2 152	2 224	2 149
09206	不整脈及び伝導障害	6 451	7 550	11 233	12 257	14 441	14 689	15 121
09207	心不全	16 627	19 983	22 962	25 327	26 916	26 961	28 254
09208	その他の心疾患	1 479	1 695	2 236	2 584	2 865	2 924	3 232
09300	脳血管疾患	69 587	63 127	63 657	60 186	54 995	53 576	52 706
09301	くも膜下出血	5 477	5 544	5 689	5 258	4 713	4 643	4 556
09302	脳内出血	17 637	16 793	18 281	18 802	17 831	17 541	17 538
09303	脳梗塞	42 724	39 068	38 009	34 548	31 093	30 070	29 384
09304	その他の脳血管疾患	3 749	1 722	1 678	1 578	1 358	1 322	1 228
09400	大動脈瘤及び解離	3 832	4 813	6 407	8 252	8 607	8 616	9 268
09500	その他の循環器系の疾患	2 351	2 370	3 080	3 260	3 306	3 418	3 462
10000	呼吸器系の疾患	71 195	75 544	92 157	105 262	115 235	118 495	120 238
10100	インフルエンザ	602	280	863	96	559	1 068	748
10200	肺炎	42 419	46 722	57 310	63 569	64 780	65 609	65 636
10300	急性気管支炎	840	607	373	228	175	181	198
10400	慢性閉塞性肺疾患	9 452	9 593	11 018	12 681	13 002	12 642	12 649
10500	喘息	4 052	2 300	1 565	898	590	573	567
10600	その他の呼吸器系の疾患	13 830	16 042	21 028	27 790	36 129	38 422	40 440
11000	消化器系の疾患	22 008	21 752	22 978	24 410	25 115	25 336	25 606
11100	胃潰瘍及び十二指腸潰瘍	2 274	2 161	1 897	1 835	1 609	1 511	1 527
11200	ヘルニア及び腸閉塞	1 835	1 944	2 312	2 694	3 231	3 290	3 279
11300	肝疾患	11 576	11 068	11 007	10 619	10 031	10 016	10 112
11301	肝硬変（アルコール性を除く）	7 478	6 401	5 683	4 907	4 232	4 114	4 153
11302	その他の肝疾患	4 098	4 667	5 324	5 712	5 799	5 902	5 959
11400	その他の消化器系の疾患	6 323	6 579	7 762	9 262	10 244	10 519	10 688
12000	皮膚及び皮下組織の疾患	285	290	370	510	640	612	618
13000	筋骨格系及び結合組織の疾患	1 278	1 438	1 566	2 093	2 294	2 308	2 552
14000	腎尿路生殖器系の疾患	9 954	9 947	11 793	14 362	16 283	16 439	17 438
14100	糸球体疾患及び腎尿細管間質性疾患	1 254	1 086	1 105	1 484	1 589	1 668	1 953
14200	腎不全	7 800	8 029	9 463	11 035	11 935	11 908	12 231
14201	急性腎不全	2 086	1 880	1 802	1 860	1 639	1 631	1 566

214

General mortality

性別死亡数及び率（人口10万対）（つづき）
by sex and causes（the condensed list of causes of death for Japan）：Japan－CON.

男
Male

死　亡　率　Death rates							死因簡単分類コード Code[a]	死　因 Causes of death
1995 平成7年	2000 12年	2005 17年	2010 22年	2014 26年	2015 27年	2016 28年		
3.4	3.4	4.0	4.7	5.3	5.8	5.7	09204	慢性非リウマチ性心内膜疾患
3.6	3.5	3.7	3.6	3.5	3.6	3.5	09205	心　筋　症
10.6	12.3	18.2	19.9	23.7	24.1	24.8	09206	不整脈及び伝導障害
27.3	32.5	37.3	41.1	44.1	44.2	46.4	09207	心　不　全
2.4	2.8	3.6	4.2	4.7	4.8	5.3	09208	その他の心疾患
114.2	102.7	103.3	97.7	90.1	87.8	86.6	09300	脳血管疾患
9.0	9.0	9.2	8.5	7.7	7.6	7.5	09301	くも膜下出血
29.0	27.3	29.7	30.5	29.2	28.7	28.8	09302	脳　内　出　血
70.1	63.5	61.7	56.1	50.9	49.3	48.3	09303	脳　梗　塞
6.2	2.8	2.7	2.6	2.2	2.2	2.0	09304	その他の脳血管疾患
6.3	7.8	10.4	13.4	14.1	14.1	15.2	09400	大動脈瘤及び解離
3.9	3.9	5.0	5.3	5.4	5.6	5.7	09500	その他の循環器系の疾患
116.9	122.9	149.6	171.0	188.8	194.2	197.5	10000	呼吸器系の疾患
1.0	0.5	1.4	0.2	0.9	1.8	1.2	10100	インフルエンザ
69.6	76.0	93.0	103.2	106.1	107.5	107.8	10200	肺　炎
1.4	1.0	0.6	0.4	0.3	0.3	0.3	10300	急性気管支炎
15.5	15.6	17.9	20.6	21.3	20.7	20.8	10400	慢性閉塞性肺疾患
6.7	3.7	2.5	1.5	1.0	0.9	0.9	10500	喘　息
22.7	26.1	34.1	45.1	59.2	63.0	66.4	10600	その他の呼吸器系の疾患
36.1	35.4	37.3	39.6	41.1	41.5	42.1	11000	消化器系の疾患
3.7	3.5	3.1	3.0	2.6	2.5	2.5	11100	胃潰瘍及び十二指腸潰瘍
3.0	3.2	3.8	4.4	5.3	5.4	5.4	11200	ヘルニア及び腸閉塞
19.0	18.0	17.9	17.2	16.4	16.4	16.6	11300	肝　疾　患
12.3	10.4	9.2	8.0	6.9	6.7	6.8	11301	肝硬変（アルコール性を除く）
6.7	7.6	8.6	9.3	9.5	9.7	9.8	11302	その他の肝疾患
10.4	10.7	12.6	15.0	16.8	17.2	17.6	11400	その他の消化器系の疾患
0.5	0.5	0.6	0.8	1.0	1.0	1.0	12000	皮膚及び皮下組織の疾患
2.1	2.3	2.5	3.4	3.8	3.8	4.2	13000	筋骨格系及び結合組織の疾患
16.3	16.2	19.1	23.3	26.7	26.9	28.6	14000	腎尿路生殖器系の疾患
2.1	1.8	1.8	2.4	2.6	2.7	3.2	14100	糸球体疾患及び腎尿細管間質性疾患
12.8	13.1	15.4	17.9	19.6	19.5	20.1	14200	腎　不　全
3.4	3.1	2.9	3.0	2.7	2.7	2.6	14201	急性腎不全

215

死　亡

表 5.13　年次別にみた死因簡単分類・
Table 5.13　Trends in deaths and death rates（per 100,000 population）

男
Male

死因簡単分類コード Code[a]	死因 Causes of death	死　亡　数 Deaths						
		1995 平成7年	2000 12年	2005 17年	2010 22年	2014 26年	2015 27年	2016 28年
14202	慢性腎不全	3 522	4 116	5 566	6 955	7 853	7 849	8 185
14203	詳細不明の腎不全	2 192	2 033	2 095	2 220	2 443	2 428	2 480
14300	その他の腎尿路生殖器系の疾患	900	832	1 225	1 843	2 759	2 863	3 254
15000	妊娠，分娩及び産じょく	・	・	・	・	・	・	・
16000	周産期に発生した病態	902	616	462	371	269	279	258
16100	妊娠期間及び胎児発育に関連する障害	44	41	29	43	27	22	21
16200	出産外傷	19	7	-	2	8	5	-
16300	周産期に特異的な呼吸障害及び心血管障害	440	337	235	197	138	137	150
16400	周産期に特異的な感染症	91	45	36	33	22	18	28
16500	胎児及び新生児の出血性障害及び血液障害	138	112	93	44	29	49	28
16600	その他の周産期に発生した病態	170	74	69	52	45	48	31
17000	先天奇形，変形及び染色体異常	1 687	1 357	1 163	1 114	993	926	951
17100	神経系の先天奇形	83	76	60	54	53	43	34
17200	循環器系の先天奇形	961	718	616	559	431	409	405
17201	心臓の先天奇形	710	553	480	426	307	295	266
17202	その他の循環器系の先天奇形	251	165	136	133	124	114	139
17300	消化系の先天奇形	66	51	54	48	49	58	52
17400	その他の先天奇形及び変形	442	395	335	316	321	295	320
17500	染色体異常，他に分類されないもの	135	117	98	137	139	121	140
18000	症状，徴候及び異常臨床所見・異常検査所見で他に分類されないもの	9 220	9 098	11 302	19 734	28 916	31 873	35 030
18100	老　衰	6 684	6 017	6 683	10 787	18 316	20 894	23 077
18200	乳幼児突然死症候群	341	217	120	84	90	61	54
18300	その他の症状，徴候及び異常臨床所見・異常検査所見で他に分類されないもの	2 195	2 864	4 499	8 863	10 510	10 918	11 899
20000	傷病及び死亡の外因	44 387	49 308	49 775	48 346	42 877	41 961	40 454
20100	不慮の事故	28 229	25 162	24 591	23 975	22 562	22 121	22 066
20101	交通事故	10 772	9 072	7 015	4 871	3 923	3 886	3 665
20102	転倒・転落	3 663	3 798	3 989	4 335	4 520	4 461	4 488
20103	不慮の溺死及び溺水	3 170	3 332	3 404	3 786	3 879	3 911	4 002
20104	不慮の窒息	4 198	4 375	5 058	5 078	5 006	4 764	4 806
20105	煙，火及び火炎への曝露	849	883	972	841	666	567	542
20106	有害物質による不慮の中毒及び有害物質への曝露	396	415	609	558	419	382	358
20107	その他の不慮の事故	5 181	3 287	3 544	4 506	4 149	4 150	4 205
20200	自　殺	14 231	21 656	22 236	21 028	16 875	16 202	14 639
20300	他　殺	413	426	317	232	181	138	148
20400	その他の外因	1 514	2 064	2 631	3 111	3 259	3 500	3 601
22000	特殊目的用コード	…	…	…	-	-	-	-
22100	重症急性呼吸器症候群〔SARS〕	…	…	…	-	-	-	-

General mortality

性別死亡数及び率（人口10万対）（つづき）
by sex and causes (the condensed list of causes of death for Japan)：Japan－CON.

男
Male

死　亡　率 Death rates							死因簡単分類コードCode[a]	死　因 Causes of death
1995 平成7年	2000 12年	2005 17年	2010 22年	2014 26年	2015 27年	2016 28年		
5.8	6.7	9.0	11.3	12.9	12.9	13.4	14202	慢性腎不全
3.6	3.3	3.4	3.6	4.0	4.0	4.1	14203	詳細不明の腎不全
1.5	1.4	2.0	3.0	4.5	4.7	5.3	14300	その他の腎尿路生殖器系の疾患
・	・	・	・	・	・	・	15000	妊娠，分娩及び産じょく
1.5	1.0	0.7	0.6	0.4	0.5	0.4	16000	周産期に発生した病態
0.1	0.1	0.0	0.1	0.0	0.0	0.0	16100	妊娠期間及び胎児発育に関連する障害
0.0	0.0	-	0.0	0.0	0.0	-	16200	出産外傷
0.7	0.5	0.4	0.3	0.2	0.2	0.2	16300	周産期に特異的な呼吸障害及び心血管障害
0.1	0.1	0.1	0.1	0.0	0.0	0.0	16400	周産期に特異的な感染症
0.2	0.2	0.2	0.1	0.0	0.1	0.0	16500	胎児及び新生児の出血性障害及び血液障害
0.3	0.1	0.1	0.1	0.1	0.1	0.1	16600	その他の周産期に発生した病態
2.8	2.2	1.9	1.8	1.6	1.5	1.6	17000	先天奇形，変形及び染色体異常
0.1	0.1	0.1	0.1	0.1	0.1	0.1	17100	神経系の先天奇形
1.6	1.2	1.0	0.9	0.7	0.7	0.7	17200	循環器系の先天奇形
1.2	0.9	0.8	0.7	0.5	0.5	0.4	17201	心臓の先天奇形
0.4	0.3	0.2	0.2	0.2	0.2	0.2	17202	その他の循環器系の先天奇形
0.1	0.1	0.1	0.1	0.1	0.1	0.1	17300	消化器系の先天奇形
0.7	0.6	0.5	0.5	0.5	0.5	0.5	17400	その他の先天奇形及び変形
0.2	0.2	0.2	0.2	0.2	0.2	0.2	17500	染色体異常，他に分類されないもの
15.1	14.8	18.3	32.1	47.4	52.2	57.6	18000	症状，徴候及び異常臨床所見・異常検査所見で他に分類されないもの
11.0	9.8	10.8	17.5	30.0	34.2	37.9	18100	老　衰
0.6	0.4	0.2	0.1	0.1	0.1	0.1	18200	乳幼児突然死症候群
3.6	4.7	7.3	14.4	17.2	17.9	19.5	18300	その他の症状，徴候及び異常臨床所見・異常検査所見で他に分類されないもの
72.9	80.2	80.8	78.5	70.2	68.8	66.5	20000	傷病及び死亡の外因
46.3	40.9	39.9	38.9	37.0	36.3	36.3	20100	不慮の事故
17.7	14.8	11.4	7.9	6.4	6.4	6.0	20101	交通事故
6.0	6.2	6.5	7.0	7.4	7.3	7.4	20102	転倒・転落
5.2	5.4	5.5	6.1	6.4	6.4	6.6	20103	不慮の溺死及び溺水
6.9	7.1	8.2	8.2	8.2	7.8	7.9	20104	不慮の窒息
1.4	1.4	1.6	1.4	1.1	0.9	0.9	20105	煙，火及び火炎への曝露
0.7	0.7	1.0	0.9	0.7	0.6	0.6	20106	有害物質による不慮の中毒及び有害物質への曝露
8.5	5.3	5.8	7.3	6.8	6.8	6.9	20107	その他の不慮の事故
23.4	35.2	36.1	34.2	27.6	26.6	24.1	20200	自　殺
0.7	0.7	0.5	0.4	0.3	0.2	0.2	20300	他　殺
2.5	3.4	4.3	5.1	5.3	5.7	5.9	20400	その他の外因
…	…	…	-	-	-	-	22000	特殊目的用コード
…	…	…	-	-	-	-	22100	重症急性呼吸器症候群〔SARS〕

死　亡

表5.13　年次別にみた死因簡単分類・
Table 5.13　Trends in deaths and death rates（per 100,000 population）

女
Female

死因簡単分類コード Code[a]	死因 Causes of death	死亡数 Deaths						
		1995 平成7年	2000 12年	2005 17年	2010 22年	2014 26年	2015 27年	2016 28年
	死亡総数 Deaths Total	420 863	435 750	498 826	563 312	612 670	623 737	633 015
01000	感染症及び寄生虫症	8 254	8 951	11 327	13 068	13 248	12 933	12 969
01100	腸管感染症	621	688	1 019	1 314	1 369	1 296	1 416
01200	結　核	911	780	717	791	849	787	759
01201	呼吸器結核	823	680	604	646	706	659	628
01202	その他の結核	88	100	113	145	143	128	131
01300	敗血症	2 636	3 319	4 459	5 564	5 940	5 872	5 913
01400	ウイルス肝炎	2 130	2 282	2 949	2 973	2 596	2 490	2 171
01401	B型ウイルス肝炎	312	301	262	211	198	173	190
01402	C型ウイルス肝炎	1 536	1 758	2 505	2 609	2 278	2 208	1 896
01403	その他のウイルス肝炎	282	223	182	153	120	109	85
01500	ヒト免疫不全ウイルス［HIV］病	4	3	7	5	5	6	6
01600	その他の感染症及び寄生虫症	1 952	1 879	2 176	2 421	2 489	2 482	2 704
02000	新生物	106 644	120 588	134 142	147 027	154 985	156 211	158 678
02100	悪性新生物	103 399	116 344	129 338	142 064	149 706	150 838	153 201
02101	口唇，口腔及び咽頭の悪性新生物	1 119	1 456	1 528	1 962	2 147	2 122	2 279
02102	食道の悪性新生物	1 385	1 550	1 717	1 875	1 947	1 965	1 950
02103	胃の悪性新生物	18 061	17 852	17 668	17 193	16 420	15 870	15 677
02104	結腸の悪性新生物	9 866	11 498	13 685	15 093	16 819	17 275	17 405
02105	直腸S状結腸移行部及び直腸の悪性新生物	4 096	4 582	4 999	5 224	5 489	5 606	5 668
02106	肝及び肝内胆管の悪性新生物	8 934	10 379	11 065	11 255	10 335	9 881	10 018
02107	胆のう及びその他の胆道の悪性新生物	7 557	8 240	8 741	9 145	9 065	9 086	8 995
02108	膵の悪性新生物	7 054	8 714	10 643	13 448	15 305	15 680	16 415
02109	喉頭の悪性新生物	87	88	84	86	70	72	88
02110	気管，気管支及び肺の悪性新生物	12 356	14 671	16 874	19 418	20 891	21 170	21 408
02111	皮膚の悪性新生物	418	484	579	738	860	760	799
02112	乳房の悪性新生物	7 763	9 171	10 721	12 455	13 240	13 584	14 015
02113	子宮の悪性新生物	4 865	5 202	5 381	5 930	6 429	6 429	6 345
02114	卵巣の悪性新生物	3 892	3 993	4 467	4 654	4 840	4 676	4 758
02115	前立腺の悪性新生物	・	・	・	・	・	・	・
02116	膀胱の悪性新生物	1 231	1 496	1 888	2 085	2 452	2 548	2 640
02117	中枢神経系の悪性新生物	668	705	743	832	982	1 039	1 167

General mortality

性別死亡数及び率（人口10万対）（つづき）
by sex and causes（the condensed list of causes of death for Japan）：Japan－CON.

女
Female

死　亡　率 Death rates							死因簡単分類コード Code[a]	死　因 Causes of death
1995 平成7年	2000 12年	2005 17年	2010 22年	2014 26年	2015 27年	2016 28年		
664.0	679.5	772.3	869.2	951.5	970.1	986.7		死　亡　総　数 Deaths Total
13.0	14.0	17.5	20.2	20.6	20.1	20.2	01000	感染症及び寄生虫症
1.0	1.1	1.6	2.0	2.1	2.0	2.2	01100	腸管感染症
1.4	1.2	1.1	1.2	1.3	1.2	1.2	01200	結　　核
1.3	1.1	0.9	1.0	1.1	1.0	1.0	01201	呼吸器結核
0.1	0.2	0.2	0.2	0.2	0.2	0.2	01202	その他の結核
4.2	5.2	6.9	8.6	9.2	9.1	9.2	01300	敗　血　症
3.4	3.6	4.6	4.6	4.0	3.9	3.4	01400	ウイルス肝炎
0.5	0.5	0.4	0.3	0.3	0.3	0.3	01401	B型ウイルス肝炎
2.4	2.7	3.9	4.0	3.5	3.4	3.0	01402	C型ウイルス肝炎
0.4	0.3	0.3	0.2	0.2	0.2	0.1	01403	その他のウイルス肝炎
0.0	0.0	0.0	0.0	0.0	0.0	0.0	01500	ヒト免疫不全ウイルス［HIV］病
3.1	2.9	3.4	3.7	3.9	3.9	4.2	01600	その他の感染症及び寄生虫症
168.3	188.1	207.7	226.9	240.7	243.0	247.3	02000	新　生　物
163.1	181.4	200.3	219.2	232.5	234.6	238.8	02100	悪性新生物
1.8	2.3	2.4	3.0	3.3	3.3	3.6	02101	口唇，口腔及び咽頭の悪性新生物
2.2	2.4	2.7	2.9	3.0	3.1	3.0	02102	食道の悪性新生物
28.5	27.8	27.4	26.5	25.5	24.7	24.4	02103	胃の悪性新生物
15.6	17.9	21.2	23.3	26.1	26.9	27.1	02104	結腸の悪性新生物
6.5	7.1	7.7	8.1	8.5	8.7	8.8	02105	直腸S状結腸移行部及び直腸の悪性新生物
14.1	16.2	17.1	17.4	16.1	15.4	15.6	02106	肝及び肝内胆管の悪性新生物
11.9	12.8	13.5	14.1	14.1	14.1	14.0	02107	胆のう及びその他の胆道の悪性新生物
11.1	13.6	16.5	20.7	23.8	24.4	25.6	02108	膵の悪性新生物
0.1	0.1	0.1	0.1	0.1	0.1	0.1	02109	喉頭の悪性新生物
19.5	22.9	26.1	30.0	32.4	32.9	33.4	02110	気管，気管支及び肺の悪性新生物
0.7	0.8	0.9	1.1	1.3	1.2	1.2	02111	皮膚の悪性新生物
12.2	14.3	16.6	19.2	20.6	21.1	21.8	02112	乳房の悪性新生物
7.7	8.1	8.3	9.1	10.0	10.0	9.9	02113	子宮の悪性新生物
6.1	6.2	6.9	7.2	7.5	7.3	7.4	02114	卵巣の悪性新生物
・	・	・	・	・	・	・	02115	前立腺の悪性新生物
1.9	2.3	2.9	3.2	3.8	4.0	4.1	02116	膀胱の悪性新生物
1.1	1.1	1.2	1.3	1.5	1.6	1.8	02117	中枢神経系の悪性新生物

219

死　亡

表 5.13　年次別にみた死因簡単分類・
Table 5.13　Trends in deaths and death rates（per 100,000 population）

女
Female

死因簡単分類コード Code[a]	死　因 Causes of death	死　亡　数　Deaths						
		1995 平成 7 年	2000 12年	2005 17年	2010 22年	2014 26年	2015 27年	2016 28年
02118	悪性リンパ腫	2 607	3 340	3 708	4 483	5 053	5 173	5 442
02119	白　血　病	2 484	2 796	2 972	3 218	3 300	3 527	3 403
02120	その他のリンパ組織, 造血組織及び関連組織の悪性新生物	1 443	1 651	1 928	2 087	2 004	2 130	2 203
02121	その他の悪性新生物	7 513	8 476	9 947	10 883	12 058	12 245	12 526
02200	その他の新生物	3 245	4 244	4 804	4 963	5 279	5 373	5 477
02201	中枢神経系のその他の新生物	1 135	1 356	1 532	1 337	1 369	1 291	1 338
02202	中枢神経系を除くその他の新生物	2 110	2 888	3 272	3 626	3 910	4 082	4 139
03000	血液及び造血器の疾患並びに免疫機構の障害	2 274	2 268	2 301	2 388	2 451	2 419	2 538
03100	貧　　血	986	1 038	1 018	1 118	1 177	1 216	1 275
03200	その他の血液及び造血器の疾患並びに免疫機構の障害	1 288	1 230	1 283	1 270	1 274	1 203	1 263
04000	内分泌, 栄養及び代謝疾患	9 873	8 369	9 752	10 822	10 504	10 446	10 597
04100	糖　尿　病	7 118	5 814	6 490	6 802	6 404	6 202	6 237
04200	その他の内分泌, 栄養及び代謝疾患	2 755	2 555	3 262	4 020	4 100	4 244	4 360
05000	精神及び行動の障害	2 092	2 365	2 910	5 417	8 705	9 102	9 767
05100	血管性及び詳細不明の認知症	1 754	1 982	2 382	4 663	7 566	7 968	8 517
05200	その他の精神及び行動の障害	338	383	528	754	1 139	1 134	1 250
06000	神経系の疾患	4 098	4 544	6 354	9 810	15 352	17 068	18 417
06100	髄　膜　炎	173	148	162	138	126	140	123
06200	脊髄性筋萎縮症及び関連症候群	542	597	720	837	961	935	1 157
06300	パーキンソン病	1 328	1 463	1 906	2 691	3 445	3 827	3 857
06400	アルツハイマー病	322	507	1 166	2 652	6 420	7 229	8 222
06500	その他の神経系の疾患	1 733	1 829	2 400	3 492	4 400	4 937	5 058
07000	眼及び付属器の疾患	-	10	2	3	1	1	3
08000	耳及び乳様突起の疾患	12	13	6	11	4	7	9
09000	循環器系の疾患	156 309	153 709	170 207	178 864	179 972	178 777	178 272
09100	高血圧性疾患	5 195	3 900	3 690	4 243	4 295	4 121	4 121
09101	高血圧性心疾患及び心腎疾患	3 216	2 411	2 214	2 305	2 141	2 037	1 955
09102	その他の高血圧性疾患	1 979	1 489	1 476	1 938	2 154	2 084	2 166
09200	心疾患（高血圧性を除く）	69 488	74 585	89 146	100 557	104 647	103 971	104 587
09201	慢性リウマチ性心疾患	1 897	1 749	1 691	1 673	1 588	1 573	1 525
09202	急性心筋梗塞	24 132	20 925	21 431	19 132	17 190	16 085	15 456
09203	その他の虚血性心疾患	11 381	11 383	13 102	15 335	14 775	14 512	14 575

性別死亡数及び率（人口10万対）（つづき）
by sex and causes（the condensed list of causes of death for Japan）：Japan－CON.

女
Female

死　亡　率 Death rates							死因簡単分類コード Code[a]	死　因 Causes of death
1995 平成7年	2000 12年	2005 17年	2010 22年	2014 26年	2015 27年	2016 28年		
4.1	5.2	5.7	6.9	7.8	8.0	8.5	02118	悪性リンパ腫
3.9	4.4	4.6	5.0	5.1	5.5	5.3	02119	白　血　病
2.3	2.6	3.0	3.2	3.1	3.3	3.4	02120	その他のリンパ組織，造血組織及び関連組織の悪性新生物
11.9	13.2	15.4	16.8	18.7	19.0	19.5	02121	その他の悪性新生物
5.1	6.6	7.4	7.7	8.2	8.4	8.5	02200	その他の新生物
1.8	2.1	2.4	2.1	2.1	2.0	2.1	02201	中枢神経系のその他の新生物
3.3	4.5	5.1	5.6	6.1	6.3	6.5	02202	中枢神経系を除くその他の新生物
3.6	3.5	3.6	3.7	3.8	3.8	4.0	03000	血液及び造血器の疾患並びに免疫機構の障害
1.6	1.6	1.6	1.7	1.8	1.9	2.0	03100	貧　　血
2.0	1.9	2.0	2.0	2.0	1.9	2.0	03200	その他の血液及び造血器の疾患並びに免疫機構の障害
15.6	13.1	15.1	16.7	16.3	16.2	16.5	04000	内分泌，栄養及び代謝疾患
11.2	9.1	10.0	10.5	9.9	9.6	9.7	04100	糖　尿　病
4.3	4.0	5.1	6.2	6.4	6.6	6.8	04200	その他の内分泌，栄養及び代謝疾患
3.3	3.7	4.5	8.4	13.5	14.2	15.2	05000	精神及び行動の障害
2.8	3.1	3.7	7.2	11.8	12.4	13.3	05100	血管性及び詳細不明の認知症
0.5	0.6	0.8	1.2	1.8	1.8	1.9	05200	その他の精神及び行動の障害
6.5	7.1	9.8	15.1	23.8	26.5	28.7	06000	神経系の疾患
0.3	0.2	0.3	0.2	0.2	0.2	0.2	06100	髄　膜　炎
0.9	0.9	1.1	1.3	1.5	1.5	1.8	06200	脊髄性筋萎縮症及び関連症候群
2.1	2.3	3.0	4.2	5.4	6.0	6.0	06300	パーキンソン病
0.5	0.8	1.8	4.1	10.0	11.2	12.8	06400	アルツハイマー病
2.7	2.9	3.7	5.4	6.8	7.7	7.9	06500	その他の神経系の疾患
-	0.0	0.0	0.0	0.0	0.0	0.0	07000	眼及び付属器の疾患
0.0	0.0	0.0	0.0	0.0	0.0	0.0	08000	耳及び乳様突起の疾患
246.6	239.7	263.5	276.0	279.5	278.1	277.9	09000	循環器系の疾患
8.2	6.1	5.7	6.5	6.7	6.4	6.4	09100	高血圧性疾患
5.1	3.8	3.4	3.6	3.3	3.2	3.0	09101	高血圧性心疾患及び心腎疾患
3.1	2.3	2.3	3.0	3.3	3.2	3.4	09102	その他の高血圧性疾患
109.6	116.3	138.0	155.2	162.5	161.7	163.0	09200	心疾患（高血圧性を除く）
3.0	2.7	2.6	2.6	2.5	2.4	2.4	09201	慢性リウマチ性心疾患
38.1	32.6	33.2	29.5	26.7	25.0	24.1	09202	急性心筋梗塞
18.0	17.8	20.3	23.7	22.9	22.6	22.7	09203	その他の虚血性心疾患

死　亡

表5.13　年次別にみた死因簡単分類・
Table 5.13　Trends in deaths and death rates (per 100,000 population)

女
Female

死因簡単分類コード Code[a]	死　因 Causes of death	死　亡　数 Deaths						
		1995 平成7年	2000 12年	2005 17年	2010 22年	2014 26年	2015 27年	2016 28年
09204	慢性非リウマチ性心内膜疾患	3 302	3 889	5 049	6 209	6 953	7 128	7 551
09205	心筋症	1 267	1 129	1 359	1 523	1 689	1 607	1 651
09206	不整脈及び伝導障害	6 390	7 547	11 284	12 862	15 298	15 611	15 924
09207	心不全	19 552	26 477	33 365	41 531	44 740	44 899	45 291
09208	その他の心疾患	1 567	1 486	1 865	2 292	2 414	2 556	2 614
09300	脳血管疾患	76 965	69 402	69 190	63 275	59 212	58 397	56 614
09301	くも膜下出血	8 947	9 271	9 194	8 333	7 949	7 833	7 762
09302	脳内出血	15 550	14 258	15 081	14 893	14 719	14 572	14 437
09303	脳梗塞	46 707	43 583	42 955	38 337	34 965	34 453	32 893
09304	その他の脳血管疾患	5 761	2 290	1 960	1 712	1 579	1 539	1 522
09400	大動脈瘤及び解離	2 382	3 401	4 985	6 957	7 816	8 271	8 877
09500	その他の循環器系の疾患	2 279	2 421	3 196	3 832	4 002	4 017	4 073
10000	呼吸器系の疾患	55 466	58 957	73 842	82 347	87 393	89 905	88 365
10100	インフルエンザ	642	295	955	65	571	1 194	715
10200	肺炎	37 210	40 216	49 931	55 319	54 870	55 344	53 664
10300	急性気管支炎	1 034	786	589	353	330	264	253
10400	慢性閉塞性肺疾患	3 640	3 248	3 398	3 612	3 182	3 114	3 037
10500	喘息	3 201	2 173	1 633	1 167	960	938	887
10600	その他の呼吸器系の疾患	9 739	12 239	17 336	21 831	27 480	29 051	29 809
11000	消化器系の疾患	16 718	16 516	18 824	21 093	22 829	22 939	23 131
11100	胃潰瘍及び十二指腸潰瘍	2 040	1 708	1 593	1 398	1 186	1 155	1 130
11200	ヘルニア及び腸閉塞	2 297	2 523	2 948	3 291	3 610	3 629	3 692
11300	肝疾患	5 442	5 011	5 423	5 597	5 661	5 643	5 661
11301	肝硬変（アルコール性を除く）	3 823	3 439	3 704	3 690	3 568	3 535	3 549
11302	その他の肝疾患	1 619	1 572	1 719	1 907	2 093	2 108	2 112
11400	その他の消化器系の疾患	6 939	7 274	8 860	10 807	12 372	12 512	12 648
12000	皮膚及び皮下組織の疾患	581	564	599	809	993	1 036	1 034
13000	筋骨格系及び結合組織の疾患	2 792	2 981	3 037	3 513	3 698	3 792	3 893
14000	腎尿路生殖器系の疾患	11 427	12 030	15 159	18 512	20 474	20 626	21 159
14100	糸球体疾患及び腎尿細管間質性疾患	1 934	1 518	1 923	2 396	2 765	2 821	3 078
14200	腎不全	8 387	9 231	11 065	12 690	12 841	12 652	12 381
14201	急性腎不全	2 192	2 083	2 210	2 284	2 048	1 940	1 833

General mortality

性別死亡数及び率（人口10万対）（つづき）
by sex and causes（the condensed list of causes of death for Japan）：Japan－CON.

女
Female

死　亡　率 Death rates							死因簡単分類コード Code[a]	死　因 Causes of death
1995 平成7年	2000 12年	2005 17年	2010 22年	2014 26年	2015 27年	2016 28年		
5.2	6.1	7.8	9.6	10.8	11.1	11.8	09204	慢性非リウマチ性心内膜疾患
2.0	1.8	2.1	2.3	2.6	2.5	2.6	09205	心　筋　症
10.1	11.8	17.5	19.8	23.8	24.3	24.8	09206	不整脈及び伝導障害
30.8	41.3	51.7	64.1	69.5	69.8	70.6	09207	心　不　全
2.5	2.3	2.9	3.5	3.7	4.0	4.1	09208	その他の心疾患
121.4	108.2	107.1	97.6	92.0	90.8	88.2	09300	脳血管疾患
14.1	14.5	14.2	12.9	12.3	12.2	12.1	09301	くも膜下出血
24.5	22.2	23.3	23.0	22.9	22.7	22.5	09302	脳　内　出　血
73.7	68.0	66.5	59.2	54.3	53.6	51.3	09303	脳　梗　塞
9.1	3.6	3.0	2.6	2.5	2.4	2.4	09304	その他の脳血管疾患
3.8	5.3	7.7	10.7	12.1	12.9	13.8	09400	大動脈瘤及び解離
3.6	3.8	4.9	5.9	6.2	6.2	6.3	09500	その他の循環器系の疾患
87.5	91.9	114.3	127.1	135.7	139.8	137.7	10000	呼吸器系の疾患
1.0	0.5	1.5	0.1	0.9	1.9	1.1	10100	インフルエンザ
58.7	62.7	77.3	85.4	85.2	86.1	83.6	10200	肺　　炎
1.6	1.2	0.9	0.5	0.5	0.4	0.4	10300	急性気管支炎
5.7	5.1	5.3	5.6	4.9	4.8	4.7	10400	慢性閉塞性肺疾患
5.1	3.4	2.5	1.8	1.5	1.5	1.4	10500	喘　　息
15.4	19.1	26.8	33.7	42.7	45.2	46.5	10600	その他の呼吸器系の疾患
26.4	25.8	29.1	32.5	35.5	35.7	36.1	11000	消化器系の疾患
3.2	2.7	2.5	2.2	1.8	1.8	1.8	11100	胃潰瘍及び十二指腸潰瘍
3.6	3.9	4.6	5.1	5.6	5.6	5.8	11200	ヘルニア及び腸閉塞
8.6	7.8	8.4	8.6	8.8	8.8	8.8	11300	肝　疾　患
6.0	5.4	5.7	5.7	5.5	5.5	5.5	11301	肝硬変（アルコール性を除く）
2.6	2.5	2.7	2.9	3.3	3.3	3.3	11302	その他の肝疾患
10.9	11.3	13.7	16.7	19.2	19.5	19.7	11400	その他の消化器系の疾患
0.9	0.9	0.9	1.2	1.5	1.6	1.6	12000	皮膚及び皮下組織の疾患
4.4	4.6	4.7	5.4	5.7	5.9	6.1	13000	筋骨格系及び結合組織の疾患
18.0	18.8	23.5	28.6	31.8	32.1	33.0	14000	腎尿路生殖器系の疾患
3.1	2.4	3.0	3.7	4.3	4.4	4.8	14100	糸球体疾患及び腎尿細管間質性疾患
13.2	14.4	17.1	19.6	19.9	19.7	19.3	14200	腎　不　全
3.5	3.2	3.4	3.5	3.2	3.0	2.9	14201	急性腎不全

223

死　亡

表 5.13　年次別にみた死因簡単分類・
Table 5.13　Trends in deaths and death rates（per 100,000 population）

女
Female

死因簡単分類コード Code[a]	死　因 Causes of death	死　亡　数 Deaths						
		1995 平成7年	2000 12年	2005 17年	2010 22年	2014 26年	2015 27年	2016 28年
14202	慢性腎不全	3 577	4 572	5 973	7 411	7 864	7 890	7 803
14203	詳細不明の腎不全	2 618	2 576	2 882	2 995	2 929	2 822	2 745
14300	その他の腎尿路生殖器系の疾患	1 106	1 281	2 171	3 426	4 868	5 153	5 700
15000	妊娠，分娩及び産じょく	90	84	66	49	33	44	36
16000	周産期に発生した病態	645	509	380	268	263	218	268
16100	妊娠期間及び胎児発育に関連する障害	34	33	38	22	32	17	22
16200	出産外傷	11	1	7	-	5	1	3
16300	周産期に特異的な呼吸障害及び心血管障害	346	278	190	152	128	114	138
16400	周産期に特異的な感染症	46	40	28	24	22	17	15
16500	胎児及び新生児の出血性障害及び血液障害	107	96	68	42	35	35	40
16600	その他の周産期に発生した病態	101	61	49	28	41	34	50
17000	先天奇形，変形及び染色体異常	1 598	1 345	1 161	1 080	1 049	1 096	1 069
17100	神経系の先天奇形	88	71	59	51	49	46	51
17200	循環器系の先天奇形	882	721	599	569	514	543	506
17201	心臓の先天奇形	675	568	451	433	352	375	324
17202	その他の循環器系の先天奇形	207	153	148	136	162	168	182
17300	消化器系の先天奇形	69	49	43	49	62	55	49
17400	その他の先天奇形及び変形	377	342	328	247	263	273	265
17500	染色体異常，他に分類されないもの	182	162	132	164	161	179	198
18000	症状，徴候及び異常臨床所見・異常検査所見で他に分類されないもの	16 500	17 450	23 152	40 612	64 044	71 173	77 416
18100	老　衰	14 809	15 196	19 677	34 555	57 073	63 916	69 729
18200	乳幼児突然死症候群	238	146	76	63	55	35	55
18300	その他の症状，徴候及び異常臨床所見・異常検査所見で他に分類されないもの	1 453	2 108	3 399	5 994	6 916	7 222	7 632
20000	傷病及び死亡の外因	25 490	24 497	25 605	27 619	26 672	25 944	25 394
20100	不慮の事故	17 094	14 322	15 272	16 757	16 467	16 185	16 240
20101	交通事故	4 375	3 785	3 013	2 351	1 794	1 760	1 613
20102	転倒・転落	2 248	2 447	2 713	3 182	3 426	3 531	3 542
20103	不慮の溺死及び溺水	2 418	2 646	2 818	3 162	3 629	3 573	3 703
20104	不慮の窒息	2 906	3 419	4 261	4 801	4 800	4 592	4 679
20105	煙，火及び火炎への曝露	534	533	621	497	420	373	349
20106	有害物質による不慮の中毒及び有害物質への曝露	172	190	282	304	258	230	207
20107	その他の不慮の事故	4 441	1 302	1 564	2 460	2 140	2 126	2 147
20200	自　殺	7 189	8 595	8 317	8 526	7 542	6 950	6 378
20300	他　殺	314	342	283	205	176	176	142
20400	その他の外因	893	1 238	1 733	2 131	2 487	2 633	2 634
22000	特殊目的用コード	…	…	…	-	-	-	-
22100	重症急性呼吸器症候群〔SARS〕	…	…	…	-	-	-	-

General mortality

性別死亡数及び率（人口10万対）（つづき）
by sex and causes（the condensed list of causes of death for Japan）：Japan－CON.

女
Female

死　亡　率 Death rates							死因簡単分類コード Code[a]	死　因 Causes of death
1995 平成7年	2000 12年	2005 17年	2010 22年	2014 26年	2015 27年	2016 28年		
5.6	7.1	9.2	11.4	12.2	12.3	12.2	14202	慢性腎不全
4.1	4.0	4.5	4.6	4.5	4.4	4.3	14203	詳細不明の腎不全
1.7	2.0	3.4	5.3	7.6	8.0	8.9	14300	その他の腎尿路生殖器系の疾患
0.1	0.1	0.1	0.1	0.1	0.1	0.1	15000	妊娠，分娩及び産じょく
1.0	0.8	0.6	0.4	0.4	0.3	0.4	16000	周産期に発生した病態
0.1	0.1	0.1	0.0	0.0	0.0	0.0	16100	妊娠期間及び胎児発育に関連する障害
0.0	0.0	0.0	-	0.0	0.0	0.0	16200	出産外傷
0.5	0.4	0.3	0.2	0.2	0.2	0.2	16300	周産期に特異的な呼吸障害及び心血管障害
0.1	0.1	0.0	0.0	0.0	0.0	0.0	16400	周産期に特異的な感染症
0.2	0.1	0.1	0.1	0.1	0.1	0.1	16500	胎児及び新生児の出血性障害及び血液障害
0.2	0.1	0.1	0.0	0.1	0.1	0.1	16600	その他の周産期に発生した病態
2.5	2.1	1.8	1.7	1.6	1.7	1.7	17000	先天奇形，変形及び染色体異常
0.1	0.1	0.1	0.1	0.1	0.1	0.1	17100	神経系の先天奇形
1.4	1.1	0.9	0.9	0.8	0.8	0.8	17200	循環器系の先天奇形
1.1	0.9	0.7	0.7	0.5	0.6	0.5	17201	心臓の先天奇形
0.3	0.2	0.2	0.2	0.3	0.3	0.3	17202	その他の循環器系の先天奇形
0.1	0.1	0.1	0.1	0.1	0.1	0.1	17300	消化器系の先天奇形
0.6	0.5	0.5	0.4	0.4	0.4	0.4	17400	その他の先天奇形及び変形
0.3	0.3	0.2	0.3	0.3	0.3	0.3	17500	染色体異常，他に分類されないもの
26.0	27.2	35.8	62.7	99.5	110.7	120.7	18000	症状，徴候及び異常臨床所見・異常検査所見で他に分類されないもの
23.4	23.7	30.5	53.3	88.6	99.4	108.7	18100	老　衰
0.4	0.2	0.1	0.1	0.1	0.1	0.1	18200	乳幼児突然死症候群
2.3	3.3	5.3	9.2	10.7	11.2	11.9	18300	その他の症状，徴候及び異常臨床所見・異常検査所見で他に分類されないもの
40.2	38.2	39.6	42.6	41.4	40.4	39.6	20000	傷病及び死亡の外因
27.0	22.3	23.6	25.9	25.6	25.2	25.3	20100	不慮の事故
6.9	5.9	4.7	3.6	2.8	2.7	2.5	20101	交通事故
3.5	3.8	4.2	4.9	5.3	5.5	5.5	20102	転倒・転落
3.8	4.1	4.4	4.9	5.6	5.6	5.8	20103	不慮の溺死及び溺水
4.6	5.3	6.6	7.4	7.5	7.1	7.3	20104	不慮の窒息
0.8	0.8	1.0	0.8	0.7	0.6	0.5	20105	煙，火及び火炎への曝露
0.3	0.3	0.4	0.5	0.4	0.4	0.3	20106	有害物質による不慮の中毒及び有害物質への曝露
7.0	2.0	2.4	3.8	3.3	3.3	3.3	20107	その他の不慮の事故
11.3	13.4	12.9	13.2	11.7	10.8	9.9	20200	自　殺
0.5	0.5	0.4	0.3	0.3	0.3	0.2	20300	他　殺
1.4	1.9	2.7	3.3	3.9	4.1	4.1	20400	その他の外因
…	…	…	-	-	-	-	22000	特殊目的用コード
…	…	…	-	-	-	-	22100	重症急性呼吸器症候群〔SARS〕

死　亡

表5.14　死因年次推移分類別にみた
Table 5.14　Trends in age-adjusted death rates（per 100,000

死因年次推移分類コード Code[a]	死因[2]・性 Causes of death and sex		1950 昭和25年	1955 30年	1960 35年	1965 40年	1970 45年	1975 50年	1980 55年	1985 60年	1990 平成2年	1995 7年
	死　亡　総　数[3] Deaths Total	男 M.	1 858.6	1 482.0	1 476.1	1 369.9	1 234.6	1 036.5	923.5	812.9	747.9	719.6
		女 F.	1 457.8	1 099.3	1 042.3	931.5	823.3	685.1	579.8	482.9	423.0	384.7
Hi 01	結　　　　核	男 M.	192.5	84.3	64.5	46.9	32.3	19.6	10.8	6.8	4.6	3.2
		女 F.	141.6	52.9	32.2	19.3	11.7	6.5	3.0	1.8	1.1	0.9
Hi 02	悪　性　新　生　物	男 M.	148.2	167.9	188.2	195.6	199.2	198.9	210.9	214.8	215.6	226.1
		女 F.	121.4	125.4	132.0	130.3	126.9	121.1	118.8	113.1	107.7	108.3
Hi 03	糖　　尿　　病	男 M.	4.3	4.2	5.6	8.4	11.5	11.7	9.4	8.5	7.5	10.1
		女 F.	3.8	4.0	5.2	7.4	9.5	9.6	7.7	7.0	5.7	6.6
Hi 04	高　血　圧　性　疾　患	男 M.	32.5	24.3	34.6	39.0	31.7	28.2	18.0	10.8	5.9	4.3
		女 F.	26.6	19.1	27.3	30.7	26.8	24.8	16.3	10.2	5.8	3.9
Hi 05	心疾患（高血圧性を除く）[4]	男 M.	126.2	125.4	153.3	156.0	161.7	150.0	158.0	146.9	139.1	99.7
		女 F.	105.4	96.8	111.9	111.1	114.5	106.3	103.9	94.6	88.5	58.4
Hi 06	脳　血　管　疾　患	男 M.	297.9	302.1	341.1	361.0	333.8	265.0	202.0	134.0	97.9	99.3
		女 F.	236.3	224.8	242.7	243.8	222.6	183.0	140.9	95.3	68.6	64.0
Hi 07	肺　　　　炎	男 M.	73.7	54.2	68.3	57.0	50.5	49.3	48.5	54.4	67.1	60.6
		女 F.	56.0	39.5	45.7	36.3	32.2	30.0	25.2	26.2	30.1	28.5
Hi 08	慢性気管支炎及び肺気腫	男 M.	22.4	11.4	7.8	8.1	9.8	9.3	9.2	10.5	9.9	11.6
		女 F.	12.2	5.4	4.0	3.8	3.6	3.1	2.7	2.7	2.3	2.4
Hi 09	喘　　　　息	男 M.	50.7	34.1	31.1	26.5	18.9	12.2	9.7	7.7	5.8	5.9
		女 F.	28.0	17.2	15.2	12.6	9.2	6.0	4.3	3.6	3.0	3.0
Hi 10	胃潰瘍及び十二指腸潰瘍	男 M.	59.8	39.5	30.2	22.9	17.3	12.4	8.1	4.9	3.3	3.2
		女 F.	22.1	14.3	11.4	8.5	6.8	5.2	3.8	2.8	1.7	1.6
Hi 11	肝　　疾　　患	男 M.	21.6	27.9	30.7	28.8	32.0	30.7	28.5	25.0	21.2	16.4
		女 F.	13.9	17.3	16.9	14.2	14.7	11.7	9.8	9.1	7.9	5.6
Hi 12	腎　　不　　全	男 M.	…	…	…	…	…	…	8.5	11.9	13.1	11.1
		女 F.	…	…	…	…	…	…	6.0	7.9	8.6	6.9
Hi 13	老　　　　衰	男 M.	243.9	198.6	148.8	110.9	72.8	43.2	35.8	22.8	14.4	9.3
		女 F.	216.3	178.2	136.4	109.3	76.5	46.2	37.4	23.0	14.5	9.4
Hi 14	不　慮　の　事　故	男 M.	62.1	63.1	74.9	73.7	74.1	51.2	41.4	38.4	36.5	42.3
		女 F.	20.1	19.2	22.7	22.8	23.3	17.0	13.9	12.5	12.9	18.8
Hi 15	（再掲）交　通　事　故	男 M.	16.2	22.0	35.5	35.9	40.4	25.0	19.2	19.0	18.6	16.5
		女 F.	4.5	5.5	8.8	9.4	11.7	7.0	5.5	5.6	6.1	5.5
Hi 16	自　　　　殺	男 M.	35.1	38.5	30.0	21.8	20.6	24.1	24.3	26.9	20.0	21.3
		女 F.	20.7	22.4	20.6	14.4	14.7	15.6	13.4	12.5	10.8	9.3

注：1）　年齢調整死亡率の基準人口は、昭和60年モデル人口である。なお、計算方法は、68ページ　3）死亡を参照されたい。
　　　2）　表側の死因名等はICD-10の死因年次推移分類による。また、死因の内容の変遷については、74ページの表2.1を参照されたい。
　　　3）　死亡総数には死因年次推移分類以外の死因を含む。
　　　4）　平成7年の心疾患の減少は、新しい死亡診断書（死体検案書）（平成7年1月施行）における「死亡の原因欄には、疾患の終末期の状態としての心不全、呼吸不全等は書かないでください。」という注意書きの、事前周知の影響によるものと考えられる。

General mortality

性別年齢調整死亡率[1]（人口10万対）
population）by sex and causes of death : Japan

2000 12年	2005 17年	2006 18年	2007 19年	2008 20年	2009 21年	2010 22年	2011 23年	2012 24年	2013 25年	2014 26年	2015 27年	2016 28年
634.2	593.2	571.3	561.9	557.4	541.0	544.3	547.6	524.1	510.3	496.7	486.0	477.2
323.9	298.6	289.8	284.7	283.0	272.5	274.9	286.4	270.6	265.4	259.7	255.0	251.3
2.2	1.5	1.4	1.3	1.3	1.1	1.0	1.0	0.9	0.8	0.8	0.7	0.7
0.5	0.4	0.4	0.4	0.4	0.4	0.3	0.3	0.3	0.3	0.3	0.2	0.2
214.0	197.7	193.6	191.5	188.9	183.3	182.4	179.4	175.7	172.5	168.9	165.3	161.7
103.5	97.3	95.8	94.5	94.2	92.2	92.2	91.8	90.3	89.7	89.4	87.7	87.3
7.8	7.3	7.2	7.2	7.1	6.7	6.7	6.7	6.4	5.9	5.7	5.5	5.4
4.4	3.9	3.7	3.6	3.6	3.3	3.3	3.2	3.1	2.8	2.7	2.5	2.4
2.5	2.0	1.9	2.0	2.0	1.9	2.0	2.0	2.0	1.9	1.8	1.7	1.8
2.2	1.6	1.5	1.5	1.4	1.4	1.4	1.4	1.4	1.3	1.2	1.1	1.1
85.8	83.7	79.7	77.0	77.1	74.2	74.2	73.9	72.4	69.1	67.7	65.4	64.5
48.5	45.3	43.6	42.3	41.7	39.6	39.7	39.5	38.7	37.0	35.5	34.2	33.1
74.2	61.9	57.8	55.4	53.6	50.4	49.5	47.3	44.8	42.0	39.8	37.8	36.2
45.7	36.1	33.4	31.6	30.3	28.1	26.9	26.3	24.6	23.3	21.9	21.0	20.0
53.1	51.8	48.8	48.2	48.2	44.8	46.0	46.1	43.7	41.8	39.3	38.3	36.9
23.3	21.6	20.9	20.2	20.3	18.6	18.9	19.2	18.1	17.3	16.3	15.8	15.0
9.5	7.7	7.0	6.7	6.3	5.8	5.6	5.1	4.7	4.3	3.9	3.5	3.2
1.6	1.2	1.1	1.0	0.9	0.9	0.8	0.8	0.7	0.6	0.6	0.6	0.5
2.8	1.6	1.3	1.1	1.0	0.8	0.8	0.7	0.6	0.5	0.4	0.4	0.4
1.6	0.9	0.8	0.8	0.7	0.6	0.5	0.5	0.5	0.4	0.4	0.4	0.3
2.6	1.9	1.9	1.7	1.6	1.6	1.6	1.5	1.4	1.3	1.2	1.1	1.1
1.1	0.8	0.7	0.7	0.7	0.6	0.6	0.6	0.6	0.5	0.4	0.4	0.4
14.0	12.6	12.4	11.9	11.6	11.3	11.2	11.0	10.7	10.4	9.9	9.8	9.7
4.4	4.2	3.9	4.0	4.0	3.8	3.8	3.7	3.5	3.5	3.5	3.5	3.5
9.2	8.8	8.7	8.4	8.5	8.4	8.3	8.4	8.2	7.9	7.6	7.3	7.2
5.7	5.3	5.2	5.0	5.0	4.7	4.8	4.7	4.6	4.4	4.1	4.0	3.7
6.3	5.6	5.5	5.6	6.3	6.2	6.9	7.5	8.3	9.0	9.2	10.1	10.5
6.8	6.6	6.6	6.9	7.7	7.9	8.9	9.7	10.8	11.9	12.3	13.4	14.0
33.6	28.9	26.6	25.0	24.5	23.5	24.2	33.0	22.3	21.1	20.3	19.3	18.6
12.6	11.3	10.6	10.4	9.9	9.6	10.0	19.3	9.4	8.9	8.5	8.0	7.7
13.2	9.7	8.6	7.5	6.9	6.5	6.3	6.0	5.5	5.2	4.9	4.8	4.5
4.4	3.2	2.8	2.7	2.2	2.1	2.2	2.0	1.9	1.7	1.5	1.5	1.4
30.7	31.6	30.3	30.9	30.5	31.5	29.8	28.3	26.4	25.9	24.2	23.0	21.1
10.7	10.7	10.9	11.2	11.3	11.1	10.9	11.8	10.2	10.1	9.7	8.9	8.2

Note : a) Code see page 74.

死 亡

〔性・年齢（５歳階級）別にみた死因〕

〔Causes of death by sex and
age（5-year age groups）〕

表5.15　性・年齢別にみた死因年次推移分類
Table 5.15　Trends in deaths and death rates (per 100,000

死亡総数[1]
Deaths Total

死 亡 数

年　　齢 Age	1950 昭和25年	1955 30年	1960 35年	1965 40年	1970 45年	1975 50年	1980 55年	1985 60年
								総　数
総数 Total	904 876	693 523	706 599	700 438	712 962	702 275	722 801	752 283
0〜4歳	222 903	99 399	64 692	42 572	32 879	25 884	16 298	10 834
5〜9 Years	19 774	14 240	8 209	4 533	3 809	3 205	2 773	1 791
10〜14	10 212	6 548	5 545	3 621	2 625	2 045	1 627	1 649
15〜19	21 222	10 992	9 829	7 374	6 926	4 750	4 043	4 212
20〜24	35 871	19 383	14 537	10 401	10 380	7 336	4 850	4 669
25〜29	32 906	19 362	15 735	11 168	10 371	8 864	6 273	4 725
30〜34	26 416	16 659	15 575	13 449	11 463	9 787	8 772	6 733
35〜39	28 174	16 452	15 518	16 099	16 121	12 810	11 462	11 127
40〜44	29 334	20 742	17 427	17 455	20 458	19 787	16 124	15 884
45〜49	33 919	26 955	25 676	22 542	23 148	26 002	26 126	22 707
50〜54	40 380	36 042	35 175	33 232	29 580	29 358	34 173	35 851
55〜59	48 436	44 993	48 623	45 941	44 464	37 320	38 000	45 575
60〜64	61 352	55 659	61 896	64 302	61 959	55 304	48 885	50 845
65〜69	75 817	69 952	74 289	81 000	85 239	76 624	73 654	64 730
70〜74	84 089	80 172	89 301	92 415	102 131	100 941	99 336	95 991
75〜79	67 055	77 338	90 324	97 834	101 517	109 869	120 044	121 250
80〜84	42 750	49 530	70 775	78 785	83 478	92 528	110 279	123 573
85〜89	18 202	22 255	32 886	43 130	47 008	55 663	67 292	86 351
90〜94	4 974	5 890	9 172	12 684	16 200	19 692	26 830	34 768
95〜99	700	857	1 294	1 771	2 587	3 705	5 135	7 772
100〜	55	77	99	106	202	363	497	825
不詳 Not stated	335	26	22	24	417	438	328	421
								男
総数	467 073	365 246	377 526	378 716	387 880	377 827	390 644	407 769
0〜4歳	118 289	53 699	36 227	24 383	19 085	14 904	9 352	6 042
5〜9	10 587	8 172	4 787	2 825	2 384	2 035	1 748	1 155
10〜14	5 048	3 610	3 263	2 260	1 652	1 262	1 030	1 011
15〜19	10 655	6 399	6 168	5 026	4 963	3 470	2 967	3 179
20〜24	18 652	11 335	8 828	6 708	6 813	4 850	3 420	3 397
25〜29	15 891	10 740	9 356	6 744	6 503	5 580	4 095	3 167
30〜34	12 541	8 202	8 820	8 287	7 170	6 083	5 546	4 237
35〜39	14 131	8 017	8 149	9 747	10 349	8 137	7 302	7 110
40〜44	15 679	10 847	9 298	9 827	12 836	12 971	10 512	10 234
45〜49	19 144	15 238	14 165	12 610	13 261	16 696	17 601	15 063
50〜54	23 308	21 269	20 848	19 393	17 013	16 991	22 341	24 347
55〜59	28 706	27 138	30 157	28 288	26 712	22 026	22 980	30 747
60〜64	35 028	33 421	38 199	40 357	38 080	33 116	29 212	30 884
65〜69	41 034	39 908	44 071	49 032	52 135	46 112	43 901	38 240
70〜74	42 419	41 481	48 424	52 399	58 277	57 697	57 166	55 100
75〜79	30 634	35 900	42 750	48 811	52 086	56 734	63 893	65 593
80〜84	17 008	20 222	29 362	32 748	36 421	41 379	51 097	59 125
85〜89	6 344	7 572	11 678	15 111	16 602	20 715	26 362	34 749
90〜94	1 523	1 828	2 626	3 704	4 538	5 705	8 497	11 718
95〜99	204	209	310	412	626	899	1 246	2 127
100〜	16	19	23	25	38	82	100	192
不詳	232	20	17	19	336	383	276	352
								女
総数	437 803	328 277	329 073	321 722	325 082	324 448	332 157	344 514
0〜4歳	104 614	45 700	28 465	18 189	13 794	10 980	6 946	4 792
5〜9	9 187	6 068	3 422	1 708	1 425	1 170	1 025	636
10〜14	5 164	2 938	2 282	1 361	973	783	597	638
15〜19	10 567	4 593	3 661	2 348	1 963	1 280	1 076	1 033
20〜24	17 219	8 048	5 709	3 693	3 567	2 486	1 430	1 272
25〜29	17 015	8 622	6 379	4 424	3 868	3 284	2 178	1 558
30〜34	13 875	8 457	6 755	5 162	4 293	3 704	3 226	2 496
35〜39	14 043	8 435	7 369	6 352	5 772	4 673	4 160	4 017
40〜44	13 655	9 895	8 129	7 628	7 622	6 816	5 612	5 650
45〜49	14 775	11 717	11 511	9 932	9 887	9 306	8 525	7 644
50〜54	17 072	14 773	14 327	13 839	12 567	12 367	11 832	11 504
55〜59	19 730	17 855	18 466	17 653	17 752	15 294	15 020	14 828
60〜64	26 324	22 238	23 697	23 945	23 879	22 188	19 673	19 961
65〜69	34 783	30 044	30 218	31 968	33 104	30 512	29 753	26 490
70〜74	41 670	38 691	40 877	40 016	43 854	43 244	42 170	40 891
75〜79	36 421	41 438	47 574	49 023	49 431	53 135	56 151	55 657
80〜84	25 742	29 308	41 413	46 037	47 057	51 149	59 182	64 448
85〜89	11 858	14 683	21 208	28 019	30 406	34 948	40 930	51 602
90〜94	3 451	4 062	6 546	8 980	11 662	13 987	18 333	23 050
95〜99	496	648	984	1 359	1 961	2 806	3 889	5 645
100〜	39	58	76	81	164	281	397	633
不詳	103	6	5	5	81	55	52	69

注：死因名等はICD-10の死因年次推移分類による。また、死因の内容の変遷については、74ページの表2.1を参照されたい。
1）死亡総数には死因年次推移分類以外の死因を含む。
2）死亡率については、1950年〜2000年の90〜94歳は、90歳以上の数値である。
3）Hi06脳血管疾患の昭和25年は、B46.b（352の一部、B22の後遺症及び1年以上経過したもの）を含むため、昭和25年報告書とは一致しない。

228

General mortality

別死亡数及び率（人口10万対）
population）by sex, age and causes of death : Japan

Deaths

1990 平成2年	1995 7年	2000 12年	2005 17年	2010 22年	2014 26年	2015 27年	2016 28年	年　　齢 Age
Total								
820 305	922 139	961 653	1 083 796	1 197 012	1 273 004	1 290 444	1 307 748	総数 Total
7 983	7 040	5 269	4 102	3 382	2 883	2 692	2 618	0〜4歳
1 377	1 235	738	655	480	460	452	391	5〜9 Years
1 242	1 184	744	590	553	501	470	440	10〜14
4 353	3 362	2 397	1 802	1 422	1 205	1 220	1 166	15〜19
4 795	5 087	4 035	3 370	2 753	2 320	2 101	2 083	20〜24
4 277	4 596	4 817	4 170	3 437	2 873	2 616	2 479	25〜29
5 038	5 129	5 596	5 952	4 837	3 896	3 549	3 354	30〜34
8 551	6 839	7 046	7 469	7 555	5 879	5 402	5 193	35〜39
15 311	12 814	10 479	10 238	10 162	10 065	9 770	9 263	40〜44
21 728	24 136	19 736	15 754	14 532	13 726	13 540	13 923	45〜49
30 258	32 946	35 843	28 964	22 014	19 841	19 717	19 480	50〜54
47 541	44 732	45 992	49 579	39 326	30 315	28 735	28 331	55〜59
62 728	68 310	60 680	62 258	66 096	57 310	52 217	48 223	60〜64
69 931	89 089	89 058	80 829	83 087	85 193	88 287	93 505	65〜69
89 813	102 443	116 528	120 825	110 248	114 866	114 323	107 826	70〜74
127 523	125 428	131 000	159 362	163 088	156 782	153 465	153 008	75〜79
139 549	157 863	147 060	174 185	211 257	221 045	222 455	223 763	80〜84
111 120	134 363	148 980	165 385	207 287	249 725	256 258	260 536	85〜89
52 814	72 295	90 913	127 573	151 959	186 121	197 174	209 379	90〜94
12 355	19 831	29 230	50 503	75 386	84 117	90 723	95 935	95〜99
1 569	2 780	4 789	9 578	17 513	23 411	24 823	26 427	100〜
449	637	723	653	638	470	455	425	不詳 Not stated
Male								
443 718	501 276	525 903	584 970	633 700	660 334	666 707	674 733	総数
4 532	3 929	2 933	2 291	1 873	1 542	1 473	1 351	0〜4歳
844	752	438	409	261	276	253	229	5〜9
760	716	493	361	350	318	267	254	10〜14
3 204	2 413	1 721	1 220	941	840	836	816	15〜19
3 466	3 640	2 875	2 303	1 962	1 665	1 515	1 471	20〜24
2 916	3 203	3 271	2 887	2 412	1 961	1 786	1 713	25〜29
3 264	3 297	3 749	3 915	3 177	2 574	2 325	2 226	30〜34
5 449	4 413	4 621	4 915	4 867	3 715	3 455	3 282	35〜39
9 769	8 236	6 840	6 806	6 629	6 449	6 214	5 835	40〜44
14 218	15 616	13 141	10 577	9 566	8 750	8 656	8 888	45〜49
20 161	21 905	24 103	19 546	14 638	12 954	12 838	12 526	50〜54
32 925	30 491	31 848	34 233	27 134	20 277	19 460	19 068	55〜59
42 742	47 188	42 214	43 403	46 155	39 570	36 141	33 464	60〜64
42 664	59 828	60 962	55 261	57 468	59 068	61 424	65 077	65〜69
51 737	60 927	76 413	80 198	73 470	77 300	76 916	72 534	70〜74
69 320	68 504	73 947	99 338	102 673	99 061	96 964	97 102	75〜79
67 916	77 924	73 533	89 502	119 801	125 619	126 762	127 978	80〜84
45 623	56 495	62 730	70 110	89 905	116 956	120 810	124 528	85〜89
17 914	24 961	30 830	42 590	49 199	58 659	64 596	70 767	90〜94
3 547	5 655	7 642	12 825	17 849	19 021	19 914	21 273	95〜99
367	639	975	1 736	2 860	3 390	3 743	4 015	100〜
380	544	624	544	510	369	359	336	不詳
Female								
376 587	420 863	435 750	498 826	563 312	612 670	623 737	633 015	総数
3 451	3 111	2 336	1 811	1 509	1 341	1 219	1 267	0〜4歳
533	483	300	246	219	184	199	162	5〜9
482	468	251	229	203	183	203	186	10〜14
1 149	949	676	582	481	365	384	350	15〜19
1 329	1 447	1 160	1 067	791	655	586	612	20〜24
1 361	1 393	1 546	1 283	1 025	912	830	766	25〜29
1 774	1 832	1 847	2 037	1 660	1 322	1 224	1 128	30〜34
3 102	2 426	2 425	2 554	2 688	2 164	1 947	1 911	35〜39
5 542	4 578	3 639	3 432	3 533	3 616	3 556	3 428	40〜44
7 510	8 520	6 595	5 177	4 966	4 976	4 884	5 035	45〜49
10 097	11 041	11 740	9 418	7 376	6 887	6 879	6 954	50〜54
14 616	14 241	14 144	15 346	12 192	10 038	9 275	9 263	55〜59
19 986	21 122	18 466	18 855	19 941	17 740	16 076	14 759	60〜64
27 267	29 261	28 096	25 568	25 619	26 125	26 863	28 428	65〜69
38 076	41 516	40 115	40 627	36 778	37 566	37 407	35 292	70〜74
58 203	56 924	57 053	60 024	60 415	57 721	56 501	55 906	75〜79
71 633	79 939	73 527	84 683	91 456	95 426	95 693	95 785	80〜84
65 497	77 868	86 250	95 275	117 382	132 769	135 448	136 008	85〜89
34 900	47 334	60 083	84 983	102 760	127 462	132 578	138 612	90〜94
8 808	14 176	21 588	37 678	57 537	65 096	70 809	74 662	95〜99
1 202	2 141	3 814	7 842	14 653	20 021	21 080	22 412	100〜
69	93	99	109	128	101	96	89	不詳

死　亡

表 5.15　性・年齢別にみた死因年次推移分類
Table 5.15　Trends in deaths and death rates (per 100,000

死亡総数 1)
Deaths Total

死　亡　率

年　齢 Age	1950 昭和25年	1955 30年	1960 35年	1965 40年	1970 45年	1975 50年	1980 55年	1985 60年
								総　数
総数 Total	1 087.6	776.8	756.4	712.7	691.4	631.2	621.4	625.5
0～4歳	1 989.2	1 074.8	824.7	523.4	375.9	260.5	192.7	145.3
5～9 Years	207.7	129.0	89.2	57.8	47.0	36.1	27.8	21.1
10～14	117.4	68.9	50.3	39.4	33.7	24.9	18.3	16.5
15～19	247.7	127.4	105.6	68.0	77.0	60.2	49.2	47.2
20～24	464.3	230.7	174.8	114.7	98.0	81.4	62.3	57.1
25～29	532.0	254.6	191.7	133.5	114.8	82.6	69.9	60.9
30～34	507.8	272.3	207.2	162.9	137.6	106.5	81.9	74.5
35～39	558.1	321.6	257.0	214.7	197.3	152.9	125.3	104.2
40～44	654.3	419.4	347.2	292.8	280.0	241.6	194.4	175.6
45～49	847.0	617.2	533.1	458.0	396.4	354.8	324.2	277.1
50～54	1 191.6	936.3	837.2	713.4	619.2	510.8	476.6	455.6
55～59	1 761.9	1 403.6	1 335.4	1 147.9	1 010.2	802.9	680.7	654.3
60～64	2 663.0	2 229.4	2 111.3	1 922.6	1 670.1	1 297.2	1 100.4	948.0
65～69	4 281.7	3 556.2	3 438.7	3 161.2	2 866.4	2 230.4	1 865.8	1 554.0
70～74	6 561.2	5 756.7	5 710.5	5 297.3	4 800.0	3 931.4	3 297.9	2 717.5
75～79	9 779.7	8 831.6	9 461.2	8 927.2	8 019.4	6 712.6	5 911.1	4 980.5
80～84	15 501.3	13 110.6	14 655.5	14 918.1	12 872.9	11 461.4	10 106.8	8 540.5
85～89	23 025.1	19 985.6	21 106.1	21 656.2	20 498.4	18 042.0	16 440.8	14 725.6
90～94 2)	35 029.0	29 973.2	32 823.8	28 683.1	28 872.3	29 126.2	27 253.3	23 364.8
95～99	…	…	…	…	…	…	…	…
100～	…	…	…	…	…	…	…	…
								男
総数	1 144.5	832.7	822.9	785.0	766.6	690.4	682.9	690.6
0～4歳	2 068.5	1 136.2	902.8	587.6	425.8	292.6	215.6	158.8
5～9	219.4	145.0	101.8	70.7	57.6	44.7	34.2	26.6
10～14	114.7	75.0	58.1	48.4	41.5	30.0	22.6	19.9
15～19	246.8	147.4	131.9	91.7	109.4	86.5	70.7	69.8
20～24	486.3	270.1	214.0	149.2	129.0	107.0	87.0	81.4
25～29	563.1	284.5	228.5	162.2	144.8	103.5	90.7	80.7
30～34	531.3	293.2	235.4	199.8	172.4	132.3	102.9	93.3
35～39	594.7	345.6	294.9	260.1	252.2	194.2	159.8	131.9
40～44	713.0	466.6	408.8	360.0	351.9	315.8	254.0	227.7
45～49	948.3	713.6	627.7	566.8	499.1	458.8	438.2	371.7
50～54	1 355.7	1 102.4	1 021.6	892.5	795.0	654.2	632.7	624.6
55～59	2 082.2	1 688.0	1 673.4	1 465.3	1 316.7	1 070.5	921.4	906.7
60～64	3 156.9	2 724.3	2 657.2	2 483.4	2 180.9	1 720.9	1 511.3	1 314.9
65～69	5 155.5	4 342.3	4 291.3	4 022.8	3 741.9	2 949.0	2 531.1	2 159.4
70～74	7 851.1	6 986.0	6 981.9	6 641.2	6 081.1	5 045.4	4 356.8	3 707.7
75～79	11 443.8	10 495.3	11 348.4	10 802.0	9 813.4	8 267.6	7 553.8	6 581.0
80～84	17 792.8	15 182.6	17 359.2	17 517.4	15 117.7	13 470.6	12 263.1	10 799.1
85～89	25 886.5	22 368.0	24 231.7	25 131.8	23 239.7	20 562.4	19 034.3	18 136.2
90～94 2)	41 011.8	35 271.9	35 823.2	30 164.6	29 773.4	30 858.0	29 681.6	25 429.3
95～99	…	…	…	…	…	…	…	…
100～	…	…	…	…	…	…	…	…
								女
総数	1 032.8	722.8	692.2	643.1	619.0	574.0	561.8	562.7
0～4歳	1 906.6	1 010.7	742.8	456.6	323.5	226.8	168.5	131.2
5～9	195.6	112.2	76.0	44.3	36.0	27.1	21.1	15.3
10～14	120.1	62.6	42.3	30.2	25.4	19.5	13.8	13.1
15～19	248.6	107.2	79.1	43.7	44.0	33.0	26.8	23.7
20～24	442.7	191.3	136.1	80.8	67.1	55.5	37.1	31.8
25～29	505.9	225.2	155.0	105.2	85.1	61.5	48.8	40.7
30～34	488.2	254.8	179.1	125.6	103.0	80.6	60.6	55.6
35～39	525.6	301.7	225.0	169.3	141.9	111.6	90.8	76.0
40～44	597.8	377.6	296.2	236.0	208.3	167.0	135.0	124.1
45～49	744.1	525.0	449.7	368.2	310.6	252.2	211.0	184.6
50～54	1 022.6	769.3	663.1	556.9	476.5	392.6	325.1	289.7
55～59	1 439.8	1 117.5	1 004.1	852.2	748.1	590.4	486.3	414.9
60～64	2 204.1	1 751.3	1 586.1	1 392.7	1 215.9	948.6	783.9	663.0
65～69	3 568.2	2 866.9	2 666.1	2 379.6	2 094.6	1 630.1	1 344.4	1 106.4
70～74	5 621.1	4 843.1	4 697.2	4 187.7	3 750.1	3 036.7	2 480.6	1 998.4
75～79	8 713.9	7 765.1	8 231.2	7 611.8	6 724.1	5 590.0	4 738.6	3 871.3
80～84	14 285.7	11 982.3	13 198.1	13 493.9	11 546.0	10 227.3	8 774.7	7 165.7
85～89	21 739.4	18 945.1	19 706.4	20 153.1	19 258.1	16 820.0	15 114.3	13 067.1
90～94 2)	32 928.5	28 149.7	31 788.4	28 134.0	28 546.3	28 499.9	26 316.5	22 490.8
95～99	…	…	…	…	…	…	…	…
100～	…	…	…	…	…	…	…	…

General mortality

別死亡数及び率（人口10万対）（つづき）
population） by sex, age and causes of death : Japan－CON.

Death rates

1990 平成2年	1995 7年	2000 12年	2005 17年	2010 22年	2014 26年	2015 27年	2016 28年	年　　齢 Age
Total								
668.4	741.9	765.6	858.8	947.1	1 014.9	1 029.7	1 046.0	総数 Total
123.4	118.3	89.9	73.9	64.4	55.9	54.5	53.5	0～4歳
18.5	19.0	12.3	11.1	8.6	8.7	8.6	7.5	5～9 Years
14.6	15.9	11.4	9.8	9.4	8.8	8.4	8.0	10～14
43.7	39.6	32.2	27.6	23.6	20.3	20.4	19.6	15～19
55.0	52.1	48.6	46.9	43.7	38.7	35.7	35.3	20～24
53.6	53.4	50.0	51.5	48.0	44.5	41.6	40.4	25～29
65.3	64.4	65.0	62.0	58.9	53.5	49.4	47.7	30～34
95.6	88.7	88.3	86.9	78.0	69.1	65.6	65.5	35～39
144.2	143.7	136.0	128.5	117.5	104.4	100.9	97.0	40～44
241.7	228.9	223.1	205.9	182.4	161.9	157.1	152.5	45～49
375.0	371.5	344.9	331.3	289.3	258.1	249.3	250.3	50～54
616.3	565.3	528.7	484.9	454.3	399.9	382.1	379.7	55～59
931.3	917.4	786.9	730.1	657.4	642.5	615.1	595.7	60～64
1 373.7	1 397.9	1 255.8	1 088.9	1 009.5	935.5	909.2	914.6	65～69
2 357.4	2 191.5	1 978.4	1 821.1	1 577.8	1 455.3	1 474.8	1 462.5	70～74
4 230.4	3 827.8	3 164.6	3 029.1	2 730.8	2 510.9	2 424.6	2 354.0	75～79
7 618.5	6 882.0	5 635.6	5 109.4	4 841.7	4 552.9	4 438.4	4 332.0	80～84
13 341.6	11 847.5	9 735.1	8 947.0	8 473.8	8 177.0	8 138.1	7 974.5	85～89
23 067.3	21 468.2	17 836.3	15 167.7	14 806.4	14 295.0	14 502.5	14 195.2	90～94²⁾
…	…	…	23 894.8	25 328.5	23 965.0	25 148.0	25 113.9	95～99
…	…	…	37 771.1	39 892.0	39 018.3	40 201.1	40 656.9	100～
Male								
736.5	822.9	855.3	949.4	1 029.2	1 081.8	1 092.6	1 108.5	総数
136.6	129.0	97.7	80.6	69.6	58.3	58.3	53.9	0～4歳
22.2	22.6	14.3	13.5	9.2	10.3	9.4	8.5	5～9
17.4	18.9	14.8	11.8	11.6	11.0	9.4	9.1	10～14
62.7	55.4	45.2	36.4	30.4	27.7	27.2	26.7	15～19
78.1	73.1	67.6	62.4	60.8	54.1	50.3	48.6	20～24
72.3	73.3	66.8	70.1	66.2	59.4	55.6	54.8	25～29
83.9	81.7	85.9	80.5	76.0	69.5	63.7	62.2	30～34
121.1	113.5	114.5	113.1	98.8	85.8	82.4	81.4	35～39
183.2	183.8	176.2	169.3	151.3	131.7	126.2	120.2	40～44
317.9	295.2	296.2	275.6	238.2	204.5	198.3	192.1	45～49
505.2	498.6	464.7	448.1	384.5	335.6	322.4	319.6	50～54
870.7	784.7	745.0	675.9	631.5	538.0	519.0	512.0	55～59
1 321.5	1 311.6	1 128.7	1 046.2	934.9	903.6	864.3	838.6	60～64
1 948.7	2 002.8	1 818.3	1 559.7	1 460.9	1 345.2	1 307.1	1 315.6	65～69
3 323.7	3 154.7	2 865.5	2 637.3	2 270.9	2 104.0	2 131.4	2 111.2	70～74
5 793.4	5 461.1	4 561.5	4 401.7	3 959.4	3 591.8	3 454.8	3 354.6	75～79
10 010.3	9 484.5	8 052.4	7 328.5	7 006.3	6 481.9	6 307.1	6 124.0	80～84
16 535.9	15 648.6	13 163.8	12 638.9	12 030.9	11 388.1	11 340.4	11 144.9	85～89
26 796.0	26 734.7	22 373.4	20 217.3	20 252.2	18 861.4	19 239.9	18 771.1	90～94²⁾
…	…	…	30 937.2	31 876.6	30 679.0	31 376.4	31 750.7	95～99
…	…	…	46 157.9	48 813.8	42 375.0	44 767.4	44 611.1	100～
Female								
602.8	664.0	679.5	772.3	869.2	951.5	970.1	986.7	総数
109.5	107.2	81.7	66.9	58.8	53.4	50.5	53.0	0～4歳
14.7	15.2	10.3	8.6	8.1	7.2	7.7	6.3	5～9
11.6	12.9	7.9	7.8	7.1	6.6	7.5	7.0	10～14
23.6	22.9	18.7	18.4	16.4	12.6	13.2	12.1	15～19
31.0	30.2	28.7	30.5	25.7	22.5	20.4	21.3	20～24
34.5	32.8	32.7	32.2	29.2	28.9	26.9	25.5	25～29
46.4	46.6	43.5	43.1	41.2	37.0	34.7	32.6	30～34
69.8	63.5	61.5	60.2	56.5	51.7	48.1	49.1	35～39
104.9	103.2	95.2	86.9	82.8	76.2	74.6	73.0	40～44
166.2	162.1	149.6	135.8	125.7	118.5	114.8	111.8	45～49
247.6	246.8	225.6	214.9	194.1	179.9	175.2	180.0	50～54
371.7	353.7	319.7	297.4	279.7	263.5	246.0	247.8	55～59
570.8	548.9	464.9	430.7	389.6	390.6	373.2	359.6	60～64
939.7	864.2	751.5	659.0	596.3	554.0	536.1	538.8	65～69
1 689.8	1 513.4	1 244.5	1 130.4	980.2	890.2	902.9	896.4	70～74
3 201.6	2 814.8	2 265.4	1 998.0	1 787.9	1 655.3	1 603.9	1 550.6	75～79
6 211.4	5 429.7	4 334.5	3 870.6	3 434.2	3 272.5	3 187.4	3 114.3	80～84
11 759.2	10 072.4	8 184.7	7 364.1	6 909.3	6 546.8	6 500.8	6 326.7	85～89
21 606.0	19 574.7	16 310.0	13 480.3	13 117.6	12 874.9	12 949.0	12 624.0	90～94²⁾
…	…	…	22 176.4	23 811.1	22 524.6	23 818.2	23 627.2	95～99
…	…	…	36 310.6	38 518.1	39 256.9	39 486.0	39 319.3	100～

死　亡

表 5.15　性・年齢別にみた死因年次推移分類
Table 5.15　Trends in deaths and death rates (per 100,000

Hi01　結　核
Tuberculosis

死　亡　数

年　齢 Age	1950 昭和25年	1955 30年	1960 35年	1965 40年	1970 45年	1975 50年	1980 55年	1985 60年
								総　数
総数　Total	121 769	46 735	31 959	22 366	15 899	10 567	6 439	4 692
0〜4歳	7 079	1 458	407	117	63	22	8	3
5〜9 Years	2 958	646	158	34	14	3	-	-
10〜14	2 422	601	195	52	14	3	-	2
15〜19	9 764	1 570	433	122	41	13	3	2
20〜24	19 643	3 647	1 024	327	122	39	14	3
25〜29	18 123	5 446	2 069	672	210	79	28	12
30〜34	12 806	4 972	2 825	1 196	433	142	57	21
35〜39	11 081	3 973	2 847	1 711	781	282	114	45
40〜44	8 831	3 854	2 548	1 777	1 059	508	203	102
45〜49	7 400	3 793	2 732	1 630	1 118	725	348	169
50〜54	6 390	3 752	2 860	1 963	1 210	765	519	293
55〜59	5 429	3 548	3 075	2 244	1 480	889	554	421
60〜64	4 439	3 337	3 107	2 588	1 826	1 121	620	481
65〜69	3 020	2 884	2 934	2 661	2 383	1 474	939	588
70〜74	1 570	1 975	2 504	2 423	2 304	1 713	1 032	719
75〜79	593	960	1 568	1 814	1 634	1 542	1 062	866
80〜84	160	257	537	801	867	861	658	606
85〜89	28	44	118	207	281	306	215	283
90〜94	10	16	17	24	48	62	61	64
95〜99	1	1	1	2	2	4	1	7
100〜	-	-	-	-	-	1	1	-
不詳 Not stated	22	1	-	1	9	13	2	7
								男
総数	65 089	26 601	19 769	14 781	10 914	7 406	4 715	3 442
0〜4歳	3 548	717	199	66	25	10	4	-
5〜9	1 393	337	75	20	6	2	-	-
10〜14	854	240	88	22	11	1	-	-
15〜19	4 119	658	207	66	25	5	2	-
20〜24	9 765	1 701	440	146	69	19	7	3
25〜29	8 911	2 736	1 012	308	97	44	15	6
30〜34	6 462	2 444	1 483	656	227	72	37	17
35〜39	6 168	2 056	1 510	954	457	170	63	25
40〜44	5 348	2 229	1 432	1 028	628	324	136	72
45〜49	4 642	2 395	1 691	1 027	693	475	247	125
50〜54	4 111	2 501	1 935	1 343	788	529	388	218
55〜59	3 508	2 373	2 155	1 640	1 068	622	397	315
60〜64	2 873	2 246	2 206	1 902	1 375	829	458	353
65〜69	1 938	1 928	2 103	1 974	1 827	1 096	710	429
70〜74	987	1 284	1 778	1 730	1 670	1 266	807	554
75〜79	335	581	1 050	1 251	1 174	1 108	806	659
80〜84	92	144	331	507	586	600	457	427
85〜89	12	21	67	124	155	184	142	180
90〜94	6	9	7	15	23	32	36	46
95〜99	1	-	-	1	2	4	1	6
100〜	-	-	-	-	-	1	1	-
不詳	16	1	-	1	8	13	2	7
								女
総数	56 680	20 134	12 190	7 585	4 985	3 161	1 724	1 250
0〜4歳	3 531	741	208	51	38	12	4	3
5〜9	1 565	309	83	14	8	1	-	-
10〜14	1 568	361	107	30	3	2	-	2
15〜19	5 645	912	226	56	16	8	1	2
20〜24	9 878	1 946	584	181	53	20	7	-
25〜29	9 212	2 710	1 057	364	113	35	13	6
30〜34	6 344	2 528	1 342	540	206	70	20	4
35〜39	4 913	1 917	1 337	757	324	112	51	20
40〜44	3 483	1 625	1 116	749	431	184	67	30
45〜49	2 758	1 398	1 041	603	425	250	101	44
50〜54	2 279	1 251	925	620	422	236	131	75
55〜59	1 921	1 175	920	604	412	267	157	106
60〜64	1 566	1 091	901	686	451	292	162	128
65〜69	1 082	956	831	687	556	378	229	159
70〜74	583	691	726	693	634	447	225	165
75〜79	258	379	518	563	460	434	256	207
80〜84	68	113	206	294	281	261	201	179
85〜89	16	23	51	83	126	122	73	103
90〜94	4	7	10	9	25	30	25	18
95〜99	-	1	1	1	1	-	1	1
100〜	-	-	-	-	-	-	-	-
不詳	6	-	-	-	1	-	-	-

232

General mortality

別死亡数及び率（人口10万対）（つづき）
population）by sex, age and causes of death : Japan－CON.

Deaths

1990 平成2年	1995 7年	2000 12年	2005 17年	2010 22年	2014 26年	2015 27年	2016 28年	年齢 Age
Total								
3 664	3 178	2 656	2 296	2 129	2 100	1 956	1 892	総数 Total
-	1	1	-	-	-	-	1	0～4歳
1	-	-	-	-	-	-	-	5～9 Years
-	-	1	-	-	-	-	-	10～14
1	-	-	-	-	-	1	-	15～19
7	5	1	2	1	1	-	-	20～24
8	4	4	2	1	-	1	1	25～29
19	16	9	5	4	1	1	2	30～34
33	18	17	6	9	2	4	4	35～39
63	40	22	7	7	10	6	3	40～44
111	81	55	27	14	5	14	8	45～49
174	135	101	61	23	13	7	14	50～54
245	181	147	112	53	25	20	12	55～59
373	283	141	90	77	60	43	30	60～64
475	384	242	138	104	82	70	85	65～69
528	490	367	203	158	141	107	89	70～74
638	524	421	415	272	233	199	185	75～79
582	526	496	515	483	436	376	359	80～84
282	339	376	400	518	597	574	534	85～89
96	122	195	232	287	370	398	413	90～94
15	20	46	67	102	107	117	138	95～99
1	-	9	9	13	15	17	12	100～
12	9	5	5	3	2	1	2	不詳 Not stated
Male								
2 745	2 267	1 876	1 579	1 338	1 251	1 169	1 133	総数
-	-	-	-	-	-	-	1	0～4歳
1	-	-	-	-	-	-	-	5～9
-	-	1	-	-	-	-	-	10～14
-	-	-	-	-	-	-	-	15～19
6	3	-	2	1	1	-	-	20～24
5	4	2	1	1	-	1	1	25～29
13	10	6	3	4	-	1	2	30～34
22	15	16	5	8	2	2	2	35～39
51	33	20	4	5	8	5	-	40～44
93	76	54	25	11	5	14	8	45～49
142	117	91	52	18	10	7	12	50～54
199	142	137	103	48	20	13	12	55～59
284	219	112	78	67	54	38	24	60～64
354	276	188	107	74	62	59	73	65～69
395	352	273	151	112	98	81	69	70～74
494	361	304	285	179	151	135	127	75～79
428	347	315	354	306	252	242	214	80～84
184	222	228	237	291	343	321	314	85～89
58	67	100	128	150	194	198	211	90～94
3	14	22	38	53	48	48	58	95～99
1	-	2	1	7	1	5	4	100～
12	9	5	5	3	2	-	1	不詳
Female								
919	911	780	717	791	849	787	759	総数
-	1	1	-	-	-	-	-	0～4歳
-	-	-	-	-	-	-	-	5～9
-	-	-	-	-	-	-	-	10～14
1	-	-	-	-	-	1	-	15～19
1	2	1	-	-	-	-	-	20～24
3	2	2	1	-	-	-	-	25～29
6	6	3	2	-	1	1	-	30～34
11	3	1	1	1	-	2	2	35～39
12	7	2	3	2	2	1	3	40～44
18	5	1	2	3	-	-	-	45～49
32	18	10	9	5	3	-	2	50～54
46	39	10	9	5	5	7	-	55～59
89	64	29	12	10	6	5	6	60～64
121	108	54	31	30	20	11	12	65～69
133	138	94	52	46	43	26	20	70～74
144	163	117	130	93	82	64	58	75～79
154	179	181	161	177	184	134	145	80～84
98	117	148	163	227	254	253	220	85～89
38	55	95	104	137	176	200	202	90～94
12	6	24	29	49	59	69	80	95～99
-	-	7	8	6	14	12	8	100～
-	-	-	-	-	-	1	1	不詳

死　亡

表 5.15　性・年齢別にみた死因年次推移分類
Table 5.15　Trends in deaths and death rates (per 100,000

Hi01　結　核
Tuberculosis

死　亡　率

年　齢 Age	1950 昭和25年	1955 30年	1960 35年	1965 40年	1970 45年	1975 50年	1980 55年	1985 60年
								総　数
総数 Total	146.4	52.3	34.2	22.8	15.4	9.5	5.5	3.9
0〜4歳	63.2	15.8	5.2	1.4	0.7	0.2	0.1	0.0
5〜9 Years	31.1	5.9	1.7	0.4	0.2	0.0	-	-
10〜14	27.8	6.3	1.8	0.6	0.2	0.0	-	-
15〜19	114.0	18.2	4.7	1.1	0.5	0.2	0.0	0.0
20〜24	254.3	43.4	12.3	3.6	1.2	0.4	0.2	0.0
25〜29	293.0	71.6	25.2	8.0	2.3	0.7	0.3	0.2
30〜34	246.2	81.3	37.6	14.5	5.2	1.5	0.5	0.2
35〜39	219.5	77.7	47.2	22.8	9.6	3.4	1.2	0.4
40〜44	197.0	77.9	50.8	29.8	14.5	6.2	2.4	1.1
45〜49	184.8	86.9	56.7	33.1	19.1	9.9	4.3	2.1
50〜54	188.6	97.5	68.1	42.1	25.3	13.3	7.2	3.7
55〜59	197.5	110.7	84.5	56.1	33.6	19.1	9.9	6.0
60〜64	192.7	133.7	106.0	77.4	49.2	26.3	14.0	9.0
65〜69	170.6	146.6	135.8	103.9	80.1	42.9	23.8	14.1
70〜74	122.5	141.8	160.1	138.9	108.3	66.7	34.3	20.4
75〜79	86.5	109.6	164.2	165.5	129.1	94.2	52.3	35.6
80〜84	58.0	68.0	111.2	151.7	133.7	106.7	60.3	41.9
85〜89	35.4	39.5	75.7	103.9	122.5	99.2	52.5	48.3
90〜94[2]	67.3	74.7	55.9	51.2	76.0	82.1	52.9	38.3
95〜99	...	...	...	...	...	...	...	...
100〜	...	...	...	...	...	...	...	...
								男
総数	159.5	60.6	43.1	30.6	21.6	13.5	8.2	5.8
0〜4歳	62.0	15.2	5.0	1.6	0.6	0.2	0.1	-
5〜9	28.9	6.0	1.6	0.5	0.1	0.0	-	-
10〜14	19.4	5.0	1.6	0.5	0.3	0.0	-	-
15〜19	95.4	15.2	4.4	1.2	0.6	0.1	0.0	-
20〜24	254.6	40.5	10.7	3.2	1.3	0.4	0.2	0.1
25〜29	315.8	72.5	24.7	7.4	2.2	0.8	0.3	0.2
30〜34	273.8	87.4	39.6	15.8	5.5	1.6	0.7	0.4
35〜39	259.6	88.6	54.6	25.5	11.1	4.1	1.4	0.5
40〜44	243.2	95.9	63.0	37.7	17.2	7.9	3.3	1.6
45〜49	229.9	112.2	74.9	46.2	26.1	13.1	6.1	3.1
50〜54	239.1	129.6	94.8	61.8	36.8	20.4	11.0	5.6
55〜59	254.4	147.6	119.6	85.0	52.6	30.2	15.9	9.3
60〜64	258.9	183.1	153.5	117.0	78.7	43.1	23.7	15.0
65〜69	243.5	209.8	204.8	162.0	131.1	70.1	40.9	24.2
70〜74	182.7	216.2	256.4	219.3	174.3	110.7	61.5	37.3
75〜79	125.1	169.9	278.7	276.8	221.2	161.5	95.3	66.1
80〜84	96.2	108.1	195.7	271.2	243.2	195.3	109.7	78.0
85〜89	49.0	62.0	139.0	206.2	217.0	182.6	102.5	93.9
90〜94[2]	164.7	154.4	84.7	116.6	143.1	170.8	111.6	94.2
95〜99	...	...	...	...	...	...	...	...
100〜	...	...	...	...	...	...	...	...
								女
総数	133.7	44.3	25.6	15.2	9.5	5.6	2.9	2.0
0〜4歳	64.4	16.4	5.4	1.3	0.9	0.2	0.1	0.1
5〜9	33.3	5.7	1.8	0.4	0.2	0.0	-	-
10〜14	36.5	7.7	2.0	0.7	0.1	0.0	-	-
15〜19	132.8	21.3	4.9	1.0	0.4	0.2	0.0	0.0
20〜24	254.0	46.3	13.9	4.0	1.0	0.4	0.2	-
25〜29	273.9	70.8	25.7	8.7	2.5	0.7	0.3	0.2
30〜34	223.2	76.2	35.6	13.1	4.9	1.5	0.4	0.1
35〜39	183.9	68.6	40.8	20.2	8.0	2.7	1.1	0.4
40〜44	152.5	62.0	40.7	23.2	11.8	4.5	1.6	0.7
45〜49	138.9	62.6	40.7	22.4	13.4	6.8	2.5	1.1
50〜54	136.5	65.1	42.8	24.9	16.0	7.5	3.6	1.9
55〜59	140.2	73.5	50.0	29.2	17.4	10.3	5.1	3.0
60〜64	131.1	85.9	60.3	39.9	23.0	12.5	6.5	4.3
65〜69	111.0	91.2	73.3	51.1	35.2	20.2	10.3	6.6
70〜74	78.6	86.5	83.4	72.5	54.2	31.4	13.2	8.1
75〜79	61.7	71.0	89.6	87.4	62.6	45.7	21.6	14.4
80〜84	37.7	46.2	65.7	86.2	68.9	52.2	29.8	19.9
85〜89	29.3	29.7	47.4	59.7	79.8	58.7	27.0	26.1
90〜94[2]	33.0	47.2	46.0	27.0	51.8	50.1	30.3	14.6
95〜99	...	...	...	...	...	...	...	...
100〜	...	...	...	...	...	...	...	...

234　結　核

別死亡数及び率（人口10万対）（つづき）
population）by sex, age and causes of death : Japan－CON.

Death rates

1990 平成2年	1995 7年	2000 12年	2005 17年	2010 22年	2014 26年	2015 27年	2016 28年	年　齢 Age
Total								
3.0	2.6	2.1	1.8	1.7	1.7	1.6	1.5	総数 Total
-	0.0	0.0	-	-	-	-	0.0	0～4歳
0.0	-	-	-	-	-	-	-	5～9 Years
-	-	0.0	-	-	-	-	-	10～14
0.0	-	-	-	-	-	0.0	-	15～19
0.1	0.1	0.0	0.0	0.0	0.0	-	-	20～24
0.1	0.0	0.0	0.0	0.0	-	0.0	0.0	25～29
0.2	0.2	0.1	0.1	0.0	0.0	0.0	0.0	30～34
0.4	0.2	0.2	0.1	0.1	0.0	0.0	0.1	35～39
0.6	0.4	0.3	0.1	0.1	0.1	0.1	0.0	40～44
1.2	0.8	0.6	0.4	0.2	0.1	0.2	0.1	45～49
2.2	1.5	1.0	0.7	0.3	0.2	0.1	0.2	50～54
3.2	2.3	1.7	1.1	0.6	0.3	0.3	0.2	55～59
5.5	3.8	1.8	1.1	0.8	0.7	0.5	0.4	60～64
9.3	6.0	3.4	1.9	1.3	0.9	0.7	0.8	65～69
13.9	10.5	6.2	3.1	2.3	1.8	1.4	1.2	70～74
21.2	16.0	10.2	7.9	4.6	3.7	3.1	2.8	75～79
31.8	22.9	19.0	15.1	11.1	9.0	7.5	7.0	80～84
33.9	29.9	24.6	21.6	21.2	19.5	18.2	16.3	85～89
38.7	32.1	35.7	27.6	28.0	28.4	29.3	28.0	90～94[2]
...	...	...	31.7	34.3	30.5	32.4	36.1	95～99
...	...	...	35.5	29.6	25.0	27.5	18.5	100～
Male								
4.6	3.7	3.1	2.6	2.2	2.0	1.9	1.9	総数
-	-	-	-	-	-	-	0.0	0～4歳
0.0	-	-	-	-	-	-	-	5～9
-	-	0.0	-	-	-	-	-	10～14
-	-	-	-	-	-	-	-	15～19
0.1	0.1	-	0.1	0.0	0.0	-	-	20～24
0.1	0.1	0.0	0.0	0.0	-	0.0	0.0	25～29
0.3	0.2	0.1	0.1	0.1	0.0	-	0.1	30～34
0.5	0.4	0.4	0.1	0.2	0.0	0.0	0.0	35～39
1.0	0.7	0.5	0.1	0.1	0.2	0.1	-	40～44
2.1	1.4	1.2	0.7	0.3	0.1	0.3	0.2	45～49
3.6	2.7	1.8	1.2	0.5	0.3	0.2	0.3	50～54
5.3	3.7	3.2	2.0	1.1	0.5	0.3	0.3	55～59
8.8	6.1	3.0	1.9	1.4	1.2	0.9	0.6	60～64
16.2	9.2	5.6	3.0	1.9	1.4	1.3	1.5	65～69
25.4	18.2	10.2	5.0	3.5	2.7	2.2	2.0	70～74
41.3	28.8	18.8	12.6	6.9	5.5	4.8	4.4	75～79
63.1	42.2	34.5	29.0	18.0	13.0	12.0	10.2	80～84
66.7	61.5	47.8	42.7	38.9	33.4	30.1	28.1	85～89
76.1	69.3	70.3	60.8	61.7	62.4	59.0	56.0	90～94[2]
...	...	...	91.7	94.7	77.4	75.6	86.6	95～99
...	...	...	26.6	119.5	12.5	59.8	44.4	100～
Female								
1.5	1.4	1.2	1.1	1.2	1.3	1.2	1.2	総数
-	0.0	0.0	-	-	-	-	-	0～4歳
-	-	-	-	-	-	-	-	5～9
-	-	-	-	-	-	-	-	10～14
0.0	-	-	-	-	-	0.0	-	15～19
0.0	0.0	0.0	-	-	-	-	-	20～24
0.1	-	0.0	0.0	-	-	-	-	25～29
0.2	0.2	0.1	0.0	-	0.0	0.0	-	30～34
0.2	0.1	0.0	0.0	0.0	-	0.0	0.1	35～39
0.2	0.2	0.1	0.1	0.0	0.0	0.0	0.1	40～44
0.4	0.1	0.0	0.1	0.1	-	-	-	45～49
0.8	0.4	0.2	0.2	0.1	0.1	-	0.1	50～54
1.2	1.0	0.2	0.2	0.1	0.1	0.2	-	55～59
2.5	1.7	0.7	0.3	0.2	0.1	0.1	0.1	60～64
4.2	3.2	1.4	0.8	0.7	0.4	0.2	0.2	65～69
5.9	5.0	2.9	1.4	1.2	1.0	0.6	0.5	70～74
7.9	8.1	4.6	4.3	2.8	2.4	1.8	1.6	75～79
13.4	12.2	10.7	7.4	6.6	6.3	4.5	4.7	80～84
17.6	15.1	14.0	12.6	13.4	12.5	12.1	10.2	85～89
24.1	18.8	24.0	16.5	17.5	17.8	19.5	18.4	90～94[2]
...	...	...	17.1	20.3	20.4	23.2	25.3	95～99
...	...	...	37.0	15.8	27.5	22.5	14.0	100～

死　亡

表5.15　性・年齢別にみた死因年次推移分類
Table 5.15　Trends in deaths and death rates (per 100,000

Hi02　悪性新生物
Malignant neoplasms

死　亡　数

年　齢 Age	1950 昭和25年	1955 30年	1960 35年	1965 40年	1970 45年	1975 50年	1980 55年	1985 60年
								総　数
総数 Total	64 428	77 721	93 773	106 536	119 977	136 383	161 764	187 714
0～4歳	553	567	604	618	667	691	464	295
5～9 Years	219	410	383	410	397	430	473	340
10～14	215	346	486	426	339	351	390	388
15～19	316	380	521	675	578	443	459	447
20～24	366	464	596	750	852	688	486	421
25～29	608	794	932	1 090	1 204	1 282	1 019	727
30～34	1 104	1 269	1 695	1 932	1 882	2 026	2 040	1 530
35～39	2 187	2 174	2 547	3 034	3 182	3 027	3 175	3 238
40～44	3 788	3 916	3 789	4 035	4 894	5 080	4 693	4 955
45～49	5 376	5 783	6 342	5 916	6 596	7 850	8 384	7 640
50～54	7 239	8 095	8 797	9 458	8 695	9 801	12 717	13 439
55～59	8 767	10 021	11 950	12 505	13 018	12 846	14 627	18 977
60～64	10 288	11 656	14 032	16 018	16 948	17 633	18 239	21 137
65～69	10 263	12 326	14 424	17 351	20 013	21 702	24 088	24 151
70～74	7 778	10 406	13 215	15 046	18 760	22 574	26 771	29 767
75～79	3 847	6 317	8 523	10 820	13 191	17 434	23 472	28 856
80～84	1 181	2 243	3 780	4 829	6 509	8 970	14 199	20 122
85～89	276	469	1 003	1 378	1 896	2 963	4 953	8 954
90～94	37	78	145	224	306	525	1 017	2 047
95～99	12	7	9	21	38	52	93	266
100～	-				6	9	3	14
不詳 Not stated	8	-	-	-	6	6	2	3
								男
総数	32 670	41 223	50 898	58 899	67 074	76 922	93 501	110 660
0～4歳	323	325	349	354	382	397	260	158
5～9	128	247	225	243	230	252	291	205
10～14	128	190	268	247	186	199	217	215
15～19	176	231	289	396	332	262	270	281
20～24	177	241	285	392	463	384	254	242
25～29	217	341	409	520	571	611	491	352
30～34	355	485	702	821	862	887	933	685
35～39	692	778	923	1 326	1 477	1 401	1 493	1 559
40～44	1 395	1 515	1 478	1 645	2 297	2 493	2 311	2 434
45～49	2 350	2 701	2 802	2 662	3 034	4 096	4 757	4 183
50～54	3 642	4 220	4 702	4 771	4 392	4 873	7 569	8 322
55～59	4 880	5 655	6 973	7 071	7 249	7 116	8 322	12 339
60～64	5 804	6 995	8 513	9 861	10 119	10 415	10 801	12 840
65～69	5 676	7 240	8 814	10 785	12 567	13 352	14 752	14 821
70～74	4 188	5 784	7 676	8 905	11 279	13 810	16 366	18 199
75～79	1 910	3 115	4 395	5 951	7 396	10 079	13 822	17 251
80～84	497	961	1 685	2 307	3 275	4 717	7 712	11 194
85～89	116	175	361	562	835	1 363	2 405	4 391
90～94	9	20	45	76	111	195	442	894
95～99	3	4	4	4	11	12	31	85
100～	-	-	-	-	2	3	1	7
不詳	4	-	-	-	4	5	1	3
								女
総数	31 758	36 498	42 875	47 637	52 903	59 461	68 263	77 054
0～4歳	230	242	255	264	285	294	204	137
5～9	91	163	158	167	167	178	182	135
10～14	87	156	218	179	153	152	173	173
15～19	140	149	232	279	246	181	189	166
20～24	189	223	311	358	389	304	232	179
25～29	391	453	523	570	633	671	528	375
30～34	749	784	993	1 111	1 020	1 139	1 107	845
35～39	1 495	1 396	1 624	1 708	1 705	1 626	1 682	1 679
40～44	2 393	2 401	2 311	2 390	2 597	2 587	2 382	2 521
45～49	3 026	3 082	3 540	3 254	3 562	3 754	3 627	3 457
50～54	3 597	3 875	4 095	4 687	4 303	4 928	5 148	5 117
55～59	3 887	4 366	4 977	5 434	5 769	5 730	6 305	6 638
60～64	4 484	4 661	5 519	6 157	6 829	7 218	7 438	8 297
65～69	4 587	5 086	5 610	6 566	7 446	8 350	9 336	9 330
70～74	3 590	4 622	5 539	6 141	7 481	8 764	10 405	11 568
75～79	1 937	3 202	4 128	4 869	5 795	7 355	9 650	11 605
80～84	684	1 282	2 095	2 522	3 234	4 253	6 487	8 928
85～89	160	294	642	816	1 061	1 600	2 548	4 563
90～94	28	58	100	148	195	330	575	1 153
95～99	9	3	5	17	27	40	62	181
100～	-	-	-	-	4	6	2	7
不詳	4	-	-	-	2	1	1	-

236

General mortality

別死亡数及び率（人口10万対）（つづき）
population）by sex, age and causes of death : Japan－CON.

Deaths

1990 平成2年	1995 7年	2000 12年	2005 17年	2010 22年	2014 26年	2015 27年	2016 28年	年　齢 Age
Total								
217 413	263 022	295 484	325 941	353 499	368 103	370 346	372 986	総数 Total
224	171	135	121	100	98	78	76	0～4歳
225	196	137	120	107	103	100	84	5～9 Years
280	215	131	108	116	101	107	95	10～14
419	340	237	166	150	141	147	120	15～19
465	408	348	284	217	175	176	159	20～24
612	624	608	423	372	325	323	315	25～29
1 109	1 046	1 051	983	760	698	654	641	30～34
2 611	1 976	1 838	1 670	1 598	1 392	1 284	1 326	35～39
5 250	4 343	3 417	2 859	2 779	2 901	2 848	2 675	40～44
8 030	9 354	7 385	5 373	4 731	4 683	4 519	4 753	45～49
12 091	13 682	15 217	11 764	8 690	7 760	7 764	7 696	50～54
20 997	19 600	20 787	22 297	17 815	13 851	13 123	12 605	55～59
28 002	31 211	28 149	29 322	31 925	27 860	25 325	23 343	60～64
28 670	39 670	41 873	37 370	39 677	42 177	43 689	46 004	65～69
30 559	38 633	49 047	51 693	48 049	51 669	51 643	48 833	70～74
33 102	37 058	44 742	57 251	60 681	59 128	58 149	58 317	75～79
26 330	34 911	37 959	48 129	61 822	65 792	66 526	67 401	80～84
13 991	20 938	28 071	33 423	44 223	54 211	55 978	57 874	85～89
3 866	7 317	11 716	17 538	21 811	26 395	28 727	30 746	90～94
551	1 226	2 402	4 552	6 996	7 504	7 981	8 605	95～99
25	97	220	480	856	1 108	1 174	1 301	100～
4	6	14	15	24	31	31	17	不詳 Not stated
Male								
130 395	159 623	179 140	196 603	211 435	218 397	219 508	219 785	総数
125	88	78	65	55	53	42	43	0～4歳
124	124	83	77	55	63	61	50	5～9
165	125	74	61	63	65	52	48	10～14
275	221	139	103	93	96	86	78	15～19
272	260	196	163	134	96	112	95	20～24
328	352	297	216	197	148	153	155	25～29
482	476	485	401	321	306	260	261	30～34
1 187	890	771	689	624	565	521	535	35～39
2 625	2 116	1 625	1 234	1 185	1 210	1 225	1 115	40～44
4 397	4 977	3 858	2 727	2 257	2 133	2 035	2 141	45～49
7 259	8 058	8 753	6 562	4 678	3 948	3 923	3 791	50～54
14 088	12 707	13 262	13 771	10 735	7 962	7 622	7 268	55～59
19 302	21 634	19 032	19 672	20 891	17 837	16 179	14 842	60～64
18 140	27 531	29 153	25 537	26 942	28 346	29 367	30 772	65～69
18 681	24 549	33 482	35 297	32 435	34 920	34 860	32 933	70～74
19 628	22 156	27 321	37 755	39 917	38 619	37 820	37 864	75～79
14 581	19 388	21 116	27 244	37 844	40 053	40 650	40 840	80～84
6 849	10 312	13 714	16 285	21 993	28 945	30 115	31 187	85～89
1 652	3 154	4 778	7 089	8 564	10 394	11 729	12 810	90～94
227	461	855	1 525	2 212	2 372	2 392	2 640	95～99
4	38	55	119	219	244	279	302	100～
4	6	13	11	21	22	25	15	不詳
Female								
87 018	103 399	116 344	129 338	142 064	149 706	150 838	153 201	総数
99	83	57	56	45	45	36	33	0～4歳
101	72	54	43	52	40	39	34	5～9
115	90	57	47	53	36	55	47	10～14
144	119	98	63	57	45	61	42	15～19
193	148	152	121	83	79	64	64	20～24
284	272	311	207	175	177	170	160	25～29
627	570	566	582	439	392	394	380	30～34
1 424	1 086	1 067	981	974	827	763	791	35～39
2 625	2 227	1 792	1 625	1 594	1 691	1 623	1 560	40～44
3 633	4 377	3 527	2 646	2 474	2 550	2 484	2 612	45～49
4 832	5 624	6 464	5 202	4 012	3 812	3 841	3 905	50～54
6 909	6 893	7 525	8 526	7 080	5 889	5 501	5 337	55～59
8 700	9 577	9 117	9 650	11 034	10 023	9 146	8 501	60～64
10 530	12 139	12 720	11 833	12 735	13 831	14 322	15 232	65～69
11 878	14 084	15 565	16 396	15 614	16 749	16 783	15 900	70～74
13 474	14 902	17 421	19 496	20 764	20 509	20 329	20 453	75～79
11 749	15 523	16 843	20 885	23 978	25 739	25 876	26 561	80～84
7 142	10 626	14 357	17 138	22 230	25 266	25 863	26 687	85～89
2 214	4 163	6 938	10 449	13 247	16 001	16 998	17 936	90～94
324	765	1 547	3 027	4 784	5 132	5 589	5 965	95～99
21	59	165	361	637	864	895	999	100～
-	-	1	4	3	9	6	2	不詳

死　亡

表 5.15　性・年齢別にみた死因年次推移分類
Table 5.15　Trends in deaths and death rates (per 100,000

Hi02　悪性新生物
Malignant neoplasms

死　亡　率

年　齢 Age	1950 昭和25年	1955 30年	1960 35年	1965 40年	1970 45年	1975 50年	1980 55年	1985 60年
								総　数
総数 Total	77.4	87.1	100.4	108.4	116.3	122.6	139.1	156.1
0〜4歳	4.9	6.1	7.7	7.6	7.6	7.0	5.5	4.0
5〜9 Years	2.3	3.7	4.2	5.2	4.9	4.8	4.7	4.0
10〜14	2.5	3.6	4.4	4.6	4.3	4.3	4.4	3.9
15〜19	3.7	4.4	5.6	6.2	6.4	5.6	5.6	5.0
20〜24	4.7	5.5	7.2	8.3	8.0	7.6	6.2	5.1
25〜29	9.8	10.4	11.4	13.0	13.3	11.9	11.4	9.4
30〜34	21.2	20.7	22.5	23.4	22.6	22.0	19.1	16.9
35〜39	43.3	42.5	42.2	40.5	38.9	36.1	34.7	30.3
40〜44	84.5	79.2	75.5	67.7	67.0	62.0	56.6	54.8
45〜49	134.2	132.4	131.7	120.2	113.0	107.1	104.0	93.2
50〜54	213.6	210.3	209.4	203.0	182.0	170.5	177.4	170.8
55〜59	318.9	312.6	328.2	312.5	295.7	276.4	262.0	272.5
60〜64	446.5	466.9	478.6	478.9	456.8	413.6	410.6	394.4
65〜69	579.6	626.6	667.7	677.2	673.0	631.7	610.2	579.8
70〜74	606.9	747.2	845.1	862.5	881.7	879.2	888.8	842.7
75〜79	561.1	721.4	892.8	987.3	1 042.0	1 065.1	1 155.8	1 185.3
80〜84	428.2	593.7	782.7	914.4	1 003.7	1 111.1	1 301.3	1 390.7
85〜89	349.1	421.2	643.7	691.9	826.8	960.4	1 210.1	1 526.9
90〜94[2]	299.6	373.3	478.5	482.6	532.2	718.3	934.4	1 253.8
95〜99	…	…	…	…	…	…	…	…
100〜	…	…	…	…	…	…	…	…
								男
総数	80.1	94.0	110.9	122.1	132.6	140.6	163.5	187.4
0〜4歳	5.6	6.9	8.7	8.5	8.5	7.8	6.0	4.2
5〜9	2.7	4.4	4.8	6.1	5.6	5.5	5.7	4.7
10〜14	2.9	3.9	4.8	5.3	4.7	4.7	4.8	4.2
15〜19	4.1	5.3	6.2	7.2	7.3	6.5	6.4	6.2
20〜24	4.6	5.7	6.9	8.7	8.8	8.5	6.5	5.8
25〜29	7.7	9.0	10.0	12.5	12.7	11.3	10.9	9.0
30〜34	15.0	17.3	18.7	19.8	20.7	19.3	17.3	15.1
35〜39	29.1	33.5	33.4	35.4	36.0	33.4	32.7	28.9
40〜44	63.4	65.2	65.0	60.3	63.0	60.7	55.8	54.2
45〜49	116.4	126.5	124.2	119.7	114.2	112.6	118.4	103.2
50〜54	211.8	218.7	230.4	219.6	205.2	187.6	214.3	213.5
55〜59	354.0	351.7	386.9	366.3	357.3	345.8	333.7	363.9
60〜64	523.1	570.2	592.2	606.8	579.5	541.2	558.8	546.7
65〜69	713.1	787.8	858.2	884.8	902.0	853.9	850.5	836.9
70〜74	775.1	974.1	1 106.7	1 128.7	1 176.9	1 207.6	1 247.3	1 224.6
75〜79	713.5	910.7	1 166.7	1 317.0	1 393.5	1 468.8	1 634.1	1 730.8
80〜84	519.9	721.5	996.2	1 234.0	1 359.4	1 535.6	1 850.9	2 044.6
85〜89	473.3	517.0	749.1	934.7	1 168.8	1 353.0	1 736.5	2 291.8
90〜94[2]	282.4	411.7	593.2	582.8	709.7	969.2	1 429.3	1 786.2
95〜99	…	…	…	…	…	…	…	…
100〜	…	…	…	…	…	…	…	…
								女
総数	74.9	80.4	90.2	95.2	100.7	105.2	115.5	125.9
0〜4歳	4.2	5.4	6.7	6.6	6.7	6.1	4.9	3.8
5〜9	1.9	3.0	3.5	4.3	4.2	4.1	3.7	3.2
10〜14	2.0	3.3	4.0	4.0	4.0	3.8	4.0	3.5
15〜19	3.3	3.5	5.0	5.2	5.5	4.7	4.7	3.8
20〜24	4.9	5.3	7.4	7.8	7.3	6.8	6.0	4.5
25〜29	11.6	11.8	12.7	13.5	13.9	12.6	11.8	9.8
30〜34	26.4	23.6	26.3	27.0	24.5	24.8	20.8	18.8
35〜39	56.0	49.9	49.6	45.5	41.9	38.8	36.7	31.8
40〜44	104.8	91.6	84.2	74.0	71.0	63.4	57.3	55.4
45〜49	152.4	138.1	138.3	120.6	111.9	101.7	89.8	83.5
50〜54	215.5	201.8	189.5	188.6	163.2	156.4	141.5	128.9
55〜59	283.6	273.2	270.6	262.3	243.1	221.2	204.2	185.7
60〜64	375.4	367.1	369.4	358.1	347.7	308.6	296.4	275.6
65〜69	470.6	485.3	495.0	488.7	471.1	446.1	421.8	389.7
70〜74	484.3	578.6	636.5	642.7	639.7	615.4	612.1	565.3
75〜79	463.4	600.0	714.2	756.0	788.3	773.8	814.4	807.2
80〜84	379.6	524.1	667.7	739.2	793.5	850.4	961.8	992.7
85〜89	293.3	379.3	596.5	586.9	672.0	770.1	940.9	1 155.5
90〜94[2]	305.7	360.1	438.8	445.5	467.9	627.6	743.5	1 028.4
95〜99	…	…	…	…	…	…	…	…
100〜	…	…	…	…	…	…	…	…

238

General mortality

別死亡数及び率（人口10万対）（つづき）
population）by sex, age and causes of death : Japan−CON.

Death rates

1990 平成2年	1995 7年	2000 12年	2005 17年	2010 22年	2014 26年	2015 27年	2016 28年	年　　齢 Age
Total								
177.2	211.6	235.2	258.3	279.7	293.5	295.5	298.3	総数 Total
3.5	2.9	2.3	2.2	1.9	1.9	1.6	1.6	0〜4歳
3.0	3.0	2.3	2.0	1.9	2.0	1.9	1.6	5〜9 Years
3.3	2.9	2.0	1.8	2.0	1.8	1.9	1.7	10〜14
4.2	4.0	3.2	2.5	2.5	2.4	2.5	2.0	15〜19
5.3	4.2	4.2	3.9	3.4	2.9	3.0	2.7	20〜24
7.7	7.2	6.3	5.2	5.2	5.0	5.1	5.1	25〜29
14.4	13.1	12.2	10.2	9.3	9.6	9.1	9.1	30〜34
29.2	25.6	23.0	19.4	16.5	16.4	15.6	16.7	35〜39
49.4	48.7	44.3	35.9	32.1	30.1	29.4	28.0	40〜44
89.3	88.7	83.5	70.2	59.4	55.2	52.4	52.1	45〜49
149.9	154.3	146.4	134.5	114.2	100.9	98.2	98.9	50〜54
272.2	247.7	239.0	218.1	205.8	182.7	174.5	168.9	55〜59
415.7	419.2	365.0	343.9	317.5	312.3	298.3	288.4	60〜64
563.2	622.5	590.5	503.4	482.1	463.1	449.9	450.0	65〜69
802.1	826.5	832.7	779.1	687.7	654.6	666.2	662.4	70〜74
1 098.1	1 130.9	1 080.8	1 088.2	1 016.1	947.0	918.7	897.2	75〜79
1 437.4	1 521.9	1 454.6	1 411.8	1 416.9	1 355.1	1 327.3	1 304.9	80〜84
1 679.8	1 846.2	1 834.3	1 808.1	1 807.8	1 775.1	1 777.7	1 771.4	85〜89
1 535.3	1 954.4	2 047.0	2 085.2	2 125.2	2 027.3	2 112.9	2 084.5	90〜94[2]
…	…	…	2 153.7	2 350.5	2 137.9	2 212.3	2 252.6	95〜99
…	…	…	1 892.9	1 949.8	1 846.7	1 901.3	2 001.5	100〜
Male								
216.4	262.0	291.3	319.1	343.4	357.8	359.7	361.1	総数
3.8	2.9	2.6	2.3	2.0	2.0	1.7	1.7	0〜4歳
3.3	3.7	2.7	2.5	1.9	2.3	2.3	1.9	5〜9
3.8	3.3	2.2	2.0	2.1	1.8	1.7	1.7	10〜14
5.4	5.1	3.6	3.1	3.0	3.2	2.8	2.6	15〜19
6.1	5.2	4.6	4.4	4.2	3.1	3.7	3.1	20〜24
8.1	8.1	6.1	5.2	5.4	4.5	4.8	5.0	25〜29
12.4	11.8	11.1	8.2	7.7	8.3	7.1	7.3	30〜34
26.4	22.9	19.1	15.9	12.7	13.1	12.4	13.3	35〜39
49.2	47.2	41.9	30.7	27.0	24.7	24.9	23.0	40〜44
98.3	94.1	87.0	71.1	56.2	49.8	46.6	46.3	45〜49
181.9	183.4	168.8	150.5	122.9	102.3	98.5	96.7	50〜54
372.5	327.0	310.2	271.9	249.9	211.2	203.3	195.2	55〜59
596.8	601.3	508.9	474.2	423.2	407.3	386.9	372.0	60〜64
828.6	921.6	869.5	720.8	684.9	645.5	624.9	622.1	65〜69
1 200.1	1 271.1	1 255.6	1 160.7	1 002.5	950.5	966.0	958.6	70〜74
1 640.4	1 766.3	1 685.3	1 672.9	1 539.3	1 400.3	1 347.5	1 308.1	75〜79
2 149.1	2 359.8	2 312.4	2 230.8	2 225.9	2 066.7	2 022.6	1 954.3	80〜84
2 482.4	2 856.3	2 877.9	2 935.7	2 943.0	2 818.4	2 826.9	2 791.2	85〜89
2 311.6	3 124.7	3 226.1	3 365.1	3 525.3	3 342.1	3 493.5	3 397.9	90〜94[2]
…	…	…	3 678.7	3 950.4	3 825.8	3 768.8	3 940.3	95〜99
…	…	…	3 164.1	3 737.8	3 050.0	3 336.9	3 355.6	100〜
Female								
139.3	163.1	181.4	200.3	219.2	232.5	234.6	238.8	総数
3.1	2.9	2.0	2.1	1.8	1.8	1.5	1.4	0〜4歳
2.8	2.3	1.9	1.5	1.9	1.6	1.5	1.3	5〜9
2.8	2.5	1.8	1.6	1.8	1.3	2.0	1.8	10〜14
3.0	2.9	2.7	2.0	1.9	1.6	2.1	1.5	15〜19
4.5	3.1	3.8	3.5	2.7	2.7	2.2	2.2	20〜24
7.2	6.4	6.6	5.2	5.0	5.6	5.5	5.3	25〜29
16.4	14.5	13.3	12.3	10.9	11.0	11.2	11.0	30〜34
32.0	28.4	27.1	23.1	20.5	19.8	18.9	20.3	35〜39
49.7	50.2	46.9	41.2	37.3	35.6	34.1	33.2	40〜44
80.4	83.3	80.0	69.4	62.6	60.7	58.4	58.0	45〜49
118.5	125.7	124.2	118.7	105.6	99.6	97.8	101.1	50〜54
175.7	171.2	170.1	165.3	162.4	154.6	145.9	142.8	55〜59
248.5	248.9	229.6	220.4	215.6	220.7	212.3	207.1	60〜64
362.9	358.5	340.2	305.0	296.4	293.3	285.8	288.7	65〜69
527.1	513.4	482.9	456.2	416.1	396.9	405.1	403.9	70〜74
741.2	736.9	691.7	648.9	614.5	588.2	577.1	567.3	75〜79
1 018.8	1 054.4	992.9	954.6	900.4	882.7	861.9	863.6	80〜84
1 282.3	1 374.5	1 362.4	1 324.6	1 308.5	1 245.9	1 241.3	1 241.4	85〜89
1 231.1	1 533.7	1 650.4	1 657.5	1 691.0	1 616.3	1 660.2	1 633.5	90〜94[2]
…	…	…	1 781.6	1 979.8	1 775.8	1 880.0	1 887.7	95〜99
…	…	…	1 671.5	1 674.5	1 694.1	1 676.5	1 752.6	100〜

239

死　亡

表 5.15　性・年齢別にみた死因年次推移分類
Table 5.15　Trends in deaths and death rates (per 100,000

Hi03　糖尿病
Diabetes mellitus

死　亡　数

年　　齢 Age	1950 昭和25年	1955 30年	1960 35年	1965 40年	1970 45年	1975 50年	1980 55年	1985 60年
								総　数
総数 Total	2 034	2 191	3 195	5 115	7 642	9 032	8 504	9 244
0 ～ 4 歳	3	6	4	5	4	3	3	3
5 ～ 9 Years	6	5	4	13	8	5	3	1
10～14	13	11	11	22	15	9	3	4
15～19	39	27	24	42	38	20	20	8
20～24	58	63	43	55	60	28	20	17
25～29	58	61	89	70	67	64	39	26
30～34	46	48	63	72	113	72	72	53
35～39	62	51	61	97	123	132	102	100
40～44	116	94	78	96	174	224	152	158
45～49	149	127	135	157	234	337	341	236
50～54	213	197	232	325	380	418	427	461
55～59	277	263	377	494	650	577	508	651
60～64	338	320	516	811	1 020	1 030	775	800
65～69	296	372	595	946	1 475	1 609	1 201	1 062
70～74	241	285	510	952	1 550	1 837	1 649	1 585
75～79	88	179	302	615	1 068	1 497	1 634	1 841
80～84	21	62	125	278	508	866	1 091	1 458
85～89	8	15	25	58	137	271	370	632
90～94	2	5	1	7	16	31	87	139
95～99	-	-	-	-	1	2	7	9
100～					1			
不詳 Not stated	-	-	-	-	-	-	-	-
								男
総数	1 005	1 020	1 482	2 463	3 753	4 377	4 055	4 322
0 ～ 4 歳	2	4	2	3	2	3	1	1
5 ～ 9	2	2	1	9	4	1	2	1
10～14	5	5	4	9	12	5	2	2
15～19	15	13	8	13	13	9	9	6
20～24	23	20	8	21	16	14	10	9
25～29	24	28	22	29	27	22	19	16
30～34	22	20	23	34	48	33	38	28
35～39	27	17	25	51	78	80	65	54
40～44	61	35	25	40	107	148	105	97
45～49	73	65	66	78	114	216	225	169
50～54	109	110	114	163	175	230	274	324
55～59	145	137	196	246	319	291	268	388
60～64	168	143	245	419	515	509	403	404
65～69	155	166	296	463	737	746	564	503
70～74	118	133	242	471	780	885	705	717
75～79	44	84	139	263	509	661	729	753
80～84	7	29	54	126	227	386	459	546
85～89	5	6	12	23	67	124	141	254
90～94	-	3	-	2	3	14	33	48
95～99	-	-	-	-	-	-	3	2
100～	-	-	-	-	-	-	-	
不詳	-	-	-	-	-	-	-	
								女
総数	1 029	1 171	1 713	2 652	3 889	4 655	4 449	4 922
0 ～ 4 歳	1	2	2	2	2	-	2	2
5 ～ 9	4	3	3	4	4	4	1	-
10～14	8	6	7	13	3	4	1	2
15～19	24	14	16	29	25	11	11	2
20～24	35	43	35	34	44	14	10	8
25～29	34	33	67	41	40	42	20	10
30～34	24	28	40	38	65	39	34	25
35～39	35	34	36	46	45	52	37	46
40～44	55	59	53	56	67	76	47	61
45～49	76	62	69	79	120	121	116	67
50～54	104	87	118	162	205	188	153	137
55～59	132	126	181	248	331	286	240	263
60～64	170	177	271	392	505	521	372	396
65～69	141	206	299	483	738	863	637	559
70～74	123	152	268	481	770	952	944	868
75～79	44	95	163	352	559	836	905	1 088
80～84	14	33	71	152	281	480	632	912
85～89	3	9	13	35	70	147	229	378
90～94	2	2	1	5	13	17	54	91
95～99	-	-	-	-	1	2	4	7
100～	-	-	-	-	1	-	-	-
不詳	-	-	-	-	-	-	-	-

240

General mortality

別死亡数及び率（人口10万対）（つづき）
population）by sex, age and causes of death : Japan－CON.

Deaths

1990 平成2年	1995 7年	2000 12年	2005 17年	2010 22年	2014 26年	2015 27年	2016 28年	年齢 Age
Total								
9 470	14 225	12 303	13 621	14 422	13 669	13 327	13 480	総数 Total
1	1	1	-	-	-	-	-	0～4歳
-	2	-	-	-	-	-	-	5～9 Years
-	4	4	1	4	2	-	1	10～14
12	13	5	7	3	1	4	-	15～19
12	20	14	9	4	15	5	7	20～24
28	24	24	19	14	5	10	9	25～29
29	38	41	46	26	18	16	16	30～34
72	75	59	55	63	47	42	32	35～39
142	152	133	117	110	106	99	96	40～44
203	380	257	191	161	151	149	151	45～49
351	549	456	377	263	238	216	235	50～54
657	809	683	733	554	380	382	360	55～59
856	1 329	1 036	1 000	999	744	645	601	60～64
1 022	1 674	1 413	1 315	1 209	1 155	1 140	1 185	65～69
1 361	1 849	1 816	1 918	1 732	1 444	1 433	1 298	70～74
1 787	2 240	1 898	2 300	2 298	2 063	1 905	1 938	75～79
1 684	2 624	1 947	2 281	2 693	2 569	2 460	2 560	80～84
924	1 743	1 655	1 781	2 284	2 463	2 544	2 581	85～89
296	602	706	1 108	1 414	1 622	1 597	1 667	90～94
31	87	142	320	528	561	573	620	95～99
1	9	11	42	61	83	106	122	100～
1	1	2	1	2	2	1	1	不詳 Not stated
Male								
4 491	7 107	6 489	7 131	7 620	7 265	7 125	7 243	総数
-	1	-	-	-	-	-	-	0～4歳
-	-	-	-	-	-	-	-	5～9
-	2	4	-	4	1	-	1	10～14
10	11	5	6	2	-	3	-	15～19
9	11	10	5	1	12	2	4	20～24
20	18	14	13	10	4	5	7	25～29
19	22	31	33	19	14	8	11	30～34
44	53	45	41	46	35	33	26	35～39
94	104	103	86	86	84	73	69	40～44
138	275	192	142	124	117	121	112	45～49
262	387	350	295	206	179	179	190	50～54
472	581	491	551	434	290	312	287	55～59
532	910	763	719	750	550	503	461	60～64
506	1 022	974	916	860	843	865	879	65～69
578	915	1 089	1 246	1 125	962	979	881	70～74
754	935	888	1 210	1 364	1 295	1 156	1 226	75～79
627	983	735	946	1 329	1 378	1 302	1 400	80～84
308	647	559	548	763	970	1 037	1 087	85～89
108	195	201	319	384	414	406	472	90～94
9	32	32	47	100	105	124	107	95～99
1	2	1	7	11	10	16	22	100～
-	1	2	1	2	2	1	1	不詳
Female								
4 979	7 118	5 814	6 490	6 802	6 404	6 202	6 237	総数
1	-	1	-	-	-	-	-	0～4歳
-	2	-	-	-	-	-	-	5～9
-	2	2	1	-	1	-	-	10～14
2	2	-	1	1	1	1	-	15～19
3	9	4	4	3	3	3	3	20～24
8	6	10	6	4	1	5	2	25～29
10	16	10	13	7	4	8	5	30～34
28	22	14	14	17	12	9	6	35～39
48	48	30	31	24	22	26	27	40～44
65	105	65	49	37	34	28	39	45～49
89	162	106	82	57	59	37	45	50～54
185	228	192	182	120	90	70	73	55～59
324	419	273	281	249	194	142	140	60～64
516	652	439	399	349	312	275	306	65～69
783	934	727	672	607	482	454	417	70～74
1 033	1 305	1 010	1 090	934	768	749	712	75～79
1 057	1 641	1 212	1 335	1 364	1 191	1 158	1 160	80～84
616	1 096	1 096	1 233	1 521	1 493	1 507	1 494	85～89
188	407	505	789	1 030	1 208	1 191	1 195	90～94
22	55	110	273	428	456	449	513	95～99
-	7	10	35	50	73	90	100	100～
1	-	-	-	-	-	-	-	不詳

死　亡

表 5.15　性・年齢別にみた死因年次推移分類
Table 5.15　Trends in deaths and death rates (per 100,000

Hi03　糖尿病
Diabetes mellitus

死　亡　率

年　齢 Age	1950 昭和25年	1955 30年	1960 35年	1965 40年	1970 45年	1975 50年	1980 55年	1985 60年
								総　数
総数 Total	2.4	2.5	3.4	5.2	7.4	8.1	7.3	7.7
0〜4歳	0.0	0.1	0.1	0.1	0.0	0.0	0.0	0.0
5〜9 Years	0.1	0.0	0.0	0.2	0.1	0.1	0.0	0.0
10〜14	0.1	0.1	0.1	0.2	0.2	0.1	0.0	0.0
15〜19	0.5	0.3	0.3	0.4	0.4	0.3	0.2	0.1
20〜24	0.8	0.7	0.5	0.6	0.6	0.3	0.3	0.2
25〜29	0.9	0.8	1.1	0.8	0.7	0.6	0.4	0.3
30〜34	0.9	0.8	0.8	0.9	1.4	0.8	0.7	0.6
35〜39	1.2	1.0	1.0	1.3	1.5	1.6	1.1	0.9
40〜44	2.6	1.9	1.6	1.6	2.4	2.7	1.8	1.7
45〜49	3.7	2.9	2.8	3.2	4.0	4.6	4.2	2.9
50〜54	6.3	5.1	5.5	7.0	8.0	7.3	6.0	5.9
55〜59	10.1	8.2	10.4	12.3	14.8	12.4	9.1	9.3
60〜64	14.7	12.8	17.6	24.2	27.5	24.2	17.4	14.9
65〜69	16.7	18.9	27.5	36.9	49.6	46.8	30.4	25.5
70〜74	18.8	20.5	32.6	54.6	72.8	71.5	54.7	44.9
75〜79	12.8	20.4	31.6	56.1	84.4	91.5	80.5	75.6
80〜84	7.6	16.4	25.9	52.6	78.3	107.3	100.0	100.8
85〜89	10.1	13.5	16.0	29.1	59.7	87.8	90.4	107.8
90〜94[2]	12.2	22.0	3.1	13.8	27.4	40.5	78.9	79.7
95〜99	…	…	…	…	…	…	…	…
100〜	…	…	…	…	…	…	…	…
								男
総数	2.5	2.3	3.2	5.1	7.4	8.0	7.1	7.3
0〜4歳	0.0	0.1	0.0	0.1	0.0	0.1	0.0	0.0
5〜9	0.0	0.0	0.0	0.2	0.1	0.0	0.0	0.0
10〜14	0.1	0.1	0.1	0.2	0.3	0.1	0.0	0.0
15〜19	0.3	0.3	0.2	0.2	0.3	0.2	0.2	0.1
20〜24	0.6	0.5	0.2	0.5	0.3	0.3	0.3	0.2
25〜29	0.9	0.7	0.5	0.7	0.6	0.4	0.4	0.4
30〜34	0.9	0.7	0.6	0.8	1.2	0.7	0.7	0.6
35〜39	1.1	0.7	0.9	1.4	1.9	1.9	1.4	1.0
40〜44	2.8	1.5	1.1	1.5	2.9	3.6	2.5	2.2
45〜49	3.6	3.0	2.9	3.5	4.3	5.9	5.6	4.2
50〜54	6.3	5.7	5.6	7.5	8.2	8.9	7.8	8.3
55〜59	10.5	8.5	10.9	12.7	15.7	14.1	10.7	11.4
60〜64	15.1	11.7	17.0	25.8	29.5	26.5	20.8	17.2
65〜69	19.5	18.1	28.8	38.0	52.9	47.7	32.5	28.4
70〜74	21.8	22.4	34.9	59.7	81.4	77.4	53.7	48.2
75〜79	16.4	24.6	36.9	58.2	95.9	96.3	86.2	75.5
80〜84	7.3	21.8	31.9	67.4	94.2	125.7	110.2	99.7
85〜89	20.4	17.7	24.9	38.3	93.8	123.1	101.8	132.6
90〜94[2]	-	51.5	-	14.6	17.2	64.6	108.6	90.6
95〜99	…	…	…	…	…	…	…	…
100〜	…	…	…	…	…	…	…	…
								女
総数	2.4	2.6	3.6	5.3	7.4	8.2	7.5	8.0
0〜4歳	0.0	0.0	0.1	0.1	0.0	-	0.0	0.1
5〜9	0.1	0.1	0.1	0.1	0.1	0.1	0.0	-
10〜14	0.2	0.1	0.1	0.3	0.1	0.1	0.0	0.0
15〜19	0.6	0.3	0.3	0.5	0.6	0.3	0.3	0.0
20〜24	0.9	1.0	0.8	0.7	0.8	0.3	0.3	0.2
25〜29	1.0	0.9	1.6	1.0	0.9	0.8	0.4	0.3
30〜34	0.8	0.8	1.1	0.9	1.6	0.8	0.6	0.6
35〜39	1.3	1.2	1.1	1.2	1.1	1.2	0.8	0.9
40〜44	2.4	2.3	1.9	1.7	1.8	1.9	1.1	1.3
45〜49	3.8	2.8	2.7	2.9	3.8	3.3	2.9	1.6
50〜54	6.2	4.5	5.5	6.5	7.8	6.0	4.2	3.5
55〜59	9.6	7.9	9.8	12.0	13.9	11.0	7.8	7.4
60〜64	14.2	13.9	18.1	22.8	25.7	22.3	14.8	13.2
65〜69	14.5	19.7	26.4	36.0	46.7	46.1	28.8	23.3
70〜74	16.6	19.0	30.8	50.3	65.8	66.9	55.5	42.4
75〜79	10.5	17.8	28.2	54.7	76.0	87.9	76.4	75.7
80〜84	7.8	13.5	22.6	44.6	68.9	96.0	93.7	101.4
85〜89	5.5	11.6	12.1	25.2	44.3	70.7	84.6	95.7
90〜94[2]	16.5	11.8	4.2	13.5	31.1	31.7	67.5	75.2
95〜99	…	…	…	…	…	…	…	…
100〜	…	…	…	…	…	…	…	…

General mortality

別死亡数及び率（人口10万対）（つづき）
population）by sex, age and causes of death : Japan－CON.

Death rates

1990 平成2年	1995 7年	2000 12年	2005 17年	2010 22年	2014 26年	2015 27年	2016 28年	年齢 Age
Total								
7.7	11.4	9.8	10.8	11.4	10.9	10.6	10.8	総数 Total
0.0	0.0	0.0	-	-	-	-	-	0～4歳
-	0.0	-	-	-	-	-	-	5～9 Years
-	0.1	0.1	0.0	0.1	0.0	-	0.0	10～14
0.1	0.2	0.1	0.1	0.0	0.0	0.1	-	15～19
0.1	0.2	0.2	0.1	0.1	0.3	0.1	0.1	20～24
0.4	0.3	0.2	0.2	0.2	0.1	0.2	0.1	25～29
0.4	0.5	0.5	0.5	0.3	0.2	0.2	0.2	30～34
0.8	1.0	0.7	0.6	0.7	0.6	0.5	0.4	35～39
1.3	1.7	1.7	1.5	1.3	1.1	1.0	1.0	40～44
2.3	3.6	2.9	2.5	2.0	1.8	1.7	1.7	45～49
4.4	6.2	4.4	4.3	3.5	3.1	2.7	3.0	50～54
8.5	10.2	7.9	7.2	6.4	5.0	5.1	4.8	55～59
12.7	17.8	13.4	11.7	9.9	8.3	7.6	7.4	60～64
20.1	26.3	19.9	17.7	14.7	12.7	11.7	11.6	65～69
35.7	39.6	30.8	28.9	24.8	18.3	18.5	17.6	70～74
59.3	68.4	45.9	43.7	38.5	33.0	30.1	29.8	75～79
91.9	114.4	74.6	66.9	61.7	52.9	49.1	49.6	80～84
110.9	153.7	108.1	96.3	93.4	80.6	80.8	79.0	85～89
113.4	157.9	122.6	131.7	137.8	124.6	117.5	113.0	90～94[2]
...	...	...	151.4	177.4	159.8	158.8	162.3	95～99
...	...	...	165.6	138.9	138.3	171.7	187.7	100～
Male								
7.5	11.7	10.6	11.6	12.4	11.9	11.7	11.9	総数
-	0.0	-	-	-	-	-	-	0～4歳
-	-	-	-	-	-	-	-	5～9
-	0.1	0.1	-	0.1	0.0	-	0.0	10～14
0.2	0.3	0.1	0.2	0.1	-	0.1	-	15～19
0.2	0.2	0.2	0.1	0.0	0.4	0.1	0.1	20～24
0.5	0.4	0.3	0.3	0.3	0.1	0.2	0.2	25～29
0.5	0.5	0.7	0.7	0.5	0.4	0.2	0.3	30～34
1.0	1.4	1.1	0.9	0.9	0.8	0.8	0.6	35～39
1.8	2.3	2.7	2.1	2.0	1.7	1.5	1.4	40～44
3.1	5.2	4.3	3.7	3.1	2.7	2.8	2.4	45～49
6.6	8.8	6.7	6.8	5.4	4.6	4.5	4.8	50～54
12.5	15.0	11.5	10.9	10.1	7.7	8.3	7.7	55～59
16.4	25.3	20.4	17.3	15.2	12.6	12.0	11.6	60～64
23.1	34.2	29.1	25.9	21.9	19.2	18.4	17.8	65～69
37.1	47.4	40.8	41.0	34.8	26.2	27.1	25.6	70～74
63.0	74.5	54.8	53.6	52.6	47.0	41.2	42.4	75～79
92.4	119.6	80.5	77.5	78.2	71.1	64.8	67.0	80～84
111.6	179.2	117.3	98.8	102.1	94.4	97.3	97.3	85～89
144.9	195.9	132.7	151.4	158.1	133.1	120.9	125.2	90～94[2]
...	...	...	113.4	178.6	169.4	195.4	159.7	95～99
...	...	...	186.1	187.7	125.0	191.4	244.4	100～
Female								
8.0	11.2	9.1	10.0	10.5	9.9	9.6	9.7	総数
0.0	-	0.0	-	-	-	-	-	0～4歳
-	0.1	0.1	-	-	-	-	-	5～9
-	0.1	-	0.0	-	0.0	-	-	10～14
0.0	0.0	-	0.0	0.0	0.0	0.0	-	15～19
0.1	0.2	0.1	0.1	0.1	0.1	0.1	0.1	20～24
0.2	0.1	0.2	0.2	0.1	0.0	0.2	0.1	25～29
0.3	0.4	0.2	0.3	0.2	0.1	0.2	0.1	30～34
0.6	0.6	0.4	0.3	0.4	0.3	0.2	0.2	35～39
0.9	1.1	0.8	0.8	0.6	0.5	0.5	0.6	40～44
1.4	2.0	1.5	1.3	0.9	0.8	0.7	0.9	45～49
2.2	3.6	2.0	1.9	1.5	1.5	0.9	1.2	50～54
4.7	5.7	4.3	3.5	2.8	2.4	1.9	2.0	55～59
9.3	10.9	6.9	6.4	4.9	4.3	3.3	3.4	60～64
17.8	19.3	11.7	10.3	8.1	6.6	5.5	5.8	65～69
34.7	34.0	22.6	18.7	16.2	11.4	11.0	10.6	70～74
56.8	64.5	40.1	36.3	27.6	22.0	21.3	19.7	75～79
91.7	111.5	71.4	61.0	51.2	40.8	38.6	37.7	80～84
110.6	141.8	104.0	95.3	89.5	73.6	72.3	69.5	85～89
101.0	144.2	119.2	125.2	131.5	122.0	116.3	108.8	90～94[2]
...	...	...	160.7	177.1	157.8	151.0	162.3	95～99
...	...	...	162.1	131.4	143.1	168.6	175.4	100～

243

死　亡

表 5.15　性・年齢別にみた死因年次推移分類
Table 5.15　Trends in deaths and death rates (per 100,000

Hi04　高血圧性疾患
Hypertensive diseases

死　亡　数

年　齢 Age	1950 昭和25年	1955 30年	1960 35年	1965 40年	1970 45年	1975 50年	1980 55年	1985 60年
								総　数
総数 Total	9 935	9 073	15 115	18 987	18 303	19 831	15 911	12 700
0〜4歳	4	-	-	-	-	-	1	-
5〜9 Years	2	-	-	-	-	-	-	-
10〜14	7	6	6	3	1	2	-	-
15〜19	8	14	12	9	8	2	-	-
20〜24	12	12	25	34	27	13	2	6
25〜29	18	28	47	33	46	24	13	7
30〜34	26	37	80	75	53	44	28	17
35〜39	41	44	94	128	124	79	29	27
40〜44	80	123	140	170	190	159	80	52
45〜49	171	228	364	331	230	222	132	76
50〜54	300	371	558	535	409	294	204	149
55〜59	505	502	904	894	678	465	273	223
60〜64	862	791	1 376	1 557	1 223	871	475	285
65〜69	1 557	1 323	2 054	2 406	2 111	1 623	1 008	521
70〜74	2 217	1 752	2 918	3 398	3 177	3 041	1 827	1 231
75〜79	2 050	1 992	3 166	4 205	3 854	4 362	3 373	2 216
80〜84	1 328	1 209	2 287	3 288	3 621	4 654	4 135	3 303
85〜89	587	526	893	1 544	1 969	2 897	2 970	2 969
90〜94	143	100	176	344	524	933	1 173	1 324
95〜99	16	12	15	32	53	137	175	276
100〜	1	3	-	1	4	9	12	17
不詳 Not stated	-	-	-	-	1	-	1	1
								男
総数	4 639	4 385	7 360	9 176	8 423	8 683	6 654	4 991
0〜4歳	2	-	-	-	-	-	-	-
5〜9	1	-	-	-	-	-	-	-
10〜14	3	2	2	1	1	2	-	-
15〜19	5	8	9	7	8	1	-	-
20〜24	6	8	16	19	10	9	1	-
25〜29	10	16	34	18	31	15	8	3
30〜34	12	21	51	51	32	29	17	6
35〜39	18	19	58	83	91	58	19	21
40〜44	40	67	72	93	119	101	50	30
45〜49	87	114	208	172	128	160	85	44
50〜54	151	231	339	303	231	169	126	94
55〜59	289	285	532	525	420	271	157	141
60〜64	471	469	832	934	660	506	263	156
65〜69	805	719	1 111	1 382	1 178	858	543	271
70〜74	1 084	858	1 453	1 778	1 589	1 504	902	589
75〜79	903	875	1 386	1 938	1 730	1 958	1 485	980
80〜84	502	476	897	1 246	1 366	1 796	1 642	1 266
85〜89	200	183	307	516	666	962	999	966
90〜94	42	29	52	102	149	244	317	372
95〜99	8	5	1	8	13	37	38	47
100〜	-	-	-	-	-	3	1	4
不詳	-	-	-	-	1	-	1	1
								女
総数	5 296	4 688	7 755	9 811	9 880	11 148	9 257	7 709
0〜4歳	2	-	-	-	-	-	1	-
5〜9	1	-	-	-	-	-	-	-
10〜14	4	4	4	2	-	-	-	-
15〜19	3	6	3	2	-	1	-	-
20〜24	6	4	9	15	17	4	1	6
25〜29	8	12	13	15	15	9	5	4
30〜34	14	16	29	24	21	15	11	11
35〜39	23	25	36	45	33	21	10	6
40〜44	40	56	68	77	71	58	30	22
45〜49	84	114	156	159	102	62	47	32
50〜54	149	140	219	232	178	125	78	55
55〜59	216	217	372	369	258	194	116	82
60〜64	391	322	544	623	563	365	212	129
65〜69	752	604	943	1 024	933	765	465	250
70〜74	1 133	894	1 465	1 620	1 588	1 537	925	642
75〜79	1 147	1 117	1 780	2 267	2 124	2 404	1 888	1 236
80〜84	826	733	1 390	2 042	2 255	2 858	2 493	2 037
85〜89	387	343	586	1 028	1 303	1 935	1 971	2 003
90〜94	101	71	124	242	375	689	856	952
95〜99	8	7	14	24	40	100	137	229
100〜	1	3	-	1	4	6	11	13
不詳	-	-	-	-	-	-	-	-

General mortality

別死亡数及び率（人口10万対）（つづき）
population) by sex, age and causes of death : Japan－CON.

Deaths

1990 平成2年	1995 7年	2000 12年	2005 17年	2010 22年	2014 26年	2015 27年	2016 28年	年齢 Age
Total								
9 246	8 222	6 063	5 835	6 760	6 932	6 726	**6 841**	総数 Total
-	-	-	-	-	-	-	-	0～4歳
-	-	-	-	-	-	-	-	5～9 Years
-	-	-	-	-	-	-	-	10～14
1	-	-	-	1	-	-	-	15～19
-	1	-	1	1	-	-	-	20～24
2	-	3	4	2	-	2	-	25～29
6	8	3	7	2	3	5	9	30～34
17	14	9	14	8	13	11	7	35～39
25	27	16	8	23	13	25	16	40～44
65	63	36	31	29	35	23	41	45～49
82	103	85	57	52	61	51	50	50～54
168	157	93	99	115	75	72	91	55～59
256	240	143	167	202	170	146	149	60～64
393	384	262	200	254	249	278	290	65～69
649	548	382	339	324	339	326	333	70～74
1 368	969	564	633	595	573	526	486	75～79
2 113	1 703	1 031	913	1 045	998	968	989	80～84
2 382	2 038	1 511	1 190	1 429	1 568	1 463	1 419	85～89
1 364	1 459	1 336	1 348	1 466	1 607	1 589	1 643	90～94
324	449	511	689	960	915	915	998	95～99
30	57	78	135	250	313	325	317	100～
1	2	-	-	2	-	1	3	不詳 Not stated
Male								
3 399	3 027	2 163	2 145	2 517	2 637	2 605	2 720	総数
-	-	-	-	-	-	-	-	0～4歳
-	-	-	-	-	-	-	-	5～9
-	-	-	-	-	-	-	-	10～14
1	-	-	-	-	-	-	-	15～19
-	1	-	-	1	-	-	-	20～24
2	-	3	3	1	-	1	-	25～29
4	6	3	5	-	3	5	8	30～34
11	9	7	13	7	11	11	5	35～39
14	18	11	6	17	12	23	12	40～44
41	41	28	26	25	27	19	35	45～49
57	79	67	49	39	48	45	49	50～54
97	119	67	79	101	64	62	83	55～59
159	158	97	122	167	141	121	123	60～64
197	247	151	133	187	203	223	222	65～69
302	262	225	206	208	226	219	229	70～74
582	409	246	326	342	304	299	290	75～79
791	632	368	351	445	471	477	484	80～84
735	579	463	380	470	585	554	555	85～89
330	366	305	300	322	364	380	406	90～94
70	97	110	129	159	145	135	178	95～99
5	3	12	17	24	33	30	39	100～
1	1	-	-	2	-	1	2	不詳
Female								
5 847	5 195	3 900	3 690	4 243	4 295	4 121	4 121	総数
-	-	-	-	-	-	-	-	0～4歳
-	-	-	-	-	-	-	-	5～9
-	-	-	-	-	-	-	-	10～14
-	-	-	-	1	-	-	-	15～19
-	-	-	1	-	-	-	-	20～24
-	-	-	1	1	-	1	-	25～29
2	2	-	2	2	-	-	1	30～34
6	5	2	1	1	2	-	2	35～39
11	9	5	2	6	1	2	4	40～44
24	22	8	5	4	8	4	6	45～49
25	24	18	8	13	13	6	1	50～54
71	38	26	20	14	11	10	8	55～59
97	82	46	45	35	29	25	26	60～64
196	137	111	67	67	46	55	68	65～69
347	286	157	133	116	113	107	104	70～74
786	560	318	307	253	269	227	196	75～79
1 322	1 071	663	562	600	527	491	505	80～84
1 647	1 459	1 048	810	959	983	909	864	85～89
1 034	1 093	1 031	1 048	1 144	1 243	1 209	1 237	90～94
254	352	401	560	801	770	780	820	95～99
25	54	66	118	226	280	295	278	100～
-	-	1	-	-	-	-	1	不詳

死　亡

表 5.15　性・年齢別にみた死因年次推移分類
Table 5.15　Trends in deaths and death rates (per 100,000

Hi04　高血圧性疾患
Hypertensive diseases

死　亡　率

年　　齢 Age	1950 昭和25年	1955 30年	1960 35年	1965 40年	1970 45年	1975 50年	1980 55年	1985 60年
								総　数
総数 Total	11.9	10.2	16.2	19.3	17.7	17.8	13.7	10.6
0〜4歳	0.0	-	-	-	-	-	0.0	-
5〜9 Years	0.0	-	-	-	-	-	-	-
10〜14	0.1	0.1	0.1	0.0	0.0	0.0	-	-
15〜19	0.1	0.2	0.1	0.1	0.1	0.0	-	-
20〜24	0.2	0.1	0.3	0.4	0.3	0.1	0.0	0.1
25〜29	0.3	0.4	0.6	0.4	0.5	0.2	0.1	0.1
30〜34	0.5	0.6	1.1	0.9	0.6	0.5	0.3	0.2
35〜39	0.8	0.9	1.6	1.7	1.5	0.9	0.3	0.3
40〜44	1.8	2.5	2.8	2.9	2.6	1.9	1.0	0.6
45〜49	4.3	5.2	7.6	6.7	3.9	3.0	1.6	0.9
50〜54	8.9	9.6	13.3	11.5	8.6	5.1	2.8	1.9
55〜59	18.4	15.7	24.8	22.3	15.4	10.0	4.9	3.2
60〜64	37.4	31.7	46.9	46.6	33.0	20.4	10.7	5.3
65〜69	87.9	67.3	95.1	93.9	71.0	47.2	25.5	12.5
70〜74	173.0	125.8	186.6	194.8	149.3	118.4	60.7	34.8
75〜79	299.0	227.5	331.6	383.7	304.4	266.5	166.1	91.0
80〜84	481.5	320.0	473.6	622.6	558.4	576.5	379.0	228.3
85〜89	742.5	472.4	573.1	775.3	858.6	939.0	725.6	506.3
90〜94[2]	978.3	505.1	593.4	742.6	883.4	1 322.7	1 141.8	871.2
95〜99	…	…	…	…	…	…	…	…
100〜	…	…	…	…	…	…	…	…
								男
総数	11.4	10.0	16.0	19.0	16.6	15.9	11.6	8.5
0〜4歳	0.0	-	-	-	-	-	-	-
5〜9	0.0	-	-	-	-	-	-	-
10〜14	0.1	0.0	0.0	0.0	0.0	0.0	-	-
15〜19	0.1	0.2	0.2	0.1	0.2	0.0	-	-
20〜24	0.2	0.2	0.4	0.4	0.2	0.2	0.0	-
25〜29	0.4	0.4	0.8	0.4	0.7	0.3	0.2	0.1
30〜34	0.5	0.8	1.4	1.2	0.8	0.6	0.3	0.1
35〜39	0.8	0.8	2.1	2.2	2.2	1.4	0.4	0.4
40〜44	1.8	2.9	3.2	3.4	3.3	2.5	1.2	0.7
45〜49	4.3	5.3	9.2	7.7	4.8	4.4	2.1	1.1
50〜54	8.8	12.0	16.6	13.9	10.8	6.5	3.6	2.4
55〜59	21.0	17.7	29.5	27.2	20.7	13.2	6.3	4.2
60〜64	42.4	38.2	57.9	57.5	37.8	26.3	13.6	6.6
65〜69	101.1	78.2	108.2	113.4	84.5	54.9	31.3	15.3
70〜74	200.6	144.5	209.5	225.4	165.8	131.5	68.7	39.6
75〜79	337.3	255.8	367.9	428.9	325.9	285.3	175.6	98.3
80〜84	525.2	357.4	530.3	666.5	567.0	584.7	394.1	231.2
85〜89	816.1	540.6	637.0	858.2	932.3	954.9	721.3	504.2
90〜94[2]	1 176.5	583.3	641.6	801.3	927.2	1 310.7	1 073.5	766.3
95〜99	…	…	…	…	…	…	…	…
100〜	…	…	…	…	…	…	…	…
								女
総数	12.5	10.3	16.3	19.6	18.8	19.7	15.7	12.6
0〜4歳	0.0	-	-	-	-	-	0.0	-
5〜9	0.0	-	-	-	-	-	-	-
10〜14	0.1	0.1	0.1	0.0	-	-	-	-
15〜19	0.1	0.1	0.1	0.0	-	0.0	-	-
20〜24	0.2	0.1	0.2	0.3	0.3	0.1	0.0	0.1
25〜29	0.2	0.3	0.3	0.4	0.3	0.2	0.1	0.1
30〜34	0.5	0.5	0.8	0.6	0.5	0.3	0.2	0.2
35〜39	0.9	0.9	1.1	1.2	0.8	0.5	0.2	0.1
40〜44	1.8	2.1	2.5	2.4	1.9	1.4	0.7	0.5
45〜49	4.2	5.1	6.1	5.9	3.2	1.7	1.2	0.8
50〜54	8.9	7.3	10.1	9.3	6.7	4.0	2.1	1.4
55〜59	15.8	13.6	20.2	17.8	10.9	7.5	3.8	2.3
60〜64	32.7	25.4	36.4	36.2	28.7	15.6	8.4	4.3
65〜69	77.1	57.6	83.2	76.2	59.0	40.9	21.0	10.4
70〜74	152.8	111.9	168.3	169.5	135.8	107.9	54.4	31.4
75〜79	274.4	209.3	308.0	352.0	288.9	252.9	159.3	86.0
80〜84	458.4	299.7	443.0	598.5	553.3	571.5	369.6	226.5
85〜89	709.5	442.6	544.5	739.4	825.3	931.3	727.8	507.2
90〜94[2]	908.7	478.2	576.8	720.9	867.5	1 327.0	1 168.1	915.6
95〜99	…	…	…	…	…	…	…	…
100〜	…	…	…	…	…	…	…	…

246

General mortality

別死亡数及び率（人口10万対）（つづき）
population）by sex, age and causes of death : Japan－CON.

Death rates

1990 平成2年	1995 7年	2000 12年	2005 17年	2010 22年	2014 26年	2015 27年	2016 28年	年齢 Age
Total								
7.5	6.6	4.8	4.6	5.3	5.5	5.4	5.5	総数 Total
-	-	-	-	-	-		-	0～4歳
-		-	-	-	-		-	5～9 Years
-		-	-	-	-		-	10～14
0.0	-	-	-	0.0	-		-	15～19
-	0.0	-	0.0	0.0	-	0.0	-	20～24
0.0	-	0.0	0.0	0.0	-	0.0	-	25～29
0.1	0.1	0.0	0.1	0.0	0.0	0.1	0.1	30～34
0.2	0.2	0.1	0.2	0.1	0.2	0.1	0.1	35～39
0.2	0.3	0.2	0.1	0.3	0.1	0.3	0.2	40～44
0.7	0.6	0.4	0.4	0.4	0.4	0.3	0.4	45～49
1.0	1.2	0.8	0.7	0.7	0.8	0.6	0.6	50～54
2.2	2.0	1.1	1.0	1.3	1.0	1.0	1.2	55～59
3.8	3.2	1.9	2.0	2.0	1.9	1.7	1.8	60～64
7.7	6.0	3.7	2.7	3.1	2.7	2.9	2.8	65～69
17.0	11.7	6.5	5.1	4.6	4.3	4.2	4.5	70～74
45.4	29.6	13.6	12.0	10.0	9.2	8.3	7.5	75～79
115.4	74.2	39.5	26.8	23.9	20.6	19.3	19.1	80～84
286.0	179.7	98.7	64.4	58.4	51.3	46.5	43.4	85～89
593.8	444.5	274.8	160.3	142.8	123.4	116.9	111.4	90～94[2]
…	…	…	326.0	322.5	260.7	253.6	261.3	95～99
…	…	…	532.4	569.5	521.7	526.3	487.7	100～
Male								
5.6	5.0	3.5	3.5	4.1	4.3	4.3	4.5	総数
-	-	-	-	-	-		-	0～4歳
-		-	-	-	-		-	5～9
-		-	-	-	-		-	10～14
0.0	-	-	-	-	-		-	15～19
-	0.0	-	-	0.0	-		-	20～24
0.0	-	0.1	0.1	0.0	-	0.0	-	25～29
0.1	0.1	0.1	0.1	-	0.1	0.1	0.2	30～34
0.2	0.2	0.2	0.3	0.1	0.3	0.3	0.1	35～39
0.3	0.4	0.3	0.1	0.4	0.2	0.5	0.2	40～44
0.9	0.8	0.6	0.7	0.6	0.6	0.4	0.8	45～49
1.4	1.8	1.3	1.1	1.0	1.2	1.1	1.3	50～54
2.6	3.1	1.6	1.6	2.4	1.7	1.7	2.2	55～59
4.9	4.4	2.6	2.9	3.4	3.2	2.9	3.1	60～64
9.0	8.3	4.5	3.8	4.8	4.6	4.7	4.5	65～69
19.4	13.6	8.4	6.8	6.4	6.2	6.1	6.7	70～74
48.6	32.6	15.2	14.4	13.2	11.0	10.7	10.0	75～79
116.6	76.9	40.3	28.7	26.2	24.3	23.7	23.2	80～84
266.4	160.4	97.2	68.5	62.9	57.0	52.0	49.7	85～89
497.2	398.6	242.2	142.4	132.5	117.0	113.2	107.7	90～94[2]
…	…	…	311.2	284.0	233.9	212.7	265.7	95～99
…	…	…	452.0	409.6	412.5	358.8	433.3	100～
Female								
9.4	8.2	6.1	5.7	6.5	6.7	6.4	6.4	総数
-	-	-	-	-	-		-	0～4歳
-		-	-	-	-		-	5～9
-		-	-	-	-		-	10～14
-		-	-	0.0	-		-	15～19
-		-	0.0	-	-		-	20～24
-		-	0.0	0.0	-	0.0	-	25～29
0.1	0.1	-	0.0	0.0	-	-	0.0	30～34
0.1	0.1	0.1	0.0	0.0	0.0	-	0.1	35～39
0.2	0.2	0.1	0.1	0.1	0.0	0.0	0.1	40～44
0.5	0.4	0.2	0.1	0.1	0.2	0.1	0.1	45～49
0.6	0.5	0.3	0.2	0.3	0.3	0.2	0.0	50～54
1.8	0.9	0.6	0.4	0.3	0.3	0.3	0.2	55～59
2.8	2.1	1.2	1.0	0.7	0.6	0.6	0.6	60～64
6.8	4.0	3.0	1.7	1.6	1.0	1.1	1.3	65～69
15.4	10.4	4.9	3.7	3.1	2.7	2.6	2.6	70～74
43.2	27.7	12.6	10.2	7.5	7.7	6.4	5.4	75～79
114.6	72.7	39.1	25.7	22.5	18.1	16.4	16.4	80～84
295.7	188.7	99.4	62.6	56.4	48.5	43.6	40.2	85～89
631.7	461.0	285.8	166.2	146.0	125.6	118.1	112.7	90～94[2]
…	…	…	329.6	331.5	266.4	262.4	259.5	95～99
…	…	…	546.4	594.1	549.0	552.6	487.7	100～

247

死　亡

表5.15　性・年齢別にみた死因年次推移分類
Table 5.15　Trends in deaths and death rates (per 100,000

Hi05　心疾患（高血圧性を除く）
Heart diseases
(excluding hypertensive heart diseases)

死　亡　数

年　　齢 Age	1950 昭和25年	1955 30年	1960 35年	1965 40年	1970 45年	1975 50年	1980 55年	1985 60年
								総　　数
総数 Total	53 377	54 351	68 400	75 672	89 411	99 226	123 505	141 097
0〜4歳	674	410	422	421	412	473	451	388
5〜9 Years	570	356	225	64	59	77	127	83
10〜14	790	605	444	202	115	105	130	134
15〜19	1 144	827	679	359	281	206	244	223
20〜24	1 323	1 086	829	595	536	440	345	373
25〜29	1 641	1 229	1 021	745	735	622	593	471
30〜34	1 573	1 259	1 254	1 023	961	856	894	789
35〜39	2 023	1 464	1 316	1 403	1 454	1 274	1 281	1 274
40〜44	2 417	1 876	1 616	1 623	1 997	2 030	2 019	1 910
45〜49	2 985	2 378	2 312	2 129	2 374	2 618	3 212	2 832
50〜54	3 636	3 329	3 331	3 188	3 137	3 264	4 376	4 510
55〜59	4 678	4 392	4 909	4 806	5 123	4 426	5 368	6 147
60〜64	6 289	5 646	6 727	7 082	7 623	7 063	7 498	7 783
65〜69	7 772	7 443	8 460	9 524	11 036	10 564	12 149	11 132
70〜74	7 526	8 557	10 788	11 409	14 012	15 073	17 741	18 388
75〜79	4 948	7 603	11 160	12 998	14 977	17 712	23 025	25 290
80〜84	2 413	4 069	8 387	10 662	13 378	16 656	22 560	28 078
85〜89	772	1 498	3 602	5 700	7 944	10 926	14 527	20 766
90〜94	167	287	815	1 530	2 786	3 985	5 759	8 454
95〜99	23	33	92	201	428	771	1 095	1 839
100〜	2	4	10	7	28	66	90	196
不詳 Not stated	11	-	1	1	15	19	21	37
								男
総数	26 108	27 282	34 755	38 827	45 988	50 395	64 103	71 766
0〜4歳	346	223	229	217	225	254	258	212
5〜9	281	185	111	36	33	48	68	50
10〜14	343	287	214	112	62	61	77	79
15〜19	550	404	341	185	174	135	175	138
20〜24	532	461	406	302	314	287	260	273
25〜29	578	502	465	379	449	412	408	334
30〜34	592	477	539	578	590	585	639	572
35〜39	787	588	559	782	909	836	920	922
40〜44	1 061	846	749	776	1 214	1 393	1 441	1 400
45〜49	1 538	1 198	1 163	1 018	1 300	1 724	2 330	2 023
50〜54	2 040	1 869	1 859	1 793	1 776	1 955	3 053	3 263
55〜59	2 657	2 571	2 940	2 898	3 015	2 710	3 465	4 342
60〜64	3 417	3 247	4 005	4 301	4 637	4 177	4 577	4 865
65〜69	4 113	4 134	4 861	5 579	6 475	6 235	7 129	6 341
70〜74	3 770	4 422	5 828	6 368	7 703	8 318	9 845	9 932
75〜79	2 194	3 550	5 288	6 420	7 539	8 700	11 694	12 747
80〜84	980	1 669	3 574	4 530	5 784	7 118	10 042	12 778
85〜89	260	550	1 365	2 031	2 850	4 048	5 549	8 047
90〜94	54	93	232	474	804	1 161	1 850	2 878
95〜99	6	5	23	44	114	205	286	488
100〜	1	1	3	3	9	15	20	48
不詳	8	-	1	1	12	18	17	34
								女
総数	27 269	27 069	33 645	36 845	43 423	48 831	59 402	69 331
0〜4歳	328	187	193	204	187	219	193	176
5〜9	289	171	114	28	26	29	59	33
10〜14	447	318	230	90	53	44	53	55
15〜19	594	423	338	174	107	71	69	85
20〜24	791	625	423	293	222	153	85	100
25〜29	1 063	727	556	366	286	210	185	137
30〜34	981	782	715	445	371	271	255	217
35〜39	1 236	876	757	621	545	438	361	352
40〜44	1 356	1 030	867	847	783	637	578	510
45〜49	1 447	1 180	1 149	1 111	1 074	894	882	809
50〜54	1 596	1 460	1 472	1 395	1 361	1 309	1 323	1 247
55〜59	2 021	1 821	1 969	1 908	2 108	1 716	1 903	1 805
60〜64	2 872	2 399	2 722	2 781	2 986	2 886	2 921	2 918
65〜69	3 659	3 309	3 599	3 945	4 561	4 329	5 020	4 791
70〜74	3 756	4 135	4 960	5 041	6 309	6 755	7 896	8 456
75〜79	2 754	4 053	5 872	6 578	7 438	9 012	11 331	12 543
80〜84	1 433	2 400	4 813	6 132	7 594	9 538	12 518	15 300
85〜89	512	948	2 237	3 669	5 094	6 878	8 978	12 719
90〜94	113	194	583	1 056	1 982	2 824	3 909	5 576
95〜99	17	28	69	157	314	566	809	1 351
100〜	1	3	7	4	19	51	70	148
不詳	3	-	-	-	3	1	4	3

248

General mortality

別死亡数及び率（人口10万対）（つづき）
population）by sex, age and causes of death : Japan－CON.

Deaths

1990 平成2年	1995 7年	2000 12年	2005 17年	2010 22年	2014 26年	2015 27年	2016 28年	年齢 Age
Total								
165 478	139 206	146 741	173 125	189 360	196 925	196 113	198 006	総数 Total
337	223	196	195	125	91	100	81	0～4歳
69	59	31	33	26	19	26	16	5～9 Years
113	84	57	44	42	26	18	19	10～14
250	179	125	107	62	62	52	45	15～19
359	277	233	196	115	119	82	108	20～24
448	314	387	307	196	142	152	156	25～29
680	483	569	531	383	327	232	248	30～34
1 079	712	724	822	756	551	514	495	35～39
1 986	1 334	1 137	1 230	1 106	1 219	1 142	1 095	40～44
2 923	2 627	2 138	1 902	1 735	1 719	1 750	1 819	45～49
4 156	3 453	3 929	3 527	2 636	2 562	2 550	2 476	50～54
6 570	5 173	5 094	6 145	4 674	3 689	3 425	3 488	55～59
9 461	8 141	7 383	7 950	8 069	7 133	6 404	5 824	60～64
11 813	11 437	11 133	10 739	10 232	10 190	10 564	11 292	65～69
17 204	14 861	15 768	16 612	14 244	14 492	13 959	13 353	70～74
27 937	20 317	20 260	24 014	23 432	21 572	20 720	20 436	75～79
33 607	27 716	25 043	29 569	33 939	33 764	33 452	33 028	80～84
28 575	24 564	28 155	31 159	37 908	43 276	43 226	43 241	85～89
14 142	13 167	17 763	25 933	30 749	35 377	36 332	38 374	90～94
3 307	3 581	5 711	10 256	15 541	16 544	17 217	17 898	95～99
418	453	861	1 807	3 353	4 009	4 165	4 475	100～
44	51	44	47	37	42	31	39	不詳 Not stated
Male								
81 774	69 718	72 156	83 979	88 803	92 278	92 142	93 419	総数
173	126	109	114	72	45	50	47	0～4歳
38	37	19	19	14	12	17	10	5～9
70	52	41	24	28	19	11	11	10～14
157	126	86	79	41	45	34	33	15～19
260	212	178	144	83	98	60	76	20～24
316	240	300	235	162	105	118	106	25～29
496	354	433	413	298	249	182	203	30～34
804	559	566	611	584	424	403	378	35～39
1 462	1 021	891	986	866	967	904	830	40～44
2 193	1 978	1 686	1 494	1 391	1 357	1 384	1 453	45～49
3 081	2 612	3 103	2 775	2 075	2 063	2 028	2 005	50～54
4 787	3 829	3 943	4 852	3 722	2 921	2 761	2 858	55～59
6 491	5 776	5 449	6 020	6 283	5 592	5 036	4 640	60～64
7 053	7 603	7 630	7 517	7 473	7 580	7 862	8 507	65～69
9 316	8 343	9 910	10 690	9 418	9 786	9 345	9 077	70～74
13 862	10 048	10 215	13 710	13 566	12 832	12 586	12 312	75～79
14 855	12 227	10 720	13 167	16 897	17 275	17 340	17 196	80～84
10 885	9 249	10 129	11 229	13 797	17 454	17 828	18 135	85～89
4 477	4 229	5 221	7 341	8 410	9 516	10 224	11 280	90～94
867	939	1 325	2 215	3 106	3 321	3 326	3 542	95～99
88	113	165	305	491	582	619	688	100～
43	45	37	39	26	35	24	32	不詳
Female								
83 704	69 488	74 585	89 146	100 557	104 647	103 971	104 587	総数
164	97	87	81	53	46	50	34	0～4歳
31	22	12	14	12	7	9	6	5～9
43	32	16	20	14	7	7	8	10～14
93	53	39	28	21	17	18	12	15～19
99	65	55	52	32	21	22	32	20～24
132	74	87	72	34	37	34	50	25～29
184	129	136	118	85	78	50	45	30～34
275	153	158	211	172	127	111	117	35～39
524	313	246	244	240	252	238	265	40～44
730	649	452	408	344	362	366	366	45～49
1 075	841	826	752	561	499	522	471	50～54
1 783	1 344	1 151	1 293	952	768	664	630	55～59
2 970	2 365	1 934	1 930	1 786	1 541	1 368	1 184	60～64
4 760	3 834	3 503	3 222	2 759	2 610	2 702	2 785	65～69
7 888	6 518	5 858	5 922	4 826	4 706	4 614	4 276	70～74
14 075	10 269	10 045	10 304	9 866	8 740	8 134	8 124	75～79
18 752	15 489	14 323	16 402	17 042	16 489	16 112	15 832	80～84
17 690	15 315	18 026	19 930	24 111	25 822	25 398	25 106	85～89
9 665	8 938	12 542	18 592	22 339	25 861	26 108	27 094	90～94
2 440	2 642	4 386	8 041	12 435	13 223	13 891	14 356	95～99
330	340	696	1 502	2 862	3 427	3 546	3 787	100～
1	6	7	8	11	7	7	7	不詳

死亡

表5.15 性・年齢別にみた死因年次推移分類
Table 5.15 Trends in deaths and death rates (per 100,000

Hi05 心疾患（高血圧性を除く）
Heart diseases
(excluding hypertensive heart diseases)

死 亡 率

年　　齢 Age	1950 昭和25年	1955 30年	1960 35年	1965 40年	1970 45年	1975 50年	1980 55年	1985 60年
								総　数
総数 Total	64.2	60.9	73.2	77.0	86.7	89.2	106.2	117.3
0～4歳	6.0	4.4	5.4	5.2	4.7	4.8	5.3	5.2
5～9 Years	6.0	3.2	2.4	0.8	0.7	0.9	1.3	1.0
10～14	9.1	6.4	4.0	2.2	1.5	1.3	1.5	1.3
15～19	13.4	9.6	7.3	3.3	3.1	2.6	3.0	2.5
20～24	17.1	12.9	10.0	6.6	5.1	4.9	4.4	4.6
25～29	26.5	16.2	12.4	8.9	8.1	5.8	6.6	6.1
30～34	30.2	20.6	16.7	12.4	11.5	9.3	8.3	8.7
35～39	40.1	28.6	21.8	18.7	17.8	15.2	14.0	11.9
40～44	53.9	37.9	32.2	27.2	27.3	24.8	24.3	21.1
45～49	74.5	54.5	48.0	43.3	40.7	35.7	39.9	34.6
50～54	107.3	86.5	79.3	68.4	65.7	56.8	61.0	57.3
55～59	170.2	137.0	134.8	120.1	116.4	95.2	96.2	88.3
60～64	273.0	226.1	229.5	211.8	205.5	165.7	168.8	145.2
65～69	438.9	378.4	391.6	371.7	371.1	307.5	307.8	267.3
70～74	587.2	614.4	689.9	654.0	658.5	587.1	589.0	520.6
75～79	721.6	868.2	1 169.0	1 186.0	1 183.1	1 082.1	1 133.8	1 038.8
80～84	875.0	1 077.1	1 736.7	2 018.9	2 063.0	2 063.2	2 067.6	1 940.6
85～89	976.6	1 345.2	2 311.7	2 862.0	3 464.1	3 541.4	3 549.2	3 541.3
90～94[2]	1 174.0	1 423.1	2 849.0	3 423.6	4 929.4	5 911.1	5 829.8	5 651.4
95～99	…	…	…	…	…	…	…	…
100～	…	…	…	…	…	…	…	…
								男
総数	64.0	62.2	75.8	80.5	90.9	92.1	112.1	121.5
0～4歳	6.1	4.7	5.7	5.2	5.0	5.0	5.9	5.6
5～9	5.8	3.3	2.4	0.9	0.8	1.1	1.3	1.2
10～14	7.8	6.0	3.8	2.4	1.6	1.4	1.7	1.6
15～19	12.7	9.3	7.3	3.4	3.8	3.4	4.2	3.0
20～24	13.9	11.0	9.8	6.7	5.9	6.3	6.6	6.5
25～29	20.5	13.3	11.4	9.1	10.0	7.6	9.0	8.5
30～34	25.1	17.1	14.4	13.9	14.2	12.7	11.9	12.6
35～39	33.1	25.4	20.2	20.9	22.2	20.0	20.1	17.1
40～44	48.3	36.4	32.9	28.4	33.3	33.9	34.8	31.2
45～49	76.2	56.1	51.5	45.8	48.9	47.4	58.0	49.9
50～54	118.7	96.9	91.1	82.5	83.0	75.3	86.5	83.7
55～59	192.7	159.9	163.1	150.1	148.6	131.7	138.9	128.0
60～64	308.0	264.7	278.6	264.7	265.6	217.1	236.8	207.1
65～69	516.8	449.8	473.3	457.7	464.7	398.7	411.0	358.1
70～74	697.8	744.7	840.3	807.1	803.8	727.4	750.3	668.3
75～79	819.6	1 037.8	1 403.7	1 420.8	1 420.4	1 267.8	1 382.5	1 278.9
80～84	1 025.2	1 253.1	2 113.0	2 423.2	2 400.8	2 317.2	2 410.0	2 333.9
85～89	1 060.9	1 624.7	2 832.4	3 377.9	3 989.5	4 018.2	4 006.6	4 199.9
90～94[2]	1 435.3	1 698.4	3 123.5	3 795.2	5 305.6	6 373.7	6 501.4	6 184.8
95～99	…	…	…	…	…	…	…	…
100～	…	…	…	…	…	…	…	…
								女
総数	64.3	59.6	70.8	73.6	82.7	86.4	100.5	113.2
0～4歳	6.0	4.1	5.0	5.1	4.4	4.5	4.7	4.8
5～9	6.2	3.2	2.5	0.7	0.7	0.7	1.2	0.8
10～14	10.4	6.8	4.3	2.0	1.4	1.1	1.2	1.1
15～19	14.0	9.9	7.3	3.2	2.4	1.8	1.7	1.9
20～24	20.3	14.9	10.1	6.4	4.2	3.4	2.2	2.5
25～29	31.6	19.0	13.5	8.7	6.3	3.9	4.1	3.6
30～34	34.5	23.6	19.0	10.8	8.9	5.9	4.8	4.8
35～39	46.3	31.3	23.1	16.6	13.4	10.5	7.9	6.7
40～44	59.4	39.3	31.6	26.2	21.4	15.6	13.9	11.2
45～49	72.9	52.9	44.9	41.2	33.7	24.2	21.8	19.5
50～54	95.6	76.0	68.1	56.1	51.6	41.6	36.4	31.4
55～59	147.5	114.0	107.1	92.1	88.8	66.2	61.6	50.5
60～64	240.5	188.9	182.2	161.7	152.0	123.4	116.4	96.9
65～69	375.4	315.8	317.5	293.6	288.6	231.3	226.8	200.1
70～74	506.7	517.6	570.0	527.5	539.5	474.4	464.5	413.3
75～79	658.9	759.5	1 016.0	1 021.4	1 011.8	948.1	956.2	872.4
80～84	795.3	981.2	1 533.9	1 797.3	1 863.3	1 907.1	1 856.0	1 701.1
85～89	938.7	1 223.2	2 078.6	2 639.0	3 226.4	3 310.3	3 315.3	3 220.8
90～94[2]	1 082.2	1 328.4	2 754.2	3 285.9	4 793.3	5 743.7	5 570.7	5 425.6
95～99	…	…	…	…	…	…	…	…
100～	…	…	…	…	…	…	…	…

250

General mortality

別死亡数及び率（人口10万対）（つづき）
population）by sex, age and causes of death : Japan－CON.

Death rates

1990 平成2年	1995 7年	2000 12年	2005 17年	2010 22年	2014 26年	2015 27年	2016 28年	年　　齢 Age
Total								
134.8	112.0	116.8	137.2	149.8	157.0	156.5	**158.4**	総数 Total
5.2	3.7	3.3	3.5	2.4	1.8	2.0	**1.7**	0〜4歳
0.9	0.9	0.5	0.6	0.5	0.4	0.5	**0.3**	5〜9 Years
1.3	1.1	0.9	0.7	0.7	0.5	0.3	**0.3**	10〜14
2.5	2.1	1.7	1.6	1.0	1.0	0.9	**0.8**	15〜19
4.1	2.8	2.8	2.7	1.8	2.0	1.4	**1.8**	20〜24
5.6	3.6	4.0	3.8	2.7	2.2	2.4	**2.5**	25〜29
8.8	6.1	6.6	5.5	4.7	4.5	3.2	**3.5**	30〜34
12.1	9.2	9.1	9.6	7.8	6.5	6.2	**6.2**	35〜39
18.7	15.0	14.8	15.4	12.8	12.6	11.8	**11.5**	40〜44
32.5	24.9	24.2	24.9	21.8	20.3	20.3	**19.9**	45〜49
51.5	38.9	37.8	40.3	34.6	33.3	32.2	**31.8**	50〜54
85.2	65.4	58.6	60.1	54.0	48.7	45.5	**46.7**	55〜59
140.5	109.3	95.7	93.2	80.3	80.0	75.4	**71.9**	60〜64
232.0	179.5	157.0	144.7	124.3	111.9	108.8	**110.5**	65〜69
451.6	317.9	267.7	250.4	203.9	183.6	180.1	**181.1**	70〜74
926.8	620.0	489.4	456.4	392.3	345.5	327.4	**314.4**	75〜79
1 834.7	1 208.3	959.7	867.3	777.8	695.4	667.4	**639.4**	80〜84
3 430.8	2 165.9	1 839.8	1 685.6	1 549.7	1 417.0	1 372.7	**1 323.5**	85〜89
6 175.5	3 891.0	3 474.3	3 083.3	2 996.1	2 717.1	2 672.3	**2 601.6**	90〜94[2]
…	…	…	4 852.5	5 221.5	4 713.4	4 772.5	**4 685.3**	95〜99
…	…	…	7 126.0	7 637.6	6 681.7	6 745.3	**6 884.6**	100〜
Male								
135.7	114.4	117.3	136.3	144.2	151.2	151.0	**153.5**	総数
5.2	4.1	3.6	4.0	2.7	1.7	2.0	**1.9**	0〜4歳
1.0	1.1	0.6	0.6	0.5	0.4	0.6	**0.4**	5〜9
1.6	1.4	1.2	0.8	0.9	0.7	0.4	**0.4**	10〜14
3.1	2.9	2.3	2.4	1.3	1.5	1.1	**1.1**	15〜19
5.9	4.3	4.2	3.9	2.6	3.2	2.0	**2.5**	20〜24
7.8	5.5	6.1	5.7	4.4	3.2	3.7	**3.4**	25〜29
12.7	8.8	9.9	8.5	7.1	6.7	5.0	**5.7**	30〜34
17.9	14.4	14.0	14.1	11.9	9.8	9.6	**9.4**	35〜39
27.4	22.8	22.9	24.5	19.8	19.7	18.4	**17.1**	40〜44
49.0	37.4	38.0	38.9	34.6	31.7	31.7	**31.4**	45〜49
77.2	59.4	59.8	63.6	54.5	53.4	50.9	**51.2**	50〜54
126.6	98.5	92.2	95.8	86.6	77.5	73.6	**76.7**	55〜59
200.7	160.5	145.7	145.1	127.3	127.7	120.4	**116.3**	60〜64
322.2	254.5	227.6	212.2	190.0	172.6	167.3	**172.0**	65〜69
598.5	432.0	371.6	351.5	291.1	266.4	259.0	**264.2**	70〜74
1 158.5	801.0	630.1	607.5	523.1	465.3	448.4	**425.3**	75〜79
2 189.5	1 488.2	1 173.9	1 078.1	993.8	891.4	862.8	**822.9**	80〜84
3 945.2	2 561.9	2 125.6	2 024.3	1 846.3	1 699.5	1 673.5	**1 623.0**	85〜89
6 668.3	4 517.2	3 806.3	3 484.7	3 461.9	3 059.8	3 045.2	**2 992.0**	90〜94[2]
…	…	…	5 343.1	5 547.0	5 356.5	5 240.4	**5 286.6**	95〜99
…	…	…	8 109.5	8 380.3	7 275.0	7 403.4	**7 644.4**	100〜
Female								
134.0	109.6	116.3	138.0	155.2	162.5	161.7	**163.0**	総数
5.2	3.3	3.0	3.0	2.1	1.8	2.1	**1.4**	0〜4歳
0.9	0.7	0.4	0.5	0.4	0.3	0.4	**0.2**	5〜9
1.0	0.9	0.5	0.7	0.5	0.3	0.3	**0.3**	10〜14
1.9	1.3	1.1	0.9	0.7	0.6	0.6	**0.4**	15〜19
2.3	1.4	1.4	1.5	1.0	0.7	0.8	**1.1**	20〜24
3.3	1.7	1.8	1.8	1.0	1.2	1.1	**1.7**	25〜29
4.8	3.3	3.2	2.5	2.1	2.2	1.4	**1.3**	30〜34
6.2	4.0	4.0	5.0	3.6	3.0	2.7	**3.0**	35〜39
9.9	7.1	6.4	6.2	5.6	5.3	5.0	**5.6**	40〜44
16.2	12.3	10.3	10.7	8.7	8.6	8.6	**8.1**	45〜49
26.4	18.8	15.9	17.2	14.8	13.0	13.3	**12.2**	50〜54
45.3	33.4	26.0	25.1	21.8	20.2	17.6	**16.9**	55〜59
84.8	61.5	48.7	44.1	34.9	33.9	31.8	**28.8**	60〜64
164.1	113.2	93.7	83.0	64.2	55.3	53.9	**52.8**	65〜69
350.1	237.6	181.7	164.8	128.6	111.5	111.4	**108.6**	70〜74
774.2	507.8	398.9	343.0	292.0	250.6	230.9	**225.3**	75〜79
1 626.0	1 052.1	844.4	749.7	639.9	565.5	536.7	**514.8**	80〜84
3 176.0	1 981.0	1 710.6	1 540.4	1 419.2	1 273.3	1 219.0	**1 167.9**	85〜89
5 982.4	3 665.8	3 362.6	2 949.1	2 851.6	2 612.2	2 550.0	**2 467.6**	90〜94[2]
…	…	…	4 732.8	5 146.1	4 575.4	4 672.6	**4 543.0**	95〜99
…	…	…	6 954.7	7 523.3	6 719.6	6 642.2	**6 643.9**	100〜

251

死　亡

表 5.15　性・年齢別にみた死因年次推移分類
Table 5.15　Trends in deaths and death rates (per 100,000

Hi06　脳血管疾患 [3)]
Cerebrovascular diseases

死　亡　数

年齢 Age	1950 昭和25年	1955 30年	1960 35年	1965 40年	1970 45年	1975 50年	1980 55年	1985 60年
								総　数
総数 Total	105 728	121 504	150 109	172 773	181 315	174 367	162 317	134 994
0～4歳	133	58	60	80	115	144	94	63
5～9 Years	76	41	41	28	31	27	32	19
10～14	93	53	57	58	39	33	36	27
15～19	149	101	118	104	111	67	45	54
20～24	245	203	160	169	194	120	87	94
25～29	292	259	283	257	318	267	200	145
30～34	427	382	494	620	602	565	483	316
35～39	932	811	892	1 251	1 487	1 220	1 130	876
40～44	1 844	2 018	1 923	2 169	2 763	2 790	2 090	1 749
45～49	3 806	4 444	4 429	4 013	3 775	4 326	4 112	2 752
50～54	6 623	8 065	8 221	7 559	6 010	5 300	5 473	4 690
55～59	9 702	11 613	13 436	12 202	10 440	7 567	6 384	5 840
60～64	14 189	15 896	18 725	19 880	17 020	13 335	9 376	7 091
65～69	19 240	20 792	23 864	27 135	26 545	20 832	16 583	10 322
70～74	21 602	23 403	28 396	32 462	34 882	31 161	25 353	18 090
75～79	15 670	19 497	25 835	32 103	35 346	36 500	34 435	25 944
80～84	7 821	10 011	16 302	21 549	26 242	29 344	31 935	28 783
85～89	2 402	3 244	5 657	9 040	11 810	15 721	17 709	19 742
90～94	400	560	1 102	1 881	3 129	4 280	5 809	6 963
95～99	57	49	107	205	385	670	882	1 298
100～	3	4	7	6	20	52	50	115
不詳 Not stated	22	-	-	2	51	46	19	21
								男
総数	52 188	62 737	78 965	92 723	96 910	89 924	81 650	65 287
0～4歳	66	33	37	43	75	78	60	38
5～9	39	24	17	20	20	18	26	13
10～14	52	24	37	29	22	15	18	14
15～19	67	66	72	68	63	34	26	30
20～24	140	114	89	93	98	68	50	57
25～29	152	134	158	154	204	169	131	87
30～34	216	174	302	434	400	382	333	210
35～39	413	414	493	863	1 106	864	785	586
40～44	854	1 086	1 116	1 380	1 980	2 007	1 452	1 169
45～49	1 868	2 371	2 474	2 360	2 337	2 995	2 747	1 771
50～54	3 396	4 489	4 746	4 536	3 553	3 141	3 585	3 022
55～59	5 318	6 793	8 342	7 606	6 380	4 435	3 782	3 772
60～64	7 763	9 391	11 478	12 497	10 501	7 863	5 342	4 046
65～69	9 957	11 597	13 807	16 130	16 012	12 307	9 440	5 704
70～74	10 657	11 745	14 752	18 064	19 655	17 230	13 923	9 696
75～79	7 053	8 841	12 003	15 678	17 820	18 202	17 373	12 842
80～84	3 112	4 121	6 707	8 914	11 388	12 866	13 986	12 426
85～89	894	1 130	1 980	3 265	4 219	5 789	6 612	7 249
90～94	143	174	327	539	918	1 232	1 733	2 159
95～99	17	15	25	48	110	176	215	355
100～	1	1	3	-	1	13	12	23
不詳	10	-	-	2	48	40	19	18
								女
総数	53 540	58 767	71 144	80 050	84 405	84 443	80 667	69 707
0～4歳	67	25	23	37	40	66	34	25
5～9	37	17	24	8	11	9	6	6
10～14	41	29	20	29	17	18	18	13
15～19	82	35	46	36	48	33	19	24
20～24	105	89	71	76	96	52	37	37
25～29	140	125	125	103	114	98	69	58
30～34	211	208	192	186	202	183	150	106
35～39	519	397	399	388	381	356	345	290
40～44	990	932	807	789	783	783	638	580
45～49	1 938	2 073	1 955	1 653	1 438	1 331	1 365	981
50～54	3 227	3 576	3 475	3 023	2 457	2 159	1 888	1 668
55～59	4 384	4 820	5 094	4 596	4 060	3 132	2 602	2 068
60～64	6 426	6 505	7 247	7 383	6 519	5 472	4 034	3 045
65～69	9 283	9 195	10 057	11 005	10 533	8 525	7 143	4 618
70～74	10 945	11 658	13 644	14 398	15 227	13 931	11 430	8 394
75～79	8 617	10 656	13 832	16 425	17 526	18 298	17 062	13 102
80～84	4 709	5 890	9 595	12 635	14 854	16 478	17 949	16 357
85～89	1 508	2 114	3 677	5 775	7 591	9 932	11 097	12 493
90～94	257	386	775	1 342	2 211	3 048	4 076	4 804
95～99	40	34	82	157	275	494	667	943
100～	2	3	4	6	19	39	38	92
不詳	12	-	-	-	3	6	-	3

General mortality

別死亡数及び率（人口10万対）（つづき）
population）by sex, age and causes of death : Japan－CON.

Deaths

1990 平成2年	1995 7年	2000 12年	2005 17年	2010 22年	2014 26年	2015 27年	2016 28年	年　　齢 Age
Total								
121 944	146 552	132 529	132 847	123 461	114 207	111 973	109 320	総数 Total
47	38	23	10	13	10	5	9	0～4歳
11	10	13	10	8	14	10	7	5～9 Years
19	23	19	14	15	18	15	13	10～14
34	41	29	22	19	15	17	17	15～19
76	74	51	52	39	34	24	26	20～24
124	112	112	110	92	60	51	47	25～29
233	273	229	217	193	133	130	118	30～34
620	483	458	510	466	311	311	307	35～39
1 618	1 177	858	844	841	844	817	826	40～44
2 468	2 475	1 907	1 467	1 294	1 165	1 208	1 203	45～49
3 557	3 499	3 456	2 647	1 946	1 720	1 673	1 628	50～54
5 137	4 747	4 322	4 439	3 185	2 249	2 171	2 148	55～59
6 884	7 447	5 833	5 455	5 180	3 912	3 632	3 324	60～64
8 292	10 638	9 125	7 569	6 615	6 020	5 979	6 273	65～69
12 726	14 667	14 000	12 630	9 741	8 765	8 573	7 667	70～74
21 318	21 482	18 842	19 254	16 421	13 705	12 830	12 451	75～79
25 587	31 341	24 774	24 456	23 735	21 435	20 567	20 087	80～84
21 606	28 602	26 791	25 160	24 831	25 105	24 705	23 746	85～89
9 457	15 219	16 272	19 555	18 672	18 994	18 993	19 285	90～94
1 904	3 765	4 773	7 290	8 541	7 885	8 330	8 257	95～99
187	393	617	1 103	1 590	1 794	1 915	1 860	100～
39	46	25	33	24	19	17	21	不詳 Not stated
Male								
57 627	69 587	63 127	63 657	60 186	54 995	53 576	52 706	総数
28	19	12	6	4	4	3	4	0～4歳
6	6	6	5	4	3	6	3	5～9
10	17	5	9	6	9	7	9	10～14
21	25	16	11	14	10	10	10	15～19
48	45	33	32	21	24	13	14	20～24
84	68	71	76	66	36	32	34	25～29
163	169	153	143	138	97	81	81	30～34
440	327	309	365	317	227	210	213	35～39
1 044	766	558	579	611	595	565	548	40～44
1 590	1 617	1 293	1 001	873	815	840	828	45～49
2 338	2 323	2 268	1 806	1 296	1 153	1 158	1 122	50～54
3 444	3 111	2 878	3 055	2 337	1 599	1 561	1 474	55～59
4 426	4 888	3 956	3 691	3 634	2 743	2 586	2 360	60～64
4 599	6 766	5 929	5 009	4 537	4 213	4 208	4 410	65～69
6 629	8 074	8 583	8 044	6 458	5 886	5 723	5 127	70～74
10 350	10 685	9 808	11 298	10 074	8 538	7 872	7 780	75～79
11 072	14 028	11 204	11 496	12 722	11 591	11 078	10 980	80～84
7 870	10 920	10 043	9 519	9 814	10 666	10 485	10 326	85～89
2 911	4 616	4 795	5 694	5 311	5 097	5 336	5 640	90～94
471	990	1 065	1 640	1 698	1 456	1 573	1 500	95～99
47	83	119	148	232	218	214	229	100～
36	44	23	30	19	15	15	14	不詳
Female								
64 317	76 965	69 402	69 190	63 275	59 212	58 397	56 614	総数
19	19	11	4	9	6	2	5	0～4歳
5	4	7	5	4	11	4	4	5～9
9	6	14	5	9	9	8	4	10～14
13	16	13	11	5	5	7	7	15～19
28	29	18	20	18	10	11	12	20～24
40	44	41	34	26	24	19	13	25～29
70	104	76	74	55	36	49	37	30～34
180	156	149	145	149	84	101	94	35～39
574	411	300	265	230	249	252	278	40～44
878	858	614	466	421	350	368	375	45～49
1 219	1 176	1 188	841	650	567	515	506	50～54
1 693	1 636	1 444	1 384	848	650	610	674	55～59
2 458	2 559	1 877	1 764	1 546	1 169	1 046	964	60～64
3 693	3 872	3 196	2 560	2 078	1 807	1 771	1 863	65～69
6 097	6 593	5 417	4 586	3 283	2 879	2 850	2 540	70～74
10 968	10 797	9 034	7 956	6 347	5 167	4 958	4 671	75～79
14 515	17 313	13 570	12 960	11 013	9 844	9 489	9 107	80～84
13 736	17 682	16 748	15 641	15 017	14 439	14 220	13 420	85～89
6 546	10 603	11 477	13 861	13 361	13 897	13 657	13 645	90～94
1 433	2 775	3 708	5 650	6 843	6 429	6 757	6 757	95～99
140	310	498	955	1 358	1 576	1 701	1 631	100～
3	2	2	3	5	4	2	7	不詳

死　亡

表 5.15　性・年齢別にみた死因年次推移分類
Table 5.15　Trends in deaths and death rates (per 100,000

Hi06　脳血管疾患[3]
Cerebrovascular diseases

死　亡　率

年　齢 Age	1950 昭和25年	1955 30年	1960 35年	1965 40年	1970 45年	1975 50年	1980 55年	1985 60年
								総　数
総数 Total	127.1	136.1	160.7	175.8	175.8	156.7	139.5	112.2
0 ～ 4 歳	1.2	0.6	0.8	1.0	1.3	1.4	1.1	0.8
5 ～ 9 Years	0.8	0.4	0.4	0.4	0.4	0.3	0.3	0.2
10～14	1.1	0.6	0.5	0.6	0.5	0.4	0.4	0.3
15～19	1.7	1.2	1.3	1.0	1.2	0.8	0.5	0.6
20～24	3.2	2.4	1.9	1.9	1.8	1.3	1.1	1.1
25～29	4.7	3.4	3.4	3.1	3.5	2.5	2.2	1.9
30～34	8.2	6.2	6.6	7.5	7.2	6.1	4.5	3.5
35～39	18.5	15.9	14.8	16.7	18.2	14.6	12.3	8.2
40～44	41.1	40.8	38.3	36.4	37.8	34.1	25.2	19.3
45～49	95.0	101.8	92.0	81.5	64.6	59.0	51.0	33.6
50～54	195.4	209.5	195.7	162.3	125.8	92.2	76.3	59.6
55～59	352.9	362.3	369.0	304.9	237.2	162.8	114.4	83.8
60～64	615.9	636.7	638.7	594.4	458.8	312.8	211.0	132.3
65～69	1 086.6	1 057.0	1 104.6	1 059.0	892.7	606.4	420.1	247.8
70～74	1 685.5	1 680.5	1 815.8	1 860.8	1 639.4	1 213.6	841.7	512.1
75～79	2 285.4	2 226.4	2 706.1	2 929.3	2 792.2	2 230.0	1 695.6	1 065.7
80～84	2 835.9	2 649.9	3 375.7	4 080.4	4 046.7	3 634.8	2 926.8	1 989.3
85～89	3 038.5	2 913.2	3 630.6	4 539.1	5 149.9	5 095.6	4 326.7	3 366.6
90～94[2]	2 812.6	2 692.5	3 777.9	4 120.9	5 373.4	6 131.7	5 659.4	4 512.9
95～99	…	…	…	…	…	…	…	…
100～	…	…	…	…	…	…	…	…
								男
総数	127.9	143.0	172.1	192.2	191.5	164.3	142.7	110.6
0 ～ 4 歳	1.2	0.7	0.9	1.0	1.7	1.5	1.4	1.0
5 ～ 9	0.8	0.4	0.4	0.5	0.5	0.4	0.5	0.3
10～14	1.2	0.5	0.7	0.6	0.6	0.4	0.4	0.3
15～19	1.6	1.5	1.5	1.2	1.4	0.8	0.6	0.7
20～24	3.6	2.7	2.2	2.1	1.9	1.5	1.3	1.4
25～29	5.4	3.5	3.9	3.7	4.5	3.1	2.9	2.2
30～34	9.2	6.2	8.1	10.5	9.6	8.3	6.2	4.6
35～39	17.4	17.8	17.8	23.0	27.0	20.6	17.2	10.9
40～44	38.8	46.7	49.1	50.6	54.3	48.9	35.1	26.0
45～49	92.5	111.0	109.6	106.1	88.0	82.3	68.4	43.7
50～54	197.5	232.7	232.6	208.8	166.0	120.9	101.5	77.5
55～59	385.7	422.5	462.9	394.0	314.5	215.5	151.6	111.2
60～64	699.6	765.5	798.4	769.0	601.4	408.6	276.4	172.3
65～69	1 251.0	1 261.8	1 344.4	1 323.4	1 149.2	787.1	544.3	322.1
70～74	1 972.5	1 978.0	2 127.0	2 289.5	2 051.0	1 506.7	1 061.1	652.4
75～79	2 634.8	2 584.6	3 186.3	3 469.6	3 357.4	2 652.5	2 053.9	1 288.5
80～84	3 255.6	3 094.0	3 965.3	4 768.2	4 726.9	4 188.4	3 356.6	2 269.6
85～89	3 647.9	3 338.1	4 108.5	5 430.2	5 905.8	5 746.4	4 774.1	3 783.4
90～94[2]	3 788.2	3 259.6	4 297.8	4 275.9	5 889.4	6 558.4	5 910.4	4 596.0
95～99	…	…	…	…	…	…	…	…
100～	…	…	…	…	…	…	…	…
								女
総数	126.3	129.4	149.6	160.0	160.7	149.4	136.4	113.9
0 ～ 4 歳	1.2	0.6	0.6	0.9	0.9	1.4	0.8	0.7
5 ～ 9	0.8	0.3	0.5	0.2	0.3	0.2	0.1	0.1
10～14	1.0	0.6	0.4	0.6	0.4	0.4	0.4	0.3
15～19	1.9	0.8	1.0	0.7	1.1	0.9	0.5	0.6
20～24	2.7	2.1	1.7	1.7	1.8	1.2	1.0	0.9
25～29	4.2	3.3	3.0	2.4	2.5	1.8	1.5	1.5
30～34	7.4	6.3	5.1	4.5	4.8	4.0	2.8	2.4
35～39	19.4	14.2	12.2	10.3	9.4	8.5	7.5	5.5
40～44	43.3	35.6	29.4	24.4	21.4	19.2	15.3	12.7
45～49	97.6	92.9	76.4	61.3	45.2	36.1	33.8	23.7
50～54	193.3	186.2	160.8	121.6	93.2	68.5	51.9	42.0
55～59	319.9	301.7	277.0	221.9	171.1	120.9	84.3	57.9
60～64	538.0	512.3	485.1	429.4	331.9	233.9	160.7	101.1
65～69	952.3	877.4	887.3	819.2	666.5	455.4	322.8	192.9
70～74	1 476.4	1 459.3	1 567.8	1 506.7	1 302.1	978.3	672.3	410.2
75～79	2 061.7	1 996.8	2 393.2	2 550.3	2 384.1	1 925.0	1 439.9	911.3
80～84	2 613.3	2 408.1	3 057.9	3 703.4	3 644.6	3 294.8	2 661.2	1 818.7
85～89	2 764.6	2 727.6	3 416.7	4 153.7	4 807.9	4 780.1	4 097.8	3 163.6
90～94[2]	2 470.1	2 497.3	3 598.4	4 063.5	5 186.7	5 977.4	5 562.5	4 477.8
95～99	…	…	…	…	…	…	…	…
100～	…	…	…	…	…	…	…	…

254

General mortality

別死亡数及び率（人口10万対）（つづき）
population）by sex, age and causes of death : Japan－CON.

Death rates

1990 平成2年	1995 7年	2000 12年	2005 17年	2010 22年	2014 26年	2015 27年	2016 28年	年　齢 Age
Total								
99.4	117.9	105.5	105.3	97.7	91.1	89.4	87.4	総数 Total
0.7	0.6	0.4	0.2	0.2	0.2	0.1	0.2	0〜4歳
0.1	0.2	0.2	0.2	0.1	0.3	0.2	0.1	5〜9 Years
0.2	0.3	0.3	0.2	0.3	0.3	0.3	0.2	10〜14
0.3	0.5	0.4	0.3	0.3	0.3	0.3	0.3	15〜19
0.9	0.8	0.6	0.7	0.6	0.6	0.4	0.4	20〜24
1.6	1.3	1.2	1.4	1.3	0.9	0.8	0.8	25〜29
3.0	3.4	2.7	2.3	2.3	1.8	1.8	1.7	30〜34
6.9	6.3	5.7	5.9	4.8	3.7	3.8	3.9	35〜39
15.2	13.2	11.1	10.6	9.7	8.8	8.4	8.6	40〜44
27.5	23.5	21.6	19.2	16.2	13.7	14.0	13.2	45〜49
44.1	39.5	33.3	30.3	25.6	22.4	21.2	20.9	50〜54
66.6	60.0	49.7	43.4	36.8	29.7	28.9	28.8	55〜59
102.2	100.0	75.6	64.0	51.5	43.9	42.8	41.1	60〜64
162.9	166.9	128.7	102.0	80.4	66.1	61.6	61.4	65〜69
334.0	313.8	237.7	190.4	139.4	111.0	110.6	104.0	70〜74
707.2	655.6	455.2	366.0	275.0	219.5	202.7	191.6	75〜79
1 396.9	1 366.3	949.4	717.4	544.0	441.5	410.4	388.9	80〜84
2 594.1	2 522.0	1 750.7	1 361.1	1 015.1	822.0	784.6	726.8	85〜89
3 991.4	4 383.2	3 092.6	2 325.0	1 819.3	1 458.8	1 397.0	1 307.5	90〜94[2]
…	…	…	3 449.2	2 869.6	2 246.4	2 309.0	2 161.5	95〜99
…	…	…	4 349.7	3 621.8	2 990.0	3 101.4	2 861.5	100〜
Male								
95.6	114.2	102.7	103.3	97.7	90.1	87.8	86.6	総数
0.8	0.6	0.4	0.2	0.1	0.2	0.1	0.2	0〜4歳
0.2	0.2	0.2	0.2	0.1	0.2	0.2	0.1	5〜9
0.2	0.4	0.1	0.3	0.2	0.3	0.2	0.3	10〜14
0.4	0.6	0.4	0.3	0.5	0.3	0.3	0.3	15〜19
1.1	0.9	0.8	0.9	0.7	0.8	0.4	0.5	20〜24
2.1	1.6	1.5	1.8	1.8	1.1	1.0	1.1	25〜29
4.2	4.2	3.5	2.9	3.3	2.6	2.2	2.3	30〜34
9.8	8.4	7.7	8.4	6.4	5.2	5.0	5.3	35〜39
19.6	17.1	14.4	14.4	13.9	12.1	11.5	11.3	40〜44
35.6	30.6	29.1	26.1	21.7	19.0	19.2	17.9	45〜49
58.6	52.9	43.7	41.4	34.0	29.9	29.1	28.6	50〜54
91.1	80.1	67.3	60.3	54.4	42.4	41.6	39.6	55〜59
136.8	135.9	105.8	89.0	73.6	62.6	61.8	59.1	60〜64
210.1	226.5	176.8	141.4	115.3	95.9	89.5	89.2	65〜69
425.9	418.1	321.9	264.5	199.6	160.2	158.6	149.2	70〜74
865.0	851.8	605.0	500.6	388.5	309.6	280.5	268.8	75〜79
1 631.9	1 707.4	1 226.9	941.3	748.3	598.1	551.2	525.4	80〜84
2 852.5	3 024.7	2 107.5	1 716.0	1 313.3	1 038.6	984.2	924.2	85〜89
4 209.4	4 866.2	3 391.1	2 702.9	2 186.2	1 638.9	1 589.3	1 496.0	90〜94[2]
…	…	…	3 956.1	3 032.5	2 348.4	2 478.4	2 238.6	95〜99
…	…	…	3 935.1	3 959.7	2 725.0	2 559.5	2 544.4	100〜
Female								
103.0	121.4	108.2	107.1	97.6	92.0	90.8	88.2	総数
0.6	0.7	0.4	0.1	0.4	0.2	0.1	0.2	0〜4歳
0.1	0.1	0.2	0.2	0.1	0.4	0.2	0.2	5〜9
0.2	0.2	0.4	0.2	0.3	0.3	0.3	0.1	10〜14
0.3	0.4	0.4	0.3	0.2	0.2	0.2	0.2	15〜19
0.7	0.6	0.4	0.6	0.6	0.3	0.4	0.4	20〜24
1.0	1.0	0.9	0.9	0.7	0.8	0.6	0.4	25〜29
1.8	2.6	1.8	1.6	1.4	1.0	1.4	1.1	30〜34
4.0	4.1	3.8	3.4	3.1	2.0	2.5	2.4	35〜39
10.9	9.3	7.8	6.7	5.4	5.2	5.3	5.9	40〜44
19.4	16.3	13.9	12.2	10.7	8.3	8.7	8.3	45〜49
29.9	26.3	22.8	19.2	17.1	14.8	13.1	13.1	50〜54
43.1	40.6	32.6	26.8	19.5	17.1	16.2	18.0	55〜59
70.2	66.5	47.3	40.3	30.2	25.7	24.3	23.5	60〜64
127.3	114.4	85.5	66.0	48.4	38.3	35.3	35.3	65〜69
270.6	240.3	168.1	127.6	87.5	68.2	68.8	64.5	70〜74
603.3	533.9	358.7	264.8	187.8	148.2	140.7	129.6	75〜79
1 258.6	1 175.9	800.0	592.4	413.5	337.6	316.1	296.1	80〜84
2 466.1	2 287.2	1 589.3	1 208.9	883.9	712.0	682.5	624.3	85〜89
3 906.0	4 209.5	2 992.2	2 198.7	1 705.6	1 403.7	1 333.9	1 242.7	90〜94[2]
…	…	…	3 325.5	2 831.9	2 224.6	2 272.9	2 138.3	95〜99
…	…	…	4 421.9	3 569.7	3 090.2	3 186.2	2 861.4	100〜

255

死　亡

表 5.15　性・年齢別にみた死因年次推移分類
Table 5.15　Trends in deaths and death rates（per 100,000

Hi07　肺　炎
Pneumonia

死　亡　数

年齢 Age	1950 昭和25年	1955 30年	1960 35年	1965 40年	1970 45年	1975 50年	1980 55年	1985 60年
								総　数
総数 Total	54 169	34 309	37 534	29 868	27 929	30 441	33 051	45 075
0～4歳	34 461	18 711	15 112	7 364	3 802	2 146	826	402
5～9 Years	1 375	922	542	264	214	161	95	49
10～14	557	312	271	186	130	115	69	45
15～19	595	299	336	241	191	140	82	61
20～24	759	358	353	244	209	172	74	85
25～29	605	373	389	233	219	195	121	67
30～34	525	306	402	266	206	203	125	99
35～39	607	296	378	281	310	251	132	152
40～44	636	304	354	297	389	350	208	184
45～49	722	377	503	313	440	443	355	295
50～54	863	524	707	517	595	548	455	543
55～59	1 204	790	1 088	903	1 009	805	725	859
60～64	1 704	1 164	1 754	1 488	1 708	1 499	1 136	1 447
65～69	2 447	1 785	2 402	2 352	2 813	2 661	2 610	2 566
70～74	2 882	2 451	3 472	3 402	4 028	4 478	4 660	5 472
75～79	2 262	2 647	4 107	4 381	4 473	5 692	6 880	9 238
80～84	1 350	1 763	3 347	4 131	3 911	5 600	7 360	11 097
85～89	484	731	1 527	2 258	2 347	3 484	4 799	8 159
90～94	110	176	438	650	790	1 231	1 923	3 410
95～99	16	18	48	87	122	233	383	743
100～	-	2	4	10	20	29	28	89
不詳 Not stated	5	-	-	-	3	5	5	13
								男
総数	28 090	17 965	20 152	15 962	15 030	16 371	18 633	25 520
0～4歳	17 829	9 848	8 227	4 020	2 059	1 140	454	215
5～9	627	444	270	139	108	85	44	20
10～14	270	154	136	100	56	59	39	19
15～19	280	152	160	140	98	75	53	33
20～24	329	165	140	108	108	87	31	53
25～29	224	146	159	101	103	85	63	35
30～34	193	108	196	126	94	97	68	48
35～39	254	112	165	148	175	153	66	87
40～44	289	126	171	142	211	214	131	118
45～49	397	212	270	143	253	266	242	197
50～54	502	286	397	289	323	328	305	379
55～59	731	462	664	549	601	466	449	610
60～64	1 015	693	1 153	917	1 066	903	742	957
65～69	1 458	1 062	1 476	1 481	1 806	1 708	1 735	1 663
70～74	1 603	1 388	2 053	2 047	2 405	2 743	2 954	3 583
75～79	1 210	1 412	2 148	2 404	2 441	3 166	4 206	5 733
80～84	635	837	1 548	1 926	1 890	2 840	3 882	6 182
85～89	185	287	652	927	938	1 450	2 285	3 903
90～94	48	64	152	224	257	420	756	1 394
95～99	7	7	13	29	30	66	112	260
100～	-	-	2	2	5	15	11	19
不詳	4	-	-	-	3	5	5	12
								女
総数	26 079	16 344	17 382	13 906	12 899	14 070	14 418	19 555
0～4歳	16 632	8 863	6 885	3 344	1 743	1 006	372	187
5～9	748	478	272	125	106	76	51	29
10～14	287	158	135	86	74	56	30	26
15～19	315	147	176	101	93	65	29	28
20～24	430	193	213	136	101	85	43	32
25～29	381	227	230	132	116	110	58	32
30～34	332	198	206	140	112	106	57	51
35～39	353	184	213	133	135	98	66	65
40～44	347	178	183	155	178	136	77	66
45～49	325	165	233	170	187	177	113	98
50～54	361	238	310	228	272	220	150	164
55～59	473	328	424	354	408	339	276	249
60～64	689	471	601	571	642	596	394	490
65～69	989	723	926	871	1 007	953	875	903
70～74	1 279	1 063	1 419	1 355	1 623	1 735	1 706	1 889
75～79	1 052	1 235	1 959	1 977	2 032	2 526	2 674	3 505
80～84	715	926	1 799	2 205	2 021	2 760	3 478	4 915
85～89	299	444	875	1 331	1 409	2 034	2 514	4 256
90～94	62	112	286	426	533	811	1 167	2 016
95～99	9	11	35	58	92	167	271	483
100～	-	2	2	8	15	14	17	70
不詳	1	-	-	-	-	-	-	1

256

General mortality

別死亡数及び率（人口10万対）（つづき）
population）by sex, age and causes of death : Japan－CON.

Deaths

1990 平成2年	1995 7年	2000 12年	2005 17年	2010 22年	2014 26年	2015 27年	2016 28年	年齢 Age
Total								
68 194	79 629	86 938	107 241	118 888	119 650	120 953	119 300	総数 Total
261	224	162	118	113	89	74	63	0～4歳
51	38	21	17	22	10	25	19	5～9 Years
42	47	32	26	14	21	11	13	10～14
59	50	35	29	18	10	13	13	15～19
71	80	35	38	31	19	22	18	20～24
77	74	44	58	43	26	29	31	25～29
86	90	84	66	70	37	63	47	30～34
146	128	112	116	102	94	68	75	35～39
219	225	153	149	162	143	123	125	40～44
362	444	301	244	198	229	201	224	45～49
571	673	600	535	403	410	379	366	50～54
1 151	1 022	1 042	1 084	893	719	639	677	55～59
2 184	2 170	1 913	1 945	1 921	1 887	1 593	1 560	60～64
3 449	3 816	3 673	3 335	3 265	3 385	3 469	3 696	65～69
6 590	6 299	7 159	7 262	6 537	6 526	6 375	6 032	70～74
12 577	10 988	11 301	13 929	13 464	12 440	12 008	11 681	75～79
16 716	18 418	17 456	20 443	24 028	22 908	22 781	22 231	80～84
14 494	19 352	21 562	24 623	28 884	31 566	31 841	31 171	85～89
7 129	11 544	15 135	21 937	23 568	24 867	26 494	26 418	90～94
1 722	3 386	5 204	9 433	12 318	11 371	11 803	11 906	95～99
220	542	899	1 843	2 824	2 878	2 936	2 924	100～
17	19	15	11	10	15	6	10	不詳 Not stated
Male								
38 596	42 419	46 722	57 310	63 569	64 780	65 609	65 636	総数
157	126	90	66	64	51	48	34	0～4歳
35	22	11	11	9	5	11	8	5～9
18	21	21	15	7	12	8	7	10～14
39	34	18	12	10	5	6	4	15～19
40	53	23	27	14	10	14	8	20～24
39	47	21	36	28	18	14	20	25～29
48	46	42	42	48	23	38	32	30～34
76	92	77	67	68	63	41	55	35～39
150	160	106	102	117	89	83	83	40～44
253	309	214	180	139	146	146	163	45～49
403	479	433	410	298	300	268	262	50～54
822	735	757	809	673	547	495	497	55～59
1 582	1 544	1 408	1 483	1 461	1 433	1 230	1 208	60～64
2 324	2 712	2 652	2 466	2 470	2 611	2 664	2 853	65～69
4 313	4 013	5 103	5 231	4 755	4 795	4 754	4 475	70～74
7 986	6 610	7 062	9 664	9 459	8 671	8 389	8 270	75～79
9 507	10 071	9 900	12 040	15 411	14 800	14 614	14 465	80～84
7 139	9 320	10 598	12 199	14 738	17 344	17 725	17 612	85～89
2 986	4 750	6 277	8 956	9 399	9 867	10 908	11 281	90～94
603	1 122	1 663	3 038	3 771	3 406	3 502	3 655	95～99
61	136	234	445	600	573	647	634	100～
15	17	13	11	10	11	4	10	不詳
Female								
29 598	37 210	40 216	49 931	55 319	54 870	55 344	53 664	総数
104	98	72	52	49	38	26	29	0～4歳
16	16	10	6	13	5	14	11	5～9
24	26	12	11	7	9	3	6	10～14
20	16	17	17	8	5	7	9	15～19
31	27	12	11	17	9	8	10	20～24
38	27	23	22	15	8	15	11	25～29
38	44	42	24	22	14	25	15	30～34
70	36	35	49	34	31	27	20	35～39
69	65	47	47	45	54	40	42	40～44
109	135	87	64	59	83	55	61	45～49
168	194	167	125	105	110	111	104	50～54
329	287	285	275	220	172	144	180	55～59
602	626	505	462	460	454	363	352	60～64
1 125	1 104	1 021	869	795	774	805	843	65～69
2 277	2 286	2 056	2 031	1 762	1 731	1 621	1 557	70～74
4 591	4 378	4 239	4 265	4 005	3 769	3 619	3 411	75～79
7 209	8 347	7 556	8 403	8 617	8 108	8 167	7 766	80～84
7 355	10 032	10 964	12 424	14 146	14 222	14 116	13 559	85～89
4 143	6 794	8 858	12 981	14 169	15 000	15 586	15 137	90～94
1 119	2 264	3 541	6 395	8 547	7 965	8 301	8 251	95～99
159	406	665	1 398	2 224	2 305	2 289	2 290	100～
2	2	2	-	-	4	2	-	不詳

257

死　亡

表5.15　性・年齢別にみた死因年次推移分類
Table 5.15　Trends in deaths and death rates (per 100,000

Hi07　肺　炎
Pneumonia

死　亡　率

年　齢 Age	1950 昭和25年	1955 30年	1960 35年	1965 40年	1970 45年	1975 50年	1980 55年	1985 60年
								総　数
総数 Total	65.1	38.4	40.2	30.4	27.1	27.4	28.4	37.5
0〜4歳	307.5	202.3	192.6	90.5	43.5	21.6	9.8	5.4
5〜9 Years	14.4	8.3	5.9	3.4	2.6	1.8	1.0	0.6
10〜14	6.4	3.3	2.5	2.0	1.7	1.4	0.8	0.5
15〜19	6.9	3.5	3.6	2.2	2.1	1.8	1.0	0.7
20〜24	9.8	4.3	4.2	2.7	2.0	1.9	1.0	1.0
25〜29	9.8	4.9	4.7	2.8	2.4	1.8	1.3	0.9
30〜34	10.1	5.0	5.3	3.2	2.5	2.2	1.2	1.1
35〜39	12.0	5.8	6.3	3.7	3.8	3.0	1.4	1.4
40〜44	14.2	6.1	7.1	5.0	5.3	4.3	2.5	2.0
45〜49	18.0	8.6	10.4	6.4	7.5	6.0	4.4	3.6
50〜54	25.5	13.6	16.8	11.1	12.5	9.5	6.3	6.9
55〜59	43.8	24.6	29.9	22.6	22.9	17.3	13.0	12.3
60〜64	74.0	46.6	59.8	44.5	46.0	35.2	25.6	27.0
65〜69	138.2	90.7	111.2	91.8	94.6	77.5	66.1	61.6
70〜74	224.9	176.0	222.0	195.0	189.3	174.4	154.7	154.9
75〜79	329.9	302.3	430.2	399.8	353.3	347.8	338.8	379.5
80〜84	489.5	466.7	693.1	782.2	603.1	693.7	674.5	767.0
85〜89	612.2	656.5	980.0	1 133.8	1 023.4	1 129.3	1 172.5	1 391.4
90〜94[1]	770.4	860.9	1 522.4	1 471.5	1 417.1	1 830.2	1 959.5	2 285.6
95〜99	...	...	...	...	...	...	...	...
100〜	...	...	...	...	...	...	...	...
								男
総数	68.8	41.0	43.9	33.1	29.7	29.9	32.6	43.2
0〜4歳	311.8	208.4	205.0	96.9	45.9	22.4	10.5	5.7
5〜9	13.0	7.9	5.7	3.5	2.6	1.9	0.9	0.5
10〜14	6.1	3.2	2.4	2.1	1.4	1.4	0.9	0.4
15〜19	6.5	3.5	3.4	2.6	2.2	1.9	1.3	0.7
20〜24	8.6	3.9	3.4	2.4	2.0	1.9	0.8	1.3
25〜29	7.9	3.9	3.9	2.4	2.3	1.6	1.4	0.9
30〜34	8.2	3.9	5.2	3.0	2.3	2.1	1.3	1.1
35〜39	10.7	4.8	6.0	3.9	4.3	3.7	1.4	1.6
40〜44	13.1	5.4	7.5	5.2	5.8	5.2	3.2	2.6
45〜49	19.7	9.9	12.0	6.4	9.5	7.3	6.0	4.9
50〜54	29.2	14.8	19.5	13.3	15.1	12.6	8.6	9.7
55〜59	53.0	28.7	36.8	28.4	29.6	22.6	18.0	18.0
60〜64	91.5	56.5	80.2	56.4	61.1	46.9	38.4	40.7
65〜69	183.2	115.6	143.7	121.5	129.6	109.2	100.0	93.9
70〜74	296.7	233.8	296.0	259.4	251.0	239.9	225.1	241.1
75〜79	452.0	412.8	570.2	532.0	459.9	461.4	497.3	575.2
80〜84	664.3	628.4	915.2	1 030.2	784.5	924.5	931.7	1 129.1
85〜89	754.9	847.8	1 352.9	1 541.7	1 313.0	1 439.3	1 649.9	2 037.1
90〜94[2]	1 294.1	1 218.0	2 021.8	1 857.5	1 671.2	2 312.3	2 650.6	3 030.8
95〜99	...	...	...	...	...	...	...	...
100〜	...	...	...	...	...	...	...	...
								女
総数	61.5	36.0	36.6	27.8	24.6	24.9	24.4	31.9
0〜4歳	303.1	196.0	179.7	83.9	40.9	20.8	9.0	5.1
5〜9	15.9	8.8	6.0	3.2	2.7	1.8	1.0	0.7
10〜14	6.7	3.4	2.5	1.9	1.9	1.4	0.7	0.5
15〜19	7.4	3.4	3.8	1.9	2.1	1.7	0.7	0.6
20〜24	11.1	4.6	5.1	3.0	1.9	1.9	1.1	0.8
25〜29	11.3	5.9	5.6	3.1	2.6	2.1	1.3	0.8
30〜34	11.7	6.0	5.5	3.4	2.7	2.3	1.1	1.1
35〜39	13.2	6.6	6.5	3.5	3.3	2.3	1.4	1.2
40〜44	15.2	6.8	6.7	4.8	4.9	3.3	1.9	1.4
45〜49	16.4	7.4	9.1	6.3	5.9	4.8	2.8	2.4
50〜54	21.6	12.4	14.3	9.2	10.3	7.0	4.1	4.1
55〜59	34.5	20.5	23.1	17.1	17.2	13.1	8.9	7.0
60〜64	57.7	37.1	40.2	33.2	32.7	25.5	15.7	16.3
65〜69	101.5	69.0	81.7	64.8	63.7	50.9	39.5	37.7
70〜74	172.5	133.1	163.1	141.8	138.8	121.8	100.4	92.3
75〜79	251.7	231.4	338.9	307.0	276.4	265.7	225.7	243.8
80〜84	396.8	378.6	573.3	646.3	495.9	551.9	515.7	546.5
85〜89	548.2	572.9	813.0	957.3	892.4	978.9	928.4	1 077.7
90〜94[2]	586.5	738.0	1 349.9	1 328.4	1 325.1	1 655.8	1 692.8	1 970.1
95〜99	...	...	...	...	...	...	...	...
100〜	...	...	...	...	...	...	...	...

General mortality

別死亡数及び率（人口10万対）（つづき）
population）by sex, age and causes of death : Japan－CON.

Death rates

1990 平成2年	1995 7年	2000 12年	2005 17年	2010 22年	2014 26年	2015 27年	2016 28年	年　齢 Age
Total								
55. 6	64. 1	69. 2	85. 0	94. 1	95. 4	96. 5	95. 4	総数 Total
4. 0	3. 8	2. 8	2. 1	2. 2	1. 7	1. 5	1. 3	0〜4歳
0. 7	0. 6	0. 4	0. 3	0. 4	0. 2	0. 5	0. 4	5〜9 Years
0. 5	0. 6	0. 5	0. 4	0. 2	0. 4	0. 2	0. 2	10〜14
0. 6	0. 6	0. 5	0. 4	0. 3	0. 2	0. 2	0. 2	15〜19
0. 8	0. 8	0. 4	0. 5	0. 5	0. 3	0. 4	0. 3	20〜24
1. 0	0. 9	0. 5	0. 7	0. 6	0. 4	0. 5	0. 5	25〜29
1. 1	1. 1	1. 0	0. 7	0. 9	0. 5	0. 9	0. 7	30〜34
1. 6	1. 7	1. 4	1. 3	1. 1	1. 1	0. 8	0. 9	35〜39
2. 1	2. 5	2. 0	1. 9	1. 9	1. 5	1. 3	1. 3	40〜44
4. 0	4. 2	3. 4	3. 2	2. 5	2. 7	2. 3	2. 5	45〜49
7. 1	7. 6	5. 8	6. 1	5. 3	5. 3	4. 8	4. 7	50〜54
14. 9	12. 9	12. 0	10. 6	10. 3	9. 5	8. 5	9. 1	55〜59
32. 4	29. 1	24. 8	22. 8	19. 1	21. 2	18. 8	19. 3	60〜64
67. 7	59. 9	51. 8	44. 9	39. 7	37. 2	35. 7	36. 2	65〜69
173. 0	134. 8	121. 5	109. 5	93. 6	82. 7	82. 2	81. 8	70〜74
417. 2	335. 3	273. 0	264. 8	225. 4	199. 2	189. 7	179. 7	75〜79
912. 6	802. 9	668. 9	599. 7	550. 7	471. 8	454. 5	430. 4	80〜84
1 740. 2	1 706. 4	1 409. 0	1 332. 1	1 180. 8	1 033. 6	1 011. 2	954. 1	85〜89
3 135. 3	3 499. 8	3 032. 1	2 608. 2	2 296. 4	1 909. 9	1 948. 7	1 791. 1	90〜94²⁾
···	···	···	4 463. 1	4 138. 7	3 239. 6	3 271. 7	3 116. 8	95〜99
···	···	···	7 267. 9	6 432. 7	4 796. 7	4 754. 9	4 498. 5	100〜
Male								
64. 1	69. 6	76. 0	93. 0	103. 2	106. 1	107. 5	107. 8	総数
4. 7	4. 1	3. 0	2. 3	2. 4	1. 9	1. 9	1. 4	0〜4歳
0. 9	0. 7	0. 4	0. 4	0. 3	0. 2	0. 4	0. 3	5〜9
0. 4	0. 6	0. 6	0. 5	0. 2	0. 4	0. 3	0. 3	10〜14
0. 8	0. 8	0. 5	0. 4	0. 3	0. 2	0. 2	0. 1	15〜19
0. 9	1. 1	0. 5	0. 7	0. 4	0. 3	0. 5	0. 3	20〜24
1. 0	1. 1	0. 4	0. 9	0. 8	0. 5	0. 4	0. 6	25〜29
1. 2	1. 1	1. 0	0. 9	1. 1	0. 6	1. 0	0. 9	30〜34
1. 7	2. 4	1. 9	1. 5	1. 4	1. 5	1. 0	1. 4	35〜39
2. 8	3. 6	2. 7	2. 5	2. 7	1. 8	1. 7	1. 7	40〜44
5. 7	5. 8	4. 8	4. 7	3. 5	3. 4	3. 3	3. 5	45〜49
10. 1	10. 9	8. 3	9. 4	7. 8	7. 8	6. 7	6. 7	50〜54
21. 7	18. 9	17. 7	16. 0	15. 7	14. 5	13. 2	13. 3	55〜59
48. 9	42. 9	37. 6	35. 7	29. 6	32. 7	29. 4	30. 3	60〜64
106. 2	90. 8	79. 1	69. 6	62. 8	59. 5	56. 7	57. 7	65〜69
277. 1	207. 8	191. 4	172. 0	147. 6	130. 5	131. 7	130. 3	70〜74
667. 4	526. 9	435. 6	428. 2	364. 8	314. 4	298. 9	285. 7	75〜79
1 401. 3	1 225. 8	1 084. 1	985. 8	906. 4	763. 7	727. 1	692. 2	80〜84
2 587. 5	2 581. 6	2 224. 0	2 199. 1	1 972. 2	1 688. 8	1 663. 8	1 576. 2	85〜89
4 480. 7	5 139. 1	4 636. 1	4 251. 4	3 869. 0	3 172. 7	3 248. 9	2 992. 3	90〜94²⁾
···	···	···	7 328. 4	6 734. 7	5 493. 5	5 517. 7	5 455. 2	95〜99
···	···	···	11 832. 0	10 240. 7	7 162. 5	7 738. 3	7 044. 4	100〜
Female								
47. 4	58. 7	62. 7	77. 3	85. 4	85. 2	86. 1	83. 6	総数
3. 3	3. 4	2. 5	1. 9	1. 9	1. 5	1. 1	1. 2	0〜4歳
0. 4	0. 5	0. 3	0. 2	0. 5	0. 2	0. 5	0. 4	5〜9
0. 6	0. 7	0. 4	0. 4	0. 2	0. 3	0. 1	0. 2	10〜14
0. 4	0. 4	0. 5	0. 5	0. 3	0. 2	0. 2	0. 3	15〜19
0. 7	0. 6	0. 3	0. 3	0. 6	0. 3	0. 3	0. 3	20〜24
1. 0	0. 6	0. 5	0. 6	0. 4	0. 4	0. 5	0. 4	25〜29
1. 0	1. 1	1. 0	0. 5	0. 5	0. 4	0. 7	0. 4	30〜34
1. 6	0. 9	0. 9	1. 2	0. 7	0. 7	0. 7	0. 5	35〜39
1. 3	1. 5	1. 2	1. 2	1. 1	1. 1	0. 8	0. 9	40〜44
2. 4	2. 6	2. 0	1. 7	1. 5	2. 0	1. 3	1. 4	45〜49
4. 1	4. 3	3. 2	2. 9	2. 8	2. 9	2. 8	2. 7	50〜54
8. 4	7. 1	6. 4	5. 3	5. 0	4. 5	3. 8	4. 8	55〜59
17. 2	16. 3	12. 7	10. 6	9. 0	10. 0	8. 4	8. 6	60〜64
38. 8	32. 6	27. 3	22. 4	18. 5	16. 4	16. 1	16. 0	65〜69
101. 1	83. 3	63. 8	56. 5	47. 0	41. 0	39. 1	39. 5	70〜74
252. 5	216. 5	168. 3	142. 0	118. 5	108. 1	102. 7	94. 6	75〜79
625. 1	566. 9	445. 4	384. 1	323. 6	278. 1	272. 0	252. 5	80〜84
1 320. 5	1 297. 7	1 040. 4	960. 3	832. 7	701. 3	677. 5	630. 7	85〜89
2 608. 0	2 910. 5	2 492. 5	2 059. 1	1 808. 7	1 515. 2	1 522. 3	1 378. 6	90〜94²⁾
···	···	···	3 764. 0	3 537. 1	2 756. 1	2 792. 2	2 611. 1	95〜99
···	···	···	6 473. 1	5 846. 2	4 519. 6	4 287. 6	4 017. 5	100〜

259

死　亡

表 5.15　性・年齢別にみた死因年次推移分類
Table 5.15　Trends in deaths and death rates (per 100,000

Hi08　慢性気管支炎及び肺気腫
Chronic bronchitis and emphysema

死　亡　数

年　齢 Age	1950 昭和25年	1955 30年	1960 35年	1965 40年	1970 45年	1975 50年	1980 55年	1985 60年
								総　数
総数 Total	7 055	3 446	2 664	3 016	3 970	4 392	5 100	6 953
0～4歳	562	86	24	21	12	6	3	-
5～9 Years	47	4	6	4	7	6	7	-
10～14	24	6	2	2	3	1	5	1
15～19	77	12	11	7	3	1	2	4
20～24	96	15	11	5	4	4	3	2
25～29	110	20	14	10	9	5	3	-
30～34	88	30	14	6	16	7	7	6
35～39	80	19	19	16	13	11	9	4
40～44	107	36	17	17	25	17	17	18
45～49	155	38	21	24	30	22	26	24
50～54	257	87	42	40	53	63	57	49
55～59	473	148	114	103	129	110	101	142
60～64	813	283	168	237	320	256	231	269
65～69	1 184	526	319	383	552	526	557	549
70～74	1 321	793	518	550	831	845	932	1 205
75～79	935	759	635	658	862	1 078	1 272	1 685
80～84	506	396	492	579	670	824	1 050	1 629
85～89	187	154	182	269	335	451	595	968
90～94	29	31	50	80	80	135	191	318
95～99	4	2	5	5	16	20	27	72
100～	-	1	-	-	-	4	5	8
不詳 Not stated	-	-	-	-	-	-	-	8
								男
総数	4 042	2 075	1 538	1 811	2 607	2 972	3 550	4 973
0～4歳	322	53	15	12	8	1	1	-
5～9	13	2	5	4	3	4	5	-
10～14	9	4	1	2	2	-	3	1
15～19	30	7	5	6	2	1	1	1
20～24	44	4	6	1	3	4	1	2
25～29	47	11	8	4	6	3	2	-
30～34	35	11	8	2	6	4	5	2
35～39	30	8	8	5	6	3	4	3
40～44	51	19	9	10	15	9	9	7
45～49	92	23	10	14	20	14	17	17
50～54	152	45	25	19	32	42	35	38
55～59	277	99	70	73	92	81	66	108
60～64	522	176	112	161	240	184	167	201
65～69	728	339	209	257	385	400	404	405
70～74	797	502	319	374	587	630	692	885
75～79	542	468	360	399	567	758	918	1 263
80～84	251	218	270	318	398	523	745	1 211
85～89	87	77	77	114	191	236	368	635
90～94	13	9	19	34	33	64	96	165
95～99	-	-	2	2	11	9	11	27
100～	-	-	-	-	-	2	-	2
不詳	-	-	-	-	-	-	-	-
								女
総数	3 013	1 371	1 126	1 205	1 363	1 420	1 550	1 980
0～4歳	240	33	9	9	4	5	2	-
5～9	34	2	1	-	4	2	2	-
10～14	15	2	1	1	1	1	2	-
15～19	47	5	6	1	1	-	1	3
20～24	52	11	5	4	1	-	2	-
25～29	63	9	6	6	3	2	1	-
30～34	53	19	6	4	10	3	2	4
35～39	50	11	11	11	7	8	5	1
40～44	56	17	8	7	10	8	8	11
45～49	63	15	11	10	10	8	9	7
50～54	105	42	17	21	21	21	22	11
55～59	196	49	44	30	37	29	35	34
60～64	291	107	56	76	80	72	64	68
65～69	456	187	110	126	167	126	153	144
70～74	524	291	199	176	244	215	240	320
75～79	393	291	275	259	295	320	354	422
80～84	255	178	222	261	272	301	305	418
85～89	100	77	105	155	144	215	227	333
90～94	16	22	31	46	47	71	95	153
95～99	4	2	3	3	5	11	16	45
100～	-	1	-	-	-	2	5	6
不詳	-	-	-	-	-	-	-	-

260

別死亡数及び率（人口10万対）（つづき）
population）by sex, age and causes of death : Japan－CON.

Deaths

1990 平成2年	1995 7年	2000 12年	2005 17年	2010 22年	2014 26年	2015 27年	2016 28年	年齢 Age
Total								
7 834	10 977	10 877	10 985	9 929	7 988	7 580	7 105	総数 Total
2	1	-	2	4	1	1	-	0～4歳
3	2	2	-	3	-	1	-	5～9 Years
2	3	2	-	-	-	-	-	10～14
4	1	-	-	1	1	-	1	15～19
2	1	3	4	-	-	2	-	20～24
-	-	1	5	-	4	1	-	25～29
3	5	4	7	1	1	2	3	30～34
7	7	5	2	6	4	5	3	35～39
3	5	8	7	4	4	9	10	40～44
17	20	16	14	16	13	11	11	45～49
19	40	33	30	25	18	27	11	50～54
96	97	71	102	67	46	42	44	55～59
265	310	207	185	173	146	142	113	60～64
504	755	587	455	360	292	336	320	65～69
1 119	1 360	1 447	1 121	737	669	633	575	70～74
1 855	2 270	2 137	2 284	1 629	1 102	1 030	987	75～79
1 942	2 864	2 598	2 707	2 622	1 904	1 731	1 603	80～84
1 325	2 099	2 329	2 282	2 368	2 127	1 971	1 759	85～89
534	888	1 078	1 329	1 305	1 203	1 187	1 192	90～94
119	227	305	386	518	377	381	389	95～99
12	22	43	61	88	75	68	84	100～
1	-	1	1	2	1	-	-	不詳 Not stated
Male								
5 664	8 018	8 237	8 525	7 711	6 321	5 949	5 594	総数
-	1	-	1	2	1	1	-	0～4歳
3	1	1	-	1	-	1	-	5～9
1	2	2	-	-	-	-	-	10～14
4	1	-	1	1	1	-	1	15～19
1	1	2	2	-	-	1	-	20～24
-	-	1	3	-	3	1	-	25～29
1	4	3	2	1	1	2	2	30～34
4	5	4	2	3	1	3	1	35～39
2	4	7	5	4	3	5	4	40～44
10	13	12	11	13	10	5	8	45～49
15	32	26	25	21	16	20	5	50～54
72	74	56	87	61	42	35	34	55～59
217	254	178	169	151	127	118	96	60～64
392	637	504	390	321	252	292	273	65～69
869	1 107	1 270	985	638	590	544	503	70～74
1 402	1 744	1 746	1 952	1 387	930	881	854	75～79
1 441	2 135	2 010	2 204	2 163	1 604	1 442	1 332	80～84
870	1 400	1 601	1 669	1 812	1 703	1 573	1 404	85～89
309	487	672	832	837	811	813	839	90～94
48	109	130	163	262	203	194	209	95～99
2	7	11	21	31	22	18	29	100～
1	-	1	1	2	1	-	-	不詳
Female								
2 170	2 959	2 640	2 460	2 218	1 667	1 631	1 511	総数
2	-	-	1	2	-	-	-	0～4歳
-	1	1	-	2	-	-	-	5～9
1	1	-	-	-	-	-	-	10～14
-	-	-	-	-	-	-	-	15～19
1	-	1	2	-	-	1	-	20～24
-	-	-	2	-	1	-	-	25～29
2	1	1	5	-	-	-	1	30～34
3	2	1	-	3	3	2	2	35～39
1	1	1	2	-	1	4	6	40～44
7	7	4	3	3	3	6	3	45～49
4	8	7	5	4	2	7	6	50～54
24	23	15	15	6	4	7	10	55～59
48	56	29	16	22	19	24	17	60～64
112	118	83	65	39	40	44	47	65～69
250	253	177	136	99	79	89	72	70～74
453	526	391	332	242	172	149	133	75～79
501	729	588	503	459	300	289	271	80～84
455	699	728	613	556	424	398	355	85～89
225	401	406	497	468	392	374	353	90～94
71	118	175	223	256	174	187	180	95～99
10	15	32	40	57	53	50	55	100～
-	-	-	-	-	-	-	-	不詳

死亡

表5.15　性・年齢別にみた死因年次推移分類
Table 5.15　Trends in deaths and death rates (per 100,000

Hi08　慢性気管支炎及び肺気腫
Chronic bronchitis and emphysema　　　　　　　　　　　　　　死亡率

年齢 Age	1950 昭和25年	1955 30年	1960 35年	1965 40年	1970 45年	1975 50年	1980 55年	1985 60年
								総数
総数 Total	8.5	3.9	2.9	3.1	3.8	3.9	4.4	5.8
0～4歳	5.0	0.9	0.3	0.3	0.1	0.1	0.0	-
5～9 Years	0.5	0.0	0.1	0.1	0.1	0.1	0.1	-
10～14	0.3	0.1	0.0	0.0	0.0	0.0	0.1	0.0
15～19	0.9	0.1	0.1	0.1	0.0	0.0	0.0	0.0
20～24	1.2	0.2	0.1	0.1	0.0	0.0	0.0	0.0
25～29	1.8	0.3	0.2	0.1	0.1	0.0	0.0	-
30～34	1.7	0.5	0.2	0.1	0.2	0.1	0.1	0.1
35～39	1.6	0.4	0.3	0.2	0.2	0.1	0.1	0.1
40～44	2.4	0.7	0.3	0.3	0.3	0.2	0.2	0.2
45～49	3.9	0.9	0.4	0.5	0.5	0.3	0.3	0.3
50～54	7.6	2.3	1.0	0.9	1.1	1.1	0.8	0.6
55～59	17.2	4.6	3.1	2.6	2.9	2.4	1.8	2.0
60～64	35.3	11.3	5.7	7.1	8.6	6.0	5.2	5.0
65～69	66.9	26.7	14.8	14.9	18.6	15.3	14.1	13.2
70～74	103.1	56.9	33.1	31.5	39.1	32.9	30.9	34.1
75～79	136.4	86.7	66.5	60.0	68.1	65.9	62.6	69.2
80～84	183.5	104.8	101.9	109.6	103.3	102.1	96.2	112.6
85～89	236.6	138.8	116.8	135.1	146.1	146.2	145.4	165.1
90～94[2]	201.8	149.3	170.9	167.4	146.0	194.9	187.2	214.4
95～99	...	...	...	...	...	...	...	...
100～	...	...	...	...	...	...	...	...
								男
総数	9.9	4.7	3.4	3.8	5.2	5.4	6.2	8.4
0～4歳	5.6	1.1	0.4	0.3	0.2	0.0	0.0	-
5～9	0.3	0.0	0.1	0.1	0.1	0.1	0.1	-
10～14	0.2	0.1	0.0	0.0	0.1	-	0.1	0.0
15～19	0.7	0.2	0.1	0.1	0.0	0.0	0.0	0.0
20～24	1.1	0.1	0.1	0.0	0.1	0.1	0.0	0.0
25～29	1.7	0.3	0.2	0.1	0.1	0.1	0.0	-
30～34	1.5	0.4	0.2	0.0	0.1	0.1	0.1	0.0
35～39	1.3	0.3	0.3	0.1	0.1	0.1	0.1	0.1
40～44	2.3	0.8	0.4	0.4	0.4	0.2	0.2	0.2
45～49	4.6	1.1	0.4	0.6	0.8	0.4	0.4	0.4
50～54	8.8	2.3	1.2	0.9	1.5	1.6	1.0	1.0
55～59	20.1	6.2	3.9	3.8	4.5	3.9	2.6	3.2
60～64	47.0	14.3	7.8	9.9	13.7	9.6	8.6	8.6
65～69	91.5	36.9	20.4	21.1	27.6	25.6	23.3	22.9
70～74	147.5	84.5	46.0	47.4	61.3	55.1	52.7	59.6
75～79	202.5	136.8	95.6	88.3	106.8	110.5	108.5	126.7
80～84	262.6	163.7	159.6	170.1	165.2	170.3	178.8	221.2
85～89	355.0	227.5	159.8	189.6	267.4	234.3	265.7	331.4
90～94[2]	305.9	154.4	254.2	262.2	251.8	346.1	322.7	351.4
95～99	...	...	...	...	...	...	...	...
100～	...	...	...	...	...	...	...	...
								女
総数	7.1	3.0	2.4	2.4	2.6	2.5	2.6	3.2
0～4歳	4.4	0.7	0.2	0.2	0.1	0.1	0.0	-
5～9	0.7	0.0	0.0	-	0.1	0.0	0.0	-
10～14	0.3	0.0	0.0	0.0	0.0	0.0	0.0	-
15～19	1.1	0.1	0.1	0.0	0.0	-	0.0	0.1
20～24	1.3	0.3	0.1	0.1	0.0	-	0.1	-
25～29	1.9	0.2	0.1	0.1	0.1	0.0	0.0	-
30～34	1.9	0.6	0.2	0.1	0.2	0.1	0.0	0.1
35～39	1.9	0.4	0.3	0.3	0.2	0.2	0.1	0.0
40～44	2.5	0.6	0.3	0.2	0.3	0.2	0.2	0.2
45～49	3.2	0.7	0.4	0.4	0.3	0.2	0.2	0.2
50～54	6.3	2.2	0.8	0.8	0.8	0.7	0.6	0.3
55～59	14.3	3.1	2.4	1.4	1.6	1.1	1.1	1.0
60～64	24.4	8.4	3.7	4.4	4.1	3.1	2.6	2.3
65～69	46.8	17.8	9.7	9.4	10.6	6.7	6.9	6.0
70～74	70.7	36.4	22.9	18.4	20.9	15.1	14.1	15.6
75～79	94.0	54.5	47.6	40.2	40.1	33.7	29.9	29.4
80～84	141.5	72.8	70.7	76.5	66.7	60.2	45.2	46.5
85～89	183.3	99.4	97.6	111.5	91.2	103.5	83.8	84.3
90～94[2]	165.2	147.6	142.1	132.3	107.7	140.2	135.0	156.4
95～99	...	...	...	...	...	...	...	...
100～	...	...	...	...	...	...	...	...

General mortality

別死亡数及び率（人口10万対）（つづき）
population) by sex, age and causes of death : Japan－CON.

Death rates

1990 平成2年	1995 7年	2000 12年	2005 17年	2010 22年	2014 26年	2015 27年	2016 28年	年　齢 Age
Total								
6.4	8.8	8.7	8.7	7.9	6.4	6.0	5.7	総数 Total
0.0	0.0		0.0	0.1	0.0	0.0	-	0～4歳
0.0	0.0	0.0	-	0.1	-	0.0	-	5～9 Years
0.0	0.0	0.0	-	-	-	-	-	10～14
0.0	0.0	-	0.0	0.0	0.0	-	0.0	15～19
0.0	0.0		0.1	-	-	0.0	-	20～24
-	-	0.0	0.1	-	0.1	0.0	-	25～29
0.0	0.1	0.0	0.1	0.0	0.0	0.0	0.0	30～34
0.1	0.1	0.1	0.0	0.1	0.0	0.1	0.0	35～39
0.0	0.1	0.1	0.1	0.0	0.0	0.1	0.1	40～44
0.2	0.2	0.2	0.2	0.2	0.2	0.1	0.1	45～49
0.2	0.5	0.3	0.3	0.3	0.2	0.3	0.1	50～54
1.2	1.2	0.8	1.0	0.8	0.6	0.6	0.6	55～59
3.9	4.2	2.7	2.2	1.7	1.6	1.7	1.4	60～64
9.9	11.8	8.3	6.1	4.4	3.2	3.5	3.1	65～69
29.4	29.1	24.6	16.9	10.5	8.5	8.2	7.8	70～74
61.5	69.3	51.6	43.4	27.3	17.6	16.3	15.2	75～79
106.0	124.9	99.6	79.4	60.1	39.2	34.5	31.0	80～84
159.1	185.1	152.2	123.5	96.8	69.6	62.6	53.8	85～89
229.9	257.2	203.6	158.0	127.2	92.4	87.3	80.8	90～94[2]
...	...	...	182.6	174.0	107.4	105.6	101.8	95～99
...	...	...	240.6	200.5	125.0	110.1	129.2	100～
Male								
9.4	13.2	13.4	13.8	12.5	10.4	9.7	9.2	総数
-	0.0	-	0.0	0.1	0.0	0.0	-	0～4歳
0.1	0.0	0.0	-	0.0	-	0.0	-	5～9
0.0	0.1	-	-	-	-	-	-	10～14
0.1	0.0	0.1	0.0	0.0	0.0	-	0.0	15～19
0.0	0.0	0.0	0.1	-	-	0.0	-	20～24
-	-	0.0	0.1	-	0.1	0.0	-	25～29
0.0	0.1	0.1	0.0	0.0	0.0	0.1	0.1	30～34
0.1	0.1	0.1	0.0	0.1	0.0	0.1	0.0	35～39
0.0	0.1	0.2	0.1	0.1	0.1	0.1	0.1	40～44
0.2	0.2	0.3	0.3	0.3	0.2	0.1	0.2	45～49
0.4	0.7	0.5	0.6	0.6	0.4	0.5	0.1	50～54
1.9	1.9	1.3	1.7	1.4	1.1	0.9	0.9	55～59
6.7	7.1	4.8	4.1	3.1	2.9	2.8	2.4	60～64
17.9	21.3	15.0	11.0	8.2	5.7	6.2	5.5	65～69
55.8	57.3	47.6	32.4	19.7	16.1	15.1	14.6	70～74
117.2	139.0	107.7	86.5	53.5	33.7	31.4	29.5	75～79
212.4	259.9	220.1	180.5	127.2	82.8	71.7	63.7	80～84
315.3	387.8	336.0	300.9	242.5	165.8	147.7	125.7	85～89
440.7	515.8	461.1	394.9	344.5	260.8	242.2	222.5	90～94[2]
...	...	...	393.2	467.9	327.4	305.7	311.9	95～99
...	...	...	558.4	529.1	275.0	215.3	322.2	100～
Female								
3.5	4.7	4.1	3.8	3.4	2.6	2.5	2.4	総数
0.1	-	-	0.0	0.1	-	-	-	0～4歳
-	0.0	0.0	-	0.1	-	-	-	5～9
0.0	0.0	-	-	-	-	-	-	10～14
-	-	-	-	-	-	-	-	15～19
0.0	-	0.0	0.1	-	-	0.0	-	20～24
-	-	-	0.1	-	0.0	-	-	25～29
0.1	0.0	0.0	0.1	-	-	-	0.0	30～34
0.1	0.1	0.0	-	0.1	0.1	0.0	0.1	35～39
0.0	0.0	0.0	0.1	-	0.0	0.1	0.1	40～44
0.2	0.1	0.1	0.1	0.1	0.1	0.1	0.1	45～49
0.1	0.2	0.1	0.1	0.1	0.1	0.2	0.2	50～54
0.6	0.6	0.3	0.3	0.1	0.1	0.2	0.3	55～59
1.4	1.5	0.7	0.4	0.4	0.4	0.6	0.4	60～64
3.9	3.5	2.2	1.7	0.9	0.8	0.9	0.9	65～69
11.1	9.2	5.5	3.8	2.6	1.9	2.1	1.8	70～74
24.9	26.0	15.5	11.1	7.2	4.9	4.2	3.7	75～79
43.4	49.5	34.7	23.0	17.2	10.3	9.6	8.8	80～84
81.7	90.4	69.1	47.4	32.7	20.9	19.1	16.5	85～89
147.2	164.2	117.0	78.8	59.7	39.6	36.5	32.1	90～94[2]
...	...	...	131.3	105.9	60.2	62.9	57.0	95～99
...	...	...	185.2	149.8	103.9	93.7	96.5	100～

263

死　亡

表 5.15　性・年齢別にみた死因年次推移分類
Table 5.15　Trends in deaths and death rates (per 100,000

Hi09　喘　息
Asthma

死　亡　数

年　齢 Age	1950 昭和25年	1955 30年	1960 35年	1965 40年	1970 45年	1975 50年	1980 55年	1985 60年
								総　数
総数 Total	16 233	11 309	11 221	10 812	9 113	6 928	6 370	6 340
0～4歳	995	487	293	165	122	85	84	51
5～9 Years	43	43	39	47	77	33	49	30
10～14	43	14	28	66	97	38	31	56
15～19	64	33	45	63	74	35	18	46
20～24	110	79	83	62	75	38	28	54
25～29	123	101	138	121	88	43	25	40
30～34	161	95	129	177	121	53	46	50
35～39	209	104	122	179	168	81	54	71
40～44	279	138	137	187	161	120	78	69
45～49	403	218	235	220	222	146	119	134
50～54	662	375	306	359	258	186	181	206
55～59	1 122	630	606	572	450	289	228	311
60～64	1 951	1 040	966	972	751	540	373	333
65～69	3 074	1 848	1 449	1 415	1 221	693	667	564
70～74	3 356	2 382	2 110	1 772	1 582	1 175	1 034	917
75～79	2 270	2 140	2 237	1 998	1 584	1 369	1 335	1 229
80～84	1 026	1 112	1 556	1 540	1 291	1 183	1 156	1 163
85～89	294	389	596	744	573	608	627	725
90～94	44	69	136	141	171	188	193	244
95～99	4	12	9	10	22	25	42	44
100～	-	-	1	2	4	-	2	3
不詳 Not stated	-	-	-	-	1	-	-	
								男
総数	9 461	6 737	6 756	6 591	5 528	4 107	3 870	3 776
0～4歳	547	266	164	86	73	48	44	27
5～9	19	23	21	28	47	17	21	20
10～14	24	8	17	45	70	28	19	30
15～19	28	15	18	38	44	18	13	32
20～24	54	41	50	36	43	16	18	35
25～29	57	51	90	72	54	21	15	28
30～34	69	42	79	104	68	27	24	26
35～39	91	40	67	103	96	41	27	41
40～44	157	68	70	109	79	76	51	31
45～49	246	125	128	116	112	80	69	76
50～54	426	247	200	211	147	92	100	121
55～59	745	433	420	375	271	174	137	184
60～64	1 235	700	641	686	485	341	228	182
65～69	1 929	1 225	1 005	989	829	453	403	340
70～74	1 987	1 470	1 354	1 193	1 071	787	679	581
75～79	1 224	1 218	1 327	1 208	997	855	880	765
80～84	480	561	787	792	705	673	699	725
85～89	125	179	258	346	264	273	336	404
90～94	18	19	58	53	65	75	94	111
95～99	-	6	1	1	7	12	12	16
100～	-	-	-	-	-	-	1	1
不詳	-	-	-	-	1	-	-	
								女
総数	6 772	4 572	4 465	4 221	3 585	2 821	2 500	2 564
0～4歳	448	221	129	79	49	37	40	24
5～9	24	20	18	19	30	16	28	10
10～14	19	6	11	21	27	10	12	26
15～19	36	18	27	25	30	17	5	14
20～24	56	38	33	26	32	22	10	19
25～29	66	50	48	49	34	22	10	12
30～34	92	53	50	73	53	26	22	24
35～39	118	64	55	76	72	40	27	30
40～44	122	70	67	78	82	44	27	38
45～49	157	93	107	104	110	66	50	58
50～54	236	128	106	148	111	94	81	85
55～59	377	197	186	197	179	115	91	127
60～64	716	340	325	286	266	199	145	151
65～69	1 145	623	444	426	392	240	264	224
70～74	1 369	912	756	579	511	388	355	336
75～79	1 046	922	910	790	587	514	455	464
80～84	546	551	769	748	586	510	457	438
85～89	169	210	338	398	309	335	291	321
90～94	26	50	78	88	106	113	99	133
95～99	4	6	8	9	15	13	30	28
100～	-	-	-	2	4	-	1	2
不詳	-	-	-	-	-	-	-	

264

General mortality

別死亡数及び率（人口10万対）（つづき）
population) by sex, age and causes of death : Japan－CON.

Deaths

1990 平成2年	1995 7年	2000 12年	2005 17年	2010 22年	2014 26年	2015 27年	2016 28年	年　齢 Age
Total								
5 947	7 253	4 473	3 198	2 065	1 550	1 511	1 454	総数 Total
27	37	25	14	4	3	2	4	0～4歳
18	15	11	2	1	2	1	1	5～9 Years
38	36	10	3	1	1	-	-	10～14
84	54	14	4	4	-	2	1	15～19
82	75	31	11	5	2	1	-	20～24
77	81	33	17	4	5	6	2	25～29
48	72	40	33	15	7	7	4	30～34
65	53	43	26	27	11	11	13	35～39
117	89	43	35	18	18	12	18	40～44
128	134	67	35	22	22	19	20	45～49
167	187	88	56	30	28	24	22	50～54
244	260	133	95	46	31	28	28	55～59
396	399	180	110	69	48	31	41	60～64
527	625	337	193	93	55	81	74	65～69
690	889	539	312	157	87	98	83	70～74
1 042	1 081	655	475	249	159	163	144	75～79
1 064	1 441	809	535	340	248	243	236	80～84
766	1 046	791	579	425	310	334	285	85～89
295	515	438	438	345	322	281	289	90～94
65	141	155	185	176	151	133	147	95～99
7	22	31	40	34	40	34	42	100～
-	1	-	-	-	-	-	-	不詳 Not stated
Male								
3 412	4 052	2 300	1 565	898	590	573	567	総数
14	18	19	13	4	1	-	3	0～4歳
11	11	9	-	1	1	1	1	5～9
25	22	7	-	1	1	-	-	10～14
56	38	10	3	3	-	1	-	15～19
56	57	19	6	3	2	1	-	20～24
51	57	23	13	2	5	3	2	25～29
36	47	20	24	9	4	6	2	30～34
33	33	26	16	18	5	9	9	35～39
64	55	27	24	9	9	7	9	40～44
75	75	35	18	16	11	8	13	45～49
82	119	53	32	20	19	13	11	50～54
138	145	83	45	23	16	19	17	55～59
247	249	109	69	34	20	16	21	60～64
295	400	206	110	62	33	43	44	65～69
379	525	326	188	76	49	57	47	70～74
625	619	357	286	131	72	79	70	75～79
626	791	407	271	169	115	112	95	80～84
424	518	358	247	173	120	102	103	85～89
146	213	162	139	108	69	70	77	90～94
29	49	38	54	31	29	22	37	95～99
-	10	6	7	5	9	4	6	100～
-	1	-	-	-	-	-	-	不詳
Female								
2 535	3 201	2 173	1 633	1 167	960	938	887	総数
13	19	6	1	-	2	2	1	0～4歳
7	4	2	2	-	1	-	-	5～9
13	14	3	3	-	-	-	-	10～14
28	16	4	1	1	-	1	1	15～19
26	18	12	5	2	-	-	-	20～24
26	24	10	4	2	-	3	-	25～29
12	25	20	9	6	3	1	2	30～34
32	20	17	10	9	6	2	4	35～39
53	34	16	11	9	9	5	9	40～44
53	59	32	17	6	11	11	7	45～49
85	68	35	24	10	9	11	11	50～54
106	115	50	50	23	15	9	11	55～59
149	150	71	41	35	28	15	20	60～64
232	225	131	83	31	22	38	30	65～69
311	364	213	124	81	38	41	36	70～74
417	462	298	189	118	87	84	74	75～79
438	650	402	264	171	133	131	141	80～84
342	528	433	332	252	190	232	182	85～89
149	302	276	299	237	253	211	212	90～94
36	92	117	131	145	122	111	110	95～99
7	12	25	33	29	31	30	36	100～
-	-	-	-	-	-	-	-	不詳

死　亡

表 5.15　性・年齢別にみた死因年次推移分類
Table 5.15　Trends in deaths and death rates (per 100,000

Hi09　喘　息
Asthma

死　亡　率

年　齢 Age	1950 昭和25年	1955 30年	1960 35年	1965 40年	1970 45年	1975 50年	1980 55年	1985 60年
								総　数
総数 Total	19.5	12.7	12.0	11.0	8.8	6.2	5.5	5.3
0～4歳	8.9	5.3	3.7	2.0	1.4	0.9	1.0	0.7
5～9 Years	0.5	0.4	0.4	0.6	1.0	0.4	0.5	0.4
10～14	0.5	0.1	0.3	0.7	1.2	0.5	0.3	0.6
15～19	0.7	0.4	0.5	0.6	0.8	0.4	0.2	0.5
20～24	1.4	0.9	1.0	0.7	0.7	0.4	0.4	0.7
25～29	2.0	1.3	1.7	1.4	1.0	0.4	0.3	0.5
30～34	3.1	1.6	1.7	2.1	1.5	0.6	0.4	0.6
35～39	4.1	2.0	2.0	2.4	2.1	1.0	0.6	0.7
40～44	6.2	2.8	2.7	3.1	2.2	1.5	0.9	0.8
45～49	10.1	5.0	4.9	4.5	3.8	2.0	1.5	1.6
50～54	19.5	9.7	7.3	7.7	5.4	3.2	2.5	2.6
55～59	40.8	19.7	16.6	14.3	10.2	6.2	4.1	4.5
60～64	84.7	41.7	33.0	29.1	20.2	12.7	8.4	6.2
65～69	173.6	93.9	67.1	55.2	41.1	20.2	16.9	13.5
70～74	261.9	171.0	134.9	101.6	74.4	45.8	34.3	26.0
75～79	331.1	244.4	234.3	182.3	125.1	83.6	65.7	50.5
80～84	372.0	294.3	322.2	291.6	199.1	146.5	105.9	80.4
85～89	371.9	349.3	382.5	373.6	249.9	197.1	153.2	123.6
90～94[2]	293.5	355.8	453.6	301.4	299.5	261.1	199.0	156.8
95～99	…	…	…	…	…	…	…	…
100～	…	…	…	…	…	…	…	…
								男
総数	23.2	15.4	14.7	13.7	10.9	7.5	6.8	6.4
0～4歳	9.6	5.6	4.1	2.1	1.6	0.9	1.0	0.7
5～9	0.4	0.4	0.4	0.7	1.1	0.4	0.4	0.5
10～14	0.5	0.2	0.3	1.0	1.8	0.7	0.4	0.6
15～19	0.6	0.3	0.4	0.7	1.0	0.4	0.3	0.7
20～24	1.4	1.0	1.2	0.8	0.8	0.4	0.5	0.8
25～29	2.0	1.4	2.2	1.7	1.2	0.4	0.3	0.7
30～34	2.9	1.5	2.1	2.5	1.6	0.6	0.4	0.6
35～39	3.8	1.7	2.4	2.7	2.3	1.0	0.6	0.8
40～44	7.1	2.9	3.1	4.0	2.2	1.9	1.2	0.7
45～49	12.2	5.9	5.7	5.2	4.2	2.2	1.7	1.9
50～54	24.8	12.8	9.8	9.7	6.9	3.5	2.8	3.1
55～59	54.0	26.9	23.3	19.4	13.4	8.5	5.5	5.4
60～64	111.3	57.1	44.6	42.2	27.8	17.7	11.8	7.7
65～69	242.4	133.3	97.9	81.1	59.5	29.0	23.2	19.2
70～74	367.8	247.6	195.2	151.2	111.8	68.8	51.7	39.1
75～79	457.2	356.1	352.3	267.3	187.8	124.6	104.0	76.8
80～84	502.1	421.2	465.3	423.7	292.6	219.1	167.8	132.4
85～89	510.1	528.8	535.3	575.4	369.6	271.0	242.6	210.9
90～94[2]	423.5	428.9	726.4	393.4	412.1	401.5	322.7	231.9
95～99	…	…	…	…	…	…	…	…
100～	…	…	…	…	…	…	…	…
								女
総数	16.0	10.1	9.4	8.4	6.8	5.0	4.2	4.2
0～4歳	8.2	4.9	3.4	2.0	1.1	0.8	1.0	0.7
5～9	0.5	0.4	0.4	0.5	0.8	0.4	0.6	0.2
10～14	0.4	0.1	0.2	0.5	0.7	0.2	0.3	0.5
15～19	0.8	0.4	0.6	0.5	0.7	0.4	0.1	0.3
20～24	1.4	0.9	0.8	0.6	0.6	0.5	0.3	0.5
25～29	2.0	1.3	1.2	1.2	0.7	0.4	0.2	0.3
30～34	3.2	1.6	1.3	1.8	1.3	0.6	0.4	0.5
35～39	4.4	2.3	1.7	2.0	1.8	1.0	0.6	0.6
40～44	5.3	2.7	2.4	2.4	2.2	1.1	0.6	0.8
45～49	7.9	4.2	4.2	3.9	3.5	1.8	1.2	1.4
50～54	14.1	6.7	4.9	6.0	4.2	3.0	2.2	2.1
55～59	27.5	12.3	10.1	9.5	7.5	4.4	2.9	3.6
60～64	60.0	26.8	21.8	16.6	13.5	8.5	5.8	5.0
65～69	117.5	59.4	39.2	31.7	24.8	12.8	11.9	9.4
70～74	184.7	114.2	86.9	60.6	43.7	27.2	20.9	16.4
75～79	250.3	172.8	157.4	122.7	79.9	54.1	38.4	32.3
80～84	303.0	225.3	245.1	219.2	143.8	102.0	67.8	48.7
85～89	309.8	271.0	314.1	286.3	195.7	161.2	107.5	81.3
90～94[2]	247.8	330.6	359.4	267.3	258.8	210.3	151.3	125.0
95～99	…	…	…	…	…	…	…	…
100～	…	…	…	…	…	…	…	…

266

別死亡数及び率（人口10万対）（つづき）
population）by sex, age and causes of death : Japan－CON.

Death rates

1990 平成2年	1995 7年	2000 12年	2005 17年	2010 22年	2014 26年	2015 27年	2016 28年	年齢 Age
Total								
4.8	5.8	3.6	2.5	1.6	1.2	1.2	1.2	総数 Total
0.4	0.6	0.4	0.3	0.1	0.1	0.0	0.1	0～4歳
0.2	0.2	0.2	0.0	0.0	0.0	0.0	0.0	5～9 Years
0.4	0.5	0.2	0.1	0.0	0.0	-	-	10～14
0.8	0.6	0.2	0.1	0.1	-	0.0	0.0	15～19
0.9	0.8	0.4	0.2	0.1	0.0	0.0	-	20～24
1.0	0.9	0.3	0.2	0.1	0.1	0.1	0.0	25～29
0.6	0.9	0.5	0.3	0.2	0.1	0.1	0.1	30～34
0.7	0.7	0.5	0.3	0.3	0.1	0.1	0.2	35～39
1.1	1.0	0.6	0.4	0.2	0.2	0.1	0.2	40～44
1.4	1.3	0.8	0.5	0.3	0.3	0.2	0.2	45～49
2.1	2.1	0.8	0.6	0.4	0.4	0.3	0.3	50～54
3.2	3.3	1.5	0.9	0.5	0.4	0.4	0.4	55～59
5.9	5.4	2.3	1.3	0.7	0.5	0.4	0.5	60～64
10.4	9.8	4.8	2.6	1.1	0.6	0.8	0.7	65～69
18.1	19.0	9.2	4.7	2.2	1.1	1.3	1.1	70～74
34.6	33.0	15.8	9.0	4.2	2.5	2.6	2.2	75～79
58.1	62.8	31.0	15.7	7.8	5.1	4.8	4.6	80～84
92.0	92.2	51.7	31.3	17.4	10.2	10.6	8.7	85～89
126.8	153.4	89.1	52.1	33.6	24.7	20.7	19.6	90～94[2]
...	...	...	87.5	59.1	43.0	36.9	38.5	95～99
...	...	...	157.7	77.4	66.7	55.1	64.6	100～
Male								
5.7	6.7	3.7	2.5	1.5	1.0	0.9	0.9	総数
0.4	0.6	0.6	0.5	0.1	0.0	-	0.1	0～4歳
0.3	0.3	0.3	-	0.0	0.0	0.0	0.0	5～9
0.6	0.6	0.2	-	0.0	0.0	-	-	10～14
1.1	0.9	0.3	0.1	0.1	-	0.0	-	15～19
1.3	1.1	0.4	0.2	0.1	0.1	0.0	-	20～24
1.3	1.3	0.5	0.3	0.1	0.2	0.1	0.1	25～29
0.9	1.2	0.5	0.5	0.2	0.1	0.2	0.1	30～34
0.7	0.8	0.6	0.4	0.4	0.1	0.2	0.2	35～39
1.2	1.2	0.7	0.6	0.2	0.2	0.1	0.2	40～44
1.7	1.4	0.8	0.5	0.4	0.3	0.2	0.3	45～49
2.1	2.7	1.0	0.7	0.5	0.5	0.3	0.3	50～54
3.6	3.7	1.9	0.9	0.5	0.4	0.5	0.5	55～59
7.6	6.9	2.9	1.7	0.7	0.5	0.4	0.5	60～64
13.5	13.4	6.1	3.1	1.6	0.8	0.9	0.9	65～69
24.3	27.2	12.2	6.2	2.3	1.3	1.6	1.4	70～74
52.2	49.3	22.0	12.7	5.1	2.6	2.8	2.4	75～79
92.3	96.3	44.6	22.2	9.9	5.9	5.6	4.5	80～84
153.7	143.5	75.1	44.5	23.2	11.7	9.6	9.2	85～89
214.8	232.7	116.8	66.0	44.5	22.2	20.8	20.4	90～94[2]
...	...	...	130.3	55.4	46.8	34.7	55.2	95～99
...	...	...	186.1	85.3	112.5	47.8	66.7	100～
Female								
4.1	5.1	3.4	2.5	1.8	1.5	1.5	1.4	総数
0.4	0.7	0.2	0.0	-	0.1	0.1	0.0	0～4歳
0.2	0.1	0.1	0.1	-	0.0	-	-	5～9
0.3	0.4	0.1	0.1	-	-	-	-	10～14
0.6	0.4	0.1	0.0	0.0	-	0.0	0.0	15～19
0.6	0.4	0.3	0.1	0.1	-	-	-	20～24
0.7	0.6	0.2	0.1	0.1	-	0.1	-	25～29
0.3	0.6	0.5	0.2	0.1	0.1	0.0	0.1	30～34
0.7	0.5	0.4	0.2	0.2	0.1	0.0	0.1	35～39
1.0	0.8	0.4	0.3	0.2	0.2	0.1	0.2	40～44
1.2	1.1	0.7	0.4	0.2	0.3	0.3	0.2	45～49
2.1	1.5	0.7	0.5	0.3	0.2	0.3	0.3	50～54
2.7	2.9	1.1	1.0	0.5	0.4	0.2	0.3	55～59
4.3	3.9	1.8	0.9	0.7	0.6	0.3	0.5	60～64
8.0	6.6	3.5	2.1	0.7	0.5	0.8	0.6	65～69
13.8	13.3	6.6	3.5	2.2	0.9	1.0	0.9	70～74
22.9	22.8	11.8	6.3	3.5	2.5	2.4	2.1	75～79
38.0	44.1	23.7	12.1	6.4	4.6	4.4	4.6	80～84
61.4	68.3	41.1	25.7	14.8	9.4	11.1	8.5	85～89
92.4	124.9	79.8	47.4	30.3	25.6	20.6	19.3	90～94[2]
...	...	...	77.1	60.0	42.2	37.3	34.8	95～99
...	...	...	152.8	76.2	60.8	56.2	63.2	100～

死　亡

表 5.15　性・年齢別にみた死因年次推移分類
Table 5.15　Trends in deaths and death rates（per 100,000

Hi10　胃潰瘍及び十二指腸潰瘍
Gastric ulcer and duodenal ulcer

死　亡　数

年　齢 Age	1950 昭和25年	1955 30年	1960 35年	1965 40年	1970 45年	1975 50年	1980 55年	1985 60年
								総　数
総数 Total	19 323	13 387	11 057	9 165	7 997	6 865	5 530	4 493
0〜4歳	98	36	21	37	71	7	7	2
5〜9 Years	61	15	12	7	3	3	2	4
10〜14	41	16	13	13	6	4	2	1
15〜19	174	70	66	41	22	18	13	9
20〜24	382	204	106	65	60	37	17	6
25〜29	435	236	158	98	67	41	18	13
30〜34	544	322	225	180	104	58	35	16
35〜39	843	395	235	249	207	130	52	37
40〜44	1 202	593	323	239	276	238	102	52
45〜49	1 607	859	510	343	286	299	174	81
50〜54	2 034	1 175	746	515	309	309	229	169
55〜59	2 387	1 508	1 064	705	547	333	251	233
60〜64	2 757	1 761	1 396	1 002	791	564	349	233
65〜69	2 732	2 046	1 621	1 333	1 136	833	540	328
70〜74	2 203	1 927	1 794	1 444	1 316	1 052	869	536
75〜79	1 197	1 388	1 491	1 452	1 265	1 266	1 032	813
80〜84	478	607	909	956	973	997	1 022	927
85〜89	112	196	293	396	437	503	595	718
90〜94	28	30	66	81	110	146	177	251
95〜99	3	3	8	9	7	22	40	51
100〜	-	-	-	-	2	4	3	9
不詳 Not stated	5	-	-	-	2	1	1	4
								男
総数	13 656	9 422	7 640	6 367	5 419	4 472	3 349	2 428
0〜4歳	55	22	15	21	48	4	5	1
5〜9	37	5	8	5	3	1	2	2
10〜14	24	10	7	8	3	3	2	1
15〜19	113	44	48	28	17	15	10	5
20〜24	243	139	73	55	45	25	13	3
25〜29	276	168	122	72	46	36	16	10
30〜34	361	205	156	148	88	39	29	12
35〜39	593	278	170	215	179	109	46	34
40〜44	900	446	233	195	242	202	95	39
45〜49	1 285	661	384	275	235	253	149	69
50〜54	1 535	927	602	425	243	243	194	140
55〜59	1 903	1 198	841	567	426	264	202	191
60〜64	2 043	1 330	1 103	802	603	431	253	163
65〜69	1 919	1 503	1 219	1 018	855	611	378	230
70〜74	1 413	1 252	1 180	1 010	908	692	551	304
75〜79	670	835	875	872	774	774	616	461
80〜84	224	300	450	460	506	531	487	403
85〜89	48	89	130	166	165	190	236	275
90〜94	9	9	21	23	29	43	56	67
95〜99	1	1	3	2	2	5	6	12
100〜	-	-	-	-	-	-	2	2
不詳	4	-	-	-	2	1	1	4
								女
総数	5 667	3 965	3 417	2 798	2 578	2 393	2 181	2 065
0〜4歳	43	14	6	16	23	3	2	1
5〜9	24	10	4	2	-	2	-	2
10〜14	17	6	6	5	3	1	-	-
15〜19	61	26	18	13	5	3	3	4
20〜24	139	65	33	10	15	12	4	3
25〜29	159	68	36	26	21	5	2	3
30〜34	183	117	69	32	16	19	6	4
35〜39	250	117	65	34	28	21	6	3
40〜44	302	147	90	44	34	36	7	13
45〜49	322	198	126	68	51	46	25	12
50〜54	499	248	144	90	66	66	35	29
55〜59	484	310	223	138	121	69	49	42
60〜64	714	431	293	200	188	133	96	70
65〜69	813	543	402	315	281	222	162	98
70〜74	790	675	614	434	408	360	318	232
75〜79	527	553	616	580	491	492	416	352
80〜84	254	307	459	496	467	466	535	524
85〜89	64	107	163	230	272	313	359	443
90〜94	19	21	45	58	81	103	121	184
95〜99	2	2	5	7	5	17	34	39
100〜	-	-	-	-	2	4	1	7
不詳	1	-	-	-	-	-	-	

General mortality

別死亡数及び率（人口10万対）（つづき）
population）by sex, age and causes of death : Japan－CON.

Deaths

1990 平成2年	1995 7年	2000 12年	2005 17年	2010 22年	2014 26年	2015 27年	2016 28年	年齢 Age
Total								
3 615	4 314	3 869	3 490	3 233	2 795	2 666	2 657	総数 Total
2	4	2	4	2	3	3	1	0～4歳
-	-	2	-	-	1	1	1	5～9 Years
-	1	-	1	2	-	-	-	10～14
3	2	1	3	-	-	-	3	15～19
3	3	2	3	1	1	1	3	20～24
4	4	-	4	1	1	1	-	25～29
11	12	11	2	1	1	3	5	30～34
22	23	12	10	9	6	6	5	35～39
52	54	34	19	17	16	17	17	40～44
72	100	88	46	30	32	32	23	45～49
101	132	135	89	57	33	44	49	50～54
177	164	159	168	120	105	79	77	55～59
208	299	226	201	215	151	114	97	60～64
245	344	341	249	239	229	198	240	65～69
356	385	435	349	314	250	252	248	70～74
615	560	507	524	433	348	321	292	75～79
734	815	626	545	552	499	490	475	80～84
610	809	705	590	612	534	530	507	85～89
315	462	425	483	404	393	395	430	90～94
75	126	130	169	191	151	148	155	95～99
9	13	24	28	28	38	30	26	100～
1	2	4	3	5	3	1	3	不詳 Not stated
Male								
1 933	2 274	2 161	1 897	1 835	1 609	1 511	1 527	総数
1	2	2	3	1	2	3	1	0～4歳
-	-	1	-	-	-	-	1	5～9
-	1	-	-	2	-	-	-	10～14
3	2	1	1	-	-	-	2	15～19
2	2	1	3	-	1	-	2	20～24
1	3	-	3	-	-	1	-	25～29
10	8	9	-	1	1	3	5	30～34
16	19	11	6	7	5	5	4	35～39
39	45	31	19	15	12	16	12	40～44
68	85	76	37	26	27	26	17	45～49
84	112	118	79	51	30	33	46	50～54
132	127	134	145	105	93	74	61	55～59
171	246	177	162	174	119	96	80	60～64
165	259	265	189	178	185	145	207	65～69
222	246	303	241	221	184	185	186	70～74
339	308	303	332	288	229	205	186	75～79
335	358	313	262	329	304	293	270	80～84
232	270	253	236	258	245	258	250	85～89
95	149	125	133	125	130	144	156	90～94
17	29	30	37	45	34	19	34	95～99
-	1	4	6	4	5	4	4	100～
1	2	4	3	5	3	1	3	不詳
Female								
1 682	2 040	1 708	1 593	1 398	1 186	1 155	1 130	総数
1	2	-	1	1	1	-	-	0～4歳
-	-	1	-	-	1	1	-	5～9
-	-	-	1	-	-	-	-	10～14
-	-	-	2	-	-	-	1	15～19
1	1	1	-	1	-	1	1	20～24
3	1	-	1	1	1	-	-	25～29
1	4	2	2	-	-	-	-	30～34
6	4	1	4	2	1	1	1	35～39
13	9	3	-	2	4	1	5	40～44
4	15	12	9	4	5	6	6	45～49
17	20	17	10	6	3	11	3	50～54
45	37	25	23	15	12	5	16	55～59
37	53	49	39	41	32	18	17	60～64
80	85	76	60	61	44	53	33	65～69
134	139	132	108	93	66	67	62	70～74
276	252	204	192	145	119	116	106	75～79
399	457	313	283	223	195	197	205	80～84
378	539	452	354	354	289	272	257	85～89
220	313	300	350	279	263	251	274	90～94
58	97	100	132	146	117	129	121	95～99
9	12	20	22	24	33	26	22	100～
-	-	-	-	-	-	-	-	不詳

死　亡

表 5.15　性・年齢別にみた死因年次推移分類
Table 5.15　Trends in deaths and death rates (per 100,000

Hi10　胃潰瘍及び十二指腸潰瘍
Gastric ulcer and duodenal ulcer

死　亡　率

年　　齢 Age	1950 昭和25年	1955 30年	1960 35年	1965 40年	1970 45年	1975 50年	1980 55年	1985 60年
								総　数
総数 Total	23.2	15.0	11.8	9.3	7.8	6.2	4.8	3.7
0〜4歳	0.9	0.4	0.3	0.5	0.8	0.1	0.1	0.0
5〜9 Years	0.6	0.1	0.1	0.1	0.0	0.0	0.0	0.0
10〜14	0.5	0.2	0.1	0.1	0.1	0.0	0.0	0.0
15〜19	2.0	0.8	0.7	0.4	0.2	0.2	0.2	0.1
20〜24	4.9	2.4	1.3	0.7	0.6	0.4	0.2	0.1
25〜29	7.0	3.1	1.9	1.2	0.7	0.4	0.2	0.2
30〜34	10.5	5.3	3.0	2.2	1.2	0.6	0.3	0.2
35〜39	16.7	7.7	3.9	3.3	2.5	1.6	0.6	0.3
40〜44	26.8	12.0	6.4	4.0	3.8	2.9	1.2	0.6
45〜49	40.1	19.7	10.6	7.0	4.9	4.1	2.2	1.0
50〜54	60.0	30.5	17.8	11.1	6.5	5.4	3.2	2.1
55〜59	86.8	47.0	29.2	17.6	12.4	7.2	4.5	3.3
60〜64	119.7	70.5	47.6	30.0	21.3	13.2	7.9	4.3
65〜69	154.3	104.0	75.0	52.0	38.2	24.2	13.7	7.9
70〜74	171.9	138.4	114.7	82.8	61.8	41.0	28.9	15.2
75〜79	174.6	158.5	156.2	132.5	99.9	77.3	50.8	33.4
80〜84	173.3	160.7	188.2	181.0	150.0	123.5	93.7	64.1
85〜89	141.7	176.0	188.0	198.8	190.6	163.0	145.4	122.4
90〜94[1]	189.5	144.9	229.9	177.3	180.9	210.8	184.7	167.6
95〜99	…	…	…	…	…	…	…	…
100〜	…	…	…	…	…	…	…	…
								男
総数	33.5	21.5	16.7	13.2	10.7	8.2	5.9	4.1
0〜4歳	1.0	0.5	0.4	0.5	1.1	0.1	0.1	0.0
5〜9	0.8	0.1	0.2	0.1	0.1	0.0	0.0	0.0
10〜14	0.5	0.2	0.1	0.2	0.1	0.1	0.0	0.0
15〜19	2.6	1.0	1.0	0.5	0.4	0.4	0.2	0.1
20〜24	6.3	3.3	1.8	1.2	0.9	0.6	0.3	0.1
25〜29	9.8	4.4	3.0	1.7	1.0	0.7	0.4	0.3
30〜34	15.3	7.3	4.2	3.6	2.1	0.8	0.5	0.3
35〜39	25.0	12.0	6.2	5.7	4.4	2.6	1.0	0.6
40〜44	40.9	19.2	10.2	7.1	6.6	4.9	2.3	0.9
45〜49	63.7	31.0	17.0	12.4	8.8	7.0	3.7	1.7
50〜54	89.3	48.0	29.5	19.6	11.4	9.4	5.5	3.6
55〜59	138.0	74.5	46.7	29.4	21.0	12.8	8.1	5.6
60〜64	184.1	108.4	76.7	49.4	34.5	22.4	13.1	6.9
65〜69	241.1	163.5	118.7	83.5	61.4	39.1	21.8	13.0
70〜74	261.5	210.9	170.1	128.0	94.7	60.5	42.0	20.5
75〜79	250.3	244.1	232.3	193.0	145.8	112.8	72.8	46.3
80〜84	234.3	225.2	266.0	246.1	210.0	172.9	116.9	73.6
85〜89	195.9	262.9	269.7	276.1	231.0	188.6	170.4	143.5
90〜94[2]	235.3	171.6	290.6	182.1	177.4	221.5	193.0	146.7
95〜99	…	…	…	…	…	…	…	…
100〜	…	…	…	…	…	…	…	…
								女
総数	13.4	8.7	7.2	5.6	4.9	4.2	3.7	3.4
0〜4歳	0.8	0.3	0.2	0.4	0.5	0.1	0.0	0.0
5〜9	0.5	0.2	0.1	0.1	-	0.0	-	0.0
10〜14	0.4	0.1	0.1	0.1	0.1	0.0	-	-
15〜19	1.4	0.6	0.4	0.2	0.1	0.1	0.1	0.1
20〜24	3.6	1.5	0.8	0.2	0.3	0.3	0.1	0.1
25〜29	4.7	1.8	0.9	0.6	0.5	0.1	0.0	0.1
30〜34	6.4	3.5	1.8	0.8	0.4	0.4	0.1	0.1
35〜39	9.4	4.2	2.0	0.9	0.7	0.5	0.1	0.1
40〜44	13.2	5.6	3.3	1.4	0.9	0.9	0.2	0.3
45〜49	16.2	8.9	4.9	2.5	1.6	1.2	0.6	0.3
50〜54	29.9	12.9	6.7	3.6	2.5	2.1	1.0	0.7
55〜59	35.3	19.4	12.1	6.7	5.1	2.7	1.6	1.2
60〜64	59.8	33.9	19.6	11.6	9.6	5.7	3.8	2.3
65〜69	83.4	51.8	35.5	23.4	17.8	11.9	7.3	4.1
70〜74	106.6	84.5	70.6	45.4	34.9	25.3	18.7	11.3
75〜79	126.1	103.6	106.6	90.1	66.8	51.8	35.1	24.5
80〜84	141.0	125.5	146.3	145.4	114.6	93.2	79.3	58.3
85〜89	117.3	138.1	151.5	165.4	172.3	150.6	132.6	112.2
90〜94[2]	173.5	135.8	209.0	175.5	182.2	207.0	181.5	176.4
95〜99	…	…	…	…	…	…	…	…
100〜	…	…	…	…	…	…	…	…

270

General mortality

別死亡数及び率（人口10万対）（つづき）
population）by sex, age and causes of death : Japan－CON.

Death rates

1990 平成2年	1995 7年	2000 12年	2005 17年	2010 22年	2014 26年	2015 27年	2016 28年	年　　齢 Age
Total								
2.9	3.5	3.1	2.8	2.6	2.2	2.1	2.1	総数 Total
0.0	0.1	0.0	0.1	0.0	0.1	0.1	0.0	0～4歳
-	-	0.0	-	-	0.0	0.0	0.0	5～9 Years
-	0.0	-	0.0	0.0	-	-	-	10～14
0.0	0.0	0.0	0.0	-	-	-	0.1	15～19
0.0	0.0	0.0	0.0	0.0	0.0	0.0	0.1	20～24
0.1	0.0	-	0.0	0.0	0.0	0.0	-	25～29
0.1	0.2	0.1	0.0	0.0	0.0	0.0	0.1	30～34
0.2	0.3	0.2	0.1	0.1	0.1	0.1	0.1	35～39
0.5	0.6	0.4	0.2	0.2	0.2	0.2	0.2	40～44
0.8	0.9	1.0	0.6	0.4	0.4	0.4	0.3	45～49
1.3	1.5	1.3	1.0	0.7	0.4	0.6	0.6	50～54
2.3	2.1	1.8	1.6	1.4	1.4	1.1	1.0	55～59
3.1	4.0	2.9	2.4	2.1	1.7	1.3	1.2	60～64
4.8	5.4	4.8	3.4	2.9	2.5	2.0	2.3	65～69
9.3	8.2	7.4	5.3	4.5	3.2	3.3	3.4	70～74
20.4	17.1	12.2	10.0	7.3	5.6	5.1	4.5	75～79
40.1	35.5	24.0	16.0	12.7	10.3	9.8	9.2	80～84
73.2	71.3	46.1	31.9	25.0	17.5	16.8	15.5	85～89
137.9	135.9	82.7	57.4	39.4	30.2	29.1	29.2	90～94[2]
...	...	...	80.0	64.2	43.0	41.0	40.6	95～99
...	...	...	110.4	63.8	63.3	48.6	40.0	100～
Male								
3.2	3.7	3.5	3.1	3.0	2.6	2.5	2.5	総数
0.0	0.1	0.1	0.1	0.0	0.1	0.1	0.0	0～4歳
-	-	0.0	0.0	0.1	-	-	0.0	5～9
-	0.0	-	-	-	-	-	-	10～14
0.1	0.0	0.0	0.0	-	-	-	0.1	15～19
0.0	0.0	0.0	0.1	-	0.0	-	0.1	20～24
0.0	0.1	-	0.1	-	-	0.0	-	25～29
0.3	0.2	0.2	-	0.0	0.0	0.1	0.1	30～34
0.4	0.5	0.3	0.1	0.1	0.1	0.1	0.1	35～39
0.7	1.0	0.8	0.5	0.3	0.2	0.3	0.2	40～44
1.5	1.6	1.7	1.0	0.6	0.6	0.6	0.4	45～49
2.1	2.5	2.3	1.8	1.3	0.8	0.8	1.2	50～54
3.5	3.3	3.1	2.9	2.4	2.5	2.0	1.6	55～59
5.3	6.8	4.7	3.9	3.5	2.7	2.3	2.0	60～64
7.5	8.7	7.9	5.3	4.5	4.2	3.1	4.2	65～69
14.3	12.7	11.4	7.9	6.8	5.0	5.1	5.4	70～74
28.3	24.6	18.7	14.7	11.1	8.3	7.3	6.4	75～79
49.4	43.6	34.3	21.5	19.4	15.7	14.6	12.9	80～84
84.1	74.8	53.1	42.5	34.5	23.9	24.2	22.4	85～89
137.5	153.1	90.2	63.1	51.5	41.8	42.9	41.4	90～94[2]
...	...	...	89.3	80.4	54.8	29.9	50.7	95～99
...	...	...	159.5	68.3	62.5	47.8	44.4	100～
Female								
2.7	3.2	2.7	2.5	2.2	1.8	1.8	1.8	総数
0.0	0.1	-	0.0	0.0	0.0	-	-	0～4歳
-	-	0.0	-	-	0.0	0.0	-	5～9
-	-	-	0.0	-	-	-	-	10～14
-	-	-	0.1	-	-	-	0.0	15～19
0.0	0.0	0.0	-	0.0	-	0.0	0.0	20～24
0.1	0.0	-	0.0	0.0	0.0	-	-	25～29
0.0	0.1	0.0	0.0	-	-	-	-	30～34
0.1	0.1	0.0	0.1	0.0	0.0	0.0	0.0	35～39
0.2	0.2	0.1	-	0.0	0.1	0.0	0.1	40～44
0.1	0.3	0.3	0.2	0.1	0.1	0.1	0.1	45～49
0.4	0.4	0.3	0.2	0.2	0.1	0.3	0.1	50～54
1.1	0.9	0.6	0.4	0.3	0.3	0.1	0.4	55～59
1.1	1.4	1.2	0.9	0.8	0.7	0.4	0.4	60～64
2.8	2.5	2.0	1.5	1.4	0.9	1.1	0.6	65～69
5.9	5.1	4.1	3.0	2.5	1.6	1.6	1.6	70～74
15.2	12.5	8.1	6.4	4.3	3.4	3.3	2.9	75～79
34.6	31.0	18.5	12.9	8.4	6.7	6.6	6.7	80～84
67.9	69.7	42.9	27.4	20.8	14.3	13.1	12.0	85～89
138.1	129.8	80.1	55.5	35.6	26.6	24.5	25.0	90～94[2]
...	...	...	77.7	60.4	40.5	43.4	38.3	95～99
...	...	...	101.9	63.1	64.7	48.7	38.6	100～

死　亡

表 5.15　性・年齢別にみた死因年次推移分類
Table 5.15　Trends in deaths and death rates (per 100,000

Hi11　肝疾患
Diseases of liver

死　亡　数

年　齢 Age	1950 昭和25年	1955 30年	1960 35年	1965 40年	1970 45年	1975 50年	1980 55年	1985 60年
								総　数
総数 Total	8 630	11 827	13 389	13 663	17 097	18 101	18 978	19 803
0～4歳	337	267	151	108	111	73	27	17
5～9 Years	116	116	86	34	29	12	15	3
10～14	82	81	85	42	35	18	12	9
15～19	113	135	107	87	65	20	10	13
20～24	205	224	183	145	136	40	33	9
25～29	205	263	261	210	187	119	54	47
30～34	224	272	345	362	360	270	211	119
35～39	313	360	404	543	856	743	521	434
40～44	470	569	546	664	1 161	1 498	1 143	901
45～49	618	771	863	912	1 181	1 761	2 196	1 589
50～54	787	1 104	1 218	1 186	1 384	1 698	2 403	2 784
55～59	913	1 240	1 364	1 512	1 900	1 738	2 019	2 776
60～64	1 103	1 369	1 472	1 628	2 077	2 122	2 059	2 234
65～69	1 177	1 557	1 646	1 707	2 194	2 203	2 115	2 047
70～74	1 058	1 569	1 805	1 709	2 111	2 177	2 083	2 253
75～79	597	1 188	1 515	1 436	1 754	1 717	1 911	2 060
80～84	238	557	939	925	1 071	1 224	1 360	1 495
85～89	62	156	320	369	376	500	596	730
90～94	10	27	65	72	93	126	180	240
95～99	1	2	12	12	7	20	26	37
100～	-	-	2	-	1	3	-	-
不詳 Not stated	1	-	-	-	8	19	4	6
								男
総数	4 887	6 749	8 013	8 582	11 047	12 461	13 348	13 591
0～4歳	189	124	73	66	58	35	18	12
5～9	76	64	40	19	16	8	7	3
10～14	54	50	48	20	21	9	6	2
15～19	65	75	62	52	36	10	3	7
20～24	112	126	89	66	65	23	22	5
25～29	113	145	159	113	95	81	41	33
30～34	108	131	213	261	251	225	167	87
35～39	155	186	254	392	679	619	453	361
40～44	267	339	353	448	926	1 309	992	771
45～49	377	484	549	606	821	1 481	1 947	1 360
50～54	463	682	825	819	972	1 277	1 968	2 389
55～59	553	750	897	1 046	1 286	1 242	1 480	2 181
60～64	639	846	946	1 094	1 359	1 474	1 366	1 517
65～69	671	946	1 051	1 071	1 423	1 455	1 375	1 237
70～74	588	853	1 049	1 069	1 267	1 310	1 252	1 290
75～79	308	604	767	802	1 008	986	1 129	1 098
80～84	115	261	469	454	556	626	754	749
85～89	30	65	139	145	157	227	283	364
90～94	4	18	25	38	40	38	70	102
95～99	-	-	5	1	3	6	11	17
100～	-	-	-	-	-	1	-	-
不詳	-	-	-	-	8	19	4	6
								女
総数	3 743	5 078	5 376	5 081	6 050	5 640	5 630	6 212
0～4歳	148	143	78	42	53	38	9	5
5～9	40	52	46	15	13	4	8	-
10～14	28	31	37	22	14	9	6	7
15～19	48	60	45	35	29	10	7	6
20～24	93	98	94	79	71	17	11	4
25～29	92	118	102	97	92	38	13	14
30～34	116	141	132	101	109	45	44	32
35～39	158	174	150	151	177	124	68	73
40～44	203	230	193	216	235	189	151	130
45～49	241	287	314	306	360	280	249	229
50～54	324	422	393	367	412	421	435	395
55～59	360	490	467	466	614	496	539	595
60～64	464	523	526	534	718	648	693	717
65～69	506	611	595	636	771	748	740	810
70～74	470	716	756	640	844	867	831	963
75～79	289	584	748	634	746	731	782	962
80～84	123	296	470	471	515	598	606	746
85～89	32	91	181	224	219	273	313	366
90～94	6	9	40	34	53	88	110	138
95～99	1	2	7	11	4	14	15	20
100～	-	-	2	-	1	2	-	-
不詳	1	-	-	-	-	-	-	-

General mortality

別死亡数及び率（人口10万対）（つづき）
population） by sex, age and causes of death : Japan－CON.

Deaths

1990 平成2年	1995 7年	2000 12年	2005 17年	2010 22年	2014 26年	2015 27年	2016 28年	年齢 Age
Total								
19 700	17 018	16 079	16 430	16 216	15 692	15 659	15 773	総数 Total
16	15	18	15	14	6	10	17	0～4歳
5	1	1	3	3	-	1	3	5～9 Years
4	3	5	5	2	1	2	3	10～14
13	4	5	5	2	1	6	3	15～19
14	12	10	4	6	8	4	5	20～24
31	40	33	22	18	11	19	9	25～29
86	106	93	84	72	55	48	54	30～34
295	260	229	209	199	165	122	124	35～39
778	622	451	441	408	376	391	376	40～44
1 342	1 200	952	744	715	632	646	669	45～49
1 927	1 671	1 646	1 283	1 027	943	983	897	50～54
2 950	2 125	1 930	1 872	1 470	1 109	1 107	1 150	55～59
2 889	2 582	2 175	2 084	1 963	1 697	1 582	1 552	60～64
2 201	2 167	2 270	2 076	2 039	1 844	1 967	2 105	65～69
2 126	1 649	1 958	2 278	2 123	2 066	2 002	1 763	70～74
2 135	1 570	1 576	1 959	2 156	2 114	2 077	2 116	75～79
1 642	1 509	1 222	1 612	1 906	2 080	2 146	2 201	80～84
901	997	924	1 006	1 316	1 619	1 555	1 640	85～89
277	384	442	541	561	730	750	829	90～94
50	80	111	163	185	191	215	218	95～99
6	8	15	25	25	40	22	35	100～
12	13	13	5	6	4	4	4	不詳 Not stated
Male								
13 256	11 576	11 068	11 007	10 619	10 031	10 016	10 112	総数
7	6	11	8	8	5	6	10	0～4歳
5	-	1	2	1	-	-	3	5～9
1	1	3	1	1	-	1	2	10～14
9	2	2	-	-	1	2	1	15～19
12	9	6	2	5	5	3	5	20～24
23	32	28	14	11	7	13	5	25～29
71	79	75	52	44	31	34	33	30～34
242	207	185	150	151	117	76	81	35～39
668	524	370	356	308	282	293	278	40～44
1 157	1 019	806	618	579	493	517	525	45～49
1 608	1 429	1 413	1 069	858	767	795	708	50～54
2 390	1 775	1 628	1 574	1 197	913	893	933	55～59
2 137	2 001	1 788	1 700	1 608	1 353	1 280	1 246	60～64
1 378	1 533	1 683	1 606	1 574	1 440	1 513	1 631	65～69
1 129	905	1 211	1 511	1 414	1 419	1 392	1 215	70～74
1 064	741	764	1 085	1 275	1 238	1 222	1 299	75～79
796	716	529	684	902	1 041	1 070	1 114	80～84
425	422	367	354	451	660	626	694	85～89
104	132	149	174	179	212	228	276	90～94
14	28	36	37	44	38	45	45	95～99
4	2	1	5	3	5	3	6	100～
12	13	12	5	6	4	4	2	不詳
Female								
6 444	5 442	5 011	5 423	5 597	5 661	5 643	5 661	総数
9	9	7	7	6	1	4	7	0～4歳
-	1	-	1	2	-	1	-	5～9
3	2	2	2	1	1	1	1	10～14
4	2	3	2	2	-	4	2	15～19
2	3	4	2	1	3	1	-	20～24
8	8	5	8	7	4	6	4	25～29
15	27	18	32	28	24	14	21	30～34
53	53	44	59	48	48	46	43	35～39
110	98	81	85	100	94	98	98	40～44
185	181	146	126	136	139	129	144	45～49
319	242	233	214	169	176	188	189	50～54
560	350	302	298	273	196	214	217	55～59
752	581	387	384	355	344	302	306	60～64
823	634	587	470	465	404	454	474	65～69
997	744	747	767	709	647	610	548	70～74
1 071	829	812	874	881	876	855	817	75～79
846	793	693	928	1 004	1 039	1 076	1 087	80～84
476	575	557	652	865	959	929	946	85～89
173	252	293	367	382	518	522	553	90～94
36	52	75	126	141	153	170	173	95～99
2	6	14	20	22	35	19	29	100～
-	-	1	-	-	-	-	2	不詳

死　亡

表 5.15　性・年齢別にみた死因年次推移分類
Table 5.15　Trends in deaths and death rates（per 100,000

Hi11　肝疾患
Diseases of liver

死　亡　率

年　　齢 Age	1950 昭和25年	1955 30年	1960 35年	1965 40年	1970 45年	1975 50年	1980 55年	1985 60年
								総　数
総数 Total	10.4	13.2	14.3	13.9	16.6	16.3	16.3	16.5
0〜4歳	3.0	2.9	1.9	1.3	1.3	0.7	0.3	0.2
5〜9 Years	1.2	1.1	0.9	0.4	0.4	0.1	0.2	0.0
10〜14	0.9	0.9	0.8	0.5	0.4	0.2	0.1	0.1
15〜19	1.3	1.6	1.1	0.8	0.7	0.3	0.1	0.1
20〜24	2.7	2.7	2.2	1.6	1.3	0.4	0.4	0.1
25〜29	3.3	3.5	3.2	2.5	2.1	1.1	0.6	0.6
30〜34	4.3	4.4	4.6	4.4	4.3	2.9	2.0	1.3
35〜39	6.2	7.0	6.7	7.2	10.5	8.9	5.7	4.1
40〜44	10.5	11.5	10.9	11.1	15.9	18.3	13.8	10.0
45〜49	15.4	17.7	17.9	18.5	20.2	24.0	27.3	19.4
50〜54	23.2	28.7	29.0	25.5	29.0	29.5	33.5	35.4
55〜59	33.2	38.7	37.5	37.8	43.2	37.4	36.2	39.9
60〜64	47.9	54.8	50.2	48.7	56.0	49.8	46.3	41.7
65〜69	66.5	79.2	76.2	66.6	73.8	64.1	53.6	49.1
70〜74	82.6	112.7	115.4	98.0	99.2	84.8	69.2	63.8
75〜79	87.1	135.7	158.7	131.0	138.6	104.9	94.1	84.6
80〜84	86.3	147.4	194.4	175.2	165.2	151.6	124.6	103.3
85〜89	78.4	140.1	205.4	185.3	164.0	162.1	145.6	124.5
90〜94[2]	67.3	127.4	245.4	165.5	153.6	182.7	172.9	149.2
95〜99	…	…	…	…	…	…	…	…
100〜	…	…	…	…	…	…	…	…
								男
総数	12.0	15.4	17.5	17.8	21.8	22.8	23.3	23.0
0〜4歳	3.3	2.6	1.8	1.6	1.3	0.7	0.4	0.3
5〜9	1.6	1.1	0.9	0.5	0.4	0.2	0.1	0.1
10〜14	1.2	1.0	0.9	0.4	0.5	0.2	0.1	0.0
15〜19	1.5	1.7	1.3	0.9	0.8	0.2	0.1	0.2
20〜24	2.9	3.0	2.2	1.5	1.2	0.5	0.6	0.1
25〜29	4.0	3.8	3.9	2.7	2.1	1.5	0.9	0.8
30〜34	4.6	4.7	5.7	6.3	6.0	4.9	3.1	1.9
35〜39	6.5	8.0	9.2	10.5	16.5	14.8	9.9	6.7
40〜44	12.1	14.6	15.5	16.4	25.4	31.9	24.0	17.2
45〜49	18.7	22.7	24.3	27.2	30.9	40.7	48.5	33.6
50〜54	26.9	35.4	40.4	37.7	45.4	49.2	55.7	61.3
55〜59	40.1	46.7	49.8	54.2	63.4	60.4	59.3	64.3
60〜64	57.6	69.0	65.8	67.3	77.8	76.6	70.7	64.6
65〜69	84.3	102.9	102.3	87.9	102.1	93.1	79.3	69.9
70〜74	108.8	143.7	151.2	135.5	132.2	114.6	95.4	86.8
75〜79	115.1	176.6	203.6	177.5	189.9	143.7	133.5	110.2
80〜84	120.3	196.0	277.3	242.9	230.8	203.8	181.0	136.8
85〜89	122.4	192.0	288.4	241.2	219.8	225.3	204.3	190.0
90〜94[2]	94.1	308.8	363.2	284.1	246.1	207.7	244.3	215.6
95〜99	…	…	…	…	…	…	…	…
100〜	…	…	…	…	…	…	…	…
								女
総数	8.8	11.2	11.3	10.2	11.5	10.0	9.5	10.1
0〜4歳	2.7	3.2	2.0	1.1	1.2	0.8	0.2	0.1
5〜9	0.9	1.0	1.0	0.4	0.3	0.1	0.2	-
10〜14	0.7	0.7	0.7	0.5	0.4	0.2	0.1	0.1
15〜19	1.1	1.4	1.0	0.7	0.7	0.3	0.2	0.1
20〜24	2.4	2.3	2.2	1.7	1.3	0.4	0.3	0.1
25〜29	2.7	3.1	2.5	2.3	2.0	0.7	0.3	0.4
30〜34	4.1	4.2	3.5	2.5	2.6	1.0	0.8	0.7
35〜39	5.9	6.2	4.6	4.0	4.4	3.0	1.5	1.4
40〜44	8.9	8.8	7.0	6.7	6.4	4.6	3.6	2.9
45〜49	12.1	12.9	12.3	11.3	11.3	7.6	6.2	5.5
50〜54	19.4	22.0	18.2	14.8	15.6	13.4	12.0	9.9
55〜59	26.3	30.7	25.4	22.5	25.9	19.1	17.5	16.6
60〜64	38.9	41.2	35.2	31.1	36.6	27.7	27.6	23.8
65〜69	51.9	58.3	52.5	47.3	48.8	40.0	33.4	33.8
70〜74	63.4	89.6	86.9	67.0	72.2	60.9	48.9	47.1
75〜79	69.1	109.4	129.4	98.4	101.5	76.9	66.0	66.9
80〜84	68.3	121.0	149.8	138.1	126.4	119.6	89.8	82.9
85〜89	58.7	117.4	168.2	161.1	138.7	131.4	115.6	92.7
90〜94[2]	57.8	64.9	204.8	121.5	120.1	173.6	145.4	121.2
95〜99	…	…	…	…	…	…	…	…
100〜	…	…	…	…	…	…	…	…

274

General mortality

別死亡数及び率（人口10万対）（つづき）
population) by sex, age and causes of death : Japan－CON.

Death rates

1990 平成2年	1995 7年	2000 12年	2005 17年	2010 22年	2014 26年	2015 27年	2016 28年	年齢 Age
Total								
16.1	13.7	12.8	13.0	12.8	12.5	12.5	**12.6**	総数 Total
0.2	0.3	0.3	0.3	0.3	0.1	0.2	**0.3**	0～4 歳
0.1	0.0	0.0	0.1	0.1	-	0.0	**0.1**	5～9 Years
0.0	0.0	0.1	0.0	0.0	0.0	0.0	**0.1**	10～14
0.1	0.0	0.1	0.0	0.0	0.0	0.0	**0.1**	15～19
0.2	0.1	0.1	0.1	0.1	0.1	0.1	**0.1**	20～24
0.4	0.5	0.3	0.3	0.3	0.2	0.3	**0.1**	25～29
1.1	1.3	1.1	0.9	0.9	0.8	0.7	**0.8**	30～34
3.3	3.4	2.9	2.4	2.1	1.9	1.5	**1.6**	35～39
7.3	7.0	5.9	5.5	4.7	3.9	4.0	**3.9**	40～44
14.9	11.4	10.8	9.7	9.0	7.5	7.5	**7.3**	45～49
23.9	18.8	15.8	14.7	13.5	12.3	12.4	**11.5**	50～54
38.2	26.9	22.2	18.3	17.0	14.6	14.7	**15.4**	55～59
42.9	34.7	28.2	24.4	19.5	19.0	18.6	**19.2**	60～64
43.2	34.0	32.0	28.0	24.8	20.2	20.3	**20.6**	65～69
55.8	35.3	33.2	34.3	30.4	26.2	25.8	**23.9**	70～74
70.8	47.9	38.1	37.2	36.1	33.9	32.8	**32.6**	75～79
89.6	65.8	46.8	47.3	43.7	42.8	42.8	**42.6**	80～84
108.2	87.9	60.4	54.4	53.8	53.0	49.4	**50.2**	85～89
115.1	106.8	81.1	64.3	54.7	56.1	55.2	**56.2**	90～94[2]
…	…	…	77.1	62.2	54.4	59.6	**57.1**	95～99
…	…	…	98.6	56.9	66.7	35.6	**53.8**	100～
Male								
22.0	19.0	18.0	17.9	17.2	16.4	16.4	**16.6**	総数
0.2	0.2	0.4	0.3	0.3	0.2	0.2	**0.4**	0～4 歳
0.1	-	0.0	0.1	0.0	-		**0.1**	5～9
0.0	0.0	0.1	0.0	0.0		0.0	**0.1**	10～14
0.2	0.0	0.1		-	0.0	0.1	**0.0**	15～19
0.3	0.2	0.1	0.1	0.2	0.2	0.1	**0.2**	20～24
0.6	0.7	0.6	0.3	0.3	0.2	0.4	**0.2**	25～29
1.8	2.0	1.7	1.1	1.1	0.8	0.9	**0.9**	30～34
5.4	5.3	4.6	3.5	3.1	2.7	1.8	**2.0**	35～39
12.5	11.7	9.5	8.9	7.0	5.8	6.0	**5.7**	40～44
25.9	19.3	18.2	16.1	14.4	11.5	11.8	**11.3**	45～49
40.3	32.5	27.2	24.5	22.5	19.9	20.0	**18.1**	50～54
63.2	45.7	38.1	31.1	27.9	24.2	23.8	**25.1**	55～59
66.1	55.6	47.8	41.0	32.6	30.9	30.6	**31.2**	60～64
62.9	51.3	50.2	45.3	40.0	32.8	32.2	**33.0**	65～69
72.5	46.9	45.4	49.7	43.7	38.6	38.6	**35.4**	70～74
88.9	59.1	47.1	48.1	49.2	44.9	43.5	**44.9**	75～79
117.3	87.1	57.9	56.0	53.1	53.7	53.2	**53.3**	80～84
154.0	116.9	77.0	63.8	60.4	64.3	58.8	**62.1**	85～89
149.8	138.6	105.5	82.6	73.7	68.2	67.9	**73.2**	90～94[2]
…	…	…	89.3	78.6	61.3	70.9	**67.2**	95～99
…	…	…	132.9	51.2	62.5	35.9	**66.7**	100～
Female								
10.3	8.6	7.8	8.4	8.6	8.8	8.8	**8.8**	総数
0.3	0.3	0.2	0.3	0.2	0.0	0.2	**0.3**	0～4 歳
-	0.0		0.0	0.1	-	0.0	**-**	5～9
0.1	0.1	0.1	0.0	0.0	0.0	0.0	**0.0**	10～14
0.1	0.0	0.1	0.1	0.1	-	0.1	**0.1**	15～19
0.0	0.1	0.1	0.1	0.0	0.1	0.0	**-**	20～24
0.2	0.2	0.1	0.2	0.2	0.1	0.2	**0.1**	25～29
0.4	0.7	0.4	0.7	0.7	0.7	0.4	**0.6**	30～34
1.2	1.4	1.1	1.4	1.0	1.1	1.1	**1.1**	35～39
2.1	2.2	2.1	2.2	2.3	2.0	2.1	**2.1**	40～44
4.1	3.4	3.3	3.3	3.4	3.3	3.0	**3.2**	45～49
7.8	5.4	4.5	4.9	4.4	4.6	4.8	**4.9**	50～54
14.2	8.7	6.8	5.8	6.3	5.1	5.7	**5.8**	55～59
21.5	15.1	9.7	8.8	6.9	7.6	7.0	**7.5**	60～64
28.4	18.7	15.7	12.1	10.8	8.6	9.1	**9.0**	65～69
44.2	27.1	23.2	21.3	18.9	15.3	14.7	**13.9**	70～74
58.9	41.0	32.2	29.1	26.1	25.1	24.3	**22.7**	75～79
73.4	53.9	40.9	42.4	37.7	35.6	35.8	**35.3**	80～84
85.5	74.4	52.9	50.4	50.9	47.3	44.6	**44.0**	85～89
101.5	95.3	72.9	58.2	48.8	52.3	51.0	**50.4**	90～94[2]
…	…	…	74.2	58.4	52.9	57.2	**54.7**	95～99
…	…	…	92.6	57.8	68.6	35.6	**50.9**	100～

死　亡

表 5.15　性・年齢別にみた死因年次推移分類
Table 5.15　Trends in deaths and death rates (per 100,000

Hi12　腎不全
Renal failure

死　亡　数

年　齢 Age	1950 昭和25年	1955 30年	1960 35年	1965 40年	1970 45年	1975 50年	1980 55年	1985 60年
								総　数
総数 Total	...	...	...	...	...	...	7 048	11 508
0～4歳	...	...	...	...	...	...	59	113
5～9 Years	...	...	...	...	...	...	5	3
10～14	...	...	...	...	...	...	6	4
15～19	...	...	...	...	...	...	11	13
20～24	...	...	...	...	...	...	24	21
25～29	...	...	...	...	...	...	77	37
30～34	...	...	...	...	...	...	108	74
35～39	...	...	...	...	...	...	113	119
40～44	...	...	...	...	...	...	148	141
45～49	...	...	...	...	...	...	240	231
50～54	...	...	...	...	...	...	328	378
55～59	...	...	...	...	...	...	406	554
60～64	...	...	...	...	...	...	532	645
65～69	...	...	...	...	...	...	859	1 000
70～74	...	...	...	...	...	...	1 166	1 697
75～79	...	...	...	...	...	...	1 281	2 301
80～84	...	...	...	...	...	...	969	2 216
85～89	...	...	...	...	...	...	527	1 384
90～94	...	...	...	...	...	...	156	480
95～99	...	...	...	...	...	...	29	88
100～	...	...	...	...	...	...	4	6
不詳 Not stated	...	...	...	...	...	...	-	3
								男
総数	...	...	...	...	...	...	3 611	5 809
0～4歳	...	...	...	...	...	...	27	52
5～9	...	...	...	...	...	...	4	3
10～14	...	...	...	...	...	...	5	2
15～19	...	...	...	...	...	...	6	10
20～24	...	...	...	...	...	...	18	11
25～29	...	...	...	...	...	...	52	22
30～34	...	...	...	...	...	...	69	45
35～39	...	...	...	...	...	...	62	74
40～44	...	...	...	...	...	...	85	93
45～49	...	...	...	...	...	...	140	139
50～54	...	...	...	...	...	...	182	240
55～59	...	...	...	...	...	...	200	323
60～64	...	...	...	...	...	...	274	337
65～69	...	...	...	...	...	...	443	548
70～74	...	...	...	...	...	...	636	883
75～79	...	...	...	...	...	...	641	1 159
80～84	...	...	...	...	...	...	488	1 064
85～89	...	...	...	...	...	...	211	580
90～94	...	...	...	...	...	...	58	184
95～99	...	...	...	...	...	...	9	34
100～	...	...	...	...	...	...	1	4
不詳	...	...	...	...	...	...	-	2
								女
総数	...	...	...	...	...	...	3 437	5 699
0～4歳	...	...	...	...	...	...	32	61
5～9	...	...	...	...	...	...	1	-
10～14	...	...	...	...	...	...	1	2
15～19	...	...	...	...	...	...	5	3
20～24	...	...	...	...	...	...	6	10
25～29	...	...	...	...	...	...	25	15
30～34	...	...	...	...	...	...	39	29
35～39	...	...	...	...	...	...	51	45
40～44	...	...	...	...	...	...	63	48
45～49	...	...	...	...	...	...	100	92
50～54	...	...	...	...	...	...	146	138
55～59	...	...	...	...	...	...	206	231
60～64	...	...	...	...	...	...	258	308
65～69	...	...	...	...	...	...	416	452
70～74	...	...	...	...	...	...	530	814
75～79	...	...	...	...	...	...	640	1 142
80～84	...	...	...	...	...	...	481	1 152
85～89	...	...	...	...	...	...	316	804
90～94	...	...	...	...	...	...	98	296
95～99	...	...	...	...	...	...	20	54
100～	...	...	...	...	...	...	3	2
不詳	...	...	...	...	...	...	-	1

General mortality

別死亡数及び率（人口10万対）（つづき）
population）by sex, age and causes of death : Japan－CON.

Deaths

1990 平成2年	1995 7年	2000 12年	2005 17年	2010 22年	2014 26年	2015 27年	2016 28年	年　齢 Age
Total								
15 575	16 187	17 260	20 528	23 725	24 776	24 560	24 612	総数 Total
82	11	18	11	9	5	1	4	0～4歳
2	2	-	4	-	3	-	2	5～9 Years
5	5	1	1	2	1	-	3	10～14
13	6	6	7	2	1	-	3	15～19
18	11	2	4	8	4	1	1	20～24
25	18	15	4	7	4	8	4	25～29
45	38	22	21	12	14	8	7	30～34
85	30	27	37	24	20	14	15	35～39
133	99	56	50	35	38	38	34	40～44
195	167	123	94	72	72	79	72	45～49
347	233	252	212	127	130	118	120	50～54
538	413	351	403	287	226	201	202	55～59
923	668	572	552	606	575	519	461	60～64
1 231	1 145	1 056	978	972	961	989	1 054	65～69
1 700	1 640	1 635	1 691	1 627	1 643	1 598	1 412	70～74
2 920	2 472	2 380	2 780	2 952	2 737	2 641	2 585	75～79
3 388	3 660	3 330	3 930	4 741	4 826	4 734	4 624	80～84
2 572	3 282	3 965	4 422	5 599	6 287	6 246	6 409	85～89
1 105	1 762	2 570	3 684	4 264	4 844	4 980	5 108	90～94
220	471	762	1 421	2 001	2 018	2 032	2 106	95～99
27	50	115	220	376	366	352	384	100～
1	4	2	2	2	1	1	2	不詳 Not stated
Male								
7 632	7 800	8 029	9 463	11 035	11 935	11 908	12 231	総数
41	7	11	8	3	3	1	2	0～4歳
1	1	-	3	-	2	-	1	5～9
1	4	-	-	2	-	-	2	10～14
9	4	3	4	-	1	-	1	15～19
12	5	-	-	4	4	1	-	20～24
14	14	10	3	6	3	3	1	25～29
27	24	12	10	9	7	4	3	30～34
54	19	22	27	17	13	8	7	35～39
82	68	44	34	29	25	27	25	40～44
122	103	86	66	48	52	56	56	45～49
216	163	166	157	93	100	87	86	50～54
365	279	247	287	197	156	147	135	55～59
589	436	357	352	431	408	361	339	60～64
668	731	673	648	661	647	694	764	65～69
898	913	993	1 049	989	1 113	1 060	948	70～74
1 481	1 265	1 228	1 606	1 758	1 727	1 612	1 608	75～79
1 537	1 681	1 485	1 832	2 502	2 624	2 585	2 672	80～84
1 042	1 313	1 598	1 767	2 251	2 847	2 883	3 090	85～89
400	606	865	1 200	1 441	1 596	1 742	1 850	90～94
65	144	208	359	523	524	562	551	95～99
7	16	19	50	69	82	74	89	100～
1	4	2	1	2	1	1	1	不詳
Female								
7 943	8 387	9 231	11 065	12 690	12 841	12 652	12 381	総数
41	4	7	3	6	2	-	2	0～4歳
1	1	-	1	-	1	-	1	5～9
4	1	1	1	-	1	-	1	10～14
4	2	3	3	2	-	-	2	15～19
6	6	2	4	4	-	-	1	20～24
11	4	5	1	1	1	5	3	25～29
18	14	10	11	3	7	4	4	30～34
31	11	5	10	7	7	6	8	35～39
51	31	12	16	6	13	11	9	40～44
73	64	37	28	24	20	23	16	45～49
131	70	86	55	34	30	31	34	50～54
173	134	104	116	90	70	54	67	55～59
334	232	215	200	175	167	158	122	60～64
563	414	383	330	311	314	295	290	65～69
802	727	642	642	638	530	538	464	70～74
1 439	1 207	1 152	1 174	1 194	1 010	1 029	977	75～79
1 851	1 979	1 845	2 098	2 239	2 202	2 149	1 952	80～84
1 530	1 969	2 367	2 655	3 348	3 440	3 363	3 319	85～89
705	1 156	1 705	2 484	2 823	3 248	3 238	3 258	90～94
155	327	554	1 062	1 478	1 494	1 470	1 555	95～99
20	34	96	170	307	284	278	295	100～
-	-	-	1	-	-	-	1	不詳

277

死　亡

表 5.15　性・年齢別にみた死因年次推移分類
Table 5.15　Trends in deaths and death rates (per 100,000

Hi12　腎不全
Renal failure

死　亡　率

年　　齢 Age	1950 昭和25年	1955 30年	1960 35年	1965 40年	1970 45年	1975 50年	1980 55年	1985 60年
								総　数
総数 Total	…	…	…	…	…	…	6.1	9.6
0 ～ 4 歳	…	…	…	…	…	…	0.7	1.5
5 ～ 9 Years	…	…	…	…	…	…	0.1	0.0
10～14	…	…	…	…	…	…	0.1	0.0
15～19	…	…	…	…	…	…	0.1	0.1
20～24	…	…	…	…	…	…	0.3	0.3
25～29	…	…	…	…	…	…	0.9	0.5
30～34	…	…	…	…	…	…	1.0	0.8
35～39	…	…	…	…	…	…	1.2	1.1
40～44	…	…	…	…	…	…	1.8	1.6
45～49	…	…	…	…	…	…	3.0	2.8
50～54	…	…	…	…	…	…	4.6	4.8
55～59	…	…	…	…	…	…	7.3	8.0
60～64	…	…	…	…	…	…	12.0	12.0
65～69	…	…	…	…	…	…	21.8	24.0
70～74	…	…	…	…	…	…	38.7	48.0
75～79	…	…	…	…	…	…	63.1	94.5
80～84	…	…	…	…	…	…	88.8	153.2
85～89	…	…	…	…	…	…	128.8	236.0
90～94[2)	…	…	…	…	…	…	158.7	309.3
95～99	…	…	…	…	…	…	…	…
100～	…	…	…	…	…	…	…	…
								男
総数	…	…	…	…	…	…	6.3	9.8
0 ～ 4 歳	…	…	…	…	…	…	0.6	1.4
5 ～ 9	…	…	…	…	…	…	0.1	0.1
10～14	…	…	…	…	…	…	0.1	0.0
15～19	…	…	…	…	…	…	0.1	0.2
20～24	…	…	…	…	…	…	0.5	0.3
25～29	…	…	…	…	…	…	1.2	0.6
30～34	…	…	…	…	…	…	1.3	1.0
35～39	…	…	…	…	…	…	1.4	1.4
40～44	…	…	…	…	…	…	2.1	2.1
45～49	…	…	…	…	…	…	3.5	3.4
50～54	…	…	…	…	…	…	5.2	6.2
55～59	…	…	…	…	…	…	8.0	9.5
60～64	…	…	…	…	…	…	14.2	14.3
65～69	…	…	…	…	…	…	25.5	30.9
70～74	…	…	…	…	…	…	48.5	59.4
75～79	…	…	…	…	…	…	75.8	116.3
80～84	…	…	…	…	…	…	117.1	194.3
85～89	…	…	…	…	…	…	152.3	302.7
90～94[2)	…	…	…	…	…	…	205.1	402.2
95～99	…	…	…	…	…	…	…	…
100～	…	…	…	…	…	…	…	…
								女
総数	…	…	…	…	…	…	5.8	9.3
0 ～ 4 歳	…	…	…	…	…	…	0.8	1.7
5 ～ 9	…	…	…	…	…	…	0.0	-
10～14	…	…	…	…	…	…	0.0	0.0
15～19	…	…	…	…	…	…	0.1	0.1
20～24	…	…	…	…	…	…	0.2	0.2
25～29	…	…	…	…	…	…	0.6	0.4
30～34	…	…	…	…	…	…	0.7	0.6
35～39	…	…	…	…	…	…	1.1	0.9
40～44	…	…	…	…	…	…	1.5	1.1
45～49	…	…	…	…	…	…	2.5	2.2
50～54	…	…	…	…	…	…	4.0	3.5
55～59	…	…	…	…	…	…	6.7	6.5
60～64	…	…	…	…	…	…	10.3	10.2
65～69	…	…	…	…	…	…	18.8	18.9
70～74	…	…	…	…	…	…	31.2	39.8
75～79	…	…	…	…	…	…	54.0	79.4
80～84	…	…	…	…	…	…	71.3	128.1
85～89	…	…	…	…	…	…	116.7	203.6
90～94[2)	…	…	…	…	…	…	140.8	269.9
95～99	…	…	…	…	…	…	…	…
100～	…	…	…	…	…	…	…	…

General mortality

別死亡数及び率（人口10万対）（つづき）
population）by sex, age and causes of death : Japan－CON.

Death rates

1990 平成2年	1995 7年	2000 12年	2005 17年	2010 22年	2014 26年	2015 27年	2016 28年	年齢 Age
Total								
12.7	13.0	13.7	16.3	18.8	19.8	19.6	19.7	総数 Total
1.3	0.2	0.3	0.2	0.2	0.1	0.0	0.1	0～4歳
0.0	0.0	-	0.1	-	0.1	-	0.0	5～9 Years
0.1	0.1	0.0	0.0	0.0	0.0	-	0.1	10～14
0.1	0.1	0.1	0.1	0.0	0.0	-	0.1	15～19
0.2	0.1	0.0	0.1	0.1	0.1	0.0	0.0	20～24
0.3	0.2	0.2	0.0	0.1	0.1	0.1	0.1	25～29
0.6	0.5	0.3	0.2	0.1	0.2	0.1	0.1	30～34
1.0	0.4	0.3	0.4	0.2	0.2	0.2	0.2	35～39
1.3	1.1	0.7	0.6	0.4	0.4	0.4	0.4	40～44
2.2	1.6	1.4	1.2	0.9	0.8	0.9	0.8	45～49
4.3	2.6	2.4	2.4	1.7	1.7	1.5	1.5	50～54
7.0	5.2	4.0	3.9	3.3	3.0	2.7	2.7	55～59
13.7	9.0	7.4	6.5	6.0	6.4	6.1	5.7	60～64
24.2	18.0	14.9	13.2	11.8	10.6	10.2	10.3	65～69
44.6	35.1	27.8	25.5	23.3	20.8	20.6	19.2	70～74
96.9	75.4	57.5	52.8	49.4	43.8	41.7	39.8	75～79
185.0	159.6	127.6	115.3	108.7	99.4	94.5	89.5	80～84
308.8	289.4	259.1	239.2	228.9	205.9	198.4	196.2	85～89
467.3	516.4	492.1	438.0	415.5	372.0	366.3	346.3	90～94[2]
...	...	...	672.3	672.3	574.9	563.3	551.3	95～99
...	...	...	867.6	856.5	610.0	570.1	590.8	100～
Male								
12.7	12.8	13.1	15.4	17.9	19.6	19.5	20.1	総数
1.2	0.2	0.4	0.3	0.1	0.1	0.0	0.1	0～4歳
0.0	0.0	-	0.1	-	0.1	-	0.0	5～9
0.0	0.1	-	-	0.1	-	-	0.1	10～14
0.2	0.1	0.1	0.1	-	0.0	-	0.0	15～19
0.3	0.1	-	-	0.1	0.1	0.0	-	20～24
0.3	0.3	0.2	0.1	0.2	0.1	0.1	0.0	25～29
0.7	0.6	0.3	0.2	0.2	0.2	0.1	0.1	30～34
1.2	0.5	0.5	0.6	0.3	0.3	0.2	0.2	35～39
1.5	1.5	1.1	0.8	0.7	0.5	0.5	0.5	40～44
2.7	1.9	1.9	1.7	1.2	1.2	1.3	1.2	45～49
5.4	3.7	3.2	3.6	2.4	2.6	2.2	2.2	50～54
9.7	7.2	5.8	5.7	4.6	4.1	3.9	3.6	55～59
18.2	12.1	9.5	8.5	8.7	9.3	8.6	8.5	60～64
30.5	24.5	20.1	18.3	16.8	14.7	14.8	15.4	65～69
57.7	47.3	37.2	34.5	30.6	30.3	29.4	27.6	70～74
123.8	100.8	75.8	71.2	67.8	62.6	57.4	55.6	75～79
226.5	204.6	162.6	150.0	147.2	135.4	128.6	127.9	80～84
377.7	363.7	335.3	318.5	301.2	277.2	270.6	276.5	85～89
579.4	655.2	619.4	569.6	593.2	513.2	518.9	490.7	90～94[2]
...	...	...	866.0	934.0	845.2	885.5	822.4	95～99
...	...	...	1 329.4	1 177.7	1 025.0	885.1	988.9	100～
Female								
12.7	13.2	14.4	17.1	19.6	19.9	19.7	19.3	総数
1.3	0.1	0.2	0.1	0.2	0.1	-	0.1	0～4歳
0.0	0.0	-	0.0	-	0.0	-	0.0	5～9
0.1	0.0	0.0	0.0	-	0.0	-	0.0	10～14
0.1	0.0	0.1	0.1	0.1	-	-	0.1	15～19
0.1	0.1	0.0	0.1	0.1	-	-	0.0	20～24
0.3	0.1	0.1	0.0	0.0	0.0	0.2	0.1	25～29
0.5	0.4	0.2	0.2	0.1	0.2	0.1	0.1	30～34
0.7	0.3	0.1	0.2	0.1	0.2	0.1	0.2	35～39
1.0	0.7	0.3	0.4	0.1	0.3	0.2	0.2	40～44
1.6	1.2	0.8	0.7	0.6	0.5	0.5	0.4	45～49
3.2	1.6	1.7	1.3	0.9	0.8	0.8	0.9	50～54
4.4	3.3	2.4	2.2	2.1	1.8	1.4	1.8	55～59
9.5	6.0	5.4	4.6	3.4	3.7	3.7	3.0	60～64
19.4	12.2	10.2	8.5	7.2	6.7	5.9	5.5	65～69
35.6	26.5	19.9	17.9	17.0	12.6	13.0	11.8	70～74
79.2	59.7	45.7	39.1	35.3	29.0	29.2	27.1	75～79
160.5	134.4	108.8	95.9	84.1	75.5	71.6	63.5	80～84
274.7	254.7	224.6	205.2	197.1	169.6	161.4	154.4	85～89
423.4	466.5	449.3	394.0	360.4	328.1	316.3	296.7	90～94[2]
...	...	...	625.1	611.7	517.0	494.5	492.1	95～99
...	...	...	787.1	807.0	556.9	520.7	517.5	100～

死　亡

表 5.15　性・年齢別にみた死因年次推移分類
Table 5.15　Trends in deaths and death rates (per 100,000

Hi13　老　衰
Senility

死　亡　数

年　齢 Age	1950 昭和25年	1955 30年	1960 35年	1965 40年	1970 45年	1975 50年	1980 55年	1985 60年
								総　数
総数　Total	58 412	59 932	54 139	49 092	39 277	29 916	32 154	27 804
0～4歳	-	-	-	-	-	-	-	-
5～9 Years	-	-	-	-	-	-	-	-
10～14	-	-	-	-	-	-	-	-
15～19	-	-	-	-	-	-	-	-
20～24	-	-	-	-	-	-	-	-
25～29	-	-	-	-	-	-	-	-
30～34	-	-	-	-	-	-	-	-
35～39	-	-	-	-	-	-	-	-
40～44	-	-	-	1	-	-	-	-
45～49	-	9	3	-	-	1	-	-
50～54	28	31	13	3	2	1	4	1
55～59	259	160	76	38	34	4	5	2
60～64	1 076	665	384	226	122	51	18	18
65～69	4 058	2 762	1 518	999	602	299	222	129
70～74	10 622	8 361	5 312	3 493	2 355	1 460	1 107	632
75～79	15 120	16 344	12 240	9 515	6 395	4 272	3 940	2 441
80～84	15 400	17 079	17 521	15 287	11 588	8 326	8 679	6 704
85～89	8 548	10 460	11 976	13 252	11 384	9 023	9 830	9 190
90～94	2 843	3 427	4 296	5 311	5 600	5 151	6 475	6 362
95～99	403	582	740	896	1 115	1 200	1 651	2 058
100～	38	51	60	71	79	128	222	267
不詳 Not stated	17	1	-	-	1	-	1	
								男
総数	23 474	23 581	20 547	17 504	13 580	10 287	11 244	9 669
0～4歳	-	-	-	-	-	-	-	-
5～9	-	-	-	-	-	-	-	-
10～14	-	-	-	-	-	-	-	-
15～19	-	-	-	-	-	-	-	-
20～24	-	-	-	-	-	-	-	-
25～29	-	-	-	-	-	-	-	-
30～34	-	-	-	-	-	-	-	-
35～39	-	-	-	-	-	-	-	-
40～44	-	-	-	-	-	-	-	-
45～49	-	2	1	-	-	1	-	-
50～54	17	13	4	-	2	-	1	-
55～59	117	69	27	18	10	2	2	2
60～64	511	316	201	118	68	29	8	7
65～69	1 916	1 311	745	480	299	159	125	68
70～74	4 869	3 798	2 530	1 645	1 115	705	540	314
75～79	6 353	7 004	5 034	4 009	2 713	1 839	1 704	1 092
80～84	5 887	6 541	6 664	5 485	4 290	3 093	3 408	2 702
85～89	2 839	3 313	4 004	4 122	3 447	2 891	3 292	3 091
90～94	833	1 064	1 152	1 415	1 401	1 316	1 775	1 823
95～99	112	136	174	197	224	234	352	513
100～	12	14	11	15	11	18	36	57
不詳	8	-	-	-	-	-	1	
								女
総数	34 938	36 351	33 592	31 588	25 697	19 629	20 910	18 135
0～4歳	-	-	-	-	-	-	-	-
5～9	-	-	-	-	-	-	-	-
10～14	-	-	-	-	-	-	-	-
15～19	-	-	-	-	-	-	-	-
20～24	-	-	-	-	-	-	-	-
25～29	-	-	-	-	-	-	-	-
30～34	-	-	-	-	-	-	-	-
35～39	-	-	-	-	-	-	-	-
40～44	-	-	-	1	-	-	-	-
45～49	-	7	2	-	-	-	-	-
50～54	11	18	9	3	-	1	3	1
55～59	142	91	49	20	24	2	3	
60～64	565	349	183	108	54	22	10	11
65～69	2 142	1 451	773	519	303	140	97	61
70～74	5 753	4 563	2 782	1 848	1 240	755	567	318
75～79	8 767	9 340	7 206	5 506	3 682	2 433	2 236	1 349
80～84	9 513	10 538	10 857	9 802	7 298	5 233	5 271	4 002
85～89	5 709	7 147	7 972	9 130	7 937	6 132	6 538	6 099
90～94	2 010	2 363	3 144	3 896	4 199	3 835	4 700	4 539
95～99	291	446	566	699	891	966	1 299	1 545
100～	26	37	49	56	68	110	186	210
不詳	9	1	-	-	1	-	-	

General mortality

別死亡数及び率（人口10万対）（つづき）
population）by sex, age and causes of death : Japan－CON.

Deaths

1990 平成2年	1995 7年	2000 12年	2005 17年	2010 22年	2014 26年	2015 27年	2016 28年	年齢 Age
Total								
24 187	21 493	21 213	26 360	45 342	75 389	84 810	92 806	総数 Total
-	-	-	-	-	-	-	-	0～4歳
-	-	-	-	-	-	-	-	5～9 Years
-	-	-	-	-	-	-	-	10～14
-	-	-	-	-	-	-	-	15～19
-	-	-	-	-	-	-	-	20～24
-	-	-	-	-	-	-	-	25～29
-	-	-	-	-	-	-	-	30～34
-	-	-	-	-	-	-	-	35～39
-	-	-	-	-	-	-	-	40～44
-	-	-	-	-	-	-	-	45～49
-	-	-	-	-	-	-	-	50～54
-	-	-	-	-	-	-	-	55～59
6	9	5	2	8	21	19	25	60～64
74	60	59	59	69	112	144	142	65～69
319	204	199	186	276	432	560	602	70～74
1 393	846	668	727	1 021	1 794	2 018	2 055	75～79
4 489	3 153	2 200	2 339	3 842	6 466	7 372	7 805	80～84
7 903	6 234	5 488	5 367	8 984	16 008	17 863	19 265	85～89
7 162	7 201	7 346	9 084	14 125	24 477	27 389	30 171	90～94
2 392	3 108	4 128	6 435	12 165	17 774	20 371	22 834	95～99
448	677	1 119	2 161	4 852	8 303	9 074	9 907	100～
1	1	1	-	-	2	-	-	不詳 Not stated
Male								
8 054	6 684	6 017	6 683	10 787	18 316	20 894	23 077	総数
-	-	-	-	-	-	-	-	0～4歳
-	-	-	-	-	-	-	-	5～9
-	-	-	-	-	-	-	-	10～14
-	-	-	-	-	-	-	-	15～19
-	-	-	-	-	-	-	-	20～24
-	-	-	-	-	-	-	-	25～29
-	-	-	-	-	-	-	-	30～34
-	-	-	-	-	-	-	-	35～39
-	-	-	-	-	-	-	-	40～44
-	-	-	-	-	-	-	-	45～49
-	-	-	-	-	-	-	-	50～54
-	-	-	-	-	-	-	-	55～59
3	6	4	-	7	13	12	15	60～64
38	38	42	35	43	73	95	92	65～69
144	91	107	101	173	244	324	357	70～74
644	374	308	362	515	925	1 023	1 037	75～79
1 784	1 234	855	852	1 565	2 747	3 142	3 293	80～84
2 593	2 045	1 726	1 562	2 567	5 075	5 784	6 440	85～89
2 092	2 033	1 942	2 224	3 187	5 322	6 092	6 999	90～94
647	737	848	1 224	2 125	2 960	3 301	3 671	95～99
108	126	184	323	605	957	1 121	1 173	100～
1	-	1	-	-	-	-	-	不詳
Female								
16 133	14 809	15 196	19 677	34 555	57 073	63 916	69 729	総数
-	-	-	-	-	-	-	-	0～4歳
-	-	-	-	-	-	-	-	5～9
-	-	-	-	-	-	-	-	10～14
-	-	-	-	-	-	-	-	15～19
-	-	-	-	-	-	-	-	20～24
-	-	-	-	-	-	-	-	25～29
-	-	-	-	-	-	-	-	30～34
-	-	-	-	-	-	-	-	35～39
-	-	-	-	-	-	-	-	40～44
-	-	-	-	-	-	-	-	45～49
-	-	-	-	-	-	-	-	50～54
-	-	-	-	-	-	-	-	55～59
3	3	1	2	1	8	7	10	60～64
36	22	17	24	26	39	49	50	65～69
175	113	92	85	103	188	236	245	70～74
749	472	360	365	506	869	995	1 018	75～79
2 705	1 919	1 345	1 487	2 277	3 719	4 230	4 512	80～84
5 310	4 189	3 762	3 805	6 417	10 933	12 079	12 825	85～89
5 070	5 168	5 404	6 860	10 938	19 155	21 297	23 172	90～94
1 745	2 371	3 280	5 211	10 040	14 814	17 070	19 163	95～99
340	551	935	1 838	4 247	7 346	7 953	8 734	100～
-	1	-	-	-	2	-	-	不詳

死　亡

表 5.15　性・年齢別にみた死因年次推移分類
Table 5.15　Trends in deaths and death rates（per 100,000

Hi13　老　衰
Senility

死　亡　率

年　　齢 Age	1950 昭和25年	1955 30年	1960 35年	1965 40年	1970 45年	1975 50年	1980 55年	1985 60年
								総　数
総数 Total	70.2	67.1	58.0	50.0	38.1	26.9	27.6	23.1
0～4歳	-	-	-	-	-	-	-	-
5～9 Years	-	-	-	-	-	-	-	-
10～14	-	-	-	-	-	-	-	-
15～19	-	-	-	-	-	-	-	-
20～24	-	-	-	-	-	-	-	-
25～29	-	-	-	-	-	-	-	-
30～34	-	-	-	-	-	-	-	-
35～39	-	-	-	-	-	-	-	-
40～44	-	-	-	0.0	-	-	-	-
45～49	-	0.2	0.1	-	-	0.0	-	-
50～54	0.8	0.8	0.3	0.1	0.0	0.0	0.1	0.0
55～59	9.4	5.0	2.1	0.9	0.8	0.1	0.1	0.0
60～64	46.7	26.6	13.1	6.8	3.3	1.2	0.4	0.3
65～69	229.2	140.4	70.3	39.0	20.2	8.7	5.6	3.1
70～74	828.8	600.4	339.7	200.2	110.7	56.9	36.8	17.9
75～79	2 205.2	1 866.4	1 282.1	868.2	505.2	261.0	194.0	100.3
80～84	5 584.1	4 520.8	3 628.1	2 894.6	1 787.0	1 031.3	795.4	463.3
85～89	10 813.0	9 393.4	7 686.1	6 654.0	4 964.1	2 924.6	2 401.7	1 567.2
90～94[1]	20 079.5	17 832.8	15 832.5	12 366.8	10 330.1	7 942.3	7 008.5	4 680.5
95～99	…	…	…	…	…	…	…	…
100～	…	…	…	…	…	…	…	…
								男
総数	57.5	53.8	44.8	36.3	26.8	18.8	19.7	16.4
0～4歳	-	-	-	-	-	-	-	-
5～9	-	-	-	-	-	-	-	-
10～14	-	-	-	-	-	-	-	-
15～19	-	-	-	-	-	-	-	-
20～24	-	-	-	-	-	-	-	-
25～29	-	-	-	-	-	-	-	-
30～34	-	-	-	-	-	-	-	-
35～39	-	-	-	-	-	-	-	-
40～44	-	-	-	-	-	-	-	-
45～49	-	0.1	0.0	-	-	0.0	-	-
50～54	1.0	0.7	0.2	-	0.1	-	0.0	-
55～59	8.5	4.3	1.5	0.9	0.5	0.1	0.1	0.1
60～64	46.1	25.8	14.0	7.3	3.9	1.5	0.4	0.3
65～69	240.7	142.6	72.5	39.4	21.5	10.2	7.2	3.8
70～74	901.2	639.6	364.8	208.5	116.3	61.7	41.2	21.1
75～79	2 373.3	2 047.6	1 336.3	887.2	511.2	268.0	201.5	109.6
80～84	6 158.7	4 911.0	3 939.8	2 934.0	1 780.7	1 006.9	817.9	493.5
85～89	11 584.4	9 786.7	8 308.3	6 855.5	4 825.2	2 869.7	2 376.9	1 613.3
90～94[1]	22 517.6	20 826.9	16 186.4	11 851.7	9 363.6	7 236.8	6 522.5	4 335.1
95～99	…	…	…	…	…	…	…	…
100～	…	…	…	…	…	…	…	…
								女
総数	82.4	80.0	70.7	63.1	48.9	34.7	35.4	29.6
0～4歳	-	-	-	-	-	-	-	-
5～9	-	-	-	-	-	-	-	-
10～14	-	-	-	-	-	-	-	-
15～19	-	-	-	-	-	-	-	-
20～24	-	-	-	-	-	-	-	-
25～29	-	-	-	-	-	-	-	-
30～34	-	-	-	-	-	-	-	-
35～39	-	-	-	-	-	-	-	-
40～44	-	-	-	0.0	-	-	-	-
45～49	-	0.3	0.1	-	-	-	-	-
50～54	0.7	0.9	0.4	0.1	-	0.0	0.1	0.0
55～59	10.4	5.7	2.7	1.0	1.0	0.1	0.1	-
60～64	47.3	27.5	12.2	6.3	2.7	0.9	0.4	0.4
65～69	219.7	138.5	68.2	38.6	19.2	7.5	4.4	2.5
70～74	776.1	571.2	319.7	193.4	106.0	53.0	33.4	15.5
75～79	2 097.6	1 750.2	1 246.8	854.9	500.9	256.0	188.7	93.8
80～84	5 279.3	4 308.3	3 460.1	2 873.1	1 790.7	1 046.3	781.5	445.0
85～89	10 466.4	9 221.6	7 407.5	6 566.9	5 027.0	2 951.2	2 414.3	1 544.4
90～94[1]	19 223.5	16 802.5	15 710.3	12 557.7	10 679.8	8 197.4	7 196.0	4 826.7
95～99	…	…	…	…	…	…	…	…
100～	…	…	…	…	…	…	…	…

282

General mortality

別死亡数及び率（人口10万対）（つづき）
population）by sex, age and causes of death : Japan－CON.

Death rates

1990 平成2年	1995 7年	2000 12年	2005 17年	2010 22年	2014 26年	2015 27年	2016 28年	年　　齢 Age
Total								
19.7	17.3	16.9	20.9	35.9	60.1	67.7	74.2	総数 Total
-	-	-	-	-	-	-	-	0～4歳
-	-	-	-	-	-	-	-	5～9 Years
-	-	-	-	-	-	-	-	10～14
-	-	-	-	-	-	-	-	15～19
-	-	-	-	-	-	-	-	20～24
-	-	-	-	-	-	-	-	25～29
-	-	-	-	-	-	-	-	30～34
-	-	-	-	-	-	-	-	35～39
-	-	-	-	-	-	-	-	40～44
-	-	-	-	-	-	-	-	45～49
-	-	-	-	-	-	-	-	50～54
-	-	-	-	-	-	-	-	55～59
0.1	0.1	0.1	0.0	0.1	0.2	0.2	0.3	60～64
1.5	0.9	0.8	0.8	0.8	1.2	1.5	1.4	65～69
8.4	4.4	3.4	2.8	3.9	5.5	7.2	8.2	70～74
46.2	25.8	16.1	13.8	17.1	28.7	31.9	31.6	75～79
245.1	137.5	84.3	68.6	88.1	133.2	147.1	151.1	80～84
948.9	549.7	358.6	290.3	367.3	524.2	567.3	589.7	85～89
3 457.1	2 485.1	1 797.9	1 080.0	1 376.3	1 880.0	2 014.5	2 045.5	90～94[2]
…	…	…	3 044.6	4 087.2	5 063.8	5 646.7	5 977.5	95～99
…	…	…	8 522.0	11 052.1	13 838.3	14 695.5	15 241.5	100～
Male								
13.4	11.0	9.8	10.8	17.5	30.0	34.2	37.9	総数
-	-	-	-	-	-	-	-	0～4歳
-	-	-	-	-	-	-	-	5～9
-	-	-	-	-	-	-	-	10～14
-	-	-	-	-	-	-	-	15～19
-	-	-	-	-	-	-	-	20～24
-	-	-	-	-	-	-	-	25～29
-	-	-	-	-	-	-	-	30～34
-	-	-	-	-	-	-	-	35～39
-	-	-	-	-	-	-	-	40～44
-	-	-	-	-	-	-	-	45～49
-	-	-	-	-	-	-	-	50～54
-	-	-	-	-	-	-	-	55～59
0.1	0.2	0.1	-	0.1	0.3	0.3	0.4	60～64
1.7	1.3	1.3	1.0	1.1	1.7	2.0	1.9	65～69
9.3	4.7	4.0	3.3	5.3	6.6	9.0	10.4	70～74
53.8	29.8	19.0	16.0	19.9	33.5	36.4	35.8	75～79
262.9	150.2	93.6	69.8	92.0	141.7	156.3	157.6	80～84
939.8	566.4	362.2	281.6	343.5	494.2	542.9	576.4	85～89
3 495.0	2 477.2	1 686.8	1 055.7	1 311.9	1 711.3	1 814.5	1 856.5	90～94[1]
…	…	…	2 952.6	3 795.0	4 774.2	5 201.0	5 479.1	95～99
…	…	…	8 588.1	10 326.0	11 962.5	13 407.5	13 033.3	100～
Female								
25.8	23.4	23.7	30.5	53.3	88.6	99.4	108.7	総数
-	-	-	-	-	-	-	-	0～4歳
-	-	-	-	-	-	-	-	5～9
-	-	-	-	-	-	-	-	10～14
-	-	-	-	-	-	-	-	15～19
-	-	-	-	-	-	-	-	20～24
-	-	-	-	-	-	-	-	25～29
-	-	-	-	-	-	-	-	30～34
-	-	-	-	-	-	-	-	35～39
-	-	-	-	-	-	-	-	40～44
-	-	-	-	-	-	-	-	45～49
-	-	-	-	-	-	-	-	50～54
-	-	-	-	-	-	-	-	55～59
0.1	0.1	0.0	0.0	0.0	0.2	0.2	0.2	60～64
1.2	0.6	0.5	0.6	0.6	0.8	1.0	0.9	65～69
7.8	4.1	2.9	2.4	2.7	4.5	5.7	6.2	70～74
41.2	23.3	14.3	12.1	15.0	24.9	28.2	28.2	75～79
234.6	130.3	79.3	68.0	85.5	127.5	140.9	146.7	80～84
953.4	541.9	357.0	294.1	377.7	539.1	579.7	596.6	85～89
3 442.2	2 487.9	1 835.2	1 088.2	1 396.3	1 934.8	2 080.1	2 110.4	90～94[2]
…	…	…	3 067.1	4 155.0	5 126.0	5 741.9	6 064.2	95～99
…	…	…	8 510.4	11 164.0	14 403.9	14 897.2	15 322.8	100～

283

死　亡

表5.15　性・年齢別にみた死因年次推移分類
Table 5.15　Trends in deaths and death rates (per 100,000

Hi14　不慮の事故
Accidents

死　亡　数

年　齢 Age	1950 昭和25年	1955 30年	1960 35年	1965 40年	1970 45年	1975 50年	1980 55年	1985 60年
								総　数
総数 Total	32 850	33 265	38 964	40 188	43 802	33 710	29 217	29 597
0～4歳	9 604	7 473	5 647	4 609	4 287	3 680	2 345	1 453
5～9 Years	3 321	3 395	2 695	1 913	1 738	1 426	1 138	728
10～14	1 176	1 347	1 430	1 036	777	530	370	407
15～19	1 904	1 609	2 626	2 653	3 172	2 075	1 884	2 249
20～24	2 626	2 802	3 490	3 382	3 822	2 227	1 531	1 703
25～29	1 826	2 477	3 365	2 805	2 807	1 888	1 274	1 082
30～34	1 490	1 700	2 602	2 862	2 543	1 663	1 316	1 065
35～39	1 557	1 447	2 065	2 692	2 871	1 677	1 396	1 384
40～44	1 496	1 569	1 794	2 260	2 857	2 118	1 573	1 548
45～49	1 478	1 618	1 952	2 143	2 286	2 185	1 920	1 793
50～54	1 342	1 562	1 939	2 236	2 252	1 832	1 967	2 173
55～59	1 104	1 416	1 864	2 178	2 507	1 771	1 740	2 139
60～64	1 028	1 221	1 745	2 255	2 508	1 931	1 585	1 749
65～69	891	1 090	1 582	1 997	2 565	2 069	1 903	1 817
70～74	829	942	1 511	1 772	2 432	2 101	2 124	2 151
75～79	601	892	1 261	1 513	1 999	1 962	2 061	2 336
80～84	361	475	906	1 156	1 396	1 389	1 674	1 973
85～89	117	176	377	539	702	819	925	1 231
90～94	29	43	92	168	199	259	373	482
95～99	4	6	18	15	23	58	81	99
100～	1	-	-	-	4	5	11	8
不詳 Not stated	65	5	3	4	55	45	26	27
								男
総数	23 783	24 908	29 787	30 674	33 112	24 865	21 153	21 318
0～4歳	5 414	4 336	3 390	2 770	2 623	2 319	1 476	910
5～9	2 450	2 596	1 983	1 386	1 264	1 037	817	544
10～14	825	913	1 091	801	607	406	284	304
15～19	1 584	1 348	2 237	2 318	2 814	1 836	1 600	1 938
20～24	2 302	2 456	3 088	3 001	3 288	1 881	1 321	1 447
25～29	1 580	2 249	3 043	2 482	2 460	1 658	1 089	917
30～34	1 270	1 482	2 334	2 562	2 240	1 445	1 120	861
35～39	1 340	1 233	1 770	2 334	2 455	1 440	1 157	1 123
40～44	1 282	1 323	1 522	1 900	2 403	1 795	1 290	1 261
45～49	1 267	1 401	1 610	1 765	1 864	1 802	1 635	1 489
50～54	1 149	1 344	1 574	1 807	1 769	1 470	1 579	1 744
55～59	911	1 172	1 465	1 698	1 942	1 367	1 325	1 728
60～64	774	952	1 333	1 730	1 873	1 459	1 173	1 266
65～69	576	742	1 137	1 414	1 797	1 471	1 353	1 252
70～74	449	569	951	1 123	1 563	1 361	1 386	1 382
75～79	319	475	648	833	1 108	1 092	1 172	1 369
80～84	177	224	413	496	654	627	833	1 033
85～89	47	76	158	197	280	270	386	531
90～94	10	14	33	49	53	76	116	167
95～99	2	1	5	4	8	11	15	24
100～	1	-	-	-	1	1	2	2
不詳	54	2	2	4	46	41	24	26
								女
総数	9 067	8 357	9 177	9 514	10 690	8 845	8 064	8 279
0～4歳	4 190	3 137	2 257	1 839	1 664	1 361	869	543
5～9	871	799	712	527	474	389	321	184
10～14	351	434	339	235	170	124	86	103
15～19	320	261	389	335	358	239	284	311
20～24	324	346	402	381	534	346	210	256
25～29	246	228	322	323	347	230	185	165
30～34	220	218	268	300	303	218	196	204
35～39	217	214	295	358	416	237	239	261
40～44	214	246	272	360	454	323	283	287
45～49	211	217	342	378	422	383	285	304
50～54	193	218	365	429	483	362	388	429
55～59	193	244	399	480	565	404	415	411
60～64	254	269	412	525	635	472	412	483
65～69	315	348	445	583	768	598	550	565
70～74	380	373	560	649	869	740	738	769
75～79	282	417	613	680	891	870	889	967
80～84	184	251	493	660	742	762	841	940
85～89	70	100	219	342	422	549	539	700
90～94	19	29	59	119	146	183	257	315
95～99	2	5	13	11	15	47	66	75
100～	-	-	-	-	3	4	9	6
不詳	11	3	1	-	9	4	2	1

284

General mortality

別死亡数及び率（人口10万対）（つづき）
population）by sex, age and causes of death : Japan－CON.

Deaths

1990 平成2年	1995 7年	2000 12年	2005 17年	2010 22年	2014 26年	2015 27年	2016 28年	年　齢 Age
Total								
32 122	45 323	39 484	39 863	40 732	39 029	38 306	38 306	総数 Total
1 071	959	525	410	264	191	190	158	0～4歳
523	525	242	230	125	102	87	68	5～9 Years
320	370	166	150	121	85	74	66	10～14
2 493	1 769	1 052	615	424	312	288	306	15～19
2 091	2 258	1 386	859	553	382	365	373	20～24
1 081	1 319	1 072	775	514	388	301	291	25～29
851	977	891	825	570	413	356	346	30～34
1 143	946	823	844	670	490	455	444	35～39
1 530	1 428	984	860	765	656	634	553	40～44
1 656	2 122	1 433	1 058	866	800	704	694	45～49
1 875	2 578	2 113	1 614	1 079	909	888	815	50～54
2 296	2 904	2 337	2 350	1 654	1 213	1 130	1 104	55～59
2 388	3 542	2 713	2 549	2 437	1 903	1 761	1 531	60～64
2 151	3 770	3 269	2 883	2 982	2 705	2 594	2 750	65～69
2 395	4 219	4 087	4 138	3 827	3 617	3 512	3 282	70～74
2 833	4 686	4 469	5 353	5 513	5 070	4 961	4 851	75～79
2 681	5 026	4 708	5 437	6 782	6 810	6 884	6 668	80～84
1 757	3 682	4 167	4 607	5 985	6 823	6 715	6 957	85～89
754	1 693	2 233	3 066	3 682	4 194	4 360	4 849	90～94
174	393	624	1 035	1 557	1 562	1 687	1 772	95～99
14	41	96	135	305	359	316	392	100～
45	116	94	70	57	45	44	36	不詳 Not stated
Male								
22 199	28 229	25 162	24 591	23 975	22 562	22 121	22 066	総数
656	585	349	242	168	108	116	96	0～4歳
369	351	158	165	87	71	63	44	5～9
232	239	128	106	93	57	53	49	10～14
2 027	1 367	855	473	312	242	231	239	15～19
1 723	1 740	1 128	678	425	307	294	281	20～24
925	1 025	896	609	395	296	238	227	25～29
697	749	741	667	436	324	272	282	30～34
959	749	635	684	496	373	354	345	35～39
1 227	1 082	764	683	572	518	484	442	40～44
1 311	1 558	1 134	812	688	627	526	527	45～49
1 462	1 891	1 638	1 247	839	695	657	615	50～54
1 789	2 057	1 768	1 779	1 285	904	879	846	55～59
1 797	2 480	2 026	1 887	1 784	1 411	1 317	1 156	60～64
1 396	2 431	2 288	1 998	2 069	1 881	1 870	1 940	65～69
1 459	2 355	2 635	2 713	2 470	2 393	2 306	2 126	70～74
1 636	2 388	2 432	3 350	3 300	3 072	2 962	3 017	75～79
1 387	2 511	2 456	2 800	3 836	3 821	3 934	3 827	80～84
790	1 752	1 933	2 059	2 796	3 384	3 338	3 492	85～89
272	687	905	1 207	1 377	1 550	1 681	1 927	90～94
41	127	191	345	439	431	456	488	95～99
2	8	27	28	67	65	59	77	100～
42	97	75	59	41	32	31	23	不詳
Female								
9 923	17 094	14 322	15 272	16 757	16 467	16 185	16 240	総数
415	374	176	168	96	83	74	62	0～4歳
154	174	84	65	38	31	24	24	5～9
88	131	38	44	28	28	21	17	10～14
466	402	197	142	112	70	57	67	15～19
368	518	258	181	128	75	71	92	20～24
156	294	176	166	119	92	63	64	25～29
154	228	150	158	134	89	84	64	30～34
184	197	188	160	174	117	101	99	35～39
303	346	220	177	193	138	150	111	40～44
345	564	299	246	178	173	178	167	45～49
413	687	475	367	240	214	231	200	50～54
507	847	569	571	369	309	251	258	55～59
591	1 062	687	662	653	492	444	375	60～64
755	1 339	981	885	913	824	724	810	65～69
936	1 864	1 452	1 425	1 357	1 224	1 206	1 156	70～74
1 197	2 298	2 037	2 003	2 213	1 998	1 999	1 834	75～79
1 294	2 515	2 252	2 637	2 946	2 989	2 950	2 841	80～84
967	1 930	2 234	2 548	3 189	3 439	3 377	3 465	85～89
482	1 006	1 328	1 859	2 305	2 644	2 679	2 922	90～94
133	266	433	690	1 118	1 131	1 231	1 284	95～99
12	33	69	107	238	294	257	315	100～
3	19	19	11	16	13	13	13	不詳

死　亡

表 5.15　性・年齢別にみた死因年次推移分類
Table 5.15　Trends in deaths and death rates (per 100,000

Hi14　不慮の事故
Accidents

死　亡　率

年　　齢 Age	1950 昭和25年	1955 30年	1960 35年	1965 40年	1970 45年	1975 50年	1980 55年	1985 60年
								総　数
総数 Total	39.5	37.3	41.7	40.9	42.5	30.3	25.1	24.6
0〜4歳	85.7	80.8	72.0	56.7	49.0	37.0	27.7	19.5
5〜9 Years	34.9	30.7	29.3	24.4	21.5	16.1	11.4	8.6
10〜14	13.5	14.2	13.0	11.3	10.0	6.4	4.2	4.1
15〜19	22.2	18.7	28.2	24.4	35.3	26.3	22.9	25.2
20〜24	34.0	33.3	42.0	37.3	36.1	24.7	19.7	20.8
25〜29	29.5	32.6	41.0	33.5	31.1	17.6	14.2	14.0
30〜34	28.6	27.8	34.6	34.7	30.5	18.1	12.3	11.8
35〜39	30.8	28.3	34.2	35.9	35.1	20.0	15.3	13.0
40〜44	33.4	31.7	35.7	37.9	39.1	25.9	19.0	17.1
45〜49	36.9	37.0	40.5	43.5	39.1	29.8	23.8	21.9
50〜54	39.6	40.6	46.2	48.0	47.1	31.9	27.4	27.6
55〜59	40.2	44.2	51.2	54.4	57.0	38.1	31.2	30.7
60〜64	44.6	48.9	59.5	67.4	67.6	45.3	35.7	32.6
65〜69	50.3	55.4	73.2	77.9	86.3	60.2	48.2	43.6
70〜74	64.7	67.6	96.6	101.6	114.3	81.8	70.5	60.9
75〜79	87.7	101.9	132.1	138.1	157.9	119.9	101.5	96.0
80〜84	130.9	125.7	187.6	218.9	215.3	172.1	153.4	136.4
85〜89	148.0	158.1	242.0	270.6	306.1	265.5	226.0	209.9
90〜94[2]	207.9	215.2	341.8	360.5	343.6	394.7	390.4	317.3
95〜99	…	…	…	…	…	…	…	…
100〜	…	…	…	…	…	…	…	…
								男
総数	58.3	56.8	64.9	63.6	65.4	45.4	37.0	36.1
0〜4歳	94.7	91.7	84.5	66.8	58.5	45.5	34.0	23.9
5〜9	50.8	46.1	42.2	34.7	30.5	22.8	16.0	12.5
10〜14	18.7	19.0	19.4	17.2	15.3	9.7	6.2	6.0
15〜19	36.7	31.1	47.8	42.3	62.0	45.8	38.1	42.5
20〜24	60.0	58.5	74.9	66.7	62.3	41.5	33.6	34.7
25〜29	56.0	59.6	74.3	59.7	54.8	30.7	24.1	23.4
30〜34	53.8	53.0	62.3	61.8	53.9	31.4	20.8	19.0
35〜39	56.4	53.2	64.1	62.3	59.8	34.4	25.3	20.8
40〜44	58.3	56.9	66.9	69.6	65.9	43.7	31.2	28.1
45〜49	62.8	65.6	71.3	79.3	70.2	49.5	40.7	36.7
50〜54	66.8	69.7	77.1	83.2	82.7	56.6	44.7	44.7
55〜59	66.1	72.9	81.3	88.0	95.7	66.4	53.1	51.0
60〜64	69.8	77.6	92.7	106.5	107.3	75.8	60.7	53.9
65〜69	72.4	80.7	110.7	116.0	129.0	94.1	78.0	70.7
70〜74	83.1	95.8	137.1	142.3	163.1	119.0	105.6	93.0
75〜79	119.2	138.9	172.0	184.3	208.8	159.1	138.6	137.4
80〜84	185.2	168.2	244.2	265.3	271.5	204.1	199.9	188.7
85〜89	191.8	224.5	327.8	327.6	391.9	268.0	278.7	277.1
90〜94[2]	305.9	257.3	460.0	386.1	354.9	406.1	401.1	349.6
95〜99	…	…	…	…	…	…	…	…
100〜	…	…	…	…	…	…	…	…
								女
総数	21.4	18.4	19.3	19.0	20.4	15.6	13.6	13.5
0〜4歳	76.4	69.4	58.9	46.2	39.0	28.1	21.1	14.9
5〜9	18.5	14.8	15.8	13.7	12.0	9.0	6.6	4.4
10〜14	8.2	9.2	6.3	5.2	4.4	3.1	2.0	2.1
15〜19	7.5	6.1	8.4	6.2	8.0	6.2	7.1	7.1
20〜24	8.3	8.2	9.6	8.3	10.0	7.7	5.5	6.4
25〜29	7.3	6.0	7.8	7.7	7.6	4.3	4.1	4.3
30〜34	7.7	6.6	7.1	7.3	7.3	4.7	3.7	4.5
35〜39	8.1	7.7	9.0	9.5	10.2	5.7	5.2	4.9
40〜44	9.4	9.4	9.9	11.1	12.4	7.9	6.8	6.3
45〜49	10.6	9.7	13.4	14.0	13.3	10.4	7.1	7.3
50〜54	11.6	11.4	16.9	17.3	18.3	11.5	10.7	10.8
55〜59	14.1	15.3	21.7	23.2	23.8	15.6	13.4	11.5
60〜64	21.3	21.2	27.6	30.5	32.3	20.2	16.4	16.0
65〜69	32.3	33.2	39.3	43.4	48.6	31.9	24.9	23.6
70〜74	51.3	46.7	64.4	67.9	74.3	52.0	43.4	37.6
75〜79	67.5	78.1	106.1	105.6	121.2	91.5	75.0	67.3
80〜84	102.1	102.6	157.1	193.5	182.1	152.4	124.7	104.5
85〜89	128.3	129.0	203.5	246.0	267.3	264.2	199.0	177.3
90〜94[2]	173.5	200.7	300.9	351.0	339.6	390.6	386.3	303.7
95〜99	…	…	…	…	…	…	…	…
100〜	…	…	…	…	…	…	…	…

別死亡数及び率（人口10万対）（つづき）
population）by sex, age and causes of death : Japan－CON.

Death rates

1990 平成2年	1995 7年	2000 12年	2005 17年	2010 22年	2014 26年	2015 27年	2016 28年	年　齢 Age
Total								
26.2	36.5	31.4	31.6	32.2	31.1	30.6	**30.6**	総数 Total
16.6	16.1	9.0	7.4	5.0	3.7	3.8	**3.2**	0～4歳
7.0	8.1	4.0	3.9	2.3	1.9	1.7	**1.3**	5～9 Years
3.8	5.0	2.6	2.5	2.1	1.5	1.3	**1.2**	10～14
25.0	20.8	14.2	9.4	7.0	5.3	4.8	**5.1**	15～19
24.0	23.1	16.7	11.9	8.8	6.4	6.2	**6.3**	20～24
13.6	15.3	11.1	9.6	7.2	6.0	4.8	**4.7**	25～29
11.0	12.3	10.3	8.6	6.9	5.7	5.0	**4.9**	30～34
12.8	12.3	10.3	9.8	6.9	5.8	5.5	**5.6**	35～39
14.4	16.0	12.8	10.8	8.8	6.8	6.5	**5.8**	40～44
18.4	20.1	16.2	13.8	10.9	9.4	8.2	**7.6**	45～49
23.2	29.1	20.3	18.5	14.2	11.8	11.2	**10.5**	50～54
29.8	36.7	26.9	23.0	19.1	16.0	15.0	**14.8**	55～59
35.5	47.6	35.2	29.9	24.2	21.3	20.7	**18.9**	60～64
42.3	59.2	46.1	38.8	36.2	29.7	26.7	**26.9**	65～69
62.9	90.3	69.4	62.4	54.8	45.8	45.3	**44.5**	70～74
94.0	143.0	108.0	101.7	92.3	81.2	78.4	**74.6**	75～79
146.4	219.1	180.4	159.5	155.4	140.3	137.3	**129.1**	80～84
211.0	324.7	272.3	249.2	244.7	223.4	213.3	**212.9**	85～89
325.6	481.1	421.6	364.5	358.8	322.1	320.7	**328.7**	90～94[2]
…	…	…	489.7	523.1	445.0	467.6	**463.9**	95～99
…	…	…	532.4	694.7	598.3	511.8	**603.1**	100～
Male								
36.8	46.3	40.9	39.9	38.9	37.0	36.3	**36.3**	総数
19.8	19.2	11.6	8.5	6.2	4.1	4.6	**3.8**	0～4歳
9.7	10.6	5.2	5.5	3.1	2.6	2.3	**1.6**	5～9
5.3	6.3	3.8	3.5	3.1	2.0	1.9	**1.8**	10～14
39.7	31.4	22.4	14.1	10.1	8.0	7.5	**7.8**	15～19
38.8	34.9	26.5	18.4	13.2	10.0	9.8	**9.3**	20～24
22.9	23.5	18.3	14.8	10.8	9.0	7.4	**7.3**	25～29
17.9	18.6	17.0	13.7	10.4	8.7	7.4	**7.9**	30～34
21.3	19.3	15.7	15.7	10.1	8.6	8.4	**8.6**	35～39
23.0	24.1	19.7	17.0	13.1	10.6	9.8	**9.1**	40～44
29.3	29.5	25.6	21.2	17.1	14.7	12.0	**11.4**	45～49
36.6	43.0	31.6	28.6	22.0	18.0	16.5	**15.7**	50～54
47.3	52.9	41.4	35.1	29.9	24.0	23.4	**22.7**	55～59
55.6	68.9	54.2	45.5	36.1	32.2	31.5	**29.0**	60～64
63.8	81.4	68.2	56.4	52.6	42.8	39.8	**39.2**	65～69
93.7	121.9	98.8	89.2	76.3	65.1	63.9	**61.9**	70～74
136.7	190.4	150.0	148.4	127.3	111.4	105.5	**104.2**	75～79
204.4	305.6	268.9	229.3	225.6	197.2	195.7	**183.1**	80～84
286.3	485.3	405.6	371.2	374.2	329.5	313.3	**312.5**	85～89
386.7	703.1	636.9	573.0	566.8	498.4	500.7	**511.1**	90～94[2]
…	…	…	832.2	784.0	695.2	718.5	**728.4**	95～99
…	…	…	744.5	1 143.5	812.5	705.7	**855.6**	100～
Female								
15.9	27.0	22.3	23.6	25.9	25.6	25.2	**25.3**	総数
13.2	12.9	6.2	6.2	3.7	3.3	3.1	**2.6**	0～4歳
4.2	5.5	2.9	2.3	1.4	1.2	0.9	**0.9**	5～9
2.1	3.6	1.2	1.5	1.0	1.0	0.8	**0.6**	10～14
9.6	9.7	5.4	4.5	3.8	2.4	2.0	**2.3**	15～19
8.6	10.8	6.4	5.2	4.2	2.6	2.5	**3.2**	20～24
4.0	6.9	3.7	4.2	3.4	2.9	2.0	**2.1**	25～29
4.0	5.8	3.5	3.3	3.3	2.5	2.4	**1.9**	30～34
4.1	5.2	4.8	3.8	3.7	2.8	2.5	**2.5**	35～39
5.7	7.8	5.8	4.5	4.5	2.9	3.1	**2.4**	40～44
7.6	10.7	6.8	6.5	4.5	4.1	4.2	**3.7**	45～49
10.1	15.4	9.1	8.4	6.3	5.6	5.9	**5.2**	50～54
12.9	21.0	12.9	11.1	8.5	8.1	6.7	**6.9**	55～59
16.9	27.6	17.3	15.1	12.8	10.8	10.3	**9.1**	60～64
26.0	39.5	26.2	22.8	21.3	17.5	14.4	**15.4**	65～69
41.5	67.9	45.0	39.7	36.2	29.0	29.1	**29.4**	70～74
65.8	113.6	80.9	66.7	65.5	57.3	56.7	**50.9**	75～79
112.2	170.8	132.8	120.5	110.6	102.5	98.3	**92.4**	80～84
173.6	249.7	212.0	196.9	187.7	169.6	162.1	**161.2**	85～89
301.6	401.3	349.2	294.9	294.2	267.1	261.7	**266.1**	90～94[2]
…	…	…	406.1	462.7	391.3	414.1	**406.3**	95～99
…	…	…	495.4	625.6	576.5	481.4	**552.6**	100～

死　亡

表 5.15　性・年齢別にみた死因年次推移分類
Table 5.15　Trends in deaths and death rates (per 100,000

（再掲）Hi15　交通事故
（Regrouped）Transport accidents

死　亡　数

年　齢 Age	1950 昭和25年	1955 30年	1960 35年	1965 40年	1970 45年	1975 50年	1980 55年	1985 60年
								総　数
総数 Total	7 542	10 500	17 757	19 516	24 096	16 191	13 302	14 401
0～4歳	1 007	1 108	1 266	1 139	1 190	996	565	332
5～9 Years	608	751	1 025	847	981	744	556	362
10～14	287	429	526	421	397	252	185	231
15～19	649	705	1 465	1 700	2 375	1 669	1 585	1 978
20～24	810	1 125	1 941	2 021	2 556	1 401	1 083	1 330
25～29	544	988	1 855	1 664	1 732	1 041	710	700
30～34	454	662	1 357	1 603	1 445	880	711	619
35～39	479	583	1 049	1 483	1 677	889	737	766
40～44	485	669	972	1 237	1 655	1 147	787	860
45～49	462	666	1 085	1 144	1 342	1 117	928	897
50～54	429	634	1 074	1 215	1 366	994	935	1 088
55～59	351	589	999	1 167	1 518	953	845	1 080
60～64	317	472	925	1 174	1 522	967	753	839
65～69	251	424	808	960	1 511	1 048	814	821
70～74	197	326	654	776	1 299	870	893	890
75～79	121	230	429	525	887	713	647	819
80～84	51	110	245	309	450	352	390	554
85～89	13	28	70	108	145	123	135	181
90～94	1	-	11	21	20	16	32	41
95～99	1	-	1	1	4	4	5	3
100～	1	-	-	-	-	-	-	-
不詳 Not stated	24	1	-	1	24	15	6	10
								男
総数	5 795	8 244	14 170	15 499	18 629	12 466	10 111	10 832
0～4歳	608	688	755	691	734	657	375	222
5～9	433	528	706	576	669	514	380	262
10～14	207	251	390	317	303	186	132	161
15～19	513	571	1 260	1 501	2 130	1 492	1 357	1 709
20～24	705	988	1 749	1 812	2 186	1 174	930	1 125
25～29	470	903	1 713	1 504	1 522	914	607	598
30～34	393	587	1 228	1 445	1 273	763	603	493
35～39	421	495	898	1 292	1 410	740	588	603
40～44	407	552	840	1 029	1 373	949	613	666
45～49	398	581	889	916	1 071	876	760	704
50～54	358	540	861	942	1 019	775	710	825
55～59	284	478	772	892	1 135	718	615	824
60～64	229	368	696	892	1 109	715	537	579
65～69	149	301	584	678	1 031	731	578	538
70～74	103	209	423	513	824	576	598	557
75～79	65	132	242	296	512	431	400	494
80～84	24	60	116	153	227	176	226	334
85～89	5	11	44	42	71	56	81	107
90～94	1	-	4	6	9	7	16	21
95～99	1	-	-	1	-	3	-	1
100～	1	-	-	-	-	-	-	-
不詳	20	1	-	1	21	13	5	9
								女
総数	1 747	2 256	3 587	4 017	5 467	3 725	3 191	3 569
0～4歳	399	420	511	448	456	339	190	110
5～9	175	223	319	271	312	230	176	100
10～14	80	178	136	104	94	66	53	70
15～19	136	134	205	199	245	177	228	269
20～24	105	137	192	209	370	227	153	205
25～29	74	85	142	160	210	127	103	102
30～34	61	75	129	158	172	117	108	126
35～39	58	88	151	191	267	149	149	163
40～44	78	117	132	208	282	198	174	194
45～49	64	85	196	228	271	241	168	193
50～54	71	94	213	273	347	219	225	263
55～59	67	111	227	275	383	235	230	256
60～64	88	104	229	282	413	252	216	260
65～69	102	123	224	282	480	317	236	283
70～74	94	117	231	263	475	294	295	333
75～79	56	98	187	229	375	282	247	325
80～84	27	50	129	156	223	176	164	220
85～89	8	17	26	66	74	67	54	74
90～94	-	-	7	15	11	9	16	20
95～99	-	-	1	-	4	1	5	2
100～	-	-	-	-	-	-	-	-
不詳	4	-	-	-	3	2	1	1

288

General mortality

別死亡数及び率（人口10万対）（つづき）
population）by sex, age and causes of death : Japan－CON.

Deaths

1990 平成2年	1995 7年	2000 12年	2005 17年	2010 22年	2014 26年	2015 27年	2016 28年	年齢 Age
Total								
15 828	15 147	12 857	10 028	7 222	5 717	5 646	5 278	総数 Total
293	194	120	82	53	31	40	31	0～4歳
274	216	119	109	56	50	37	34	5～9 Years
183	117	86	71	45	34	25	26	10～14
2 248	1 406	869	461	292	214	199	204	15～19
1 749	1 600	1 074	602	332	222	205	216	20～24
795	789	737	441	249	181	158	147	25～29
536	498	549	444	250	155	158	144	30～34
666	447	424	418	255	172	207	190	35～39
849	643	491	382	271	230	224	218	40～44
877	905	628	393	266	254	238	226	45～49
941	980	892	608	329	269	274	224	50～54
1 080	1 066	936	801	446	313	297	269	55～59
1 127	1 221	1 076	826	600	437	394	316	60～64
994	1 179	1 076	864	624	537	520	536	65～69
1 014	1 274	1 215	1 030	810	596	577	546	70～74
1 052	1 142	1 137	1 070	896	702	713	623	75～79
783	949	853	833	841	726	755	685	80～84
277	405	440	417	443	444	448	449	85～89
69	87	110	142	134	127	149	165	90～94
5	9	14	23	23	19	25	27	95～99
-	-	-	1	3	3	-	2	100～
16	20	11	10	4	1	3	-	不詳 Not stated
Male								
11 481	10 772	9 072	7 015	4 871	3 923	3 886	3 665	総数
191	131	83	43	35	15	22	18	0～4歳
181	151	78	80	35	34	29	21	5～9
128	81	66	47	36	20	20	21	10～14
1 832	1 151	711	362	214	166	163	171	15～19
1 430	1 296	880	484	269	185	169	171	20～24
679	656	631	371	205	146	140	121	25～29
439	407	477	380	207	133	131	131	30～34
546	382	342	360	219	147	173	153	35～39
655	505	384	321	224	193	180	179	40～44
670	681	501	311	229	217	198	192	45～49
677	738	677	474	266	234	230	183	50～54
769	765	669	593	339	254	242	218	55～59
784	854	752	589	426	332	289	232	60～64
620	775	708	541	391	336	381	384	65～69
614	756	729	639	489	370	360	345	70～74
628	630	599	681	492	415	393	380	75～79
442	514	484	455	480	399	426	383	80～84
146	228	221	198	242	255	247	259	85～89
32	48	61	69	58	62	77	85	90～94
3	4	8	8	10	8	13	16	95～99
-	-	-	-	1	1	-	2	100～
15	19	11	9	4	1	3	-	不詳
Female								
4 347	4 375	3 785	3 013	2 351	1 794	1 760	1 613	総数
102	63	37	39	18	16	18	13	0～4歳
93	65	41	29	21	16	8	13	5～9
55	36	20	24	9	14	5	5	10～14
416	255	158	99	78	48	36	33	15～19
319	304	194	118	63	37	36	45	20～24
116	133	106	70	44	35	18	26	25～29
97	91	72	64	43	22	27	13	30～34
120	65	82	58	36	25	34	37	35～39
194	138	107	61	47	37	44	39	40～44
207	224	127	82	37	37	40	34	45～49
264	242	215	134	63	35	44	41	50～54
311	301	267	208	107	59	55	51	55～59
343	367	324	237	174	105	105	84	60～64
374	404	368	323	233	201	139	152	65～69
400	518	486	391	321	226	217	201	70～74
424	512	538	389	404	287	320	243	75～79
341	435	369	378	361	327	329	302	80～84
131	177	219	219	201	189	201	190	85～89
37	39	49	73	76	65	72	80	90～94
2	5	6	15	13	11	12	11	95～99
-	-	-	1	2	2	-	-	100～
1	1	-	1	-	-	-	-	不詳

死　亡

表 5.15　性・年齢別にみた死因年次推移分類
Table 5.15　Trends in deaths and death rates (per 100,000

（再掲）Hi15　交通事故
（Regrouped）Transport accidents

死　亡　率

年　齢 Age	1950 昭和25年	1955 30年	1960 35年	1965 40年	1970 45年	1975 50年	1980 55年	1985 60年
								総　数
総数 Total	9.1	11.8	19.0	19.9	23.4	14.6	11.4	12.0
0〜4歳	9.0	12.0	16.1	14.0	13.6	10.0	6.7	4.5
5〜9 Years	6.4	6.8	11.1	10.8	12.1	8.4	5.6	4.3
10〜14	3.3	4.5	4.8	4.6	5.1	3.1	2.1	2.3
15〜19	7.6	8.2	15.7	15.7	26.4	21.1	19.3	22.2
20〜24	10.5	13.4	23.3	22.3	24.1	15.6	13.9	16.3
25〜29	8.8	13.0	22.6	19.9	19.2	9.7	7.9	9.0
30〜34	8.7	10.8	18.1	19.4	17.4	9.6	6.6	6.9
35〜39	9.5	11.4	17.4	19.8	20.5	10.6	8.1	7.2
40〜44	10.8	13.5	19.4	20.8	22.7	14.0	9.5	9.5
45〜49	11.5	15.3	22.5	23.2	23.0	15.2	11.5	10.9
50〜54	12.7	16.5	25.6	26.1	28.6	17.3	13.0	13.8
55〜59	12.8	18.4	27.4	29.2	34.5	20.5	15.1	15.5
60〜64	13.8	18.9	31.6	35.1	41.0	22.7	16.9	15.7
65〜69	14.2	21.6	37.4	37.5	50.8	30.5	20.6	19.7
70〜74	15.4	23.4	41.8	44.5	61.1	33.9	29.6	25.2
75〜79	17.6	26.3	44.9	47.9	70.1	43.6	31.9	33.6
80〜84	18.5	29.1	50.7	58.5	69.4	43.6	35.7	38.3
85〜89	16.4	25.1	44.9	54.2	63.2	39.9	33.0	30.9
90〜94²⁾	18.3	-	37.3	43.3	36.5	24.5	31.1	23.7
95〜99	…	…	…	…	…	…	…	…
100〜	…	…	…	…	…	…	…	…
								男
総数	14.2	18.8	30.9	32.1	36.8	22.8	17.7	18.3
0〜4歳	10.6	14.6	18.8	16.7	16.4	12.9	8.6	5.8
5〜9	9.0	9.4	15.0	14.4	16.2	11.3	7.4	6.0
10〜14	4.7	5.2	6.9	6.8	7.6	4.4	2.9	3.2
15〜19	11.9	13.2	26.9	27.4	46.9	37.2	32.3	37.5
20〜24	18.4	23.5	42.4	40.3	41.4	25.9	23.7	27.0
25〜29	16.7	23.9	41.8	36.2	33.9	16.9	13.4	15.2
30〜34	16.7	21.0	32.8	34.8	30.6	16.6	11.2	10.9
35〜39	17.7	21.3	32.5	32.5	34.5	17.7	12.9	11.2
40〜44	18.5	23.7	36.9	37.7	37.6	23.1	14.8	14.8
45〜49	19.7	27.2	39.4	41.2	40.3	24.1	18.9	17.4
50〜54	20.8	28.0	42.2	43.4	47.6	29.8	20.1	21.2
55〜59	20.6	29.7	42.8	46.2	55.9	34.9	24.7	24.3
60〜64	20.6	30.0	48.4	54.9	63.5	37.2	27.8	24.7
65〜69	18.7	32.8	56.9	55.6	74.0	46.7	33.3	30.4
70〜74	19.1	35.2	61.0	65.0	86.0	50.4	45.6	37.5
75〜79	24.3	38.6	64.2	65.5	96.5	62.8	47.3	49.6
80〜84	25.1	45.0	68.6	81.8	94.2	57.3	54.2	61.0
85〜89	20.4	32.5	91.3	69.9	99.4	55.6	58.5	55.8
90〜94²⁾	70.6	-	48.4	51.0	51.5	46.2	48.2	39.9
95〜99	…	…	…	…	…	…	…	…
100〜	…	…	…	…	…	…	…	…
								女
総数	4.1	5.0	7.5	8.0	10.4	6.6	5.4	5.8
0〜4歳	7.3	9.3	13.3	11.2	10.7	7.0	4.6	3.0
5〜9	3.7	4.1	7.1	7.0	7.9	5.3	3.6	2.4
10〜14	1.9	3.8	2.5	2.3	2.5	1.6	1.2	1.4
15〜19	3.2	3.1	4.4	3.7	5.5	4.6	5.7	6.2
20〜24	2.7	3.3	4.6	4.6	7.0	5.1	4.0	5.1
25〜29	2.2	2.2	3.5	3.8	4.6	2.4	2.3	2.7
30〜34	2.1	2.3	3.4	3.8	4.1	2.5	2.0	2.8
35〜39	2.2	3.1	4.6	5.1	6.6	3.6	3.3	3.1
40〜44	3.4	4.5	4.8	6.4	7.7	4.9	4.2	4.3
45〜49	3.2	3.8	7.7	8.5	8.5	6.5	4.2	4.7
50〜54	4.3	4.9	9.9	11.0	13.2	7.0	6.2	6.6
55〜59	4.9	6.9	12.3	13.3	16.1	9.1	7.4	7.2
60〜64	7.4	8.2	15.3	16.4	21.0	10.8	8.6	8.6
65〜69	10.5	11.7	19.8	21.0	30.4	16.9	10.7	11.8
70〜74	12.7	14.6	26.5	27.5	40.6	20.6	17.4	16.3
75〜79	13.4	18.4	32.4	35.6	51.0	29.7	20.8	22.6
80〜84	15.0	20.4	41.1	45.7	54.7	35.2	24.3	24.5
85〜89	14.7	21.9	24.2	47.5	46.9	32.2	19.9	18.7
90〜94²⁾	-	-	33.4	40.5	31.1	16.7	24.4	16.9
95〜99	…	…	…	…	…	…	…	…
100〜	…	…	…	…	…	…	…	…

General mortality

別死亡数及び率（人口10万対）（つづき）
population）by sex, age and causes of death : Japan－CON.

Death rates

1990 平成2年	1995 7年	2000 12年	2005 17年	2010 22年	2014 26年	2015 27年	2016 28年	年齢 Age
Total								
12.9	12.2	10.2	7.9	5.7	4.6	4.5	4.2	総数 Total
4.5	3.3	2.0	1.5	1.0	0.6	0.8	0.6	0～4歳
3.7	3.3	2.0	1.8	1.0	1.0	0.7	0.6	5～9 Years
2.2	1.6	1.3	1.2	0.8	0.6	0.4	0.5	10～14
22.6	16.6	11.7	7.1	4.8	3.6	3.3	3.4	15～19
20.1	16.4	12.9	8.4	5.3	3.7	3.5	3.7	20～24
10.0	9.2	7.7	5.4	3.5	2.8	2.5	2.4	25～29
6.9	6.2	6.4	4.6	3.0	2.1	2.2	2.0	30～34
7.4	5.8	5.3	4.9	2.6	2.0	2.5	2.4	35～39
8.0	7.2	6.4	4.8	3.1	2.4	2.3	2.3	40～44
9.8	8.6	7.1	5.1	3.3	3.0	2.8	2.5	45～49
11.7	11.1	8.6	7.0	4.3	3.5	3.5	2.9	50～54
14.0	13.5	10.8	7.8	5.2	4.1	3.9	3.6	55～59
16.7	16.4	14.0	9.7	6.0	4.9	4.6	3.9	60～64
19.5	18.5	15.2	11.6	7.6	5.9	5.4	5.2	65～69
26.6	27.3	20.6	15.5	11.6	7.6	7.4	7.4	70～74
34.9	34.9	27.5	20.3	15.0	11.2	11.3	9.6	75～79
42.7	41.4	32.7	24.4	19.3	15.0	15.1	13.3	80～84
33.3	35.7	28.8	22.6	18.1	14.5	14.2	13.7	85～89
25.6	21.7	17.7	16.9	13.1	9.8	11.0	11.2	90～94²⁾
…	…	…	10.9	7.7	5.4	6.9	7.1	95～99
…	…	…	3.9	6.8	5.0	-	3.1	100～
Male								
19.1	17.7	14.8	11.4	7.9	6.4	6.4	6.0	総数
5.8	4.3	2.8	1.5	1.3	0.6	0.9	0.7	0～4歳
4.8	4.5	2.5	2.6	1.2	1.3	1.1	0.8	5～9
2.9	2.1	2.0	1.5	1.2	0.7	0.7	0.8	10～14
35.9	26.4	18.7	10.8	6.9	5.5	5.3	5.6	15～19
32.2	26.0	20.7	13.1	8.3	6.0	5.6	5.7	20～24
16.8	15.0	12.9	9.0	5.6	4.4	4.4	3.9	25～29
11.3	10.1	10.9	7.8	5.0	3.6	3.6	3.7	30～34
12.1	9.8	8.5	8.3	4.4	3.4	4.1	3.8	35～39
12.3	11.3	9.9	8.0	5.1	3.9	3.7	3.7	40～44
15.0	12.9	11.3	8.1	5.7	5.1	4.5	4.2	45～49
17.0	16.8	13.1	10.9	7.0	6.1	5.8	4.7	50～54
20.3	19.7	15.7	11.7	7.9	6.7	6.5	5.9	55～59
24.2	23.7	20.1	14.2	8.6	7.6	6.9	5.8	60～64
28.3	25.9	21.1	15.3	9.9	7.7	8.1	7.8	65～69
39.4	39.1	27.3	21.0	15.1	10.1	10.0	10.0	70～74
52.5	50.2	36.9	30.2	19.0	15.0	14.0	13.1	75～79
65.1	62.6	53.0	37.3	28.2	20.6	21.2	18.3	80～84
52.9	63.2	46.4	35.7	32.4	24.8	23.2	23.2	85～89
43.0	44.5	39.1	32.8	23.9	19.9	22.9	22.5	90～94²⁾
…	…	…	19.3	17.9	12.9	20.5	23.9	95～99
…	…	…	-	17.1	12.5	-	22.2	100～
Female								
7.0	6.9	5.9	4.7	3.6	2.8	2.7	2.5	総数
3.2	2.2	1.3	1.4	0.7	0.6	0.7	0.5	0～4歳
2.6	2.1	1.4	1.0	0.8	0.6	0.3	0.5	5～9
1.3	1.0	0.6	0.8	0.3	0.5	0.2	0.2	10～14
8.6	6.2	4.4	3.1	2.7	1.7	1.2	1.1	15～19
7.4	6.4	4.8	3.4	2.0	1.3	1.3	1.6	20～24
2.9	3.1	2.2	1.8	1.3	1.1	0.6	0.9	25～29
2.5	2.3	1.7	1.4	1.1	0.6	0.8	0.4	30～34
2.7	1.7	2.1	1.4	0.8	0.6	0.8	0.9	35～39
3.7	3.1	2.8	1.5	1.1	0.8	0.9	0.8	40～44
4.6	4.3	2.9	2.2	0.9	0.9	0.9	0.8	45～49
6.5	5.4	4.1	3.1	1.7	0.9	1.1	1.1	50～54
7.9	7.5	6.0	4.0	2.5	1.5	1.5	1.4	55～59
9.8	9.5	8.2	5.4	3.4	2.3	2.4	2.0	60～64
12.9	11.9	9.8	8.3	5.4	4.3	2.8	2.9	65～69
17.8	18.9	15.1	10.9	8.6	5.4	5.2	5.1	70～74
23.3	25.3	21.4	12.9	12.0	8.2	9.1	6.7	75～79
29.6	29.5	21.8	17.3	13.6	11.2	11.0	9.8	80～84
23.5	22.9	20.8	16.9	11.8	9.3	9.6	8.8	85～89
18.8	13.5	10.5	11.6	9.7	6.6	7.0	7.3	90～94²⁾
…	…	…	8.8	5.4	3.8	4.0	3.5	95～99
…	…	…	4.6	5.3	3.9	-	-	100～

死　亡

表5.15　性・年齢別にみた死因年次推移分類
Table 5.15　Trends in deaths and death rates (per 100,000

Hi16　自　殺
Suicide

死　亡　数

年　齢 Age	1950 昭和25年	1955 30年	1960 35年	1965 40年	1970 45年	1975 50年	1980 55年	1985 60年
								総　数
総数 Total	16 311	22 477	20 143	14 444	15 728	19 975	20 542	23 383
0～4歳	-	-		-		-	-	
5～9 Years	-	3	1			1	2	4
10～14	2	88	62	46	55	88	53	81
15～19	1 310	2 735	2 217	806	702	768	599	453
20～24	2 804	5 496	4 269	1 884	1 853	1 933	1 401	1 177
25～29	1 649	3 139	2 845	1 670	1 688	2 218	1 745	1 303
30～34	1 034	1 448	1 495	1 202	1 275	1 786	1 864	1 496
35～39	919	1 015	940	990	1 254	1 550	1 799	1 920
40～44	862	936	775	701	977	1 668	1 830	2 270
45～49	1 033	1 055	954	764	869	1 500	1 983	2 614
50～54	1 021	1 082	1 057	891	894	1 195	1 695	2 740
55～59	1 103	1 128	1 087	962	1 052	1 080	1 341	2 125
60～64	1 150	1 070	1 151	1 087	1 074	1 263	1 099	1 473
65～69	1 201	1 046	1 104	1 090	1 194	1 276	1 273	1 314
70～74	1 010	974	948	935	1 111	1 318	1 350	1 394
75～79	672	730	688	727	846	1 149	1 187	1 341
80～84	297	350	398	480	474	711	777	974
85～89	110	140	124	159	228	271	324	458
90～94	20	25	17	38	50	59	80	104
95～99	4	2	-	4	6	4	14	14
100～	-	-	-	-	-	1	-	2
不詳 Not stated	110	15	11	8	126	136	126	126
								男
総数	9 820	13 836	11 506	8 330	8 761	11 744	12 769	15 356
0～4歳	-	-		-		-	-	
5～9	-	3		-		1	2	4
10～14	-	55	40	32	40	64	39	55
15～19	757	1 615	1 182	480	394	506	400	310
20～24	1 722	3 528	2 422	1 049	994	1 177	954	829
25～29	1 016	2 067	1 804	991	987	1 403	1 195	933
30～34	576	848	858	746	763	1 145	1 294	1 049
35～39	533	568	515	592	790	1 023	1 237	1 364
40～44	534	549	422	421	599	1 128	1 292	1 651
45～49	656	686	534	460	482	989	1 402	1 958
50～54	683	725	640	518	490	677	1 113	1 989
55～59	773	768	707	631	602	612	810	1 509
60～64	751	679	711	684	626	707	628	867
65～69	677	623	619	638	637	641	604	681
70～74	569	515	504	466	552	604	637	706
75～79	324	380	325	344	394	507	528	653
80～84	117	163	165	206	205	321	336	435
85～89	43	44	44	54	91	97	150	196
90～94	8	6	4	11	16	20	30	50
95～99	2	1	-	-	2	3	6	5
100～	-	-	-	-	-	1	-	1
不詳	79	13	10	7	97	118	112	111
								女
総数	6 491	8 641	8 637	6 114	6 967	8 231	7 773	8 027
0～4歳	-	-	1	-		-	-	
5～9								
10～14	2	33	22	14	15	24	14	26
15～19	553	1 120	1 035	326	308	262	199	143
20～24	1 082	1 968	1 847	835	859	756	447	348
25～29	633	1 072	1 041	679	701	815	550	370
30～34	458	600	637	456	512	641	570	447
35～39	386	447	425	398	464	527	562	556
40～44	328	387	353	280	378	540	538	619
45～49	377	369	420	304	387	511	581	656
50～54	338	357	417	373	404	518	582	751
55～59	330	360	380	331	450	468	531	616
60～64	399	391	440	403	448	556	471	606
65～69	524	423	485	452	557	635	669	633
70～74	441	459	444	469	559	714	713	688
75～79	348	350	363	383	452	642	659	688
80～84	180	187	233	274	269	390	441	539
85～89	67	96	80	105	137	174	174	262
90～94	12	19	13	27	34	39	50	54
95～99	2	1	-	4	4	1	8	9
100～	-	-	-	-	-	-	-	1
不詳	31	2	1	1	29	18	14	15

General mortality

別死亡数及び率（人口10万対）（つづき）
population）by sex, age and causes of death : Japan－CON.

Deaths

1990 平成2年	1995 7年	2000 12年	2005 17年	2010 22年	2014 26年	2015 27年	2016 28年	年　齢 Age
Total								
20 088	21 420	30 251	30 553	29 554	24 417	23 152	21 017	総数 Total
-	-	-	-	-	2	1	-	0～4歳
-	-	-	1	-	2	1	-	5～9 Years
47	66	74	44	63	100	89	71	10～14
381	423	473	511	451	434	447	430	15～19
928	1 115	1 331	1 374	1 372	1 178	1 052	1 001	20～24
1 065	1 202	1 740	1 785	1 630	1 423	1 234	1 165	25～29
1 095	1 157	1 740	2 217	1 920	1 520	1 398	1 253	30～34
1 278	1 164	1 717	2 098	2 345	1 762	1 573	1 445	35～39
1 728	1 558	1 830	2 308	2 325	2 042	1 984	1 739	40～44
1 981	2 227	2 713	2 573	2 465	2 046	1 965	1 888	45～49
2 019	2 539	3 934	3 208	2 615	2 015	2 008	1 853	50～54
1 937	2 228	3 915	3 917	2 940	1 995	1 822	1 684	55～59
1 651	1 937	2 967	2 905	3 124	1 995	1 807	1 563	60～64
1 348	1 437	2 348	2 112	2 432	2 142	2 025	1 870	65～69
1 325	1 250	1 788	1 855	1 847	1 853	1 876	1 513	70～74
1 373	1 100	1 295	1 403	1 606	1 503	1 447	1 337	75～79
1 074	1 000	1 063	1 039	1 143	1 207	1 232	1 085	80～84
584	581	721	625	712	740	727	694	85～89
171	225	271	316	323	304	311	304	90～94
17	32	59	66	83	77	73	53	95～99
-	2	5	8	5	7	13	9	100～
86	177	267	188	153	72	68	60	不詳 Not stated
Male								
12 316	14 231	21 656	22 236	21 028	16 875	16 202	14 639	総数
-	-	-	-	-	-	-	-	0～4歳
-	-	-	1	-	1	1	-	5～9
30	43	58	28	42	67	61	43	10～14
244	287	335	321	301	312	310	301	15～19
631	763	938	922	1 014	868	781	745	20～24
705	875	1 194	1 277	1 201	1 042	914	877	25～29
757	817	1 259	1 585	1 342	1 088	1 034	936	30～34
917	850	1 332	1 587	1 719	1 241	1 163	1 032	35～39
1 195	1 166	1 430	1 806	1 755	1 507	1 459	1 305	40～44
1 361	1 659	2 175	2 096	1 862	1 465	1 410	1 400	45～49
1 349	1 830	3 086	2 584	2 011	1 496	1 474	1 353	50～54
1 277	1 598	3 101	3 104	2 306	1 464	1 339	1 219	55～59
1 006	1 334	2 176	2 155	2 327	1 422	1 295	1 107	60～64
716	862	1 612	1 499	1 639	1 408	1 390	1 235	65～69
655	632	1 098	1 245	1 192	1 181	1 215	942	70～74
604	533	634	813	987	932	915	850	75～79
474	447	506	549	640	705	758	657	80～84
248	264	339	306	354	423	424	387	85～89
72	98	117	146	159	158	157	163	90～94
7	15	18	36	46	31	34	26	95～99
-	1	4	7	1	3	8	5	100～
68	157	244	169	130	61	60	56	不詳
Female								
7 772	7 189	8 595	8 317	8 526	7 542	6 950	6 378	総数
-	-	-	-	-	-	-	-	0～4歳
-	-	-	-	-	1	-	-	5～9
17	23	16	16	21	33	28	28	10～14
137	136	138	190	150	122	137	129	15～19
297	352	393	452	358	310	271	256	20～24
360	327	546	508	429	381	320	288	25～29
338	340	481	632	578	432	364	317	30～34
361	314	385	511	626	521	410	413	35～39
533	392	400	502	570	535	525	434	40～44
620	568	538	477	603	581	555	488	45～49
670	709	848	624	604	519	534	500	50～54
660	630	814	813	634	531	483	465	55～59
645	603	791	750	797	573	512	456	60～64
632	575	736	613	793	734	635	635	65～69
670	618	690	610	655	672	661	571	70～74
769	567	661	590	619	571	532	487	75～79
600	553	557	490	503	502	474	428	80～84
336	317	382	319	358	317	303	307	85～89
99	127	154	170	164	146	154	141	90～94
10	17	41	30	37	46	39	27	95～99
-	1	1	1	4	4	5	4	100～
18	20	23	19	23	11	8	4	不詳

293

死　亡

表 5.15　性・年齢別にみた死因年次推移分類
Table 5.15　Trends in deaths and death rates（per 100,000

Hi16　自　殺
Suicide

死　亡　率

年齢 Age	1950 昭和25年	1955 30年	1960 35年	1965 40年	1970 45年	1975 50年	1980 55年	1985 60年
総数								
総数 Total	19.6	25.2	21.6	14.7	15.3	18.0	17.7	19.4
0～4歳	-	-	-	-		-	-	
5～9 Years	-	0.0	0.0			0.0	0.0	0.0
10～14	0.0	0.9	0.6	0.5	0.7	1.1	0.6	0.8
15～19	15.3	31.7	23.8	7.4	7.8	9.7	7.3	5.1
20～24	36.3	65.4	51.3	20.8	17.5	21.5	18.0	14.4
25～29	26.7	41.3	34.7	20.0	18.7	20.7	19.4	16.8
30～34	19.9	23.7	19.9	14.6	15.3	19.4	17.4	16.6
35～39	18.2	19.8	15.6	13.2	15.3	18.5	19.7	18.0
40～44	19.2	18.9	15.4	11.8	13.4	20.4	22.1	25.1
45～49	25.8	24.2	19.8	15.5	14.9	20.5	24.6	31.9
50～54	30.1	28.1	25.2	19.1	18.7	20.8	23.6	34.8
55～59	40.1	35.2	29.9	24.0	23.9	23.2	24.0	30.5
60～64	49.9	42.9	39.3	32.5	28.9	29.6	24.7	27.5
65～69	67.8	53.2	51.1	42.5	40.2	37.1	32.2	31.5
70～74	78.8	69.9	60.6	53.6	52.2	51.3	44.8	39.5
75～79	98.0	83.4	72.1	66.3	66.8	70.2	58.4	55.1
80～84	107.7	92.6	82.4	90.9	73.1	88.1	71.2	67.3
85～89	139.1	125.7	79.6	79.8	99.4	87.8	79.2	78.1
90～94[2]	146.7	118.6	52.8	82.7	85.1	78.5	78.9	64.7
95～99	...	...	...	...	...	...	...	...
100～	...	...	...	...	...	...	...	...
男								
総数	24.1	31.5	25.1	17.3	17.3	21.5	22.3	26.0
0～4歳	-	-	-	-	-	-	-	-
5～9	-	0.1	-	-	-	0.0	0.0	0.1
10～14	-	1.1	0.7	0.7	1.0	1.5	0.9	1.1
15～19	17.5	37.2	25.3	8.8	8.7	12.6	9.5	6.8
20～24	44.9	84.1	58.7	23.3	18.8	26.0	24.3	19.9
25～29	36.0	54.7	44.1	23.8	22.0	26.0	26.5	23.8
30～34	24.4	30.3	22.9	18.0	18.3	24.9	24.0	23.1
35～39	22.4	24.5	18.6	15.8	19.3	24.4	27.1	25.3
40～44	24.3	23.6	18.6	15.4	16.4	27.5	31.2	36.7
45～49	32.5	32.1	23.7	20.7	18.1	27.2	34.9	48.3
50～54	39.7	37.6	31.4	23.8	22.9	26.1	31.5	51.0
55～59	56.1	47.8	39.2	32.7	29.7	29.7	32.5	44.5
60～64	67.7	55.3	49.5	42.1	35.9	36.7	32.5	36.9
65～69	85.1	67.8	60.3	52.3	45.7	41.0	34.8	38.5
70～74	105.3	86.7	72.7	59.1	57.6	52.8	48.5	47.5
75～79	121.0	111.1	86.3	76.1	74.2	73.9	62.4	65.5
80～84	122.4	122.4	97.6	110.2	85.1	104.5	80.6	79.5
85～89	175.5	130.0	91.3	89.8	127.4	96.3	108.3	102.3
90～94[2]	235.3	120.1	48.4	80.1	103.0	110.8	108.6	101.4
95～99	...	...	...	...	...	...	...	...
100～	...	...	...	...	...	...	...	...
女								
総数	15.3	19.0	18.2	12.2	13.3	14.6	13.1	13.1
0～4歳	-	-	-	-	-	-	-	-
5～9	-	-	0.0	-	-	-	-	-
10～14	0.0	0.7	0.4	0.3	0.4	0.6	0.3	0.5
15～19	13.0	26.1	22.4	6.1	6.9	6.8	4.9	3.3
20～24	27.8	46.8	44.0	18.3	16.2	16.9	11.6	8.7
25～29	18.8	28.0	25.3	16.1	15.4	15.3	12.3	9.7
30～34	16.1	18.1	16.9	11.1	12.3	13.9	10.7	9.9
35～39	14.4	16.0	13.0	10.6	11.4	12.6	12.3	10.5
40～44	14.4	14.8	12.9	8.7	10.3	13.2	12.9	13.6
45～49	19.0	16.5	16.4	11.3	12.2	13.8	14.4	15.8
50～54	20.2	18.6	19.3	15.0	15.3	16.4	16.0	18.9
55～59	24.1	22.5	20.7	16.0	19.0	18.1	17.2	17.2
60～64	33.4	30.8	29.5	23.4	22.8	23.8	18.8	20.1
65～69	53.8	40.4	42.8	33.6	35.2	33.9	30.2	26.4
70～74	59.5	57.5	51.0	49.1	47.8	50.1	41.9	33.6
75～79	83.3	65.6	62.8	59.5	61.5	67.5	55.6	47.9
80～84	99.9	76.5	74.3	80.3	66.0	78.0	65.4	59.9
85～89	122.8	123.9	74.3	75.5	86.8	83.7	64.3	66.3
90～94[2]	115.7	118.1	54.3	83.7	78.7	66.8	67.5	49.1
95～99	...	...	...	...	...	...	...	...
100～	...	...	...	...	...	...	...	...

General mortality

別死亡数及び率（人口10万対）（つづき）
population）by sex, age and causes of death : Japan－CON.

Death rates

1990 平成2年	1995 7年	2000 12年	2005 17年	2010 22年	2014 26年	2015 27年	2016 28年	年　　齢 Age
Total								
16.4	17.2	24.1	24.2	23.4	19.5	18.5	16.8	総数 Total
-	-	-	-	-	-	-	-	0～4歳
-	-	-	0.0	-	0.0	0.0	-	5～9 Years
0.6	0.9	1.1	0.7	1.1	1.8	1.6	1.3	10～14
3.8	5.0	6.4	7.8	7.5	7.3	7.5	7.2	15～19
10.6	11.4	16.0	19.1	21.8	19.7	17.9	17.0	20～24
13.4	14.0	18.1	22.0	22.8	22.0	19.6	19.0	25～29
14.2	14.5	20.2	23.1	23.4	20.9	19.5	17.8	30～34
14.3	15.1	21.5	24.4	24.2	20.7	19.1	18.2	35～39
16.3	17.5	23.7	29.0	26.9	21.2	20.5	18.2	40～44
22.0	21.1	30.7	33.6	30.9	24.1	22.8	20.7	45～49
25.0	28.6	37.9	36.7	34.4	26.2	25.4	23.8	50～54
25.1	28.2	45.0	38.3	34.0	26.3	24.2	22.6	55～59
24.5	26.0	38.5	34.1	31.1	22.4	21.3	19.3	60～64
26.5	22.5	33.1	28.5	29.5	23.5	20.9	18.3	65～69
34.8	26.7	30.4	28.0	26.4	23.5	24.2	20.5	70～74
45.5	33.6	31.3	26.7	26.9	24.1	22.9	20.6	75～79
58.6	43.6	40.7	30.5	26.2	24.9	24.6	21.0	80～84
70.1	51.2	47.1	33.8	29.1	24.2	23.1	21.2	85～89
65.0	58.6	47.8	37.6	31.5	23.3	22.9	20.6	90～94[2]
…	…	…	31.2	27.9	21.9	20.2	13.9	95～99
…	…	…	31.5	11.4	11.7	21.1	13.8	100～
Male								
20.4	23.4	35.2	36.1	34.2	27.6	26.6	24.1	総数
-	-	-	-	-	-	-	-	0～4歳
-	-	-	0.0	-	0.0	0.0	-	5～9
0.7	1.1	1.7	0.9	1.4	2.3	2.1	1.5	10～14
4.8	6.6	8.8	9.6	9.7	10.3	10.1	9.8	15～19
14.2	15.3	22.0	25.0	31.4	28.2	25.9	24.6	20～24
17.5	20.0	24.4	31.0	33.0	31.5	28.5	28.0	25～29
19.5	20.2	28.8	32.6	32.1	29.4	28.3	26.2	30～34
20.4	21.9	33.0	36.5	34.9	28.7	27.7	25.6	35～39
22.4	26.0	36.8	44.9	40.1	30.8	29.6	26.9	40～44
30.4	31.4	49.0	54.6	46.4	34.2	32.3	30.3	45～49
33.8	41.7	59.5	59.2	52.8	38.8	37.0	34.5	50～54
33.8	41.1	72.5	61.3	53.7	38.8	35.7	32.7	55～59
31.1	37.1	58.2	51.9	47.1	32.5	31.0	27.7	60～64
32.7	28.9	48.1	42.3	41.7	32.1	29.6	25.0	65～69
42.1	32.7	41.2	40.9	36.8	32.1	33.7	27.4	70～74
50.5	42.5	39.1	36.0	38.1	33.8	32.6	29.4	75～79
69.9	54.4	55.4	45.0	37.6	36.4	37.7	31.4	80～84
89.9	73.1	71.1	55.2	47.4	41.2	39.8	34.6	85～89
97.0	97.5	78.8	69.3	65.5	50.8	46.8	43.2	90～94[2]
…	…	…	86.8	82.2	50.0	53.6	38.8	95～99
…	…	…	186.1	17.1	37.5	95.7	55.6	100～
Female								
12.4	11.3	13.4	12.9	13.2	11.7	10.8	9.9	総数
-	-	-	-	-	-	-	-	0～4歳
-	-	-	-	-	0.0	-	-	5～9
0.4	0.6	0.5	0.5	0.7	1.2	1.0	1.0	10～14
2.8	3.3	3.8	6.0	5.1	4.2	4.7	4.5	15～19
6.9	7.4	9.7	12.9	11.6	10.6	9.4	8.9	20～24
9.1	7.7	11.5	12.8	12.2	12.1	10.4	9.6	25～29
8.8	8.6	11.3	13.4	14.3	12.1	10.3	9.2	30～34
8.1	8.2	9.8	12.0	13.1	12.4	10.1	10.6	35～39
10.1	8.8	10.5	12.7	13.4	11.3	11.0	9.2	40～44
13.7	10.8	12.2	12.5	15.3	13.8	13.0	10.8	45～49
16.4	15.8	16.3	14.2	15.9	13.6	13.6	12.9	50～54
16.8	15.6	18.4	15.8	14.5	13.9	12.8	12.4	55～59
18.4	15.7	19.9	17.1	15.6	12.6	11.9	11.1	60～64
21.8	17.0	19.7	15.8	18.5	15.6	12.7	12.0	65～69
29.7	22.5	21.4	17.0	17.5	15.9	16.0	14.5	70～74
42.3	28.0	26.2	19.6	18.3	16.4	15.1	13.5	75～79
52.0	37.6	32.8	22.4	18.9	17.2	15.8	13.9	80～84
60.3	41.0	36.2	24.7	21.1	15.6	14.5	14.3	85～89
52.4	44.6	37.4	27.0	20.9	14.7	15.0	12.8	90～94[2]
…	…	…	17.7	15.3	15.9	13.1	8.5	95～99
…	…	…	4.6	10.5	7.8	9.4	7.0	100～

295

死　亡

表 5.16　性・年齢別にみた死因
Table 5.16　Death rates (per 100,000 population) by sex, age and

死因簡単分類コード[a] Code[a]	死因・性 Causes of death and sex		総数 Total	0歳[1] Year	1	2	3	4	1～4	0～4	5～9	10～14	15～19	20～24	25～29	30～34
	死亡総数 Deaths Total	総数 T.	1 046.0	197.3	32.7	17.9	11.6	9.2	17.7	53.5	7.5	8.0	19.6	35.3	40.4	47.7
		男 M.	1 108.5	195.3	34.1	18.1	13.3	9.5	18.6	53.9	8.5	9.1	26.7	48.6	54.8	62.2
		女 F.	986.7	199.5	31.3	17.7	9.8	8.8	16.7	53.0	6.3	7.0	12.1	21.3	25.5	32.6
01000	感染症及び寄生虫症	総数 T.	20.1	7.1	3.1	1.5	1.5	0.9	1.7	2.8	0.5	0.1	0.3	0.3	0.4	0.5
		男 M.	19.9	7.2	3.3	1.8	1.8	0.4	1.8	2.9	0.6	0.1	0.2	0.4	0.4	0.6
		女 F.	20.2	6.9	2.8	1.1	1.2	1.4	1.6	2.7	0.4	0.1	0.3	0.1	0.3	0.3
01100	腸管感染症	総数 T.	2.0	0.9	0.7	0.3	0.6	0.3	0.5	0.6	0.2	0.0	0.0	0.1	0.0	0.0
		男 M.	1.9	1.0	1.0	0.4	0.4	-	0.5	0.6	0.3	0.0	0.0	0.0	0.0	0.0
		女 F.	2.2	0.8	0.4	0.2	0.8	0.6	0.5	0.6	0.1	0.0	0.0	0.1	-	0.1
01200	結核	総数 T.	1.5	-	-	0.1	-	-	0.0	0.0	-	-	-	-	0.0	0.0
		男 M.	1.9	-	-	0.2	-	-	0.1	0.0	-	-	-	-	0.0	0.1
		女 F.	1.2	-	-	-	-	-	-	-	-	-	-	-	-	-
01201	呼吸器結核	総数 T.	1.3	-	-	-	-	-	-	-	-	-	-	-	0.0	0.0
		男 M.	1.7	-	-	-	-	-	-	-	-	-	-	-	0.0	0.1
		女 F.	1.0	-	-	-	-	-	-	-	-	-	-	-	-	-
01202	その他の結核	総数 T.	0.2	-	-	0.1	-	-	0.0	0.0	-	-	-	-	-	-
		男 M.	0.2	-	-	0.2	-	-	0.1	0.0	-	-	-	-	-	-
		女 F.	0.2	-	-	-	-	-	-	-	-	-	-	-	-	-
01300	敗血症	総数 T.	9.2	4.1	1.1	0.5	0.6	0.4	0.6	1.3	0.2	0.1	0.1	0.1	0.2	0.2
		男 M.	9.2	4.4	1.2	0.8	1.2	0.2	0.9	1.6	0.2	0.1	0.1	0.3	0.2	0.3
		女 F.	9.2	3.8	0.9	0.2	-	0.6	0.4	1.1	0.2	0.1	0.0	-	0.2	0.1
01400	ウイルス肝炎	総数 T.	3.1	0.2	-	-	-	-	-	0.0	-	-	0.0	-	-	0.0
		男 M.	2.8	0.2	-	-	-	-	-	0.0	-	-	-	-	-	0.1
		女 F.	3.4	0.2	-	-	-	-	-	0.0	-	-	0.0	-	-	-
01401	B型ウイルス肝炎	総数 T.	0.3	-	-	-	-	-	-	-	-	-	-	-	-	-
		男 M.	0.4	-	-	-	-	-	-	-	-	-	-	-	-	-
		女 F.	0.3	-	-	-	-	-	-	-	-	-	-	-	-	-
01402	C型ウイルス肝炎	総数 T.	2.6	-	-	-	-	-	-	-	-	-	-	-	-	0.0
		男 M.	2.2	-	-	-	-	-	-	-	-	-	-	-	-	0.0
		女 F.	3.0	-	-	-	-	-	-	-	-	-	-	-	-	-
01403	その他のウイルス肝炎	総数 T.	0.1	0.2	-	-	-	-	-	0.0	-	-	0.0	-	-	0.0
		男 M.	0.2	0.2	-	-	-	-	-	0.0	-	-	-	-	-	0.1
		女 F.	0.1	0.2	-	-	-	-	-	0.0	-	-	0.0	-	-	-
01500	ヒト免疫不全ウイルス[HIV]病	総数 T.	0.1	-	-	-	-	-	-	-	-	-	-	-	0.0	0.0
		男 M.	0.1	-	-	-	-	-	-	-	-	-	-	-	0.0	0.0
		女 F.	0.0	-	-	-	-	-	-	-	-	-	-	-	-	-
01600	その他の感染症及び寄生虫症	総数 T.	4.2	1.8	1.3	0.5	0.3	0.2	0.6	0.8	0.1	0.0	0.1	0.1	0.1	0.1
		男 M.	4.2	1.6	1.0	0.4	0.2	0.2	0.5	0.7	0.1	0.0	0.1	0.1	0.2	0.2
		女 F.	4.2	2.1	1.5	0.6	0.4	0.2	0.7	1.0	0.1	0.0	0.2	0.1	0.1	0.1
02000	新生物	総数 T.	307.5	2.7	1.5	2.4	1.3	1.5	1.7	1.9	1.9	1.9	2.2	3.0	5.4	9.6
		男 M.	370.9	2.6	2.5	2.2	1.4	1.2	1.8	2.0	2.2	1.9	2.8	3.5	5.2	7.8
		女 F.	247.3	2.7	0.4	2.6	1.2	1.8	1.5	1.8	1.5	1.8	1.7	2.4	5.7	11.4
02100	悪性新生物	総数 T.	298.3	1.7	1.4	2.1	1.2	1.4	1.5	1.6	1.6	1.7	2.0	2.7	5.1	9.1
		男 M.	361.1	1.8	2.5	2.0	1.4	1.0	1.7	1.7	1.9	1.7	2.6	3.1	5.0	7.3
		女 F.	238.8	1.7	0.2	2.1	1.0	1.8	1.3	1.4	1.3	1.8	1.5	2.2	5.3	11.0
02101	口唇, 口腔及び咽頭の悪性新生物	総数 T.	6.1	-	-	-	-	-	-	-	-	-	-	0.1	0.2	0.4
		男 M.	8.9	-	-	-	-	-	-	-	-	-	-	0.1	0.3	0.4
		女 F.	3.6	-	-	-	-	-	-	-	-	-	-	0.0	0.2	0.4
02102	食道の悪性新生物	総数 T.	9.2	-	-	-	-	-	-	-	-	-	-	-	0.0	0.0
		男 M.	15.7	-	-	-	-	-	-	-	-	-	-	-	0.1	0.0
		女 F.	3.0	-	-	-	-	-	-	-	-	-	-	-	-	0.1
02103	胃の悪性新生物	総数 T.	36.4	-	-	-	-	-	-	-	-	-	0.0	0.2	0.5	1.0
		男 M.	49.0	-	-	-	-	-	-	-	-	-	0.0	0.3	0.6	0.9
		女 F.	24.4	-	-	-	-	-	-	-	-	-	-	0.2	0.5	1.2
02104	結腸の悪性新生物	総数 T.	27.6	-	-	-	-	-	-	-	-	-	0.1	0.1	0.2	0.7
		男 M.	28.1	-	-	-	-	-	-	-	-	-	0.0	0.1	0.3	0.8
		女 F.	27.1	-	-	-	-	-	-	-	-	-	0.1	0.0	0.1	0.6

注：1)　0歳は出生10万対の死亡率である。
　　　実数については下巻死亡第2表を参照されたい。

General mortality

簡単分類別死亡率（人口10万対）
causes (the condensed list of causes of death for Japan)：Japan, 2016

平成28年

35～39	40～44	45～49	50～54	55～59	60～64	65～69	70～74	75～79	80～84	85～89	90～94	95～99	100～	65～	75～	80～	85～	死因簡単分類コード Code[a]
65.5	97.0	152.5	250.3	379.7	595.7	914.6	1 462.5	2 354.0	4 332.0	7 974.5	14 195.2	25 113.9	40 656.9	3 397.2	5 749.1	7 880.1	11 411.1	
81.4	120.2	192.1	319.6	512.0	838.6	1 315.6	2 111.2	3 354.6	6 124.0	11 144.9	18 771.1	31 750.7	44 611.1	3 904.9	6 799.3	9 523.5	14 047.6	
49.1	73.0	111.8	180.0	247.8	359.6	538.8	896.4	1 550.6	3 114.3	6 326.7	12 624.0	23 627.2	39 319.3	3 008.5	5 080.8	6 981.8	10 267.5	
0.7	1.5	2.0	4.0	6.7	10.9	16.9	29.8	50.2	99.0	167.1	244.0	318.8	290.8	66.1	111.8	150.4	201.6	01000
0.9	1.9	2.8	5.3	9.5	14.6	22.6	37.4	60.7	121.7	210.7	317.2	443.3	322.2	70.8	124.8	175.4	246.8	
0.6	1.1	1.1	2.6	4.0	7.3	11.5	23.2	41.8	83.5	144.4	218.9	291.5	280.7	62.4	103.5	136.8	182.0	
0.1	0.1	0.2	0.3	0.2	0.7	1.1	1.9	3.9	8.6	19.4	35.9	56.3	67.7	6.9	12.6	18.0	27.4	01100
0.1	0.2	0.2	0.4	0.4	0.8	1.6	2.3	4.9	10.9	24.9	43.2	73.1	55.6	6.9	13.2	19.8	31.5	
0.1	0.1	0.2	0.2	0.1	0.6	0.6	1.5	3.1	7.0	16.5	33.3	52.5	68.4	6.9	12.1	17.0	25.6	
0.1	0.0	0.1	0.2	0.2	0.4	0.8	1.2	2.8	7.0	16.3	28.0	36.1	18.5	5.3	9.7	14.1	21.1	01200
0.0	-	0.2	0.3	0.3	0.6	1.5	2.0	4.4	10.2	28.1	56.0	86.6	44.4	7.2	14.2	21.9	37.4	
0.1	0.1	-	0.1	-	0.1	0.2	0.5	1.6	4.7	10.2	18.4	25.3	14.0	3.8	6.9	9.8	14.1	
0.0	0.0	0.1	0.2	0.2	0.3	0.7	1.0	2.4	6.0	14.4	25.4	31.7	18.5	4.6	8.6	12.5	18.9	01201
0.0	-	0.2	0.3	0.3	0.6	1.3	1.7	3.9	9.3	26.0	52.5	79.1	44.4	6.5	13.0	20.2	34.8	
0.0	0.1	-	-	-	0.1	0.2	0.4	1.3	3.8	8.4	16.1	21.5	14.0	3.2	5.8	8.2	12.0	
0.0	-	0.0	0.0	-	0.0	0.1	0.2	0.4	0.9	1.9	2.6	4.5	-	0.6	1.1	1.6	2.3	01202
-	-	0.0	-	-	0.1	0.2	0.3	0.5	1.0	2.1	3.4	7.5	-	0.6	1.2	1.7	2.6	
0.0	-	-	0.1	-	0.0	0.1	0.2	0.3	0.9	1.8	2.3	3.8	-	0.7	1.1	1.6	2.1	
0.2	0.7	0.8	1.6	2.8	4.5	7.1	13.4	22.3	45.4	77.9	119.7	164.1	152.3	30.6	52.4	71.3	97.0	01300
0.2	0.9	0.9	1.9	3.7	6.3	9.6	18.6	29.2	59.6	96.8	141.9	192.5	188.9	33.3	58.8	82.2	112.3	
0.2	0.4	0.6	1.4	1.9	2.8	4.7	8.9	16.8	35.8	68.0	112.0	157.6	143.9	28.6	48.3	65.3	90.4	
0.1	0.2	0.5	1.2	2.3	3.0	3.6	6.2	9.0	17.5	19.2	17.1	13.9	15.4	9.5	14.4	17.8	18.2	01400
0.1	0.3	0.9	1.8	3.3	4.0	4.5	6.3	8.0	16.1	17.0	13.8	10.4	-	8.4	12.5	16.0	15.9	
-	0.1	0.1	0.6	1.3	2.0	2.8	6.1	9.7	18.5	20.4	18.2	14.6	17.5	10.2	15.7	18.8	19.2	
-	0.1	0.1	0.2	0.3	0.5	0.6	0.8	0.8	1.3	1.1	1.6	2.4	3.1	0.9	1.1	1.3	1.3	01401
-	0.1	0.2	0.4	0.6	0.7	0.7	0.9	0.8	1.4	1.3	2.4	3.0	-	1.0	1.2	1.5	1.6	
-	0.0	0.0	0.1	0.1	0.4	0.5	0.7	0.9	1.2	1.0	1.3	2.2	3.5	0.8	1.1	1.2	1.2	
0.0	0.1	0.4	0.9	1.8	2.4	2.8	5.0	7.6	15.7	17.6	15.1	11.3	12.3	8.2	12.8	16.0	16.3	01402
0.0	0.1	0.6	1.3	2.5	3.3	3.6	5.0	6.6	14.1	15.1	10.3	7.5	-	7.0	10.7	13.9	13.6	
-	0.1	0.1	0.5	1.2	1.5	2.1	5.1	8.4	16.7	18.8	16.7	12.0	14.0	9.0	14.1	17.2	17.5	
0.0	0.1	0.1	0.1	0.1	0.1	0.3	0.3	0.5	0.6	0.6	0.5	0.3	-	0.4	0.5	0.5	0.5	01403
0.1	0.1	0.1	0.1	0.2	0.1	0.3	0.4	0.6	0.6	0.6	1.1			0.5	0.6	0.7	0.7	
-	0.1	-	0.1	0.1	0.1	0.2	0.3	0.5	0.5	0.6	0.3	0.3	-	0.4	0.5	0.5	0.4	
0.1	0.1	0.1	0.1	0.1	0.1	0.1	0.1	0.1	-	0.1	0.1	-	-	0.1	0.1	0.0	0.1	01500
0.1	0.2	0.1	0.3	0.1	0.1	0.2	0.1	0.2	-	-	-	-	-	0.1	0.1	-	-	
-	-	-	-	-	-	0.0	0.0	0.0	-	-	0.1	0.1	-	0.0	0.0	0.0	0.1	
0.2	0.3	0.4	0.5	1.2	2.3	4.1	7.1	12.1	20.5	34.2	43.3	48.4	36.9	13.8	22.6	29.2	37.9	01600
0.2	0.3	0.5	0.6	1.7	2.8	5.2	8.1	14.1	24.9	43.9	62.3	80.6	33.3	15.0	26.1	35.6	49.8	
0.2	0.3	0.3	0.4	0.7	1.8	3.1	6.2	10.5	17.6	29.2	36.8	41.5	36.8	12.9	20.4	25.8	32.7	
17.3	28.9	53.3	100.9	171.9	293.0	457.4	676.0	920.5	1 346.9	1 849.6	2 197.6	2 410.7	2 132.3	956.2	1 381.4	1 670.6	1 992.9	02000
13.9	24.0	47.6	99.5	198.9	378.3	632.2	977.7	1 340.2	2 014.0	2 900.8	3 553.1	4 152.2	3 522.2	1 303.1	1 980.1	2 486.1	3 114.5	
20.8	34.0	59.1	102.4	145.0	210.2	293.5	412.8	583.5	893.6	1 303.2	1 732.2	2 033.9	1 875.4	690.7	1 000.4	1 224.9	1 506.3	
16.7	28.0	52.1	98.9	168.9	288.4	450.0	662.4	897.2	1 304.9	1 771.4	2 084.5	2 252.6	2 001.5	926.2	1 330.4	1 602.3	1 898.3	02100
13.3	23.0	46.3	96.7	195.2	372.0	622.1	958.6	1 308.1	1 954.3	2 791.2	3 397.9	3 940.3	3 355.6	1 267.7	1 916.9	2 398.3	2 989.3	
20.3	33.2	58.0	101.1	142.8	207.1	288.7	403.9	567.3	863.6	1 241.4	1 633.5	1 887.7	1 752.6	664.8	957.2	1 167.1	1 425.0	
0.6	0.8	1.5	2.9	5.0	7.5	10.7	14.4	18.2	21.6	29.2	35.9	47.9	52.3	17.9	23.7	27.2	32.8	02101
0.6	1.2	2.1	4.2	8.4	12.7	18.4	25.4	31.1	36.0	46.1	53.6	71.6	44.4	28.2	37.0	41.6	49.0	
0.5	0.5	0.9	1.5	1.6	2.5	3.4	4.9	7.8	11.9	20.4	29.9	42.7	52.6	10.0	15.3	19.4	25.7	
0.1	0.6	1.2	3.2	6.9	13.2	19.8	28.9	30.5	32.5	33.2	31.0	25.4	21.5	27.5	31.5	32.2	31.9	02102
0.1	0.7	1.7	4.9	11.8	22.8	36.1	55.2	58.9	66.7	71.2	68.7	53.7	33.3	52.7	64.0	67.9	69.6	
0.1	0.4	0.7	1.4	2.1	3.9	4.5	5.9	7.7	9.3	13.5	18.0	19.3	19.3	8.2	10.9	12.6	15.5	
1.8	2.7	5.4	9.1	17.7	32.9	54.6	80.1	110.8	161.5	229.3	274.1	295.0	216.9	115.6	168.2	204.2	246.7	02103
1.7	2.6	6.2	11.5	24.4	48.3	82.7	129.9	182.6	270.8	390.0	466.0	556.7	400.0	174.2	266.5	332.9	415.5	
1.8	2.7	4.6	6.6	11.1	18.0	28.1	36.5	53.2	87.2	145.8	208.2	238.6	184.2	70.7	105.6	133.8	173.4	
1.5	2.4	4.5	8.3	14.0	25.0	37.7	54.0	76.7	114.0	178.8	267.3	334.6	324.6	87.0	131.4	165.7	217.2	02104
1.3	2.3	4.6	8.7	15.5	30.1	47.9	69.8	99.9	144.3	218.9	308.2	392.5	355.6	97.6	149.7	189.0	248.6	
1.7	2.5	4.4	7.9	12.5	20.0	28.2	40.2	58.1	93.4	157.9	253.3	321.2	314.0	78.9	119.7	153.0	203.6	

Note : 1) Per 100,000 live birth.
a) Code see page 595.

死　亡

表 5.16　性・年齢別にみた死因
Table 5.16　Death rates (per 100,000 population) by sex, age and

死因簡単分類コード Code[a]	死因・性 Causes of death and sex		総数 Total	0歳[1] Year	1	2	3	4	1～4	0～4	5～9	10～14	15～19	20～24	25～29	30～34
02105	直腸S状結腸移行部及び直腸の悪性新生物	総数 T.	12.5	-	-	-			-	-	-	-	0.0	0.0	0.1	0.3
		男 M.	16.3	-	-	-			-	-	-	-	0.0	0.1	0.2	0.5
		女 F.	8.8	-	-	-			-	-	-	-	0.0	-	0.0	0.2
02106	肝及び肝内胆管の悪性新生物	総数 T.	22.8	0.2	-	0.5			0.1	0.1	0.0	0.0	0.0	-	0.0	0.2
		男 M.	30.4	0.4	-	0.2			0.1	0.1	0.0	0.0	0.0	-	0.0	0.2
		女 F.	15.6			0.9			0.2	0.2	-	0.0	-		0.1	0.1
02107	胆のう及びその他の胆道の悪性新生物	総数 T.	14.4	-	-	-			-	-	-	-	0.0	-	0.0	0.1
		男 M.	14.7	-	-	-			-	-	-	-	-	-	0.0	0.1
		女 F.	14.0	-	-	-			-	-	-	-	0.0	-	0.0	0.0
02108	膵の悪性新生物	総数 T.	26.8	-	-	-			-	-	-	-	-	0.0	0.0	0.1
		男 M.	28.0	-	-	-			-	-	-	-	-	-	0.0	0.2
		女 F.	25.6	-	-	-			-	-	-	-	-	0.1	0.0	0.0
02109	喉頭の悪性新生物	総数 T.	0.8	-	-	-			-	-	-	-	-	-	-	-
		男 M.	1.4	-	-	-			-	-	-	-	-	-	-	-
		女 F.	0.1	-	-	-			-	-	-	-	-	-	-	-
02110	気管, 気管支及び肺の悪性新生物	総数 T.	59.1	0.1	-	-			-	0.0	-	0.0		0.0	0.2	0.5
		男 M.	86.1	0.2	-	-			-	0.0	-	0.1		0.1	0.2	0.5
		女 F.	33.4	-	-	-			-	-	-	-			0.3	0.4
02111	皮膚の悪性新生物	総数 T.	1.2	-	-	-			-	-	-	-	0.0	0.1	0.1	0.1
		男 M.	1.2	-	-	-			-	-	-	-	-	0.1	0.1	0.1
		女 F.	1.2	-	-	-			-	-	-	-	0.0	0.1	0.1	0.1
02112	乳房の悪性新生物	総数 T.	11.3	-	-	-			-	-	-	-	-	0.0	0.3	1.2
		男 M.	0.2	-	-	-			-	-	-	-	-	-	-	-
		女 F.	21.8	-	-	-			-	-	-	-	-	0.0	0.6	2.4
02113	子宮の悪性新生物	女 F.	9.9	-	-	-			-	-	-	-	-	0.1	0.7	1.8
02114	卵巣の悪性新生物	女 F.	7.4	-	-	-			-	-	-	-	-	0.1	0.5	0.6
02115	前立腺の悪性新生物	男 M.	19.4	-	-	-			-	-	-	-	-	0.1	-	-
02116	膀胱の悪性新生物	総数 T.	6.7	-	-	-			-	-	-	-	-	-	0.0	0.1
		男 M.	9.5	-	-	-			-	-	-	-	-	-	0.0	0.1
		女 F.	4.1	-	-	-			-	-	-	-	-	-	-	0.1
02117	中枢神経系の悪性新生物	総数 T.	2.1	0.1	0.3	0.4	0.2	0.7	0.4	0.3	0.8	0.6	0.4	0.3	0.5	0.8
		男 M.	2.4	-	0.6	0.2	0.2	0.6	0.4	0.3	0.8	0.6	0.5	0.4	0.6	0.8
		女 F.	1.8	0.2	-	0.6	0.2	0.8	0.4	0.4	0.8	0.6	0.2	0.3	0.4	0.8
02118	悪性リンパ腫	総数 T.	9.9	-	-	-			-	-	-	0.1	0.1	0.3	0.2	0.3
		男 M.	11.3	-	-	-			-	-	-	0.1	0.1	0.4	0.4	0.2
		女 F.	8.5	-	-	-			-	-	-	0.1	0.0	0.1	0.1	0.4
02119	白血病	総数 T.	7.0	1.0	0.5	0.3	0.6	0.2	0.4	0.5	0.4	0.4	0.6	0.5	0.7	1.0
		男 M.	8.9	1.0	0.8	0.4	0.6	0.2	0.5	0.6	0.5	0.4	0.8	0.6	0.9	1.1
		女 F.	5.3	1.1	0.2	0.2	0.6	0.2	0.3	0.5	0.2	0.4	0.3	0.4	0.5	0.9
02120	その他のリンパ組織, 造血組織及び関連組織の悪性新生物	総数 T.	3.6	-	-	-			-	-	-	-	0.0	-	-	-
		男 M.	3.7	-	-	-			-	-	-	-	-	-	-	-
		女 F.	3.4	-	-	-			-	-	-	-	0.0	-	-	-
02121	その他の悪性新生物	総数 T.	22.6	0.3	0.5	0.8	0.4	0.5	0.6	0.5	0.4	0.6	0.9	0.9	1.2	1.3
		男 M.	25.8	0.2	1.0	1.2	0.6	0.2	0.8	0.6	0.5	0.5	1.0	1.1	1.3	1.6
		女 F.	19.5	0.4	-	0.4	0.2	0.8	0.4	0.4	0.3	0.6	0.7	0.8	1.1	1.0
02200	その他の新生物	総数 T.	9.2	0.9	0.1	0.3	0.1	0.1	0.2	0.3	0.3	0.1	0.2	0.3	0.3	0.5
		男 M.	9.9	0.8	-	0.2	-	0.2	0.1	0.2	0.4	0.2	0.2	0.4	0.3	0.5
		女 F.	8.5	1.1	0.2	0.4	0.2	-	0.2	0.4	0.2	0.0	0.2	0.2	0.3	0.4
02201	中枢神経系のその他の新生物	総数 T.	2.0	0.1	0.1	0.2	0.1	-	0.1	0.1	0.3	0.1	0.1	0.2	0.2	0.2
		男 M.	1.9	-	-	-	-	-	-	-	0.4	0.1	0.1	0.2	0.2	0.3
		女 F.	2.1	0.2	0.2	0.4	0.2	-	0.2	0.2	0.2	0.0	0.1	0.1	0.2	0.1

簡単分類別死亡率（人口10万対）（つづき）
causes (the condensed list of causes of death for Japan)：Japan, 2016－CON.

平成28年

35～39	40～44	45～49	50～54	55～59	60～64	65～69	70～74	75～79	80～84	85～89	90～94	95～99	100～	65～	75～	80～	85～	死因簡単分類コード Code[a)]
0.7	1.4	2.9	5.7	10.9	17.1	23.3	30.3	35.1	45.6	57.1	67.4	73.6	60.0	36.1	46.4	53.5	61.3	02105
0.9	1.7	3.5	7.1	14.8	25.4	35.9	45.5	53.6	68.9	86.7	96.0	140.3	100.0	52.0	67.5	78.5	91.3	
0.6	1.2	2.4	4.3	7.1	9.2	11.5	17.0	20.2	29.8	41.7	57.6	59.2	52.6	23.9	32.9	39.8	48.2	
0.5	1.0	2.0	5.1	11.3	20.9	33.5	51.8	77.7	118.2	135.6	133.2	110.2	72.3	73.3	106.9	125.2	132.2	02106
0.6	1.4	3.2	8.1	18.9	34.4	54.3	80.9	116.8	177.1	213.5	204.8	214.9	133.3	106.2	158.6	191.6	211.0	
0.3	0.6	0.8	1.9	3.6	7.7	14.1	26.5	46.3	78.2	95.1	108.6	87.7	61.4	48.2	74.0	88.9	98.0	
0.1	0.5	0.9	2.2	3.7	8.9	15.6	25.2	43.2	73.1	113.3	145.6	172.3	164.6	48.3	78.3	100.3	127.4	02107
0.1	0.4	1.0	2.5	4.2	11.1	19.9	33.3	56.5	94.9	144.2	179.0	219.4	200.0	54.9	92.6	121.2	156.1	
0.2	0.5	0.8	2.0	3.2	6.8	11.5	18.1	32.5	58.2	97.3	134.1	161.7	156.1	43.3	69.2	88.9	115.0	
0.6	1.3	3.8	8.2	15.9	27.0	44.8	66.5	89.1	114.8	143.1	159.0	164.4	118.5	84.0	115.4	131.8	148.8	02108
0.7	1.7	5.1	10.5	20.3	34.4	57.3	82.3	105.8	132.9	160.2	193.1	200.0	177.8	94.8	129.8	148.8	169.9	
0.5	0.8	2.5	5.9	11.6	19.9	33.2	52.7	75.7	102.5	134.2	147.3	156.3	107.0	75.7	106.2	122.6	139.7	
0.0	-	0.1	0.1	0.4	0.8	1.3	1.6	2.4	3.6	4.6	5.6	2.6	1.5	2.4	3.5	4.1	4.7	02109
0.0	-	0.1	0.2	0.8	1.4	2.6	3.3	5.0	7.8	11.8	18.6	9.0	-	5.1	7.9	10.1	13.2	
0.0	-	0.0	0.1	-	0.1	0.2	0.1	0.3	0.7	0.8	1.2	1.3	1.8	0.4	0.7	0.9	1.0	
1.4	2.7	5.6	12.4	25.8	53.8	95.7	150.3	189.4	272.1	352.7	364.4	352.6	284.6	190.6	265.7	313.7	355.1	02110
1.9	3.5	7.4	17.6	38.9	83.3	152.5	247.4	317.2	478.2	686.5	767.6	765.7	611.1	310.3	462.4	577.2	709.0	
0.9	1.7	3.7	7.2	12.8	25.2	42.4	65.5	86.8	132.0	179.1	226.0	263.9	228.1	98.9	140.6	169.6	201.5	
0.1	0.2	0.3	0.4	0.5	0.9	1.2	1.8	3.0	4.1	8.3	14.8	33.0	80.0	3.9	6.4	8.5	12.8	02111
0.1	0.3	0.3	0.5	0.7	1.1	1.6	2.5	4.2	5.6	11.2	17.5	34.3	77.8	4.2	7.0	9.3	14.1	
0.1	0.2	0.3	0.4	0.4	0.7	0.8	1.3	2.1	3.0	6.7	13.8	32.6	78.9	3.6	6.0	8.0	12.3	
2.6	4.7	8.2	14.1	17.1	19.0	20.1	20.5	21.6	26.6	35.0	57.8	83.2	112.3	25.3	30.6	36.3	46.0	02112
-	0.0	0.0	0.1	0.1	0.2	0.3	0.3	0.7	1.0	2.1	2.4	1.5	-	0.7	1.1	1.5	2.2	
5.3	9.5	16.5	28.3	34.0	37.2	38.7	38.1	38.4	44.1	52.0	76.8	100.3	128.1	44.2	49.4	55.3	64.9	
3.4	5.2	7.7	12.0	13.6	13.8	15.3	16.4	19.3	22.9	31.1	32.6	32.9	28.1	20.5	24.7	27.7	31.7	02113
1.4	2.9	5.5	9.2	11.8	11.3	12.7	12.0	13.6	18.9	21.8	21.6	28.2	21.1	15.5	18.2	20.7	22.3	02114
-	0.0	0.2	0.9	2.3	7.3	17.4	37.7	66.5	128.9	248.8	373.2	532.8	644.4	76.2	140.7	199.3	293.1	02115
0.1	0.3	0.4	1.0	1.7	3.8	6.6	11.1	17.1	33.5	57.7	79.7	99.0	104.6	22.8	37.7	50.6	67.6	02116
0.1	0.4	0.6	1.3	2.7	6.3	11.3	18.9	28.0	57.1	111.6	182.2	252.2	255.6	35.7	63.0	90.7	135.4	
0.1	0.2	0.2	0.6	0.7	1.3	2.3	4.3	8.4	17.4	29.7	44.5	66.1	78.9	12.9	21.6	28.6	38.1	
0.9	1.0	1.2	1.7	2.1	3.1	3.5	4.4	5.5	6.1	6.0	4.0	3.4	3.1	4.7	5.6	5.7	5.2	02117
1.2	1.1	1.4	2.0	2.7	3.5	4.4	5.6	6.6	7.5	8.2	5.6	4.5	22.2	5.9	7.1	7.5	7.5	
0.5	1.0	0.8	1.3	1.5	2.7	2.6	3.3	4.7	5.2	4.8	3.5	3.2	-	3.8	4.7	4.7	4.2	
0.5	0.7	1.3	2.2	4.7	7.4	11.5	20.0	29.8	54.3	67.9	71.4	59.9	29.2	31.7	49.0	61.1	67.8	02118
0.7	1.0	1.7	2.8	6.1	9.9	15.0	27.1	40.4	72.8	98.6	109.3	111.9	22.2	39.9	65.3	85.1	101.3	
0.3	0.5	0.8	1.6	3.2	5.0	8.2	13.8	21.3	41.7	52.0	58.4	48.7	29.8	25.4	38.6	48.0	53.3	
1.0	1.4	2.0	2.8	4.2	6.8	11.1	15.7	23.7	30.1	34.2	31.9	27.5	16.9	20.6	28.5	31.5	32.8	02119
1.0	1.6	2.3	3.6	5.6	8.8	15.8	22.2	34.6	45.7	52.5	53.6	43.3	55.6	29.0	42.4	48.6	52.4	
0.9	1.2	1.6	2.0	2.8	4.9	6.6	10.0	14.9	19.6	24.6	24.4	24.1	10.5	14.2	19.6	22.1	24.3	
0.1	0.1	0.4	0.7	1.5	2.8	4.9	7.2	11.7	17.9	25.5	24.5	18.8	12.3	11.6	17.6	21.3	24.6	02120
0.1	0.2	0.5	0.8	1.9	2.9	5.5	8.4	14.3	22.7	33.0	38.2	31.3	22.2	13.3	21.7	27.6	34.1	
-	0.1	0.3	0.6	1.2	2.7	4.3	6.1	9.6	14.7	21.6	19.9	16.1	10.5	10.3	14.9	17.8	20.4	
1.8	2.3	3.9	7.8	11.6	21.0	31.2	46.0	63.7	98.2	140.1	181.2	205.2	193.8	69.5	103.1	127.8	157.2	02121
2.1	3.0	4.5	9.4	15.1	28.1	43.1	62.8	85.4	135.4	195.8	260.2	304.5	200.0	86.9	132.6	170.0	216.0	
1.5	1.6	3.4	6.1	8.1	14.2	20.1	31.2	46.3	72.9	111.2	154.1	183.5	189.5	56.2	84.3	104.7	131.8	
0.5	0.9	1.2	2.1	3.0	4.7	7.4	13.7	23.3	42.0	78.1	113.2	158.1	130.8	30.1	51.0	68.4	94.6	02200
0.6	1.0	1.3	2.8	3.7	6.3	10.1	19.1	32.1	59.7	109.6	155.2	211.9	166.7	35.5	63.2	87.8	125.3	
0.5	0.8	1.1	1.3	2.2	3.1	4.8	8.9	16.3	30.0	61.8	98.7	146.2	122.8	25.9	43.2	57.8	81.3	
0.3	0.5	0.5	0.8	1.0	1.4	2.0	3.1	4.7	8.4	14.4	19.3	23.8	12.3	5.9	9.4	12.4	16.5	02201
0.4	0.5	0.6	1.1	1.2	1.7	2.3	3.6	5.1	9.2	16.7	21.8	31.3	-	5.8	9.6	13.2	18.5	
0.3	0.4	0.4	0.5	0.9	1.2	1.7	2.8	4.3	7.8	13.2	18.5	22.2	14.0	5.9	9.3	12.0	15.6	

死　亡

表 5.16　性・年齢別にみた死因
Table 5.16　Death rates (per 100,000 population) by sex, age and

死因簡単分類コード Code[a]	死因・性 Causes of death and sex		総数 Total	0歳[1] Year	1	2	3	4	1～4	0～4	5～9	10～14	15～19	20～24	25～29	30～34
02202	中枢神経系を除くその他の新生物	総数 T.	7.2	0.8	-	0.1	-	0.1	0.1	0.2	-	0.0	0.1	0.1	0.1	0.2
		男 M.	8.0	0.8	-	0.2	-	0.2	0.1	0.2	-	0.1	0.1	0.2	0.1	0.1
		女 F.	6.5	0.8	-	-	-	-	-	0.2	-	-	0.1	0.1	0.1	0.3
03000	血液及び造血器の疾患並びに免疫機構の障害	総数 T.	3.6	1.7	0.1	0.4	0.1	0.1	0.2	0.5	0.1	0.1	0.1	0.1	0.1	0.1
		男 M.	3.3	3.0	-	0.4	-	0.2	0.2	0.7	0.1	0.0	0.2	0.1	0.1	0.1
		女 F.	4.0	0.4	0.2	0.4	0.2	-	0.2	0.3	-	0.1	0.1	0.1	0.1	0.1
03100	貧　血	総数 T.	1.7	0.1	-	-	-	-	-	0.0	-	0.1	0.0	0.0	0.0	0.0
		男 M.	1.4	0.2	-	-	-	-	-	0.0	-	0.0	0.1	-	0.0	0.1
		女 F.	2.0	-	-	-	-	-	-	-	-	0.1	-	0.0	-	0.0
03200	その他の血液及び造血器の疾患並びに免疫機構の障害	総数 T.	1.9	1.6	0.1	0.4	0.1	0.1	0.2	0.5	0.1	0.0	0.1	0.1	0.0	0.1
		男 M.	1.9	2.8	-	0.4	-	0.2	0.2	0.7	0.1	-	0.1	0.1	0.0	0.1
		女 F.	2.0	0.4	0.2	0.4	0.2	-	0.2	0.3	-	0.1	0.1	0.1	0.1	0.1
04000	内分泌，栄養及び代謝疾患	総数 T.	17.1	2.6	0.5	0.3	0.3	-	0.3	0.7	0.1	0.1	0.1	0.4	0.5	0.6
		男 M.	17.6	3.0	0.4	0.2	0.2	-	0.2	0.8	0.2	0.1	0.1	0.5	0.7	0.8
		女 F.	16.5	2.1	0.6	0.4	0.4	-	0.4	0.7	-	0.0	0.2	0.3	0.4	0.4
04100	糖　尿　病	総数 T.	10.8	-	-	-	-	-	-		-	0.0	-	0.1	0.1	0.2
		男 M.	11.9	-	-	-	-	-	-		-	0.0	-	0.1	0.2	0.3
		女 F.	9.7	-	-	-	-	-	-		-	-	-	0.1	0.1	0.1
04200	その他の内分泌，栄養及び代謝疾患	総数 T.	6.3	2.6	0.5	0.3	0.3	-	0.3	0.7	0.1	0.1	0.1	0.3	0.4	0.4
		男 M.	5.7	3.0	0.4	0.2	0.2	-	0.2	0.8	0.2	0.1	0.1	0.3	0.4	0.4
		女 F.	6.8	2.1	0.6	0.4	0.4	-	0.4	0.7	-	0.0	0.2	0.2	0.3	0.3
05000	精神及び行動の障害	総数 T.	11.3	-	-	-	-	-	-		-	0.0	-	0.1	0.2	0.5
		男 M.	7.3	-	-	-	-	-	-		-	-	-	0.1	0.1	0.3
		女 F.	15.2	-	-	-	-	-	-		-	0.1	-	0.1	0.3	0.7
05100	血管性及び詳細不明の認知症	総数 T.	9.5	-	-	-	-	-	-		-	-	-	-	-	-
		男 M.	5.5	-	-	-	-	-	-		-	-	-	-	-	-
		女 F.	13.3	-	-	-	-	-	-		-	-	-	-	-	-
05200	その他の精神及び行動の障害	総数 T.	1.8	-	-	-	-	-	-		-	0.0	-	0.1	0.2	0.5
		男 M.	1.7	-	-	-	-	-	-		-	-	-	0.1	0.1	0.3
		女 F.	1.9	-	-	-	-	-	-		-	0.1	-	0.1	0.3	0.7
06000	神経系の疾患	総数 T.	26.7	3.4	2.9	1.0	1.0	0.6	1.4	1.8	0.7	0.6	0.9	1.2	1.2	1.2
		男 M.	24.5	3.0	1.2	0.4	1.2	0.6	0.9	1.3	0.7	0.6	1.3	1.5	1.4	1.5
		女 F.	28.7	3.8	4.5	1.7	0.8	0.6	1.9	2.3	0.7	0.6	0.5	1.0	0.9	0.8
06100	髄　膜　炎	総数 T.	0.2	0.5	-	-	-	-	-	0.1	-	-	-	0.0	-	0.0
		男 M.	0.3	0.4	-	-	-	-	-	0.1	-	-	-	-	-	0.1
		女 F.	0.2	0.6	-	-	-	-	-	0.1	-	-	0.1	-	-	-
06200	脊髄性筋萎縮症及び関連症候群	総数 T.	2.1	0.2	-	-	-	-	-	0.0	-	0.0	0.0	0.0	-	0.0
		男 M.	2.5	0.2	-	-	-	-	-	0.0	-	0.0	0.0	0.0	-	0.0
		女 F.	1.8	0.2	-	-	-	-	-	0.0	-	-	-	-	-	-
06300	パーキンソン病	総数 T.	6.0	-	-	-	-	-	-		-	-	-	-	-	-
		男 M.	6.1	-	-	-	-	-	-		-	-	-	-	-	-
		女 F.	6.0	-	-	-	-	-	-		-	-	-	-	-	-
06400	アルツハイマー病	総数 T.	9.6	-	-	-	-	-	-		-	-	-	-	-	-
		男 M.	6.2	-	-	-	-	-	-		-	-	-	-	-	-
		女 F.	12.8	-	-	-	-	-	-		-	-	-	-	-	-
06500	その他の神経系の疾患	総数 T.	8.7	2.7	2.9	1.0	1.0	0.6	1.4	1.6	0.7	0.6	0.9	1.2	1.2	1.1
		男 M.	9.6	2.4	1.2	0.4	1.2	0.6	0.9	1.2	0.7	0.6	1.3	1.4	1.4	1.4
		女 F.	7.9	2.9	4.5	1.7	0.8	0.6	1.9	2.1	0.7	0.6	0.5	0.9	0.9	0.8
07000	眼及び付属器の疾患	総数 T.	0.0	-	-	-	-	-	-	-	-	-	0.0	-	-	-
		男 M.	0.0	-	-	-	-	-	-	-	-	-	0.0	-	-	-
		女 F.	0.0	-	-	-	-	-	-	-	-	-	-	-	-	-
08000	耳及び乳様突起の疾患	総数 T.	0.0	-	-	-	-	-	-	-	-	-	-	-	-	-
		男 M.	0.0	-	-	-	-	-	-	-	-	-	-	-	-	-
		女 F.	0.0	-	-	-	-	-	-	-	-	-	-	-	-	-
09000	循環器系の疾患	総数 T.	271.8	4.8	2.1	1.3	0.9	0.5	1.2	1.9	0.4	0.6	1.1	2.6	3.5	5.7
		男 M.	265.5	4.8	2.1	1.8	1.0	1.0	1.5	2.1	0.5	0.8	1.5	3.4	4.8	8.7
		女 F.	277.9	4.8	2.2	0.6	0.8	-	0.9	1.7	0.4	0.4	0.7	1.7	2.1	2.6

簡単分類別死亡率（人口10万対）（つづき）
causes（the condensed list of causes of death for Japan）：Japan, 2016－CON.

平成28年

35～39	40～44	45～49	50～54	55～59	60～64	65～69	70～74	75～79	80～84	85～89	90～94	95～99	100～	65～	75～	80～	85～	死因簡単分類コード Code[a]
0.2	0.5	0.7	1.2	1.9	3.2	5.4	10.5	18.6	33.6	63.7	93.8	134.3	118.5	24.2	41.6	55.9	78.1	02202
0.2	0.5	0.7	1.6	2.6	4.6	7.8	15.5	27.0	50.5	92.9	133.4	180.6	166.7	29.7	53.6	74.6	106.8	
0.2	0.5	0.7	0.8	1.3	1.9	3.1	6.1	11.9	22.2	48.6	80.2	124.1	108.8	20.0	33.9	45.7	65.7	
0.2	0.3	0.5	0.8	0.8	1.7	2.8	4.5	7.9	17.8	29.8	50.6	78.8	87.7	12.0	20.8	29.0	40.0	03000
0.2	0.2	0.7	0.9	0.9	1.8	3.7	5.6	9.4	20.7	36.2	57.3	86.6	111.1	11.8	21.3	30.6	43.8	
0.2	0.3	0.3	0.6	0.8	1.6	2.0	3.5	6.7	15.8	26.5	48.4	76.9	82.5	12.1	20.6	28.0	38.4	
0.1	0.1	0.2	0.3	0.3	0.6	1.0	1.5	3.0	7.5	15.1	30.6	49.7	61.5	5.7	10.4	15.1	22.6	03100
0.0	0.1	0.3	0.4	0.4	0.7	1.3	1.7	3.5	8.3	16.5	34.0	56.7	88.9	5.1	9.7	14.5	22.8	
0.1	0.1	0.1	0.3	0.2	0.5	0.8	1.2	2.6	7.0	14.4	29.4	48.1	56.1	6.2	10.9	15.4	22.6	
0.2	0.1	0.3	0.4	0.5	1.1	1.8	3.0	4.9	10.3	14.7	20.1	29.1	26.2	6.3	10.4	13.8	17.4	03200
0.2	0.1	0.4	0.5	0.5	1.2	2.4	3.9	5.9	12.4	19.7	23.3	29.9	22.2	6.8	11.6	16.1	21.0	
0.1	0.2	0.2	0.3	0.6	1.1	1.2	2.3	4.1	8.8	12.0	18.9	28.8	26.3	5.9	9.6	12.6	15.8	
1.2	1.7	2.9	4.5	7.0	10.7	15.7	24.1	42.6	74.1	130.5	209.3	337.2	453.8	54.9	92.1	123.2	172.1	04000
1.4	2.3	4.0	6.6	10.5	16.2	23.5	34.1	58.6	97.3	158.5	227.1	368.7	555.6	60.2	101.5	135.5	186.2	
0.9	1.0	1.9	2.3	3.6	5.3	8.5	15.4	29.8	58.3	115.9	203.2	329.4	429.8	50.9	86.2	116.5	166.0	
0.4	1.0	1.7	3.0	4.8	7.4	11.6	17.6	29.8	49.6	79.0	113.0	162.3	187.7	34.7	56.3	72.9	96.1	04100
0.6	1.4	2.4	4.8	7.7	11.6	17.8	25.6	42.4	67.0	97.3	125.2	159.7	244.4	40.7	65.8	84.4	107.5	
0.2	0.6	0.9	1.2	2.0	3.4	5.8	10.6	19.7	37.7	69.5	108.8	162.3	175.4	30.2	50.2	66.6	91.2	
0.8	0.7	1.3	1.5	2.2	3.3	4.1	6.5	12.8	24.5	51.5	96.3	174.9	266.2	20.2	35.8	50.3	75.9	04200
0.7	0.9	1.6	1.8	2.8	4.7	5.7	8.5	16.2	30.3	61.2	101.9	209.0	311.1	19.5	35.7	51.1	78.7	
0.8	0.5	1.0	1.1	1.6	1.9	2.7	4.9	10.0	20.6	46.4	94.4	167.1	254.4	20.7	35.9	49.9	74.7	
0.3	0.6	0.9	1.2	1.5	2.3	3.1	5.7	12.7	37.1	102.8	260.3	587.4	1 009.2	39.4	76.1	116.0	194.5	05000
0.2	0.6	0.8	1.6	1.9	3.5	4.2	7.3	15.3	41.1	98.7	220.2	435.8	666.7	27.1	54.7	85.9	145.5	
0.3	0.6	0.9	0.8	1.1	1.2	2.0	4.2	10.6	34.3	104.9	274.0	617.7	1 045.6	48.8	89.8	132.4	215.8	
-	0.0		-	0.1	0.3	0.9	3.0	9.1	31.3	93.2	242.1	551.3	961.5	34.4	68.5	105.9	180.1	05100
-			-	0.1	0.5	1.2	4.0	11.2	34.6	89.4	204.8	417.9	644.4	22.5	48.2	77.4	134.3	
-	0.0		-	0.0	0.1	0.5	2.2	7.4	29.0	95.1	254.9	577.8	994.7	43.6	81.5	121.4	199.9	
0.3	0.6	0.9	1.2	1.5	2.0	2.2	2.6	3.6	5.7	9.6	18.2	36.1	47.7	4.9	7.6	10.1	14.5	05200
0.2	0.6	0.8	1.6	1.9	3.0	3.0	3.3	4.1	6.5	9.3	15.4	17.9	22.2	4.6	6.5	8.5	11.2	
0.3	0.6	0.9	0.8	1.1	1.1	1.5	2.1	3.2	5.3	9.8	19.1	39.9	50.9	5.2	8.3	11.0	15.9	
1.3	1.7	2.4	4.5	6.7	11.3	19.4	36.1	68.0	130.7	225.7	346.5	521.7	575.4	89.0	154.4	208.6	286.2	06000
1.8	2.1	2.9	5.3	8.4	14.5	24.0	44.8	86.1	165.2	261.0	353.8	500.0	322.2	88.9	161.1	220.4	293.8	
0.8	1.2	2.0	3.6	5.1	8.1	15.1	28.5	53.5	107.2	207.4	344.0	524.7	605.3	89.1	150.1	202.2	282.8	
0.0	0.1	0.1	0.1	0.2	0.3	0.3	0.3	0.7	0.9	1.7	1.2	1.3	1.5	0.6	1.0	1.2	1.5	06100
0.0	0.0	0.0	0.2	0.3	0.6	0.4	0.4	0.8	1.0	2.8	1.6	4.5	-	0.8	1.3	1.6	2.5	
-	0.1		0.1	0.1	0.1	0.2	0.2	0.7	0.8	1.1	1.0	0.6	1.8	0.5	0.9	0.9	1.0	
0.1	0.2	0.4	0.8	1.3	2.5	4.5	6.7	8.8	9.0	5.6	3.5	1.8	-	6.5	7.6	6.8	4.6	06200
0.1	0.3	0.4	1.0	1.3	3.1	5.7	8.3	11.2	12.1	7.7	5.6	4.5	-	8.4	10.5	9.9	7.0	
0.1	0.1	0.4	0.5	1.3	2.0	3.4	5.3	7.0	6.9	4.5	2.7	1.3	-	5.0	5.8	5.1	3.6	
-	-	0.0	0.1	0.4	0.9	2.4	7.8	20.2	42.0	61.7	62.4	47.1	29.2	21.6	39.3	51.2	60.4	06300
-	-	0.0	0.2	0.5	1.4	3.1	10.3	26.5	56.1	75.8	72.9	53.7	11.1	24.1	47.3	63.7	73.8	
-	-		0.1	0.2	0.4	1.7	5.6	15.2	32.4	54.3	58.7	45.6	31.6	19.6	34.2	44.4	54.6	
-	0.0		0.1	0.2	0.7	1.8	4.8	12.7	38.7	103.6	221.4	409.2	486.2	34.5	67.4	101.7	164.3	06400
-	0.0		0.1	0.2	0.9	2.0	5.2	14.3	42.0	100.8	196.6	358.2	255.6	24.8	52.2	82.2	135.6	
-	0.0		0.1	0.2	0.5	1.6	4.4	11.4	36.5	105.1	229.9	418.7	514.0	42.0	77.0	112.3	176.8	
1.2	1.4	2.0	3.4	4.7	6.8	10.4	16.6	25.5	40.1	53.2	58.2	62.3	58.5	25.8	39.2	47.7	55.3	06500
1.7	1.7	2.4	3.9	6.1	8.6	12.8	20.5	33.3	54.0	73.9	77.2	79.1	55.6	30.8	49.9	62.9	74.8	
0.7	1.0	1.6	2.9	3.3	5.1	8.2	13.2	19.3	30.6	42.4	51.6	58.5	57.9	22.0	32.3	39.4	46.8	
-	-	-	-	0.0		0.0		0.0			0.1	0.3		0.0	0.0	0.0	0.1	07000
-	-	-	-	0.0		0.0				0.1				0.0	0.0	0.0	0.1	
-	-	-	-			0.0		0.0			0.1	0.3		0.0	0.0	0.0	0.1	
-	-		0.0	0.0		0.0	0.0	0.1		0.4	0.3			0.0	0.1	0.1	0.2	08000
-	-		0.0	0.0		0.0	0.1			0.3				0.0	0.1	0.1	0.1	
-	-			0.0			0.0	0.1		0.5	0.3			0.0	0.1	0.1	0.2	
11.4	22.5	37.3	59.2	85.7	126.3	194.2	320.5	562.1	1 139.8	2 257.6	4 277.9	7 456.5	10 595.4	903.1	1 587.8	2 231.6	3 318.2	09000
16.3	31.8	55.5	89.8	132.7	195.1	292.7	459.9	766.4	1 485.9	2 801.5	4 914.6	8 173.1	10 922.2	936.0	1 671.0	2 386.4	3 584.8	
6.2	12.8	18.5	28.1	38.9	59.4	101.9	198.7	398.1	904.6	1 974.9	4 059.3	7 281.0	10 357.9	877.9	1 534.9	2 147.1	3 202.6	

表 5.16　性・年齢別にみた死因
Table 5.16　Death rates (per 100,000 population) by sex, age and

死因簡単分類コード Code[a]	死因・性 Causes of death and sex		総数 Total	0歳[1] Year	1	2	3	4	1～4	0～4	5～9	10～14	15～19	20～24	25～29	30～34
09100	高血圧性疾患	総数 T.	5.5	-	-	-	-	-	-	-	-	-	-	-	-	0.1
		男 M.	4.5	-	-	-	-	-	-	-	-	-	-	-	-	0.2
		女 F.	6.4	-	-	-	-	-	-	-	-	-	-	-	-	0.0
09101	高血圧性心疾患及び心腎疾患	総数 T.	2.5	-	-	-	-	-	-	-	-	-	-	-	-	0.1
		男 M.	1.9	-	-	-	-	-	-	-	-	-	-	-	-	0.1
		女 F.	3.0	-	-	-	-	-	-	-	-	-	-	-	-	-
09102	その他の高血圧性疾患	総数 T.	3.0	-	-	-	-	-	-	-	-	-	-	-	-	0.1
		男 M.	2.6	-	-	-	-	-	-	-	-	-	-	-	-	0.1
		女 F.	3.4	-	-	-	-	-	-	-	-	-	-	-	-	0.0
09200	心疾患（高血圧性を除く）	総数 T.	158.4	4.2	2.0	0.9	0.8	0.4	1.0	1.7	0.3	0.3	0.8	1.8	2.5	3.5
		男 M.	153.5	4.2	2.1	1.4	1.0	0.8	1.3	1.9	0.4	0.4	1.1	2.5	3.4	5.7
		女 F.	163.0	4.2	1.9	0.4	0.6	-	0.7	1.4	0.2	0.3	0.4	1.1	1.7	1.3
09201	慢性リウマチ性心疾患	総数 T.	1.8										0.0			0.0
		男 M.	1.2												-	0.1
		女 F.	2.4										0.0			-
09202	急性心筋梗塞	総数 T.	28.7									0.1	0.0	0.1	0.2	0.7
		男 M.	33.6									0.0	0.0	0.2	0.3	1.1
		女 F.	24.1									0.1	-	-	0.1	0.2
09203	その他の虚血性心疾患	総数 T.	27.6		-	0.1	-		0.0	0.0	0.0		0.0	0.2	0.3	0.6
		男 M.	32.8		-	-	-		-	-	-		0.0	0.3	0.4	1.0
		女 F.	22.7		-	0.2	-		0.1	0.0	0.0		0.0	0.2	0.2	0.2
09204	慢性非リウマチ性心内膜疾患	総数 T.	8.8										0.0	0.0	0.0	0.0
		男 M.	5.7										0.0	0.0	0.0	0.0
		女 F.	11.8										-	-	0.0	-
09205	心筋症	総数 T.	3.0	1.8	0.4	0.2	0.2	0.1	0.2	0.6	0.1	0.1	0.2	0.3	0.3	0.2
		男 M.	3.5	1.4	0.4	0.2	0.2	0.2	0.3	0.5	0.1	0.1	0.3	0.3	0.4	0.3
		女 F.	2.6	2.3	0.4	0.2	0.2	-	0.2	0.6	-	0.0	0.1	0.2	0.1	0.1
09206	不整脈及び伝導障害	総数 T.	24.8	0.4	0.1	0.2	0.2		0.1	0.2	0.1	0.1	0.2	0.5	0.9	0.9
		男 M.	24.8	0.6	-	0.4	0.2		0.2	0.2	0.1	0.1	0.4	0.8	1.3	1.5
		女 F.	24.8	0.2	0.2	-	0.2		0.1	0.1	0.1	0.0	0.1	0.1	0.5	0.3
09207	心不全	総数 T.	58.8	0.3	0.4	0.1	0.1	0.1	0.2	0.2	0.0	0.1	0.1	0.4	0.5	0.5
		男 M.	46.4	-	0.2	0.2	0.2	0.2	0.2	0.2	0.0	0.0	0.2	0.4	0.7	0.9
		女 F.	70.6	0.6	0.6	-	-		0.2	0.2	-	0.1	-	0.3	0.4	0.1
09208	その他の心疾患	総数 T.	4.7	1.6	1.1	0.3	0.3	0.2	0.5	0.7	0.1	0.1	0.2	0.4	0.3	0.6
		男 M.	5.3	2.2	1.4	0.6	0.4	0.4	0.7	1.0	0.1	0.1	0.2	0.5	0.5	0.8
		女 F.	4.1	1.1	0.6	-	0.2	-	0.2	0.4	0.1	0.1	0.1	0.2	0.3	0.3
09300	脳血管疾患	総数 T.	87.4	0.4	0.1	0.3	-	0.1	0.1	0.2	0.1	0.2	0.3	0.4	0.8	1.7
		男 M.	86.6	0.2	-	0.4	-	0.2	0.2	0.2	0.1	0.3	0.3	0.5	1.1	2.3
		女 F.	88.2	0.6	0.2	0.2	-	-	0.1	0.2	0.2	0.1	0.2	0.4	0.4	1.1
09301	くも膜下出血	総数 T.	9.9	0.1	-	0.1	-	-	0.0	0.0	0.0	0.1	0.1	0.2	0.4	0.8
		男 M.	7.5	-	-	-	-	-	-	-	0.0	0.1	0.2	0.3	0.5	1.0
		女 F.	12.1	0.2	-	0.2	-	-	0.1	0.1	0.0	0.1	0.1	0.1	0.3	0.6
09302	脳内出血	総数 T.	25.6	0.2	0.1	0.2	-	0.1	0.1	0.1	0.1	0.1	0.1	0.1	0.3	0.7
		男 M.	28.8	-		0.4		0.2	0.2	0.1	0.1	0.2	0.1	0.1	0.4	1.0
		女 F.	22.5	0.4	0.2	-	-		0.1	0.1	0.1	0.1	0.1	0.1	0.1	0.3
09303	脳梗塞	総数 T.	49.8	0.1	-	-	-	-	-	0.0	-	-	0.0	0.1	0.0	0.1
		男 M.	48.3	0.2	-	-	-	-	-	0.0	-	-	0.0	-	0.0	0.1
		女 F.	51.3	-	-	-	-	-	-	-	-	-	-	0.1	0.0	0.1
09304	その他の脳血管疾患	総数 T.	2.2										0.0	0.0	0.0	0.1
		男 M.	2.0										0.0	-	-	0.2
		女 F.	2.4										0.0	0.0	0.0	0.0
09400	大動脈瘤及び解離	総数 T.	14.5										0.0	0.1	0.0	0.2
		男 M.	15.2										0.0	0.2	0.1	0.3
		女 F.	13.8										0.0	0.1	0.0	0.0
09500	その他の循環器系の疾患	総数 T.	6.0	0.2	-	-	0.1		-	0.0	0.1		-	0.2	0.1	0.2
		男 M.	5.7	0.4	-	-	-		-	0.1	0.1		0.1	0.3	0.2	0.3
		女 F.	6.3	-	-	-	0.2		0.1	0.0	-		-	0.1	-	0.1

簡単分類別死亡率（人口10万対）（つづき）
causes (the condensed list of causes of death for Japan)：Japan, 2016－CON.

平成28年

35～39	40～44	45～49	50～54	55～59	60～64	65～69	70～74	75～79	80～84	85～89	90～94	95～99	100～	65～	75～	80～	85～	死因簡単分類コード[a] Code[a]
0.1	0.2	0.4	0.6	1.2	1.8	2.8	4.5	7.5	19.1	43.4	111.4	261.3	487.7	18.8	34.7	51.8	84.3	09100
0.1	0.2	0.8	1.3	2.2	3.1	4.5	6.7	10.0	23.2	49.7	107.7	265.7	433.3	16.1	29.8	45.4	75.0	
0.1	0.1	0.1	0.0	0.2	0.6	1.3	2.6	5.4	16.4	40.2	112.7	259.5	487.7	20.9	37.9	55.3	88.4	
0.0	0.1	0.2	0.3	0.5	0.8	1.3	2.0	3.2	8.1	20.2	54.4	119.1	173.8	8.5	15.8	23.7	39.1	09101
0.1	0.1	0.4	0.5	1.0	1.3	2.1	3.0	3.7	8.7	20.2	49.3	120.9	166.7	6.7	12.1	18.8	32.4	
-	0.0	0.0	-	0.1	0.3	0.6	1.1	2.7	7.7	20.2	56.1	118.4	171.9	9.9	18.1	26.3	42.1	
0.1	0.1	0.2	0.4	0.7	1.1	1.5	2.5	4.3	11.0	23.2	57.0	142.1	313.8	10.3	19.0	28.2	45.2	09102
0.0	0.2	0.3	0.7	1.3	1.8	2.4	3.6	6.4	14.5	29.4	58.4	144.8	266.7	9.4	17.7	26.6	42.7	
0.1	0.0	0.1	0.0	0.1	0.3	0.7	1.6	2.7	8.7	20.0	56.6	141.1	315.8	11.0	19.8	29.0	46.3	
6.2	11.5	19.9	31.8	46.7	71.9	110.5	181.1	314.4	639.4	1 323.5	2 601.6	4 685.3	6 884.6	528.6	934.1	1 323.1	2 003.5	09200
9.4	17.1	31.4	51.2	76.7	116.3	172.0	264.2	425.3	822.9	1 623.0	2 992.0	5 286.6	7 644.4	540.5	963.5	1 389.1	2 142.6	
3.0	5.6	8.1	12.2	16.9	28.8	52.8	108.6	225.3	514.8	1 167.9	2 467.6	4 543.0	6 643.9	519.4	915.4	1 287.0	1 943.1	
0.0	0.0	0.0	0.1	0.1	0.5	0.8	2.2	4.1	7.6	17.9	31.3	56.0	58.5	6.4	11.6	16.3	25.0	09201
0.0	0.0	0.0	0.1	0.2	0.6	1.0	1.8	4.1	7.6	15.0	30.5	34.3	44.4	4.7	9.0	12.8	19.7	
0.1	0.0	-	0.0	0.1	0.3	0.6	2.5	4.1	7.5	19.4	31.5	60.4	59.6	7.7	13.3	18.2	27.3	
1.3	3.1	5.7	9.9	14.6	20.9	29.9	45.0	70.7	126.7	212.7	335.3	442.4	433.8	91.1	148.3	197.1	267.2	09202
2.1	4.9	9.8	16.9	25.6	35.2	48.6	68.1	102.3	171.6	285.9	445.6	607.5	477.8	111.2	181.1	243.5	339.1	
0.6	1.1	1.6	2.8	3.6	7.1	12.4	24.7	45.3	96.1	174.6	297.4	406.0	419.3	75.6	127.5	171.7	236.0	
1.3	2.7	5.2	7.5	11.5	18.9	29.1	45.9	73.1	123.0	201.5	306.5	435.6	604.6	88.9	144.0	188.4	253.6	09203
2.0	4.1	8.4	12.2	19.4	31.5	47.3	71.7	103.0	171.1	290.4	440.3	616.4	944.4	112.2	182.5	245.3	344.1	
0.6	1.3	1.8	2.8	3.6	6.8	12.1	23.3	49.0	90.4	155.3	260.6	395.9	540.4	71.0	119.5	157.4	214.3	
0.1	0.1	0.2	0.3	0.6	1.1	2.2	5.3	11.3	34.2	92.5	206.0	361.5	446.2	31.5	60.7	91.7	148.9	09204
0.1	0.2	0.2	0.5	0.9	1.5	2.8	6.4	13.4	36.3	90.4	162.3	295.5	366.7	22.5	45.8	71.4	118.0	
0.1	0.0	0.2	0.2	0.3	0.8	1.6	4.3	9.7	32.7	93.5	221.0	374.4	450.9	38.4	70.2	102.8	162.4	
0.4	0.5	0.9	1.4	1.6	2.3	3.5	5.3	7.9	12.7	20.3	26.8	36.6	23.1	9.1	14.1	18.1	23.4	09205
0.6	0.9	1.3	2.2	2.4	3.5	5.4	7.8	11.1	17.2	25.2	30.5	49.3	33.3	11.0	17.0	21.7	27.6	
0.2	0.2	0.4	0.6	0.8	1.2	1.6	3.0	5.4	9.7	17.8	25.5	33.9	21.1	7.6	12.3	16.1	21.6	
1.5	2.3	3.4	5.2	7.9	12.3	18.3	28.2	50.2	103.3	212.4	391.1	638.7	812.3	81.9	144.0	202.9	302.0	09206
2.2	3.4	5.1	8.3	13.0	19.8	28.4	40.3	67.1	135.4	265.8	471.6	734.3	1 000.0	86.3	154.1	222.9	339.4	
0.7	1.3	1.8	2.1	2.8	4.9	8.8	17.7	36.7	81.5	184.6	363.4	616.5	768.4	78.6	137.6	191.9	285.7	
0.9	1.6	2.9	5.0	7.3	12.2	21.0	41.9	85.6	212.3	537.4	1 263.7	2 661.5	4 444.6	206.1	390.2	581.5	948.9	09207
1.4	2.1	4.4	7.5	10.5	18.5	30.1	57.5	108.9	259.3	614.1	1 362.6	2 873.1	4 666.7	176.6	349.6	539.9	913.5	
0.4	1.1	1.5	2.5	4.0	6.0	12.4	28.3	66.8	180.3	497.5	1 229.7	2 608.2	4 331.6	228.7	416.1	604.2	964.3	
0.7	1.1	1.6	2.4	3.2	3.7	5.7	7.4	11.5	19.7	28.9	41.0	52.9	61.5	13.6	21.1	27.1	34.5	09208
0.9	1.5	2.2	3.6	4.8	5.8	8.4	10.4	15.5	24.4	36.1	48.5	76.1	111.1	15.9	24.5	31.6	41.2	
0.4	0.6	0.9	1.1	1.7	1.7	3.2	4.7	8.2	16.5	25.2	38.4	47.8	52.6	11.8	18.9	24.7	31.6	
3.9	8.6	13.2	20.9	28.8	41.1	61.4	104.0	191.6	388.9	726.8	1 307.5	2 161.5	2 861.5	289.2	508.3	707.2	1 024.0	09300
5.3	11.3	17.9	28.6	39.6	59.1	89.2	149.2	268.8	525.4	924.2	1 496.0	2 238.8	2 544.4	307.9	556.2	783.5	1 126.9	
2.4	5.9	8.3	13.1	18.0	23.5	35.3	64.5	129.6	296.1	624.3	1 242.7	2 138.3	2 861.4	274.8	477.9	665.5	979.3	
2.0	4.3	5.8	8.0	8.8	10.0	12.3	16.5	22.6	38.3	53.3	68.4	81.4	63.1	26.2	38.8	49.0	59.7	09301
2.7	4.8	7.0	8.7	10.3	11.2	11.4	13.8	16.5	24.4	36.1	45.6	59.7	77.8	17.7	24.5	30.9	39.6	
1.3	3.6	4.6	7.2	7.3	8.9	13.2	18.9	27.6	47.7	62.2	76.2	85.8	59.6	32.7	47.9	58.9	68.5	
1.4	3.7	6.2	10.5	15.4	20.8	27.2	39.9	65.5	119.0	178.9	262.8	301.8	300.0	78.9	127.4	166.3	213.2	09302
2.1	5.6	9.4	16.1	22.6	31.9	42.3	58.4	90.2	157.6	224.4	313.5	313.4	266.7	93.2	149.9	197.2	249.8	
0.7	1.7	2.8	4.7	8.2	9.9	13.0	23.8	45.7	92.9	155.2	245.4	298.4	300.0	68.0	113.1	149.4	197.4	
0.3	0.5	0.9	1.8	3.9	8.8	20.0	45.0	98.6	222.6	476.7	946.1	1 726.2	2 409.2	176.9	329.8	475.0	726.1	09303
0.3	0.6	1.1	3.0	5.7	13.8	32.6	73.7	156.2	333.0	643.9	1 106.4	1 814.9	2 066.7	190.1	369.9	539.0	813.1	
0.3	0.3	0.6	0.6	2.0	3.9	8.2	19.9	52.4	147.6	389.7	891.1	1 701.9	2 421.1	166.9	304.4	440.0	688.4	
0.1	0.2	0.3	0.6	0.8	1.5	1.9	2.6	4.8	9.0	18.0	30.2	52.1	89.2	7.1	12.3	16.9	24.9	09304
0.1	0.2	0.3	0.8	1.0	2.2	2.8	3.4	6.0	10.5	19.8	30.5	50.7	133.3	6.9	11.8	16.4	24.3	
0.1	0.2	0.3	0.5	0.5	0.8	1.0	2.0	3.9	7.9	17.1	30.1	52.2	80.7	7.3	12.5	17.2	25.1	
0.6	1.2	2.0	3.6	6.2	8.5	14.9	23.3	36.2	68.0	119.1	170.2	193.7	146.2	47.4	77.7	103.8	139.4	09400
1.1	2.2	3.4	5.8	10.0	12.6	20.8	29.4	46.3	83.6	149.9	229.7	234.3	122.2	52.4	88.5	121.8	172.5	
0.1	0.2	0.5	1.3	2.3	4.6	9.4	17.9	28.1	57.4	103.1	149.7	184.5	147.4	43.6	70.9	94.0	125.1	
0.5	1.0	1.7	2.2	2.8	2.9	4.7	7.6	12.4	24.4	44.7	87.3	154.7	215.4	19.1	32.9	45.7	67.0	09500
0.5	1.0	2.0	3.0	4.2	4.0	6.3	10.5	15.9	30.8	54.8	89.1	147.8	177.8	19.0	33.0	46.6	67.7	
0.6	1.0	1.4	1.5	1.4	1.9	3.1	5.0	9.7	20.0	39.5	86.6	155.7	217.5	19.2	32.8	45.3	66.7	

死 亡

表 5.16 性・年齢別にみた死因
Table 5.16 Death rates (per 100,000 population) by sex, age and

死因簡単分類コード Code[a]	死因・性 Causes of death and sex		総数 Total	0歳[1] Year	1	2	3	4	1～4	0～4	5～9	10～14	15～19	20～24	25～29	30～34
10000	呼吸器系の疾患	総数 T.	166.9	9.8	4.1	2.2	1.7	1.7	2.4	3.9	0.8	0.6	0.6	0.7	1.0	1.3
		男 M.	197.5	11.4	4.6	1.8	2.6	1.9	2.7	4.4	0.7	0.6	0.6	0.6	1.4	1.7
		女 F.	137.7	8.2	3.7	2.6	0.8	1.4	2.1	3.3	0.8	0.7	0.6	0.8	0.6	0.8
10100	インフルエンザ	総数 T.	1.2	0.2	0.6	0.3	0.4	0.6	0.5	0.4	0.1	0.2	0.1	0.0	0.0	0.1
		男 M.	1.2	0.2	0.6	0.6	0.6	0.6	0.6	0.5	0.1	0.2	0.1	0.0	0.0	0.1
		女 F.	1.1	0.2	0.6	-	0.2	0.6	0.4	0.3	0.1	0.1	0.0	0.0	0.0	0.1
10200	肺　　　炎	総数 T.	95.4	2.9	1.4	0.4	1.0	0.8	0.9	1.3	0.4	0.2	0.2	0.3	0.5	0.7
		男 M.	107.8	3.0	1.2	0.2	1.6	0.8	1.0	1.4	0.3	0.3	0.1	0.3	0.6	0.9
		女 F.	83.6	2.7	1.5	0.6	0.4	0.8	0.8	1.2	0.4	0.2	0.3	0.3	0.4	0.4
10300	急性気管支炎	総数 T.	0.4	0.6	0.2	0.3			0.1	0.2	0.1	0.0				
		男 M.	0.3	1.2	0.4	0.2			0.2	0.4	0.1	0.0				
		女 F.	0.4				0.4		0.1	0.1	0.1					
10400	慢性閉塞性肺疾患	総数 T.	12.5	-	-	-	-	-	-	-	-	-	0.0	0.0	-	0.1
		男 M.	20.8	-	-	-	-	-	-	-	-	-	0.0	0.0	-	0.1
		女 F.	4.7										-	-	-	0.0
10500	喘　　　息	総数 T.	1.2	-	0.2	0.1	-	0.1	0.1	0.1	0.0		0.0		0.0	0.1
		男 M.	0.9		0.2	0.2		0.2	0.2	0.1	0.0				0.1	0.1
		女 F.	1.4		0.2				0.1	0.1	0.0		0.0			0.1
10600	その他の呼吸器系の疾患	総数 T.	56.2	6.1	1.7	1.0	0.3	0.2	0.8	1.9	0.2	0.2	0.3	0.3	0.4	0.4
		男 M.	66.4	7.0	2.1	0.6	0.4	0.4	0.9	2.1	0.1	0.1	0.3	0.3	0.6	0.6
		女 F.	46.5	5.3	1.3	1.5	0.2	-	0.7	1.6	0.2	0.3	0.2	0.4	0.2	0.2
11000	消化器系の疾患	総数 T.	39.0	6.4	0.7	0.4	0.7	0.3	0.5	1.7	0.2	0.2	0.3	0.4	0.6	1.3
		男 M.	42.1	5.6	1.0	0.4	1.2	0.2	0.7	1.7	0.3	0.3	0.4	0.6	0.7	1.6
		女 F.	36.1	7.4	0.4	0.4	0.2	0.4	0.4	1.8	0.1	0.1	0.3	0.2	0.5	1.0
11100	胃潰瘍及び十二指腸潰瘍	総数 T.	2.1		-	0.1	-	-	0.0	0.0	0.0		0.1	0.1	-	0.1
		男 M.	2.5		-	0.2	-	-	0.1	0.0	0.0		0.1	0.1	-	0.1
		女 F.	1.8						-	-	-		0.0	0.0		
11200	ヘルニア及び腸閉塞	総数 T.	5.6	1.2	0.2	0.1	0.3	-	0.2	0.4	0.0	0.0	0.1	0.1	0.1	0.1
		男 M.	5.4	1.2	0.4	-	0.4	-	0.2	0.4	0.0	0.0	0.1	0.1	0.2	0.1
		女 F.	5.8	1.3	-	0.2	0.2	-	0.1	0.3	0.0	0.0	0.0	0.1	-	0.1
11300	肝　　疾　　患	総数 T.	12.6	1.1	0.4	0.1	0.1	-	0.2	0.3	0.1	0.1	0.1	0.1	0.1	0.8
		男 M.	16.6	1.0	0.6	0.2	0.2	-	0.3	0.4	0.1	0.1	0.0	0.2	0.2	0.9
		女 F.	8.8	1.3	0.2	-	-	-	0.1	0.1	-	-	0.1	-	0.1	0.6
11301	肝硬変(アルコール性を除く)	総数 T.	6.2	0.2	0.3	-	-	-	0.1	0.1	-	-	-	0.0	0.0	0.1
		男 M.	6.8	0.2	0.4	-	-	-	0.1	0.1	-	-	-	0.0	0.1	0.1
		女 F.	5.5	0.2	0.2	-	-	-	0.1	0.1	-	-	-	-	-	0.1
11302	その他の肝疾患	総数 T.	6.5	0.9	0.1	0.1	0.1	-	0.1	0.2	0.1	0.1	0.1	0.1	0.1	0.7
		男 M.	9.8	0.8	0.2	0.2	0.2	-	0.2	0.3	0.1	0.1	0.0	0.1	0.1	0.8
		女 F.	3.3	1.1	-	-	-	-	-	0.2	-	0.0	0.1	-	0.1	0.5
11400	その他の消化器系の疾患	総数 T.	18.7	4.1	0.1	0.1	0.3	0.3	0.2	1.0	0.1	0.1	0.2	0.2	0.4	0.4
		男 M.	17.6	3.4	-	-	0.6	0.2	0.2	0.8	0.1	0.1	0.2	0.3	0.4	0.4
		女 F.	19.7	4.8	0.2	0.2	-	0.4	0.2	1.1	0.1	0.0	0.2	0.1	0.4	0.3
12000	皮膚及び皮下組織の疾患	総数 T.	1.3	-	-	0.1	-	-	0.0	0.0	-	-	-	-	0.0	0.0
		男 M.	1.0	-	-	0.2	-	-	0.1	0.0	-	-	-	-	0.1	0.1
		女 F.	1.6						-	-					-	
13000	筋骨格系及び結合組織の疾患	総数 T.	5.2	0.1	-	-	-	0.1	0.0	0.0	0.0	0.1	0.0	0.1	0.1	0.2
		男 M.	4.2	0.2	-	-	-	-	-	0.0	0.0	0.1	0.0	-	0.1	0.1
		女 F.	6.1	-	-	-	-	0.2	0.1	0.0	-	0.1	-	0.2	0.1	0.2
14000	腎尿路生殖器系の疾患	総数 T.	30.9	0.4	0.1	0.1	0.1	0.2	0.1	0.2	0.1	0.1	0.1	0.1	0.1	0.2
		男 M.	28.6	0.4	0.2	0.2	0.2	0.2	0.2	0.2	0.1	0.1	0.1	0.0	0.1	0.1
		女 F.	33.0	0.4	-	-	-	0.2	0.1	0.1	0.2	0.0	0.1	0.1	0.2	0.3
14100	糸球体疾患及び腎尿細管間質性疾患	総数 T.	4.0	0.1	0.1	-	-	-	0.0	0.0	-	-	-	0.0	-	0.0
		男 M.	3.2	-	0.2	-	-	-	0.1	0.0	0.0	0.0	-	0.0	-	
		女 F.	4.8	0.2	-	-	-	-	-	0.0	-	-	-	0.0	-	0.1
14200	腎　　不　　全	総数 T.	19.7	0.2	-	0.1	-	0.1	0.1	0.1	0.0	0.1	0.1	0.0	0.1	0.1
		男 M.	20.1	0.2	-	0.2	-	-	0.1	0.1	0.0	0.1	0.0	-	0.0	0.1
		女 F.	19.3	0.2	-	-	-	0.2	0.1	0.1	0.0	0.0	0.1	0.0	0.1	0.1

簡単分類別死亡率（人口10万対）（つづき）
causes (the condensed list of causes of death for Japan)：Japan, 2016－CON.

平成28年

35～39	40～44	45～49	50～54	55～59	60～64	65～69	70～74	75～79	80～84	85～89	90～94	95～99	100～	65～	75～	80～	85～	死因簡単分類コード Code[a]
1.9	2.9	4.7	8.9	16.8	36.7	70.8	163.9	349.8	783.7	1 633.0	2 931.0	4 878.8	7 044.6	587.3	1 085.8	1 547.7	2 308.1	10000
2.8	3.6	6.6	12.2	24.7	57.3	113.3	263.3	564.4	1 290.8	2 804.2	5 144.6	8 883.6	11 322.2	774.3	1 541.1	2 313.5	3 674.5	
1.0	2.1	2.7	5.5	9.0	16.6	30.9	77.2	177.5	439.1	1 024.2	2 170.9	4 014.2	6 245.6	444.2	796.1	1 129.2	1 715.4	
0.2	0.2	0.2	0.4	0.4	0.7	0.8	1.2	2.2	5.0	8.8	15.6	33.8	50.8	3.6	6.4	9.0	13.1	10100
0.2	0.3	0.3	0.5	0.4	0.8	1.3	1.7	2.8	6.8	13.2	22.0	50.7	66.7	4.1	7.6	11.3	17.3	
0.1	0.2	0.1	0.3	0.3	0.5	0.4	0.9	1.6	3.7	6.4	13.4	30.1	47.4	3.2	5.6	7.8	11.2	
0.9	1.3	2.5	4.7	9.1	19.3	36.2	81.8	179.7	430.4	954.1	1 791.1	3 116.8	4 498.5	336.9	630.8	914.0	1 395.3	10200
1.4	1.7	3.5	6.7	13.3	30.3	57.7	130.3	285.7	692.2	1 576.2	2 992.3	5 455.2	7 044.4	423.4	853.1	1 301.8	2 113.2	
0.5	0.9	1.4	2.7	4.8	8.6	16.0	39.5	94.6	252.5	630.7	1 378.6	2 611.1	4 017.5	270.6	489.4	702.0	1 083.9	
-	-	-	0.0	0.0	0.1	0.1	0.2	0.6	1.1	3.1	8.0	15.7	43.1	1.2	2.4	3.5	5.9	10300
-	-	-	0.0	0.0	0.1	0.1	0.3	0.8	1.5	4.3	9.8	26.9	33.3	1.2	2.5	3.8	6.8	
-	-	-	0.0	0.0	0.1	0.1	0.1	0.4	0.7	2.5	7.4	13.3	43.9	1.3	2.3	3.4	5.6	
0.0	0.1	0.2	0.3	1.2	2.8	6.7	17.9	34.6	71.5	123.5	167.7	186.1	212.3	44.4	78.9	106.7	141.8	10400
0.0	0.1	0.2	0.4	2.0	4.9	12.1	33.6	67.1	149.0	292.4	479.3	603.0	622.2	82.6	161.6	236.3	352.4	
0.1	0.1	0.1	0.2	0.4	0.8	1.7	4.3	8.5	18.9	35.7	60.7	97.2	143.9	15.2	26.3	35.9	50.4	
0.2	0.2	0.2	0.3	0.4	0.5	0.7	1.1	2.2	4.6	8.7	19.6	38.5	64.6	3.8	6.8	9.6	14.7	10500
0.2	0.2	0.3	0.3	0.5	0.5	0.9	1.4	2.4	4.5	9.2	20.4	55.2	66.7	3.2	5.9	8.7	14.2	
0.1	0.2	0.2	0.3	0.3	0.5	0.6	0.9	2.1	4.6	8.5	19.3	34.8	63.2	4.2	7.3	10.2	14.9	
0.6	1.0	1.7	3.2	5.8	13.3	26.2	61.6	130.6	271.2	534.8	929.0	1 488.0	2 175.4	197.4	360.5	504.9	737.4	10600
1.0	1.3	2.3	4.4	8.4	20.7	41.3	96.0	205.6	436.7	908.8	1 620.7	2 692.5	3 488.9	259.8	510.5	751.6	1 170.7	
0.2	0.6	1.0	1.9	3.2	6.2	12.1	31.6	70.4	158.7	340.4	691.5	1 227.8	1 929.8	149.6	265.1	370.0	549.4	
2.3	5.6	10.0	16.0	22.4	29.4	37.8	54.5	88.1	158.3	280.9	477.6	756.3	972.3	120.5	199.6	269.6	380.4	11000
3.0	8.1	15.0	24.9	35.4	46.9	59.1	78.6	119.9	206.7	350.3	551.5	832.8	944.4	134.2	220.1	299.3	422.6	
1.6	3.0	4.8	7.0	9.4	12.4	17.8	33.4	62.5	125.4	244.8	452.2	737.7	959.6	110.0	186.6	253.4	362.0	
0.1	0.2	0.3	0.6	1.0	1.2	2.3	3.4	4.5	9.2	15.5	29.2	40.6	40.0	6.9	11.2	15.4	21.5	11100
0.1	0.2	0.4	1.2	1.6	2.0	4.2	5.4	6.4	12.9	22.4	41.4	50.7	44.4	8.7	13.7	19.5	28.3	
0.0	0.1	0.1	0.1	0.4	0.4	0.6	1.6	2.9	6.7	12.0	25.0	38.3	38.6	5.5	9.6	13.1	18.6	
0.1	0.2	0.4	0.7	1.0	1.8	2.9	6.1	11.8	25.5	53.3	92.5	140.8	166.2	19.1	34.6	49.0	72.3	11200
0.1	0.3	0.6	0.9	1.3	2.6	4.0	8.6	16.4	35.6	68.0	110.9	156.7	188.9	20.2	38.4	55.8	82.8	
0.2	0.1	0.2	0.6	0.7	1.0	1.8	3.9	8.0	18.7	45.6	86.2	137.0	159.6	18.3	32.2	45.2	67.7	
1.6	3.9	7.3	11.5	15.4	19.2	20.6	23.9	32.6	42.6	50.2	56.2	57.1	53.8	31.7	41.8	47.5	52.4	11300
2.0	5.7	11.3	18.1	25.1	31.2	33.0	35.4	44.9	53.3	62.1	73.2	67.2	66.0	42.0	52.4	58.3	65.0	
1.1	2.1	3.2	4.9	5.8	7.5	9.0	13.9	22.7	35.3	44.0	50.4	54.7	50.9	23.7	35.0	41.6	47.0	
0.4	1.0	2.2	3.9	5.9	7.6	9.0	12.1	18.7	26.9	31.3	31.1	23.8	10.8	17.4	24.8	28.7	30.4	11301
0.5	1.4	3.4	5.7	8.8	11.2	12.7	15.3	21.4	28.4	32.8	37.1	35.8	11.1	19.4	26.6	30.8	33.9	
0.3	0.7	1.0	2.0	2.9	4.1	5.6	9.3	16.5	25.8	30.5	29.1	21.2	10.5	15.9	23.6	27.5	28.9	
1.2	2.9	5.1	7.6	9.6	11.6	11.5	11.8	13.9	15.7	18.9	25.1	33.2	43.1	14.2	16.9	18.9	22.0	11302
1.5	4.4	7.9	12.4	16.2	20.0	20.3	20.1	23.5	24.9	29.3	36.1	31.3	55.6	22.6	25.8	27.6	31.1	
0.8	1.4	2.2	2.8	2.9	3.3	3.4	4.6	6.2	9.5	13.5	21.3	33.5	40.4	7.8	11.3	14.1	18.0	
0.6	1.2	2.0	3.2	4.9	7.2	12.0	21.1	39.3	81.0	161.9	299.7	517.8	712.3	62.9	112.0	157.7	234.1	11400
0.8	1.8	2.7	4.8	7.4	11.1	17.9	29.3	52.2	104.8	197.8	326.0	558.2	644.4	63.4	115.6	165.6	246.5	
0.3	0.7	1.2	1.5	2.4	3.5	6.4	13.9	28.8	64.8	143.2	290.6	507.6	710.5	62.5	109.8	153.4	228.7	
0.0	0.1	0.1	0.2	0.3	0.5	0.9	1.2	2.4	5.1	11.1	22.8	49.2	95.4	4.5	8.1	11.7	18.3	12000
0.0	0.1	0.2	0.3	0.5	0.8	1.0	1.7	2.8	6.3	10.5	21.0	25.4	77.8	3.6	6.6	9.6	14.0	
0.0	0.1	0.1	0.1	0.2	0.3	0.8	0.8	2.0	4.3	11.4	23.4	54.1	96.5	5.1	9.1	12.9	20.1	
0.4	0.4	0.7	1.0	2.0	3.1	5.4	9.4	15.9	25.6	36.0	49.4	65.2	93.8	16.9	27.1	34.1	42.7	13000
0.3	0.3	0.5	0.9	2.0	3.2	5.3	9.9	15.5	25.5	36.6	53.8	71.6	77.8	15.1	25.2	32.8	42.5	
0.5	0.5	0.8	1.2	2.0	2.9	5.4	8.9	16.2	25.6	35.7	47.9	63.6	94.7	18.2	28.3	34.9	42.8	
0.3	0.6	1.2	2.3	4.0	8.4	15.3	28.9	61.2	141.1	306.4	550.2	900.5	1 030.8	108.0	198.8	285.1	428.4	14000
0.4	0.8	1.6	3.1	5.2	11.6	21.5	38.7	80.3	181.3	395.6	706.6	1 183.6	1 422.2	110.5	215.4	322.2	509.8	
0.3	0.5	0.7	1.5	2.9	5.2	9.5	20.3	45.8	113.8	260.1	496.5	837.7	950.9	106.0	188.2	264.8	393.2	
0.1	0.1	0.1	0.4	0.6	1.2	2.0	3.8	8.4	18.9	40.8	66.2	112.0	123.1	14.0	25.7	36.6	54.3	14100
0.1	0.1	0.1	0.4	0.7	1.7	2.6	4.2	10.2	19.3	44.3	71.4	117.9	133.3	12.2	23.7	34.4	54.4	
0.1	0.1	0.2	0.3	0.5	0.8	1.5	3.3	6.9	18.6	38.9	64.5	110.4	119.3	15.3	27.0	37.8	54.2	
0.2	0.4	0.8	1.5	2.7	5.7	10.3	19.2	39.8	89.5	196.2	346.3	551.3	590.8	68.7	125.9	179.9	269.9	14200
0.2	0.5	1.2	2.2	3.6	8.5	15.4	27.6	55.6	127.9	276.5	490.7	822.4	988.9	77.5	150.4	225.5	355.4	
0.2	0.2	0.4	0.9	1.8	3.0	5.5	11.8	27.1	63.5	154.4	296.7	492.1	517.5	62.1	110.2	155.0	232.8	

死　亡

表 5.16　性・年齢別にみた死因
Table 5.16　Death rates (per 100,000 population) by sex, age and

死因簡単分類コード Code[a]	死因・性 Causes of death and sex		総数 Total	0歳[1] Year	1	2	3	4	1～4	0～4	5～9	10～14	15～19	20～24	25～29	30～34
14201	急性腎不全	総数 T.	2.7	0.1	-	-	-	-	-	0.0	-	-	0.0	-	0.0	0.1
		男　M.	2.6	0.2	-	-	-	-	-	0.0	-	-	-	-	-	0.1
		女　F.	2.9	-	-	-	-	-	-	-	-	-	0.1	-	0.0	0.1
14202	慢性腎不全	総数 T.	12.8	-	-	-	-	-	-	-	0.0	0.0	0.0	-	0.0	-
		男　M.	13.4	-	-	-	-	-	-	-	0.0	0.0	0.0	-	0.0	-
		女　F.	12.2	-	-	-	-	-	-	-	0.0	-	-	-	0.0	-
14203	詳細不明の腎不全	総数 T.	4.2	0.1	-	0.1	-	0.1	0.1	0.1	-	0.0	-	0.0	0.0	0.0
		男　M.	4.1	-	-	0.2	-	-	0.1	0.0	-	0.0	-	-	-	0.0
		女　F.	4.3	0.2	-	-	-	0.2	0.1	0.1	-	0.0	-	0.0	0.0	0.1
14300	その他の腎尿路生殖器系の疾患	総数 T.	7.2	0.1	-	-	0.1	0.1	0.1	0.1	0.1	-	0.0	-	0.1	0.0
		男　M.	5.3	0.2	-	-	0.2	0.2	0.1	0.1	-	-	0.0	-	0.1	-
		女　F.	8.9	-	-	-	-	-	-	-	0.1	-	0.0	0.1	0.1	0.1
15000	妊娠，分娩及び産じょく	女　F.	0.1	-	-	-	-	-	-	-	-	-	-	0.1	0.3	0.4
16000	周産期に発生した病態	総数 T.	0.4	52.1	0.6	0.3	0.1	-	0.3	10.6	0.1	0.0	0.0	0.0	0.0	-
		男　M.	0.4	50.0	0.6	0.4	-	-	0.3	10.2	0.0	-	-	0.0	-	-
		女　F.	0.4	54.3	0.6	0.2	0.2	-	0.3	11.0	0.1	0.0	-	-	-	-
16100	妊娠期間及び胎児発育に関連する障害	総数 T.	0.0	4.4	-	-	-	-	-	0.9	-	-	-	-	-	-
		男　M.	0.0	4.2	-	-	-	-	-	0.8	-	-	-	-	-	-
		女　F.	0.0	4.6	-	-	-	-	-	0.9	-	-	-	-	-	-
16200	出産外傷	総数 T.	0.0	0.3	-	-	-	-	-	0.1	-	-	-	-	-	-
		男　M.	-	-												
		女　F.	0.0	0.6	-	-	-	-	-	0.1	-	-	-	-	-	-
16300	周産期に特異的な呼吸障害及び心血管障害	総数 T.	0.2	28.9	0.3	0.1	-	-	0.1	5.8	-	-	-	0.0	0.0	-
		男　M.	0.2	28.9	0.6	0.2	-	-	0.2	5.9	-	-	-	-	0.0	-
		女　F.	0.2	28.8	-	-	-	-	-	5.7	-	-	0.0	-	-	-
16400	周産期に特異的な感染症	総数 T.	0.0	4.4	-	-	-	-	-	0.9	-	-	-	-	-	-
		男　M.	0.0	5.6	-	-	-	-	-	1.1	-	-	-	-	-	-
		女　F.	0.0	3.2	-	-	-	-	-	0.6	-	-	-	-	-	-
16500	胎児及び新生児の出血性障害及び血液障害	総数 T.	0.1	6.9	-	-	-	-	-	1.4	-	-	0.0	-	-	-
		男　M.	0.0	5.6	-	-	-	-	-	1.1	-	-	-	-	-	-
		女　F.	0.1	8.2	-	-	-	-	-	1.6	-	-	-	-	-	-
16600	その他の周産期に発生した病態	総数 T.	0.1	7.3	0.3	0.2	0.1	-	0.2	1.6	0.1	0.0	-	-	-	-
		男　M.	0.1	5.8	-	0.2	-	-	0.1	1.2	0.0	0.0	-	-	-	-
		女　F.	0.1	8.8	0.6	0.2	0.2	-	0.3	2.0	0.1	0.0	-	-	-	-
17000	先天奇形，変形及び染色体異常	総数 T.	1.6	67.9	8.3	4.2	1.5	1.6	3.8	16.6	0.6	0.5	0.4	0.6	0.4	0.5
		男　M.	1.6	64.4	7.2	4.3	1.4	1.8	3.6	15.8	0.6	0.3	0.5	0.7	0.4	0.5
		女　F.	1.7	71.6	9.5	4.1	1.6	1.4	4.1	17.5	0.6	0.7	0.3	0.5	0.3	0.4
17100	神経系の先天奇形	総数 T.	0.1	3.0	0.2	0.1	0.4	0.3	0.3	0.8	0.1	0.1	0.1	0.1	0.0	0.1
		男　M.	0.1	2.2	0.2	-	0.4	0.4	0.3	0.6	0.1	-	0.1	-	0.0	0.1
		女　F.	0.1	3.8	0.2	0.2	0.4	0.2	0.3	1.0	0.1	0.1	0.1	0.1	-	0.1
17200	循環器系の先天奇形	総数 T.	0.7	25.1	3.6	1.9	0.6	0.8	1.7	6.4	0.2	0.2	0.3	0.3	0.2	0.3
		男　M.	0.7	23.9	2.7	1.8	0.8	0.8	1.5	6.0	0.2	0.2	0.3	0.4	0.3	0.3
		女　F.	0.8	26.3	4.5	1.9	0.4	0.8	1.9	6.7	0.2	0.3	0.2	0.2	0.1	0.3
17201	心臓の先天奇形	総数 T.	0.5	16.5	3.0	1.3	0.5	0.6	1.3	4.3	0.1	0.2	0.2	0.2	0.1	0.2
		男　M.	0.4	15.1	2.3	1.2	0.6	0.6	1.2	4.0	0.2	0.1	0.3	0.3	0.2	0.3
		女　F.	0.5	17.9	3.7	1.3	0.4	0.6	1.5	4.7	0.1	0.3	0.1	0.2	0.1	0.2
17202	その他の循環器系の先天奇形	総数 T.	0.3	8.6	0.6	0.6	0.1	0.2	0.4	2.0	0.1	0.0	0.0	0.1	0.0	0.0
		男　M.	0.2	8.8	0.4	0.6	0.2	0.2	0.4	2.0	0.0	-	0.1	0.1	-	-
		女　F.	0.3	8.4	0.9	0.6	-	0.2	0.4	2.0	0.1	-	0.1	0.1	-	0.1
17300	消化器系の先天奇形	総数 T.	0.1	2.0	0.3	0.4	-	-	0.2	0.6	0.0	-	0.0	0.0	0.0	-
		男　M.	0.1	2.0	0.4	0.6	-	-	0.3	0.6	-	-	0.0	0.0	0.0	-
		女　F.	0.1	2.1	0.2	0.2	-	-	0.1	0.5	0.0	-	0.0	0.0	0.0	0.1
17400	その他の先天奇形及び変形	総数 T.	0.5	16.5	1.3	0.6	0.1	0.2	0.5	3.7	0.1	0.1	0.1	0.2	0.1	0.1
		男　M.	0.5	18.3	1.9	0.6	0.2	0.2	0.7	4.2	0.1	0.1	0.1	0.2	0.1	0.2
		女　F.	0.4	14.5	0.6	0.6	-	0.2	0.4	3.2	0.1	0.1	-	0.1	0.1	0.1

簡単分類別死亡率（人口10万対）（つづき）
causes (the condensed list of causes of death for Japan)：Japan, 2016－CON.

平成28年

35～39	40～44	45～49	50～54	55～59	60～64	65～69	70～74	75～79	80～84	85～89	90～94	95～99	100～	65～	75～	80～	85～	死因簡単分類コード Code[a]
0.0	0.1	0.1	0.2	0.5	0.8	1.3	2.3	5.4	12.4	26.4	48.5	83.5	87.7	9.4	17.5	25.0	37.6	14201
0.0	0.1	0.2	0.3	0.8	1.3	2.0	3.6	7.5	16.9	33.7	56.2	94.0	100.0	9.7	18.8	27.7	42.0	
0.1	0.0	0.0	0.1	0.3	0.2	0.7	1.2	3.7	9.3	22.7	45.8	81.0	84.2	9.2	16.6	23.6	35.7	
0.1	0.2	0.5	1.0	1.8	4.0	7.4	13.5	26.8	59.5	126.3	216.7	328.0	341.5	44.6	80.8	114.6	169.5	14202
0.1	0.4	0.8	1.5	2.3	5.8	11.1	19.3	37.1	86.2	182.7	318.8	540.3	644.4	51.9	99.8	149.3	233.3	
0.1	0.1	0.3	0.5	1.2	2.3	4.0	8.5	18.6	41.4	97.0	181.6	282.0	287.7	39.1	68.7	95.7	141.8	
0.1	0.0	0.1	0.4	0.4	0.9	1.6	3.3	7.5	17.7	43.4	81.2	139.8	161.5	14.7	27.6	40.2	62.7	14203
0.0	0.0	0.2	0.5	0.6	1.4	2.4	4.7	10.9	24.8	60.2	115.6	188.1	244.4	15.9	31.9	48.5	80.1	
0.1	0.0	0.0	0.3	0.2	0.5	0.8	2.1	4.8	12.8	34.7	69.3	129.1	145.6	13.8	24.9	35.7	55.2	
0.1	0.2	0.2	0.4	0.7	1.4	2.9	6.0	13.0	32.7	69.5	137.7	237.2	316.9	25.2	47.2	68.6	104.3	14300
0.1	0.2	0.3	0.5	0.9	1.4	3.5	6.9	14.5	34.1	74.7	144.6	243.3	300.0	20.8	41.3	62.4	100.0	
0.1	0.2	0.2	0.3	0.6	1.5	2.4	5.2	11.8	31.7	66.8	135.3	235.1	314.0	28.6	50.9	72.0	106.2	
0.1	0.1	-	-	-	-	-	0.0	-	-	0.0	-	-	-	0.0	0.0	0.0	0.0	15000
-	-	-	-	-	-	-	-	-	-	-	-	-	-	-	-	-	-	16000
-	-	-	-	-	-	-	-	-	-	-	-	-	-	-	-	-	-	16100
-	-	-	-	-	-	-	-	-	-	-	-	-	-	-	-	-	-	16200
-	-	-	-	-	-	-	-	-	-	-	-	-	-	-	-	-	-	16300
-	-	-	-	-	-	-	-	-	-	-	-	-	-	-	-	-	-	16400
-	-	-	-	-	-	-	-	-	-	-	-	-	-	-	-	-	-	16500
-	-	-	-	-	-	-	-	-	-	-	-	-	-	-	-	-	-	16600
0.4	0.5	0.4	0.6	0.5	1.0	1.0	1.2	1.7	2.7	5.2	6.2	8.6	15.4	2.2	3.3	4.3	5.9	17000
0.5	0.4	0.4	0.7	0.5	1.1	1.1	1.3	1.8	2.8	6.3	8.2	9.0	11.1	2.1	3.3	4.6	6.9	
0.3	0.6	0.4	0.6	0.6	0.9	0.9	1.2	1.7	2.6	4.7	5.5	8.5	15.8	2.2	3.3	4.1	5.4	
0.0	0.0	-	0.1	0.0	0.0	0.0	-	0.0	0.0	0.1	0.1	-	-	0.0	0.1	0.1	0.1	17100
0.0	-	-	0.1	-	0.0	0.0	-	0.0	-	0.2	-	-	-	0.0	0.0	0.1	0.1	
0.0	0.1	-	0.1	0.0	0.0	-	-	0.1	0.1	-	0.2	-	-	0.0	0.1	0.1	0.1	
0.3	0.3	0.2	0.2	0.1	0.3	0.3	0.5	0.9	1.4	3.4	4.1	6.3	15.4	1.2	2.0	2.7	3.9	17200
0.3	0.3	0.2	0.2	0.2	0.3	0.2	0.4	0.9	1.1	3.8	4.5	7.5	11.1	0.9	1.8	2.4	4.1	
0.2	0.2	0.2	0.2	0.1	0.2	0.3	0.6	0.9	1.6	3.2	4.0	6.0	15.8	1.3	2.1	2.8	3.9	
0.2	0.2	0.2	0.2	0.1	0.2	0.2	0.4	0.6	0.9	1.5	1.4	1.6	-	0.6	0.9	1.2	1.5	17201
0.2	0.3	0.2	0.2	0.1	0.3	0.1	0.2	0.6	0.7	1.8	1.1	-	-	0.5	0.9	1.1	1.5	
0.2	0.2	0.2	0.2	0.1	0.2	0.2	0.5	0.5	1.1	1.3	1.5	1.9	-	0.7	1.0	1.3	1.4	
0.0	0.0	0.0	0.0	0.0	0.0	0.1	0.1	0.3	0.4	1.9	2.7	4.7	15.4	0.6	1.0	1.5	2.5	17202
0.1	0.0	0.1	0.0	0.1	0.1	0.1	0.1	0.3	0.4	2.0	3.4	7.5	11.1	0.5	0.9	1.3	2.6	
-	0.0	-	0.0	-	-	0.1	0.1	0.3	0.5	1.8	2.5	4.1	15.8	0.6	1.1	1.5	2.4	
0.0	0.0	0.0	0.1	0.0	0.1	0.1	0.1	0.1	0.1	0.4	0.3	-	-	0.1	0.2	0.2	0.3	17300
-	-	0.0	0.1	0.0	0.1	0.1	0.1	0.1	0.2	0.4	0.8	-	-	0.2	0.2	0.3	0.5	
0.0	0.0	0.0	-	0.0	0.0	0.1	0.1	0.2	0.1	0.3	0.2	-	-	0.1	0.2	0.2	0.2	
0.1	0.1	0.2	0.2	0.2	0.4	0.5	0.6	0.7	1.2	1.4	1.6	2.4	-	0.8	1.1	1.3	1.5	17400
0.2	0.1	0.1	0.2	0.2	0.5	0.6	0.7	0.8	1.5	1.9	2.9	1.5	-	0.9	1.3	1.8	2.1	
0.1	0.1	0.2	0.2	0.3	0.3	0.3	0.5	0.6	0.9	1.2	1.1	2.5	-	0.7	0.9	1.1	1.2	

死　亡

表 5.16　性・年齢別にみた死因
Table 5.16　Death rates (per 100,000 population) by sex, age and

死因簡単分類コード Code[a]	死因・性 Causes of death and sex		総数 Total	0歳[1] Year	1	2	3	4	1～4	0～4	5～9	10～14	15～19	20～24	25～29	30～34
17500	染色体異常，他に分類されないもの	総数 T.	0.3	21.3	3.0	1.1	0.4	0.3	1.2	5.2	0.2	0.1	0.0	0.0	0.0	0.0
		男 M.	0.2	17.9	2.1	1.2	-	0.4	0.9	4.3	0.2	-	0.0	0.1	-	-
		女 F.	0.3	24.8	3.9	1.1	0.8	0.2	1.5	6.1	0.2	0.1	0.0	-	0.0	0.0
18000	症状，徴候及び異常臨床所見・異常検査所見で他に分類されないもの	総数 T.	89.9	27.7	3.8	1.4	0.4	0.5	1.5	6.7	0.3	0.2	0.3	1.1	1.6	1.8
		男 M.	57.6	28.1	3.9	1.4	0.6	0.8	1.7	6.9	0.4	0.1	0.4	1.5	2.2	2.4
		女 F.	120.7	27.4	3.7	1.3	0.2	0.2	1.3	6.5	0.1	0.2	0.1	0.6	1.0	1.2
18100	老　衰	総数 T.	74.2	-	-	-	-	-	-	-	-	-	-	-	-	-
		男 M.	37.9	-	-	-	-	-	-	-	-	-	-	-	-	-
		女 F.	108.7	-	-	-	-	-	-	-	-	-	-	-	-	-
18200	乳幼児突然死症候群	総数 T.	0.1	11.2	-	-	-	-	-	2.2	-	-	-	-	-	-
		男 M.	0.1	10.8	-	-	-	-	-	2.2	-	-	-	-	-	-
		女 F.	0.1	11.6	-	-	-	-	-	2.3	-	-	-	-	-	-
18300	その他の症状，徴候及び異常臨床所見・異常検査所見で他に分類されないもの	総数 T.	15.6	16.6	3.8	1.4	0.4	0.5	1.5	4.5	0.3	0.2	0.3	1.1	1.6	1.8
		男 M.	19.5	17.3	3.9	1.4	0.6	0.8	1.7	4.8	0.4	0.1	0.4	1.5	2.2	2.4
		女 F.	11.9	15.8	3.7	1.3	0.2	0.2	1.3	4.2	0.1	0.2	0.1	0.6	1.0	1.2
20000	傷病及び死亡の外因	総数 T.	52.7	10.6	4.9	2.4	2.0	1.2	2.6	4.2	1.7	2.9	13.1	24.7	25.2	24.2
		男 M.	66.5	11.8	7.0	2.4	2.0	1.4	3.2	4.9	2.0	3.9	18.6	35.7	37.2	35.9
		女 F.	39.6	9.5	2.6	2.3	2.0	1.0	2.0	3.5	1.4	1.8	7.2	13.0	12.7	12.1
20100	不慮の事故	総数 T.	30.6	7.5	4.4	1.9	1.6	0.9	2.2	3.2	1.3	1.2	5.1	6.3	4.7	4.9
		男 M.	36.3	8.4	6.6	1.4	1.8	1.2	2.7	3.8	1.6	1.8	7.8	9.3	7.3	7.9
		女 F.	25.3	6.5	2.2	2.3	1.4	0.6	1.6	2.6	0.9	0.6	2.3	3.2	2.1	1.9
20101	交通事故	総数 T.	4.2	0.3	1.1	0.9	0.7	0.2	0.7	0.6	0.6	0.5	3.4	3.7	2.4	2.0
		男 M.	6.0	0.6	1.0	0.8	0.8	0.4	0.8	0.7	0.8	0.8	5.6	5.7	3.9	3.7
		女 F.	2.5	-	1.1	1.1	0.6	-	0.7	0.5	0.5	0.2	1.1	1.6	0.9	0.4
20102	転倒・転落	総数 T.	6.4		0.2	-	0.3	0.1	0.2	0.1	0.1	0.1	0.3	0.7	0.5	0.5
		男 M.	7.4		0.4	-	0.4	0.2	0.3	0.2	0.1	0.2	0.4	0.9	0.7	0.8
		女 F.	5.5		-	-	0.2	-	0.1	0.0	-	0.1	0.2	0.4	0.3	0.2
20103	不慮の溺死及び溺水	総数 T.	6.2	0.4	1.7	0.3	0.4	0.3	0.7	0.6	0.3	0.4	0.9	0.6	0.5	0.5
		男 M.	6.6	-	2.5	0.2	0.6	0.4	0.9	0.7	0.4	0.5	1.2	0.7	0.6	0.8
		女 F.	5.8	0.8	0.9	0.4	0.2	0.2	0.4	0.5	0.2	0.3	0.6	0.4	0.3	0.3
20104	不慮の窒息	総数 T.	7.6	6.3	1.4	0.4	0.2	0.1	0.5	1.7	0.1	0.1	0.2	0.2	0.3	0.5
		男 M.	7.9	7.8	2.5	-	-	0.2	0.7	2.1	0.0	0.1	0.2	0.3	0.5	0.7
		女 F.	7.3	4.8	0.2	0.9	0.4	-	0.4	1.3	0.2	0.1	0.1	0.1	0.1	0.2
20105	煙，火及び火炎への曝露	総数 T.	0.7	-	0.1	0.1		0.2	0.1	0.1	-	0.1	0.0	0.0	0.1	0.1
		男 M.	0.9	-	0.2	0.2		-	0.1	0.1	0.2	0.1	-	0.2	0.1	0.1
		女 F.	0.5	-	-	-		0.4	0.1	0.1	-	-	0.0	0.1	0.1	0.1
20106	有害物質による不慮の中毒及び有害物質への曝露	総数 T.	0.5	0.1		-	-	-	-	0.0	-	0.0	0.1	0.5	0.3	0.6
		男 M.	0.6	-		-	-	-	-	-	-	0.0	0.2	0.6	0.2	0.7
		女 F.	0.3	0.2		-	-	-	-	0.0	-	-	0.1	0.4	0.3	0.4
20107	その他の不慮の事故	総数 T.	5.1	0.3	-	0.1	-	-	0.0	0.1	0.0	0.1	0.2	0.6	0.6	0.7
		男 M.	6.9	-	-	0.2	-	-	0.1	0.0	0.1	0.1	0.3	1.0	1.2	1.1
		女 F.	3.3	0.6	-	-	-	-	-	0.1	-	-	0.1	0.1	0.1	0.3
20200	自殺	総数 T.	16.8	-	-	-	-	-	-	-	-	1.3	7.2	17.0	19.0	17.8
		男 M.	24.1	-	-	-	-	-	-	-	-	1.5	9.8	24.6	28.0	26.2
		女 F.	9.9	-	-	-	-	-	-	-	-	1.0	4.5	8.9	9.6	9.2
20300	他殺	総数 T.	0.2	0.7		0.2	0.2	0.1	0.1	0.2	0.2	0.1	0.2	0.1	0.2	0.2
		男 M.	0.2	0.6		0.4	0.2	-	0.2	0.2	0.1	0.2	0.2	0.0	0.1	0.2
		女 F.	0.2	0.8		-	0.2	0.2	0.1	0.3	0.3	-	0.1	0.1	0.3	0.2
20400	その他の外因	総数 T.	5.0	2.5	0.4	0.3	0.2	0.2	0.3	0.7	0.2	0.3	0.6	1.3	1.3	1.3
		男 M.	5.9	2.8	0.4	0.6	-	0.2	0.3	0.8	0.2	0.4	0.8	1.8	1.8	1.6
		女 F.	4.1	2.1	0.4	-	0.4	0.2	0.3	0.6	0.2	0.1	0.3	0.8	0.7	0.9
22000	特殊目的用コード	総数 T.	-	-	-	-	-	-	-	-	-	-	-	-	-	-
		男 M.	-	-	-	-	-	-	-	-	-	-	-	-	-	-
		女 F.	-													
22100	重症急性呼吸器症候群〔SARS〕	総数 T.	-	-	-	-	-	-	-	-	-	-	-	-	-	-
		男 M.	-	-	-	-	-	-	-	-	-	-	-	-	-	-
		女 F.	-													

308

簡単分類別死亡率（人口10万対）（つづき）
causes (the condensed list of causes of death for Japan)：Japan, 2016－CON.

平成28年

General mortality

35～39	40～44	45～49	50～54	55～59	60～64	65～69	70～74	75～79	80～84	85～89	90～94	95～99	100～	65～	75～	80～	85～	死因簡単分類コード Code[a]
0.0	0.1	0.0	0.1	0.1	0.2	0.1	0.0	0.0	-	-	-	-	-	0.0	0.0	-	-	17500
-	0.0	0.0	0.1	0.1	0.2	0.1	0.1	-	-	-	-	-	-	0.0	-	-	-	
0.0	0.1	0.0	0.2	0.1	0.2	0.2	0.0	0.0	-	-	-	-	-	0.1	0.0	-	-	
2.4	3.7	5.6	8.9	12.2	18.3	23.3	34.3	65.0	203.6	676.7	2 174.6	6 171.5	15 473.8	312.0	608.5	949.6	1 691.9	18000
3.4	5.2	8.7	14.0	20.4	31.0	38.8	51.5	83.1	225.4	687.3	2 028.1	5 723.9	13 300.0	208.6	419.2	684.9	1 296.5	
1.4	2.1	2.4	3.9	4.0	6.0	8.9	19.4	50.5	188.8	671.2	2 224.9	6 246.8	15 545.6	391.1	728.9	1 094.2	1 863.5	
-	-	-	-	-	0.3	1.4	8.2	31.6	151.1	589.7	2 045.5	5 977.5	15 241.5	269.3	546.0	868.9	1 583.3	18100
-	-	-	-	-	0.4	1.9	10.4	35.8	157.6	576.4	1 856.5	5 479.1	13 033.1	154.4	345.0	589.5	1 164.3	
-	-	-	-	-	0.2	0.9	6.2	28.2	146.7	596.6	2 110.4	6 064.2	15 322.8	357.3	673.9	1 021.6	1 765.0	
-	-	-	-	-	-	-	-	-	-	-	-	-	-	-	-	-	-	18200
-	-	-	-	-	-	-	-	-	-	-	-	-	-	-	-	-	-	
-	-	-	-	-	-	-	-	-	-	-	-	-	-	-	-	-	-	
2.4	3.7	5.6	8.9	12.2	18.0	22.0	26.2	33.4	52.5	87.0	129.1	194.0	232.3	42.7	62.4	80.7	108.7	18300
3.4	5.2	8.7	14.0	20.4	30.6	36.9	41.1	47.3	67.9	111.0	171.6	244.8	266.7	54.2	74.2	95.4	132.1	
1.4	2.1	2.4	3.9	4.0	5.7	8.0	13.1	22.2	42.1	74.6	114.5	182.6	222.8	33.8	55.0	72.6	98.5	
25.4	26.1	30.7	37.2	41.0	42.3	50.7	72.4	105.8	166.6	262.1	396.7	572.0	786.2	125.1	193.4	248.3	329.7	20000
36.3	38.7	44.8	54.5	60.5	62.8	72.7	99.5	150.0	239.3	386.7	613.8	861.2	1 033.3	158.4	254.0	336.2	465.2	
14.0	13.0	16.2	19.8	21.5	22.3	30.0	48.7	70.4	117.2	197.3	322.2	508.9	733.3	99.7	154.8	200.3	270.8	
5.6	5.8	7.6	10.5	14.8	18.9	26.9	44.5	74.6	129.1	212.9	328.7	463.9	603.1	91.5	151.2	199.3	269.2	20100
8.6	9.1	11.4	15.7	22.7	29.0	39.2	61.9	104.2	183.1	312.5	511.1	728.4	855.6	113.1	195.7	268.1	381.1	
2.5	2.4	3.7	5.2	6.9	9.1	15.4	29.4	50.9	92.4	161.2	266.1	406.3	552.6	75.0	122.9	161.7	220.6	
2.4	2.3	2.5	2.9	3.6	3.9	5.2	7.4	9.6	13.3	13.7	11.2	7.1	3.1	8.8	11.6	12.8	12.4	20101
3.8	3.7	4.2	4.7	5.9	5.8	7.8	10.0	13.1	18.3	23.2	22.5	23.9	22.2	12.4	17.2	20.4	23.1	
0.9	0.8	0.8	1.1	1.4	2.0	2.9	5.1	6.7	9.8	8.8	7.3	3.5	-	6.0	8.0	8.7	7.8	
0.6	0.7	1.0	1.6	2.5	3.5	4.5	6.5	12.9	24.9	50.7	100.4	184.8	264.6	20.6	36.4	51.2	77.3	20102
0.9	1.1	1.6	2.7	4.4	6.1	7.5	11.2	21.1	38.2	72.4	143.5	241.8	322.2	24.8	45.0	63.9	98.1	
0.3	0.3	0.3	0.5	0.7	1.0	1.7	2.5	6.4	15.9	39.4	85.6	172.2	250.9	17.3	31.0	44.2	68.3	
0.5	0.8	0.9	1.3	2.3	3.2	6.2	12.7	21.9	32.2	42.1	40.9	23.8	15.4	19.6	30.7	36.2	40.1	20103
0.7	1.3	1.1	1.9	3.4	4.7	8.0	15.1	25.8	37.3	51.4	70.3	46.3	22.2	22.2	36.6	45.1	55.5	
0.3	0.3	0.7	0.8	1.3	1.6	4.5	10.7	18.8	28.8	37.3	30.8	19.0	14.0	17.5	26.9	31.2	33.3	
0.5	0.5	1.3	1.8	2.9	3.7	5.4	9.8	16.6	31.9	64.2	107.5	163.4	230.8	24.6	42.6	58.9	85.9	20104
0.7	0.7	1.8	2.0	3.8	4.8	7.3	13.2	22.7	45.1	89.7	141.1	237.3	300.0	27.7	50.7	72.8	109.5	
0.2	0.4	0.7	1.5	1.9	2.6	3.6	6.9	11.7	22.9	50.9	96.0	147.2	215.8	22.2	37.5	51.4	75.6	
0.1	0.2	0.3	0.5	0.6	0.8	1.0	1.2	1.7	3.0	3.5	3.9	3.1	-	1.9	2.7	3.3	3.5	20105
0.1	0.4	0.5	0.7	0.9	1.3	1.4	1.7	2.1	4.4	4.8	5.8	7.5	-	2.4	3.6	4.7	5.2	
0.1	0.0	0.2	0.3	0.3	0.2	0.7	0.9	1.3	2.1	2.7	3.2	2.2	-	1.5	2.1	2.5	2.8	
0.6	0.5	0.8	0.6	0.5	0.5	0.3	0.4	0.6	0.7	0.8	0.8		-	0.5	0.7	0.7	0.7	20106
0.9	0.6	1.1	0.9	0.6	0.6	0.5	0.5	0.9	1.1	1.0	1.3		-	0.7	1.0	1.1	1.0	
0.4	0.4	0.6	0.3	0.5	0.3	0.1	0.3	0.4	0.4	0.7	0.6		-	0.3	0.5	0.5	0.6	
0.9	0.8	0.9	1.8	2.3	3.4	4.2	6.4	11.4	23.1	38.0	64.1	81.7	89.2	15.7	26.6	36.2	49.3	20107
1.5	1.3	1.3	2.9	3.7	5.6	6.8	10.2	18.6	38.7	70.1	126.5	171.6	188.9	22.9	41.8	60.1	88.6	
0.2	0.1	0.4	0.7	0.9	1.3	1.9	3.1	5.6	12.5	21.4	42.6	62.3	71.9	10.1	17.0	23.1	32.2	
18.2	18.2	20.7	23.8	22.6	19.3	18.3	20.5	20.6	21.0	21.2	20.6	13.9	13.8	19.9	20.7	20.7	20.4	20200
25.6	26.9	30.3	34.5	32.7	27.7	25.0	27.4	29.4	31.4	34.6	43.2	38.8	55.6	28.6	31.9	33.8	37.0	
10.6	9.2	10.8	12.9	12.4	11.1	12.0	14.5	13.5	13.9	14.3	12.8	8.5	7.0	13.3	13.5	13.5	13.2	
0.1	0.2	0.2	0.2	0.3	0.2	0.3	0.4	0.3	0.5	0.3	0.4	1.0	-	0.3	0.4	0.4	0.4	20300
0.1	0.3	0.2	0.3	0.4	0.3	0.2	0.3	0.2	0.5	0.4	0.5	3.0	-	0.3	0.4	0.5	0.5	
0.2	0.2	0.2	0.1	0.2	0.1	0.3	0.4	0.3	0.5	0.3	0.4	0.6	-	0.3	0.4	0.4	0.3	
1.4	1.8	2.2	2.8	3.3	3.8	5.2	7.0	10.4	16.0	27.6	47.0	93.2	169.2	13.4	21.1	27.9	39.7	20400
2.1	2.4	2.9	4.0	4.7	5.8	8.3	9.8	16.1	24.2	39.2	58.9	91.0	122.2	16.4	26.0	33.8	46.6	
0.7	1.2	1.5	1.6	2.0	1.9	2.4	4.5	5.7	10.5	21.5	42.9	93.4	173.7	11.1	18.0	24.7	36.7	
-	-	-	-	-	-	-	-	-	-	-	-	-	-	-	-	-	-	22000
-	-	-	-	-	-	-	-	-	-	-	-	-	-	-	-	-	-	
-	-	-	-	-	-	-	-	-	-	-	-	-	-	-	-	-	-	
-	-	-	-	-	-	-	-	-	-	-	-	-	-	-	-	-	-	22100

死　亡

表5.17 性・年齢別

死亡数, 死亡率（人口10万対）, 割合（%）²⁾　**総数**

年齢	第1位 死因	第1位 死亡数 死亡率 (割合)	第2位 死因	第2位 死亡数 死亡率 (割合)	第3位 死因	第3位 死亡数 死亡率 (割合)	第4位 死因	第4位 死亡数 死亡率 (割合)	第5位 死因	第5位 死亡数 死亡率 (割合)
総数	悪性新生物	372 986 / 298.3 / (28.5)	心疾患	198 006 / 158.4 / (15.1)	肺炎	119 300 / 95.4 / (9.1)	脳血管疾患	109 320 / 87.4 / (8.4)	老衰	92 806 / 74.2 / (7.1)
0歳³⁾	先天奇形,変形及び染色体異常	663 / 67.9 / (34.4)	周産期に特異的な呼吸障害等	282 / 28.9 / (14.6)	乳幼児突然死症候群	109 / 11.2 / (5.7)	不慮の事故	73 / 7.5 / (3.8)	胎児及び新生児の出血性障害等	67 / 6.9 / (3.5)
1～4	先天奇形,変形及び染色体異常	150 / 3.8 / (21.7)	不慮の事故	85 / 2.2 / (12.3)	悪性新生物	59 / 1.5 / (8.6)	心疾患	40 / 1.0 / (5.8)	肺炎	35 / 0.9 / (5.1)
5～9	悪性新生物	84 / 1.6 / (21.5)	不慮の事故	68 / 1.3 / (17.4)	先天奇形,変形及び染色体異常	32 / 0.6 / (8.2)	肺炎	19 / 0.4 / (4.9)	心疾患	16 / 0.3 / (4.1)
10～14	悪性新生物	95 / 1.7 / (21.6)	自殺	71 / 1.3 / (16.1)	不慮の事故	66 / 1.2 / (15.0)	先天奇形,変形及び染色体異常	27 / 0.5 / (6.1)	心疾患	19 / 0.3 / (4.3)
15～19	自殺	430 / 7.2 / (36.9)	不慮の事故	306 / 5.1 / (26.2)	悪性新生物	120 / 2.0 / (10.3)	心疾患	45 / 0.8 / (3.9)	先天奇形,変形及び染色体異常	26 / 0.4 / (2.2)
20～24	自殺	1 001 / 17.0 / (48.1)	不慮の事故	373 / 6.3 / (17.9)	悪性新生物	159 / 2.7 / (7.6)	心疾患	108 / 1.8 / (5.2)	先天奇形,変形及び染色体異常	36 / 0.6 / (1.7)
25～29	自殺	1 165 / 19.0 / (47.0)	悪性新生物	315 / 5.1 / (12.7)	不慮の事故	291 / 4.7 / (11.7)	心疾患	156 / 2.5 / (6.3)	脳血管疾患	47 / 0.8 / (1.9)
30～34	自殺	1 253 / 17.8 / (37.4)	悪性新生物	641 / 9.1 / (19.1)	不慮の事故	346 / 4.9 / (10.3)	心疾患	248 / 3.5 / (7.4)	脳血管疾患	118 / 1.7 / (3.5)
35～39	自殺	1 445 / 18.2 / (27.8)	悪性新生物	1 326 / 16.7 / (25.5)	心疾患	495 / 6.2 / (9.5)	不慮の事故	444 / 5.6 / (8.5)	脳血管疾患	307 / 3.9 / (5.9)
40～44	悪性新生物	2 675 / 28.0 / (28.9)	自殺	1 739 / 18.2 / (18.8)	心疾患	1 095 / 11.5 / (11.8)	脳血管疾患	826 / 8.6 / (8.9)	不慮の事故	553 / 5.8 / (6.0)
45～49	悪性新生物	4 753 / 52.1 / (34.1)	自殺	1 888 / 20.7 / (13.6)	心疾患	1 819 / 19.9 / (13.1)	脳血管疾患	1 203 / 13.2 / (8.6)	不慮の事故	694 / 7.6 / (5.0)
50～54	悪性新生物	7 696 / 98.9 / (39.5)	心疾患	2 476 / 31.8 / (12.7)	自殺	1 853 / 23.8 / (9.5)	脳血管疾患	1 628 / 20.9 / (8.4)	肝疾患	897 / 11.5 / (4.6)
55～59	悪性新生物	12 605 / 168.9 / (44.5)	心疾患	3 488 / 46.7 / (12.3)	脳血管疾患	2 148 / 28.8 / (7.6)	自殺	1 684 / 22.6 / (5.9)	肝疾患	1 150 / 15.4 / (4.1)
60～64	悪性新生物	23 343 / 288.4 / (48.4)	心疾患	5 824 / 71.9 / (12.1)	脳血管疾患	3 324 / 41.1 / (6.9)	自殺	1 563 / 19.3 / (3.2)	肺炎	1 560 / 19.3 / (3.2)
65～69	悪性新生物	46 004 / 450.0 / (49.2)	心疾患	11 292 / 110.5 / (12.1)	脳血管疾患	6 273 / 61.4 / (6.7)	肺炎	3 696 / 36.2 / (4.0)	不慮の事故	2 750 / 26.9 / (2.9)
70～74	悪性新生物	48 833 / 662.4 / (45.3)	心疾患	13 353 / 181.1 / (12.4)	脳血管疾患	7 667 / 104.0 / (7.1)	肺炎	6 032 / 81.8 / (5.6)	不慮の事故	3 282 / 44.5 / (3.0)
75～79	悪性新生物	58 317 / 897.2 / (38.1)	心疾患	20 436 / 314.4 / (13.4)	脳血管疾患	12 451 / 191.6 / (8.1)	肺炎	11 681 / 179.7 / (7.6)	不慮の事故	4 851 / 74.6 / (3.2)
80～84	悪性新生物	67 401 / 1 304.9 / (30.1)	心疾患	33 028 / 639.4 / (14.8)	肺炎	22 231 / 430.4 / (9.9)	脳血管疾患	20 087 / 388.9 / (9.0)	老衰	7 805 / 151.1 / (3.5)
85～89	悪性新生物	57 874 / 1 771.4 / (22.2)	心疾患	43 241 / 1 323.5 / (16.6)	肺炎	31 171 / 954.1 / (12.0)	脳血管疾患	23 746 / 726.8 / (9.1)	老衰	19 265 / 589.7 / (7.4)
90～94	心疾患	38 374 / 2 601.6 / (18.3)	悪性新生物	30 746 / 2 084.5 / (14.7)	老衰	30 171 / 2 045.5 / (14.4)	肺炎	26 418 / 1 791.1 / (12.6)	脳血管疾患	19 285 / 1 307.5 / (9.2)
95～99	老衰	22 834 / 5 977.5 / (23.8)	心疾患	17 898 / 4 685.3 / (18.7)	肺炎	11 906 / 3 116.8 / (12.4)	悪性新生物	8 605 / 2 252.6 / (9.0)	脳血管疾患	8 257 / 2 161.5 / (8.6)
100～	老衰	9 907 / 15 241.5 / (37.5)	心疾患	4 475 / 6 884.6 / (16.9)	肺炎	2 924 / 4 498.5 / (11.1)	脳血管疾患	1 860 / 2 861.5 / (7.0)	悪性新生物	1 301 / 2 001.5 / (4.9)
（再掲）										
65～	悪性新生物	319 081 / 926.2 / (27.3)	心疾患	182 097 / 528.6 / (15.6)	肺炎	116 059 / 336.9 / (9.9)	脳血管疾患	99 626 / 289.2 / (8.5)	老衰	92 781 / 269.3 / (7.9)
75～	悪性新生物	224 244 / 1 330.4 / (23.1)	心疾患	157 452 / 934.1 / (16.2)	肺炎	106 331 / 630.8 / (11.0)	老衰	92 037 / 546.0 / (9.5)	脳血管疾患	85 686 / 508.3 / (8.8)
80～	悪性新生物	165 927 / 1 602.3 / (20.3)	心疾患	137 016 / 1 323.1 / (16.8)	肺炎	94 650 / 914.0 / (11.6)	老衰	89 982 / 868.9 / (11.0)	脳血管疾患	73 235 / 707.2 / (9.0)

注：1）〔1〕死因順位の選び方については巻末の参考表「1各種分類表」の「表6－1(1)」を参照されたい。
　　〔2〕乳児（0歳）の死因については乳児死因順位に用いる分類項目によるもので、死因順位の選び方については巻末の参考表「1各種分類表」の「表6－1(2)」を参照されたい。
　　〔3〕死因名は次のように省略した。
　　　　心疾患　←　心疾患（高血圧性を除く）
　　　　周産期に特異的な呼吸障害等　←　周産期に特異的な呼吸障害及び心血管障害
　　　　胎児及び新生児の出血性障害等　←　胎児及び新生児の出血性障害及び血液障害
　　　　妊娠期間等に関連する障害　←　妊娠期間及び胎児発育に関連する障害
　　　　血管性等の認知症　←　血管性及び詳細不明の認知症
　　〔4〕「敗血症」には、"新生児の細菌性敗血症"を含まない。
　　〔5〕死因順位は死亡数の多いものから定めた。死亡数が同数の場合は、同一順位に死因名を列記し、次位を空欄とした。

General mortality

に　み　た　死　因　順　位 [1]

総　数　　　　　　　　　　　　　　　　　　　　　　　　　　　　平成28年

第 6 位 死因	死亡数 死亡率 (割合)	第 7 位 死因	死亡数 死亡率 (割合)	第 8 位 死因	死亡数 死亡率 (割合)	第 9 位 死因	死亡数 死亡率 (割合)	第 10 位 死因	死亡数 死亡率 (割合)
不慮の事故	38 306 30.6 (2.9)	腎不全	24 612 19.7 (1.9)	自殺	21 017 16.8 (1.6)	大動脈瘤及び解離	18 145 14.5 (1.4)	肝疾患	15 773 12.6 (1.2)
妊娠期間等に関連する障害	43 4.4 (2.2)			心疾患	41 4.2 (2.1)	敗血症	40 4.1 (2.1)	肺炎	28 2.9 (1.5)
周産期に特異的な感染症 敗血症	25 0.6 (3.6)	腸管感染症 インフルエンザ	19 0.5 (2.8)			周産期に発生した病態	10 0.3 (1.4)	その他の新生物 ヘルニア及び腸閉塞 肝疾患	6 0.2 (0.9)
その他の新生物	15 0.3 (3.8)	腸管感染症 他殺	11 0.2 (2.8)			敗血症	9 0.2 (2.3)	脳血管疾患 インフルエンザ	7 0.1 (1.8)
脳血管疾患 肺炎	13 0.2 (3.0)			インフルエンザ	10 0.2 (2.3)	その他の新生物	7 0.1 (1.6)	他殺	6 0.1 (1.4)
脳血管疾患	17 0.3 (1.5)	その他の新生物 肺炎	13 0.2 (1.1)			他殺	9 0.2 (0.8)	敗血症	5 0.1 (0.4)
脳血管疾患	26 0.4 (1.2)	肺炎	18 0.3 (0.9)	その他の新生物	17 0.3 (0.8)	敗血症	8 0.1 (0.4)	糖尿病 大動脈瘤及び解離	7 0.1 (0.3)
肺炎	31 0.5 (1.3)	先天奇形,変形及び染色体異常	22 0.4 (0.9)	その他の新生物	18 0.3 (0.7)	敗血症	12 0.2 (0.5)	他殺	11 0.2 (0.4)
肝疾患	54 0.8 (1.6)	肺炎	47 0.7 (1.4)	その他の新生物 先天奇形,変形及び染色体異常	32 0.5 (1.0)			糖尿病	16 0.2 (0.5)
肝疾患	124 1.6 (2.4)	肺炎	75 0.9 (1.4)	大動脈瘤及び解離	48 0.6 (0.9)	その他の新生物	43 0.5 (0.8)	先天奇形,変形及び染色体異常	33 0.4 (0.6)
肝疾患	376 3.9 (4.1)	肺炎	125 1.3 (1.3)	大動脈瘤及び解離	115 1.2 (1.2)	糖尿病	96 1.0 (1.0)	その他の新生物	88 0.9 (1.0)
肝疾患	669 7.3 (4.8)	肺炎	224 2.5 (1.6)	大動脈瘤及び解離	181 2.0 (1.3)	糖尿病	151 1.7 (1.1)	その他の新生物	110 1.2 (0.8)
不慮の事故	815 10.5 (4.2)	肺炎	366 4.7 (1.9)	大動脈瘤及び解離	280 3.6 (1.4)	糖尿病	235 3.0 (1.2)	その他の新生物	160 2.1 (0.8)
不慮の事故	1 104 14.8 (3.9)	肺炎	677 9.1 (2.4)	大動脈瘤及び解離	461 6.2 (1.6)	糖尿病	360 4.8 (1.3)	その他の新生物	221 3.0 (0.8)
肝疾患	1 552 19.2 (3.2)	不慮の事故	1 531 18.9 (3.2)	大動脈瘤及び解離	690 8.5 (1.4)	糖尿病	601 7.4 (1.2)	腎不全	461 5.7 (1.0)
肝疾患	2 105 20.6 (2.3)	自殺	1 870 18.3 (2.0)	大動脈瘤及び解離	1 525 14.9 (1.6)	糖尿病	1 185 11.6 (1.2)	腎不全	1 054 10.3 (1.1)
肝疾患	1 763 23.9 (1.6)	大動脈瘤及び解離	1 715 23.3 (1.6)	自殺	1 513 20.5 (1.4)	腎不全	1 412 19.2 (1.3)	慢性閉塞性肺疾患	1 323 17.9 (1.2)
腎不全	2 585 39.8 (1.7)	大動脈瘤及び解離	2 353 36.2 (1.5)	慢性閉塞性肺疾患	2 246 34.6 (1.5)	肝疾患	2 116 32.6 (1.4)	老衰	2 055 31.6 (1.1)
不慮の事故	6 668 129.1 (3.0)	腎不全	4 624 89.5 (2.1)	慢性閉塞性肺疾患	3 694 71.5 (1.7)	大動脈瘤及び解離	3 512 68.0 (1.6)	糖尿病	2 560 49.6 (1.1)
不慮の事故	6 957 212.9 (2.7)	腎不全	6 409 196.2 (2.5)	慢性閉塞性肺疾患	4 035 123.5 (1.5)	大動脈瘤及び解離	3 891 119.1 (1.5)	アルツハイマー病	3 386 103.6 (1.3)
腎不全	5 108 346.3 (2.4)	不慮の事故	4 849 328.7 (2.3)	血管性等の認知症	3 571 242.1 (1.7)	アルツハイマー病	3 265 221.4 (1.6)	大動脈瘤及び解離	2 510 170.2 (1.2)
血管性等の認知症 腎不全	2 106 551.3 (2.2)			不慮の事故	1 772 463.9 (1.7)	アルツハイマー病	1 563 409.2 (1.6)	高血圧性疾患	998 261.3 (1.0)
血管性等の認知症	625 961.5 (2.4)	不慮の事故	392 603.1 (1.5)	腎不全	384 590.8 (1.5)	高血圧性疾患	317 487.7 (1.2)	アルツハイマー病	316 486.2 (1.2)
不慮の事故	31 521 91.5 (2.7)	腎不全	23 682 68.7 (2.0)	大動脈瘤及び解離	16 341 47.4 (1.4)	慢性閉塞性肺疾患	15 309 44.4 (1.3)	糖尿病	11 971 34.7 (1.0)
不慮の事故	25 489 151.2 (2.6)	腎不全	21 216 125.9 (2.2)	慢性閉塞性肺疾患	13 298 78.9 (1.4)	大動脈瘤及び解離	13 101 77.7 (1.3)	血管性等の認知症	11 553 68.5 (1.2)
不慮の事故	20 638 199.3 (2.5)	腎不全	18 631 179.9 (2.3)	慢性閉塞性肺疾患	11 052 106.7 (1.4)	血管性等の認知症	10 963 105.9 (1.3)	大動脈瘤及び解離	10 748 103.8 (1.3)

2)　割合（％）は、それぞれの年齢別死亡数を100とした場合の割合である。
3)　0歳の死亡率は出生10万対の率である。

死　亡

表5.17　性・年齢別

死亡数，死亡率（人口10万対），割合（%）[2]　男

年　齢	第1位 死因	第1位 死亡数 死亡率 (割合)	第2位 死因	第2位 死亡数 死亡率 (割合)	第3位 死因	第3位 死亡数 死亡率 (割合)	第4位 死因	第4位 死亡数 死亡率 (割合)	第5位 死因	第5位 死亡数 死亡率 (割合)
総　数	悪性新生物	219 785 / 361.1 / (32.6)	心疾患	93 419 / 153.5 / (13.8)	肺炎	65 636 / 107.8 / (9.7)	脳血管疾患	52 706 / 86.6 / (7.8)	老衰	23 077 / 37.9 / (3.4)
0 歳[3]	先天奇形, 変形及び染色体異常	323 / 64.4 / (33.0)	周産期に特異的な呼吸障害等	145 / 28.9 / (14.8)	乳幼児突然死症候群	54 / 10.8 / (5.5)	不慮の事故	42 / 8.4 / (4.3)	周産期に特異的な感染症／胎児及び新生児の出血性障害等	28 / 5.6 / (2.9)
1～4	先天奇形, 変形及び染色体異常	72 / 3.6 / (19.4)	不慮の事故	54 / 2.7 / (14.6)	悪性新生物	34 / 1.7 / (9.2)	心疾患	26 / 1.3 / (7.0)	肺炎	19 / 1.0 / (5.1)
5～9	悪性新生物	50 / 1.9 / (21.8)	不慮の事故	44 / 1.6 / (19.2)	先天奇形, 変形及び染色体異常	16 / 0.6 / (7.0)	その他の新生物／心疾患	10 / 0.4 / (4.4)		
10～14	不慮の事故	49 / 1.8 / (19.3)	悪性新生物	48 / 1.7 / (18.9)	自殺	43 / 1.5 / (16.9)	心疾患	11 / 0.4 / (4.3)	脳血管疾患／先天奇形, 変形及び染色体異常	9 / 0.3 / (3.5)
15～19	自殺	301 / 9.8 / (36.9)	不慮の事故	239 / 7.8 / (29.3)	悪性新生物	78 / 2.6 / (9.6)	心疾患	33 / 1.1 / (4.0)	先天奇形, 変形及び染色体異常	16 / 0.5 / (2.0)
20～24	自殺	745 / 24.6 / (50.6)	不慮の事故	281 / 9.3 / (19.1)	悪性新生物	95 / 3.1 / (6.5)	心疾患	76 / 2.5 / (5.2)	先天奇形, 変形及び染色体異常	21 / 0.7 / (1.4)
25～29	自殺	877 / 28.0 / (51.2)	不慮の事故	227 / 7.3 / (13.3)	悪性新生物	155 / 5.0 / (9.0)	心疾患	106 / 3.4 / (6.2)	脳血管疾患	34 / 1.1 / (2.0)
30～34	自殺	936 / 26.2 / (42.0)	不慮の事故	282 / 7.9 / (12.7)	悪性新生物	261 / 7.3 / (11.7)	心疾患	203 / 5.7 / (9.1)	脳血管疾患	81 / 2.3 / (3.6)
35～39	自殺	1 032 / 25.6 / (31.4)	悪性新生物	535 / 13.3 / (16.3)	心疾患	378 / 9.4 / (11.5)	不慮の事故	345 / 8.6 / (10.5)	脳血管疾患	213 / 5.3 / (6.5)
40～44	自殺	1 305 / 26.9 / (22.4)	悪性新生物	1 115 / 23.0 / (19.1)	心疾患	830 / 17.1 / (14.2)	脳血管疾患	548 / 11.3 / (9.4)	不慮の事故	442 / 9.1 / (7.6)
45～49	悪性新生物	2 141 / 46.3 / (24.1)	心疾患	1 453 / 31.4 / (16.3)	自殺	1 400 / 30.3 / (15.8)	脳血管疾患	828 / 17.9 / (9.3)	不慮の事故	527 / 11.4 / (5.9)
50～54	悪性新生物	3 791 / 96.7 / (30.3)	心疾患	2 005 / 51.2 / (16.0)	自殺	1 353 / 34.5 / (10.8)	脳血管疾患	1 122 / 28.6 / (9.0)	肝疾患	708 / 18.1 / (5.7)
55～59	悪性新生物	7 268 / 195.2 / (38.1)	心疾患	2 858 / 76.7 / (15.0)	脳血管疾患	1 474 / 39.6 / (7.7)	自殺	1 219 / 32.7 / (6.4)	肝疾患	933 / 25.1 / (4.9)
60～64	悪性新生物	14 842 / 372.0 / (44.4)	心疾患	4 640 / 116.3 / (13.9)	脳血管疾患	2 360 / 59.1 / (7.1)	肝疾患	1 246 / 31.2 / (3.7)	肺炎	1 208 / 30.3 / (3.6)
65～69	悪性新生物	30 772 / 622.1 / (47.3)	心疾患	8 507 / 172.0 / (13.1)	脳血管疾患	4 410 / 89.2 / (6.8)	肺炎	2 853 / 57.7 / (4.4)	不慮の事故	1 940 / 39.2 / (3.0)
70～74	悪性新生物	32 933 / 958.6 / (45.4)	心疾患	9 077 / 264.2 / (12.5)	脳血管疾患	5 127 / 149.2 / (7.1)	肺炎	4 475 / 130.3 / (6.2)	不慮の事故	2 126 / 61.9 / (2.9)
75～79	悪性新生物	37 864 / 1 308.1 / (39.0)	心疾患	12 312 / 425.3 / (12.7)	肺炎	8 270 / 285.7 / (8.5)	脳血管疾患	7 780 / 268.8 / (8.0)	不慮の事故	3 017 / 104.2 / (3.1)
80～84	悪性新生物	40 840 / 1 954.3 / (31.9)	心疾患	17 196 / 822.9 / (13.4)	肺炎	14 465 / 692.2 / (11.3)	脳血管疾患	10 980 / 525.4 / (8.6)	不慮の事故	3 827 / 183.1 / (3.0)
85～89	悪性新生物	31 187 / 2 791.2 / (25.0)	心疾患	18 135 / 1 623.0 / (14.6)	肺炎	17 612 / 1 576.2 / (14.1)	脳血管疾患	10 326 / 924.2 / (8.3)	老衰	6 440 / 576.4 / (5.2)
90～94	悪性新生物	12 810 / 3 397.9 / (18.1)	肺炎	11 281 / 2 992.3 / (15.9)	心疾患	11 280 / 2 992.0 / (15.9)	老衰	6 999 / 1 856.5 / (9.9)	脳血管疾患	5 640 / 1 496.0 / (8.0)
95～99	老衰	3 671 / 5 479.1 / (17.3)	肺炎	3 655 / 5 455.2 / (17.2)	心疾患	3 542 / 5 286.6 / (16.7)	悪性新生物	2 640 / 3 940.3 / (12.4)	脳血管疾患	1 500 / 2 238.8 / (7.1)
100～	老衰	1 173 / 13 033.3 / (29.2)	心疾患	688 / 7 644.4 / (17.1)	肺炎	634 / 7 044.4 / (15.8)	悪性新生物	302 / 3 355.6 / (7.5)	脳血管疾患	229 / 2 544.4 / (5.7)
(再掲) 65～	悪性新生物	189 348 / 1 267.7 / (32.5)	心疾患	80 737 / 540.5 / (13.8)	肺炎	63 245 / 423.4	脳血管疾患	45 992 / 307.9 / (7.9)	老衰	23 062 / 154.4 / (4.0)
75～	悪性新生物	125 643 / 1 916.9 / (28.2)	心疾患	63 153 / 963.5 / (14.2)	肺炎	55 917 / 853.1 / (12.5)	脳血管疾患	36 455 / 556.2 / (8.2)	老衰	22 613 / 345.0 / (5.1)
80～	悪性新生物	87 779 / 2 398.3 / (25.2)	心疾患	50 841 / 1 389.1 / (14.6)	肺炎	47 647 / 1 301.8 / (13.7)	脳血管疾患	28 675 / 783.5 / (8.2)	老衰	21 576 / 589.5 / (6.2)

注：1）～3）　310～311ページの同番号の注を参照されたい。

General mortality

に み た 死 因 順 位 [1]（つづき）

男 平成28年

第 6 位	死亡数 死亡率（割合）	第 7 位	死亡数 死亡率（割合）	第 8 位	死亡数 死亡率（割合）	第 9 位	死亡数 死亡率（割合）	第 10 位	死亡数 死亡率（割合）
死　因		死　因		死　因		死　因		死　因	
不 慮 の 事 故	22 066 36.3 (3.3)	自　　　殺	14 639 24.1 (2.2)	慢性閉塞性肺疾患	12 649 20.8 (1.9)	腎 不 全	12 231 20.1 (1.8)	肝 疾 患	10 112 16.6 (1.5)
		敗 血 症	22 4.4 (2.2)	心 疾 患 / 妊娠期間等に関連する障害	21 4.2 (2.1)			肺　　　炎	15 3.0 (1.5)
敗 血 症	17 0.9 (4.6)	インフルエンザ	12 0.6 (3.2)	腸 管 感 染 症	9 0.5 (2.4)	肝 疾 患 / 周産期に発生した病態	5 0.3 (1.3)		
腸管感染症 / 肺　炎	8 0.3 (3.5)			敗 血 症	5 0.2 (2.2)	インフルエンザ / 他　殺	4 0.1 (1.7)		
		肺　　　炎	7 0.3 (2.8)	その他の新生物 / インフルエンザ / 他　殺	6 0.2 (2.4)				
脳 血 管 疾 患	10 0.3 (1.2)	その他の新生物	7 0.2 (0.9)	他　　　殺	6 0.2 (0.7)	敗 血 症 / 肺　炎	4 0.1 (0.5)		
脳 血 管 疾 患	14 0.5 (1.0)	その他の新生物	11 0.4 (0.7)	敗 血 症 / 肺　炎	8 0.3 (0.5)			大動脈瘤及び解離 / 肝 疾 患	5 0.2 (0.3)
肺　　　炎	20 0.6 (1.2)	先天奇形, 変形及び染色体異常	12 0.4 (0.7)	その他の新生物	8 0.3 (0.5)	糖 尿 病 / ヘルニア及び腸閉塞	7 0.2 (0.4)		
肝 疾 患	33 0.9 (1.5)	肺　　　炎	32 0.9 (1.4)	その他の新生物 / 先天奇形, 変形及び染色体異常	17 0.5 (0.8)			糖 尿 病 / 大動脈瘤及び解離	11 0.3 (0.5)
肝 疾 患	81 2.0 (2.5)	肺　　　炎	55 1.4 (1.7)	大動脈瘤及び解離	43 1.1 (1.3)	糖 尿 病	26 0.6 (0.8)	その他の新生物	25 0.6 (0.6)
肝 疾 患	278 5.7 (4.8)	大動脈瘤及び解離	105 2.2 (1.8)	肺　　　炎	83 1.7 (1.4)	糖 尿 病	69 1.4 (1.2)	その他の新生物	49 1.0 (0.8)
肝 疾 患	525 11.3 (5.9)	肺　　　炎	163 3.5 (1.8)	大動脈瘤及び解離	159 3.4 (1.8)	糖 尿 病	112 2.4 (1.3)	その他の新生物	61 1.3 (0.7)
不 慮 の 事 故	615 15.7 (4.9)	肺　　　炎	262 6.7 (2.1)	大動脈瘤及び解離	229 5.8 (1.8)	糖 尿 病	190 4.8 (1.5)	その他の新生物	108 2.8 (0.9)
不 慮 の 事 故	846 22.7 (4.4)	肺　　　炎	497 13.3 (2.6)	大動脈瘤及び解離	374 10.0 (2.0)	糖 尿 病	287 7.7 (1.5)	その他の新生物	139 3.7 (0.7)
不 慮 の 事 故	1 156 29.0 (3.5)	自　　　殺	1 107 27.7 (3.3)	大動脈瘤及び解離	503 12.6 (1.5)	糖 尿 病	461 11.6 (1.4)	腎 不 全	339 8.5 (1.0)
肝 疾 患	1 631 33.0 (2.5)	自　　　殺	1 235 25.0 (1.9)	大動脈瘤及び解離	1 027 20.8 (1.6)	糖 尿 病	879 17.8 (1.4)	腎 不 全	764 15.4 (1.2)
肝 疾 患	1 215 35.4 (1.7)	慢性閉塞性肺疾患	1 155 33.6 (1.6)	大動脈瘤及び解離	1 009 29.4 (1.4)	腎 不 全	948 27.6 (1.3)	自　　　殺	942 27.4 (1.3)
慢性閉塞性肺疾患	1 941 67.1 (2.0)	腎 不 全	1 608 55.6 (1.7)	大動脈瘤及び解離	1 341 46.3 (1.4)	肝 疾 患	1 299 44.9 (1.3)	糖 尿 病	1 226 42.4 (1.3)
老　　　衰	3 293 157.6 (2.6)	慢性閉塞性肺疾患	3 114 149.0 (2.4)	腎 不 全	2 672 127.9 (2.1)	大動脈瘤及び解離	1 748 83.6 (1.4)	糖 尿 病	1 400 67.0 (1.1)
不 慮 の 事 故	3 492 312.5 (2.8)	慢性閉塞性肺疾患	3 267 292.4 (2.6)	腎 不 全	3 090 276.5 (2.5)	大動脈瘤及び解離	1 675 149.9 (1.3)	その他の新生物	1 225 109.6 (1.0)
不 慮 の 事 故	1 927 511.1 (2.6)	腎 不 全	1 850 490.7 (2.6)	慢性閉塞性肺疾患	1 807 479.3 (2.6)	大動脈瘤及び解離	866 229.7 (1.2)	血管性等の認知症	772 204.8 (1.1)
腎 不 全	551 822.4 (2.6)	不 慮 の 事 故	488 728.4 (2.3)	慢性閉塞性肺疾患	404 603.0 (1.9)	血管性等の認知症	280 417.9 (1.3)	アルツハイマー病	240 358.2 (1.1)
腎 不 全	89 988.9 (2.2)	不 慮 の 事 故	77 855.6 (1.9)	血管性等の認知症	58 644.4 (1.4)	慢性閉塞性肺疾患	56 622.2 (1.4)	高 血 圧 性 疾 患	39 433.3 (1.0)
不 慮 の 事 故	16 894 113.1 (2.9)	慢性閉塞性肺疾患	12 342 82.6 (2.1)	腎 不 全	11 572 77.5 (2.0)	大動脈瘤及び解離	7 834 52.4 (1.3)	肝 疾 患	6 280 42.0 (1.1)
不 慮 の 事 故	12 828 195.7 (2.9)	慢性閉塞性肺疾患	10 589 161.6 (2.4)	腎 不 全	9 860 150.4 (2.2)	大動脈瘤及び解離	5 798 88.5 (1.3)	糖 尿 病	4 314 65.8 (1.0)
不 慮 の 事 故	9 811 268.1 (2.8)	慢性閉塞性肺疾患	8 648 236.3 (2.5)	腎 不 全	8 252 225.5 (2.4)	大動脈瘤及び解離	4 457 121.8 (1.3)	その他の新生物	3 214 87.8 (0.9)

死　亡

表5.17　性・年齢別

死亡数，死亡率（人口10万対），割合（%）[2]　女

年　齢	第1位 死因	死亡数 死亡率 (割合)	第2位 死因	死亡数 死亡率 (割合)	第3位 死因	死亡数 死亡率 (割合)	第4位 死因	死亡数 死亡率 (割合)	第5位 死因	死亡数 死亡率 (割合)
総　数	悪性新生物	153 201 238.8 (24.2)	心疾患	104 587 163.0 (16.5)	老衰	69 729 108.7 (11.0)	脳血管疾患	56 614 88.2 (8.9)	肺炎	53 664 83.6 (8.5)
0歳[3]	先天奇形，変形及び染色体異常	340 71.6 (35.9)	周産期に特異的な呼吸障害等	137 28.8 (14.5)	乳幼児突然死症候群	55 11.6 (5.8)	胎児及び新生児の出血性障害等	39 8.2 (4.1)	不慮の事故	31 6.5 (3.3)
1～4	先天奇形，変形及び染色体異常	78 4.1 (24.5)	不慮の事故	31 1.6 (9.7)	悪性新生物	25 1.3 (7.8)	肺炎	16 0.8 (5.0)	心疾患	14 0.7 (4.4)
5～9	悪性新生物	34 1.3 (21.0)	不慮の事故	24 0.9 (14.8)	先天奇形，変形及び染色体異常	16 0.6 (9.9)	肺炎	11 0.4 (6.8)	他殺	7 0.3 (4.3)
10～14	悪性新生物	47 1.8 (25.3)	自殺	28 1.0 (15.1)	先天奇形，変形及び染色体異常	18 0.7 (9.7)	不慮の事故	17 0.6 (9.1)	心疾患	8 0.3 (4.3)
15～19	自殺	129 4.5 (36.9)	不慮の事故	67 2.3 (19.1)	悪性新生物	42 1.5 (12.0)	心疾患	12 0.4 (3.4)	先天奇形，変形及び染色体異常	10 0.3 (2.9)
20～24	自殺	256 8.9 (41.8)	不慮の事故	92 3.2 (15.0)	悪性新生物	64 2.2 (10.5)	心疾患	32 1.1 (5.2)	先天奇形，変形及び染色体異常	15 0.5 (2.5)
25～29	自殺	288 9.6 (37.6)	悪性新生物	160 5.3 (20.9)	不慮の事故	64 2.1 (8.4)	心疾患	50 1.7 (6.5)	脳血管疾患	13 0.4 (1.7)
30～34	悪性新生物	380 11.0 (33.7)	自殺	317 9.2 (28.1)	不慮の事故	64 1.9 (5.7)	心疾患	45 1.3 (4.0)	脳血管疾患	37 1.1 (3.3)
35～39	悪性新生物	791 20.3 (41.4)	自殺	413 10.6 (21.6)	心疾患	117 3.0 (6.1)	不慮の事故	99 2.5 (5.2)	脳血管疾患	94 2.4 (4.9)
40～44	悪性新生物	1 560 33.2 (45.5)	自殺	434 9.2 (12.7)	脳血管疾患	278 5.9 (8.1)	心疾患	265 5.6 (7.7)	不慮の事故	111 2.4 (3.2)
45～49	悪性新生物	2 612 58.0 (51.9)	自殺	488 10.8 (9.7)	脳血管疾患	375 8.3 (7.4)	心疾患	366 8.1 (7.3)	不慮の事故	167 3.7 (3.3)
50～54	悪性新生物	3 905 101.1 (56.2)	脳血管疾患	506 13.1 (7.3)	自殺	500 12.9 (7.2)	心疾患	471 12.2 (6.8)	不慮の事故	200 5.2 (2.9)
55～59	悪性新生物	5 337 142.8 (57.6)	脳血管疾患	674 18.0 (7.3)	心疾患	630 16.9 (6.8)	自殺	465 12.4 (5.0)	不慮の事故	258 6.9 (2.8)
60～64	悪性新生物	8 501 207.1 (57.6)	心疾患	1 184 28.8 (8.0)	脳血管疾患	964 23.5 (6.5)	自殺	456 11.1 (3.1)	不慮の事故	375 9.1 (2.5)
65～69	悪性新生物	15 232 288.7 (53.6)	心疾患	2 785 52.8 (9.8)	脳血管疾患	1 863 35.3 (6.6)	肺炎	843 16.0 (3.0)	不慮の事故	810 15.4 (2.8)
70～74	悪性新生物	15 900 403.9 (45.1)	心疾患	4 276 108.6 (12.1)	脳血管疾患	2 540 64.5 (7.2)	肺炎	1 557 39.5 (4.4)	不慮の事故	1 156 29.4 (3.3)
75～79	悪性新生物	20 453 567.3 (36.6)	心疾患	8 124 225.3 (14.5)	脳血管疾患	4 671 129.6 (8.4)	肺炎	3 411 94.6 (6.1)	不慮の事故	1 834 50.9 (3.3)
80～84	悪性新生物	26 561 863.6 (27.7)	心疾患	15 832 514.8 (16.5)	脳血管疾患	9 107 296.1 (9.5)	肺炎	7 766 252.5 (8.1)	老衰	4 512 146.7 (4.7)
85～89	悪性新生物	26 687 1 241.4 (19.6)	心疾患	25 106 1 167.9 (18.5)	肺炎	13 559 630.7 (10.0)	脳血管疾患	13 420 624.3 (9.9)	老衰	12 825 596.6 (9.4)
90～94	心疾患	27 094 2 467.6 (19.5)	老衰	23 172 2 110.4 (16.7)	悪性新生物	17 936 1 633.5 (12.9)	肺炎	15 137 1 378.6 (10.9)	脳血管疾患	13 645 1 242.7 (9.8)
95～99	老衰	19 163 6 064.2 (25.7)	心疾患	14 356 4 543.0 (19.3)	肺炎	8 251 2 611.1 (11.1)	脳血管疾患	6 757 2 138.3 (9.1)	悪性新生物	5 965 1 887.7 (8.0)
100～	老衰	8 734 15 322.8 (39.0)	心疾患	3 787 6 643.9 (16.9)	肺炎	2 290 4 017.5 (10.2)	脳血管疾患	1 631 2 861.4 (7.3)	悪性新生物	999 1 752.6 (4.5)
(再掲) 65～	悪性新生物	129 733 664.8 (22.1)	心疾患	101 360 519.4 (17.3)	老衰	69 719 357.3 (11.9)	脳血管疾患	53 634 274.8 (9.1)	肺炎	52 814 270.6 (9.0)
75～	悪性新生物	98 601 957.2 (18.8)	心疾患	94 299 915.4 (18.0)	老衰	69 424 673.9 (13.3)	肺炎	50 414 489.4 (9.6)	脳血管疾患	49 231 477.9 (9.4)
80～	心疾患	86 175 1 287.0 (18.4)	悪性新生物	78 148 1 167.1 (16.7)	老衰	68 406 1 021.6 (14.6)	肺炎	47 003 702.0 (10.1)	脳血管疾患	44 560 665.5 (9.5)

注：1)～3)　310～311ページの同番号の注を参照されたい。

General mortality

に み た 死 因 順 位[1]（つづき）

女   平成28年

第 6 位 死因	死亡数 死亡率 (割合)	第 7 位 死因	死亡数 死亡率 (割合)	第 8 位 死因	死亡数 死亡率 (割合)	第 9 位 死因	死亡数 死亡率 (割合)	第 10 位 死因	死亡数 死亡率 (割合)
不慮の事故	16 240 / 25.3 / (2.6)	腎不全	12 381 / 19.3 / (2.0)	大動脈瘤及び解離	8 877 / 13.8 / (1.4)	血管性等の認知症	8 517 / 13.3 / (1.3)	アルツハイマー病	8 222 / 12.8 / (1.3)
妊娠期間等に関連する障害	22 / 4.6 / (2.3)	心疾患	20 / 4.2 / (2.1)	敗血症	18 / 3.8 / (1.9)	周産期に特異的な感染症	15 / 3.2 / (1.6)	肺炎	13 / 2.7 / (1.4)
腸管感染症	10 / 0.5 / (3.1)	敗血症	8 / 0.4 / (2.5)	インフルエンザ	7 / 0.4 / (2.2)	周産期に発生した病態	5 / 0.3 / (1.6)	その他の新生物	4 / 0.2 / (1.3)
心疾患	6 / 0.2 / (3.7)	その他の新生物	5 / 0.3 / (3.1)	｛敗血症／脳血管疾患｝	4 / 0.2 / (2.5)			｛腸管感染症／インフルエンザ｝	3 / 0.1 / (1.9)
肺炎	6 / 0.2 / (3.2)	｛脳血管疾患／インフルエンザ｝	4 / 0.1 / (2.2)			｛敗血症／貧血／筋骨格系及び結合組織の疾患｝	／ 0.1 / (1.1)		
肺炎	9 / 0.3 / (2.6)	脳血管疾患	7 / 0.2 / (2.0)	その他の新生物	6 / 0.2 / (1.7)	他殺	3 / 0.1 / (0.9)	｛肝疾患／腎不全｝	2 / 0.1 / (0.6)
脳血管疾患	12 / 0.4 / (2.0)	肺炎	10 / 0.3 / (1.6)	その他の新生物	6 / 0.2 / (1.0)	筋骨格系及び結合組織の疾患	5 / 0.2 / (0.8)	他殺	4 / 0.1 / (0.7)
肺炎	11 / 0.4 / (1.4)	｛その他の新生物／先天奇形,変形及び染色体異常｝	10 / 0.3 / (1.3)			他殺	9 / 0.3 / (1.2)	妊娠,分娩及び産じょく	8 / 0.3 / (1.0)
肝疾患	21 / 0.6 / (1.9)	｛その他の新生物／肺炎／先天奇形,変形及び染色体異常｝	15 / 0.4 / (1.3)					妊娠,分娩及び産じょく	13 / 0.4 / (1.2)
肝疾患	43 / 1.1 / (2.3)	肺炎	20 / 0.5 / (1.0)	｛その他の新生物／筋骨格系及び結合組織の疾患｝	18 / 0.5 / (0.9)			先天奇形,変形及び染色体異常	12 / 0.3 / (0.6)
肝疾患	98 / 2.1 / (2.9)	肺炎	42 / 0.9 / (1.2)	その他の新生物	39 / 0.8 / (1.1)	糖尿病	27 / 0.6 / (0.8)	先天奇形,変形及び染色体異常	26 / 0.6 / (0.8)
肝疾患	144 / 3.2 / (2.9)	肺炎	61 / 1.4 / (1.2)	その他の新生物	49 / 1.1 / (1.0)	糖尿病	39 / 0.9 / (0.8)	筋骨格系及び結合組織の疾患	36 / 0.8 / (0.7)
肝疾患	189 / 4.9 / (2.7)	肺炎	104 / 2.7 / (1.5)	敗血症	53 / 1.4 / (0.8)	その他の新生物	52 / 1.3 / (0.7)	大動脈瘤及び解離	51 / 1.3 / (0.7)
肝疾患	217 / 5.8 / (2.3)	肺炎	180 / 4.8 / (1.9)	大動脈瘤及び解離	87 / 2.3 / (0.9)	その他の新生物	82 / 2.2 / (0.9)	｛糖尿病／筋骨格系及び結合組織の疾患｝	73 / 2.0 / (0.8)
肺炎	352 / 8.6 / (2.4)	肝疾患	306 / 7.5 / (2.1)	大動脈瘤及び解離	187 / 4.6 / (1.3)	糖尿病	140 / 3.4 / (0.9)	その他の新生物	126 / 3.1 / (0.9)
自殺	635 / 12.0 / (2.2)	大動脈瘤及び解離	498 / 9.4 / (1.8)	肝疾患	474 / 9.0 / (1.7)	糖尿病	306 / 5.8 / (1.1)	腎不全	290 / 5.5 / (1.0)
大動脈瘤及び解離	706 / 17.9 / (2.0)	自殺	571 / 14.5 / (1.6)	肝疾患	548 / 13.9 / (1.6)	腎不全	464 / 11.8 / (1.3)	糖尿病	417 / 10.6 / (1.2)
老衰	1 018 / 28.2 / (1.8)	大動脈瘤及び解離	1 012 / 28.1 / (1.8)	腎不全	977 / 27.1 / (1.7)	肝疾患	817 / 22.7 / (1.5)	糖尿病	712 / 19.7 / (1.2)
不慮の事故	2 841 / 92.4 / (3.0)	腎不全	1 952 / 63.5 / (2.0)	大動脈瘤及び解離	1 764 / 57.4 / (1.8)	糖尿病	1 160 / 37.7 / (1.2)	アルツハイマー病	1 122 / 36.5 / (1.2)
不慮の事故	3 465 / 161.2 / (2.5)	腎不全	3 319 / 154.4 / (2.5)	アルツハイマー病	2 260 / 105.1 / (1.7)	大動脈瘤及び解離	2 216 / 103.1 / (1.6)	血管性等の認知症	2 045 / 95.1 / (1.5)
腎不全	3 258 / 296.7 / (2.4)	不慮の事故	2 922 / 266.1 / (2.4)	血管性等の認知症	2 799 / 254.9 / (2.0)	アルツハイマー病	2 524 / 229.9 / (1.8)	大動脈瘤及び解離	1 644 / 149.7 / (1.2)
血管性等の認知症	1 826 / 577.8 / (2.4)	腎不全	1 555 / 492.1 / (2.1)	アルツハイマー病	1 323 / 418.7 / (1.8)	不慮の事故	1 284 / 406.3 / (1.7)	高血圧性疾患	820 / 259.5 / (1.1)
血管性等の認知症	567 / 994.7 / (2.5)	不慮の事故	315 / 552.6 / (1.4)	腎不全	295 / 517.5 / (1.3)	アルツハイマー病	293 / 514.0 / (1.3)	高血圧性疾患	278 / 487.7 / (1.2)
不慮の事故	14 627 / 75.0 / (2.5)	腎不全	12 110 / 62.1 / (2.1)	血管性等の認知症	8 511 / 43.6 / (1.4)	大動脈瘤及び解離	8 507 / 43.6 / (1.4)	アルツハイマー病	8 191 / 42.0 / (1.4)
不慮の事故	12 661 / 122.9 / (2.4)	腎不全	11 356 / 110.2 / (2.2)	血管性等の認知症	8 396 / 81.5 / (1.6)	アルツハイマー病	7 933 / 77.0 / (1.5)	大動脈瘤及び解離	7 303 / 70.9 / (1.3)
不慮の事故	10 827 / 161.7 / (2.3)	腎不全	10 379 / 155.0 / (2.2)	血管性等の認知症	8 130 / 121.4 / (1.7)	アルツハイマー病	7 522 / 112.3 / (1.6)	大動脈瘤及び解離	6 291 / 94.0 / (1.3)

死 亡

Table 5.17 Leading causes of death

Deaths, Death rates (per 100,000 population), Proportion (%)　**Total**

Age	1 Causes of death	Deaths Rates (%)	2 Causes of death	Deaths Rates (%)	3 Causes of death	Deaths Rates (%)	4 Causes of death	Deaths Rates (%)	5 Causes of death	Deaths Rates (%)
Total	Malignant neoplasms	372 986 / 298.3 / (28.5)	Heart dis.	198 006 / 158.4 / (15.1)	Pneumonia	119 300 / 95.4 / (9.1)	C.V.D.	109 320 / 87.4 / (8.4)	Senility	92 806 / 74.2 / (7.1)
0 Year	Congenital malformations, etc.	663 / 67.9 / (34.4)	Respiratory and cardiovascular disorders	282 / 28.9 / (14.6)	SIDS	109 / 11.2 / (5.7)	Accidents	73 / 7.5 / (3.8)	Haemorrhagic and haematological disorders	67 / 6.9 / (3.5)
1~4	Congenital malformations, etc.	150 / 3.8 / (21.7)	Accidents	85 / 2.2 / (12.3)	Malignant neoplasms	59 / 1.5 / (8.6)	Heart dis.	40 / 1.0 / (5.8)	Pneumonia	35 / 0.9 / (5.1)
5~9	Malignant neoplasms	84 / 1.6 / (21.5)	Accidents	68 / 1.3 / (17.4)	Congenital malformations, etc.	32 / 0.6 / (8.2)	Pneumonia	19 / 0.4 / (4.9)	Heart dis.	16 / 0.3 / (4.1)
10~14	Malignant neoplasms	95 / 1.7 / (21.6)	Suicide	71 / 1.3 / (16.1)	Accidents	66 / 1.2 / (15.0)	Congenital malformations, etc.	27 / 0.5 / (6.1)	Heart dis.	19 / 0.3 / (4.3)
15~19	Suicide	430 / 7.2 / (36.9)	Accidents	306 / 5.1 / (26.2)	Malignant neoplasms	120 / 2.0 / (10.3)	Heart dis.	45 / 0.8 / (3.9)	Congenital malformations, etc.	26 / 0.4 / (2.2)
20~24	Suicide	1 001 / 17.0 / (48.1)	Accidents	373 / 6.3 / (17.9)	Malignant neoplasms	159 / 2.7 / (7.6)	Heart dis.	108 / 1.8 / (5.2)	Congenital malformations, etc.	36 / 0.6 / (1.7)
25~29	Suicide	1 165 / 19.0 / (47.0)	Malignant neoplasms	315 / 5.1 / (12.7)	Accidents	291 / 4.7 / (11.7)	Heart dis.	156 / 2.5 / (6.3)	C.V.D.	47 / 0.8 / (1.9)
30~34	Suicide	1 253 / 17.8 / (37.4)	Malignant neoplasms	641 / 9.1 / (19.1)	Accidents	346 / 4.9 / (10.3)	Heart dis.	248 / 3.5 / (7.4)	C.V.D.	118 / 1.7 / (3.5)
35~39	Suicide	1 445 / 18.2 / (27.8)	Malignant neoplasms	1 326 / 16.7 / (25.5)	Heart dis.	495 / 6.2 / (9.5)	Accidents	444 / 5.6 / (8.5)	C.V.D.	307 / 3.9 / (5.9)
40~44	Malignant neoplasms	2 675 / 28.0 / (28.9)	Suicide	1 739 / 18.2 / (18.8)	Heart dis.	1 095 / 11.5 / (11.8)	C.V.D.	826 / 8.6 / (8.9)	Accidents	553 / 5.8 / (6.0)
45~49	Malignant neoplasms	4 753 / 52.1 / (34.1)	Suicide	1 888 / 20.7 / (13.6)	Heart dis.	1 819 / 19.9 / (13.1)	C.V.D.	1 203 / 13.2 / (8.6)	Accidents	694 / 7.6 / (5.0)
50~54	Malignant neoplasms	7 696 / 98.9 / (39.5)	Heart dis.	2 476 / 31.8 / (12.7)	Suicide	1 853 / 23.8 / (9.5)	C.V.D.	1 628 / 20.9 / (8.4)	Dis. of liver	897 / 11.5 / (4.6)
55~59	Malignant neoplasms	12 605 / 168.9 / (44.5)	Heart dis.	3 488 / 46.7 / (12.3)	C.V.D.	2 148 / 28.8 / (7.6)	Suicide	1 684 / 22.6 / (5.9)	Dis. of liver	1 150 / 15.4 / (4.1)
60~64	Malignant neoplasms	23 343 / 288.4 / (48.4)	Heart dis.	5 824 / 71.9 / (12.1)	C.V.D.	3 324 / 41.1 / (6.9)	Suicide	1 563 / 19.3 / (3.2)	Pneumonia	1 560 / 19.3 / (3.2)
65~69	Malignant neoplasms	46 004 / 450.0 / (49.2)	Heart dis.	11 292 / 110.5 / (12.1)	C.V.D.	6 273 / 61.4 / (6.7)	Pneumonia	3 696 / 36.2 / (4.0)	Accidents	2 750 / 26.9 / (2.9)
70~74	Malignant neoplasms	48 833 / 662.4 / (45.3)	Heart dis.	13 353 / 181.1 / (12.4)	C.V.D.	7 667 / 104.0 / (7.1)	Pneumonia	6 032 / 81.8 / (5.6)	Accidents	3 282 / 44.5 / (3.0)
75~79	Malignant neoplasms	58 317 / 897.2 / (38.1)	Heart dis.	20 436 / 314.4 / (13.4)	C.V.D.	12 451 / 191.6 / (8.1)	Pneumonia	11 681 / 179.7 / (7.6)	Accidents	4 851 / 74.6 / (3.2)
80~84	Malignant neoplasms	67 401 / 1 304.9 / (30.1)	Heart dis.	33 028 / 639.4 / (14.8)	Pneumonia	22 231 / 430.4 / (9.9)	C.V.D.	20 087 / 388.9 / (9.0)	Senility	7 805 / 151.1 / (3.5)
85~89	Malignant neoplasms	57 874 / 1 771.4 / (22.2)	Heart dis.	43 241 / 1 323.5 / (16.6)	Pneumonia	31 171 / 954.1 / (12.0)	C.V.D.	23 746 / 726.8 / (9.1)	Senility	19 265 / 589.7 / (7.4)
90~94	Heart dis.	38 374 / 2 601.6 / (18.3)	Malignant neoplasms	30 746 / 2 084.5 / (14.7)	Senility	30 171 / 2 045.5 / (14.4)	Pneumonia	26 418 / 1 791.1 / (12.6)	C.V.D.	19 285 / 1 307.5 / (9.2)
95~99	Senility	22 834 / 5 977.5 / (23.8)	Heart dis.	17 898 / 4 685.3 / (18.7)	Pneumonia	11 906 / 3 116.8 / (12.4)	Malignant neoplasms	8 605 / 2 252.6 / (9.0)	C.V.D.	8 257 / 2 161.5 / (8.6)
100~	Senility	9 907 / 15 241.5 / (37.5)	Heart dis.	4 475 / 6 884.6 / (16.9)	Pneumonia	2 924 / 4 498.5 / (11.1)	C.V.D.	1 860 / 2 861.5 / (7.0)	Malignant neoplasms	1 301 / 2 001.5 / (4.9)
(Regrouped) 65~	Malignant neoplasms	319 081 / 926.2 / (27.3)	Heart dis.	182 097 / 528.6 / (15.6)	Pneumonia	116 059 / 336.9 / (9.9)	C.V.D.	99 626 / 289.2 / (8.5)	Senility	92 781 / 269.3 / (7.9)
75~	Malignant neoplasms	224 244 / 1 330.4 / (23.1)	Heart dis.	157 452 / 934.1 / (16.2)	Pneumonia	106 331 / 630.8 / (11.0)	Senility	92 037 / 546.0 / (9.5)	C.V.D.	85 686 / 508.3 / (8.8)
80~	Malignant neoplasms	165 927 / 1 602.3 / (20.3)	Heart dis.	137 016 / 1 323.1 / (16.8)	Pneumonia	94 650 / 914.0 / (11.6)	Senility	89 982 / 868.9 / (11.0)	C.V.D.	73 235 / 707.2 / (9.0)

Note : C.V.D. ← Cerebrovascular diseases
Congenital malformations, etc. ← Congenital malformations, deformations and chromosomal abnormalities
Benign neoplasms ← In situ neoplasms and benign neoplasms and neoplasms of uncertain or unknown behaviour
D.M. ← Diabetes mellitus
Respiratory and cardiovascular disorders ← Respiratory and cardiovascular disorders specific to the perinatal period
SIDS ← Sudden infant death syndrome
Haemorrhagic and haematological disorders ← Haemorrhagic and haematological disorders of fetus and newborn

General mortality

by sex and age : Japan, 2016

Total

6		7		8		9		10	
Causes of death	Deaths Rates (%)	Causes of death	Deaths Rates (%)	Causes of death	Deaths Rates (%)	Causes of death	Deaths Rates (%)	Causes of death	Deaths Rates (%)
Accidents	38 306 30.6 (2.9)	Renal failure	24 612 19.7 (1.9)	Suicide	21 017 16.8 (1.6)	Aortic aneurysm	18 145 14.5 (1.4)	Dis. of liver	15 773 12.6 (1.2)
Disorders related to length of gestation and fetal growth / Infections specific to the perinatal period	43 4.4 (2.2)			Heart dis.	41 4.2 (2.1)	Septicaemia	40 4.1 (2.1)	Pneumonia	28 2.9 (1.5)
Septicaemia	25 0.6 (3.6)	Intestinal infectious diseases / Influenza	19 0.5 (2.8)			Certain conditions originating in the perinatal period	10 0.3 (1.4)	Benign neoplasms / Hernia and intestinal obstruction / Dis. of liver	6 0.2 (0.9)
Benign neoplasms	15 0.3 (3.8)	Intestinal infectious diseases / Homicide	11 0.2 (2.8)			Septicaemia	9 0.2 (2.3)	C.V.D. / Influenza	7 0.1 (1.8)
C.V.D. / Pneumonia	13 0.2 (3.0)			Influenza	10 0.2 (2.3)	Benign neoplasms	7 0.1 (1.6)	Homicide	6 0.1 (1.4)
C.V.D.	17 0.3 (1.5)	Benign neoplasms / Pneumonia	13 0.2 (1.1)			Homicide	9 0.2 (0.8)	Septicaemia	5 0.1 (0.4)
C.V.D.	26 0.4 (1.2)	Pneumonia	18 0.3 (0.9)	Benign neoplasms	17 0.3 (0.8)	Septicaemia	8 0.1 (0.4)	D.M. / Aortic aneurysm	7 0.1 (0.3)
Pneumonia	31 0.5 (1.3)	Congenital malformations, etc.	22 0.4 (0.9)	Benign neoplasms	18 0.3 (0.7)	Septicaemia	12 0.2 (0.5)	Homicide	11 0.2 (0.4)
Dis. of liver	54 0.8 (1.6)	Pneumonia	47 0.7 (1.4)	Benign neoplasms / Congenital malformations, etc.	32 0.5 (1.0)			D.M.	16 0.2 (0.5)
Dis. of liver	124 1.6 (2.4)	Pneumonia	75 0.9 (1.4)	Aortic aneurysm	48 0.6 (0.9)	Benign neoplasms	43 0.5 (0.8)	Congenital malformations, etc.	33 0.4 (0.6)
Dis. of liver	376 3.9 (4.1)	Pneumonia	125 1.3 (1.3)	Aortic aneurysm	115 1.2 (1.2)	D.M.	96 1.0 (1.0)	Benign neoplasms	88 0.9 (1.0)
Dis. of liver	669 7.3 (4.8)	Pneumonia	224 2.5 (1.6)	Aortic aneurysm	181 2.0 (1.3)	D.M.	151 1.7 (1.1)	Benign neoplasms	110 1.2 (0.8)
Accidents	815 10.5 (4.2)	Pneumonia	366 4.7 (1.9)	Aortic aneurysm	280 3.6 (1.4)	D.M.	235 3.0 (1.2)	Benign neoplasms	160 2.1 (0.8)
Accidents	1 104 14.8 (3.9)	Pneumonia	677 9.1 (2.4)	Aortic aneurysm	461 6.2 (1.6)	D.M.	360 4.8 (1.3)	Benign neoplasms	221 3.0 (0.8)
Dis. of liver	1 552 19.2 (3.2)	Accidents	1 531 18.9 (3.2)	Aortic aneurysm	690 8.5 (1.4)	D.M.	601 7.4 (1.2)	Renal failure	461 5.7 (1.0)
Dis. of liver	2 105 20.6 (2.3)	Suicide	1 870 18.3 (2.0)	Aortic aneurysm	1 525 14.9 (1.6)	D.M.	1 185 11.6 (1.3)	Renal failure	1 054 10.3 (1.1)
Dis. of liver	1 763 23.9 (1.6)	Aortic aneurysm	1 715 23.3 (1.6)	Suicide	1 513 20.5 (1.4)	Renal failure	1 412 19.2 (1.3)	Chronic obstructive pulmonary dis.	1 323 17.9 (1.2)
Renal failure	2 585 39.8 (1.7)	Aortic aneurysm	2 353 36.2 (1.5)	Chronic obstructive pulmonary dis.	2 246 34.6 (1.5)	Dis. of liver	2 116 32.6 (1.4)	Senility	2 055 31.6 (1.3)
Accidents	6 668 129.1 (3.0)	Renal failure	4 624 89.5 (2.1)	Chronic obstructive pulmonary dis.	3 694 71.5 (1.7)	Aortic aneurysm	3 512 68.0 (1.6)	D.M.	2 560 49.6 (1.1)
Accidents	6 957 212.9 (2.7)	Renal failure	6 409 196.2 (2.5)	Chronic obstructive pulmonary dis.	4 035 123.5 (1.5)	Aortic aneurysm	3 891 119.1 (1.5)	Alzheimer's disease	3 386 103.6 (1.3)
Renal failure	5 108 346.3 (2.4)	Accidents	4 849 328.7 (2.3)	Vascular dementia	3 571 242.1 (1.7)	Alzheimer's disease	3 265 221.4 (1.6)	Aortic aneurysm	2 510 170.2 (1.2)
Vascular dementia / Renal failure	2 106 551.3 (2.2)			Accidents	1 772 463.9 (1.8)	Alzheimer's disease	1 563 409.2 (1.6)	Hypertensive dis.	998 261.3 (1.0)
Vascular dementia	625 961.5 (2.4)	Accidents	392 603.1 (1.5)	Renal failure	384 590.8 (1.5)	Hypertensive dis.	317 487.7 (1.2)	Alzheimer's disease	316 486.2 (1.2)
Accidents	31 521 91.5 (2.7)	Renal failure	23 682 68.7 (2.0)	Aortic aneurysm	16 341 47.4 (1.4)	Chronic obstructive pulmonary dis.	15 309 44.4 (1.3)	D.M.	11 971 34.7 (1.0)
Accidents	25 489 151.2 (2.6)	Renal failure	21 216 125.9 (2.2)	Chronic obstructive pulmonary dis.	13 298 78.9 (1.4)	Aortic aneurysm	13 101 77.7 (1.4)	Vascular dementia	11 553 68.5 (1.2)
Accidents	20 638 199.3 (2.5)	Renal failure	18 631 179.9 (2.3)	Chronic obstructive pulmonary dis.	11 052 106.7 (1.4)	Vascular dementia	10 963 105.9 (1.3)	Aortic aneurysm	10 748 103.8 (1.3)

Aortic aneurysm ← Aortic aneurysm and dissection
Vascular dementia ← Vascular dementia and unspecified dementia
Heart dis. ← Heart diseases(excluding hypertensive heart diseases)

死 亡

Table 5.17 Leading causes of death

Deaths, Death rates (per 100,000 population), Proportion (%)　Male

Age	1 Causes of death / Deaths Rates (%)	2 Causes of death / Deaths Rates (%)	3 Causes of death / Deaths Rates (%)	4 Causes of death / Deaths Rates (%)	5 Causes of death / Deaths Rates (%)
Total	Malignant neoplasms 219 785 / 361.1 / (32.6)	Heart dis. 93 419 / 153.5 / (13.8)	Pneumonia 65 636 / 107.8 / (9.7)	C.V.D. 52 706 / 86.6 / (7.8)	Senility 23 077 / 37.9 / (3.4)
0 Year	Congenital malformations, etc. 323 / 64.4 / (33.0)	Respiratory and cardiovascular disorders 145 / 28.9 / (14.8)	SIDS 54 / 10.8 / (5.5)	Accidents 42 / 8.4 / (4.3)	Infections specific to the perinatal period / Haemorrhagic and haematological disorders 28 / 5.6 / (2.9)
1～4	Congenital malformations, etc. 72 / 3.6 / (19.4)	Accidents 54 / 2.7 / (14.6)	Malignant neoplasms 34 / 1.7 / (9.2)	Heart dis. 26 / 1.3 / (7.0)	Pneumonia 19 / 1.0 / (5.1)
5～9	Malignant neoplasms 50 / 1.9 / (21.8)	Accidents 44 / 1.6 / (19.2)	Congenital malformations, etc. 16 / 0.6 / (7.0)	Benign neoplasms / Heart dis. 10 / 0.4 / (4.4)	
10～14	Accidents 49 / 1.8 / (19.3)	Malignant neoplasms 48 / 1.7 / (18.9)	Suicide 43 / 1.5 / (16.9)	Heart dis. 11 / 0.4 / (4.3)	C.V.D. / Congenital malformations, etc. 9 / 0.3 / (3.5)
15～19	Suicide 301 / 9.8 / (36.9)	Accidents 239 / 7.8 / (29.3)	Malignant neoplasms 78 / 2.6 / (9.6)	Heart dis. 33 / 1.1 / (4.0)	Congenital malformations, etc. 16 / 0.5 / (2.0)
20～24	Suicide 745 / 24.6 / (50.6)	Accidents 281 / 9.3 / (19.1)	Malignant neoplasms 95 / 3.1 / (6.5)	Heart dis. 76 / 2.5 / (5.2)	Congenital malformations, etc. 21 / 0.7 / (1.4)
25～29	Suicide 877 / 28.0 / (51.2)	Accidents 227 / 7.3 / (13.3)	Malignant neoplasms 155 / 5.0 / (9.0)	Heart dis. 106 / 3.4 / (6.2)	C.V.D. 34 / 1.1 / (2.0)
30～34	Suicide 936 / 26.2 / (42.0)	Accidents 282 / 7.9 / (12.7)	Malignant neoplasms 261 / 7.3 / (11.7)	Heart dis. 203 / 5.7 / (9.1)	C.V.D. 81 / 2.3 / (3.6)
35～39	Suicide 1 032 / 25.6 / (31.4)	Malignant neoplasms 535 / 13.3 / (16.3)	Heart dis. 378 / 9.4 / (11.5)	Accidents 345 / 8.6 / (10.5)	C.V.D. 213 / 5.3 / (6.5)
40～44	Suicide 1 305 / 26.9 / (22.4)	Malignant neoplasms 1 115 / 23.0 / (19.1)	Heart dis. 830 / 17.1 / (14.2)	C.V.D. 548 / 11.3 / (9.4)	Accidents 442 / 9.1 / (7.6)
45～49	Malignant neoplasms 2 141 / 46.3 / (24.1)	Heart dis. 1 453 / 31.4 / (16.3)	Suicide 1 400 / 30.3 / (15.8)	C.V.D. 828 / 17.9 / (9.3)	Accidents 527 / 11.4 / (5.9)
50～54	Malignant neoplasms 3 791 / 96.7 / (30.3)	Heart dis. 2 005 / 51.2 / (16.0)	Suicide 1 353 / 34.5 / (10.8)	C.V.D. 1 122 / 28.6 / (9.0)	Dis. of liver 708 / 18.1 / (5.7)
55～59	Malignant neoplasms 7 268 / 195.2 / (38.1)	Heart dis. 2 858 / 76.7 / (15.0)	C.V.D. 1 474 / 39.6 / (7.7)	Suicide 1 219 / 32.7 / (6.4)	Dis. of liver 933 / 25.1 / (4.9)
60～64	Malignant neoplasms 14 842 / 372.0 / (44.4)	Heart dis. 4 640 / 116.3 / (13.9)	C.V.D. 2 360 / 59.1 / (7.1)	Dis. of liver 1 246 / 31.2 / (3.7)	Pneumonia 1 208 / 30.3 / (3.6)
65～69	Malignant neoplasms 30 772 / 622.1 / (47.3)	Heart dis. 8 507 / 172.0 / (13.1)	C.V.D. 4 410 / 89.2 / (6.8)	Pneumonia 2 853 / 57.7 / (4.4)	Accidents 1 940 / 39.2 / (3.0)
70～74	Malignant neoplasms 32 933 / 958.6 / (45.4)	Heart dis. 9 077 / 264.2 / (12.5)	C.V.D. 5 127 / 149.2 / (7.1)	Pneumonia 4 475 / 130.3 / (6.2)	Accidents 2 126 / 61.9 / (2.9)
75～79	Malignant neoplasms 37 864 / 1 308.1 / (39.0)	Heart dis. 12 312 / 425.3 / (12.7)	Pneumonia 8 270 / 285.7 / (8.5)	C.V.D. 7 780 / 268.8 / (8.0)	Accidents 3 017 / 104.2 / (3.1)
80～84	Malignant neoplasms 40 840 / 1 954.3 / (31.9)	Heart dis. 17 196 / 822.9 / (13.4)	Pneumonia 14 465 / 692.2 / (11.3)	C.V.D. 10 980 / 525.4 / (8.6)	Accidents 3 827 / 183.1 / (3.0)
85～89	Malignant neoplasms 31 187 / 2 791.2 / (25.0)	Heart dis. 18 135 / 1 623.0 / (14.6)	Pneumonia 17 612 / 1 576.2 / (14.1)	C.V.D. 10 326 / 924.2 / (8.3)	Senility 6 440 / 576.4 / (5.2)
90～94	Malignant neoplasms 12 810 / 3 397.9 / (18.1)	Pneumonia 11 281 / 2 992.3 / (15.9)	Heart dis. 11 280 / 2 992.0 / (15.9)	Senility 6 999 / 1 856.5 / (9.9)	C.V.D. 5 640 / 1 496.0 / (8.0)
95～99	Senility 3 671 / 5 479.1 / (17.3)	Pneumonia 3 655 / 5 455.2 / (17.2)	Heart dis. 3 542 / 5 286.6 / (16.7)	Malignant neoplasms 2 640 / 3 940.3 / (12.4)	C.V.D. 1 500 / 2 238.8 / (7.1)
100～	Senility 1 173 / 13 033.3 / (29.2)	Heart dis. 688 / 7 644.4 / (17.1)	Pneumonia 634 / 7 044.4 / (15.8)	Malignant neoplasms 302 / 3 355.6 / (7.5)	C.V.D. 229 / 2 544.4 / (5.7)
(Regrouped) 65～	Malignant neoplasms 189 348 / 1 267.7 / (32.5)	Heart dis. 80 737 / 540.5 / (13.8)	Pneumonia 63 245 / 423.4 / (10.8)	C.V.D. 45 992 / 307.9 / (7.9)	Senility 23 062 / 154.4 / (4.0)
75～	Malignant neoplasms 125 643 / 1 916.9 / (28.2)	Heart dis. 63 153 / 963.5 / (14.2)	Pneumonia 55 917 / 853.1 / (12.5)	C.V.D. 36 455 / 556.2 / (8.2)	Senility 22 613 / 345.0 / (5.1)
80～	Malignant neoplasms 87 779 / 2 398.3 / (25.2)	Heart dis. 50 841 / 1 389.1 / (14.6)	Pneumonia 47 647 / 1 301.8 / (13.7)	C.V.D. 28 675 / 783.5 / (8.2)	Senility 21 576 / 589.5 / (6.2)

General mortality

by sex and age : Japan, 2016－CON.

Male

6		7		8		9		10	
Causes of death	Deaths Rates (%)	Causes of death	Deaths Rates (%)	Causes of death	Deaths Rates (%)	Causes of death	Deaths Rates (%)	Causes of death	Deaths Rates (%)
Accidents	22 066 / 36.3 / (3.3)	Suicide	14 639 / 24.1 / (2.2)	Chronic obstructive pulmonary dis.	12 649 / 20.8 / (1.9)	Renal failure	12 231 / 20.1 / (1.8)	Dis. of liver	10 112 / 16.6 / (1.5)
		Septicaemia	22 / 4.4 / (2.2)	Heart dis. / Disorders related to length of gestation and fetal growth	21 / 4.2 / (2.1)			Pneumonia	15 / 3.0 / (1.5)
Septicaemia	17 / 0.9 / (4.6)	Influenza	12 / 0.6 / (3.2)	Intestinal infectious diseases	9 / 0.5 / (2.4)	Dis. of liver / Certain conditions originating in the perinatal period	5 / 0.3 / (1.3)		
Intestinal infectious diseases / Pneumonia	8 / 0.3 / (3.5)			Septicaemia	5 / 0.2 / (2.2)	Influenza / Homicide	4 / 0.1 / (1.7)		
		Pneumonia	7 / 0.3 / (2.8)	Benign neoplasms / Influenza / Homicide	6 / 0.2 / (2.4)				
C.V.D.	10 / 0.3 / (1.2)	Benign neoplasms	7 / 0.2 / (0.9)	Homicide	6 / 0.2 / (0.7)	Septicaemia / Pneumonia	4 / 0.1 / (0.5)		
C.V.D.	14 / 0.5 / (1.0)	Benign neoplasms	11 / 0.4 / (0.7)	Septicaemia / Pneumonia	8 / 0.3 / (0.5)			Aortic aneurysm / Dis. of liver	5 / 0.2 / (0.3)
Pneumonia	20 / 0.6 / (1.2)	Congenital malformations, etc.	12 / 0.4 / (0.7)	Benign neoplasms	8 / 0.3 / (0.5)	D.M. / Hernia and intestinal obstruction	7 / 0.2 / (0.4)		
Dis. of liver	33 / 0.9 / (1.5)	Pneumonia	32 / 0.9 / (1.4)	Benign neoplasms / Congenital malformations, etc.	17 / 0.5 / (0.8)			D.M. / Aortic aneurysm	11 / 0.3 / (0.5)
Dis. of liver	81 / 2.0 / (2.5)	Pneumonia	55 / 1.4 / (1.7)	Aortic aneurysm	43 / 1.1 / (1.3)	D.M.	26 / 0.6 / (0.8)	Benign neoplasms	25 / 0.6 / (0.8)
Dis. of liver	278 / 5.7 / (4.8)	Aortic aneurysm	105 / 2.2 / (1.8)	Pneumonia	83 / 1.7 / (1.4)	D.M.	69 / 1.4 / (1.2)	Benign neoplasms	49 / 1.0 / (0.8)
Dis. of liver	525 / 11.3 / (5.9)	Pneumonia	163 / 3.5 / (1.8)	Aortic aneurysm	159 / 3.4 / (1.8)	D.M.	112 / 2.4 / (1.3)	Benign neoplasms	61 / 1.3 / (0.7)
Accidents	615 / 15.7 / (4.9)	Pneumonia	262 / 6.7 / (2.1)	Aortic aneurysm	229 / 5.8 / (1.8)	D.M.	190 / 4.8 / (1.5)	Benign neoplasms	108 / 2.8 / (0.9)
Accidents	846 / 22.7 / (4.4)	Pneumonia	497 / 13.3 / (2.6)	Aortic aneurysm	374 / 10.0 / (2.0)	D.M.	287 / 7.7 / (1.5)	Benign neoplasms	139 / 3.7 / (0.7)
Accidents	1 156 / 29.0 / (3.5)	Suicide	1 107 / 27.7 / (3.3)	Aortic aneurysm	503 / 12.6 / (1.5)	D.M.	461 / 11.6 / (1.4)	Renal failure	339 / 8.5 / (1.0)
Dis. of liver	1 631 / 33.0 / (2.5)	Suicide	1 235 / 25.0 / (1.9)	Aortic aneurysm	1 027 / 20.8 / (1.6)	D.M.	879 / 17.8 / (1.4)	Renal failure	764 / 15.4 / (1.2)
Dis. of liver	1 215 / 35.4 / (1.7)	Chronic obstructive pulmonary dis.	1 155 / 33.6 / (1.6)	Aortic aneurysm	1 009 / 29.4 / (1.4)	Renal failure	948 / 27.6 / (1.3)	Suicide	942 / 27.4 / (1.3)
Chronic obstructive pulmonary dis.	1 941 / 67.1 / (2.0)	Renal failure	1 608 / 55.6 / (1.7)	Aortic aneurysm	1 341 / 46.3 / (1.4)	Dis. of liver	1 299 / 44.9 / (1.3)	D.M.	1 226 / 42.4 / (1.3)
Senility	3 293 / 157.6 / (2.6)	Chronic obstructive pulmonary dis.	3 114 / 149.0 / (2.4)	Renal failure	2 672 / 127.9 / (2.1)	Aortic aneurysm	1 748 / 83.6 / (1.4)	D.M.	1 400 / 67.0 / (1.1)
Accidents	3 492 / 312.5 / (2.8)	Chronic obstructive pulmonary dis.	3 267 / 292.4 / (2.6)	Renal failure	3 090 / 276.5 / (2.5)	Aortic aneurysm	1 675 / 149.9 / (1.3)	Benign neoplasms	1 225 / 109.6 / (1.0)
Accidents	1 927 / 511.1 / (2.7)	Renal failure	1 850 / 490.7 / (2.6)	Chronic obstructive pulmonary dis.	1 807 / 479.3 / (2.6)	Aortic aneurysm	866 / 229.7 / (1.2)	Vascular dementia	772 / 204.8 / (1.1)
Renal failure	551 / 822.4 / (2.6)	Accidents	488 / 728.4 / (2.3)	Chronic obstructive pulmonary dis.	404 / 603.0 / (1.9)	Vascular dementia	280 / 417.9 / (1.3)	Alzheimer's disease	240 / 358.2 / (1.1)
Renal failure	89 / 988.9 / (2.2)	Accidents	77 / 855.6 / (1.9)	Vascular dementia	58 / 644.4 / (1.4)	Chronic obstructive pulmonary dis.	56 / 622.2 / (1.4)	Hypertensive dis.	39 / 433.3 / (1.0)
Accidents	16 894 / 113.1 / (2.9)	Chronic obstructive pulmonary dis.	12 342 / 82.6 / (2.1)	Renal failure	11 572 / 77.5 / (2.0)	Aortic aneurysm	7 834 / 52.4 / (1.3)	Dis. of liver	6 280 / 42.0 / (1.1)
Accidents	12 828 / 195.7 / (2.9)	Chronic obstructive pulmonary dis.	10 589 / 161.6 / (2.4)	Renal failure	9 860 / 150.4 / (2.2)	Aortic aneurysm	5 798 / 88.5 / (1.3)	D.M.	4 314 / 65.8 / (1.0)
Accidents	9 811 / 268.1 / (2.8)	Chronic obstructive pulmonary dis.	8 648 / 236.3 / (2.5)	Renal failure	8 252 / 225.5 / (2.4)	Aortic aneurysm	4 457 / 121.8 / (1.3)	Benign neoplasms	3 214 / 87.8 / (0.9)

死 亡

Table 5.17 Leading causes of death

Deaths, Death rates (per 100,000 population), Proportion (%)   **Female**

Age	1 Causes of death	1 Deaths Rates (%)	2 Causes of death	2 Deaths Rates (%)	3 Causes of death	3 Deaths Rates (%)	4 Causes of death	4 Deaths Rates (%)	5 Causes of death	5 Deaths Rates (%)
Total	Malignant neoplasms	153 201 238.8 (24.2)	Heart dis.	104 587 163.0 (16.5)	Senility	69 729 108.7 (11.0)	C.V.D.	56 614 88.2 (8.9)	Pneumonia	53 664 83.6 (8.5)
0 Year	Congenital malformations, etc.	340 71.6 (35.9)	Respiratory and cardiovascular disorders	137 28.8 (14.5)	SIDS	55 11.6 (5.8)	Haemorrhagic and haematological disorders	39 8.2 (4.1)	Accidents	31 6.5 (3.3)
1～4	Congenital malformations, etc.	78 4.1 (24.5)	Accidents	31 1.6 (9.7)	Malignant neoplasms	25 1.3 (7.8)	Pneumonia	16 0.8 (5.0)	Heart dis.	14 0.7 (4.4)
5～9	Malignant neoplasms	34 1.3 (21.0)	Accidents	24 0.9 (14.8)	Congenital malformations, etc.	16 0.6 (9.9)	Pneumonia	11 0.4 (6.8)	Homicide	7 0.3 (4.3)
10～14	Malignant neoplasms	47 1.8 (25.3)	Suicide	28 1.0 (15.1)	Congenital malformations, etc.	18 0.7 (9.7)	Accidents	17 0.6 (9.1)	Heart dis.	8 0.3 (4.3)
15～19	Suicide	129 4.5 (36.9)	Accidents	67 2.3 (19.1)	Malignant neoplasms	42 1.5 (12.0)	Heart dis.	12 0.4 (3.4)	Congenital malformations, etc.	10 0.3 (2.9)
20～24	Suicide	256 8.9 (41.8)	Accidents	92 3.2 (15.0)	Malignant neoplasms	64 2.2 (10.5)	Heart dis.	32 1.1 (5.2)	Congenital malformations, etc.	15 0.5 (2.5)
25～29	Suicide	288 9.6 (37.6)	Malignant neoplasms	160 5.3 (20.9)	Accidents	64 2.1 (8.4)	Heart dis.	50 1.7 (6.5)	C.V.D.	13 0.4 (1.7)
30～34	Malignant neoplasms	380 11.0 (33.7)	Suicide	317 9.2 (28.1)	Accidents	64 1.9 (5.7)	Heart dis.	45 1.3 (4.0)	C.V.D.	37 1.1 (3.3)
35～39	Malignant neoplasms	791 20.3 (41.4)	Suicide	413 10.6 (21.6)	Heart dis.	117 3.0 (6.1)	Accidents	99 2.5 (5.2)	C.V.D.	94 2.4 (4.9)
40～44	Malignant neoplasms	1 560 33.2 (45.5)	Suicide	434 9.2 (12.7)	C.V.D.	278 5.9 (8.1)	Heart dis.	265 5.6 (7.7)	Accidents	111 2.4 (3.2)
45～49	Malignant neoplasms	2 612 58.0 (51.9)	Suicide	488 10.8 (9.7)	C.V.D.	375 8.3 (7.4)	Heart dis.	366 8.1 (7.3)	Accidents	167 3.7 (3.3)
50～54	Malignant neoplasms	3 905 101.1 (56.2)	C.V.D.	506 13.1 (7.3)	Suicide	500 12.9 (7.2)	Heart dis.	471 12.2 (6.8)	Accidents	200 5.2 (2.9)
55～59	Malignant neoplasms	5 337 142.8 (57.6)	C.V.D.	674 18.0 (7.3)	Heart dis.	630 16.9 (6.8)	Suicide	465 12.4 (5.0)	Accidents	258 6.9 (2.8)
60～64	Malignant neoplasms	8 501 207.1 (57.6)	Heart dis.	1 184 28.8 (8.0)	C.V.D.	964 23.5 (6.5)	Suicide	456 11.1 (3.1)	Accidents	375 9.1 (2.5)
65～69	Malignant neoplasms	15 232 288.7 (53.6)	Heart dis.	2 785 52.8 (9.8)	C.V.D.	1 863 35.3 (6.6)	Pneumonia	843 16.0 (3.0)	Accidents	810 15.4 (2.8)
70～74	Malignant neoplasms	15 900 403.9 (45.1)	Heart dis.	4 276 108.6 (12.1)	C.V.D.	2 540 64.5 (7.2)	Pneumonia	1 557 39.5 (4.4)	Accidents	1 156 29.4 (3.3)
75～79	Malignant neoplasms	20 453 567.3 (36.6)	Heart dis.	8 124 225.3 (14.5)	C.V.D.	4 671 129.6 (8.4)	Pneumonia	3 411 94.6 (6.1)	Accidents	1 834 50.9 (3.3)
80～84	Malignant neoplasms	26 561 863.6 (27.7)	Heart dis.	15 832 514.8 (16.5)	C.V.D.	9 107 296.1 (9.5)	Pneumonia	7 766 252.5 (8.1)	Senility	4 512 146.7 (4.7)
85～89	Malignant neoplasms	26 687 1 241.4 (19.6)	Heart dis.	25 106 1 167.9 (18.5)	Pneumonia	13 559 630.7 (10.0)	C.V.D.	13 420 624.3 (9.9)	Senility	12 825 596.6 (9.4)
90～94	Heart dis.	27 094 2 467.6 (19.5)	Senility	23 172 2 110.4 (16.7)	Malignant neoplasms	17 936 1 633.5 (12.9)	Pneumonia	15 137 1 378.6 (10.9)	C.V.D.	13 645 1 242.7 (9.8)
95～99	Senility	19 163 6 064.2 (25.7)	Heart dis.	14 356 4 543.0 (19.2)	Pneumonia	8 251 2 611.1 (11.1)	C.V.D.	6 757 2 138.3 (9.1)	Malignant neoplasms	5 965 1 887.7 (8.0)
100～	Senility	8 734 15 322.8 (39.0)	Heart dis.	3 787 6 643.9 (16.9)	Pneumonia	2 290 4 017.5 (10.2)	C.V.D.	1 631 2 861.4 (7.3)	Malignant neoplasms	999 1 752.6 (4.5)
(Regrouped) 65～	Malignant neoplasms	129 733 664.8 (22.1)	Heart dis.	101 360 519.4 (17.3)	Senility	69 719 357.3 (11.9)	C.V.D.	53 634 274.8 (9.1)	Pneumonia	52 814 270.6 (9.0)
75～	Malignant neoplasms	98 601 957.2 (18.8)	Heart dis.	94 299 915.4 (18.0)	Senility	69 424 673.9 (13.3)	Pneumonia	50 414 489.4 (9.4)	C.V.D.	49 231 477.9 (9.4)
80～	Heart dis.	86 175 1 287.0 (18.4)	Malignant neoplasms	78 148 1 167.1 (16.7)	Senility	68 406 1 021.6 (14.6)	Pneumonia	47 003 702.0 (10.1)	C.V.D.	44 560 665.5 (9.5)

General mortality

by sex and age : Japan, 2016—CON.

Female

6		7		8		9		10	
Causes of death	Deaths Rates (%)	Causes of death	Deaths Rates (%)	Causes of death	Deaths Rates (%)	Causes of death	Deaths Rates (%)	Causes of death	Deaths Rates (%)
Accidents	16 240 25.3 (2.6)	Renal failure	12 381 19.3 (2.0)	Aortic aneurysm	8 877 13.8 (1.4)	Vascular dementia	8 517 13.3 (1.3)	Alzheimer's disease	8 222 12.8 (1.3)
Disorders related to length of gestation and fetal growth	22 4.6 (2.3)	Heart dis.	20 4.2 (2.1)	Septicaemia	18 3.8 (1.9)	Infections specific to the perinatal period	15 3.2 (1.6)	Pneumonia	13 2.7 (1.4)
Intestinal infectious diseases	10 0.5 (3.1)	Septicaemia	8 0.4 (2.5)	Influenza	7 0.4 (2.2)	Certain conditions originating in the perinatal period	5 0.3 (1.6)	Benign neoplasms	4 0.2 (1.3)
Heart dis.	6 0.2 (3.7)	Benign neoplasms	5 0.2 (3.1)	Septicaemia / C.V.D.	4 0.2 (2.5)	Septicaemia / Anaemias / Dis. of the musculoskeletal system and connective tissue	2 0.1 (1.1)	Intestinal infectious diseases / Influenza	3 0.1 (1.9)
Pneumonia	6 0.2 (3.2)	C.V.D. / Influenza	4 0.1 (2.2)						
Pneumonia	9 0.3 (2.6)	C.V.D.	7 0.2 (2.0)	Benign neoplasms	6 0.2 (1.7)	Homicide	3 0.1 (0.9)	Dis. of liver / Renal failure	2 0.1 (0.6)
C.V.D.	12 0.4 (2.0)	Pneumonia	10 0.3 (1.6)	Benign neoplasms	6 0.2 (1.0)	Dis. of the musculoskeletal system and connective tissue	5 0.2 (0.8)	Homicide	4 0.1 (0.7)
Pneumonia	11 0.4 (1.4)	Benign neoplasms / Congenital malformations, etc.	10 0.3 (1.3)			Homicide	9 0.3 (1.2)	Pregnancy, childbirth and the puerperium	8 0.3 (1.0)
Dis. of liver	21 0.6 (1.9)	Benign neoplasms / Pneumonia / Congenital malformations, etc.	15 0.4 (1.3)	Benign neoplasms / Dis. of the musculoskeletal system and connective tissue	18 0.5 (0.9)			Pregnancy, childbirth and the puerperium	13 0.4 (1.2)
Dis. of liver	43 1.1 (2.3)	Pneumonia	20 0.5 (1.0)					Congenital malformations, etc.	12 0.3 (0.6)
Dis. of liver	98 2.1 (1.2)	Pneumonia	42 0.9 (1.2)	Benign neoplasms	39 0.8 (1.1)	D.M.	27 0.6 (0.8)	Congenital malformations, etc.	26 0.6 (0.8)
Dis. of liver	144 3.2 (2.9)	Pneumonia	61 1.4 (1.2)	Benign neoplasms	49 1.1 (1.0)	D.M.	39 0.9 (0.8)	Dis. of the musculoskeletal system and connective tissue	36 0.8 (0.7)
Dis. of liver	189 4.9 (2.7)	Pneumonia	104 2.7 (1.5)	Septicaemia	53 1.4 (0.8)	Benign neoplasms	52 1.3 (0.7)	Aortic aneurysm	51 1.3 (0.7)
Dis. of liver	217 5.8 (2.3)	Pneumonia	180 4.8 (1.9)	Aortic aneurysm	87 2.3 (0.9)	Benign neoplasms	82 2.2 (0.9)	D.M. / Dis. of the musculoskeletal system and connective tissue	73 2.0 (0.8)
Pneumonia	352 8.6 (2.4)	Dis. of liver	306 7.5 (2.1)	Aortic aneurysm	187 4.6 (1.3)	D.M.	140 3.4 (0.9)	Benign neoplasms	126 3.1 (0.9)
Suicide	635 12.0 (2.2)	Aortic aneurysm	498 9.4 (1.8)	Dis. of liver	474 9.0 (1.7)	D.M.	306 5.8 (1.1)	Renal failure	290 5.5 (1.0)
Aortic aneurysm	706 17.9 (2.0)	Suicide	571 14.5 (1.6)	Dis. of liver	548 13.9 (1.6)	Renal failure	464 11.8 (1.3)	D.M.	417 10.6 (1.2)
Senility	1 018 28.2 (1.8)	Aortic aneurysm	1 012 28.1 (1.8)	Renal failure	977 27.1 (1.7)	Dis. of liver	817 22.7 (1.5)	D.M.	712 19.7 (1.3)
Accidents	2 841 92.4 (3.0)	Renal failure	1 952 63.5 (1.8)	Aortic aneurysm	1 764 57.4 (1.8)	D.M.	1 160 37.7 (1.2)	Alzheimer's disease	1 122 36.5 (1.2)
Accidents	3 465 161.2 (2.5)	Renal failure	3 319 154.4 (2.4)	Alzheimer's disease	2 260 105.1 (1.7)	Aortic aneurysm	2 216 103.1 (1.6)	Vascular dementia	2 045 95.1 (1.5)
Renal failure	3 258 296.7 (2.4)	Accidents	2 922 266.1 (2.1)	Vascular dementia	2 799 254.9 (2.0)	Alzheimer's disease	2 524 229.9 (1.8)	Aortic aneurysm	1 644 149.7 (1.2)
Vascular dementia	1 826 577.8 (2.4)	Renal failure	1 555 492.1 (2.1)	Alzheimer's disease	1 323 418.7 (1.8)	Accidents	1 284 406.3 (1.7)	Hypertensive dis.	820 259.5 (1.1)
Vascular dementia	567 994.7 (2.5)	Accidents	315 552.6 (1.4)	Renal failure	295 517.5 (1.3)	Alzheimer's disease	293 514.0 (1.3)	Hypertensive dis.	278 487.7 (1.2)
Accidents	14 627 75.0 (2.5)	Renal failure	12 110 62.1 (2.1)	Vascular dementia	8 511 43.6 (1.4)	Aortic aneurysm	8 507 43.6 (1.4)	Alzheimer's disease	8 191 42.0 (1.4)
Accidents	12 661 122.9 (2.2)	Renal failure	11 356 110.2 (2.2)	Vascular dementia	8 396 81.5 (1.6)	Alzheimer's disease	7 933 77.0 (1.5)	Aortic aneurysm	7 303 70.9 (1.4)
Accidents	10 827 161.7 (2.3)	Renal failure	10 379 155.0 (2.2)	Vascular dementia	8 130 121.4 (1.7)	Alzheimer's disease	7 522 112.3 (1.6)	Aortic aneurysm	6 291 94.0 (1.3)

死　亡

〔月別にみた死因〕
〔Causes of death by month〕

表5.18　月別にみた死因
Table 5.18　Death rates (per 100,000 population) by causes

死因簡単分類コード Code[a]	死因 Causes of death	総数 Total	1月 January	2月 February	3月 March	4月 April
	死亡総数　Deaths Total	1 046.0	1 174.4	1 154.3	1 094.8	1 026.0
01000	感染症及び寄生虫症	20.1	22.4	22.2	21.5	19.7
01100	腸管感染症	2.0	2.6	2.5	2.4	2.0
01200	結核	1.5	1.7	1.5	1.5	1.3
01201	呼吸器結核	1.3	1.5	1.4	1.2	1.2
01202	その他の結核	0.2	0.2	0.1	0.2	0.1
01300	敗血症	9.2	10.1	10.3	9.4	9.1
01400	ウイルス肝炎	3.1	3.6	3.4	3.7	3.2
01401	B型ウイルス肝炎	0.3	0.4	0.4	0.5	0.3
01402	C型ウイルス肝炎	2.6	3.0	2.8	3.1	2.7
01403	その他のウイルス肝炎	0.1	0.2	0.3	0.2	0.2
01500	ヒト免疫不全ウイルス[HIV]病	0.1	0.0	0.1	0.2	0.0
01600	その他の感染症及び寄生虫症	4.2	4.3	4.4	4.4	4.1
02000	新生物	307.5	311.0	308.7	306.0	304.0
02100	悪性新生物	298.3	301.8	299.3	296.9	295.0
02101	口唇,口腔及び咽頭の悪性新生物	6.1	6.4	6.0	6.3	5.7
02102	食道の悪性新生物	9.2	9.4	8.9	9.4	9.0
02103	胃の悪性新生物	36.4	37.1	36.8	35.9	36.5
02104	結腸の悪性新生物	27.6	26.8	27.6	27.6	26.8
02105	直腸S状結腸移行部及び直腸の悪性新生物	12.5	12.3	12.3	12.5	11.5
02106	肝及び肝内胆管の悪性新生物	22.8	23.6	22.5	23.6	23.2
02107	胆のう及びその他の胆道の悪性新生物	14.4	14.3	14.5	14.2	13.6
02108	膵の悪性新生物	26.8	26.1	27.0	26.5	26.7
02109	喉頭の悪性新生物	0.8	0.9	0.8	0.7	0.7
02110	気管,気管支及び肺の悪性新生物	59.1	61.0	60.3	59.5	59.7
02111	皮膚の悪性新生物	1.2	1.0	1.3	1.3	1.2
02112	乳房の悪性新生物	11.3	11.9	11.4	10.6	11.0
02113	子宮の悪性新生物2)	9.9	9.7	9.7	10.0	9.3
02114	卵巣の悪性新生物2)	7.4	8.1	7.6	6.7	7.4
02115	前立腺の悪性新生物3)	19.4	19.7	19.4	18.3	18.1
02116	膀胱の悪性新生物	6.7	7.5	6.9	6.7	6.7
02117	中枢神経系の悪性新生物	2.1	2.0	2.0	2.1	2.1
02118	悪性リンパ腫	9.9	9.8	9.6	9.5	9.7
02119	白血病	7.0	7.0	7.0	7.2	7.4
02120	その他のリンパ組織,造血組織及び関連組織の悪性新生物	3.6	3.6	3.7	3.4	3.5
02121	その他の悪性新生物	22.6	22.4	22.3	22.4	22.4
02200	その他の新生物	9.2	9.1	9.3	9.0	9.0
02201	中枢神経系のその他の新生物	2.0	2.2	2.1	1.9	2.0
02202	中枢神経系を除くその他の新生物	7.2	7.0	7.2	7.1	7.0
03000	血液及び造血器の疾患並びに免疫機構の障害	3.6	4.1	3.9	3.6	3.7
03100	貧血	1.7	2.0	1.8	1.7	1.6
03200	その他の血液及び造血器の疾患並びに免疫機構の障害	1.9	2.1	2.1	2.0	2.1
04000	内分泌,栄養及び代謝疾患	17.1	20.5	19.7	18.0	17.1
04100	糖尿病	10.8	13.0	12.7	11.4	11.3
04200	その他の内分泌,栄養及び代謝疾患	6.3	7.5	7.0	6.6	5.8
05000	精神及び行動の障害	11.3	12.9	12.2	11.0	11.1
05100	血管性及び詳細不明の認知症	9.5	10.7	10.2	9.1	9.5
05200	その他の精神及び行動の障害	1.8	2.2	2.0	1.9	1.7
06000	神経系の疾患	26.7	27.8	27.6	26.8	25.8
06100	髄膜炎	0.2	0.3	0.2	0.3	0.3
06200	脊髄性筋萎縮症及び関連症候群	2.1	2.1	2.3	1.8	2.0
06300	パーキンソン病	6.0	6.6	6.0	5.6	5.7
06400	アルツハイマー病	9.6	9.6	10.1	9.8	9.1
06500	その他の神経系の疾患	8.7	9.1	9.0	9.3	8.8
07000	眼及び付属器の疾患	0.0	-	-	-	-
08000	耳及び乳様突起の疾患	0.0	0.0	0.0	0.0	0.0
09000	循環器系の疾患	271.8	334.4	321.8	297.1	266.3
09100	高血圧性疾患	5.5	6.8	6.4	6.0	5.4
09101	高血圧性心疾患及び心腎疾患	2.5	3.1	2.8	2.8	2.7
09102	その他の高血圧性疾患	3.0	3.8	3.6	3.2	2.7
09200	心疾患（高血圧性を除く）	158.4	202.1	192.4	175.0	154.2
09201	慢性リウマチ性心疾患	1.8	2.0	2.5	1.8	2.0
09202	急性心筋梗塞	28.7	38.8	37.2	32.0	27.7
09203	その他の虚血性心疾患	27.6	38.5	34.7	31.7	25.7

注:1)　各月の率は年率に換算したものである。計算方法は、68ページ　3)死亡を参照されたい。
　　2)　率については、女性人口10万対である。
　　3)　率については、男性人口10万対である。
　　　実数については下巻死亡第3表を参照されたい。

General mortality

簡単分類別死亡率 [1] （人口10万対）
(the condensed list of causes of death for Japan) by month：Japan, 2016

平成28年

5 月 May	6 月 June	7 月 July	8 月 August	9 月 September	10 月 October	11 月 November	12 月 December
974.4	930.8	936.1	975.1	976.3	1 034.1	1 111.2	1 158.0
18.7	18.5	17.8	18.1	19.0	19.5	20.9	22.5
1.9	1.7	1.5	1.7	1.8	1.8	2.0	2.6
1.4	1.5	1.5	1.3	1.7	1.7	1.4	1.6
1.2	1.3	1.4	1.2	1.5	1.5	1.2	1.4
0.2	0.2	0.1	0.1	0.3	0.2	0.2	0.2
8.3	8.5	8.1	8.4	8.8	9.4	9.7	10.3
3.1	2.8	2.7	2.7	2.8	2.6	3.2	3.1
0.4	0.3	0.3	0.3	0.3	0.2	0.4	0.3
2.5	2.4	2.3	2.4	2.4	2.2	2.6	2.7
0.2	0.1	0.2	0.1	0.1	0.2	0.2	0.1
0.1	0.1	0.0	0.0	0.1	0.0	0.0	0.0
3.9	4.0	3.9	3.9	3.9	4.1	4.6	4.9
299.7	300.1	304.4	306.0	309.1	313.2	315.8	309.7
291.0	291.5	295.6	297.1	299.9	303.3	306.2	300.0
5.9	5.5	6.0	6.5	6.2	6.2	6.6	6.3
9.1	8.7	9.3	9.0	9.2	9.5	9.4	9.3
34.6	35.6	35.6	36.0	36.9	36.8	38.2	36.7
27.0	27.0	28.5	28.5	28.3	27.2	28.3	27.6
12.6	12.4	11.9	12.3	13.2	12.6	12.9	12.9
22.5	21.5	22.9	22.3	22.6	23.1	23.1	22.6
14.2	14.8	14.4	14.2	14.9	14.6	14.4	14.2
26.7	26.8	26.9	27.6	26.4	27.4	26.3	26.7
0.7	0.6	0.6	0.8	0.7	0.7	0.9	0.7
57.5	57.0	57.4	58.2	58.7	60.2	59.7	59.1
1.2	1.1	1.2	1.4	1.3	1.3	1.4	1.1
11.0	10.7	11.9	11.3	11.3	11.6	11.3	11.5
9.3	10.0	9.5	10.0	10.4	9.6	10.3	10.7
6.8	7.5	7.7	7.4	7.8	7.2	7.4	7.4
18.8	18.5	18.9	18.5	19.2	20.7	21.9	20.5
6.2	6.9	6.5	6.6	6.6	6.7	7.0	6.6
2.0	2.0	2.0	2.2	2.3	2.3	2.1	2.3
10.2	9.7	9.6	9.9	9.5	10.6	10.4	9.6
6.8	7.4	6.8	7.0	6.9	7.3	7.0	6.8
3.4	3.3	3.6	3.4	3.7	3.7	3.9	3.4
22.0	22.7	22.3	22.0	22.5	22.8	23.5	23.3
8.8	8.6	8.9	8.9	9.2	9.9	9.6	9.7
1.8	1.9	2.0	1.7	2.0	2.0	2.0	2.0
7.0	6.7	6.9	7.2	7.2	7.9	7.5	7.7
3.3	3.4	3.3	3.3	3.3	4.0	3.9	3.7
1.4	1.5	1.5	1.5	1.5	1.9	2.0	1.8
1.9	1.9	1.8	1.8	1.9	2.0	1.9	1.9
15.5	14.4	14.4	15.9	14.9	16.5	18.0	19.7
10.1	9.3	9.1	9.7	9.0	10.4	11.2	12.1
5.4	5.1	5.3	6.2	5.9	6.1	6.7	7.6
10.6	9.5	9.8	10.2	11.0	11.7	13.3	12.7
9.1	8.1	8.0	8.5	9.2	9.9	11.2	10.7
1.5	1.4	1.8	1.7	1.8	1.8	2.1	2.0
24.2	23.7	24.2	25.7	26.7	27.5	29.2	30.7
0.1	0.1	0.3	0.2	0.1	0.2	0.2	0.3
2.6	3.0	1.8	2.0	1.9	1.7	2.2	2.3
5.1	5.2	5.9	6.2	6.4	5.9	6.7	7.0
8.6	8.5	8.5	8.6	9.7	10.4	10.9	10.9
7.7	6.8	7.8	8.7	8.5	9.2	9.2	10.2
-	-	0.0	-	0.0	-	-	0.0
0.0	0.0	0.0	-	0.0	0.0	0.0	0.0
243.8	229.2	226.6	236.4	231.6	256.7	294.3	322.5
4.7	4.7	4.4	4.8	4.5	5.0	6.1	6.7
2.2	2.1	2.0	2.0	2.0	2.1	2.9	3.1
2.5	2.6	2.4	2.7	2.5	2.9	3.3	3.6
140.3	132.4	129.5	135.7	130.2	144.8	171.9	191.5
1.7	1.7	1.5	1.6	1.6	1.7	2.0	1.8
23.9	23.2	22.2	24.4	23.2	25.7	30.3	36.2
24.0	22.1	22.0	23.2	20.8	24.2	30.0	34.3

Note：a) Code see page 595.

死　亡

表 5.18　月別にみた死因
Table 5.18　Death rates (per 100,000 population) by causes

死因簡単分類コード Code[a]	死　　　　因 Causes of death	総　数 Total	1　月 January	2　月 February	3　月 March	4　月 April
09204	慢性非リウマチ性心内膜疾患	8.8	10.1	10.4	9.3	9.1
09205	心　　　筋　　　症	3.0	3.3	3.5	2.8	3.3
09206	不整脈及び伝導障害	24.8	32.6	30.8	27.0	24.7
09207	心　　不　　全	58.8	70.7	67.6	64.8	57.2
09208	そ　の　他　の　心　疾　患	4.7	6.1	5.9	5.5	4.4
09300	脳　　血　　管　　疾　　患	87.4	101.2	98.6	93.7	86.6
09301	く　も　膜　下　出　血	9.9	11.5	11.2	10.8	9.9
09302	脳　　内　　出　　血	25.6	30.6	29.1	28.1	25.4
09303	脳　　　梗　　　塞	49.8	56.6	55.7	52.3	49.2
09304	そ　の　他　の　脳血管疾患	2.2	2.5	2.6	2.5	2.2
09400	大動脈瘤及び解離	14.5	17.4	16.9	16.4	14.0
09500	その他の循環器系の疾患	6.0	6.9	7.4	6.0	6.1
10000	呼　吸　器　系　の　疾　患	166.9	189.0	195.2	178.4	163.9
10100	イ　ン　フ　ル　エ　ン　ザ	1.2	0.9	4.9	4.2	1.7
10200	肺　　　　　　　　炎	95.4	110.8	113.4	100.7	93.8
10300	急　性　気　管　支　炎	0.4	0.5	0.5	0.5	0.2
10400	慢性閉塞性肺疾患	12.5	13.9	14.2	13.7	12.5
10500	喘　　　　　　　　息	1.2	1.6	1.3	1.4	1.1
10600	その他の呼吸器系の疾患	56.2	61.3	60.9	57.8	54.6
11000	消　化　器　系　の　疾　患	39.0	44.1	43.5	40.5	37.8
11100	胃潰瘍及び十二指腸潰瘍	2.1	2.8	2.7	2.2	2.2
11200	ヘ　ル　ニ　ア　及　び　腸閉塞	5.6	6.0	5.7	6.0	4.9
11300	肝　　　　疾　　　　患	12.6	14.7	14.6	12.9	12.4
11301	肝硬変（アルコール性を除く）	6.2	7.5	7.3	6.5	6.5
11302	そ　の　他　の　肝　疾　患	6.5	7.3	7.3	6.3	6.0
11400	その他の消化器系の疾患	18.7	20.5	20.5	19.5	18.2
12000	皮膚及び皮下組織の疾患	1.3	1.4	1.5	1.3	1.2
13000	筋骨格系及び結合組織の疾患	5.2	5.3	5.7	5.5	4.7
14000	腎　尿　路　生　殖　器　系　の　疾　患	30.9	35.4	34.0	32.3	30.3
14100	糸球体疾患及び腎尿細管間質性疾患	4.0	4.4	4.3	4.4	3.9
14200	腎　　　不　　　全	19.7	23.9	22.0	20.9	19.4
14201	急　性　腎　不　全	2.7	3.5	3.1	2.7	2.7
14202	慢　性　腎　不　全	12.8	15.1	14.0	14.0	12.6
14203	詳　細　不　明　の　腎不全	4.2	5.3	4.8	4.2	4.1
14300	その他の腎尿路生殖器系の疾患	7.2	7.2	7.7	7.0	7.0
15000	妊娠，分娩及び産じょく[2]	0.1	0.1	0.1	0.1	0.1
16000	周産期に発生した病態	0.4	0.6	0.4	0.5	0.6
16100	妊娠期間及び胎児発育に関連する障害	0.0	0.0	0.1	0.1	0.0
16200	出　　産　　外　　傷	0.0	-	-	-	0.0
16300	周産期に特異的な呼吸障害及び心血管障害	0.2	0.3	0.2	0.3	0.3
16400	周産期に特異的な感染症	0.0	0.0	0.0	0.0	0.0
16500	胎児及び新生児の出血性障害及び血液障害	0.1	0.0	0.1	0.1	0.1
16600	その他の周産期に発生した病態	0.1	0.2	0.0	0.0	0.1
17000	先天奇形，変形及び染色体異常	1.6	1.6	2.0	1.8	1.6
17100	神　経　系　の　先　天　奇　形	0.1	0.0	0.1	0.0	0.1
17200	循　環　器　系　の　先　天　奇　形	0.7	0.7	0.9	0.8	0.8
17201	心　臓　の　先　天　奇　形	0.5	0.5	0.5	0.5	0.6
17202	その他の循環器系の先天奇形	0.3	0.3	0.4	0.3	0.2
17300	消　化　器　系　の　先　天　奇　形	0.1	0.1	0.2	0.1	0.0
17400	その他の先天奇形及び変形	0.5	0.5	0.4	0.5	0.4
17500	染色体異常,他に分類されないもの	0.3	0.2	0.4	0.4	0.2
18000	症状,徴候及び異常臨床所見・異常検査所見で他に分類されないもの	89.9	99.8	96.7	91.4	85.1
18100	老　　　　　　　　衰	74.2	80.6	78.0	75.5	70.1
18200	乳　幼　児　突　然　死　症　候　群	0.1	0.1	0.2	0.1	0.1
18300	その他の症状,徴候及び異常臨床所見・異常検査所見で他に分類されないもの	15.6	19.1	18.5	15.8	14.9
20000	傷　病　及　び　死　亡　の　外　因	52.7	64.3	59.2	59.1	53.1
20100	不　　慮　　の　　事　　故	30.6	41.7	36.7	34.3	30.5
20101	交　　通　　事　　故	4.2	4.3	3.9	4.1	4.3
20102	転　　倒　・　転　　落	6.4	6.8	6.5	6.7	6.6
20103	不　慮　の　溺　死　及　び　溺水	6.2	11.1	9.6	8.6	6.5
20104	不　　慮　　の　　窒　　息	7.6	11.3	9.1	8.4	7.1
20105	煙，火及び火炎への曝露	0.7	1.1	1.1	1.1	0.9
20106	有害物質による不慮の中毒及び有害物質への曝露	0.5	0.6	0.6	0.5	0.5
20107	その他の不慮の事故	5.1	6.5	5.9	5.0	4.5
20200	自　　　　　　　　殺	16.8	17.1	16.9	19.1	17.4
20300	他　　　　　　　　殺	0.2	0.2	0.3	0.2	0.2
20400	そ　の　他　の　外　因	5.0	5.3	5.3	5.4	5.1
22000	特　殊　目　的　用　コ　ー　ド	-	-	-	-	-
22100	重症急性呼吸器症候群〔SARS〕	-	-	-	-	-

324

General mortality

簡単分類別死亡率 [1] （人口10万対）（つづき）
(the condensed list of causes of death for Japan) by month：Japan, 2016－CON. 平成28年

5 月 May	6 月 June	7 月 July	8 月 August	9 月 September	10 月 October	11 月 November	12 月 December
7.8	7.8	7.5	7.6	7.8	8.2	10.0	10.4
2.9	2.8	2.9	3.0	2.7	2.8	3.1	3.5
21.4	19.8	19.8	20.8	20.1	23.0	27.2	30.5
54.4	51.4	49.5	51.2	50.3	55.0	64.4	69.0
4.1	3.6	4.0	3.9	3.6	4.3	5.0	5.7
80.5	75.0	76.2	78.9	79.3	86.1	93.3	99.4
8.4	8.2	9.1	8.9	9.0	9.4	10.5	11.2
23.5	22.2	20.7	22.3	22.2	25.1	27.6	30.0
46.5	42.8	44.5	45.9	46.1	49.6	52.7	55.5
2.0	1.7	2.0	1.7	1.9	2.1	2.5	2.8
12.6	11.9	11.1	11.7	12.6	14.9	16.4	18.0
5.8	5.2	5.4	5.3	5.0	5.8	6.5	6.8
153.1	140.2	140.5	153.8	157.2	164.0	180.2	186.2
0.4	0.1	0.1	0.0	0.0	0.1	0.5	1.2
86.3	79.8	78.0	87.7	90.1	93.8	104.1	106.4
0.4	0.2	0.2	0.3	0.3	0.3	0.4	0.3
11.3	11.1	11.3	11.9	12.1	12.1	12.7	13.9
1.1	0.9	1.0	1.2	1.0	1.0	1.0	1.2
53.7	48.1	49.9	52.7	53.6	56.6	61.5	63.2
36.4	34.8	33.3	35.9	36.7	40.3	41.6	42.8
1.9	1.7	1.6	1.8	1.7	2.2	2.2	2.6
4.9	5.0	5.0	5.6	5.2	5.8	6.0	6.7
12.1	11.3	10.9	11.2	12.0	12.6	13.1	13.5
6.1	5.2	5.3	5.3	5.8	5.9	6.2	6.3
6.1	6.1	5.6	5.8	6.3	6.6	6.9	7.2
17.5	16.8	15.8	17.4	17.8	19.7	20.3	19.9
1.5	1.2	1.3	1.1	1.2	1.3	1.4	1.5
5.1	5.0	5.1	4.7	5.0	4.7	5.5	5.6
29.3	27.1	26.7	28.0	28.3	31.2	33.4	34.1
3.9	3.5	3.3	4.1	3.9	4.2	4.3	4.1
18.5	17.3	16.7	17.2	17.9	19.2	21.1	22.0
2.5	2.2	2.2	2.2	2.5	2.7	3.4	3.0
12.3	11.3	11.0	11.4	11.6	12.5	13.3	14.1
3.7	3.9	3.5	3.5	3.7	4.1	4.4	4.9
6.9	6.2	6.7	6.8	6.6	7.8	7.9	8.1
0.0	0.1	0.0	0.1	0.1	0.1	0.1	0.0
0.5	0.3	0.3	0.4	0.4	0.4	0.4	0.3
0.0	0.0	0.0	0.0	0.0	0.1	0.0	0.0
0.0	0.0	-	-	-	-	-	-
0.3	0.2	0.2	0.2	0.3	0.2	0.2	0.2
0.0	0.0	0.0	0.0	0.0	0.0	0.0	0.0
0.1	0.1	0.0	0.0	0.1	0.0	0.1	0.0
0.1	0.1	0.1	0.1	0.0	0.1	0.0	0.0
1.5	1.7	1.7	1.4	1.5	1.4	1.7	1.7
0.0	0.0	0.1	0.1	0.1	0.1	0.1	0.1
0.6	0.8	0.7	0.7	0.6	0.7	0.7	0.7
0.4	0.6	0.5	0.4	0.4	0.4	0.4	0.5
0.2	0.2	0.2	0.2	0.2	0.2	0.3	0.3
0.1	0.1	0.1	0.0	0.1	0.1	0.1	0.0
0.5	0.5	0.5	0.4	0.4	0.3	0.5	0.5
0.2	0.2	0.3	0.2	0.3	0.2	0.3	0.3
81.7	76.8	80.2	86.2	85.8	92.6	97.8	104.5
67.9	63.4	65.0	69.0	71.4	78.4	83.1	87.8
0.1	0.1	0.1	0.1	0.1	0.0	0.0	0.1
13.7	13.3	15.1	17.2	14.3	14.2	14.7	16.7
49.5	44.8	46.3	47.8	44.5	49.1	54.0	59.7
26.1	22.7	24.4	27.6	23.5	27.1	33.0	39.9
4.1	3.4	3.8	4.2	4.2	4.7	4.4	5.1
5.8	5.6	5.9	6.4	6.2	6.2	6.7	7.7
4.5	3.6	3.2	3.1	2.5	4.2	7.2	9.8
6.8	5.8	5.7	6.7	5.8	7.1	8.0	9.2
0.5	0.3	0.3	0.3	0.3	0.5	0.9	1.1
0.5	0.3	0.4	0.3	0.3	0.3	0.6	0.5
3.8	3.6	5.0	6.6	4.2	4.0	5.2	6.5
18.6	17.3	16.7	15.5	16.2	16.9	15.6	14.3
0.2	0.2	0.3	0.3	0.2	0.2	0.2	0.2
4.7	4.6	4.9	4.5	4.7	4.9	5.2	5.3
-	-	-	-	-	-	-	-
-	-	-	-	-	-	-	-

死　亡

〔地域別にみた死因〕
〔Causes of death by prefecture〕

表 5.19　都道府県（21大都市再掲）別にみた死因
Table 5.19　Death rates (per 100,000 population) by causes each prefecture and 21 major cities, 2016

都道府県 Prefecture	死亡総数 Deaths Total	01000 感染症及び 寄生虫症	01100 腸管 感染症	01200 結核	01201 呼吸器 結核	01202 その他の 結核	01300 敗血症	01400 ウイルス 肝炎	01401 B型 ウイルス 肝炎	01402 C型 ウイルス 肝炎
全国　Total	1 046.0	20.1	2.0	1.5	1.3	0.2	9.2	3.1	0.3	2.6
01 北海道	1 162.1	22.7	2.1	1.0	0.8	0.1	12.0	2.8	0.5	2.0
02 青森	1 341.8	20.8	1.9	2.2	2.0	0.2	10.2	3.1	0.2	2.6
03 岩手	1 342.8	19.6	2.9	1.4	1.2	0.2	7.9	1.9	0.2	1.7
04 宮城	1 012.4	15.5	2.2	1.1	1.0	0.1	7.4	1.9	0.2	1.7
05 秋田	1 513.8	25.1	2.8	0.7	0.5	0.2	13.5	2.6	0.3	2.3
06 山形	1 371.4	18.5	2.7	1.3	1.0	0.3	7.6	3.0	0.3	2.5
07 福島	1 277.9	19.1	1.9	1.0	1.0	-	8.9	3.0	0.3	2.5
08 茨城	1 098.0	20.8	1.5	1.2	1.0	0.1	10.1	4.1	0.3	3.7
09 栃木	1 105.5	19.7	1.5	1.5	1.3	0.2	8.5	4.5	0.4	3.9
10 群馬	1 148.8	22.0	2.3	1.2	1.0	0.3	10.1	4.3	0.1	4.2
11 埼玉	885.3	17.5	1.2	1.2	1.1	0.1	8.7	3.0	0.3	2.6
12 千葉	919.0	16.4	1.7	1.3	1.2	0.1	7.6	2.5	0.3	2.2
13 東京	858.7	16.9	1.3	1.6	1.4	0.2	7.7	2.3	0.2	2.0
14 神奈川	860.9	15.3	1.4	1.1	1.0	0.1	7.7	1.9	0.1	1.7
15 新潟	1 268.0	15.6	1.9	1.1	0.9	0.2	7.1	1.3	0.3	0.9
16 富山	1 226.3	22.0	3.0	1.6	1.6	-	9.4	3.1	0.4	2.6
17 石川	1 089.6	21.0	2.7	1.2	1.1	0.1	8.4	4.1	0.4	3.2
18 福井	1 195.3	25.4	2.5	1.8	1.3	0.5	11.7	4.7	0.8	3.8
19 山梨	1 169.3	23.2	3.5	1.1	0.7	0.4	11.0	4.2	0.1	4.0
20 長野	1 218.9	19.1	2.9	1.2	0.9	0.2	7.0	3.7	0.4	3.1
21 岐阜	1 132.0	22.0	2.4	2.0	1.9	0.1	9.3	3.4	0.4	2.9
22 静岡	1 084.6	20.0	1.7	1.5	1.4	0.1	8.5	2.8	0.2	2.4
23 愛知	890.6	18.7	1.6	1.7	1.5	0.2	8.8	2.4	0.4	1.9
24 三重	1 117.2	21.8	3.3	1.2	1.0	0.2	9.9	3.0	0.2	2.7
25 滋賀	898.5	16.0	2.1	0.9	0.6	0.4	8.5	1.6	-	1.4
26 京都	1 009.4	19.5	1.6	1.9	1.6	0.3	9.0	2.8	0.4	2.3
27 大阪	973.1	22.3	1.9	2.7	2.6	0.2	9.6	4.0	0.4	3.5
28 兵庫	1 019.2	21.4	2.1	1.7	1.5	0.2	9.6	3.5	0.3	3.1
29 奈良	1 043.4	18.7	1.9	1.2	1.1	0.1	8.0	3.4	0.6	2.5
30 和歌山	1 329.7	31.3	2.6	1.7	1.2	0.5	14.3	5.8	0.4	5.2
31 鳥取	1 299.8	21.9	3.4	1.8	1.4	0.4	8.3	3.0	0.4	2.5
32 島根	1 398.0	24.4	4.8	1.8	0.9	0.9	8.9	3.1	0.1	2.8
33 岡山	1 135.7	20.9	2.2	1.5	1.4	0.1	8.9	3.7	0.3	3.2
34 広島	1 071.6	20.8	2.5	1.0	0.9	0.1	8.5	3.5	0.4	3.1
35 山口	1 329.9	28.7	2.7	2.3	1.8	0.5	13.5	3.9	0.4	3.5
36 徳島	1 321.0	28.2	4.4	1.7	1.7	-	11.9	3.8	0.4	3.4
37 香川	1 235.3	22.8	2.1	1.1	1.0	0.1	9.6	4.0	0.4	3.0
38 愛媛	1 298.2	22.7	2.9	1.5	1.2	0.3	7.9	5.1	0.4	4.5
39 高知	1 435.2	34.5	4.2	2.8	2.5	0.3	17.8	4.7	0.4	4.3
40 福岡	1 009.2	21.4	2.5	1.3	1.1	0.2	9.6	4.1	0.3	3.6
41 佐賀	1 180.2	27.9	2.4	2.7	2.1	0.6	11.4	6.2	0.8	5.1
42 長崎	1 257.1	26.6	2.5	1.1	1.1	-	13.8	3.3	0.9	2.2
43 熊本	1 211.3	23.9	2.8	2.0	1.9	0.1	9.7	4.2	0.6	3.3
44 大分	1 240.3	23.9	3.6	1.4	1.0	0.3	9.6	4.5	1.0	3.5
45 宮崎	1 254.5	22.3	2.9	1.4	1.2	0.2	10.0	1.9	0.5	1.4
46 鹿児島	1 325.8	27.5	3.1	2.0	1.7	0.4	13.9	3.0	0.1	2.8
47 沖縄	820.3	21.8	3.2	1.0	0.8	0.1	13.2	1.3	0.5	0.5
21大都市（再掲） 21 major cities (Regrouped)										
50 東京都の区部	819.5	16.8	1.3	1.5	1.3	0.2	7.7	2.4	0.2	2.1
51 札幌	945.0	20.4	1.5	0.7	0.7	0.1	11.1	2.5	0.5	1.8
52 仙台	791.6	12.4	1.1	0.8	0.7	0.1	6.3	1.8	0.2	1.7
53 さいたま	798.2	16.9	0.9	0.9	0.8	0.1	9.7	2.6	0.3	2.2
54 千葉	832.9	13.0	1.6	0.9	0.9	-	5.2	2.0	0.4	1.5
55 横浜	842.0	15.0	1.5	1.2	1.1	0.1	7.5	1.7	0.1	1.4
56 川崎	697.0	11.7	0.6	0.9	0.7	0.1	5.6	1.9	0.1	1.7
57 相模原	777.1	12.6	1.4	0.7	0.6	0.1	5.8	2.5	0.1	2.4
58 新潟	1 064.4	14.6	1.5	1.5	1.4	0.1	7.1	1.2	0.1	1.1
59 静岡	1 103.3	18.9	1.4	1.7	1.6	0.1	8.0	2.4	0.3	1.9
60 浜松	985.2	17.1	2.4	1.5	1.4	0.1	5.9	2.4	0.1	2.3
61 名古屋	920.7	20.7	1.7	2.2	1.9	0.3	10.0	2.3	0.3	1.6
62 京都	946.8	19.0	1.6	2.2	1.9	0.3	8.6	2.5	0.3	2.1
63 大阪	1 029.4	26.2	2.0	4.2	4.0	0.2	10.6	5.2	0.6	4.4
64 堺	948.8	18.6	1.7	2.0	1.9	0.1	8.1	3.1	0.2	2.9
65 神戸	999.3	21.3	1.8	1.6	1.4	0.2	9.1	3.9	0.4	3.3
66 岡山	904.3	15.7	1.7	1.7	1.7	-	6.1	3.2	0.1	2.8
67 広島	832.0	17.1	1.8	0.9	0.8	0.2	7.4	2.6	0.5	2.0
68 北九州	1 125.4	24.1	1.8	1.6	1.4	0.2	11.6	4.2	0.4	3.0
69 福岡	741.4	16.0	1.9	0.8	0.4	0.4	7.5	2.6	0.4	2.6
70 熊本	934.6	18.4	1.4	1.6	1.6	-	7.3	3.1	0.3	2.6

注：実数については下巻死亡第4表を参照されたい。

General mortality

簡単分類別死亡率（人口10万対）
(the condensed list of causes of death for Japan)[a] : Japan,

平成28年

01403	01500	01600	02000	02100	02101	02102	02103	02104	02105	02106	02107
その他の ウイルス 肝炎	ヒト免疫 不全ウイルス [HIV] 病	その他の 感染症及び 寄生虫症	新生物	悪性 新生物	口唇, 口腔 及び咽頭の 悪性新生物	食道の 悪性新生物	胃の悪性 新生物	結腸の 悪性新生物	直腸S状 結腸移行部 及び直腸の 悪性新生物	肝及び 肝内胆管の 悪性新生物	胆のう及び その他の 胆道の 悪性新生物
0.1	0.1	4.2	307.5	298.3	6.1	9.2	36.4	27.6	12.5	22.8	14.4
0.2	0.0	4.8	371.5	360.0	6.9	10.5	39.5	34.1	15.1	23.3	17.9
0.3	-	3.3	401.8	390.2	8.8	11.2	47.8	41.6	20.2	28.1	23.8
0.1	0.1	5.4	370.0	358.0	6.2	8.4	42.8	35.5	20.7	21.1	20.4
0.1	-	2.8	297.1	287.9	6.3	8.9	36.1	27.5	11.4	18.4	15.4
-	-	5.6	432.6	421.3	10.8	16.7	62.6	41.5	17.0	25.3	26.4
0.2	-	4.0	382.2	370.4	6.7	11.5	53.1	39.7	13.8	22.3	22.9
0.2	0.1	4.2	349.4	339.2	7.0	9.7	46.8	33.6	14.3	21.3	22.3
0.1	0.1	3.7	316.8	307.4	6.0	8.2	41.5	27.6	14.8	22.0	16.3
0.2	0.1	3.6	311.6	301.7	5.6	8.7	40.5	29.1	13.3	22.6	13.6
0.1	0.1	4.0	313.6	302.8	5.4	10.1	36.9	29.3	15.5	22.7	16.0
0.2	0.1	3.4	274.8	267.1	5.5	9.5	33.3	24.8	11.1	18.1	11.7
0.1	0.1	3.1	282.7	273.7	6.7	8.7	34.1	25.2	11.6	19.1	12.8
0.1	0.1	3.9	265.4	257.6	5.9	9.4	30.1	24.1	11.2	16.7	11.0
0.1	0.0	3.2	267.8	260.3	5.9	9.7	31.4	25.3	11.2	17.6	10.7
0.1	0.0	4.1	357.1	346.5	7.6	11.9	49.2	32.8	15.5	17.3	21.1
0.2	-	4.9	343.6	331.9	5.9	9.4	46.9	33.9	14.7	23.5	19.4
0.4	-	4.5	317.2	308.5	4.9	8.0	39.6	29.6	11.8	24.0	14.6
0.1	-	4.8	325.8	315.9	5.2	6.1	39.9	31.3	12.8	22.3	18.3
-	-	3.4	311.2	301.6	6.0	9.2	36.9	29.1	13.4	29.0	18.0
0.2	-	4.3	318.2	308.3	4.2	9.1	38.0	32.5	11.4	20.6	18.5
0.2	0.1	4.8	313.3	304.7	5.3	7.1	40.9	29.5	14.0	19.9	13.4
0.2	0.0	5.5	304.8	295.9	5.7	9.4	33.8	27.8	13.5	22.3	13.5
0.1	0.0	4.0	268.4	260.6	5.1	7.3	33.7	24.6	11.2	18.6	11.8
0.1	-	4.5	304.7	294.0	5.7	7.6	37.1	28.6	11.2	21.7	13.7
0.2	0.1	2.7	269.6	261.6	4.4	6.4	36.1	22.1	9.7	17.9	12.7
0.1	0.1	4.1	308.4	300.0	6.3	9.1	36.9	26.3	11.8	24.4	13.8
0.1	0.0	4.0	308.0	299.2	6.2	9.8	36.4	25.5	12.3	27.3	12.0
0.1	0.1	4.4	310.7	302.7	5.8	9.7	38.2	26.6	11.0	27.1	12.8
0.3	-	4.2	318.9	308.8	5.9	10.4	41.4	26.4	10.9	24.1	13.1
0.2	0.1	6.7	362.2	350.8	6.8	11.2	43.2	29.9	16.0	32.8	13.6
0.2	0.2	5.3	370.5	359.5	7.4	11.3	44.7	29.0	16.6	27.7	20.7
0.1	-	5.8	389.0	376.0	7.6	11.3	46.3	32.2	17.1	33.8	20.3
0.3	-	4.6	304.4	293.9	6.6	7.8	35.8	23.6	9.8	26.1	13.3
0.0	-	5.3	308.0	297.6	6.1	8.3	35.3	25.7	10.9	29.0	12.3
0.1	0.1	6.2	365.5	355.0	8.6	10.6	45.1	35.3	13.3	30.2	17.5
-	-	6.3	344.2	332.2	4.7	6.4	39.0	26.4	13.9	31.6	20.2
0.2	0.1	5.8	324.4	313.5	5.9	7.5	40.9	24.9	11.1	29.5	15.4
0.1	0.1	5.2	344.9	332.2	7.2	7.7	42.8	29.1	12.2	30.2	16.4
-	0.1	4.9	374.9	363.1	8.8	8.8	46.1	28.3	13.1	34.0	18.1
0.3	0.0	4.0	315.4	307.3	5.9	8.2	35.3	28.5	12.8	31.1	14.6
0.2	0.1	5.1	342.8	334.3	6.2	7.0	37.9	30.3	11.5	37.6	18.6
0.2	-	5.9	361.6	350.4	7.0	10.5	37.8	32.6	14.1	31.1	19.9
0.3	-	5.2	324.1	313.8	6.7	7.8	29.2	26.0	10.4	31.2	18.5
0.1	0.1	4.8	324.8	312.7	6.3	7.8	32.3	23.3	13.7	29.8	17.0
-	-	6.0	344.7	333.6	7.1	10.6	37.7	29.4	14.1	27.9	18.0
0.1	0.1	5.5	346.0	334.4	7.2	10.5	29.5	31.7	11.9	31.8	19.8
0.3	0.1	3.1	221.9	215.4	6.0	7.2	16.6	22.6	10.9	14.2	10.6
0.1	0.1	3.8	255.3	248.0	5.8	9.2	28.4	23.0	10.5	16.0	10.4
0.2	0.1	4.5	315.6	306.6	6.4	9.6	30.6	29.1	12.2	18.8	12.0
-	-	2.3	244.1	237.1	4.6	8.5	28.5	24.7	8.8	15.7	12.0
0.1	0.1	2.7	235.7	228.4	5.1	9.6	23.9	21.6	8.8	13.7	9.8
-	0.2	3.1	262.1	256.0	6.7	7.7	32.4	24.8	12.0	17.4	10.6
0.1	-	3.1	261.9	254.7	6.4	9.1	31.1	25.5	10.7	17.9	11.2
0.1	-	2.6	216.2	209.7	5.0	8.3	22.9	17.9	9.3	12.8	6.9
-	-	2.2	251.5	243.4	4.8	8.7	28.0	24.5	11.6	16.3	10.8
-	-	3.3	320.8	310.2	7.1	11.3	38.4	29.0	12.8	15.7	16.6
0.3	-	5.4	320.7	311.8	6.3	12.5	34.6	27.5	13.8	26.4	12.5
-	-	4.9	272.1	263.1	5.4	6.9	28.9	27.5	10.2	17.7	14.1
0.1	-	4.6	275.8	267.9	5.1	8.2	33.0	27.1	11.7	18.7	10.8
0.1	0.1	3.9	294.5	286.4	6.4	8.1	34.7	26.0	10.0	25.5	12.9
0.2	-	4.1	319.3	310.4	6.7	11.2	36.5	25.8	13.7	30.5	13.2
-	-	3.7	310.6	301.7	5.7	9.7	39.7	27.6	12.3	27.3	11.2
0.2	0.1	4.8	309.2	302.0	5.6	10.4	33.9	28.1	12.1	27.3	11.7
0.3	-	3.1	259.6	250.5	5.7	7.4	29.8	20.4	8.9	22.2	10.0
-	-	4.3	258.1	251.4	6.7	6.4	29.3	20.0	8.4	22.2	9.6
0.7	-	4.9	360.6	351.6	6.5	7.5	40.9	34.5	15.6	36.4	16.0
-	-	2.9	239.8	234.4	5.1	8.0	26.8	22.1	10.2	20.4	9.9
0.3	-	5.0	275.3	267.8	5.3	8.0	25.3	24.6	8.2	26.5	14.3

Note : a)　Code see page 595.
　　　 b)　See page 44.

死　亡

表5.19　都道府県（21大都市再掲）別にみた死因
Table 5.19　Death rates (per 100,000 population) by causes each prefecture and 21 major cities, 2016－CON.

都　道　府　県 Prefecture	02108 膵の悪性 新生物	02109 喉頭の 悪性新生物	02110 気管, 気管 支及び肺の 悪性新生物	02111 皮膚の 悪性新生物	02112 乳房の 悪性新生物	02113 子宮の 悪性新生物 （女性人口 10万対）	02114 卵巣の 悪性新生物 （女性人口 10万対）	02115 前立腺の 悪性新生物 （男性人口 10万対）	02116 膀胱の 悪性新生物	02117 中枢神経系の 悪性新生物
全　　国　　Total	26.8	0.8	59.1	1.2	11.3	9.9	7.4	19.4	6.7	2.1
01 北　海　道 b)	37.5	0.9	76.5	1.7	13.2	10.7	8.3	22.9	7.9	2.3
02 青　　　森	35.2	1.3	71.6	2.2	13.6	11.4	10.2	26.9	9.5	1.9
03 岩　　　手	32.5	0.7	65.6	2.1	12.4	11.2	9.3	24.1	10.7	3.1
04 宮　　　城	27.9	1.0	54.8	1.1	11.8	9.5	8.5	21.4	7.6	1.9
05 秋　　　田	37.7	1.1	76.2	1.7	12.2	12.0	9.4	26.6	11.0	2.6
06 山　　　形	32.2	1.3	71.6	1.4	10.5	11.0	8.7	26.0	7.9	2.7
07 福　　　島	29.1	0.5	65.5	2.3	12.5	11.3	7.1	23.9	6.7	1.7
08 茨　　　城	26.5	0.8	60.0	1.6	11.8	10.2	7.9	20.6	6.0	2.2
09 栃　　　木	27.4	1.0	55.7	0.9	11.6	12.4	7.1	21.2	7.4	2.0
10 群　　　馬	24.9	1.0	56.5	1.3	11.2	10.7	6.4	23.9	7.0	2.1
11 埼　　　玉	22.7	0.6	53.2	0.9	11.5	9.8	8.1	17.6	5.9	1.7
12 千　　　葉	23.9	0.7	55.7	1.4	10.8	8.7	7.7	18.0	5.8	2.2
13 東　　　京	23.4	0.6	50.0	1.0	11.3	9.2	7.6	18.8	6.0	1.7
14 神　奈　川	23.4	0.6	50.1	1.0	12.4	8.9	7.2	17.2	5.7	2.1
15 新　　　潟	33.2	1.4	66.8	1.0	11.0	9.6	8.2	22.6	7.3	2.2
16 富　　　山	30.4	1.0	57.3	1.1	10.6	8.1	6.7	22.0	8.6	1.5
17 石　　　川	28.8	0.8	61.9	1.3	10.9	9.2	7.5	15.6	7.5	2.0
18 福　　　井	32.5	0.6	61.1	1.0	10.4	9.1	8.8	20.2	7.9	1.9
19 山　　　梨	26.4	0.7	55.4	2.1	9.5	7.0	5.3	18.5	5.9	1.7
20 長　　　野	30.4	0.9	51.0	1.7	10.8	12.2	7.3	26.8	8.6	2.3
21 岐　　　阜	29.8	0.9	61.2	1.8	10.6	9.8	7.2	17.5	7.7	2.3
22 静　　　岡	27.7	0.6	58.3	1.4	11.6	11.0	6.4	19.5	7.8	2.0
23 愛　　　知	23.5	0.9	53.5	0.8	9.9	9.2	6.8	14.9	6.0	1.8
24 三　　　重	23.6	0.7	63.8	1.2	10.5	10.3	8.0	16.4	7.4	1.6
25 滋　　　賀	24.6	0.9	54.6	1.4	8.8	6.1	6.7	15.6	6.1	2.1
26 京　　　都	27.0	0.8	62.5	1.2	10.2	10.0	6.5	16.7	6.5	2.2
27 大　　　阪	25.8	0.8	63.4	1.1	11.2	9.9	6.5	16.3	6.6	2.1
28 兵　　　庫	26.2	0.7	61.5	1.1	10.7	10.1	6.6	16.5	6.6	2.3
29 奈　　　良	29.9	0.7	61.5	1.5	11.6	8.3	6.5	19.1	6.2	1.9
30 和　歌　山	31.1	1.3	71.9	2.3	11.1	11.4	8.4	24.6	6.5	2.2
31 鳥　　　取	30.4	0.7	71.7	1.4	11.1	11.9	7.1	23.2	7.4	3.4
32 島　　　根	39.5	0.7	65.4	1.3	11.5	7.3	8.5	22.2	10.5	3.2
33 岡　　　山	28.3	0.8	61.6	1.2	9.4	7.8	7.5	20.2	7.2	1.9
34 広　　　島	27.4	0.7	59.0	0.8	11.7	7.3	8.4	19.5	6.9	2.5
35 山　　　口	28.7	1.1	68.3	1.4	11.8	8.7	6.9	23.4	8.7	2.8
36 徳　　　島	29.4	0.8	68.0	1.5	14.1	6.4	7.4	21.6	7.0	1.9
37 香　　　川	28.8	0.5	66.5	0.7	7.5	10.3	7.8	18.8	5.1	2.5
38 愛　　　媛	31.3	0.3	66.3	1.4	12.6	12.3	7.1	20.8	6.4	2.4
39 高　　　知	33.6	0.6	71.0	1.5	12.3	12.4	10.0	23.7	7.5	3.8
40 福　　　岡	24.4	0.6	60.1	1.3	12.2	11.6	6.2	18.7	6.9	2.5
41 佐　　　賀	30.2	0.4	60.3	1.1	12.1	11.7	8.7	25.7	6.8	3.2
42 長　　　崎	29.5	0.7	69.9	1.4	13.0	11.1	7.4	21.2	8.5	2.4
43 熊　　　本	28.0	0.5	61.9	1.2	11.7	9.9	7.9	25.0	7.3	1.7
44 大　　　分	30.0	1.0	62.4	1.6	10.5	10.7	8.3	20.9	6.3	2.7
45 宮　　　崎	30.3	0.5	63.0	1.6	9.1	13.0	8.7	29.2	5.4	2.9
46 鹿　児　島	26.7	0.6	64.8	1.5	9.9	10.6	7.8	25.8	7.3	3.1
47 沖　　　縄	14.1	0.6	41.0	1.3	9.0	12.3	4.8	13.8	3.2	2.0
21 大 都 市 （再掲） 21 major cities(Regrouped)										
50 東 京 都 の 区 部	22.7	0.6	49.6	1.0	11.0	8.7	7.0	16.7	5.7	1.5
51 札　　　幌	32.2	0.5	68.1	1.4	13.0	9.8	7.8	17.7	7.0	2.1
52 仙　　　台	20.6	0.9	42.9	0.7	11.8	7.9	8.1	16.9	6.7	2.2
53 さ い た ま	21.3	0.4	46.2	1.2	11.1	6.5	7.6	16.0	4.9	1.3
54 千　　　葉	23.0	1.5	52.1	1.4	9.1	5.9	7.6	15.5	5.1	3.0
55 横　　　浜	22.5	0.6	48.3	1.2	11.5	8.0	6.7	15.4	5.9	1.4
56 川　　　崎	18.2	0.5	42.2	0.7	11.6	7.8	6.7	16.7	5.1	1.9
57 相　模　原	20.8	0.4	48.9	1.0	11.9	11.1	7.5	16.6	4.0	1.7
58 新　　　潟	31.2	0.6	62.6	1.0	8.1	8.1	6.7	20.9	6.3	2.6
59 静　　　岡	28.5	0.3	60.4	1.0	12.8	7.8	9.7	17.8	7.7	2.6
60 浜　　　松	24.6	0.6	49.8	0.9	11.0	10.7	5.0	18.2	6.6	2.0
61 名　古　屋	24.0	1.2	55.7	1.0	11.9	9.5	8.0	14.8	5.9	2.0
62 京　　　都	24.7	0.7	60.1	1.0	9.6	10.8	5.8	15.6	6.2	2.3
63 大　　　阪	25.8	1.1	67.1	0.9	11.2	8.7	7.1	15.2	7.4	1.6
64 堺	24.6	0.8	62.9	0.8	10.3	10.3	6.2	20.0	5.4	1.7
65 神　　　戸	27.3	0.8	63.0	1.2	10.2	9.1	6.5	16.1	5.9	2.6
66 岡　　　山	26.6	0.4	48.4	1.0	7.6	8.0	7.2	15.0	7.8	2.1
67 広　　　島	23.4	0.8	51.9	1.0	11.0	6.8	6.8	16.5	5.4	1.8
68 北　九　州	26.4	0.8	71.9	1.4	14.3	10.9	6.7	19.5	8.6	2.7
69 福　　　岡	17.8	0.1	44.2	1.2	11.2	10.5	4.8	14.6	4.5	2.3
70 熊　　　本	21.9	0.3	53.9	0.5	10.9	9.7	7.4	19.0	5.5	1.5

General mortality

簡単分類別死亡率（人口10万対）（つづき）
(the condensed list of causes of death for Japan)[a]: Japan,

平成28年

02118 悪性リンパ腫	02119 白血病	02120 その他のリンパ組織，造血組織及び関連組織の悪性新生物	02121 その他の悪性新生物	02200 その他の新生物	02201 中枢神経系のその他の新生物	02202 中枢神経系を除くその他の新生物	03000 血液及び造血器の疾患並びに免疫機構の障害	03100 貧血	03200 その他の血液及び造血器の疾患並びに免疫機構の障害	04000 内分泌，栄養及び代謝疾患	04100 糖尿病
9.9	7.0	3.6	22.6	9.2	2.0	7.2	3.6	1.7	1.9	17.1	10.8
11.4	7.8	3.8	28.6	11.5	2.7	8.8	4.3	1.7	2.6	18.9	13.7
10.1	7.2	3.4	28.6	11.6	2.5	9.1	4.2	2.4	1.8	24.4	17.1
11.3	8.6	4.8	28.8	12.0	3.2	8.9	4.4	1.7	2.8	22.1	13.8
8.3	5.0	3.5	21.3	9.1	2.0	7.1	2.8	1.2	1.6	15.9	9.7
13.6	8.1	4.2	28.7	11.3	2.3	9.0	5.0	2.7	2.3	28.2	16.9
10.1	8.3	4.9	26.7	11.8	1.6	10.2	4.9	2.6	2.3	20.6	10.9
10.7	6.8	4.0	23.3	10.2	2.0	8.2	4.6	1.6	3.0	24.7	16.3
11.0	7.4	3.3	20.8	9.4	1.9	7.5	3.5	1.9	1.6	17.2	11.9
9.4	5.8	4.4	22.1	10.0	1.9	8.1	4.0	1.5	2.5	18.3	12.5
9.2	6.0	4.4	22.7	10.8	2.4	8.4	4.0	1.9	2.1	18.8	13.0
8.7	6.0	3.2	21.0	7.7	1.9	5.8	3.1	1.4	1.7	14.3	9.8
7.9	5.6	2.9	21.5	9.0	2.1	6.9	3.2	1.5	1.7	13.0	8.6
8.8	5.5	3.0	20.0	7.8	1.7	6.1	3.0	1.4	1.6	15.2	9.0
8.2	5.9	2.7	19.9	7.5	1.5	5.9	2.9	1.6	1.4	12.0	7.8
10.5	7.7	3.9	26.0	10.6	2.8	7.9	3.7	1.8	1.9	19.5	12.5
12.4	5.9	4.8	26.3	11.6	2.8	8.9	4.1	1.7	2.4	22.4	14.7
11.1	6.3	4.3	24.9	8.7	1.5	7.2	2.8	1.4	1.4	15.6	9.8
9.7	8.5	5.4	21.8	9.8	2.5	7.4	3.5	2.1	1.4	20.5	13.6
11.9	7.2	3.9	20.0	9.7	2.3	7.3	3.8	1.8	2.0	18.2	14.3
11.1	6.4	5.2	22.5	9.9	1.9	7.9	4.9	2.3	2.6	19.7	12.3
10.3	6.7	3.4	22.8	8.6	1.9	6.7	3.6	1.7	1.9	16.1	8.8
9.2	6.7	4.2	22.1	8.9	1.6	7.3	3.8	1.7	2.2	20.2	13.7
8.4	6.1	2.7	19.1	7.8	1.7	6.1	2.8	1.3	1.5	14.0	7.7
9.8	6.0	4.2	22.0	10.6	2.5	8.1	2.4	1.1	1.2	18.3	11.5
10.1	5.9	3.9	19.8	8.0	2.0	6.0	3.1	1.1	1.9	14.6	8.0
10.0	6.5	3.9	23.9	8.4	1.5	7.0	4.1	2.0	2.1	18.1	10.3
9.7	7.0	2.8	22.9	8.8	1.8	7.0	3.6	1.6	2.0	16.2	9.8
10.9	6.8	3.2	24.9	8.0	1.8	6.2	3.9	1.9	2.0	18.1	11.3
12.3	7.6	3.6	23.0	10.1	2.6	7.5	3.3	1.8	1.6	16.5	10.2
12.4	8.2	4.1	24.1	11.4	2.1	9.3	4.6	1.9	2.7	22.3	12.4
13.4	8.5	6.9	26.1	11.0	1.6	9.4	4.1	2.3	1.8	22.1	14.7
13.3	9.4	6.6	27.2	13.0	1.5	11.5	3.8	1.3	2.5	20.3	9.5
11.3	6.0	4.4	21.2	10.5	2.0	8.6	3.7	1.6	2.1	16.5	10.5
10.0	6.3	3.8	23.4	10.4	2.1	8.3	2.9	1.4	1.5	17.6	12.5
12.5	9.9	4.2	25.9	10.6	2.5	8.1	4.6	2.3	2.3	16.3	11.2
12.9	7.5	4.4	24.9	12.1	2.0	10.1	4.7	2.1	2.5	20.6	14.2
12.0	7.8	4.7	23.9	10.9	1.9	9.0	4.0	2.0	2.1	20.1	14.1
11.1	8.6	4.0	22.1	12.7	3.2	9.4	3.8	2.1	1.7	20.3	12.1
11.1	7.8	4.9	29.0	11.8	2.8	9.1	7.0	1.8	5.2	21.0	13.0
10.4	7.7	3.4	23.1	8.1	1.7	6.4	3.3	1.6	1.7	18.3	10.9
11.2	9.1	3.9	24.0	8.5	2.5	5.9	5.1	3.5	1.6	20.6	11.2
11.2	13.3	4.6	23.5	11.2	1.5	9.7	6.0	2.7	3.4	17.5	9.3
11.0	11.5	4.6	23.6	10.3	1.3	9.0	4.4	2.2	2.2	17.8	11.1
10.9	11.0	4.1	22.1	12.1	3.0	9.0	5.0	2.1	2.9	21.7	14.1
10.5	13.6	3.6	23.0	11.1	3.6	7.5	5.3	3.3	2.0	21.0	13.4
12.1	16.0	4.4	23.8	11.6	2.9	8.7	6.1	2.7	3.4	22.9	14.4
7.1	11.1	3.2	19.4	6.5	1.9	4.6	4.1	1.8	2.3	15.6	9.8
8.4	5.3	2.9	19.5	7.3	1.6	5.7	2.8	1.2	1.6	14.8	8.5
9.5	7.5	2.9	26.0	9.0	2.0	7.0	3.9	1.2	2.8	14.7	10.1
6.5	4.6	3.1	17.8	7.1	1.4	5.7	1.9	0.6	1.3	14.6	8.8
7.6	6.5	2.2	18.0	7.3	2.4	4.9	2.5	1.2	1.3	10.5	6.4
8.3	5.0	2.3	19.0	6.2	0.6	5.5	2.7	1.4	1.2	12.9	8.2
8.0	5.4	2.7	19.6	7.2	1.5	5.7	2.9	1.8	1.2	11.1	7.1
6.7	4.8	2.1	17.3	6.5	1.0	5.5	2.4	1.1	1.3	9.9	6.1
6.1	4.6	2.1	19.5	8.2	2.2	6.0	3.2	1.0	2.2	11.2	7.3
9.4	7.3	3.3	25.2	10.7	2.5	8.2	3.8	1.5	2.4	17.2	11.4
11.7	7.4	4.6	23.6	8.8	1.3	7.5	2.8	1.4	1.4	18.7	13.7
8.7	7.3	4.6	19.4	9.0	2.0	7.0	2.9	0.9	2.0	17.9	12.9
7.9	5.8	2.7	19.1	7.9	1.7	6.2	3.2	1.5	1.7	13.8	7.5
9.6	5.6	3.1	23.7	8.1	1.2	6.8	3.3	1.6	1.7	17.4	10.3
10.1	6.4	2.4	23.2	8.9	2.0	7.0	3.3	1.7	1.6	17.7	9.7
9.7	7.6	3.1	23.2	8.9	1.7	7.3	3.7	1.1	2.6	13.6	8.8
12.2	6.4	3.2	24.3	7.2	1.7	5.5	3.0	1.4	1.6	19.9	12.7
9.6	5.4	4.2	18.0	9.2	1.0	8.2	2.4	0.7	1.7	12.8	8.4
8.9	6.3	3.3	19.4	6.7	1.1	5.6	2.3	1.3	0.9	11.9	8.4
11.5	7.7	4.3	26.0	9.0	1.9	7.1	3.2	1.7	1.6	20.6	11.8
8.6	5.6	2.7	18.9	5.3	1.4	4.0	1.7	0.8	0.8	13.8	8.7
11.1	8.9	4.6	18.5	7.4	0.9	6.5	3.5	2.0	1.5	13.8	7.7

死　亡

表5.19　都道府県（21大都市再掲）別にみた死因
Table 5.19　Death rates (per 100,000 population) by causes each prefecture and 21 major cities, 2016—CON.

都道府県 Prefecture	04200 その他の内分泌，栄養及び代謝疾患	05000 精神及び行動の障害	05100 血管性及び詳細不明の認知症	05200 その他の精神及び行動の障害	06000 神経系の疾患	06100 髄膜炎	06200 脊髄性筋萎縮症及び関連症候群	06300 パーキンソン病	06400 アルツハイマー病	06500 その他の神経系の疾患
全　　国　Total	6.3	11.3	9.5	1.8	26.7	0.2	2.1	6.0	9.6	8.7
01 北　海　　道 b)	5.2	11.5	9.7	1.8	27.9	0.2	2.0	5.4	10.2	10.1
02 青　　　森	7.4	20.2	17.7	2.5	30.2	0.2	2.2	5.1	15.0	7.6
03 岩　　　手	8.3	13.1	10.6	2.5	36.1	0.6	2.7	8.1	14.7	10.1
04 宮　　　城	6.2	12.7	10.5	2.2	31.3	0.4	2.1	5.4	13.1	10.3
05 秋　　　田	11.3	22.0	19.7	2.4	42.3	0.2	1.9	9.0	20.4	10.8
06 山　　　形	9.7	19.4	15.5	3.9	44.0	0.1	2.3	7.8	23.3	10.5
07 福　　　島	8.5	17.8	15.1	2.7	32.5	0.2	2.6	7.2	14.3	8.1
08 茨　　　城	5.2	10.0	8.5	1.5	21.6	0.2	2.0	5.5	6.0	8.0
09 栃　　　木	5.8	16.0	14.4	1.6	28.0	0.3	2.4	4.9	12.4	8.0
10 群　　　馬	5.9	11.5	10.1	1.4	27.9	0.3	1.7	5.8	12.2	8.0
11 埼　　　玉	4.4	7.1	5.8	1.2	19.3	0.1	1.7	4.0	6.3	7.2
12 千　　　葉	4.4	8.1	6.8	1.3	19.3	0.2	2.0	4.9	5.3	6.9
13 東　　　京	6.2	8.5	7.3	1.2	22.7	0.2	1.8	5.6	7.4	7.7
14 神　奈　　川	4.2	9.0	7.5	1.5	22.8	0.3	2.0	5.3	7.8	7.3
15 新　　　潟	7.0	23.3	21.1	2.2	50.0	0.2	2.8	8.9	25.2	12.9
16 富　　　山	7.7	19.2	17.2	2.0	34.1	0.2	1.7	7.1	15.0	10.1
17 石　　　川	5.8	14.1	11.9	2.2	29.3	0.4	2.5	4.7	11.8	9.9
18 福　　　井	6.9	12.2	10.2	1.9	31.3	0.1	1.9	6.6	11.5	11.1
19 山　　　梨	3.9	15.0	13.0	2.1	33.1	0.4	1.6	6.1	15.6	9.4
20 長　　　野	7.4	21.5	18.1	3.4	39.3	0.1	3.4	9.4	14.9	11.5
21 岐　　　阜	7.3	12.6	10.2	2.4	27.3	0.2	2.7	6.2	10.0	8.1
22 静　　　岡	6.5	14.2	12.2	2.0	29.1	0.3	2.3	7.9	9.4	9.1
23 愛　　　知	6.3	9.7	7.6	2.1	20.5	0.3	2.0	5.1	5.5	7.6
24 三　　　重	6.8	16.2	14.7	1.5	25.2	0.1	2.1	6.9	8.8	7.2
25 滋　　　賀	6.6	10.5	8.6	1.9	30.9	0.2	2.3	6.5	12.5	9.4
26 京　　　都	7.7	12.2	10.4	1.8	28.3	0.2	2.7	7.4	8.2	9.7
27 大　　　阪	6.3	8.2	6.7	1.5	20.6	0.3	2.0	5.5	4.9	7.9
28 兵　　　庫	6.7	12.2	10.8	1.4	27.6	0.2	2.0	6.6	9.3	9.4
29 奈　　　良	6.3	11.4	8.9	2.4	24.4	0.2	1.9	6.7	6.4	9.1
30 和　歌　　山	9.9	11.7	8.4	3.3	23.9	0.3	2.5	6.2	6.0	8.9
31 鳥　　　取	7.4	12.2	9.7	2.5	45.8	0.5	1.1	8.1	24.4	11.7
32 島　　　根	10.8	27.0	23.5	3.5	50.3	0.4	2.3	6.3	28.4	12.9
33 岡　　　山	5.9	10.9	8.9	2.1	31.2	0.2	2.4	7.6	11.4	9.5
34 広　　　島	5.0	11.4	10.1	1.3	28.3	0.1	2.3	5.8	11.0	9.0
35 山　　　口	5.1	9.3	7.3	2.0	35.4	0.1	2.7	8.8	13.8	10.1
36 徳　　　島	6.4	13.8	11.4	2.4	26.5	0.3	2.3	7.0	7.1	9.9
37 香　　　川	6.0	9.5	8.6	0.9	30.5	0.3	2.0	6.0	13.8	8.4
38 愛　　　媛	8.2	13.3	11.1	2.3	30.8	0.1	2.5	7.7	11.4	9.2
39 高　　　知	8.1	8.4	5.3	3.1	30.5	-	3.1	7.5	9.9	10.0
40 福　　　岡	7.4	10.1	7.9	2.2	25.8	0.3	2.3	5.7	8.8	8.9
41 佐　　　賀	9.5	12.9	10.7	2.2	28.8	0.4	1.9	5.0	12.3	9.2
42 長　　　崎	8.2	12.8	10.2	2.7	33.1	0.1	3.0	8.0	11.0	11.0
43 熊　　　本	6.7	12.9	10.1	2.8	33.7	0.2	2.7	7.0	13.1	10.7
44 大　　　分	7.6	17.5	14.3	3.2	36.1	-	2.9	6.4	15.1	11.7
45 宮　　　崎	7.6	9.4	7.8	1.6	29.9	0.3	2.5	6.0	12.3	8.9
46 鹿　児　　島	8.6	7.6	5.8	1.8	33.4	0.4	1.8	7.1	12.3	11.8
47 沖　　　縄	5.7	7.5	5.5	2.0	19.1	0.2	1.9	4.8	3.6	8.6
21 大 都 市 （再掲） 21 major cities(Regrouped)										
50 東 京 都 の 区 部	6.3	7.5	6.6	0.9	21.2	0.2	1.5	5.4	6.8	7.2
51 札　　　幌	4.5	8.3	7.0	1.3	24.4	0.3	1.7	4.8	8.4	9.2
52 仙　　　台	5.7	8.7	6.7	1.9	29.3	-	1.4	5.3	13.0	9.6
53 さ　い　た　ま	4.2	6.7	5.9	0.8	19.5	-	1.6	4.1	6.6	7.2
54 千　　　葉	4.7	10.5	8.7	1.7	21.1	0.3	1.7	6.2	5.1	7.8
55 横　　　浜	4.0	8.4	7.2	1.2	23.0	0.3	1.9	5.4	8.1	7.3
56 川　　　崎	3.8	8.3	7.2	1.1	18.2	0.3	1.2	5.6	5.2	5.8
57 相　模　　原	3.9	7.2	6.0	1.2	14.5	0.1	1.7	3.2	4.8	4.7
58 新　　　潟	5.8	17.3	15.5	1.9	39.4	-	2.6	7.7	17.5	11.6
59 静　　　岡	5.0	9.8	9.3	0.6	27.4	0.1	1.6	7.3	10.0	8.4
60 浜　　　松	5.0	15.8	13.8	2.0	30.9	0.4	2.4	8.0	11.2	8.9
61 名　古　　屋	6.3	9.7	7.4	2.3	20.1	0.4	2.0	5.2	5.6	6.9
62 京　　　都	7.1	12.2	10.4	1.8	27.7	0.3	2.3	6.9	9.2	9.0
63 大　　　阪	8.0	8.2	6.8	1.4	20.7	0.5	1.9	6.0	4.4	7.9
64 堺	4.8	7.2	6.0	1.2	18.3	0.2	2.0	4.2	4.2	7.6
65 神　　　戸	7.2	11.3	9.9	1.4	28.2	0.3	1.9	7.4	8.7	9.9
66 岡　　　山	4.6	10.0	7.1	2.9	32.0	0.1	1.1	9.2	11.5	10.1
67 広　　　島	3.4	7.1	5.7	1.4	22.9	-	1.8	5.5	7.8	7.8
68 北　九　　州	8.8	11.9	9.9	2.0	28.6	0.5	2.4	6.7	9.8	9.1
69 福　　　岡	5.1	8.6	6.7	1.9	20.0	0.1	1.5	4.5	6.7	7.1
70 熊　　　本	6.1	11.2	8.4	2.8	25.7	-	2.4	5.8	8.8	8.6

General mortality

簡単分類別死亡率（人口10万対）（つづき）
(the condensed list of causes of death for Japan)[a]: Japan,

平成28年

07000 眼及び付属器の疾患	08000 耳及び乳様突起の疾患	09000 循環器系の疾患	09100 高血圧性疾患	09101 高血圧性心疾患及び心腎疾患	09102 その他の高血圧性疾患	09200 心疾患（高血圧性を除く）	09201 慢性リウマチ性心疾患	09202 急性心筋梗塞	09203 その他の虚血性心疾患	09204 慢性非リウマチ性心内膜疾患	09205 心筋症
0.0	0.0	271.8	5.5	2.5	3.0	158.4	1.8	28.7	27.6	8.8	3.0
-	-	304.8	5.1	2.6	2.5	173.9	2.3	27.9	22.5	9.6	3.9
-	-	356.6	5.3	2.5	2.8	199.1	2.4	39.1	19.7	8.4	2.9
-	0.1	415.9	6.9	4.2	2.7	234.1	2.9	32.9	15.0	11.6	3.2
0.0	-	285.3	5.8	1.8	4.0	158.3	1.6	22.1	25.7	10.2	5.3
-	0.1	402.5	8.4	2.5	6.0	208.3	3.9	23.1	21.9	12.0	4.0
0.1	0.1	380.3	5.9	2.3	3.5	210.0	2.8	59.6	21.9	12.7	3.7
-	-	367.5	7.9	2.7	5.1	208.6	5.6	63.9	18.1	12.6	4.2
-	0.0	298.0	4.8	2.1	2.7	168.2	2.3	43.9	21.7	10.6	3.4
-	-	317.2	5.1	1.8	3.3	177.5	2.4	40.3	54.8	8.7	2.2
-	-	330.2	6.7	2.5	4.2	187.8	2.0	25.9	19.6	10.5	4.1
0.0	0.0	231.2	3.5	1.4	2.2	139.9	1.5	26.2	40.5	6.6	2.1
-	-	254.9	5.0	1.8	3.2	157.2	1.5	25.3	16.9	6.8	2.1
0.0	0.0	217.6	4.2	2.3	1.9	128.7	1.5	18.0	48.7	7.4	2.6
0.0	-	214.5	3.1	1.2	1.9	125.6	1.4	22.7	17.8	7.6	2.3
-	-	336.4	6.6	2.2	4.4	182.8	2.3	33.0	14.3	12.6	3.3
-	0.1	319.4	7.8	1.9	5.9	172.7	1.7	39.6	18.5	10.1	3.2
-	-	291.5	5.3	1.8	3.4	165.9	2.5	31.7	19.7	10.8	3.4
-	-	310.6	6.1	2.8	3.2	178.2	1.8	42.2	22.5	9.2	3.5
-	-	301.7	6.1	2.8	3.3	162.0	2.1	35.1	19.3	11.2	3.8
-	-	341.5	7.9	3.6	4.3	181.9	2.7	37.3	21.7	11.7	3.3
-	0.1	297.2	4.0	1.1	2.9	175.2	1.7	39.5	16.3	9.3	3.4
-	0.1	278.6	6.3	2.2	4.1	149.6	1.6	28.3	19.0	9.8	3.2
-	-	201.6	3.5	1.1	2.4	113.2	0.9	21.3	19.8	6.5	1.8
-	-	287.9	6.9	2.8	4.1	164.8	1.2	38.2	26.7	11.1	3.0
-	-	231.0	4.3	2.2	2.2	144.8	1.7	34.3	21.7	7.6	2.9
-	0.0	272.7	3.6	1.9	1.6	171.2	2.2	20.6	53.2	8.7	3.0
-	-	240.1	8.4	6.3	2.0	152.9	1.3	21.9	50.6	6.5	3.4
-	-	257.0	4.9	2.4	2.6	153.1	1.5	33.3	23.1	8.5	3.1
-	-	284.6	5.6	2.0	3.6	187.2	1.8	19.0	14.8	6.6	2.5
-	-	348.3	5.4	3.0	2.4	222.0	1.7	37.9	56.8	14.4	3.6
-	-	347.3	5.3	1.8	3.5	194.7	2.1	58.8	18.9	12.9	3.9
-	-	359.8	7.7	2.3	5.4	198.4	2.8	24.3	17.0	15.2	5.6
-	-	300.5	4.5	1.7	2.8	179.8	1.4	54.4	11.4	8.2	2.9
-	-	279.2	5.5	2.4	3.1	170.7	1.3	31.4	33.7	8.9	3.2
-	-	367.6	6.2	3.7	2.5	220.0	1.7	29.5	16.3	9.6	3.8
-	-	322.5	9.5	5.0	4.6	186.7	2.1	28.8	16.8	13.5	3.8
-	-	333.1	7.5	1.8	5.7	206.7	3.2	25.6	17.0	9.5	3.2
-	-	363.6	4.9	2.0	2.9	233.0	2.4	26.2	18.4	10.2	3.2
-	0.1	398.2	5.7	1.9	3.8	244.7	2.2	62.7	28.1	14.5	3.5
0.0	-	219.0	7.9	2.8	5.1	114.5	1.2	21.1	15.6	7.3	2.5
-	-	294.8	12.4	6.2	6.2	160.9	2.1	20.9	14.1	11.2	2.9
-	0.1	323.0	8.0	3.8	4.2	189.2	3.3	39.6	17.5	11.8	4.9
-	-	318.0	5.2	2.0	3.1	188.2	2.1	19.5	15.9	9.0	5.8
-	0.1	319.3	7.4	4.4	3.0	181.9	2.9	44.8	23.7	13.1	4.3
-	-	347.3	5.8	2.5	3.3	204.4	3.2	31.9	20.4	12.0	3.0
-	-	359.7	6.7	3.2	3.6	195.1	2.4	45.1	18.0	14.1	3.4
-	-	204.1	6.0	1.7	4.3	117.0	2.7	27.8	22.9	10.6	3.5
-	0.0	207.1	4.3	2.5	1.8	124.7	1.6	15.2	50.0	7.5	2.6
-	-	235.6	3.6	2.1	1.5	123.3	2.1	17.7	16.0	8.2	3.1
0.1	-	211.8	6.6	2.1	4.5	111.5	0.9	15.0	20.5	7.6	2.9
-	-	203.1	2.3	0.9	1.3	122.2	1.0	19.1	42.0	7.4	2.6
-	-	227.6	5.3	0.7	4.6	134.7	0.5	23.0	14.2	6.3	2.0
0.0	-	206.1	2.3	0.9	1.4	122.5	1.7	24.9	9.7	6.8	2.0
-	-	174.5	2.6	1.1	1.4	99.8	1.3	19.3	16.6	6.2	2.5
-	-	209.1	2.2	1.7	0.6	130.5	1.2	16.8	48.3	4.8	1.8
-	-	280.2	4.0	1.2	2.7	157.0	1.7	20.0	13.5	10.9	2.6
-	-	281.2	7.3	3.3	4.0	163.1	1.0	24.4	14.5	10.7	4.6
-	0.1	251.4	5.6	1.0	4.6	127.7	1.5	24.0	22.2	8.5	2.6
-	-	204.3	3.4	1.0	2.4	117.1	1.2	18.3	26.2	6.2	2.0
-	0.1	257.6	3.3	1.6	1.6	163.9	1.8	18.9	52.8	7.5	2.6
-	-	249.3	14.0	11.5	2.4	147.6	0.9	20.2	44.1	7.4	4.7
-	-	230.3	9.4	7.0	2.4	140.0	1.2	24.1	48.6	5.5	3.6
-	-	238.8	4.8	2.5	2.2	142.8	2.0	26.2	31.2	7.7	3.6
-	-	233.1	3.3	1.8	1.5	135.2	1.1	45.5	11.2	6.8	1.9
-	-	215.5	3.9	1.8	2.1	132.1	1.3	21.6	28.7	7.4	3.0
-	-	254.0	8.5	2.2	6.3	134.3	1.6	26.0	22.5	7.9	2.9
0.1	-	155.2	6.2	1.7	4.6	82.2	0.8	14.9	12.5	5.1	2.1
-	-	234.6	3.5	1.1	2.4	145.5	1.1	15.0	16.9	6.9	3.6

死　亡

表 5.19　都道府県（21大都市再掲）別にみた死因
Table 5.19　Death rates (per 100,000 population) by causes each prefecture and 21 major cities, 2016−CON.

都道府県 Prefecture	09206 不整脈及び伝導障害	09207 心不全	09208 その他の心疾患	09300 脳血管疾患	09301 くも膜下出血	09302 脳内出血	09303 脳梗塞	09304 その他の脳血管疾患	09400 大動脈瘤及び解離	09500 その他の循環器系の疾患
全　国　Total	24.8	58.8	4.7	87.4	9.9	25.6	49.8	2.2	14.5	6.0
01 北　海　道 b)	29.8	74.6	3.2	92.6	11.4	27.2	51.9	2.1	16.3	16.9
02 青　　森	47.1	76.7	2.8	124.8	12.7	34.6	74.9	2.6	20.0	7.4
03 岩　　手	96.4	69.2	3.0	151.1	16.0	44.6	86.7	3.9	15.7	8.1
04 宮　　城	36.3	53.1	3.9	99.9	9.8	33.4	54.7	1.9	15.6	5.7
05 秋　　田	31.3	108.0	4.1	161.6	15.3	45.3	94.0	7.0	15.8	8.3
06 山　　形	30.3	75.9	3.2	138.8	13.3	31.6	92.2	1.6	19.4	6.2
07 福　　島	26.9	73.2	4.0	125.9	13.8	31.9	77.7	2.4	18.0	7.2
08 茨　　城	20.9	62.2	3.3	105.8	12.1	31.7	60.1	1.9	14.4	4.9
09 栃　　木	19.2	46.6	3.2	113.9	13.3	34.7	63.7	2.3	15.5	5.2
10 群　　馬	20.1	63.2	42.3	108.3	11.1	31.3	63.6	2.4	17.1	10.3
11 埼　　玉	15.1	45.4	2.5	72.0	9.1	22.4	38.6	1.8	11.7	4.1
12 千　　葉	44.6	56.9	3.1	74.7	9.2	21.8	42.1	1.6	13.5	4.6
13 東　　京	12.0	36.0	2.5	66.2	8.2	21.8	35.0	1.3	14.2	4.4
14 神　奈　川	10.1	57.3	6.4	67.8	8.4	22.1	36.2	1.1	12.9	5.1
15 新　　潟	36.6	74.4	6.1	126.5	11.9	34.4	78.5	1.7	15.0	5.5
16 富　　山	20.5	76.5	2.6	113.8	14.8	26.7	69.5	2.9	18.5	6.5
17 石　　川	30.5	65.2	2.1	99.9	10.8	25.1	61.8	2.3	14.4	6.1
18 福　　井	23.3	73.3	2.3	105.4	10.0	29.3	64.0	2.2	16.3	4.5
19 山　　梨	24.1	63.1	3.3	108.7	15.2	29.6	62.1	1.8	17.6	7.3
20 長　　野	31.0	70.3	3.8	126.0	12.1	34.7	75.4	3.8	19.1	6.7
21 岐　　阜	30.0	72.0	3.0	95.3	11.5	27.5	54.8	1.6	16.1	6.6
22 静　　岡	26.1	57.9	3.6	99.9	10.9	33.6	51.5	3.9	16.6	6.2
23 愛　　知	19.1	41.3	2.5	66.3	8.2	20.5	35.6	1.9	13.2	5.4
24 三　　重	28.5	52.6	3.6	93.1	9.1	27.2	53.8	3.0	17.5	5.5
25 滋　　賀	15.9	57.6	2.9	65.2	9.3	18.4	35.8	1.8	12.1	4.6
26 京　　都	15.7	65.1	2.7	79.7	7.6	24.6	44.9	2.5	13.0	5.2
27 大　　阪	12.5	53.9	2.9	64.2	7.3	17.6	37.5	1.8	9.7	4.9
28 兵　　庫	16.8	62.7	4.1	80.0	9.8	23.0	44.5	2.7	13.0	6.0
29 奈　　良	71.7	65.5	5.3	75.6	6.8	19.7	45.7	3.3	12.0	4.2
30 和　歌　山	19.3	84.9	3.4	97.5	9.9	24.1	60.4	3.1	15.9	7.5
31 鳥　　取	23.0	73.3	1.8	121.0	12.4	35.2	71.4	2.1	20.0	6.4
32 島　　根	60.1	70.0	3.5	128.8	11.3	33.6	81.9	2.0	18.1	6.7
33 岡　　山	16.5	82.8	2.2	95.9	10.9	26.3	56.9	1.8	13.3	6.9
34 広　　島	17.1	73.0	2.1	84.0	8.8	26.2	47.2	1.8	14.0	5.0
35 山　　口	21.2	73.4	64.4	115.6	8.2	29.3	71.5	6.6	19.5	6.4
36 徳　　島	51.3	67.3	3.1	104.7	11.3	26.4	63.8	3.2	15.4	6.2
37 香　　川	78.4	67.1	2.6	100.6	11.3	27.2	60.6	1.6	13.2	5.1
38 愛　　媛	63.8	105.3	3.5	107.2	11.3	29.0	64.2	2.8	13.0	5.5
39 高　　知	27.9	102.9	2.9	121.4	11.8	32.2	74.7	2.8	18.0	8.4
40 福　　岡	18.5	45.5	2.8	75.8	8.7	20.9	43.3	2.9	15.4	5.3
41 佐　　賀	42.4	64.1	3.4	100.1	10.8	26.5	59.6	3.3	16.3	5.1
42 長　　崎	33.3	75.9	2.9	99.4	9.1	27.2	60.6	2.5	18.9	7.6
43 熊　　本	66.2	65.6	4.2	99.2	11.7	28.4	56.8	2.3	19.2	6.3
44 大　　分	31.3	59.0	2.8	106.3	11.0	27.9	63.5	3.8	17.4	6.3
45 宮　　崎	53.8	76.5	3.6	116.2	12.1	34.9	67.3	1.9	14.1	6.8
46 鹿　児　島	27.7	79.0	5.3	128.3	13.6	34.4	77.5	2.8	21.9	7.7
47 沖　　縄	13.2	30.0	6.4	65.3	9.0	22.7	31.3	2.4	10.6	5.1
21 大 都 市 （再掲） 21 major cities(Regrouped)										
50 東京都の区部	11.8	33.6	2.5	61.9	7.1	20.4	33.4	1.0	12.3	3.9
51 札　　幌	19.4	53.8	3.0	74.0	9.2	23.3	40.0	1.5	13.6	21.1
52 仙　　台	29.6	30.5	4.6	74.6	7.0	29.0	36.3	2.2	14.6	4.5
53 さ　い　たま	12.2	35.5	2.4	63.9	8.8	21.6	32.4	1.1	11.0	3.8
54 千　　葉	28.3	56.2	4.3	70.7	9.4	22.5	37.1	1.7	12.5	4.3
55 横　　浜	9.6	61.0	6.8	64.0	8.0	20.9	34.4	0.8	12.2	5.0
56 川　　崎	8.7	40.2	5.1	57.4	8.2	18.7	29.1	1.3	10.3	4.5
57 相　　模　原	9.0	45.3	3.6	62.7	8.0	19.4	33.8	1.5	10.7	3.0
58 新　　潟	41.6	62.5	4.2	103.0	8.8	26.8	66.2	1.2	12.6	3.6
59 静　　岡	40.0	63.4	4.6	90.6	11.5	29.8	47.0	2.3	14.8	5.4
60 浜　　松	16.1	48.1	4.8	95.1	7.9	32.1	52.1	3.0	15.6	7.4
61 名　古　屋	21.0	39.3	3.0	61.9	7.5	20.9	31.2	2.3	16.0	5.9
62 京　　都	14.5	63.3	2.4	71.8	7.7	20.7	40.5	2.9	13.0	4.9
63 大　　阪	13.2	53.4	3.7	70.1	6.9	19.7	40.7	2.7	11.4	6.3
64 堺	10.0	44.5	2.5	67.7	11.7	16.8	38.2	1.0	8.4	4.9
65 神　　戸	17.6	50.8	3.7	72.0	6.6	22.9	41.2	1.4	12.8	6.4
66 岡　　山	13.3	53.1	2.2	75.2	10.5	20.0	42.7	1.9	14.3	5.1
67 広　　島	13.6	54.9	1.6	63.5	7.2	21.5	33.9	0.9	12.5	3.4
68 北　九　州	21.4	47.6	4.3	87.6	11.8	24.8	47.9	3.0	18.8	4.8
69 福　　岡	13.8	30.7	2.3	51.5	6.6	14.5	29.0	1.4	10.9	4.4
70 熊　　本	47.8	50.7	3.5	63.9	8.9	19.1	35.3	0.7	16.9	4.7

General mortality

簡単分類別死亡率（人口10万対）（つづき）
(the condensed list of causes of death for Japan)[a] : Japan,

平成28年

10000	10100	10200	10300	10400	10500	10600	11000	11100	11200	11300	11301
呼吸器系の疾患	インフルエンザ	肺炎	急性気管支炎	慢性閉塞性肺疾患	喘息	その他の呼吸器系の疾患	消化器系の疾患	胃潰瘍及び十二指腸潰瘍	ヘルニア及び腸閉塞	肝疾患	肝硬変（アルコール性を除く）
166.9	1.2	95.4	0.4	12.5	1.2	56.2	39.0	2.1	5.6	12.6	6.2
176.4	1.6	109.5	0.5	13.0	1.1	50.8	42.6	1.6	6.2	12.7	6.5
202.3	0.9	136.4	0.6	13.1	1.1	50.2	48.8	2.4	9.2	16.0	8.0
193.9	0.8	110.7	1.4	16.2	0.8	64.1	43.2	2.4	6.1	13.1	5.7
135.0	1.1	72.9	0.3	10.9	1.0	48.8	34.6	1.6	5.5	10.6	5.0
219.4	1.7	127.9	0.9	12.9	1.4	74.6	53.8	3.4	8.5	14.4	5.5
202.5	1.1	116.4	0.5	15.4	1.5	67.7	47.6	2.6	9.2	11.7	5.6
189.5	1.5	109.2	0.7	17.5	1.5	59.2	49.7	3.1	7.5	13.6	6.1
177.6	1.0	113.4	0.2	13.6	1.3	48.0	40.7	1.7	6.3	12.4	6.5
160.3	1.2	96.5	0.3	12.5	1.0	48.8	40.2	2.1	6.2	12.0	6.7
187.8	1.5	113.6	0.6	15.6	0.9	55.6	48.5	2.5	7.5	13.8	7.3
145.0	1.0	91.3	0.2	9.6	0.7	42.2	31.7	1.5	4.5	10.9	5.7
140.9	0.8	88.7	0.3	9.2	0.8	41.0	31.9	1.5	4.8	10.3	5.3
131.1	1.1	75.6	0.2	10.0	1.1	43.1	33.5	2.5	4.6	12.9	5.2
127.7	0.9	69.3	0.1	10.1	0.8	46.5	33.8	2.3	4.4	13.0	7.8
169.7	1.8	100.2	0.3	12.7	0.6	54.1	42.2	1.4	7.5	10.6	4.4
206.8	1.1	124.7	0.4	12.7	0.4	67.5	40.0	2.5	5.9	11.3	5.5
169.3	0.9	97.5	0.3	13.2	1.6	55.9	39.6	2.5	6.8	10.6	6.0
208.5	1.7	117.5	0.1	15.7	1.6	72.0	37.8	2.1	6.2	11.7	5.8
176.9	1.0	97.9	0.4	16.3	1.2	60.1	47.4	2.6	6.7	15.5	7.1
170.4	1.2	87.2	0.4	14.1	1.3	66.2	44.7	2.8	6.8	12.3	5.9
188.3	1.2	97.6	0.2	12.6	1.1	75.6	38.8	2.1	5.7	12.0	5.9
156.7	0.9	81.1	0.4	12.7	0.9	60.8	39.1	2.3	5.2	11.9	6.0
138.5	1.1	72.7	0.3	9.5	0.8	54.1	32.9	1.8	4.3	10.2	5.1
177.9	1.4	101.4	0.1	15.3	1.3	58.5	39.8	2.5	4.8	9.9	4.3
138.6	0.8	74.1	0.4	11.9	0.9	50.5	32.0	1.3	4.1	10.2	4.8
153.9	1.1	83.2	0.6	13.1	1.0	55.0	35.4	1.4	5.2	10.4	4.8
174.2	1.3	101.3	0.2	13.2	1.3	56.8	40.1	2.3	4.7	15.8	7.9
159.8	1.1	86.3	0.3	14.0	1.4	56.7	38.9	2.4	5.4	13.4	6.5
175.6	1.5	100.9	0.4	13.1	1.3	58.4	37.5	1.9	6.5	12.9	6.3
224.1	0.9	126.7	0.1	20.5	0.8	75.0	48.6	2.2	6.3	14.4	8.4
180.2	1.2	101.2	0.4	15.0	1.1	61.3	41.5	2.8	7.4	13.6	6.9
201.0	0.7	98.8	1.0	18.0	1.9	80.6	48.0	2.8	6.1	13.5	6.6
205.4	1.2	120.9	0.3	14.0	1.6	67.3	42.8	2.4	7.1	11.9	6.1
175.1	1.0	98.8	0.3	12.8	1.0	61.2	36.3	1.8	5.1	12.1	6.0
239.2	1.2	151.5	0.8	15.6	2.0	68.1	47.4	2.2	7.1	13.6	7.2
253.1	2.0	141.8	0.5	18.0	2.0	88.7	56.7	2.0	7.2	16.4	10.3
216.9	1.0	84.5	0.5	17.1	2.6	111.1	44.6	2.4	7.1	13.3	6.7
214.9	1.2	119.0	0.7	15.2	2.3	76.6	46.6	2.3	6.2	14.9	6.6
258.2	3.1	163.6	1.7	16.3	1.7	71.9	57.7	1.8	8.1	16.2	6.5
181.8	0.9	101.6	0.3	12.1	1.3	65.6	38.1	1.9	5.4	12.2	5.9
208.6	1.1	124.0	0.7	17.0	1.3	64.4	47.5	1.6	6.3	13.6	6.6
216.4	1.4	122.9	0.2	12.6	1.5	77.8	46.6	1.7	7.1	13.4	5.7
213.4	1.2	109.3	0.6	14.4	1.2	86.6	44.3	1.9	7.3	11.4	5.6
231.7	1.4	127.5	0.2	17.0	2.2	83.6	47.0	3.2	8.3	14.7	7.1
222.1	1.2	133.3	0.8	14.9	1.9	69.9	47.6	1.9	8.2	14.6	5.7
241.8	2.1	147.0	1.0	20.0	1.8	69.9	51.7	3.1	7.2	14.4	6.6
134.8	1.8	61.1	0.4	14.3	2.4	54.9	43.9	2.7	3.5	18.4	7.3
123.7	1.1	70.7	0.2	9.8	1.1	40.7	32.3	2.6	4.2	12.8	4.9
144.6	1.2	88.7	0.4	10.3	0.9	43.2	33.5	1.4	4.8	11.0	5.9
101.1	0.6	50.9	-	7.9	0.6	41.1	27.6	1.6	3.7	8.9	4.1
125.5	0.6	79.5	0.2	6.7	0.3	38.1	30.0	0.9	4.0	11.5	5.0
126.8	0.7	79.7	-	7.0	0.7	38.7	28.2	1.5	4.5	9.0	5.2
123.7	0.8	66.1	0.1	10.0	1.0	45.8	33.0	2.2	4.2	13.1	8.7
108.6	0.5	58.8	0.1	7.9	0.5	40.8	29.4	1.7	3.1	12.2	6.6
117.3	0.8	64.0	0.4	11.9	0.6	39.6	30.1	1.8	4.7	11.2	5.7
148.9	1.7	83.6	0.4	10.7	0.6	51.9	36.6	1.2	7.1	8.1	3.3
159.4	1.0	76.8	0.3	15.2	0.9	65.2	41.7	2.4	6.3	11.5	6.6
137.0	0.5	65.9	0.8	10.0	0.6	59.2	32.4	1.9	3.8	11.9	6.4
147.5	1.1	77.4	0.5	10.3	0.9	57.4	35.0	2.2	4.3	10.7	4.6
142.6	0.8	76.5	0.8	12.9	1.1	50.4	34.0	1.5	5.4	10.1	3.9
184.3	1.3	108.7	0.2	14.2	1.7	58.1	46.9	2.9	5.5	20.1	11.0
173.3	1.4	102.3	0.2	14.6	1.2	53.6	37.8	1.9	3.6	13.7	6.6
158.2	1.3	82.2	0.4	12.8	1.6	59.9	40.7	2.9	5.1	15.6	7.7
146.0	1.1	83.4	0.4	9.6	1.0	50.6	33.3	1.5	5.8	10.0	5.4
129.6	0.8	71.2	0.3	9.4	0.9	46.8	27.2	1.2	4.4	8.4	4.5
194.6	1.0	102.3	0.4	14.4	1.6	74.8	44.0	2.0	6.0	14.3	7.2
129.9	0.4	70.0	0.1	7.9	0.9	50.7	28.0	1.4	3.5	10.0	4.7
160.7	0.9	74.7	0.4	10.4	0.4	73.8	33.2	1.4	6.6	8.6	3.9

死　亡

表 5.19　都道府県（21大都市再掲）別にみた死因
Table 5.19　Death rates (per 100,000 population) by causes each prefecture and 21 major cities, 2016－CON.

都　道　府　県 Prefecture	11302 その他の 肝疾患	11400 その他の 消化器系 の疾患	12000 皮膚及び 皮下組織 の疾患	13000 筋骨格系 及び結合 組織の疾患	14000 腎尿路生 殖器系の 疾　患	14100 糸球体疾患 及　　び 腎尿細管間 質性疾患	14200 腎不全	14201 急　性 腎不全	14202 慢　性 腎不全	14203 詳細不明 の腎不全
全　　国　Total	6.5	18.7	1.3	5.2	30.9	4.0	19.7	2.7	12.8	4.2
01 北　　海　　道 b)	6.2	22.1	0.9	4.6	42.6	4.3	29.8	5.1	19.2	5.5
02 青　　　　森	8.0	21.2	1.6	4.2	47.7	6.4	32.2	3.9	21.0	7.4
03 岩　　　　手	7.4	21.5	1.0	5.5	33.9	4.0	22.7	3.3	14.3	5.1
04 宮　　　　城	5.6	16.9	1.0	4.0	28.3	3.7	17.4	1.8	12.7	2.9
05 秋　　　　田	8.9	27.5	1.7	4.4	48.0	8.0	27.7	3.6	19.0	5.2
06 山　　　　形	6.1	24.1	1.4	5.2	38.8	4.1	27.3	3.3	18.5	5.4
07 福　　　　島	7.5	25.4	1.4	7.1	32.2	4.8	20.3	3.0	13.5	3.8
08 茨　　　　城	5.9	20.2	1.4	6.6	32.6	3.7	20.0	2.7	12.8	4.6
09 栃　　　　木	5.3	19.9	1.3	6.0	32.3	3.9	21.4	2.7	14.2	4.4
10 群　　　　馬	6.5	24.7	1.1	6.2	31.7	3.5	19.4	2.9	11.9	4.6
11 埼　　　　玉	5.2	14.8	1.0	4.0	24.0	2.4	15.8	2.1	10.3	3.4
12 千　　　　葉	5.1	15.3	1.1	4.2	23.8	2.6	14.7	2.2	8.7	3.9
13 東　　　　京	7.7	13.5	1.2	4.1	22.7	2.7	13.8	1.9	8.8	3.0
14 神　奈　川	5.2	14.2	1.0	4.1	21.8	2.9	12.6	1.9	7.7	3.0
15 新　　　　潟	6.2	22.7	1.3	6.6	34.4	4.5	21.1	2.1	14.2	4.8
16 富　　　　山	5.8	20.3	1.9	5.5	33.7	5.1	20.0	2.8	12.8	4.5
17 石　　　　川	4.6	19.7	1.1	4.3	29.4	4.6	17.9	2.1	12.7	3.1
18 福　　　　井	5.8	17.9	1.6	6.9	36.0	5.6	23.2	3.6	14.4	5.2
19 山　　　　梨	8.4	22.6	1.7	5.3	33.6	3.3	23.1	2.4	15.8	4.9
20 長　　　　野	6.5	22.7	1.2	6.4	34.0	5.7	20.4	2.2	13.3	4.9
21 岐　　　　阜	6.1	19.0	2.1	5.7	32.7	4.9	21.6	3.3	13.7	4.6
22 静　　　　岡	5.9	19.7	1.5	6.0	30.8	3.2	21.4	2.2	14.6	4.6
23 愛　　　　知	5.0	16.7	1.3	4.1	23.1	3.0	14.9	2.0	10.0	2.9
24 三　　　　重	5.6	22.6	2.4	5.3	37.1	4.8	23.9	2.6	15.0	6.3
25 滋　　　　賀	6.1	16.4	1.9	5.1	28.0	4.7	18.4	1.7	11.4	5.2
26 京　　　　都	5.7	18.3	1.1	5.7	30.5	4.4	19.0	3.2	11.4	4.4
27 大　　　　阪	8.0	17.3	1.2	5.0	30.5	4.0	19.2	2.8	12.5	4.0
28 兵　　　　庫	6.9	17.8	1.0	5.6	30.5	3.6	20.8	3.4	12.8	4.6
29 奈　　　　良	6.6	16.2	1.5	4.8	28.7	3.0	18.9	2.7	11.4	4.8
30 和　歌　山	6.0	25.6	2.3	6.4	44.0	5.4	29.4	3.3	18.5	7.6
31 鳥　　　　取	6.7	17.7	1.6	6.0	41.0	5.3	28.8	3.7	20.5	4.6
32 島　　　　根	6.9	25.6	1.6	8.0	46.3	10.8	25.0	2.0	18.9	4.1
33 岡　　　　山	5.9	21.4	1.6	6.2	33.8	5.2	22.0	3.1	13.8	5.1
34 広　　　　島	6.1	17.4	1.1	5.4	33.4	4.9	22.4	2.6	14.9	4.8
35 山　　　　口	6.4	24.4	2.2	6.3	45.2	6.8	30.3	4.1	19.5	6.7
36 徳　　　　島	6.0	31.1	1.5	6.6	48.9	7.1	32.4	4.0	22.0	6.4
37 香　　　　川	6.5	21.9	1.1	6.5	35.6	5.9	24.2	3.7	15.1	5.3
38 愛　　　　媛	8.3	23.1	1.8	6.7	39.3	6.0	26.4	4.2	16.8	5.4
39 高　　　　知	9.6	31.6	2.5	6.8	55.6	7.1	35.0	5.2	20.3	9.5
40 福　　　　岡	6.3	18.6	1.6	5.5	31.6	4.7	18.6	3.0	11.9	3.8
41 佐　　　　賀	7.0	26.0	1.7	5.5	35.6	7.0	20.5	2.3	14.0	4.2
42 長　　　　崎	7.7	24.4	1.3	7.3	43.4	7.1	25.8	3.5	17.7	4.6
43 熊　　　　本	5.9	23.7	1.5	6.2	40.3	4.9	26.3	3.3	18.2	4.8
44 大　　　　分	7.6	20.8	1.3	6.9	45.4	6.8	29.7	3.8	20.7	5.1
45 宮　　　　崎	8.9	22.9	1.9	6.1	36.7	4.8	26.0	4.4	17.9	3.8
46 鹿　　児　　島	7.8	27.0	1.4	6.7	44.6	5.1	30.4	3.8	22.1	4.5
47 沖　　　　縄	11.1	19.3	1.7	5.4	30.3	5.8	13.9	1.8	9.7	2.5
21 大 都 市 （再掲） 21 major cities(Regrouped)										
50 東京都の区部	7.9	12.6	1.3	3.9	22.3	2.6	13.5	1.8	8.5	3.1
51 札　　　　幌	5.1	16.2	0.9	4.0	31.3	2.7	22.3	3.5	14.5	4.3
52 仙　　　　台	4.8	13.5	0.6	3.4	18.1	2.6	10.9	1.7	7.6	1.7
53 さ　い　ま	6.4	13.6	1.1	4.9	24.6	2.5	15.6	1.7	10.0	3.9
54 千　　　　葉	3.8	13.1	0.4	4.1	19.9	2.2	12.8	1.7	6.5	4.6
55 横　　　　浜	4.4	13.5	0.9	4.0	20.9	2.8	12.2	2.0	7.2	3.0
56 川　　　　崎	5.6	12.4	0.5	3.6	16.4	1.8	9.7	1.5	6.3	1.9
57 相　模　原	5.5	12.3	0.8	2.9	21.5	4.0	13.2	1.7	8.2	3.3
58 新　　　　潟	4.7	20.2	0.6	5.0	29.2	4.3	17.5	1.1	11.6	4.7
59 静　　　　岡	5.0	21.5	1.1	4.7	29.3	3.0	20.1	2.4	13.5	4.1
60 浜　　　　松	5.5	14.8	1.4	6.5	24.0	3.0	17.7	1.8	12.2	3.8
61 名　古　屋	6.0	17.8	1.3	4.1	25.0	3.0	15.7	2.3	10.7	2.8
62 京　　　　都	6.2	17.0	0.9	4.4	25.8	3.4	16.1	2.6	9.3	4.2
63 大　　　　阪	9.1	18.5	1.4	4.6	34.3	4.1	21.6	2.6	15.1	3.9
64 堺	7.2	18.6	1.2	3.9	29.7	3.8	19.7	2.6	11.9	5.1
65 神　　　　戸	7.9	17.1	1.1	5.8	27.8	3.4	18.0	3.1	10.0	4.9
66 岡　　　　山	4.6	16.0	2.2	5.8	25.4	3.5	17.2	1.9	12.1	3.2
67 広　　　　島	3.9	13.1	0.4	4.8	20.3	3.4	13.2	1.8	9.1	2.3
68 北　九　州	7.1	21.8	1.8	8.6	33.2	4.7	20.9	3.9	12.8	4.3
69 福　　　　岡	5.3	13.1	0.9	3.7	20.7	4.2	11.9	2.4	7.2	2.3
70 熊　　　　本	4.7	16.6	0.9	4.6	29.2	3.0	20.0	2.7	13.4	3.9

334

General mortality

簡単分類別死亡率（人口10万対）（つづき）
(the condensed list of causes of death for Japan)[a]: Japan,

平成28年

14300 その他の腎尿路生殖器系の疾患	15000 妊娠，分娩及び産じょく（女性人口10万対）	16000 周産期に発生した病態	16100 妊娠期間及び胎児発育に関連する障害	16200 出産外傷	16300 周産期に特異的な呼吸障害及び心血管障害	16400 周産期に特異的な感染症	16500 胎児及び新生児の出血性障害及び血液障害	16600 その他の周産期に発生した病態	17000 先天奇形，変形及び染色体異常	17100 神経系の先天奇形	17200 循環器系の先天奇形
7.2	0.1	0.4	0.0	0.0	0.2	0.0	0.1	0.1	1.6	0.1	0.7
8.5	-	0.5	0.0	-	0.3	0.0	0.1	0.0	1.6	0.1	0.8
9.0	0.1	0.5	0.2	-	0.1	-	0.2	-	1.3	-	0.6
7.2	0.2	0.2	-	-	0.1	0.1	-	0.1	1.6	-	0.5
7.3	0.1	0.6	0.1	-	0.2	0.0	0.0	0.2	1.6	-	0.8
12.2	-	0.3	-	-	0.2	-	0.1	-	1.9	0.2	0.6
7.4	-	0.9	-	-	0.2	0.4	0.3	0.1	1.9	-	1.0
7.1	-	0.3	-	-	0.1	0.1	-	0.2	2.2	0.1	1.0
8.9	0.1	0.3	0.1	-	0.1	0.0	-	0.1	1.9	0.1	0.6
7.0	0.1	0.6	-	-	0.3	0.1	0.2	0.1	1.6	0.1	1.0
8.8	0.1	0.2	0.1	-	0.1	-	0.1	0.1	2.5	0.1	1.0
5.8	0.0	0.4	-	-	0.2	0.0	0.1	0.1	1.6	0.1	0.8
6.5	0.1	0.5	0.0	-	0.3	0.1	0.0	0.1	1.3	0.0	0.6
6.3	0.0	0.5	0.0	-	0.3	0.0	0.1	0.1	1.6	0.1	0.8
6.3	0.0	0.5	0.1	-	0.3	0.0	0.1	0.1	1.5	0.1	0.6
8.8	-	0.3	0.0	-	0.1	0.1	-	-	1.1	-	0.4
8.7	-	0.6	-	-	0.4	-	0.1	0.1	1.7	0.1	0.7
6.8	-	0.5	0.3	-	0.3	-	-	-	1.8	0.1	0.7
7.3	-	0.8	-	-	0.5	-	0.3	-	1.4	-	0.6
7.2	-	0.5	-	-	0.2	-	-	0.2	1.5	0.1	0.6
7.9	0.1	0.6	0.0	-	0.3	0.0	0.1	0.1	2.2	0.1	1.0
6.1	-	0.5	-	-	0.3	-	0.1	0.2	1.6	0.2	0.8
6.3	0.1	0.3	0.0	-	0.1	0.0	0.1	-	1.8	0.1	0.6
5.3	0.1	0.4	0.0	-	0.3	0.0	0.1	0.0	1.7	0.1	0.6
8.4	0.1	0.2	-	-	0.1	0.1	-	0.1	1.5	-	0.8
4.9	0.1	0.2	-	-	0.1	-	-	0.1	2.4	0.1	1.5
7.1	0.1	0.5	-	-	0.4	-	0.0	0.0	1.3	0.0	0.8
7.3	0.1	0.3	0.0	0.0	0.2	0.0	0.0	0.0	1.3	0.1	0.6
6.2	0.1	0.3	-	0.0	0.2	0.0	-	0.0	1.4	0.1	0.6
6.7	-	0.6	-	-	0.4	-	0.1	0.1	2.0	-	1.2
9.3	-	0.2	-	-	-	0.2	-	-	2.0	0.2	1.2
6.9	-	1.2	-	-	1.1	-	0.2	-	1.6	-	0.5
10.5	-	0.6	-	-	0.6	-	-	-	1.3	-	0.6
6.6	0.1	0.3	-	-	0.3	-	-	0.1	1.4	0.1	0.5
6.1	-	0.3	0.1	-	0.1	-	0.1	0.0	1.7	0.0	0.9
8.1	-	0.2	-	-	0.1	-	0.1	0.1	2.5	-	1.6
9.4	-	0.1	-	-	-	-	-	0.1	2.7	-	1.1
5.5	-	0.2	-	-	-	0.2	-	-	0.8	-	0.4
7.0	-	0.1	-	-	-	0.1	-	-	1.2	-	0.4
13.5	-	0.1	-	-	-	-	-	0.1	1.7	-	0.6
8.2	0.0	0.3	0.1	-	0.1	0.0	0.0	0.1	1.7	0.0	0.7
8.0	0.2	0.6	0.1	-	0.5	-	-	-	1.0	0.1	0.7
10.6	-	0.4	0.1	-	0.1	-	-	0.1	1.3	0.1	0.2
9.1	0.1	0.5	0.1	-	0.3	-	-	0.1	2.0	0.1	1.1
9.0	0.2	0.6	-	-	0.3	-	0.1	0.2	1.3	-	0.4
6.0	0.2	0.5	-	-	0.3	0.1	0.1	0.1	2.2	0.1	0.7
9.1	-	0.6	-	-	0.2	0.1	0.1	0.2	1.9	-	0.9
10.5	-	0.6	0.1	-	0.4	-	-	0.1	1.9	0.1	0.8
6.1	0.0	0.5	0.0	-	0.3	0.0	0.1	0.1	1.6	0.1	0.8
6.3	-	0.3	0.1	-	0.3	-	-	-	1.3	0.1	0.8
4.6	-	1.0	0.1	-	0.4	0.1	0.1	0.4	1.1	-	0.6
6.5	-	0.5	-	-	0.3	-	0.1	0.1	2.0	0.1	0.9
4.9	0.2	0.6	0.1	-	0.2	0.1	-	0.2	1.4	-	0.8
5.9	-	0.5	0.0	-	0.3	0.0	0.0	0.1	1.3	0.1	0.5
4.9	-	0.6	0.1	-	0.3	-	0.1	0.1	1.9	-	0.7
4.3	-	0.7	0.1	-	0.2	-	0.1	0.1	1.0	-	0.3
7.4	-	0.4	0.1	-	0.2	-	-	-	1.0	-	0.5
6.3	-	0.1	-	-	-	-	-	0.1	2.3	0.3	0.7
3.3	-	0.4	-	-	0.3	-	-	0.1	1.5	-	0.6
6.2	-	0.3	0.0	-	0.2	-	-	0.0	2.0	-	0.7
6.2	0.3	0.4	-	-	0.3	-	0.1	-	1.2	0.1	0.6
8.6	0.1	0.3	0.0	0.1	0.2	-	-	0.1	1.6	0.1	0.7
6.2	-	0.1	-	-	0.1	-	-	-	1.1	-	0.4
6.4	0.1	0.3	-	-	0.1	0.1	-	-	1.7	0.1	0.8
4.7	0.3	0.4	-	-	0.4	-	-	-	1.2	-	0.4
4.2	-	0.3	0.1	-	-	-	0.1	0.1	2.0	-	1.1
7.5	-	0.4	-	-	0.2	0.1	-	0.1	2.1	0.1	0.6
4.6	-	0.3	-	-	-	-	0.1	0.1	1.9	-	1.0
6.2	0.3	0.1	-	-	-	-	-	0.1	1.8	0.1	1.2

死　亡

表 5.19　都道府県（21大都市再掲）別にみた死因
Table 5.19　Death rates (per 100,000 population) by causes each prefecture and 21 major cities, 2016－CON.

都　道　府　県　Prefecture	17201 心臓の先天奇形	17202 その他の循環器系の先天奇形	17300 消化器系の先天奇形	17400 その他の先天奇形及び変形	17500 染色体異常，他に分類されないもの	18000 症状，徴候及び異常臨床所見・異常検査所見で他に分類されないもの	18100 老　衰	18200 乳幼児突然死症候群	18300 その他の症状，徴候及び異常臨床所見・異常検査所見で他に分類されないもの	20000 傷病及び死亡の外因
全　国　Total	0.5	0.3	0.1	0.5	0.3	89.9	74.2	0.1	15.6	52.7
01 北　海　　道	0.5	0.4	0.1	0.5	0.1	77.5	63.7	0.3	13.5	53.9
02 青　　　森	0.5	0.2	-	0.5	0.2	110.7	87.0	-	23.7	66.6
03 岩　　　手	0.4	0.1	-	0.8	0.3	110.9	96.7	-	14.3	71.3
04 宮　　　城	0.6	0.2	0.2	0.3	0.3	95.9	87.5	0.3	8.2	50.7
05 秋　　　田	0.5	0.1	0.2	0.5	0.4	139.7	106.7	-	33.1	86.9
06 山　　　形	0.5	0.5	-	0.7	0.2	137.9	130.2	-	7.8	65.0
07 福　　　島	0.7	0.3	0.1	0.6	0.5	114.4	99.9	0.1	14.4	65.4
08 茨　　　城	0.5	0.1	0.1	0.8	0.3	97.2	78.0	0.0	19.1	51.7
09 栃　　　木	0.7	0.3	0.1	0.3	0.1	98.7	85.1	-	13.6	49.6
10 群　　　馬	0.7	0.3	0.2	0.9	0.4	80.9	74.2	-	6.7	61.6
11 埼　　　玉	0.5	0.3	0.1	0.5	0.2	70.6	49.0	0.1	21.6	39.7
12 千　　　葉	0.4	0.2	0.0	0.4	0.2	75.1	64.4	0.1	10.6	42.4
13 東　　　京	0.5	0.3	0.1	0.5	0.2	76.8	59.1	0.1	17.6	38.0
14 神　奈　川	0.4	0.2	0.1	0.4	0.4	74.9	70.5	0.1	4.3	51.1
15 新　　　潟	0.2	0.2	0.1	0.4	0.1	136.8	116.1	0.2	20.5	70.1
16 富　　　山	0.5	0.2	-	0.8	0.2	99.3	85.8	-	13.5	71.9
17 石　　　川	0.6	0.1	-	0.7	0.3	94.1	78.1	-	16.1	58.2
18 福　　　井	0.5	0.1	0.1	0.3	0.4	101.0	91.5	0.1	9.5	72.0
19 山　　　梨	0.4	0.2	0.2	0.2	0.2	134.5	109.7	-	24.8	61.6
20 長　　　野	0.6	0.4	0.2	0.5	0.3	129.9	114.9	-	15.0	65.3
21 岐　　　阜	0.6	0.2	0.1	0.3	0.3	108.8	96.3	0.1	12.5	61.4
22 静　　　岡	0.3	0.3	0.0	0.6	0.6	124.5	112.0	-	12.5	52.9
23 愛　　　知	0.4	0.2	0.1	0.5	0.3	107.9	71.7	0.1	36.1	44.8
24 三　　　重	0.7	0.1	0.1	0.5	0.2	117.2	103.5	-	13.6	59.2
25 滋　　　賀	1.2	0.3	0.1	0.4	0.2	64.8	57.5	-	7.3	49.7
26 京　　　都	0.4	0.4	-	0.3	0.2	77.7	69.2	-	8.5	39.9
27 大　　　阪	0.4	0.2	0.0	0.4	0.1	53.1	44.3	-	8.8	48.6
28 兵　　　庫	0.4	0.3	0.1	0.4	0.2	76.8	68.0	0.1	8.7	53.8
29 奈　　　良	0.8	0.4	0.1	0.2	0.5	70.8	65.9	-	4.9	44.2
30 和　歌　山	0.9	0.2	0.3	-	0.3	127.4	113.8	-	13.6	70.3
31 鳥　　　取	0.2	0.4	0.2	0.7	0.2	146.3	119.4	0.4	26.5	56.5
32 島　　　根	0.6	-	-	0.3	0.4	146.1	133.0	0.1	12.9	70.3
33 岡　　　山	0.3	0.2	-	0.5	0.3	98.9	84.3	0.1	14.6	57.1
34 広　　　島	0.5	0.4	0.0	0.4	0.4	98.3	81.5	0.1	16.7	51.9
35 山　　　口	0.9	0.7	0.2	0.4	0.3	97.8	86.7	0.2	10.9	61.7
36 徳　　　島	0.5	0.5	-	1.1	0.5	118.5	97.9	-	20.6	72.4
37 香　　　川	0.4	-	-	0.2	0.2	118.5	108.2	-	10.3	66.5
38 愛　　　媛	0.1	0.3	-	0.6	0.2	119.2	109.1	0.1	10.0	69.0
39 高　　　知	0.6	-	-	0.8	0.3	101.8	82.2	0.4	19.2	76.2
40 福　　　岡	0.5	0.3	0.1	0.5	0.4	79.5	48.8	0.1	30.5	55.8
41 佐　　　賀	0.5	0.2	-	-	0.1	90.4	66.3	-	24.2	56.4
42 長　　　崎	0.1	0.1	0.2	0.4	0.4	96.1	73.5	0.1	22.5	63.3
43 熊　　　本	0.6	0.5	0.2	0.2	0.5	106.4	91.2	0.1	15.2	61.8
44 大　　　分	0.2	0.3	-	0.6	0.3	92.0	80.4	0.2	11.4	65.8
45 宮　　　崎	0.5	0.3	-	1.1	0.3	93.1	82.4	0.2	10.5	64.5
46 鹿　児　島	0.5	0.4	0.3	0.6	0.1	108.0	89.6	0.1	18.2	65.8
47 沖　　　縄	0.4	0.5	0.2	0.6	0.2	60.3	52.3	0.4	7.6	47.4
21 大 都 市 (再掲) 21 major cities(Regrouped)										
50 東 京 都 の 区 部	0.5	0.3	0.1	0.4	0.2	71.1	54.6	0.1	16.5	37.4
51 札　　　幌	0.4	0.4	0.1	0.3	0.2	61.4	45.6	0.4	15.5	44.7
52 仙　　　台	0.4	0.2	0.1	0.3	0.2	74.4	67.7	0.5	6.2	41.4
53 さ　い　た　ま	0.5	0.5	0.2	0.7	0.2	75.2	50.8	-	24.4	39.5
54 千　　　葉	0.6	0.2	0.1	0.2	0.3	65.5	49.6	-	15.9	35.7
55 横　　　浜	0.4	0.1	0.1	0.3	0.3	77.8	74.1	0.2	3.5	51.2
56 川　　　崎	0.5	0.3	0.1	0.7	0.5	53.1	49.8	0.2	3.1	41.7
57 相　模　原	0.1	0.1	-	0.3	0.4	51.0	46.4	0.1	4.4	42.5
58 新　　　潟	0.2	0.2	0.1	0.4	-	94.3	69.1	0.1	25.0	55.0
59 静　　　岡	0.4	0.3	0.1	0.4	0.7	134.0	119.4	-	14.7	51.0
60 浜　　　松	0.3	0.4	-	0.3	0.6	128.2	121.0	-	7.3	45.5
61 名　古　屋	0.5	0.2	0.0	0.8	0.3	114.3	70.6	-	43.7	43.6
62 京　　　都	0.3	0.3	-	0.3	0.3	70.2	62.0	-	8.2	35.5
63 大　　　阪	0.5	0.2	0.0	0.4	0.3	52.9	40.9	-	12.1	58.4
64 堺	0.1	0.2	0.1	0.5	0.1	54.1	44.5	-	9.5	45.3
65 神　　　戸	0.5	0.3	0.1	0.5	0.3	74.7	65.4	-	9.3	57.4
66 岡　　　山	0.4	-	-	0.6	0.3	77.4	66.4	-	11.0	46.7
67 広　　　島	0.7	0.4	0.1	0.4	0.4	75.0	57.9	-	17.1	37.2
68 北　九　州	0.3	0.3	0.1	0.7	0.5	78.3	49.7	0.3	28.3	59.5
69 福　　　岡	0.8	0.3	0.1	0.1	0.6	57.0	32.8	0.1	24.1	44.0
70 熊　　　本	0.8	0.4	0.1	0.1	0.1	77.2	66.1	-	11.1	44.3

簡単分類別死亡率（人口10万対）（つづき）
(the condensed list of causes of death for Japan)[a] : Japan,

General mortality

平成28年

20100 不慮の事故	20101 交通事故	20102 転倒・転落	20103 不慮の溺死及び溺水	20104 不慮の窒息	20105 煙，火及び火炎への曝露	20106 有害物質による不慮の中毒及び有害物質への曝露	20107 その他の不慮の事故	20200 自殺	20300 他殺	20400 その他の外因	22000 特殊目的用コード	22100 重症急性呼吸器症候群〔SARS〕
30.6	4.2	6.4	6.2	7.6	0.7	0.5	5.1	16.8	0.2	5.0	-	-
31.1	3.9	6.3	5.2	8.1	1.1	1.2	5.2	17.5	0.4	5.0	-	-
41.8	6.0	6.1	9.2	11.0	1.8	0.5	7.1	21.0	0.3	3.5	-	-
43.7	7.6	8.4	4.9	13.0	1.3	0.5	8.0	22.9	0.2	4.5	-	-
27.9	3.7	5.4	5.3	7.7	1.0	0.5	4.3	18.0	0.3	4.5	-	-
54.5	6.6	9.6	12.5	14.2	1.1	0.5	10.0	23.8	0.3	8.2	-	-
38.2	3.5	6.9	9.8	11.8	0.5	0.6	5.1	19.9	0.3	6.6	-	-
41.8	5.8	9.0	6.6	10.8	1.7	0.6	7.2	18.4	0.1	5.2	-	-
30.4	6.5	5.9	4.3	7.8	0.7	0.3	4.7	17.1	0.2	4.0	-	-
26.7	5.3	6.9	2.0	7.0	1.0	0.4	4.2	18.9	0.3	3.8	-	-
34.9	4.6	7.5	9.8	7.3	0.6	0.1	5.2	20.2	0.3	6.1	-	-
20.3	3.5	4.8	2.0	5.4	0.6	0.3	3.7	16.7	0.2	2.6	-	-
22.7	4.1	5.9	2.4	5.3	0.8	0.3	3.8	16.7	0.2	2.8	-	-
19.0	1.9	5.3	3.0	4.3	0.3	0.5	3.7	15.5	0.1	3.5	-	-
28.7	2.4	4.4	12.3	5.4	0.3	0.2	3.6	14.6	0.5	7.4	-	-
43.2	5.9	8.5	8.1	11.7	1.7	0.4	6.9	21.8	0.1	5.0	-	-
48.7	6.1	8.0	16.5	10.5	1.0	0.3	6.4	17.7	0.1	5.3	-	-
39.4	6.1	7.5	7.4	11.1	1.0	0.2	6.1	15.5	0.2	3.1	-	-
49.2	7.6	8.0	11.5	14.4	0.9	0.6	6.1	17.0	0.3	5.6	-	-
38.3	5.5	8.2	9.5	7.6	0.7	0.2	6.5	17.0	0.1	6.2	-	-
43.4	5.9	7.3	10.6	10.2	0.9	0.4	8.0	16.5	0.1	5.3	-	-
40.2	5.3	8.0	9.6	9.6	1.2	0.8	5.6	17.5	0.2	3.6	-	-
31.0	4.6	7.4	5.2	7.3	0.9	0.3	5.3	16.6	0.4	5.0	-	-
26.4	3.9	6.2	6.3	5.7	0.6	0.3	3.3	14.4	0.2	3.9	-	-
37.7	6.4	8.4	6.8	9.6	0.5	0.3	5.7	14.9	0.2	6.4	-	-
30.5	5.1	5.7	6.6	7.1	0.9	0.4	4.7	16.1	0.2	2.9	-	-
20.9	3.3	5.0	1.1	5.5	0.5	0.5	5.0	14.2	0.2	4.5	-	-
25.9	3.3	5.2	5.3	6.0	0.4	0.5	5.2	17.8	0.3	4.7	-	-
31.5	3.8	6.0	6.8	7.8	0.5	0.3	6.2	16.4	0.2	5.7	-	-
25.5	3.9	6.5	3.1	5.9	0.8	0.4	4.9	13.6	0.1	4.9	-	-
35.8	5.7	7.6	4.7	10.9	0.4	0.6	5.9	21.7	0.5	12.2	-	-
35.5	4.4	8.3	5.7	9.5	0.7	-	6.9	14.5	0.2	6.4	-	-
42.0	4.4	10.2	6.7	12.9	0.9	0.4	6.4	19.0	0.3	9.1	-	-
36.6	6.1	7.9	6.0	9.1	1.4	0.6	5.6	15.7	0.5	4.3	-	-
31.8	4.8	7.0	5.7	8.8	0.6	0.4	4.5	15.4	0.3	4.4	-	-
35.8	5.9	9.6	3.7	9.5	0.2	0.6	6.4	15.8	0.2	9.8	-	-
45.2	8.4	9.2	9.4	9.1	1.2	0.5	7.2	18.0	0.1	9.1	-	-
42.1	8.9	10.1	4.7	10.5	0.5	0.6	6.8	16.2	0.4	7.8	-	-
44.0	7.3	10.2	6.9	11.8	1.1	0.6	6.1	18.3	0.2	6.4	-	-
51.3	7.1	11.7	7.5	14.8	1.3	0.3	8.6	18.4	0.3	6.3	-	-
33.7	4.1	5.4	10.0	8.7	0.5	0.5	4.6	16.3	0.3	5.6	-	-
35.1	4.9	6.6	6.3	10.4	0.7	0.7	5.5	15.4	0.1	5.8	-	-
40.1	3.5	8.8	9.6	10.7	0.6	0.7	6.0	14.9	0.1	8.2	-	-
38.8	5.0	7.8	5.2	10.0	0.7	0.7	9.4	18.2	0.2	4.7	-	-
44.2	5.0	9.7	9.7	10.9	0.7	0.3	8.0	16.9	0.1	4.7	-	-
39.3	6.0	8.2	7.8	10.5	1.0	0.4	5.5	18.8	0.2	6.2	-	-
43.9	4.8	8.5	6.8	13.0	1.7	0.7	8.4	16.1	0.1	5.7	-	-
20.0	3.5	4.1	1.7	6.4	0.3	0.8	3.2	18.9	0.4	8.2	-	-
19.0	1.9	5.3	3.3	4.2	0.3	0.6	3.3	15.1	0.0	3.3	-	-
22.9	2.6	5.4	3.6	5.7	0.6	1.4	3.7	16.1	0.4	5.3	-	-
20.7	3.5	4.1	3.1	6.5	0.4	0.5	2.8	16.3	0.2	4.1	-	-
20.0	2.8	5.8	1.3	5.8	0.6	0.4	3.3	16.5	0.2	2.8	-	-
19.4	3.1	5.0	1.7	4.4	0.7	-	4.4	13.7	0.1	2.6	-	-
28.9	2.4	4.2	12.8	5.5	0.2	0.1	3.6	14.7	0.3	7.3	-	-
22.9	1.9	3.4	9.3	4.7	0.3	0.5	2.8	12.0	0.2	6.6	-	-
19.7	1.8	3.7	7.3	4.0	0.3	0.2	2.2	13.6	2.2	7.1	-	-
33.8	4.6	6.1	6.9	8.9	2.2	0.2	4.8	16.5	-	4.7	-	-
28.2	4.3	7.5	3.7	7.1	0.9	0.1	4.6	17.5	0.4	4.8	-	-
26.7	4.5	6.4	4.6	6.3	0.6	0.3	4.0	13.3	0.5	5.0	-	-
24.8	2.7	6.5	6.5	4.7	0.7	0.3	3.5	14.4	0.2	4.3	-	-
18.3	1.9	4.8	1.1	5.0	0.4	0.6	4.5	12.7	0.3	4.2	-	-
30.2	2.7	5.6	7.7	6.7	0.4	1.0	6.1	21.5	0.3	6.4	-	-
25.7	4.1	4.4	4.9	6.4	0.4	0.2	5.3	16.0	0.1	3.6	-	-
33.0	3.1	7.0	9.1	7.4	0.7	0.2	5.5	17.6	0.3	6.4	-	-
30.9	4.7	7.2	5.5	7.6	1.4	0.8	3.6	12.6	0.3	2.9	-	-
21.2	3.3	4.4	3.4	6.3	0.4	0.4	3.2	12.5	0.2	3.3	-	-
36.3	3.0	6.9	10.9	10.0	0.8	0.5	4.1	15.9	0.3	7.0	-	-
24.3	3.0	3.7	7.1	6.1	0.4	0.7	3.3	15.0	0.1	4.6	-	-
25.3	3.4	5.3	3.0	8.1	0.9	0.7	3.9	16.1	0.1	2.8	-	-

表 5.20　都道府県（21大都市再掲）別
Table 5.20　Leading causes of death：Japan,

都道府県 Prefecture	第1位 死因 Causes of death	割合(%) Proportion	第2位 死因 Causes of death	割合(%) Proportion	第3位 死因 Causes of death	割合(%) Proportion	第4位 死因 Causes of death	割合(%) Proportion	第5位 死因 Causes of death	割合(%) Proportion
全国 Total [a]	悪性新生物	28.5	心疾患	15.1	肺炎	9.1	脳血管疾患	8.4	老衰	7.1
01 北海道	悪性新生物	31.0	心疾患	15.0	肺炎	9.4	脳血管疾患	8.0	老衰	5.5
02 青森	悪性新生物	29.1	心疾患	14.8	肺炎	10.2	脳血管疾患	9.3	老衰	6.5
03 岩手	悪性新生物	26.7	心疾患	17.4	脳血管疾患	11.3	肺炎	8.2	老衰	7.2
04 宮城	悪性新生物	28.4	心疾患	15.6	脳血管疾患	9.9	老衰	8.6	肺炎	7.2
05 秋田	悪性新生物	27.8	心疾患	13.8	脳血管疾患	10.7	肺炎	8.4	老衰	7.0
06 山形	悪性新生物	27.0	心疾患	15.3	脳血管疾患	10.1	老衰	9.5	肺炎	8.5
07 福島	悪性新生物	26.5	心疾患	16.3	脳血管疾患	9.8	老衰	8.5	肺炎	7.8
08 茨城	悪性新生物	28.0	心疾患	15.3	肺炎	10.3	脳血管疾患	9.6	老衰	7.1
09 栃木	悪性新生物	27.3	心疾患	16.1	脳血管疾患	10.3	肺炎	8.7	老衰	7.7
10 群馬	悪性新生物	26.4	心疾患	16.3	肺炎	9.9	脳血管疾患	9.4	老衰	6.5
11 埼玉	悪性新生物	30.2	心疾患	15.8	肺炎	10.3	脳血管疾患	8.1	老衰	5.5
12 千葉	悪性新生物	29.8	心疾患	17.1	肺炎	9.7	脳血管疾患	8.1	老衰	7.0
13 東京	悪性新生物	30.0	心疾患	15.0	肺炎	8.8	老衰	7.7	脳血管疾患	6.9
14 神奈川	悪性新生物	30.2	心疾患	14.6	老衰	8.2	肺炎	8.0	脳血管疾患	7.9
15 新潟	悪性新生物	27.3	心疾患	14.4	脳血管疾患	10.0	老衰	9.2	肺炎	7.9
16 富山	悪性新生物	27.1	心疾患	14.1	肺炎	10.2	脳血管疾患	9.3	老衰	7.0
17 石川	悪性新生物	28.3	心疾患	15.2	肺炎	9.2	脳血管疾患	9.0	老衰	7.2
18 福井	悪性新生物	26.4	心疾患	14.9	肺炎	9.8	脳血管疾患	8.8	老衰	7.7
19 山梨	悪性新生物	25.8	心疾患	13.9	老衰	9.4	脳血管疾患	9.3	肺炎	8.4
20 長野	悪性新生物	25.3	心疾患	14.9	脳血管疾患	10.3	老衰	9.4	肺炎	7.2
21 岐阜	悪性新生物	26.9	心疾患	15.5	肺炎	8.6	老衰	8.5	脳血管疾患	8.4
22 静岡	悪性新生物	27.3	心疾患	13.8	老衰	10.3	脳血管疾患	9.2	肺炎	7.5
23 愛知	悪性新生物	29.3	心疾患	12.7	肺炎	8.2	老衰	8.1	脳血管疾患	7.4
24 三重	悪性新生物	26.3	心疾患	14.8	老衰	9.3	肺炎	9.1	脳血管疾患	8.3
25 滋賀	悪性新生物	29.1	心疾患	16.1	肺炎	8.3	脳血管疾患	7.3	老衰	6.4
26 京都	悪性新生物	29.7	心疾患	17.0	肺炎	8.2	脳血管疾患	7.9	老衰	6.9
27 大阪	悪性新生物	30.7	心疾患	15.7	肺炎	10.4	脳血管疾患	6.6	老衰	4.6
28 兵庫	悪性新生物	29.7	心疾患	15.0	肺炎	8.5	脳血管疾患	7.9	老衰	6.7
29 奈良	悪性新生物	29.6	心疾患	17.9	肺炎	9.7	脳血管疾患	7.3	老衰	6.3
30 和歌山	悪性新生物	26.4	心疾患	16.7	肺炎	9.5	老衰	8.6	脳血管疾患	7.3
31 鳥取	悪性新生物	27.7	心疾患	15.0	脳血管疾患	9.3	老衰	9.2	肺炎	7.8
32 島根	悪性新生物	26.9	心疾患	14.2	老衰	9.2	脳血管疾患	9.2	肺炎	7.1
33 岡山	悪性新生物	25.9	心疾患	15.8	肺炎	10.6	脳血管疾患	8.4	老衰	7.4
34 広島	悪性新生物	27.8	心疾患	15.9	肺炎	9.2	脳血管疾患	7.8	老衰	7.6
35 山口	悪性新生物	26.7	心疾患	16.5	肺炎	11.4	脳血管疾患	8.7	老衰	6.5
36 徳島	悪性新生物	25.1	心疾患	14.1	肺炎	10.7	脳血管疾患	7.9	老衰	7.4
37 香川	悪性新生物	25.4	心疾患	16.7	老衰	8.8	脳血管疾患	8.1	肺炎	6.8
38 愛媛	悪性新生物	25.6	心疾患	17.9	肺炎	9.2	老衰	8.4	脳血管疾患	8.3
39 高知	悪性新生物	25.3	心疾患	17.0	肺炎	11.4	脳血管疾患	8.5	老衰	5.7
40 福岡	悪性新生物	30.4	心疾患	11.3	肺炎	10.1	脳血管疾患	7.5	老衰	4.8
41 佐賀	悪性新生物	28.3	心疾患	13.6	肺炎	10.5	脳血管疾患	8.5	老衰	5.6
42 長崎	悪性新生物	27.9	心疾患	15.1	肺炎	9.8	脳血管疾患	7.9	老衰	5.8
43 熊本	悪性新生物	25.9	心疾患	15.5	肺炎	9.0	老衰	8.2	脳血管疾患	7.5
44 大分	悪性新生物	25.2	心疾患	14.7	肺炎	10.3	脳血管疾患	8.6	老衰	6.5
45 宮崎	悪性新生物	26.6	心疾患	16.3	肺炎	10.6	脳血管疾患	9.3	老衰	6.6
46 鹿児島	悪性新生物	25.2	心疾患	14.7	肺炎	11.1	脳血管疾患	9.7	老衰	6.8
47 沖縄	悪性新生物	26.3	心疾患	14.3	脳血管疾患	8.0	肺炎	7.4	老衰	6.4
21 大都市（再掲） 21 major cities (Regrouped)										
50 東京都の区部	悪性新生物	30.3	心疾患	15.2	肺炎	8.6	脳血管疾患	7.5	老衰	6.7
51 札幌	悪性新生物	32.4	心疾患	13.0	肺炎	9.4	脳血管疾患	7.8	老衰	4.8
52 仙台	悪性新生物	29.9	心疾患	14.1	脳血管疾患	9.4	老衰	8.6	肺炎	6.4
53 さいたま	悪性新生物	28.6	心疾患	15.3	肺炎	10.0	脳血管疾患	8.0	老衰	6.4
54 千葉	悪性新生物	30.7	心疾患	16.2	肺炎	9.6	脳血管疾患	8.5	老衰	6.0
55 横浜	悪性新生物	30.3	心疾患	14.5	老衰	8.8	肺炎	7.8	脳血管疾患	7.6
56 川崎	悪性新生物	30.1	心疾患	14.3	肺炎	8.4	脳血管疾患	8.2	老衰	7.1
57 相模原	悪性新生物	31.3	心疾患	16.8	肺炎	8.2	脳血管疾患	8.1	老衰	6.0
58 新潟	悪性新生物	29.1	心疾患	14.7	脳血管疾患	9.7	肺炎	7.9	老衰	6.5
59 静岡	悪性新生物	28.3	心疾患	14.8	老衰	10.8	脳血管疾患	8.2	肺炎	7.0
60 浜松	悪性新生物	26.7	心疾患	13.0	老衰	12.3	脳血管疾患	9.7	肺炎	6.7
61 名古屋	悪性新生物	29.1	心疾患	12.7	肺炎	8.4	老衰	7.7	脳血管疾患	6.7
62 京都	悪性新生物	30.3	心疾患	17.3	肺炎	8.4	脳血管疾患	7.6	老衰	6.0
63 大阪	悪性新生物	30.2	心疾患	14.3	肺炎	10.6	脳血管疾患	6.8	老衰	6.0
64 堺	悪性新生物	31.8	心疾患	14.8	肺炎	10.8	脳血管疾患	7.1	老衰	4.7
65 神戸	悪性新生物	30.2	心疾患	14.3	肺炎	8.2	脳血管疾患	7.2	老衰	6.5
66 岡山	悪性新生物	27.7	心疾患	15.0	肺炎	9.2	脳血管疾患	8.3	老衰	7.3
67 広島	悪性新生物	30.2	心疾患	15.9	肺炎	8.6	脳血管疾患	7.6	老衰	7.0
68 北九州	悪性新生物	31.2	心疾患	11.9	肺炎	9.1	脳血管疾患	7.8	老衰	4.4
69 福岡	悪性新生物	31.6	心疾患	11.1	肺炎	9.4	脳血管疾患	7.0	老衰	4.4
70 熊本	悪性新生物	28.7	心疾患	15.6	肺炎	8.0	老衰	7.1	脳血管疾患	6.8

注：1)　死因順位の選び方については、巻末の参考表「1 各種分類表」の「表6－1(1)」を参照されたい。
　　　死因順位は死亡数の多いものから定めた。死亡数が同数の場合は、同一順位に死因名を列記し、次位を空欄とした。
　　全国には住所地外国・不詳を含む。
　　百分率は、それぞれの都道府県別死亡数を100とした率である。
　　「心疾患」は「心疾患（高血圧性を除く）」、「血管性等の認知症」は「血管性及び詳細不明の認知症」である。

General mortality

にみた死因順位 [1)]
each prefecture and 21 major cities, 2016

平成28年

第6位 死因 Causes of death	割合(%) Proportion	第7位 死因 Causes of death	割合(%) Proportion	第8位 死因 Causes of death	割合(%) Proportion	第9位 死因 Causes of death	割合(%) Proportion	第10位 死因 Causes of death	割合(%) Proportion	都道府県 Prefecture
不慮の事故	2.9	腎不全	1.9	自殺	1.6	大動脈瘤及び解離	1.4	肝疾患	1.2	全国 Total [a)]
不慮の事故	2.7	腎不全	2.6	自殺	1.5	大動脈瘤及び解離	1.4	糖尿病	1.2	01 北海道
不慮の事故	3.1	腎不全	2.4	自殺	1.6	血管性等の認知症	1.5	血管性等の認知症	1.3	02 青森
不慮の事故	3.3	自殺	1.7	腎不全	1.7	慢性閉塞性肺疾患	1.2	大動脈瘤及び解離	1.3	03 岩手
不慮の事故	2.8	自殺	1.8	腎不全	1.7	大動脈瘤及び解離	1.5	アルツハイマー病	1.3	04 宮城
不慮の事故	3.6	腎不全	1.8	自殺	1.6	アルツハイマー病	1.3	血管性等の認知症	1.3	05 秋田
不慮の事故	2.8	腎不全	2.0	アルツハイマー病	1.7	自殺	1.4	大動脈瘤及び解離	1.4	06 山形
不慮の事故	3.3	腎不全	1.6	自殺	1.4	大動脈瘤及び解離	1.4	慢性閉塞性肺疾患	1.4	07 福島
不慮の事故	2.8	腎不全	1.6	自殺	1.6	慢性閉塞性肺疾患	1.3	慢性閉塞性肺疾患	1.2	08 茨城
不慮の事故	2.4	腎不全	1.9	自殺	1.7	大動脈瘤及び解離	1.4	血管性等の認知症	1.3	09 栃木
不慮の事故	3.0	自殺	1.8	腎不全	1.7	大動脈瘤及び解離	1.5	慢性閉塞性肺疾患	1.4	10 群馬
不慮の事故	2.3	自殺	1.9	腎不全	1.8	大動脈瘤及び解離	1.3	肝疾患	1.2	11 埼玉
不慮の事故	2.5	自殺	1.8	腎不全	1.8	大動脈瘤及び解離	1.5	肝疾患	1.1	12 千葉
不慮の事故	2.2	自殺	1.8	大動脈瘤及び解離	1.6	腎不全	1.6	肝疾患	1.5	13 東京
不慮の事故	3.3	自殺	1.7	肝疾患	1.5	大動脈瘤及び解離	1.5	腎不全	1.5	14 神奈川
不慮の事故	3.4	アルツハイマー病	2.0	自殺	1.7	血管性等の認知症	1.7	腎不全	1.7	15 新潟
不慮の事故	4.0	腎不全	1.6	大動脈瘤及び解離	1.5	自殺	1.4	血管性等の認知症	1.4	16 富山
不慮の事故	3.6	腎不全	1.6	自殺	1.4	大動脈瘤及び解離	1.3	慢性閉塞性肺疾患	1.2	17 石川
不慮の事故	4.1	腎不全	1.9	自殺	1.4	大動脈瘤及び解離	1.3	慢性閉塞性肺疾患	1.3	18 福井
不慮の事故	3.3	腎不全	2.0	大動脈瘤及び解離	1.5	自殺	1.5	慢性閉塞性肺疾患	1.4	19 山梨
不慮の事故	3.6	腎不全	1.7	大動脈瘤及び解離	1.6	血管性等の認知症	1.5	自殺	1.4	20 長野
不慮の事故	3.5	腎不全	1.9	自殺	1.5	大動脈瘤及び解離	1.4	慢性閉塞性肺疾患	1.1	21 岐阜
不慮の事故	2.9	腎不全	2.0	大動脈瘤及び解離	1.5	自殺	1.5	糖尿病	1.3	22 静岡
不慮の事故	3.0	腎不全	1.7	自殺	1.6	大動脈瘤及び解離	1.5	肝疾患	1.1	23 愛知
不慮の事故	3.4	腎不全	2.1	大動脈瘤及び解離	1.6	慢性閉塞性肺疾患	1.4	自殺	1.3	24 三重
不慮の事故	3.4	腎不全	2.0	自殺	1.8	アルツハイマー病	1.4	大動脈瘤及び解離	1.4	25 滋賀
不慮の事故	2.1	腎不全	1.9	自殺	1.4	慢性閉塞性肺疾患	1.3	大動脈瘤及び解離	1.3	26 京都
不慮の事故	2.7	腎不全	2.0	自殺	1.8	肝疾患	1.6	慢性閉塞性肺疾患	1.4	27 大阪
不慮の事故	3.1	腎不全	2.0	自殺	1.6	慢性閉塞性肺疾患	1.4	肝疾患	1.3	28 兵庫
不慮の事故	2.4	腎不全	1.8	自殺	1.3	慢性閉塞性肺疾患	1.3	肝疾患	1.2	29 奈良
不慮の事故	2.7	腎不全	2.2	自殺	1.6	慢性閉塞性肺疾患	1.5	大動脈瘤及び解離	1.2	30 和歌山
不慮の事故	2.7	腎不全	2.2	アルツハイマー病	1.9	大動脈瘤及び解離	1.5	慢性閉塞性肺疾患	1.2	31 鳥取
不慮の事故	3.0	アルツハイマー病	2.0	血管性等の認知症	1.7	自殺	1.4	大動脈瘤及び解離	1.4	32 島根
不慮の事故	3.2	腎不全	1.9	自殺	1.4	大動脈瘤及び解離	1.2	慢性閉塞性肺疾患	1.2	33 岡山
不慮の事故	3.0	腎不全	2.1	自殺	1.4	大動脈瘤及び解離	1.3	慢性閉塞性肺疾患	1.2	34 広島
不慮の事故	2.7	腎不全	2.3	大動脈瘤及び解離	1.5	自殺	1.2	慢性閉塞性肺疾患	1.2	35 山口
不慮の事故	3.4	腎不全	2.5	慢性閉塞性肺疾患 / 自殺	1.4			肝疾患	1.2	36 徳島
不慮の事故	3.4	腎不全	2.0	慢性閉塞性肺疾患	1.4	自殺	1.3	糖尿病	1.1	37 香川
不慮の事故	3.4	腎不全	2.0	自殺	1.4	慢性閉塞性肺疾患	1.2	肝疾患	1.2	38 愛媛
不慮の事故	3.6	腎不全	2.4	自殺	1.3	大動脈瘤及び解離	1.3	敗血症	1.2	39 高知
不慮の事故	3.3	腎不全	1.8	自殺	1.6	大動脈瘤及び解離	1.5	肝疾患	1.2	40 福岡
不慮の事故	3.0	腎不全	1.7	慢性閉塞性肺疾患	1.4	自殺	1.2			41 佐賀
不慮の事故	3.2	腎不全	2.1	大動脈瘤及び解離	1.5	自殺	1.2	敗血症	1.1	42 長崎
不慮の事故	3.2	腎不全	2.2	大動脈瘤及び解離	1.6	自殺	1.5	慢性閉塞性肺疾患	1.2	43 熊本
不慮の事故	3.6	腎不全	2.4	大動脈瘤及び解離	1.4	自殺	1.4	自殺	1.4	44 大分
不慮の事故	3.1	腎不全	2.1	自殺	1.5	慢性閉塞性肺疾患	1.2	肝疾患	1.2	45 宮崎
不慮の事故	3.3	腎不全	2.3	大動脈瘤及び解離	1.7	慢性閉塞性肺疾患	1.5	自殺	1.2	46 鹿児島
不慮の事故	2.4	自殺	2.3	肝疾患	2.2	慢性閉塞性肺疾患	1.7	腎不全	1.7	47 沖縄
										21 大都市(再掲) 21 major cities(Regrouped)
不慮の事故	2.3	自殺	1.8	腎不全	1.6	肝疾患	1.6	大動脈瘤及び解離	1.5	50 東京都の区部
不慮の事故	2.4	腎不全	2.4	自殺	1.7	大動脈瘤及び解離	1.4	敗血症	1.2	51 札幌
不慮の事故	2.6	自殺	2.1	大動脈瘤及び解離	1.8	アルツハイマー病	1.6	腎不全	1.4	52 仙台
不慮の事故	2.5	自殺	2.1	腎不全	2.0	肝疾患	1.4	大動脈瘤及び解離	1.4	53 さいたま
不慮の事故	2.3	自殺	1.6	腎不全	1.5	大動脈瘤及び解離	1.5	肝疾患	1.1	54 千葉
不慮の事故	3.4	自殺	1.8	肝疾患	1.7	大動脈瘤及び解離	1.5	腎不全	1.4	55 横浜
不慮の事故	3.3	肝疾患	1.8	自殺	1.7	大動脈瘤及び解離	1.5	腎不全	1.4	56 川崎
不慮の事故	2.5	自殺	1.7	腎不全	1.7	慢性閉塞性肺疾患	1.5	肝疾患	1.4	57 相模原
不慮の事故	3.2	アルツハイマー病 / 腎不全	1.6			自殺	1.5	血管性等の認知症	1.5	58 新潟
不慮の事故	2.6	腎不全	1.8	自殺	1.6	慢性閉塞性肺疾患	1.4	大動脈瘤及び解離	1.3	59 静岡
不慮の事故	2.7	腎不全	1.8	大動脈瘤及び解離	1.6	血管性等の認知症	1.4	自殺	1.3	60 浜松
不慮の事故	2.7	大動脈瘤及び解離	1.7	腎不全	1.7	自殺	1.6	肝疾患	1.2	61 名古屋
不慮の事故	1.9	大動脈瘤及び解離	1.7	腎不全	1.5	自殺	1.4	肝疾患	1.3	62 京都
不慮の事故	2.9	腎不全	2.1	自殺	2.1	肝疾患	1.9	慢性閉塞性肺疾患	1.4	63 大阪
不慮の事故	2.7	腎不全	2.1	自殺	1.7	慢性閉塞性肺疾患	1.5	肝疾患	1.4	64 堺
不慮の事故	3.3	腎不全	1.8	自殺	1.8	肝疾患	1.6	大動脈瘤及び解離	1.3	65 神戸
不慮の事故	3.4	腎不全	1.9	大動脈瘤及び解離	1.6	自殺	1.4	アルツハイマー病	1.3	66 岡山
不慮の事故	2.6	腎不全	1.6	自殺	1.5	大動脈瘤及び解離	1.5	慢性閉塞性肺疾患	1.1	67 広島
不慮の事故	3.2	腎不全	1.9	大動脈瘤及び解離	1.7	自殺	1.4	慢性閉塞性肺疾患	1.4	68 北九州
不慮の事故	3.3	自殺	2.0	腎不全	1.6	大動脈瘤及び解離	1.5	肝疾患	1.3	69 福岡
不慮の事故	2.7	腎不全	2.1	大動脈瘤及び解離	1.8	自殺	1.7	慢性閉塞性肺疾患	1.1	70 熊本

Note : a) See Page 44.

死 亡

〔死亡の場所別にみた死因〕
〔Causes of death by place of occurrence〕

表 5.21 死亡の場所別にみた主な死因 [1] の
Table 5.21 Trends in deaths and percent distribution from

死亡総数
Deaths Total

年　次 Year		死　亡　数　Deaths								百　分　率　Percentage							
		総　数 Total	病　院 Hospital	診療所 Clinic	介護老人 保健施設 HSFE[a]	助産所 Maternity home	老人[2] ホーム Home for the elderly	自　宅 Home	その他 Others	総　数 Total	病院 Hospital	診療所 Clinic	介護老人 保健施設 HSFE[a]	助産所 Maternity home	老人[2] ホーム Home for the elderly	自宅 Home	その他 Others
		総　数　Total															
1960	昭和35年	706 599	128 306	25 941	・	791	・	499 406	52 155	100.0	18.2	3.7	・	0.1	・	70.7	7.4
65	40	700 438	172 091	27 477	・	774	・	455 081	45 015	100.0	24.6	3.9	・	0.1	・	65.0	6.4
70	45	712 962	234 915	31 949	・	428	・	403 870	41 800	100.0	32.9	4.5	・	0.1	・	56.6	5.9
75	50	702 275	293 352	34 556	・	193	・	334 980	39 194	100.0	41.8	4.9	・	0.0	・	47.7	5.6
80	55	722 801	376 838	35 102	・	30	・	274 966	35 865	100.0	52.1	4.9	・	0.0	・	38.0	5.0
85	60	752 283	473 691	32 353	・	10	・	212 763	33 466	100.0	63.0	4.3	・	0.0	・	28.3	4.4
90	平成 2 年	820 305	587 438	27 968	351	2	・	177 657	26 889	100.0	71.6	3.4	0.0	0.0	・	21.7	3.3
95	7	922 139	682 943	27 555	2 080	2	14 256	168 756	26 547	100.0	74.1	3.0	0.2	0.0	1.5	18.3	2.9
2000	12	961 653	751 581	27 087	4 818	2	17 807	133 534	26 824	100.0	78.2	2.8	0.5	0.0	1.9	13.9	2.8
05	17	1 083 796	864 338	28 581	7 346	3	23 278	132 702	27 548	100.0	79.8	2.6	0.7	0.0	2.1	12.2	2.5
10	22	1 197 012	931 905	28 869	15 651	1	42 099	150 783	27 704	100.0	77.9	2.4	1.3	0.0	3.5	12.6	2.3
14	26	1 273 004	956 913	26 574	26 037	2	73 338	162 599	27 541	100.0	75.2	2.1	2.0	0.0	5.8	12.8	2.2
15	27	1 290 444	962 597	25 482	29 127	-	81 680	163 973	27 585	100.0	74.6	2.0	2.3	-	6.3	12.7	2.1
16	**28**	**1 307 748**	**965 779**	**24 861**	**30 713**	**1**	**90 067**	**169 400**	**26 927**	**100.0**	**73.9**	**1.9**	**2.3**	**0.0**	**6.9**	**13.0**	**2.1**
		男　Male															
1960	昭和35年	377 526	78 318	15 270	・	418	・	250 531	32 989	100.0	20.7	4.0	・	0.1	・	66.4	8.7
65	40	378 716	104 842	16 336	・	410	・	228 389	28 739	100.0	27.7	4.3	・	0.1	・	60.3	7.6
70	45	387 880	139 884	18 843	・	230	・	201 657	27 266	100.0	36.1	4.9	・	0.1	・	52.0	7.0
75	50	377 827	170 021	19 481	・	72	・	162 856	25 397	100.0	45.0	5.2	・	0.0	・	43.1	6.7
80	55	390 644	215 038	19 229	・	7	・	132 784	23 586	100.0	55.0	4.9	・	0.0	・	34.0	6.0
85	60	407 769	266 203	16 897	・	3	・	102 240	22 426	100.0	65.3	4.1	・	0.0	・	25.1	5.5
90	平成 2 年	443 718	328 903	14 251	162	1	・	82 292	18 109	100.0	74.1	3.2	0.0	0.0	・	18.5	4.1
95	7	501 276	381 841	13 719	834	-	4 533	81 324	19 025	100.0	76.2	2.7	0.2	-	0.9	16.2	3.8
2000	12	525 903	417 214	12 781	1 731	2	4 755	69 213	20 207	100.0	79.3	2.4	0.3	0.0	0.9	13.2	3.8
05	17	584 970	471 449	13 092	2 238	2	5 845	71 724	20 620	100.0	80.6	2.2	0.4	0.0	1.0	12.3	3.5
10	22	633 700	503 632	12 926	4 607	1	10 500	83 111	18 923	100.0	79.5	2.0	0.7	0.0	1.7	13.1	3.0
14	26	660 334	513 562	12 017	7 960	-	19 738	90 340	16 717	100.0	77.8	1.8	1.2	-	3.0	13.7	2.5
15	27	666 707	516 266	11 564	8 921	-	22 150	91 340	16 466	100.0	77.4	1.7	1.3	-	3.3	13.7	2.5
16	**28**	**674 733**	**519 104**	**11 352**	**9 803**	**1**	**24 542**	**94 109**	**15 822**	**100.0**	**76.9**	**1.7**	**1.5**	**0.0**	**3.6**	**13.9**	**2.3**
		女　Female															
1960	昭和35年	329 073	49 988	10 671	・	373	・	248 875	19 166	100.0	15.2	3.2	・	0.1	・	75.6	5.8
65	40	321 722	67 249	11 141	・	364	・	226 692	16 276	100.0	20.9	3.5	・	0.1	・	70.5	5.1
70	45	325 082	95 031	13 106	・	198	・	202 213	14 534	100.0	29.2	4.0	・	0.1	・	62.2	4.5
75	50	324 448	123 331	15 075	・	121	・	172 124	13 797	100.0	38.0	4.6	・	0.0	・	53.1	4.3
80	55	332 157	161 800	15 873	・	23	・	142 182	12 279	100.0	48.7	4.8	・	0.0	・	42.8	3.7
85	60	344 514	207 488	15 456	・	7	・	110 523	11 040	100.0	60.2	4.5	・	0.0	・	32.1	3.2
90	平成 2 年	376 587	258 535	13 717	189	1	・	95 365	8 780	100.0	68.7	3.6	0.1	0.0	・	25.3	2.3
95	7	420 863	301 102	13 836	1 246	2	9 723	87 432	7 522	100.0	71.5	3.3	0.3	0.0	2.3	20.8	1.8
2000	12	435 750	334 367	14 306	3 087	-	13 052	64 321	6 617	100.0	76.7	3.3	0.7	-	3.0	14.8	1.5
05	17	498 826	392 889	15 489	5 108	1	17 433	60 978	6 928	100.0	78.8	3.1	1.0	0.0	3.5	12.2	1.4
10	22	563 312	428 273	15 943	11 044	-	31 599	67 672	8 781	100.0	76.0	2.8	2.0	-	5.6	12.0	1.6
14	26	612 670	443 351	14 557	18 077	2	53 600	72 259	10 824	100.0	72.4	2.4	3.0	0.0	8.7	11.8	1.8
15	27	623 737	446 331	13 918	20 206	-	59 530	72 633	11 119	100.0	71.6	2.2	3.2	-	9.5	11.6	1.8
16	**28**	**633 015**	**446 675**	**13 509**	**20 910**	**-**	**65 525**	**75 291**	**11 105**	**100.0**	**70.6**	**2.1**	**3.3**	**-**	**10.4**	**11.9**	**1.8**

注：1） 死因はICD-10の死因年次推移分類のうちの主なものによる。また、死因の内容の変遷については、74ページの表2.1を参照されたい。
2） 平成 2 年までは老人ホームでの死亡は、自宅又はその他に含まれる。

性・年次別死亡数及び百分率
leading causes of death by sex and place of occurrence : Japan

Hi02　悪性新生物
Malignant neoplasms

年次 Year		死亡数 Deaths								百分率 Percentage							
		総数 Total	病院 Hospital	診療所 Clinic	介護老人保健施設 HSFE a)	助産所 Maternity home	老人ホーム 2) Home for the elderly	自宅 Home	その他 Others	総数 Total	病院 Hospital	診療所 Clinic	介護老人保健施設 HSFE a)	助産所 Maternity home	老人ホーム 2) Home for the elderly	自宅 Home	その他 Others
総数 Total																	
1960	昭和35年	93 773	29 601	2 302	•	-	•	59 676	2 194	100.0	31.6	2.5	•	-	•	63.6	2.3
65	40	106 536	46 820	3 521	•	2	•	54 305	1 888	100.0	43.9	3.3	•	0.0	•	51.0	1.8
70	45	119 977	67 909	4 988	•	16	•	45 591	1 473	100.0	56.6	4.2	•	0.0	•	38.0	1.2
75	50	136 383	96 083	6 502	•	15	•	32 625	1 158	100.0	70.5	4.8	•	0.0	•	23.9	0.8
80	55	161 764	129 460	7 969	•	1	•	23 343	991	100.0	80.0	4.9	•	0.0	•	14.4	0.6
85	60	187 714	162 120	7 740	•	-	•	17 062	792	100.0	86.4	4.1	•	-	•	9.1	0.4
90	平成2年	217 413	196 126	6 793	16	-	•	13 895	583	100.0	90.2	3.1	0.0	-	•	6.4	0.3
95	7	263 022	236 165	7 013	111	-	697	18 285	751	100.0	89.8	2.7	0.0	-	0.3	7.0	0.3
2000	12	295 484	268 842	6 852	316	-	1 166	17 645	663	100.0	91.0	2.3	0.1	-	0.4	6.0	0.2
05	17	325 941	297 362	7 001	462	-	1 739	18 505	872	100.0	91.2	2.1	0.1	-	0.5	5.7	0.3
10	22	353 499	312 304	7 112	1 279	-	3 643	27 508	1 653	100.0	88.3	2.0	0.4	-	1.0	7.8	0.5
14	26	368 103	312 827	6 540	2 172	-	7 448	36 446	2 670	100.0	85.0	1.8	0.6	-	2.0	9.9	0.7
15	27	370 346	311 904	6 224	2 564	-	8 300	38 514	2 840	100.0	84.2	1.7	0.7	-	2.2	10.4	0.8
16	**28**	**372 986**	**310 643**	**6 145**	**2 732**	**-**	**9 574**	**41 031**	**2 861**	**100.0**	**83.3**	**1.6**	**0.7**	**-**	**2.6**	**11.0**	**0.8**
男　Male																	
1960	昭和35年	50 898	17 272	1 310	•	-	•	31 380	936	100.0	33.9	2.6	•	-	•	61.7	1.8
65	40	58 899	27 413	1 973	•	1	•	28 736	776	100.0	46.5	3.3	•	0.0	•	48.8	1.3
70	45	67 074	39 328	2 874	•	8	•	24 239	625	100.0	58.6	4.3	•	0.0	•	36.1	0.9
75	50	76 922	55 304	3 631	•	-	•	17 446	541	100.0	71.9	4.7	•	-	•	22.7	0.7
80	55	93 501	75 968	4 476	•	-	•	12 584	473	100.0	81.2	4.8	•	-	•	13.5	0.5
85	60	110 660	96 307	4 414	•	-	•	9 554	385	100.0	87.0	4.0	•	-	•	8.6	0.3
90	平成2年	130 395	118 434	3 862	9	-	•	7 788	302	100.0	90.8	3.0	0.0	-	•	6.0	0.2
95	7	159 623	144 077	4 049	48	-	267	10 781	401	100.0	90.3	2.5	0.0	-	0.2	6.8	0.3
2000	12	179 140	164 025	3 852	125	-	376	10 416	346	100.0	91.6	2.2	0.1	-	0.2	5.8	0.2
05	17	196 603	180 599	3 877	178	-	572	10 935	442	100.0	91.9	2.0	0.1	-	0.3	5.6	0.2
10	22	211 435	188 733	3 778	515	-	1 342	16 311	756	100.0	89.3	1.8	0.2	-	0.6	7.7	0.4
14	26	218 397	188 002	3 549	899	-	3 013	21 700	1 234	100.0	86.1	1.6	0.4	-	1.4	9.9	0.6
15	27	219 508	187 241	3 491	1 102	-	3 414	22 907	1 353	100.0	85.3	1.6	0.5	-	1.6	10.4	0.6
16	**28**	**219 785**	**185 628**	**3 349**	**1 172**	**-**	**4 000**	**24 311**	**1 325**	**100.0**	**84.5**	**1.5**	**0.5**	**-**	**1.8**	**11.1**	**0.6**
女　Female																	
1960	昭和35年	42 875	12 329	992	•	-	•	28 296	1 258	100.0	28.8	2.3	•	-	•	66.0	2.9
65	40	47 637	19 407	1 548	•	1	•	25 569	1 112	100.0	40.7	3.2	•	0.0	•	53.7	2.3
70	45	52 903	28 581	2 114	•	8	•	21 352	848	100.0	54.0	4.0	•	0.0	•	40.4	1.6
75	50	59 461	40 779	2 871	•	15	•	15 179	617	100.0	68.6	4.8	•	0.0	•	25.5	1.0
80	55	68 263	53 492	3 493	•	1	•	10 759	518	100.0	78.4	5.1	•	0.0	•	15.8	0.8
85	60	77 054	65 813	3 326	•	-	•	7 508	407	100.0	85.4	4.3	•	-	•	9.7	0.5
90	平成2年	87 018	77 692	2 931	7	-	•	6 107	281	100.0	89.3	3.4	0.0	-	•	7.0	0.3
95	7	103 399	92 088	2 964	63	-	430	7 504	350	100.0	89.1	2.9	0.1	-	0.4	7.3	0.3
2000	12	116 344	104 817	3 000	191	-	790	7 229	317	100.0	90.1	2.6	0.2	-	0.7	6.2	0.3
05	17	129 338	116 763	3 124	284	-	1 167	7 570	430	100.0	90.3	2.4	0.2	-	0.9	5.9	0.3
10	22	142 064	123 571	3 334	764	-	2 301	11 197	897	100.0	87.0	2.3	0.5	-	1.6	7.9	0.6
14	26	149 706	124 825	2 991	1 273	-	4 435	14 746	1 436	100.0	83.4	2.0	0.9	-	3.0	9.8	1.0
15	27	150 838	124 663	2 733	1 462	-	4 886	15 607	1 487	100.0	82.6	1.8	1.0	-	3.2	10.3	1.0
16	**28**	**153 201**	**125 015**	**2 796**	**1 560**	**-**	**5 574**	**16 720**	**1 536**	**100.0**	**81.6**	**1.8**	**1.0**	**-**	**3.6**	**10.9**	**1.0**

Note：a) Health services facilities for the elderly

死　亡

表5.21　死亡の場所別にみた主な死因[1]の
Table 5.21 Trends in deaths and percent distribution from

Hi05　心疾患（高血圧性を除く）
Heart diseases（excluding hypertensive heart diseases）

年次 Year	死亡数 Deaths 総数 Total	病院 Hospital	診療所 Clinic	介護老人保健施設 HSFE[a]	助産所 Maternity home	老人ホーム[2] Home for the elderly	自宅 Home	その他 Others	百分率 Percentage 総数 Total	病院 Hospital	診療所 Clinic	介護老人保健施設 HSFE[a]	助産所 Maternity home	老人ホーム[2] Home for the elderly	自宅 Home	その他 Others
								総数　Total								
1960 昭和35年	68 400	7 229	1 409	・	10	・	56 331	3 421	100.0	10.6	2.1	・	0.0	・	82.4	5.0
65 40	75 672	11 445	1 962	・	11	・	58 375	3 879	100.0	15.1	2.6	・	0.0	・	77.1	5.1
70 45	89 411	19 929	3 269	・	21	・	61 974	4 218	100.0	22.3	3.7	・	0.0	・	69.3	4.7
75 50	99 226	29 531	4 579	・	9	・	60 225	4 882	100.0	29.8	4.6	・	0.0	・	60.7	4.9
80 55	123 505	49 705	6 370	・	1	・	61 386	6 043	100.0	40.2	5.2	・	0.0	・	49.7	4.9
85 60	141 097	73 440	6 583	・	2	・	55 365	5 707	100.0	52.0	4.7	・	0.0	・	39.2	4.0
90 平成2年	165 478	102 727	6 122	158	-	・	51 931	4 540	100.0	62.1	3.7	0.1	-	・	31.4	2.7
95 7	139 206	90 143	4 320	538	-	2 736	38 147	3 322	100.0	64.8	3.1	0.4	-	2.0	27.4	2.4
2000 12	146 741	99 317	4 258	1 294	-	3 525	35 172	3 175	100.0	67.7	2.9	0.9	-	2.4	24.0	2.2
05 17	173 125	118 309	4 424	1 770	-	4 197	40 978	3 447	100.0	68.3	2.6	1.0	-	2.4	23.7	2.0
10 22	189 360	127 297	4 381	3 084	-	6 678	44 417	3 503	100.0	67.2	2.3	1.6	-	3.5	23.5	1.8
14 26	196 925	130 163	3 930	4 264	-	9 751	45 055	3 762	100.0	66.1	2.0	2.2	-	5.0	22.9	1.9
15 27	196 113	129 660	3 808	4 511	-	10 231	44 343	3 560	100.0	66.1	1.9	2.3	-	5.2	22.6	1.8
16 28	**198 006**	**131 015**	**3 702**	**4 646**	**-**	**10 758**	**44 408**	**3 477**	**100.0**	**66.2**	**1.9**	**2.3**	**-**	**5.4**	**22.4**	**1.8**
								男　Male								
1960 昭和35年	34 755	3 939	785	・	6	・	28 119	1 906	100.0	11.3	2.3	・	0.0	・	80.9	5.5
65 40	38 827	6 216	1 078	・	5	・	29 298	2 230	100.0	16.0	2.8	・	0.0	・	75.5	5.7
70 45	45 988	10 696	1 784	・	13	・	30 935	2 560	100.0	23.3	3.9	・	0.0	・	67.3	5.6
75 50	50 395	15 842	2 368	・	1	・	29 206	2 978	100.0	31.4	4.7	・	0.0	・	58.0	5.9
80 55	64 103	26 202	3 344	・	-	・	30 715	3 842	100.0	40.9	5.2	・	-	・	47.9	6.0
85 60	71 766	37 487	3 195	・	-	・	27 530	3 554	100.0	52.2	4.5	・	-	・	38.4	5.0
90 平成2年	81 774	51 187	2 850	71	-	・	24 679	2 987	100.0	62.6	3.5	0.1	-	・	30.2	3.7
95 7	69 718	45 572	1 897	198	-	865	18 768	2 418	100.0	65.4	2.7	0.3	-	1.2	26.9	3.5
2000 12	72 156	48 614	1 703	435	-	927	18 048	2 429	100.0	67.4	2.4	0.6	-	1.3	25.0	3.4
05 17	83 979	55 923	1 692	539	-	1 013	22 267	2 545	100.0	66.6	2.0	0.6	-	1.2	26.5	3.0
10 22	88 803	58 048	1 611	813	-	1 559	24 402	2 370	100.0	65.4	1.8	0.9	-	1.8	27.5	2.7
14 26	92 278	59 683	1 482	1 144	-	2 475	25 202	2 292	100.0	64.7	1.6	1.2	-	2.7	27.3	2.5
15 27	92 142	59 486	1 402	1 285	-	2 686	25 175	2 108	100.0	64.6	1.5	1.4	-	2.9	27.3	2.3
16 28	**93 419**	**60 577**	**1 457**	**1 341**	**-**	**2 788**	**25 185**	**2 071**	**100.0**	**64.8**	**1.6**	**1.4**	**-**	**3.0**	**27.0**	**2.2**
								女　Female								
1960 昭和35年	33 645	3 290	624	・	4	・	28 212	1 515	100.0	9.8	1.9	・	0.0	・	83.9	4.5
65 40	36 845	5 229	884	・	6	・	29 077	1 649	100.0	14.2	2.4	・	0.0	・	78.9	4.5
70 45	43 423	9 233	1 485	・	8	・	31 039	1 658	100.0	21.3	3.4	・	0.0	・	71.5	3.8
75 50	48 831	13 689	2 211	・	8	・	31 019	1 904	100.0	28.0	4.5	・	0.0	・	63.5	3.9
80 55	59 402	23 503	3 026	・	1	・	30 671	2 201	100.0	39.6	5.1	・	0.0	・	51.6	3.7
85 60	69 331	35 953	3 388	・	2	・	27 835	2 153	100.0	51.9	4.9	・	0.0	・	40.1	3.1
90 平成2年	83 704	51 540	3 272	87	-	・	27 252	1 553	100.0	61.6	3.9	0.1	-	・	32.6	1.9
95 7	69 488	44 571	2 423	340	-	1 871	19 379	904	100.0	64.1	3.5	0.5	-	2.7	27.9	1.3
2000 12	74 585	50 703	2 555	859	-	2 598	17 124	746	100.0	68.0	3.4	1.2	-	3.5	23.0	1.0
05 17	89 146	62 386	2 732	1 231	-	3 184	18 711	902	100.0	70.0	3.1	1.4	-	3.6	21.0	1.0
10 22	100 557	69 249	2 770	2 271	-	5 119	20 015	1 133	100.0	68.9	2.8	2.3	-	5.1	19.9	1.1
14 26	104 647	70 480	2 448	3 120	-	7 276	19 853	1 470	100.0	67.4	2.3	3.0	-	7.0	19.0	1.4
15 27	103 971	70 174	2 406	3 226	-	7 545	19 168	1 452	100.0	67.5	2.3	3.1	-	7.3	18.4	1.4
16 28	**104 587**	**70 438**	**2 245**	**3 305**	**-**	**7 970**	**19 223**	**1 406**	**100.0**	**67.3**	**2.1**	**3.2**	**-**	**7.6**	**18.4**	**1.3**

General mortality

性・年次別死亡数及び百分率（つづき）
leading causes of death by sex and place of occurrence : Japan－CON.

Hi06　脳血管疾患
Cerebrovascular diseases

年　次 Year		死　亡　数 Deaths								百　分　率 Percentage							
		総　数 Total	病　院 Hospital	診療所 Clinic	介護老人保健施設 HSFE a)	助産所 Maternity home	老人ホーム 2) Home for the elderly	自　宅 Home	その他 Others	総　数 Total	病　院 Hospital	診療所 Clinic	介護老人保健施設 HSFE a)	助産所 Maternity home	老人ホーム 2) Home for the elderly	自　宅 Home	その他 Others
総　数　Total																	
1960	昭和35年	150 109	8 557	1 586	・	-	・	132 860	7 106	100.0	5.7	1.1	・	-	・	88.5	4.7
65	40	172 773	17 972	2 861	・	3	・	144 544	7 393	100.0	10.4	1.7	・	0.0	・	83.7	4.3
70	45	181 315	34 374	4 848	・	23	・	136 134	5 936	100.0	19.0	2.7	・	0.0	・	75.1	3.3
75	50	174 367	52 626	6 801	・	10	・	109 858	5 072	100.0	30.2	3.9	・	0.0	・	63.0	2.9
80	55	162 317	71 510	7 258	・	-	・	79 609	3 940	100.0	44.1	4.5	・	-	・	49.0	2.4
85	60	134 994	75 634	5 890	・	-	・	50 622	2 848	100.0	56.0	4.4	・	-	・	37.5	2.1
90	平成 2 年	121 944	78 788	4 486	70	-	・	36 865	1 735	100.0	64.6	3.7	0.1	-	・	30.2	1.4
95	7	146 552	102 174	4 895	433	-	3 630	33 989	1 431	100.0	69.7	3.3	0.3	-	2.5	23.2	1.0
2000	12	132 529	102 130	4 542	1 037	-	4 219	19 471	1 130	100.0	77.1	3.4	0.8	-	3.2	14.7	0.9
05	17	132 847	105 396	4 349	1 482	-	4 703	15 848	1 069	100.0	79.3	3.3	1.1	-	3.5	11.9	0.8
10	22	123 461	95 642	3 622	2 653	-	6 365	14 013	1 166	100.0	77.5	2.9	2.1	-	5.2	11.4	0.9
14	26	114 207	86 127	2 701	3 623	-	8 795	11 731	1 230	100.0	75.4	2.4	3.2	-	7.7	10.3	1.1
15	27	111 973	83 945	2 434	3 955	-	9 088	11 343	1 208	100.0	75.0	2.2	3.5	-	8.1	10.1	1.1
16	28	109 320	81 439	2 236	4 059	-	9 297	11 072	1 217	100.0	74.5	2.0	3.7	-	8.5	10.1	1.1
男　Male																	
1960	昭和35年	78 965	5 522	1 029	・	-	・	68 463	3 951	100.0	7.0	1.3	・	-	・	86.7	5.0
65	40	92 723	11 489	1 848	・	1	・	75 412	3 973	100.0	12.4	2.0	・	0.0	・	81.3	4.3
70	45	96 910	20 318	2 878	・	14	・	70 545	3 155	100.0	21.0	3.0	・	0.0	・	72.8	3.3
75	50	89 924	29 444	3 880	・	1	・	54 075	2 524	100.0	32.7	4.3	・	0.0	・	60.1	2.8
80	55	81 650	38 003	3 750	・	-	・	37 909	1 988	100.0	46.5	4.6	・	-	・	46.4	2.4
85	60	65 287	37 839	2 807	・	-	・	23 172	1 469	100.0	58.0	4.3	・	-	・	35.5	2.3
90	平成 2 年	57 627	38 784	2 037	32	-	・	15 816	958	100.0	67.3	3.5	0.1	-	・	27.4	1.7
95	7	69 587	50 419	2 270	192	-	1 195	14 635	876	100.0	72.5	3.3	0.3	-	1.7	21.0	1.3
2000	12	63 127	50 069	1 995	392	-	1 175	8 755	741	100.0	79.3	3.2	0.6	-	1.9	13.9	1.2
05	17	63 657	51 700	1 868	500	-	1 288	7 647	654	100.0	81.2	2.9	0.8	-	2.0	12.0	1.0
10	22	60 186	47 950	1 620	921	-	1 824	7 160	711	100.0	79.7	2.7	1.5	-	3.0	11.9	1.2
14	26	54 995	42 934	1 188	1 352	-	2 698	6 173	650	100.0	78.1	2.2	2.5	-	4.9	11.2	1.2
15	27	53 576	41 553	1 096	1 432	-	2 862	6 009	624	100.0	77.6	2.0	2.7	-	5.3	11.2	1.2
16	28	52 706	40 732	1 026	1 515	-	2 881	5 909	643	100.0	77.3	1.9	2.9	-	5.5	11.2	1.2
女　Female																	
1960	昭和35年	71 144	3 035	557	・	-	・	64 397	3 155	100.0	4.3	0.8	・	-	・	90.5	4.4
65	40	80 050	6 483	1 013	・	2	・	69 132	3 420	100.0	8.1	1.3	・	0.0	・	86.4	4.3
70	45	84 405	14 056	1 970	・	9	・	65 589	2 781	100.0	16.7	2.3	・	0.0	・	77.7	3.3
75	50	84 443	23 182	2 921	・	9	・	55 783	2 548	100.0	27.5	3.5	・	0.0	・	66.1	3.0
80	55	80 667	33 507	3 508	・	-	・	41 700	1 952	100.0	41.5	4.3	・	-	・	51.7	2.4
85	60	69 707	37 795	3 083	・	-	・	27 450	1 379	100.0	54.2	4.4	・	-	・	39.4	2.0
90	平成 2 年	64 317	40 004	2 449	38	-	・	21 049	777	100.0	62.2	3.8	0.1	-	・	32.7	1.2
95	7	76 965	51 755	2 625	241	-	2 435	19 354	555	100.0	67.2	3.4	0.3	-	3.2	25.1	0.7
2000	12	69 402	52 061	2 547	645	-	3 044	10 716	389	100.0	75.0	3.7	0.9	-	4.4	15.4	0.6
05	17	69 190	53 696	2 481	982	-	3 415	8 201	415	100.0	77.6	3.6	1.4	-	4.9	11.9	0.6
10	22	63 275	47 692	2 002	1 732	-	4 541	6 853	455	100.0	75.4	3.2	2.7	-	7.2	10.8	0.7
14	26	59 212	43 193	1 513	2 271	-	6 097	5 558	580	100.0	72.9	2.6	3.8	-	10.3	9.4	1.0
15	27	58 397	42 392	1 338	2 523	-	6 226	5 334	584	100.0	72.6	2.3	4.3	-	10.7	9.1	1.0
16	28	56 614	40 707	1 210	2 544	-	6 416	5 163	574	100.0	71.9	2.1	4.5	-	11.3	9.1	1.0

343

死　亡

表 5.21　死亡の場所別にみた主な死因[1] の
Table 5.21 Trends in deaths and percent distribution from

Hi07　肺炎
Pneumonia

年次 Year		死亡数 Deaths								百分率 Percentage							
		総数 Total	病院 Hospital	診療所 Clinic	介護老人保健施設 HSFE[a]	助産所 Maternity home	老人ホーム[2] Home for the elderly	自宅 Home	その他 Others	総数 Total	病院 Hospital	診療所 Clinic	介護老人保健施設 HSFE[a]	助産所 Maternity home	老人ホーム[2] Home for the elderly	自宅 Home	その他 Others
総数 Total																	
1960	昭和35年	37 534	6 556	2 465	·	74	·	26 828	1 611	100.0	17.5	6.6	·	0.2	·	71.5	4.3
65	40	29 868	6 621	1 910	·	58	·	20 337	942	100.0	22.2	6.4	·	0.2	·	68.1	3.2
70	45	27 929	8 809	1 618	·	16	·	16 760	726	100.0	31.5	5.8	·	0.1	·	60.0	2.6
75	50	30 441	12 067	1 759	·	7	·	15 666	942	100.0	39.6	5.8	·	0.0	·	51.5	3.1
80	55	33 051	17 441	1 808	·	1	·	13 045	756	100.0	52.8	5.5	·	0.0	·	39.5	2.3
85	60	45 075	31 271	2 239	·	-	·	10 772	793	100.0	69.4	5.0	·	-	·	23.9	1.8
90	平成2年	68 194	55 202	2 597	23	-	·	9 794	578	100.0	80.9	3.8	0.0	-	·	14.4	0.8
95	7	79 629	65 447	2 930	210	-	2 140	8 594	308	100.0	82.2	3.7	0.3	-	2.7	10.8	0.4
2000	12	86 938	76 380	3 069	356	-	1 940	4 990	203	100.0	87.9	3.5	0.4	-	2.2	5.7	0.2
05	17	107 241	96 842	3 568	584	-	2 324	3 660	263	100.0	90.3	3.3	0.5	-	2.2	3.4	0.2
10	22	118 888	106 578	3 613	1 066	-	3 597	3 511	523	100.0	89.6	3.0	0.9	-	3.0	3.0	0.4
14	26	119 650	105 092	3 225	1 947	-	4 919	3 697	770	100.0	87.8	2.7	1.6	-	4.1	3.1	0.6
15	27	120 953	106 375	3 066	2 121	-	5 122	3 510	759	100.0	87.9	2.5	1.8	-	4.2	2.9	0.6
16	**28**	**119 300**	**104 392**	**3 038**	**2 126**	**-**	**5 250**	**3 740**	**754**	**100.0**	**87.5**	**2.5**	**1.8**	**-**	**4.4**	**3.1**	**0.6**
男 Male																	
1960	昭和35年	20 152	3 699	1 347	·	38	·	14 203	865	100.0	18.4	6.7	·	0.2	·	70.5	4.3
65	40	15 962	3 697	1 050	·	32	·	10 719	464	100.0	23.2	6.6	·	0.2	·	67.2	2.9
70	45	15 030	5 049	916	·	9	·	8 705	351	100.0	33.6	6.1	·	0.1	·	57.9	2.3
75	50	16 371	7 031	972	·	1	·	7 939	428	100.0	42.9	5.9	·	0.0	·	48.5	2.6
80	55	18 633	10 607	1 034	·	-	·	6 643	349	100.0	56.9	5.5	·	-	·	35.7	1.9
85	60	25 520	18 653	1 266	·	-	·	5 237	364	100.0	73.1	5.0	·	-	·	20.5	1.4
90	平成2年	38 596	32 285	1 417	12	-	·	4 611	271	100.0	83.6	3.7	0.0	-	·	11.9	0.7
95	7	42 419	36 167	1 465	103	-	703	3 811	170	100.0	85.3	3.5	0.2	-	1.7	9.0	0.4
2000	12	46 722	42 228	1 456	149	-	584	2 209	96	100.0	90.4	3.1	0.3	-	1.2	4.7	0.2
05	17	57 310	52 958	1 684	208	-	665	1 647	148	100.0	92.4	2.9	0.4	-	1.2	2.9	0.3
10	22	63 569	58 496	1 665	405	-	1 138	1 625	240	100.0	92.0	2.6	0.6	-	1.8	2.6	0.4
14	26	64 780	58 455	1 542	819	-	1 746	1 855	363	100.0	90.2	2.4	1.3	-	2.7	2.9	0.6
15	27	65 609	59 240	1 480	891	-	1 900	1 738	360	100.0	90.3	2.3	1.4	-	2.9	2.6	0.5
16	**28**	**65 636**	**58 895**	**1 521**	**894**	**-**	**2 031**	**1 936**	**359**	**100.0**	**89.7**	**2.3**	**1.4**	**-**	**3.1**	**2.9**	**0.5**
女 Female																	
1960	昭和35年	17 382	2 857	1 118	·	36	·	12 625	746	100.0	16.4	6.4	·	0.2	·	72.6	4.3
65	40	13 906	2 924	860	·	26	·	9 618	478	100.0	21.0	6.2	·	0.2	·	69.2	3.4
70	45	12 899	3 760	702	·	7	·	8 055	375	100.0	29.1	5.4	·	0.1	·	62.4	2.9
75	50	14 070	5 036	787	·	6	·	7 727	514	100.0	35.8	5.6	·	0.0	·	54.9	3.7
80	55	14 418	6 834	774	·	1	·	6 402	407	100.0	47.4	5.4	·	0.0	·	44.4	2.8
85	60	19 555	12 618	973	·	-	·	5 535	429	100.0	64.5	5.0	·	-	·	28.3	2.2
90	平成2年	29 598	22 917	1 180	11	-	·	5 183	307	100.0	77.4	4.0	0.0	-	·	17.5	1.0
95	7	37 210	29 280	1 465	107	-	1 437	4 783	138	100.0	78.7	3.9	0.3	-	3.9	12.9	0.4
2000	12	40 216	34 152	1 613	207	-	1 356	2 781	107	100.0	84.9	4.0	0.5	-	3.4	6.9	0.3
05	17	49 931	43 884	1 884	376	-	1 659	2 013	115	100.0	87.9	3.8	0.8	-	3.3	4.0	0.2
10	22	55 319	48 082	1 948	661	-	2 459	1 886	283	100.0	86.9	3.5	1.2	-	4.4	3.4	0.5
14	26	54 870	46 637	1 683	1 128	-	3 173	1 842	407	100.0	85.0	3.1	2.1	-	5.8	3.4	0.7
15	27	55 344	47 135	1 586	1 230	-	3 222	1 772	399	100.0	85.2	2.9	2.2	-	5.8	3.2	0.7
16	**28**	**53 664**	**45 497**	**1 517**	**1 232**	**-**	**3 219**	**1 804**	**395**	**100.0**	**84.8**	**2.8**	**2.3**	**-**	**6.0**	**3.4**	**0.7**

General mortality

性・年次別死亡数及び百分率（つづき）
leading causes of death by sex and place of occurrence : Japan−CON.

Hi14　不慮の事故
Accidents

年　次 Year		死　亡　数 Deaths								百　分　率 Percentage							
		総　数 Total	病　院 Hospital	診療所 Clinic	介護老人保健施設 HSFE a)	助産所 Maternity home	老人ホーム Home for the elderly 2)	自　宅 Home	その他 Others	総　数 Total	病院 Hospital	診療所 Clinic	介護老人保健施設 HSFE a)	助産所 Maternity home	老人ホーム Home for the elderly 2)	自宅 Home	その他 Others
総　数　Total																	
1960	昭和35年	38 964	11 758	4 303	・	-	・	5 892	17 011	100.0	30.2	11.0	・	-	・	15.1	43.7
65	40	40 188	14 527	4 324	・	7	・	5 331	15 999	100.0	36.1	10.8	・	0.0	・	13.3	39.8
70	45	43 802	18 676	4 401	・	8	・	5 043	15 674	100.0	42.6	10.0	・	0.0	・	11.5	35.8
75	50	33 710	14 146	2 639	・	3	・	4 641	12 281	100.0	42.0	7.8	・	0.0	・	13.8	36.4
80	55	29 217	13 207	1 705	・	-	・	4 296	10 009	100.0	45.2	5.8	・	-	・	14.7	34.3
85	60	29 597	15 972	991	・	-	・	3 626	9 008	100.0	54.0	3.3	・	-	・	12.3	30.4
90	平成 2 年	32 122	20 387	585	6	-	・	3 655	7 489	100.0	63.5	1.8	0.0	-	・	11.4	23.3
95	7	45 323	26 142	618	49	-	181	9 721	8 612	100.0	57.7	1.4	0.1	-	0.4	21.4	19.0
2000	12	39 484	26 793	518	138	-	255	5 138	6 642	100.0	67.9	1.3	0.3	-	0.6	13.0	16.8
05	17	39 863	27 703	409	159	-	323	5 595	5 674	100.0	69.5	1.0	0.4	-	0.8	14.0	14.2
10	22	40 732	28 898	442	224	-	435	6 168	4 565	100.0	70.9	1.1	0.5	-	1.1	15.1	11.2
14	26	39 029	27 908	360	306	-	633	6 020	3 802	100.0	71.5	0.9	0.8	-	1.6	15.4	9.7
15	27	38 306	27 156	384	375	-	689	5 999	3 703	100.0	70.9	1.0	1.0	-	1.8	15.7	9.7
16	28	38 306	27 250	373	348	-	740	6 155	3 440	100.0	71.1	1.0	0.9	-	1.9	16.1	9.0
男　　Male																	
1960	昭和35年	29 787	9 403	3 321	・	-	・	3 336	13 727	100.0	31.6	11.1	・	-	・	11.2	46.1
65	40	30 674	11 415	3 328	・	1	・	2 921	13 009	100.0	37.2	10.8	・	0.0	・	9.5	42.4
70	45	33 112	14 310	3 269	・	5	・	2 786	12 742	100.0	43.2	9.9	・	0.0	・	8.4	38.5
75	50	24 865	10 471	1 896	・	1	・	2 562	9 935	100.0	42.1	7.6	・	0.0	・	10.3	40.0
80	55	21 153	9 506	1 155	・	-	・	2 416	8 076	100.0	44.9	5.5	・	-	・	11.4	38.2
85	60	21 318	11 466	644	・	-	・	1 982	7 226	100.0	53.8	3.0	・	-	・	9.3	33.9
90	平成 2 年	22 199	14 073	374	2	-	・	1 881	5 869	100.0	63.4	1.7	0.0	-	・	8.5	26.4
95	7	28 229	16 970	344	31	-	64	4 370	6 450	100.0	60.1	1.2	0.1	-	0.2	15.5	22.8
2000	12	25 162	17 018	289	63	-	86	2 620	5 086	100.0	67.6	1.1	0.3	-	0.3	10.4	20.2
05	17	24 591	17 020	216	66	-	120	2 887	4 282	100.0	69.2	0.9	0.3	-	0.5	11.7	17.4
10	22	23 975	17 078	215	77	-	133	3 202	3 270	100.0	71.2	0.9	0.3	-	0.6	13.4	13.6
14	26	22 562	16 254	169	104	-	205	3 069	2 761	100.0	72.0	0.7	0.5	-	0.9	13.6	12.2
15	27	22 121	15 895	199	121	-	223	2 957	2 726	100.0	71.9	0.9	0.5	-	1.0	13.4	12.3
16	28	22 066	15 911	155	126	-	232	3 116	2 526	100.0	72.1	0.7	0.6	-	1.1	14.1	11.4
女　　Female																	
1960	昭和35年	9 177	2 355	982	・	-	・	2 556	3 284	100.0	25.7	10.7	・	-	・	27.9	35.8
65	40	9 514	3 112	996	・	6	・	2 410	2 990	100.0	32.7	10.5	・	0.1	・	25.3	31.4
70	45	10 690	4 366	1 132	・	3	・	2 257	2 932	100.0	40.8	10.6	・	0.0	・	21.1	27.4
75	50	8 845	3 675	743	・	2	・	2 079	2 346	100.0	41.5	8.4	・	0.0	・	23.5	26.5
80	55	8 064	3 701	550	・	-	・	1 880	1 933	100.0	45.9	6.8	・	-	・	23.3	24.0
85	60	8 279	4 506	347	・	-	・	1 644	1 782	100.0	54.4	4.2	・	-	・	19.9	21.5
90	平成 2 年	9 923	6 314	211	4	-	・	1 774	1 620	100.0	63.6	2.1	0.0	-	・	17.9	16.3
95	7	17 094	9 172	274	18	-	117	5 351	2 162	100.0	53.7	1.6	0.1	-	0.7	31.3	12.6
2000	12	14 322	9 775	229	75	-	169	2 518	1 556	100.0	68.3	1.6	0.5	-	1.2	17.6	10.9
05	17	15 272	10 683	193	93	-	203	2 708	1 392	100.0	70.0	1.3	0.6	-	1.3	17.7	9.1
10	22	16 757	11 820	227	147	-	302	2 966	1 295	100.0	70.5	1.4	0.9	-	1.8	17.7	7.7
14	26	16 467	11 654	191	202	-	428	2 951	1 041	100.0	70.8	1.2	1.2	-	2.6	17.9	6.3
15	27	16 185	11 261	185	254	-	466	3 042	977	100.0	69.6	1.1	1.6	-	2.9	18.8	6.0
16	28	16 240	11 339	218	222	-	508	3 039	914	100.0	69.8	1.3	1.4	-	3.1	18.7	5.6

345

死　亡

表5.22　死亡の場所別にみた主な死因[1]の
Table 5.22 Deaths and percent distribution from leading causes

死亡総数
Deaths Total

平成28年

年　齢 Age	死　亡　数 Deaths								百　分　率 Percentage							
	総　数 Total	病　院 Hospital	診療所 Clinic	介護老人 保健施設 HSFE[a)	助産所 Maternity home	老　人 ホーム Home for the elderly	自　宅 Home	その他 Others	総　数 Total	病　院 Hospital	診療所 Clinic	介護老人 保健施設 HSFE[a)	助産所 Maternity home	老　人 ホーム Home for the elderly	自　宅 Home	その他 Others
総　数　Total	1 307 748	965 779	24 861	30 713	1	90 067	169 400	26 927	100.0	73.9	1.9	2.3	0.0	6.9	13.0	2.1
0～4　歳	2 618	2 274	27	-	1	-	280	36	100.0	86.9	1.0	-	0.0	-	10.7	1.4
5～14 Years	831	669	1	-	-	-	121	40	100.0	80.5	0.1	-	-	-	14.6	4.8
15～24	3 249	1 674	8	-	-	-	853	714	100.0	51.5	0.2	-	-	-	26.3	22.0
25～44	20 289	11 789	105	2	-	7	5 365	3 021	100.0	58.1	0.5	0.0	-	0.0	26.4	14.9
45～64	109 957	80 605	963	117	-	397	22 802	5 073	100.0	73.3	0.9	0.1	-	0.4	20.7	4.6
65～79	354 339	282 032	4 779	2 535	-	7 370	51 967	5 656	100.0	79.6	1.3	0.7	-	2.1	14.7	1.6
80～	816 040	586 626	18 977	28 059	-	82 290	88 009	12 079	100.0	71.9	2.3	3.4	-	10.1	10.8	1.5
不詳 Not stated	425	110	1	-	-	3	3	308	100.0	25.9	0.2	-	-	0.7	0.7	72.5
（再掲） （Regrouped）																
70～	1 076 874	795 283	22 711	30 310	-	88 697	124 117	15 756	100.0	73.9	2.1	2.8	-	8.2	11.5	1.5
男　　Male																
総　数　Total	674 733	519 104	11 352	9 803	1	24 542	94 109	15 822	100.0	76.9	1.7	1.5	0.0	3.6	13.9	2.3
0～4　歳	1 351	1 152	15	-	1	-	162	21	100.0	85.3	1.1	-	0.1	-	12.0	1.6
5～14 Years	483	385	1	-	-	-	74	23	100.0	79.7	0.2	-	-	-	15.3	4.8
15～24	2 287	1 118	6	-	-	-	599	564	100.0	48.9	0.3	-	-	-	26.2	24.7
25～44	13 056	6 823	62	1	-	5	3 700	2 465	100.0	52.3	0.5	0.0	-	0.0	28.3	18.9
45～64	73 946	52 227	636	86	-	271	16 640	4 086	100.0	70.6	0.9	0.1	-	0.4	22.5	5.5
65～79	234 713	187 028	3 149	1 554	-	4 067	34 853	4 062	100.0	79.7	1.3	0.7	-	1.7	14.8	1.7
80～	348 561	270 290	7 482	8 162	-	20 196	38 079	4 352	100.0	77.5	2.1	2.3	-	5.8	10.9	1.2
不詳 Not stated	336	81	1	-	-	3	2	249	100.0	24.1	0.3	-	-	0.9	0.6	74.1
（再掲） （Regrouped）																
70～	518 197	406 791	9 878	9 524	-	23 640	61 479	6 885	100.0	78.5	1.9	1.8	-	4.6	11.9	1.3
女　　Female																
総　数　Total	633 015	446 675	13 509	20 910	-	65 525	75 291	11 105	100.0	70.6	2.1	3.3	-	10.4	11.9	1.8
0～4　歳	1 267	1 122	12	-	-	-	118	15	100.0	88.6	0.9	-	-	-	9.3	1.2
5～14 Years	348	284	-	-	-	-	47	17	100.0	81.6	-	-	-	-	13.5	4.9
15～24	962	556	2	-	-	-	254	150	100.0	57.8	0.2	-	-	-	26.4	15.6
25～44	7 233	4 966	43	1	-	2	1 665	556	100.0	68.7	0.6	0.0	-	0.0	23.0	7.7
45～64	36 011	28 378	327	31	-	126	6 162	987	100.0	78.8	0.9	0.1	-	0.3	17.1	2.7
65～79	119 626	95 004	1 630	981	-	3 303	17 114	1 594	100.0	79.4	1.4	0.8	-	2.8	14.3	1.3
80～	467 479	316 336	11 495	19 897	-	62 094	49 930	7 727	100.0	67.7	2.5	4.3	-	13.3	10.7	1.7
不詳 Not stated	89	29	-	-	-	-	1	59	100.0	32.6	-	-	-	-	1.1	66.3
（再掲） （Regrouped）																
70～	558 677	388 492	12 833	20 786	-	65 057	62 638	8 871	100.0	69.5	2.3	3.7	-	11.6	11.2	1.6

注：1)　死因はICD-10の死因年次推移分類のうちの主なものによる。

General mortality

性・年齢別死亡数及び百分率
of death by sex, age and place of occurrence : Japan, 2016

Hi02　悪性新生物
Malignant neoplasms

平成28年

年　齢 Age	死　亡　数 Deaths								百　分　率 Percentage							
	総　数 Total	病　院 Hospital	診療所 Clinic	介護老人 保健施設 HSFE a)	助産所 Maternity home	老　人 ホーム Home for the elderly	自　宅 Home	その他 Others	総　数 Total	病　院 Hospital	診療所 Clinic	介護老人 保健施設 HSFE a)	助産所 Maternity home	老　人 ホーム Home for the elderly	自　宅 Home	その他 Others
総　数　Total																
総　数　Total	372 986	310 643	6 145	2 732	-	9 574	41 031	2 861	100.0	83.3	1.6	0.7	-	2.6	11.0	0.8
0～4 歳	76	71	-	-	-	-	4	1	100.0	93.4	-	-	-	-	5.3	1.3
5～14 Years	179	141	-	-	-	-	37	1	100.0	78.8	-	-	-	-	20.7	0.6
15～24	279	235	2	-	-	-	42	-	100.0	84.2	0.7	-	-	-	15.1	-
25～44	4 957	4 296	42	1	-	3	583	32	100.0	86.7	0.8	0.0	-	0.1	11.8	0.6
45～64	48 397	42 831	477	14	-	113	4 754	208	100.0	88.5	1.0	0.0	-	0.2	9.8	0.4
65～79	153 154	131 805	1 916	368	-	1 515	16 810	740	100.0	86.1	1.3	0.2	-	1.0	11.0	0.5
80～	165 927	131 249	3 708	2 349	-	7 943	18 801	1 877	100.0	79.1	2.2	1.4	-	4.8	11.3	1.1
不詳 Not stated	17	15	-	-	-	-	-	2	100.0	88.2	-	-	-	-	-	11.8
（再掲） （Regrouped）																
70～	273 077	223 008	5 129	2 678	-	9 204	30 647	2 411	100.0	81.7	1.9	1.0	-	3.4	11.2	0.9
男　　Male																
総　数　Total	219 785	185 628	3 349	1 172	-	4 000	24 311	1 325	100.0	84.5	1.5	0.5	-	1.8	11.1	0.6
0～4 歳	43	42	-	-	-	-	1	-	100.0	97.7	-	-	-	-	2.3	-
5～14 Years	98	77	-	-	-	-	21	-	100.0	78.6	-	-	-	-	21.4	-
15～24	173	146	1	-	-	-	26	-	100.0	84.4	0.6	-	-	-	15.0	-
25～44	2 066	1 826	19	1	-	2	205	13	100.0	88.4	0.9	0.0	-	0.1	9.9	0.6
45～64	28 042	25 127	257	11	-	62	2 479	106	100.0	89.6	0.9	0.0	-	0.2	8.8	0.4
65～79	101 569	87 575	1 269	229	-	897	11 171	428	100.0	86.2	1.2	0.2	-	0.9	11.0	0.4
80～	87 779	70 822	1 803	931	-	3 039	10 408	776	100.0	80.7	2.1	1.1	-	3.5	11.9	0.9
不詳 Not stated	15	13	-	-	-	-	-	2	100.0	86.7	-	-	-	-	-	13.3
（再掲） （Regrouped）																
70～	158 576	131 434	2 727	1 131	-	3 770	18 425	1 089	100.0	82.9	1.7	0.7	-	2.4	11.6	0.7
女　　Female																
総　数　Total	153 201	125 015	2 796	1 560	-	5 574	16 720	1 536	100.0	81.6	1.8	1.0	-	3.6	10.9	1.0
0～4 歳	33	29	-	-	-	-	3	1	100.0	87.9	-	-	-	-	9.1	3.0
5～14 Years	81	64	-	-	-	-	16	1	100.0	79.0	-	-	-	-	19.8	1.2
15～24	106	89	1	-	-	-	16	-	100.0	84.0	0.9	-	-	-	15.1	-
25～44	2 891	2 470	23	-	-	1	378	19	100.0	85.4	0.8	-	-	0.0	13.1	0.7
45～64	20 355	17 704	220	3	-	51	2 275	102	100.0	87.0	1.1	0.0	-	0.3	11.2	0.5
65～79	51 585	44 230	647	139	-	618	5 639	312	100.0	85.7	1.3	0.3	-	1.2	10.9	0.6
80～	78 148	60 427	1 905	1 418	-	4 904	8 393	1 101	100.0	77.3	2.4	1.8	-	6.3	10.7	1.4
不詳 Not stated	2	2	-	-	-	-	-	-	100.0	100.0	-	-	-	-	-	-
（再掲） （Regrouped）																
70～	114 501	91 574	2 402	1 547	-	5 434	12 222	1 322	100.0	80.0	2.1	1.4	-	4.7	10.7	1.2

Note：a) Health services facilities for the elderly

死　亡

表5.22　死亡の場所別にみた主な死因[1]の
Table 5.22 Deaths and percent distribution from leading causes

Hi05　心疾患（高血圧性を除く）
Heart diseases（excluding hypertensive heart diseases）

平成28年

年　齢 Age	死　亡　数 Deaths								百　分　率 Percentage							
	総　数 Total	病　院 Hospital	診療所 Clinic	介護老人 保健施設 HSFE[a]	助産所 Maternity home	老　人 ホーム Home for the elderly	自　宅 Home	その他 Others	総　数 Total	病　院 Hospital	診療所 Clinic	介護老人 保健施設 HSFE[a]	助産所 Maternity home	老　人 ホーム Home for the elderly	自　宅 Home	その他 Others
総　数　Total	198 006	131 015	3 702	4 646	-	10 758	44 408	3 477	100.0	66.2	1.9	2.3	-	5.4	22.4	1.8
0～4　歳	81	78	1	-	-	-	2	-	100.0	96.3	1.2	-	-	-	2.5	-
5～14　Years	35	30	-	-	-	-	4	1	100.0	85.7	-	-	-	-	11.4	2.9
15～24	153	86	1	-	-	-	59	7	100.0	56.2	0.7	-	-	-	38.6	4.6
25～44	1 994	1 116	14	-	-	-	759	105	100.0	56.0	0.7	-	-	-	38.1	5.3
45～64	13 607	7 245	101	20	-	36	5 597	608	100.0	53.2	0.7	0.1	-	0.3	41.1	4.5
65～79	45 081	27 816	581	373	-	810	14 568	933	100.0	61.7	1.3	0.8	-	1.8	32.3	2.1
80～	137 016	94 631	3 004	4 253	-	9 910	23 418	1 800	100.0	69.1	2.2	3.1	-	7.2	17.1	1.3
不詳 Not stated	39	13	-	-	-	2	1	23	100.0	33.3	-	-	-	5.1	2.6	59.0
（再掲） （Regrouped）																
70～	170 805	116 018	3 466	4 592	-	10 616	33 704	2 409	100.0	67.9	2.0	2.7	-	6.2	19.7	1.4
男　　Male																
総　数　Total	93 419	60 577	1 457	1 341	-	2 788	25 185	2 071	100.0	64.8	1.6	1.4	-	3.0	27.0	2.2
0～4　歳	47	45	1	-	-	-	1	-	100.0	95.7	2.1	-	-	-	2.1	-
5～14　Years	21	18	-	-	-	-	3	-	100.0	85.7	-	-	-	-	14.3	-
15～24	109	59	1	-	-	-	42	7	100.0	54.1	0.9	-	-	-	38.5	6.4
25～44	1 517	834	9	-	-	-	591	83	100.0	55.0	0.6	-	-	-	39.0	5.5
45～64	10 956	5 708	82	14	-	25	4 582	545	100.0	52.1	0.7	0.1	-	0.2	41.8	5.0
65～79	29 896	18 277	371	206	-	428	9 870	744	100.0	61.1	1.2	0.7	-	1.4	33.0	2.5
80～	50 841	35 627	993	1 121	-	2 333	10 095	672	100.0	70.1	2.0	2.2	-	4.6	19.9	1.3
不詳 Not stated	32	9	-	-	-	2	1	20	100.0	28.1	-	-	-	6.3	3.1	62.5
（再掲） （Regrouped）																
70～	72 230	49 189	1 275	1 310	-	2 693	16 630	1 133	100.0	68.1	1.8	1.8	-	3.7	23.0	1.6
女　　Female																
総　数　Total	104 587	70 438	2 245	3 305	-	7 970	19 223	1 406	100.0	67.3	2.1	3.2	-	7.6	18.4	1.3
0～4　歳	34	33	-	-	-	-	1	-	100.0	97.1	-	-	-	-	2.9	-
5～14　Years	14	12	-	-	-	-	1	1	100.0	85.7	-	-	-	-	7.1	7.1
15～24	44	27	-	-	-	-	17	-	100.0	61.4	-	-	-	-	38.6	-
25～44	477	282	5	-	-	-	168	22	100.0	59.1	1.0	-	-	-	35.2	4.6
45～64	2 651	1 537	19	6	-	11	1 015	63	100.0	58.0	0.7	0.2	-	0.4	38.3	2.4
65～79	15 185	9 539	210	167	-	382	4 698	189	100.0	62.8	1.4	1.1	-	2.5	30.9	1.2
80～	86 175	59 004	2 011	3 132	-	7 577	13 323	1 128	100.0	68.5	2.3	3.6	-	8.8	15.5	1.3
不詳 Not stated	7	4	-	-	-	-	-	3	100.0	57.1	-	-	-	-	-	42.9
（再掲） （Regrouped）																
70～	98 575	66 829	2 191	3 282	-	7 923	17 074	1 276	100.0	67.8	2.2	3.3	-	8.0	17.3	1.3

General mortality

性・年齢別死亡数及び百分率（つづき）
of death by sex, age and place of occurrence : Japan, 2016－CON.

Hi06　脳血管疾患
Cerebrovascular diseases

平成28年

年　齢 Age	死　亡　数 Deaths								百　分　率 Percentage							
	総　数 Total	病　院 Hospital	診療所 Clinic	介護老人保健施設 HSFE a)	助産所 Maternity home	老　人ホーム Home for the elderly	自　宅 Home	その他 Others	総　数 Total	病院 Hospital	診療所 Clinic	介護老人保健施設 HSFE a)	助産所 Maternity home	老　人ホーム Home for the elderly	自宅 Home	その他 Others
総　数　Total	109 320	81 439	2 236	4 059	-	9 297	11 072	1 217	100.0	74.5	2.0	3.7	-	8.5	10.1	1.1
0～4 歳	9	9	-	-	-	-	-	-	100.0	100.0	-	-	-	-	-	-
5～14 Years	20	20	-	-	-	-	-	-	100.0	100.0	-	-	-	-	-	-
15～24	43	36	-	-	-	-	7	-	100.0	83.7	-	-	-	-	16.3	-
25～44	1 298	999	7	-	-	-	260	32	100.0	77.0	0.5	-	-	-	20.0	2.5
45～64	8 303	6 193	96	35	-	61	1 735	183	100.0	74.6	1.2	0.4	-	0.7	20.9	2.2
65～79	26 391	20 824	434	518	-	1 053	3 280	282	100.0	78.9	1.6	2.0	-	4.0	12.4	1.1
80～	73 235	53 341	1 699	3 506	-	8 183	5 790	716	100.0	72.8	2.3	4.8	-	11.2	7.9	1.0
不詳 Not stated	21	17	-	-	-	-	-	4	100.0	81.0	-	-	-	-	-	19.0
（再掲）(Regrouped)																
70～	93 353	69 313	2 042	3 954	-	9 082	8 071	891	100.0	74.2	2.2	4.2	-	9.7	8.6	1.0
男　Male																
総　数　Total	52 706	40 732	1 026	1 515	-	2 881	5 909	643	100.0	77.3	1.9	2.9	-	5.5	11.2	1.2
0～4 歳	4	4	-	-	-	-	-	-	100.0	100.0	-	-	-	-	-	-
5～14 Years	12	12	-	-	-	-	-	-	100.0	100.0	-	-	-	-	-	-
15～24	24	19	-	-	-	-	5	-	100.0	79.2	-	-	-	-	20.8	-
25～44	876	640	3	-	-	-	208	25	100.0	73.1	0.3	-	-	-	23.7	2.9
45～64	5 784	4 162	74	27	-	46	1 322	153	100.0	72.0	1.3	0.5	-	0.8	22.9	2.6
65～79	17 317	13 635	318	362	-	679	2 109	214	100.0	78.7	1.8	2.1	-	3.9	12.2	1.2
80～	28 675	22 247	631	1 126	-	2 156	2 265	250	100.0	77.6	2.2	3.9	-	7.5	7.9	0.9
不詳 Not stated	14	13	-	-	-	-	-	1	100.0	92.9	-	-	-	-	-	7.1
（再掲）(Regrouped)																
70～	41 582	32 545	872	1 434	-	2 717	3 641	373	100.0	78.3	2.1	3.4	-	6.5	8.8	0.9
女　Female																
総　数　Total	56 614	40 707	1 210	2 544	-	6 416	5 163	574	100.0	71.9	2.1	4.5	-	11.3	9.1	1.0
0～4 歳	5	5	-	-	-	-	-	-	100.0	100.0	-	-	-	-	-	-
5～14 Years	8	8	-	-	-	-	-	-	100.0	100.0	-	-	-	-	-	-
15～24	19	17	-	-	-	-	2	-	100.0	89.5	-	-	-	-	10.5	-
25～44	422	359	4	-	-	-	52	7	100.0	85.1	0.9	-	-	-	12.3	1.7
45～64	2 519	2 031	22	8	-	15	413	30	100.0	80.6	0.9	0.3	-	0.6	16.4	1.2
65～79	9 074	7 189	116	156	-	374	1 171	68	100.0	79.2	1.3	1.7	-	4.1	12.9	0.7
80～	44 560	31 094	1 068	2 380	-	6 027	3 525	466	100.0	69.8	2.4	5.3	-	13.5	7.9	1.0
不詳 Not stated	7	4	-	-	-	-	-	3	100.0	57.1	-	-	-	-	-	42.9
（再掲）(Regrouped)																
70～	51 771	36 768	1 170	2 520	-	6 365	4 430	518	100.0	71.0	2.3	4.9	-	12.3	8.6	1.0

349

死　亡

表5.22　死亡の場所別にみた主な死因[1]　の
Table 5.22 Deaths and percent distribution from leading causes

Hi07　肺炎
Pneumonia

平成28年

年　齢 Age	死　亡　数 Deaths								百　分　率 Percentage							
	総　数 Total	病　院 Hospital	診療所 Clinic	介護老人保健施設 HSFE [a]	助産所 Maternity home	老　人ホーム Home for the elderly	自　宅 Home	その他 Others	総　数 Total	病　院 Hospital	診療所 Clinic	介護老人保健施設 HSFE [a]	助産所 Maternity home	老　人ホーム Home for the elderly	自　宅 Home	その他 Others
総　数　Total	119 300	104 392	3 038	2 126	-	5 250	3 740	754	100.0	87.5	2.5	1.8	-	4.4	3.1	0.6
0～4　歳	63	53	-	-	-	-	10	-	100.0	84.1	-	-	-	-	15.9	-
5～14 Years	32	29	-	-	-	-	3	-	100.0	90.6	-	-	-	-	9.4	-
15～24	31	30	-	-	-	-	1	-	100.0	96.8	-	-	-	-	3.2	-
25～44	278	220	4	-	-	1	48	5	100.0	79.1	1.4	-	-	0.4	17.3	1.8
45～64	2 827	2 516	42	10	-	30	206	23	100.0	89.0	1.5	0.4	-	1.1	7.3	0.8
65～79	21 409	19 483	409	197	-	578	645	97	100.0	91.0	1.9	0.9	-	2.7	3.0	0.5
80～	94 650	82 054	2 582	1 919	-	4 640	2 827	628	100.0	86.7	2.7	2.0	-	4.9	3.0	0.7
不詳 Not stated	10	7	1	-	-	1	-	1	100.0	70.0	10.0	-	-	10.0	-	10.0
（再掲）(Regrouped)																
70～	112 363	98 143	2 926	2 091	-	5 152	3 341	710	100.0	87.3	2.6	1.9	-	4.6	3.0	0.6
男　　Male																
総　数　Total	65 636	58 895	1 521	894	-	2 031	1 936	359	100.0	89.7	2.3	1.4	-	3.1	2.9	0.5
0～4　歳	34	28	-	-	-	-	6	-	100.0	82.4	-	-	-	-	17.6	-
5～14 Years	15	15	-	-	-	-	-	-	100.0	100.0	-	-	-	-	-	-
15～24	12	11	-	-	-	-	1	-	100.0	91.7	-	-	-	-	8.3	-
25～44	190	148	2	-	-	1	35	4	100.0	77.9	1.1	-	-	0.5	18.4	2.1
45～64	2 130	1 901	36	5	-	22	145	21	100.0	89.2	1.7	0.2	-	1.0	6.8	1.0
65～79	15 598	14 235	312	145	-	376	455	75	100.0	91.3	2.0	0.9	-	2.4	2.9	0.5
80～	47 647	42 550	1 170	744	-	1 631	1 294	258	100.0	89.3	2.5	1.6	-	3.4	2.7	0.5
不詳 Not stated	10	7	1	-	-	1	-	1	100.0	70.0	10.0	-	-	10.0	-	10.0
（再掲）(Regrouped)																
70～	60 392	54 165	1 428	869	-	1 958	1 652	320	100.0	89.7	2.4	1.4	-	3.2	2.7	0.5
女　　Female																
総　数　Total	53 664	45 497	1 517	1 232	-	3 219	1 804	395	100.0	84.8	2.8	2.3	-	6.0	3.4	0.7
0～4　歳	29	25	-	-	-	-	4	-	100.0	86.2	-	-	-	-	13.8	-
5～14 Years	17	14	-	-	-	-	3	-	100.0	82.4	-	-	-	-	17.6	-
15～24	19	19	-	-	-	-	-	-	100.0	100.0	-	-	-	-	-	-
25～44	88	72	2	-	-	-	13	1	100.0	81.8	2.3	-	-	-	14.8	1.1
45～64	697	615	6	5	-	8	61	2	100.0	88.2	0.9	0.7	-	1.1	8.8	0.3
65～79	5 811	5 248	97	52	-	202	190	22	100.0	90.3	1.7	0.9	-	3.5	3.3	0.4
80～	47 003	39 504	1 412	1 175	-	3 009	1 533	370	100.0	84.0	3.0	2.5	-	6.4	3.3	0.8
不詳 Not stated	-	-	-	-	-	-	-	-								
（再掲）(Regrouped)																
70～	51 971	43 978	1 498	1 222	-	3 194	1 689	390	100.0	84.6	2.9	2.4	-	6.1	3.2	0.8

350

General mortality

性・年齢別死亡数及び百分率（つづき）
of death by sex, age and place of occurrence : Japan, 2016－CON.

Hi14　不慮の事故
Accidents

平成28年

年　齢 Age	死　亡　数　Deaths								百　分　率　Percentage							
	総　数 Total	病　院 Hospital	診療所 Clinic	介護老人 保健施設 HSFE a)	助産所 Maternity home	老　人 ホーム Home for the elderly	自　宅 Home	その他 Others	総　数 Total	病　院 Hospital	診療所 Clinic	介護老人 保健施設 HSFE a)	助産所 Maternity home	老　人 ホーム Home for the elderly	自　宅 Home	その他 Others
総　数　Total	38 306	27 250	373	348	-	740	6 155	3 440	100.0	71.1	1.0	0.9	-	1.9	16.1	9.0
0～4 歳	158	104	3	-	-	-	40	11	100.0	65.8	1.9	-	-	-	25.3	7.0
5～14 Years	134	107	-	-	-	-	11	16	100.0	79.9	-	-	-	-	8.2	11.9
15～24	679	475	3	-	-	-	45	156	100.0	70.0	0.4	-	-	-	6.6	23.0
25～44	1 634	984	5	-	-	-	209	436	100.0	60.2	0.3	-	-	-	12.8	26.7
45～64	4 144	2 536	15	2	-	2	799	790	100.0	61.2	0.4	0.0	-	0.0	19.3	19.1
65～79	10 883	7 516	74	39	-	83	2 072	1 099	100.0	69.1	0.7	0.4	-	0.8	19.0	10.1
80～	20 638	15 523	273	307	-	655	2 978	902	100.0	75.2	1.3	1.5	-	3.2	14.4	4.4
不詳 Not stated	36	5	-	-	-	-	1	30	100.0	13.9	-	-	-	-	2.8	83.3
（再掲） （Regrouped）																
70～	28 771	21 225	330	341	-	727	4 523	1 625	100.0	73.8	1.1	1.2	-	2.5	15.7	5.6
男　　Male																
総　数　Total	22 066	15 911	155	126	-	232	3 116	2 526	100.0	72.1	0.7	0.6	-	1.1	14.1	11.4
0～4 歳	96	61	-	-	-	-	27	8	100.0	63.5	-	-	-	-	28.1	8.3
5～14 Years	93	73	-	-	-	-	7	13	100.0	78.5	-	-	-	-	7.5	14.0
15～24	520	369	2	-	-	-	21	128	100.0	71.0	0.4	-	-	-	4.0	24.6
25～44	1 296	783	4	-	-	-	139	370	100.0	60.4	0.3	-	-	-	10.7	28.5
45～64	3 144	1 908	9	2	-	2	562	661	100.0	60.7	0.3	0.1	-	0.1	17.9	21.0
65～79	7 083	4 991	41	23	-	52	1 151	825	100.0	70.5	0.6	0.3	-	0.7	16.3	11.6
80～	9 811	7 723	99	101	-	178	1 209	501	100.0	78.7	1.0	1.0	-	1.8	12.3	5.1
不詳 Not stated	23	3	-	-	-	-	-	20	100.0	13.0	-	-	-	-	-	87.0
（再掲） （Regrouped）																
70～	14 954	11 438	128	119	-	223	2 018	1 028	100.0	76.5	0.9	0.8	-	1.5	13.5	6.9
女　　Female																
総　数　Total	16 240	11 339	218	222	-	508	3 039	914	100.0	69.8	1.3	1.4	-	3.1	18.7	5.6
0～4 歳	62	43	3	-	-	-	13	3	100.0	69.4	4.8	-	-	-	21.0	4.8
5～14 Years	41	34	-	-	-	-	4	3	100.0	82.9	-	-	-	-	9.8	7.3
15～24	159	106	1	-	-	-	24	28	100.0	66.7	0.6	-	-	-	15.1	17.6
25～44	338	201	1	-	-	-	70	66	100.0	59.5	0.3	-	-	-	20.7	19.5
45～64	1 000	628	6	-	-	-	237	129	100.0	62.8	0.6	-	-	-	23.7	12.9
65～79	3 800	2 525	33	16	-	31	921	274	100.0	66.4	0.9	0.4	-	0.8	24.2	7.2
80～	10 827	7 800	174	206	-	477	1 769	401	100.0	72.0	1.6	1.9	-	4.4	16.3	3.7
不詳 Not stated	13	2	-	-	-	-	1	10	100.0	15.4	-	-	-	-	7.7	76.9
（再掲） （Regrouped）																
70～	13 817	9 787	202	222	-	504	2 505	597	100.0	70.8	1.5	1.6	-	3.6	18.1	4.3

死　亡

〔世帯の主な仕事別にみた死因〕
〔Causes of death by type of occupation of household〕

表5.23　世帯の主な仕事別にみた
Table 5.23　Deaths and percent distribution by causes and type of occupation of household :

世帯の主な仕事 Type of occupation of household	死亡総数[1] Deaths Total	Se 01 結　　核	Se 02 悪性新生物	Se 03 食道の 悪性新生物	Se 04 胃の悪性 新生物	Se 05 結腸の 悪性新生物	Se 06 直腸Ｓ状 結腸移行部 及び直腸の 悪性新生物	Se 07 肝及び 肝内胆管の 悪性新生物
死						**亡**		
総　数[2]　Total	1 307 748	1 892	372 986	11 483	45 531	34 521	15 578	28 528
農　家　世　帯　Agriculture[b]	66 702	67	17 877	425	2 557	1 540	630	1 240
自　営　業　者　世　帯　Self employed	62 167	73	21 481	763	2 685	1 933	986	1 774
常用勤労者世帯（Ⅰ）　Employee[c]	82 472	93	27 568	869	3 516	2 457	1 185	1 940
常用勤労者世帯（Ⅱ）　Employee[d] or director	46 788	47	16 294	471	1 846	1 430	688	1 099
そ　の　他　の　世　帯　Other	77 358	93	24 667	750	2 964	2 220	1 112	1 715
無　職　の　世　帯　Not working	883 255	1 393	239 144	7 339	28 763	22 628	9 878	18 741
百						**分**		
総　数[2]　Total	100. 0	0. 1	28. 5	0. 9	3. 5	2. 6	1. 2	2. 2
農　家　世　帯　Agriculture[b]	100. 0	0. 1	26. 8	0. 6	3. 8	2. 3	0. 9	1. 9
自　営　業　者　世　帯　Self employed	100. 0	0. 1	34. 6	1. 2	4. 3	3. 1	1. 6	2. 9
常用勤労者世帯（Ⅰ）　Employee[c]	100. 0	0. 1	33. 4	1. 1	4. 3	3. 0	1. 4	2. 4
常用勤労者世帯（Ⅱ）　Employee[d] or director	100. 0	0. 1	34. 8	1. 0	3. 9	3. 1	1. 5	2. 3
そ　の　他　の　世　帯　Other	100. 0	0. 1	31. 9	1. 0	3. 8	2. 9	1. 4	2. 2
無　職　の　世　帯　Not working	100. 0	0. 2	27. 1	0. 8	3. 3	2. 6	1. 1	2. 1

注：1)　選択死因以外の死亡数を含む。
　　2)　総数には世帯の主な仕事不詳を含む。

352

General mortality

選択死因分類別死亡数及び百分率
（the selected list of causes of death for Japan)[a]

Japan, 2016

平成28年

掲	)						
Se 08	Se 09	Se 10	Se 11	Se 12	Se 13	Se 14	Se 15
胆のう及び その他の 胆道の 悪性新生物	膵 の 悪性新生物	気管，気管支 及び肺の 悪性新生物	乳房の 悪性新生物	子宮の 悪性新生物	白血病	糖尿病	高血圧性 疾患
数			**Deaths**				
17 965	33 475	73 838	14 132	6 345	8 801	13 480	6 841
1 099	1 682	3 501	431	247	415	536	372
948	2 013	4 053	866	442	542	618	306
1 239	2 506	5 246	1 477	652	719	748	323
670	1 594	2 899	1 026	387	472	408	182
1 153	2 305	4 606	1 176	542	620	719	378
11 709	21 076	48 337	8 082	3 641	5 413	9 525	4 746
率			**Percentage**				
1.4	2.6	5.6	1.1	0.5	0.7	1.0	0.5
1.6	2.5	5.2	0.6	0.4	0.6	0.8	0.6
1.5	3.2	6.5	1.4	0.7	0.9	1.0	0.5
1.5	3.0	6.4	1.8	0.8	0.9	0.9	0.4
1.4	3.4	6.2	2.2	0.8	1.0	0.9	0.4
1.5	3.0	6.0	1.5	0.7	0.8	0.9	0.5
1.3	2.4	5.5	0.9	0.4	0.6	1.1	0.5

Note：a) See page 596.
b) Agriculture only or that with other work.
c) Employee at office (excluding governmental office) with 1－99 employee (excluding daily or less than one year contracts).
d) Employee at office excluding c) above.

死　亡

表 5.23　世帯の主な仕事別にみた
Table 5.23　Deaths and percent distribution by causes and type of occupation of household：

世帯の主な仕事 Type of occupation of household	Se 16 心疾患 （高血圧 性を除く）	（再　掲）				Se 21 脳血管 疾　患	（再　掲）			Se 25 大動脈瘤 及び解離
		Se 17 急　性 心筋梗塞	Se 18 その他の 虚血性 心疾患	Se 19 不整脈 及　び 伝導障害	Se 20 心不全		Se 22 くも膜下 出　血	Se 23 脳内出血	Se 24 脳梗塞	
死							亡			
総　　　数[2)] 　　　Total	198 006	35 926	34 534	31 045	73 545	109 320	12 318	31 975	62 277	18 145
農　家　世　帯 Agriculture[b)]	10 718	1 981	1 206	2 050	4 194	6 089	672	1 663	3 637	933
自　営　業　者　世　帯 Self employed	9 155	1 973	1 609	1 486	2 944	4 910	784	1 617	2 401	1 057
常用勤労者世帯（Ⅰ） Employee[c)]	11 976	2 730	2 038	2 047	3 730	7 171	1 423	2 407	3 194	1 436
常用勤労者世帯（Ⅱ） Employee[d)] or director	6 445	1 449	1 052	1 091	1 987	3 667	778	1 162	1 624	781
そ　の　他　の　世　帯 Other	11 521	2 561	2 112	1 894	3 571	6 576	1 165	2 178	3 080	1 317
無　職　の　世　帯 Not working	134 910	22 785	23 534	20 681	52 544	73 750	6 609	20 804	44 372	11 408
百							分			
総　　　数[2)] 　　　Total	15.1	2.7	2.6	2.4	5.6	8.4	0.9	2.4	4.8	1.4
農　家　世　帯 Agriculture[b)]	16.1	3.0	1.8	3.1	6.3	9.1	1.0	2.5	5.5	1.4
自　営　業　者　世　帯 Self employed	14.7	3.2	2.6	2.4	4.7	7.9	1.3	2.6	3.9	1.7
常用勤労者世帯（Ⅰ） Employee[c)]	14.5	3.3	2.5	2.5	4.5	8.7	1.7	2.9	3.9	1.7
常用勤労者世帯（Ⅱ） Employee[d)] or director	13.8	3.1	2.2	2.3	4.2	7.8	1.7	2.5	3.5	1.7
そ　の　他　の　世　帯 Other	14.9	3.3	2.7	2.4	4.6	8.5	1.5	2.8	4.0	1.7
無　職　の　世　帯 Not working	15.3	2.6	2.7	2.3	5.9	8.3	0.7	2.4	5.0	1.3

General mortality

選択死因分類別死亡数及び百分率（つづき）
（the selected list of causes of death for Japan）[a]

Japan, 2016－CON.

平成28年

							(再掲)	
Se 26	Se 27	Se 28	Se 29	Se 30	Se 31	Se 32	Se 33	Se 34
肺　　炎	慢性閉塞性肺　疾　患	喘　　息	肝　疾　患	腎　不　全	老　　衰	不慮の事故	交　通　事　故	自　　殺

数　　　　　　　　　　　Deaths

Se 26	Se 27	Se 28	Se 29	Se 30	Se 31	Se 32	Se 33	Se 34
119 300	15 686	1 454	15 773	24 612	92 806	38 306	5 278	21 017
6 099	882	61	615	1 195	5 437	2 467	417	987
4 277	640	53	929	989	3 361	2 171	426	1 556
5 364	792	81	1 161	1 285	3 635	3 404	935	3 129
3 141	478	44	583	740	2 023	1 673	412	1 799
5 458	840	81	1 063	1 188	3 974	2 868	666	2 679
87 193	10 975	1 015	10 199	17 629	68 923	23 128	2 039	8 879

率　　　　　　　　　　　Percentage

Se 26	Se 27	Se 28	Se 29	Se 30	Se 31	Se 32	Se 33	Se 34
9. 1	1. 2	0. 1	1. 2	1. 9	7. 1	2. 9	0. 4	1. 6
9. 1	1. 3	0. 1	0. 9	1. 8	8. 2	3. 7	0. 6	1. 5
6. 9	1. 0	0. 1	1. 5	1. 6	5. 4	3. 5	0. 7	2. 5
6. 5	1. 0	0. 1	1. 4	1. 6	4. 4	4. 1	1. 1	3. 8
6. 7	1. 0	0. 1	1. 2	1. 6	4. 3	3. 6	0. 9	3. 8
7. 1	1. 1	0. 1	1. 4	1. 5	5. 1	3. 7	0. 9	3. 5
9. 9	1. 2	0. 1	1. 2	2. 0	7. 8	2. 6	0. 2	1. 0

死亡

〔主な死因〕悪性新生物
〔Selected causes of death〕

表5.24　悪性新生物の主な部位別にみた
Table 5.24　Trends in deaths and death rates (per 100,000

総数
Total

死因簡単分類コード Code[a]	死因 Causes of death	1950 昭和25年	1955 30年	1960 35年	1965 40年	1970 45年	1975 50年	1980 55年	1985 60年
		死					亡		
02100	悪　性　新　生　物	64 428	77 721	93 773	106 536	119 977	136 383	161 764	187 714
02101	口唇，口腔及び咽頭の悪性新生物	699	650	761	894	1 112	1 448	1 825	2 089
02102	食　道　の　悪　性　新　生　物	2 763	2 973	3 467	3 958	4 823	4 997	5 733	6 197
02103	胃　の　悪　性　新　生　物	31 211	37 306	42 750	46 385	48 823	49 857	50 443	48 902
02104	結　腸　の　悪　性　新　生　物	1 457	1 628	2 039	2 804	3 818	5 573	7 932	11 225
02105	直腸S状結腸移行部及び直腸の悪性新生物	2 271	2 611	2 998	3 796	4 681	5 880	6 807	7 813
02106	肝及び肝内胆管の悪性新生物	} 6 179	} 8 577	8 818	8 505	9 442	10 373	13 968	18 972
02107	胆のう及びその他の胆道の悪性新生物			1 144	2 041	3 104	4 484	6 599	9 470
02108	膵　の　悪　性　新　生　物	526	1 102	1 975	3 066	4 399	5 635	7 835	10 441
02109	喉　頭　の　悪　性　新　生　物	800	717	738	792	943	862	866	835
02110	気管，気管支及び肺の悪性新生物	1 119	2 711	5 171	7 725	10 489	14 759	21 294	28 590
02111	皮　膚　の　悪　性　新　生　物	517	563	610	626	707	704	619	679
02112	乳　房　の　悪　性　新　生　物	1 448	1 589	1 703	1 995	2 509	3 289	4 185	4 958
02113	子　宮　の　悪　性　新　生　物[1]	8 356	7 289	7 068	6 689	6 373	6 075	5 465	4 912
02114	卵　巣　の　悪　性　新　生　物	346	473	647	840	1 129	1 516	2 098	2 675
02115	前　立　腺　の　悪　性　新　生　物	83	273	480	683	883	1 267	1 736	2 640
02116	膀　胱　の　悪　性　新　生　物	…	…	1 108	1 291	1 570	1 830	2 361	2 577
02117	中枢神経系の悪性新生物[2]	…	…	265	324	346	453	903	1 068
02118	悪　性　リ　ン　パ　腫	…	…	…	…	…	…	…	…
02119	白　　　血　　　病	1 226	2 038	2 628	3 159	3 559	4 164	4 567	5 179
02120	その他のリンパ組織，造血組織及び関連組織の悪性新生物	…	…	…	…	…	…	…	…
（再掲）02104, 02105	大　腸　の　悪　性　新　生　物[3]	3 728	4 239	5 037	6 600	8 499	11 453	14 739	19 038
		死					亡		
02100	悪　性　新　生　物	77.4	87.1	100.4	108.4	116.3	122.6	139.1	156.1
02101	口唇，口腔及び咽頭の悪性新生物	0.8	0.7	0.8	0.9	1.1	1.3	1.6	1.7
02102	食　道　の　悪　性　新　生　物	3.3	3.3	3.7	4.0	4.7	4.5	4.9	5.2
02103	胃　の　悪　性　新　生　物	37.5	41.8	45.8	47.2	47.3	44.8	43.4	40.7
02104	結　腸　の　悪　性　新　生　物	1.8	1.8	2.2	2.9	3.7	5.0	6.8	9.3
02105	直腸S状結腸移行部及び直腸の悪性新生物	2.7	2.9	3.2	3.9	4.5	5.3	5.9	6.5
02106	肝及び肝内胆管の悪性新生物	} 7.4	} 9.6	9.4	8.7	9.2	9.3	12.0	15.8
02107	胆のう及びその他の胆道の悪性新生物			1.2	2.1	3.0	4.0	5.7	7.9
02108	膵　の　悪　性　新　生　物	0.6	1.2	2.1	3.1	4.3	5.1	6.7	8.7
02109	喉　頭　の　悪　性　新　生　物	1.0	0.8	0.8	0.8	0.9	0.8	0.7	0.7
02110	気管，気管支及び肺の悪性新生物	1.3	3.0	5.5	7.9	10.2	13.3	18.3	23.8
02111	皮　膚　の　悪　性　新　生　物	0.6	0.6	0.7	0.6	0.7	0.6	0.5	0.6
02112	乳　房　の　悪　性　新　生　物	1.7	1.8	1.8	2.0	2.4	3.0	3.6	4.1
02113	子　宮　の　悪　性　新　生　物[1][4]	19.7	16.0	14.9	13.4	12.1	10.7	9.2	8.0
02114	卵　巣　の　悪　性　新　生　物[4]	0.8	1.0	1.4	1.7	2.1	2.7	3.5	4.4
02115	前　立　腺　の　悪　性　新　生　物[5]	0.2	0.6	1.0	1.4	1.7	2.3	3.0	4.5
02116	膀　胱　の　悪　性　新　生　物	…	…	1.2	1.3	1.5	1.6	2.0	2.1
02117	中枢神経系の悪性新生物[2]	…	…	0.3	0.3	0.3	0.4	0.8	0.9
02118	悪　性　リ　ン　パ　腫	…	…	…	…	…	…	…	…
02119	白　　　血　　　病	1.5	2.3	2.8	3.2	3.5	3.7	3.9	4.3
02120	その他のリンパ組織，造血組織及び関連組織の悪性新生物	…	…	…	…	…	…	…	…
（再掲）02104, 02105	大　腸　の　悪　性　新　生　物[3]	4.5	4.7	5.4	6.7	8.2	10.3	12.7	15.8

注：1)　平成6年以前の「子宮」は、胎盤を含む。
　　2)　昭和42年以前の「中枢神経系」は、松果体を含まない。
　　3)　結腸と直腸S状結腸移行部及び直腸を示す。ただし、昭和42年までは直腸肛門部を含む。
　　4)　率については、女性人口10万対である。
　　5)　率については、男性人口10万対である。

General mortality

性・年次別死亡数及び率（人口10万対）
population）from malignant neoplasms by sex and site : Japan

総 数
Total

	1990 平成2年	1995 7年	2000 12年	2005 17年	2010 22年	2011 23年	2012 24年	2013 25年	2014 26年	2015 27年	2016 28年	死因簡単分類 コード Code[a]
数 Deaths												
	217 413	263 022	295 484	325 941	353 499	357 305	360 963	364 872	368 103	370 346	**372 986**	02100
	2 607	4 099	5 066	5 679	6 802	6 888	7 167	7 179	7 415	7 380	**7 675**	02101
	7 274	8 638	10 256	11 182	11 867	11 970	11 592	11 543	11 576	11 739	**11 483**	02102
	47 471	50 076	50 650	50 311	50 136	49 830	49 129	48 632	47 903	46 679	**45 531**	02103
	15 509	20 286	23 637	27 121	30 040	31 050	32 177	32 682	33 297	34 338	**34 521**	02104
	9 123	10 988	12 311	13 709	14 198	14 694	15 099	14 972	15 188	15 361	**15 578**	02105
	24 233	31 707	33 981	34 268	32 765	31 875	30 690	30 175	29 543	28 889	**28 528**	02106
	11 871	13 746	15 153	16 586	17 585	18 186	18 209	18 225	18 117	18 152	**17 965**	02107
	13 318	16 019	19 094	22 927	28 017	28 829	29 916	30 672	31 716	31 866	**33 475**	02108
	847	959	1 046	1 090	1 002	954	953	963	978	971	**944**	02109
	36 486	45 745	53 724	62 063	69 813	70 293	71 518	72 734	73 396	74 378	**73 838**	02110
	685	869	986	1 207	1 404	1 453	1 556	1 525	1 657	1 505	**1 553**	02111
	5 882	7 819	9 248	10 808	12 545	12 838	12 617	13 230	13 323	13 705	**14 132**	02112
	4 600	4 865	5 202	5 381	5 930	6 075	6 113	6 033	6 429	6 429	**6 345**	02113
	3 279	3 892	3 993	4 467	4 654	4 705	4 688	4 717	4 840	4 676	**4 758**	02114
	3 460	5 399	7 514	9 265	10 722	10 823	11 143	11 560	11 507	11 326	**11 803**	02115
	3 048	3 931	4 680	6 029	6 804	7 008	7 299	7 685	7 760	8 130	**8 432**	02116
	1 242	1 574	1 574	1 681	1 959	2 144	2 201	2 217	2 326	2 445	**2 650**	02117
	…	6 342	7 918	8 537	10 172	10 336	10 831	11 298	11 480	11 829	**12 325**	02118
	5 633	6 129	6 766	7 283	8 078	8 156	7 900	8 133	8 196	8 631	**8 801**	02119
	…	3 008	3 425	3 932	4 287	4 120	4 121	4 163	4 237	4 174	**4 443**	02120
	24 632	31 274	35 948	40 830	44 238	45 744	47 276	47 654	48 485	49 699	**50 099**	（再掲） 02104, 02105
率 Death rates												
	177.2	211.6	235.2	258.3	279.7	283.2	286.6	290.3	293.5	295.5	**298.3**	02100
	2.1	3.3	4.0	4.5	5.4	5.5	5.7	5.7	5.9	5.9	**6.1**	02101
	5.9	6.9	8.2	8.9	9.4	9.5	9.2	9.2	9.2	9.4	**9.2**	02102
	38.7	40.3	40.3	39.9	39.7	39.5	39.0	38.7	38.2	37.2	**36.4**	02103
	12.6	16.3	18.8	21.5	23.8	24.6	25.5	26.0	26.5	27.4	**27.6**	02104
	7.4	8.8	9.8	10.9	11.2	11.6	12.0	11.9	12.1	12.3	**12.5**	02105
	19.7	25.5	27.1	27.2	25.9	25.3	24.4	24.0	23.6	23.1	**22.8**	02106
	9.7	11.1	12.1	13.1	13.9	14.4	14.5	14.5	14.4	14.5	**14.4**	02107
	10.9	12.9	15.2	18.2	22.2	22.8	23.8	24.4	25.3	25.4	**26.8**	02108
	0.7	0.8	0.8	0.9	0.8	0.8	0.8	0.8	0.8	0.8	**0.8**	02109
	29.7	36.8	42.8	49.2	55.2	55.7	56.8	57.9	58.5	59.4	**59.1**	02110
	0.6	0.7	0.8	1.0	1.1	1.2	1.2	1.2	1.3	1.2	**1.2**	02111
	4.8	6.3	7.4	8.6	9.9	10.2	10.0	10.5	10.6	10.9	**11.3**	02112
	7.4	7.7	8.1	8.3	9.1	9.4	9.5	9.4	10.0	10.0	**9.9**	02113
	5.2	6.1	6.2	6.9	7.2	7.3	7.3	7.3	7.5	7.3	**7.4**	02114
	5.7	8.9	12.2	15.0	17.4	17.6	18.2	18.9	18.9	18.6	**19.4**	02115
	2.5	3.2	3.7	4.8	5.4	5.6	5.8	6.1	6.2	6.5	**6.7**	02116
	1.0	1.3	1.3	1.3	1.6	1.7	1.7	1.8	1.9	2.0	**2.1**	02117
	…	5.1	6.3	6.8	8.0	8.2	8.6	9.0	9.2	9.4	**9.9**	02118
	4.6	4.9	5.4	5.8	6.4	6.5	6.3	6.5	6.5	6.9	**7.0**	02119
	…	2.4	2.7	3.1	3.4	3.3	3.3	3.3	3.4	3.3	**3.6**	02120
	20.1	25.2	28.6	32.4	35.0	36.3	37.5	37.9	38.7	39.7	**40.1**	（再掲） 02104, 02105

Note：a) Code see page 595.

死　亡

表5.24　悪性新生物の主な部位別にみた
Table 5.24　Trends in deaths and death rates (per 100,000

男
Male

死亡

死因簡単分類コード Code[a]	死因 Causes of death	1950 昭和25年	1955 30年	1960 35年	1965 40年	1970 45年	1975 50年	1980 55年	1985 60年
02100	悪 性 新 生 物	32 670	41 223	50 898	58 899	67 074	76 922	93 501	110 660
02101	口唇，口腔及び咽頭の悪性新生物	432	414	484	561	738	943	1 233	1 462
02102	食 道 の 悪 性 新 生 物	1 961	2 102	2 472	2 870	3 673	3 862	4 490	5 046
02103	胃 の 悪 性 新 生 物	19 023	22 899	26 283	28 636	29 653	30 403	30 845	30 146
02104	結 腸 の 悪 性 新 生 物	620	723	910	1 272	1 766	2 662	3 842	5 522
02105	直腸S状結腸移行部及び直腸の悪性新生物	1 199	1 356	1 480	1 993	2 537	3 137	3 882	4 590
02106	肝及び肝内胆管の悪性新生物	}3 601	}4 877	5 204	5 006	5 868	6 677	9 741	13 780
02107	胆のう及びその他の胆道の悪性新生物			556	991	1 340	1 905	2 791	3 949
02108	膵 の 悪 性 新 生 物	328	625	1 150	1 748	2 549	3 155	4 483	5 953
02109	喉 頭 の 悪 性 新 生 物	575	536	557	624	773	738	736	747
02110	気管，気管支及び肺の悪性新生物	789	1 893	3 638	5 404	7 502	10 711	15 438	20 837
02111	皮 膚 の 悪 性 新 生 物	292	300	300	325	381	371	327	367
02112	乳 房 の 悪 性 新 生 物	29	17	20	29	23	27	44	36
02113	子 宮 の 悪 性 新 生 物[1]	·	·	·	·	·	·	·	·
02114	卵 巣 の 悪 性 新 生 物	·	·	·	·	·	·	·	·
02115	前 立 腺 の 悪 性 新 生 物	83	273	480	683	883	1 267	1 736	2 640
02116	膀 胱 の 悪 性 新 生 物	...	...	673	837	1 030	1 174	1 606	1 705
02117	中 枢 神 経 系 の 悪 性 新 生 物[2]	...	...	150	199	183	253	509	593
02118	悪 性 リ ン パ 腫	...	...	...	...	...	...	...	...
02119	白 血 病	718	1 214	1 473	1 765	2 005	2 321	2 624	2 983
02120	その他のリンパ組織，造血組織及び関連組織の悪性新生物	...	...	...	...	...	...	...	...
（再掲） 02104, 02105	大 腸 の 悪 性 新 生 物[3]	1 819	2 079	2 390	3 265	4 303	5 799	7 724	10 112

死亡

死因簡単分類コード Code[a]	死因 Causes of death	1950 昭和25年	1955 30年	1960 35年	1965 40年	1970 45年	1975 50年	1980 55年	1985 60年
02100	悪 性 新 生 物	80.1	94.0	110.9	122.1	132.6	140.6	163.5	187.4
02101	口唇，口腔及び咽頭の悪性新生物	1.1	0.9	1.1	1.2	1.5	1.7	2.2	2.5
02102	食 道 の 悪 性 新 生 物	4.8	4.8	5.4	5.9	7.3	7.1	7.8	8.5
02103	胃 の 悪 性 新 生 物	46.6	52.2	57.3	59.4	58.6	55.6	53.9	51.1
02104	結 腸 の 悪 性 新 生 物	1.5	1.6	2.0	2.6	3.5	4.9	6.7	9.4
02105	直腸S状結腸移行部及び直腸の悪性新生物	2.9	3.1	3.2	4.1	5.0	5.7	6.8	7.8
02106	肝及び肝内胆管の悪性新生物	}8.8	}11.1	11.3	10.4	11.6	12.2	17.0	23.3
02107	胆のう及びその他の胆道の悪性新生物			1.2	2.1	2.6	3.5	4.9	6.7
02108	膵 の 悪 性 新 生 物	0.8	1.4	2.5	3.6	5.0	5.8	7.8	10.1
02109	喉 頭 の 悪 性 新 生 物	1.4	1.2	1.2	1.3	1.5	1.3	1.3	1.3
02110	気管，気管支及び肺の悪性新生物	1.9	4.3	7.9	11.2	14.8	19.6	27.0	35.3
02111	皮 膚 の 悪 性 新 生 物	0.7	0.7	0.7	0.7	0.8	0.7	0.6	0.6
02112	乳 房 の 悪 性 新 生 物	0.1	0.0	0.0	0.1	0.0	0.0	0.1	0.1
02113	子 宮 の 悪 性 新 生 物[1]	·	·	·	·	·	·	·	·
02114	卵 巣 の 悪 性 新 生 物	·	·	·	·	·	·	·	·
02115	前 立 腺 の 悪 性 新 生 物	0.2	0.6	1.0	1.4	1.7	2.3	3.0	4.5
02116	膀 胱 の 悪 性 新 生 物	...	...	1.5	1.7	2.0	2.1	2.8	2.9
02117	中 枢 神 経 系 の 悪 性 新 生 物[2]	...	...	0.3	0.4	0.4	0.5	0.9	1.0
02118	悪 性 リ ン パ 腫	...	...	...	...	...	...	...	...
02119	白 血 病	1.8	2.8	3.2	3.7	4.0	4.2	4.6	5.1
02120	その他のリンパ組織，造血組織及び関連組織の悪性新生物	...	...	...	...	...	...	...	...
（再掲） 02104, 02105	大 腸 の 悪 性 新 生 物[3]	4.5	4.7	5.2	6.8	8.5	10.6	13.5	17.1

性・年次別死亡数及び率（人口10万対）（つづき）
population）from malignant neoplasms by sex and site : Japan－CON.

男
Male

1990 平成2年	1995 7年	2000 12年	2005 17年	2010 22年	2011 23年	2012 24年	2013 25年	2014 26年	2015 27年	2016 28年	死因簡単分類コード Code[a]
数 Deaths											
130 395	159 623	179 140	196 603	211 435	213 190	215 110	216 975	218 397	219 508	219 785	02100
1 866	2 980	3 610	4 151	4 840	4 901	5 166	5 128	5 268	5 258	5 396	02101
6 004	7 253	8 706	9 465	9 992	10 141	9 724	9 667	9 629	9 774	9 533	02102
29 909	32 015	32 798	32 643	32 943	32 785	32 206	31 978	31 483	30 809	29 854	02103
7 791	10 420	12 139	13 436	14 947	15 469	16 006	16 233	16 478	17 063	17 116	02104
5 495	6 892	7 729	8 710	8 974	9 393	9 523	9 575	9 699	9 755	9 910	02105
17 786	22 773	23 602	23 203	21 510	20 972	20 060	19 816	19 208	19 008	18 510	02106
5 069	6 189	6 913	7 845	8 440	8 886	8 964	8 929	9 052	9 066	8 970	02107
7 317	8 965	10 380	12 284	14 569	14 825	15 517	15 873	16 411	16 186	17 060	02108
770	872	958	1 006	916	876	870	895	908	899	856	02109
26 872	33 389	39 053	45 189	50 395	50 782	51 372	52 054	52 505	53 208	52 430	02110
381	451	502	628	666	706	735	773	797	745	754	02111
34	56	77	87	90	107	88	82	83	121	117	02112
·	·	·	·	·	·	·	·	·	·	·	02113
·	·	·	·	·	·	·	·	·	·	·	02114
3 460	5 399	7 514	9 265	10 722	10 823	11 143	11 560	11 507	11 326	11 803	02115
2 110	2 700	3 184	4 141	4 719	4 784	5 003	5 266	5 308	5 582	5 792	02116
695	906	869	938	1 127	1 222	1 257	1 213	1 344	1 406	1 483	02117
···	3 735	4 578	4 829	5 689	5 771	6 069	6 316	6 427	6 656	6 883	02118
3 225	3 645	3 970	4 311	4 860	4 775	4 779	4 806	4 896	5 104	5 398	02119
···	1 565	1 774	2 004	2 200	2 131	2 119	2 085	2 233	2 044	2 240	02120
13 286	17 312	19 868	22 146	23 921	24 862	25 529	25 808	26 177	26 818	27 026	（再掲）02104, 02105
率 Death rates											
216.4	262.0	291.3	319.1	343.4	346.9	350.8	354.6	357.8	359.7	361.1	02100
3.1	4.9	5.9	6.7	7.9	8.0	8.4	8.4	8.6	8.6	8.9	02101
10.0	11.9	14.2	15.4	16.2	16.5	15.9	15.8	15.8	16.0	15.7	02102
49.6	52.6	53.3	53.0	53.5	53.3	52.5	52.3	51.6	50.5	49.0	02103
12.9	17.1	19.7	21.8	24.3	25.2	26.1	26.5	27.0	28.0	28.1	02104
9.1	11.3	12.6	14.1	14.6	15.3	15.5	15.6	15.9	16.0	16.3	02105
29.5	37.4	38.4	37.7	34.9	34.1	32.7	32.4	31.5	31.1	30.4	02106
8.4	10.2	11.2	12.7	13.7	14.5	14.6	14.6	14.8	14.9	14.7	02107
12.1	14.7	16.9	19.9	23.7	24.1	25.3	25.9	26.9	26.5	28.0	02108
1.3	1.4	1.6	1.6	1.5	1.4	1.4	1.5	1.5	1.5	1.4	02109
44.6	54.8	63.5	73.3	81.8	82.6	83.8	85.1	86.0	87.2	86.1	02110
0.6	0.7	0.8	1.0	1.1	1.1	1.2	1.3	1.3	1.2	1.2	02111
0.1	0.1	0.1	0.1	0.1	0.2	0.1	0.1	0.1	0.2	0.2	02112
·	·	·	·	·	·	·	·	·	·	·	02113
·	·	·	·	·	·	·	·	·	·	·	02114
5.7	8.9	12.2	15.0	17.4	17.6	18.2	18.9	18.9	18.6	19.4	02115
3.5	4.4	5.2	6.7	7.7	7.8	8.2	8.6	8.7	9.1	9.5	02116
1.2	1.5	1.4	1.5	1.8	2.0	2.0	2.0	2.2	2.3	2.4	02117
···	6.1	7.4	7.8	9.2	9.4	9.9	10.3	10.5	10.9	11.3	02118
5.4	6.0	6.5	7.0	7.9	7.8	7.8	7.9	8.0	8.4	8.9	02119
···	2.6	2.9	3.3	3.6	3.5	3.5	3.4	3.7	3.3	3.7	02120
22.1	28.4	32.3	35.9	38.9	40.5	41.6	42.2	42.9	43.9	44.4	（再掲）02104, 02105

死　亡

表 5.24　悪性新生物の主な部位別にみた
Table 5.24　Trends in deaths and death rates (per 100,000

女
Female

死因簡単分類コード Code[a]	死　因 Causes of death	1950 昭和25年	1955 30年	1960 35年	1965 40年	1970 45年	1975 50年	1980 55年	1985 60年
		死						亡	
02100	悪　性　新　生　物	31 758	36 498	42 875	47 637	52 903	59 461	68 263	77 054
02101	口唇，口腔及び咽頭の悪性新生物	267	236	277	333	374	505	592	627
02102	食 道 の 悪 性 新 生 物	802	871	995	1 088	1 150	1 135	1 243	1 151
02103	胃 の 悪 性 新 生 物	12 188	14 407	16 467	17 749	19 170	19 454	19 598	18 756
02104	結 腸 の 悪 性 新 生 物	837	905	1 129	1 532	2 052	2 911	4 090	5 703
02105	直腸S状結腸移行部及び直腸の悪性新生物	1 072	1 255	1 518	1 803	2 144	2 743	2 925	3 223
02106	肝及び肝内胆管の悪性新生物	} 2 578	} 3 700	3 614	3 499	3 574	3 696	4 227	5 192
02107	胆のう及びその他の胆道の悪性新生物			588	1 050	1 764	2 579	3 808	5 521
02108	膵 の 悪 性 新 生 物	198	477	825	1 318	1 850	2 480	3 352	4 488
02109	喉 頭 の 悪 性 新 生 物	225	181	181	168	170	124	130	88
02110	気管，気管支及び肺の悪性新生物	330	818	1 533	2 321	2 987	4 048	5 856	7 753
02111	皮 膚 の 悪 性 新 生 物	225	263	310	301	326	333	292	312
02112	乳 房 の 悪 性 新 生 物	1 419	1 572	1 683	1 966	2 486	3 262	4 141	4 922
02113	子 宮 の 悪 性 新 生 物[1]	8 356	7 289	7 068	6 689	6 373	6 075	5 465	4 912
02114	卵 巣 の 悪 性 新 生 物	346	473	647	840	1 129	1 516	2 098	2 675
02115	前 立 腺 の 悪 性 新 生 物	・	・	・	・	・	・	・	・
02116	膀 胱 の 悪 性 新 生 物	…	…	435	454	540	656	755	872
02117	中枢神経系の悪性新生物[2]	…	…	115	125	163	200	394	475
02118	悪 性 リ ン パ 腫	…	…	…	…	…	…	…	…
02119	白 血 病	508	824	1 155	1 394	1 554	1 843	1 943	2 196
02120	その他のリンパ組織，造血組織及び 関 連 組 織 の 悪 性 新 生 物	…	…	…	…	…	…	…	…
(再掲) 02104, 02105	大 腸 の 悪 性 新 生 物[3]	1 909	2 160	2 647	3 335	4 196	5 654	7 015	8 926
		死						亡	
02100	悪　性　新　生　物	74.9	80.4	90.2	95.2	100.7	105.2	115.5	125.9
02101	口唇，口腔及び咽頭の悪性新生物	0.6	0.5	0.6	0.7	0.7	0.9	1.0	1.0
02102	食 道 の 悪 性 新 生 物	1.9	1.9	2.1	2.2	2.2	2.0	2.1	1.9
02103	胃 の 悪 性 新 生 物	28.8	31.7	34.6	35.5	36.5	34.4	33.2	30.6
02104	結 腸 の 悪 性 新 生 物	2.0	2.0	2.4	3.1	3.9	5.1	6.9	9.3
02105	直腸S状結腸移行部及び直腸の悪性新生物	2.5	2.8	3.2	3.6	4.1	4.9	4.9	5.3
02106	肝及び肝内胆管の悪性新生物	} 6.1	} 8.1	7.6	7.0	6.8	6.5	7.1	8.5
02107	胆のう及びその他の胆道の悪性新生物			1.2	2.1	3.4	4.6	6.4	9.0
02108	膵 の 悪 性 新 生 物	0.5	1.1	1.7	2.6	3.5	4.4	5.7	7.3
02109	喉 頭 の 悪 性 新 生 物	0.5	0.4	0.4	0.3	0.3	0.2	0.2	0.1
02110	気管，気管支及び肺の悪性新生物	0.8	1.8	3.2	4.6	5.7	7.2	9.9	12.7
02111	皮 膚 の 悪 性 新 生 物	0.5	0.6	0.7	0.6	0.6	0.6	0.5	0.5
02112	乳 房 の 悪 性 新 生 物	3.3	3.5	3.5	3.9	4.7	5.8	7.0	8.0
02113	子 宮 の 悪 性 新 生 物[1]	19.7	16.0	14.9	13.4	12.1	10.7	9.2	8.0
02114	卵 巣 の 悪 性 新 生 物	0.8	1.0	1.4	1.7	2.1	2.7	3.5	4.4
02115	前 立 腺 の 悪 性 新 生 物	・	・	・	・	・	・	・	・
02116	膀 胱 の 悪 性 新 生 物	…	…	0.9	0.9	1.0	1.2	1.3	1.4
02117	中枢神経系の悪性新生物[2]	…	…	0.2	0.2	0.3	0.4	0.7	0.8
02118	悪 性 リ ン パ 腫	…	…	…	…	…	…	…	…
02119	白 血 病	1.2	1.8	2.4	2.8	3.0	3.3	3.3	3.6
02120	その他のリンパ組織，造血組織及び 関 連 組 織 の 悪 性 新 生 物	…	…	…	…	…	…	…	…
(再掲) 02104, 02105	大 腸 の 悪 性 新 生 物[3]	4.5	4.8	5.6	6.7	8.0	10.0	11.9	14.6

性・年次別死亡数及び率（人口10万対）（つづき）
population）from malignant neoplasms by sex and site : Japan－CON.

女
Female

1990 平成2年	1995 7年	2000 12年	2005 17年	2010 22年	2011 23年	2012 24年	2013 25年	2014 26年	2015 27年	2016 28年	死因簡単分類コード Code[a]
数 Deaths											
87 018	103 399	116 344	129 338	142 064	144 115	145 853	147 897	149 706	150 838	**153 201**	02100
741	1 119	1 456	1 528	1 962	1 987	2 001	2 051	2 147	2 122	**2 279**	02101
1 270	1 385	1 550	1 717	1 875	1 829	1 868	1 876	1 947	1 965	**1 950**	02102
17 562	18 061	17 852	17 668	17 193	17 045	16 923	16 654	16 420	15 870	**15 677**	02103
7 718	9 866	11 498	13 685	15 093	15 581	16 171	16 449	16 819	17 275	**17 405**	02104
3 628	4 096	4 582	4 999	5 224	5 301	5 576	5 397	5 489	5 606	**5 668**	02105
6 447	8 934	10 379	11 065	11 255	10 903	10 630	10 359	10 335	9 881	**10 018**	02106
6 802	7 557	8 240	8 741	9 145	9 300	9 245	9 296	9 065	9 086	**8 995**	02107
6 001	7 054	8 714	10 643	13 448	14 004	14 399	14 799	15 305	15 680	**16 415**	02108
77	87	88	84	86	78	83	68	70	72	**88**	02109
9 614	12 356	14 671	16 874	19 418	19 511	20 146	20 680	20 891	21 170	**21 408**	02110
304	418	484	579	738	747	821	752	860	760	**799**	02111
5 848	7 763	9 171	10 721	12 455	12 731	12 529	13 148	13 240	13 584	**14 015**	02112
4 600	4 865	5 202	5 381	5 930	6 075	6 113	6 033	6 429	6 429	**6 345**	02113
3 279	3 892	3 993	4 467	4 654	4 705	4 688	4 717	4 840	4 676	**4 758**	02114
·	·	·	·	·	·	·	·	·	·	·	02115
938	1 231	1 496	1 888	2 085	2 224	2 296	2 419	2 452	2 548	**2 640**	02116
547	668	705	743	832	922	944	1 004	982	1 039	**1 167**	02117
···	2 607	3 340	3 708	4 483	4 565	4 762	4 982	5 053	5 173	**5 442**	02118
2 408	2 484	2 796	2 972	3 218	3 381	3 121	3 327	3 300	3 527	**3 403**	02119
···	1 443	1 651	1 928	2 087	1 989	2 002	2 078	2 004	2 130	**2 203**	02120
11 346	13 962	16 080	18 684	20 317	20 882	21 747	21 846	22 308	22 881	**23 073**	（再掲）02104, 02105
率 Death rates											
139.3	163.1	181.4	200.3	219.2	222.7	225.7	229.2	232.5	234.6	**238.8**	02100
1.2	1.8	2.3	2.4	3.0	3.1	3.1	3.2	3.3	3.3	**3.6**	02101
2.0	2.2	2.4	2.7	2.9	2.8	2.9	2.9	3.0	3.1	**3.0**	02102
28.1	28.5	27.8	27.4	26.5	26.3	26.2	25.8	25.5	24.7	**24.4**	02103
12.4	15.6	17.9	21.2	23.3	24.1	25.0	25.5	26.1	26.9	**27.1**	02104
5.8	6.5	7.1	7.7	8.1	8.2	8.6	8.4	8.5	8.7	**8.8**	02105
10.3	14.1	16.2	17.1	17.4	16.8	16.4	16.1	16.1	15.4	**15.6**	02106
10.9	11.9	12.8	13.5	14.1	14.4	14.3	14.4	14.1	14.1	**14.0**	02107
9.6	11.1	13.6	16.5	20.7	21.6	22.3	22.9	23.8	24.4	**25.6**	02108
0.1	0.1	0.1	0.1	0.1	0.1	0.1	0.1	0.1	0.1	**0.1**	02109
15.4	19.5	22.9	26.1	30.0	30.1	31.2	32.1	32.4	32.9	**33.4**	02110
0.5	0.7	0.8	0.9	1.1	1.2	1.3	1.2	1.3	1.2	**1.2**	02111
9.4	12.2	14.3	16.6	19.2	19.7	19.4	20.4	20.6	21.1	**21.8**	02112
7.4	7.7	8.1	8.3	9.1	9.4	9.5	9.4	10.0	10.0	**9.9**	02113
5.2	6.1	6.2	6.9	7.2	7.3	7.3	7.3	7.5	7.3	**7.4**	02114
·	·	·	·	·	·	·	·	·	·	·	02115
1.5	1.9	2.3	2.9	3.2	3.4	3.6	3.7	3.8	4.0	**4.1**	02116
0.9	1.1	1.1	1.2	1.3	1.4	1.5	1.6	1.5	1.6	**1.8**	02117
···	4.1	5.2	5.7	6.9	7.1	7.4	7.7	7.8	8.0	**8.5**	02118
3.9	3.9	4.4	4.6	5.0	5.2	4.8	5.2	5.1	5.5	**5.3**	02119
···	2.3	2.6	3.0	3.2	3.1	3.1	3.2	3.1	3.3	**3.4**	02120
18.2	22.0	25.1	28.9	31.3	32.3	33.6	33.9	34.6	35.6	**36.0**	（再掲）02104, 02105

死　亡

表5.25　悪性新生物の主な部位別にみた性・
Table 5.25　Trends in death rates (per 100,000 population)

男（7－1）　　02103[a]　胃の悪性新生物
Male　　　　Malignant neoplasm of stomach

年　齢 Age	1950 昭和25年	1955 30年	1960 35年	1965 40年	1970 45年	1975 50年	1980 55年	1985 60年	1990 平成2年	1995 7年	2000 12年	2005 17年	2010 22年	2014 26年	2015 27年	2016 28年
総　数 Total	46.6	52.2	57.3	59.4	58.6	55.6	53.9	51.1	49.6	52.6	53.3	53.0	53.5	51.6	50.5	49.0
0～4 歳	0.1	-	-	0.0	-	-	-	-	-	-	-	-	-	-	-	-
5～9 Years	0.1	0.0	-	-	-	-	-	-	-	-	-	-	-	-	0.0	-
10～14	0.2	-	0.0	0.0	-	0.0	-	-	-	0.0	-	0.0	-	0.0	-	-
15～19	0.2	0.2	0.3	0.3	0.4	0.2	0.1	0.1	0.2	0.1	0.1	0.1	0.1	0.1	-	0.0
20～24	0.7	0.7	1.1	1.6	1.5	1.3	0.7	0.5	0.4	0.4	0.4	0.3	0.1	0.2	0.3	0.3
25～29	2.3	2.8	3.1	3.8	3.6	3.0	2.3	2.2	1.2	1.1	0.6	0.6	0.7	0.6	0.6	0.6
30～34	7.0	7.0	8.0	8.5	8.3	6.7	5.7	4.3	2.6	1.9	1.6	1.3	1.1	1.1	0.8	0.9
35～39	15.1	17.0	17.0	16.4	15.3	13.4	11.5	8.4	7.0	5.3	3.5	2.8	2.0	1.8	1.6	1.7
40～44	35.8	36.7	34.7	28.6	27.5	24.4	19.3	16.0	12.1	11.0	7.8	4.6	3.8	3.2	2.9	2.6
45～49	69.6	73.4	67.2	58.8	52.2	45.0	39.4	29.4	24.6	19.4	16.3	11.3	7.6	6.3	5.9	6.2
50～54	128.3	128.0	121.9	110.5	93.0	74.0	69.8	56.5	44.4	37.0	31.0	26.3	18.3	12.2	13.2	11.5
55～59	219.3	211.3	206.2	189.9	158.4	139.5	105.5	95.9	79.1	66.7	57.5	45.3	39.3	28.4	26.5	24.4
60～64	324.6	336.2	317.8	307.2	265.6	218.3	186.4	147.6	131.8	112.1	91.1	77.4	66.3	59.4	52.6	48.3
65～69	435.3	456.4	467.2	449.8	409.0	341.1	289.0	230.5	186.4	174.4	156.2	124.0	107.1	93.6	87.4	82.7
70～74	463.6	546.2	597.8	568.1	545.5	489.1	417.0	333.2	273.5	252.1	225.3	189.9	163.1	137.6	136.9	129.9
75～79	397.1	509.3	607.6	666.1	651.7	602.0	560.7	471.7	385.5	364.4	299.7	264.6	236.7	209.1	196.1	182.6
80～84	273.0	359.6	490.1	553.1	604.4	650.8	632.4	597.8	517.5	495.7	435.5	366.4	329.8	296.0	284.1	270.8
85～89	248.9	230.4	352.7	400.8	438.1	531.1	580.5	669.6	625.9	653.7	580.6	523.0	468.1	406.1	397.9	390.0
90～94[1]	47.1	257.3	193.7	196.7	200.3	350.8	401.1	487.3	563.5	689.4	671.5	645.1	620.7	500.6	512.3	466.0
95～99	…	…	…	…	…	…	…	…	…	…	…	646.5	634.0	543.5	504.2	556.7
100～	…	…	…	…	…	…	…	…	…	…	…	292.5	597.4	325.0	394.7	400.0

女（9－1）　　02103　胃の悪性新生物
Female　　　　Malignant neoplasm of stomach

年　齢 Age	1950 昭和25年	1955 30年	1960 35年	1965 40年	1970 45年	1975 50年	1980 55年	1985 60年	1990 平成2年	1995 7年	2000 12年	2005 17年	2010 22年	2014 26年	2015 27年	2016 28年
総　数 Total	28.8	31.7	34.6	35.5	36.5	34.4	33.2	30.6	28.1	28.5	27.8	27.4	26.5	25.5	24.7	24.4
0～4 歳	0.0	-	-	-	-	-	-	-	-	-	-	-	-	-	-	-
5～9 Years	0.1	-	0.0	-	-	-	-	-	-	-	-	-	-	-	-	-
10～14	0.0	0.0	0.0	0.0	-	-	-	0.0	-	-	-	-	-	-	-	-
15～19	0.2	0.2	0.2	0.2	0.5	0.2	0.1	-	0.1	-	0.1	0.1	-	-	0.1	0.1
20～24	1.0	1.0	1.3	1.4	1.6	1.4	1.1	0.5	0.6	0.2	0.2	0.3	0.3	0.2	0.2	0.2
25～29	3.4	3.1	3.7	4.7	5.1	4.6	4.0	3.2	1.9	1.5	1.0	0.5	0.4	0.5	0.4	0.5
30～34	8.5	8.7	10.3	10.5	9.1	10.1	8.1	6.5	4.7	3.2	2.3	1.8	1.0	1.5	1.5	1.2
35～39	15.5	17.7	18.2	17.9	16.0	15.0	13.5	10.6	8.7	6.2	4.1	3.7	2.6	2.5	1.9	1.8
40～44	29.7	29.9	31.2	26.5	25.6	21.4	17.9	15.2	12.8	10.1	8.0	5.0	3.8	3.9	3.0	2.7
45～49	45.4	44.0	45.0	42.2	37.5	31.2	24.8	21.0	15.8	15.8	13.5	8.4	5.8	5.0	5.0	4.6
50～54	69.8	69.3	64.7	63.9	54.2	45.1	35.6	28.1	23.0	18.4	17.1	13.8	10.3	7.8	7.1	6.6
55～59	108.7	104.8	96.7	88.6	82.4	64.0	52.9	39.8	30.0	26.6	22.3	18.7	16.3	13.5	11.6	11.1
60～64	158.3	153.6	142.1	128.9	119.1	97.2	80.9	63.2	45.2	37.2	32.5	25.6	22.5	20.9	18.6	18.0
65～69	219.4	223.0	208.7	192.9	175.0	145.6	116.5	88.4	68.6	56.4	43.8	37.3	30.5	29.2	27.0	28.1
70～74	235.0	264.2	282.8	275.0	254.4	211.3	173.9	132.2	98.1	85.3	66.1	56.3	46.7	37.2	39.0	36.5
75～79	229.4	284.1	321.3	316.1	321.2	279.0	250.9	199.2	150.0	125.8	103.6	84.0	68.6	61.1	56.5	53.2
80～84	169.8	253.9	307.2	315.1	332.0	319.1	307.7	265.4	225.9	202.1	166.2	133.1	111.4	97.8	91.2	87.2
85～89	146.7	170.3	249.0	246.0	266.0	273.4	312.0	329.2	303.8	283.7	254.7	224.6	182.2	155.0	149.0	145.8
90～94[1]	74.3	124.0	183.9	170.1	153.2	205.3	235.0	286.0	281.4	324.1	303.6	283.0	267.8	224.8	215.9	208.2
95～99	…	…	…	…	…	…	…	…	…	…	…	313.1	301.3	230.8	247.6	238.6
100～	…	…	…	…	…	…	…	…	…	…	…	287.1	239.2	221.6	192.9	184.2

注：1)　昭和25年～平成12年の90～94歳は90歳以上の数値である。

General mortality

年齢・年次別死亡率（人口10万対）
from malignant neoplasms by sex, age and site : Japan

男（7－2）　　02105　直腸Ｓ状結腸移行部及び直腸の悪性新生物
Male　　Malignant neoplasm of rectosigmoid junction and rectum

年　　齢 Age	1950 昭和25年	1955 30年	1960 35年	1965 40年	1970 45年	1975 50年	1980 55年	1985 60年	1990 平成2年	1995 7年	2000 12年	2005 17年	2010 22年	2014 26年	2015 27年	2016 28年
総　数 Total	2.9	3.1	3.2	4.1	5.0	5.7	6.8	7.8	9.1	11.3	12.6	14.1	14.6	15.9	16.0	16.3
0～4 歳	-	0.0	-	0.0	-	-	-	-	-	-	-	-	-	-	-	-
5～9 Years	-	-	-	-	-	-	-	-	-	-	-	-	-	-	-	-
10～14	-	0.0	-	0.0	-	-	-	-	-	-	-	-	-	-	-	-
15～19	0.1	0.0	0.1	0.1	0.1	0.0	-	-	0.0	-	-	-	-	0.0	-	0.0
20～24	0.1	0.1	0.2	0.6	0.4	0.2	0.1	0.1	0.0	0.0	0.2	0.1	0.1	0.0	0.1	0.1
25～29	0.6	0.3	0.1	0.5	1.1	0.6	0.4	0.3	0.1	0.2	0.2	0.0	0.0	0.1	0.2	0.2
30～34	0.8	0.6	0.7	0.9	1.2	1.5	0.9	0.6	0.6	0.4	0.5	0.3	0.4	0.4	0.4	0.5
35～39	1.3	1.2	0.6	1.0	2.1	2.2	2.1	1.6	1.4	1.1	0.7	0.9	0.6	1.0	0.7	0.9
40～44	1.9	2.3	2.0	1.9	2.8	3.2	3.5	3.3	2.8	2.2	2.2	2.2	2.1	1.7	1.8	1.7
45～49	4.8	3.8	2.7	4.2	4.4	4.8	5.9	5.5	5.9	5.3	5.1	4.4	3.7	3.4	3.7	3.5
50～54	7.0	4.9	4.9	6.4	7.1	6.4	9.0	10.3	10.4	10.9	10.3	9.9	8.5	7.6	7.4	7.1
55～59	11.5	9.6	8.9	10.7	11.8	12.2	11.9	16.0	17.2	19.3	18.3	16.6	16.1	14.7	14.6	14.8
60～64	17.8	17.2	17.4	17.7	19.0	19.9	19.3	20.7	24.6	29.4	27.6	25.9	23.9	27.4	25.9	25.4
65～69	25.0	25.8	23.6	29.3	30.4	31.9	31.8	31.3	33.1	40.9	40.0	36.4	35.0	36.6	34.3	35.9
70～74	34.4	39.2	41.1	39.5	43.8	47.2	50.9	46.4	43.9	48.4	49.0	50.0	45.9	44.9	44.8	45.5
75～79	38.5	46.2	44.6	52.9	59.3	65.3	68.2	67.9	59.7	57.6	56.9	61.3	55.1	57.3	55.6	53.6
80～84	20.9	38.3	46.7	71.7	70.6	84.0	89.0	90.2	91.1	89.7	81.0	76.6	73.7	65.5	68.7	68.9
85～89	16.3	35.4	49.8	64.9	70.0	75.4	94.6	103.3	102.2	110.2	98.4	104.0	84.4	84.2	86.8	86.7
90～94[1]	-	17.2	24.2	21.9	45.8	41.5	129.7	81.5	128.9	124.9	121.9	131.5	100.4	98.7	104.2	96.0
95～99	…	…	…	…	…	…	…	…	…	…	…	127.8	116.1	109.7	119.7	140.3
100～	…	…	…	…	…	…	…	…	…	…	…	265.9	153.6	87.5	71.8	100.0

女（9－2）　　02105　直腸Ｓ状結腸移行部及び直腸の悪性新生物
Female　　Malignant neoplasm of rectosigmoid junction and rectum

年　　齢 Age	1950 昭和25年	1955 30年	1960 35年	1965 40年	1970 45年	1975 50年	1980 55年	1985 60年	1990 平成2年	1995 7年	2000 12年	2005 17年	2010 22年	2014 26年	2015 27年	2016 28年
総　数 Total	2.5	2.8	3.2	3.6	4.1	4.9	4.9	5.3	5.8	6.5	7.1	7.7	8.1	8.5	8.7	8.8
0～4 歳	0.0	0.0	0.0	-	0.0	-	-	-	-	-	-	-	-	-	-	-
5～9 Years	-	-	-	-	-	-	-	-	-	-	-	-	-	-	-	-
10～14	-	-	0.0	0.0	-	-	-	-	-	-	-	-	-	-	0.0	-
15～19	-	0.1	0.1	-	0.0	-	0.0	-	-	0.0	-	-	0.0	-	-	0.0
20～24	0.1	0.2	0.1	0.4	0.1	0.1	0.1	0.0	0.0	0.0	0.1	-	-	-	0.0	-
25～29	0.4	0.3	0.3	0.6	0.9	0.4	0.3	0.2	0.1	0.1	0.1	0.1	0.2	0.0	0.2	0.0
30～34	1.0	0.3	0.5	0.9	1.3	1.3	0.8	0.5	0.5	0.5	0.3	0.4	0.2	0.4	0.2	0.2
35～39	1.7	1.1	1.1	1.2	1.6	2.0	1.6	0.9	1.0	0.7	0.6	0.8	0.8	0.7	0.4	0.6
40～44	3.0	2.9	2.0	2.3	2.3	2.5	2.8	2.3	1.6	2.1	1.3	1.3	1.1	1.3	1.1	1.2
45～49	4.5	3.5	4.0	3.9	3.3	4.3	3.9	3.9	4.3	3.5	3.1	2.7	2.1	2.4	2.2	2.4
50～54	6.9	6.7	6.0	5.6	7.0	6.1	5.9	5.8	6.5	5.5	5.6	5.5	4.9	4.5	4.0	4.3
55～59	10.2	10.1	9.6	9.2	8.2	9.6	7.8	7.9	8.1	7.7	8.2	7.3	6.7	7.2	6.4	7.1
60～64	12.6	13.5	13.3	11.6	11.9	12.1	11.1	11.1	11.1	10.6	11.9	10.1	9.4	10.5	9.9	9.2
65～69	18.2	17.1	18.5	19.9	19.0	18.6	15.4	15.2	14.5	15.0	13.8	13.6	12.5	11.9	12.0	11.5
70～74	18.6	21.8	29.0	28.5	26.8	30.8	25.7	23.1	19.8	18.6	20.1	18.0	15.4	14.9	16.2	17.0
75～79	15.3	27.2	33.7	36.5	41.4	40.9	39.6	32.4	28.5	27.5	24.3	22.8	20.6	20.9	21.1	20.2
80～84	16.1	25.3	29.6	41.6	44.2	54.0	52.5	44.1	40.9	40.5	34.4	35.1	31.7	27.3	29.8	29.8
85～89	14.7	15.5	23.2	28.8	43.7	51.0	54.3	59.3	58.9	55.0	49.4	46.2	44.9	42.6	40.7	41.7
90～94[1]	16.5	23.6	29.3	27.0	20.7	46.7	45.4	69.0	60.1	64.6	65.6	58.8	59.0	58.2	58.0	57.6
95～99	…	…	…	…	…	…	…	…	…	…	…	67.7	76.1	56.7	73.7	59.2
100～	…	…	…	…	…	…	…	…	…	…	…	92.6	57.8	84.3	76.8	52.6

Note : a) Code see page 595.

363

死　亡

表 5.25　悪性新生物の主な部位別にみた性・
Table 5.25　Trends in death rates（per 100,000 population）

男（7－3）　　　02106　肝及び肝内胆管の悪性新生物
Male　　　　　　Malignant neoplasm of liver and intrahepatic bile ducts

年　　齢 Age	1950 昭和25年	1955 30年	1960 35年	1965 40年	1970 45年	1975 50年	1980 55年	1985 60年	1990 平成2年	1995 7年	2000 12年	2005 17年	2010 22年	2014 26年	2015 27年	2016 28年
総　数 Total	8.8	11.1	11.3	10.4	11.6	12.2	17.0	23.3	29.5	37.4	38.4	37.7	34.9	31.5	31.1	30.4
0～4　歳	0.1	0.2	0.2	0.3	0.4	0.5	0.3	0.4	0.2	0.2	0.2	0.1	0.1	0.2	0.0	0.1
5～9　Years	0.0	0.1	0.1	0.1	0.2	0.1	0.1	0.0	-	0.2	0.1	0.2	-	-	-	0.0
10～14	0.0	0.0	0.1	0.1	0.1	0.0	0.1	0.1	0.0	0.1	0.1	-	0.1	0.0	0.0	0.0
15～19	0.2	0.1	0.2	0.1	0.0	0.1	0.1	0.1	0.1	0.2	0.1	0.1	0.0	0.1	-	0.0
20～24	0.2	0.2	0.4	0.2	0.3	0.3	0.2	0.1	0.1	0.1	0.1	0.1	0.1	-	0.1	-
25～29	0.3	0.5	0.5	0.5	0.4	0.3	0.4	0.3	0.2	0.4	0.4	0.2	0.1	0.1	0.1	0.0
30～34	1.4	1.4	1.1	0.9	0.9	1.4	1.3	1.0	0.7	0.6	0.7	0.4	0.5	0.2	0.1	0.2
35～39	2.5	3.7	2.4	2.8	3.0	2.6	2.9	3.6	2.7	2.2	1.5	1.7	0.8	0.7	0.5	0.6
40～44	7.4	7.7	6.3	6.3	6.4	6.8	6.3	7.4	7.2	6.6	4.8	3.0	2.3	1.6	1.4	1.4
45～49	13.4	16.1	12.5	13.1	12.2	13.3	20.7	17.6	15.4	15.8	12.4	8.3	5.7	4.2	3.8	3.2
50～54	27.0	28.7	28.6	20.5	23.5	22.9	37.3	51.0	35.0	33.9	27.6	22.4	14.4	10.1	9.3	8.1
55～59	38.9	43.1	42.6	33.0	36.9	38.2	50.0	72.9	94.7	65.0	51.3	38.1	29.3	20.4	20.0	18.9
60～64	61.6	69.7	64.1	53.3	50.4	50.3	69.6	87.7	114.9	141.8	89.4	65.8	49.9	39.4	35.6	34.4
65～69	79.8	94.6	83.9	71.7	76.2	73.1	79.6	98.3	118.4	159.6	164.8	102.4	76.1	57.6	56.0	54.3
70～74	79.6	114.7	115.3	90.0	94.0	91.0	107.2	115.5	127.7	163.4	173.0	175.6	113.3	83.8	87.9	80.9
75～79	84.4	110.8	127.2	114.9	116.8	98.1	113.6	135.3	137.5	169.2	172.4	188.4	183.3	133.7	122.9	116.8
80～84	48.1	101.4	87.5	125.2	115.4	112.6	132.0	144.5	157.4	180.5	186.9	189.5	198.2	196.3	187.2	177.1
85～89	65.3	50.2	74.7	86.5	107.8	112.2	114.8	138.8	154.4	180.9	177.5	182.6	198.2	206.3	213.5	213.5
90～94[1]	47.1	34.3	84.7	58.3	103.0	69.2	75.4	119.6	154.7	158.2	162.8	180.4	188.1	213.2	205.8	204.8
95～99	…	…	…	…	…	…	…	…	…	…	…	183.3	200.0	198.4	206.4	214.9
100～	…	…	…	…	…	…	…	…	…	…	…	106.4	136.5	100.0	143.5	133.3

女（9－3）　　　02106　肝及び肝内胆管の悪性新生物
Female　　　　　Malignant neoplasm of liver and intrahepatic bile ducts

年　　齢 Age	1950 昭和25年	1955 30年	1960 35年	1965 40年	1970 45年	1975 50年	1980 55年	1985 60年	1990 平成2年	1995 7年	2000 12年	2005 17年	2010 22年	2014 26年	2015 27年	2016 28年
総　数 Total	6.1	8.1	7.6	7.0	6.8	6.5	7.1	8.5	10.3	14.1	16.2	17.1	17.4	16.1	15.4	15.6
0～4　歳	0.2	0.2	0.3	0.4	0.3	0.2	0.2	0.3	0.2	0.2	0.1	-	0.1	0.1	0.2	0.2
5～9　Years	0.1	0.0	0.0	0.0	0.1	0.1	0.0	0.0	0.0	0.1	-	0.0	0.0	-	0.0	-
10～14	0.1	0.0	0.0	0.1	0.0	0.1	0.0	0.1	0.0	-	-	-	-	0.0	0.0	0.0
15～19	-	0.0	0.1	0.1	0.1	0.1	0.0	0.0	0.0	-	0.0	-	-	0.0	0.1	-
20～24	0.1	0.1	0.3	0.2	0.2	0.2	0.0	0.0	0.1	0.1	0.1	-	0.0	-	-	0.1
25～29	0.3	0.3	0.3	0.3	0.2	0.3	0.1	0.2	0.2	0.0	0.2	0.1	0.1	0.1	0.1	0.1
30～34	1.0	1.3	0.7	0.9	0.6	0.3	0.3	0.4	0.3	0.2	0.3	0.1	0.1	0.1	0.0	0.1
35～39	1.5	2.4	2.0	1.5	1.2	1.1	1.0	0.7	0.4	0.3	0.5	0.3	0.3	0.3	0.3	0.3
40～44	4.8	5.6	4.3	3.0	2.7	2.3	1.9	1.4	0.9	1.0	0.7	0.7	0.4	0.4	0.5	0.6
45～49	8.2	10.5	7.9	6.5	5.2	4.2	3.2	3.3	2.1	2.2	1.6	1.0	1.0	0.9	0.8	0.8
50～54	15.9	18.0	13.1	11.0	9.3	7.6	6.0	6.4	4.9	5.0	4.2	3.4	2.1	1.6	1.8	1.9
55～59	23.2	26.5	20.8	18.0	15.4	12.5	12.1	13.0	12.8	11.6	9.1	6.5	5.0	4.1	3.4	3.6
60～64	37.6	43.3	36.7	28.3	23.8	20.2	19.0	22.3	24.2	30.3	21.4	15.0	11.6	8.5	7.7	7.7
65～69	47.1	60.6	49.8	45.4	36.8	32.1	30.5	30.8	37.0	45.8	45.3	31.1	22.6	15.7	14.1	14.1
70～74	52.1	76.9	70.0	57.5	53.8	46.8	45.3	44.0	49.0	60.3	64.5	61.7	42.8	29.7	27.8	26.5
75～79	56.9	78.5	80.3	74.8	72.1	58.8	60.9	60.7	57.9	74.4	77.7	80.3	72.2	55.9	46.9	46.3
80～84	40.5	62.1	71.4	65.1	61.3	65.2	69.8	69.4	70.8	79.7	89.9	92.6	89.4	85.0	78.7	78.2
85～89	29.3	41.3	68.8	53.9	65.9	59.7	70.2	79.0	92.6	92.9	97.6	95.6	107.2	93.7	97.4	95.1
90～94[1]	33.0	41.3	46.0	43.2	41.4	41.7	38.4	54.4	68.3	86.4	91.2	93.4	100.7	102.6	101.2	108.6
95～99	…	…	…	…	…	…	…	…	…	…	…	86.5	99.3	96.2	99.6	87.7
100～	…	…	…	…	…	…	…	…	…	…	…	46.3	65.7	64.7	71.2	61.4

注：昭和25、30年は、「胆路および肝臓」である。

年齢・年次別死亡率（人口10万対）（つづき）
from malignant neoplasms by sex, age and site : Japan－CON.

男（7－4）　　02108　膵の悪性新生物
Male　　　　Malignant neoplasm of pancreas

年　　齢 Age	1950 昭和25年	1955 30年	1960 35年	1965 40年	1970 45年	1975 50年	1980 55年	1985 60年	1990 平成2年	1995 7年	2000 12年	2005 17年	2010 22年	2014 26年	2015 27年	2016 28年
総数 Total	0.8	1.4	2.5	3.6	5.0	5.8	7.8	10.1	12.1	14.7	16.9	19.9	23.7	26.9	26.5	**28.0**
0～4 歳	-	0.0	-	-	0.0	-	-	-	-	-	-	-	-	-	-	-
5～9 Years	-	-	-	-	-	-	0.0	-	-	-	-	-	-	-	-	-
10～14	0.0	-	-	-	0.1	0.0	-	-	-	-	-	-	-	-	-	-
15～19	-	-	0.0	0.1	0.0	0.0	0.0	-	-	0.0	-	-	-	0.0	-	-
20～24	0.1	0.0	0.1	0.1	0.2	0.1	0.1	0.0	0.0	0.1	-	0.0	0.0	-	-	-
25～29	-	0.1	0.2	0.2	0.2	0.3	0.3	0.0	0.0	0.1	0.1	0.0	-	-	0.0	**0.0**
30～34	0.3	0.3	0.3	0.6	0.6	0.4	0.4	0.4	0.3	0.4	0.5	0.1	0.1	0.2	0.2	**0.2**
35～39	0.6	0.6	0.9	0.9	1.4	1.1	1.4	0.9	1.3	1.0	0.9	0.7	0.8	0.7	0.8	**0.7**
40～44	1.4	1.5	1.9	1.9	2.4	2.2	3.1	2.8	2.8	2.8	2.4	2.4	1.7	2.1	2.2	**1.7**
45～49	1.7	2.3	4.4	4.5	4.1	5.2	6.1	6.3	6.3	5.9	6.1	5.5	5.4	6.0	4.5	**5.1**
50～54	2.7	5.0	6.6	9.1	10.1	9.7	10.9	11.5	11.0	12.0	11.9	11.4	10.2	9.5	9.4	**10.5**
55～59	4.7	7.0	11.1	13.4	18.1	17.0	19.1	20.8	18.5	20.7	21.2	22.6	22.1	20.4	19.4	**20.3**
60～64	6.2	9.3	13.9	20.6	25.5	26.6	32.3	32.1	33.0	33.0	33.5	35.9	37.3	37.2	36.1	**34.4**
65～69	4.0	11.8	20.4	25.5	36.7	38.8	45.2	51.4	49.0	53.2	50.0	51.8	55.0	58.6	54.6	**57.3**
70～74	3.7	9.9	17.3	30.2	42.7	47.6	57.6	70.1	71.5	71.3	71.4	71.3	74.6	77.4	76.0	**82.3**
75～79	1.5	5.6	19.6	28.5	35.8	52.0	71.2	91.0	99.5	100.9	95.7	92.6	99.9	105.0	100.8	**105.8**
80～84	2.1	2.3	10.1	23.0	34.0	41.7	67.9	91.5	115.1	130.8	122.0	123.6	130.8	135.1	132.4	**132.9**
85～89	4.1	3.0	6.2	11.6	30.8	34.7	58.5	98.6	122.5	130.5	143.5	146.2	155.1	157.0	161.5	**160.2**
90～94[1]	-	-	-	21.9	17.2	18.5	39.2	85.1	139.9	145.4	140.7	155.2	162.6	182.0	177.2	**193.1**
95～99	…	…	…	…	…	…	…	…	…	…	…	135.1	171.4	193.5	165.4	**200.0**
100～	…	…	…	…	…	…	…	…	…	…	…	132.9	187.7	175.0	143.5	**177.8**

女（9－4）　　02108　膵の悪性新生物
Female　　　Malignant neoplasm of pancreas

年　　齢 Age	1950 昭和25年	1955 30年	1960 35年	1965 40年	1970 45年	1975 50年	1980 55年	1985 60年	1990 平成2年	1995 7年	2000 12年	2005 17年	2010 22年	2014 26年	2015 27年	2016 28年
総数 Total	0.5	1.1	1.7	2.6	3.5	4.4	5.7	7.3	9.6	11.1	13.6	16.5	20.7	23.8	24.4	**25.6**
0～4 歳	-	0.0	-	-	-	-	-	-	-	-	-	-	-	-	-	-
5～9 Years	-	-	-	-	-	-	-	-	-	-	-	-	-	-	-	-
10～14	0.0	-	-	-	-	-	-	-	-	-	-	-	0.0	0.0	-	-
15～19	-	-	0.0	0.0	-	0.0	0.0	-	0.0	-	-	-	-	-	-	-
20～24	0.1	-	0.0	0.0	0.1	0.1	-	0.1	0.0	-	-	0.0	-	-	-	**0.1**
25～29	0.1	0.1	0.1	0.2	0.2	0.1	0.2	0.2	0.1	0.1	0.1	0.1	0.1	0.2	0.0	**0.0**
30～34	0.2	0.2	0.4	0.3	0.5	0.3	0.3	0.3	0.4	0.2	0.2	0.1	0.2	0.3	0.2	**0.0**
35～39	0.3	0.7	0.4	0.5	0.8	0.6	0.5	0.6	1.0	0.4	0.5	0.6	0.4	0.4	0.5	**0.5**
40～44	0.6	1.5	1.3	1.7	1.5	1.4	1.3	1.6	1.2	1.2	1.4	1.4	1.6	1.3	1.1	**0.8**
45～49	1.0	1.8	2.6	3.0	2.9	3.5	3.0	3.0	2.8	2.7	3.2	2.7	2.8	2.6	2.7	**2.5**
50～54	1.1	2.6	5.0	5.3	6.0	6.6	5.9	5.0	5.0	5.5	5.6	6.2	6.0	5.9	5.4	**5.9**
55～59	3.0	5.0	7.4	10.3	9.4	10.0	9.3	9.4	9.7	8.6	10.7	10.8	11.5	12.0	10.5	**11.6**
60～64	3.3	5.4	8.2	14.0	15.5	15.5	17.7	17.2	16.1	17.5	16.1	18.4	20.8	20.8	20.3	**19.9**
65～69	2.4	8.1	12.7	17.2	21.0	23.2	26.7	26.1	27.5	24.4	27.3	28.7	32.2	34.6	33.4	**33.2**
70～74	1.6	5.8	11.6	15.9	27.4	31.0	40.3	43.6	42.2	41.1	40.9	43.2	45.4	48.2	48.7	**52.7**
75～79	1.4	5.1	9.5	18.5	27.2	36.6	42.1	55.6	63.3	60.0	61.6	60.8	66.9	67.7	71.1	**75.7**
80～84	0.6	2.9	7.3	11.4	17.7	29.0	43.6	61.7	82.7	85.6	81.2	84.6	93.0	99.1	99.3	**102.5**
85～89	3.7	3.9	-	7.2	12.0	18.8	36.2	62.0	98.6	103.1	108.7	113.5	125.6	129.4	133.6	**134.2**
90～94[1]	-	-	4.2	-	4.1	8.3	18.6	48.3	94.3	104.3	128.2	123.4	137.2	146.9	148.9	**147.3**
95～99	…	…	…	…	…	…	…	…	…	…	…	121.2	150.6	145.7	151.4	**156.3**
100～	…	…	…	…	…	…	…	…	…	…	…	78.7	120.9	105.9	138.6	**107.0**

死　亡

表5.25　悪性新生物の主な部位別にみた性・
Table 5.25　Trends in death rates (per 100,000 population)

男（7－5）　02110　気管，気管支及び肺の悪性新生物
Male　　Malignant neoplasm of trachea, bronchus and lung

年齢 Age	1950 昭和25年	1955 30年	1960 35年	1965 40年	1970 45年	1975 50年	1980 55年	1985 60年	1990 平成2年	1995 7年	2000 12年	2005 17年	2010 22年	2014 26年	2015 27年	2016 28年
総数 Total	1.9	4.3	7.9	11.2	14.8	19.6	27.0	35.3	44.6	54.8	63.5	73.3	81.8	86.0	87.2	86.1
0～4 歳	0.0	0.0	0.0	0.0	0.0	0.0	0.0	0.0	-	-	-	-	-	-	-	0.0
5～9 Years	-	-	0.0	-	-	-	-	-	-	-	0.0	0.0	-	-	0.0	-
10～14	0.1	0.1	-	0.1	-	-	0.0	-	-	-	0.0	-	-	-	-	0.1
15～19	0.2	0.1	0.2	0.1	0.1	0.0	0.1	0.0	0.0	0.1	0.1	0.0	0.1	0.0	0.0	-
20～24	0.1	0.2	0.2	0.4	0.2	0.2	0.1	0.1	0.1	0.1	0.1	0.1	0.2	0.1	0.0	0.1
25～29	0.2	0.3	0.4	0.5	0.4	0.4	0.5	0.3	0.4	0.3	0.2	0.2	0.2	0.2	0.1	0.2
30～34	0.1	0.5	0.7	0.8	0.8	0.9	0.9	0.9	1.0	1.2	1.3	0.8	0.5	0.4	0.3	0.5
35～39	0.4	0.8	1.1	1.8	1.6	1.9	2.5	2.9	3.3	2.6	2.4	1.9	1.9	1.4	1.4	1.9
40～44	0.9	2.0	2.7	3.6	4.6	4.9	5.0	6.1	6.8	6.4	7.4	5.8	3.9	4.0	4.2	3.5
45～49	2.1	4.9	7.7	8.5	8.5	11.4	11.2	11.1	12.9	14.3	14.3	13.4	10.8	9.3	8.8	7.4
50～54	4.9	10.1	15.8	18.7	20.1	20.8	26.4	25.2	23.0	25.9	28.2	26.5	24.3	20.6	20.0	17.6
55～59	7.7	15.5	30.5	32.0	40.7	43.9	48.8	53.6	53.4	47.1	51.7	52.6	50.6	44.8	41.7	38.9
60～64	13.7	29.5	46.5	66.3	71.5	79.7	96.0	98.8	113.0	104.5	89.6	97.7	92.2	92.8	88.2	83.3
65～69	21.9	43.2	71.4	93.1	125.0	139.4	157.2	179.1	190.2	202.3	173.1	147.4	163.2	159.0	155.4	152.5
70～74	20.4	51.5	86.9	118.5	156.6	210.5	252.7	284.5	300.3	316.1	307.2	270.2	237.1	237.1	252.1	247.4
75～79	21.3	36.3	81.8	126.1	160.9	238.3	329.1	403.1	419.7	454.6	451.9	445.5	384.4	340.1	331.7	317.2
80～84	8.4	27.0	62.1	105.9	127.0	191.7	321.4	430.0	515.0	575.6	596.2	601.7	596.0	518.8	503.4	478.2
85～89	-	17.7	33.2	44.9	86.8	140.0	246.9	442.6	531.3	611.0	660.0	706.1	729.0	717.0	703.7	686.5
90～94[1]	23.5	-	60.5	14.6	40.1	69.2	223.1	275.4	384.2	563.7	576.3	664.6	793.6	736.0	783.3	767.6
95～99	…	…	…	…	…	…	…	…	…	…	…	617.5	698.3	698.4	783.1	765.7
100～	…	…	…	…	…	…	…	…	…	…	…	425.4	751.0	675.0	442.5	611.1

女（9－5）　02110　気管，気管支及び肺の悪性新生物
Female　　Malignant neoplasm of trachea, bronchus and lung

年齢 Age	1950 昭和25年	1955 30年	1960 35年	1965 40年	1970 45年	1975 50年	1980 55年	1985 60年	1990 平成2年	1995 7年	2000 12年	2005 17年	2010 22年	2014 26年	2015 27年	2016 28年
総数 Total	0.8	1.8	3.2	4.6	5.7	7.2	9.9	12.7	15.4	19.5	22.9	26.1	30.0	32.4	32.9	33.4
0～4 歳	-	0.0	0.0	-	-	0.0	0.0	0.0	-	0.0	0.0	-	0.1	-	-	-
5～9 Years	-	0.1	0.0	-	-	0.0	-	-	-	-	-	-	-	-	-	-
10～14	0.1	0.0	0.0	-	0.0	-	-	-	0.0	0.0	-	-	-	0.0	-	-
15～19	0.1	0.1	0.1	0.1	0.1	-	-	-	-	-	-	0.0	0.0	0.0	-	-
20～24	0.0	0.1	0.2	0.2	0.1	-	0.1	0.1	-	0.1	-	-	0.1	0.1	0.1	-
25～29	0.1	0.2	0.1	0.3	0.2	0.3	0.3	0.2	0.2	0.1	0.2	0.4	0.1	0.2	0.1	0.3
30～34	0.2	0.6	0.8	0.9	0.8	0.7	0.8	0.4	0.7	0.9	0.7	0.7	0.5	0.3	0.3	0.4
35～39	0.4	1.1	1.3	1.8	1.2	1.7	1.7	1.8	2.0	1.7	1.9	1.5	1.2	0.8	1.0	0.9
40～44	0.8	1.9	1.8	2.7	2.9	2.4	2.9	3.3	3.1	3.8	3.8	2.1	2.3	2.1	2.1	1.7
45～49	1.1	3.0	4.9	3.9	5.2	5.4	5.1	5.3	5.7	7.2	5.9	5.1	4.5	4.6	3.8	3.7
50～54	2.7	4.4	6.4	9.3	8.0	9.4	9.6	9.4	10.4	12.3	12.8	10.9	8.6	7.4	7.2	7.2
55～59	3.6	6.6	10.5	14.1	14.2	15.9	15.9	16.4	15.7	18.2	18.2	17.8	15.9	15.3	14.7	12.8
60～64	4.1	9.4	16.7	20.7	24.5	23.3	27.4	28.0	25.3	26.5	26.9	26.3	28.0	27.6	25.1	25.2
65～69	5.0	13.2	22.1	27.8	32.0	35.8	42.1	43.6	42.7	41.8	42.8	38.5	42.8	45.2	43.4	42.4
70～74	5.9	14.1	23.3	35.9	41.3	51.1	63.7	66.1	69.3	64.4	62.6	63.1	61.6	62.7	64.4	65.5
75～79	4.5	9.4	25.4	41.8	46.7	58.5	84.4	96.8	99.6	109.0	97.6	92.6	90.8	89.0	89.5	86.8
80～84	3.3	6.5	19.8	31.7	47.6	55.2	90.4	117.9	119.8	142.9	144.6	140.9	134.0	134.2	132.8	132.0
85～89	-	5.2	14.9	19.4	27.2	56.3	69.8	121.3	155.1	170.7	188.7	187.9	190.4	178.8	178.7	179.1
90～94[1]	8.3	-	20.9	8.1	20.7	33.4	61.7	95.1	137.1	178.1	209.1	226.8	230.4	219.9	226.4	226.0
95～99	…	…	…	…	…	…	…	…	…	…	…	226.6	285.1	248.4	267.8	263.9
100～	…	…	…	…	…	…	…	…	…	…	…	282.4	228.7	203.9	204.2	228.1

年齢・年次別死亡率（人口10万対）（つづき）
from malignant neoplasms by sex, age and site : Japan−CON.

男（7−6）　　02119　白血病
Male　　Leukaemia

年齢 Age	1950 昭和25年	1955 30年	1960 35年	1965 40年	1970 45年	1975 50年	1980 55年	1985 60年	1990 平成2年	1995 7年	2000 12年	2005 17年	2010 22年	2014 26年	2015 27年	2016 28年
総数 Total	1.8	2.8	3.2	3.7	4.0	4.2	4.6	5.1	5.4	6.0	6.5	7.0	7.9	8.0	8.4	8.9
0〜4 歳	2.4	4.1	4.5	4.4	4.6	3.9	2.8	1.3	1.4	1.1	1.0	0.9	1.0	0.8	0.5	0.6
5〜9 Years	1.5	2.8	2.9	3.7	3.5	3.5	3.3	2.6	1.4	1.5	0.9	0.9	0.4	0.7	0.6	0.5
10〜14	1.5	2.3	2.8	3.0	2.2	2.3	2.6	2.2	2.0	1.5	0.9	0.8	0.8	0.7	0.7	0.4
15〜19	1.7	2.5	2.8	3.3	3.2	2.8	2.5	2.7	2.2	2.4	1.2	1.1	0.9	0.8	0.8	0.8
20〜24	1.2	2.1	2.4	2.7	2.5	2.6	2.0	2.2	2.3	1.8	1.2	1.4	1.2	0.9	1.0	0.6
25〜29	1.3	2.3	2.2	2.6	2.7	2.4	2.8	2.1	2.1	1.9	1.6	0.9	1.3	1.0	0.9	0.9
30〜34	1.7	2.2	2.4	2.4	2.9	3.4	2.4	2.8	2.2	1.9	1.5	1.4	1.0	1.2	1.1	1.1
35〜39	1.7	2.6	2.5	3.2	3.5	3.5	3.5	3.4	3.1	2.4	2.6	1.9	1.0	0.8	1.0	1.0
40〜44	1.9	3.4	3.5	3.0	3.8	4.0	4.0	3.8	3.5	3.5	3.3	1.7	2.0	1.7	1.5	1.6
45〜49	2.1	3.0	3.7	4.6	5.0	4.9	4.9	4.8	4.3	4.1	4.0	3.2	2.6	2.4	2.1	2.3
50〜54	2.3	2.8	4.0	4.9	5.1	5.6	5.7	5.8	6.0	5.4	5.9	4.0	4.4	3.2	2.9	3.6
55〜59	1.9	3.3	5.4	5.2	6.2	6.4	7.1	7.5	8.3	8.2	6.9	7.0	6.1	5.6	5.5	5.6
60〜64	2.5	3.2	4.6	7.1	7.4	8.5	8.4	10.2	11.9	11.0	10.8	10.5	10.1	9.1	9.5	8.8
65〜69	2.0	3.0	5.0	7.0	8.9	10.2	12.5	14.6	13.2	16.4	17.2	15.4	15.7	13.6	14.3	15.8
70〜74	0.7	2.9	5.6	5.2	9.7	11.7	16.8	20.4	18.2	21.1	21.7	23.0	22.2	22.1	21.6	22.2
75〜79	1.9	1.8	3.2	5.1	8.1	13.1	19.6	25.8	24.5	27.7	28.7	31.2	34.1	31.1	33.0	34.6
80〜84	1.0	0.8	4.1	2.1	4.2	10.4	21.1	25.6	33.0	33.7	35.9	39.0	43.6	41.6	43.3	45.7
85〜89	-	-	-	3.3	2.8	6.9	18.8	24.5	31.5	41.5	43.4	47.2	49.6	48.7	50.5	52.5
90〜94[1]	-	-	12.1	-	5.7	4.6	12.1	21.7	30.7	56.5	38.0	47.9	47.7	45.0	55.4	53.6
95〜99	...	...	...	...	...	...	...	...	...	...	...	41.0	42.9	50.0	39.4	43.3
100〜	...	...	...	...	...	...	...	...	...	...	...	26.6	68.3	62.5	59.8	55.6

女（9−6）　　02119　白血病
Female　　Leukaemia

年齢 Age	1950 昭和25年	1955 30年	1960 35年	1965 40年	1970 45年	1975 50年	1980 55年	1985 60年	1990 平成2年	1995 7年	2000 12年	2005 17年	2010 22年	2014 26年	2015 27年	2016 28年
総数 Total	1.2	1.8	2.4	2.8	3.0	3.3	3.3	3.6	3.9	3.9	4.4	4.6	5.0	5.1	5.5	5.3
0〜4 歳	2.0	2.7	3.7	3.5	3.6	3.1	2.0	1.4	1.4	1.2	0.9	0.7	0.5	0.4	0.5	0.5
5〜9 Years	1.0	1.8	2.2	2.7	2.8	2.7	2.3	1.7	1.4	0.9	0.7	0.6	0.5	0.5	0.5	0.2
10〜14	1.1	1.8	2.1	2.4	2.3	1.9	1.9	1.6	1.2	0.9	0.4	0.8	0.8	0.5	0.7	0.4
15〜19	1.0	1.4	2.0	2.6	2.3	2.2	2.2	1.7	1.2	0.9	1.0	0.8	0.6	0.4	0.6	0.3
20〜24	1.0	1.4	2.1	1.8	2.0	2.0	1.7	1.3	1.2	1.3	1.1	0.9	0.6	0.5	0.4	0.4
25〜29	1.1	1.9	1.7	2.0	1.8	2.1	1.5	1.5	1.3	1.0	1.0	0.9	0.9	0.8	0.6	0.5
30〜34	0.7	1.2	2.6	2.1	1.6	2.5	2.2	1.9	1.6	1.4	1.1	0.9	0.8	0.5	0.9	0.9
35〜39	1.3	1.7	2.4	2.8	2.7	2.4	2.5	2.3	2.5	1.8	1.3	0.9	0.9	0.8	0.7	0.9
40〜44	1.0	2.3	2.6	2.9	3.0	3.1	3.4	3.0	2.6	2.3	2.1	1.4	1.1	1.0	1.0	1.2
45〜49	1.5	2.2	3.3	3.3	4.2	3.5	3.3	3.6	3.7	3.0	2.9	2.1	1.8	1.4	1.3	1.6
50〜54	1.6	1.9	2.3	3.7	3.0	4.1	4.5	4.7	4.3	3.7	3.6	2.5	2.2	1.8	2.4	2.0
55〜59	1.2	2.3	2.9	4.1	5.6	5.6	4.3	5.4	5.6	5.3	4.5	4.2	3.6	2.7	3.2	2.8
60〜64	1.4	1.9	2.9	4.6	5.0	5.4	6.0	6.4	6.5	5.8	6.2	5.4	4.9	4.8	4.6	4.9
65〜69	1.1	1.7	3.3	3.8	5.2	6.8	7.1	7.6	8.2	6.9	8.9	7.9	7.1	7.0	6.9	6.6
70〜74	0.8	1.3	1.8	3.3	5.6	6.4	8.4	9.9	10.6	11.3	11.3	10.4	10.5	10.6	11.2	10.0
75〜79	-	0.4	2.2	3.1	2.6	8.6	9.4	12.9	12.0	13.9	14.3	15.4	16.0	14.6	17.0	14.9
80〜84	-	-	1.0	1.2	3.4	4.6	8.7	12.5	17.9	15.8	17.6	19.7	19.6	21.1	20.0	19.6
85〜89	-	-	-	-	-	4.8	5.9	12.7	15.1	19.1	20.2	22.4	23.4	21.9	24.4	24.6
90〜94[1]	-	-	-	-	-	-	5.8	10.0	9.6	17.2	21.0	23.6	23.6	23.5	26.0	24.4
95〜99	...	...	...	...	...	...	...	...	...	...	...	17.1	25.7	28.0	23.2	24.1
100〜	...	...	...	...	...	...	...	...	...	...	...	13.9	15.8	11.8	16.9	10.5

死　亡

表 5.25　悪性新生物の主な部位別にみた性・
Table 5.25　Trends in death rates (per 100,000 population)

男（7 − 7）　02104, 02105　大腸の悪性新生物
Male　Malignant neoplasm of colon and rectosigmoid junction and rectum

年　　齢 Age	1950 昭和25年	1955 30年	1960 35年	1965 40年	1970 45年	1975 50年	1980 55年	1985 60年	1990 平成2年	1995 7年	2000 12年	2005 17年	2010 22年	2014 26年	2015 27年	2016 28年
総　数 Total	4.5	4.7	5.2	6.8	8.5	10.6	13.5	17.1	22.1	28.4	32.3	35.9	38.9	42.9	43.9	**44.4**
0 〜 4 歳	0.1	0.0	0.0	0.0	-	0.0	-	-	-	-	-	-	-	-	-	-
5 〜 9 Years	-	0.0	0.0	-	-	-	-	-	-	-	0.0	-	-	-	-	-
10〜14	0.0	0.0	0.0	0.1	-	0.0	0.0	0.0	0.0	-	0.0	0.1	0.0	0.0	-	-
15〜19	0.2	0.1	0.2	0.3	0.2	0.2	0.1	-	0.1	0.0	0.1	0.1	0.0	0.1	0.0	0.1
20〜24	0.2	0.2	0.4	0.7	0.9	0.5	0.3	0.4	0.3	0.2	0.3	0.2	0.4	0.3	0.4	0.2
25〜29	0.8	0.7	0.6	1.1	1.8	1.2	0.9	0.7	0.6	0.6	0.6	0.3	0.3	0.4	0.5	0.5
30〜34	1.1	1.1	1.1	1.8	2.3	2.3	2.1	1.7	1.5	1.5	1.3	1.2	1.2	0.9	1.2	1.2
35〜39	2.1	2.1	1.4	2.1	3.6	4.0	4.3	2.9	3.0	2.5	2.0	2.3	1.6	2.3	2.3	2.2
40〜44	3.3	3.4	3.2	3.7	5.1	6.3	6.2	6.3	6.0	5.0	5.1	4.6	4.6	4.3	4.8	3.9
45〜49	6.6	6.6	4.9	7.0	7.9	8.8	10.9	11.0	12.1	11.1	10.3	9.2	8.2	8.2	7.7	8.1
50〜54	10.5	7.9	8.3	11.2	12.2	13.2	16.4	20.3	21.5	23.0	21.1	20.0	17.1	15.8	16.3	15.8
55〜59	17.4	14.7	14.9	17.9	20.9	24.1	25.2	34.2	38.8	40.6	39.0	33.7	32.7	31.1	30.7	30.3
60〜64	27.8	27.3	26.8	28.8	30.8	36.4	39.9	47.3	59.7	65.2	62.5	56.0	53.3	59.9	56.0	55.5
65〜69	38.1	38.7	37.9	46.0	53.1	58.7	64.9	67.4	80.6	97.5	93.7	85.6	79.4	84.5	80.1	83.8
70〜74	49.4	58.8	62.1	65.3	71.3	83.7	101.5	106.7	109.9	129.7	131.5	123.1	114.1	113.7	116.2	115.3
75〜79	56.4	62.6	69.0	81.4	100.0	118.3	136.1	156.0	150.4	173.1	167.9	173.6	159.4	159.5	157.1	153.5
80〜84	36.6	54.8	71.5	101.6	110.2	148.4	182.4	205.8	236.9	255.5	244.2	233.1	231.6	215.2	219.4	213.2
85〜89	32.6	59.1	80.9	98.1	98.0	142.9	180.5	249.5	288.1	332.1	329.7	334.8	316.3	300.8	317.3	305.6
90〜94[1]	-	17.2	109.0	36.4	68.7	106.2	183.9	175.7	321.6	417.4	431.6	421.5	401.3	382.0	420.6	404.2
95〜99	…	…	…	…	…	…	…	…	…	…	…	513.8	517.9	456.5	513.6	532.8
100〜	…	…	…	…	…	…	…	…	…	…	…	585.0	477.9	375.0	430.6	455.6

女（9 − 7）　02104, 02105　大腸の悪性新生物
Female　Malignant neoplasm of colon and rectosigmoid junction and rectum

年　　齢 Age	1950 昭和25年	1955 30年	1960 35年	1965 40年	1970 45年	1975 50年	1980 55年	1985 60年	1990 平成2年	1995 7年	2000 12年	2005 17年	2010 22年	2014 26年	2015 27年	2016 28年
総　数 Total	4.5	4.8	5.6	6.7	8.0	10.0	11.9	14.6	18.2	22.0	25.1	28.9	31.3	34.6	35.6	**36.0**
0 〜 4 歳	0.1	0.1	0.1	-	0.0	-	-	-	-	-	-	-	-	-	-	-
5 〜 9 Years	-	-	-	0.1	-	-	-	-	-	-	-	-	-	-	-	-
10〜14	-	-	0.0	0.0	-	0.0	0.0	-	0.0	-	0.0	-	-	-	0.0	-
15〜19	-	0.1	0.1	0.0	-	0.1	0.1	0.0	-	0.0	0.0	0.1	0.0	0.0	0.1	0.1
20〜24	0.2	0.4	0.2	0.9	0.3	0.2	0.4	0.2	0.4	0.1	0.3	0.1	0.1	0.2	0.1	0.0
25〜29	0.6	0.5	0.6	0.9	1.4	1.0	0.8	0.8	0.3	0.3	0.4	0.4	0.4	0.2	0.6	0.2
30〜34	1.5	0.9	1.0	1.6	2.1	2.5	1.7	1.3	1.4	1.0	1.1	1.2	0.9	0.9	0.6	0.8
35〜39	2.6	2.0	2.4	2.1	3.0	3.8	3.4	2.6	2.7	2.6	1.8	2.1	2.1	2.0	1.9	2.3
40〜44	4.9	4.6	3.4	4.0	4.5	5.4	5.3	5.8	4.8	5.1	3.8	4.2	4.1	4.2	3.9	3.7
45〜49	6.7	5.7	6.3	7.0	6.6	8.3	8.4	9.3	10.2	9.3	7.8	7.4	6.5	6.8	6.5	6.8
50〜54	10.8	10.5	9.3	10.9	12.2	12.9	13.7	15.4	15.5	15.9	15.3	14.3	12.2	12.8	11.6	12.2
55〜59	17.6	15.6	16.0	15.6	15.8	19.4	19.2	21.2	23.6	22.9	23.3	21.4	19.7	20.6	19.2	19.5
60〜64	24.2	22.6	22.6	22.3	23.6	25.4	28.2	30.6	33.1	33.6	32.8	30.3	27.7	31.2	30.2	29.2
65〜69	33.8	31.8	32.7	35.1	37.3	39.4	40.1	43.3	46.5	46.9	45.0	44.4	38.5	40.1	39.3	39.7
70〜74	36.7	41.3	51.0	55.2	65.1	64.8	63.2	65.3	67.5	66.9	68.3	60.6	57.1	53.6	56.7	57.2
75〜79	31.6	46.8	58.5	71.4	83.8	85.8	95.7	95.7	96.4	97.6	92.4	89.9	82.3	82.5	82.3	78.3
80〜84	32.7	42.1	58.0	73.6	89.1	110.8	121.1	132.1	141.3	152.6	141.2	140.8	128.0	122.0	126.7	123.2
85〜89	23.8	32.3	51.1	62.6	78.5	96.7	129.2	153.7	186.2	214.6	207.4	210.3	208.4	208.3	200.5	199.6
90〜94[1]	33.0	35.4	33.4	45.9	37.3	90.1	105.9	156.4	201.8	262.9	288.9	311.4	306.9	303.4	318.9	310.8
95〜99	…	…	…	…	…	…	…	…	…	…	…	343.3	387.8	351.2	385.5	380.4
100〜	…	…	…	…	…	…	…	…	…	…	…	277.8	318.1	337.3	389.6	366.7

注：結腸と直腸S状結腸移行部及び直腸を示す。ただし、昭和42年までは直腸肛門部を含む。

General mortality

年齢・年次別死亡率（人口10万対）（つづき）
from malignant neoplasms by sex, age and site : Japan－CON.

女（9－8）　02112　乳房の悪性新生物
Female　　Malignant neoplasm of breast

年　　齢 Age	1950 昭和25年	1955 30年	1960 35年	1965 40年	1970 45年	1975 50年	1980 55年	1985 60年	1990 平成2年	1995 7年	2000 12年	2005 17年	2010 22年	2014 26年	2015 27年	2016 28年
総　数 Total	3.3	3.5	3.5	3.9	4.7	5.8	7.0	8.0	9.4	12.2	14.3	16.6	19.2	20.6	21.1	21.8
0～4 歳	-	-	-	-	-	-	-	-	-	-	-	-	-	-	-	-
5～9 Years	-	-	-	-	-	-	-	-	-	-	-	-	-	-	-	-
10～14	-	0.0	-	-	-	0.0	-	-	-	0.0	-	-	-	-	-	-
15～19	-	0.0	0.0	0.0	-	-	-	-	-	-	-	-	-	-	0.0	-
20～24	0.1	0.1	0.0	0.0	0.1	0.2	0.1	0.1	0.0	0.1	0.1	0.1	0.0	0.0	0.2	0.0
25～29	0.4	0.5	0.4	0.5	0.6	0.5	1.0	0.8	0.8	0.6	0.5	0.5	0.5	0.4	0.7	0.6
30～34	1.8	1.8	1.6	1.7	2.0	2.3	2.5	3.0	2.6	2.4	2.3	2.6	2.0	1.9	2.4	2.4
35～39	3.6	4.3	4.1	4.0	4.2	4.6	5.5	5.5	6.4	7.3	7.3	6.0	5.0	5.5	4.3	5.3
40～44	7.0	6.4	6.4	6.8	7.2	8.6	8.6	9.5	10.8	12.4	12.5	12.2	10.7	8.7	9.6	9.5
45～49	9.0	8.7	9.5	9.4	10.6	12.3	13.3	13.1	15.8	18.6	20.2	19.6	17.6	16.3	16.6	16.5
50～54	10.9	10.1	9.6	12.6	13.2	17.1	17.2	18.0	19.2	26.6	28.4	28.8	28.8	26.0	26.7	28.3
55～59	13.6	11.6	11.5	12.6	14.2	16.4	19.9	20.7	22.5	25.3	29.9	34.5	37.9	34.9	32.8	34.0
60～64	15.2	13.6	10.3	11.9	14.0	15.8	17.2	19.9	20.2	24.0	26.5	31.1	35.8	38.5	38.9	37.2
65～69	15.0	14.7	11.9	12.9	12.5	14.6	18.2	19.1	19.6	25.0	26.3	28.1	34.2	37.2	37.3	38.7
70～74	14.8	16.9	15.6	12.6	15.3	14.8	18.0	19.7	20.1	22.0	24.7	27.6	31.1	36.6	37.7	38.1
75～79	17.0	18.4	17.8	12.7	14.4	15.4	18.2	18.0	18.5	24.7	27.8	30.7	33.9	36.6	37.6	38.4
80～84	15.5	18.0	21.7	17.0	23.3	18.2	20.2	19.2	20.9	26.4	27.9	34.9	38.4	39.7	40.7	44.1
85～89	14.7	23.2	28.8	15.8	31.0	22.6	22.9	26.6	23.2	30.0	35.1	37.9	50.4	51.5	54.2	52.0
90～94[1]	16.5	23.6	25.1	37.8	26.9	30.0	24.4	26.1	23.6	39.4	41.0	49.3	64.0	67.6	71.4	76.8
95～99	…	…	…	…	…	…	…	…	…	…	…	61.2	77.4	88.6	89.1	100.3
100～	…	…	…	…	…	…	…	…	…	…	…	46.3	99.9	100.0	121.8	128.1

女（9－9）　02113　子宮の悪性新生物
Female　　Malignant neoplasm of uterus

年　　齢 Age	1950 昭和25年	1955 30年	1960 35年	1965 40年	1970 45年	1975 50年	1980 55年	1985 60年	1990 平成2年	1995 7年	2000 12年	2005 17年	2010 22年	2014 26年	2015 27年	2016 28年
総　数 Total	19.7	16.0	14.9	13.4	12.1	10.7	9.2	8.0	7.4	7.7	8.1	8.3	9.1	10.0	10.0	9.9
0～4 歳	0.0	0.0	0.0	-	0.0	-	-	-	-	-	-	-	-	-	-	-
5～9 Years	-	-	0.0	-	-	-	-	-	-	-	-	-	-	-	-	-
10～14	-	0.1	-	0.1	-	-	-	0.0	-	-	-	-	-	-	-	-
15～19	0.1	0.1	0.2	0.1	0.2	-	-	0.0	-	-	-	-	-	-	-	-
20～24	0.8	0.5	0.8	0.6	0.2	0.3	0.2	0.1	0.3	-	0.2	0.1	0.0	0.1	0.1	0.1
25～29	3.0	2.3	2.3	1.7	1.2	0.5	0.6	0.5	0.5	0.5	0.6	0.7	0.6	0.7	0.6	0.7
30～34	8.8	5.1	4.5	3.8	2.6	1.7	1.1	1.3	1.0	1.6	1.8	1.6	2.1	1.9	2.1	1.8
35～39	23.5	12.4	9.9	7.3	5.6	2.9	2.2	1.9	2.4	2.3	3.6	2.9	3.2	3.2	3.4	3.4
40～44	43.8	27.0	19.0	13.7	11.9	7.1	4.7	3.9	3.2	3.8	4.0	5.5	5.3	5.4	4.8	5.2
45～49	62.7	43.7	34.5	23.5	19.5	14.8	9.5	7.1	5.4	5.9	7.1	6.8	7.2	9.1	8.4	7.7
50～54	76.8	58.8	46.9	36.5	26.8	22.1	14.9	10.9	7.9	8.3	9.0	10.2	10.4	12.1	12.1	12.0
55～59	80.3	65.6	55.7	46.6	37.1	28.7	21.0	14.2	12.3	11.0	12.4	11.8	12.6	14.0	14.3	13.6
60～64	84.1	70.2	64.7	57.0	49.3	36.9	27.8	20.6	14.3	13.4	12.1	12.1	13.8	14.6	14.6	13.8
65～69	85.5	71.9	68.0	63.3	52.5	47.5	35.7	26.8	20.0	16.1	13.7	13.8	14.3	15.5	15.4	15.3
70～74	72.2	79.9	71.9	65.5	61.9	57.0	43.8	32.7	25.2	21.7	18.5	16.5	16.2	16.4	17.5	16.4
75～79	53.6	65.8	71.6	70.2	62.3	59.5	54.2	42.2	34.1	27.2	23.5	19.8	18.9	18.5	18.5	19.3
80～84	52.2	50.3	51.9	66.2	59.4	56.6	64.5	55.7	47.2	39.1	32.8	26.4	25.2	25.3	23.6	22.9
85～89	20.2	36.1	49.2	41.7	52.6	53.4	55.0	54.7	51.7	54.5	42.2	32.5	32.8	30.9	28.9	31.1
90～94[1]	33.0	53.1	16.7	29.7	33.1	48.4	48.9	47.5	52.0	60.0	53.8	43.9	39.6	35.4	36.9	32.6
95～99	…	…	…	…	…	…	…	…	…	…	…	49.4	42.2	34.9	39.0	32.9
100～	…	…	…	…	…	…	…	…	…	…	…	37.0	34.2	29.4	22.5	28.1

死　亡

表5.26　悪性新生物の主な部位別にみた性・
Table 5.26　Trends in age-adjusted death rates (per 100,000 population)

男
Male

死因簡単分類コード Code[a]	死因 Causes of death	1950 昭和25年	1955 30年	1960 35年	1965 40年	1970 45年	1975 50年	1980 55年	1985 60年	1990 平成2年
02100	悪性新生物	148.2	167.9	188.2	195.6	199.2	198.9	210.9	214.8	215.6
02101	口唇，口腔及び咽頭の悪性新生物	2.1	1.7	1.8	1.9	2.2	2.4	2.7	2.8	3.0
02102	食道の悪性新生物	9.5	9.3	9.6	10.1	11.4	10.3	10.3	9.8	9.8
02103	胃の悪性新生物	87.3	94.4	98.5	96.0	88.9	79.4	69.9	58.7	49.5
02104	結腸の悪性新生物	2.9	3.1	3.6	4.3	5.2	7.0	8.7	10.8	12.9
02105	直腸S状結腸移行部及び直腸の悪性新生物	5.6	6.0	5.9	7.0	7.7	8.3	8.8	8.9	9.0
02106	肝及び肝内胆管の悪性新生物	} 16.6	} 20.2	19.4	17.0	17.6	17.1	21.3	25.7	28.4
02107	胆のう及びその他の胆道の悪性新生物			2.1	3.4	4.1	5.1	6.5	7.9	8.5
02108	膵の悪性新生物	1.4	2.4	4.1	5.6	7.4	8.0	10.0	11.5	12.1
02109	喉頭の悪性新生物	2.7	2.3	2.2	2.2	2.4	2.0	1.7	1.5	1.3
02110	気管，気管支及び肺の悪性新生物	3.6	7.8	13.6	18.1	22.5	28.1	35.5	41.2	45.0
02111	皮膚の悪性新生物	1.5	1.3	1.3	1.2	1.3	1.0	0.8	0.7	0.6
02115	前立腺の悪性新生物	0.5	1.3	2.2	2.8	3.2	3.8	4.4	5.5	6.0
02116	膀胱の悪性新生物	…	…	2.9	3.2	3.4	3.4	3.9	3.5	3.6
02117	中枢神経系の悪性新生物[1]	…	…	0.4	0.5	0.4	0.5	1.0	1.1	1.1
02118	悪性リンパ腫	…	…	…	…	…	…	…	…	…
02119	白血病	1.8	2.7	3.4	3.9	4.3	4.7	5.1	5.4	5.3
02120	その他のリンパ組織，造血組織及び関連組織の悪性新生物	…	…	…	…	…	…	…	…	…
（再掲）02104, 02105	大腸の悪性新生物[2]	8.6	9.0	9.5	11.3	12.9	15.2	17.6	19.6	21.9

女
Female

死因簡単分類コード Code[a]	死因 Causes of death	1950 昭和25年	1955 30年	1960 35年	1965 40年	1970 45年	1975 50年	1980 55年	1985 60年	1990 平成2年
02100	悪性新生物	121.4	125.4	132.0	130.3	126.9	121.1	118.8	113.1	107.7
02101	口唇，口腔及び咽頭の悪性新生物	1.1	0.8	0.9	0.9	0.9	1.0	1.0	0.9	0.9
02102	食道の悪性新生物	3.2	3.2	3.3	3.2	2.9	2.4	2.2	1.6	1.5
02103	胃の悪性新生物	48.0	50.8	51.8	49.4	46.5	39.8	34.1	27.4	21.6
02104	結腸の悪性新生物	3.3	3.2	3.6	4.3	5.0	6.0	7.1	8.3	9.3
02105	直腸S状結腸移行部及び直腸の悪性新生物	4.2	4.5	4.8	5.1	5.2	5.7	5.1	4.7	4.5
02106	肝及び肝内胆管の悪性新生物	} 10.3	} 13.2	11.6	9.9	8.8	7.6	7.4	7.5	7.8
02107	胆のう及びその他の胆道の悪性新生物			1.9	3.0	4.3	5.3	6.6	7.9	8.0
02108	膵の悪性新生物	0.8	1.6	2.5	3.6	4.5	5.1	5.8	6.5	7.1
02109	喉頭の悪性新生物	0.9	0.6	0.6	0.5	0.4	0.3	0.2	0.1	0.1
02110	気管，気管支及び肺の悪性新生物	1.3	2.8	4.8	6.5	7.3	8.3	10.2	11.2	11.6
02111	皮膚の悪性新生物	0.9	1.0	1.0	0.9	0.8	0.7	0.5	0.4	0.4
02112	乳房の悪性新生物	5.4	5.3	5.1	5.2	5.8	6.5	7.2	7.6	8.2
02113	子宮の悪性新生物[3]	31.0	24.6	21.3	18.0	15.1	12.4	9.5	7.3	5.8
02114	卵巣の悪性新生物	1.2	1.4	1.7	2.1	2.5	3.0	3.7	4.1	4.4
02116	膀胱の悪性新生物	…	…	1.4	1.3	1.4	1.4	1.3	1.2	1.0
02117	中枢神経系の悪性新生物[1]	…	…	0.3	0.3	0.3	0.4	0.7	0.7	0.8
02118	悪性リンパ腫	…	…	…	…	…	…	…	…	…
02119	白血病	1.1	1.8	2.5	2.9	3.1	3.4	3.3	3.4	3.4
02120	その他のリンパ組織，造血組織及び関連組織の悪性新生物	…	…	…	…	…	…	…	…	…
（再掲）02104, 02105	大腸の悪性新生物[2]	7.5	7.7	8.4	9.4	10.3	11.7	12.2	13.0	13.8

注：年齢調整死亡率の基準人口は、昭和60年モデル人口である。なお、計算方法は、68ページ　3）死亡を参照されたい。
　1）　昭和42年以前の「中枢神経系」は、松果体を含まない。
　2）　結腸と直腸S状結腸移行部及び直腸を示す。ただし、昭和42年までは直腸肛門部を含む。
　3）　平成6年以前の「子宮」は、胎盤を含む。

年次別年齢調整死亡率（人口10万対）
from malignant neoplasms by sex and site : Japan

男
Male

1995 7年	2000 12年	2005 17年	2006 18年	2007 19年	2008 20年	2009 21年	2010 22年	2011 23年	2012 24年	2013 25年	2014 26年	2015 27年	2016 28年	死因簡単分類コード Code[a]
226.1	214.0	197.7	193.6	191.5	188.9	183.3	182.4	179.4	175.7	172.5	168.9	165.3	**161.7**	02100
4.2	4.4	4.4	4.5	4.6	4.7	4.5	4.5	4.5	4.6	4.4	4.5	4.3	**4.5**	02101
10.1	10.4	9.7	9.7	9.7	9.6	9.2	9.1	9.0	8.5	8.2	8.0	7.9	**7.6**	02102
45.4	39.1	32.7	31.9	31.1	30.0	29.0	28.2	27.4	26.1	25.2	24.1	22.9	**21.6**	02103
14.8	14.4	13.4	13.3	13.2	13.2	12.5	12.8	13.0	13.0	12.8	12.8	12.9	**12.6**	02104
9.7	9.3	9.0	8.8	8.7	8.6	8.0	8.2	8.5	8.4	8.3	8.2	8.1	**8.1**	02105
31.6	28.2	23.7	22.4	21.5	20.9	19.7	19.0	18.0	16.7	16.0	15.0	14.5	**13.7**	02106
8.8	8.2	7.6	7.4	7.2	7.2	7.2	6.9	7.0	6.8	6.6	6.5	6.3	**6.0**	02107
12.7	12.4	12.6	12.5	12.6	12.9	12.9	13.0	13.0	13.3	13.3	13.3	12.8	**13.3**	02108
1.2	1.1	1.0	0.9	0.9	0.8	0.8	0.8	0.7	0.7	0.7	0.7	0.6	**0.6**	02109
47.5	46.3	44.6	44.0	44.0	43.5	42.5	42.4	41.7	41.0	40.4	39.7	39.2	**37.6**	02110
0.6	0.6	0.6	0.6	0.6	0.6	0.6	0.6	0.6	0.6	0.6	0.6	0.6	**0.6**	02111
7.7	8.6	8.5	8.4	8.2	8.1	7.7	8.0	7.8	7.6	7.7	7.3	7.0	**7.1**	02115
3.9	3.7	3.9	3.8	3.7	3.7	3.6	3.6	3.6	3.6	3.7	3.6	3.7	**3.7**	02116
1.4	1.2	1.1	1.2	1.1	1.2	1.2	1.3	1.4	1.4	1.4	1.5	1.5	**1.6**	02117
5.4	5.6	4.9	5.0	5.0	5.0	5.1	5.0	4.9	5.0	5.0	4.9	4.9	**5.0**	02118
5.4	5.2	4.8	4.7	4.8	4.7	4.7	4.7	4.5	4.4	4.3	4.3	4.3	**4.5**	02119
2.2	2.1	2.0	1.8	1.9	1.9	1.8	1.8	1.7	1.7	1.6	1.7	1.5	**1.6**	02120
24.4	23.7	22.4	22.1	21.9	21.7	20.5	21.0	21.4	21.4	21.1	21.0	21.0	**20.7**	（再掲）02104, 02105

女
Female

1995 7年	2000 12年	2005 17年	2006 18年	2007 19年	2008 20年	2009 21年	2010 22年	2011 23年	2012 24年	2013 25年	2014 26年	2015 27年	2016 28年	死因簡単分類コード Code[a]
108.3	103.5	97.3	95.8	94.5	94.2	92.2	92.2	91.8	90.3	89.7	89.4	87.7	**87.3**	02100
1.1	1.3	1.1	1.2	1.2	1.2	1.2	1.2	1.2	1.2	1.1	1.2	1.1	**1.2**	02101
1.3	1.3	1.3	1.2	1.3	1.2	1.2	1.2	1.2	1.2	1.2	1.2	1.2	**1.2**	02102
18.5	15.3	12.5	12.0	11.5	11.0	10.7	10.2	9.9	9.6	9.2	9.0	8.3	**8.0**	02103
9.9	9.5	9.3	9.0	8.8	8.6	8.6	8.6	8.7	8.7	8.8	8.8	8.8	**8.6**	02104
4.3	4.1	3.8	3.7	3.8	3.7	3.5	3.5	3.4	3.6	3.4	3.5	3.4	**3.4**	02105
9.1	8.8	7.7	7.4	7.3	7.0	6.6	6.4	6.0	5.6	5.2	5.1	4.6	**4.6**	02106
7.2	6.3	5.4	5.3	5.1	4.9	4.8	4.7	4.5	4.4	4.3	4.0	3.9	**3.8**	02107
7.0	7.2	7.5	7.4	7.6	7.9	8.0	8.2	8.4	8.4	8.4	8.5	8.4	**8.6**	02108
0.1	0.1	0.1	0.0	0.1	0.1	0.0	0.0	0.0	0.1	0.0	0.0	0.0	**0.0**	02109
12.5	12.3	11.7	11.7	11.7	11.7	11.4	11.5	11.4	11.4	11.4	11.4	11.1	**11.0**	02110
0.4	0.4	0.4	0.4	0.4	0.4	0.4	0.4	0.4	0.5	0.4	0.4	0.4	**0.4**	02111
9.9	10.7	11.4	11.7	11.6	11.9	11.8	11.9	12.1	11.5	12.0	11.8	12.0	**12.2**	02112
5.4	5.3	5.1	5.1	5.1	5.2	5.0	5.3	5.4	5.4	5.3	5.7	5.6	**5.5**	02113
4.6	4.3	4.4	4.3	4.2	4.3	4.3	4.3	4.3	4.2	4.1	4.2	4.0	**4.0**	02114
1.1	1.0	1.0	1.0	1.0	1.0	1.0	0.9	1.0	1.0	1.0	1.0	1.0	**1.0**	02116
0.9	0.9	0.8	0.8	0.7	0.9	0.8	0.9	0.9	1.0	1.0	1.0	0.9	**1.1**	02117
2.8	3.0	2.7	2.6	2.6	2.6	2.6	2.7	2.6	2.7	2.7	2.6	2.7	**2.7**	02118
3.0	3.0	2.6	2.6	2.6	2.5	2.5	2.5	2.5	2.3	2.4	2.2	2.4	**2.2**	02119
1.4	1.4	1.4	1.3	1.3	1.3	1.2	1.2	1.1	1.1	1.1	1.1	1.1	**1.1**	02120
14.1	13.6	13.2	12.7	12.6	12.3	12.1	12.1	12.1	12.3	12.2	12.2	12.1	**12.0**	（再掲）02104, 02105

Note : a) Code see page 595.

死　亡

〔主な死因〕脳血管疾患

表 5.27　脳血管疾患の病類別にみた性・
Table 5.27　Trends in deaths, percent distribution, crude
from cerebrovascular diseases by sex and

死因簡単分類 コード Code[a]	死　因　・　性 Causes of death and sex			1951 昭和26年	1955 30年	1960 35年	1965 40年	1970 45年	1975 50年	1980 55年	1985 60年	1990 平成2年
											死	亡
09300	脳　血　管　疾　患[3]	総数	T.	105 858	121 504	150 109	172 773	181 315	174 367	162 317	134 994	121 944
		男	M.	52 388	62 737	78 965	92 723	96 910	89 924	81 650	65 287	57 627
		女	F.	53 470	58 767	71 144	80 050	84 405	84 443	80 667	69 707	64 317
09301	く　も　膜　下　出　血	総数	T.	1 587	2 649	3 634	4 533	5 278	6 575	8 066	10 257	12 281
		男	M.	767	1 324	1 824	2 323	2 677	3 164	3 633	4 133	4 856
		女	F.	820	1 325	1 810	2 210	2 601	3 411	4 433	6 124	7 425
09302	脳　内　出　血[4]	総数	T.	98 441	104 793	115 230	104 099	85 518	64 744	50 225	35 955	29 558
		男	M.	48 759	54 121	60 726	56 577	46 864	34 981	26 785	18 939	15 827
		女	F.	49 682	50 672	54 504	47 522	38 654	29 763	23 440	17 016	13 731
09303	脳　梗　塞	総数	T.	3 425	7 968	19 999	42 654	59 003	68 547	75 311	67 350	64 575
		男	M.	1 697	4 109	10 435	22 225	30 604	34 130	37 175	32 460	30 419
		女	F.	1 728	3 859	9 564	20 429	28 399	34 417	38 136	34 890	34 156
											百	分
09300	脳　血　管　疾　患[3]	総数	T.	100.0	100.0	100.0	100.0	100.0	100.0	100.0	100.0	100.0
		男	M.	100.0	100.0	100.0	100.0	100.0	100.0	100.0	100.0	100.0
		女	F.	100.0	100.0	100.0	100.0	100.0	100.0	100.0	100.0	100.0
09301	く　も　膜　下　出　血	総数	T.	1.5	2.2	2.4	2.6	2.9	3.8	5.0	7.6	10.1
		男	M.	1.5	2.1	2.3	2.5	2.8	3.5	4.4	6.3	8.4
		女	F.	1.5	2.3	2.5	2.8	3.1	4.0	5.5	8.8	11.5
09302	脳　内　出　血[4]	総数	T.	93.0	86.2	76.8	60.3	47.2	37.1	30.9	26.6	24.2
		男	M.	93.1	86.3	76.9	61.0	48.4	38.9	32.8	29.0	27.5
		女	F.	92.9	86.2	76.6	59.4	45.8	35.2	29.1	24.4	21.3
09303	脳　梗　塞	総数	T.	3.2	6.6	13.3	24.7	32.5	39.3	46.4	49.9	53.0
		男	M.	3.2	6.5	13.2	24.0	31.6	38.0	45.5	49.7	52.8
		女	F.	3.2	6.6	13.4	25.5	33.6	40.8	47.3	50.1	53.1
											粗	死
09300	脳　血　管　疾　患[3]	総数	T.	125.2	136.1	160.7	175.8	175.8	156.7	139.5	112.2	99.4
		男	M.	126.3	143.0	172.1	192.2	191.5	164.3	142.7	110.6	95.6
		女	F.	124.1	129.4	149.6	160.0	160.7	149.4	136.4	113.9	103.0
09301	く　も　膜　下　出　血	総数	T.	1.9	3.0	3.9	4.6	5.1	5.9	6.9	8.5	10.0
		男	M.	1.8	3.0	4.0	4.8	5.3	5.8	6.4	7.0	8.1
		女	F.	1.9	2.9	3.8	4.4	5.0	6.0	7.5	10.0	11.9
09302	脳　内　出　血[4]	総数	T.	116.4	117.4	123.3	105.9	82.9	58.2	43.2	29.9	24.1
		男	M.	117.5	123.4	132.4	117.3	92.6	63.9	46.8	32.0	26.3
		女	F.	115.3	111.6	114.6	95.0	73.6	52.7	39.6	27.8	22.0
09303	脳　梗　塞	総数	T.	4.0	8.9	21.4	43.4	57.2	61.6	64.7	56.0	52.6
		男	M.	4.1	9.4	22.7	46.1	60.5	62.4	65.0	55.0	50.5
		女	F.	4.0	8.5	20.1	40.8	54.1	60.9	64.5	57.0	54.7
										年　齢　調　整		死
09300	脳　血　管　疾　患[3]	男	M.	285.3	302.1	341.1	361.0	333.8	265.0	202.0	134.0	97.9
		女	F.	229.4	224.8	242.7	243.8	222.6	183.0	140.9	95.3	68.6
09301	く　も　膜　下　出　血	男	M.	2.9	4.8	6.1	7.0	7.1	7.3	7.4	7.5	7.8
		女	F.	2.9	4.4	5.5	6.0	6.1	6.9	7.7	9.1	9.4
09302	脳　内　出　血[4]	男	M.	266.7	260.1	258.5	212.2	152.0	95.7	61.9	36.9	26.1
		女	F.	213.9	194.1	185.5	143.4	100.1	63.3	40.8	24.0	15.7
09303	脳　梗　塞	男	M.	8.9	20.8	50.0	96.0	115.5	108.7	96.9	68.9	52.7
		女	F.	7.1	14.8	33.5	64.1	77.1	76.1	66.7	46.6	34.6

注：1）　粗死亡率は、年齢調整死亡率と並記したので粗死亡率と表現したが、単に死亡率とよんでいるものである。
　　2）　年齢調整死亡率の基準人口は、昭和60年モデル人口である。なお、計算方法は、68ページ　3）死亡を参照されたい。
　　3）　平成6年以前の「脳血管疾患」は、一過性脳虚血を含む。
　　4）　昭和53年以前の「脳内出血」は、非外傷性頭蓋内出血を含む。

372

General mortality

年次別死亡数・百分率・粗死亡率[1] 及び年齢調整死亡率[2] （人口10万対）
death rates and age-adjusted death rates (per 100,000 population)
disease type : Japan

	1995 7年	2000 12年	2005 17年	2006 18年	2007 19年	2008 20年	2009 21年	2010 22年	2011 23年	2012 24年	2013 25年	2014 26年	2015 27年	2016 28年
数 Deaths														
	146 552	132 529	132 847	128 268	127 041	127 023	122 350	123 461	123 867	121 602	118 347	114 207	111 973	109 320
	69 587	63 127	63 657	61 348	60 992	61 121	59 293	60 186	59 616	58 625	56 718	54 995	53 576	52 706
	76 965	69 402	69 190	66 920	66 049	65 902	63 057	63 275	64 251	62 977	61 629	59 212	58 397	56 614
	14 424	14 815	14 883	14 466	14 243	14 075	13 923	13 591	13 460	13 004	12 479	12 662	12 476	12 318
	5 477	5 544	5 689	5 456	5 349	5 317	5 229	5 258	4 980	4 913	4 723	4 713	4 643	4 556
	8 947	9 271	9 194	9 010	8 894	8 758	8 694	8 333	8 480	8 091	7 756	7 949	7 833	7 762
	33 187	31 051	33 362	33 290	33 135	33 682	33 002	33 695	34 062	33 605	32 962	32 550	32 113	31 975
	17 637	16 793	18 281	18 309	18 403	18 646	18 394	18 802	18 656	18 497	17 963	17 831	17 541	17 538
	15 550	14 258	15 081	14 981	14 732	15 036	14 608	14 893	15 406	15 108	14 999	14 719	14 572	14 437
	89 431	82 651	80 964	77 008	76 247	76 016	72 238	72 885	73 273	71 962	69 967	66 058	64 523	62 277
	42 724	39 068	38 009	35 972	35 660	35 656	34 183	34 548	34 521	33 822	32 638	31 093	30 070	29 384
	46 707	43 583	42 955	41 036	40 587	40 360	38 055	38 337	38 752	38 140	37 329	34 965	34 453	32 893
率 Percentage														
	100.0	100.0	100.0	100.0	100.0	100.0	100.0	100.0	100.0	100.0	100.0	100.0	100.0	100.0
	100.0	100.0	100.0	100.0	100.0	100.0	100.0	100.0	100.0	100.0	100.0	100.0	100.0	100.0
	100.0	100.0	100.0	100.0	100.0	100.0	100.0	100.0	100.0	100.0	100.0	100.0	100.0	100.0
	9.8	11.2	11.2	11.3	11.2	11.1	11.4	11.0	10.9	10.7	10.5	11.1	11.1	11.3
	7.9	8.8	8.9	8.9	8.8	8.7	8.8	8.7	8.4	8.4	8.3	8.6	8.7	8.6
	11.6	13.4	13.3	13.5	13.5	13.3	13.8	13.2	13.2	12.8	12.6	13.4	13.4	13.7
	22.6	23.4	25.1	26.0	26.1	26.5	27.0	27.3	27.5	27.6	27.9	28.5	28.7	29.2
	25.3	26.6	28.7	29.8	30.2	30.5	31.0	31.2	31.3	31.6	31.7	32.4	32.7	33.3
	20.2	20.5	21.8	22.4	22.3	22.8	23.2	23.5	24.0	24.0	24.3	24.9	25.0	25.5
	61.0	62.4	60.9	60.0	60.0	59.8	59.0	59.0	59.2	59.2	59.1	57.8	57.6	57.0
	61.4	61.9	59.7	58.6	58.5	58.3	57.7	57.4	57.9	57.7	57.5	56.5	56.1	55.8
	60.7	62.8	62.1	61.3	61.4	61.2	60.4	60.6	60.3	60.6	60.6	59.1	59.0	58.1
亡率 （人口10万対） Death rates (per 100,000 population)														
	117.9	105.5	105.3	101.7	100.8	100.9	97.2	97.7	98.2	96.5	94.1	91.1	89.4	87.4
	114.2	102.7	103.3	99.6	99.2	99.5	96.7	97.7	97.0	95.6	92.7	90.1	87.8	86.6
	121.4	108.2	107.1	103.6	102.3	102.1	97.8	97.6	99.3	97.4	95.5	92.0	90.8	88.2
	11.6	11.8	11.8	11.5	11.3	11.2	11.1	10.8	10.7	10.3	9.9	10.1	10.0	9.9
	9.0	9.0	9.2	8.9	8.7	8.7	8.5	8.5	8.1	8.0	7.7	7.7	7.6	7.5
	14.1	14.5	14.2	14.0	13.8	13.6	13.5	12.9	13.1	12.5	12.0	12.3	12.2	12.1
	26.7	24.7	26.4	26.4	26.3	26.7	26.2	26.7	27.0	26.7	26.2	26.0	25.6	25.6
	29.0	27.3	29.7	29.7	29.9	30.4	30.0	30.5	30.4	30.2	29.4	29.2	28.7	28.8
	24.5	22.2	23.3	23.2	22.8	23.3	22.7	23.0	23.8	23.4	23.2	22.9	22.7	22.5
	71.9	65.8	64.2	61.0	60.5	60.4	57.4	57.7	58.1	57.1	55.7	52.7	51.5	49.8
	70.1	63.5	61.7	58.4	58.0	58.0	55.7	56.1	56.2	55.1	53.3	50.9	49.3	48.3
	73.7	68.0	66.5	63.5	62.9	62.6	59.0	59.2	59.9	59.0	57.9	54.3	53.6	51.3
亡率 （人口10万対） Age-adjusted death rates (per 100,000 population)														
	99.3	74.2	61.9	57.8	55.4	53.6	50.4	49.5	47.3	44.8	42.0	39.8	37.8	36.2
	64.0	45.7	36.1	33.4	31.6	30.3	28.1	26.9	26.3	24.6	23.3	21.9	21.0	20.0
	7.9	7.1	6.7	6.3	6.1	6.0	5.8	5.7	5.3	5.2	4.9	4.8	4.7	4.6
	9.6	8.4	7.2	6.8	6.6	6.3	6.1	5.7	5.7	5.2	4.9	4.9	4.8	4.7
	25.0	20.3	19.0	18.6	18.2	17.9	17.3	17.1	16.5	15.8	15.0	14.6	14.1	13.7
	14.3	10.8	9.3	8.9	8.5	8.4	7.9	7.6	7.6	7.2	6.9	6.6	6.3	6.1
	61.1	44.7	34.5	31.3	29.6	28.4	26.0	25.4	24.3	22.7	21.0	19.4	18.1	17.0
	35.8	25.0	18.6	16.8	15.6	14.7	13.3	12.8	12.3	11.6	10.8	9.8	9.3	8.6

Note : a) Code see page 595.

死亡

〔主な死因〕心疾患（高血圧性を除く）

表 5.28 心疾患の病類別にみた性・年次別死亡数・
Table 5.28 Trends in deaths, percent distribution, crude (per 100,000 population) from heart diseases

死因簡単分類コード Code[a]	死因・性 Causes of death and sex			1950 昭和25年	1955 30年	1960 35年	1965 40年	1970 45年	1975 50年	1980 55年	1985 60年	1990 平成2年
											死	亡
09200	心疾患(高血圧性を除く)[3]	総数	T.	53 377	54 351	68 400	75 672	89 411	99 226	123 505	141 097	165 478
		男	M.	26 108	27 282	34 755	38 827	45 988	50 395	64 103	71 766	81 774
		女	F.	27 269	27 069	33 645	36 845	43 423	48 831	59 402	69 331	83 704
09201	慢性リウマチ性心疾患	総数	T.	5 010	3 092	5 671	4 751	4 195	3 948	1 716	1 644	1 360
		男	M.	1 937	1 149	2 116	1 645	1 594	1 576	582	516	436
		女	F.	3 073	1 943	3 555	3 106	2 601	2 372	1 134	1 128	924
09202	急性心筋梗塞	総数	T.	…	…	…	…	21 714	23 827	29 393	30 558	31 933
		男	M.	…	…	…	…	12 984	14 051	17 511	17 656	17 883
		女	F.	…	…	…	…	8 730	9 776	11 882	12 902	14 050
09203	その他の虚血性心疾患	総数	T.	…	…	…	…	17 372	19 993	18 954	18 926	19 504
		男	M.	…	…	…	…	9 457	10 055	9 376	9 213	9 466
		女	F.	…	…	…	…	7 915	9 938	9 578	9 713	10 038
09204	慢性非リウマチ性心内膜疾患	総数	T.	21 451	18 013	11 953	7 606	4 577	2 959	3 510	3 554	4 201
		男	M.	9 330	7 801	5 070	3 133	1 713	1 092	1 519	1 452	1 680
		女	F.	12 121	10 212	6 883	4 473	2 864	1 867	1 991	2 102	2 521
09205	心筋症	総数	T.	…	…	…	…	26	182	776	1 417	2 097
		男	M.	…	…	…	…	22	123	492	904	1 387
		女	F.	…	…	…	…	4	59	284	513	710
09206	不整脈及び伝導障害	総数	T.	176	343	737	1 019	1 220	1 707	3 826	4 977	6 350
		男	M.	73	185	383	534	644	896	1 990	2 533	3 057
		女	F.	103	158	354	485	576	811	1 836	2 444	3 293
09207	心不全	総数	T.	4 575	9 869	14 840	21 206	31 736	40 608	59 560	75 310	96 078
		男	M.	2 328	4 881	7 122	10 118	15 035	19 482	29 448	36 993	45 881
		女	F.	2 247	4 988	7 718	11 088	16 701	21 126	30 112	38 317	50 197
											百	分
09200	心疾患(高血圧性を除く)[3]	総数	T.	100.0	100.0	100.0	100.0	100.0	100.0	100.0	100.0	100.0
		男	M.	100.0	100.0	100.0	100.0	100.0	100.0	100.0	100.0	100.0
		女	F.	100.0	100.0	100.0	100.0	100.0	100.0	100.0	100.0	100.0
09201	慢性リウマチ性心疾患	総数	T.	9.4	5.7	8.3	6.3	4.7	4.0	1.4	1.2	0.8
		男	M.	7.4	4.2	6.1	4.2	3.5	3.1	0.9	0.7	0.5
		女	F.	11.3	7.2	10.6	8.4	6.0	4.9	1.9	1.6	1.1
09202	急性心筋梗塞	総数	T.	…	…	…	…	24.3	24.0	23.8	21.7	19.3
		男	M.	…	…	…	…	28.2	27.9	27.3	24.6	21.9
		女	F.	…	…	…	…	20.1	20.0	20.0	18.6	16.8
09203	その他の虚血性心疾患	総数	T.	…	…	…	…	19.4	20.1	15.3	13.4	11.8
		男	M.	…	…	…	…	20.6	20.0	14.6	12.8	11.6
		女	F.	…	…	…	…	18.2	20.4	16.1	14.0	12.0
09204	慢性非リウマチ性心内膜疾患	総数	T.	40.2	33.1	17.5	10.1	5.1	3.0	2.8	2.5	2.5
		男	M.	35.7	28.6	14.6	8.1	3.7	2.2	2.4	2.0	2.1
		女	F.	44.4	37.7	20.5	12.1	6.6	3.8	3.4	3.0	3.0
09205	心筋症	総数	T.	…	…	…	…	0.0	0.2	0.6	1.0	1.3
		男	M.	…	…	…	…	0.0	0.2	0.8	1.3	1.7
		女	F.	…	…	…	…	0.0	0.1	0.5	0.7	0.8
09206	不整脈及び伝導障害	総数	T.	0.3	0.6	1.1	1.3	1.4	1.7	3.1	3.5	3.8
		男	M.	0.3	0.7	1.1	1.4	1.4	1.8	3.1	3.5	3.7
		女	F.	0.4	0.6	1.1	1.3	1.3	1.7	3.1	3.5	3.9
09207	心不全	総数	T.	8.6	18.2	21.7	28.0	35.5	40.9	48.2	53.4	58.1
		男	M.	8.9	17.9	20.5	26.1	32.7	38.7	45.9	51.5	56.1
		女	F.	8.2	18.4	22.9	30.1	38.5	43.3	50.7	55.3	60.0

注：1) 粗死亡率は、年齢調整死亡率と並記したので粗死亡率と表現したが、単に死亡率とよんでいるものである。
2) 年齢調整死亡率の基準人口は、昭和60年モデル人口である。なお、計算方法は、68ページ 3)死亡を参照されたい。
3) 平成6年以前の「心疾患」には肺塞栓及びその他の肺血管の疾患を含み、心臓併発症を伴うリウマチ熱及び心臓併発症を伴うリウマチ性舞踏病を含まない。

百分率・粗死亡率[1] 及び年齢調整死亡率[2] （人口10万対）
death rates and age-adjusted death rates
by sex and disease type : Japan

1995	2000	2005	2006	2007	2008	2009	2010	2011	2012	2013	2014	2015	2016
7年	12年	17年	18年	19年	20年	21年	22年	23年	24年	25年	26年	27年	28年

数　Deaths

1995	2000	2005	2006	2007	2008	2009	2010	2011	2012	2013	2014	2015	2016
139 206	146 741	173 125	173 024	175 539	181 928	180 745	189 360	194 926	198 836	196 723	196 925	196 113	198 006
69 718	72 156	83 979	82 811	83 090	86 139	85 543	88 803	91 298	92 976	91 445	92 278	92 142	93 419
69 488	74 585	89 146	90 213	92 449	95 789	95 202	100 557	103 628	105 860	105 278	104 647	103 971	104 587
2 755	2 522	2 520	2 445	2 431	2 433	2 298	2 416	2 422	2 493	2 330	2 308	2 313	2 266
858	773	829	796	735	727	737	743	747	769	704	720	740	741
1 897	1 749	1 691	1 649	1 696	1 706	1 561	1 673	1 675	1 724	1 626	1 588	1 573	1 525
52 533	45 885	47 193	45 067	43 780	43 580	43 209	42 629	43 265	42 107	39 956	38 991	37 222	35 926
28 401	24 960	25 762	24 554	23 927	23 722	23 913	23 497	23 966	23 406	22 212	21 801	21 137	20 470
24 132	20 925	21 431	20 513	19 853	19 858	19 296	19 132	19 299	18 701	17 744	17 190	16 085	15 456
23 040	24 298	29 310	30 362	31 360	33 002	32 272	34 588	34 576	35 472	34 853	34 894	34 451	34 534
11 659	12 915	16 208	16 742	17 096	18 434	17 882	19 253	19 646	20 095	19 872	20 119	19 939	19 959
11 381	11 383	13 102	13 620	14 264	14 568	14 390	15 335	14 930	15 377	14 981	14 775	14 512	14 575
5 357	5 995	7 532	7 481	8 074	8 465	8 371	9 125	9 437	9 913	10 139	10 217	10 656	11 044
2 055	2 106	2 483	2 418	2 635	2 664	2 634	2 916	2 927	3 124	3 155	3 264	3 528	3 493
3 302	3 889	5 049	5 063	5 439	5 801	5 737	6 209	6 510	6 789	6 984	6 953	7 128	7 551
3 455	3 303	3 625	3 655	3 547	3 683	3 584	3 749	3 692	3 737	3 809	3 841	3 831	3 800
2 188	2 174	2 266	2 166	2 082	2 224	2 121	2 226	2 143	2 207	2 172	2 152	2 224	2 149
1 267	1 129	1 359	1 489	1 465	1 459	1 463	1 523	1 549	1 530	1 637	1 689	1 607	1 651
12 841	15 097	22 517	21 290	21 721	23 510	23 214	25 119	27 346	28 378	28 676	29 739	30 300	31 045
6 451	7 550	11 233	10 487	10 728	11 619	11 410	12 257	13 277	13 919	13 894	14 441	14 689	15 121
6 390	7 547	11 284	10 803	10 993	11 891	11 804	12 862	14 069	14 459	14 782	15 298	15 611	15 924
36 179	46 460	56 327	58 418	60 273	62 708	63 101	66 858	69 368	71 616	71 922	71 656	71 860	73 545
16 627	19 983	22 962	23 342	23 558	24 332	24 364	25 327	26 011	26 781	26 733	26 916	26 961	28 254
19 552	26 477	33 365	35 076	36 715	38 376	38 737	41 531	43 357	44 835	45 189	44 740	44 899	45 291

率　Percentage

1995	2000	2005	2006	2007	2008	2009	2010	2011	2012	2013	2014	2015	2016
100.0	100.0	100.0	100.0	100.0	100.0	100.0	100.0	100.0	100.0	100.0	100.0	100.0	100.0
100.0	100.0	100.0	100.0	100.0	100.0	100.0	100.0	100.0	100.0	100.0	100.0	100.0	100.0
100.0	100.0	100.0	100.0	100.0	100.0	100.0	100.0	100.0	100.0	100.0	100.0	100.0	100.0
2.0	1.7	1.5	1.4	1.4	1.3	1.3	1.3	1.2	1.3	1.2	1.2	1.2	1.1
1.2	1.1	1.0	1.0	0.9	0.8	0.9	0.8	0.8	0.8	0.8	0.8	0.8	0.8
2.7	2.3	1.9	1.8	1.8	1.8	1.6	1.7	1.6	1.6	1.5	1.5	1.5	1.5
37.7	31.3	27.3	26.0	24.9	24.0	23.9	22.5	22.2	21.2	20.3	19.8	19.0	18.1
40.7	34.6	30.7	29.7	28.8	27.5	28.0	26.5	26.3	25.2	24.3	23.6	22.9	21.9
34.7	28.1	24.0	22.7	21.5	20.7	20.3	19.0	18.6	17.7	16.9	16.4	15.5	14.8
16.6	16.6	16.9	17.5	17.9	18.1	17.9	18.3	17.7	17.8	17.7	17.7	17.6	17.4
16.7	17.9	19.3	20.2	20.6	21.4	20.9	21.7	21.5	21.6	21.7	21.8	21.6	21.4
16.4	15.3	14.7	15.1	15.4	15.2	15.1	15.3	14.4	14.5	14.2	14.1	14.0	13.9
3.8	4.1	4.4	4.3	4.6	4.7	4.6	4.8	4.8	5.0	5.2	5.2	5.4	5.6
2.9	2.9	3.0	2.9	3.2	3.1	3.1	3.3	3.2	3.4	3.5	3.5	3.8	3.7
4.8	5.2	5.7	5.6	5.9	6.1	6.0	6.2	6.3	6.4	6.6	6.6	6.9	7.2
2.5	2.3	2.1	2.1	2.0	2.0	2.0	2.0	1.9	1.9	1.9	2.0	2.0	1.9
3.1	3.0	2.7	2.6	2.5	2.6	2.5	2.5	2.3	2.4	2.4	2.3	2.4	2.3
1.8	1.5	1.5	1.7	1.6	1.5	1.5	1.5	1.5	1.4	1.6	1.6	1.5	1.6
9.2	10.3	13.0	12.3	12.4	12.9	12.8	13.3	14.0	14.3	14.6	15.1	15.5	15.7
9.3	10.5	13.4	12.7	12.9	13.5	13.3	13.8	14.5	15.0	15.2	15.6	15.9	16.2
9.2	10.1	12.7	12.0	11.9	12.4	12.4	12.8	13.6	13.7	14.0	14.6	15.0	15.2
26.0	31.7	32.5	33.8	34.3	34.5	34.9	35.3	35.6	36.0	36.6	36.4	36.6	37.1
23.8	27.7	27.3	28.2	28.4	28.2	28.5	28.5	28.5	28.8	29.2	29.2	29.3	30.2
28.1	35.5	37.4	38.9	39.7	40.1	40.7	41.3	41.8	42.4	42.9	42.8	43.2	43.3

Note : a) Code see page 595.

死　亡

表5.28　心疾患の病類別にみた性・年次別死亡数・
Table 5.28　Trends in deaths, percent distribution, crude
(per 100,000 population) from heart diseases

死因簡単分類コード Code[a]	死因・性 Causes of death and sex			1950 昭和25年	1955 30年	1960 35年	1965 40年	1970 45年	1975 50年	1980 55年	1985 60年	1990 平成2年
										粗　死　亡		
09200	心疾患(高血圧性を除く)[3]	総数 男 女	T. M. F.	64.2 64.0 64.3	60.9 62.2 59.6	73.2 75.8 70.8	77.0 80.5 73.6	86.7 90.9 82.7	89.2 92.1 86.4	106.2 112.1 100.5	117.3 121.5 113.2	134.8 135.7 134.0
09201	慢性リウマチ性心疾患	総数 男 女	T. M. F.	6.0 4.7 7.2	3.5 2.6 4.3	6.1 4.6 7.5	4.8 3.4 6.2	4.1 3.2 5.0	3.5 2.9 4.2	1.5 1.0 1.9	1.4 0.9 1.8	1.1 0.7 1.5
09202	急性心筋梗塞	総数 男 女	T. M. F.	… … …	… … …	… … …	… … …	21.1 25.7 16.6	21.4 25.7 17.3	25.3 30.6 20.1	25.4 29.9 21.1	26.0 29.7 22.5
09203	その他の虚血性心疾患	総数 男 女	T. M. F.	… … …	… … …	… … …	… … …	16.8 18.7 15.1	18.0 18.4 17.6	16.3 16.4 16.2	15.7 15.6 15.9	15.9 15.7 16.1
09204	慢性非リウマチ性心内膜疾患	総数 男 女	T. M. F.	25.8 22.9 28.6	20.2 17.8 22.5	12.8 11.1 14.5	7.7 6.5 8.9	4.4 3.4 5.5	2.7 2.0 3.3	3.0 2.7 3.4	3.0 2.5 3.4	3.4 2.8 4.0
09205	心筋症	総数 男 女	T. M. F.	… … …	… … …	… … …	… … …	0.0 0.0 0.0	0.2 0.2 0.1	0.7 0.9 0.5	1.2 1.5 0.8	1.7 2.3 1.1
09206	不整脈及び伝導障害	総数 男 女	T. M. F.	0.2 0.2 0.2	0.4 0.4 0.3	0.8 0.8 0.7	1.0 1.1 1.0	1.2 1.3 1.1	1.5 1.6 1.4	3.3 3.5 3.1	4.1 4.3 4.0	5.2 5.1 5.3
09207	心不全	総数 男 女	T. M. F.	5.5 5.7 5.3	11.1 11.1 11.0	15.9 15.5 16.2	21.6 21.0 22.2	30.8 29.7 31.8	36.5 35.6 37.4	51.2 51.5 50.9	62.6 62.7 62.6	78.3 76.2 80.4
										年　齢　調　整　死　亡		
09200	心疾患(高血圧性を除く)[3]	男 女	M. F.	126.2 105.4	125.4 96.8	153.3 111.9	156.0 111.1	161.7 114.5	150.0 106.3	158.0 103.9	146.9 94.6	139.1 88.5
09201	慢性リウマチ性心疾患	男 女	M. F.	8.3 11.0	4.6 6.3	8.0 10.8	5.6 8.4	4.6 6.2	4.0 4.9	1.3 2.0	1.0 1.7	0.7 1.1
09202	急性心筋梗塞	男 女	M. F.	… …	… …	… …	… …	41.9 22.5	38.7 20.9	41.1 20.7	35.3 17.9	30.1 15.4
09203	その他の虚血性心疾患	男 女	M. F.	… …	… …	… …	… …	33.8 21.2	31.6 21.9	24.4 16.8	19.4 13.0	16.2 10.2
09204	慢性非リウマチ性心内膜疾患	男 女	M. F.	41.4 44.5	33.0 34.4	20.6 21.4	11.3 12.5	5.5 7.0	3.0 3.9	3.5 3.5	2.9 2.9	2.9 2.7
09205	心筋症	男 女	M. F.	… …	… …	… …	… …	0.0 0.0	0.2 0.1	1.0 0.5	1.7 0.8	2.3 0.9
09206	不整脈及び伝導障害	男 女	M. F.	0.3 0.4	0.8 0.6	1.6 1.2	2.1 1.4	2.1 1.5	2.7 1.7	4.9 3.2	5.4 3.4	5.3 3.5
09207	心不全	男 女	M. F.	13.2 9.8	26.5 19.6	36.1 27.4	45.2 34.8	57.2 45.4	60.3 46.6	74.2 52.8	76.4 51.9	78.3 52.4

376

百分率・粗死亡率[1] 及び年齢調整死亡率[2] （人口10万対）（つづき）
death rates and age-adjusted death rates
by sex and disease type : Japan－CON.

1995 7年	2000 12年	2005 17年	2006 18年	2007 19年	2008 20年	2009 21年	2010 22年	2011 23年	2012 24年	2013 25年	2014 26年	2015 27年	2016 28年
率（人口10万対） Death rates (per 100,000 population)													
112.0	116.8	137.2	137.2	139.2	144.4	143.7	149.8	154.5	157.9	156.5	157.0	156.5	158.4
114.4	117.3	136.3	134.5	135.1	140.2	139.5	144.2	148.6	151.6	149.5	151.2	151.0	153.5
109.6	116.3	138.0	139.7	143.2	148.5	147.6	155.2	160.1	163.8	163.2	162.5	161.7	163.0
2.2	2.0	2.0	1.9	1.9	1.9	1.8	1.9	1.9	2.0	1.9	1.8	1.8	1.8
1.4	1.3	1.3	1.3	1.2	1.2	1.2	1.2	1.2	1.3	1.2	1.2	1.2	1.2
3.0	2.7	2.6	2.6	2.6	2.6	2.4	2.6	2.6	2.7	2.5	2.5	2.4	2.4
42.3	36.5	37.4	35.7	34.7	34.6	34.3	33.7	34.3	33.4	31.8	31.1	29.7	28.7
46.6	40.6	41.8	39.9	38.9	38.6	39.0	38.2	39.0	38.2	36.3	35.7	34.6	33.6
38.1	32.6	33.2	31.8	30.7	30.8	29.9	29.5	29.8	28.9	27.5	26.7	25.0	24.1
18.5	19.3	23.2	24.1	24.9	26.2	25.6	27.4	27.4	28.2	27.7	27.8	27.5	27.6
19.1	21.0	26.3	27.2	27.8	30.0	29.2	31.3	32.0	32.8	32.5	33.0	32.7	32.8
18.0	17.8	20.3	21.1	22.1	22.6	22.3	23.7	23.1	23.8	23.2	22.9	22.6	22.7
4.3	4.8	6.0	5.9	6.4	6.7	6.7	7.2	7.5	7.9	8.1	8.1	8.5	8.8
3.4	3.4	4.0	3.9	4.3	4.3	4.3	4.7	4.8	5.1	5.2	5.3	5.8	5.7
5.2	6.1	7.8	7.8	8.4	9.0	8.9	9.6	10.1	10.5	10.8	10.8	11.1	11.8
2.8	2.6	2.9	2.9	2.8	2.9	2.8	3.0	2.9	3.0	3.0	3.1	3.1	3.0
3.6	3.5	3.7	3.5	3.4	3.6	3.5	3.6	3.5	3.6	3.5	3.5	3.6	3.5
2.0	1.8	2.1	2.3	2.3	2.3	2.3	2.3	2.4	2.4	2.5	2.6	2.5	2.6
10.3	12.0	17.8	16.9	17.2	18.7	18.5	19.9	21.7	22.5	22.8	23.7	24.2	24.8
10.6	12.3	18.2	17.0	17.4	18.9	18.6	19.9	21.6	22.7	22.7	23.7	24.1	24.8
10.1	11.8	17.5	16.7	17.0	18.4	18.3	19.8	21.7	22.4	22.9	23.8	24.3	24.8
29.1	37.0	44.6	46.3	47.8	49.8	50.2	52.9	55.0	56.9	57.2	57.1	57.3	58.8
27.3	32.5	37.3	37.9	38.3	39.6	39.7	41.1	42.3	43.7	43.7	44.1	44.2	46.4
30.8	41.3	51.7	54.3	56.9	59.5	60.1	64.1	67.0	69.4	70.0	69.5	69.8	70.6
率（人口10万対） Age－adjusted death rates (per 100,000 population)													
99.7	85.8	83.7	79.7	77.0	77.1	74.2	74.2	73.9	72.4	69.1	67.7	65.4	64.5
58.4	48.5	45.3	43.6	42.3	41.7	39.6	39.7	39.5	38.7	37.0	35.5	34.2	33.1
1.2	0.9	0.8	0.7	0.6	0.6	0.6	0.6	0.5	0.5	0.5	0.5	0.5	0.4
1.7	1.2	0.9	0.8	0.8	0.7	0.6	0.7	0.6	0.6	0.6	0.5	0.5	0.5
40.5	29.7	25.9	24.0	22.5	21.8	21.3	20.4	20.3	19.3	17.9	17.2	16.2	15.5
20.8	14.2	11.5	10.7	9.9	9.5	8.8	8.4	8.3	7.8	7.1	6.7	6.1	5.7
16.6	15.3	16.3	16.4	16.2	16.8	15.9	16.6	16.5	16.4	15.8	15.6	15.1	14.7
9.1	7.4	7.0	7.1	7.1	7.0	6.6	6.9	6.5	6.4	6.2	6.0	5.6	5.6
2.9	2.4	2.3	2.1	2.2	2.1	2.0	2.1	2.0	2.1	2.0	2.0	2.1	1.9
2.7	2.3	2.2	2.1	2.1	2.2	2.0	2.0	2.1	2.0	2.0	1.9	1.9	1.9
3.2	2.8	2.5	2.3	2.1	2.3	2.2	2.1	2.0	2.0	1.9	1.9	1.9	1.8
1.4	1.0	1.0	1.0	1.0	0.9	0.9	0.9	0.9	0.9	0.9	0.8	0.8	0.8
9.3	9.1	11.4	10.3	10.2	10.6	10.1	10.5	11.0	11.0	10.7	10.8	10.6	10.7
5.4	5.0	6.1	5.4	5.3	5.5	5.2	5.3	5.7	5.6	5.5	5.5	5.4	5.3
23.8	23.5	22.0	21.4	20.7	20.5	19.7	19.5	19.1	18.7	17.9	17.3	16.5	16.7
15.8	16.0	15.2	15.0	14.8	14.6	14.0	14.2	14.0	13.9	13.4	12.7	12.4	12.0

死 亡

〔主な死因〕感染症

表 5.29　感染症分類別にみた

Table 5.29　Trends in deaths and death rates（per 100,000 population）

感染症分類コード Code[a]	死　因 Causes of death	死　亡　数 Deaths					死　亡　率 Death rates（per 100,000 population）				
		2012 平成24年	2013 25年	2014 26年	2015 27年	**2016 28年**	2012 平成24年	2013 25年	2014 26年	2015 27年	**2016 28年**
	総　数　　　Total	8 333	8 290	7 473	8 528	**7 826**	6.6	6.6	6.0	6.8	**6.3**
In101	エボラ出血熱	-	-	-	-	**-**	-	-	-	-	**-**
In102	クリミア・コンゴ出血熱	-	-	-	-	**-**	-	-	-	-	**-**
In103	痘そう	-	-	-	-	**-**	-	-	-	-	**-**
In104	南米出血熱	-	-	-	-	**-**	-	-	-	-	**-**
In105	ペスト	-	-	-	-	**-**	-	-	-	-	**-**
In106	マールブルグ病	-	-	-	-	**-**	-	-	-	-	**-**
In107	ラッサ熱	-	-	-	-	**-**	-	-	-	-	**-**
In201	急性灰白髄炎	-	-	-	-	**-**	-	-	-	-	**-**
In202	結核	2 110	2 087	2 100	1 956	**1 892**	1.7	1.7	1.7	1.6	**1.5**
In203	ジフテリア	-	-	-	-	**-**	-	-	-	-	**-**
In204	重症急性呼吸器症候群 （病原体がベータコロナウイルス属 SARSコロナウイルスであるものに限る。）	-	-	-	-	**-**	-	-	-	-	**-**
In205	鳥インフルエンザ （特定鳥インフルエンザ（H5N1）に限る。）	-	-	-	-	**-**	-	-	-	-	**-**
In206	鳥インフルエンザ （特定鳥インフルエンザ（H7N9）に限る。）	…	…	…	-	**-**	…	…	…	-	**-**
In207	中東呼吸器症候群 （病原体がベータコロナウイルス属 MERSコロナウイルスであるものに限る。）	…	…	…	-	**-**	…	…	…	-	**-**
In301	コレラ	-	-	-	-	**1**	-	-	-	-	**0.0**
In302	細菌性赤痢	-	-	-	-	**-**	-	-	-	-	**-**
In303	腸管出血性大腸菌感染症	8	10	1	7	**12**	0.0	0.0	0.0	0.0	**0.0**
In304	腸チフス	-	-	-	-	**-**	-	-	-	-	**-**
In305	パラチフス	-	-	-	-	**-**	-	-	-	-	**-**
In401	E型肝炎	2	1	3	-	**1**	0.0	0.0	0.0	-	**0.0**
In402	ウエストナイル熱	-	-	-	-	**-**	-	-	-	-	**-**
In403	A型肝炎	3	5	5	8	**5**	0.0	0.0	0.0	0.0	**0.0**
In404	エキノコックス症	4	2	-	1	**-**	0.0	0.0	-	0.0	**-**
In405	黄熱	-	-	-	-	**-**	-	-	-	-	**-**
In406	オウム病	-	-	-	-	**-**	-	-	-	-	**-**
In407	オムスク出血熱	-	-	-	-	**-**	-	-	-	-	**-**
In408	回帰熱	-	-	-	-	**-**	-	-	-	-	**-**
In409	キャサヌル森林病	-	-	-	-	**-**	-	-	-	-	**-**
In410	Q熱	-	-	-	-	**-**	-	-	-	-	**-**
In411	狂犬病	-	-	-	-	**-**	-	-	-	-	**-**
In412	コクシジオイデス症	-	-	-	-	**-**	-	-	-	-	**-**
In413	サル痘	-	-	-	-	**-**	-	-	-	-	**-**
In414	腎症候性出血熱	-	-	-	-	**-**	-	-	-	-	**-**

注：1　感染症の分類名は、「感染症の予防及び感染症の患者に対する医療に関する法律」（平成10年法律第114号。以下「感染症法」という。）、感染症法施行令（平成10年政令第420号）及び感染症法施行規則（平成10年厚生省令第99号）に規定された疾病名であるため、必ずしもICD-10とは一致していない。
　　　　なお、本表は感染症法等の改正（平成28年2月15日施行）に基づく分類で表章しており、1月からの数値を計上しているが、遡及できない分類については「…」と表記している。
　　2　感染症法第44条の2第3項の規定に基づき、平成23年4月1日以降、「新型インフルエンザ（A/H1N1）」を通常の季節性インフルエンザとして取り扱うこととなったので、同日以降の当該インフルエンザによる死亡数は、「In504 インフルエンザ」に含まれる。
　　1）平成24〜26年は、遡及できない死因基本分類（A04.8）を集計の対象から除いている。

General mortality

年次別死亡数及び率（人口10万対）
by causes（the list of infectious diseases）：Japan

感染症分類コード Code[a]	死　因 Causes of death	死　亡　数 Deaths					死　亡　率 Death rates（per 100,000 population）				
		2012 平成24年	2013 25年	2014 26年	2015 27年	**2016** **28年**	2012 平成24年	2013 25年	2014 26年	2015 27年	**2016** **28年**
In415	西部ウマ脳炎	-	-	-	-	**-**	-	-	-	-	**-**
In416	ダニ媒介脳炎	-	-	-	-	**1**	-	-	-	-	**0.0**
In417	炭疽	-	-	-	-	**-**	-	-	-	-	**-**
In418	つつが虫病	3	1	1	2	**2**	0.0	0.0	0.0	0.0	**0.0**
In419	デング熱	-	-	-	-	**-**	-	-	-	-	**-**
In420	東部ウマ脳炎	-	-	-	-	**-**	-	-	-	-	**-**
In421	鳥インフルエンザ （特定鳥インフルエンザを除く。）	-	-	-	-	**-**	-	-	-	-	**-**
In422	ニパウイルス感染症	-	-	-	-	**-**	-	-	-	-	**-**
In423	日本紅斑熱	2	1	-	4	**2**	0.0	0.0	-	0.0	**0.0**
In424	日本脳炎	-	2	-	1	**1**	-	0.0	-	0.0	**0.0**
In425	ハンタウイルス肺症候群	-	-	-	-	**-**	-	-	-	-	**-**
In426	Ｂウイルス病	-	-	-	-	**-**	-	-	-	-	**-**
In427	鼻疽	-	-	-	-	**-**	-	-	-	-	**-**
In428	ブルセラ症	-	-	-	-	**-**	-	-	-	-	**-**
In429	ベネズエラウマ脳炎	-	-	-	-	**-**	-	-	-	-	**-**
In430	ヘンドラウイルス感染症	-	-	-	-	**-**	-	-	-	-	**-**
In431	発しんチフス	-	-	-	-	**-**	-	-	-	-	**-**
In432	ボツリヌス症（乳児ボツリヌス症を除く。）	1	-	-	-	**-**	0.0	-	-	-	**-**
In433	乳児ボツリヌス症	-	-	-	-	**-**	-	-	-	-	**-**
In434	マラリア	-	-	-	1	**2**	-	-	-	0.0	**0.0**
In435	野兎病	-	-	-	-	**-**	-	-	-	-	**-**
In436	ライム病	-	-	-	-	**-**	-	-	-	-	**-**
In437	リッサウイルス感染症	-	-	-	-	**-**	-	-	-	-	**-**
In438	リフトバレー熱	-	-	-	-	**-**	-	-	-	-	**-**
In439	類鼻疽	-	-	-	-	**-**	-	-	-	-	**-**
In440	レジオネラ症	58	64	65	59	**67**	0.0	0.1	0.1	0.0	**0.1**
In441	レプトスピラ症	1	-	1	1	**-**	0.0	-	0.0	0.0	**-**
In442	ロッキー山紅斑熱	-	-	-	-	**-**	-	-	-	-	**-**
In443	チクングニア熱	-	-	-	-	**-**	-	-	-	-	**-**
In444	重症熱性血小板減少症候群 （病原体がフレボウイルス属 ＳＦＴＳウイルスであるものに限る。）	-	8	13	11	**8**	-	0.0	0.0	0.0	**0.0**
In445	ジカウイルス感染症	…	…	…	…	**-**	…	…	…	…	**-**
In501	アメーバ赤痢	3	3	3	5	**4**	0.0	0.0	0.0	0.0	**0.0**
In502	ＲＳウイルス感染症	34	16	22	19	**22**	0.0	0.0	0.0	0.0	**0.0**
In503	咽頭結膜熱	-	-	-	-	**-**	-	-	-	-	**-**
In504	インフルエンザ （鳥インフルエンザ及び 新型インフルエンザ等感染症を除く。）	1 275	1 514	1 130	2 262	**1 463**	1.0	1.2	0.9	1.8	**1.2**
In505	急性ウイルス性肝炎 （Ｅ型肝炎及びＡ型肝炎を除く。）	304	310	240	248	**212**	0.2	0.2	0.2	0.2	**0.2**
In506	Ａ群溶血性レンサ球菌咽頭炎	1	-	-	-	**1**	0.0	-	-	-	**0.0**
In507	感染性胃腸炎[1]	2 641	2 533	2 372	2 293	**2 502**	2.1	2.0	1.9	1.8	**2.0**

Note : a) Code see page 599.

死　亡

表5.29　感染症分類別にみた年次別死亡数及び率（人口10万対）（つづき）
Table 5.29　Trends in deaths and death rates（per 100,000 population）by causes（the list of infectious diseases）: Japan－CON.

感染症分類コード Code[a]	死因 Causes of death	死亡数 Deaths					死亡率 Death rates (per 100,000 population)				
		2012 平成24年	2013 25年	2014 26年	2015 27年	2016 28年	2012 平成24年	2013 25年	2014 26年	2015 27年	2016 28年
In508	急性出血性結膜炎	-	-	-	-	-	-	-	-	-	-
In509	急性脳炎 （ウエストナイル脳炎、西部ウマ脳炎、ダニ媒介脳炎、東部ウマ脳炎、日本脳炎、ベネズエラウマ脳炎及びリフトバレー熱を除く。）	111	99	82	92	96	0.1	0.1	0.1	0.1	0.1
In510	クラミジア肺炎（オウム病を除く。）	5	10	9	6	8	0.0	0.0	0.0	0.0	0.0
In511	クリプトスポリジウム症	-	-	-	-	-	-	-	-	-	-
In512	クロイツフェルト・ヤコブ病	241	252	245	263	259	0.2	0.2	0.2	0.2	0.2
In513	劇症型溶血性レンサ球菌感染症	23	20	12	30	29	0.0	0.0	0.0	0.0	0.0
In514	後天性免疫不全症候群	50	45	45	56	66	0.0	0.0	0.0	0.0	0.1
In515	細菌性髄膜炎 （侵襲性インフルエンザ菌感染症、侵襲性髄膜炎菌感染症、侵襲性肺炎球菌感染症を除く。）	162	136	146	149	138	0.1	0.1	0.1	0.1	0.1
In516	ジアルジア症	-	-	-	-	-	-	-	-	-	-
In517	水痘	5	10	5	10	3	0.0	0.0	0.0	0.0	0.0
In518	侵襲性髄膜炎菌感染症	-	2	-	-	2	-	0.0	-	-	0.0
In519	性器クラミジア感染症	-	-	-	-	-	-	-	-	-	-
In520	性器ヘルペスウイルス感染症	-	-	-	-	-	-	-	-	-	-
In521	尖圭コンジローマ	-	-	-	-	1	-	-	-	-	0.0
In522	先天性風しん症候群	-	2	1	-	-	-	0.0	0.0	-	-
In523	手足口病	-	-	-	-	-	-	-	-	-	-
In524	伝染性紅斑	-	-	-	-	-	-	-	-	-	-
In525	突発性発しん	-	-	-	-	-	-	-	-	-	-
In526	梅毒	9	6	18	9	9	0.0	0.0	0.0	0.0	0.0
In527	破傷風	8	5	9	9	8	0.0	0.0	0.0	0.0	0.0
In528	バンコマイシン耐性黄色ブドウ球菌感染症	-	-	-	-	-	-	-	-	-	-
In529	バンコマイシン耐性腸球菌感染症	-	-	-	-	-	-	-	-	-	-
In530	百日咳	3	1	1	1	1	0.0	0.0	0.0	0.0	0.0
In531	風しん	-	1	-	-	1	-	0.0	-	-	0.0
In532	ペニシリン耐性肺炎球菌感染症	-	-	-	-	-	-	-	-	-	-
In533	ヘルパンギーナ	-	-	-	-	-	-	-	-	-	-
In534	マイコプラズマ肺炎	47	40	27	24	46	0.0	0.0	0.0	0.0	0.0
In535	麻しん	-	1	-	-	-	-	0.0	-	-	-
In537	無菌性髄膜炎	13	13	7	12	12	0.0	0.0	0.0	0.0	0.0
In538	メチシリン耐性黄色ブドウ球菌感染症	1 157	1 024	841	893	852	0.9	0.8	0.7	0.7	0.7
In539	薬剤耐性緑膿菌感染症	22	9	8	8	12	0.0	0.0	0.0	0.0	0.0
In540	流行性角結膜炎	-	-	-	-	-	-	-	-	-	-
In541	流行性耳下腺炎	-	2	2	1	2	-	0.0	0.0	0.0	0.0
In542	淋菌感染症	-	-	1	-	-	-	-	0.0	-	-
In543	薬剤耐性アシネトバクター感染症	-	-	1	-	-	-	-	0.0	-	-
In544	侵襲性インフルエンザ菌感染症	…	1	-	3	2	…	0.0	-	0.0	0.0
In545	侵襲性肺炎球菌感染症	…	30	35	58	47	…	0.0	0.0	0.0	0.0
In546	カルバペネム耐性腸内細菌科細菌感染症	…	…	…	1	1	…	…	…	0.0	0.0
In547	播種性クリプトコックス症	27	23	21	25	33	0.0	0.0	0.0	0.0	0.0
In601	新型インフルエンザ等感染症	-	-	-	-	-	-	-	-	-	-

General mortality

○感染症分類（平成25年改正）と死因基本分類との対照表

感染症法等の改正（平成25年3月4日施行）に伴う追加分

感染症 分類コード	感 染 症 分 類 名	死 因 基 本 分 類 コード	変 更 内 容
In 444	重症熱性血小板減少症候群 （病原体がフレボウイルス属SFTSウイルスであるものに限る）	A98.8A	追加

感染症法等の改正（平成25年4月1日施行）に伴う追加・変更分

感染症 分類コード	感 染 症 分 類 名	死 因 基 本 分 類 コード	変 更 内 容
In 515	細菌性髄膜炎	A02.2A, A32.1, G00（G00.0, G00.1を除く）	A02.2A, A32.1, G00から変更
In 518	侵襲性髄膜炎菌感染症	A39.0, A39.2, A39.4	髄膜炎菌性髄膜炎から名称変更 A39.0から変更
In 544	侵襲性インフルエンザ菌感染症	A41.3, G00.0, P36.8A	追加 （G00.0はIn515細菌性髄膜炎から分離）
In 545	侵襲性肺炎球菌感染症	A40.3B, G00.1, P36.1C	追加 （G00.1はIn515細菌性髄膜炎から分離）

○感染症分類（平成27年改正）と死因基本分類との対照表

感染症法等の改正（平成26年9月19日施行）に伴う追加分

感染症 分類コード	感 染 症 分 類 名	死 因 基 本 分 類 コード	変 更 内 容
In546	カルバペネム耐性腸内細菌科細菌感染症	A04.8B, A41.5D, A49.8F, J15.8D	追加 （A04.8BはIn507感染性胃腸炎から分離）
In547	播種性クリプトコックス症	B45.1, B45.7	追加
In507	感染性胃腸炎	A01（A01.0, A01.1を除く）， A04（A04.3, A04.8A, A04.8Bを除く）， A07（A07.1, A07.2を除く），A08, A09	A01（A01.0, A01.1を除く）， A04（A04.3を除く）， A07（A07.1, A07.2を除く），A08, A09から変更
In538	メチシリン耐性黄色ブドウ球菌感染症	A04.8A, A41.0A, A49.0A, J15.2A	A41.0A, A49.0A, J15.2Aから変更 （A04.8AはIn507感染性胃腸炎から分離）

感染症法等の改正（平成27年1月21日施行）に伴う追加・変更分

感染症 分類コード	感 染 症 分 類 名	死 因 基 本 分 類 コード	変 更 内 容
In204	重症急性呼吸器症候群 （病原体がベータコロナウイルス属SARSコロナウイルスであるものに限る。）	U04	重症急性呼吸器症候群 （病原体がコロナウイルス属SARSコロナウイルスであるものに限る。）から名称変更
In205	鳥インフルエンザ （特定鳥インフルエンザ（H5N1）に限る。）	J10.0C, J10.1C, J10.8C	鳥インフルエンザ （鳥インフルエンザ（H5N1）に限る。）から名称変更
In206	鳥インフルエンザ （特定鳥インフルエンザ（H7N9）に限る。）	J10.0E, J10.1E, J10.8E	追加
In207	中東呼吸器症候群 （病原体がベータコロナウイルス属MERSコロナウイルスであるものに限る。）	J12.8E	追加
In421	鳥インフルエンザ （特定鳥インフルエンザを除く。）	J10.0A, J10.1A, J10.8A	鳥インフルエンザ （鳥インフルエンザ（H5N1）を除く。）から名称変更

○感染症分類（平成28年改正）と死因基本分類との対照表

感染症法等の改正（平成28年2月15日施行）等に伴う追加・変更・削除分

感染症 分類コード	感 染 症 分 類 名	死 因 基 本 分 類 コード	変 更 内 容
In 445	ジカウイルス感染症	A92.8A	追加
In 515	細菌性髄膜炎（侵襲性インフルエンザ菌感染症、侵襲性髄膜炎菌感染症、侵襲性肺炎球菌感染症を除く。）	A02.2A, A32.1, G00（G00.0, G00.1を除く）	細菌性髄膜炎から名称変更
In 535	麻しん	B05	麻しん（成人麻しんを除く。）から名称変更 In536成人麻しんを含めた分類に変更
In 536	成人麻しん	B05	削除

381

死 亡
〔主な死因〕不慮の事故

表 5.30 不慮の事故の種類別にみた
Table 5.30 Trends in deaths and death rates

死因基本分類コード Code	死　因 Causes of death	死　亡　数 Deaths						
		1995 平成7年	2000 12年	2005 17年	2010 22年	2014 26年	2015 27年	2016 28年
V01－X59	総　数　　　Total	45 323	39 484	39 863	40 732	39 029	38 306	38 306
V01－V98	交　通　事　故	15 147	12 857	10 028	7 222	5 717	5 646	5 278
W00－W17	転　倒　・　転　落	5 911	6 245	6 702	7 517	7 946	7 992	8 030
W01	スリップ，つまづき及びよろめきによる同一平面上での転倒	2 692	3 269	3 879	4 843	5 516	5 636	5 788
W10	階段及びステップからの転落及びその上での転倒	720	653	687	666	696	694	695
W13	建物又は建造物からの転落	940	819	747	685	526	486	509
W17	そ　の　他　の　転　落	766	785	724	628	646	627	541
W20－W49	生物によらない機械的な力への曝露	998	804	576	587	512	490	493
W20	投げられ，投げ出され又は落下する物体による打撲	337	264	228	199	146	170	155
W50－W64	生物による機械的な力への曝露	25	27	30	17	14	6	15
W65－W74	不　慮　の　溺　死　及　び　溺　水	5 588	5 978	6 222	6 948	7 508	7 484	7 705
W65－W66	浴槽内での及び浴槽への転落による溺死及び溺水	3 190	3 518	3 756	4 467	5 362	5 293	5 673
W69－W70	自然の水域内での及び自然の水域への転落による溺死及び溺水	1 413	1 492	1 268	1 218	944	965	862
W75－W84	そ　の　他　の　不　慮　の　窒　息	7 104	7 794	9 319	9 879	9 806	9 356	9 485
W78	胃　内　容　物　の　誤　えん	1 206	1 207	1 433	1 554	1 564	1 533	1 429
W79	気道閉塞を生じた食物の誤えん	3 846	3 985	4 485	4 869	4 874	4 686	4 870
W80	気道閉塞を生じたその他の物体の誤えん	651	631	772	804	855	739	817
W84	詳　細　不　明　の　窒　息	1 041	1 664	2 340	2 435	2 253	2 166	2 170
W85－W99	電流，放射線並びに極端な気温及び気圧への曝露	65	60	59	31	45	44	48
X00－X09	煙，　火及び火炎への曝露	1 383	1 416	1 593	1 338	1 086	940	891
X00	建物又は建造物内の管理されていない火への曝露	959	1 074	1 234	1 077	832	752	711
X10－X19	熱及び高温物質との接触	238	180	167	131	110	96	93
X20－X29	有　毒　動　植　物　と　の　接　触	45	43	32	26	20	29	23
X30－X39	自　然　の　力　へ　の　曝　露	6 429	1 042	1 380	2 805	1 900	1 970	1 809
X30	自然の過度の高温への曝露	318	207	328	1 731	529	968	621
X31	自然の過度の低温への曝露	761	810	997	1 040	1 216	977	1 093
X34	地　震　に　よ　る　受　傷　者	5 326	1	1	-	-	-	51
X40－X49	有害物質による不慮の中毒及び有害物質への曝露	568	605	891	862	677	612	565
X50－X57	無理ながんばり，旅行及び欠乏状態	66	90	83	43	29	22	22
X58－X59	その他及び詳細不明の要因への不慮の曝露	1 756	2 343	2 781	3 326	3 659	3 619	3 849

General mortality

年次別死亡数及び率（人口10万対）
(per 100,000 population) from accidents by external causes : Japan

死　亡　率　Death rates (per 100,000 population)							死因基本分類コード Code	死　因 Causes of death
1995 平成7年	2000 12年	2005 17年	2010 22年	2014 26年	2015 27年	2016 28年		
36.5	31.4	31.6	32.2	31.1	30.6	30.6	V01－X59	総　数　　　　　Total
12.2	10.2	7.9	5.7	4.6	4.5	4.2	V01－V98	交　通　事　故
4.8	5.0	5.3	5.9	6.3	6.4	6.4	W00－W17	転　倒　・　転　落
2.2	2.6	3.1	3.8	4.4	4.5	4.6	W01	スリップ，つまづき及びよろめきによる同一平面上での転倒
0.6	0.5	0.5	0.5	0.6	0.6	0.6	W10	階段及びステップからの転落及びその上での転倒
0.8	0.7	0.6	0.5	0.4	0.4	0.4	W13	建物又は建造物からの転落
0.6	0.6	0.6	0.5	0.5	0.5	0.4	W17	そ　の　他　の　転　落
0.8	0.6	0.5	0.5	0.4	0.4	0.4	W20－W49	生物によらない機械的な力への曝露
0.3	0.2	0.2	0.2	0.1	0.1	0.1	W20	投げられ，投げ出され又は落下する物体による打撲
0.0	0.0	0.0	0.0	0.0	0.0	0.0	W50－W64	生物による機械的な力への曝露
4.5	4.8	4.9	5.5	6.0	6.0	6.2	W65－W74	不　慮　の　溺　死　及　び　溺　水
2.6	2.8	3.0	3.5	4.3	4.2	4.5	W65－W66	浴槽内での及び浴槽への転落による溺死及び溺水
1.1	1.2	1.0	1.0	0.8	0.8	0.7	W69－W70	自然の水域内での及び自然の水域への転落による溺死及び溺水
5.7	6.2	7.4	7.8	7.8	7.5	7.6	W75－W84	そ　の　他　の　不　慮　の　窒　息
1.0	1.0	1.1	1.2	1.2	1.2	1.1	W78	胃　内　容　物　の　誤えん
3.1	3.2	3.6	3.9	3.9	3.7	3.9	W79	気道閉塞を生じた食物の誤えん
0.5	0.5	0.6	0.6	0.7	0.6	0.7	W80	気道閉塞を生じたその他の物体の誤えん
0.8	1.3	1.9	1.9	1.8	1.7	1.7	W84	詳　細　不　明　の　窒　息
0.1	0.0	0.0	0.0	0.0	0.0	0.0	W85－W99	電流，放射線並びに極端な気温及び気圧への曝露
1.1	1.1	1.3	1.1	0.9	0.8	0.7	X00－X09	煙，火及び火炎への曝露
0.8	0.9	1.0	0.9	0.7	0.6	0.6	X00	建物又は建造物内の管理されていない火への曝露
0.2	0.1	0.1	0.1	0.1	0.1	0.1	X10－X19	熱及び高温物質との接触
0.0	0.0	0.0	0.0	0.0	0.0	0.0	X20－X29	有　毒　動　植　物　と　の　接　触
5.2	0.8	1.1	2.2	1.5	1.6	1.4	X30－X39	自　然　の　力　へ　の　曝　露
0.3	0.2	0.3	1.4	0.4	0.8	0.5	X30	自然の過度の高温への曝露
0.6	0.6	0.8	0.8	1.0	0.8	0.9	X31	自然の過度の低温への曝露
4.3	0.0	0.0	-	-	-	0.0	X34	地　震　に　よ　る　受　傷　者
0.5	0.5	0.7	0.7	0.5	0.5	0.5	X40－X49	有害物質による不慮の中毒及び有害物質への曝露
0.1	0.1	0.1	0.0	0.0	0.0	0.0	X50－X57	無理ながんばり，旅行及び欠乏状態
1.4	1.9	2.2	2.6	2.9	2.9	3.1	X58－X59	その他及び詳細不明の要因への不慮の曝露

死　亡

表5.31　不慮の事故の種類別にみた年齢別死亡数
Table 5.31　Deaths from accidents by age and external causes : Japan, 2016

平成28年

死因基本分類コード Code	死　因 Causes of death	総数 Total	0歳 Year	1〜4	5〜9	10〜14	15〜29	30〜44	45〜64	65〜79	80〜	不詳 Not stated
V01−X59	総　数　　　　Total	38 306	73	85	68	66	970	1 343	4 144	10 883	20 638	36
V01−V98	交　通　事　故	5 278	3	28	34	26	567	552	1 035	1 705	1 328	-
W00−W17	転　倒　・　転　落	8 030	-	6	3	8	86	152	690	1 780	5 302	3
W01	スリップ，つまづき及びよろめきによる同一平面上での転倒	5 788	-	1	2	-	10	43	266	986	4 480	-
W10	階段及びステップからの転落及びその上での転倒	695	-	-	-	-	4	16	119	256	299	1
W13	建物又は建造物からの転落	509	-	4	1	6	47	53	129	159	109	1
W17	そ　の　他　の　転　落	541	-	1	-	-	18	28	114	222	157	1
W20−W49	生物によらない機械的な力への曝露	493	-	-	1	-	32	68	146	157	89	-
W20	投げられ，投げ出され又は落下する物体による打撲	155	-	-	-	-	11	14	54	61	15	-
W50−W64	生物による機械的な力への曝露	15	-	-	-	-	-	3	2	8	2	-
W65−W74	不　慮　の　溺　死　及　び　溺　水	7 705	4	26	18	20	119	150	617	2 994	3 744	13
W65−W66	浴槽内での及び浴槽への転落による溺死及び溺水	5 673	3	15	3	10	43	42	322	2 217	3 016	2
W69−W70	自然の水域内での及び自然の水域への転落による溺死及び溺水	862	1	-	13	9	68	87	199	313	162	10
W75−W84	そ　の　他　の　不　慮　の　窒　息	9 485	62	20	6	6	45	123	763	2 356	6 103	1
W78	胃　内　容　物　の　誤　えん	1 429	19	7	2	-	17	33	130	300	921	-
W79	気道閉塞を生じた食物の誤えん	4 870	10	6	-	1	6	44	433	1 358	3 012	-
W80	気道閉塞を生じたその他の物体の誤えん	817	3	2	1	3	4	11	59	208	526	-
W84	詳　細　不　明　の　窒　息	2 170	6	3	2	-	8	19	100	438	1 593	1
W85−W99	電流，放射線並びに極端な気温及び気圧への曝露	48	-	-	-	-	6	5	9	20	8	-
X00−X09	煙，　火及び火炎への曝露	891	-	4	5	2	16	37	173	306	338	10
X00	建物又は建造物内の管理されていない火への曝露	711	-	4	5	2	15	30	139	259	247	10
X10−X19	熱及び高温物質との接触	93	-	1	-	-	1	3	6	28	54	-
X20−X29	有毒動植物との接触	23	-	-	-	-	-	-	4	10	9	-
X30−X39	自　然　の　力　へ　の　曝　露	1 809	1	-	-	2	28	72	290	531	880	5
X30	自然の過度の高温への曝露	621	1	-	-	2	6	27	93	166	326	-
X31	自然の過度の低温への曝露	1 093	-	-	-	-	12	39	178	333	526	5
X34	地　震　に　よ　る　受　傷　者	51	-	-	-	-	6	2	8	18	17	-
X40−X49	有害物質による不慮の中毒及び有害物質への曝露	565	1	-	-	1	54	140	200	95	73	1
X50−X57	無理ながんばり，旅行及び欠乏状態	22	-	-	-	-	-	2	3	9	6	2
X58−X59	その他及び詳細不明の要因への不慮の曝露	3 849	2	-	1	1	14	35	200	887	2 706	3

384

General mortality

表 5.32　不慮の事故の種類別にみた年齢別死亡数百分率
Table 5.32　Percent distribution of deaths from accidents by age and external causes : Japan, 2016

平成28年

死因基本分類コード Code	死因 Causes of death	総数[1] Total	0歳 Year	1～4	5～9	10～14	15～29	30～44	45～64	65～79	80～
V01－X59	総　数　　　　Total	100.0	100.0	100.0	100.0	100.0	100.0	100.0	100.0	100.0	100.0
V01－V98	交　通　事　故	13.8	4.1	32.9	50.0	39.4	58.5	41.1	25.0	15.7	6.4
W00－W17	転　倒　・　転　落	21.0	-	7.1	4.4	12.1	8.9	11.3	16.7	16.4	25.7
W01	スリップ，つまづき及びよろめきによる同一平面上での転倒	15.1	-	1.2	2.9	-	1.0	3.2	6.4	9.1	21.7
W10	階段及びステップからの転落及びその上での転倒	1.8	-	-	-	-	0.4	1.2	2.9	2.4	1.4
W13	建物又は建造物からの転落	1.3	-	4.7	1.5	9.1	4.8	3.9	3.1	1.5	0.5
W17	そ　の　他　の　転　落	1.4	-	1.2	-	-	1.9	2.1	2.8	2.0	0.8
W20－W49	生物によらない機械的な力への曝露	1.3	-	-	1.5	-	3.3	5.1	3.5	1.4	0.4
W20	投げられ，投げ出され又は落下する物体による打撲	0.4	-	-	-	-	1.1	1.0	1.3	0.6	0.1
W50－W64	生物による機械的な力への曝露	0.0	-	-	-	-	-	0.2	0.0	0.1	0.0
W65－W74	不　慮　の　溺　死　及　び　溺　水	20.1	5.5	30.6	26.5	30.3	12.3	11.2	14.9	27.5	18.1
W65－W66	浴槽内での及び浴槽への転落による溺死及び溺水	14.8	4.1	17.6	4.4	15.2	4.4	3.1	7.8	20.4	14.6
W69－W70	自然の水域内での及び自然の水域への転落による溺死及び溺水	2.3	1.4	-	19.1	13.6	7.0	6.5	4.8	2.9	0.8
W75－W84	そ　の　他　の　不　慮　の　窒　息	24.8	84.9	23.5	8.8	9.1	4.6	9.2	18.4	21.6	29.6
W78	胃　内　容　物　の　誤　えん	3.7	26.0	8.2	2.9	-	1.8	2.5	3.1	2.8	4.5
W79	気　道　閉　塞　を　生　じ　た　食　物　の　誤　えん	12.7	13.7	7.1	-	1.5	0.6	3.3	10.4	12.5	14.6
W80	気道閉塞を生じたその他の物体の誤えん	2.1	4.1	2.4	1.5	4.5	0.4	0.8	1.4	1.9	2.5
W84	詳　細　不　明　の　窒　息	5.7	8.2	3.5	2.9	-	0.8	1.4	2.4	4.0	7.7
W85－W99	電流，放射線並びに極端な気温及び気圧への曝露	0.1	-	-	-	-	0.6	0.4	0.2	0.2	0.0
X00－X09	煙，　火及び火炎への曝露	2.3	-	4.7	7.4	3.0	1.6	2.8	4.2	2.8	1.6
X00	建物又は建造物内の管理されていない火への曝露	1.9	-	4.7	7.4	3.0	1.5	2.2	3.4	2.4	1.2
X10－X19	熱　及　び　高　温　物　質　と　の　接　触	0.2	-	1.2	-	-	0.1	0.2	0.1	0.3	0.3
X20－X29	有　毒　動　植　物　と　の　接　触	0.1	-	-	-	-	-	-	0.1	0.1	0.0
X30－X39	自　然　の　力　へ　の　曝　露	4.7	1.4	-	-	3.0	2.9	5.4	7.0	4.9	4.3
X30	自　然　の　過　度　の　高　温　へ　の　曝　露	1.6	1.4	-	-	3.0	0.6	2.0	2.2	1.5	1.6
X31	自　然　の　過　度　の　低　温　へ　の　曝　露	2.9	-	-	-	-	1.2	2.9	4.3	3.1	2.5
X34	地　震　に　よ　る　受　傷　者	0.1	-	-	-	-	0.6	0.1	0.2	0.2	0.1
X40－X49	有害物質による不慮の中毒及び有害物質への曝露	1.5	1.4	-	-	1.5	5.6	10.4	4.8	0.9	0.4
X50－X57	無理ながんばり，旅行及び欠乏状態	0.1	-	-	-	-	0.2	0.2	0.2	0.1	0.0
X58－X59	その他及び詳細不明の要因への不慮の曝露	10.0	2.7	-	1.5	1.5	1.4	2.6	4.8	8.2	13.1

注：1）　総数には年齢不詳を含む。

死　亡

表 5.33　交通事故の種類別にみた
Table 5.33　Trends in deaths and percent distribution

死因基本分類コード Code	交通事故の種類 Kinds of accident	死　亡　数 Deaths						
		1995 平成7年	2000 12年	2005 17年	2010 22年	2014 26年	2015 27年	2016 28年
V01－V98	総　　数　　Total	15 147	12 857	10 028	7 222	5 717	5 646	5 278
V01－V06, V09	歩行者	4 335	3 680	3 033	2 418	2 048	2 059	1 871
V10－V19	自転車乗員	1 998	1 605	1 318	1 088	773	748	706
V20－V29	オートバイ乗員	2 551	1 984	1 422	1 050	803	765	765
V30－V39	オート三輪車乗員	4	4	3	-	1	3	1
V40－V49	乗用車乗員	4 281	3 638	2 376	1 587	1 303	1 289	1 179
V50－V59	軽トラック乗員又はバン乗員	470	374	318	231	151	127	154
V60－V69	大型輸送車両乗員	284	217	165	110	73	87	68
V70－V79	バス乗員	12	5	6	4	7	4	21
V80－V89	その他の陸上交通事故	918	1 067	1 170	580	431	444	385
V90－V94	水上交通事故	260	252	192	132	121	100	110
V95－V97	航空及び宇宙交通事故	32	30	25	22	6	20	18
V98	その他及び詳細不明	2	1	-	-	-	-	-

年次別死亡数及び百分率
from transportation accidents by external causes : Japan

百分率 Percentage							死因基本分類コード Code	交通事故の種類 Kinds of accident
1995 平成7年	2000 12年	2005 17年	2010 22年	2014 26年	2015 27年	2016 28年		
100.0	100.0	100.0	100.0	100.0	100.0	100.0	V01－V98	総　数　　Total
28.6	28.6	30.2	33.5	35.8	36.5	35.4	V01－V06,V09	歩行者
13.2	12.5	13.1	15.1	13.5	13.2	13.4	V10－V19	自転車乗員
16.8	15.4	14.2	14.5	14.0	13.5	14.5	V20－V29	オートバイ乗員
0.0	0.0	0.0	-	0.0	0.1	0.0	V30－V39	オート三輪車乗員
28.3	28.3	23.7	22.0	22.8	22.8	22.3	V40－V49	乗用車乗員
3.1	2.9	3.2	3.2	2.6	2.2	2.9	V50－V59	軽トラック乗員又はバン乗員
1.9	1.7	1.6	1.5	1.3	1.5	1.3	V60－V69	大型輸送車両乗員
0.1	0.0	0.1	0.1	0.1	0.1	0.4	V70－V79	バス乗員
6.1	8.3	11.7	8.0	7.5	7.9	7.3	V80－V89	その他の陸上交通事故
1.7	2.0	1.9	1.8	2.1	1.8	2.1	V90－V94	水上交通事故
0.2	0.2	0.2	0.3	0.1	0.4	0.3	V95－V97	航空及び宇宙交通事故
0.0	0.0	-	-	-	-	-	V98	その他及び詳細不明

死　亡

表 5.34　交通事故以外の不慮の事故の傷害発生の場所別にみた年齢別死亡数及び百分率
Table 5.34　Deaths and percent distribution from nontransportation accidents by age and place of occurrence：Japan, 2016

平成28年

死因基本分類コード Code	傷害発生の場所 Place of occurrence	総 数[1] Total	0歳 Year	1〜4	5〜14	15〜44	45〜64	65〜79	80〜
		死 亡 数　Deaths							
W00-X59	総　　数　　Total	33 028	70	57	74	1 194	3 109	9 178	19 310
.0	家(庭)	14 175	60	45	34	463	1 415	4 670	7 476
.1	居住施設	2 057	-	1	1	19	61	362	1 613
.2	学校，施設及び公共の地域	1 106	1	2	3	21	172	382	524
.3	スポーツ施設及び競技施設	34	-	1	1	6	11	11	4
.4	街路及びハイウェイ	632	-	1	1	40	110	224	256
.5	商業及びサービス施設	862	-	-	2	72	149	381	255
.6	工業用地域及び建築現場	404	-	-	-	140	154	97	13
.7	農場	281	-	-	1	10	45	91	134
.8	その他の明示された場所	2 363	3	2	23	299	503	868	650
.9	詳細不明の場所	11 114	6	5	8	124	489	2 092	8 385
		百 分 率　Percentage							
W00-X59	総　　数　　Total	100.0	100.0	100.0	100.0	100.0	100.0	100.0	100.0
.0	家(庭)	42.9	85.7	78.9	45.9	38.8	45.5	50.9	38.7
.1	居住施設	6.2	-	1.8	1.4	1.6	2.0	3.9	8.4
.2	学校，施設及び公共の地域	3.3	1.4	3.5	4.1	1.8	5.5	4.2	2.7
.3	スポーツ施設及び競技施設	0.1	-	1.8	1.4	0.5	0.4	0.1	0.0
.4	街路及びハイウェイ	1.9	-	1.8	1.4	3.4	3.5	2.4	1.3
.5	商業及びサービス施設	2.6	-	-	2.7	6.0	4.8	4.2	1.3
.6	工業用地域及び建築現場	1.2	-	-	-	11.7	5.0	1.1	0.1
.7	農場	0.9	-	-	1.4	0.8	1.4	1.0	0.7
.8	その他の明示された場所	7.2	4.3	3.5	31.1	25.0	16.2	9.5	3.4
.9	詳細不明の場所	33.7	8.6	8.8	10.8	10.4	15.7	22.8	43.4

注：1）　総数には年齢不詳を含む。

General mortality

表5.35　家庭における主な不慮の事故の種類別にみた年齢別死亡数及び百分率
Table 5.35　Deaths and percent distribution from accidents at home by age and external causes : Japan, 2016

平成28年

死因基本分類コード Code	死　因 Causes of death	総数[1] Total	0歳 Year	1～4	5～9	10～14	15～29	30～44	45～64	65～79	80～
		死　亡　数　Deaths									
W00－X59	総　数[2]　　　Total	14 175	60	45	14	20	155	308	1 415	4 670	7 476
W00－W17	転倒・転落	2 748	-	6	1	5	33	52	289	834	1 528
W01	スリップ，つまづき及びよろめきによる同一平面上での転倒	1 608	-	1	-	-	8	21	114	422	1 042
W10	階段及びステップからの転落及びその上での転倒	484	-	-	-	-	-	7	77	174	226
W13	建物又は建造物からの転落	300	-	4	1	5	24	23	69	94	80
W65－W74	不慮の溺死及び溺水	5 491	3	18	3	9	41	36	295	2 075	3 011
W65	浴槽内での溺死及び溺水	5 100	2	15	3	8	40	32	279	1 937	2 784
W66	浴槽への転落による溺死及び溺水	38	1	-	-	1	-	-	1	13	22
W75－W84	その他の不慮の窒息	3 817	57	16	4	4	22	67	373	1 094	2 180
W78	胃内容物の誤えん	596	18	5	2	-	8	28	83	129	323
W79	気道閉塞を生じた食物の誤えん	2 659	8	5	-	1	3	25	234	825	1 558
W80	気道閉塞を生じたその他の物体の誤えん	183	3	1	1	1	2	3	16	52	104
X00－X09	煙，火及び火炎への曝露	787	-	4	5	2	15	34	155	280	282
X00	建物又は建造物内の管理されていない火への曝露	705	-	4	5	2	15	30	138	255	246
X05－X06	夜着，その他の着衣及び衣服の発火又は溶解への曝露	27	-	-	-	-	-	-	4	5	18
X10－X19	熱及び高温物質との接触	77	-	1	-	-	-	-	6	23	47
X11	蛇口からの熱湯との接触	62	-	1	-	-	-	-	4	16	41
X40－X49	有害物質による不慮の中毒及び有害物質への曝露	332	-	-	-	-	32	87	117	56	39
X47	その他のガス及び蒸気による不慮の中毒及び曝露	74	-	-	-	-	17	18	19	16	3
X48	農薬による不慮の中毒及び曝露	36	-	-	-	-	-	1	2	12	21
		百　分　率　Percentage									
W00－X59	総　数　　　Total	100.0	100.0	100.0	100.0	100.0	100.0	100.0	100.0	100.0	100.0
W00－W17	転倒・転落	19.4	-	13.3	7.1	25.0	21.3	16.9	20.4	17.9	20.4
W01	スリップ，つまづき及びよろめきによる同一平面上での転倒	11.3	-	2.2	-	-	5.2	6.8	8.1	9.0	13.9
W10	階段及びステップからの転落及びその上での転倒	3.4	-	-	-	-	-	2.3	5.4	3.7	3.0
W13	建物又は建造物からの転落	2.1	-	8.9	7.1	25.0	15.5	7.5	4.9	2.0	1.1
W65－W74	不慮の溺死及び溺水	38.7	5.0	40.0	21.4	45.0	26.5	11.7	20.8	44.4	40.3
W65	浴槽内での溺死及び溺水	36.0	3.3	33.3	21.4	40.0	25.8	10.4	19.7	41.5	37.2
W66	浴槽への転落による溺死及び溺水	0.3	1.7	-	-	5.0	-	-	0.1	0.3	0.3
W75－W84	その他の不慮の窒息	26.9	95.0	35.6	28.6	20.0	14.2	21.8	26.4	23.4	29.2
W78	胃内容物の誤えん	4.2	30.0	11.1	14.3	-	5.2	9.1	5.9	2.8	4.3
W79	気道閉塞を生じた食物の誤えん	18.8	13.3	11.1	-	5.0	1.9	8.1	16.5	17.7	20.8
W80	気道閉塞を生じたその他の物体の誤えん	1.3	5.0	2.2	7.1	5.0	1.3	1.0	1.1	1.1	1.4
X00－X09	煙，火及び火炎への曝露	5.6	-	8.9	35.7	10.0	9.7	11.0	11.0	6.0	3.8
X00	建物又は建造物内の管理されていない火への曝露	5.0	-	8.9	35.7	10.0	9.7	9.7	9.8	5.5	3.3
X05－X06	夜着，その他の着衣及び衣服の発火又は溶解への曝露	0.2	-	-	-	-	-	-	0.3	0.1	0.2
X10－X19	熱及び高温物質との接触	0.5	-	2.2	-	-	-	-	0.4	0.5	0.6
X11	蛇口からの熱湯との接触	0.4	-	2.2	-	-	-	-	0.3	0.3	0.5
X40－X49	有害物質による不慮の中毒及び有害物質への曝露	2.3	-	-	-	-	20.6	28.2	8.3	1.2	0.5
X47	その他のガス及び蒸気による不慮の中毒及び曝露	0.5	-	-	-	-	11.0	5.8	1.3	0.3	0.0
X48	農薬による不慮の中毒及び曝露	0.3	-	-	-	-	-	0.3	0.1	0.3	0.3

注：1)　総数には年齢不詳を含む。
　　2)　内訳は主な項目のため、たしあげても総数にはならない。

死　亡

〔主な死因〕自殺

表5.36　自殺の手段別にみた
Table 5.36　Trends in deaths and percent distribution

死因基本分類コード Code	死　因 Causes of death	総　数 Total													
		死　亡　数 Deaths							百　分　率 Percentage						
		1995 平成7年	2000 12年	2005 17年	2010 22年	2014 26年	2015 27年	2016 28年	1995 平成7年	2000 12年	2005 17年	2010 22年	2014 26年	2015 27年	2016 28年
X60-X84	総　数　Total	21 420	30 251	30 553	29 554	24 417	23 152	21 017	100.0	100.0	100.0	100.0	100.0	100.0	100.0
X60	非オピオイド系鎮痛薬, 解熱薬及び抗リウマチ薬	8	10	7	8	7	6	5	0.0	0.0	0.0	0.0	0.0	0.0	0.0
X61	抗てんかん薬, 鎮静・催眠薬, パーキンソン病治療薬及び向精神薬	235	359	375	307	240	200	191	1.1	1.2	1.2	1.0	1.0	0.9	0.9
X62	麻薬及び精神変容薬〔幻覚発現薬〕	-	1	3	-	2	1	2		0.0	0.0	-	0.0	0.0	0.0
X63	自律神経系に作用するその他の薬物	1	1	3	-	2	3	-	0.0	0.0	0.0	-	0.0	0.0	-
X64	その他及び詳細不明の薬物, 薬剤及び生物学的製剤	111	164	197	187	158	176	165	0.5	0.5	0.6	0.6	0.6	0.8	0.8
X65	アルコール	1	4	5	4	10	3	6	0.0	0.0	0.0	0.0	0.0	0.0	0.0
X66	有機溶剤及びハロゲン化炭化水素類及びそれらの蒸気	11	14	15	11	5	10	10	0.1	0.0	0.0	0.0	0.0	0.0	0.0
X67	その他のガス及び蒸気	1 070	1 424	4 494	3 923	2 245	2 086	1 841	5.0	4.7	14.7	13.3	9.2	9.0	8.8
X68	農薬	835	795	506	373	254	226	180	3.9	2.6	1.7	1.3	1.0	1.0	0.9
X69	その他及び詳細不明の化学物質及び有害物質	57	48	42	44	21	25	17	0.3	0.2	0.1	0.1	0.1	0.1	0.1
X70	縊首, 絞首及び窒息	13 379	20 846	19 365	19 628	17 154	16 230	14 481	62.5	68.9	63.4	66.4	70.3	70.1	68.9
X71	溺死及び溺水	1 168	1 178	919	831	667	631	592	5.5	3.9	3.0	2.8	2.7	2.7	2.8
X72	拳銃の発射	12	10	14	11	5	3	5	0.1	0.0	0.0	0.0	0.0	0.0	0.0
X73	ライフル, 散弾銃及び大型銃器の発射	22	43	23	8	5	6	7	0.1	0.1	0.1	0.0	0.0	0.0	0.0
X74	その他及び詳細不明の銃器の発射	6	9	6	7	4	1	2	0.0	0.0	0.0	0.0	0.0	0.0	0.0
X75	爆発物	2	-	1	-	-	-	-	0.0	-	0.0	-	-	-	-
X76	煙, 火及び火炎	620	743	575	362	296	281	241	2.9	2.5	1.9	1.2	1.2	1.2	1.1
X77	スチーム, 高温蒸気及び高温物体	-	-	-	-	2	-	-				-	0.0	-	-
X78	鋭利な物体	615	793	727	601	556	523	517	2.9	2.6	2.4	2.0	2.3	2.3	2.5
X79	鈍器	6	2	1	2	-	-	2	0.0	0.0	0.0	0.0	-	-	0.0
X80	高所からの飛び降り	2 159	2 881	2 333	2 391	2 011	1 927	1 944	10.1	9.5	7.6	8.1	8.2	8.3	9.2
X81	移動中の物体の前への飛び込み又は横臥	827	639	666	614	533	532	542	3.9	2.1	2.2	2.1	2.2	2.3	2.6
X82	モーター車両の衝突	25	4	1	3	3	1	3	0.1	0.0	0.0	0.0	0.0	0.0	0.0
X83	その他の明示された手段	205	205	189	97	120	116	110	1.0	0.7	0.6	0.3	0.5	0.5	0.5
X84	詳細不明の手段	45	78	86	142	117	165	154	0.2	0.3	0.3	0.5	0.5	0.7	0.7

性・年次別死亡数及び百分率
from suicide by sex and external causes : Japan

男 Male 死亡数 Deaths							百分率 Percentage							死因基本分類コード Code	死因 Causes of death
1995 平成7年	2000 12年	2005 17年	2010 22年	2014 26年	2015 27年	2016 28年	1995 平成7年	2000 12年	2005 17年	2010 22年	2014 26年	2015 27年	2016 28年		
14 231	21 656	22 236	21 028	16 875	16 202	14 639	100.0	100.0	100.0	100.0	100.0	100.0	100.0	X60-X84	総　数　Total
5	6	2	5	4	1	3	0.0	0.0	0.0	0.0	0.0	0.0	0.0	X60	非オピオイド系鎮痛薬, 解熱薬及び抗リウマチ薬
121	194	166	141	97	94	85	0.9	0.9	0.7	0.7	0.6	0.6	0.6	X61	抗てんかん薬, 鎮静・催眠薬, パーキンソン病治療薬及び向精神薬
-	-	2	-	-	1	1	-	-	0.0	-	-	0.0	0.0	X62	麻薬及び精神変容薬［幻覚発現薬］
1	-	2	-	1	1	-	0.0	-	0.0	-	0.0	0.0	-	X63	自律神経系に作用するその他の薬物
55	106	96	98	76	84	76	0.4	0.5	0.4	0.5	0.5	0.5	0.5	X64	その他及び詳細不明の薬物, 薬剤及び生物学的製剤
-	3	2	3	8	2	4	-	0.0	0.0	0.0	0.0	0.0	0.0	X65	アルコール
8	10	11	9	3	7	6	0.1	0.0	0.0	0.0	0.0	0.0	0.0	X66	有機溶剤及びハロゲン化炭化水素類及びそれらの蒸気
946	1 288	3 886	3 275	1 864	1 723	1 503	6.6	5.9	17.5	15.6	11.0	10.6	10.3	X67	その他のガス及び蒸気
461	472	313	223	143	126	98	3.2	2.2	1.4	1.1	0.8	0.8	0.7	X68	農薬
33	25	25	25	12	10	7	0.2	0.1	0.1	0.1	0.1	0.1	0.0	X69	その他及び詳細不明の化学物質及び有害物質
9 229	15 513	14 343	14 273	12 098	11 668	10 399	64.9	71.6	64.5	67.9	71.7	72.0	71.0	X70	縊首, 絞首及び窒息
463	525	413	365	294	297	277	3.3	2.4	1.9	1.7	1.7	1.8	1.9	X71	溺死及び溺水
12	10	14	11	5	3	5	0.1	0.0	0.1	0.1	0.0	0.0	0.0	X72	拳銃の発射
21	42	21	8	5	6	7	0.1	0.2	0.1	0.0	0.0	0.0	0.0	X73	ライフル, 散弾銃及び大型銃器の発射
5	9	6	7	4	1	2	0.0	0.0	0.0	0.0	0.0	0.0	0.0	X74	その他及び詳細不明の銃器の発射
2	-	1	-	-	-	-	0.0	-	0.0	-	-	-	-	X75	爆発物
377	493	385	227	189	176	158	2.6	2.3	1.7	1.1	1.1	1.1	1.1	X76	煙, 火及び火炎
-	-	-	-	-	-	-								X77	スチーム, 高温蒸気及び高温物体
465	600	549	411	408	359	355	3.3	2.8	2.5	2.0	2.4	2.2	2.4	X78	鋭利な物体
2	2	1	2	-	-	1	0.0	0.0	0.0	0.0	-	-	0.0	X79	鈍器
1 339	1 772	1 405	1 415	1 157	1 113	1 145	9.4	8.2	6.3	6.7	6.9	6.9	7.8	X80	高所からの飛び降り
476	383	411	377	341	349	334	3.3	1.8	1.8	1.8	2.0	2.2	2.3	X81	移動中の物体の前への飛び込み又は横臥
14	2	1	3	3	-	2	0.1	0.0	0.0	0.0	0.0	-	0.0	X82	モーター車両の衝突
167	148	129	62	94	85	79	1.2	0.7	0.6	0.3	0.6	0.5	0.5	X83	その他の明示された手段
29	53	52	88	69	96	92	0.2	0.2	0.2	0.4	0.4	0.6	0.6	X84	詳細不明の手段

死 亡

表5.36　自殺の手段別にみた性・年次別死亡数及び百分率（つづき）
Table 5.36　Trends in deaths and percent distribution from suicide by sex and external causes : Japan−CON.

死因基本分類コード Code	死因 Causes of death	女　Female													
		死亡数 Deaths							百分率 Percentage						
		1995 平成7年	2000 12年	2005 17年	2010 22年	2014 26年	2015 27年	2016 28年	1995 平成7年	2000 12年	2005 17年	2010 22年	2014 26年	2015 27年	2016 28年
X60−X84	総　数　Total	7 189	8 595	8 317	8 526	7 542	6 950	6 378	100.0	100.0	100.0	100.0	100.0	100.0	100.0
X60	非オピオイド系鎮痛薬，解熱薬及び抗リウマチ薬	3	4	5	3	3	5	2	0.0	0.0	0.1	0.0	0.0	0.1	0.0
X61	抗てんかん薬，鎮静・催眠薬，パーキンソン病治療薬及び向精神薬	114	165	209	166	143	106	106	1.6	1.9	2.5	1.9	1.9	1.5	1.7
X62	麻薬及び精神変容薬［幻覚発現薬］	-	1	1	-	2	-	1	-	0.0	0.0	-	0.0	-	0.0
X63	自律神経系に作用するその他の薬物	-	1	1	-	1	2	-	-	0.0	0.0	-	0.0	0.0	-
X64	その他及び詳細不明の薬物，薬剤及び生物学的製剤	56	58	101	89	82	92	89	0.8	0.7	1.2	1.0	1.1	1.3	1.4
X65	アルコール	1	1	3	1	2	1	2	0.0	0.0	0.0	0.0	0.0	0.0	0.0
X66	有機溶剤及びハロゲン化炭化水素類及びそれらの蒸気	3	4	4	2	2	3	4	0.0	0.0	0.0	0.0	0.0	0.0	0.1
X67	その他のガス及び蒸気	124	136	608	648	381	363	338	1.7	1.6	7.3	7.6	5.1	5.2	5.3
X68	農薬	374	323	193	150	111	100	82	5.2	3.8	2.3	1.8	1.5	1.4	1.3
X69	その他及び詳細不明の化学物質及び有害物質	24	23	17	19	9	15	10	0.3	0.3	0.2	0.2	0.1	0.2	0.2
X70	縊首，絞首及び窒息	4 150	5 333	5 022	5 355	5 056	4 562	4 082	57.7	62.0	60.4	62.8	67.0	65.6	64.0
X71	溺死及び溺水	705	653	506	466	373	334	315	9.8	7.6	6.1	5.5	4.9	4.8	4.9
X72	拳銃の発射	-	-	-	-	-	-	-	-	-	-	-	-	-	-
X73	ライフル，散弾銃及び大型銃器の発射	1	1	2	-	-	-	-	0.0	0.0	0.0	-	-	-	-
X74	その他及び詳細不明の銃器の発射	1	-	-	-	-	-	-	0.0	-	-	-	-	-	-
X75	爆発物	-	-	-	-	-	-	-	-	-	-	-	-	-	-
X76	煙，火及び火炎	243	250	190	135	107	105	83	3.4	2.9	2.3	1.6	1.4	1.5	1.3
X77	スチーム，高温蒸気及び高温物体	-	-	-	-	2	-	-	-	-	-	-	0.0	-	-
X78	鋭利な物体	150	193	178	190	148	164	162	2.1	2.2	2.1	2.2	2.0	2.4	2.5
X79	鈍器	4	-	-	-	-	-	1	0.1	-	-	-	-	-	0.0
X80	高所からの飛び降り	820	1 109	928	976	854	814	799	11.4	12.9	11.2	11.4	11.3	11.7	12.5
X81	移動中の物体の前への飛び込み又は横臥	351	256	255	237	192	183	208	4.9	3.0	3.1	2.8	2.5	2.6	3.3
X82	モーター車両の衝突	11	2	-	-	-	1	1	0.2	0.0	-	-	-	0.0	0.0
X83	その他の明示された手段	38	57	60	35	26	31	31	0.5	0.7	0.7	0.4	0.3	0.4	0.5
X84	詳細不明の手段	16	25	34	54	48	69	62	0.2	0.3	0.4	0.6	0.6	1.0	1.0

死　亡

〔主な死因〕妊産婦死亡

表5.37　妊産婦死亡の死因別にみた年次別死亡数及び率（出産10万対）
Table 5.37　Trends in maternal deaths and maternal mortality rates (per 100,000 total births) by causes of death : Japan

死因基本分類コード Code	死因 Causes of death	妊　産　婦　死　亡　数 Maternal deaths									
		1995 平成7年	2000 12年	2005 17年	2010 22年	2011 23年	2012 24年	2013 25年	2014 26年	2015 27年	2016 28年
	総　数　　　Total	85	78	62	45	41	42	36	28	39	34
O00－O92	直　接　産　科　的　死　亡	67	62	45	34	26	35	28	18	30	27
O00	子　宮　外　妊　娠	2	5	1	3	2	-	1	-	-	2
O10－O16	妊娠，分娩及び産じょくにおける浮腫，たんぱく尿及び高血圧性障害	19	8	5	2	3	8	8	1	3	4
O44－O45	前置胎盤及び（常位）胎盤早期剥離	3	12	8	4	3	4	1		3	3
O46	分娩前出血，他に分類されないもの	-	-	-	-	-	-	-	1	-	-
O72	分　娩　後　出　血	4	11	6	3	4	3	7	6	11	2
O88	産　科　的　塞　栓　症	20	14	12	11	9	11	4	6	6	8
O01－O07 O20－O43 O47－O71 O73－O87 O89－O92	その他の直接産科的死亡	19	12	13	11	5	9	7	4	7	8
O98－O99	間　接　産　科　的　死　亡	18	15	17	11	15	7	8	9	8	7
O95	原　因　不　明　の　産　科　的　死　亡	-	1	-	-	-	-	-	1	1	-
A34	産　科　的　破　傷　風	-	-	-	-	-	-	-	-	-	-
B20－B24	ヒト免疫不全ウイルス病（妊娠，分娩及び産じょくによる死亡）	-	-	-	-	-	-	-	-	-	-

死因基本分類コード Code	死因 Causes of death	妊産婦死亡率（出産10万対） Maternal mortality rates (per 100,000 total births)									
		1995 平成7年	2000 12年	2005 17年	2010 22年	2011 23年	2012 24年	2013 25年	2014 26年	2015 27年	2016 28年
	総　数　　　Total	6.9	6.3	5.7	4.1	3.8	4.0	3.4	2.7	3.8	3.4
O00－O92	直　接　産　科　的　死　亡	5.5	5.0	4.1	3.1	2.4	3.3	2.7	1.8	2.9	2.7
O00	子　宮　外　妊　娠	0.2	0.4	0.1	0.3	0.2	-	0.1	-	-	0.2
O10－O16	妊娠，分娩及び産じょくにおける浮腫，たんぱく尿及び高血圧性障害	1.5	0.7	0.5	0.2	0.3	0.8	0.8	0.1	0.3	0.4
O44－O45	前置胎盤及び（常位）胎盤早期剥離	0.2	1.0	0.7	0.4	0.3	0.4	0.1		0.3	0.3
O46	分娩前出血，他に分類されないもの	-	-	-	-	-	-	-	0.1	-	-
O72	分　娩　後　出　血	0.3	0.9	0.5	0.3	0.4	0.3	0.7	0.6	1.1	0.2
O88	産　科　的　塞　栓　症	1.6	1.1	1.1	1.0	0.8	1.0	0.4	0.6	0.6	0.8
O01－O07 O20－O43 O47－O71 O73－O87 O89－O92	その他の直接産科的死亡	1.5	1.0	1.2	1.0	0.5	0.8	0.7	0.4	0.7	0.8
O98－O99	間　接　産　科　的　死　亡	1.5	1.2	1.6	1.0	1.4	0.7	0.8	0.9	0.8	0.7
O95	原　因　不　明　の　産　科　的　死　亡	-	0.1	-	-	-	-	-	0.1	0.1	-
A34	産　科　的　破　傷　風	-	-	-	-	-	-	-	-	-	-
B20－B24	ヒト免疫不全ウイルス病（妊娠，分娩及び産じょくによる死亡）	-	-	-	-	-	-	-	-	-	-

注：妊産婦死亡については、「第2章 調査結果の利用上の解説」65ページを参照されたい。

General mortality

表5.38　後発妊産婦死亡の死因別にみた年次別死亡数及び率 （出産10万対）
Table 5.38　Trends in late maternal deaths and late maternal mortality rates (per 100,000 total births) by causes of death：Japan

死因基本分類コード Code	死　因 Causes of death	後発妊産婦死亡数（妊娠終了満42日以後1年未満） Late maternal deaths									
		1995 平成7年	2000 12年	2005 17年	2010 22年	2011 23年	2012 24年	2013 25年	2014 26年	2015 27年	2016 28年
	総　　数　　　Total	3	2	-	-	-	-	1	-	1	-
O96	あらゆる産科的原因による母体死亡	3	2	-	-	-	-	1	-	1	-
A34	産　科　的　破　傷　風	-	-	-	-	-	-	-	-	-	-
B20－B24	ヒ ト 免 疫 不 全 ウ イ ル ス 病 （妊娠，分娩及び産じょくによる死亡）	-	-	-	-	-	-	-	-	-	-

死因基本分類コード Code	死　因 Causes of death	後発妊産婦死亡率 （出産10万対） Late maternal mortality rates（per 100,000 total births）									
		1995 平成7年	2000 12年	2005 17年	2010 22年	2011 23年	2012 24年	2013 25年	2014 26年	2015 27年	2016 28年
	総　　数　　　Total	0.2	0.2	-	-	-	-	0.1	-	0.1	-
O96	あらゆる産科的原因による母体死亡	0.2	0.2	-	-	-	-	0.1	-	0.1	-
A34	産　科　的　破　傷　風	-	-	-	-	-	-	-	-	-	-
B20－B24	ヒ ト 免 疫 不 全 ウ イ ル ス 病 （妊娠，分娩及び産じょくによる死亡）	-	-	-	-	-	-	-	-	-	-

注：後発妊産婦死亡については、「第2章 調査結果の利用上の解説」65ページを参照されたい。

死　亡

表5.39　都道府県別にみた年次別
Table 5.39　Trends in maternal deaths and maternal mortality rates

都道府県 Prefecture	妊産婦死亡数 Maternal deaths												
	1980 昭和55年	1985 60年	1990 平成2年	1995 7年	2000 12年	2005 17年	2010 22年	2011 23年	2012 24年	2013 25年	2014 26年	2015 27年	**2016 28年**
全国[1] Total	323	226	105	85	78	62	45	41	42	36	28	39	**34**
01[a] 北海道	13	7	4	4	-	2	2	2	2	2	3	1	-
02 青　森	7	3	2	3	-	-	2	-	1	-	1	-	1
03 岩　手	6	4	1	2	2	-	1	1	1	-	1	-	1
04 宮　城	4	6	5	2	-	-	-	-	-	1	1	-	1
05 秋　田	2	1	2	-	-	1	-	1	-	-	-	1	-
06 山　形	-	3	1	1	2	-	1	-	1	-	1	-	-
07 福　島	4	5	1	1	2	1	2	-	-	-	-	1	-
08 茨　城	8	5	1	3	3	2	-	-	-	2	2	-	-
09 栃　木	6	7	4	-	-	1	-	-	1	-	-	-	1
10 群　馬	4	3	1	-	1	-	-	-	1	-	-	-	-
11 埼　玉	16	9	14	7	10	4	5	3	2	1	3	3	1
12 千　葉	14	7	3	2	4	2	3	3	1	2	2	3	2
13 東　京	40	22	11	6	4	2	8	3	7	3	3	2	3
14 神奈川	15	14	8	6	4	5	2	3	5	2	2	4	2
15 新　潟	3	3	2	3	4	2	-	-	1	2	1	-	-
16 富　山	2	3	-	-	-	-	-	-	-	-	-	2	-
17 石　川	-	1	1	1	-	-	-	-	-	1	-	-	-
18 福　井	-	3	-	-	2	1	-	-	-	-	-	2	-
19 山　梨	3	5	-	-	-	-	-	1	-	1	-	-	-
20 長　野	10	3	2	2	2	2	-	-	2	-	-	1	1
21 岐　阜	4	2	1	4	1	3	-	-	-	-	1	-	-
22 静　岡	7	6	4	2	3	1	-	3	3	2	-	3	1
23 愛　知	12	15	3	4	7	11	2	2	1	5	1	3	3
24 三　重	3	1	1	-	2	2	-	1	-	-	-	-	1
25 滋　賀	2	1	2	3	-	2	-	-	1	-	-	1	1
26 京　都	7	7	2	3	3	-	-	2	1	-	-	2	2
27 大　阪	32	15	9	9	3	3	3	5	-	5	1	1	4
28 兵　庫	17	9	1	3	3	1	3	1	3	-	1	3	3
29 奈　良	2	2	2	-	1	-	-	-	2	-	-	2	-
30 和歌山	2	2	-	1	-	-	-	-	-	1	-	-	-
31 鳥　取	2	-	-	1	-	-	-	-	1	-	-	-	-
32 島　根	5	3	-	1	-	-	-	-	-	-	-	-	-
33 岡　山	2	2	1	-	1	-	1	-	-	1	1	2	1
34 広　島	8	7	2	1	-	1	-	1	-	1	-	-	-
35 山　口	7	4	2	1	1	1	2	2	-	-	-	-	-
36 徳　島	3	-	-	-	1	1	1	-	-	-	-	-	-
37 香　川	-	2	-	1	-	1	1	-	-	-	-	-	-
38 愛　媛	4	2	1	1	-	-	-	1	-	-	-	1	-
39 高　知	2	2	-	-	2	-	-	-	-	-	-	-	-
40 福　岡	12	6	4	2	2	3	-	3	3	1	1	1	1
41 佐　賀	2	-	-	-	2	2	1	-	-	-	-	-	1
42 長　崎	4	4	4	2	1	1	-	2	-	-	-	-	-
43 熊　本	1	2	2	1	2	1	-	-	2	1	-	-	1
44 大　分	7	8	-	-	-	-	-	-	-	-	-	-	1
45 宮　崎	4	2	1	1	2	-	2	-	-	-	-	-	1
46 鹿児島	12	5	-	1	1	2	1	1	-	-	-	1	-
47 沖　縄	2	3	-	-	-	1	1	-	-	2	1	-	-

注：1)　全国には住所地外国・不詳を含む。

妊産婦死亡数及び率（出産10万対）
（per 100,000 total births）by each prefecture : Japan

1980 昭和55年	1985 60年	1990 平成2年	1995 7年	2000 12年	2005 17年	2010 22年	2011 23年	2012 24年	2013 25年	2014 26年	2015 27年	2016 28年	都道府県 Prefecture
19.5	15.1	8.2	6.9	6.3	5.7	4.1	3.8	4.0	3.4	2.7	3.8	**3.4**	全国[1] Total
16.0	9.8	6.9	7.7	-	4.6	4.8	4.9	5.0	5.1	7.9	2.6	-	01[a] 北海道
30.6	14.9	13.1	20.7	-	-	20.0	-	10.6	-	11.0	-	**11.4**	02 青森
28.9	22.0	6.7	14.8	15.5	-	10.0	10.5	10.5	-	11.1	-	**11.7**	03 岩手
12.2	20.2	20.3	8.6	-	-	-	-	-	5.2	5.4	-	**5.6**	04 宮城
11.7	7.0	17.4	-	-	12.6	-	14.6	-	-	-	16.7	-	05 秋田
-	19.1	7.6	8.4	17.6	-	11.3	-	11.9	-	12.3	-	-	06 山形
12.9	17.4	4.2	4.5	9.5	5.5	12.0	-	-	-	-	6.9	-	07 福島
21.2	14.3	3.3	10.3	10.3	8.0	-	-	-	8.7	8.9	-	-	08 茨城
22.2	28.2	19.1	-	-	5.6	-	-	6.1	-	-	-	**6.7**	09 栃木
15.3	12.6	5.0	-	5.0	-	-	-	6.5	-	-	-	-	10 群馬
20.5	12.9	21.3	10.0	14.6	6.5	8.2	5.0	3.4	1.7	5.2	5.2	**1.8**	11 埼玉
20.5	11.1	5.4	3.6	7.0	3.8	5.7	5.8	2.0	4.0	4.2	6.2	**4.3**	12 千葉
27.2	16.7	10.1	6.0	3.9	2.0	7.2	2.8	6.4	2.7	2.7	1.7	**2.6**	13 東京
15.3	15.7	9.7	7.2	4.7	6.4	2.5	3.9	6.5	2.6	2.7	5.3	**2.8**	14 神奈川
8.8	9.9	8.0	12.9	17.8	10.5	-	-	5.6	11.4	5.9	-	-	15 新潟
14.2	24.0	-	-	-	-	-	-	-	-	-	25.9	-	16 富山
-	7.2	8.3	8.8	-	-	-	-	-	10.4	-	-	-	17 石川
-	28.6	-	-	24.2	13.6	-	-	-	-	-	31.4	-	18 福井
28.6	48.7	-	-	-	-	-	15.2	-	15.8	-	-	-	19 山梨
35.3	12.0	9.0	9.2	9.2	10.5	-	-	11.7	-	-	6.3	**6.5**	20 長野
14.9	8.1	4.7	19.3	4.8	16.5	-	-	-	-	6.5	-	-	21 岐阜
14.2	13.1	10.4	5.5	8.1	3.1	-	9.4	9.5	6.5	-	10.4	**3.5**	22 静岡
13.1	17.9	4.1	5.4	9.1	16.0	2.8	2.8	1.4	7.3	1.5	4.5	**4.6**	23 愛知
13.4	4.9	5.4	-	11.0	12.7	-	6.5	-	-	-	-	**7.4**	24 三重
12.0	6.5	14.2	21.9	-	15.1	-	-	7.4	-	-	7.8	**8.1**	25 滋賀
20.7	23.5	7.9	12.5	12.2	-	-	9.4	4.9	-	-	10.0	**10.1**	26 京都
27.0	14.2	9.9	10.1	3.3	3.8	3.9	6.6	-	6.8	1.4	1.4	**5.7**	27 大阪
23.7	14.1	1.8	5.6	5.4	2.1	6.1	2.1	6.3	-	2.2	6.7	**6.8**	28 兵庫
12.0	13.1	14.4	-	7.3	-	-	-	18.5	-	-	19.9	-	29 奈良
14.3	15.8	-	9.8	-	-	-	-	-	13.7	-	-	-	30 和歌山
23.2	-	-	16.8	-	-	-	-	20.5	-	-	-	-	31 鳥取
47.9	31.7	-	14.4	-	-	-	-	-	-	-	-	-	32 島根
7.8	8.4	5.0	-	5.1	-	5.8	-	-	6.0	6.2	12.5	**6.3**	33 岡山
20.5	19.9	6.7	3.5	-	3.9	-	3.8	-	4.0	-	-	-	34 広島
33.5	21.6	13.9	7.3	7.4	8.4	16.9	17.4	-	-	-	-	-	35 山口
27.0	-	-	-	13.5	16.4	16.5	-	-	-	-	-	-	36 徳島
-	16.6	-	10.5	-	11.2	11.6	-	-	-	-	-	-	37 香川
19.3	10.8	6.5	7.0	-	-	-	8.6	-	-	-	9.6	-	38 愛媛
20.2	20.3	-	-	28.2	-	-	-	-	-	-	-	-	39 高知
17.6	9.6	7.9	4.1	4.1	6.7	-	6.3	6.4	2.1	2.2	2.2	**2.2**	40 福岡
15.2	-	-	-	21.9	25.8	12.7	-	-	-	-	-	**14.4**	41 佐賀
16.8	18.2	23.0	12.9	6.8	7.9	-	16.6	-	-	-	-	-	42 長崎
3.9	8.1	10.0	5.3	11.1	6.2	-	-	12.2	6.1	-	-	**6.5**	43 熊本
40.4	52.0	-	-	-	-	-	-	-	-	-	-	**10.8**	44 大分
22.1	12.3	7.8	8.1	17.3	-	19.0	-	-	-	-	-	**10.9**	45 宮崎
45.9	20.2	-	5.7	5.9	12.9	6.4	6.4	-	-	6.8	-	-	46 鹿児島
9.6	14.1	-	-	-	6.0	5.7	-	-	11.3	5.9	-	-	47 沖縄

Note : a) See page 44.

乳児死亡

〔乳児死亡の年次推移〕
〔Trends in infant deaths〕

第6章 乳児死亡
Chapter 6 Infant mortality

表6.1 年次別にみた乳児死亡数・率（出生千対）・乳児死亡性比

Table 6.1 Trends in infant deaths, infant mortality rates (per 1,000 live

年　　　次 [1] Year		出　生　数 Live births	乳　児　死　亡　数 Infant deaths				乳児死亡率 Infant mortality rates	乳児死亡性比 Sex ratio of infant deaths	総死亡中乳児死亡の占める割合（%） Proportion of infant deaths
			総　数 Total	男 Male	女 Female	不　詳 Not stated			
1899	明治32年	1 386 981	213 359	115 077	98 278	4	153.8	117.1	22.9
1900	33	1 420 534	220 211	118 470	101 740	1	155.0	116.4	24.2
01	34	1 501 591	225 107	120 640	104 465	2	149.9	115.5	24.3
02	35	1 510 835	232 652	125 398	107 252	2	154.0	116.9	24.3
03	36	1 489 816	226 982	122 045	104 935	2	152.4	116.3	24.4
04	37	1 440 371	218 756	117 247	101 508	1	151.9	115.5	22.9
05	38	1 452 770	220 450	118 305	102 141	4	151.7	115.8	21.9
06	39	1 394 295	214 148	113 942	100 203	3	153.6	113.7	22.4
07	40	1 614 472	244 300	130 983	113 315	2	151.3	115.6	24.0
08	41	1 662 815	262 801	140 659	122 141	1	158.0	115.2	25.5
09	42	1 693 850	283 436	151 099	132 334	3	167.3	114.2	26.0
1910	43	1 712 857	276 136	147 338	128 797	1	161.2	114.4	25.9
11	44	1 747 803	276 798	147 466	129 330	2	158.4	114.0	26.5
12	大正元年	1 737 674	268 025	143 105	124 919	1	154.2	114.6	25.8
13	2	1 757 441	267 281	142 528	124 752	1	152.1	114.2	26.0
14	3	1 808 402	286 678	152 577	134 100	1	158.5	113.8	26.0
15	4	1 799 326	288 634	153 903	134 731	-	160.4	114.2	26.4
16	5	1 804 822	307 283	164 838	142 445	-	170.3	115.7	25.9
17	6	1 812 413	313 872	168 123	145 749	-	173.2	115.4	26.2
18	7	1 791 992	337 919	180 982	156 937	-	188.6	115.3	22.6
19	8	1 778 685	303 202	162 144	141 058	-	170.5	114.9	23.7
1920	9	2 025 564	335 613	179 956	155 657	-	165.7	115.6	23.6
21	10	1 990 876	335 143	180 420	154 723	-	168.3	116.6	26.0
22	11	1 969 314	327 604	175 657	151 947	-	166.4	115.6	25.5
23	12	2 043 297	333 930	179 388	154 541	1	163.4	116.1	25.1
24	13	1 998 520	312 267	168 308	143 959	-	156.2	116.9	24.9
25	14	2 086 091	297 008	160 311	136 697	-	142.4	117.3	24.5
26	昭和元年	2 104 405	289 275	156 181	133 093	1	137.5	117.3	24.9
27	2	2 060 737	292 084	157 823	134 261	-	141.7	117.5	24.1
28	3	2 135 852	293 881	158 849	135 032	-	137.6	117.6	23.8
29	4	2 077 026	295 178	159 519	135 659	-	142.1	117.6	23.4
1930	5	2 085 101	258 703	140 143	118 559	1	124.1	118.2	22.1
31	6	2 102 784	276 584	149 995	126 589	-	131.5	118.5	22.3
32	7	2 182 742	256 505	138 555	117 950	-	117.5	117.5	21.8
33	8	2 121 253	257 251	139 571	117 680	-	121.3	118.6	21.5
34	9	2 043 783	255 063	138 736	116 327	-	124.8	119.3	20.7
35	10	2 190 704	233 706	126 936	106 768	2	106.7	118.9	20.1
36	11	2 101 969	245 357	133 899	111 456	2	116.7	120.1	19.9
37	12	2 180 734	230 701	125 589	105 112	-	105.8	119.5	19.1
38	13	1 928 321	220 695	120 397	100 298	-	114.4	120.0	17.5
39	14	1 901 573	202 018	110 490	91 528	-	106.2	120.7	15.9
1940	15	2 115 867	190 509	103 900	86 609	-	90.0	120.0	16.1
41	16	2 277 283	191 420	104 271	87 149	-	84.1	119.6	16.7
42	17	2 233 660	190 897	103 824	87 073	-	85.5	119.2	16.4
43	18	2 253 535	195 219	106 297	88 922	-	86.6	119.5	16.0
47	22	2 678 792	205 360	111 597	93 763	-	76.7	119.0	18.0
48	23	2 681 624	165 406	90 779	74 627	-	61.7	121.6	17.4
49	24	2 696 638	168 467	91 422	77 045	-	62.5	118.7	17.8
1950	25	2 337 507	140 515	76 247	64 268	-	60.1	118.6	15.4
51	26	2 137 689	122 869	66 864	56 005	-	57.5	119.4	14.6
52	27	2 005 162	99 114	54 049	45 065	-	49.4	119.9	13.0
53	28	1 868 040	91 424	49 839	41 585	-	48.9	119.8	11.8
54	29	1 769 580	78 944	43 171	35 773	-	44.6	120.7	10.9

注：1) 昭和19～21年は資料不備のため省略した。
　　 昭和22～47年は沖縄県を含まない。

398

Infant mortality

及び総死亡中乳児死亡の占める割合
births), sex ratio and proportion of infant deaths to total deaths : Japan

年　　次[1] Year		出 生 数 Live births	乳 児 死 亡 数 Infant deaths				乳児死亡率 Infant mortality rates	乳児死亡性比 Sex ratio of infant deaths	総死亡中乳児死亡の占める割合（％） Proportion of infant deaths
			総　数 Total	男 Male	女 Female	不　詳 Not stated			
1955	昭和30年	1 730 692	68 801	37 628	31 173	-	39.8	120.7	9.9
56	31	1 665 278	67 691	37 309	30 382	-	40.6	122.8	9.3
57	32	1 566 713	62 678	34 828	27 850	-	40.0	125.1	8.3
58	33	1 653 469	57 052	31 671	25 381	-	34.5	124.8	8.3
59	34	1 626 088	54 768	30 646	24 122	-	33.7	127.0	7.9
1960	35	1 606 041	49 293	27 714	21 579	-	30.7	128.4	7.0
61	36	1 589 372	45 465	25 893	19 572	-	28.6	132.3	6.5
62	37	1 618 616	42 797	24 159	18 638	-	26.4	129.6	6.0
63	38	1 659 521	38 442	21 763	16 679	-	23.2	130.5	5.7
64	39	1 716 761	34 967	19 922	15 045	-	20.4	132.4	5.2
65	40	1 823 697	33 742	19 322	14 420	-	18.5	134.0	4.8
66	41	1 360 974	26 217	15 024	11 193	-	19.3	134.2	3.9
67	42	1 935 647	28 928	16 628	12 300	-	14.9	135.2	4.3
68	43	1 871 839	28 600	16 676	11 924	-	15.3	139.9	4.2
69	44	1 889 815	26 874	15 544	11 330	-	14.2	137.2	3.9
1970	45	1 934 239	25 412	14 747	10 665	-	13.1	138.3	3.6
71	46	2 000 973	24 805	14 292	10 513	-	12.4	135.9	3.6
72	47	2 038 682	23 773	13 840	9 933	-	11.7	139.3	3.5
73	48	2 091 983	23 683	13 698	9 985	-	11.3	137.2	3.3
74	49	2 029 989	21 888	12 654	9 234	-	10.8	137.0	3.1
75	50	1 901 440	19 103	10 975	8 128	-	10.0	135.0	2.7
76	51	1 832 617	17 105	9 843	7 262	-	9.3	135.5	2.4
77	52	1 755 100	15 666	8 988	6 678	-	8.9	134.6	2.3
78	53	1 708 643	14 327	8 216	6 111	-	8.4	134.4	2.1
79	54	1 642 580	12 923	7 387	5 536	-	7.9	133.4	1.9
1980	55	1 576 889	11 841	6 754	5 087	-	7.5	132.8	1.6
81	56	1 529 455	10 891	6 148	4 743	-	7.1	129.6	1.5
82	57	1 515 392	9 969	5 685	4 284	-	6.6	132.7	1.4
83	58	1 508 687	9 406	5 267	4 139	-	6.2	127.3	1.3
84	59	1 489 780	8 920	5 075	3 845	-	6.0	132.0	1.2
85	60	1 431 577	7 899	4 332	3 567	-	5.5	121.4	1.1
86	61	1 382 946	7 251	4 008	3 243	-	5.2	123.6	1.0
87	62	1 346 658	6 711	3 734	2 977	-	5.0	125.4	0.9
88	63	1 314 006	6 265	3 434	2 831	-	4.8	121.3	0.8
89	平成元年	1 246 802	5 724	3 118	2 606	-	4.6	119.6	0.7
1990	2	1 221 585	5 616	3 123	2 493	-	4.6	125.3	0.7
91	3	1 223 245	5 418	2 915	2 503	-	4.4	116.5	0.7
92	4	1 208 989	5 477	3 103	2 374	-	4.5	130.7	0.6
93	5	1 188 282	5 169	2 847	2 322	-	4.3	122.6	0.6
94	6	1 238 328	5 261	2 994	2 267	-	4.2	132.1	0.6
95	7	1 187 064	5 054	2 808	2 246	-	4.3	125.0	0.5
96	8	1 206 555	4 546	2 532	2 014	-	3.8	125.7	0.5
97	9	1 191 665	4 403	2 414	1 989	-	3.7	121.4	0.5
98	10	1 203 147	4 380	2 364	2 016	-	3.6	117.3	0.5
99	11	1 177 669	4 010	2 224	1 786	-	3.4	124.5	0.4
2000	12	1 190 547	3 830	2 107	1 723	-	3.2	122.3	0.4
01	13	1 170 662	3 599	1 989	1 610	-	3.1	123.5	0.4
02	14	1 153 855	3 497	1 903	1 594	-	3.0	119.4	0.4
03	15	1 123 610	3 364	1 787	1 577	-	3.0	113.3	0.3
04	16	1 110 721	3 122	1 716	1 406	-	2.8	122.0	0.3
05	17	1 062 530	2 958	1 641	1 317	-	2.8	124.6	0.3
06	18	1 092 674	2 864	1 556	1 308	-	2.6	119.0	0.3
07	19	1 089 818	2 828	1 534	1 294	-	2.6	118.5	0.3
08	20	1 091 156	2 798	1 488	1 310	-	2.6	113.6	0.2
09	21	1 070 035	2 556	1 441	1 115	-	2.4	129.2	0.2
2010	22	1 071 304	2 450	1 355	1 095	-	2.3	123.7	0.2
11	23	1 050 806	2 463	1 269	1 194	-	2.3	106.3	0.2
12	24	1 037 231	2 299	1 222	1 077	-	2.2	113.5	0.2
13	25	1 029 816	2 185	1 193	992	-	2.1	120.3	0.2
14	26	1 003 539	2 080	1 110	970	-	2.1	114.4	0.2
15	27	1 005 677	1 916	1 042	874	-	1.9	119.2	0.1
16	28	976 978	1 928	980	948	-	2.0	103.4	0.1

399

乳児死亡

表 6.2 年次別にみた新生児死亡数・率（出生千対）・新生児死亡性比
Table 6.2 Trends in neonatal deaths, neonatal mortality rates (per 1,000 live births),

年　　次[1] Year		新　生　児　死　亡　数[2] Neonatal deaths				新生児死亡率 Neonatal mortality rates	新生児死亡性比 Sex ratio of neonatal deaths	乳児死亡中新生児死亡の占める割合（%） Proportion of neonatal deaths
		総　数 Total	男 Male	女 Female	不　　詳 Not stated			
1899	明治32年	108 077	58 283	49 793	1	77.9	117.1	50.7
1900	33	112 259	60 081	52 177	1	79.0	115.1	51.0
01	34	115 794	61 920	53 872	2	77.1	114.9	51.4
02	35	116 654	62 413	54 240	1	77.2	115.1	50.1
03	36	112 909	60 292	52 616	1	75.8	114.6	49.7
04	37	106 477	56 297	50 179	1	73.9	112.2	48.7
05	38	103 382	55 077	48 305	-	71.2	114.0	46.9
06	39	105 307	55 618	49 688	1	75.5	111.9	49.2
07	40	118 617	63 124	55 491	2	73.5	113.8	48.6
08	41	123 867	66 151	57 716	-	74.5	114.6	47.1
09	42	129 629	68 788	60 839	2	76.5	113.1	45.7
1910	43	126 910	67 556	59 353	1	74.1	113.8	46.0
11	44	127 302	67 783	59 517	2	72.8	113.9	46.0
12	大正元年	123 902	66 253	57 648	1	71.3	114.9	46.2
13	2	124 213	66 111	58 101	1	70.7	113.8	46.5
14	3	125 745	67 215	58 530	-	69.5	114.8	43.9
15	4	125 337	66 711	58 626	-	69.7	113.8	43.4
16	5	132 000	71 173	60 827	-	73.1	117.0	43.0
17	6	139 717	75 180	64 537	-	77.1	116.5	44.5
18	7	145 710	78 161	67 549	-	81.3	115.7	43.1
19	8	129 072	69 460	59 612	-	72.6	116.5	42.6
1920	9	139 681	75 068	64 613	-	69.0	116.2	41.6
21	10	136 342	73 782	62 560	-	68.5	117.9	40.7
22	11	132 856	71 710	61 146	-	67.5	117.3	40.6
23	12	135 504	73 843	61 660	1	66.3	119.8	40.6
24	13	126 385	68 810	57 575	-	63.2	119.5	40.5
25	14	121 238	65 983	55 255	-	58.1	119.4	40.8
26	昭和元年	119 642	65 264	54 377	1	56.9	120.0	41.4
27	2	116 240	63 349	52 891	-	56.4	119.8	39.8
28	3	115 682	63 232	52 450	-	54.2	120.6	39.4
29	4	115 009	62 716	52 293	-	55.4	119.9	39.0
1930	5	104 101	57 067	47 033	1	49.9	121.3	40.2
31	6	108 812	59 549	49 263	-	51.7	120.9	39.3
32	7	104 573	57 383	47 190	-	47.9	121.6	40.8
33	8	102 887	56 414	46 473	-	48.5	121.4	40.0
34	9	103 408	56 828	46 580	-	50.6	122.0	40.5
35	10	97 994	53 945	44 048	1	44.7	122.5	41.9
36	11	101 043	55 715	45 327	1	48.1	122.9	41.2
37	12	95 465	52 807	42 658	-	43.8	123.8	41.4
38	13	89 159	49 030	40 129	-	46.2	122.2	40.4
39	14	84 204	46 812	37 392	-	44.3	125.2	41.7
1940	15	81 869	45 439	36 430	-	38.7	124.7	43.0
41	16	77 829	43 177	34 652	-	34.2	124.6	40.7
42	17	76 177	41 847	34 330	-	34.1	121.9	39.9
43	18	76 588	42 548	34 040	-	33.8	125.0	39.0
47	22	84 204	46 545	37 659	-	31.4	123.6	41.0
48	23	73 855	41 206	32 649	-	27.5	126.2	44.7
49	24	72 432	40 271	32 161	-	26.9	125.2	43.0
1950	25	64 142	35 484	28 658	-	27.4	123.8	45.6
51	26	58 686	32 488	26 198	-	27.5	124.0	47.8
52	27	51 015	28 257	22 758	-	25.4	124.2	51.5
53	28	47 580	26 351	21 229	-	25.5	124.1	52.0
54	29	42 726	23 725	19 001	-	24.1	124.9	54.1

注：1) 昭和18年のみ樺太を含む数字である。なお、昭和18年の樺太を含む出生数は2 267 292、乳児死亡数は196 311である。
昭和19〜21年は資料不備のため省略した。
昭和22〜47年は沖縄県を含まない。
2) 昭和18年以前は1か月未満の死亡であり、昭和22年以降は28日未満の死亡である。

400

Infant mortality

及び乳児死亡中新生児死亡の占める割合
sex ratio and proportion of neonatal deaths to infant deaths : Japan

年　　次[1] Year		新　　生　　児　　死　　亡　　数[2] Neonatal deaths				新生児死亡率 Neonatal mortality rates	新生児死亡性比 Sex ratio of neonatal deaths	乳児死亡中新生児死亡の占める割合（%） Proportion of neonatal deaths
		総　　数 Total	男 Male	女 Female	不　　詳 Not stated			
1955	昭和30年	38 646	21 395	17 251	-	22.3	124.0	56.2
56	31	38 232	21 368	16 864	-	23.0	126.7	56.5
57	32	33 847	18 967	14 880	-	21.6	127.5	54.0
58	33	32 237	18 152	14 085	-	19.5	128.9	56.5
59	34	30 235	17 202	13 033	-	18.6	132.0	55.2
1960	35	27 362	15 544	11 818	-	17.0	131.5	55.5
61	36	26 255	15 101	11 154	-	16.5	135.4	57.7
62	37	24 777	14 100	10 677	-	15.3	132.1	57.9
63	38	22 965	13 154	9 811	-	13.8	134.1	59.7
64	39	21 344	12 304	9 040	-	12.4	136.1	61.0
65	40	21 260	12 315	8 945	-	11.7	137.7	63.0
66	41	16 296	9 430	6 866	-	12.0	137.3	62.2
67	42	19 248	11 170	8 078	-	9.9	138.3	66.5
68	43	18 326	10 828	7 498	-	9.8	144.4	64.1
69	44	17 116	10 074	7 042	-	9.1	143.1	63.7
1970	45	16 742	9 929	6 813	-	8.7	145.7	65.9
71	46	16 450	9 633	6 817	-	8.2	141.3	66.3
72	47	15 817	9 439	6 378	-	7.8	148.0	66.5
73	48	15 473	9 157	6 316	-	7.4	145.0	65.3
74	49	14 472	8 604	5 868	-	7.1	146.6	66.1
75	50	12 912	7 560	5 352	-	6.8	141.3	67.6
76	51	11 638	6 896	4 742	-	6.4	145.4	68.0
77	52	10 773	6 290	4 483	-	6.1	140.3	68.8
78	53	9 628	5 605	4 023	-	5.6	139.3	67.2
79	54	8 590	4 980	3 610	-	5.2	138.0	66.5
1980	55	7 796	4 522	3 274	-	4.9	138.1	65.8
81	56	7 188	4 111	3 077	-	4.7	133.6	66.0
82	57	6 425	3 702	2 723	-	4.2	136.0	64.4
83	58	5 894	3 305	2 589	-	3.9	127.7	62.7
84	59	5 527	3 130	2 397	-	3.7	130.6	62.0
85	60	4 910	2 705	2 205	-	3.4	122.7	62.2
86	61	4 296	2 384	1 912	-	3.1	124.7	59.2
87	62	3 933	2 206	1 727	-	2.9	127.7	58.6
88	63	3 592	1 943	1 649	-	2.7	117.8	57.3
89	平成元年	3 214	1 737	1 477	-	2.6	117.6	56.1
1990	2	3 179	1 767	1 412	-	2.6	125.1	56.6
91	3	2 978	1 591	1 387	-	2.4	114.7	55.0
92	4	2 905	1 631	1 274	-	2.4	128.0	53.0
93	5	2 765	1 513	1 252	-	2.3	120.8	53.5
94	6	2 889	1 663	1 226	-	2.3	135.6	54.9
95	7	2 615	1 467	1 148	-	2.2	127.8	51.7
96	8	2 438	1 358	1 080	-	2.0	125.7	53.6
97	9	2 307	1 241	1 066	-	1.9	116.4	52.4
98	10	2 353	1 286	1 067	-	2.0	120.5	53.7
99	11	2 137	1 166	971	-	1.8	120.1	53.3
2000	12	2 106	1 149	957	-	1.8	120.1	55.0
01	13	1 909	1 056	853	-	1.6	123.8	53.0
02	14	1 937	1 046	891	-	1.7	117.4	55.4
03	15	1 879	976	903	-	1.7	108.1	55.9
04	16	1 622	907	715	-	1.5	126.9	52.0
05	17	1 510	823	687	-	1.4	119.8	51.0
06	18	1 444	782	662	-	1.3	118.1	50.4
07	19	1 434	764	670	-	1.3	114.0	50.7
08	20	1 331	706	625	-	1.2	113.0	47.6
09	21	1 254	705	549	-	1.2	128.4	49.1
2010	22	1 167	657	510	-	1.1	128.8	47.6
11	23	1 147	581	566	-	1.1	102.7	46.6
12	24	1 065	542	523	-	1.0	103.6	46.3
13	25	1 026	567	459	-	1.0	123.5	47.0
14	26	952	509	443	-	0.9	114.9	45.8
15	27	902	482	420	-	0.9	114.8	47.1
16	28	874	447	427	-	0.9	104.7	45.3

乳児死亡

〔生存期間別にみた乳児死亡〕
〔Infant deaths by age〕

表6.3　生存期間別にみた性別乳児死亡率（出生10万対）・乳児死亡率性比及び百分率
Table 6.3　Infant mortality rates (per 100,000 live births) and percent distribution by sex and age (days, weeks and months) : Japan, 2016

平成28年

日　齢・月　齢 Age	乳　児　死　亡　率 Infant mortality rates			乳児死亡率性比 Sex ratio of infant mortality rates	生存期間別 百分率 Percentage
	総　数 Total	男 Male	女 Female		
総　数　Total	197. 3	195. 3	199. 5	97. 9	100. 0
4　週　未　満　Under 4 weeks	89. 5	89. 1	89. 9	99. 1	45. 3
1　週　未　満　Under 1 week	69. 2	68. 9	69. 5	99. 3	35. 1
1 日（24 時 間）未 満　Under 1 day(24 hours)	45. 1	46. 4	43. 8	106. 0	22. 9
1日　Day	8. 8	8. 8	8. 8	99. 2	4. 5
2日	5. 2	5. 0	5. 5	91. 0	2. 6
3日	3. 4	3. 4	3. 4	100. 6	1. 7
4日	2. 1	2. 0	2. 3	86. 1	1. 1
5日	1. 7	1. 2	2. 3	51. 6	0. 9
6日	2. 8	2. 2	3. 4	65. 1	1. 4
1　〜　2　週　未　満　1 week and over, less than 2 weeks	9. 5	9. 8	9. 3	105. 4	4. 8
2　〜　3　週　未　満　2 weeks and over, less than 3 weeks	5. 7	5. 4	6. 1	88. 1	2. 9
3　〜　4　週　未　満　3 weeks and over, less than 4 weeks	5. 0	5. 0	5. 1	98. 6	2. 5
4　週　〜　2　か　月　未　満　4 weeks and over, less than 2 months	23. 2	22. 5	24. 0	93. 8	11. 8
2　か　月　Months	15. 1	14. 5	15. 8	92. 1	7. 7
3　か　月	12. 2	12. 0	12. 4	96. 3	6. 2
4　か　月	10. 2	8. 4	12. 2	68. 5	5. 2
5　か　月	11. 4	12. 2	10. 5	115. 5	5. 8
6　か　月	8. 6	9. 6	7. 6	126. 2	4. 4
7　か　月	7. 3	7. 0	7. 6	92. 0	3. 7
8　か　月	6. 7	7. 6	5. 7	133. 2	3. 4
9　か　月	4. 8	4. 2	5. 5	76. 5	2. 4
10　か　月	3. 7	4. 2	3. 2	132. 5	1. 9
11　か　月	4. 7	4. 2	5. 3	79. 5	2. 4

乳児死亡

表6.4　生存期間別にみた性・
Table 6.4　Trends in infant mortality rates (per 100,000 live

日　齢・月　齢 Age	1950 昭和25年	1955 30年	1960 35年	1965 40年	1970 45年	1975 50年	1980 55年	1985 60年	1990 平成2年	1995 7年
									総　数	
総　数　Total	6 011.3	3 975.3	3 069.2	1 850.2	1 313.8	1 004.7	750.9	551.8	459.7	425.8
4　週　未　満　Under 4 weeks	2 744.0	2 233.0	1 703.7	1 165.8	865.6	679.1	494.4	343.0	260.2	220.3
1　週　未　満　Under 1 week	1 505.2	1 307.0	1 061.0	819.7	662.3	538.8	390.3	261.0	191.3	154.3
1　日　未　満　Under 1 day	360.3	335.2	271.2	236.7	219.1	213.3	178.1	130.7	103.6	84.7
1　～　2　週　未　満　1 week and over, less than 2 weeks	565.6	470.7	341.3	189.7	115.3	77.8	57.1	42.3	30.9	30.3
2　～　3　週　未　満　2 weeks and over, less than 3 weeks	401.2	276.5	180.3	95.7	53.1	39.0	28.2	21.7	22.3	19.9
3　～　4　週　未　満　3 weeks and over, less than 4 weeks	272.1	178.8	121.1	60.6	34.8	23.5	18.8	18.0	15.6	15.8
4　週　～　3　か　月　未　満　4 weeks and over, less than 3 months	1 265.1	763.5	565.7	266.5	154.4	113.5	89.5	72.9	74.0	74.2
3　か　月　～　6　か　月　未　満　3 months and over, less than 6 months	825.4	473.6	390.5	189.7	133.3	95.8	78.4	64.8	62.9	65.1
6　か　月　～　9　か　月　未　満　6 months and over, less than 9 months	608.3	290.8	241.5	133.0	93.8	67.3	49.6	39.4	37.2	39.0
9　か　月　～　1　年　未　満　9 months and over, less than 1 year	566.9	214.5	167.8	95.2	67.1	49.0	39.0	31.7	25.4	27.1
									男	
総　数　Total	6 337.5	4 229.4	3 360.2	2 065.7	1 474.1	1 120.9	832.4	589.2	498.1	461.4
4　週　未　満　Under 4 weeks	2 949.4	2 404.8	1 884.7	1 316.6	992.5	772.1	557.3	367.9	281.8	241.1
1　週　未　満　Under 1 week	1 636.3	1 434.6	1 187.1	941.4	769.1	613.3	444.8	281.1	211.0	168.4
1　日　未　満　Under 1 day	389.9	376.7	298.1	274.3	248.4	238.2	201.7	135.6	111.5	90.5
1　～　2　週　未　満　1 week and over, less than 2 weeks	593.0	488.2	372.4	199.5	128.5	89.5	62.1	44.9	31.7	34.7
2　～　3　週　未　満　2 weeks and over, less than 3 weeks	429.0	291.3	195.7	105.3	54.6	43.9	30.4	23.7	24.1	20.9
3　～　4　週　未　満　3 weeks and over, less than 4 weeks	291.2	190.7	129.5	70.3	40.3	25.4	20.0	18.2	15.0	17.1
4　週　～　3　か　月　未　満　4 weeks and over, less than 3 months	1 322.7	792.8	609.5	295.4	167.2	119.2	96.5	73.0	80.7	79.0
3　か　月　～　6　か　月　未　満　3 months and over, less than 6 months	862.5	499.8	421.6	206.6	141.1	105.7	88.5	72.4	66.5	70.0
6　か　月　～　9　か　月　未　満　6 months and over, less than 9 months	629.6	301.6	261.3	143.8	101.6	69.5	51.0	42.3	41.8	42.2
9　か　月　～　1　年　未　満　9 months and over, less than 1 year	571.7	230.3	183.2	103.4	71.7	54.4	39.1	33.6	27.3	29.1
									女	
総　数　Total	5 665.4	3 706.6	2 762.0	1 623.3	1 142.1	881.2	664.6	512.3	419.3	388.2
4　週　未　満　Under 4 weeks	2 526.3	2 051.2	1 512.6	1 006.9	729.5	580.3	427.7	316.7	237.5	198.4
1　週　未　満　Under 1 week	1 366.2	1 172.1	927.8	691.5	547.8	459.7	332.5	239.8	170.5	139.5
1　日　未　満　Under 1 day	328.9	291.3	242.7	197.1	187.6	186.8	153.0	125.5	95.4	78.5
1　～　2　週　未　満　1 week and over, less than 2 weeks	536.6	452.2	308.6	179.3	101.2	65.4	51.9	39.6	30.1	25.8
2　～　3　週　未　満　2 weeks and over, less than 3 weeks	371.7	260.8	164.0	85.7	51.6	33.8	25.9	19.5	20.5	18.8
3　～　4　週　未　満　3 weeks and over, less than 4 weeks	251.9	166.1	112.3	50.4	28.9	21.4	17.5	17.7	16.3	14.3
4　週　～　3　か　月　未　満　4 weeks and over, less than 3 months	1 204.0	732.4	519.5	236.1	140.0	107.6	82.0	72.7	66.9	69.1
3　か　月　～　6　か　月　未　満　3 months and over, less than 6 months	786.0	445.9	357.6	171.9	124.9	5.3	67.8	56.9	59.0	60.0
6　か　月　～　9　か　月　未　満　6 months and over, less than 9 months	585.7	279.3	220.7	121.7	85.6	64.9	48.1	36.3	32.5	35.6
9　か　月　～　1　年　未　満　9 months and over, less than 1 year	561.8	197.7	151.5	86.7	62.1	43.2	38.9	29.7	23.4	25.1

404

年次別乳児死亡率（出生10万対）
births）by sex and age（days,weeks and months）: Japan

	2000 12年	2005 17年	2006 18年	2007 19年	2008 20年	2009 21年	2010 22年	2011 23年	2012 24年	2013 25年	2014 26年	2015 27年	2016 28年
Total													
	321.7	278.4	262.1	259.5	256.4	238.9	228.7	234.4	221.6	212.2	207.3	190.5	197.3
	176.9	142.1	132.2	131.6	122.0	117.2	108.9	109.2	102.7	99.6	94.9	89.7	89.5
	127.6	102.7	96.4	96.5	88.8	81.7	82.0	78.4	76.2	73.0	70.8	66.1	69.2
	75.6	65.0	58.9	61.8	58.7	54.5	55.3	52.2	54.5	49.1	47.4	44.9	45.1
	23.3	19.0	15.0	15.6	14.8	15.5	11.2	14.5	10.0	10.3	10.1	11.4	9.5
	15.0	11.7	11.7	10.3	10.9	11.3	8.8	9.8	8.7	9.0	6.8	5.8	5.7
	11.1	8.8	9.1	9.2	7.5	8.7	7.0	6.5	7.8	7.3	7.2	6.4	5.0
	54.3	45.3	46.5	44.0	47.5	42.1	41.8	42.0	41.6	40.0	39.5	34.4	38.4
	42.9	45.1	40.5	41.0	42.7	38.8	37.7	39.0	34.7	36.8	34.7	33.7	33.8
	30.5	26.3	26.6	27.1	26.4	24.6	22.6	28.5	26.0	22.2	23.5	19.9	22.5
	17.1	19.7	16.4	15.8	17.9	16.3	17.6	15.8	16.7	13.5	14.7	12.8	13.2
Male													
	344.2	301.1	277.6	274.0	265.9	262.5	246.0	235.8	229.8	226.1	215.3	202.2	195.3
	187.7	151.0	139.5	136.5	126.2	128.4	119.3	107.9	101.9	107.5	98.7	93.5	89.1
	137.1	111.6	101.2	99.3	90.3	90.7	92.2	77.7	76.9	78.6	72.4	69.5	68.9
	81.2	68.8	60.0	63.1	57.7	62.3	61.4	51.8	54.2	52.9	48.7	47.7	46.4
	23.7	16.9	16.8	17.1	16.1	16.0	10.7	14.5	11.1	11.2	11.3	10.9	9.8
	15.8	12.7	12.1	11.3	10.9	12.8	9.1	8.9	8.3	9.5	7.8	6.8	5.4
	11.1	9.9	9.5	8.8	8.9	8.9	7.3	6.9	5.6	8.1	7.4	6.4	5.0
	57.3	50.3	48.5	49.7	51.7	49.0	46.8	42.0	44.4	43.0	38.8	35.7	37.1
	49.5	50.6	42.1	45.2	44.9	42.3	37.4	40.7	36.9	37.7	37.0	38.4	32.5
	32.2	26.8	29.6	28.2	25.7	26.0	23.1	29.2	31.0	23.7	26.0	22.1	24.1
	17.5	22.4	17.8	14.5	17.5	16.8	19.4	16.0	15.6	14.2	14.7	12.4	12.6
Female													
	297.9	254.5	245.8	244.2	246.4	214.0	210.3	233.0	213.1	197.5	198.8	178.3	199.5
	165.5	132.8	124.4	126.4	117.6	105.4	98.0	110.4	103.5	91.4	90.8	85.7	89.9
	117.6	93.3	91.3	93.6	87.3	72.2	71.1	79.2	75.4	67.1	69.3	62.6	69.5
	69.7	61.1	57.9	60.4	59.6	46.3	48.8	52.7	54.8	45.2	46.1	42.0	43.8
	22.8	21.3	13.2	14.0	13.4	15.0	11.7	14.4	8.9	9.4	8.8	12.0	9.3
	14.0	10.6	11.3	9.2	10.9	9.8	8.5	10.7	9.1	8.6	5.7	4.7	6.1
	11.1	7.5	8.6	9.6	6.0	8.4	6.7	6.0	10.1	6.4	7.0	6.3	5.1
	51.2	40.0	44.3	38.1	43.1	34.7	36.5	41.9	38.6	36.8	40.2	33.0	39.8
	36.0	39.2	38.7	36.6	40.4	35.1	38.0	37.3	32.4	35.8	32.2	28.8	35.2
	28.7	25.7	23.5	25.9	27.1	23.0	22.1	27.7	20.8	20.7	20.9	17.5	20.8
	16.6	16.8	14.8	17.2	18.2	15.7	15.8	15.6	17.8	12.7	14.8	13.3	13.9

乳児死亡

〔月別にみた乳児死亡〕
〔Infant deaths by month〕

表6.5 月別にみた年次別
Table 6.5 Trends in infant deaths and infant

年 次 Year		総 数 [2] Total	1 月 January	2 月 February	3 月 March	4 月 April	5 月 May
						乳	児 死
1947	昭和22年	205 360	21 088	24 154	23 936	17 965	15 096
50	25	140 515	19 497	16 822	16 601	11 422	10 179
55	30	68 801	9 751	7 923	7 170	6 088	5 137
60	35	49 293	6 745	5 793	5 622	4 377	3 745
65	40	33 742	3 869	3 528	3 600	2 843	2 552
70	45	25 412	2 710	2 155	2 277	2 072	2 096
75	50	19 103	1 744	1 618	1 651	1 572	1 603
80	55	11 841	1 047	979	1 038	929	1 000
85	60	7 899	694	642	691	622	701
90	平成2年	5 616	507	399	506	432	476
95	7	5 054	498	443	460	412	442
2000	12	3 830	342	341	326	347	305
05	17	2 958	276	214	244	261	284
06	18	2 864	261	230	266	235	267
07	19	2 828	248	224	235	260	243
08	20	2 798	246	241	256	236	236
09	21	2 556	219	205	219	221	226
10	22	2 450	224	215	223	197	226
11	23	2 463	220	201	256	217	233
12	24	2 299	193	196	208	204	179
13	25	2 185	195	151	196	174	194
14	26	2 080	172	172	176	181	164
15	27	1 916	158	157	165	166	161
16	**28**	**1 928**	**171**	**180**	**167**	**175**	**161**
						乳	児 死
1947	昭和22年	76.7	122.9	149.3	127.5	94.9	74.8
50	25	60.1	87.3	84.1	75.9	54.6	47.6
55	30	39.8	64.9	58.8	48.2	42.1	34.3
60	35	30.7	49.2	45.4	41.2	33.2	27.5
65	40	18.5	26.5	26.6	24.4	19.8	17.2
70	45	13.1	16.9	14.9	14.2	13.3	13.0
75	50	10.0	10.2	10.5	9.7	9.6	9.5
80	55	7.5	7.5	7.5	7.5	6.9	7.3
85	60	5.5	5.5	5.7	5.5	5.2	5.6
90	平成2年	4.6	4.8	4.2	4.8	4.2	4.5
95	7	4.3	4.9	4.9	4.6	4.2	4.4
2000	12	3.2	3.4	3.6	3.2	3.6	3.0
05	17	2.8	3.1	2.6	2.7	3.0	3.1
06	18	2.6	2.8	2.7	2.9	2.6	2.9
07	19	2.6	2.7	2.7	2.5	2.9	2.6
08	20	2.6	2.7	2.8	2.8	2.6	2.6
09	21	2.4	2.4	2.5	2.4	2.5	2.5
10	22	2.3	2.5	2.6	2.5	2.2	2.5
11	23	2.3	2.5	2.5	2.9	2.5	2.6
12	24	2.2	2.2	2.4	2.4	2.4	2.0
13	25	2.1	2.2	1.9	2.2	2.1	2.2
14	26	2.1	2.0	2.2	2.1	2.2	1.9
15	27	1.9	1.8	2.0	1.9	2.0	1.9
16	**28**	**2.0**	**2.1**	**2.3**	**2.0**	**2.2**	**1.9**

注：1) 各月の率は年率に換算したものである。計算方法は、69ページ 4）乳児死亡を参照されたい。
　　なお、平成7年から年間出生数を用いて算出している。
　　2) 昭和22年、25年には月不詳があり、総数に含む。

Infant mortality

乳児死亡数及び率 1)（出生千対）
mortality rates (per 1,000 live births) by month : Japan

	6 月 June	7 月 July	8 月 August	9 月 September	10 月 October	11 月 November	12 月 December
亡 数 Infant deaths							
	13 816	16 416	15 406	11 081	11 396	14 664	20 341
	9 361	9 455	7 887	7 161	8 253	9 712	14 160
	4 816	4 178	3 654	3 652	4 243	5 301	6 888
	3 270	2 959	2 684	2 634	2 924	3 454	5 086
	2 432	2 598	2 403	2 112	2 324	2 369	3 112
	2 009	2 269	1 986	1 807	1 905	1 893	2 233
	1 588	1 843	1 603	1 434	1 461	1 400	1 586
	1 009	1 022	1 000	931	907	922	1 057
	654	685	662	582	666	605	695
	487	458	465	456	461	484	485
	406	411	411	355	428	367	421
	290	283	318	304	315	324	335
	227	256	235	215	251	239	256
	239	223	247	221	229	216	230
	228	214	256	208	237	209	266
	251	222	229	199	229	212	241
	221	226	198	190	202	214	215
	192	183	191	199	199	198	203
	197	177	167	169	195	196	235
	180	181	165	187	191	202	213
	164	194	169	201	163	194	190
	182	165	174	167	158	171	198
	152	149	161	152	177	155	163
	149	**157**	**152**	**157**	**160**	**148**	**151**
亡 率 Infant mortality rates							
	68. 9	77. 2	70. 8	51. 8	50. 9	67. 2	89. 4
	45. 7	45. 2	38. 1	36. 1	40. 8	50. 1	71. 3
	33. 3	28. 1	24. 6	25. 5	28. 7	37. 2	46. 9
	24. 9	21. 8	19. 8	20. 0	21. 5	26. 2	37. 4
	16. 8	17. 3	15. 9	14. 3	15. 1	15. 8	20. 1
	12. 9	14. 0	12. 2	11. 5	11. 7	12. 0	13. 6
	9. 8	11. 0	9. 7	9. 0	9. 0	8. 9	9. 8
	7. 6	7. 5	7. 3	7. 1	6. 7	7. 1	7. 9
	5. 4	5. 5	5. 4	4. 9	5. 4	5. 1	5. 7
	4. 8	4. 4	4. 4	4. 5	4. 4	4. 8	4. 7
	4. 2	4. 1	4. 1	3. 6	4. 2	3. 8	4. 2
	3. 0	2. 8	3. 2	3. 1	3. 1	3. 3	3. 3
	2. 6	2. 8	2. 6	2. 5	2. 8	2. 7	2. 8
	2. 7	2. 4	2. 7	2. 5	2. 5	2. 4	2. 5
	2. 5	2. 3	2. 8	2. 3	2. 6	2. 3	2. 9
	2. 8	2. 4	2. 5	2. 2	2. 5	2. 4	2. 6
	2. 5	2. 5	2. 2	2. 2	2. 2	2. 4	2. 4
	2. 2	2. 0	2. 1	2. 3	2. 2	2. 2	2. 2
	2. 3	2. 0	1. 9	2. 0	2. 2	2. 3	2. 6
	2. 1	2. 1	1. 9	2. 2	2. 2	2. 4	2. 4
	1. 9	2. 2	1. 9	2. 4	1. 9	2. 3	2. 2
	2. 2	1. 9	2. 0	2. 0	1. 9	2. 1	2. 3
	1. 8	1. 7	1. 9	1. 8	2. 1	1. 9	1. 9
	1. 9	**1. 9**	**1. 8**	**2. 0**	**1. 9**	**1. 8**	**1. 8**

乳児死亡

表 6.6　出生年月別にみた出生数・乳児死亡数及び率（出生千対）
Table 6.6　Live births, infant deaths and infant mortality rates (per 1,000 live births) by months of birth : Japan

出　生　年　月 Months of birth			出　生　数 Live births	乳 児 死 亡 数 Infant deaths	乳 児 死 亡 率 Infant mortality rates
2012	平成24年　年計	Total	1 037 231	2 221	2.1
13	25		1 029 816	2 194	2.1
14	26		1 003 539	2 043	2.0
15	27		1 005 677	1 918	1.9
2012	平成24年 1 月	January	87 680	180	2.1
	2	February	81 469	177	2.2
	3	March	83 749	187	2.2
	4	April	81 718	200	2.4
	5	May	85 841	176	2.1
	6	June	83 451	169	2.0
	7	July	90 537	190	2.1
	8	August	90 906	191	2.1
	9	September	89 758	184	2.0
	10	October	90 438	218	2.4
	11	November	85 577	195	2.3
	12	December	86 107	154	1.8
2013	平成25年 1 月	January	85 853	186	2.2
	2	February	77 066	173	2.2
	3	March	82 997	174	2.1
	4	April	81 856	173	2.1
	5	May	85 297	192	2.3
	6	June	82 397	167	2.0
	7	July	91 467	180	2.0
	8	August	92 118	203	2.2
	9	September	90 618	193	2.1
	10	October	90 667	170	1.9
	11	November	83 126	197	2.4
	12	December	86 354	186	2.2
2014	平成26年 1 月	January	83 572	168	2.0
	2	February	73 897	149	2.0
	3	March	79 340	163	2.1
	4	April	78 834	174	2.2
	5	May	83 310	162	1.9
	6	June	81 401	176	2.2
	7	July	89 516	176	2.0
	8	August	87 732	174	2.0
	9	September	90 309	168	1.9
	10	October	88 592	173	2.0
	11	November	80 993	196	2.4
	12	December	86 043	164	1.9
2015	平成27年 1 月	January	84 740	147	1.7
	2	February	75 989	161	2.1
	3	March	81 942	163	2.0
	4	April	83 408	143	1.7
	5	May	83 827	151	1.8
	6	June	83 200	145	1.7
	7	July	88 612	181	2.0
	8	August	86 344	178	2.1
	9	September	86 832	173	2.0
	10	October	85 825	181	2.1
	11	November	80 659	135	1.7
	12	December	84 299	160	1.9

注：乳児死亡数は、当該年月に出生した者が 1 年未満で死亡した場合の累計であり、死亡年月による累計とは異なる。

Infant mortality

〔死亡の場所別にみた乳児死亡〕
〔Infant deaths by place of occurrence〕

表 6.7 死亡の場所別にみた年次別乳児死亡数及び百分率
Table 6.7 Trends in infant deaths and percent distribution by place of occurrence : Japan

年　次 Year		総　数 Total	施　設　内 Hospitalized				施　設　外 Nonhosp.		
			総　数 Total	病　院 Hospital	診療所 Clinic	助産所 Maternity home	総　数 Total	自　宅 Home	その他 Others
乳　児　死　亡　数　Infant deaths									
1950	昭和25年	140 515	11 610	6 804	4 603	203	128 905	128 905	
55	30	68 801	13 050	8 025	4 657	368	55 751	51 199	4 552
60	35	49 293	21 763	14 113	6 896	754	27 530	24 462	3 068
65	40	33 742	24 021	16 594	6 732	695	9 721	8 550	1 171
70	45	25 412	21 520	15 929	5 281	310	3 892	3 384	508
75	50	19 103	17 104	13 338	3 640	126	1 999	1 647	352
80	55	11 841	10 767	9 125	1 618	24	1 074	882	192
85	60	7 899	7 205	6 573	625	7	694	551	143
90	平成 2 年	5 616	5 072	4 787	283	2	544	448	96
95	7	5 054	4 545	4 370	173	2	509	409	100
2000	12	3 830	3 480	3 373	105	2	350	290	60
01	13	3 599	3 271	3 178	93	-	328	273	55
02	14	3 497	3 205	3 123	82	-	292	249	43
03	15	3 364	3 102	3 031	69	2	262	214	48
04	16	3 122	2 849	2 782	65	2	273	241	32
05	17	2 958	2 671	2 593	75	3	287	243	44
06	18	2 864	2 622	2 576	46	-	242	209	33
07	19	2 828	2 554	2 493	60	1	274	236	38
08	20	2 798	2 502	2 452	50	-	296	252	44
09	21	2 556	2 313	2 257	54	2	243	220	23
10	22	2 450	2 211	2 167	43	1	239	202	37
11	23	2 463	2 162	2 110	51	1	301	199	102
12	24	2 299	2 059	2 010	49	-	240	208	32
13	25	2 185	1 960	1 921	39	-	225	206	19
14	26	2 080	1 844	1 816	26	2	236	211	25
15	27	1 916	1 721	1 691	30	-	195	170	25
16	**28**	**1 928**	**1 703**	**1 678**	**24**	**1**	**225**	**203**	**22**
百　分　率　Percentage									
1950	昭和25年	100.0	8.3	4.8	3.3	0.1	91.7	91.7	
55	30	100.0	19.0	11.7	6.8	0.5	81.0	74.1	6.6
60	35	100.0	44.2	28.6	14.0	1.5	55.8	49.6	6.2
65	40	100.0	71.2	49.2	20.0	2.1	28.8	25.3	3.5
70	45	100.0	84.7	62.7	20.8	1.2	15.3	13.3	2.0
75	50	100.0	89.5	69.8	19.1	0.7	10.5	8.6	1.8
80	55	100.0	90.9	77.1	13.7	0.2	9.1	7.4	1.6
85	60	100.0	91.2	83.2	7.9	0.1	8.8	7.0	1.8
90	平成 2 年	100.0	90.3	85.2	5.0	0.0	9.7	8.0	1.7
95	7	100.0	89.9	86.5	3.4	0.0	10.1	8.1	2.0
2000	12	100.0	90.9	88.1	2.7	0.1	9.1	7.6	1.6
01	13	100.0	90.9	88.3	2.6	-	9.1	7.6	1.5
02	14	100.0	91.6	89.3	2.3	-	8.4	7.1	1.2
03	15	100.0	92.2	90.1	2.1	0.1	7.8	6.4	1.4
04	16	100.0	91.3	89.1	2.1	0.1	8.7	7.7	1.0
05	17	100.0	90.3	87.7	2.5	0.1	9.7	8.2	1.5
06	18	100.0	91.6	89.9	1.6	-	8.4	7.3	1.2
07	19	100.0	90.3	88.2	2.1	0.0	9.7	8.3	1.3
08	20	100.0	89.4	87.6	1.8	-	10.6	9.0	1.6
09	21	100.0	90.5	88.3	2.1	0.1	9.5	8.6	0.9
10	22	100.0	90.2	88.4	1.8	0.0	9.8	8.2	1.5
11	23	100.0	87.8	85.7	2.1	0.0	12.2	8.1	4.1
12	24	100.0	89.6	87.4	2.1	-	10.4	9.0	1.4
13	25	100.0	89.7	87.9	1.8	-	10.3	9.4	0.9
14	26	100.0	88.7	87.3	1.3	0.1	11.3	10.1	1.2
15	27	100.0	89.8	88.3	1.6	-	10.2	8.9	1.3
16	**28**	**100.0**	**88.3**	**87.0**	**1.2**	**0.1**	**11.7**	**10.5**	**1.1**

409

乳児死亡

表6.8　死亡の場所別にみた都道府県（21大都市再掲）別乳児死亡数百分率
Table 6.8　Percent distribution of infant deaths by place of occurrence : Japan, each prefecture and 21 major cities, 2016

平成28年

都　道　府　県 Prefecture	総　数 Total	施　設　内 Hospitalized				施　設　外 Nonhosp.		
		総　数 Total	病　院 Hospital	診療所 Clinic	助産所 Maternity home	総　数 Total	自　宅 Home	その他 Others
全　国　　　　　Total	100.0	88.3	87.0	1.2	0.1	11.7	10.5	1.1
市　部 Total for Urban residence	100.0	88.5	87.4	1.1	0.1	11.5	10.4	1.1
郡　部 Total for Rural residence	100.0	86.7	83.5	3.2	-	13.3	12.7	0.6
01 北　海　　道 a)	100.0	94.7	94.7	-	-	5.3	3.9	1.3
02 青　　　森	100.0	100.0	100.0	-	-	-	-	-
03 岩　　　手	100.0	70.6	70.6	-	-	29.4	29.4	-
04 宮　　　城	100.0	90.0	90.0	-	-	10.0	10.0	-
05 秋　　　田	100.0	100.0	100.0	-	-	-	-	-
06 山　　　形	100.0	100.0	100.0	-	-	-	-	-
07 福　　　島	100.0	85.2	81.5	3.7	-	14.8	14.8	-
08 茨　　　城	100.0	100.0	97.5	2.5	-	-	-	-
09 栃　　　木	100.0	100.0	92.3	7.7	-	-	-	-
10 群　　　馬	100.0	95.5	90.9	4.5	-	4.5	4.5	-
11 埼　　　玉	100.0	93.2	91.5	1.7	-	6.8	5.1	1.7
12 千　　　葉	100.0	91.6	89.5	2.1	-	8.4	7.4	1.1
13 東　　　京	100.0	94.1	93.2	0.9	-	5.9	5.0	0.9
14 神　奈　川	100.0	87.8	87.8	-	-	12.2	11.6	0.7
15 新　　　潟	100.0	100.0	100.0	-	-	-	-	-
16 富　　　山	100.0	93.8	87.5	6.3	-	6.3	6.3	-
17 石　　　川	100.0	78.9	78.9	-	-	21.1	21.1	-
18 福　　　井	100.0	100.0	100.0	-	-	-	-	-
19 山　　　梨	100.0	100.0	100.0	-	-	-	-	-
20 長　　　野	100.0	93.1	86.2	3.4	3.4	6.9	6.9	-
21 岐　　　阜	100.0	88.6	88.6	-	-	11.4	8.6	2.9
22 静　　　岡	100.0	78.3	78.3	-	-	21.7	19.6	2.2
23 愛　　　知	100.0	92.3	90.6	1.7	-	7.7	7.7	-
24 三　　　重	100.0	81.8	81.8	-	-	18.2	13.6	4.5
25 滋　　　賀	100.0	95.0	90.0	5.0	-	5.0	5.0	-
26 京　　　都	100.0	73.2	73.2	-	-	26.8	26.8	-
27 大　　　阪	100.0	78.4	77.5	0.9	-	21.6	18.9	2.7
28 兵　　　庫	100.0	73.1	70.1	3.0	-	26.9	25.4	1.5
29 奈　　　良	100.0	80.0	80.0	-	-	20.0	20.0	-
30 和　歌　山	100.0	100.0	100.0	-	-	-	-	-
31 鳥　　　取	100.0	84.6	84.6	-	-	15.4	7.7	7.7
32 島　　　根	100.0	90.9	90.9	-	-	9.1	9.1	-
33 岡　　　山	100.0	73.3	70.0	3.3	-	26.7	26.7	-
34 広　　　島	100.0	83.7	83.7	-	-	16.3	16.3	-
35 山　　　口	100.0	79.2	79.2	-	-	20.8	20.8	-
36 徳　　　島	100.0	87.5	87.5	-	-	12.5	12.5	-
37 香　　　川	100.0	50.0	50.0	-	-	50.0	37.5	12.5
38 愛　　　媛	100.0	68.8	68.8	-	-	31.3	25.0	6.3
39 高　　　知	100.0	77.8	77.8	-	-	22.2	22.2	-
40 福　　　岡	100.0	83.1	82.0	1.1	-	16.9	14.6	2.2
41 佐　　　賀	100.0	84.6	84.6	-	-	15.4	15.4	-
42 長　　　崎	100.0	100.0	100.0	-	-	-	-	-
43 熊　　　本	100.0	86.2	79.3	6.9	-	13.8	10.3	3.4
44 大　　　分	100.0	100.0	100.0	-	-	-	-	-
45 宮　　　崎	100.0	88.0	84.0	4.0	-	12.0	8.0	4.0
46 鹿　児　島	100.0	100.0	100.0	-	-	-	-	-
47 沖　　　縄	100.0	83.9	83.9	-	-	16.1	16.1	-
21 大 都 市（再掲） 21 major cities （Regrouped）								
50 東京都の区部	100.0	95.3	94.7	0.7	-	4.7	4.0	0.7
51 札　　　幌	100.0	96.6	96.6	-	-	3.4	3.4	-
52 仙　　　台	100.0	88.5	88.5	-	-	11.5	11.5	-
53 さ い た ま	100.0	96.7	93.3	3.3	-	3.3	3.3	-
54 千　　　葉	100.0	93.3	93.3	-	-	6.7	6.7	-
55 横　　　浜	100.0	82.8	82.8	-	-	17.2	17.2	-
56 川　　　崎	100.0	90.6	90.6	-	-	9.4	9.4	-
57 相　模　原	100.0	93.3	93.3	-	-	6.7	6.7	-
58 新　　　潟	100.0	100.0	100.0	-	-	-	-	-
59 静　　　岡	100.0	72.7	72.7	-	-	27.3	27.3	-
60 浜　　　松	100.0	83.3	83.3	-	-	16.7	16.7	-
61 名　古　屋	100.0	97.1	97.1	-	-	2.9	2.9	-
62 京　　　都	100.0	68.2	68.2	-	-	31.8	31.8	-
63 大　　　阪	100.0	81.1	81.1	-	-	18.9	16.2	2.7
64 堺	100.0	77.8	66.7	11.1	-	22.2	22.2	-
65 神　　　戸	100.0	81.3	75.0	6.3	-	18.8	18.8	-
66 岡　　　山	100.0	72.7	63.6	9.1	-	27.3	27.3	-
67 広　　　島	100.0	80.0	80.0	-	-	20.0	20.0	-
68 北　九　州	100.0	77.3	77.3	-	-	22.7	18.2	4.5
69 福　　　岡	100.0	83.3	83.3	-	-	16.7	16.7	-
70 熊　　　本	100.0	90.9	81.8	9.1	-	9.1	9.1	-

Note : a) See page 44.

〔世帯の主な仕事別にみた乳児死亡〕
〔Infant deaths by type of occupation of household〕

表6.9　世帯の主な仕事別にみた生存期間別乳児死亡数・率
（世帯の主な仕事別出生千対）及び百分率

Table 6.9　Infant deaths, infant mortality rates （per 1,000 live births） and percent distribution by type of occupation of household : Japan, 2016

平成28年

日　齢・月　齢 Age	総　数[1] Total	農家世帯 Agriculture[a]	自営業者世帯 Self employed	常用勤労者世帯（Ⅰ） Employee[b]	常用勤労者世帯（Ⅱ） Employee[c] or director	その他の世帯 Other	無職の世帯 Not working
乳　児　死　亡　数　　Infant deaths							
総　数　Total	1 928	30	117	529	510	260	264
4　週　未　満　Under 4 weeks	874	12	57	244	312	91	75
1　週　未　満　Under 1 week	676	10	46	189	256	68	51
1　日　未　満　Under 1 day	441	7	32	122	165	46	29
4　週～3か月未満　4 weeks and over, less than 3 months	375	2	24	106	79	61	65
3か月～6か月未満　3 months and over, less than 6 months	330	8	18	95	58	47	59
6か月～9か月未満　6 months and over, less than 9 months	220	5	11	51	42	33	43
9か月～1年未満　9 months and over, less than 1 year	129	3	7	33	19	28	22
乳　児　死　亡　率　　Infant mortality rates							
総　数　Total	2.0	2.5	1.7	1.7	1.1	3.2	15.7
4　週　未　満　Under 4 weeks	0.9	1.0	0.8	0.8	0.7	1.1	4.5
1　週　未　満　Under 1 week	0.7	0.8	0.7	0.6	0.6	0.8	3.0
1　日　未　満　Under 1 day	0.5	0.6	0.5	0.4	0.4	0.6	1.7
4　週～3か月未満　4 weeks and over, less than 3 months	0.4	0.2	0.3	0.3	0.2	0.8	3.9
3か月～6か月未満　3 months and over, less than 6 months	0.3	0.7	0.3	0.3	0.1	0.6	3.5
6か月～9か月未満　6 months and over, less than 9 months	0.2	0.4	0.2	0.2	0.1	0.4	2.6
9か月～1年未満　9 months and over, less than 1 year	0.1	0.3	0.1	0.1	0.0	0.3	1.3
百　　分　　率　　Percentage							
総　数　Total	100.0	100.0	100.0	100.0	100.0	100.0	100.0
4　週　未　満　Under 4 weeks	45.3	40.0	48.7	46.1	61.2	35.0	28.4
1　週　未　満　Under 1 week	35.1	33.3	39.3	35.7	50.2	26.2	19.3
1　日　未　満　Under 1 day	22.9	23.3	27.4	23.1	32.4	17.7	11.0
4　週～3か月未満　4 weeks and over, less than 3 months	19.5	6.7	20.5	20.0	15.5	23.5	24.6
3か月～6か月未満　3 months and over, less than 6 months	17.1	26.7	15.4	18.0	11.4	18.1	22.3
6か月～9か月未満　6 months and over, less than 9 months	11.4	16.7	9.4	9.6	8.2	12.7	16.3
9か月～1年未満　9 months and over, less than 1 year	6.7	10.0	6.0	6.2	3.7	10.8	8.3

注：1)　総数には世帯の主な仕事不詳を含む。
Note：a) Agriculture only or that with other work.
　　　b) Employee at office (excluding governmental office) with 1－99 employee (excluding daily or less than one year contracts).
　　　c) Employee at office excluding b) above.

411

乳児死亡

〔地域別にみた乳児死亡〕
〔Infant deaths by prefecture〕

表 6.10　都道府県別にみた
Table 6.10　Trends in infant deaths

都道府県[1] Prefecture	1947 昭和22年	1950 25　年	1955 30　年	1960 35　年	1965 40　年	1970 45　年	1975 50　年	1980 55　年	1985 60　年	1990 平成2年	1995 7　年	2000 12　年
全　　国　Total	205 360	140 515	68 801	49 293	33 742	25 412	19 103	11 841	7 899	5 616	5 054	3 830
01[a] 北　海　道	11 716	8 178	3 995	2 831	1 881	1 201	1 007	632	409	237	203	115
02 青　　　森	4 883	4 404	2 043	1 370	822	468	291	180	109	86	77	64
03 岩　　　手	4 524	4 105	2 245	1 346	707	406	292	178	87	52	46	29
04 宮　　　城	4 184	3 170	1 601	1 054	583	412	334	261	136	107	80	58
05 秋　　　田	4 640	3 403	1 623	860	465	282	205	129	78	56	48	23
06 山　　　形	4 042	2 773	1 288	784	341	264	161	122	71	46	47	47
07 福　　　島	5 335	4 263	2 422	1 624	742	445	408	260	189	102	92	88
08 茨　　　城	5 615	4 147	2 099	1 473	866	608	467	335	213	137	125	87
09 栃　　　木	3 797	2 631	1 343	863	588	430	333	227	130	112	96	74
10 群　　　馬	3 609	2 445	1 241	822	589	418	347	199	118	93	92	61
11 埼　　　玉	5 622	4 119	2 304	1 523	1 348	1 232	1 015	558	369	280	257	210
12 千　　　葉	5 722	3 860	2 020	1 364	1 029	945	778	472	291	225	196	177
13 東　　　京	9 813	6 363	3 408	3 358	3 053	2 630	1 654	934	622	438	423	354
14 神　奈　川	4 503	2 689	1 559	1 412	1 382	1 362	1 049	678	437	354	361	279
15 新　　　潟	6 237	4 237	2 008	1 301	865	501	397	252	182	83	78	62
16 富　　　山	3 956	2 333	970	631	384	274	184	105	81	63	52	42
17 石　　　川	3 241	2 190	951	616	346	237	186	125	66	52	56	32
18 福　　　井	2 185	1 640	724	457	305	169	135	57	73	42	44	30
19 山　　　梨	1 662	1 125	444	338	212	166	101	78	58	42	52	33
20 長　　　野	3 804	2 464	1 173	783	553	386	270	223	150	95	69	54
21 岐　　　阜	3 828	2 684	1 240	914	672	527	340	196	147	79	74	53
22 静　　　岡	5 365	4 043	2 015	1 319	866	672	542	305	236	157	164	96
23 愛　　　知	7 715	5 207	2 598	1 957	1 630	1 417	1 029	614	432	304	276	241
24 三　　　重	4 099	2 514	1 068	787	522	347	244	165	118	92	87	57
25 滋　　　賀	2 247	1 411	706	459	343	231	191	103	82	56	65	51
26 京　　　都	3 705	2 079	909	747	587	481	353	209	143	118	97	78
27 大　　　阪	8 287	5 118	2 524	2 228	2 281	1 932	1 411	771	558	417	340	257
28 兵　　　庫	7 326	4 534	2 228	1 741	1 286	1 069	790	481	326	233	226	189
29 奈　　　良	2 186	1 252	608	394	260	214	167	127	82	61	51	30
30 和　歌　山	2 180	1 387	668	563	352	280	205	113	79	51	49	26
31 鳥　　　取	1 507	991	439	300	174	115	93	62	49	31	32	13
32 島　　　根	2 471	1 651	707	495	269	149	105	95	47	50	32	16
33 岡　　　山	4 283	2 505	1 101	810	439	311	250	136	115	103	76	58
34 広　　　島	4 603	2 781	1 541	1 082	707	606	463	286	166	148	122	76
35 山　　　口	3 531	2 189	1 041	801	482	353	259	158	115	70	59	44
36 徳　　　島	2 702	1 949	867	535	271	168	132	86	57	38	43	26
37 香　　　川	2 793	1 677	849	549	317	229	214	88	51	46	34	31
38 愛　　　媛	3 990	2 612	1 253	834	482	332	250	154	128	73	61	38
39 高　　　知	2 177	1 437	651	486	250	174	126	75	68	52	38	31
40 福　　　岡	8 748	5 715	2 539	1 828	1 154	869	568	442	324	223	230	162
41 佐　　　賀	3 063	1 944	845	607	303	200	139	86	70	44	32	25
42 長　　　崎	4 275	3 274	1 534	1 310	697	407	246	153	91	57	64	45
43 熊　　　本	4 284	3 017	1 454	1 168	678	407	339	224	125	84	67	54
44 大　　　分	3 705	2 467	1 180	739	457	297	206	144	61	52	39	37
45 宮　　　崎	2 843	2 156	1 069	723	488	297	205	145	81	65	49	41
46 鹿　児　島	4 357	3 325	1 693	1 094	709	446	319	233	150	81	56	53
47 沖　　　縄	…	…	…	…	…	…	270	159	115	123	83	75
外　　　国 Foreign countries	…	…	…	…	…	…	…	…	…	…	-	1
不　　　詳 Place of residence not stated	-	57	13	13	5	46	33	26	14	6	14	7

注：1）　昭和22年は事件発生地により、25年以降は住所地により表章している。

Infant mortality

年次別乳児死亡数
by each prefecture : Japan

2005 17 年	2006 18 年	2007 19 年	2008 20 年	2009 21 年	2010 22 年	2011 23 年	2012 24 年	2013 25 年	2014 26 年	2015 27 年	2016 28 年	都道府県[1)] Prefecture
2 958	2 864	2 828	2 798	2 556	2 450	2 463	2 299	2 185	2 080	1 916	**1 928**	全　国　Total
115	116	111	99	89	84	84	88	85	61	73	76	01 北海道 [a)]
29	32	26	21	33	21	23	24	14	17	20	18	02 青森
34	26	23	36	35	26	43	27	12	17	27	17	03 岩手
54	41	48	41	38	47	85	42	49	35	28	40	04 宮城
17	21	14	20	17	15	15	11	10	15	4	13	05 秋田
18	31	23	21	27	25	28	23	30	19	18	24	06 山形
42	41	44	45	47	49	34	30	24	27	34	27	07 福島
68	65	80	61	53	60	56	61	56	58	53	40	08 茨城
58	56	50	60	43	34	38	38	29	56	23	26	09 栃木
55	40	41	39	44	35	33	45	35	19	22	22	10 群馬
137	163	147	164	140	133	109	114	114	118	111	118	11 埼玉
147	136	135	133	137	117	117	135	110	104	101	95	12 千葉
257	290	278	261	246	212	216	236	215	205	189	222	13 東京
239	236	226	217	187	203	209	174	149	149	142	147	14 神奈川
50	46	43	48	35	31	32	20	37	33	33	20	15 新潟
29	24	27	25	20	25	16	17	21	17	11	16	16 富山
30	25	36	25	19	30	14	19	15	21	13	19	17 石川
20	17	22	18	15	15	12	14	12	12	11	16	18 福井
18	22	13	10	18	7	9	13	14	11	12	10	19 山梨
42	39	36	34	38	25	32	31	36	23	20	29	20 長野
54	60	43	58	38	41	49	27	40	37	30	35	21 岐阜
99	87	81	80	65	68	70	58	64	61	53	46	22 静岡
202	188	192	207	183	153	176	142	133	137	140	117	23 愛知
33	45	59	41	37	37	37	48	44	27	29	22	24 三重
45	41	48	35	31	39	28	29	37	20	23	20	25 滋賀
54	48	51	54	44	52	40	40	52	35	50	41	26 京都
198	204	204	213	176	161	170	154	136	138	125	111	27 大阪
132	118	105	115	97	105	96	79	72	91	74	67	28 兵庫
38	29	23	30	43	24	14	25	19	24	17	30	29 奈良
26	22	27	18	18	16	23	15	15	18	13	12	30 和歌山
15	10	15	11	9	24	10	9	6	16	15	13	31 鳥取
18	16	13	11	11	13	11	11	13	13	8	11	32 島根
54	32	37	55	36	29	39	38	32	26	23	30	33 岡山
64	67	48	68	62	64	53	57	43	46	53	43	34 広島
32	31	22	27	27	31	24	26	21	26	22	24	35 山口
18	19	21	15	18	16	30	25	24	19	14	16	36 徳島
24	25	13	22	23	22	23	15	19	12	11	8	37 香川
32	17	25	16	29	19	13	28	25	16	14	16	38 愛媛
15	18	25	21	9	15	18	13	14	12	8	9	39 高知
109	90	110	105	107	105	116	94	103	99	99	89	40 福岡
13	15	17	22	11	18	12	12	23	9	7	13	41 佐賀
33	37	37	21	40	38	32	27	27	24	19	19	42 長崎
43	35	45	39	33	42	31	39	41	25	19	29	43 熊本
23	24	27	26	27	27	32	24	18	21	17	22	44 大分
32	24	24	33	24	14	30	27	27	24	16	25	45 宮崎
46	53	46	38	31	34	36	28	37	38	37	32	46 鹿児島
40	39	42	34	41	46	40	46	30	47	34	31	47 沖縄
4	1	2	1	3	1	2	-	2	2	-	2	外　国 Foreign countries
3	2	3	4	2	2	3	1	1	-	1	-	不　詳 Place of residence not stated

Note : a) See page 44.

乳児死亡

表 6.11　都道府県別にみた
Table 6.11　Trends in infant mortality rates

都道府県[1] Prefecture	1947 昭和22年	1950 25　年	1955 30　年	1960 35　年	1965 40　年	1970 45　年	1975 50　年	1980 55　年	1985 60　年	1990 平成2年	1995 7　年	2000 12　年
全　国　Total	76.7	60.1	39.8	30.7	18.5	13.1	10.0	7.5	5.5	4.6	4.3	3.2
01 北　海　道 [a]	82.8	55.6	38.5	30.2	19.5	13.1	11.2	8.4	6.2	4.4	4.1	2.5
02 青　　　森	99.7	95.5	58.0	45.8	29.1	17.7	12.1	8.3	5.7	5.9	5.5	5.0
03 岩　　　手	98.2	89.9	64.7	48.4	28.7	18.4	13.2	9.1	5.0	3.6	3.5	2.3
04 宮　　　城	75.4	59.6	41.6	33.6	19.9	13.5	10.2	8.4	4.9	4.6	3.6	2.6
05 秋　　　田	97.0	79.8	53.4	36.5	23.4	15.9	11.7	7.9	5.7	5.1	4.8	2.6
06 山　　　形	92.0	68.1	47.2	35.2	18.1	15.3	9.3	7.2	4.8	3.7	4.1	4.3
07 福　　　島	74.9	63.1	49.5	41.4	22.6	14.9	13.0	8.8	6.9	4.5	4.3	4.3
08 茨　　　城	81.2	69.4	47.1	41.3	24.4	15.8	11.5	9.2	6.4	4.8	4.4	3.1
09 栃　　　木	69.2	56.2	40.2	33.1	22.8	15.6	11.2	8.8	5.5	5.6	5.1	3.9
10 群　　　馬	66.1	54.6	38.4	32.2	21.1	14.2	11.7	7.9	5.1	4.8	4.7	3.1
11 埼　　　玉	72.8	65.8	48.2	35.1	20.2	13.5	10.6	7.4	5.5	4.4	3.8	3.2
12 千　　　葉	77.4	67.2	46.2	34.5	19.0	13.0	10.1	7.2	4.8	4.2	3.6	3.2
13 東　　　京	62.4	42.9	26.7	20.4	13.5	11.5	8.9	6.7	4.9	4.2	4.4	3.5
14 神　奈　川	60.3	40.9	30.1	23.3	14.2	11.0	8.8	7.2	5.1	4.5	4.5	3.4
15 新　　　潟	72.4	58.8	38.9	31.6	21.5	13.4	10.6	7.7	6.2	3.4	3.4	2.8
16 富　　　山	95.5	83.7	52.6	39.1	23.5	15.7	10.6	7.7	6.8	6.3	5.2	4.1
17 石　　　川	86.9	83.6	52.8	38.5	20.8	13.1	9.9	8.3	5.0	4.5	5.0	2.8
18 福　　　井	85.9	77.3	48.8	35.5	23.9	13.9	10.9	5.3	7.3	4.8	5.3	3.7
19 山　　　梨	63.2	52.7	28.4	26.4	16.7	13.5	8.5	7.8	5.9	4.9	5.9	3.9
20 長　　　野	61.4	49.3	32.9	25.5	17.5	12.3	8.5	8.2	6.2	4.4	3.3	2.5
21 岐　　　阜	74.4	64.7	42.3	32.1	20.9	16.3	10.8	7.6	6.2	3.9	3.7	2.6
22 静　　　岡	65.8	57.5	37.0	26.6	15.7	11.6	9.3	6.5	5.4	4.2	4.6	2.7
23 愛　　　知	73.9	59.3	39.8	26.7	16.0	12.2	9.2	7.0	5.4	4.3	3.8	3.2
24 三　　　重	88.7	67.5	42.0	32.6	19.3	13.3	9.4	7.7	6.0	5.1	5.0	3.2
25 滋　　　賀	86.9	65.9	46.9	34.1	24.0	14.8	10.8	6.5	5.5	4.1	4.9	3.6
26 京　　　都	68.8	50.4	32.5	25.6	16.0	11.7	8.8	6.5	5.0	4.9	4.2	3.3
27 大　　　阪	79.9	54.5	34.4	23.4	15.5	11.4	9.4	6.9	5.6	4.8	3.9	2.9
28 兵　　　庫	75.2	55.4	35.7	26.9	15.6	11.7	9.1	7.0	5.3	4.3	4.4	3.5
29 奈　　　良	91.1	67.3	46.5	32.8	17.8	12.2	9.3	8.0	5.6	4.6	3.8	2.3
30 和　歌　山	70.8	58.4	38.3	35.4	19.5	15.6	12.5	8.4	6.5	5.0	5.0	2.7
31 鳥　　　取	77.9	61.5	36.9	31.3	20.3	14.4	10.6	7.6	6.5	4.8	5.6	2.3
32 島　　　根	76.0	63.9	41.2	35.1	22.8	14.1	9.6	9.5	5.2	6.7	4.7	2.5
33 岡　　　山	80.0	62.1	38.7	32.0	17.2	10.8	8.3	5.6	5.1	5.4	4.1	3.0
34 広　　　島	67.9	52.7	40.9	31.4	18.1	13.6	9.9	7.7	5.0	5.1	4.4	2.8
35 山　　　口	71.7	51.2	36.2	32.1	19.6	14.4	10.8	8.0	6.5	5.1	4.5	3.4
36 徳　　　島	85.4	76.5	48.1	40.2	21.5	14.2	11.0	8.2	5.9	4.8	5.8	3.6
37 香　　　川	81.5	68.1	51.0	40.5	23.1	15.8	13.8	6.8	4.4	4.8	3.7	3.2
38 愛　　　媛	75.6	57.3	41.0	33.3	19.7	14.5	10.7	7.8	7.3	5.0	4.4	2.9
39 高　　　知	76.0	62.4	40.6	38.4	20.8	14.7	10.7	8.0	7.3	7.2	5.5	4.6
40 福　　　岡	80.8	52.4	33.2	27.2	16.8	12.5	8.0	6.9	5.5	4.6	4.9	3.4
41 佐　　　賀	95.8	64.8	37.9	35.1	21.0	15.2	10.6	6.9	6.0	4.6	3.7	2.9
42 長　　　崎	80.6	60.0	35.6	35.9	23.1	15.2	9.6	6.9	4.5	3.5	4.3	3.2
43 熊　　　本	70.0	54.5	34.5	35.4	23.4	16.2	13.2	9.2	5.4	4.4	3.7	3.1
44 大　　　分	87.5	67.2	44.6	36.7	24.7	16.9	11.2	8.8	4.2	4.5	3.5	3.4
45 宮　　　崎	73.6	61.0	40.0	33.0	26.5	17.5	11.3	8.5	5.3	5.4	4.2	3.7
46 鹿　児　島	74.1	60.4	33.9	28.9	24.2	18.4	13.0	9.5	6.4	4.3	3.4	3.3
47 沖　　　縄	…	…	…	…	…	…	12.1	7.8	5.6	7.2	5.0	4.5

注：1)　昭和22年は事件発生地により、25年以降は住所地により表章している。

年次別乳児死亡率（出生千対）
(per 1,000 live births) by each prefecture : Japan

2005 17 年	2006 18 年	2007 19 年	2008 20 年	2009 21 年	2010 22 年	2011 23 年	2012 24 年	2013 25 年	2014 26 年	2015 27 年	2016 28 年	都道府県[1] Prefecture
2.8	2.6	2.6	2.6	2.4	2.3	2.3	2.2	2.1	2.1	1.9	2.0	全　国　Total
2.8	2.7	2.7	2.4	2.2	2.1	2.1	2.3	2.2	1.6	2.0	2.2	01 北　海　道 a)
2.8	3.0	2.6	2.1	3.5	2.2	2.4	2.6	1.5	1.9	2.3	2.1	02 青　　　森
3.2	2.5	2.2	3.5	3.5	2.7	4.6	2.9	1.3	1.9	3.1	2.0	03 岩　　　手
2.8	2.1	2.4	2.1	2.0	2.5	4.7	2.2	2.6	1.9	1.6	2.3	04 宮　　　城
2.2	2.7	1.9	2.7	2.4	2.2	2.3	1.7	1.6	2.5	0.7	2.3	05 秋　　　田
1.9	3.3	2.5	2.3	3.1	2.9	3.3	2.8	3.7	2.4	2.3	3.2	06 山　　　形
2.4	2.3	2.6	2.7	2.9	3.0	2.3	2.2	1.6	1.9	2.4	2.0	07 福　　　島
2.8	2.6	3.2	2.5	2.2	2.5	2.4	2.7	2.5	2.7	2.4	1.9	08 茨　　　城
3.3	3.2	2.9	3.5	2.5	2.1	2.4	2.4	1.9	3.6	1.5	1.8	09 栃　　　木
3.2	2.3	2.4	2.3	2.7	2.2	2.1	3.0	2.4	1.3	1.5	1.6	10 群　　　馬
2.3	2.7	2.4	2.7	2.3	2.2	1.9	2.0	2.0	2.1	2.0	2.2	11 埼　　　玉
2.9	2.6	2.6	2.5	2.6	2.3	2.3	2.8	2.3	2.2	2.1	2.1	12 千　　　葉
2.7	2.9	2.7	2.5	2.3	2.0	2.0	2.2	2.0	1.9	1.7	2.0	13 東　　　京
3.1	3.0	2.9	2.7	2.4	2.6	2.8	2.3	2.0	2.0	1.9	2.1	14 神　奈　川
2.7	2.4	2.3	2.6	2.0	1.7	1.8	1.1	2.2	2.0	2.0	1.3	15 新　　　潟
3.2	2.7	3.1	2.9	2.4	3.1	2.0	2.2	2.7	2.2	1.5	2.2	16 富　　　山
3.0	2.4	3.5	2.5	1.9	3.1	1.5	2.0	1.6	2.3	1.4	2.1	17 石　　　川
2.8	2.3	3.1	2.5	2.1	2.2	1.8	2.1	1.9	1.9	1.8	2.6	18 福　　　井
2.5	3.1	1.9	1.4	2.7	1.1	1.4	2.1	2.3	1.8	2.0	1.7	19 山　　　梨
2.3	2.1	1.9	1.9	2.2	1.5	1.9	1.9	2.2	1.5	1.3	1.9	20 長　　　野
3.0	3.3	2.4	3.3	2.2	2.4	2.9	1.6	2.5	2.4	1.9	2.4	21 岐　　　阜
3.1	2.6	2.4	2.4	2.0	2.1	2.2	1.9	2.1	2.1	1.9	1.7	22 静　　　岡
3.0	2.7	2.7	2.9	2.6	2.2	2.6	2.1	2.0	2.1	2.1	1.8	23 愛　　　知
2.2	2.8	3.8	2.6	2.4	2.4	2.5	3.3	3.0	2.0	2.1	1.7	24 三　　　重
3.5	3.0	3.6	2.6	2.4	2.9	2.1	2.2	2.8	1.6	1.8	1.7	25 滋　　　賀
2.5	2.2	2.4	2.5	2.1	2.4	1.9	2.0	2.6	1.8	2.5	2.1	26 京　　　都
2.6	2.6	2.7	2.8	2.3	2.1	2.3	2.1	1.9	2.0	1.8	1.6	27 大　　　阪
2.8	2.4	2.2	2.4	2.0	2.2	2.0	1.7	1.6	2.1	1.7	1.5	28 兵　　　庫
3.4	2.5	2.0	2.7	4.0	2.2	1.3	2.4	1.9	2.5	1.7	3.2	29 奈　　　良
3.3	2.8	3.5	2.3	2.4	2.1	3.1	2.0	2.1	2.5	1.8	1.8	30 和　歌　山
3.0	1.9	3.0	2.3	1.8	5.0	2.0	1.9	1.3	3.5	3.2	2.9	31 鳥　　　取
3.2	2.7	2.2	1.9	2.0	2.3	2.0	2.0	2.3	2.4	1.4	2.1	32 島　　　根
3.2	1.9	2.2	3.2	2.2	1.7	2.3	2.3	2.0	1.6	1.5	1.9	33 岡　　　山
2.6	2.6	1.9	2.7	2.4	2.5	2.1	2.3	1.7	1.9	2.2	1.9	34 広　　　島
2.8	2.7	1.9	2.3	2.4	2.7	2.1	2.4	2.0	2.5	2.1	2.4	35 山　　　口
3.0	3.0	3.5	2.5	3.1	2.7	5.1	4.4	4.2	3.5	2.5	3.0	36 徳　　　島
2.8	2.9	1.5	2.6	2.7	2.6	2.8	1.8	2.4	1.5	1.4	1.1	37 香　　　川
2.8	1.4	2.1	1.4	2.5	1.7	1.1	2.5	2.3	1.5	1.4	1.6	38 愛　　　媛
2.5	3.0	4.4	3.6	1.7	2.7	3.4	2.5	2.7	2.4	1.6	1.9	39 高　　　知
2.5	2.0	2.4	2.2	2.3	2.2	2.5	2.1	2.2	2.2	2.2	2.0	40 福　　　岡
1.7	2.0	2.2	2.8	1.5	2.4	1.6	1.6	3.2	1.3	1.0	1.9	41 佐　　　賀
2.7	3.0	3.0	1.7	3.4	3.2	2.7	2.3	2.3	2.1	1.7	1.7	42 長　　　崎
2.7	2.2	2.8	2.4	2.0	2.6	1.9	2.4	2.6	1.6	1.2	1.9	43 熊　　　本
2.4	2.4	2.7	2.5	2.7	2.7	3.2	2.5	1.9	2.3	1.9	2.4	44 大　　　分
3.3	2.4	2.3	3.2	2.4	1.4	3.0	2.7	2.7	2.5	1.7	2.8	45 宮　　　崎
3.1	3.5	3.0	2.5	2.1	2.2	2.4	1.9	2.5	2.7	2.6	2.3	46 鹿　児　島
2.5	2.4	2.5	2.0	2.4	2.7	2.4	2.7	1.7	2.9	2.0	1.9	47 沖　　　縄

Note : a) See page 44.

乳児死亡

表 6.12 都道府県（21大都市再掲）別にみた生存期間別乳児死亡率（出生10万対）及び乳児死亡中新生児死亡・早期新生児死亡の占める割合

Table 6.12 Infant mortality rates (per 100,000 live births) by age and proportion of neonatal deaths : Japan, each prefecture and 21 major cities, 2016

平成28年

都道府県 Prefecture	総 数 Total	4週未満 Under 4 weeks	（再掲）1週未満 Under 1 week (Regrouped)	（再掲）1日未満 Under 1 day (Regrouped)	4週～3か月未満 4 weeks and over, less than 3 months	3か月～6か月未満 3 months and over, less than 6 months	6か月～9か月未満 6 months and over, less than 9 months	9か月～1年未満 9 months and over, less than 1 year	乳児死亡中4週未満の占める割合(%) Proportion of under 4 weeks	乳児死亡中1週未満の占める割合(%) Proportion of under 1 week
全 国 Total [a]	197.3	89.5	69.2	45.1	38.4	33.8	22.5	13.2	45.3	35.1
01 北海道	216.4	94.0	79.7	51.2	56.9	22.8	28.5	14.2	43.4	36.8
02 青森	208.7	92.7	69.6	58.0	11.6	34.8	69.6	-	44.4	33.3
03 岩手	203.8	83.9	48.0	24.0	12.0	71.9	12.0	24.0	41.2	23.5
04 宮城	230.6	138.4	115.3	69.2	46.1	28.8	11.5	5.8	60.0	50.0
05 秋田	229.4	105.9	88.2	70.6	17.6	35.3	17.6	52.9	46.2	38.5
06 山形	318.0	225.3	119.3	39.8	39.8	13.3	13.3	26.5	70.8	37.5
07 福島	196.4	87.3	50.9	36.4	58.2	21.8	14.6	14.6	44.4	25.9
08 茨城	191.6	100.6	62.3	47.9	19.2	43.1	23.9	4.8	52.5	32.5
09 栃木	177.8	82.1	82.1	54.7	47.9	20.5	13.7	13.7	46.2	46.2
10 群馬	161.0	87.8	73.2	29.3	36.6	22.0	7.3	7.3	54.5	45.5
11 埼玉	216.7	95.5	73.5	49.6	33.1	44.1	31.2	12.9	44.1	33.9
12 千葉	209.3	99.1	74.9	55.1	33.0	46.3	19.8	11.0	47.4	35.8
13 東京	198.3	86.6	71.5	47.3	39.3	31.3	25.9	15.2	43.7	36.0
14 神奈川	208.1	113.2	87.8	58.0	43.9	21.2	15.6	14.2	54.4	42.2
15 新潟	127.1	57.2	31.8	12.7	38.1	12.7	19.1	-	45.0	25.0
16 富山	219.1	164.3	123.3	54.8	41.1	13.7	-	-	75.0	56.3
17 石川	212.8	78.4	67.2	67.2	44.8	67.2	22.4	-	36.8	31.6
18 福井	261.8	130.9	130.9	65.4	16.4	49.1	32.7	32.7	50.0	50.0
19 山梨	171.9	68.7	51.6	34.4	17.2	34.4	34.4	17.2	40.0	30.0
20 長野	191.2	105.5	98.9	52.7	39.6	6.6	33.0	6.6	55.2	51.7
21 岐阜	236.0	128.1	101.1	67.4	27.0	60.7	20.2	-	54.3	42.9
22 静岡	166.4	83.2	57.9	43.4	28.9	21.7	18.1	14.5	50.0	34.8
23 愛知	182.2	88.7	70.1	46.7	28.0	35.8	20.2	9.3	48.7	38.5
24 三重	166.6	90.9	60.6	30.3	22.7	15.1	30.3	7.6	54.5	36.4
25 滋賀	165.7	82.8	66.3	49.7	24.9	41.4	16.6	-	50.0	40.0
26 京都	212.1	108.7	88.0	46.6	46.6	41.4	-	15.5	51.2	41.5
27 大阪	161.3	66.8	49.4	29.1	30.5	24.7	24.7	14.5	41.4	30.6
28 兵庫	154.5	41.5	36.9	20.7	41.5	25.4	18.4	27.7	26.9	23.9
29 奈良	318.1	127.3	106.0	63.6	84.8	63.6	10.6	31.8	40.0	33.3
30 和歌山	180.2	45.1	30.0	-	75.1	45.1	15.0	-	25.0	16.7
31 鳥取	293.1	180.3	135.3	135.3	22.5	-	22.5	67.6	61.5	46.2
32 島根	207.5	75.5	37.7	18.9	18.9	18.9	56.6	37.7	36.4	18.2
33 岡山	193.8	71.1	71.1	58.2	51.7	19.4	45.2	6.5	36.7	36.7
34 広島	189.1	83.6	52.8	30.8	22.0	39.6	30.8	13.2	44.2	27.9
35 山口	243.8	61.0	40.6	30.5	30.5	71.1	30.5	50.8	25.0	16.7
36 徳島	299.3	112.2	93.5	18.7	130.9	56.1	-	-	37.5	31.3
37 香川	106.5	53.3	39.9	39.9	-	26.6	26.6	-	50.0	37.5
38 愛媛	161.4	20.2	10.1	-	70.6	40.4	30.3	-	12.5	6.3
39 高知	188.3	41.8	41.8	41.8	62.8	62.8	-	20.9	22.2	22.2
40 福岡	202.1	68.1	59.0	47.7	50.0	50.0	31.8	2.3	33.7	29.2
41 佐賀	190.9	58.7	44.0	29.4	14.7	58.7	44.0	14.7	30.8	23.1
42 長崎	174.5	110.2	64.3	55.1	9.2	27.6	18.4	9.2	63.2	36.8
43 熊本	194.7	107.4	67.1	53.7	20.1	47.0	6.7	13.4	55.2	34.5
44 大分	242.9	121.4	110.4	66.2	66.2	11.0	33.1	11.0	50.0	45.5
45 宮崎	280.0	123.2	89.6	67.2	89.6	11.2	22.4	33.6	44.0	32.0
46 鹿児島	233.8	65.8	51.1	29.2	65.8	65.8	14.6	21.9	28.1	21.9
47 沖縄	186.6	84.3	66.2	36.1	36.1	48.1	12.0	6.0	45.2	35.5
21 大 都 市（再掲）21 major cities (Regrouped)										
50 東京都の区部	187.0	84.8	68.6	42.4	37.4	29.9	24.9	10.0	45.3	36.7
51 札幌	206.8	85.6	64.2	42.8	57.1	14.3	14.3	35.7	41.4	31.0
52 仙台	292.0	168.5	134.8	67.4	67.4	44.9	11.2	-	57.7	46.2
53 さいたま	284.4	161.2	104.3	66.4	37.9	37.9	37.9	9.5	56.7	36.7
54 千葉	216.5	115.5	86.6	72.2	14.4	72.2	-	14.4	53.3	40.0
55 横浜	200.8	110.8	96.9	51.9	41.5	27.7	10.4	10.4	55.2	48.3
56 川崎	226.0	113.0	70.6	56.5	35.3	21.2	21.2	35.3	50.0	31.3
57 相模原	288.7	154.0	77.0	77.0	77.0	19.2	19.2	19.2	53.3	26.7
58 新潟	84.2	33.7	33.7	16.8	50.5	-	-	-	40.0	40.0
59 静岡	215.4	58.8	58.8	39.2	58.8	39.2	58.8	-	27.3	27.3
60 浜松	91.5	45.7	45.7	45.7	-	-	15.2	30.5	50.0	50.0
61 名古屋	179.1	102.3	71.6	46.1	46.1	20.5	5.1	5.1	57.1	40.0
62 京都	201.4	91.6	82.4	45.8	36.6	45.8	-	27.5	45.5	40.9
63 大阪	167.4	72.4	58.8	40.7	31.7	22.6	27.2	13.6	43.2	35.1
64 堺	131.5	58.4	43.8	14.6	14.6	14.6	43.8	-	44.4	33.3
65 神戸	135.8	33.9	33.9	17.0	33.9	33.9	17.0	17.0	25.0	25.0
66 岡山	175.6	79.8	79.8	63.9	31.9	31.9	31.9	-	45.5	45.5
67 広島	189.4	66.3	47.4	28.4	9.5	66.3	37.9	9.5	35.0	25.0
68 北九州	288.7	118.1	78.7	52.5	78.7	39.4	39.4	13.1	40.9	27.3
69 福岡	165.7	41.4	34.5	27.6	48.3	48.3	27.6	-	25.0	20.8
70 熊本	161.8	117.7	44.1	29.4	14.7	-	14.7	14.7	72.7	27.3

注：実数については中巻乳児死亡第2表を参照されたい。
Note : a) See page 44.

乳児死亡

〔乳児死亡の原因〕
〔Causes of infant death〕

表 6.13　年次別にみた乳児死因簡単分類別
Table 6.13　Trends in infant deaths and infant mortality rates

乳児死因簡単分類コード Code[a]	死　　因 Causes of death	乳　児　死　亡　数 Infant deaths						
		1995 平成7年	2000 12年	2005 17年	2010 22年	2014 26年	2015 27年	2016 28年
	総　数　　Total	5 054	3 830	2 958	2 450	2 080	1 916	1 928
Ba01	腸管感染症	12	11	18	11	6	11	9
Ba02	敗血症	107	85	71	46	40	21	40
Ba03	麻疹	2	1	-	-	-	-	-
Ba04	ウイルス肝炎	6	7	3	2	3	-	2
Ba05	その他の感染症及び寄生虫症	20	24	25	22	11	18	18
Ba06	悪性新生物	27	18	21	14	10	10	17
Ba07	白血病	11	11	6	3	4	2	10
Ba08	その他の悪性新生物	16	7	15	11	6	8	7
Ba09	その他の新生物	15	12	28	14	15	24	9
Ba10	栄養失調症及びその他の栄養欠乏症	5	2	3	1	-	1	1
Ba11	代謝障害	44	43	35	28	18	7	23
Ba12	髄膜炎	23	12	5	10	5	3	5
Ba13	脊髄性筋萎縮症及び関連症候群	18	9	3	2	4	4	2
Ba14	脳性麻痺	6	3	2	2	1	2	-
Ba15	心疾患（高血圧性を除く）	143	117	138	68	52	50	41
Ba16	脳血管疾患	23	15	7	6	7	3	4
Ba17	インフルエンザ	5	-	-	2	3	-	2
Ba18	肺炎	114	73	48	42	33	24	28
Ba19	喘息	16	4	4	-	1	1	-
Ba20	ヘルニア及び腸閉塞	7	6	8	10	7	6	12
Ba21	肝疾患	11	16	9	9	5	6	11
Ba22	腎不全	8	17	4	5	2	-	2
Ba23	周産期に発生した病態	1 504	1 108	822	629	513	487	509
Ba24	妊娠期間及び胎児発育に関連する障害	76	73	66	65	59	39	43
Ba25	出産外傷	24	7	7	2	13	6	3
Ba26	出生時仮死	164	153	126	92	76	74	77
Ba27	新生児の呼吸窮迫	188	97	56	22	24	18	33
Ba28	周産期に発生した肺出血	47	37	21	10	23	9	10
Ba29	周産期に発生した心血管障害	98	65	42	70	42	46	43
Ba30	その他の周産期に特異的な呼吸障害及び心血管障害	267	251	169	147	96	101	119
Ba31	新生児の細菌性敗血症	103	61	41	46	29	24	36
Ba32	その他の周産期に特異的な感染症	30	23	19	11	14	9	7
Ba33	胎児及び新生児の出血性障害及び血液障害	241	207	159	85	63	83	67
Ba34	その他の周産期に発生した病態	266	134	116	79	74	78	71
Ba35	先天奇形，変形及び染色体異常	1 786	1 385	1 025	916	751	715	663
Ba36	神経系の先天奇形	83	66	56	42	47	34	29
Ba37	心臓の先天奇形	647	470	339	303	213	212	161
Ba38	その他の循環器系の先天奇形	270	177	122	110	93	78	84
Ba39	呼吸器系の先天奇形	213	174	139	69	54	63	52
Ba40	消化器系の先天奇形	64	39	26	29	18	17	20
Ba41	筋骨格系の先天奇形及び変形	126	95	65	63	63	48	42
Ba42	その他の先天奇形及び変形	119	132	100	75	72	73	67
Ba43	染色体異常，他に分類されないもの	264	232	178	225	191	190	208
Ba44	乳幼児突然死症候群	526	317	174	140	145	96	109
Ba45	その他のすべての疾患	260	279	296	325	337	312	317
Ba46	不慮の事故	329	217	174	113	78	81	73
Ba47	交通事故	18	16	11	9	2	3	3
Ba48	転倒・転落	8	8	7	4	3	1	-
Ba49	不慮の溺死及び溺水	22	7	9	6	2	4	4
Ba50	胃内容物の誤えん及び気道閉塞を生じた食物等の誤えん	107	71	62	43	22	27	32
Ba51	その他の不慮の窒息	124	89	71	42	42	42	30
Ba52	煙，火及び火炎への曝露	5	6	6	3	-	1	-
Ba53	有害物質による不慮の中毒及び有害物質への曝露	1	-	-	-	-	-	1
Ba54	その他の不慮の事故	44	20	8	6	7	3	3
Ba55	他殺	32	29	21	14	13	12	7
Ba56	その他の外因	5	20	14	19	20	22	24

注：「敗血症」には，“新生児の細菌性敗血症”を含まない。

Infant mortality

乳児死亡数及び率 （出生10万対）
(per 100,000 live births) by causes (the list of causes of infant death) : Japan

乳 児 死 亡 率（出生10万対）Infant mortality rates （per 100,000 live births）							乳児死因簡単分類コードCode[a]	死　　因Causes of death
1995平成7年	200012年	200517年	201022年	201426年	201527年	201628年		
425.8	321.7	278.4	228.7	207.3	190.5	197.3		総　　数　　Total
1.0	0.9	1.7	1.0	0.6	1.1	0.9	Ba01	腸管感染症
9.0	7.1	6.7	4.3	4.0	2.1	4.1	Ba02	敗　血　症
0.2	0.1	-	-	-	-	-	Ba03	麻　疹
0.5	0.6	0.3	0.2	0.3	-	0.2	Ba04	ウイルス肝炎
1.7	2.0	2.4	2.1	1.1	1.8	1.8	Ba05	その他の感染症及び寄生虫症
2.3	1.5	2.0	1.3	1.0	1.0	1.7	Ba06	悪性新生物
0.9	0.9	0.6	0.3	0.4	0.2	1.0	Ba07	白　血　病
1.3	0.6	1.4	1.0	0.6	0.8	0.7	Ba08	その他の悪性新生物
1.3	1.0	2.6	1.3	1.5	2.4	0.9	Ba09	その他の新生物
0.4	0.2	0.3	0.1	-	0.1	0.1	Ba10	栄養失調症及びその他の栄養欠乏症
3.7	3.6	3.3	2.6	1.8	0.7	2.4	Ba11	代　謝　障　害
1.9	1.0	0.5	0.9	0.5	0.3	0.5	Ba12	髄　膜　炎
1.5	0.8	0.3	0.2	0.4	0.4	0.2	Ba13	脊髄性筋萎縮症及び関連症候群
0.5	0.3	0.2	0.2	0.1	0.2	-	Ba14	脳　性　麻　痺
12.0	9.8	13.0	6.3	5.2	5.0	4.2	Ba15	心疾患（高血圧性を除く）
1.9	1.3	0.7	0.6	0.7	0.3	0.4	Ba16	脳血管疾患
0.4	-	-	0.2	0.3	-	0.2	Ba17	インフルエンザ
9.6	6.1	4.5	3.9	3.3	2.4	2.9	Ba18	肺　　炎
1.3	0.3	0.4	-	0.1	0.1	-	Ba19	喘　　息
0.6	0.5	0.8	0.9	0.7	0.6	1.2	Ba20	ヘルニア及び腸閉塞
0.9	1.3	0.8	0.8	0.5	0.6	1.1	Ba21	肝　疾　患
0.7	1.4	0.4	0.5	0.2	-	0.2	Ba22	腎　不　全
126.7	93.1	77.4	58.7	51.1	48.4	52.1	Ba23	周産期に発生した病態
6.4	6.1	6.2	6.1	5.9	3.9	4.4	Ba24	妊娠期間及び胎児発育に関連する障害
2.0	0.6	0.7	0.2	1.3	0.6	0.3	Ba25	出　産　外　傷
13.8	12.9	11.9	8.6	7.6	7.4	7.9	Ba26	出生時仮死
15.8	8.1	5.3	2.1	2.4	1.8	3.4	Ba27	新生児の呼吸窮迫
4.0	3.1	2.0	0.9	2.3	0.9	1.0	Ba28	周産期に発生した肺出血
8.3	5.5	4.0	6.5	4.2	4.6	4.4	Ba29	周産期に発生した心血管障害
22.5	21.1	15.9	13.7	9.6	10.0	12.2	Ba30	その他の周産期に特異的な呼吸障害及び心血管障害
8.7	5.1	3.9	4.3	2.9	2.4	3.7	Ba31	新生児の細菌性敗血症
2.5	1.9	1.8	1.0	1.4	0.9	0.7	Ba32	その他の周産期に特異的な感染症
20.3	17.4	15.0	7.9	6.3	8.3	6.9	Ba33	胎児及び新生児の出血性障害及び血液障害
22.4	11.3	10.9	7.4	7.4	7.8	7.3	Ba34	その他の周産期に発生した病態
150.5	116.3	96.5	85.5	74.8	71.1	67.9	Ba35	先天奇形，変形及び染色体異常
7.0	5.5	5.3	3.9	4.7	3.4	3.0	Ba36	神経系の先天奇形
54.5	39.5	31.9	28.3	21.2	21.1	16.5	Ba37	心臓の先天奇形
22.7	14.9	11.5	10.3	9.3	9.5	8.6	Ba38	その他の循環器系の先天奇形
17.9	14.6	13.1	6.4	5.4	6.3	5.3	Ba39	呼吸器系の先天奇形
5.4	3.3	2.4	2.7	1.8	1.7	2.0	Ba40	消化器系の先天奇形
10.6	8.0	6.1	5.9	6.3	4.8	4.3	Ba41	筋骨格系の先天奇形及び変形
10.0	11.1	9.4	7.0	7.2	7.3	6.9	Ba42	その他の先天奇形及び変形
22.2	19.5	16.8	21.0	19.0	18.9	21.3	Ba43	染色体異常，他に分類されないもの
44.3	26.6	16.4	13.1	14.4	9.5	11.2	Ba44	乳幼児突然死症候群
21.9	23.4	27.9	30.3	33.6	31.0	32.4	Ba45	その他のすべての疾患
27.7	18.2	16.4	10.5	7.8	8.1	7.5	Ba46	不慮の事故
1.5	1.3	1.0	0.8	0.2	0.3	0.3	Ba47	交　通　事　故
0.7	0.7	0.7	0.4	0.3	0.1	-	Ba48	転倒・転落
1.9	0.6	0.8	0.6	0.2	0.4	0.4	Ba49	不慮の溺死及び溺水
9.0	6.0	5.8	4.0	2.2	2.7	3.3	Ba50	胃内容物の誤えん及び気道閉塞を生じた食物等の誤えん
10.4	7.5	6.7	3.9	4.2	4.2	3.1	Ba51	その他の不慮の窒息
0.4	0.5	0.6	0.3	-	0.1	-	Ba52	煙，火及び火炎への曝露
0.1	-	-	-	-	-	0.1	Ba53	有害物質による不慮の中毒及び有害物質への曝露
3.7	1.7	0.8	0.6	0.7	0.3	0.3	Ba54	その他の不慮の事故
2.7	2.4	2.0	1.3	1.3	1.2	0.7	Ba55	他　　殺
0.4	1.7	1.3	1.8	2.0	2.2	2.5	Ba56	その他の外因

Note : a) Code see page 598.

乳児死亡

表 6.14 生存期間別にみた乳児死因簡単分類別
Table 6.14 Infant deaths and infant mortality rates (per 100,000 live births)

乳児死因簡単分類コード Code[a]	死　因 Causes of death	生存期間別乳児死亡数 Infant deaths				生存期間別乳児死亡率（出生10万対） Infant mortality rates			
		総　数 Total	4週未満 Under 4 weeks	（再掲） 1週未満 Under 1 week (Regrouped)	4週以上 1年未満 4 weeks and over, less than 1 year	総　数 Total	4週未満 Under 4 weeks	（再掲） 1週未満 Under 1 week (Regrouped)	4週以上 1年未満 4 weeks and over, less than 1 year
	総　数　Total	1 928	874	676	1 054	197.3	89.5	69.2	107.9
Ba01	腸管感染症	9	-	-	9	0.9	-	-	0.9
Ba02	敗 血 症	40	14	-	26	4.1	1.4	-	2.7
Ba03	麻　疹	-	-	-	-	-	-	-	-
Ba04	ウイルス肝炎	2	-	-	2	0.2	-	-	0.2
Ba05	その他の感染症及び寄生虫症	18	2	-	16	1.8	0.2	-	1.6
Ba06	悪性新生物	17	-	-	17	1.7	-	-	1.7
Ba07	白 血 病	10	-	-	10	1.0	-	-	1.0
Ba08	その他の悪性新生物	7	-	-	7	0.7	-	-	0.7
Ba09	その他の新生物	9	3	3	6	0.9	0.3	0.3	0.6
Ba10	栄養失調症及びその他の栄養欠乏症	1	-	-	1	0.1	-	-	0.1
Ba11	代 謝 障 害	23	7	5	16	2.4	0.7	0.5	1.6
Ba12	髄 膜 炎	5	2	1	3	0.5	0.2	0.1	0.3
Ba13	脊髄性筋萎縮症及び関連症候群	2	-	-	2	0.2	-	-	0.2
Ba14	脳 性 麻 痺	-	-	-	-	-	-	-	-
Ba15	心 疾 患（高血圧性を除く）	41	3	2	38	4.2	0.3	0.2	3.9
Ba16	脳血管疾患	4	1	-	3	0.4	0.1	-	0.3
Ba17	インフルエンザ	2	-	-	2	0.2	-	-	0.2
Ba18	肺　炎	28	2	-	26	2.9	0.2	-	2.7
Ba19	喘　息	-	-	-	-	-	-	-	-
Ba20	ヘルニア及び腸閉塞	12	-	-	12	1.2	-	-	1.2
Ba21	肝 疾 患	11	-	-	11	1.1	-	-	1.1
Ba22	腎 不 全	2	-	-	2	0.2	-	-	0.2
Ba23	周産期に発生した病態	509	451	390	58	52.1	46.2	39.9	5.9
Ba24	妊娠期間及び胎児発育に関連する障害	43	38	35	5	4.4	3.9	3.6	0.5
Ba25	出 産 外 傷	3	3	2	-	0.3	0.3	0.2	-
Ba26	出生時仮死	77	74	67	3	7.9	7.6	6.9	0.3
Ba27	新生児の呼吸窮迫	33	32	30	1	3.4	3.3	3.1	0.1
Ba28	周産期に発生した肺出血	10	10	9	-	1.0	1.0	0.9	-

注：「敗血症」には、"新生児の細菌性敗血症"を含まない。

Infant mortality

乳児死亡数及び率（出生10万対）
by age and causes（the list of causes of infant death）: Japan, 2016

平成28年

乳児死因 簡単分類 コード Code[a]	死　　　因 Causes of death	生 存 期 間 別 乳 児 死 亡 数 Infant deaths				生存期間別乳児死亡率（出生10万対） Infant mortality rates			
		総　数 Total	4週未満 Under 4 weeks	（再掲） 1週未満 Under 1 week (Regrouped)	4週以上 1年未満 4 weeks and over, less than 1 year	総　数 Total	4週未満 Under 4 weeks	（再掲） 1週未満 Under 1 week (Regrouped)	4週以上 1年未満 4 weeks and over, less than 1 year
Ba29	周産期に発生した心血管障害	43	40	36	3	4.4	4.1	3.7	0.3
Ba30	その他の周産期に特異的な呼吸障害及び心血管障害	119	99	91	20	12.2	10.1	9.3	2.0
Ba31	新生児の細菌性敗血症	36	33	26	3	3.7	3.4	2.7	0.3
Ba32	その他の周産期に特異的な感染症	7	7	5	-	0.7	0.7	0.5	-
Ba33	胎児及び新生児の出血性障害及び血液障害	67	62	47	5	6.9	6.3	4.8	0.5
Ba34	その他の周産期に発生した病態	71	53	42	18	7.3	5.4	4.3	1.8
Ba35	先天奇形，変形及び染色体異常	663	344	266	319	67.9	35.2	27.2	32.7
Ba36	神経系の先天奇形	29	20	20	9	3.0	2.0	2.0	0.9
Ba37	心臓の先天奇形	161	51	30	110	16.5	5.2	3.1	11.3
Ba38	その他の循環器系の先天奇形	84	38	23	46	8.6	3.9	2.4	4.7
Ba39	呼吸器系の先天奇形	52	45	36	7	5.3	4.6	3.7	0.7
Ba40	消化器系の先天奇形	20	8	7	12	2.0	0.8	0.7	1.2
Ba41	筋骨格系の先天奇形及び変形	42	37	30	5	4.3	3.8	3.1	0.5
Ba42	その他の先天奇形及び変形	67	49	47	18	6.9	5.0	4.8	1.8
Ba43	染色体異常，他に分類されないもの	208	96	73	112	21.3	9.8	7.5	11.5
Ba44	乳幼児突然死症候群	109	3	-	106	11.2	0.3	-	10.8
Ba45	その他のすべての疾患	317	33	3	284	32.4	3.4	0.3	29.1
Ba46	不慮の事故	73	3	1	70	7.5	0.3	0.1	7.2
Ba47	交　通　事　故	3	-	-	3	0.3	-	-	0.3
Ba48	転倒・転落	-	-	-	-	-	-	-	-
Ba49	不慮の溺死及び溺水	4	-	-	4	0.4	-	-	0.4
Ba50	胃内容物の誤えん及び気道閉塞を生じた食物等の誤えん	32	1	-	31	3.3	0.1	-	3.2
Ba51	その他の不慮の窒息	30	2	1	28	3.1	0.2	0.1	2.9
Ba52	煙，火及び火炎への曝露	-	-	-	-	-	-	-	-
Ba53	有害物質による不慮の中毒及び有害物質への曝露	1	-	-	1	0.1	-	-	0.1
Ba54	その他の不慮の事故	3	-	-	3	0.3	-	-	0.3
Ba55	他　　　殺	7	1	1	6	0.7	0.1	0.1	0.6
Ba56	その他の外因	24	5	4	19	2.5	0.5	0.4	1.9

Note : a) Code see page 598.

乳児死亡

表 6.15　生存期間別にみた乳児死因簡単分類別乳児死亡数百分率及び
Table 6.15　Percent distribution of infant deaths by age and

乳児死因 簡単分類 コード Code[a)]	死　　因 Causes of death	死因別乳児死亡数百分率 Percentage of infant deaths by causes				生存期間別乳児死亡数百分率 Percentage of infant deaths by age			
		総　数 Total	4週未満 Under 4 weeks	（再掲） 1週未満 Under 1 week (Regrouped)	4週以上 1年未満 4 weeks and over, less than 1 year	総　数 Total	4週未満 Under 4 weeks	（再掲） 1週未満 Under 1 week (Regrouped)	4週以上 1年未満 4 weeks and over, less than 1 year
	総　　数　　Total	100.0	100.0	100.0	100.0	100.0	45.3	35.1	54.7
Ba01	腸管感染症	0.5	-	-	0.9	100.0	-	-	100.0
Ba02	敗　血　症	2.1	1.6	-	2.5	100.0	35.0	-	65.0
Ba03	麻　　疹	-	-	-	-	-	-	-	-
Ba04	ウイルス肝炎	0.1	-	-	0.2	100.0	-	-	100.0
Ba05	その他の感染症及び寄生虫症	0.9	0.2	-	1.5	100.0	11.1	-	88.9
Ba06	悪性新生物	0.9	-	-	1.6	100.0	-	-	100.0
Ba07	白　血　病	0.5	-	-	0.9	100.0	-	-	100.0
Ba08	その他の悪性新生物	0.4	-	-	0.7	100.0	-	-	100.0
Ba09	その他の新生物	0.5	0.3	0.4	0.6	100.0	33.3	33.3	66.7
Ba10	栄養失調症及びその他の栄養欠乏症	0.1	-	-	0.1	100.0	-	-	100.0
Ba11	代 謝 障 害	1.2	0.8	0.7	1.5	100.0	30.4	21.7	69.6
Ba12	髄　膜　炎	0.3	0.2	0.1	0.3	100.0	40.0	20.0	60.0
Ba13	脊髄性筋萎縮症及び関連症候群	0.1	-	-	0.2	100.0	-	-	100.0
Ba14	脳 性 麻 痺	-	-	-	-	-	-	-	-
Ba15	心　疾　患（高血圧性を除く）	2.1	0.3	0.3	3.6	100.0	7.3	4.9	92.7
Ba16	脳血管疾患	0.2	0.1	-	0.3	100.0	25.0	-	75.0
Ba17	インフルエンザ	0.1	-	-	0.2	100.0	-	-	100.0
Ba18	肺　　炎	1.5	0.2	-	2.5	100.0	7.1	-	92.9
Ba19	喘　　息	-	-	-	-	-	-	-	-
Ba20	ヘルニア及び腸閉塞	0.6	-	-	1.1	100.0	-	-	100.0
Ba21	肝 疾 患	0.6	-	-	1.0	100.0	-	-	100.0
Ba22	腎 不 全	0.1	-	-	0.2	100.0	-	-	100.0
Ba23	周産期に発生した病態	26.4	51.6	57.7	5.5	100.0	88.6	76.6	11.4
Ba24	妊娠期間及び胎児発育に関連する障害	2.2	4.3	5.2	0.5	100.0	88.4	81.4	11.6
Ba25	出 産 外 傷	0.2	0.3	0.3	-	100.0	100.0	66.7	-
Ba26	出生時仮死	4.0	8.5	9.9	0.3	100.0	96.1	87.0	3.9
Ba27	新生児の呼吸窮迫	1.7	3.7	4.4	0.1	100.0	97.0	90.9	3.0
Ba28	周産期に発生した肺出血	0.5	1.1	1.3	-	100.0	100.0	90.0	-

注：「敗血症」には、"新生児の細菌性敗血症"を含まない。

Infant mortality

乳児死因簡単分類別にみた生存期間別乳児死亡数百分率
causes（the list of causes of infant death）：Japan, 2016

平成28年

乳児死因簡単分類コード Code[a]	死　因 Causes of death	死因別乳児死亡数百分率 Percentage of infant deaths by causes				生存期間別乳児死亡数百分率 Percentage of infant deaths by age			
		総　数 Total	4週未満 Under 4 weeks	（再掲） 1週未満 Under 1 week (Regrouped)	4週以上 1年未満 4 weeks and over, less than 1 year	総　数 Total	4週未満 Under 4 weeks	（再掲） 1週未満 Under 1 week (Regrouped)	4週以上 1年未満 4 weeks and over, less than 1 year
Ba29	周産期に発生した心血管障害	2.2	4.6	5.3	0.3	100.0	93.0	83.7	7.0
Ba30	その他の周産期に特異的な呼吸障害及び心血管障害	6.2	11.3	13.5	1.9	100.0	83.2	76.5	16.8
Ba31	新生児の細菌性敗血症	1.9	3.8	3.8	0.3	100.0	91.7	72.2	8.3
Ba32	その他の周産期に特異的な感染症	0.4	0.8	0.7	-	100.0	100.0	71.4	-
Ba33	胎児及び新生児の出血性障害及び血液障害	3.5	7.1	7.0	0.5	100.0	92.5	70.1	7.5
Ba34	その他の周産期に発生した病態	3.7	6.1	6.2	1.7	100.0	74.6	59.2	25.4
Ba35	先天奇形，変形及び染色体異常	34.4	39.4	39.3	30.3	100.0	51.9	40.1	48.1
Ba36	神経系の先天奇形	1.5	2.3	3.0	0.9	100.0	69.0	69.0	31.0
Ba37	心臓の先天奇形	8.4	5.8	4.4	10.4	100.0	31.7	18.6	68.3
Ba38	その他の循環器系の先天奇形	4.4	4.3	3.4	4.4	100.0	45.2	27.4	54.8
Ba39	呼吸器系の先天奇形	2.7	5.1	5.3	0.7	100.0	86.5	69.2	13.5
Ba40	消化器系の先天奇形	1.0	0.9	1.0	1.1	100.0	40.0	35.0	60.0
Ba41	筋骨格系の先天奇形及び変形	2.2	4.2	4.4	0.5	100.0	88.1	71.4	11.9
Ba42	その他の先天奇形及び変形	3.5	5.6	7.0	1.7	100.0	73.1	70.1	26.9
Ba43	染色体異常，他に分類されないもの	10.8	11.0	10.8	10.6	100.0	46.2	35.1	53.8
Ba44	乳幼児突然死症候群	5.7	0.3	-	10.1	100.0	2.8	-	97.2
Ba45	その他のすべての疾患	16.4	3.8	0.4	26.9	100.0	10.4	0.9	89.6
Ba46	不慮の事故	3.8	0.3	0.1	6.6	100.0	4.1	1.4	95.9
Ba47	交　通　事　故	0.2	-	-	0.3	100.0	-	-	100.0
Ba48	転倒・転落	-	-	-	-	-	-	-	-
Ba49	不慮の溺死及び溺水	0.2	-	-	0.4	100.0	-	-	100.0
Ba50	胃内容物の誤えん及び気道閉塞を生じた食物等の誤えん	1.7	0.1	-	2.9	100.0	3.1	-	96.9
Ba51	その他の不慮の窒息	1.6	0.2	0.1	2.7	100.0	6.7	3.3	93.3
Ba52	煙，火及び火炎への曝露	-	-	-	-	-	-	-	-
Ba53	有害物質による不慮の中毒及び有害物質への曝露	0.1	-	-	0.1	100.0	-	-	100.0
Ba54	その他の不慮の事故	0.2	-	-	0.3	100.0	-	-	100.0
Ba55	他　　　殺	0.4	0.1	0.1	0.6	100.0	14.3	14.3	85.7
Ba56	その他の外因	1.2	0.6	0.6	1.8	100.0	20.8	16.7	79.2

Note：a) Code see page 598.

423

乳児死亡

表6.16　年次別にみた乳児・

死亡数，死亡率（出生10万対），割合（％）[2]

年次[3]	第1位 死因	死亡数 死亡率 (割合)	第2位 死因	死亡数 死亡率 (割合)	第3位 死因	死亡数 死亡率 (割合)	第4位 死因	死亡数 死亡率 (割合)	第5位 死因	死亡数 死亡率 (割合)
昭和45年	先天異常	3 914 202.4 (15.4)	出生時損傷等	3 757 194.2 (14.8)	肺炎及び気管支炎	3 295 170.4 (13.0)	詳細不明の未熟児	2 547 131.7 (10.0)	その他の新生児の異常	2 109 109.0 (8.3)
50	先天異常	4 072 214.2 (21.3)	出生時損傷等	3 314 174.3 (17.3)	肺炎及び気管支炎	1 720 90.5 (9.0)	詳細不明の未熟児	1 446 76.0 (7.6)	その他の新生児の異常	1 255 66.0 (6.6)
55	出産時外傷等	3 885 246.4 (32.8)	先天異常	3 131 198.6 (26.4)	不慮の事故及び有害作用	659 41.8 (5.6)	詳細不明の未熟児	658 41.7 (5.6)	肺炎及び気管支炎	588 37.3 (5.0)
60	先天異常	2 414 168.6 (30.6)	出産時外傷等	2 406 168.1 (30.5)	不慮の事故及び有害作用	451 31.5 (5.7)	肺炎及び気管支炎	268 18.7 (3.4)	心疾患	234 16.3 (3.0)
平成2年	先天異常	2 028 166.0 (36.1)	出産時外傷等	1 185 97.0 (21.1)	不慮の事故及び有害作用	346 28.3 (6.2)	心疾患	180 14.7 (3.2)	敗血症（新生児敗血症を含む）	169 13.8 (3.0)
7	先天奇形，変形及び染色体異常	1 786 150.5 (35.3)	周産期に特異的な呼吸障害等	764 64.4 (15.1)	乳幼児突然死症候群	526 44.3 (10.4)	不慮の事故	329 27.7 (6.5)	胎児及び新生児の出血性障害等	241 20.3 (4.8)
12	先天奇形，変形及び染色体異常	1 385 116.3 (36.2)	周産期に特異的な呼吸障害等	603 50.6 (15.7)	乳幼児突然死症候群	317 26.6 (8.3)	不慮の事故	217 18.2 (5.7)	胎児及び新生児の出血性障害等	207 17.4 (5.4)
17	先天奇形，変形及び染色体異常	1 025 96.5 (34.7)	周産期に特異的な呼吸障害等	414 39.0 (14.0)	［乳幼児突然死症候群／不慮の事故］	174 16.4 (5.9)			胎児及び新生児の出血性障害等	159 15.0 (5.4)
22	先天奇形，変形及び染色体異常	916 85.5 (37.4)	周産期に特異的な呼吸障害等	341 31.8 (13.9)	乳幼児突然死症候群	140 13.1 (5.7)	不慮の事故	113 10.5 (4.6)	胎児及び新生児の出血性障害等	85 7.9 (3.5)
23	先天奇形，変形及び染色体異常	862 82.0 (35.0)	周産期に特異的な呼吸障害等	322 30.6 (13.1)	不慮の事故	199 18.9 (8.1)	乳幼児突然死症候群	132 12.6 (5.4)	胎児及び新生児の出血性障害等	85 8.1 (3.5)
24	先天奇形，変形及び染色体異常	815 78.6 (35.5)	周産期に特異的な呼吸障害等	314 30.3 (13.7)	乳幼児突然死症候群	144 13.9 (6.3)	不慮の事故	93 9.0 (4.0)	胎児及び新生児の出血性障害等	81 7.8 (3.5)
25	先天奇形，変形及び染色体異常	811 78.8 (37.1)	周産期に特異的な呼吸障害等	308 29.9 (14.1)	乳幼児突然死症候群	124 12.0 (5.7)	不慮の事故	89 8.6 (4.1)	胎児及び新生児の出血性障害等	76 7.4 (3.5)
26	先天奇形，変形及び染色体異常	751 74.8 (36.1)	周産期に特異的な呼吸障害等	261 26.0 (12.5)	乳幼児突然死症候群	145 14.4 (7.0)	不慮の事故	78 7.8 (3.8)	胎児及び新生児の出血性障害等	63 6.3 (3.0)
27	先天奇形，変形及び染色体異常	715 71.1 (37.3)	周産期に特異的な呼吸障害等	248 24.7 (12.9)	乳幼児突然死症候群	96 9.5 (5.0)	胎児及び新生児の出血性障害等	83 8.3 (4.3)	不慮の事故	81 8.1 (4.2)
28	先天奇形，変形及び染色体異常	663 67.9 (34.4)	周産期に特異的な呼吸障害等	282 28.9 (14.6)	乳幼児突然死症候群	109 11.2 (5.7)	不慮の事故	73 7.5 (3.8)	胎児及び新生児の出血性障害等	67 6.9 (3.5)

注：1）　死因順位の選び方については、巻末の参考表「1各種分類表」の平成7年以降は「表6－1(2)」、平成6年以前は「表6－2(2)」を参照されたい。
　　2）　死亡率は出生10万対、割合は乳児又は新生児死亡数を100とした場合の百分率である。
　　3）　昭和45、50年の「出生時損傷等」は、「出生時損傷，難産及びその他の無酸素症，低酸素症」である。
　　　　　昭和55年～平成2年の「出産時外傷等」は、「出産時外傷，低酸素症，分娩仮死及びその他の呼吸器病態」である。

新生児の死因順位 [1]

Infant mortality

第 6 位 死因	死亡数死亡率（割合）	第 7 位 死因	死亡数死亡率（割合）	第 8 位 死因	死亡数死亡率（割合）	第 9 位 死因	死亡数死亡率（割合）	第 10 位 死因	死亡数死亡率（割合）
死亡									
不慮の事故	1 142 59.0 (4.5)	母体の妊娠時の疾患による新生児の障害	1 081 55.9 (4.3)	新生児の出血性疾患	972 50.3 (3.8)	胃腸炎	921 47.6 (3.6)	腸閉塞及びヘルニア	424 21.9 (1.7)
母体の妊娠時の疾患による新生児の障害	956 50.3 (5.0)	不慮の事故	919 48.3 (4.8)	新生児の出血性疾患	612 32.2 (3.2)	心疾患	353 18.6 (1.8)	胃腸炎	336 17.7 (1.8)
心疾患	266 16.9 (2.2)	敗血症（新生児敗血症を含む）	231 14.6 (2.0)	その他の外因	161 10.2 (1.4)	髄膜炎 新生児の出血及び新生児出血性疾患	132 8.4 (1.1)		
敗血症（新生児敗血症を含む）	230 16.1 (2.9)	詳細不明の未熟児	185 12.9 (2.3)	その他の外因	132 9.2 (1.7)	髄膜炎	74 5.2 (0.9)	悪性新生物	55 3.8 (0.7)
肺炎及び気管支炎	148 12.1 (2.6)	その他の外因	89 7.3 (1.6)	詳細不明の未熟児	66 5.4 (1.2)	悪性新生物	50 4.1 (0.9)	新生児の出血及び新生児出血性疾患	28 2.3 (0.5)
心疾患	143 12.0 (2.8)	周産期に特異的な感染症	133 11.2 (2.6)	肺炎	114 9.6 (2.3)	敗血症	107 9.0 (2.1)	妊娠期間及び胎児発育に関連する障害	76 6.4 (1.5)
心疾患	117 9.8 (3.1)	敗血症	85 7.1 (2.2)	周産期に特異的な感染症	84 7.1 (2.2)	肺炎 妊娠期間及び胎児発育に関連する障害	73 6.1 (1.9)		
心疾患	138 13.0 (4.7)	敗血症	71 6.7 (2.4)	妊娠期間及び胎児発育に関連する障害	66 6.2 (2.2)	周産期に特異的な感染症	60 5.6 (2.0)	肺炎	48 4.5 (1.6)
心疾患	68 6.3 (2.8)	妊娠期間及び胎児発育に関連する障害	65 6.1 (2.7)	周産期に特異的な感染症	57 5.3 (2.3)	敗血症	46 4.3 (1.9)	肺炎	42 3.9 (1.7)
妊娠期間及び胎児発育に関連する障害	70 6.7 (2.8)	心疾患	61 5.8 (2.5)	敗血症	58 5.5 (2.4)	周産期に特異的な感染症	47 4.5 (1.9)	肺炎	40 3.8 (1.6)
心疾患	60 5.8 (2.6)	妊娠期間及び胎児発育に関連する障害	59 5.7 (2.6)	敗血症	53 5.1 (2.3)	肺炎	42 4.0 (1.8)	周産期に特異的な感染症	37 3.6 (1.6)
心疾患	63 6.1 (2.9)	妊娠期間及び胎児発育に関連する障害	59 5.7 (2.7)	敗血症	42 4.1 (1.9)	肺炎	37 3.6 (1.7)	周産期に特異的な感染症	30 2.9 (1.4)
妊娠期間及び胎児発育に関連する障害	59 5.9 (2.8)	心疾患	52 5.2 (2.5)	周産期に特異的な感染症	43 4.3 (2.1)	敗血症	40 4.0 (1.9)	肺炎	33 3.3 (1.6)
心疾患	50 5.0 (2.6)	妊娠期間及び胎児発育に関連する障害	39 3.9 (2.0)	周産期に特異的な感染症	33 3.3 (1.7)	その他の新生物 肺炎	24 2.4 (1.3)		
妊娠期間及び胎児発育に関連する障害 周産期に特異的な感染症	43 4.4 (2.2)			心疾患	41 4.2 (2.1)	敗血症	40 4.1 (2.1)	肺炎	28 2.9 (1.5)

平成7年以降の「周産期に特異的な呼吸障害等」は、「周産期に特異的な呼吸障害及び心血管障害」である。
平成7年以降の「胎児及び新生児の出血性障害等」は、「胎児及び新生児の出血性障害及び血液障害」である。
平成7年以降の「心疾患」は、「心疾患（高血圧性を除く）」である。
平成7年以降の「敗血症」には、"新生児の細菌性敗血症"を含まない。

乳児死亡

表6.16　年次別にみた乳児・

死亡数，死亡率（出生10万対），割合（%）[2]

年次[3]	第1位 死因	死亡数 死亡率（割合）	第2位 死因	死亡数 死亡率（割合）	第3位 死因	死亡数 死亡率（割合）	第4位 死因	死亡数 死亡率（割合）	第5位 死因	死亡数 死亡率（割合）
									新生児	
昭和45年	出生時損傷等	3 742 193.5 (22.4)	詳細不明の未熟児	2 428 125.5 (14.5)	その他の新生児の異常	2 066 106.8 (12.3)	先天異常	1 903 98.4 (11.4)	肺炎及び気管支炎	1 108 57.3 (6.6)
50	出生時損傷等	3 298 173.4 (25.5)	先天異常	2 119 111.4 (16.4)	詳細不明の未熟児	1 376 72.4 (10.7)	その他の新生児の異常	1 234 64.9 (9.6)	母体の妊娠時の疾患による新生児の障害	956 50.3 (7.4)
55	出産時外傷等	3 752 237.9 (48.1)	先天異常	1 624 103.0 (20.8)	詳細不明の未熟児	650 41.2 (8.3)	肺炎及び気管支炎	173 11.0 (2.2)	敗血症（新生児敗血症を含む）	152 9.6 (1.9)
60	出産時外傷等	2 222 155.2 (45.3)	先天異常	1 326 92.6 (27.0)	詳細不明の未熟児	182 12.7 (3.7)	敗血症（新生児敗血症を含む）	152 10.6 (3.1)	肺炎及び気管支炎	78 5.4 (1.6)
平成2年	先天異常	1 183 96.8 (37.2)	出産時外傷等	1 097 89.8 (34.5)	敗血症（新生児敗血症を含む）	115 9.4 (3.6)	詳細不明の未熟児	64 5.2 (2.0)	肺炎及び気管支炎	36 2.9 (1.1)
7	先天奇形，変形及び染色体異常	996 83.9 (38.1)	周産期に特異的な呼吸障害等	685 57.7 (26.2)	胎児及び新生児の出血性障害等	231 19.5 (8.8)	周産期に特異的な感染症	124 10.4 (4.7)	妊娠期間及び胎児発育に関連する障害	71 6.0 (2.7)
12	先天奇形，変形及び染色体異常	840 70.6 (39.9)	周産期に特異的な呼吸障害等	551 46.3 (26.2)	胎児及び新生児の出血性障害等	199 16.7 (9.4)	周産期に特異的な感染症	77 6.5 (3.7)	妊娠期間及び胎児発育に関連する障害	65 5.5 (3.1)
17	先天奇形，変形及び染色体異常	572 53.8 (37.9)	周産期に特異的な呼吸障害等	378 35.6 (25.0)	胎児及び新生児の出血性障害等	148 13.9 (9.8)	妊娠期間及び胎児発育に関連する障害	62 5.8 (4.1)	周産期に特異的な感染症	51 4.8 (3.4)
22	先天奇形，変形及び染色体異常	491 45.8 (42.1)	周産期に特異的な呼吸障害等	309 28.8 (26.5)	胎児及び新生児の出血性障害等	79 7.4 (6.8)	妊娠期間及び胎児発育に関連する障害	52 4.9 (4.5)	周産期に特異的な感染症	51 4.8 (4.4)
23	先天奇形，変形及び染色体異常	448 42.6 (39.1)	周産期に特異的な呼吸障害等	293 27.9 (25.5)	胎児及び新生児の出血性障害等	77 7.3 (6.7)	妊娠期間及び胎児発育に関連する障害	62 5.9 (5.4)	周産期に特異的な感染症	45 4.3 (3.9)
24	先天奇形，変形及び染色体異常	418 40.3 (39.2)	周産期に特異的な呼吸障害等	283 27.3 (26.6)	胎児及び新生児の出血性障害等	76 7.3 (7.1)	妊娠期間及び胎児発育に関連する障害	55 5.3 (5.2)	周産期に特異的な感染症	36 3.5 (3.4)
25	先天奇形，変形及び染色体異常	440 42.7 (42.9)	周産期に特異的な呼吸障害等	266 25.8 (25.9)	胎児及び新生児の出血性障害等	65 6.3 (6.3)	妊娠期間及び胎児発育に関連する障害	45 4.4 (4.4)	周産期に特異的な感染症	29 2.8 (2.8)
26	先天奇形，変形及び染色体異常	396 39.5 (41.6)	周産期に特異的な呼吸障害等	235 23.4 (24.7)	胎児及び新生児の出血性障害等	57 5.7 (6.0)	妊娠期間及び胎児発育に関連する障害	51 5.1 (5.4)	周産期に特異的な感染症	36 3.6 (3.8)
27	先天奇形，変形及び染色体異常	383 38.1 (42.5)	周産期に特異的な呼吸障害等	226 22.5 (25.1)	胎児及び新生児の出血性障害等	73 7.3 (8.1)	妊娠期間及び胎児発育に関連する障害	36 3.6 (4.0)	周産期に特異的な感染症	30 3.0 (3.3)
28	先天奇形，変形及び染色体異常	344 35.2 (39.4)	周産期に特異的な呼吸障害等	255 26.1 (29.2)	胎児及び新生児の出血性障害等	62 6.3 (7.1)	周産期に特異的な感染症	40 4.1 (4.6)	妊娠期間及び胎児発育に関連する障害	38 3.9 (4.3)

注：1）　死因順位の選び方については、巻末の参考表「1各種分類表」の平成7年以降は「表6－1(2)」、平成6年以前は「表6－2(2)」を参照されたい。
　　2）　死亡率は出生10万対、割合は乳児又は新生児死亡数を100とした場合の百分率である。
　　3）　昭和45、50年の「出生時損傷等」は、「出生時損傷，難産及びその他の無酸素症，低酸素症」である。
　　　　昭和55年～平成2年の「出産時外傷等」は、「出産時外傷，低酸素症，分娩仮死及びその他の呼吸器病態」である。

Infant mortality

新生児の死因順位[1]（つづき）

第 6 位 死因	死亡数 死亡率 (割合)	第 7 位 死因	死亡数 死亡率 (割合)	第 8 位 死因	死亡数 死亡率 (割合)	第 9 位 死因	死亡数 死亡率 (割合)	第 10 位 死因	死亡数 死亡率 (割合)
死 亡									
母体の妊娠時の疾患による新生児の障害	1 081 55.9 (6.5)	新生児の出血性疾患	954 49.3 (5.7)	新生児溶血性疾患	298 15.4 (1.8)	心疾患	163 8.4 (1.0)	腸閉塞及びヘルニア	153 7.9 (0.9)
新生児の出血性疾患	604 31.8 (4.7)	肺炎及び気管支炎	536 28.2 (4.2)	心疾患	142 7.5 (1.1)	新生児溶血性疾患	111 5.8 (0.9)	敗血症	103 5.4 (0.8)
新生児の出血及び新生児出血性疾患	121 7.7 (1.6)	不慮の事故及び有害作用	79 5.0 (1.0)	髄膜炎	71 4.5 (0.9)	その他の外因	70 4.4 (0.9)	心疾患	42 2.7 (0.5)
その他の外因	53 3.7 (1.1)	不慮の事故及び有害作用	49 3.4 (1.0)	新生児の出血及び新生児出血性疾患	40 2.8 (0.8)	髄膜炎	33 2.3 (0.7)	心疾患	32 2.2 (0.7)
その他の外因	31 2.5 (1.0)	新生児の出血及び新生児出血性疾患	26 2.1 (0.8)	心疾患	25 2.0 (0.8)	悪性新生物	13 1.1 (0.4)	不慮の事故及び有害作用	10 0.8 (0.3)
乳幼児突然死症候群	53 4.5 (2.0)	心疾患	51 4.3 (2.0)	敗血症	37 3.1 (1.4)	代謝障害	30 2.5 (1.1)	出産外傷／不慮の事故	16 1.3 (0.6)
心疾患	47 3.9 (2.2)	敗血症	37 3.1 (1.8)	乳幼児突然死症候群	31 2.6 (1.5)	代謝障害	24 2.0 (1.1)	不慮の事故	16 1.3 (0.8)
心疾患	43 4.0 (2.8)	敗血症	35 3.3 (2.3)	代謝障害	17 1.6 (1.1)	不慮の事故	16 1.5 (1.1)	乳幼児突然死症候群	11 1.0 (0.7)
敗血症	16 1.5 (1.4)	代謝障害	13 1.2 (1.1)	乳幼児突然死症候群	9 0.8 (0.8)	他殺	8 0.7 (0.7)	肺炎	7 0.7 (0.6)
敗血症	21 2.0 (1.8)	不慮の事故	16 1.5 (1.4)	乳幼児突然死症候群	10 1.0 (0.9)	その他の新生物	9 0.9 (0.8)	代謝障害／心疾患	7 0.7 (0.6)
敗血症	17 1.6 (1.6)	その他の新生物	12 1.2 (1.1)	心疾患／乳幼児突然死症候群	10 1.0 (0.9)			代謝障害	8 0.8 (0.8)
敗血症	16 1.6 (1.6)	代謝障害／乳幼児突然死症候群	14 1.4 (1.4)			その他の新生物／心疾患／不慮の事故	7 0.7 (0.7)		
敗血症	15 1.5 (1.6)	出産外傷	12 1.2 (1.3)	その他の新生物／乳幼児突然死症候群	9 0.9 (0.9)			代謝障害	7 0.7 (0.7)
その他の新生物	13 1.3 (1.4)	乳幼児突然死症候群	10 1.0 (1.1)	出産外傷	6 0.6 (0.7)	他殺	5 0.5 (0.6)	心疾患	4 0.4 (0.4)
敗血症	**14 1.4 (1.6)**	**代謝障害**	**7 0.7 (0.8)**	その他の新生物／心疾患／出産外傷／乳幼児突然死症候群／不慮の事故	3 0.3 (0.3)				

平成7年以降の「周産期に特異的な呼吸障害等」は、「周産期に特異的な呼吸障害及び心血管障害」である。
平成7年以降の「胎児及び新生児の出血性障害等」は、「胎児及び新生児の出血性障害及び血液障害」である。
平成7年以降の「心疾患」は、「心疾患（高血圧性を除く）」である。
平成7年以降の「敗血症」には、"新生児の細菌性敗血症"を含まない。

乳児死亡

Table 6.16　Trends in leading causes of

Deaths, death rates (per 100,000 live births), proportion (%)

Year	1 Causes of death	Deaths Rates (%)	2 Causes of death	Deaths Rates (%)	3 Causes of death	Deaths Rates (%)	4 Causes of death	Deaths Rates (%)	5 Causes of death	Deaths Rates (%)
									Infant	
1970	Cong. anomalies	3 914 202.4 (15.4)	Birth injury.	3 757 194.2 (14.8)	Pneu. & Bronch.	3 295 170.4 (13.0)	Premature babies	2 547 131.7 (10.0)	Other conditions	2 109 109.0 (8.3)
75	Cong. anomalies	4 072 214.2 (21.3)	Birth injury.	3 314 174.3 (17.3)	Pneu. & Bronch.	1 720 90.5 (9.0)	Premature babies	1 446 76.0 (7.6)	Other conditions	1 255 66.0 (6.6)
80	Birth trauma, etc.	3 885 246.4 (32.8)	Cong. anomalies	3 131 198.6 (26.4)	Accidents	659 41.8 (5.6)	Premature babies	658 41.7 (5.6)	Pneu. & Bronch.	588 37.3 (5.0)
85	Cong. anomalies	2 414 168.6 (30.6)	Birth trauma, etc.	2 406 168.1 (30.5)	Accidents	451 31.5 (5.7)	Pneu. & Bronch.	268 18.7 (3.4)	Heart dis.	234 16.3 (3.0)
90	Cong. anomalies	2 028 166.0 (36.1)	Birth trauma, etc.	1 185 97.0 (21.1)	Accidents	346 28.3 (6.2)	Heart dis.	180 14.7 (3.2)	Septicaemia	169 13.8 (3.0)
95	Congenital malformations, etc.	1 786 150.5 (35.3)	Respiratory and cardiovascular disorders	764 64.4 (15.1)	SIDS	526 44.3 (10.4)	Accidents	329 27.7 (6.5)	Haemorrhagic and haematological disorders	241 20.3 (4.8)
2000	Congenital malformations, etc.	1 385 116.3 (36.2)	Respiratory and cardiovascular disorders	603 50.6 (15.7)	SIDS	317 26.6 (8.3)	Accidents	217 18.2 (5.7)	Haemorrhagic and haematological disorders	207 17.4 (5.4)
05	Congenital malformations, etc.	1 025 96.5 (34.7)	Respiratory and cardiovascular disorders	414 39.0 (14.0)	SIDS Accidents	174 16.4 (5.9)			Haemorrhagic and haematological disorders	159 15.0 (5.4)
10	Congenital malformations, etc.	916 85.5 (37.4)	Respiratory and cardiovascular disorders	341 31.8 (13.9)	SIDS	140 13.1 (5.7)	Accidents	113 10.5 (4.6)	Haemorrhagic and haematological disorders	85 7.9 (3.5)
11	Congenital malformations, etc.	862 82.0 (35.0)	Respiratory and cardiovascular disorders	322 30.6 (13.1)	Accidents	199 18.9 (8.1)	SIDS	132 12.6 (5.4)	Haemorrhagic and haematological disorders	85 8.1 (3.5)
12	Congenital malformations, etc.	815 78.6 (35.5)	Respiratory and cardiovascular disorders	314 30.3 (13.7)	SIDS	144 13.9 (6.3)	Accidents	93 9.0 (4.0)	Haemorrhagic and haematological disorders	81 7.8 (3.5)
13	Congenital malformations, etc.	811 78.8 (37.1)	Respiratory and cardiovascular disorders	308 29.9 (14.1)	SIDS	124 12.0 (5.7)	Accidents	89 8.6 (4.1)	Haemorrhagic and haematological disorders	76 7.4 (3.5)
14	Congenital malformations, etc.	751 74.8 (36.1)	Respiratory and cardiovascular disorders	261 26.0 (12.5)	SIDS	145 14.4 (7.0)	Accidents	78 7.8 (3.8)	Haemorrhagic and haematological disorders	63 6.3 (3.0)
15	Congenital malformations, etc.	715 71.1 (37.3)	Respiratory and cardiovascular disorders	248 24.7 (12.9)	SIDS	96 9.5 (5.0)	Haemorrhagic and haematological disorders	83 8.3 (4.3)	Accidents	81 8.1 (4.2)
16	Congenital malformations, etc.	663 67.9 (34.4)	Respiratory and cardiovascular disorders	282 28.9 (14.6)	SIDS	109 11.2 (5.7)	Accidents	73 7.5 (3.8)	Haemorrhagic and haematological disorders	67 6.9 (3.5)

Note : Cong. anomalies　←　Congenital anomalies
Accidents　←　Accidents and adverse effects till 1990.
Septicaemia　←　Septicaemia including newborn till 1990.
Hernia　←　Hernia of abdominal cavity and intestinal obstruction
Newborn　←　Fetus or newborn affected by maternal complications of infancy
Premature babies　←　Premature babies of unknown details
Hemolytic dis.　←　Hemolytic dis. of newborn due to isoimmumzation
SIDS　←　Sudden infant death syndrome

Infant mortality

neonatal and infant death : Japan

6		7		8		9		10	
Causes of death	Deaths Rates (%)	Causes of death	Deaths Rates (%)	Causes of death	Deaths Rates (%)	Causes of death	Deaths Rates (%)	Causes of death	Deaths Rates (%)
deaths									
Accidents	1 142 59.0 (4.5)	Newborn	1 081 55.9 (4.3)	Hemorrhagic dis.	972 50.3 (3.8)	Gastroenteritis	921 47.6 (3.6)	Hernia	424 21.9 (1.7)
Newborn	956 50.3 (5.0)	Accidents	919 48.3 (4.8)	Hemorrhagic dis.	612 32.2 (3.2)	Heart dis.	353 18.6 (1.8)	Gastroenteritis	336 17.7 (1.8)
Heart dis.	266 16.9 (2.2)	Septicaemia	231 14.6 (2.0)	Other external causes	161 10.2 (1.4)	{Meningitis, Hemorrhage of newborn and hemorrhagic diseases of newborns}	132 8.4 (1.1)		
Septicaemia	230 16.1 (2.9)	Premature babies	185 12.9 (2.3)	Other external causes	132 9.2 (1.7)	Meningitis	74 5.2 (0.9)	Malignant neoplasms	55 3.8 (0.7)
Pneu. & Bronch.	148 12.1 (2.6)	Other external causes	89 7.3 (1.6)	Premature babies	66 5.4 (1.2)	Malignant neoplasms	50 4.1 (0.9)	Hemorrhage of newborn and hemorrhagic diseases of newborns	28 2.3 (0.5)
Heart dis.	143 12.0 (2.8)	Infections specific to the perinatal period	133 11.2 (2.6)	Pneumonia	114 9.6 (2.3)	Septicaemia	107 9.0 (2.1)	Disorders related to length of gestation and fetal growth	76 6.4 (1.5)
Heart dis.	117 9.8 (3.1)	Septicaemia	85 7.1 (2.2)	Infections specific to the perinatal period	84 7.1 (2.2)	{Pneumonia, Disorders related to length of gestation and fetal growth}	73 6.1 (1.9)		
Heart dis.	138 13.0 (4.7)	Septicaemia	71 6.7 (2.4)	Disorders related to length of gestation and fetal growth	66 6.2 (2.2)	Infections specific to the perinatal period	60 5.6 (2.0)	Pneumonia	48 4.5 (1.6)
Heart dis.	68 6.3 (2.8)	Disorders related to length of gestation and fetal growth	65 6.1 (2.7)	Infections specific to the perinatal period	57 5.3 (2.3)	Septicaemia	46 4.3 (1.9)	Pneumonia	42 3.9 (1.7)
Disorders related to length of gestation and fetal growth	70 6.7 (2.8)	Heart dis.	61 5.8 (2.5)	Septicaemia	58 5.5 (2.4)	Infections specific to the perinatal period	47 4.5 (1.9)	Pneumonia	40 3.8 (1.6)
Heart dis.	60 5.8 (2.6)	Disorders related to length of gestation and fetal growth	59 5.7 (2.6)	Septicaemia	53 5.1 (2.3)	Pneumonia	42 4.0 (1.8)	Infections specific to the perinatal period	37 3.6 (1.6)
Heart dis.	63 6.1 (2.9)	Disorders related to length of gestation and fetal growth	59 5.7 (2.7)	Septicaemia	42 4.1 (1.9)	Pneumonia	37 3.6 (1.7)	Infections specific to the perinatal period	30 2.9 (1.4)
Disorders related to length of gestation and fetal growth	59 5.9 (2.8)	Heart dis.	52 5.2 (2.5)	Infections specific to the perinatal period	43 4.3 (2.1)	Septicaemia	40 4.0 (1.9)	Pneumonia	33 3.3 (1.6)
Heart dis.	50 5.0 (2.6)	Disorders related to length of gestation and fetal growth	39 3.9 (2.0)	Infections specific to the perinatal period	33 3.3 (1.7)	{Benign neoplasms, Pneumonia}	24 2.4 (1.3)		
{Disorders related to length of gestation and fetal growth, Infections specific to the perinatal period}	43 4.4 (2.2)			Heart dis.	41 4.2 (2.1)	Septicaemia	40 4.1 (2.1)	Pneumonia	28 2.9 (1.5)

Hemorrhagic dis. ← Hemorrhagic dis. of newborn (VK. deficiency of newborn)
Other conditions ← Other conditions originating in newborn period
Benign neoplasms ← Benign neoplasms and neoplasms of unspecified
Congenital malformations, etc. ← Congenital malformations, deformations and chromosomal abnormalities
Respiratory and cardiovascular disorders ← Respiratory and cardiovascular disorders specific to the perinatal period
Haemorrhagic and haematological disorders ← Haemorrhagic and haematological disorders of fetus and newborn
Heart dis. ← Heart diseases (excluding hypertensive heart diseases)

乳児死亡

Table 6.16　Trends in leading causes of

Deaths, death rates （per 100,000 live births）, proportion （%）

Year	1		2		3		4		5	
	Causes of death	Deaths Rates (%)	Causes of death	Deaths Rates (%)	Causes of death	Deaths Rates (%)	Causes of death	Deaths Rates (%)	Causes of death	Deaths Rates (%)
									Neonatal	
1970	Birth injury.	3 742 193.5 (22.4)	Premature babies	2 428 125.5 (14.5)	Other conditions	2 066 106.8 (12.3)	Cong. anomalies	1 903 98.4 (11.4)	Pneu. & Bronch.	1 108 57.3 (6.6)
75	Birth injury.	3 298 173.4 (25.5)	Cong. anomalies	2 119 111.4 (16.4)	Premature babies	1 376 72.4 (10.7)	Other conditions	1 234 64.9 (9.6)	Newborn	956 50.3 (7.4)
80	Birth trauma, etc.	3 752 237.9 (48.1)	Cong. anomalies	1 624 103.0 (20.8)	Premature babies	650 41.2 (8.3)	Pneu. & Bronch.	173 11.0 (2.2)	Septicaemia	152 9.6 (1.9)
85	Birth trauma, etc.	2 222 155.2 (45.3)	Cong. anomalies	1 326 92.6 (27.0)	Premature babies	182 12.7 (3.7)	Septicaemia	152 10.6 (3.1)	Pneu. & Bronch.	78 5.4 (1.6)
90	Cong. anomalies	1 183 96.8 (37.2)	Birth trauma, etc.	1 097 89.8 (34.5)	Septicaemia	115 9.4 (3.6)	Premature babies	64 5.2 (2.0)	Pneu. & Bronch.	36 2.9 (1.1)
95	Congenital malformations, etc.	996 83.9 (38.1)	Respiratory and cardiovascular disorders	685 57.7 (26.2)	Haemorrhagic and haematological disorders	231 19.5 (8.8)	Infections specific to the perinatal period	124 10.4 (4.7)	Disorders related to length of gestation and fetal growth	71 6.0 (2.7)
2000	Congenital malformations, etc.	840 70.6 (39.9)	Respiratory and cardiovascular disorders	551 46.3 (26.2)	Haemorrhagic and haematological disorders	199 16.7 (9.4)	Infections specific to the perinatal period	77 6.5 (3.7)	Disorders related to length of gestation and fetal growth	65 5.5 (3.1)
05	Congenital malformations, etc.	572 53.8 (37.9)	Respiratory and cardiovascular disorders	378 35.6 (25.0)	Haemorrhagic and haematological disorders	148 13.9 (9.8)	Disorders related to length of gestation and fetal growth	62 5.8 (4.1)	Infections specific to the perinatal period	51 4.8 (3.4)
10	Congenital malformations, etc.	491 45.8 (42.1)	Respiratory and cardiovascular disorders	309 28.8 (26.5)	Haemorrhagic and haematological disorders	79 7.4 (6.8)	Disorders related to length of gestation and fetal growth	52 4.9 (4.5)	Infections specific to the perinatal period	51 4.8 (4.4)
11	Congenital malformations, etc.	448 42.6 (39.1)	Respiratory and cardiovascular disorders	293 27.9 (25.5)	Haemorrhagic and haematological disorders	77 7.3 (6.7)	Disorders related to length of gestation and fetal growth	62 5.9 (5.4)	Infections specific to the perinatal period	45 4.3 (3.9)
12	Congenital malformations, etc.	418 40.3 (39.2)	Respiratory and cardiovascular disorders	283 27.3 (26.6)	Haemorrhagic and haematological disorders	76 7.3 (7.1)	Disorders related to length of gestation and fetal growth	55 5.3 (5.2)	Infections specific to the perinatal period	36 3.5 (3.4)
13	Congenital malformations, etc.	440 42.7 (42.9)	Respiratory and cardiovascular disorders	266 25.8 (25.9)	Haemorrhagic and haematological disorders	65 6.3 (6.3)	Disorders related to length of gestation and fetal growth	45 4.4 (4.4)	Infections specific to the perinatal period	29 2.8 (2.8)
14	Congenital malformations, etc.	396 39.5 (41.6)	Respiratory and cardiovascular disorders	235 23.4 (24.7)	Haemorrhagic and haematological disorders	57 5.7 (6.0)	Disorders related to length of gestation and fetal growth	51 5.1 (5.4)	Infections specific to the perinatal period	36 3.6 (3.8)
15	Congenital malformations, etc.	383 38.1 (42.5)	Respiratory and cardiovascular disorders	226 22.5 (25.1)	Haemorrhagic and haematological disorders	73 7.3 (8.1)	Disorders related to length of gestation and fetal growth	36 3.6 (4.0)	Infections specific to the perinatal period	30 3.0 (3.3)
16	Congenital malformations, etc.	344 35.2 (39.4)	Respiratory and cardiovascular disorders	255 26.1 (29.2)	Haemorrhagic and haematological disorders	62 6.3 (7.1)	Infections specific to the perinatal period	40 4.1 (4.6)	Disorders related to length of gestation and fetal growth	38 3.9 (4.3)

Note：Cong. anomalies　←　Congenital anomalies
　　　Accidents　←　Accidents and adverse effects till 1990.
　　　Septicaemia　←　Septicaemia including newborn till 1990.
　　　Hernia　←　Hernia of abdominal cavity and intestinal obstruction
　　　Newborn　←　Fetus or newborn affected by maternal complications of infancy
　　　Premature babies　←　Premature babies of unknown details
　　　Hemolytic dis.　←　Hemolytic dis. of newborn due to isoimmumzation
　　　SIDS　←　Sudden infant death syndrome

Infant mortality

neonatal and infant death : Japan－CON.

6		7		8		9		10	
Causes of death	Deaths Rates (%)	Causes of death	Deaths Rates (%)	Causes of death	Deaths Rates (%)	Causes of death	Deaths Rates (%)	Causes of death	Deaths Rates (%)
deaths									
Newborn	1 081 55.9 (6.5)	Hemorrhagic dis.	954 49.3 (5.7)	Hemolytic dis.	298 15.4 (1.8)	Heart dis.	163 8.4 (1.0)	Hernia	153 7.9 (0.9)
Hemorrhagic dis.	604 31.8 (4.7)	Pneu. & Bronch.	536 28.2 (4.2)	Heart dis.	142 7.5 (1.1)	Hemolytic dis.	111 5.8 (0.9)	Septicaemia	103 5.4 (0.8)
Hemorrhage of newborn and hemorrhagic diseases of newborns	121 7.7 (1.6)	Accidents	79 5.0 (1.0)	Meningitis	71 4.5 (0.9)	Other external causes	70 4.4 (0.9)	Heart dis.	42 2.7 (0.5)
Other external causes	53 3.7 (1.1)	Accidents	49 3.4 (1.0)	Hemorrhage of newborn and hemorrhagic diseases of newborns	40 2.8 (0.8)	Meningitis	33 2.3 (0.7)	Heart dis.	32 2.2 (0.7)
Other external causes	31 2.5 (1.0)	Hemorrhage of newborn and hemorrhagic diseases of newborns	26 2.1 (0.8)	Heart dis.	25 2.0 (0.8)	Malignant neoplasms	13 1.1 (0.4)	Accidents	10 0.8 (0.3)
SIDS	53 4.5 (2.0)	Heart dis.	51 4.3 (2.0)	Septicaemia	37 3.1 (1.4)	Metabolic disorders	30 2.5 (1.1)	Birth trauma / Accidents	16 1.3 (0.6)
Heart dis.	47 3.9 (2.2)	Septicaemia	37 3.1 (1.8)	SIDS	31 2.6 (1.5)	Metabolic disorders	24 2.0 (1.1)	Accidents	16 1.3 (0.8)
Heart dis.	43 4.0 (2.8)	Septicaemia	35 3.3 (2.3)	Metabolic disorders	17 1.6 (1.1)	Accidents	16 1.5 (1.1)	SIDS	11 1.0 (0.7)
Septicaemia	16 1.5 (1.4)	Metabolic disorders	13 1.2 (1.1)	SIDS	9 0.8 (0.8)	Homicide	8 0.7 (0.7)	Pneumonia	7 0.7 (0.6)
Septicaemia	21 2.0 (1.8)	Accidents	16 1.5 (1.4)	SIDS	10 1.0 (0.9)	Benign neoplasms	9 0.9 (0.8)	Metabolic disorders / Heart dis.	7 0.7 (0.6)
Septicaemia	17 1.6 (1.6)	Benign neoplasms	12 1.2 (1.1)	Heart dis. / SIDS	10 1.0 (0.9)			Metabolic disorders	8 0.8 (0.8)
Septicaemia	16 1.6 (1.6)	Metabolic disorders / SIDS	14 1.4 (1.4)			Benign neoplasms / Heart dis. / Accidents	7 0.7 (0.7)		
Septicaemia	15 1.5 (1.6)	Birth trauma	12 1.2 (1.3)	Benign neoplasms / SIDS	9 0.9 (0.9)			Metabolic disorders	7 0.7 (0.7)
Benign neoplasms	13 1.3 (1.4)	SIDS	10 1.0 (1.1)	Birth trauma	6 0.6 (0.7)	Homicide	5 0.5 (0.6)	Heart dis.	4 0.4 (0.4)
Septicaemia	14 1.4 (1.6)	Metabolic disorders	7 0.7 (0.8)	Benign neoplasms / Heart dis. / Birth trauma / SIDS / Accidents	3 0.3 (0.3)				

Hemorrhagic dis. ← Hemorrhagic dis. of newborn (VK. deficiency of newborn)
Other conditions ← Other conditions originating in newborn period
Benign neoplasms ← Benign neoplasms and neoplasms of unspecified
Congenital malformations, etc. ← Congenital malformations, deformations and chromosomal abnormalities
Respiratory and cardiovascular disorders ← Respiratory and cardiovascular disorders specific to the perinatal period
Haemorrhagic and haematological disorders ← Haemorrhagic and haematological disorders of fetus and newborn
Heart dis. ← Heart diseases (excluding hypertensive heart diseases)

乳児死亡

表 6.17　都道府県（21大都市再掲）別にみた乳児
Table 6.17　Infant mortality rates (per 100,000 live births) by causes (the list of

都道府県 Prefecture	総数 Total	Ba01[a)] 腸管感染症	Ba02 敗血症	Ba03 麻疹	Ba04 ウイルス肝炎	Ba05 その他の感染症及び寄生虫症	Ba06 悪性新生物	Ba07 白血病	Ba08 その他の悪性新生物	Ba09 その他の新生物	Ba10 栄養失調症及びその他の栄養欠乏症	Ba11 代謝障害	Ba12 髄膜炎	Ba13 脊髄性筋萎縮症及び関連症候群	Ba14 脳性麻痺
全　国 Total	197.3	0.9	4.1	-	0.2	1.8	1.7	1.0	0.7	0.9	0.1	2.4	0.5	0.2	-
01 北海道 [b)]	216.4	2.8	-	-	-	5.7	2.8	-	2.8	-	-	2.8	-	-	-
02 青森	208.7	-	-	-	-	-	-	-	-	-	-	-	-	-	-
03 岩手	203.8	-	-	-	-	-	-	-	-	-	-	-	-	-	-
04 宮城	230.6	-	-	-	-	-	-	-	-	-	-	5.8	-	-	-
05 秋田	229.4	-	-	-	-	17.6	17.6	17.6	-	-	-	-	-	-	-
06 山形	318.0	-	-	-	-	13.3	-	-	-	13.3	-	-	-	-	-
07 福島	196.4	-	-	-	-	14.6	-	-	-	-	-	-	-	-	-
08 茨城	191.6	-	4.8	-	-	-	-	-	-	4.8	-	-	-	-	-
09 栃木	177.8	-	-	-	-	-	-	-	-	-	-	-	-	-	-
10 群馬	161.0	7.3	-	-	-	-	-	-	-	-	-	14.6	-	-	-
11 埼玉	216.7	-	3.7	-	-	1.8	1.8	-	1.8	1.8	-	3.7	-	1.8	-
12 千葉	209.3	2.2	8.8	-	-	2.2	2.2	-	2.2	-	-	4.4	2.2	-	-
13 東京	198.3	-	2.7	-	-	0.9	0.9	-	0.9	-	-	1.8	-	-	-
14 神奈川	208.1	-	8.5	-	-	1.4	2.8	2.8	-	-	-	2.8	-	-	-
15 新潟	127.1	-	6.4	-	-	-	-	-	-	-	-	-	-	-	-
16 富山	219.1	-	-	-	-	-	-	-	-	-	-	-	13.7	-	-
17 石川	212.8	-	-	-	-	-	-	-	-	-	-	-	-	-	-
18 福井	261.8	-	-	-	-	-	-	-	-	-	-	-	-	-	-
19 山梨	171.9	-	-	-	-	-	-	-	-	-	-	-	-	-	-
20 長野	191.2	-	-	-	-	-	-	-	-	-	-	-	-	-	-
21 岐阜	236.0	6.7	6.7	-	-	-	-	-	-	-	-	-	-	-	-
22 静岡	166.4	-	3.6	-	-	-	-	-	-	-	-	-	3.6	-	-
23 愛知	182.2	-	3.1	-	-	3.1	1.6	1.6	-	-	-	4.7	-	-	-
24 三重	166.6	-	7.6	-	-	-	-	-	-	-	-	-	-	-	-
25 滋賀	165.7	-	-	-	-	-	8.3	8.3	-	-	-	-	-	-	-
26 京都	212.1	-	-	-	5.2	-	-	-	-	-	5.2	15.5	-	-	-
27 大阪	161.3	-	2.9	-	1.5	2.9	2.9	1.5	1.5	1.5	-	2.9	-	-	-
28 兵庫	154.5	-	-	-	-	-	2.3	2.3	-	2.3	-	-	-	-	-
29 奈良	318.1	-	-	-	-	-	-	-	-	-	-	-	-	-	-
30 和歌山	180.2	-	-	-	-	-	-	-	-	-	-	-	-	-	-
31 鳥取	293.1	-	-	-	-	-	22.5	22.5	-	22.5	-	-	-	-	-
32 島根	207.5	-	18.9	-	-	-	-	-	-	-	-	-	-	-	-
33 岡山	193.8	-	12.9	-	-	-	-	-	-	-	-	-	-	-	-
34 広島	189.1	4.4	4.4	-	-	-	4.4	-	-	4.4	-	-	-	-	-
35 山口	243.8	-	10.2	-	-	-	-	-	-	-	-	-	-	-	-
36 徳島	299.3	-	-	-	-	18.7	-	-	-	18.7	-	-	-	-	-
37 香川	106.5	-	-	-	-	-	-	-	-	-	-	-	-	-	-
38 愛媛	161.4	-	10.1	-	-	-	10.1	10.1	-	-	-	10.1	-	-	-
39 高知	188.3	-	20.9	-	-	-	-	-	-	-	-	-	-	-	-
40 福岡	202.1	4.5	4.5	-	-	2.3	2.3	2.3	-	4.5	-	2.3	2.3	-	-
41 佐賀	190.9	-	-	-	-	-	-	-	-	-	-	14.7	-	-	-
42 長崎	174.5	-	18.4	-	-	-	-	-	-	-	-	-	-	-	-
43 熊本	194.7	6.7	6.7	-	-	13.4	-	-	-	-	-	-	-	-	-
44 大分	242.9	-	11.0	-	-	-	-	-	-	-	-	-	-	-	-
45 宮崎	280.0	-	11.2	-	-	-	-	-	-	-	-	-	11.2	-	-
46 鹿児島	233.8	-	14.6	-	-	-	7.3	-	-	7.3	-	-	-	7.3	-
47 沖縄	186.6	6.0	-	-	-	-	-	-	-	-	-	-	-	-	-
21 大都市(再掲) 21 major cities(Regrouped)															
50 東京都の区部	187.0	-	1.2	-	-	-	1.2	-	-	1.2	-	1.2	-	-	-
51 札幌	206.8	7.1	-	-	-	7.1	-	-	-	-	-	-	-	-	-
52 仙台	292.0	-	-	-	-	-	-	-	-	-	-	-	-	-	-
53 さいたま	284.4	-	19.0	-	-	-	-	-	-	-	-	-	-	9.5	-
54 千葉	216.5	-	28.9	-	-	-	-	-	-	-	-	-	-	-	-
55 横浜	200.8	-	6.9	-	-	-	3.5	3.5	-	-	-	-	-	-	-
56 川崎	226.0	-	14.1	-	-	7.1	7.1	7.1	-	-	-	-	-	-	-
57 相模原	288.7	-	38.5	-	-	-	-	-	-	-	-	19.2	-	-	-
58 新潟	84.2	-	-	-	-	-	-	-	-	-	-	-	-	-	-
59 静岡	215.4	-	-	-	-	-	-	-	-	-	-	-	19.6	-	-
60 浜松	91.5	-	-	-	-	-	-	-	-	-	-	-	-	-	-
61 名古屋	179.1	-	-	-	-	-	5.1	5.1	-	-	-	15.4	-	-	-
62 京都	201.4	-	-	-	9.2	-	-	-	-	-	-	27.5	-	-	-
63 大阪	167.4	-	-	-	-	-	4.5	-	4.5	4.5	-	4.5	-	-	-
64 堺	131.5	-	-	-	-	-	-	-	-	-	-	-	-	-	-
65 神戸	135.8	-	-	-	-	-	-	-	-	-	-	-	-	-	-
66 岡山	175.6	-	-	-	-	-	-	-	-	-	-	-	-	-	-
67 広島	189.4	-	-	-	-	-	-	-	-	-	-	-	-	-	-
68 北九州	288.7	-	13.1	-	-	-	-	-	-	13.1	-	-	13.1	-	-
69 福岡	165.7	6.9	-	-	-	6.9	-	-	-	-	-	-	-	-	-
70 熊本	161.8	14.7	14.7	-	-	14.7	-	-	-	-	-	-	-	-	-

注：「敗血症」には、"新生児の細菌性敗血症"を含まない。
　　実数については下巻乳児死亡第2表を参照されたい。

Infant mortality

死因簡単分類別乳児死亡率（出生10万対）
causes of infant death）: Japan, each prefecture and 21 major cities, 2016

平成28年

Ba15	Ba16	Ba17	Ba18	Ba19	Ba20	Ba21	Ba22	Ba23	Ba24	Ba25	Ba26	Ba27	Ba28
心疾患（高血圧性を除く）	脳血管疾患	インフルエンザ	肺炎	喘息	ヘルニア及び腸閉塞	肝疾患	腎不全	周産期に発生した病態	妊娠期間及び胎児発育に関連する障害	出産外傷	出生時仮死	新生児の呼吸窮迫	周産期に発生した肺出血
4.2	0.4	0.2	2.9	-	1.2	1.1	0.2	52.1	4.4	0.3	7.9	3.4	1.0
2.8	-	-	8.5	-	-	2.8	-	62.6	5.7	-	5.7	8.5	2.8
23.2	-	-	-	-	-	11.6	-	69.6	23.2	-	-	-	-
12.0	-	-	12.0	-	-	-	-	36.0	-	-	-	-	-
11.5	-	-	-	-	-	-	-	80.7	11.5	-	11.5	5.8	-
-	-	-	-	-	-	-	-	52.9	-	-	-	17.6	-
-	-	-	-	-	-	-	-	132.5	-	-	13.3	-	-
-	-	-	-	-	-	-	-	36.4	-	-	7.3	-	-
4.8	-	-	-	-	-	-	-	38.3	9.6	-	4.8	4.8	-
13.7	-	-	-	-	6.8	-	-	75.2	-	-	13.7	6.8	-
-	-	-	-	-	-	-	-	29.3	7.3	-	7.3	-	-
7.3	-	-	3.7	-	1.8	-	-	49.6	-	-	7.3	1.8	1.8
2.2	-	-	-	-	-	2.2	2.2	68.3	6.6	-	11.0	4.4	-
2.7	0.9	0.9	0.9	-	1.8	3.6	-	57.2	3.6	-	8.0	2.7	1.8
5.7	-	-	4.2	-	1.4	-	-	60.9	7.1	-	14.2	4.2	1.4
-	-	-	-	-	-	-	-	38.1	6.4	-	-	6.4	-
-	-	-	-	-	-	-	-	82.2	-	-	-	13.7	-
-	-	-	-	-	-	-	-	67.2	33.6	-	11.2	11.2	-
16.4	-	-	-	-	-	-	-	98.2	-	-	16.4	-	-
17.2	-	-	-	-	-	-	-	68.7	-	-	17.2	-	-
-	-	-	-	-	-	-	-	79.1	6.6	-	13.2	-	-
13.5	-	-	-	-	-	-	-	60.7	-	-	6.7	-	6.7
-	3.6	-	-	-	-	3.6	-	32.5	3.6	-	7.2	-	-
3.1	-	-	3.1	-	1.6	-	1.6	45.2	3.1	-	12.5	6.2	1.6
-	-	-	7.6	-	-	-	-	30.3	-	-	-	7.6	-
-	-	-	-	-	-	-	-	24.9	-	-	-	-	-
10.3	-	-	5.2	-	-	-	-	62.1	-	-	10.3	5.2	5.2
4.4	1.5	-	4.4	-	2.9	1.5	-	36.3	2.9	2.9	1.5	1.5	-
4.6	-	-	4.6	-	-	-	-	39.2	-	2.3	6.9	2.3	4.6
10.6	-	-	10.6	-	-	-	-	84.8	-	-	-	-	-
-	-	-	-	-	15.0	-	-	30.0	-	-	-	-	-
-	-	-	-	-	-	-	-	157.8	-	-	45.1	45.1	-
18.9	-	-	-	-	-	-	-	75.5	-	-	-	-	-
-	-	-	-	-	6.5	-	-	38.8	-	-	19.4	-	-
-	-	-	-	-	-	-	-	39.6	8.8	-	8.8	4.4	-
10.2	10.2	-	10.2	-	-	-	-	30.5	-	-	-	-	-
-	-	-	-	-	18.7	-	-	18.7	-	-	-	-	-
-	-	-	13.3	-	-	-	-	26.6	-	-	-	-	-
10.1	-	-	10.1	-	-	-	-	10.1	-	-	-	-	-
-	-	-	-	-	2.3	2.3	-	36.3	9.1	-	2.3	2.3	-
-	-	-	-	-	-	-	-	73.4	14.7	-	14.7	14.7	-
-	-	9.2	9.2	-	-	-	-	55.1	18.4	-	-	-	-
-	-	-	6.7	-	6.7	-	-	53.7	6.7	-	26.9	-	-
11.0	-	-	22.1	-	-	-	-	66.2	-	-	11.0	11.0	-
11.2	-	-	-	-	-	-	-	67.2	-	-	-	-	-
7.3	-	-	7.3	-	-	-	-	73.1	-	-	7.3	-	-
-	-	-	-	-	-	-	-	54.2	6.0	-	12.0	-	-
2.5	-	1.2	-	-	2.5	5.0	-	54.9	3.7	-	7.5	1.2	1.2
7.1	-	-	-	-	-	-	-	42.8	7.1	-	-	7.1	-
11.2	-	-	-	-	-	-	-	123.5	11.2	-	22.5	11.2	-
-	-	-	-	-	9.5	-	-	56.9	-	-	9.5	-	-
-	-	-	-	-	-	14.4	-	57.7	14.4	-	14.4	14.4	-
3.5	-	-	3.5	-	3.5	-	-	58.8	3.5	-	13.8	3.5	-
7.1	-	-	7.1	-	-	-	-	63.6	7.1	-	7.1	7.1	7.1
-	-	-	-	-	-	-	-	96.2	19.2	-	38.5	-	-
-	-	-	-	-	-	-	-	50.5	16.8	-	-	16.8	-
-	-	-	-	-	19.6	-	-	19.6	-	-	-	-	-
-	-	-	-	-	-	-	-	30.5	-	-	-	-	-
-	-	-	-	-	-	-	-	35.8	5.1	-	15.4	5.1	-
9.2	-	-	9.2	-	-	-	-	54.9	-	-	9.2	-	-
-	-	-	4.5	-	4.5	-	-	40.7	4.5	9.1	-	-	-
-	-	-	14.6	-	-	-	-	14.6	-	-	-	-	-
-	-	-	-	-	-	-	-	33.9	-	-	8.5	-	-
-	-	-	-	-	-	-	-	47.9	-	-	31.9	-	-
-	-	-	-	-	-	-	-	28.4	9.5	-	-	-	-
-	-	-	-	-	-	13.1	-	52.5	-	-	-	-	-
-	-	-	-	-	-	-	-	27.6	-	-	-	-	-
-	-	-	-	-	-	-	-	14.7	-	-	-	-	-

Note : a) Code see page 598.
　　　 b) See page 44.

乳児死亡

表 6.17　都道府県（21大都市再掲）別にみた乳児
Table 6.17　Infant mortality rates (per 100,000 live births) by causes (the list of

都道府県 Prefecture	Ba29 周産期に発生した心血管障害	Ba30 その他の周産期に特異的な呼吸障害及び心血管障害	Ba31 新生児の細菌性敗血症	Ba32 その他の周産期に特異的な感染症	Ba33 胎児及び新生児の出血性障害及び血液障害	Ba34 その他の周産期に発生した病態	Ba35 先天奇形，変形及び染色体異常	Ba36 神経系の先天奇形	Ba37 心臓の先天奇形	Ba38 その他の循環器系の先天奇形	Ba39 呼吸器系の先天奇形	Ba40 消化器系の先天奇形	Ba41 筋骨格系の先天奇形及び変形	Ba42 その他の先天奇形及び変形
全国 Total	4.4	12.2	3.7	0.7	6.9	7.3	67.9	3.0	16.5	8.6	5.3	2.0	4.3	6.9
01 北海道	8.5	17.1	-	2.8	8.5	2.8	54.1	2.8	19.9	8.5	2.8	2.8	2.8	-
02 青森	-	11.6	-	-	34.8	-	58.0	-	11.6	11.6	11.6	-	-	-
03 岩手	-	12.0	12.0	-	-	12.0	83.9	-	12.0	-	12.0	-	12.0	24.0
04 宮城	-	11.5	-	-	5.8	5.8	86.5	-	23.1	5.8	11.5	-	5.8	5.8
05 秋田	-	17.6	-	-	-	17.6	123.5	-	17.6	17.6	-	-	-	17.6
06 山形	13.3	-	26.5	26.5	39.8	13.3	66.3	-	-	-	13.3	-	-	26.5
07 福島	-	-	7.3	-	-	21.8	65.5	-	21.8	-	-	7.3	-	7.3
08 茨城	-	9.6	4.8	-	-	4.8	71.8	4.8	4.8	4.8	-	-	19.2	9.6
09 栃木	-	20.5	6.8	-	20.5	6.8	47.9	6.8	13.7	6.8	6.8	-	-	6.8
10 群馬	-	-	-	-	7.3	7.3	87.8	-	29.3	7.3	14.6	7.3	7.3	7.3
11 埼玉	5.5	9.2	3.7	-	7.3	12.9	79.0	3.7	20.2	16.5	5.5	5.5	3.7	11.0
12 千葉	2.2	24.2	8.8	2.2	4.4	4.4	61.7	2.2	11.0	4.4	2.2	-	8.8	11.0
13 東京	5.4	15.2	3.6	-	9.8	7.1	74.1	2.7	20.5	10.7	6.3	2.7	3.6	7.1
14 神奈川	2.8	11.3	1.4	-	8.5	9.9	82.1	2.8	12.7	12.7	4.2	1.4	5.7	8.5
15 新潟	-	6.4	12.7	-	6.4	-	25.4	-	6.4	12.7	-	-	-	-
16 富山	-	41.1	-	-	13.7	13.7	82.2	13.7	-	13.7	13.7	-	13.7	-
17 石川	-	11.2	-	-	-	-	67.2	11.2	44.8	-	-	-	-	-
18 福井	16.4	32.7	-	-	32.7	-	114.5	-	49.1	-	-	16.4	-	-
19 山梨	-	17.2	-	-	-	34.4	51.6	-	-	17.2	-	-	-	-
20 長野	6.6	19.8	6.6	-	13.2	13.2	79.1	-	-	6.6	13.2	-	6.6	13.2
21 岐阜	13.5	6.7	-	-	13.5	13.5	80.9	13.5	27.0	-	-	-	6.7	-
22 静岡	3.6	3.6	3.6	-	10.8	-	61.5	3.6	-	-	7.2	-	3.6	7.2
23 愛知	-	10.9	1.6	-	6.2	3.1	68.5	9.3	10.9	6.2	12.5	4.7	1.6	7.8
24 三重	-	7.6	-	7.6	-	7.6	60.6	-	22.7	-	7.6	-	-	7.6
25 滋賀	16.6	-	-	-	-	8.3	99.4	8.3	41.4	8.3	8.3	-	-	16.6
26 京都	10.3	20.7	-	-	5.2	5.2	51.7	5.2	20.7	5.2	-	-	-	10.3
27 大阪	8.7	8.7	5.8	-	2.9	1.5	45.0	2.9	13.1	2.9	4.4	-	2.9	7.3
28 兵庫	4.6	11.5	4.6	-	-	2.3	41.5	2.3	11.5	6.9	-	-	-	6.9
29 奈良	21.2	42.4	-	-	-	10.6	127.3	-	53.0	21.2	-	-	-	10.6
30 和歌山	-	-	30.0	-	-	-	75.1	15.0	15.0	15.0	-	-	-	-
31 鳥取	22.5	22.5	-	-	22.5	-	22.5	-	-	-	-	-	-	-
32 島根	18.9	56.6	-	-	-	-	56.6	-	-	-	-	-	-	-
33 岡山	-	12.9	-	-	-	6.5	64.6	-	6.5	6.5	-	-	19.4	-
34 広島	-	4.4	-	-	8.8	4.4	74.8	-	22.0	13.2	4.4	-	4.4	8.8
35 山口	10.2	-	-	-	10.2	10.2	81.3	-	40.6	-	-	10.2	10.2	-
36 徳島	-	-	-	-	-	18.7	168.4	-	37.4	56.1	18.7	-	-	18.7
37 香川	-	-	26.6	-	-	-	26.6	-	13.3	-	-	-	-	-
38 愛媛	-	-	10.1	-	-	-	50.4	-	-	-	10.1	10.1	10.1	10.1
39 高知	-	-	-	-	-	-	62.8	-	-	-	-	-	20.9	20.9
40 福岡	-	6.8	2.3	-	4.5	9.1	65.9	-	18.2	13.6	4.5	2.3	2.3	6.8
41 佐賀	14.7	14.7	-	-	-	-	14.7	-	-	14.7	-	-	-	-
42 長崎	9.2	9.2	-	-	-	18.4	55.1	-	9.2	-	9.2	-	9.2	-
43 熊本	-	6.7	-	-	-	13.4	67.1	6.7	13.4	13.4	-	-	13.4	-
44 大分	11.0	11.0	-	-	11.0	11.0	66.2	-	-	11.0	11.0	-	11.0	-
45 宮崎	11.2	22.4	-	11.2	11.2	11.2	123.2	-	33.6	11.2	44.8	-	11.2	-
46 鹿児島	-	21.9	14.6	-	7.3	21.9	73.1	-	51.1	7.3	-	7.3	-	-
47 沖縄	6.0	18.1	-	-	-	12.0	66.2	-	18.1	18.1	6.0	12.0	6.0	-
21 大都市（再掲）21 major cities (Regrouped)														
50 東京都の区部	5.0	15.0	3.7	-	11.2	6.2	74.8	2.5	22.4	11.2	6.2	-	5.0	7.5
51 札幌	7.1	21.4	-	-	-	-	57.1	-	21.4	14.3	7.1	-	-	-
52 仙台	-	11.2	-	11.2	11.2	44.9	89.8	-	33.7	11.2	-	-	11.2	11.2
53 さいたま	19.0	9.5	-	-	9.5	9.5	132.7	9.5	19.0	47.4	9.5	9.5	9.5	9.5
54 千葉	-	-	14.4	-	-	-	86.6	-	28.9	14.4	-	-	-	14.4
55 横浜	-	20.8	3.5	-	3.5	10.4	90.0	3.5	17.3	13.8	3.5	3.5	10.4	10.4
56 川崎	7.1	7.1	-	-	7.1	14.1	84.8	-	7.1	28.3	-	-	7.1	14.1
57 相模原	-	-	-	-	19.2	19.2	77.0	-	-	-	19.2	-	-	-
58 新潟	-	16.8	-	-	-	-	16.8	-	16.8	-	-	-	-	-
59 静岡	-	-	-	-	19.6	-	78.3	-	-	-	-	-	-	19.6
60 浜松	-	15.2	-	-	15.2	-	30.5	-	-	-	-	-	-	-
61 名古屋	-	5.1	-	-	5.1	-	102.3	10.2	20.5	5.1	35.8	-	5.1	5.1
62 京都	9.2	18.3	-	-	9.2	9.2	36.6	9.2	9.2	-	-	-	-	9.2
63 大阪	13.6	13.6	-	-	-	-	72.4	9.1	18.1	9.1	-	-	4.5	13.6
64 堺	14.6	-	-	-	-	-	43.8	-	-	-	29.2	-	-	-
65 神戸	-	8.5	17.0	-	-	-	59.4	8.5	17.0	-	-	-	-	8.5
66 岡山	-	16.0	-	-	-	-	47.9	-	16.0	-	-	-	16.0	-
67 広島	-	-	-	-	-	9.5	113.6	-	37.9	28.4	-	-	-	18.9
68 北九州	-	26.2	13.1	-	-	13.1	78.7	-	13.1	26.2	13.1	-	-	13.1
69 福岡	-	-	-	-	-	13.8	75.9	-	34.5	6.9	-	-	-	-
70 熊本	-	-	-	-	-	14.7	73.6	14.7	14.7	14.7	-	-	14.7	-

Infant mortality

死因簡単分類別乳児死亡率（出生10万対）（つづき）
causes of infant death): Japan, each prefecture and 21 major cities, 2016−CON.
平成28年

Ba43	Ba44	Ba45	Ba46	Ba47	Ba48	Ba49	Ba50	Ba51	Ba52	Ba53	Ba54	Ba55	Ba56
染色体異常，他に分類されないもの	乳幼児突然死症候群	その他のすべての疾患	不慮の事故	交通事故	転倒・転落	不慮の溺死及び溺水	胃内容物の誤えん及び気道閉塞を生じた食物等の誤えん	その他の不慮の窒息	煙，火及び火炎への曝露	有害物質による不慮の中毒及び有害物質への曝露	その他の不慮の事故	他　殺	その他の外因
21.3	11.2	32.4	7.5	0.3	-	0.4	3.3	3.1	-	0.1	0.3	0.7	2.5
14.2	45.6	11.4	11.4		-	2.8	2.8	2.8	-		2.8	-	2.8
23.2	-	34.8	11.6				11.6						
24.0	-	36.0	-										24.0
34.6	34.6	5.8	5.8				5.8						
70.6	-	17.6											
26.5	-	66.3	13.3			13.3							13.3
29.1	14.6	65.5											
28.7	4.8	47.9	9.6				9.6					4.8	
6.8	-	34.2											
14.6	-	22.0											
12.9	12.9	44.1	1.8	1.8	-								1.8
22.0	11.0	33.0	6.6					6.6					
20.5	6.3	38.4	5.4	0.9			3.6	0.9					
34.0	18.4	15.6	2.8					2.8					1.4
6.4	25.4	19.1	12.7				6.4	6.4					
27.4	-	27.4	13.7					13.7					
11.2			78.4				44.8	33.6					
49.1	16.4		16.4				16.4						
34.4	-	34.4											
39.6	13.2	13.2	6.6	6.6									
33.7	6.7	40.5	13.5				6.7			6.7			6.7
39.8	-	28.9	10.8				7.2	3.6				7.2	10.8
15.6	6.2	31.1	4.7				3.1	1.6				1.6	3.1
22.7	-	37.9	7.6					7.6					15.1
16.6	-	33.1											
10.3		51.7											5.2
11.6	-	34.9	8.7				2.9	5.8				1.5	5.8
13.8	11.5	36.9	11.5				4.6	6.9					
42.4	-	74.2	10.6								10.6		
30.0	-	60.1											
22.5	45.1	22.5											
56.6	18.9		18.9								18.9		
32.3	6.5	58.2										6.5	
22.0	8.8	30.8	13.2			4.4		8.8				4.4	4.4
20.3	30.5	50.8											10.2
37.4		37.4	18.7				18.7						
13.3			26.6				13.3	13.3					13.3
10.1	20.2	10.1	20.2				10.1	10.1					
20.9	62.8	20.9	20.9			20.9							
18.2	15.9	45.4	9.1				2.3	6.8					2.3
-		58.7	29.4				14.7	14.7					
27.6	18.4	9.2	-										
20.1	6.7	26.9	-										
33.1	22.1	44.2	-										
22.4	22.4	11.2	22.4				22.4						
7.3	14.6	21.9	7.3				7.3						
6.0	30.1	24.1	-										6.0
19.9	7.5	31.2	3.7				2.5	1.2					
14.3	49.9	7.1	21.4			7.1		7.1			7.1		7.1
22.5	56.2	-	11.2				11.2						
19.0	-	56.9											
28.9	-	14.4	14.4					14.4					
27.7	27.7	-	3.5					3.5					
28.3	21.2	14.1	-										
57.7	19.2	38.5	-										
-	16.8												
58.8		39.2										19.6	19.6
30.5	-	30.5											
20.5	-	20.5											
9.2	-	45.8											9.2
18.1	-	9.1	18.1				4.5	13.6					4.5
14.6	-	29.2	14.6					14.6					14.6
25.5	-	42.4											
16.0	-	79.8											
28.4	-	28.4	18.9					18.9					
13.1	39.4	52.5	-										13.1
34.5	6.9	27.6	13.8				6.9	6.9					
14.7	-	29.4											

乳児死亡

〔病死の乳児死亡〕
〔Infant deaths by diseases〕

表6.18　体重別にみた乳児死因簡単分類別病死による
Table 6.18　Infant deaths and infant mortality rates (per 100,000 live births)

病死による乳児死亡数
Infant deaths by diseases

乳児死因簡単分類コード Code[a]	死因 Causes of death	総数 Total	1.0kg未満 Under 1.0kg	1.0kg以上1.5kg未満 1.0kg and over, less than 1.5kg	1.5〜2.0	2.0〜2.5	2.5〜3.0	3.0〜3.5	3.5〜4.0	4.0〜4.5	4.5kg以上 4.5kg and over
	総数　Total	1 824	388	150	247	283	419	252	62	9	-
Ba01	腸管感染症	9	-	-	1	2	4	2	-	-	
Ba02	敗血症	40	21	2	3	-	9	5	-	-	
Ba03	麻疹	-	-	-	-	-	-	-	-	-	
Ba04	ウイルス肝炎	2	-	-	-	-	1	-	1	-	
Ba05	その他の感染症及び寄生虫症	18	4	-	3	2	5	4	-	-	
Ba06	悪性新生物	17	1	-	-	1	3	9	1	1	
Ba07	白血病	10	-	-	-	1	-	7	1	-	
Ba08	その他の悪性新生物	7	1	-	-	-	3	2	-	1	
Ba09	その他の新生物	9	-	-	-	2	4	3	-	-	
Ba10	栄養失調症及びその他の栄養欠乏症	1	-	-	-	-	-	1	-	-	
Ba11	代謝障害	23	7	-	2	2	6	4	2	-	-
Ba12	髄膜炎	5	-	1	-	-	2	2	-	-	
Ba13	脊髄性筋萎縮症及び関連症候群	2	-	-	-	-	-	1	1	-	
Ba14	脳性麻痺	-	-	-	-	-	-	-	-	-	
Ba15	心疾患（高血圧性を除く）	41	8	-	1	6	15	11	-	-	-
Ba16	脳血管疾患	4	1	-	1	1	1	-	-	-	
Ba17	インフルエンザ	2	-	-	-	1	-	-	1	-	-
Ba18	肺炎	28	1	4	2	6	9	5	1	-	-
Ba19	喘息	-	-	-	-	-	-	-	-	-	
Ba20	ヘルニア及び腸閉塞	12	4	1	1	1	3	1	1	-	
Ba21	肝疾患	11	4	-	1	2	-	3	1	-	
Ba22	腎不全	2	2	-	-	-	-	-	-	-	

注：「敗血症」には、"新生児の細菌性敗血症"を含まない。
　　総数には体重不詳を含む。

Infant mortality

乳児死亡数及び率（出生10万対）
by diseases, causes (the list of causes of infant death) and birth weight : Japan, 2016

平成28年

乳児死因簡単分類コード Code[a]	死因 Causes of death	総数 Total	1.0kg未満 Under 1.0kg	1.0kg以上1.5kg未満 1.0kg and over, less than 1.5kg	1.5～2.0	2.0～2.5	2.5～3.0	3.0～3.5	3.5～4.0	4.0～4.5	4.5kg以上 4.5kg and over
Ba23	周産期に発生した病態	509	234	43	48	52	73	41	14	1	-
Ba24	妊娠期間及び胎児発育に関連する障害	43	41	-	1	-	-	-	-	-	-
Ba25	出産外傷	3	1	-	-	-	-	-	2	-	-
Ba26	出生時仮死	77	21	10	10	11	15	7	3	-	-
Ba27	新生児の呼吸窮迫	33	25	4	-	2	1	1	-	-	-
Ba28	周産期に発生した肺出血	10	6	1	1	-	-	2	-	-	-
Ba29	周産期に発生した心血管障害	43	15	5	3	4	8	5	3	-	-
Ba30	その他の周産期に特異的な呼吸障害及び心血管障害	119	46	12	15	14	20	9	3	-	-
Ba31	新生児の細菌性敗血症	36	20	3	2	3	3	5	-	-	-
Ba32	その他の周産期に特異的な感染症	7	5	-	-	-	1	1	-	-	-
Ba33	胎児及び新生児の出血性障害及び血液障害	67	33	6	5	10	8	3	2	-	-
Ba34	その他の周産期に発生した病態	71	21	2	11	8	17	8	1	1	-
Ba35	先天奇形，変形及び染色体異常	663	54	80	162	144	139	63	16	3	-
Ba36	神経系の先天奇形	29	1	1	9	6	8	3	1	-	-
Ba37	心臓の先天奇形	161	5	15	26	35	53	20	7	-	-
Ba38	その他の循環器系の先天奇形	84	14	4	12	13	18	19	3	1	-
Ba39	呼吸器系の先天奇形	52	2	5	4	16	17	3	3	1	-
Ba40	消化器系の先天奇形	20	4	1	3	4	3	3	2	-	-
Ba41	筋骨格系の先天奇形及び変形	42	3	8	10	7	8	4	-	1	-
Ba42	その他の先天奇形及び変形	67	7	7	13	20	13	7	-	-	-
Ba43	染色体異常，他に分類されないもの	208	18	39	85	43	19	4	-	-	-
Ba44	乳幼児突然死症候群	109	-	2	5	13	44	34	9	2	-
Ba45	その他のすべての疾患	317	47	17	17	48	101	63	14	2	-

Note : a) Code see page 598.

乳児死亡

表6.18　体重別にみた乳児死因簡単分類別病死による
Table 6.18　Infant deaths and infant mortality rates (per 100,000 live births)

病死による乳児死亡率
Infant mortality rates by diseases

乳児死因簡単分類コード Code[a]	死　因 Causes of death	総数 Total	1.0kg未満 Under 1.0kg	1.0kg以上1.5kg未満 1.0kg and over, less than 1.5kg	1.5〜2.0	2.0〜2.5	2.5〜3.0	3.0〜3.5	3.5〜4.0	4.0〜4.5	4.5kg以上 4.5kg and over
	総　数　　Total	186.7	39.7	15.4	25.3	29.0	42.9	25.8	6.3	0.9	-
Ba01	腸管感染症	0.9	-	-	0.1	0.2	0.4	0.2	-	-	-
Ba02	敗血症	4.1	2.1	0.2	0.3	-	0.9	0.5	-	-	-
Ba03	麻疹	-	-	-	-	-	-	-	-	-	-
Ba04	ウイルス肝炎	0.2	-	-	-	-	0.1	-	0.1	-	-
Ba05	その他の感染症及び寄生虫症	1.8	0.4	-	0.3	0.2	0.5	0.4	-	-	-
Ba06	悪性新生物	1.7	0.1	-	-	0.1	0.3	0.9	0.1	0.1	-
Ba07	白血病	1.0	-	-	-	0.1	-	0.7	0.1	-	-
Ba08	その他の悪性新生物	0.7	0.1	-	-	-	0.3	0.2	-	0.1	-
Ba09	その他の新生物	0.9	-	-	-	0.2	0.4	0.3	-	-	-
Ba10	栄養失調症及びその他の栄養欠乏症	0.1	-	-	-	-	-	0.1	-	-	-
Ba11	代謝障害	2.4	0.7	-	0.2	0.2	0.6	0.4	0.2	-	-
Ba12	髄膜炎	0.5	-	0.1	-	-	0.2	0.2	-	-	-
Ba13	脊髄性筋萎縮症及び関連症候群	0.2	-	-	-	-	-	0.1	0.1	-	-
Ba14	脳性麻痺	-	-	-	-	-	-	-	-	-	-
Ba15	心疾患（高血圧性を除く）	4.2	0.8	-	0.1	0.6	1.5	1.1	-	-	-
Ba16	脳血管疾患	0.4	0.1	-	0.1	0.1	0.1	-	-	-	-
Ba17	インフルエンザ	0.2	-	-	-	0.1	-	-	0.1	-	-
Ba18	肺炎	2.9	0.1	0.4	0.2	0.6	0.9	0.5	0.1	-	-
Ba19	喘息	-	-	-	-	-	-	-	-	-	-
Ba20	ヘルニア及び腸閉塞	1.2	0.4	0.1	0.1	0.1	0.3	0.1	0.1	-	-
Ba21	肝疾患	1.1	0.4	-	0.1	0.2	-	0.3	0.1	-	-
Ba22	腎不全	0.2	0.2	-	-	-	-	-	-	-	-

Infant mortality

乳児死亡数及び率（出生10万対）（つづき）
by diseases, causes (the list of causes of infant death) and birth weight : Japan, 2016−CON.

平成28年

乳児死因簡単分類コード Code[a]	死因 Causes of death	総数 Total	1.0kg未満 Under 1.0kg	1.0kg以上1.5kg未満 1.0kg and over, less than 1.5kg	1.5～2.0	2.0～2.5	2.5～3.0	3.0～3.5	3.5～4.0	4.0～4.5	4.5kg以上 4.5kg and over
Ba23	周産期に発生した病態	52.1	24.0	4.4	4.9	5.3	7.5	4.2	1.4	0.1	-
Ba24	妊娠期間及び胎児発育に関連する障害	4.4	4.2	-	0.1	-	-	-	-	-	-
Ba25	出産外傷	0.3	0.1	-	-	-	-	-	0.2		-
Ba26	出生時仮死	7.9	2.1	1.0	1.0	1.1	1.5	0.7	0.3	-	-
Ba27	新生児の呼吸窮迫	3.4	2.6	0.4	-	0.2	0.1	0.1		-	-
Ba28	周産期に発生した肺出血	1.0	0.6	0.1	0.1	-	-	0.2		-	-
Ba29	周産期に発生した心血管障害	4.4	1.5	0.5	0.3	0.4	0.8	0.5	0.3	-	-
Ba30	その他の周産期に特異的な呼吸障害及び心血管障害	12.2	4.7	1.2	1.5	1.4	2.0	0.9	0.3	-	-
Ba31	新生児の細菌性敗血症	3.7	2.0	0.3	0.2	0.3	0.3	0.5		-	-
Ba32	その他の周産期に特異的な感染症	0.7	0.5	-	-	-	0.1	0.1		-	-
Ba33	胎児及び新生児の出血性障害及び血液障害	6.9	3.4	0.6	0.5	1.0	0.8	0.3	0.2	-	-
Ba34	その他の周産期に発生した病態	7.3	2.1	0.2	1.1	0.8	1.7	0.8	0.1	0.1	-
Ba35	先天奇形，変形及び染色体異常	67.9	5.5	8.2	16.6	14.7	14.2	6.4	1.6	0.3	-
Ba36	神経系の先天奇形	3.0	0.1	0.1	0.9	0.6	0.8	0.3	0.1	-	-
Ba37	心臓の先天奇形	16.5	0.5	1.5	2.7	3.6	5.4	2.0	0.7	-	-
Ba38	その他の循環器系の先天奇形	8.6	1.4	0.4	1.2	1.3	1.8	1.9	0.3	0.1	-
Ba39	呼吸器系の先天奇形	5.3	0.2	0.5	0.4	1.6	1.7	0.3	0.3	0.1	-
Ba40	消化器系の先天奇形	2.0	0.4	0.1	0.3	0.4	0.3	0.3	0.2	-	-
Ba41	筋骨格系の先天奇形及び変形	4.3	0.3	0.8	1.0	0.7	0.8	0.4	-	0.1	-
Ba42	その他の先天奇形及び変形	6.9	0.7	0.7	1.3	2.0	1.3	0.7			-
Ba43	染色体異常，他に分類されないもの	21.3	1.8	4.0	8.7	4.4	1.9	0.4			-
Ba44	乳幼児突然死症候群	11.2	-	0.2	0.5	1.3	4.5	3.5	0.9	0.2	-
Ba45	その他のすべての疾患	32.4	4.8	1.7	1.7	4.9	10.3	6.4	1.4	0.2	-

乳児死亡

表 6.19 体重別にみた乳児死因簡単分類別病死による
Table 6.19 Neonatal deaths and neonatal mortality rates (per 100,000 live births)

病死による新生児死亡数
Neonatal deaths by diseases

乳児死因簡単分類コード Code[a)]	死因 Causes of death	総数 Total	1.0kg未満 Under 1.0kg	1.0kg以上1.5kg未満 1.0kg and over, less than 1.5kg	1.5〜2.0	2.0〜2.5	2.5〜3.0	3.0〜3.5	3.5〜4.0	4.0〜4.5	4.5kg以上 4.5kg and over
	総数　Total	865	273	97	141	120	138	64	25	2	-
Ba01	腸管感染症	-	-	-	-	-	-	-	-	-	-
Ba02	敗血症	14	13	-	1	-	-	-	-	-	-
Ba03	麻疹	-	-	-	-	-	-	-	-	-	-
Ba04	ウイルス肝炎	-	-	-	-	-	-	-	-	-	-
Ba05	その他の感染症及び寄生虫症	2	1	-	1	-	-	-	-	-	-
Ba06	悪性新生物	-	-	-	-	-	-	-	-	-	-
Ba07	白血病	-	-	-	-	-	-	-	-	-	-
Ba08	その他の悪性新生物	-	-	-	-	-	-	-	-	-	-
Ba09	その他の新生物	3	-	-	-	1	1	1	-	-	-
Ba10	栄養失調症及びその他の栄養欠乏症	-	-	-	-	-	-	-	-	-	-
Ba11	代謝障害	7	4	-	1	1	-	1	-	-	-
Ba12	髄膜炎	2	-	-	-	-	1	1	-	-	-
Ba13	脊髄性筋萎縮症及び関連症候群	-	-	-	-	-	-	-	-	-	-
Ba14	脳性麻痺	-	-	-	-	-	-	-	-	-	-
Ba15	心疾患（高血圧性を除く）	3	-	-	1	1	-	1	-	-	-
Ba16	脳血管疾患	1	1	-	-	-	-	-	-	-	-
Ba17	インフルエンザ	-	-	-	-	-	-	-	-	-	-
Ba18	肺炎	2	1	1	-	-	-	-	-	-	-
Ba19	喘息	-	-	-	-	-	-	-	-	-	-
Ba20	ヘルニア及び腸閉塞	-	-	-	-	-	-	-	-	-	-
Ba21	肝疾患	-	-	-	-	-	-	-	-	-	-
Ba22	腎不全	-	-	-	-	-	-	-	-	-	-

注：「敗血症」には、"新生児の細菌性敗血症"を含まない。
　　総数には体重不詳を含む。

Infant mortality

新生児死亡数及び率（出生10万対）
by diseases, causes (the list of causes of infant death) and birth weight : Japan, 2016

平成28年

乳児死因簡単分類コード Code[a]	死因 Causes of death	総数 Total	1.0kg未満 Under 1.0kg	1.0kg以上1.5kg未満 1.0kg and over, less than 1.5kg	1.5～2.0	2.0～2.5	2.5～3.0	3.0～3.5	3.5～4.0	4.0～4.5	4.5kg以上 4.5kg and over
Ba23	周産期に発生した病態	451	205	39	43	46	64	37	14	-	-
Ba24	妊娠期間及び胎児発育に関連する障害	38	37	-	-	-	-	-	-	-	-
Ba25	出 産 外 傷	3	1	-	-	-	-	-	2	-	-
Ba26	出生時仮死	74	20	10	10	10	14	7	3	-	-
Ba27	新生児の呼吸窮迫	32	24	4	-	2	1	1	-	-	-
Ba28	周産期に発生した肺出血	10	6	1	1	-	-	2	-	-	-
Ba29	周産期に発生した心血管障害	40	14	5	3	4	8	3	3	-	-
Ba30	その他の周産期に特異的な呼吸障害及び心血管障害	99	32	10	15	13	18	8	3	-	-
Ba31	新生児の細菌性敗血症	33	19	3	2	2	3	4	-	-	-
Ba32	その他の周産期に特異的な感染症	7	5	-	-	-	1	1	-	-	-
Ba33	胎児及び新生児の出血性障害及び血液障害	62	32	5	3	9	8	3	2	-	-
Ba34	その他の周産期に発生した病態	53	15	1	9	6	11	8	1	-	-
Ba35	先天奇形，変形及び染色体異常	344	37	55	92	68	59	19	10	2	-
Ba36	神経系の先天奇形	20	1	1	8	4	4	2	-	-	-
Ba37	心臓の先天奇形	51	3	9	12	7	12	4	4	-	-
Ba38	その他の循環器系の先天奇形	38	9	4	4	4	9	5	3	-	-
Ba39	呼吸器系の先天奇形	45	1	4	4	13	15	3	3	1	-
Ba40	消化器系の先天奇形	8	2	1	3	1	-	1	-	-	-
Ba41	筋骨格系の先天奇形及び変形	37	3	8	8	6	7	3	-	1	-
Ba42	その他の先天奇形及び変形	49	6	5	13	18	6	1	-	-	-
Ba43	染色体異常，他に分類されないもの	96	12	23	40	15	6	-	-	-	-
Ba44	乳幼児突然死症候群	3	-	-	-	1	1	1	-	-	-
Ba45	その他のすべての疾患	33	11	2	2	2	12	3	1	-	-

Note : a) Code see page 598.

乳児死亡

表6.19　体重別にみた乳児死因簡単分類別病死による
Table 6.19　Neonatal deaths and neonatal mortality rates（per 100,000 live births）

病死による新生児死亡率
Neonatal mortality rates by diseases

乳児死因簡単分類コード Code[a]	死因 Causes of death	総数 Total	1.0kg未満 Under 1.0kg	1.0kg以上1.5kg未満 1.0kg and over, less than 1.5kg	1.5～2.0	2.0～2.5	2.5～3.0	3.0～3.5	3.5～4.0	4.0～4.5	4.5kg以上 4.5kg and over
	総　数　　Total	88.5	27.9	9.9	14.4	12.3	14.1	6.6	2.6	0.2	-
Ba01	腸管感染症	-	-	-	-	-	-	-	-	-	-
Ba02	敗　血　症	1.4	1.3	-	0.1	-	-	-	-	-	-
Ba03	麻　疹	-	-	-	-	-	-	-	-	-	-
Ba04	ウイルス肝炎	-	-	-	-	-	-	-	-	-	-
Ba05	その他の感染症及び寄生虫症	0.2	0.1	-	0.1	-	-	-	-	-	-
Ba06	悪性新生物	-	-	-	-	-	-	-	-	-	-
Ba07	白　血　病	-	-	-	-	-	-	-	-	-	-
Ba08	その他の悪性新生物	-	-	-	-	-	-	-	-	-	-
Ba09	その他の新生物	0.3	-	-	-	0.1	0.1	0.1	-	-	-
Ba10	栄養失調症及びその他の栄養欠乏症	-	-	-	-	-	-	-	-	-	-
Ba11	代　謝　障　害	0.7	0.4	-	0.1	0.1	-	0.1	-	-	-
Ba12	髄　膜　炎	0.2	-	-	-	-	0.1	0.1	-	-	-
Ba13	脊髄性筋萎縮症及び関連症候群	-	-	-	-	-	-	-	-	-	-
Ba14	脳　性　麻　痺	-	-	-	-	-	-	-	-	-	-
Ba15	心　疾　患（高血圧性を除く）	0.3	-	-	0.1	0.1	-	0.1	-	-	-
Ba16	脳血管疾患	0.1	0.1	-	-	-	-	-	-	-	-
Ba17	インフルエンザ	-	-	-	-	-	-	-	-	-	-
Ba18	肺　炎	0.2	0.1	0.1	-	-	-	-	-	-	-
Ba19	喘　息	-	-	-	-	-	-	-	-	-	-
Ba20	ヘルニア及び腸閉塞	-	-	-	-	-	-	-	-	-	-
Ba21	肝　疾　患	-	-	-	-	-	-	-	-	-	-
Ba22	腎　不　全	-	-	-	-	-	-	-	-	-	-

Infant mortality

新生児死亡数及び率（出生10万対）（つづき）
by diseases, causes (the list of causes of infant death) and birth weight : Japan,2016－CON.

平成28年

乳児死因簡単分類コード Code[a]	死　因 Causes of death	総数 Total	1.0kg未満 Under 1.0kg	1.0kg以上1.5kg未満 1.0kg and over, less than 1.5kg	1.5〜2.0	2.0〜2.5	2.5〜3.0	3.0〜3.5	3.5〜4.0	4.0〜4.5	4.5kg以上 4.5kg and over
Ba23	周産期に発生した病態	46.2	21.0	4.0	4.4	4.7	6.6	3.8	1.4	-	-
Ba24	妊娠期間及び胎児発育に関連する障害	3.9	3.8	-	-	-	-	-	-	-	-
Ba25	出 産 外 傷	0.3	0.1	-	-	-	-	-	0.2	-	-
Ba26	出生時仮死	7.6	2.0	1.0	1.0	1.0	1.4	0.7	0.3	-	-
Ba27	新生児の呼吸窮迫	3.3	2.5	0.4	-	0.2	0.1	0.1	-	-	-
Ba28	周産期に発生した肺出血	1.0	0.6	0.1	0.1	-	-	0.2	-	-	-
Ba29	周産期に発生した心血管障害	4.1	1.4	0.5	0.3	0.4	0.8	0.3	0.3	-	-
Ba30	その他の周産期に特異的な呼吸障害及び心血管障害	10.1	3.3	1.0	1.5	1.3	1.8	0.8	0.3	-	-
Ba31	新生児の細菌性敗血症	3.4	1.9	0.3	0.2	0.2	0.3	0.4	-	-	-
Ba32	その他の周産期に特異的な感染症	0.7	0.5	-	-	-	0.1	0.1	-	-	-
Ba33	胎児及び新生児の出血性障害及び血液障害	6.3	3.3	0.5	0.3	0.9	0.8	0.3	0.2	-	-
Ba34	その他の周産期に発生した病態	5.4	1.5	0.1	0.9	0.6	1.1	0.8	0.1	-	-
Ba35	先天奇形，変形及び染色体異常	35.2	3.8	5.6	9.4	7.0	6.0	1.9	1.0	0.2	-
Ba36	神経系の先天奇形	2.0	0.1	0.1	0.8	0.4	0.4	0.2	-	-	-
Ba37	心臓の先天奇形	5.2	0.3	0.9	1.2	0.7	1.2	0.4	0.4	-	-
Ba38	その他の循環器系の先天奇形	3.9	0.9	0.4	0.4	0.4	0.9	0.5	0.3	-	-
Ba39	呼吸器系の先天奇形	4.6	0.1	0.4	0.4	1.3	1.5	0.3	0.3	0.1	-
Ba40	消化器系の先天奇形	0.8	0.2	0.1	0.3	0.1	-	0.1	-	-	-
Ba41	筋骨格系の先天奇形及び変形	3.8	0.3	0.8	0.8	0.6	0.7	0.3	-	0.1	-
Ba42	その他の先天奇形及び変形	5.0	0.6	0.5	1.3	1.8	0.6	0.1	-	-	-
Ba43	染色体異常，他に分類されないもの	9.8	1.2	2.4	4.1	1.5	0.6	-	-	-	-
Ba44	乳幼児突然死症候群	0.3	-	-	-	0.1	0.1	0.1	-	-	-
Ba45	その他のすべての疾患	3.4	1.1	0.2	0.2	0.2	1.2	0.3	0.1	-	-

死 産

〔死産の年次推移〕
〔Trends in foetal deaths〕

第7章 死　　　産
Chapter 7　Foetal mortality

表7.1　年次別にみた死産数

Table 7.1　Trends in foetal deaths, foetal death rates

年　　次 [1]		出 生 数	死　　産　　数 Foetal deaths				死 産 率	死産性比
Year		Live births	総　数 Total	男 Male	女 Female	不　詳 Not stated	Foetal death rates	Sex ratio of foetal deaths
1899	明治32年	1 386 981	135 727	70 759	64 493	475	89.1	109.7
1900	33	1 420 534	137 987	72 257	65 288	442	88.5	110.7
01	34	1 501 591	155 489	81 500	73 573	416	93.8	110.8
02	35	1 510 835	157 708	82 670	74 557	481	94.5	110.9
03	36	1 489 816	153 920	80 437	73 041	442	93.6	110.1
04	37	1 440 371	147 058	76 893	69 787	378	92.6	110.2
05	38	1 452 770	142 092	74 095	67 660	337	89.1	109.5
06	39	1 394 295	149 731	78 262	71 104	365	97.0	110.1
07	40	1 614 472	158 814	82 920	75 415	479	89.6	110.0
08	41	1 662 815	162 676	85 729	76 585	362	89.1	111.9
09	42	1 693 850	161 576	85 228	75 938	410	87.1	112.2
1910	43	1 712 857	157 392	83 214	73 808	370	84.2	112.7
11	44	1 747 803	155 319	82 515	72 362	442	81.6	114.0
12	大正元年	1 737 674	147 545	78 492	68 604	449	78.3	114.4
13	2	1 757 441	147 769	78 253	69 074	442	77.6	113.3
14	3	1 808 402	145 692	77 565	67 737	390	74.6	114.5
15	4	1 799 326	141 301	75 285	65 604	412	72.8	114.8
16	5	1 804 822	139 998	74 760	64 829	409	72.0	115.3
17	6	1 812 413	140 328	75 477	64 446	405	71.9	117.1
18	7	1 791 992	142 507	76 021	66 116	370	73.7	115.0
19	8	1 778 685	132 939	71 628	60 918	393	69.5	117.6
1920	9	2 025 564	144 038	77 540	66 202	296	66.4	117.1
21	10	1 990 876	138 301	74 665	63 296	340	65.0	118.0
22	11	1 969 314	132 244	71 327	60 566	351	62.9	117.8
23	12	2 043 297	133 863	72 126	61 312	425	61.5	117.6
24	13	1 998 520	125 839	67 777	57 707	355	59.2	117.5
25	14	2 086 091	124 403	67 580	56 506	317	56.3	119.6
26	昭和元年	2 104 405	124 038	67 562	56 136	340	55.7	120.4
27	2	2 060 737	116 922	63 401	53 140	381	53.7	119.3
28	3	2 135 852	120 191	65 339	54 432	420	53.3	120.0
29	4	2 077 026	116 971	63 553	52 992	426	53.3	119.9
1930	5	2 085 101	117 730	63 955	53 282	493	53.4	120.0
31	6	2 102 784	116 509	63 614	52 463	432	52.5	121.3
32	7	2 182 742	119 579	64 932	54 192	455	51.9	119.8
33	8	2 121 253	114 138	62 080	51 521	537	51.1	120.5
34	9	2 043 783	113 043	61 374	51 075	594	52.4	120.2
35	10	2 190 704	115 593	62 508	52 410	675	50.1	119.3
36	11	2 101 969	111 056	60 425	50 008	623	50.2	120.8
37	12	2 180 734	111 485	60 578	50 214	693	48.6	120.6
38	13	1 928 321	99 528	54 079	44 873	576	49.1	120.5
39	14	1 901 573	98 349	53 510	44 148	691	49.2	121.2
1940	15	2 115 867	102 034	55 042	46 296	696	46.0	118.9
41	16	2 277 283	103 400	56 274	46 318	808	43.4	121.5
42	17	2 233 660	95 448	…	…	…	41.0	…
43	18	2 253 535	92 889	…	…	…	39.6	…
47	22	2 678 792	123 837	65 437	53 181	5 219	44.2	123.0
48	23	2 681 624	143 963	75 990	61 130	6 843	50.9	124.3
49	24	2 696 638	192 677	100 696	79 493	12 488	66.7	126.7
1950	25	2 337 507	216 974	111 359	86 908	18 707	84.9	128.1
51	26	2 137 689	217 231	110 916	86 841	19 474	92.2	127.7
52	27	2 005 162	203 824	104 417	81 925	17 482	92.3	127.5
53	28	1 868 040	193 274	99 472	77 241	16 561	93.8	128.8
54	29	1 769 580	187 119	96 175	74 521	16 423	95.6	129.1

注：1）　昭和19～21年は資料不備のため省略した。
　　　　昭和22～47年は沖縄県を含まない。

444

Foetal mortality

・率（出産千対）及び死産性比
(per 1,000 total births) and sex ratio : Japan

年　　次[1] Year		出　生　数 Live births	死　　産　　数 Foetal deaths				死産率 Foetal death rates	死産性比 Sex ratio of foetal deaths
			総　数 Total	男 Male	女 Female	不　詳 Not stated		
1955	昭和30年	1 730 692	183 265	94 334	72 781	16 150	95. 8	129. 6
56	31	1 665 278	179 007	92 089	71 741	15 177	97. 1	128. 4
57	32	1 566 713	176 353	90 493	70 649	15 211	101. 2	128. 1
58	33	1 653 469	185 148	94 786	74 174	16 188	100. 7	127. 8
59	34	1 626 088	181 893	93 181	72 719	15 993	100. 6	128. 1
1960	35	1 606 041	179 281	91 160	71 775	16 346	100. 4	127. 0
61	36	1 589 372	179 895	91 093	71 239	17 563	101. 7	127. 9
62	37	1 618 616	177 363	89 210	70 095	18 058	98. 8	127. 3
63	38	1 659 521	175 424	88 245	68 698	18 481	95. 6	128. 5
64	39	1 716 761	168 046	83 697	65 730	18 619	89. 2	127. 3
65	40	1 823 697	161 617	80 559	62 379	18 679	81. 4	129. 1
66	41	1 360 974	148 248	72 739	56 602	18 907	98. 2	128. 5
67	42	1 935 647	149 389	73 485	56 848	19 056	71. 6	129. 3
68	43	1 871 839	143 259	69 743	53 349	20 167	71. 1	130. 7
69	44	1 889 815	139 211	66 770	50 202	22 239	68. 6	133. 0
1970	45	1 934 239	135 095	63 684	48 166	23 245	65. 3	132. 2
71	46	2 000 973	130 920	60 144	45 413	25 363	61. 4	132. 4
72	47	2 038 682	125 154	56 714	41 707	26 733	57. 8	136. 0
73	48	2 091 983	116 171	51 653	37 470	27 048	52. 6	137. 9
74	49	2 029 989	109 738	47 526	34 680	27 532	51. 3	137. 0
75	50	1 901 440	101 862	44 026	32 010	25 826	50. 8	137. 5
76	51	1 832 617	101 930	43 015	30 559	28 356	52. 7	140. 8
77	52	1 755 100	95 247	39 590	28 077	27 580	51. 5	141. 0
78	53	1 708 643	87 463	36 358	25 530	25 575	48. 7	142. 4
79	54	1 642 580	82 311	35 133	24 054	23 124	47. 7	146. 1
1980	55	1 576 889	77 446	33 450	22 098	21 898	46. 8	151. 4
81	56	1 529 455	79 222	33 761	21 829	23 632	49. 2	154. 7
82	57	1 515 392	78 107	33 394	21 018	23 695	49. 0	158. 9
83	58	1 508 687	71 941	30 352	19 589	22 000	45. 5	154. 9
84	59	1 489 780	72 361	31 661	19 626	21 074	46. 3	161. 3
85	60	1 431 577	69 009	30 701	18 376	19 932	46. 0	167. 1
86	61	1 382 946	65 678	29 107	17 156	19 415	45. 3	169. 7
87	62	1 346 658	63 834	28 480	15 959	19 395	45. 3	178. 5
88	63	1 314 006	59 636	26 553	14 947	18 136	43. 4	177. 6
89	平成元年	1 246 802	55 204	24 406	13 375	17 423	42. 4	182. 5
1990	2	1 221 585	53 892	23 901	12 564	17 427	42. 3	190. 2
91	3	1 223 245	50 510	22 062	11 603	16 845	39. 7	190. 1
92	4	1 208 989	48 896	21 148	10 845	16 903	38. 9	195. 0
93	5	1 188 282	45 090	19 808	9 987	15 295	36. 6	198. 3
94	6	1 238 328	42 962	18 818	9 510	14 634	33. 5	197. 9
95	7	1 187 064	39 403	17 891	8 704	12 808	32. 1	205. 5
96	8	1 206 555	39 536	17 825	8 711	13 000	31. 7	204. 6
97	9	1 191 665	39 546	17 671	8 397	13 478	32. 1	210. 4
98	10	1 203 147	38 988	17 588	8 346	13 054	31. 4	210. 7
99	11	1 177 669	38 452	17 267	8 250	12 935	31. 6	209. 3
2000	12	1 190 547	38 393	17 307	7 975	13 111	31. 2	217. 0
01	13	1 170 662	37 467	16 733	7 499	13 235	31. 0	223. 1
02	14	1 153 855	36 978	16 602	7 501	12 875	31. 1	221. 3
03	15	1 123 610	35 330	15 658	7 071	12 601	30. 5	221. 4
04	16	1 110 721	34 365	15 352	6 845	12 168	30. 0	224. 3
05	17	1 062 530	31 818	13 979	6 104	11 735	29. 1	229. 0
06	18	1 092 674	30 911	13 456	6 005	11 450	27. 5	224. 1
07	19	1 089 818	29 313	12 878	5 694	10 741	26. 2	226. 2
08	20	1 091 156	28 177	12 381	5 498	10 298	25. 2	225. 2
09	21	1 070 035	27 005	11 952	5 305	9 748	24. 6	225. 3
2010	22	1 071 304	26 560	11 796	5 216	9 548	24. 2	226. 2
11	23	1 050 806	25 751	11 420	5 061	9 270	23. 9	225. 6
12	24	1 037 231	24 800	11 015	4 995	8 790	23. 4	220. 5
13	25	1 029 816	24 102	10 456	4 824	8 822	22. 9	216. 7
14	26	1 003 539	23 524	10 255	4 652	8 617	22. 9	220. 4
15	27	1 005 677	22 617	10 102	4 660	7 855	22. 0	216. 8
16	28	976 978	20 934	9 348	4 454	7 132	21. 0	209. 9

445

死　産

表7.2　年次別にみた市部－郡部・自然－人工別死産数
Table 7.2　Trends in foetal deaths by type of extraction : Japan, urban／rural residence

年　　次 Year		全　　国[1] Total			市　　部 Urban residence			郡　　部 Rural residence		
		総　数 Total	自然死産 Spontaneous	人工死産 Artificial	総　数 Total	自然死産 Spontaneous	人工死産 Artificial	総　数 Total	自然死産 Spontaneous	人工死産 Artificial
1955	昭和30年	183 265	85 159	98 106	105 907	48 416	57 491	77 304	36 702	40 602
1960	35	179 281	93 424	85 857	120 670	64 112	56 558	58 543	29 254	29 289
65	40	161 617	94 476	67 141	118 261	70 773	47 488	43 268	23 625	19 643
66	41	148 248	83 253	64 995	109 087	62 718	46 369	39 061	20 446	18 615
67	42	149 389	90 938	58 451	111 759	69 387	42 372	37 508	21 441	16 067
68	43	143 259	87 381	55 878	108 347	67 342	41 005	34 819	19 970	14 849
69	44	139 211	85 788	53 423	105 250	66 062	39 188	33 795	19 610	14 185
1970	45	135 095	84 073	51 022	103 035	65 229	37 806	31 886	18 730	13 156
71	46	130 920	83 827	47 093	101 481	65 961	35 520	29 293	17 764	11 529
72	47	125 154	81 741	43 413	98 536	65 338	33 198	26 549	16 354	10 195
73	48	116 171	78 613	37 558	91 417	62 657	28 760	24 685	15 903	8 782
74	49	109 738	74 618	35 120	86 598	59 420	27 178	23 069	15 144	7 925
75	50	101 862	67 643	34 219	80 052	53 590	26 462	21 752	14 003	7 749
76	51	101 930	64 046	37 884	80 607	50 677	29 930	21 265	13 320	7 945
77	52	95 247	60 330	34 917	74 503	47 425	27 078	20 689	12 857	7 832
78	53	87 463	55 818	31 645	68 408	43 788	24 620	19 000	11 983	7 017
79	54	82 311	51 083	31 228	64 251	40 044	24 207	18 009	11 000	7 009
1980	55	77 446	47 651	29 795	60 425	37 222	23 203	16 971	10 387	6 584
81	56	79 222	46 296	32 926	61 782	36 104	25 678	17 325	10 115	7 210
82	57	78 107	44 135	33 972	61 199	34 588	26 611	16 860	9 511	7 349
83	58	71 941	40 108	31 833	56 197	31 225	24 972	15 720	8 865	6 855
84	59	72 361	37 976	34 385	56 649	29 713	26 936	15 672	8 232	7 440
85	60	69 009	33 114	35 895	54 309	25 999	28 310	14 674	7 097	7 577
86	61	65 678	31 050	34 628	51 444	24 124	27 320	14 214	6 908	7 306
87	62	63 834	29 956	33 878	50 092	23 390	26 702	13 725	6 552	7 173
88	63	59 636	26 804	32 832	46 816	20 874	25 942	12 796	5 915	6 881
89	平成元年	55 204	24 558	30 646	43 543	19 241	24 302	11 637	5 301	6 336
1990	2	53 892	23 383	30 509	42 809	18 483	24 326	11 061	4 887	6 174
91	3	50 510	22 317	28 193	40 113	17 622	22 491	10 375	4 684	5 691
92	4	48 896	21 689	27 207	38 975	17 074	21 901	9 889	4 598	5 291
93	5	45 090	20 205	24 885	35 767	15 974	19 793	9 292	4 216	5 076
94	6	42 962	19 754	23 208	33 972	15 655	18 317	8 957	4 083	4 874
95	7	39 403	18 262	21 141	31 302	14 544	16 758	8 073	3 703	4 370
96	8	39 536	18 329	21 207	31 456	14 657	16 799	8 049	3 653	4 396
97	9	39 546	17 453	22 093	31 505	13 854	17 651	8 012	3 583	4 429
98	10	38 988	16 936	22 052	31 084	13 608	17 476	7 875	3 313	4 562
99	11	38 452	16 711	21 741	30 505	13 343	17 162	7 916	3 352	4 564
2000	12	38 393	16 200	22 193	30 519	12 978	17 541	7 845	3 206	4 639
01	13	37 467	15 704	21 763	29 967	12 705	17 262	7 468	2 987	4 481
02	14	36 978	15 161	21 817	29 548	12 223	17 325	7 412	2 926	4 486
03	15	35 330	14 644	20 686	28 362	11 848	16 514	6 940	2 784	4 156
04	16	34 365	14 288	20 077	27 994	11 653	16 341	6 348	2 626	3 722
05	17	31 818	13 502	18 316	27 254	11 606	15 648	4 545	1 889	2 656
06	18	30 911	13 424	17 487	27 628	12 059	15 569	3 258	1 354	1 904
07	19	29 313	13 107	16 206	26 425	11 806	14 619	2 873	1 294	1 579
08	20	28 177	12 625	15 552	25 465	11 393	14 072	2 688	1 221	1 467
09	21	27 005	12 214	14 791	24 447	11 051	13 396	2 545	1 157	1 388
2010	22	26 560	12 245	14 315	24 230	11 146	13 084	2 313	1 093	1 220
11	23	25 751	11 940	13 811	23 469	10 878	12 591	2 271	1 056	1 215
12	24	24 800	11 448	13 352	22 634	10 426	12 208	2 152	1 016	1 136
13	25	24 102	10 938	13 164	22 109	10 042	12 067	1 982	892	1 090
14	26	23 524	10 905	12 619	21 586	10 032	11 554	1 928	864	1 064
15	27	22 617	10 862	11 755	20 771	9 995	10 776	1 831	862	969
16	28	20 934	10 067	10 867	19 373	9 317	10 056	1 550	745	805

注：1)　市部・郡部の計が全国と異なるのは、平成3年以前は住所地不詳が、平成4年以降は住所地外国・不詳があるためである。

Foetal mortality

表7.3　年次別にみた市部－郡部・自然－人工別死産率（出産千対）及び全死産中人工死産の占める割合

Table 7.3　Trends in foetal death rates (per 1,000 total births) by type of extraction and proportion of artificial intervention : Japan, urban／rural residence

年　　次 Year		全　　国 Total				市　　部 Urban residence				郡　　部 Rural residence			
		総　数 Total	自然死産 Spontaneous	人工死産 Artificial	全死産中人工死産の占める割合(%) Proportion of artificial	総　数 Total	自然死産 Spontaneous	人工死産 Artificial	全死産中人工死産の占める割合(%) Proportion of artificial	総　数 Total	自然死産 Spontaneous	人工死産 Artificial	全死産中人工死産の占める割合(%) Proportion of artificial
1955	昭和30年	95.8	44.5	51.3	53.5	107.0	48.9	58.1	54.3	83.7	39.7	44.0	52.5
1960	35	100.4	52.3	48.1	47.9	106.4	56.5	49.9	46.9	89.9	44.9	45.0	50.0
65	40	81.4	47.6	33.8	41.5	82.6	49.4	33.2	40.2	78.1	42.6	35.5	45.4
66	41	98.2	55.2	43.1	43.8	98.6	56.7	41.9	42.5	97.0	50.8	46.2	47.7
67	42	71.6	43.6	28.0	39.1	72.4	44.9	27.4	37.9	69.4	39.7	29.7	42.8
68	43	71.1	43.4	27.7	39.0	71.5	44.4	27.1	37.8	69.7	40.0	29.7	42.6
69	44	68.6	42.3	26.3	38.4	68.6	43.0	25.5	37.2	68.4	39.7	28.7	42.0
1970	45	65.3	40.6	24.7	37.8	65.2	41.3	23.9	36.7	65.1	38.2	26.9	41.3
71	46	61.4	39.3	22.1	36.0	61.1	39.7	21.4	35.0	62.3	37.8	24.5	39.4
72	47	57.8	37.8	20.1	34.7	57.5	38.1	19.4	33.7	59.1	36.4	22.7	38.4
73	48	52.6	35.6	17.0	32.3	52.2	35.7	16.4	31.5	54.2	34.9	19.3	35.6
74	49	51.3	34.9	16.4	32.0	51.2	35.1	16.1	31.4	51.4	33.7	17.7	34.4
75	50	50.8	33.8	17.1	33.6	50.8	34.0	16.8	33.1	50.9	32.7	18.1	35.6
76	51	52.7	33.1	19.6	37.2	53.3	33.5	19.8	37.1	50.5	31.6	18.9	37.4
77	52	51.5	32.6	18.9	36.7	51.6	32.9	18.8	36.3	50.7	31.5	19.2	37.9
78	53	48.7	31.1	17.6	36.2	49.0	31.4	17.6	36.0	47.5	30.0	17.6	36.9
79	54	47.7	29.6	18.1	37.9	48.1	30.0	18.1	37.7	46.2	28.2	18.0	38.9
1980	55	46.8	28.8	18.0	38.5	47.3	29.2	18.2	38.4	44.9	27.5	17.4	38.8
81	56	49.2	28.8	20.5	41.6	49.7	29.1	20.7	41.6	47.3	27.6	19.7	41.6
82	57	49.0	27.7	21.3	43.5	49.7	28.1	21.6	43.5	46.5	26.2	20.3	43.6
83	58	45.5	25.4	20.1	44.2	46.1	25.6	20.5	44.4	43.6	24.6	19.0	43.6
84	59	46.3	24.3	22.0	47.5	46.9	24.6	22.3	47.5	44.2	23.2	21.0	47.5
85	60	46.0	22.1	23.9	52.0	46.7	22.4	24.4	52.1	43.4	21.0	22.4	51.6
86	61	45.3	21.4	23.9	52.7	45.7	21.4	24.3	53.1	43.9	21.3	22.6	51.4
87	62	45.3	21.2	24.0	53.1	45.6	21.3	24.3	53.3	43.9	21.0	23.0	52.3
88	63	43.4	19.5	23.9	55.1	43.5	19.4	24.1	55.4	42.9	19.8	23.1	53.8
89	平成元年	42.4	18.9	23.5	55.5	42.7	18.9	23.8	55.8	41.4	18.8	22.5	54.4
1990	2	42.3	18.3	23.9	56.6	42.7	18.4	24.2	56.8	40.7	18.0	22.7	55.8
91	3	39.7	17.5	22.1	55.8	39.9	17.5	22.4	56.1	38.8	17.5	21.3	54.9
92	4	38.9	17.2	21.6	55.6	39.0	17.1	21.9	56.2	38.1	17.7	20.4	53.5
93	5	36.6	16.4	20.2	55.2	36.4	16.3	20.2	55.3	36.9	16.8	20.2	54.6
94	6	33.5	15.4	18.1	54.0	33.2	15.3	17.9	53.9	34.6	15.8	18.8	54.4
95	7	32.1	14.9	17.2	53.7	31.9	14.8	17.1	53.5	32.8	15.0	17.7	54.1
96	8	31.7	14.7	17.0	53.6	31.5	14.7	16.8	53.4	32.6	14.8	17.8	54.6
97	9	32.1	14.2	17.9	55.9	31.8	14.0	17.8	56.0	33.2	14.9	18.4	55.3
98	10	31.4	13.6	17.8	56.6	31.0	13.6	17.4	56.2	32.8	13.8	19.0	57.9
99	11	31.6	13.7	17.9	56.5	31.1	13.6	17.5	56.3	33.9	14.3	19.5	57.7
2000	12	31.2	13.2	18.1	57.8	30.7	13.1	17.7	57.5	33.3	13.6	19.7	59.1
01	13	31.0	13.0	18.0	58.1	30.6	13.0	17.7	57.6	32.4	13.0	19.5	60.0
02	14	31.1	12.7	18.3	59.0	30.5	12.6	17.9	58.6	33.4	13.2	20.2	60.5
03	15	30.5	12.6	17.8	58.6	30.0	12.6	17.5	58.2	32.6	13.1	19.5	59.9
04	16	30.0	12.5	17.5	58.4	29.6	12.3	17.3	58.4	31.6	13.1	18.6	58.6
05	17	29.1	12.3	16.7	57.6	28.8	12.3	16.6	57.4	30.5	12.7	17.8	58.4
06	18	27.5	11.9	15.6	56.6	27.3	11.9	15.4	56.4	29.2	12.2	17.1	58.4
07	19	26.2	11.7	14.5	55.3	26.1	11.6	14.4	55.3	27.4	12.4	15.1	55.0
08	20	25.2	11.3	13.9	55.2	25.0	11.2	13.8	55.3	26.3	11.9	14.4	54.6
09	21	24.6	11.1	13.5	54.8	24.5	11.1	13.4	54.8	25.8	11.7	14.1	54.5
2010	22	24.2	11.2	13.0	53.9	24.1	11.1	13.0	54.0	24.9	11.8	13.1	52.7
11	23	23.9	11.1	12.8	53.6	23.8	11.0	12.8	53.6	25.5	11.9	13.6	53.5
12	24	23.4	10.8	12.6	53.8	23.2	10.7	12.5	53.9	25.2	11.9	13.3	52.8
13	25	22.9	10.4	12.5	54.6	22.8	10.3	12.4	54.6	23.8	10.7	13.1	55.0
14	26	22.9	10.6	12.3	53.6	22.8	10.6	12.2	53.5	24.4	10.9	13.4	55.2
15	27	22.0	10.6	11.4	52.0	21.9	10.5	11.3	51.9	23.3	11.0	12.3	52.9
16	28	21.0	10.1	10.9	51.9	21.0	10.1	10.9	51.9	20.5	9.9	10.6	51.9

447

死　産

表 7.4　年次別にみた自然－人工別妊娠満22週以後の死産数・妊娠満22週以後の死産率（出産千対）及び全死産中妊娠満22週以後の死産の占める割合
Table 7.4　Trends in foetal deaths, foetal death rates at 22 completed weeks and over of gestation[a] and proportion by type of extraction : Japan

年　次 Year		総　数 Total			自然死産 Spontaneous			人工死産 Artificial		
		妊娠満22週以後死産数 Foetal deaths at 22 completed weeks and over of gestation	妊娠満22週以後死産率 Foetal death rates at 22 completed weeks and over of gestation	全死産中妊娠満22週以後の死産の占める割合（%）Proportion of foetal deaths at 22 completed weeks and over of gestation	妊娠満22週以後死産数 Foetal deaths at 22 completed weeks and over of gestation	妊娠満22週以後死産率 Foetal death rates at 22 completed weeks and over of gestation	全死産中妊娠満22週以後の死産の占める割合（%）Proportion of foetal deaths at 22 completed weeks and over of gestation	妊娠満22週以後死産数 Foetal deaths at 22 completed weeks and over of gestation	妊娠満22週以後死産率 Foetal death rates at 22 completed weeks and over of gestation	全死産中妊娠満22週以後の死産の占める割合（%）Proportion of foetal deaths at 22 completed weeks and over of gestation
1979	昭和54年	29 289	17.5	35.6	24 041	14.4	47.1	5 248	3.1	16.8
80	55	26 268	16.4	33.9	21 602	13.5	45.3	4 666	2.9	15.7
81	56	24 672	15.9	31.1	19 860	12.8	42.9	4 812	3.1	14.6
82	57	23 137	15.0	29.6	18 405	12.0	41.7	4 732	3.1	13.9
83	58	21 354	14.0	29.7	16 965	11.1	42.3	4 389	2.9	13.8
84	59	20 875	13.8	28.8	16 062	10.6	42.3	4 813	3.2	14.0
85	60	18 642	12.9	27.0	13 840	9.5	41.8	4 802	3.3	13.4
86	61	17 143	12.2	26.1	12 599	9.0	40.6	4 544	3.2	13.1
87	62	15 634	11.5	24.5	11 665	8.6	38.9	3 969	2.9	11.7
88	63	14 090	10.6	23.6	10 501	7.9	39.2	3 589	2.7	10.9
89	平成元年	12 797	10.2	23.2	9 450	7.5	38.5	3 347	2.7	10.9
1990	2	11 367	9.2	21.1	8 782	7.1	37.6	2 585	2.1	8.5
91	3	8 258	6.7	16.3	7 873	6.4	35.3	385	0.3	1.4
92	4	7 758	6.4	15.9	7 466	6.1	34.4	292	0.2	1.1
93	5	7 191	6.0	15.9	6 972	5.8	34.5	219	0.2	0.9
94	6	7 200	5.8	16.8	7 090	5.7	35.9	110	0.1	0.5
95	7	6 580	5.5	16.7	6 511	5.5	35.7	69	0.1	0.3
96	8	6 333	5.2	16.0	6 291	5.2	34.3	42	0.0	0.2
97	9	6 009	5.0	15.2	5 969	5.0	34.2	40	0.0	0.2
98	10	5 804	4.8	14.9	5 772	4.8	34.1	32	0.0	0.1
99	11	5 567	4.7	14.5	5 532	4.7	33.1	35	0.0	0.2
2000	12	5 362	4.5	14.0	5 327	4.5	32.9	35	0.0	0.2
01	13	5 114	4.3	13.6	5 091	4.3	32.4	23	0.0	0.1
02	14	4 959	4.3	13.4	4 931	4.3	32.5	28	0.0	0.1
03	15	4 626	4.1	13.1	4 616	4.1	31.5	10	0.0	0.0
04	16	4 357	3.9	12.7	4 347	3.9	30.4	10	0.0	0.0
05	17	4 058	3.8	12.8	4 048	3.8	30.0	10	0.0	0.1
06	18	4 047	3.7	13.1	4 031	3.7	30.0	16	0.0	0.1
07	19	3 854	3.5	13.1	3 842	3.5	29.3	12	0.0	0.1
08	20	3 751	3.4	13.3	3 742	3.4	29.6	9	0.0	0.1
09	21	3 645	3.4	13.5	3 633	3.4	29.7	12	0.0	0.1
2010	22	3 637	3.4	13.7	3 617	3.4	29.5	20	0.0	0.1
11	23	3 491	3.3	13.6	3 480	3.3	29.1	11	0.0	0.1
12	24	3 343	3.2	13.5	3 334	3.2	29.1	9	0.0	0.1
13	25	3 110	3.0	12.9	3 110	3.0	28.4	-	-	-
14	26	3 039	3.0	12.9	3 038	3.0	27.9	1	0.0	0.0
15	27	3 063	3.0	13.5	3 061	3.0	28.2	2	0.0	0.0
16	28	2 840	2.9	13.6	2 839	2.9	28.2	1	0.0	0.0

Note : a) Per 1,000 live births and foetal deaths at 22 completed weeks and over of gestation.

死 産

〔妊娠期間別にみた死産〕
〔Foetal deaths by period of gestation〕

表7.5　妊娠期間別にみた自然
Table 7.5　Trends in foetal deaths and percent distribution by

年　次 Year		総　数 Total	満12週～ 15週 12－15 completed weeks	16～19	20～23	24～27	28～31	32～35	36～39	40～ 40 completed weeks and over	不　詳 Not stated
		死	産	数	Total foetal deaths						
1955	昭和30年	183 265	16 099	44 932	43 468	25 469	13 100	10 046	29 814	337	-
60	35	179 281	15 493	43 126	44 881	26 269	11 886	8 611	28 641	374	-
65	40	161 617	16 195	42 097	40 226	23 144	9 721	7 001	22 901	332	-
70	45	135 095	18 902	36 720	32 049	18 317	6 911	5 593	16 239	364	-
75	50	101 862	21 832	26 844	21 294	11 615	4 576	4 106	11 268	318	9
80	55	77 446	20 237	21 838	18 414	4 705	2 828	3 013	3 842	2 548	21
85	60	69 009	22 124	20 212	15 855	3 056	1 943	2 071	2 478	1 241	29
90	平成2年	53 892	19 665	16 455	11 252	1 827	1 337	1 248	1 530	549	29
95	7	39 403	14 460	12 509	7 187	1 536	1 005	1 024	1 264	401	17
2000	12	38 393	14 968	12 236	6 863	1 276	820	873	1 051	299	7
05	17	31 818	12 974	10 073	5 489	879	587	674	882	258	2
10	22	26 560	10 430	8 420	4 663	857	533	612	819	223	3
14	26	23 524	8 894	7 684	4 445	709	493	494	657	146	2
15	27	22 617	8 187	7 461	4 416	721	483	521	664	162	2
16	28	20 934	7 602	6 856	4 112	661	419	478	662	140	4
		自	然 死	産	Spontaneous foetal deaths						
1955	昭和30年	85 159	3 242	9 824	12 192	11 735	10 764	9 140	27 991	271	-
60	35	93 424	4 568	13 556	16 179	13 229	10 099	7 918	27 523	352	-
65	40	94 476	6 290	17 621	18 707	13 631	8 809	6 690	22 409	319	-
70	45	84 073	8 971	17 632	17 128	11 808	6 594	5 477	16 102	361	-
75	50	67 643	12 071	14 642	12 602	8 284	4 466	4 050	11 203	316	9
80	55	47 651	10 085	11 084	9 731	4 602	2 775	2 984	3 826	2 545	19
85	60	33 114	8 030	7 894	6 533	2 996	1 887	2 039	2 470	1 241	24
90	平成2年	23 383	5 831	6 111	4 988	1 792	1 317	1 240	1 527	548	29
95	7	18 262	4 408	4 961	3 687	1 512	997	1 018	1 264	401	14
2000	12	16 200	4 068	4 615	3 213	1 260	815	872	1 051	299	7
05	17	13 502	3 886	3 852	2 487	874	587	674	882	258	2
10	22	12 245	3 698	3 509	2 006	845	531	611	819	223	3
14	26	10 905	3 394	3 207	1 803	709	493	494	657	146	2
15	27	10 862	3 290	3 253	1 766	721	483	521	664	162	2
16	28	10 067	3 109	2 946	1 649	660	419	478	662	140	4
		人	工 死	産	Artificial foetal deaths						
1955	昭和30年	98 106	12 857	35 108	31 276	13 734	2 336	906	1 823	66	-
60	35	85 857	10 925	29 570	28 702	13 040	1 787	693	1 118	22	-
65	40	67 141	9 905	24 476	21 519	9 513	912	311	492	13	-
70	45	51 022	9 931	19 088	14 921	6 509	317	116	137	3	-
75	50	34 219	9 761	12 202	8 692	3 331	110	56	65	2	-
80	55	29 795	10 152	10 754	8 683	103	53	29	16	3	2
85	60	35 895	14 094	12 318	9 322	60	56	32	8	-	5
90	平成2年	30 509	13 834	10 344	6 264	35	20	8	3	1	
95	7	21 141	10 052	7 548	3 500	24	8	6	-	-	3
2000	12	22 193	10 900	7 621	3 650	16	5	1	-	-	
05	17	18 316	9 088	6 221	3 002	5	-	-	-	-	
10	22	14 315	6 732	4 911	2 657	12	2	1	-	-	
14	26	12 619	5 500	4 477	2 642	-	-	-	-	-	
15	27	11 755	4 897	4 208	2 650	-	-	-	-	-	
16	28	10 867	4 493	3 910	2 463	1	-	-	-	-	

Foetal mortality

－人工・年次別死産数及び百分率
period of gestation and type of extraction : Japan

年　　次 Year		総　数 Total	満12週～ 15週 12－15 completed weeks	16～19	20～23	24～27	28～31	32～35	36～39	40～ 40 completed weeks and over	不　詳 Not stated
		百　　分　　率　　Percentage									
1955	昭和30年	100.0	8.8	24.5	23.7	13.9	7.1	5.5	16.3	0.2	-
60	35	100.0	8.6	24.1	25.0	14.7	6.6	4.8	16.0	0.2	-
65	40	100.0	10.0	26.0	24.9	14.3	6.0	4.3	14.2	0.2	-
70	45	100.0	14.0	27.2	23.7	13.6	5.1	4.1	12.0	0.3	-
75	50	100.0	21.4	26.4	20.9	11.4	4.5	4.0	11.1	0.3	0.0
80	55	100.0	26.1	28.2	23.8	6.1	3.7	3.9	5.0	3.3	0.0
85	60	100.0	32.1	29.3	23.0	4.4	2.8	3.0	3.6	1.8	0.0
90	平成2年	100.0	36.5	30.5	20.9	3.4	2.5	2.3	2.8	1.0	0.1
95	7	100.0	36.7	31.7	18.2	3.9	2.6	2.6	3.2	1.0	0.0
2000	12	100.0	39.0	31.9	17.9	3.3	2.1	2.3	2.7	0.8	0.0
05	17	100.0	40.8	31.7	17.3	2.8	1.8	2.1	2.8	0.8	0.0
10	22	100.0	39.3	31.7	17.6	3.2	2.0	2.3	3.1	0.8	0.0
14	26	100.0	37.8	32.7	18.9	3.0	2.1	2.1	2.8	0.6	0.0
15	27	100.0	36.2	33.0	19.5	3.2	2.1	2.3	2.9	0.7	0.0
16	**28**	**100.0**	**36.3**	**32.8**	**19.6**	**3.2**	**2.0**	**2.3**	**3.2**	**0.7**	**0.0**
		自　　然　　死　　産　　Spontaneous foetal deaths									
1955	昭和30年	100.0	3.8	11.5	14.3	13.8	12.6	10.7	32.9	0.3	-
60	35	100.0	4.9	14.5	17.3	14.2	10.8	8.5	29.5	0.4	-
65	40	100.0	6.7	18.7	19.8	14.4	9.3	7.1	23.7	0.3	-
70	45	100.0	10.7	21.0	20.4	14.0	7.8	6.5	19.2	0.4	-
75	50	100.0	17.8	21.6	18.6	12.2	6.6	6.0	16.6	0.5	0.0
80	55	100.0	21.2	23.3	20.4	9.7	5.8	6.3	8.0	5.3	0.0
85	60	100.0	24.2	23.8	19.7	9.0	5.7	6.2	7.5	3.7	0.1
90	平成2年	100.0	24.9	26.1	21.3	7.7	5.6	5.3	6.5	2.3	0.1
95	7	100.0	24.1	27.2	20.2	8.3	5.5	5.6	6.9	2.2	0.1
2000	12	100.0	25.1	28.5	19.8	7.8	5.0	5.4	6.5	1.8	0.0
05	17	100.0	28.8	28.5	18.4	6.5	4.3	5.0	6.5	1.9	0.0
10	22	100.0	30.2	28.7	16.4	6.9	4.3	5.0	6.7	1.8	0.0
14	26	100.0	31.1	29.4	16.5	6.5	4.5	4.5	6.0	1.3	0.0
15	27	100.0	30.3	29.9	16.3	6.6	4.4	4.8	6.1	1.5	0.0
16	**28**	**100.0**	**30.9**	**29.3**	**16.4**	**6.6**	**4.2**	**4.7**	**6.6**	**1.4**	**0.0**
		人　　工　　死　　産　　Artificial foetal deaths									
1955	昭和30年	100.0	13.1	35.8	31.9	14.0	2.4	0.9	1.9	0.1	-
60	35	100.0	12.7	34.4	33.4	15.2	2.1	0.8	1.3	0.0	-
65	40	100.0	14.8	36.5	32.1	14.2	1.4	0.5	0.7	0.0	-
70	45	100.0	19.5	37.4	29.2	12.8	0.6	0.2	0.3	0.0	-
75	50	100.0	28.5	35.7	25.4	9.7	0.3	0.2	0.2	0.0	-
80	55	100.0	34.1	36.1	29.1	0.3	0.2	0.1	0.1	0.0	0.0
85	60	100.0	39.3	34.3	26.0	0.2	0.2	0.1	0.0	-	0.0
90	平成2年	100.0	45.3	33.9	20.5	0.1	0.1	0.0	0.0	0.0	-
95	7	100.0	47.5	35.7	16.6	0.1	0.0	0.0	-	-	0.0
2000	12	100.0	49.1	34.3	16.4	0.1	0.0	0.0	-	-	-
05	17	100.0	49.6	34.0	16.4	0.0	-	-	-	-	-
10	22	100.0	47.0	34.3	18.6	0.1	0.0	0.0	-	-	-
14	26	100.0	43.6	35.5	20.9	-	-	-	-	-	-
15	27	100.0	41.7	35.8	22.5	-	-	-	-	-	-
16	**28**	**100.0**	**41.3**	**36.0**	**22.7**	**0.0**	**-**	**-**	**-**	**-**	**-**

死　産

〔月別にみた死産〕
〔Foetal deaths by month〕

表 7.6　月別にみた自然－人工・年次別
Table 7.6　Trends in foetal deaths and foetal death rates

年　　　次		総　　数 2)	1　月	2　月	3　月	4　月	5　月
	Year	Total	January	February	March	April	May
		死					産
1955	昭和30年	183 265	15 871	15 684	16 796	15 117	15 209
60	35	179 281	15 613	15 787	15 838	14 338	14 158
65	40	161 617	14 517	13 488	14 237	13 659	13 698
70	45	135 095	12 013	11 643	12 031	11 470	11 240
75	50	101 862	8 883	8 540	9 145	8 613	8 752
80	55	77 446	6 590	6 711	6 884	6 644	6 723
85	60	69 009	6 000	5 929	6 208	6 020	6 177
90	平成 2 年	53 892	4 761	4 576	5 125	4 574	4 583
95	7	39 403	3 311	3 347	3 775	3 225	3 325
2000	12	38 393	3 200	3 274	3 612	3 175	3 120
05	17	31 818	2 686	2 721	3 038	2 812	2 563
10	22	26 560	2 259	2 070	2 363	2 315	2 158
14	26	23 524	1 994	1 919	2 098	1 915	2 023
15	27	22 617	1 875	1 856	2 021	1 933	1 793
16	**28**	**20 934**	**1 728**	**1 732**	**1 909**	**1 785**	**1 825**
		自	然	死			産
1955	昭和30年	85 159	8 143	7 242	7 584	6 945	6 947
60	35	93 424	8 435	7 926	8 219	7 573	7 574
65	40	94 476	8 555	7 803	8 597	8 115	8 375
70	45	84 073	7 405	6 878	7 499	7 058	7 070
75	50	67 643	5 863	5 563	6 045	5 667	5 879
80	55	47 651	4 112	4 031	4 169	4 109	4 119
85	60	33 114	2 842	2 731	2 906	2 850	2 883
90	平成 2 年	23 383	2 120	1 870	2 156	2 005	1 931
95	7	18 262	1 533	1 394	1 666	1 533	1 558
2000	12	16 200	1 354	1 262	1 453	1 333	1 370
05	17	13 502	1 117	1 086	1 175	1 164	1 098
10	22	12 245	988	924	1 040	1 057	998
14	26	10 905	922	862	940	849	967
15	27	10 862	870	846	900	905	864
16	**28**	**10 067**	**859**	**804**	**906**	**851**	**888**
		人	工	死			産
1955	昭和30年	98 106	7 728	8 442	9 212	8 172	8 262
60	35	85 857	7 178	7 861	7 619	6 765	6 584
65	40	67 141	5 962	5 685	5 640	5 544	5 323
70	45	51 022	4 608	4 765	4 532	4 412	4 170
75	50	34 219	3 020	2 977	3 100	2 946	2 873
80	55	29 795	2 478	2 680	2 715	2 535	2 604
85	60	35 895	3 158	3 198	3 302	3 170	3 294
90	平成 2 年	30 509	2 641	2 706	2 969	2 569	2 652
95	7	21 141	1 778	1 953	2 109	1 692	1 767
2000	12	22 193	1 846	2 012	2 159	1 842	1 750
05	17	18 316	1 569	1 635	1 863	1 648	1 465
10	22	14 315	1 271	1 146	1 323	1 258	1 160
14	26	12 619	1 072	1 057	1 158	1 066	1 056
15	27	11 755	1 005	1 010	1 121	1 028	929
16	**28**	**10 867**	**869**	**928**	**1 003**	**934**	**937**

注：1)　計算方法は、69ページ 5)死産を参照されたい。
　　2)　昭和42年以前は月不詳があり、総数に含む。

死産数及び死産率[1] （出産千対）
(per 1,000 total births) by type of extraction by month : Japan

6　月 June	7　月 July	8　月 August	9　月 September	10　月 October	11　月 November	12　月 December
数　　Total foetal deaths						
13 449	15 290	15 991	15 700	14 404	14 344	15 410
13 651	15 162	15 389	15 490	14 724	14 495	14 632
13 117	13 886	13 627	13 238	13 251	12 326	12 565
10 579	11 635	10 834	11 479	11 471	10 102	10 598
8 246	8 886	8 584	8 396	8 419	7 507	7 891
6 141	6 599	6 337	6 273	6 460	5 888	6 196
5 537	5 642	5 474	5 602	5 825	5 298	5 297
4 284	4 361	4 369	4 351	4 516	4 299	4 093
3 224	3 134	3 247	3 345	3 219	3 085	3 166
3 116	3 077	3 372	3 134	3 173	3 089	3 051
2 532	2 504	2 728	2 640	2 556	2 528	2 510
2 250	2 302	2 224	2 342	2 147	1 966	2 164
1 910	2 004	1 988	1 941	2 061	1 745	1 926
1 918	1 913	1 809	1 984	1 993	1 649	1 873
1 827	**1 605**	**1 774**	**1 733**	**1 737**	**1 674**	**1 605**
数　　Spontaneous foetal deaths						
6 395	6 969	7 008	6 763	6 859	6 816	7 488
7 200	7 686	7 732	7 680	7 748	7 620	8 027
7 921	8 267	7 993	7 464	7 517	6 706	7 155
6 805	7 198	6 866	6 987	7 097	6 389	6 821
5 546	5 857	5 756	5 464	5 539	5 057	5 407
3 830	4 118	3 974	3 876	3 902	3 673	3 738
2 746	2 806	2 701	2 709	2 722	2 615	2 603
1 831	1 966	1 975	1 909	1 940	1 877	1 803
1 517	1 482	1 547	1 530	1 517	1 498	1 487
1 320	1 421	1 388	1 279	1 350	1 338	1 332
1 095	1 081	1 212	1 120	1 184	1 088	1 082
1 020	1 083	1 073	1 081	1 037	918	1 026
904	963	927	899	932	828	912
934	984	922	971	939	791	936
871	**766**	**890**	**829**	**872**	**756**	**775**
数　　Artificial foetal deaths						
7 054	8 321	8 983	8 937	7 545	7 528	7 922
6 451	7 476	7 657	7 810	6 976	6 875	6 605
5 196	5 619	5 634	5 774	5 734	5 620	5 410
3 774	4 437	3 968	4 492	4 374	3 713	3 777
2 700	3 029	2 828	2 932	2 880	2 450	2 484
2 311	2 481	2 363	2 397	2 558	2 215	2 458
2 791	2 836	2 773	2 893	3 103	2 683	2 694
2 453	2 395	2 394	2 442	2 576	2 422	2 290
1 707	1 652	1 700	1 815	1 702	1 587	1 679
1 796	1 656	1 984	1 855	1 823	1 751	1 719
1 437	1 423	1 516	1 520	1 372	1 440	1 428
1 230	1 219	1 151	1 261	1 110	1 048	1 138
1 006	1 041	1 061	1 042	1 129	917	1 014
984	929	887	1 013	1 054	858	937
956	**839**	**884**	**904**	**865**	**918**	**830**

死　産

表 7.6　月別にみた自然－人工・年次別
Table 7.6　Trends in foetal deaths and foetal death rates

年　　次 Year		総　数 [2] Total	1　月 January	2　月 February	3　月 March	4　月 April	5　月 May
		死　　　　　産					
1955	昭和30年	95.8	73.5	90.8	96.8	92.6	103.1
60	35	100.4	85.6	99.6	95.8	90.4	100.3
65	40	81.4	79.9	81.8	82.0	81.1	89.0
70	45	65.3	64.4	69.9	68.3	64.6	65.3
75	50	50.8	50.2	52.9	54.1	51.1	51.5
80	55	46.8	46.3	50.9	50.4	49.3	47.7
85	60	46.0	47.5	50.9	51.1	49.8	48.6
90	平成 2 年	42.3	43.7	47.1	48.2	44.0	41.3
95	7	32.1	31.2	35.7	37.0	32.7	31.7
2000	12	31.2	30.6	33.8	35.2	32.4	30.2
05	17	29.1	28.1	32.5	32.8	31.6	28.6
10	22	24.2	24.3	24.8	26.2	25.8	24.3
14	26	22.9	23.3	25.3	25.8	23.7	23.7
15	27	22.0	21.6	23.8	24.1	22.7	20.9
16	**28**	**21.0**	**20.6**	**22.1**	**23.0**	**21.9**	**22.1**
		自　　然　　死　　産					
1955	昭和30年	44.5	37.7	41.9	43.7	42.6	47.1
60	35	52.3	46.2	50.0	49.7	47.8	53.7
65	40	47.6	47.1	47.3	49.5	48.2	54.4
70	45	40.6	39.7	41.3	42.5	39.8	41.1
75	50	33.8	33.1	34.4	35.8	33.6	34.6
80	55	28.8	28.9	30.6	30.5	30.5	29.2
85	60	22.1	22.5	23.5	23.9	23.6	22.7
90	平成 2 年	18.3	19.5	19.3	20.3	19.3	17.4
95	7	14.9	14.5	14.9	16.3	15.5	14.9
2000	12	13.2	13.0	13.0	14.2	13.6	13.3
05	17	12.3	11.7	13.0	12.7	13.1	12.2
10	22	11.2	10.6	11.1	11.5	11.8	11.2
14	26	10.6	10.8	11.4	11.5	10.5	11.3
15	27	10.6	10.0	10.9	10.7	10.6	10.1
16	**28**	**10.1**	**10.2**	**10.2**	**10.9**	**10.4**	**10.7**
		人　　工　　死　　産					
1955	昭和30年	51.3	35.8	48.9	53.1	50.1	56.0
60	35	48.1	39.4	49.6	46.1	42.7	46.7
65	40	33.8	32.8	34.5	32.5	32.9	34.6
70	45	24.7	24.7	28.6	25.7	24.8	24.2
75	50	17.1	17.1	18.4	18.4	17.5	16.9
80	55	18.0	17.4	20.3	19.9	18.8	18.5
85	60	23.9	25.0	27.5	27.2	26.2	25.9
90	平成 2 年	23.9	24.3	27.9	27.9	24.7	23.9
95	7	17.2	16.8	20.8	20.7	17.1	16.9
2000	12	18.1	17.7	20.8	21.0	18.8	16.9
05	17	16.7	16.4	19.6	20.1	18.5	16.3
10	22	13.0	13.7	13.7	14.7	14.0	13.1
14	26	12.3	12.5	13.9	14.2	13.2	12.4
15	27	11.4	11.6	13.0	13.4	12.0	10.9
16	**28**	**10.9**	**10.3**	**11.8**	**12.1**	**11.5**	**11.3**

注：1）　計算方法は、69ページ　5）死産を参照されたい。
　　2）　昭和42年以前は月不詳があり、総数に含む。

454

Foetal mortality

死産数及び死産率[1]（出産千対）（つづき）
(per 1,000 total births) by type of extraction by month : Japan−CON.

6 月 June	7 月 July	8 月 August	9 月 September	10 月 October	11 月 November	12 月 December
率　Total foetal death rates						
101. 9	103. 3	101. 2	101. 9	95. 1	97. 4	102. 7
105. 8	107. 4	106. 0	107. 2	105. 2	105. 4	103. 1
88. 4	83. 9	79. 8	77. 0	76. 8	78. 8	79. 8
64. 6	64. 1	62. 0	68. 1	69. 8	63. 5	59. 4
51. 2	50. 3	49. 6	50. 1	51. 5	49. 9	47. 8
45. 7	45. 3	43. 8	43. 8	46. 2	46. 6	46. 3
45. 4	41. 5	41. 5	43. 7	45. 2	45. 2	42. 7
41. 1	39. 0	39. 2	40. 9	42. 0	42. 4	38. 7
31. 3	28. 7	29. 9	32. 1	32. 4	32. 1	31. 4
31. 6	29. 1	31. 5	29. 5	30. 5	31. 0	29. 8
28. 2	26. 8	28. 7	27. 7	27. 4	29. 2	27. 8
24. 5	24. 1	23. 5	24. 8	22. 7	21. 8	23. 5
22. 9	21. 9	22. 2	21. 0	22. 7	21. 1	21. 9
22. 5	21. 1	20. 5	22. 3	22. 7	20. 0	21. 7
22. 2	**18. 5**	**20. 4**	**20. 0**	**20. 4**	**21. 0**	**19. 8**
率　Spontaneous foetal death rates						
48. 5	47. 1	44. 3	43. 9	45. 3	46. 3	49. 9
55. 8	54. 5	53. 3	53. 2	55. 3	55. 4	56. 5
53. 4	50. 0	46. 8	43. 4	43. 6	42. 9	45. 5
41. 6	39. 7	39. 3	41. 4	43. 2	40. 2	38. 3
34. 4	33. 1	33. 3	32. 6	33. 9	33. 6	32. 8
28. 5	28. 3	27. 5	27. 1	27. 9	29. 1	27. 9
22. 5	20. 6	20. 5	21. 1	21. 1	22. 3	21. 0
17. 6	17. 6	17. 7	17. 9	18. 1	18. 5	17. 0
14. 7	13. 6	14. 2	14. 7	15. 3	15. 6	14. 8
13. 4	13. 4	13. 0	12. 0	13. 0	13. 4	13. 0
12. 2	11. 6	12. 7	11. 7	12. 7	12. 6	12. 0
11. 1	11. 4	11. 3	11. 4	11. 0	10. 2	11. 1
10. 9	10. 5	10. 3	9. 7	10. 3	10. 0	10. 4
11. 0	10. 9	10. 5	10. 9	10. 7	9. 6	10. 9
10. 6	**8. 8**	**10. 3**	**9. 6**	**10. 3**	**9. 5**	**9. 6**
率　Artificial foetal death rates						
53. 5	56. 2	56. 8	58. 0	49. 8	51. 1	52. 8
50. 0	53. 0	52. 7	54. 1	49. 8	50. 0	46. 5
35. 0	34. 0	33. 0	33. 6	33. 2	35. 9	34. 4
23. 1	24. 5	22. 7	26. 6	26. 6	23. 4	21. 2
16. 8	17. 1	16. 3	17. 5	17. 6	16. 3	15. 1
17. 2	17. 0	16. 3	16. 7	18. 3	17. 5	18. 4
22. 9	20. 9	21. 0	22. 6	24. 1	22. 9	21. 7
23. 6	21. 4	21. 5	22. 9	24. 0	23. 9	21. 6
16. 6	15. 2	15. 6	17. 4	17. 1	16. 5	16. 7
18. 2	15. 6	18. 5	17. 5	17. 5	17. 6	16. 8
16. 0	15. 2	15. 9	15. 9	14. 7	16. 6	15. 8
13. 4	12. 8	12. 2	13. 4	11. 8	11. 6	12. 4
12. 1	11. 4	11. 8	11. 3	12. 5	11. 1	11. 5
11. 6	10. 3	10. 1	11. 4	12. 0	10. 4	10. 9
11. 6	**9. 7**	**10. 2**	**10. 4**	**10. 2**	**11. 5**	**10. 2**

死　産

〔出産の場所別にみた死産〕
〔Foetal deaths by place of delivery〕

表 7.7　出産の場所別にみた自然
Table 7.7　Trends in foetal deaths and percent distribution

年　次 Year		総　数 Total	施　設　内 Hospitalized				施　設　外 Nonhosp.		
			総　数 Total	病　院 Hospital	診療所 Clinic	助産所 Maternity home	総　数 Total	自　宅 Home	その他 Others
			死　産　数　Total foetal deaths						
1955	昭和30年	183 265	131 253	56 016	73 449	1 788	52 012	47 271	4 741
60	35	179 281	151 134	56 312	90 772	4 050	28 147	24 587	3 560
65	40	161 617	151 716	52 626	94 397	4 693	9 901	8 622	1 279
70	45	135 095	131 666	48 858	80 147	2 661	3 429	2 855	574
75	50	101 862	100 287	40 815	58 252	1 220	1 575	1 314	261
80	55	77 446	76 621	31 079	45 151	391	825	690	135
85	60	69 009	68 471	27 661	40 676	134	538	442	96
90	平成 2 年	53 892	53 624	22 755	30 832	37	268	235	33
95	7	39 403	39 134	17 368	21 725	41	269	240	29
2000	12	38 393	38 121	17 348	20 737	36	272	235	37
05	17	31 818	31 606	15 568	16 032	6	212	187	25
10	22	26 560	26 351	14 286	12 058	7	209	186	23
14	26	23 524	23 322	13 065	10 253	4	202	175	27
15	27	22 617	22 415	12 843	9 567	5	202	173	29
16	**28**	**20 934**	**20 734**	**12 196**	**8 532**	**6**	**200**	**178**	**22**
		自　然　死　産　Spontaneous foetal deaths							
1955	昭和30年	85 159	36 324	16 334	18 430	1 560	48 835	44 580	4 255
60	35	93 424	66 189	25 954	36 369	3 866	27 235	23 855	3 380
65	40	94 476	84 741	32 030	48 115	4 596	9 735	8 491	1 244
70	45	84 073	80 726	34 314	43 789	2 623	3 347	2 831	516
75	50	67 643	66 109	30 774	34 127	1 208	1 534	1 304	230
80	55	47 651	46 828	22 579	23 859	390	823	688	135
85	60	33 114	32 576	16 886	15 556	134	538	442	96
90	平成 2 年	23 383	23 116	12 754	10 325	37	267	234	33
95	7	18 262	17 993	10 214	7 738	41	269	240	29
2000	12	16 200	15 928	9 314	6 578	36	272	235	37
05	17	13 502	13 290	8 174	5 110	6	212	187	25
10	22	12 245	12 036	7 881	4 148	7	209	186	23
14	26	10 905	10 703	7 221	3 478	4	202	175	27
15	27	10 862	10 660	7 216	3 439	5	202	173	29
16	**28**	**10 067**	**9 867**	**6 797**	**3 064**	**6**	**200**	**178**	**22**
		人　工　死　産　Artificial foetal deaths							
1955	昭和30年	98 106	94 929	39 682	55 019	228	3 177	2 691	486
60	35	85 857	84 945	30 358	54 403	184	912	732	180
65	40	67 141	66 975	20 596	46 282	97	166	131	35
70	45	51 022	50 940	14 544	36 358	38	82	24	58
75	50	34 219	34 178	10 041	24 125	12	41	10	31
80	55	29 795	29 793	8 500	21 292	1	2	2	-
85	60	35 895	35 895	10 775	25 120	-	-	-	-
90	平成 2 年	30 509	30 508	10 001	20 507	-	1	1	-
95	7	21 141	21 141	7 154	13 987	-	-	-	-
2000	12	22 193	22 193	8 034	14 159	-	-	-	-
05	17	18 316	18 316	7 394	10 922	-	-	-	-
10	22	14 315	14 315	6 405	7 910	-	-	-	-
14	26	12 619	12 619	5 844	6 775	-	-	-	-
15	27	11 755	11 755	5 627	6 128	-	-	-	-
16	**28**	**10 867**	**10 867**	**5 399**	**5 468**	**-**	**-**	**-**	**-**

Foetal mortality

－人工・年次別死産数及び百分率
by place of delivery and type of extraction : Japan

年　　次 Year		総　数 Total	施　設　内 Hospitalized				施　設　外 Nonhosp.		
			総　数 Total	病　院 Hospital	診療所 Clinic	助産所 Maternity home	総　数 Total	自　宅 Home	その他 Others
百　分　率　Percentage									
1955	昭和30年	100.0	71.6	30.6	40.1	1.0	28.4	25.8	2.6
60	35	100.0	84.3	31.4	50.6	2.3	15.7	13.7	2.0
65	40	100.0	93.9	32.6	58.4	2.9	6.1	5.3	0.8
70	45	100.0	97.5	36.2	59.3	2.0	2.5	2.1	0.4
75	50	100.0	98.5	40.1	57.2	1.2	1.5	1.3	0.3
80	55	100.0	98.9	40.1	58.3	0.5	1.1	0.9	0.2
85	60	100.0	99.2	40.1	58.9	0.2	0.8	0.6	0.1
90	平成 2 年	100.0	99.5	42.2	57.2	0.1	0.5	0.4	0.1
95	7	100.0	99.3	44.1	55.1	0.1	0.7	0.6	0.1
2000	12	100.0	99.3	45.2	54.0	0.1	0.7	0.6	0.1
05	17	100.0	99.3	48.9	50.4	0.0	0.7	0.6	0.1
10	22	100.0	99.2	53.8	45.4	0.0	0.8	0.7	0.1
14	26	100.0	99.1	55.5	43.6	0.0	0.9	0.7	0.1
15	27	100.0	99.1	56.8	42.3	0.0	0.9	0.8	0.1
16	**28**	**100.0**	**99.0**	**58.3**	**40.8**	**0.0**	**1.0**	**0.9**	**0.1**
自　然　死　産　Spontaneous foetal deaths									
1955	昭和30年	100.0	42.7	19.2	21.6	1.8	57.3	52.3	5.0
60	35	100.0	70.8	27.8	38.9	4.1	29.2	25.5	3.6
65	40	100.0	89.7	33.9	50.9	4.9	10.3	9.0	1.3
70	45	100.0	96.0	40.8	52.1	3.1	4.0	3.4	0.6
75	50	100.0	97.7	45.5	50.5	1.8	2.3	1.9	0.3
80	55	100.0	98.3	47.4	50.1	0.8	1.7	1.4	0.3
85	60	100.0	98.4	51.0	47.0	0.4	1.6	1.3	0.3
90	平成 2 年	100.0	98.9	54.5	44.2	0.2	1.1	1.0	0.1
95	7	100.0	98.5	55.9	42.4	0.2	1.5	1.3	0.2
2000	12	100.0	98.3	57.5	40.6	0.2	1.7	1.5	0.2
05	17	100.0	98.4	60.5	37.8	0.0	1.6	1.4	0.2
10	22	100.0	98.3	64.4	33.9	0.1	1.7	1.5	0.2
14	26	100.0	98.1	66.2	31.9	0.0	1.9	1.6	0.2
15	27	100.0	98.1	66.4	31.7	0.0	1.9	1.6	0.3
16	**28**	**100.0**	**98.0**	**67.5**	**30.4**	**0.1**	**2.0**	**1.8**	**0.2**
人　工　死　産　Artificial foetal deaths									
1955	昭和30年	100.0	96.8	40.4	56.1	0.2	3.2	2.7	0.5
60	35	100.0	98.9	35.4	63.4	0.2	1.1	0.9	0.2
65	40	100.0	99.8	30.7	68.9	0.1	0.2	0.2	0.1
70	45	100.0	99.8	28.5	71.3	0.1	0.2	0.0	0.1
75	50	100.0	99.9	29.3	70.5	0.0	0.1	0.0	0.1
80	55	100.0	100.0	28.5	71.5	0.0	0.0	0.0	-
85	60	100.0	100.0	30.0	70.0	-	-	-	-
90	平成 2 年	100.0	100.0	32.8	67.2	-	0.0	0.0	-
95	7	100.0	100.0	33.8	66.2	-	-	-	-
2000	12	100.0	100.0	36.2	63.8	-	-	-	-
05	17	100.0	100.0	40.4	59.6	-	-	-	-
10	22	100.0	100.0	44.7	55.3	-	-	-	-
14	26	100.0	100.0	46.3	53.7	-	-	-	-
15	27	100.0	100.0	47.9	52.1	-	-	-	-
16	**28**	**100.0**	**100.0**	**49.7**	**50.3**	**-**	**-**	**-**	**-**

死　産

〔母の年齢（5歳階級）別にみた死産〕
〔Foetal deaths by age of mother (5-year age groups)〕

表7.8　母の年齢・世帯の主な仕事別にみた自然－人工別死産率[1]（出産千対）
Table 7.8　Foetal death rates (per 1,000 total births) by age of mother, type of extraction and type of occupation of household : Japan, 2016

平成28年

世帯の主な仕事 Type of occupation of household	総　数[2] Total	15～19歳 Years	20～24	25～29	30～34	35～39	40～44	45～49
死　産　率　Total foetal death rates								
総　　　　数[2]　Total	21.0	136.5	35.2	15.1	15.2	20.3	37.0	84.7
農　家　世　帯　Agriculture[a]	20.2	154.9	30.6	18.7	14.3	15.8	37.0	125.0
自営業者世帯　Self employed	21.0	127.6	34.3	16.0	14.5	18.8	35.4	62.5
常用勤労者世帯（Ⅰ）　Employee[b]	20.4	86.6	25.0	15.1	15.9	21.3	40.5	113.6
常用勤労者世帯（Ⅱ）　Employee or director[c]	14.2	105.6	21.9	10.1	11.3	15.9	28.4	53.6
その他の世帯　Other	37.4	191.2	65.7	26.0	26.4	35.8	56.3	127.1
無職の世帯　Not working	91.8	257.0	103.4	64.8	56.2	58.4	94.5	152.2
自然死産率　Spontaneous foetal death rates								
総　　　　数[2]　Total	10.1	12.9	8.1	7.8	9.4	12.3	18.0	28.5
農　家　世　帯　Agriculture[a]	9.2	7.0	8.3	9.8	8.7	7.9	16.3	-
自営業者世帯　Self employed	9.9	17.3	7.7	7.7	8.9	10.8	17.4	18.8
常用勤労者世帯（Ⅰ）　Employee[b]	10.5	8.5	7.3	8.2	10.1	13.3	19.3	39.5
常用勤労者世帯（Ⅱ）　Employee or director[c]	8.3	11.3	7.4	6.2	7.6	10.3	15.5	19.3
その他の世帯　Other	15.1	21.1	10.1	11.3	15.1	19.6	27.5	50.8
無職の世帯　Not working	15.8	17.1	11.2	12.7	17.3	22.8	21.1	21.7
人工死産率　Artificial foetal death rates								
総　　　　数[2]　Total	10.9	123.6	27.1	7.4	5.8	8.0	19.0	56.3
農　家　世　帯　Agriculture[a]	11.1	147.9	22.2	8.9	5.5	7.9	20.7	125.0
自営業者世帯　Self employed	11.1	110.2	26.6	8.3	5.6	8.0	18.0	43.8
常用勤労者世帯（Ⅰ）　Employee[b]	9.9	78.1	17.7	6.9	5.9	8.0	21.2	74.1
常用勤労者世帯（Ⅱ）　Employee or director[c]	5.8	94.2	14.6	3.9	3.7	5.6	12.9	34.2
その他の世帯　Other	22.3	170.1	55.6	14.7	11.3	16.2	28.8	76.3
無職の世帯　Not working	76.0	239.9	92.2	52.1	38.9	35.6	73.4	130.4

注：1)　死産率＝ 世帯の主な仕事別年間のある年齢階級の母親による死産数 ／世帯の主な仕事別年間のある年齢階級の母親による出産数 ×1,000

　　2)　総数には、母の年齢15歳未満、50歳以上及び不詳を含む。また、世帯の主な仕事不詳を含む。

Note : a)　Agriculture only or that with other work.

　　　b)　Employee at office (excluding governmental office) with 1－99 employee (excluding daily or less than one year contracts).

　　　c)　Employee at office excluding b) above.

死 産

〔嫡出子－嫡出でない子別にみた死産〕
〔Foetal deaths by legitimacy status〕

表7.9　嫡出子－嫡出でない子・自然－人工別にみた妊娠期間別死産数及び百分率
Table 7.9　Foetal deaths and percent distribution by legitimacy status, type of extraction and period of gestation : Japan, 2016

平成28年

妊 娠 期 間 Period of gestation	自 然 死 産 Spontaneous		人 工 死 産 Artificial	
	嫡 出 子 Born in wedlock	嫡出でない子 Born out of wedlock	嫡 出 子 Born in wedlock	嫡出でない子 Born out of wedlock
死　産　数　　Foetal deaths				
総　　　　　　　数　　Total	9 108	959	4 923	5 944
満 12 週 ～ 満 15 週 12－15 completed weeks	2 742	367	1 650	2 843
16 ～ 19	2 648	298	1 791	2 119
20 ～ 23	1 499	150	1 481	982
24 ～ 27	614	46	1	-
28 ～ 31	395	24	-	-
32 ～ 35	448	30	-	-
36 ～ 39	633	29	-	-
40 ～ 40 completed weeks and over	129	11	-	-
不　　　　　　　詳　　Not stated	-	4	-	-
百　分　率　　Percentage				
総　　　　　　　数　　Total	100.0	100.0	100.0	100.0
満 12 週 ～ 満 15 週 12－15 completed weeks	30.1	38.3	33.5	47.8
16 ～ 19	29.1	31.1	36.4	35.6
20 ～ 23	16.5	15.6	30.1	16.5
24 ～ 27	6.7	4.8	0.0	-
28 ～ 31	4.3	2.5	-	-
32 ～ 35	4.9	3.1	-	-
36 ～ 39	6.9	3.0	-	-
40 ～ 40 completed weeks and over	1.4	1.1	-	-
不　　　　　　　詳　　Not stated	-	0.4	-	-

Foetal mortality

表7.10　嫡出子－嫡出でない子別にみた年次別妊娠満22週以後の死産数及び百分率
Table 7.10　Trends in foetal deaths at 22 completed weeks and over of gestation and percent distribution by legitimacy status : Japan

年　　次 Year		妊娠満22週以後の死産数 Foetal deaths at 22 completed weeks and over of gestation			百　　分　　率 Percentage		
		総　数 Total	嫡出子 Born in wedlock	嫡出でない子 Born out of wedlock	総　数 Total	嫡出子 Born in wedlock	嫡出でない子 Born out of wedlock
1979	昭和54年	29 284	23 061	6 223	100.0	78.7	21.3
80	55	26 268	20 646	5 622	100.0	78.6	21.4
81	56	24 672	19 152	5 520	100.0	77.6	22.4
82	57	23 137	17 857	5 280	100.0	77.2	22.8
83	58	21 354	16 217	5 137	100.0	75.9	24.1
84	59	20 875	15 463	5 412	100.0	74.1	25.9
85	60	18 642	13 789	4 853	100.0	74.0	26.0
86	61	17 143	12 515	4 628	100.0	73.0	27.0
87	62	15 634	11 512	4 122	100.0	73.6	26.4
88	63	14 090	10 477	3 613	100.0	74.4	25.6
89	平成元年	12 797	9 421	3 376	100.0	73.6	26.4
1990	2	11 367	8 750	2 617	100.0	77.0	23.0
91	3	8 258	7 308	950	100.0	88.5	11.5
92	4	7 758	6 916	842	100.0	89.1	10.9
93	5	7 191	6 462	729	100.0	89.9	10.1
94	6	7 200	6 604	596	100.0	91.7	8.3
95	7	6 580	6 070	510	100.0	92.2	7.8
96	8	6 333	5 830	503	100.0	92.1	7.9
97	9	6 009	5 520	489	100.0	91.9	8.1
98	10	5 804	5 311	493	100.0	91.5	8.5
99	11	5 567	5 135	432	100.0	92.2	7.8
2000	12	5 362	4 916	446	100.0	91.7	8.3
01	13	5 114	4 680	434	100.0	91.5	8.5
02	14	4 959	4 508	451	100.0	90.9	9.1
03	15	4 626	4 230	396	100.0	91.4	8.6
04	16	4 357	4 010	347	100.0	92.0	8.0
05	17	4 058	3 695	363	100.0	91.1	8.9
06	18	4 047	3 777	270	100.0	93.3	6.7
07	19	3 854	3 587	267	100.0	93.1	6.9
08	20	3 751	3 479	272	100.0	92.7	7.3
09	21	3 645	3 396	249	100.0	93.2	6.8
2010	22	3 637	3 391	246	100.0	93.2	6.8
11	23	3 491	3 253	238	100.0	93.2	6.8
12	24	3 343	3 111	232	100.0	93.1	6.9
13	25	3 110	2 891	219	100.0	93.0	7.0
14	26	3 039	2 806	233	100.0	92.3	7.7
15	27	3 063	2 876	187	100.0	93.9	6.1
16	28	2 840	2 653	187	100.0	93.4	6.6

死　産

〔地域別にみた死産〕
〔Foetal deaths by prefecture〕

表7.11　都道府県（21大都市再掲）別にみた
Table 7.11　Foetal deaths and percent distribution by prefecture and 21 major cities, 2016

都道府県 Prefecture	死産数 Foetal deaths 総数 Total	病院 Hospital	診療所 Clinic	助産所 Maternity home	自宅 Home	その他 Others
全国 Total	20 934	12 196	8 532	6	178	22
市部 Total for urban residence	19 373	11 331	7 854	4	166	18
郡部 Total for rural residence	1 550	858	675	2	12	3
a)						
01 北海道	901	505	390	-	6	-
02 青森	183	99	84	-	-	-
03 岩手	184	83	99	-	2	-
04 宮城	402	201	195	-	4	2
05 秋田	133	90	41	-	2	-
06 山形	165	103	62	-	-	-
07 福島	306	224	81	-	1	-
08 茨城	423	232	183	1	7	-
09 栃木	321	169	149	-	3	-
10 群馬	330	203	121	-	4	2
11 埼玉	1 181	702	470	1	7	1
12 千葉	1 001	564	426	-	10	1
13 東京	2 365	1 497	853	-	13	2
14 神奈川	1 400	771	615	-	11	3
15 新潟	320	175	142	-	2	1
16 富山	152	106	44	-	1	1
17 石川	159	102	55	-	2	-
18 福井	146	84	60	-	1	1
19 山梨	101	50	50	-	1	-
20 長野	312	210	99	-	3	-
21 岐阜	289	173	113	-	3	-
22 静岡	538	288	243	-	6	1
23 愛知	1 182	684	482	-	16	-
24 三重	272	176	91	-	5	-
25 滋賀	213	104	107	-	2	-
26 京都	401	270	128	-	3	-
27 大阪	1 480	986	487	-	6	1
28 兵庫	856	447	398	-	11	-
29 奈良	190	88	97	1	3	1
30 和歌山	155	88	66	-	1	-
31 鳥取	98	66	30	1	1	-
32 島根	136	97	38	-	1	-
33 岡山	325	217	106	-	2	-
34 広島	501	350	146	1	4	-
35 山口	195	148	45	1	1	-
36 徳島	94	68	26	-	-	-
37 香川	144	80	64	-	-	-
38 愛媛	245	161	84	-	-	-
39 高知	106	63	41	-	2	-
40 福岡	1 018	477	529	-	11	1
41 佐賀	135	59	76	-	-	-
42 長崎	247	142	103	-	2	-
43 熊本	396	176	215	-	3	2
44 大分	221	80	141	-	-	-
45 宮崎	240	119	118	-	2	1
46 鹿児島	327	173	147	-	7	-
47 沖縄	434	239	189	-	6	-
外国 Foreign countries	10	7	3	-	-	-
不詳 Place of residence not stated	1	-	-	-	-	1
21 大都市（再掲）21 major cities(Regrouped)						
50 東京都の区部	1 735	1 076	649	-	8	2
51 札幌	344	159	182	-	3	-
52 仙台	175	94	79	-	1	1
53 さいたま	216	137	76	-	2	1
54 千葉	158	70	87	-	1	-
55 横浜	568	350	211	-	6	1
56 川崎	255	140	112	-	2	1
57 相模原	122	84	37	-	1	-
58 新潟	133	62	70	-	1	-
59 静岡	121	62	57	-	1	1
60 浜松	90	52	38	-	-	-
61 名古屋	383	197	179	-	7	-
62 京都	233	172	60	-	1	-
63 大阪	494	336	156	-	2	-
64 堺	138	97	41	-	-	-
65 神戸	254	132	117	-	5	-
66 岡山	116	60	54	-	2	-
67 広島	234	158	73	-	3	-
68 北九州	181	110	68	-	3	-
69 福岡	323	140	181	-	3	-
70 熊本	184	104	77	-	3	-

注：全国には住所地外国・不詳を含む。市部・郡部の計には住所地外国・不詳を含まない。

Foetal mortality

出産の場所別死産数及び百分率
place of delivery : Japan, urban/rural residence, each

平成28年

都道府県 Prefecture	百分率 Percentage					
	総数 Total	病院 Hospital	診療所 Clinic	助産所 Maternity home	自宅 Home	その他 Others
全国 Total	100.0	58.3	40.8	0.0	0.9	0.1
市部 Total for urban residence	100.0	58.5	40.5	0.0	0.9	0.1
郡部 Total for rural residence	100.0	55.4	43.5	0.1	0.8	0.2
a)						
01 北海道	100.0	56.0	43.3	-	0.7	-
02 青森	100.0	54.1	45.9	-	-	-
03 岩手	100.0	45.1	53.8	-	1.1	-
04 宮城	100.0	50.0	48.5	-	1.0	0.5
05 秋田	100.0	67.7	30.8	-	1.5	-
06 山形	100.0	62.4	37.6	-	-	-
07 福島	100.0	73.2	26.5	-	0.3	-
08 茨城	100.0	54.8	43.3	0.2	1.7	-
09 栃木	100.0	52.6	46.4	-	0.9	-
10 群馬	100.0	61.5	36.7	-	1.2	0.6
11 埼玉	100.0	59.4	39.8	0.1	0.6	0.1
12 千葉	100.0	56.3	42.6	-	1.0	0.1
13 東京	100.0	63.3	36.1	-	0.5	0.1
14 神奈川	100.0	55.1	43.9	-	0.8	0.2
15 新潟	100.0	54.7	44.4	-	0.6	0.3
16 富山	100.0	69.7	28.9	-	0.7	0.7
17 石川	100.0	64.2	34.6	-	1.3	-
18 福井	100.0	57.5	41.1	-	0.7	0.7
19 山梨	100.0	49.5	49.5	-	1.0	-
20 長野	100.0	67.3	31.7	-	1.0	-
21 岐阜	100.0	59.9	39.1	-	1.0	-
22 静岡	100.0	53.5	45.2	-	1.1	0.2
23 愛知	100.0	57.9	40.8	-	1.4	-
24 三重	100.0	64.7	33.5	-	1.8	-
25 滋賀	100.0	48.8	50.2	-	0.9	-
26 京都	100.0	67.3	31.9	-	0.7	-
27 大阪	100.0	66.6	32.9	-	0.4	0.1
28 兵庫	100.0	52.2	46.5	-	1.3	-
29 奈良	100.0	46.3	51.1	0.5	1.6	0.5
30 和歌山	100.0	56.8	42.6	-	0.6	-
31 鳥取	100.0	67.3	30.6	1.0	1.0	-
32 島根	100.0	71.3	27.9	-	0.7	-
33 岡山	100.0	66.8	32.6	-	0.6	-
34 広島	100.0	69.9	29.1	0.2	0.8	-
35 山口	100.0	75.9	23.1	0.5	0.5	-
36 徳島	100.0	72.3	27.7	-	-	-
37 香川	100.0	55.6	44.4	-	-	-
38 愛媛	100.0	65.7	34.3	-	-	-
39 高知	100.0	59.4	38.7	-	1.9	-
40 福岡	100.0	46.9	52.0	-	1.1	0.1
41 佐賀	100.0	43.7	56.3	-	-	-
42 長崎	100.0	57.5	41.7	-	0.8	-
43 熊本	100.0	44.4	54.3	-	0.8	0.5
44 大分	100.0	36.2	63.8	-	-	-
45 宮崎	100.0	49.6	49.2	-	0.8	0.4
46 鹿児島	100.0	52.9	45.0	-	2.1	-
47 沖縄	100.0	55.1	43.5	-	1.4	-
外国 Foreign countries	100.0	70.0	30.0	-	-	-
不詳 Place of residence not stated	100.0	-	-	-	-	100.0
21 大都市(再掲) 21 major cities(Regrouped)						
50 東京都の区部	100.0	62.0	37.4	-	0.5	0.1
51 札幌	100.0	46.2	52.9	-	0.9	-
52 仙台	100.0	53.7	45.1	-	0.6	0.6
53 さいたま	100.0	63.4	35.2	-	0.9	0.5
54 千葉	100.0	44.3	55.1	-	0.6	-
55 横浜	100.0	61.6	37.1	-	1.1	0.2
56 川崎	100.0	54.9	43.9	-	0.8	0.4
57 相模原	100.0	68.9	30.3	-	0.8	-
58 新潟	100.0	46.6	52.6	-	0.8	-
59 静岡	100.0	51.2	47.1	-	0.8	0.8
60 浜松	100.0	57.8	42.2	-	-	-
61 名古屋	100.0	51.4	46.7	-	1.8	-
62 京都	100.0	73.8	25.8	-	0.4	-
63 大阪	100.0	68.0	31.6	-	0.4	-
64 堺	100.0	70.3	29.7	-	-	-
65 神戸	100.0	52.0	46.1	-	2.0	-
66 岡山	100.0	51.7	46.6	-	1.7	-
67 広島	100.0	67.5	31.2	-	1.3	-
68 北九州	100.0	60.8	37.6	-	1.7	-
69 福岡	100.0	43.3	56.0	-	0.6	-
70 熊本	100.0	56.5	41.8	-	1.6	-

Note : The number of "Total for urban residence" and "Total for rural residence" does not include "Foreign countries" and "Place of residence not stated".
a) See page 44.

死　産

表 7.12　都道府県別に
Table 7.12　Trends in foetal deaths

都道府県 Prefecture	1950 昭和25年	1955 30年	1960 35年	1965 40年	1970 45年	1975 50年	1980 55年	1985 60年
全国　Total	216 974	183 265	179 281	161 617	135 095	101 862	77 446	69 009
01[a] 北 海 道	11 449	10 827	11 866	11 167	9 914	7 272	5 790	4 988
02 青　　森	3 885	3 216	3 367	2 561	2 090	1 583	1 122	1 010
03 岩　　手	4 278	3 682	3 229	2 501	1 891	1 308	1 101	918
04 宮　　城	4 940	4 472	3 965	3 164	2 621	2 058	1 789	1 630
05 秋　　田	3 632	2 960	2 738	2 040	1 495	1 057	764	636
06 山　　形	3 938	3 194	2 555	1 776	1 365	1 040	906	809
07 福　　島	5 923	5 007	4 292	3 154	2 348	1 778	1 547	1 369
08 茨　　城	5 236	4 081	3 586	2 955	2 355	1 800	1 340	1 474
09 栃　　木	3 697	3 064	2 522	2 182	1 705	1 461	1 120	996
10 群　　馬	4 649	3 648	2 752	2 249	1 818	1 333	1 007	890
11 埼　　玉	5 040	4 233	3 794	4 237	4 277	3 795	2 792	2 630
12 千　　葉	4 360	3 890	3 693	3 857	3 894	3 385	2 617	2 408
13 東　　京	12 263	13 418	18 070	18 117	14 081	9 347	6 877	5 885
14 神 奈 川	5 290	5 573	6 124	6 774	5 810	4 890	3 628	3 250
15 新　　潟	6 820	4 560	3 855	2 799	2 212	1 787	1 340	1 147
16 富　　山	2 274	1 767	1 436	1 255	1 137	679	575	502
17 石　　川	2 012	1 564	1 460	1 165	1 078	901	702	557
18 福　　井	1 826	1 289	1 194	1 014	829	543	432	428
19 山　　梨	2 238	1 799	1 512	1 129	808	655	465	416
20 長　　野	5 887	3 871	3 069	2 353	1 919	1 539	1 145	921
21 岐　　阜	3 972	2 737	2 687	2 341	2 030	1 414	1 008	935
22 静　　岡	6 280	5 584	4 835	4 431	3 495	2 709	2 039	1 819
23 愛　　知	9 123	7 419	7 449	8 517	7 739	5 394	3 996	3 490
24 三　　重	3 427	2 733	2 594	2 145	1 912	1 349	1 007	841
25 滋　　賀	2 030	1 502	1 255	1 065	921	822	672	541
26 京　　都	4 587	3 319	3 356	3 284	2 704	2 192	1 622	1 360
27 大　　阪	11 491	10 455	13 383	15 140	13 185	9 350	6 579	5 430
28 兵　　庫	9 056	6 953	6 952	7 477	6 292	4 440	3 200	2 657
29 奈　　良	1 593	1 184	1 140	1 098	960	798	709	620
30 和 歌 山	2 194	1 965	1 801	1 493	1 234	866	590	569
31 鳥　　取	2 335	2 021	1 572	1 015	789	557	419	376
32 島　　根	2 593	2 089	1 827	1 334	907	621	470	424
33 岡　　山	4 615	3 407	2 582	2 125	1 934	1 496	1 073	1 051
34 広　　島	4 180	3 938	3 896	3 409	3 112	2 569	1 668	1 595
35 山　　口	4 285	3 402	3 368	2 629	2 194	1 439	1 086	832
36 徳　　島	2 359	1 793	1 422	1 118	971	699	552	442
37 香　　川	2 524	1 519	1 302	1 066	810	670	497	500
38 愛　　媛	3 899	3 112	2 766	2 157	1 592	1 349	1 036	923
39 高　　知	1 849	1 354	1 304	1 159	790	718	515	514
40 福　　岡	10 752	9 947	10 427	7 949	6 199	4 793	3 753	3 588
41 佐　　賀	2 501	2 001	1 729	1 386	1 083	801	670	632
42 長　　崎	4 837	4 477	4 244	3 202	2 693	1 959	1 544	1 558
43 熊　　本	4 807	4 251	3 677	2 939	2 062	1 613	1 409	1 437
44 大　　分	3 534	3 025	2 809	1 980	1 636	1 406	1 013	974
45 宮　　崎	4 035	3 483	2 939	2 125	1 863	1 327	1 074	965
46 鹿 児 島	4 352	3 426	2 818	2 496	2 167	1 692	1 596	1 417
47 沖　　縄	…	…	…	…	…	550	540	629
外　　　国 Foreign countries	…	…	…	…	…	…	…	…
不　　　詳 Place of residence not stated	127	54	68	88	174	58	50	26

464

Foetal mortality

みた年次別死産数
by each prefecture : Japan

1990 平成2年	1995 7年	2000 12年	2005 17年	2010 22年	2014 26年	2015 27年	2016 28年	都道府県 Prefecture
53 892	39 403	38 393	31 818	26 560	23 524	22 617	20 934	全国　Total
3 498	2 139	2 069	1 664	1 260	1 101	1 057	901	01a) 北 海 道
645	527	471	367	283	250	216	183	02 青　　森
694	513	480	361	291	213	216	184	03 岩　　手
1 260	893	829	640	495	421	427	402	04 宮　　城
508	410	304	247	181	165	130	133	05 秋　　田
607	444	419	274	231	173	181	165	06 山　　形
1 043	752	782	567	487	344	360	306	07 福　　島
1 147	935	933	715	600	491	489	423	08 茨　　城
895	657	626	485	398	356	326	321	09 栃　　木
725	561	599	491	399	326	332	330	10 群　　馬
2 324	1 944	1 907	1 637	1 375	1 382	1 350	1 181	11 埼　　玉
1 993	1 541	1 648	1 487	1 238	1 143	1 102	1 001	12 千　　葉
4 543	3 189	2 995	2 839	2 587	2 460	2 406	2 365	13 東　　京
2 888	2 259	2 206	2 062	1 666	1 566	1 500	1 400	14 神 奈 川
850	629	599	529	474	391	349	320	15 新　　潟
392	256	288	233	188	155	164	152	16 富　　山
507	311	313	259	213	187	188	159	17 石　　川
313	249	226	191	159	161	147	146	18 福　　井
339	239	266	195	161	143	137	101	19 山　　梨
752	610	531	479	395	341	326	312	20 長　　野
770	555	611	469	382	313	320	289	21 岐　　阜
1 464	1 086	1 088	816	716	629	539	538	22 静　　岡
2 860	2 066	2 107	1 748	1 402	1 358	1 283	1 182	23 愛　　知
717	509	496	417	335	308	284	272	24 三　　重
480	371	392	308	286	224	253	213	25 滋　　賀
1 039	777	694	600	482	447	427	401	26 京　　都
4 368	2 974	2 760	2 214	1 907	1 621	1 519	1 480	27 大　　阪
2 064	1 439	1 578	1 296	1 070	951	916	856	28 兵　　庫
532	337	379	330	275	205	214	190	29 奈　　良
423	291	299	239	176	148	177	155	30 和 歌 山
300	228	192	172	138	109	101	98	31 鳥　　取
291	196	201	170	143	124	107	136	32 島　　根
796	650	600	499	418	354	342	325	33 岡　　山
1 177	911	784	613	555	468	485	501	34 広　　島
650	451	463	328	265	210	203	195	35 山　　口
327	194	199	171	152	129	123	94	36 徳　　島
353	266	297	232	206	169	167	144	37 香　　川
703	471	430	393	341	316	246	245	38 愛　　媛
363	323	284	225	166	149	111	106	39 高　　知
2 689	1 935	1 858	1 605	1 366	1 155	1 164	1 018	40 福　　岡
494	368	371	249	233	162	163	135	41 佐　　賀
879	672	656	502	362	302	275	247	42 長　　崎
1 101	856	808	556	430	458	413	396	43 熊　　本
708	475	404	308	312	257	286	221	44 大　　分
751	582	536	421	317	294	279	240	45 宮　　崎
1 072	806	739	613	467	391	379	327	46 鹿 児 島
576	528	647	583	560	494	423	434	47 沖　　縄
…	12	17	9	12	8	11	10	外　　国 Foreign countries
22	16	12	10	5	2	4	1	不　　詳 Place of residence not stated

Note : a) See page 44.

死　産

表 7.13　都道府県別にみた
Table 7.13　Trends in foetal death rates

都道府県 Prefecture	1950 昭和25年	1955 30年	1960 35年	1965 40年	1970 45年	1975 50年	1980 55年	1985 60年
全国　Total	84.9	95.8	100.4	81.4	65.3	50.8	46.8	46.0
01[a] 北 海 道	72.2	94.6	112.2	103.6	97.4	75.0	71.2	69.9
02 青 　 森	77.7	83.7	101.3	83.2	73.4	61.8	49.0	50.2
03 岩 　 手	85.7	95.9	104.0	92.2	78.9	55.7	53.1	50.6
04 宮 　 城	84.9	104.0	112.2	97.6	79.3	59.1	54.3	55.0
05 秋 　 田	78.5	88.7	104.1	93.1	77.7	57.0	44.7	44.5
06 山 　 形	88.2	104.7	102.8	86.0	73.4	56.9	51.0	51.5
07 福 　 島	80.6	92.8	98.6	87.7	72.7	53.8	49.8	47.7
08 茨 　 城	80.6	83.8	91.4	76.9	57.5	42.6	35.5	42.2
09 栃 　 木	73.2	84.0	88.2	78.1	58.3	46.9	41.4	40.1
10 群 　 馬	94.1	101.4	97.4	74.6	58.2	43.1	38.5	37.4
11 埼 　 玉	74.6	81.3	80.4	59.8	44.8	38.0	35.8	37.6
12 千 　 葉	70.5	81.6	85.4	66.5	51.0	41.9	38.4	38.1
13 東 　 京	76.3	95.0	98.8	74.4	57.8	47.7	46.8	44.6
14 神 奈 川	74.5	97.2	91.6	65.0	44.9	39.6	37.0	36.4
15 新 　 潟	86.5	81.2	85.7	65.0	55.9	45.5	39.2	37.8
16 富 　 山	75.4	87.5	81.8	71.3	61.0	37.8	40.7	40.2
17 石 　 川	71.3	79.9	83.7	65.6	56.1	45.7	44.3	40.3
18 福 　 井	79.3	80.0	84.8	73.7	63.7	41.9	38.7	40.9
19 山 　 梨	94.8	103.4	105.7	81.5	61.8	52.3	44.4	40.5
20 長 　 野	105.4	98.1	90.7	69.4	57.6	46.3	40.4	36.7
21 岐 　 阜	87.4	85.3	86.1	67.9	59.2	42.9	37.6	37.7
22 静 　 岡	82.0	93.0	88.9	74.1	56.7	44.4	41.4	39.8
23 愛 　 知	94.1	102.0	92.3	77.1	62.4	46.1	43.6	41.7
24 三 　 重	84.3	97.0	97.1	73.5	68.1	49.6	44.8	40.9
25 滋 　 賀	86.6	90.7	85.2	69.4	55.8	44.6	40.4	35.1
26 京 　 都	100.1	106.2	103.1	82.1	61.5	52.1	48.0	45.6
27 大 　 阪	109.0	124.7	123.5	93.2	72.0	58.4	55.5	51.3
28 兵 　 庫	99.6	100.2	97.1	83.1	64.6	48.6	44.5	41.5
29 奈 　 良	78.9	83.0	86.8	70.1	52.0	42.5	42.6	40.6
30 和 歌 山	84.6	101.3	101.7	76.4	64.2	50.3	42.0	45.0
31 鳥 　 取	126.6	145.2	141.0	106.0	89.8	59.8	48.6	47.7
32 島 　 根	91.1	108.5	114.6	101.6	79.2	53.7	45.1	44.7
33 岡 　 山	102.6	106.9	92.6	77.1	63.1	47.3	42.0	44.3
34 広 　 島	73.4	94.7	101.6	80.4	65.3	52.0	42.7	45.4
35 山 　 口	91.1	105.8	118.8	96.8	81.9	56.7	52.0	45.0
36 徳 　 島	84.8	90.4	96.5	81.4	75.7	55.0	49.7	43.5
37 香 　 川	92.9	83.6	87.7	72.1	52.8	41.3	36.8	41.6
38 愛 　 媛	78.9	92.4	99.5	81.1	65.1	54.7	49.9	49.7
39 高 　 知	74.3	77.9	93.4	87.9	62.5	57.5	52.1	52.1
40 福 　 岡	89.7	115.2	134.1	103.5	81.7	63.2	55.1	57.5
41 佐 　 賀	77.0	82.5	90.9	87.6	75.9	57.7	51.0	51.2
42 長 　 崎	81.4	94.0	104.1	95.9	91.6	71.0	64.9	71.1
43 熊 　 本	79.9	91.6	100.2	92.3	75.9	59.3	54.5	58.4
44 大 　 分	87.8	102.7	122.5	96.5	85.1	71.2	58.5	63.3
45 宮 　 崎	102.5	115.2	118.2	103.3	98.8	68.2	59.5	59.5
46 鹿 児 島	73.3	64.2	69.3	78.6	81.9	64.4	61.1	57.2
47 沖 　 縄	…	…	…	…	…	24.0	25.9	29.5

466

Foetal mortality

年次別死産率（出産千対）
（per 1,000 total births）by each prefecture : Japan

1990 平成2年	1995 7年	2000 12年	2005 17年	2010 22年	2014 26年	2015 27年	2016 28年	都道府県 Prefecture
42.3	32.1	31.2	29.1	24.2	22.9	22.0	21.0	全国　Total
60.4	41.1	42.4	38.6	30.4	28.9	28.0	25.0	01[a) 北　海　道
42.2	36.3	35.2	33.7	28.3	27.5	24.4	20.8	02　青　　　森
46.4	37.9	37.2	33.1	29.0	23.6	23.9	21.6	03　岩　　　手
51.3	38.6	36.1	32.1	25.2	22.8	23.2	22.6	04　宮　　　城
44.2	39.4	32.6	31.1	26.4	26.8	21.7	22.9	05　秋　　　田
46.1	37.2	37.0	28.4	26.0	21.3	22.6	21.4	06　山　　　形
43.9	34.1	37.0	31.3	29.3	23.1	24.7	21.8	07　福　　　島
38.3	32.1	32.0	28.6	24.4	22.0	22.0	19.9	08　茨　　　城
42.8	34.0	31.9	27.2	23.6	22.5	20.9	21.5	09　栃　　　木
35.9	28.1	29.9	27.9	24.3	22.0	22.8	23.6	10　群　　　馬
35.4	27.9	27.9	26.7	22.6	24.2	23.5	21.2	11　埼　　　玉
36.0	27.6	28.9	28.6	23.4	23.9	22.9	21.6	12　千　　　葉
41.9	31.9	29.0	28.6	23.4	21.8	20.8	20.7	13　東　　　京
35.1	27.2	25.9	26.3	20.9	21.0	20.0	19.4	14　神　奈　川
34.1	27.0	26.6	27.8	25.5	23.2	20.9	19.9	15　新　　　潟
37.5	24.8	27.5	25.3	22.4	20.1	21.2	20.4	16　富　　　山
42.1	27.3	26.6	25.1	21.7	20.4	20.3	17.5	17　石　　　川
34.9	29.3	27.4	26.0	22.6	25.4	23.1	23.3	18　福　　　井
38.0	26.3	30.8	26.6	23.6	23.0	22.4	17.1	19　山　　　梨
34.0	28.0	24.4	25.2	22.4	21.1	20.4	20.2	20　長　　　野
36.6	26.8	29.3	25.8	22.1	20.3	20.3	19.1	21　岐　　　阜
38.0	29.8	29.5	24.9	22.0	21.5	18.7	19.1	22　静　　　岡
38.8	27.9	27.4	25.4	19.7	20.4	19.2	18.1	23　愛　　　知
38.5	28.3	27.2	26.5	21.5	21.9	20.0	20.2	24　三　　　重
34.1	27.1	27.1	23.3	21.0	17.3	19.7	17.3	25　滋　　　賀
41.2	32.4	28.1	27.1	22.2	22.3	21.3	20.3	26　京　　　都
47.9	33.4	30.4	28.3	24.8	22.6	21.1	21.1	27　大　　　阪
36.9	27.0	28.2	26.7	21.9	21.0	20.4	19.4	28　兵　　　庫
38.4	24.6	27.8	28.7	25.1	20.9	21.3	19.8	29　奈　　　良
40.1	28.6	30.3	29.6	22.7	20.3	24.6	22.8	30　和　歌　山
44.7	38.3	32.9	33.2	28.0	23.5	21.4	21.6	31　鳥　　　取
37.3	28.2	29.9	29.0	24.2	22.6	18.9	25.0	32　島　　　根
40.0	33.7	30.5	29.0	24.3	21.9	21.5	20.6	33　岡　　　山
39.2	31.9	27.8	24.2	21.3	19.3	20.1	21.6	34　広　　　島
45.2	32.9	34.1	27.7	22.4	20.2	19.2	19.4	35　山　　　口
39.5	25.3	26.8	28.1	25.1	22.9	21.5	17.3	36　徳　　　島
35.6	27.8	29.4	26.0	23.9	21.4	21.2	18.8	37　香　　　川
45.9	32.9	31.5	33.0	29.0	29.5	23.7	24.1	38　愛　　　媛
48.1	44.5	40.0	36.6	29.2	28.9	21.5	21.7	39　高　　　知
52.9	39.7	37.8	35.6	28.3	24.9	25.1	22.6	40　福　　　岡
49.2	40.5	40.7	32.1	29.6	22.1	22.6	19.4	41　佐　　　賀
50.5	43.5	44.5	39.7	29.3	26.0	24.3	22.2	42　長　　　崎
54.8	45.7	44.7	34.3	25.8	28.6	25.8	25.9	43　熊　　　本
57.4	40.9	35.7	30.5	30.0	27.0	30.4	23.8	44　大　　　分
58.4	47.4	46.3	41.4	30.1	30.0	29.4	26.2	45　宮　　　崎
53.7	46.2	43.4	39.7	30.0	26.7	26.1	23.3	46　鹿　児　島
32.6	30.6	37.1	34.9	31.7	29.3	24.4	25.5	47　沖　　　縄

Note : a)　See page 44.

死　産

表7.14　都道府県別にみた
Table 7.14　Trends in spontaneous foetal deaths

都道府県 Prefecture	1950 昭和25年	1955 30年	1960 35年	1965 40年	1970 45年	1975 50年	1980 55年	1985 60年
全国　Total	106 594	85 159	93 424	94 476	84 073	67 643	47 651	33 114
01[a] 北 海 道	5 239	4 088	4 776	4 700	4 382	3 704	2 797	1 766
02 青　　森	1 845	1 339	1 592	1 352	1 188	951	735	490
03 岩　　手	2 066	1 501	1 249	1 065	914	685	476	369
04 宮　　城	2 353	1 794	1 581	1 311	1 193	1 091	863	544
05 秋　　田	1 967	1 236	998	844	653	538	349	197
06 山　　形	1 639	1 150	1 018	776	587	550	386	308
07 福　　島	2 862	2 117	2 123	1 635	1 302	1 060	886	669
08 茨　　城	3 192	2 268	2 109	1 802	1 623	1 391	933	784
09 栃　　木	2 062	1 533	1 381	1 322	1 136	1 073	786	558
10 群　　馬	2 309	1 651	1 412	1 381	1 178	949	691	469
11 埼　　玉	3 200	2 609	2 491	3 077	3 307	2 976	2 021	1 521
12 千　　葉	2 784	2 316	2 408	2 750	2 938	2 689	2 041	1 479
13 東　　京	7 193	7 737	11 904	13 308	10 408	6 994	4 787	3 213
14 神 奈 川	3 231	2 892	3 828	4 896	4 342	3 725	2 656	1 906
15 新　　潟	3 047	2 111	1 962	1 516	1 297	1 163	858	550
16 富　　山	1 027	778	748	694	766	483	399	268
17 石　　川	1 089	828	923	825	852	696	482	322
18 福　　井	1 028	726	748	666	640	413	296	204
19 山　　梨	1 321	948	813	737	594	502	347	272
20 長　　野	2 372	1 706	1 553	1 359	1 168	1 047	791	504
21 岐　　阜	1 681	1 198	1 415	1 414	1 331	1 031	670	486
22 静　　岡	3 165	2 393	2 521	2 690	2 285	1 843	1 203	847
23 愛　　知	3 652	3 311	3 830	4 723	4 782	3 462	2 284	1 595
24 三　　重	1 577	1 185	1 293	1 144	1 161	858	568	385
25 滋　　賀	899	725	706	673	601	647	475	297
26 京　　都	1 935	1 618	1 821	1 955	1 741	1 571	1 053	707
27 大　　阪	5 277	5 073	7 484	9 356	8 365	6 166	4 034	2 623
28 兵　　庫	4 557	3 671	4 130	4 810	4 269	3 081	2 128	1 361
29 奈　　良	1 075	720	701	716	692	606	530	330
30 和 歌 山	1 138	937	990	962	829	619	412	312
31 鳥　　取	777	580	496	417	381	314	213	163
32 島　　根	1 141	704	669	560	444	329	263	204
33 岡　　山	2 029	1 501	1 192	1 111	1 147	961	560	433
34 広　　島	2 273	2 067	2 237	2 186	2 162	1 840	1 101	770
35 山　　口	1 887	1 404	1 512	1 258	1 213	917	645	378
36 徳　　島	1 340	990	783	709	577	451	329	199
37 香　　川	1 051	653	660	589	543	464	318	245
38 愛　　媛	1 879	1 303	1 287	1 149	935	837	649	426
39 高　　知	923	657	714	657	489	439	312	180
40 福　　岡	5 027	4 269	4 966	4 285	3 602	3 009	2 044	1 543
41 佐　　賀	1 136	903	940	832	656	509	363	242
42 長　　崎	2 112	1 849	1 978	1 513	1 301	1 002	690	548
43 熊　　本	2 393	1 973	1 754	1 549	1 137	899	689	541
44 大　　分	1 739	1 268	1 163	870	778	789	519	390
45 宮　　崎	1 542	1 126	957	781	757	644	503	357
46 鹿 児 島	2 459	1 712	1 550	1 473	1 313	1 109	995	667
47 沖　　縄	…	…	…	…	…	516	479	474
外　　国 Foreign countries	…	…	…	…	…	…	…	…
不　　詳 Place of residence not stated	104	41	58	78	114	50	42	18

468

Foetal mortality

年次別自然死産数
by each prefecture : Japan

1990 平成2年	1995 7年	2000 12年	2005 17年	2010 22年	2014 26年	2015 27年	2016 28年	都道府県 Prefecture
23 383	18 262	16 200	13 502	12 245	10 905	10 862	10 067	全国　Total
1 210	852	750	604	512	460	420	345	01[a)] 北 海 道
311	235	200	154	142	108	102	81	02 青　　森
236	219	159	153	133	117	114	95	03 岩　　手
445	351	316	237	210	180	202	174	04 宮　　城
178	180	112	100	102	86	68	73	05 秋　　田
203	153	159	109	116	88	94	83	06 山　　形
444	348	333	240	217	179	191	170	07 福　　島
528	443	376	306	261	239	249	208	08 茨　　城
430	305	280	195	169	154	138	147	09 栃　　木
361	271	239	200	193	155	160	163	10 群　　馬
1 226	1 057	941	780	690	665	670	575	11 埼　　玉
1 115	875	935	774	630	600	621	546	12 千　　葉
2 248	1 745	1 364	1 293	1 143	1 135	1 143	1 131	13 東　　京
1 462	1 288	1 119	1 023	871	771	749	665	14 神 奈 川
404	352	305	253	232	190	176	175	15 新　　潟
225	147	142	123	106	84	93	84	16 富　　山
271	181	172	137	122	107	104	85	17 石　　川
132	121	107	89	72	75	81	70	18 福　　井
201	134	148	96	68	55	58	52	19 山　　梨
355	318	246	220	181	161	161	178	20 長　　野
347	267	249	243	171	144	148	154	21 岐　　阜
629	535	466	364	379	336	264	288	22 静　　岡
1 088	956	903	777	665	641	666	615	23 愛　　知
314	230	221	178	182	157	143	143	24 三　　重
232	171	185	169	162	120	129	101	25 滋　　賀
466	374	296	227	208	210	197	190	26 京　　都
1 798	1 238	1 095	844	824	726	689	670	27 大　　阪
939	671	695	579	512	451	479	414	28 兵　　庫
257	168	197	165	138	99	106	89	29 奈　　良
192	132	117	87	78	61	61	64	30 和 歌 山
118	84	66	67	67	49	55	46	31 鳥　　取
131	92	73	61	67	65	41	78	32 島　　根
273	236	198	172	163	148	140	147	33 岡　　山
477	421	314	245	254	212	230	249	34 広　　島
258	228	197	146	127	99	103	103	35 山　　口
119	80	85	68	73	75	61	41	36 徳　　島
145	131	130	93	125	71	82	74	37 香　　川
294	209	168	166	112	120	105	102	38 愛　　媛
108	110	94	71	65	50	55	47	39 高　　知
1 051	683	593	556	582	462	496	450	40 福　　岡
171	144	141	93	103	74	82	51	41 佐　　賀
289	243	236	187	173	134	141	123	42 長　　崎
346	301	209	172	172	185	174	176	43 熊　　本
198	175	154	95	128	93	112	86	44 大　　分
216	173	135	122	103	117	124	99	45 宮　　崎
553	306	224	205	181	155	178	149	46 鹿 児 島
376	314	340	257	255	233	202	213	47 沖　　縄
…	8	7	4	3	7	2	4	外　　国 Foreign countries
13	7	9	3	3	2	3	1	不　　詳 Place of residence not stated

Note : a) See page 44.

死　産

表 7.15　都道府県別にみた
Table 7.15　Trends in spontaneous foetal death rates

都道府県 Prefecture	1950 昭和25年	1955 30年	1960 35年	1965 40年	1970 45年	1975 50年	1980 55年	1985 60年
全国　Total	41.7	44.5	52.3	47.6	40.6	33.8	28.8	22.1
01[a)] 北 海 道	33.1	35.7	45.2	43.6	43.1	38.2	34.4	24.7
02 青　　森	36.9	34.8	47.9	43.9	41.7	37.1	32.1	24.4
03 岩　　手	41.4	39.1	40.2	39.3	38.1	29.2	23.0	20.3
04 宮　　城	40.5	41.7	44.8	40.5	36.1	31.3	26.2	18.3
05 秋　　田	42.5	37.4	38.0	38.5	33.9	29.0	20.4	13.8
06 山　　形	36.7	37.7	41.0	37.6	31.6	30.1	21.7	19.6
07 福　　島	38.9	39.2	48.8	45.5	40.3	32.1	28.5	23.3
08 茨　　城	49.1	46.6	53.7	46.9	39.6	32.9	24.7	22.4
09 栃　　木	40.8	42.0	48.3	47.3	38.9	34.5	29.1	22.5
10 群　　馬	46.7	45.9	50.0	45.8	37.7	30.7	26.4	19.7
11 埼　　玉	47.3	50.1	52.8	43.4	34.7	29.8	25.9	21.8
12 千　　葉	45.0	48.6	55.7	47.4	38.5	33.3	29.9	23.4
13 東　　京	44.8	54.8	65.1	54.6	42.7	35.7	32.6	24.3
14 神 奈 川	45.5	50.4	57.3	47.0	33.5	30.2	27.1	21.3
15 新　　潟	38.7	37.6	43.6	35.2	32.8	29.6	25.1	18.1
16 富　　山	34.1	38.5	42.6	39.4	41.1	26.9	28.2	21.5
17 石　　川	38.6	42.3	52.9	46.4	44.4	35.3	30.4	23.3
18 福　　井	44.6	45.0	53.1	48.4	49.2	31.9	26.5	19.5
19 山　　梨	56.0	54.3	56.9	53.2	45.4	40.1	33.1	26.5
20 長　　野	42.5	43.2	45.9	40.1	35.1	31.5	27.9	20.1
21 岐　　阜	37.0	37.3	45.3	41.0	38.8	31.3	25.0	19.6
22 静　　岡	41.3	39.9	46.4	45.0	37.1	30.2	24.5	18.5
23 愛　　知	37.7	45.5	47.5	42.8	38.6	29.6	24.9	19.1
24 三　　重	38.8	42.0	48.4	39.2	41.4	31.5	25.3	18.7
25 滋　　賀	38.3	43.8	47.9	43.9	36.4	35.1	28.6	19.3
26 京　　都	42.2	51.8	55.9	48.9	39.6	37.3	31.2	23.7
27 大　　阪	50.1	60.5	69.0	57.6	45.7	38.5	34.0	24.8
28 兵　　庫	50.1	52.9	57.7	53.5	43.8	33.8	29.6	21.3
29 奈　　良	53.3	50.5	53.4	45.7	37.5	32.3	31.8	21.6
30 和 歌 山	43.9	48.3	55.9	49.2	43.2	36.0	29.4	24.7
31 鳥　　取	42.1	41.7	44.5	43.6	43.4	33.7	24.7	20.7
32 島　　根	40.1	36.6	42.0	42.7	38.8	28.5	25.2	21.5
33 岡　　山	45.1	47.1	42.7	40.3	37.4	30.4	21.9	18.2
34 広　　島	39.9	49.7	58.3	51.6	45.4	37.2	28.2	21.9
35 山　　口	40.1	43.7	53.3	46.3	45.3	36.1	30.9	20.4
36 徳　　島	48.2	49.9	53.1	51.6	45.0	35.5	29.7	19.6
37 香　　川	38.7	36.0	44.5	39.8	35.4	28.6	23.6	20.4
38 愛　　媛	38.0	38.7	46.3	43.2	38.2	33.9	31.3	22.9
39 高　　知	37.1	37.8	51.1	49.8	38.7	35.1	31.5	18.2
40 福　　岡	41.9	49.4	63.9	55.8	47.5	39.7	30.0	24.7
41 佐　　賀	35.0	37.2	49.4	52.6	46.0	36.7	27.6	19.6
42 長　　崎	35.5	38.8	48.5	45.3	44.2	36.3	29.0	25.0
43 熊　　本	39.8	42.5	47.8	48.6	41.8	33.0	26.6	22.0
44 大　　分	43.2	43.1	50.7	42.4	40.5	40.0	30.0	25.3
45 宮　　崎	39.2	37.3	38.5	38.0	40.2	33.1	27.8	22.0
46 鹿 児 島	41.4	32.1	38.1	46.4	49.6	42.2	38.1	26.9
47 沖　　縄	…	…	…	…	…	22.5	23.0	22.3

Foetal mortality

年次別自然死産率（出産千対）
(per 1,000 total births) by each prefecture : Japan

1990 平成2年	1995 7年	2000 12年	2005 17年	2010 22年	2014 26年	2015 27年	2016 28年	都道府県 Prefecture
18.3	14.9	13.2	12.3	11.2	10.6	10.6	10.1	全国　Total
20.9	16.4	15.4	14.0	12.4	12.1	11.1	9.6	01[a] 北 海 道
20.4	16.2	14.9	14.1	14.2	11.9	11.5	9.2	02 青　　森
15.8	16.2	12.3	14.0	13.3	13.0	12.6	11.1	03 岩　　手
18.1	15.2	13.7	11.9	10.7	9.7	11.0	9.8	04 宮　　城
15.5	17.3	12.0	12.6	14.8	14.0	11.4	12.6	05 秋　　田
15.4	12.8	14.0	11.3	13.1	10.8	11.7	10.8	06 山　　形
18.7	15.8	15.8	13.3	13.1	12.0	13.1	12.1	07 福　　島
17.6	15.2	12.9	12.3	10.6	10.7	11.2	9.8	08 茨　　城
20.6	15.8	14.3	10.9	10.0	9.7	8.8	9.8	09 栃　　木
17.9	13.6	11.9	11.3	11.8	10.4	11.0	11.7	10 群　　馬
18.7	15.2	13.8	12.7	11.3	11.6	11.7	10.3	11 埼　　玉
20.1	15.6	16.4	14.9	11.9	12.5	12.9	11.8	12 千　　葉
20.7	17.4	13.2	13.0	10.3	10.0	9.9	9.9	13 東　　京
17.8	15.5	13.1	13.1	10.9	10.3	10.0	9.2	14 神 奈 川
16.2	15.1	13.6	13.3	12.5	11.3	10.5	10.9	15 新　　潟
21.5	14.3	13.6	13.4	12.7	10.9	12.0	11.3	16 富　　山
22.5	15.9	14.6	13.3	12.4	11.7	11.2	9.4	17 石　　川
14.7	14.2	13.0	12.1	10.2	11.9	12.7	11.2	18 福　　井
22.5	14.8	17.1	13.1	10.0	8.9	9.5	8.8	19 山　　梨
16.0	14.6	11.3	11.6	10.3	9.9	10.1	11.5	20 長　　野
16.5	12.9	11.9	13.4	9.9	9.3	9.4	10.2	21 岐　　阜
16.3	14.7	12.6	11.1	11.6	11.5	9.1	10.2	22 静　　岡
14.7	12.9	11.8	11.3	9.3	9.6	10.0	9.4	23 愛　　知
16.9	12.8	12.1	11.3	11.7	11.2	10.0	10.6	24 三　　重
16.5	12.5	12.8	12.8	11.9	9.3	10.0	8.2	25 滋　　賀
18.5	15.6	12.0	10.2	9.6	10.5	9.8	9.6	26 京　　都
19.7	13.9	12.0	10.8	10.7	10.1	9.6	9.5	27 大　　阪
16.8	12.6	12.4	11.9	10.5	10.0	10.7	9.4	28 兵　　庫
18.6	12.3	14.4	14.3	12.6	10.1	10.6	9.3	29 奈　　良
18.2	13.0	11.9	10.8	10.0	8.4	8.5	9.4	30 和 歌 山
17.6	14.1	11.3	12.9	13.6	10.6	11.6	10.1	31 鳥　　取
16.8	13.2	10.9	10.4	11.4	11.9	7.2	14.3	32 島　　根
13.7	12.2	10.1	10.0	9.5	9.1	8.8	9.3	33 岡　　山
15.9	14.8	11.1	9.7	9.7	8.7	9.5	10.7	34 広　　島
17.9	16.7	14.5	12.3	10.7	9.5	9.8	10.3	35 山　　口
14.4	10.4	11.5	11.2	12.1	13.3	10.7	7.5	36 徳　　島
14.6	13.7	12.9	10.4	14.5	9.0	10.4	9.7	37 香　　川
19.2	14.6	12.3	13.9	9.5	11.2	10.1	10.0	38 愛　　媛
14.3	15.1	13.2	11.6	11.4	9.7	10.7	9.6	39 高　　知
20.7	14.0	12.1	12.3	12.1	10.0	10.7	10.0	40 福　　岡
17.0	15.8	15.5	12.0	13.1	10.1	11.3	7.3	41 佐　　賀
16.6	15.7	16.0	14.8	14.0	11.5	12.5	11.0	42 長　　崎
17.2	16.1	11.6	10.6	10.3	11.6	10.9	11.5	43 熊　　本
16.0	15.1	13.6	9.4	12.3	9.8	11.9	9.3	44 大　　分
16.8	14.1	11.7	12.0	9.8	11.9	13.0	10.8	45 宮　　崎
27.7	17.5	13.2	13.3	11.6	10.6	12.3	10.6	46 鹿 児 島
21.3	18.2	19.5	15.4	14.4	13.8	11.6	12.5	47 沖　　縄

Note : a)　See page 44.

死　産

表 7.16　都道府県別にみた
Table 7.16　Trends in artificial foetal deaths

都道府県 Prefecture	1950 昭和25年	1955 30年	1960 35年	1965 40年	1970 45年	1975 50年	1980 55年	1985 60年
全国　Total	110 380	98 106	85 857	67 141	51 022	34 219	29 795	35 895
01[a] 北 海 道	6 210	6 739	7 090	6 467	5 532	3 568	2 993	3 222
02 青　　森	2 040	1 877	1 775	1 209	902	632	387	520
03 岩　　手	2 212	2 181	1 980	1 436	977	623	625	549
04 宮　　城	2 587	2 678	2 384	1 853	1 428	967	926	1 086
05 秋　　田	1 665	1 724	1 740	1 196	842	519	415	439
06 山　　形	2 299	2 044	1 537	1 000	778	490	520	501
07 福　　島	3 061	2 890	2 169	1 519	1 046	718	661	700
08 茨　　城	2 044	1 813	1 477	1 153	732	409	407	690
09 栃　　木	1 635	1 531	1 141	860	569	388	334	438
10 群　　馬	2 340	1 997	1 340	868	640	384	316	421
11 埼　　玉	1 840	1 624	1 303	1 160	970	819	771	1 109
12 千　　葉	1 576	1 574	1 285	1 107	956	696	576	929
13 東　　京	5 070	5 681	6 166	4 809	3 673	2 353	2 090	2 672
14 神 奈 川	2 059	2 681	2 296	1 878	1 468	1 165	972	1 344
15 新　　潟	3 773	2 449	1 893	1 283	915	624	482	597
16 富　　山	1 247	989	688	561	371	196	176	234
17 石　　川	923	736	537	340	226	205	220	235
18 福　　井	798	563	446	348	189	130	136	224
19 山　　梨	917	851	699	392	214	153	118	144
20 長　　野	3 515	2 165	1 516	994	751	492	354	417
21 岐　　阜	2 291	1 539	1 272	927	699	383	338	449
22 静　　岡	3 115	3 191	2 314	1 741	1 210	866	836	972
23 愛　　知	5 471	4 108	3 619	3 794	2 957	1 932	1 712	1 895
24 三　　重	1 850	1 548	1 301	1 001	751	491	439	456
25 滋　　賀	1 131	777	549	392	320	175	197	244
26 京　　都	2 652	1 701	1 535	1 329	963	621	569	653
27 大　　阪	6 214	5 382	5 899	5 784	4 820	3 184	2 545	2 807
28 兵　　庫	4 499	3 282	2 822	2 667	2 023	1 359	1 072	1 296
29 奈　　良	518	464	439	382	268	192	179	290
30 和 歌 山	1 056	1 028	811	531	405	247	178	257
31 鳥　　取	1 558	1 441	1 076	598	408	243	206	213
32 島　　根	1 452	1 385	1 158	774	463	292	207	220
33 岡　　山	2 586	1 906	1 390	1 014	787	535	513	618
34 広　　島	1 907	1 871	1 659	1 223	950	729	567	825
35 山　　口	2 398	1 998	1 856	1 371	981	522	441	454
36 徳　　島	1 019	803	639	409	394	248	223	243
37 香　　川	1 473	866	642	477	267	206	179	255
38 愛　　媛	2 020	1 809	1 479	1 008	657	512	387	497
39 高　　知	926	697	590	502	301	279	203	334
40 福　　岡	5 725	5 678	5 461	3 664	2 597	1 784	1 709	2 045
41 佐　　賀	1 365	1 098	789	554	427	292	307	390
42 長　　崎	2 725	2 628	2 266	1 689	1 392	957	854	1 010
43 熊　　本	2 414	2 278	1 923	1 390	925	714	720	896
44 大　　分	1 795	1 757	1 646	1 110	858	617	494	584
45 宮　　崎	2 493	2 357	1 982	1 344	1 106	683	571	608
46 鹿 児 島	1 893	1 714	1 268	1 023	854	583	601	750
47 沖　　縄	…	…	…	…	…	34	61	155
外　　国 Foreign countries	…	…	…	…	…	…	…	…
不　　詳 Place of residence not stated	23	13	10	10	60	8	8	8

Foetal mortality

年次別人工死産数
by each prefecture : Japan

1990 平成2年	1995 7年	2000 12年	2005 17年	2010 22年	2014 26年	2015 27年	2016 28年	都道府県 Prefecture
30 509	21 141	22 193	18 316	14 315	12 619	11 755	10 867	全国　Total
2 288	1 287	1 319	1 060	748	641	637	556	01[a] 北 海 道
334	292	271	213	141	142	114	102	02 青　　森
458	294	321	208	158	96	102	89	03 岩　　手
815	542	513	403	285	241	225	228	04 宮　　城
330	230	192	147	79	79	62	60	05 秋　　田
404	291	260	165	115	85	87	82	06 山　　形
599	404	449	327	270	165	169	136	07 福　　島
619	492	557	409	339	252	240	215	08 茨　　城
465	352	346	290	229	202	188	174	09 栃　　木
364	290	360	291	206	171	172	167	10 群　　馬
1 098	887	966	857	685	717	680	606	11 埼　　玉
878	666	713	713	608	543	481	455	12 千　　葉
2 295	1 444	1 631	1 546	1 444	1 325	1 263	1 234	13 東　　京
1 426	971	1 087	1 039	795	795	751	735	14 神 奈 川
446	277	294	276	242	201	173	145	15 新　　潟
167	109	146	110	82	71	71	68	16 富　　山
236	130	141	122	91	80	84	74	17 石　　川
181	128	119	102	87	86	66	76	18 福　　井
138	105	118	99	93	88	79	49	19 山　　梨
397	292	285	259	214	180	165	134	20 長　　野
423	288	362	226	211	169	172	135	21 岐　　阜
835	551	622	452	337	293	275	250	22 静　　岡
1 772	1 110	1 204	971	737	717	617	567	23 愛　　知
403	279	275	239	153	151	141	129	24 三　　重
248	200	207	139	124	104	124	112	25 滋　　賀
573	403	398	373	274	237	230	211	26 京　　都
2 570	1 736	1 665	1 370	1 083	895	830	810	27 大　　阪
1 125	768	883	717	558	500	437	442	28 兵　　庫
275	169	182	165	137	106	108	101	29 奈　　良
231	159	182	152	98	87	116	91	30 和 歌 山
182	144	126	105	71	60	46	52	31 鳥　　取
160	104	128	109	76	59	66	58	32 島　　根
523	414	402	327	255	206	202	178	33 岡　　山
700	490	470	368	301	256	255	252	34 広　　島
392	223	266	182	138	111	100	92	35 山　　口
208	114	114	103	79	54	62	53	36 徳　　島
208	135	167	139	81	98	85	70	37 香　　川
409	262	262	227	229	196	141	143	38 愛　　媛
255	213	190	154	101	99	56	59	39 高　　知
1 638	1 252	1 265	1 049	784	693	668	568	40 福　　岡
323	224	230	156	130	88	81	84	41 佐　　賀
590	429	420	315	189	168	134	124	42 長　　崎
755	555	599	384	258	273	239	220	43 熊　　本
510	300	250	213	184	164	174	135	44 大　　分
535	409	401	299	214	177	155	141	45 宮　　崎
519	500	515	408	286	236	201	178	46 鹿 児 島
200	214	307	326	305	261	221	221	47 沖　　縄
…	4	10	5	9	1	9	6	外　　国 Foreign countries
9	9	3	7	2	-	1	-	不　　詳 Place of residence not stated

Note : a) See page 44.

死　産

表 7.17　都道府県別にみた
Table 7.17　Trends in artificial foetal death rates

都道府県 Prefecture	1950 昭和25年	1955 30年	1960 35年	1965 40年	1970 45年	1975 50年	1980 55年	1985 60年
全国　Total	43.2	51.3	48.1	33.8	24.7	17.1	18.0	23.9
01[a) 北　海　道	39.2	58.9	67.1	60.0	54.4	36.8	36.8	45.1
02　青　　　森	40.8	48.8	53.4	39.3	31.7	24.7	16.9	25.9
03　岩　　　手	44.3	56.8	63.8	52.9	40.8	26.5	30.1	30.2
04　宮　　　城	44.5	62.3	67.5	57.2	43.2	27.8	28.1	36.6
05　秋　　　田	36.0	51.7	66.2	54.6	43.7	28.0	24.3	30.7
06　山　　　形	51.5	67.0	61.9	48.4	41.9	26.8	29.3	31.9
07　福　　　島	41.7	53.6	49.8	42.2	32.4	21.7	21.3	24.4
08　茨　　　城	31.5	37.2	37.6	30.0	17.9	9.7	10.8	19.7
09　栃　　　木	32.4	42.0	39.9	30.8	19.5	12.5	12.3	17.6
10　群　　　馬	47.3	55.5	47.4	28.8	20.5	12.4	12.1	17.7
11　埼　　　玉	27.2	31.2	27.6	16.4	10.2	8.2	9.9	15.9
12　千　　　葉	25.5	33.0	29.7	19.1	12.5	8.6	8.4	14.7
13　東　　　京	31.6	40.2	33.7	19.7	15.1	12.0	14.2	20.2
14　神　奈　川	29.0	46.7	34.4	18.0	11.3	9.4	9.9	15.0
15　新　　　潟	47.9	43.6	42.1	29.8	23.1	15.9	14.1	19.7
16　富　　　山	41.4	49.0	39.2	31.9	19.9	10.9	12.5	18.7
17　石　　　川	32.7	37.6	30.8	19.1	11.8	10.4	13.9	17.0
18　福　　　井	34.6	34.9	31.7	25.3	14.5	10.0	12.2	21.4
19　山　　　梨	38.8	48.7	48.9	28.3	16.4	12.2	11.3	14.0
20　長　　　野	62.9	54.8	44.8	29.3	22.5	14.8	12.5	16.6
21　岐　　　阜	50.4	48.0	40.8	26.9	20.4	11.6	12.6	18.1
22　静　　　岡	40.7	53.1	42.6	29.1	19.6	14.2	17.0	21.2
23　愛　　　知	56.4	56.5	44.9	34.4	23.8	16.5	18.7	22.6
24　三　　　重	45.5	54.9	48.7	34.3	26.8	18.0	19.6	22.2
25　滋　　　賀	48.2	46.9	37.3	25.6	19.4	9.5	11.9	15.8
26　京　　　都	57.9	54.4	47.2	33.2	21.9	14.7	16.9	21.9
27　大　　　阪	59.0	64.2	54.4	35.6	26.3	19.9	21.5	26.5
28　兵　　　庫	49.5	47.3	39.4	29.6	20.8	14.9	14.9	20.3
29　奈　　　良	25.7	32.5	33.4	24.4	14.5	10.2	10.7	19.0
30　和　歌　山	40.7	53.0	45.8	27.2	21.1	14.4	12.7	20.3
31　鳥　　　取	84.5	103.5	96.5	62.5	46.4	26.1	23.9	27.0
32　島　　　根	51.0	71.9	72.6	58.9	40.5	25.3	19.8	23.2
33　岡　　　山	57.5	59.8	49.8	36.8	25.7	16.9	20.1	26.0
34　広　　　島	33.5	45.0	43.3	28.9	19.9	14.8	14.5	23.5
35　山　　　口	51.0	62.1	65.5	50.5	36.6	20.6	21.1	24.5
36　徳　　　島	36.6	40.5	43.4	29.8	30.7	19.5	20.1	23.9
37　香　　　川	54.2	47.7	43.3	32.3	17.4	12.7	13.3	21.2
38　愛　　　媛	40.9	53.7	53.2	37.9	26.9	20.8	18.6	26.8
39　高　　　知	37.2	40.1	42.2	38.1	23.8	22.3	20.5	33.9
40　福　　　岡	47.7	65.7	70.2	47.7	34.2	23.5	25.1	32.8
41　佐　　　賀	42.0	45.2	41.5	35.0	29.9	21.0	23.4	31.6
42　長　　　崎	45.8	55.2	55.6	50.6	47.3	34.7	35.9	46.1
43　熊　　　本	40.1	49.1	52.4	43.6	34.0	26.2	27.8	36.4
44　大　　　分	44.6	59.7	71.8	54.1	44.7	31.3	28.5	37.9
45　宮　　　崎	63.3	78.0	79.7	65.4	58.7	35.1	31.6	37.5
46　鹿　児　島	31.9	32.1	31.2	32.2	32.3	22.2	23.0	30.3
47　沖　　　縄	…	…	…	…	…	1.5	2.9	7.3

Foetal mortality

年次別人工死産率（出産千対）
(per 1,000 total births) by each prefecture : Japan

1990 平成 2 年	1995 7 年	2000 12年	2005 17年	2010 22年	2014 26年	2015 27年	2016 28年	都道府県 Prefecture
23.9	17.2	18.1	16.7	13.0	12.3	11.4	10.9	全国　Total
39.5	24.7	27.0	24.6	18.1	16.8	16.9	15.4	01[a] 北 海 道
21.9	20.1	20.2	19.6	14.1	15.6	12.9	11.6	02 青　　森
30.6	21.7	24.9	19.1	15.7	10.6	11.3	10.4	03 岩　　手
33.2	23.4	22.3	20.2	14.5	13.0	12.2	12.8	04 宮　　城
28.7	22.1	20.6	18.5	11.5	12.8	10.3	10.3	05 秋　　田
30.7	24.3	22.9	17.1	12.9	10.4	10.9	10.6	06 山　　形
25.2	18.3	21.3	18.1	16.3	11.1	11.6	9.7	07 福　　島
20.7	16.9	19.1	16.4	13.8	11.3	10.8	10.1	08 茨　　城
22.3	18.2	17.7	16.2	13.6	12.8	12.0	11.6	09 栃　　木
18.0	14.5	18.0	16.5	12.5	11.5	11.8	11.9	10 群　　馬
16.7	12.7	14.1	14.0	11.3	12.5	11.8	10.9	11 埼　　玉
15.9	11.9	12.5	13.7	11.5	11.3	10.0	9.8	12 千　　葉
21.1	14.4	15.8	15.6	13.0	11.7	10.9	10.8	13 東　　京
17.3	11.7	12.8	13.3	10.0	10.7	10.0	10.2	14 神 奈 川
17.9	11.9	13.1	14.5	13.0	11.9	10.4	9.0	15 新　　潟
16.0	10.6	14.0	11.9	9.8	9.2	9.2	9.1	16 富　　山
19.6	11.4	12.0	11.8	9.3	8.7	9.1	8.1	17 石　　川
20.2	15.1	14.4	13.9	12.4	13.6	10.3	12.1	18 福　　井
15.5	11.6	13.7	13.5	13.7	14.2	12.9	8.3	19 山　　梨
17.9	13.4	13.1	13.6	12.1	11.1	10.3	8.7	20 長　　野
20.1	13.9	17.3	12.4	12.2	10.9	10.9	8.9	21 岐　　阜
21.7	15.1	16.9	13.8	10.3	10.0	9.5	8.9	22 静　　岡
24.0	15.0	15.7	14.1	10.3	10.8	9.2	8.7	23 愛　　知
21.6	15.5	15.1	15.2	9.8	10.8	9.9	9.6	24 三　　重
17.6	14.6	14.3	10.5	9.1	8.0	9.6	9.1	25 滋　　賀
22.7	16.8	16.1	16.8	12.6	11.8	11.4	10.7	26 京　　都
28.2	19.5	18.3	17.5	14.1	12.5	11.5	11.5	27 大　　阪
20.1	14.4	15.8	14.8	11.4	11.0	9.7	10.0	28 兵　　庫
19.9	12.4	13.3	14.3	12.5	10.8	10.8	10.5	29 奈　　良
21.9	15.6	18.4	18.8	12.6	11.9	16.1	13.4	30 和 歌 山
27.1	24.2	21.6	20.3	14.4	12.9	9.7	11.5	31 鳥　　取
20.5	14.9	19.0	18.6	12.9	10.8	11.7	10.7	32 島　　根
26.3	21.5	20.4	19.0	14.8	12.7	12.7	11.3	33 岡　　山
23.3	17.2	16.7	14.5	11.5	10.6	10.6	10.8	34 広　　島
27.3	16.3	19.6	15.4	11.7	10.7	9.5	9.2	35 山　　口
25.2	14.9	15.4	16.9	13.0	9.6	10.9	9.7	36 徳　　島
21.0	14.1	16.5	15.6	9.4	12.4	10.8	9.1	37 香　　川
26.7	18.3	19.2	19.0	19.5	18.3	13.6	14.1	38 愛　　媛
33.8	29.3	26.8	25.1	17.8	19.2	10.8	12.1	39 高　　知
32.2	25.7	25.7	23.3	16.3	14.9	14.4	12.6	40 福　　岡
32.1	24.6	25.2	20.1	16.5	12.0	11.2	12.1	41 佐　　賀
33.9	27.8	28.5	24.9	15.3	14.5	11.9	11.1	42 長　　崎
37.6	29.6	33.1	23.7	15.5	17.0	14.9	14.4	43 熊　　本
41.3	25.9	22.1	21.1	17.7	17.2	18.5	14.5	44 大　　分
41.6	33.3	34.6	29.4	20.3	18.1	16.3	15.4	45 宮　　崎
26.0	28.6	30.3	26.4	18.3	16.1	13.9	12.7	46 鹿 児 島
11.3	12.4	17.6	19.5	17.3	15.5	12.7	13.0	47 沖　　縄

Note : a) See page 44.

死　産

〔死産の原因〕
〔Causes of foetal death〕

表 7.18　死産原因別にみた
Table 7.18　Foetal deaths and percent

死因基本分類コード Code	死産原因 Causes of foetal death	死産数 Foetal deaths	百分率 Percentage
	総　　数　　　　Total	20 934	100.0
	自　然　死　産　　Spontaneous	10 067	48.1
ⅩⅥ	周産期に発生した病態	9 442	45.1
(P00-P04)	母体側要因並びに妊娠及び分娩の合併症により影響を受けた胎児及び新生児	5 915	28.3
P00	現在の妊娠とは無関係の場合もありうる母体の病態により影響を受けた胎児及び新生児	3 244	15.5
P01	母体の妊娠合併症により影響を受けた胎児及び新生児	1 194	5.7
P02	胎盤，臍帯及び卵膜の合併症により影響を受けた胎児及び新生児	1 429	6.8
P03	その他の分娩合併症により影響を受けた胎児及び新生児	48	0.2
P04	胎盤又は母乳を介して有害な影響を受けた胎児及び新生児	-	-
(P05-P08)	妊娠期間及び胎児発育に関連する障害	59	0.3
P05	胎児発育遅延及び胎児栄養失調	37	0.2
P07	妊娠期間短縮及び低出産体重に関連する障害，他に分類されないもの	22	0.1
P08	遷延妊娠及び高出産体重に関連する障害	-	-
(P10-P15)	出　産　外　傷	-	-
P10	出産損傷による頭蓋内裂傷及び出血	-	-
P11	中枢神経系のその他の出産損傷	-	-
P12	頭皮の出産損傷	-	-
P13	骨格の出産損傷	-	-
P14	末梢神経系の出産損傷	-	-
P15	その他の出産損傷	-	-
(P20-P29)	周産期に特異的な呼吸障害及び心血管障害	79	0.4
P20	子宮内低酸素症	9	0.0
P21	出生時仮死	-	-
P22	新生児の呼吸窮迫	-	-
P23	先天性肺炎	-	-
P24	新生児吸引症候群	-	-
P25	周産期に発生した間質性気腫及び関連病態	-	-
P26	周産期に発生した肺出血	-	-
P27	周産期に発生した慢性呼吸器疾患	-	-
P28	周産期に発生したその他の呼吸器病態	7	0.0
P29	周産期に発生した心血管障害	63	0.3
(P35-P39)	周産期に特異的な感染症	53	0.3
P35	先天性ウイルス疾患	18	0.1
P36	新生児の細菌性敗血症	-	-
P37	その他の先天性感染症及び寄生虫症	-	-
P38	軽度出血を伴う又は伴わない新生児の臍炎	-	-
P39	周産期に特異的なその他の感染症	35	0.2
(P50-P61)	胎児及び新生児の出血性障害及び血液障害	98	0.5
P50	胎　児　失　血	94	0.4
P51	新生児の臍出血	-	-
P52	胎児及び新生児の頭蓋内非外傷性出血	2	0.0
P53	胎児及び新生児の出血性疾患	-	-
P54	その他の新生児出血	-	-
P55	胎児及び新生児の溶血性疾患	-	-
P56	溶血性疾患による胎児水腫	-	-
P57	核　黄　疸	-	-
P58	その他の多量の溶血による新生児黄疸	-	-
P59	その他及び詳細不明の原因による新生児黄疸	1	0.0
P60	胎児及び新生児の播種性血管内凝固	-	-
P61	その他の周産期の血液障害	1	0.0

死産数及び百分率
distribution by causes : Japan, 2016

Foetal mortality

平成28年

死因基本 分類コード Code	死 産 原 因 Causes of foetal death	死 産 数 Foetal deaths	百 分 率 Percentage
(P70-P72)	胎児及び新生児に特異的な一過性の内分泌障害及び代謝障害	19	0.1
P70	胎児及び新生児に特異的な一過性糖質代謝障害	19	0.1
P72	その他の一過性新生児内分泌障害	-	-
(P76-P78)	胎児及び新生児の消化器系障害	-	-
P76	新生児のその他の腸閉塞	-	-
P77	胎児及び新生児のえ死性腸炎	-	-
P78	その他の周産期の消化器系障害	-	-
(P80-P83)	胎児及び新生児の外皮及び体温調節に関連する病態	414	2.0
P80	新生児低体温	-	-
P81	新生児のその他の体温調節機能障害	-	-
P83	胎児及び新生児に特異的な外皮のその他の病態	414	2.0
(P90-P97)	周産期に発生したその他の障害	2 805	13.4
P90	新生児のけいれん	-	-
P91	新生児の脳のその他の機能障害	-	-
P92	新生児の哺乳上の問題	-	-
P93	胎児及び新生児に投与された薬物による反応及び中毒	-	-
P94	新生児の筋緊張障害	-	-
P95	原因不明の胎児死亡	2 773	13.2
P96	周産期に発生したその他の病態	32	0.2
P97	母体保護法による人工妊娠中絶，母体の病態によらないもの	・	・
ⅩⅦ	先天奇形，変形及び染色体異常	584	2.8
(Q00-Q07)	神経系の先天奇形	88	0.4
Q00	無脳症及び類似先天奇形	58	0.3
Q01	脳　　　瘤	1	0.0
Q02	小　頭　症	1	0.0
Q03	先天性水頭症	8	0.0
Q04	脳のその他の先天奇形	17	0.1
Q05	二　分　脊　椎	1	0.0
Q06	脊髄のその他の先天奇形	-	-
Q07	神経系のその他の先天奇形	2	0.0
(Q10-Q18)	眼，耳，顔面及び頚部の先天奇形	7	0.0
Q10	眼瞼，涙器及び眼窩の先天奇形	-	-
Q11	無眼球，小眼球及び巨大眼球	-	-
Q12	先天水晶体奇形	-	-
Q13	前眼部の先天奇形	-	-
Q14	眼球後極部の先天奇形	-	-
Q15	眼のその他の先天奇形	-	-
Q16	聴覚障害の原因となる耳の先天奇形	-	-
Q17	耳のその他の先天奇形	3	0.0
Q18	顔面及び頚部のその他の先天奇形	4	0.0
(Q20-Q28)	循環器系の先天奇形	57	0.3
Q20	心臓の房室及び結合部の先天奇形	-	-
Q21	心中隔の先天奇形	6	0.0
Q22	肺動脈弁及び三尖弁の先天奇形	6	0.0
Q23	大動脈弁及び僧帽弁の先天奇形	1	0.0
Q24	心臓のその他の先天奇形	42	0.2
Q25	大型動脈の先天奇形	2	0.0
Q26	大型静脈の先天奇形	-	-
Q27	末梢血管系のその他の先天奇形	-	-
Q28	循環器系のその他の先天奇形	-	-

死　産

表 7.18　死産原因別にみた
Table 7.18　Foetal deaths and percent

死因基本 分類コード Code	死　産　原　因 Causes of foetal death	死　産　数 Foetal deaths	百　分　率 Percentage
(Q30-Q34)	呼吸器系の先天奇形	6	0.0
Q30	鼻の先天奇形	-	-
Q31	喉頭の先天奇形	-	-
Q32	気管及び気管支の先天奇形	1	0.0
Q33	肺の先天奇形	4	0.0
Q34	呼吸器系のその他の先天奇形	1	0.0
(Q35-Q37)	唇裂及び口蓋裂	3	0.0
Q35	口　蓋　裂	1	0.0
Q36	唇　　　裂	-	-
Q37	唇裂を伴う口蓋裂	2	0.0
(Q38-Q45)	消化器系のその他の先天奇形	10	0.0
Q38	舌，口及び咽頭のその他の先天奇形	-	-
Q39	食道の先天奇形	2	0.0
Q40	上部消化管のその他の先天奇形	-	-
Q41	小腸の先天欠損，閉鎖及び狭窄	5	0.0
Q42	大腸の先天欠損，閉鎖及び狭窄	1	0.0
Q43	腸のその他の先天奇形	-	-
Q44	胆のう，胆管及び肝の先天奇形	2	0.0
Q45	消化器系のその他の先天奇形	-	-
(Q50-Q56)	生殖器の先天奇形	-	-
Q50	卵巣，卵管及び広間膜の先天奇形	-	-
Q51	子宮及び子宮頚の先天奇形	-	-
Q52	女性性器のその他の先天奇形	-	-
Q53	停　留　精　巣	-	-
Q54	尿　道　下　裂	-	-
Q55	男性生殖器のその他の先天奇形	-	-
Q56	性不確定及び仮性半陰陽	-	-
(Q60-Q64)	腎尿路系の先天奇形	24	0.1
Q60	腎の無発生及びその他の減形成	10	0.0
Q61	のう胞性腎疾患	4	0.0
Q62	腎盂の先天性閉塞性欠損及び尿管の先天奇形	1	0.0
Q63	腎のその他の先天奇形	1	0.0
Q64	尿路系のその他の先天奇形	8	0.0
(Q65-Q79)	筋骨格系の先天奇形及び変形	58	0.3
Q65	股関節部の先天変形	-	-
Q66	足の先天変形	-	-
Q67	頭部，顔面，脊柱及び胸部の先天筋骨格変形	1	0.0
Q68	その他の先天筋骨格変形	-	-
Q69	多　　　指	1	0.0
Q70	合　　　指	-	-
Q71	上肢の減形成	-	-
Q72	下肢の減形成	-	-
Q73	詳細不明の肢の減形成	-	-
Q74	肢のその他の先天奇形	-	-
Q75	頭蓋及び顔面骨のその他の先天奇形	8	0.0
Q76	脊柱及び骨性胸郭の先天奇形	-	-
Q77	骨軟骨異形成，長管骨及び脊椎の成長障害を伴うもの	3	0.0
Q78	その他の骨軟骨異形成	1	0.0
Q79	筋骨格系の先天奇形，他に分類されないもの	44	0.2

Foetal mortality

死産数及び百分率（つづき）
distribution by causes : Japan, 2016－CON.

平成28年

死因基本 分類コード Code	死 産 原 因 Causes of foetal death	死 産 数 Foetal deaths	百 分 率 Percentage
(Q80－Q89)	その他の先天奇形	139	0.7
Q80	先天性魚りんせん	-	-
Q81	表皮水疱症	-	-
Q82	皮膚のその他の先天奇形	2	0.0
Q83	乳房の先天奇形	-	-
Q84	外皮のその他の先天奇形	-	-
Q85	母斑症，他に分類されないもの	-	-
Q86	既知の外因による先天奇形症候群，他に分類されないもの	-	-
Q87	多系統に及ぶその他の明示された先天奇形症候群	3	0.0
Q89	その他の先天奇形，他に分類されないもの	134	0.6
(Q90－Q99)	染色体異常，他に分類されないもの	192	0.9
Q90	ダウン症候群	26	0.1
Q91	エドワーズ症候群及びパトー症候群	69	0.3
Q92	常染色体のその他のトリソミー及び部分トリソミー，他に分類されないもの	2	0.0
Q93	常染色体のモノソミー及び欠失，他に分類されないもの	-	-
Q95	均衡型再配列及びマーカー，他に分類されないもの	-	-
Q96	ターナー症候群	6	0.0
Q97	その他の性染色体異常，女性表現型，他に分類されないもの	-	-
Q98	その他の性染色体異常，男性表現型，他に分類されないもの	-	-
Q99	その他の染色体異常，他に分類されないもの	89	0.4
I	感染症及び寄生虫症	-	-
II	新 生 物	40	0.2
III	血液及び造血器の疾患並びに免疫機構の障害	-	-
IV	内分泌，栄養及び代謝疾患	-	-
V	精神及び行動の障害	-	-
VI	神経系の疾患	-	-
VII	眼及び付属器の疾患	-	-
VIII	耳及び乳様突起の疾患	-	-
IX	循環器系の疾患	-	-
X	呼吸器系の疾患	-	-
XI	消化器系の疾患	1	0.0
XII	皮膚及び皮下組織の疾患	-	-
XIII	筋骨格系及び結合組織の疾患	-	-
XIV	腎尿路生殖器系の疾患	-	-
XVIII	症状，徴候及び異常臨床所見・異常検査所見で他に分類されないもの	-	-
XXII	特殊目的用コード	-	-
	人 工 死 産　　　　Artificial	10 867	51.9
(P00－P04)	母体側要因並びに妊娠及び分娩の合併症により影響を受けた胎児及び新生児	5 452	26.0
P00	現在の妊娠とは無関係の場合もありうる母体の病態により影響を受けた胎児及び新生児	4 978	23.8
P01	母体の妊娠合併症により影響を受けた胎児及び新生児	386	1.8
P02	胎盤，臍帯及び卵膜の合併症により影響を受けた胎児及び新生児	71	0.3
P03	その他の分娩合併症により影響を受けた胎児及び新生児	17	0.1
P04	胎盤又は母乳を介して有害な影響を受けた胎児及び新生児	-	-
P97	母体保護法による人工妊娠中絶，母体の病態によらないもの	5 415	25.9

注：第XV，XIX，XX章は該当があり得ないので省略した。

死　産

表 7.19　死因・母側病態－児側病態別に
Table 7.19　Foetal deaths and percent distribution of spontaneous

死因基本 分類コード Code	母　側　病　態 Maternal condition	自然死産 Spontaneous	母側病態 百分率 Percentage of maternal condition	児　側　病　態		
				総　数 Total	P05－P08 妊娠期間及び 胎児発育に 関連する障害	P10－P15 出産外傷
	総　数　　　Total	10 067	100.0	100.0	1.0	-
(P00－P04)	母体側要因並びに妊娠及び分娩の合併症により影響を受けた胎児及び新生児	6 174	61.3	100.0	0.8	
P00	現在の妊娠とは無関係の場合もありうる母体の病態により影響を受けた胎児及び新生児	3 432	34.1	100.0	0.6	
P00.0	母体の高血圧性障害により影響を受けた胎児及び新生児	46	0.5	100.0	17.4	-
P00.0A	高血圧症	23	0.2	100.0	17.4	
P00.0B	たんぱく尿を伴う高血圧性障害	18	0.2	100.0	16.7	-
P00.0C	たんぱく尿を伴わない妊娠高血圧	-	-	-	-	-
P00.0D	子癇	1	0.0	100.0	-	-
P00.0E	その他	4	0.0	100.0	25.0	-
P00.1	母体の腎及び尿路疾患により影響を受けた胎児及び新生児	1	0.0	100.0		
P00.1A	糸球体疾患	1	0.0	100.0		
P00.1B	腎尿細管間質性疾患	-	-	-	-	-
P00.1C	腎不全	-	-	-	-	-
P00.1D	尿路系のその他	-	-	-	-	-
P00.1E	その他	-	-	-	-	-
P00.2	母体の感染症及び寄生虫症により影響を受けた胎児及び新生児	229	2.3	100.0	0.4	-
P00.2A	梅毒	2	0.0	100.0		-
P00.2B	インフルエンザ	1	0.0	100.0		-
P00.2C	風疹	1	0.0	100.0		-
P00.2D	トキソプラズマ	-	-	-	-	-
P00.2E	結核	-	-	-	-	-
P00.2F	ＨＩＶ	-	-	-	-	-
P00.2G	その他	225	2.2	100.0	0.4	-
P00.3	その他の母体の循環器系疾患及び呼吸器系疾患により影響を受けた胎児及び新生児	7	0.1	100.0	-	-
P00.3A	心疾患	4	0.0	100.0	-	
P00.3B	その他の循環器系疾患	3	0.0	100.0	-	
P00.3C	呼吸器系疾患	-	-	-	-	-
P00.4	母体の栄養障害により影響を受けた胎児及び新生児	-	-	-		
P00.5	母体の損傷により影響を受けた胎児及び新生児	6	0.1	100.0	-	
P00.6	母体に対する外科的処置により影響を受けた胎児及び新生児	1	0.0	100.0		
P00.7	母体に対するその他の医学的処置により影響を受けた胎児及び新生児, 他に分類されないもの	-	-	-		
P00.8	その他の母体の病態により影響を受けた胎児及び新生児	44	0.4	100.0	2.3	-
P00.8A	悪性新生物	4	0.0	100.0		
P00.8B	良性及び性質不詳の新生物	9	0.1	100.0		
P00.8C	糖尿病	-	-	-	-	-
P00.8D	精神障害	-	-	-	-	-
P00.8E	消化器系の疾患	-	-	-	-	-
P00.8F	生殖器系の疾患	19	0.2	100.0	-	
P00.8G	その他の母体側の疾患	9	0.1	100.0	11.1	-
P00.8H	疲労	-	-	-	-	-
P00.8I	その他の診断名不明確な母体側の疾患	3	0.0	100.0	-	
P00.9	詳細不明の母体の病態により影響を受けた胎児及び新生児	3 098	30.8	100.0	0.4	-
P00.9A	身体的原因, 精神的原因	3	0.0	100.0	-	
P00.9B	詳細不明	3 095	30.7	100.0	0.4	-
P01	母体の妊娠合併症により影響を受けた胎児及び新生児	1 239	12.3	100.0	1.8	
P01.0	無力頸管により影響を受けた胎児及び新生児	229	2.3	100.0	1.7	
P01.1	前期破水により影響を受けた胎児及び新生児	721	7.2	100.0	1.2	
P01.2	羊水過少症により影響を受けた胎児及び新生児	22	0.2	100.0	4.5	
P01.3	羊水過多症により影響を受けた胎児及び新生児	7	0.1	100.0	-	
P01.4	子宮外妊娠により影響を受けた胎児及び新生児	3	0.0	100.0	-	
P01.5	多胎妊娠により影響を受けた胎児及び新生児	72	0.7	100.0	4.2	
P01.6	母体死亡により影響を受けた胎児及び新生児	-	-	-	-	
P01.7	分娩開始前の胎位異常により影響を受けた胎児及び新生児	2	0.0	100.0	-	
P01.8	その他の母体の妊娠合併症により影響を受けた胎児及び新生児	183	1.8	100.0	2.7	

Foetal mortality

みた自然死産数及び百分率
by causes on child and maternal condition : Japan, 2016

平成28年

別　百　分　率　Percentage by causes on child

P20－P29 周産期に特異的な呼吸障害及び心血管障害	P35－P39 周産期に特異的な感染症	P50－P61 胎児及び新生児の出血性障害及び血液障害	P70－P72 胎児及び新生児に特異的な一過性の内分泌障害及び代謝障害	P76－P78 胎児及び新生児の消化器系障害	P80－P83 胎児及び新生児の外皮及び体温調節に関連する病態	P90－P96 周産期に発生したその他の障害	XⅦ 先天奇形，変形及び染色体異常	Ⅰ－ⅩⅣ，ⅩⅧ ⅩⅫ その他
1.4	2.1	1.0	0.2	-	4.1	84.0	5.8	0.4
1.2	3.3	0.5	0.1	-	0.6	91.8	1.6	0.1
0.3	1.7	0.1	0.2	-	1.0	94.0	2.0	0.2
2.2	-	-	2.2	-	-	78.3	-	-
4.3	-	-	4.3	-	-	73.9	-	-
-	-	-	-	-	-	83.3	-	-
-	-	-	-	-	-	100.0	-	-
-	-	-	-	-	-	75.0	-	-
-	-	100.0	-	-	-	-	-	-
-	-	-	100.0	-	-	-	-	-
-	-	-	-	-	-	-	-	-
-	-	-	-	-	-	-	-	-
-	-	-	-	-	-	-	-	-
-	25.8	-	0.4	-	3.1	68.6	0.9	0.9
-	-	-	-	-	-	-	-	100.0
-	-	-	-	-	-	100.0	-	-
-	-	-	-	-	-	-	100.0	-
-	-	-	-	-	-	-	-	-
-	-	-	-	-	-	-	-	-
-	26.2	-	0.4	-	3.1	69.3	0.4	-
-	-	-	-	-	-	100.0	-	-
-	-	-	-	-	-	100.0	-	-
-	-	-	-	-	-	100.0	-	-
-	-	-	-	-	-	-	-	-
-	-	-	-	-	-	-	-	-
-	-	-	-	-	-	100.0	-	-
-	-	-	-	-	-	100.0	-	-
-	-	-	-	-	-	-	-	-
-	-	-	-	-	2.3	95.5	-	-
-	-	-	-	-	-	100.0	-	-
-	-	-	-	-	-	100.0	-	-
-	-	-	-	-	-	-	-	-
-	-	-	-	-	-	100.0	-	-
-	-	-	-	-	11.1	77.8	-	-
-	-	-	-	-	-	-	-	-
-	-	-	-	-	-	100.0	-	-
0.3	-	0.1	0.1	-	0.8	96.1	2.1	0.1
-	-	-	-	-	-	100.0	-	-
0.3	-	0.1	0.1	-	0.8	96.1	2.1	0.1
0.7	9.3	2.0	-	-	-	84.5	1.6	0.1
0.4	2.2	-	-	-	-	95.6	-	-
0.7	13.5	1.0	-	-	-	83.2	0.4	-
4.5	-	-	-	-	-	72.7	13.6	4.5
-	-	28.6	-	-	-	-	71.4	-
-	-	-	-	-	-	100.0	-	-
-	-	19.4	-	-	-	65.3	11.1	-
-	-	-	-	-	-	100.0	-	-
1.1	7.1	1.1	-	-	-	87.4	0.5	-

注：第ⅩⅤ，ⅩⅨ，ⅩⅩ章は該当があり得ないので省略した。

死　産

表 7.19　死因・母側病態－児側病態別に
Table 7.19　Foetal deaths and percent distribution of spontaneous

死因基本分類コード Code	母側病態 Maternal condition	自然死産 Spontaneous	母側病態百分率 Percentage of maternal condition	児側病態 総数 Total	P05-P08 妊娠期間及び胎児発育に関連する障害	P10-P15 出産外傷
P01.8A	習慣性流早死産	1	0.0	100.0	-	-
P01.8B	流死産	171	1.7	100.0	1.8	-
P01.8C	その他	11	0.1	100.0	18.2	-
P01.9	母体の妊娠合併症により影響を受けた胎児及び新生児，詳細不明	-	-	-	-	-
P02	胎盤，臍帯及び卵膜の合併症により影響を受けた胎児及び新生児	1 455	14.5	100.0	0.4	-
P02.0	前置胎盤により影響を受けた胎児及び新生児	6	0.1	100.0	-	-
P02.1	その他の様式の胎盤剥離及び出血により影響を受けた胎児及び新生児	399	4.0	100.0	0.3	-
P02.1A	常位胎盤早期剥離	271	2.7	100.0	0.4	-
P02.1B	分娩前出血，不慮の出血，母体の失血	128	1.3	100.0	-	-
P02.1C	羊水穿刺，帝王切開又は外科的分娩誘発による胎盤の障害	-	-	-	-	-
P02.1D	その他	-	-	-	-	-
P02.2	その他及び詳細不明の胎盤の形態及び機能の異常により影響を受けた胎児及び新生児	35	0.3	100.0	-	-
P02.3	胎盤輸血症候群により影響を受けた胎児及び新生児	-	-	-	-	-
P02.4	臍帯脱出により影響を受けた胎児及び新生児	47	0.5	100.0	-	-
P02.5	臍帯のその他の圧迫により影響を受けた胎児及び新生児	471	4.7	100.0	0.2	-
P02.5A	臍帯巻絡	110	1.1	100.0	-	-
P02.5B	その他	361	3.6	100.0	0.3	-
P02.6	臍帯のその他及び詳細不明の病態により影響を受けた胎児及び新生児	170	1.7	100.0	1.2	-
P02.7	絨毛羊膜炎により影響を受けた胎児及び新生児	261	2.6	100.0	0.8	-
P02.8	卵膜のその他の異常により影響を受けた胎児及び新生児	6	0.1	100.0	-	-
P02.9	卵膜の異常により影響を受けた胎児及び新生児，詳細不明	60	0.6	100.0	-	-
P03	その他の分娩合併症により影響を受けた胎児及び新生児	48	0.5	100.0	2.1	-
P03.0	骨盤位分娩及び牽出により影響を受けた胎児及び新生児	-	-	-	-	-
P03.1	分娩中のその他の胎位異常，胎向異常及び胎児骨盤不均衡により影響を受けた胎児及び新生児	2	0.0	100.0	50.0	-
P03.2	鉗子分娩により影響を受けた胎児及び新生児	-	-	-	-	-
P03.3	吸引分娩により影響を受けた胎児及び新生児	-	-	-	-	-
P03.4	帝王切開分娩により影響を受けた胎児及び新生児	-	-	-	-	-
P03.5	急産により影響を受けた胎児及び新生児	2	0.0	100.0	-	-
P03.6	異常子宮収縮により影響を受けた胎児及び新生児	3	0.0	100.0	-	-
P03.8	その他の明示された分娩合併症により影響を受けた胎児及び新生児	27	0.3	100.0	-	-
P03.9	分娩合併症により影響を受けた胎児及び新生児，詳細不明	14	0.1	100.0	-	-
P04	胎盤又は母乳を介して有害な影響を受けた胎児及び新生児	-	-	-	-	-
P04.0	妊娠及び分娩における母体の麻酔及び鎮痛治療により影響を受けた胎児及び新生児	-	-	-	-	-
P04.1	その他の母体への投薬により影響を受けた胎児及び新生児	-	-	-	-	-
P04.2	母体のタバコ使用により影響を受けた胎児及び新生児	-	-	-	-	-
P04.3	母体のアルコール使用により影響を受けた胎児及び新生児	-	-	-	-	-
P04.4	母体の嗜癖性薬物使用により影響を受けた胎児及び新生児	-	-	-	-	-
P04.5	母体の栄養性化学物質の使用により影響を受けた胎児及び新生児	-	-	-	-	-
P04.6	母体の環境化学物質の曝露により影響を受けた胎児及び新生児	-	-	-	-	-
P04.8	母体のその他の有害な影響を受けた胎児及び新生児	-	-	-	-	-
P04.9	母体の有害な影響を受けた胎児及び新生児，詳細不明	-	-	-	-	-
P97	母体保護法による人工妊娠中絶，母体の病態によらないもの	・	・	・	・	・
P97.1	経済的理由	・	・	・	・	・
P97.2	その他	・	・	・	・	・
P99	母体に原因なし	3 893	38.7	100.0	1.2	-

Foetal mortality

みた自然死産数及び百分率（つづき）
by causes on child and maternal condition : Japan, 2016－CON.

平成28年

別　百　分　率　Percentage by causes on child

P20－P29 周産期に特異的な呼吸障害及び心血管障害	P35－P39 周産期に特異的な感染症	P50－P61 胎児及び新生児の出血性障害及び血液障害	P70－P72 胎児及び新生児に特異的な一過性の内分泌障害及び代謝障害	P76－P78 胎児及び新生児の消化器系障害	P80－P83 胎児及び新生児の外皮及び体温調節に関連する病態	P90－P96 周産期に発生したその他の障害	ⅩⅦ 先天奇形，変形及び染色体異常	Ⅰ－ⅩⅣ，ⅩⅧ ⅩⅫ その他
-	-	-		-	-	-	100.0	-
0.6	7.6	1.2	-	-	-	88.9	-	-
9.1	-	-	-	-	-	72.7	-	-
-	-	-	-	-	-	-	-	-
3.6	2.1	0.2	0.1	-	0.1	92.6	0.8	-
-	16.7	-	-	-	-	83.3	-	-
1.5	2.5	0.3	-	-	-	95.2	0.3	-
1.8	1.8	-	-	-	-	95.6	0.4	-
0.8	3.9	0.8	-	-	-	94.5	-	-
-	-	-	-	-	-	-	-	-
-	-	-	-	-	-	100.0	-	-
-	-	-	-	-	-	-	-	-
-	-	-	-	-	-	95.7	4.3	-
6.6	-	-	-	-	0.4	91.9	0.8	-
5.5	-	-	-	-	0.9	92.7	0.9	-
6.9	-	-	-	-	0.3	91.7	0.8	-
6.5	-	1.2	-	-	-	90.0	1.2	-
1.9	6.5	-	0.4	-	-	90.0	0.4	-
-	-	-	-	-	-	83.3	16.7	-
-	3.3	-	-	-	-	95.0	1.7	-
-	-	-	-	-	-	97.9	-	-
-	-	-	-	-	-	-	-	-
-	-	-	-	-	-	50.0	-	-
-	-	-	-	-	-	-	-	-
-	-	-	-	-	-	100.0	-	-
-	-	-	-	-	-	100.0	-	-
-	-	-	-	-	-	100.0	-	-
-	-	-	-	-	-	100.0	-	-
-	-	-	-	-	-	-	-	-
-	-	-	-	-	-	-	-	-
-	-	-	-	-	-	-	-	-
-	-	-	-	-	-	-	-	-
-	-	-	-	-	-	-	-	-
・	・	・	・	・	・	・	・	・
・	・	・	・	・	・	・	・	・
・	・	・	・	・	・	・	・	・
1.8	0.1	1.8	0.3	-	9.7	71.6	12.5	1.0

周産期死亡

〔周産期死亡の年次推移〕
〔Trends in perinatal deaths〕

第8章　周産期死亡
Chapter 8　Perinatal mortality

表8.1　年次別にみた性・妊娠満22週以後の死産－早期新生児死亡別周産期死亡数
Table 8.1　Trends in perinatal deaths by sex : Japan

年　　次 Year		周　産　期　死　亡　数 Perinatal deaths				妊娠満22週以後の死産数 Foetal deaths at 22 completed weeks and over of gestation				早　期　新　生　児　死　亡　数 Early neonatal deaths		
		総　数 Total	男 Male	女 Female	不　詳 Not stated	総　数 Total	男 Male	女 Female	不　詳 Not stated	総　数 Total	男 Male	女 Female
1979	昭和54年	36 190	19 183	16 135	872	29 289	15 146	13 271	872	6 901	4 037	2 864
80	55	32 422	17 261	14 443	718	26 268	13 652	11 898	718	6 154	3 609	2 545
81	56	30 274	16 095	13 507	672	24 672	12 871	11 129	672	5 602	3 224	2 378
82	57	28 204	15 031	12 560	613	23 137	12 085	10 439	613	5 067	2 946	2 121
83	58	25 925	13 600	11 790	535	21 354	11 008	9 811	535	4 571	2 592	1 979
84	59	25 149	13 281	11 389	479	20 875	10 846	9 550	479	4 274	2 435	1 839
85	60	22 379	11 578	10 358	443	18 642	9 511	8 688	443	3 737	2 067	1 670
86	61	20 389	10 588	9 357	444	17 143	8 748	7 951	444	3 246	1 840	1 406
87	62	18 699	9 866	8 370	463	15 634	8 140	7 031	463	3 065	1 726	1 339
88	63	16 839	8 719	7 748	372	14 090	7 229	6 489	372	2 749	1 490	1 259
89	平成元年	15 183	7 832	6 976	375	12 797	6 529	5 893	375	2 386	1 303	1 083
1990	2	13 704	7 150	6 180	374	11 367	5 827	5 166	374	2 337	1 323	1 014
91	3	10 426	5 259	4 889	278	8 258	4 102	3 878	278	2 168	1 157	1 011
92	4	9 888	5 104	4 476	308	7 758	3 905	3 545	308	2 130	1 199	931
93	5	9 226	4 790	4 194	242	7 191	3 658	3 291	242	2 035	1 132	903
94	6	9 286	4 877	4 147	262	7 200	3 673	3 265	262	2 086	1 204	882
95	7	8 412	4 386	3 820	206	6 580	3 361	3 013	206	1 832	1 025	807
96	8	8 080	4 119	3 739	222	6 333	3 160	2 951	222	1 747	959	788
97	9	7 624	3 910	3 514	200	6 009	3 034	2 775	200	1 615	876	739
98	10	7 447	3 861	3 401	185	5 804	2 962	2 657	185	1 643	899	744
99	11	7 102	3 576	3 331	195	5 567	2 757	2 615	195	1 535	819	716
2000	12	6 881	3 532	3 164	185	5 362	2 693	2 484	185	1 519	839	680
01	13	6 476	3 313	2 988	175	5 114	2 557	2 382	175	1 362	756	606
02	14	6 333	3 218	2 923	192	4 959	2 466	2 301	192	1 374	752	622
03	15	5 929	2 976	2 765	188	4 626	2 301	2 137	188	1 303	675	628
04	16	5 541	2 853	2 533	155	4 357	2 197	2 005	155	1 184	656	528
05	17	5 149	2 658	2 337	154	4 058	2 050	1 854	154	1 091	608	483
06	18	5 100	2 531	2 378	191	4 047	1 964	1 892	191	1 053	567	486
07	19	4 906	2 479	2 278	149	3 854	1 923	1 782	149	1 052	556	496
08	20	4 720	2 439	2 139	142	3 751	1 934	1 675	142	969	505	464
09	21	4 519	2 288	2 084	147	3 645	1 790	1 708	147	874	498	376
2010	22	4 515	2 374	2 017	124	3 637	1 866	1 647	124	878	508	370
11	23	4 315	2 121	2 069	125	3 491	1 703	1 663	125	824	418	406
12	24	4 133	2 053	1 951	129	3 343	1 644	1 570	129	790	409	381
13	25	3 862	1 956	1 782	124	3 110	1 541	1 445	124	752	415	337
14	26	3 750	1 872	1 750	128	3 039	1 499	1 412	128	711	373	338
15	27	3 728	1 864	1 723	141	3 063	1 506	1 416	141	665	358	307
16	28	3 516	1 716	1 681	119	2 840	1 370	1 351	119	676	346	330

484

Perinatal mortality

表 8.2　年次別にみた性・妊娠満22週以後の死産－早期新生児死亡別周産期死亡率
Table 8.2　Trends in perinatal death rates by sex : Japan

年　　　次 Year		周産期死亡率（出産千対）Perinatal death rates[a]			妊娠満22週以後の死産率（出産千対）Foetal death rates at 22 completed weeks and over of gestation[a]			早期新生児死亡率（出生千対）Early neonatal death rates (per 1,000 live births)		
		総　数 Total	男 Male	女 Female	総　数 Total	男 Male	女 Female	総　数 Total	男 Male	女 Female
1979	昭和54年	21.6	22.3	19.9	17.5	17.6	16.4	4.2	4.8	3.6
80	55	20.2	20.9	18.6	16.4	16.5	15.3	3.9	4.4	3.3
81	56	19.5	20.1	17.9	15.9	16.1	14.8	3.7	4.1	3.2
82	57	18.3	19.0	16.8	15.0	15.3	14.0	3.3	3.8	2.9
83	58	16.9	17.3	15.9	14.0	14.0	13.2	3.0	3.3	2.7
84	59	16.6	17.1	15.5	13.8	14.0	13.0	2.9	3.2	2.5
85	60	15.4	15.5	14.7	12.9	12.8	12.3	2.6	2.8	2.4
86	61	14.6	14.7	13.8	12.2	12.1	11.7	2.3	2.6	2.1
87	62	13.7	14.1	12.7	11.5	11.6	10.6	2.3	2.5	2.0
88	63	12.7	12.8	12.0	10.6	10.6	10.1	2.1	2.2	2.0
89	平成元年	12.1	12.1	11.4	10.2	10.1	9.6	1.9	2.0	1.8
1990	2	11.1	11.3	10.3	9.2	9.2	8.6	1.9	2.1	1.7
91	3	8.5	8.3	8.2	6.7	6.5	6.5	1.8	1.8	1.7
92	4	8.1	8.2	7.6	6.4	6.2	6.0	1.8	1.9	1.6
93	5	7.7	7.8	7.2	6.0	6.0	5.7	1.7	1.9	1.6
94	6	7.5	7.6	6.8	5.8	5.7	5.4	1.7	1.9	1.5
95	7	7.0	7.2	6.6	5.5	5.5	5.2	1.5	1.7	1.4
96	8	6.7	6.6	6.3	5.2	5.1	5.0	1.4	1.5	1.3
97	9	6.4	6.4	6.0	5.0	4.9	4.8	1.4	1.4	1.3
98	10	6.2	6.2	5.8	4.8	4.8	4.5	1.4	1.5	1.3
99	11	6.0	5.9	5.8	4.7	4.5	4.5	1.3	1.4	1.2
2000	12	5.8	5.7	5.4	4.5	4.4	4.3	1.3	1.4	1.2
01	13	5.5	5.5	5.2	4.3	4.2	4.2	1.2	1.3	1.1
02	14	5.5	5.4	5.2	4.3	4.1	4.1	1.2	1.3	1.1
03	15	5.3	5.1	5.0	4.1	4.0	3.9	1.2	1.2	1.1
04	16	5.0	5.0	4.7	3.9	3.8	3.7	1.1	1.2	1.0
05	17	4.8	4.9	4.5	3.8	3.7	3.6	1.0	1.1	0.9
06	18	4.7	4.5	4.5	3.7	3.5	3.5	1.0	1.0	0.9
07	19	4.5	4.4	4.3	3.5	3.4	3.4	1.0	1.0	0.9
08	20	4.3	4.3	4.0	3.4	3.4	3.1	0.9	0.9	0.9
09	21	4.2	4.2	4.0	3.4	3.2	3.3	0.8	0.9	0.7
2010	22	4.2	4.3	3.9	3.4	3.4	3.2	0.8	0.9	0.7
11	23	4.1	3.9	4.0	3.3	3.2	3.2	0.8	0.8	0.8
12	24	4.0	3.8	3.8	3.2	3.1	3.1	0.8	0.8	0.8
13	25	3.7	3.7	3.5	3.0	2.9	2.9	0.7	0.8	0.7
14	26	3.7	3.6	3.6	3.0	2.9	2.9	0.7	0.7	0.7
15	27	3.7	3.6	3.5	3.0	2.9	2.9	0.7	0.7	0.6
16	28	3.6	3.4	3.5	2.9	2.7	2.8	0.7	0.7	0.7

Note : a) Per 1,000 live births and foetal deaths at 22 completed weeks and over of gestation.

周産期死亡

〔月別にみた周産期死亡〕
〔Perinatal deaths by month〕

表 8.3　月別にみた年次別妊娠満22週以後の
Table 8.3　Trends in perinatal deaths and

年次 Year		総数 Total	1 月 January	2 月 February	3 月 March	4 月 April	5 月 May
						周　産　期	
1980	昭和55年	32 422	2 743	2 611	2 796	2 775	2 884
85	60	22 379	1 869	1 807	1 993	1 857	2 047
90	平成2年	13 704	1 251	1 109	1 228	1 212	1 155
95	7	8 412	700	629	749	707	696
2000	12	6 881	591	537	600	553	600
05	17	5 149	447	406	438	399	450
10	22	4 515	367	348	374	367	385
14	26	3 750	313	272	308	273	343
15	27	3 728	271	286	320	302	312
16	**28**	**3 516**	**298**	**251**	**298**	**288**	**332**
					妊　娠　満　22　週　以　後　の		
1980	昭和55年	26 268	2 253	2 130	2 277	2 284	2 344
85	60	18 642	1 567	1 509	1 666	1 571	1 675
90	平成2年	11 367	1 062	962	1 033	1 002	954
95	7	6 580	551	474	585	554	522
2000	12	5 362	459	407	464	415	473
05	17	4 058	356	313	348	316	351
10	22	3 637	299	265	297	305	305
14	26	3 039	259	226	254	214	285
15	27	3 063	233	234	260	253	246
16	**28**	**2 840**	**232**	**203**	**242**	**222**	**265**
						早　期　新　生　児	
1980	昭和55年	6 154	490	481	519	491	540
85	60	3 737	302	298	327	286	372
90	平成2年	2 337	189	147	195	210	201
95	7	1 832	149	155	164	153	174
2000	12	1 519	132	130	136	138	127
05	17	1 091	91	93	90	83	99
10	22	878	68	83	77	62	80
14	26	711	54	46	54	59	58
15	27	665	38	52	60	49	66
16	**28**	**676**	**66**	**48**	**56**	**66**	**67**
						周　産　期　死　亡　率	
1980	昭和55年	20.2	19.9	20.5	21.2	21.3	21.1
85	60	15.4	15.3	16.1	17.1	15.9	16.7
90	平成2年	11.1	11.9	11.9	12.0	12.1	10.8
95	7	7.0	6.8	6.9	7.6	7.4	6.8
2000	12	5.8	5.8	5.7	6.0	5.8	6.0
05	17	4.8	4.8	5.0	4.9	4.6	5.1
10	22	4.2	4.0	4.3	4.2	4.2	4.4
14	26	3.7	3.7	3.7	3.9	3.5	4.1
15	27	3.7	3.2	3.8	3.9	3.6	3.7
16	**28**	**3.6**	**3.6**	**3.3**	**3.7**	**3.6**	**4.1**
				妊　娠　満　22　週　以　後　の　死　産　率			
1980	昭和55年	16.4	16.3	16.7	17.3	17.5	17.1
85	60	12.9	12.8	13.5	14.3	13.5	13.7
90	平成2年	9.2	10.1	10.3	10.1	10.0	8.9
95	7	5.5	5.3	5.2	5.9	5.8	5.1
2000	12	4.5	4.5	4.3	4.7	4.4	4.7
05	17	3.8	3.8	3.9	3.9	3.6	4.0
10	22	3.4	3.3	3.2	3.4	3.5	3.5
14	26	3.0	3.1	3.0	3.2	2.7	3.4
15	27	3.0	2.7	3.1	3.2	3.0	2.9
16	**28**	**2.9**	**2.8**	**2.6**	**3.0**	**2.8**	**3.3**
					早　期　新　生　児　死　亡　率		
1980	昭和55年	3.9	3.6	3.8	4.0	3.8	4.0
85	60	2.6	2.5	2.7	2.8	2.5	3.1
90	平成2年	1.9	1.8	1.6	1.9	2.1	1.9
95	7	1.5	1.5	1.7	1.7	1.6	1.7
2000	12	1.3	1.3	1.4	1.4	1.5	1.3
05	17	1.0	1.0	1.1	1.0	1.0	1.1
10	22	0.8	0.8	1.0	0.9	0.7	0.9
14	26	0.7	0.6	0.6	0.7	0.7	0.7
15	27	0.7	0.4	0.7	0.7	0.6	0.8
16	**28**	**0.7**	**0.8**	**0.6**	**0.7**	**0.8**	**0.8**

注：1）計算方法は、69ページ　6）周産期死亡を参照されたい。

Perinatal mortality

死産－早期新生児死亡別周産期死亡数及び率[1]
perinatal death rates by month : Japan

	6 月 June	7 月 July	8 月 August	9 月 September	10 月 October	11 月 November	12 月 December
死　亡　数　Perinatal deaths							
	2 750	2 778	2 786	2 627	2 619	2 480	2 573
	1 844	1 859	1 911	1 778	1 875	1 771	1 768
	1 142	1 078	1 156	1 096	1 135	1 074	1 068
	725	715	714	706	689	701	681
	567	619	585	570	558	514	587
	399	440	483	415	448	400	424
	367	401	393	419	382	353	359
	337	353	323	334	305	288	301
	319	303	346	322	347	272	328
	330	**297**	**313**	**322**	**279**	**263**	**245**
死　産　数　Foetal deaths at 22 completed weeks and over of gestation							
	2 224	2 250	2 255	2 095	2 156	1 970	2 030
	1 519	1 549	1 586	1 481	1 548	1 517	1 454
	943	896	942	888	931	888	866
	579	552	557	564	548	555	539
	445	493	454	446	446	402	458
	312	337	393	337	354	310	331
	299	319	334	331	308	286	289
	271	285	264	265	242	223	251
	269	248	287	264	273	224	272
	276	**244**	**261**	**263**	**226**	**208**	**198**
死　亡　数　Early neonatal deaths							
	526	528	531	532	463	510	543
	325	310	325	297	327	254	314
	199	182	214	208	204	186	202
	146	163	157	142	141	146	142
	122	126	131	124	112	112	129
	87	103	90	78	94	90	93
	68	82	59	88	74	67	70
	66	68	59	69	63	65	50
	50	55	59	58	74	48	56
	54	**53**	**52**	**59**	**53**	**55**	**47**
（出 産 千 対）　Perinatal death rates[a]							
	21.1	19.7	19.8	18.9	19.3	20.3	19.9
	15.6	14.1	14.9	14.3	15.0	15.6	14.7
	11.3	9.9	10.7	10.6	10.9	11.0	10.4
	7.2	6.7	6.7	7.0	7.1	7.5	6.9
	5.9	6.0	5.6	5.5	5.5	5.3	5.9
	4.6	4.8	5.2	4.5	4.9	4.7	4.8
	4.1	4.3	4.2	4.5	4.1	4.0	4.0
	4.1	3.9	3.7	3.7	3.4	3.5	3.5
	3.8	3.4	4.0	3.7	4.0	3.4	3.9
	4.1	**3.5**	**3.7**	**3.8**	**3.3**	**3.4**	**3.1**
（出 産 千 対）　Foetal death rates at 22 completed weeks and over of gestation[a]							
	17.0	15.9	16.0	15.1	15.9	16.1	15.7
	12.9	11.7	12.4	11.9	12.4	13.4	12.1
	9.4	8.3	8.7	8.6	9.0	9.1	8.4
	5.8	5.2	5.3	5.6	5.7	5.9	5.5
	4.6	4.8	4.4	4.3	4.4	4.2	4.6
	3.6	3.7	4.2	3.6	3.9	3.7	3.8
	3.3	3.4	3.6	3.6	3.3	3.2	3.2
	3.3	3.2	3.0	2.9	2.7	2.7	2.9
	3.2	2.8	3.3	3.0	3.2	2.8	3.2
	3.4	**2.9**	**3.1**	**3.1**	**2.7**	**2.7**	**2.5**
（出 生 千 対）　Early neonatal death rates (per 1,000 live births)							
	4.1	3.8	3.8	3.9	3.5	4.2	4.3
	2.8	2.4	2.6	2.4	2.7	2.3	2.6
	2.0	1.7	2.0	2.0	2.0	1.9	2.0
	1.5	1.5	1.5	1.4	1.5	1.6	1.5
	1.3	1.2	1.3	1.2	1.1	1.2	1.3
	1.0	1.1	1.0	0.8	1.0	1.1	1.1
	0.8	0.9	0.6	1.0	0.8	0.8	0.8
	0.8	0.8	0.7	0.8	0.7	0.8	0.6
	0.6	0.6	0.7	0.7	0.9	0.6	0.7
	0.7	**0.6**	**0.6**	**0.7**	**0.6**	**0.7**	**0.6**

Note : a) Per 1,000 live births and foetal deaths at 22 completed weeks and over of gestation.

周産期死亡

〔出産時の体重別にみた周産期死亡〕
〔Perinatal deaths by birth weight〕

表8.4 体重別にみた年次別妊娠満22週以後の死産－早期新生児死亡別 周産期死亡数及び百分率
Table 8.4 Trends in perinatal deaths and percent distribution by birth weight : Japan

年次 Year	総数[1] Total	1.0kg未満 Under 1.0kg	1.0kg以上1.5kg未満 1.0kg and over, less than 1.5kg	1.5~2.0	2.0~2.5	2.5~3.0	3.0~3.5	3.5~4.0	4.0~4.5	4.5kg以上 4.5kg and over	(再掲) 1.0kg以上 1.0kg and over (Regrouped)	(再掲) 2.5kg未満 Under 2.5kg (Regrouped)
周産期死亡数 Perinatal deaths												
1980 昭和55年	32 422	14 258	4 494	3 369	2 766	2 853	2 453	904	247	100	17 186	24 887
85 60	22 379	12 018	2 699	1 971	1 700	1 742	1 380	512	107	47	10 158	18 388
90 平成2年	13 704	7 649	1 491	1 165	1 081	1 084	801	266	51	18	5 957	11 386
95 7	8 412	3 747	1 037	933	880	915	610	200	39	15	4 629	6 597
2000 12	6 881	3 072	853	792	754	782	450	119	16	7	3 773	5 471
05 17	5 149	2 300	622	547	596	626	337	71	14	6	2 819	4 065
10 22	4 515	1 989	549	531	533	527	298	65	2	2	2 507	3 602
14 26	3 750	1 752	437	397	402	459	214	60	12	1	1 982	2 988
15 27	3 728	1 725	441	430	425	419	219	47	5	2	1 988	3 021
16 28	3 516	1 623	399	424	398	402	209	47	4	1	1 884	2 844
妊娠満22週以後の死産数 Foetal deaths at 22 completed weeks and over of gestation												
1980 昭和55年	26 268	13 377	3 351	2 396	1 941	1 924	1 603	566	167	77	12 025	21 065
85 60	18 642	11 128	2 152	1 510	1 232	1 183	903	310	71	31	7 392	16 022
90 平成2年	11 367	7 098	1 189	901	763	705	481	146	34	15	4 234	9 951
95 7	6 580	3 262	830	705	641	621	363	117	17	11	3 305	5 438
2000 12	5 362	2 674	677	568	545	516	291	69	8	4	2 678	4 464
05 17	4 058	1 961	489	399	461	464	221	43	10	4	2 091	3 310
10 22	3 637	1 742	430	392	403	403	213	49	2	-	1 892	2 967
14 26	3 039	1 543	357	298	298	341	152	40	8	1	1 495	2 496
15 27	3 063	1 559	358	318	331	312	150	28	4	-	1 501	2 566
16 28	2 840	1 414	320	307	303	301	163	28	3	1	1 426	2 344
早期新生児死亡数 Early neonatal deaths												
1980 昭和55年	6 154	881	1 143	973	825	929	850	338	80	23	5 161	3 822
85 60	3 737	890	547	461	468	559	477	202	36	16	2 766	2 366
90 平成2年	2 337	551	302	264	318	379	320	120	17	3	1 723	1 435
95 7	1 832	485	207	228	239	294	247	83	22	4	1 324	1 159
2000 12	1 519	398	176	224	209	266	159	50	8	3	1 095	1 007
05 17	1 091	339	133	148	135	162	116	28	4	2	728	755
10 22	878	247	119	139	130	124	85	16	-	2	615	635
14 26	711	209	80	99	104	118	62	20	4	-	487	492
15 27	665	166	83	112	94	107	69	19	1	2	487	455
16 28	676	209	79	117	95	101	46	19	1	-	458	500
周産期死亡の百分率[2] Percentage of perinatal deaths												
1980 昭和55年	100.0	45.3	14.3	10.7	8.8	9.1	7.8	2.9	0.8	0.3	54.7	79.1
85 60	100.0	54.2	12.2	8.9	7.7	7.9	6.2	2.3	0.5	0.2	45.8	82.9
90 平成2年	100.0	56.2	11.0	8.6	7.9	8.0	5.9	2.0	0.4	0.1	43.8	83.7
95 7	100.0	44.7	12.4	11.1	10.5	10.9	7.3	2.4	0.5	0.2	55.3	78.8
2000 12	100.0	44.6	12.4	11.5	11.0	11.4	6.5	1.7	0.2	0.1	54.8	79.5
05 17	100.0	44.7	12.1	10.6	11.6	12.2	6.5	1.4	0.3	0.1	54.7	78.9
10 22	100.0	44.1	12.2	11.8	11.8	11.7	6.6	1.4	0.0	0.0	55.5	79.8
14 26	100.0	46.7	11.7	10.6	10.7	12.2	5.7	1.6	0.3	0.0	52.9	79.7
15 27	100.0	46.3	11.8	11.5	11.4	11.2	5.9	1.3	0.1	0.1	53.3	81.0
16 28	100.0	46.2	11.3	12.1	11.3	11.4	5.9	1.3	0.1	0.0	53.6	80.9
妊娠満22週以後の死産の百分率[2] Percentage of foetal deaths at 22 completed weeks and over of gestation												
1980 昭和55年	100.0	52.7	13.2	9.4	7.6	7.6	6.3	2.2	0.7	0.3	47.3	82.9
85 60	100.0	60.1	11.6	8.2	6.7	6.4	4.9	1.7	0.4	0.2	39.9	86.5
90 平成2年	100.0	62.6	10.5	8.0	6.7	6.2	4.2	1.3	0.3	0.1	37.4	87.8
95 7	100.0	49.7	12.6	10.7	9.8	9.5	5.5	1.8	0.3	0.2	50.3	82.8
2000 12	100.0	49.9	12.6	10.6	10.2	9.6	5.4	1.3	0.1	0.1	49.9	83.3
05 17	100.0	48.3	12.1	9.8	11.4	11.4	5.4	1.1	0.2	0.1	51.5	81.6
10 22	100.0	47.9	11.8	10.8	11.1	11.1	5.9	1.3	0.1	-	52.0	81.6
14 26	100.0	50.8	11.7	9.8	9.8	11.2	5.0	1.3	0.3	0.0	49.2	82.1
15 27	100.0	50.9	11.7	10.4	10.8	10.2	4.9	0.9	0.1	-	49.0	83.8
16 28	100.0	49.8	11.3	10.8	10.7	10.6	5.7	1.0	0.1	0.0	50.2	82.5
早期新生児死亡の百分率[2] Percentage of early neonatal deaths												
1980 昭和55年	100.0	14.6	18.9	16.1	13.7	15.4	14.1	5.6	1.3	0.4	85.4	63.3
85 60	100.0	24.3	15.0	12.6	12.8	15.3	13.0	5.5	1.0	0.4	75.7	64.7
90 平成2年	100.0	24.2	13.3	11.6	14.0	16.7	14.1	5.3	0.7	0.1	75.8	63.1
95 7	100.0	26.8	11.4	12.6	13.2	16.3	13.7	4.6	1.2	0.2	73.2	64.1
2000 12	100.0	26.2	11.6	14.7	13.8	17.5	10.5	3.3	0.5	0.2	72.1	66.3
05 17	100.0	31.1	12.2	13.6	12.4	14.8	10.6	2.6	0.4	0.2	66.7	69.2
10 22	100.0	28.1	13.6	15.8	14.8	14.1	9.7	1.8	-	0.2	70.0	72.3
14 26	100.0	29.4	11.3	13.9	14.6	16.6	8.7	2.8	0.6	-	68.5	69.2
15 27	100.0	25.0	12.5	16.8	14.1	16.1	10.4	2.9	0.2	0.3	73.2	68.4
16 28	100.0	30.9	11.7	17.3	14.1	14.9	6.8	2.8	0.1	-	67.8	74.0

注：1) 総数には体重不詳を含む。
　　2) 昭和55年～平成7年の百分率は、体重不詳を除き算出している。

Perinatal mortality

表8.5 体重別にみた性別妊娠満22週以後の死産－早期新生児死亡別周産期死亡数・率及び百分率

Table 8.5 Perinatal deaths, perinatal death rates and percent distribution by sex and birth weight : Japan, 2016

平成28年

			総数[1] Total	1.0kg 未満 Under 1.0kg	1.0kg以上 1.5kg未満 1.0kg and over, less than 1.5kg	1.5～2.0	2.0～2.5	2.5～3.0	3.0～3.5	3.5～4.0	4.0～4.5	4.5kg 以上 4.5kg and over	(再掲) 1.0kg 以上 1.0kg and over (Regrouped)	(再掲) 2.5kg 未満 Under 2.5kg (Regrouped)
						実 数 Number								
周 産 期 死 亡 数[2]			3 516	1 623	399	424	398	402	209	47	4	1	1 884	2 844
Perinatal deaths	男	M.	1 716	762	213	205	185	201	125	23	-	-	952	1 365
	女	F.	1 681	746	185	216	213	201	84	24	4	1	928	1 360
妊娠満22週以後の死産数[2]			2 840	1 414	320	307	303	301	163	28	3	1	1 426	2 344
Foetal deaths at 22 completed weeks and over of gestation	男	M.	1 370	661	161	150	139	148	98	13	-	-	709	1 111
	女	F.	1 351	638	158	154	164	153	65	15	3	1	713	1 114
早 期 新 生 児 死 亡 数			676	209	79	117	95	101	46	19	1	-	458	500
Early neonatal deaths	男	M.	346	101	52	55	46	53	27	10	-	-	243	254
	女	F.	330	108	27	62	49	48	19	9	1	-	215	246
						率 Rates								
周産期死亡率（出産千対）			3.6	377.0	89.8	35.5	5.4	1.1	0.5	0.5	0.5	2.8	1.9	30.1
Perinatal death rates[a]	男	M.	3.4	365.5	91.5	35.1	5.7	1.1	0.6	0.4	-	-	1.9	31.9
	女	F.	3.5	354.4	87.5	35.5	5.2	1.0	0.5	0.7	1.6	7.8	2.0	26.4
妊娠満22週以後の死産率（出産千対）			2.9	328.5	72.0	25.7	4.1	0.8	0.4	0.3	0.4	2.8	1.5	24.8
Foetal death rates at 22 completed weeks and over of gestation[a]	男	M.	2.7	317.0	69.1	25.7	4.3	0.8	0.4	0.2	-	-	1.4	26.0
	女	F.	2.8	303.1	74.7	25.3	4.0	0.8	0.4	0.4	1.2	7.8	1.5	21.6
早期新生児死亡率（出生千対）			0.7	72.3	19.2	10.1	1.3	0.3	0.1	0.2	0.1	-	0.5	5.4
Early neonatal death rates (per 1,000 live births)	男	M.	0.7	70.9	24.0	9.7	1.4	0.3	0.1	0.2	-	-	0.5	6.1
	女	F.	0.7	73.6	13.8	10.5	1.2	0.2	0.1	0.2	0.4	-	0.5	4.9
						百 分 率[3] Percentage								
周 産 期 死 亡 （百分率）			100.0	46.3	11.4	12.1	11.3	11.5	6.0	1.3	0.1	0.0	53.7	81.1
Percentage of perinatal deaths	男	M.	100.0	44.5	12.4	12.0	10.8	11.7	7.3	1.3	-	-	55.5	79.6
	女	F.	100.0	44.6	11.1	12.9	12.7	12.0	5.0	1.4	0.2	0.1	55.4	81.2
妊娠満22週以後の死産（百分率）			100.0	49.8	11.3	10.8	10.7	10.6	5.7	1.0	0.1	0.0	50.2	82.5
Percentage of foetal deaths at 22 completed weeks and over of gestation	男	M.	100.0	48.2	11.8	10.9	10.1	10.8	7.2	0.9	-	-	51.8	81.1
	女	F.	100.0	47.2	11.7	11.4	12.1	11.3	4.8	1.1	0.2	0.1	52.8	82.5
早 期 新 生 児 死 亡 （百分率）			100.0	31.3	11.8	17.5	14.2	15.1	6.9	2.8	0.1		68.7	75.0
Percentage of early neonatal deaths	男	M.	100.0	29.4	15.1	16.0	13.4	15.4	7.8	2.9	-		70.6	73.8
	女	F.	100.0	33.4	8.4	19.2	15.2	14.9	5.9	2.8	0.3	-	66.6	76.2

注：1) 総数には体重不詳を含む。
　　2) 性別不詳を含む。
　　3) 百分率は体重不詳を除き算出した。
Note : a) Per 1,000 live births and foetal deaths at 22 completed weeks and over of gestation.

周産期死亡

〔母の年齢（5歳階級）別にみた周産期死亡〕
〔Perinatal deaths by age of mother（5-year age groups）〕

表8.6 母の年齢別にみた年次別妊娠満22週以後の死産－早期新生児死亡別周産期死亡数及び率
Table 8.6 Trends in perinatal deaths and perinatal death rates by age of mother : Japan

年　次 Year		総数 Total	～19歳 Years	20～24	25～29	30～34	35～39	40～44	45～
		周　産　期　死　亡　数　Perinatal deaths							
1980	昭和55年	32 422	1 796	6 713	12 606	7 708	2 617	801	102
85	60	22 379	1 691	4 466	7 599	5 224	2 552	724	91
90	平成2年	13 704	1 030	2 527	4 624	3 352	1 577	536	39
95	7	8 412	195	1 337	3 015	2 582	1 004	234	26
2000	12	6 881	208	917	2 369	2 178	958	215	13
05	17	5 149	114	571	1 460	1 841	934	200	9
10	22	4 515	79	456	1 060	1 512	1 099	282	14
14	26	3 750	75	306	826	1 178	1 005	327	21
15	27	3 728	52	280	837	1 184	1 013	339	13
16	**28**	**3 516**	**54**	**256**	**741**	**1 227**	**921**	**293**	**17**
		妊娠満22週以後の死産数　Foetal deaths at 22 completed weeks and over of gestation							
1980	昭和55年	26 268	1 694	5 553	9 780	6 172	2 234	717	95
85	60	18 642	1 619	3 820	6 088	4 243	2 119	651	90
90	平成2年	11 367	983	2 164	3 709	2 702	1 302	466	37
95	7	6 580	158	1 057	2 311	2 012	823	191	24
2000	12	5 362	179	711	1 875	1 652	767	168	10
05	17	4 058	93	454	1 155	1 443	752	154	7
10	22	3 637	62	371	872	1 220	879	220	10
14	26	3 039	59	249	681	963	809	260	18
15	27	3 063	42	237	682	1 000	831	259	11
16	**28**	**2 840**	**47**	**198**	**618**	**1 002**	**739**	**222**	**13**
		早期新生児死亡数　Early neonatal deaths							
1980	昭和55年	6 154	102	1 160	2 826	1 536	383	84	7
85	60	3 737	72	646	1 511	981	433	73	1
90	平成2年	2 337	47	363	915	650	275	70	2
95	7	1 832	37	280	704	570	181	43	2
2000	12	1 519	29	206	494	526	191	47	3
05	17	1 091	21	117	305	398	182	46	2
10	22	878	17	85	188	292	220	62	4
14	26	711	16	57	145	215	196	67	3
15	27	665	10	43	155	184	182	80	2
16	**28**	**676**	**7**	**58**	**123**	**225**	**182**	**71**	**4**
		周産期死亡率（出産千対）　Perinatal death rates[a]							
1980	昭和55年	20.2	110.3	22.2	15.4	19.5	42.6	105.0	289.0
85	60	15.4	86.7	17.8	11.0	13.5	26.7	81.6	271.6
90	平成2年	11.1	55.7	13.0	8.3	9.3	16.8	41.1	149.4
95	7	7.0	12.0	6.9	6.1	6.9	10.0	18.5	59.4
2000	12	5.8	10.4	5.7	5.0	5.5	7.5	14.3	31.6
05	17	4.8	6.8	4.4	4.3	4.5	6.1	10.0	14.9
10	22	4.2	5.8	4.1	3.4	3.9	4.9	8.1	17.5
14	26	3.7	5.7	3.5	3.1	3.3	4.4	6.6	16.3
15	27	3.7	4.3	3.3	3.2	3.2	4.4	6.4	9.9
16	**28**	**3.6**	**4.8**	**2.9**	**3.4**	**4.1**	**5.5**	**12.0**	
		妊娠満22週以後の死産率（出産千対）　Foetal death rates at 22 completed weeks and over of gestation[a]							
1980	昭和55年	16.4	104.0	18.4	11.9	15.6	36.4	94.0	269.1
85	60	12.9	83.0	15.2	8.8	11.0	22.2	73.4	268.7
90	平成2年	9.2	53.2	11.2	6.7	7.5	13.9	35.7	141.8
95	7	5.5	9.7	5.4	4.7	5.4	8.2	15.1	54.8
2000	12	4.5	9.0	4.4	4.0	4.1	6.0	11.2	24.3
05	17	3.8	5.6	3.5	3.4	3.6	4.9	7.7	11.6
10	22	3.4	4.6	3.3	2.8	3.2	4.0	6.3	12.5
14	26	3.0	4.5	2.9	2.5	2.7	5.2	14.0	
15	27	3.0	3.5	2.8	2.6	2.7	3.6	4.9	8.3
16	**28**	**2.9**	**4.2**	**2.4**	**2.5**	**2.8**	**3.3**	**4.1**	**9.2**
		早期新生児死亡率（出生千対）　Early neonatal death rates（per 1,000 live births）							
1980	昭和55年	3.9	7.0	3.9	3.5	3.9	6.5	12.2	27.1
85	60	2.6	4.0	2.6	2.2	2.6	4.6	8.9	4.1
90	平成2年	1.9	2.7	1.9	1.7	1.8	3.0	5.6	8.9
95	7	1.5	2.3	1.4	1.4	1.5	1.8	3.4	4.8
2000	12	1.3	1.5	1.3	1.0	1.3	1.5	3.2	7.5
05	17	1.0	1.3	0.9	0.9	1.0	1.2	2.3	3.3
10	22	0.8	1.3	0.8	0.6	0.8	1.0	1.8	5.1
14	26	0.7	1.2	0.7	0.5	0.6	0.9	1.4	2.4
15	27	0.7	0.8	0.5	0.6	0.5	0.8	1.5	1.5
16	**28**	**0.7**	**0.6**	**0.7**	**0.5**	**0.6**	**0.8**	**1.3**	**2.9**

注：総数には年齢不詳を含む。
Note : a) Per 1,000 live births and foetal deaths at 22 completed weeks and over of gestation.

表8.7 母の年齢別にみた世帯の主な仕事別妊娠満22週以後の死産－早期新生児死亡別周産期死亡数
Table 8.7 Perinatal deaths by age of mother and type of occupation of household : Japan, 2016

平成28年

世帯の主な仕事 Type of occupation of household	総数 Total	～19歳 Years	20～24	25～29	30～34	35～39	40～44	45～	不詳 Not stated
周　産　期　死　亡　数　Perinatal deaths									
総　　　　　数[1]　Total	3 516	54	256	741	1 227	921	293	17	7
農　家　世　帯　Agriculture[a]	36	-	3	9	11	8	5	-	-
自　営　業　者　世　帯　Self employed	253	4	21	42	78	77	30	1	-
常用勤労者世帯（Ⅰ）　Employee[b]	1 133	14	91	266	386	284	82	9	1
常用勤労者世帯（Ⅱ）　Employee or director[c]	1 383	11	74	266	521	380	125	4	2
そ　の　他　の　世　帯　Other	394	9	27	103	145	82	26	1	1
無　職　の　世　帯　Not working	133	10	18	25	25	41	13	-	1
妊娠満22週以後の死産数　Foetal deaths at 22 completed weeks and over of gestation									
総　　　　　数[1]　Total	2 840	47	198	618	1 002	739	222	13	1
農　家　世　帯　Agriculture[a]	26	-	3	9	6	5	3	-	-
自　営　業　者　世　帯　Self employed	207	4	20	35	61	61	25	1	-
常用勤労者世帯（Ⅰ）　Employee[b]	944	10	70	223	328	240	66	7	-
常用勤労者世帯（Ⅱ）　Employee or director[c]	1 127	10	62	229	424	307	92	3	-
そ　の　他　の　世　帯　Other	326	9	20	86	122	68	20	1	-
無　職　の　世　帯　Not working	82	9	5	17	15	29	7	-	-
早期新生児死亡数　Early neonatal deaths									
総　　　　　数[1]　Total	676	7	58	123	225	182	71	4	6
農　家　世　帯　Agriculture[a]	10	-	-	-	5	3	2	-	-
自　営　業　者　世　帯　Self employed	46	-	1	7	17	16	5	-	-
常用勤労者世帯（Ⅰ）　Employee[b]	189	4	21	43	58	44	16	2	1
常用勤労者世帯（Ⅱ）　Employee or director[c]	256	1	12	37	97	73	33	1	2
そ　の　他　の　世　帯　Other	68	-	7	17	23	14	6	-	1
無　職　の　世　帯　Not working	51	1	13	8	10	12	6	-	1

注：1) 総数には世帯の主な仕事不詳を含む。
Note : a) Agriculture only or that with other work.
　　　 b) Employee at office (excluding governmental office) with 1－99 employee (excluding daily or less than one year contracts).
　　　 c) Employee at office excluding b) above.

周産期死亡

表8.8　母の年齢別にみた世帯の主な仕事別妊娠満22週以後の死産－早期新生児死亡別周産期死亡率

Table 8.8　Perinatal death rates by age of mother and type of occupation of household : Japan, 2016

平成28年

世帯の主な仕事 Type of occupation of household	総数[1] Total	～19歳 Years	20～24	25～29	30～34	35～39	40～44	45～
周産期死亡率（出産千対）　Perinatal death rates[d]								
総　　　　　　　　数[1] Total	3.6	4.8	3.1	2.9	3.4	4.1	5.5	12.0
農　家　世　帯 Agriculture[a]	3.0	-	2.9	2.9	2.6	2.9	7.7	-
自 営 業 者 世 帯 Self employed	3.6	4.6	3.7	2.9	3.3	4.0	5.5	6.5
常 用 勤 労 者 世 帯 （Ⅰ） Employee[b]	3.5	3.0	2.6	3.2	3.5	4.1	5.0	23.7
常 用 勤 労 者 世 帯 （Ⅱ） Employee or director[c]	3.1	5.5	3.0	2.3	3.0	3.5	5.0	6.0
そ の 他 の 世 帯 Other	4.9	6.5	3.1	4.5	5.1	5.3	7.0	9.3
無 職 の 世 帯 Not working	7.9	7.6	4.6	6.3	6.4	14.9	14.3	-
妊娠満22週以後の死産率（出産千対） Foetal death rates at 22 completed weeks and over of gestation[d]								
総　　　　　　　　数[1] Total	2.9	4.2	2.4	2.5	2.8	3.3	4.1	9.2
農　家　世　帯 Agriculture[a]	2.2	-	2.9	2.9	1.4	1.8	4.6	-
自 営 業 者 世 帯 Self employed	3.0	4.6	3.5	2.4	2.5	3.2	4.6	6.5
常 用 勤 労 者 世 帯 （Ⅰ） Employee[b]	2.9	2.2	2.0	2.7	2.9	3.4	4.0	18.5
常 用 勤 労 者 世 帯 （Ⅱ） Employee or director[c]	2.5	5.0	2.5	2.0	2.4	2.9	3.7	4.5
そ の 他 の 世 帯 Other	4.0	6.5	2.3	3.8	4.3	4.4	5.4	9.3
無 職 の 世 帯 Not working	4.9	6.8	1.3	4.3	3.8	10.5	7.7	-
早期新生児死亡率（出生千対）　Early neonatal death rates （per 1,000 live births）								
総　　　　　　　　数[1] Total	0.7	0.6	0.7	0.5	0.6	0.8	1.3	2.9
農　家　世　帯 Agriculture[a]	0.8	-	-	-	1.2	1.1	3.1	-
自 営 業 者 世 帯 Self employed	0.7	-	0.2	0.5	0.7	0.8	0.9	-
常 用 勤 労 者 世 帯 （Ⅰ） Employee[b]	0.6	0.9	0.6	0.5	0.5	0.6	1.0	5.4
常 用 勤 労 者 世 帯 （Ⅱ） Employee or director[c]	0.6	0.5	0.5	0.3	0.6	0.7	1.3	1.5
そ の 他 の 世 帯 Other	0.8	-	0.8	0.7	0.8	0.9	1.6	-
無 職 の 世 帯 Not working	3.0	0.8	3.3	2.0	2.6	4.4	6.7	-

注：1）　母の年齢・世帯の主な仕事ともに不詳を含む。

Note : a) Agriculture only or that with other work.

　　b) Employee at office (excluding governmental office) with 1－99 employee (excluding daily or less than one year contracts).

　　c) Employee at office excluding b) above.

　　d) Per 1,000 live births and foetal deaths at 22 completed weeks and over of gestation.

Perinatal mortality

表8.9　母の年齢別にみた性別妊娠満22週以後の死産－早期新生児死亡別周産期死亡数
及び率

Table 8.9　Perinatal deaths and perinatal death rates by sex
and age of mother : Japan, 2016

平成28年

母　の　年　齢 Age of mother	周　産　期　死　亡　数 Perinatal deaths			妊娠満22週以後の死産数 Foetal deaths at 22 completed weeks and over of gestation			早期新生児死亡数 Early neonatal deaths		
	総　数[1)] Total	男 Male	女 Female	総　数[1)] Total	男 Male	女 Female	総　数 Total	男 Male	女 Female
総　　数[2)] Total	3 516	1 716	1 681	2 840	1 370	1 351	676	346	330
～19歳 Years	54	25	28	47	19	27	7	6	1
20～24	256	130	122	198	102	92	58	28	30
25～29	741	346	372	618	279	316	123	67	56
30～34	1 227	616	566	1 002	508	449	225	108	117
35～39	921	445	444	739	348	359	182	97	85
40～44	293	146	134	222	109	100	71	37	34
45～	17	6	10	13	5	7	4	1	3

母　の　年　齢 Age of mother	周産期死亡率（出産千対） Perinatal death rates[a)]			妊娠満22週以後の死産率（出産千対） Foetal death rates at 22 completed weeks and over of gestation[a)]			早期新生児死亡率（出生千対） Early neonatal death rates (per 1,000 live births)		
	総　数[1)] Total	男 Male	女 Female	総　数[1)] Total	男 Male	女 Female	総　数 Total	男 Male	女 Female
総　　数[2)] Total	3.6	3.4	3.5	2.9	2.7	2.8	0.7	0.7	0.7
～19歳 Years	4.8	4.4	5.2	4.2	3.3	5.0	0.6	1.0	0.2
20～24	3.1	3.1	3.0	2.4	2.4	2.3	0.7	0.7	0.7
25～29	2.9	2.7	3.0	2.5	2.2	2.6	0.5	0.5	0.5
30～34	3.4	3.4	3.3	2.8	2.8	2.6	0.6	0.6	0.7
35～39	4.1	3.9	4.1	3.3	3.0	3.3	0.8	0.8	0.8
40～44	5.5	5.3	5.1	4.1	4.0	3.8	1.3	1.4	1.3
45～	12.0	8.2	14.7	9.2	6.8	10.3	2.9	1.4	4.4

注：1)　総数には性別不詳を含む。
　　2)　総数には母の年齢不詳を含む。
Note : a) Per 1,000 live births and foetal deaths at 22 completed weeks and over of gestation.

周産期死亡

〔単産－複産・出産順位別にみた周産期死亡〕
〔Perinatal deaths by plurality of birth and birth order〕

表8.10 単産－複産・出産順位別[1]にみた妊娠満22週以後の死産－早期新生児死亡別 周産期死亡数及び率

Table 8.10 Perinatal deaths and perinatal death rates by plurality of birth and birth order : Japan, 2016

平成28年

出 産 順 位 Birth order	周 産 期 死 亡 数 Perinatal deaths			妊娠満22週以後の死産数 Foetal deaths at 22 completed weeks and over of gestation			早期新生児死亡数 Early neonatal deaths		
	総 数[2] Total	単 産 Single	複 産 Plural	総 数[2] Total	単 産 Single	複 産 Plural	総 数[2] Total	単 産 Single	複 産 Plural
総 数[3] Total	3 516	3 161	348	2 840	2 554	285	676	607	63
第 1 児 1st	1 622	1 537	84	1 313	1 267	45	309	270	39
2 2nd	1 114	958	156	876	739	137	238	219	19
3 3rd	514	444	70	434	368	66	80	76	4
4 4th	171	142	29	150	122	28	21	20	1
5 ～ 5th and over	84	75	9	67	58	9	17	17	-

出 産 順 位 Birth order	周産期死亡率（出産千対） Perinatal death rates[a]			妊娠満22週以後の死産率（出産千対） Foetal death rates at 22 completed weeks and over of gestation[a]			早期新生児死亡率（出生千対） Early neonatal death rates (per 1,000 live births)		
	総 数[2] Total	単 産 Single	複 産 Plural	総 数[2] Total	単 産 Single	複 産 Plural	総 数[2] Total	単 産 Single	複 産 Plural
総 数[3] Total	3.6	3.3	17.7	2.9	2.7	14.5	0.7	0.6	3.3
第 1 児 1st	3.5	3.4	15.6	2.9	2.8	8.4	0.7	0.6	7.3
2 2nd	3.1	2.8	18.2	2.5	2.1	16.0	0.7	0.6	2.3
3 3rd	4.0	3.6	16.6	3.4	3.0	15.7	0.6	0.6	1.0
4 4th	6.3	5.4	25.7	5.5	4.7	24.8	0.8	0.8	0.9
5 ～ 5th and over	9.5	8.8	25.6	7.5	6.8	25.6	1.9	2.0	-

注：1) 出産順位の児数は、同じ母の出産した児の数であって妊娠満22週以後の死産を含む。
　　2) 総数には単産－複産不詳を含む。
　　3) 総数には出産順位不詳を含む。
Note：a) Per 1,000 live births and foetal deaths at 22 completed weeks and over of gestation.

Perinatal mortality

〔地域別にみた周産期死亡〕
〔Perinatal deaths by prefecture〕

表8.11　都道府県（21大都市再掲）別にみた妊娠満22週以後の死産－早期新生児死亡別周産期死亡数・率及び周産期死亡中妊娠満22週以後の死産の占める割合

Table 8.11　Perinatal deaths, perinatal death rates and proportion of foetal deaths at 22 completed weeks and over of gestation : Japan, each prefecture and 21 major cities, 2016　平成28年

都道府県 Prefecture	周産期死亡数 Perinatal deaths	妊娠満22週以後の死産数 Foetal deaths at 22 completed weeks and over of gestation	早期新生児死亡数 Early neonatal deaths	周産期死亡率（出産千対） Perinatal death rates[a]	妊娠満22週以後の死産率（出産千対） Foetal death rates at 22 completed weeks and over of gestation[a]	早期新生児死亡率（出生千対） Early neonatal death rates (per 1,000 live births)	周産期死亡中妊娠満22週以後の死産の占める割合（％） Proportion of foetal deaths at 22 completed weeks and over of gestation
全国　Total	3 516	2 840	676	3.6	2.9	0.7	80.8
01[b] 北海道	117	89	28	3.3	2.5	0.8	76.1
02 青森	26	20	6	3.0	2.3	0.7	76.9
03 岩手	32	28	4	3.8	3.3	0.5	87.5
04 宮城	64	44	20	3.7	2.5	1.2	68.8
05 秋田	26	21	5	4.6	3.7	0.9	80.8
06 山形	33	24	9	4.4	3.2	1.2	72.7
07 福島	63	56	7	4.6	4.1	0.5	88.9
08 茨城	83	70	13	4.0	3.3	0.6	84.3
09 栃木	46	34	12	3.1	2.3	0.8	73.9
10 群馬	48	38	10	3.5	2.8	0.7	79.2
11 埼玉	185	145	40	3.4	2.7	0.7	78.4
12 千葉	188	154	34	4.1	3.4	0.7	81.9
13 東京	402	322	80	3.6	2.9	0.7	80.1
14 神奈川	258	196	62	3.6	2.8	0.9	76.0
15 新潟	59	54	5	3.7	3.4	0.3	91.5
16 富山	29	20	9	4.0	2.7	1.2	69.0
17 石川	24	18	6	2.7	2.0	0.7	75.0
18 福井	26	18	8	4.2	2.9	1.3	69.2
19 山梨	15	12	3	2.6	2.1	0.5	80.0
20 長野	56	41	15	3.7	2.7	1.0	73.2
21 岐阜	55	40	15	3.7	2.7	1.0	72.7
22 静岡	115	99	16	4.1	3.6	0.6	86.1
23 愛知	237	192	45	3.7	3.0	0.7	81.0
24 三重	75	67	8	5.7	5.0	0.6	89.3
25 滋賀	29	21	8	2.4	1.7	0.7	72.4
26 京都	70	53	17	3.6	2.7	0.9	75.7
27 大阪	239	205	34	3.5	3.0	0.5	85.8
28 兵庫	120	104	16	2.8	2.4	0.4	86.7
29 奈良	35	25	10	3.7	2.6	1.1	71.4
30 和歌山	20	18	2	3.0	2.7	0.3	90.0
31 鳥取	23	17	6	5.2	3.8	1.4	73.9
32 島根	17	15	2	3.2	2.8	0.4	88.2
33 岡山	61	50	11	3.9	3.2	0.7	82.0
34 広島	84	72	12	3.7	3.2	0.5	85.7
35 山口	43	39	4	4.4	3.9	0.4	90.7
36 徳島	18	13	5	3.4	2.4	0.9	72.2
37 香川	19	16	3	2.5	2.1	0.4	84.2
38 愛媛	31	30	1	3.1	3.0	0.1	96.8
39 高知	14	12	2	2.9	2.5	0.4	85.7
40 福岡	149	123	26	3.4	2.8	0.6	82.6
41 佐賀	17	14	3	2.5	2.1	0.4	82.4
42 長崎	46	39	7	4.2	3.6	0.6	84.8
43 熊本	48	38	10	3.2	2.5	0.7	79.2
44 大分	32	22	10	3.5	2.4	1.1	68.8
45 宮崎	31	23	8	3.5	2.6	0.9	74.2
46 鹿児島	42	35	7	3.1	2.6	0.5	83.3
47 沖縄	63	52	11	3.8	3.1	0.7	82.5
外国　Foreign countries	2	1	1	…	…	…	…
不詳　Place of residence not stated	1	1	-	…	…	…	…
21 大都市（再掲） 21 major cities (Regrouped)							
50 東京都の区部	297	242	55	3.7	3.0	0.7	81.5
51 札幌	47	38	9	3.3	2.7	0.6	80.9
52 仙台	33	21	12	3.7	2.4	1.3	63.6
53 さいたま	45	34	11	4.3	3.2	1.0	75.6
54 千葉	23	17	6	3.3	2.4	0.9	73.9
55 横浜	121	93	28	4.2	3.2	1.0	76.9
56 川崎	42	32	10	3.0	2.3	0.7	76.2
57 相模原	20	16	4	3.8	3.1	0.8	80.0
58 新潟	25	23	2	4.2	3.9	0.3	92.0
59 静岡	28	25	3	5.5	4.9	0.5	89.3
60 浜松	18	15	3	2.7	2.3	0.5	83.3
61 名古屋	70	56	14	3.6	2.9	0.7	80.0
62 京都	42	33	9	3.8	3.0	0.8	78.6
63 大阪	80	67	13	3.6	3.0	0.6	83.8
64 堺	18	15	3	2.6	2.2	0.4	83.3
65 神戸	31	27	4	2.6	2.3	0.3	87.1
66 岡山	28	23	5	4.5	3.7	0.8	82.1
67 広島	41	36	5	3.9	3.4	0.5	87.8
68 北九州	25	19	6	3.3	2.5	0.8	76.0
69 福岡	52	47	5	3.6	3.2	0.3	90.4
70 熊本	24	21	3	3.5	3.1	0.4	87.5

Note : a) Per 1,000 live births and foetal deaths at 22 completed weeks and over of gestation.
b) See page 44.

周産期死亡

表 8.12　都道府県別にみた年次別妊娠満22週以後の
Table 8.12　Trends in perinatal deaths

都道府県 Prefecture	1980 昭和55年			1985 60 年			1990 平成 2 年		
	周産期死亡数 Perinatal deaths	妊娠満22週以後の死産数 Foetal deaths at 22 completed weeks and over of gestation	早期新生児死亡数 Early neonatal deaths	周産期死亡数 Perinatal deaths	妊娠満22週以後の死産数 Foetal deaths at 22 completed weeks and over of gestation	早期新生児死亡数 Early neonatal deaths	周産期死亡数 Perinatal deaths	妊娠満22週以後の死産数 Foetal deaths at 22 completed weeks and over of gestation	早期新生児死亡数 Early neonatal deaths
全国　Total	32 422	26 268	6 154	22 379	18 642	3 737	13 704	11 367	2 337
01 北 海 道 a)	1 857	1 515	342	1 286	1 087	199	754	647	107
02 青　　森	464	368	96	352	302	50	180	141	39
03 岩　　手	437	337	100	254	219	35	169	150	19
04 宮　　城	710	553	157	459	394	65	302	254	48
05 秋　　田	317	253	64	193	150	43	129	99	30
06 山　　形	324	260	64	236	196	40	146	127	19
07 福　　島	706	567	139	501	415	86	279	243	36
08 茨　　城	806	612	194	603	501	102	343	295	48
09 栃　　木	563	451	112	369	312	57	265	215	50
10 群　　馬	492	379	113	338	272	66	252	210	42
11 埼　　玉	1 404	1 108	296	972	797	175	712	586	126
12 千　　葉	1 314	1 084	230	954	818	136	555	469	86
13 東　　京	2 734	2 265	469	1 848	1 570	278	1 111	945	166
14 神 奈 川	1 724	1 366	358	1 124	896	228	836	680	156
15 新　　潟	618	483	135	428	327	101	228	192	36
16 富　　山	258	206	52	168	129	39	102	75	27
17 石　　川	296	229	67	173	142	31	120	96	24
18 福　　井	175	146	29	151	123	28	86	65	21
19 山　　梨	261	227	34	170	151	19	113	98	15
20 長　　野	622	505	117	382	310	72	235	200	35
21 岐　　阜	517	415	102	382	306	76	193	165	28
22 静　　岡	911	769	142	634	527	107	383	320	63
23 愛　　知	1 606	1 297	309	1 154	968	186	666	566	100
24 三　　重	432	349	83	298	236	62	207	159	48
25 滋　　賀	303	240	63	204	165	39	120	93	27
26 京　　都	607	493	114	407	339	68	268	209	59
27 大　　阪	2 307	1 918	389	1 475	1 220	255	940	762	178
28 兵　　庫	1 315	1 074	241	862	696	166	541	438	103
29 奈　　良	366	296	70	227	178	49	137	107	30
30 和 歌 山	278	204	74	180	136	44	98	78	20
31 鳥　　取	148	121	27	127	107	20	72	63	9
32 島　　根	237	174	63	137	120	17	79	62	17
33 岡　　山	370	318	52	330	285	45	205	160	45
34 広　　島	683	545	138	514	439	75	308	260	48
35 山　　口	417	323	94	258	198	60	176	147	29
36 徳　　島	254	218	36	162	130	32	87	75	12
37 香　　川	202	155	47	166	141	25	91	70	21
38 愛　　媛	451	373	78	318	251	67	165	134	31
39 高　　知	222	178	44	171	143	28	89	68	21
40 福　　岡	1 335	1 122	213	1 049	908	141	632	528	104
41 佐　　賀	266	232	34	212	170	42	118	101	17
42 長　　崎	557	484	73	440	403	37	187	161	26
43 熊　　本	551	429	122	417	347	70	223	192	31
44 大　　分	446	357	89	235	210	25	168	146	22
45 宮　　崎	442	359	83	283	250	33	139	119	20
46 鹿 児 島	679	569	110	466	399	67	254	219	35
47 沖　　縄	391	312	79	287	246	41	227	170	57

注：全国には住所地外国・不詳を含む。

Perinatal mortality

死産－早期新生児死亡別周産期死亡数
by each prefecture : Japan

1995 7 年			2000 12 年			2005 17 年			2010 22 年		
Perinatal deaths	Foetal deaths at 22 completed weeks and over of gestation	Early neonatal deaths	Perinatal deaths	Foetal deaths at 22 completed weeks and over of gestation	Early neonatal deaths	Perinatal deaths	Foetal deaths at 22 completed weeks and over of gestation	Early neonatal deaths	Perinatal deaths	Foetal deaths at 22 completed weeks and over of gestation	Early neonatal deaths
8 412	6 580	1 832	6 881	5 362	1 519	5 149	4 058	1 091	4 515	3 637	878
350	278	72	259	208	51	212	166	46	171	138	33
116	80	36	103	65	38	56	38	18	39	30	9
104	92	12	75	59	16	69	55	14	59	53	6
172	141	31	125	103	22	92	75	17	72	61	11
82	66	16	38	31	7	36	31	5	44	39	5
80	62	18	76	56	20	42	37	5	35	27	8
133	110	23	141	106	35	69	54	15	75	62	13
224	173	51	149	117	32	113	90	23	112	84	28
167	128	39	125	94	31	76	47	29	63	54	9
144	109	35	105	81	24	86	66	20	71	56	15
476	385	91	397	319	78	281	242	39	252	205	47
368	313	55	389	321	68	253	199	54	213	169	44
728	584	144	566	423	143	461	370	91	424	352	72
609	467	142	521	392	129	397	311	86	379	298	81
135	115	20	146	118	28	94	79	15	85	75	10
77	55	22	60	40	20	36	28	8	33	26	7
70	52	18	68	56	12	52	40	12	54	41	13
66	50	16	60	42	18	29	25	4	20	14	6
78	61	17	65	55	10	32	27	5	28	28	-
139	113	26	111	85	26	91	76	15	62	48	14
123	94	29	112	93	19	105	85	20	65	48	17
276	227	49	201	160	41	161	123	38	134	107	27
518	398	120	424	323	101	333	259	74	281	224	57
123	84	39	105	83	22	76	65	11	67	57	10
92	71	21	96	80	16	73	52	21	77	60	17
180	150	30	137	103	34	108	83	25	97	72	25
557	428	129	486	385	101	341	263	78	303	245	58
308	233	75	288	212	76	228	176	52	175	147	28
79	56	23	67	58	9	60	46	14	42	35	7
73	52	21	51	39	12	35	30	5	34	26	8
47	35	12	21	21	-	34	27	7	29	19	10
49	37	12	32	27	5	31	24	7	23	17	6
109	78	31	77	62	15	70	58	12	59	48	11
206	166	40	130	103	27	105	77	28	100	78	22
91	73	18	71	60	11	43	32	11	46	32	14
53	34	19	41	33	8	34	27	7	26	22	4
49	34	15	48	36	12	43	33	10	37	29	8
91	69	22	68	52	16	72	55	17	39	33	6
60	48	12	37	29	8	32	26	6	19	14	5
295	217	78	251	195	56	209	161	48	200	160	40
58	48	10	50	38	12	27	22	5	35	28	7
113	90	23	85	65	20	57	46	11	53	41	12
123	98	25	90	70	20	68	51	17	56	41	15
78	62	16	64	51	13	37	27	10	52	42	10
70	51	19	54	41	13	36	26	10	31	29	2
105	89	16	92	76	16	60	49	11	67	54	13
152	118	34	116	94	22	90	78	12	70	65	5

Note : a) See page 44.

周産期死亡

表 8.12 都道府県別にみた年次別妊娠満22週以後の死産－早期新生児死亡別周産期死亡数（つづき）
Table 8.12 Trends in perinatal deaths by each prefecture : Japan－CON.

都道府県 Prefecture	2014 26 年 周産期死亡数 Perinatal deaths	2014 26 年 妊娠満22週以後の死産数 Foetal deaths at 22 completed weeks and over of gestation	2014 26 年 早期新生児死亡数 Early neonatal deaths	2015 27 年 周産期死亡数 Perinatal deaths	2015 27 年 妊娠満22週以後の死産数 Foetal deaths at 22 completed weeks and over of gestation	2015 27 年 早期新生児死亡数 Early neonatal deaths	2016 28 年 周産期死亡数 Perinatal deaths	2016 28 年 妊娠満22週以後の死産数 Foetal deaths at 22 completed weeks and over of gestation	2016 28 年 早期新生児死亡数 Early neonatal deaths
全国　Total	3 750	3 039	711	3 728	3 063	665	3 516	2 840	676
a) 01 北　海　道	148	123	25	152	126	26	117	89	28
02 青　　　森	28	20	8	40	30	10	26	20	6
03 岩　　　手	46	41	5	30	26	4	32	28	4
04 宮　　　城	69	50	19	64	53	11	64	44	20
05 秋　　　田	33	28	5	17	16	1	26	21	5
06 山　　　形	34	27	7	32	27	5	33	24	9
07 福　　　島	49	44	5	72	60	12	63	56	7
08 茨　　　城	97	72	25	91	73	18	83	70	13
09 栃　　　木	67	45	22	51	39	12	46	34	12
10 群　　　馬	61	52	9	60	50	10	48	38	10
11 埼　　　玉	221	181	40	208	175	33	185	145	40
12 千　　　葉	202	159	43	179	144	35	188	154	34
13 東　　　京	388	324	64	368	308	60	402	322	80
14 神　奈　川	274	213	61	290	230	60	258	196	62
15 新　　　潟	78	69	9	61	50	11	59	54	5
16 富　　　山	37	33	4	38	33	5	29	20	9
17 石　　　川	25	22	3	47	43	4	24	18	6
18 福　　　井	28	23	5	28	27	1	26	18	8
19 山　　　梨	20	18	2	17	15	2	15	12	3
20 長　　　野	49	41	8	47	39	8	56	41	15
21 岐　　　阜	70	53	17	56	45	11	55	40	15
22 静　　　岡	121	99	22	105	84	21	115	99	16
23 愛　　　知	231	191	40	253	202	51	237	192	45
24 三　　　重	60	49	11	53	43	10	75	67	8
25 滋　　　賀	47	38	9	57	50	7	29	21	8
26 京　　　都	71	60	11	86	59	27	70	53	17
27 大　　　阪	248	206	42	230	194	36	239	205	34
28 兵　　　庫	142	121	21	144	125	19	120	104	16
29 奈　　　良	37	27	10	51	43	8	35	25	10
30 和　歌　山	28	22	6	17	11	6	20	18	2
31 鳥　　　取	20	15	5	24	17	7	23	17	6
32 島　　　根	17	17	-	14	10	4	17	15	2
33 岡　　　山	45	37	8	55	50	5	61	50	11
34 広　　　島	71	53	18	80	63	17	84	72	12
35 山　　　口	41	32	9	44	33	11	43	39	4
36 徳　　　島	22	15	7	21	17	4	18	13	5
37 香　　　川	17	14	3	26	19	7	19	16	3
38 愛　　　媛	39	34	5	27	22	5	31	30	1
39 高　　　知	15	11	4	18	16	2	14	12	2
40 福　　　岡	170	133	37	177	142	35	149	123	26
41 佐　　　賀	26	23	3	24	22	2	17	14	3
42 長　　　崎	42	37	5	34	29	5	46	39	7
43 熊　　　本	44	36	8	44	38	6	48	38	10
44 大　　　分	31	22	9	48	41	7	32	22	10
45 宮　　　崎	26	19	7	33	30	3	31	23	8
46 鹿　児　島	47	37	10	58	46	12	42	35	7
47 沖　　　縄	65	50	15	55	47	8	63	52	11

498

周産期死亡

表 8.13　都道府県別にみた年次別妊娠満22週以後の
Table 8.13　Trends in perinatal death rates

都道府県 Prefecture	1980 昭和55年			1985 60　年			1990 平成 2 年		
	周産期死亡率 （出産千対） Perinatal death rates[a]	妊娠満22週以後の死産率 （出産千対） Foetal death rates at 22 completed weeks and over of gestation[a]	早期新生児死亡率 （出生千対） Early neonatal death rates (per1,000 live births)	周産期死亡率 （出産千対） Perinatal death rates[a]	妊娠満22週以後の死産率 （出産千対） Foetal death rates at 22 completed weeks and over of gestation[a]	早期新生児死亡率 （出生千対） Early neonatal death rates (per1,000 live births)	周産期死亡率 （出産千対） Perinatal death rates[a]	妊娠満22週以後の死産率 （出産千対） Foetal death rates at 22 completed weeks and over of gestation[a]	早期新生児死亡率 （出生千対） Early neonatal death rates (per1,000 live births)
全国　Total	20.2	16.4	3.9	15.4	12.9	2.6	11.1	9.2	1.9
01　北　海　道 [b]	24.1	19.7	4.5	19.1	16.1	3.0	13.7	11.7	2.0
02　青　　　森	21.0	16.6	4.4	18.1	15.6	2.6	12.2	9.5	2.7
03　岩　　　手	21.9	16.9	5.1	14.6	12.5	2.0	11.7	10.4	1.3
04　宮　　　城	22.4	17.5	5.0	16.2	13.9	2.3	12.8	10.8	2.1
05　秋　　　田	19.1	15.3	3.9	14.0	10.9	3.1	11.6	8.9	2.7
06　山　　　形	18.9	15.2	3.8	15.6	13.0	2.7	11.5	10.0	1.5
07　福　　　島	23.5	18.9	4.7	18.1	15.0	3.1	12.1	10.6	1.6
08　茨　　　城	21.8	16.5	5.3	17.7	14.7	3.0	11.8	10.1	1.7
09　栃　　　木	21.3	17.1	4.3	15.3	12.9	2.4	13.1	10.6	2.5
10　群　　　馬	19.3	14.9	4.5	14.6	11.7	2.9	12.8	10.7	2.2
11　埼　　　玉	18.4	14.5	3.9	14.3	11.7	2.6	11.1	9.2	2.0
12　千　　　葉	19.7	16.3	3.5	15.5	13.3	2.2	10.3	8.7	1.6
13　東　　　京	19.2	15.9	3.4	14.5	12.3	2.2	10.6	9.0	1.6
14　神　奈　川	18.0	14.3	3.8	12.9	10.3	2.6	10.4	8.5	2.0
15　新　　　潟	18.6	14.5	4.1	14.5	11.1	3.5	9.4	7.9	1.5
16　富　　　山	18.7	15.0	3.8	13.9	10.6	3.3	10.1	7.4	2.7
17　石　　　川	19.3	14.9	4.4	12.9	10.6	2.3	10.3	8.3	2.1
18　福　　　井	16.1	13.4	2.7	14.9	12.1	2.8	9.8	7.4	2.4
19　山　　　梨	25.5	22.2	3.4	17.0	15.1	1.9	13.0	11.3	1.7
20　長　　　野	22.5	18.2	4.3	15.6	12.7	3.0	10.9	9.3	1.6
21　岐　　　阜	19.7	15.8	3.9	15.8	12.7	3.2	9.4	8.1	1.4
22　静　　　岡	19.0	16.0	3.0	14.3	11.9	2.4	10.3	8.6	1.7
23　愛　　　知	18.0	14.6	3.5	14.2	11.9	2.3	9.3	7.9	1.4
24　三　　　重	19.8	16.0	3.9	14.9	11.8	3.1	11.5	8.8	2.7
25　滋　　　賀	18.7	14.8	4.0	13.6	11.0	2.6	8.8	6.8	2.0
26　京　　　都	18.6	15.1	3.5	14.1	11.8	2.4	11.0	8.6	2.4
27　大　　　阪	20.3	16.8	3.5	14.5	12.0	2.5	10.7	8.7	2.0
28　兵　　　庫	18.9	15.4	3.5	13.9	11.2	2.7	10.0	8.1	1.9
29　奈　　　良	22.5	18.2	4.4	15.3	12.0	3.3	10.2	8.0	2.3
30　和　歌　山	20.4	14.9	5.5	14.7	11.1	3.6	9.6	7.6	2.0
31　鳥　　　取	17.8	14.5	3.3	16.7	14.1	2.7	11.1	9.7	1.4
32　島　　　根	23.4	17.2	6.3	14.9	13.1	1.9	10.4	8.2	2.3
33　岡　　　山	14.9	12.8	2.1	14.4	12.4	2.0	10.6	8.3	2.4
34　広　　　島	18.0	14.4	3.7	15.1	12.9	2.2	10.6	8.9	1.7
35　山　　　口	20.7	16.1	4.7	14.4	11.1	3.4	12.7	10.6	2.1
36　徳　　　島	23.6	20.3	3.4	16.5	13.2	3.3	10.9	9.4	1.5
37　香　　　川	15.4	11.8	3.6	14.2	12.1	2.2	9.5	7.3	2.2
38　愛　　　媛	22.4	18.6	4.0	17.8	14.0	3.8	11.2	9.1	2.1
39　高　　　知	23.2	18.6	4.7	18.0	15.1	3.0	12.3	9.4	2.9
40　福　　　岡	20.4	17.1	3.3	17.6	15.2	2.4	13.0	10.8	2.2
41　佐　　　賀	20.9	18.3	2.7	17.9	14.3	3.6	12.2	10.5	1.8
42　長　　　崎	24.5	21.3	3.3	21.2	19.4	1.8	11.2	9.7	1.6
43　熊　　　本	22.2	17.2	5.0	17.7	14.7	3.0	11.6	10.0	1.6
44　大　　　分	26.8	21.4	5.5	16.1	14.4	1.7	14.3	12.4	1.9
45　宮　　　崎	25.5	20.7	4.9	18.2	16.1	2.2	11.4	9.7	1.7
46　鹿　児　島	27.0	22.7	4.5	19.6	16.8	2.9	13.3	11.5	1.9
47　沖　　　縄	19.0	15.2	3.9	13.7	11.8	2.0	13.2	9.9	3.3

500

死産－早期新生児死亡別周産期死亡率
by each prefecture : Japan

Perinatal mortality

1995 7 年			2000 12 年			2005 17 年			2010 22 年		
周産期死亡率 (出産千対) Perinatal death rates[a]	妊娠満22週以後の死産率 (出産千対) Foetal death rates at 22 completed weeks and over of gestation[a]	早期新生児死亡率 (出生千対) Early neonatal death rates (per1,000 live births)	周産期死亡率 (出産千対) Perinatal death rates[a]	妊娠満22週以後の死産率 (出産千対) Foetal death rates at 22 completed weeks and over of gestation[a]	早期新生児死亡率 (出生千対) Early neonatal death rates (per1,000 live births)	周産期死亡率 (出産千対) Perinatal death rates[a]	妊娠満22週以後の死産率 (出産千対) Foetal death rates at 22 completed weeks and over of gestation[a]	早期新生児死亡率 (出生千対) Early neonatal death rates (per1,000 live births)	周産期死亡率 (出産千対) Perinatal death rates[a]	妊娠満22週以後の死産率 (出産千対) Foetal death rates at 22 completed weeks and over of gestation[a]	早期新生児死亡率 (出生千対) Early neonatal death rates (per1,000 live births)
7.0	5.5	1.5	5.8	4.5	1.3	4.8	3.8	1.0	4.2	3.4	0.8
7.0	5.5	1.4	5.5	4.4	1.1	5.1	4.0	1.1	4.2	3.4	0.8
8.3	5.7	2.6	7.9	5.0	2.9	5.3	3.6	1.7	4.0	3.1	0.9
7.9	7.0	0.9	6.0	4.7	1.3	6.5	5.2	1.3	6.0	5.4	0.6
7.7	6.3	1.4	5.6	4.6	1.0	4.7	3.9	0.9	3.8	3.2	0.6
8.2	6.6	1.6	4.2	3.4	0.8	4.7	4.0	0.6	6.5	5.8	0.7
6.9	5.4	1.6	6.9	5.1	1.8	4.5	3.9	0.5	4.0	3.1	0.9
6.2	5.1	1.1	6.9	5.2	1.7	3.9	3.1	0.9	4.6	3.8	0.8
7.9	6.1	1.8	5.3	4.1	1.1	4.6	3.7	0.9	4.7	3.5	1.2
8.9	6.8	2.1	6.6	4.9	1.6	4.4	2.7	1.7	3.8	3.3	0.5
7.4	5.6	1.8	5.4	4.1	1.2	5.0	3.8	1.2	4.4	3.5	0.9
7.0	5.7	1.3	6.0	4.8	1.2	4.7	4.0	0.7	4.2	3.4	0.8
6.7	5.7	1.0	7.0	5.8	1.2	5.0	3.9	1.1	4.1	3.3	0.9
7.5	6.0	1.5	5.6	4.2	1.4	4.8	3.8	0.9	3.9	3.2	0.7
7.5	5.8	1.8	6.3	4.7	1.6	5.2	4.1	1.1	4.8	3.8	1.0
5.9	5.0	0.9	6.6	5.4	1.3	5.1	4.3	0.8	4.7	4.1	0.6
7.6	5.4	2.2	5.9	3.9	2.0	4.0	3.1	0.9	4.0	3.2	0.9
6.3	4.7	1.6	5.9	4.9	1.0	5.2	4.0	1.2	5.6	4.3	1.4
8.0	6.0	1.9	7.4	5.2	2.2	4.0	3.5	0.6	2.9	2.0	0.9
8.8	6.9	1.9	7.7	6.5	1.2	4.5	3.8	0.7	4.2	4.2	-
6.5	5.3	1.2	5.2	4.0	1.2	4.9	4.1	0.8	3.6	2.8	0.8
6.1	4.6	1.4	5.5	4.6	0.9	5.9	4.8	1.1	3.8	2.8	1.0
7.8	6.4	1.4	5.6	4.5	1.1	5.0	3.8	1.2	4.2	3.3	0.8
7.2	5.5	1.7	5.6	4.3	1.4	4.9	3.8	1.1	4.0	3.2	0.8
7.0	4.8	2.2	5.9	4.7	1.2	4.9	4.2	0.7	4.4	3.7	0.7
6.9	5.3	1.6	6.8	5.6	1.1	5.6	4.0	1.6	5.7	4.5	1.3
7.7	6.4	1.3	5.7	4.3	1.4	5.0	3.8	1.2	4.6	3.4	1.2
6.4	4.9	1.5	5.5	4.3	1.1	4.5	3.4	1.0	4.0	3.3	0.8
5.9	4.5	1.4	5.3	3.9	1.4	4.8	3.7	1.1	3.6	3.1	0.6
5.9	4.2	1.7	5.0	4.4	0.7	5.3	4.1	1.3	3.9	3.3	0.7
7.4	5.2	2.1	5.3	4.1	1.3	4.5	3.8	0.6	4.5	3.4	1.1
8.2	6.1	2.1	3.7	3.7	-	6.7	5.4	1.4	6.0	4.0	2.1
7.2	5.4	1.8	4.9	4.1	0.8	5.4	4.2	1.2	4.0	2.9	1.0
5.8	4.2	1.7	4.0	3.2	0.8	4.2	3.5	0.7	3.5	2.9	0.7
7.4	6.0	1.4	4.7	3.7	1.0	4.2	3.1	1.1	3.9	3.0	0.9
6.8	5.5	1.4	5.4	4.6	0.8	3.7	2.8	1.0	4.0	2.8	1.2
7.1	4.5	2.5	5.6	4.5	1.1	5.7	4.5	1.2	4.4	3.7	0.7
5.2	3.6	1.6	4.9	3.7	1.2	4.9	3.8	1.2	4.4	3.4	1.0
6.5	5.0	1.6	5.1	3.9	1.2	6.2	4.7	1.5	3.4	2.9	0.5
8.6	6.9	1.7	5.4	4.2	1.2	5.4	4.4	1.0	3.4	2.5	0.9
6.3	4.6	1.7	5.3	4.1	1.2	4.8	3.7	1.1	4.3	3.4	0.9
6.6	5.5	1.1	5.7	4.3	1.4	3.6	2.9	0.7	4.6	3.7	0.9
7.6	6.1	1.6	6.0	4.6	1.4	4.7	3.8	0.9	4.4	3.4	1.0
6.8	5.4	1.4	5.2	4.0	1.2	4.3	3.2	1.1	3.4	2.5	0.9
7.0	5.5	1.4	5.8	4.7	1.2	3.8	2.8	1.0	5.1	4.2	1.0
6.0	4.3	1.6	4.9	3.7	1.2	3.7	2.7	1.0	3.0	2.8	0.2
6.3	5.3	1.0	5.6	4.6	1.0	4.0	3.3	0.7	4.4	3.6	0.9
9.0	7.0	2.0	6.9	5.6	1.3	5.6	4.8	0.7	4.1	3.8	0.3

Note : a) Per 1,000 live births and foetal deaths at 22 completed weeks and over of gestation.

b) See page 44.

周産期死亡

表8.13 都道府県別にみた年次別妊娠満22週以後の死産－早期新生児死亡別周産期死亡率（つづき）
Table 8.13 Trends in perinatal death rates by each prefecture : Japan－CON.

都道府県 Prefecture	2014 26 年			2015 27 年			2016 28 年		
	周産期死亡率（出産千対）Perinatal death rates[a]	妊娠満22週以後の死産率（出産千対）Foetal death rates at 22 completed weeks and over of gestation[a]	早期新生児死亡率（出生千対）Early neonatal death rates (per1,000 live births)	周産期死亡率（出産千対）Perinatal death rates[a]	妊娠満22週以後の死産率（出産千対）Foetal death rates at 22 completed weeks and over of gestation[a]	早期新生児死亡率（出生千対）Early neonatal death rates (per1,000 live births)	周産期死亡率（出産千対）Perinatal death rates[a]	妊娠満22週以後の死産率（出産千対）Foetal death rates at 22 completed weeks and over of gestation[a]	早期新生児死亡率（出生千対）Early neonatal death rates (per1,000 live births)
全国 Total	3.7	3.0	0.7	3.7	3.0	0.7	3.6	2.9	0.7
01 北海道 [b]	4.0	3.3	0.7	4.1	3.4	0.7	3.3	2.5	0.8
02 青　森	3.2	2.3	0.9	4.6	3.5	1.2	3.0	2.3	0.7
03 岩　手	5.2	4.6	0.6	3.4	2.9	0.5	3.8	3.3	0.5
04 宮　城	3.8	2.8	1.1	3.5	2.9	0.6	3.7	2.5	1.2
05 秋　田	5.5	4.6	0.8	2.9	2.7	0.2	4.6	3.7	0.9
06 山　形	4.3	3.4	0.9	4.1	3.4	0.6	4.4	3.2	1.2
07 福　島	3.4	3.0	0.3	5.1	4.2	0.8	4.6	4.1	0.5
08 茨　城	4.4	3.3	1.1	4.2	3.4	0.8	4.0	3.3	0.6
09 栃　木	4.3	2.9	1.4	3.3	2.5	0.8	3.1	2.3	0.8
10 群　馬	4.2	3.6	0.6	4.2	3.5	0.7	3.5	2.8	0.7
11 埼　玉	4.0	3.2	0.7	3.7	3.1	0.6	3.4	2.7	0.7
12 千　葉	4.3	3.4	0.9	3.8	3.1	0.7	4.1	3.4	0.7
13 東　京	3.5	2.9	0.6	3.2	2.7	0.5	3.6	2.9	0.7
14 神奈川	3.7	2.9	0.8	3.9	3.1	0.8	3.6	2.8	0.9
15 新　潟	4.7	4.2	0.5	3.7	3.1	0.7	3.7	3.4	0.3
16 富　山	4.9	4.3	0.5	5.0	4.3	0.7	4.0	2.7	1.2
17 石　川	2.8	2.4	0.3	5.2	4.7	0.4	2.7	2.0	0.7
18 福　井	4.5	3.7	0.8	4.5	4.3	0.2	4.2	2.9	1.3
19 山　梨	3.3	3.0	0.3	2.8	2.5	0.3	2.6	2.1	0.5
20 長　野	3.1	2.6	0.5	3.0	2.5	0.5	3.7	2.7	1.0
21 岐　阜	4.6	3.5	1.1	3.6	2.9	0.7	3.7	2.7	1.0
22 静　岡	4.2	3.4	0.8	3.7	3.0	0.7	4.1	3.6	0.6
23 愛　知	3.5	2.9	0.6	3.8	3.1	0.8	3.7	3.0	0.7
24 三　重	4.4	3.6	0.8	3.8	3.1	0.7	5.7	5.0	0.6
25 滋　賀	3.7	3.0	0.7	4.5	3.9	0.6	2.4	1.7	0.7
26 京　都	3.6	3.1	0.6	4.4	3.0	1.4	3.6	2.7	0.9
27 大　阪	3.5	2.9	0.6	3.2	2.7	0.5	3.5	3.0	0.5
28 兵　庫	3.2	2.7	0.5	3.3	2.8	0.4	2.8	2.4	0.4
29 奈　良	3.8	2.8	1.0	5.2	4.4	0.8	3.7	2.6	1.1
30 和歌山	3.9	3.1	0.8	2.4	1.6	0.9	3.0	2.7	0.3
31 鳥　取	4.4	3.3	1.1	5.2	3.7	1.5	5.2	3.8	1.4
32 島　根	3.2	3.2	-	2.5	1.8	0.7	3.2	2.8	0.4
33 岡　山	2.8	2.3	0.5	3.5	3.2	0.3	3.9	3.2	0.7
34 広　島	3.0	2.2	0.8	3.4	2.7	0.7	3.7	3.2	0.5
35 山　口	4.0	3.1	0.9	4.2	3.2	1.1	4.4	3.9	0.4
36 徳　島	4.0	2.7	1.3	3.7	3.0	0.7	3.4	2.4	0.9
37 香　川	2.2	1.8	0.4	3.4	2.5	0.9	2.5	2.1	0.4
38 愛　媛	3.7	3.3	0.5	2.7	2.2	0.5	3.1	3.0	0.1
39 高　知	3.0	2.2	0.8	3.6	3.2	0.4	2.9	2.5	0.4
40 福　岡	3.7	2.9	0.8	3.9	3.1	0.8	3.4	2.8	0.6
41 佐　賀	3.6	3.2	0.4	3.4	3.1	0.3	2.5	2.1	0.4
42 長　崎	3.7	3.3	0.4	3.1	2.6	0.5	4.2	3.6	0.6
43 熊　本	2.8	2.3	0.5	2.8	2.4	0.4	3.2	2.5	0.7
44 大　分	3.3	2.4	1.0	5.2	4.5	0.8	3.5	2.4	1.1
45 宮　崎	2.7	2.0	0.7	3.6	3.2	0.3	3.5	2.6	0.9
46 鹿児島	3.3	2.6	0.7	4.1	3.2	0.8	3.1	2.6	0.5
47 沖　縄	4.0	3.0	0.9	3.2	2.8	0.5	3.8	3.1	0.7

周産期死亡

〔周産期死亡の原因〕
〔Causes of perinatal death〕

表8.14　死因・母側病態－児側病態別にみた妊娠満
Table 8.14　Perinatal deaths and percent distribution by maternal condition

死因基本分類コード Code	死因（児側病態）Causes on child	母側 総数 Total							側
		総数 Total	(P00-P04) 母体側要因並びに妊娠及び分娩の合併症により影響を受けた胎児及び新生児	P00 現在の妊娠とは無関係の場合もありうる母体の病態により影響を受けた胎児及び新生児	P01 母体の妊娠合併症により影響を受けた胎児及び新生児	P02 胎盤，臍帯及び卵膜の合併症により影響を受けた胎児及び新生児	P03 その他の分娩合併症により影響を受けた胎児及び新生児	P04 胎盤又は母乳を介して有害な影響を受けた胎児	P99 母体に原因なし
	周産期死亡数　Perinatal deaths	3 516	2 074	942	307	790	35	-	1 442
	母側病態別百分率	100.0	59.0	26.8	8.7	22.5	1.0		41.0
	Percentage of maternal condition	·	·	·	·	·	·	·	·
	総　数　Total	100.0	100.0	100.0	100.0	100.0	100.0	-	100.0
XVI	周産期に発生した病態	85.2	92.6	94.2	73.3	98.4	88.6	-	74.5
(P05-P08)	妊娠期間及び胎児発育に関連する障害	3.2	3.1	2.8	8.5	1.4	2.9	-	3.5
P05	胎児発育遅延及び胎児栄養失調	1.4	1.2	1.4	2.3	0.5	-	-	1.7
P07	妊娠期間短縮及び低出産体重に関連する障害, 他に分類されないもの	1.8	1.9	1.4	6.2	0.9	-	-	1.8
P08	遷延妊娠及び高出産体重に関連する障害	0.0	0.0	-	-	-	2.9	-	-
(P10-P15)	出産外傷	0.1	0.0	-	0.3	-	-	-	0.1
P10	出産損傷による頭蓋内裂傷及び出血	-	-	-	-	-	-	-	-
P11	中枢神経系のその他の出産損傷	-	-	-	-	-	-	-	-
P12	頭皮の出産損傷	0.0	-	-	-	-	-	-	0.1
P13	骨格の出産損傷	-	-	-	-	-	-	-	-
P14	末梢神経系の出産損傷								
P15	その他の出産損傷	0.0	0.0	-	0.3	-	-	-	-
(P20-P29)	周産期に特異的な呼吸障害及び心血管障害	8.6	9.6	3.8	22.5	10.6	28.6	-	7.1
P20	子宮内低酸素症	0.5	0.6	0.2	0.3	1.3	-	-	0.4
P21	出生時仮死	1.9	2.3	0.8	3.3	3.3	11.4	-	1.3
P22	新生児の呼吸窮迫	0.9	0.9	0.4	3.9	0.3	2.9	-	0.8
P23	先天性肺炎	0.1	0.0	0.1	-	-	-	-	0.1
P24	新生児吸引症候群	0.2	0.1	0.1	-	0.1	-	-	0.3
P25	周産期に発生した間質性気腫及び関連病態	0.3	0.3	0.2	1.0	0.1	-	-	0.2
P26	周産期に発生した肺出血	0.3	0.3	0.1	1.0	0.4	-	-	0.1
P27	周産期に発生した慢性呼吸器疾患	0.1	0.1	-	0.7	-	-	-	-
P28	周産期に発生したその他の呼吸器病態	2.2	2.4	1.0	9.8	1.0	8.6	-	1.9
P29	周産期に発生した心血管障害	2.2	2.5	0.8	2.6	4.2	5.7	-	1.8
(P35-P39)	周産期に特異的な感染症	1.6	2.3	1.8	8.1	0.8	-	-	0.6
P35	先天性ウイルス疾患	0.1	0.1	0.3	-	-	-	-	0.1
P36	新生児の細菌性敗血症	0.7	1.0	0.8	3.3	0.3	-	-	0.4
P37	その他の先天性感染症及び寄生虫症	-	-	-	-	-	-	-	-
P38	軽度出血を伴う又は伴わない新生児の臍炎	-	-	-	-	-	-	-	-
P39	周産期に特異的なその他の感染症	0.8	1.2	0.6	4.9	0.5	-	-	0.1
(P50-P61)	胎児及び新生児の出血性障害及び血液障害	3.2	2.7	1.2	8.5	2.0	5.7	-	4.1
P50	胎児失血	2.1	1.2	0.2	5.9	0.5	-	-	3.5
P51	新生児の臍出血	-	-	-	-	-	-	-	-
P52	胎児及び新生児の頭蓋内非外傷性出血	0.2	0.2	0.2	0.7	0.1	-	-	0.2
P53	胎児及び新生児の出血性疾患	-	-	-	-	-	-	-	-
P54	その他の新生児出血	0.3	0.5	0.3	1.0	0.5	-	-	0.1
P55	胎児及び新生児の溶血性疾患	-	-	-	-	-	-	-	-
P56	溶血性疾患による胎児水腫								
P57	核黄疸								
P58	その他の多量の溶血による新生児黄疸								
P59	その他及び詳細不明の原因による新生児黄疸	0.1	0.1	0.2	-	0.1	-	-	0.1
P60	胎児及び新生児の播種性血管内凝固	0.4	0.6	0.2	0.7	0.8	5.7	-	0.2
P61	その他の周産期の血液障害	0.1	0.0	-	0.3	-	-	-	0.1

注：実数については下巻周産期死亡第1表を参照されたい。

Perinatal mortality

22週以後の死産－早期新生児死亡別周産期死亡数及び百分率
and causes on child（the list of three-character categories）：Japan, 2016

平成28年

病　態　Maternal condition

妊娠満22週以後の死産 Foetal deaths at 22 completed weeks and over of gestation								早期新生児死亡 Early neonatal deaths							
総数 Total	(P00-P04)	P00	P01	P02	P03	P04	P99	総数 Total	(P00-P04)	P00	P01	P02	P03	P04	P99
	母体側要因並びに妊娠及び分娩の合併症により影響を受けた胎児及び新生児	現在の妊娠とは無関係の場合もありうる母体の病態により影響を受けた胎児及び新生児	母体の妊娠合併症により影響を受けた胎児及び新生児	胎盤，臍帯及び卵膜の合併症により影響を受けた胎児及び新生児	その他の分娩合併症により影響を受けた胎児及び新生児	胎盤又は母乳を介して有害な影響を受けた胎児及び新生児	母体に原因なし		母体側要因並びに妊娠及び分娩の合併症により影響を受けた胎児及び新生児	現在の妊娠とは無関係の場合もありうる母体の病態により影響を受けた胎児及び新生児	母体の妊娠合併症により影響を受けた胎児及び新生児	胎盤，臍帯及び卵膜の合併症により影響を受けた胎児及び新生児	その他の分娩合併症により影響を受けた胎児及び新生児	胎盤又は母乳を介して有害な影響を受けた胎児及び新生児	母体に原因なし
2 840	1 696	852	119	709	16	-	1 144	676	378	90	188	81	19	-	298
80.8	48.2	24.2	3.4	20.2	0.5		32.5	19.2	10.8	2.6	5.3	2.3	0.5		8.5
100.0	59.7	30.0	4.2	25.0	0.6		40.3	100.0	55.9	13.3	27.8	12.0	2.8		44.1
100.0	100.0	100.0	100.0	100.0	100.0		100.0	100.0	100.0	100.0	100.0	100.0	100.0		100.0
91.7	97.5	96.8	93.3	99.0	100.0		83.1	57.7	70.4	68.9	60.6	92.6	78.9		41.6
2.8	2.3	2.5	10.1	0.7	6.3	-	3.5	5.2	6.6	5.6	7.4	7.4	-	-	3.4
1.6	1.3	1.5	5.0	0.4			2.1	0.3	0.5	-	0.5	1.2	-	-	-
1.1	0.9	0.9	5.0	0.3			1.4	4.9	6.1	5.6	6.9	6.2	-	-	3.4
0.0	0.1	-	-	-	6.3		-	-	-	-	-	-	-	-	-
-	-	-	-	-	-		-	0.3	0.3	-	0.5	-	-	-	0.3
-	-	-	-	-	-		-	-	-	-	-	-	-	-	-
-	-	-	-	-	-		-	0.1	0.3	-	0.5	-	-	-	0.3
-	-	-	-	-	-		-	-	-	-	-	-	-	-	-
-	-	-	-	-	-		-	0.1	0.3	-	0.5	-	-	-	-
2.4	2.5	0.5	1.7	5.1	-		2.3	34.5	41.5	35.6	35.6	59.3	52.6		25.5
0.7	0.8	0.2	0.8	1.4	-		0.5	-	-	-	-	-	-		-
-	-	-	-	-	-		-	9.9	12.7	8.9	5.3	32.1	21.1		6.4
-	-	-	-	-	-		-	4.4	5.0	4.4	6.4	2.5	5.3		3.7
-	-	-	-	-	-		-	0.4	0.3	1.1	-	-	-		0.7
-	-	-	-	-	-		-	1.0	0.5	1.1	-	1.2	-		1.7
-	-	-	-	-	-		-	1.3	1.6	2.2	1.6	1.2	-		1.0
-	-	-	-	-	-		-	1.3	1.9	1.1	1.6	3.7	-		0.7
-	-	-	-	-	-		-	0.3	0.5	-	1.1	-	-		-
0.3	0.2	-	0.8	0.3	-		0.4	10.4	12.4	10.0	15.4	7.4	15.8		7.7
1.4	1.5	0.2	-	3.4	-		1.3	5.3	6.6	6.7	4.3	11.1	10.5		3.7
0.9	1.4	0.9	10.9	0.4	-		0.2	4.6	6.3	10.0	6.4	3.7	-		2.3
0.1	0.2	0.4	-	-	-		0.1	-	-	-	-	-	-		0.3
-	-	-	-	-	-		-	3.8	5.3	8.9	5.3	2.5	-		2.0
-	-	-	-	-	-		-	-	-	-	-	-	-		-
-	-	-	-	-	-		-	-	-	-	-	-	-		-
0.8	1.2	0.6	10.9	0.4	-		0.2	0.6	1.1	1.1	1.1	1.2	-		-
2.4	1.0	0.5	9.2	0.3	-		4.4	7.0	10.1	7.8	8.0	17.3	10.5		3.0
2.2	0.8	0.1	9.2	0.3	-		4.3	1.6	2.6	1.1	3.7	2.5	-		0.3
-	-	-	-	-	-		-	-	-	-	-	-	-		-
0.1	0.1	0.1	-	-	-		0.1	0.9	1.1	1.1	1.1	1.2	-		0.7
-	-	-	-	-	-		-	-	-	-	-	-	-		-
-	-	-	-	-	-		-	1.6	2.6	3.3	1.6	4.9	-		0.3
0.1	0.1	0.2	-	-	-		-	0.3	0.3	-	-	1.2	-		0.3
-	-	-	-	-	-		-	2.2	3.2	2.2	1.1	7.4	10.5		1.0
-	-	-	-	-	-		-	0.3	0.3	-	0.5	-	-		0.3

周産期死亡

表8.14 死因・母側病態－児側病態別にみた妊娠満
Table 8.14 Perinatal deaths and percent distribution by maternal condition

死因基本分類コード Code	死　因 （児　側　病　態） Causes on child	母					側	
		総　数　Total						
		総数 (P00-P04) Total	P00 母体側要因並びに妊娠及び分娩の合併症により影響を受けた胎児及び新生児	P01 現在の妊娠とは無関係の場合もありうる母体の病態により影響を受けた胎児及び新生児	P02 母体の妊娠合併症により影響を受けた胎児及び新生児	P03 胎盤，臍帯及び卵膜の合併症により影響を受けた胎児及び新生児	P04 その他の分娩合併症により影響を受けた胎児及び新生児	P99 胎盤又は母乳を介して有害な影響を受けた胎児及び新生児 ／ 母体に原因なし
(P70-P72)	胎児及び新生児に特異的な一過性の内分泌障害及び代謝障害	0.2	0.0	0.1	-	-	-	-	0.5
P70	胎児及び新生児に特異的な一過性糖質代謝障害	0.2	0.0	0.1	-	-	-	-	0.5
P72	その他の一過性新生児内分泌障害	-	-	-	-	-	-	-	-
(P76-P78)	胎児及び新生児の消化器系障害	0.2	0.1	0.2	0.3	-	-	-	0.3
P76	新生児のその他の腸閉塞	0.0	0.0	-	0.3	-	-	-	-
P77	胎児及び新生児のえ死性腸炎	0.1	0.0	0.1	-	-	-	-	0.1
P78	その他の周産期の消化器系障害	0.1	0.0	0.1	-	-	-	-	0.3
(P80-P83)	胎児及び新生児の外皮及び体温調節に関連する病態	1.6	0.4	0.6	1.0	-	-	-	3.3
P80	新 生 児 低 体 温	0.0	-	-	-	-	-	-	0.1
P81	新生児のその他の体温調節機能障害	-	-	-	-	-	-	-	-
P83	胎児及び新生児に特異的な外皮のその他の病態	1.6	0.4	0.6	1.0	-	-	-	3.3
(P90-P96)	周産期に発生したその他の障害	66.4	74.3	83.7	24.1	83.5	51.4	-	55.1
P90	新生児のけいれん	-	-	-	-	-	-	-	-
P91	新生児の脳のその他の機能障害	0.2	0.1	0.1	0.3	0.1	-	-	0.2
P92	新生児の哺乳上の問題	-	-	-	-	-	-	-	-
P93	胎児及び新生児に投与された薬物による反応及び中毒	-	-	-	-	-	-	-	-
P94	新生児の筋緊張障害	-	-	-	-	-	-	-	-
P95	原因不明の胎児死亡	65.1	73.1	82.7	22.5	82.7	42.9	-	53.5
P96	周産期に発生したその他の病態	1.1	1.0	0.8	1.3	0.8	8.6	-	1.3
XVII	先天奇形，変形及び染色体異常	14.0	7.1	5.5	26.1	1.5	11.4	-	23.9
(Q00-Q07)	神経系の先天奇形	1.1	0.7	0.3	2.6	0.3	2.9	-	1.7
Q00	無脳症及び類似先天奇形	0.5	0.3	-	1.3	0.1	2.9	-	0.8
Q01	脳　　　瘤	0.0	0.0	0.1	-	-	-	-	-
Q02	小　頭　症	0.0	0.0	-	-	0.1	-	-	-
Q03	先天性水頭症	0.1	-	-	0.3	-	-	-	0.3
Q04	脳のその他の先天奇形	0.4	0.2	0.2	1.0	-	-	-	0.6
Q05	二　分　脊　椎	-	-	-	-	-	-	-	-
Q06	脊髄のその他の先天奇形	-	-	-	-	-	-	-	-
Q07	神経系のその他の先天奇形	0.0	-	-	-	-	-	-	0.1
(Q10-Q18)	眼，耳，顔面及び頚部の先天奇形	0.1	0.0	-	-	0.1	-	-	0.1
Q10	眼瞼，涙器及び眼窩の先天奇形	-	-	-	-	-	-	-	-
Q11	無眼球，小眼球及び巨大眼球	-	-	-	-	-	-	-	-
Q12	先天水晶体奇形	-	-	-	-	-	-	-	-
Q13	前眼部の先天奇形	-	-	-	-	-	-	-	-
Q14	眼球後極部の先天奇形	-	-	-	-	-	-	-	-
Q15	眼のその他の先天奇形	-	-	-	-	-	-	-	-
Q16	聴覚障害の原因となる耳の先天奇形	-	-	-	-	-	-	-	-
Q17	耳のその他の先天奇形	0.1	0.0	-	-	0.1	-	-	0.1
Q18	顔面及び頚部のその他の先天奇形	0.0	-	-	-	-	-	-	0.1
(Q20-Q28)	循環器系の先天奇形	2.7	1.4	1.7	4.2	0.1	-	-	4.4
Q20	心臓の房室及び結合部の先天奇形	0.2	0.1	0.1	0.3	-	-	-	0.3
Q21	心中隔の先天奇形	0.3	0.3	0.5	0.3	-	-	-	0.4
Q22	肺動脈弁及び三尖弁の先天奇形	0.3	-	-	-	-	-	-	0.6
Q23	大動脈弁及び僧帽弁の先天奇形	0.2	0.1	0.1	0.3	-	-	-	0.3
Q24	心臓のその他の先天奇形	1.0	0.4	0.7	0.7	-	-	-	1.8
Q25	大型動脈の先天奇形	0.4	0.4	0.2	1.6	0.1	-	-	0.4

22週以後の死産－早期新生児死亡別周産期死亡数及び百分率（つづき）
and causes on child（the list of three-character categories）: Japan, 2016－CON.　　平成28年

病態　Maternal condition

妊娠満22週以後の死産　Foetal deaths at 22 completed weeks and over of gestation								早期新生児死亡　Early neonatal deaths							
総数 Total	(P00-P04)	P00	P01	P02	P03	P04	P99	総数 Total	(P00-P04)	P00	P01	P02	P03	P04	P99
0.3	0.1	0.1	-	-	-	-	0.6	-	-	-	-	-	-	-	-
0.3	0.1	0.1	-	-	-	-	0.6	-	-	-	-	-	-	-	-
-	-	-	-	-	-	-	-	1.2	0.8	2.2	0.5	-	-	-	1.7
-	-	-	-	-	-	-	-	0.1	0.3	-	0.5	-	-	-	-
-	-	-	-	-	-	-	-	0.3	0.3	1.1	-	-	-	-	0.3
-	-	-	-	-	-	-	-	0.7	0.3	1.1	-	-	-	-	1.3
1.7	0.2	0.5	-	-	-	-	3.8	1.3	1.3	2.2	1.6	-	-	-	1.3
-	-	-	-	-	-	-	-	0.1	-	-	-	-	-	-	0.3
1.7	0.2	0.5	-	-	-	-	3.8	1.2	1.3	2.2	1.6	-	-	-	1.0
81.3	90.0	91.9	61.3	92.5	93.8	-	68.4	3.7	3.4	5.6	0.5	4.9	15.8	-	4.0
-	-	-	-	-	-	-	-	0.9	0.8	1.1	0.5	1.2	-	-	1.0
-	-	-	-	-	-	-	-	-	-	-	-	-	-	-	-
80.6	89.4	91.4	58.0	92.1	93.8	-	67.5	-	-	-	-	-	-	-	-
0.7	0.6	0.5	3.4	0.4	-	-	0.9	2.8	2.6	4.4	-	3.7	15.8	-	3.0
8.0	2.4	2.9	6.7	1.0	-	-	16.3	39.3	28.6	30.0	38.3	6.2	21.1	-	53.0
0.6	0.2	0.2	-	0.3	-	-	1.2	3.0	2.6	1.1	4.3	-	5.3	-	3.4
0.2	0.1	-	-	0.1	-	-	0.5	1.5	1.3	-	2.1	-	5.3	-	1.7
-	-	-	-	-	-	-	-	0.1	0.3	1.1	-	-	-	-	-
0.0	0.1	-	-	0.1	-	-	-	-	-	-	-	-	-	-	-
0.1	-	-	-	-	-	-	0.3	0.3	0.3	-	0.5	-	-	-	0.3
0.2	0.1	0.2	-	-	-	-	0.3	1.0	0.8	-	1.6	-	-	-	1.3
-	-	-	-	-	-	-	-	-	-	-	-	-	-	-	-
-	-	-	-	-	-	-	-	-	-	-	-	-	-	-	-
0.0	-	-	-	-	-	-	0.1	-	-	-	-	-	-	-	-
0.1	0.1	-	-	0.1	-	-	0.2	-	-	-	-	-	-	-	-
-	-	-	-	-	-	-	-	-	-	-	-	-	-	-	-
-	-	-	-	-	-	-	-	-	-	-	-	-	-	-	-
-	-	-	-	-	-	-	-	-	-	-	-	-	-	-	-
-	-	-	-	-	-	-	-	-	-	-	-	-	-	-	-
-	-	-	-	-	-	-	-	-	-	-	-	-	-	-	-
0.1	0.1	-	-	0.1	-	-	0.1	-	-	-	-	-	-	-	-
0.0	-	-	-	-	-	-	0.1	-	-	-	-	-	-	-	-
1.4	0.8	1.2	1.7	0.1	-	-	2.4	7.8	4.5	6.7	5.9	-	-	-	12.1
-	-	-	-	-	-	-	-	0.9	0.5	1.1	0.5	-	-	-	1.3
0.2	0.3	0.6	-	-	-	-	0.1	0.9	0.3	-	0.5	-	-	-	1.7
0.2	-	-	-	-	-	-	0.4	0.6	-	-	-	-	-	-	1.3
-	-	-	-	-	-	-	-	1.0	0.5	1.1	0.5	-	-	-	1.7
1.0	0.4	0.6	1.7	-	-	-	1.8	1.0	0.5	2.2	-	-	-	-	1.7
0.1	0.1	-	-	0.1	-	-	0.1	1.8	1.9	2.2	2.7	-	-	-	1.7

周産期死亡

表 8.14　死因・母側病態－児側病態別にみた妊娠満
Table 8.14　Perinatal deaths and percent distribution by maternal condition

死因基本分類コード	死因（児側病態）	母側 総数 Total							
		総数 Total	(P00-P04) 母体側要因並びに妊娠及び分娩の合併症により影響を受けた胎児及び新生児	P00 現在の妊娠とは無関係の場合もありうる母体の病態により影響を受けた胎児及び新生児	P01 母体の妊娠合併症により影響を受けた胎児及び新生児	P02 胎盤，臍帯及び卵膜の合併症により影響を受けた胎児及び新生児	P03 その他の分娩合併症により影響を受けた胎児及び新生児	P04 胎盤又は母乳を介して有害な影響を受けた胎児及び新生児	P99 母体に原因なし
Code	Causes on child								
Q26	大型静脈の先天奇形	0.3	0.1	-	1.0	-	-	-	0.5
Q27	末梢血管系のその他の先天奇形	0.0	-	-	-	-	-	-	0.1
Q28	循環器系のその他の先天奇形	-	-	-	-	-	-	-	-
(Q30-Q34)	呼吸器系の先天奇形	1.1	0.6	0.2	2.6	-	5.7	-	1.9
Q30	鼻の先天奇形	-	-	-	-	-	-	-	-
Q31	喉頭の先天奇形	0.0	-	-	-	-	-	-	0.1
Q32	気管及び気管支の先天奇形	0.2	0.1	-	0.3	-	2.9	-	0.4
Q33	肺の先天奇形	0.9	0.4	0.2	2.0	-	2.9	-	1.5
Q34	呼吸器系のその他の先天奇形	0.0	0.0	-	0.3	-	-	-	-
(Q35-Q37)	唇裂及び口蓋裂	0.1	0.0	0.1	-	-	-	-	0.1
Q35	口蓋裂	0.0	-	-	-	-	-	-	0.1
Q36	唇裂	-	-	-	-	-	-	-	-
Q37	唇裂を伴う口蓋裂	0.1	0.0	0.1	-	-	-	-	0.1
(Q38-Q45)	消化器系のその他の先天奇形	0.5	0.4	0.2	2.0	0.1	-	-	0.6
Q38	舌，口及び咽頭のその他の先天奇形	-	-	-	-	-	-	-	-
Q39	食道の先天奇形	0.2	0.2	0.1	1.3	-	-	-	0.1
Q40	上部消化管のその他の先天奇形	-	-	-	-	-	-	-	-
Q41	小腸の先天欠損，閉鎖及び狭窄	0.2	0.1	0.1	0.3	0.1	-	-	0.2
Q42	大腸の先天欠損，閉鎖及び狭窄	0.1	0.0	-	0.3	-	-	-	0.1
Q43	腸のその他の先天奇形	-	-	-	-	-	-	-	-
Q44	胆のう，胆管及び肝の先天奇形	0.1	-	-	-	-	-	-	0.1
Q45	消化器系のその他の先天奇形	-	-	-	-	-	-	-	-
(Q50-Q56)	生殖器の先天奇形	-	-	-	-	-	-	-	-
Q50	卵巣，卵管及び広間膜の先天奇形	-	-	-	-	-	-	-	-
Q51	子宮及び子宮頚の先天奇形	-	-	-	-	-	-	-	-
Q52	女性性器のその他の先天奇形	-	-	-	-	-	-	-	-
Q53	停留精巣	-	-	-	-	-	-	-	-
Q54	尿道下裂	-	-	-	-	-	-	-	-
Q55	男性生殖器のその他の先天奇形	-	-	-	-	-	-	-	-
Q56	性不確定及び仮性半陰陽	-	-	-	-	-	-	-	-
(Q60-Q64)	腎尿路系の先天奇形	1.1	0.6	0.4	2.6	0.1	-	-	1.9
Q60	腎の無発生及びその他の減形成	0.9	0.4	0.1	2.3	0.1	-	-	1.5
Q61	のう胞性腎疾患	0.3	0.2	0.3	0.3	-	-	-	0.3
Q62	腎盂の先天性閉塞性欠損及び尿管の先天奇形	-	-	-	-	-	-	-	-
Q63	腎のその他の先天奇形	-	-	-	-	-	-	-	-
Q64	尿路系のその他の先天奇形	0.0	-	-	-	-	-	-	0.1
(Q65-Q79)	筋骨格系の先天奇形及び変形	1.4	0.9	0.7	3.3	0.1	2.9	-	2.0
Q65	股関節部の先天変形	-	-	-	-	-	-	-	-
Q66	足の先天変形	-	-	-	-	-	-	-	-
Q67	頭部，顔面，脊柱及び胸部の先天筋骨格変形	0.0	0.0	0.1	-	-	-	-	-
Q68	その他の先天筋骨格変形	-	-	-	-	-	-	-	-
Q69	多指	0.0	-	-	-	-	-	-	0.1
Q70	合指	-	-	-	-	-	-	-	-
Q71	上肢の減形成	-	-	-	-	-	-	-	-
Q72	下肢の減形成	-	-	-	-	-	-	-	-
Q73	詳細不明の肢の減形成	-	-	-	-	-	-	-	-
Q74	肢のその他の先天奇形	-	-	-	-	-	-	-	-

22週以後の死産－早期新生児死亡別周産期死亡数及び百分率（つづき）
and causes on child（the list of three-character categories）: Japan, 2016－CON.　平成28年

病　態　Maternal condition

妊娠満22週以後の死産　Foetal deaths at 22 completed weeks and over of gestation								早期新生児死亡　Early neonatal deaths							
総数 Total	(P00-P04)	P00	P01	P02	P03	P04	P99	総数 Total	(P00-P04)	P00	P01	P02	P03	P04	P99
-	-	-	-	-	-	-	-	1.5	0.8	-	1.6	-	-	-	2.3
-	-	-	-	-	-	-	-	0.1	-	-	-	-	-	-	0.3
-	-	-	-	-	-	-	-	-	-	-	-	-	-	-	-
0.1	0.1	-	0.8	-	-	-	0.3	5.3	2.9	2.2	3.7	-	10.5	-	8.4
-	-	-	-	-	-	-	-	-	-	-	-	-	-	-	-
-	-	-	-	-	-	-	-	0.1	-	-	-	-	-	-	0.3
0.0	-	-	-	-	-	-	0.1	1.0	0.5	-	0.5	-	5.3	-	1.7
0.1	0.1	-	0.8	-	-	-	0.2	4.0	2.1	2.2	2.7	-	5.3	-	6.4
-	-	-	-	-	-	-	-	0.1	0.3	-	0.5	-	-	-	-
0.1	0.1	0.1	-	-	-	-	0.2	-	-	-	-	-	-	-	-
0.0	-	-	-	-	-	-	0.1	-	-	-	-	-	-	-	-
0.1	0.1	0.1	-	-	-	-	0.1	-	-	-	-	-	-	-	-
0.4	0.2	0.2	0.8	0.1	-	-	0.5	1.0	1.3	-	2.7	-	-	-	0.7
-	-	-	-	-	-	-	-	-	-	-	-	-	-	-	-
0.1	0.1	0.1	0.8	-	-	-	-	0.7	0.8	-	1.6	-	-	-	0.7
0.2	0.1	0.1	-	0.1	-	-	0.3	0.1	0.3	-	0.5	-	-	-	-
0.0	-	-	-	-	-	-	0.1	0.1	0.3	-	0.5	-	-	-	-
0.1	-	-	-	-	-	-	0.2	-	-	-	-	-	-	-	-
0.2	-	-	-	-	-	-	0.6	4.9	3.4	4.4	4.3	1.2	-	-	6.7
0.2	-	-	-	-	-	-	0.4	3.7	2.4	1.1	3.7	1.2	-	-	5.4
0.1	-	-	-	-	-	-	0.2	1.0	1.1	3.3	0.5	-	-	-	1.0
-	-	-	-	-	-	-	-	0.1	-	-	-	-	-	-	0.3
0.6	0.3	0.4	0.8	0.1	-	-	1.1	4.4	3.7	4.4	4.8	-	5.3	-	5.4
0.0	0.1	0.1	-	-	-	-	-	-	-	-	-	-	-	-	-
0.0	-	-	-	-	-	-	0.1	-	-	-	-	-	-	-	-

周産期死亡

表8.14　死因・母側病態－児側病態別にみた妊娠満
Table 8.14　Perinatal deaths and percent distribution by maternal condition

死因基本分類コード Code	死因（児側病態） Causes on child	総数 Total (P00-P04)	P00 現在の妊娠とは無関係の場合もありうる母体の病態により影響を受けた胎児及び新生児	P01 母体の妊娠合併症により影響を受けた胎児及び新生児	P02 胎盤，臍帯及び卵膜の合併症により影響を受けた胎児及び新生児	P03 その他の分娩合併症により影響を受けた胎児及び新生児	P04 胎盤又は母乳を介して有害な影響を受けた胎児及び新生児	P99 母体に原因なし
Q75	頭蓋及び顔面骨のその他の先天奇形	0.1	0.1	0.1	0.3	-	-	0.1
Q76	脊柱及び骨性胸郭の先天奇形	0.0	0.0	0.1	-	-	-	-
Q77	骨軟骨異形成，長管骨及び脊椎の成長障害を伴うもの	0.3	0.2	-	1.3	-	-	0.6
Q78	その他の骨軟骨異形成	0.1	0.0	-	-	2.9	-	0.1
Q79	筋骨格系の先天奇形，他に分類されないもの	0.8	0.5	0.4	1.6	0.1	-	1.2
(Q80-Q89)	その他の先天奇形	1.6	0.5	0.5	1.6	0.1	-	3.1
Q80	先天性魚りんせん	0.0	-	-	-	-	-	0.1
Q81	表皮水疱症	-	-	-	-	-	-	-
Q82	皮膚のその他の先天奇形	-	-	-	-	-	-	-
Q83	乳房の先天奇形	-	-	-	-	-	-	-
Q84	外皮のその他の先天奇形	-	-	-	-	-	-	-
Q85	母斑症，他に分類されないもの	-	-	-	-	-	-	-
Q86	既知の外因による先天奇形症候群，他に分類されないもの	-	-	-	-	-	-	-
Q87	多系統に及ぶその他の明示された先天奇形症候群	0.2	0.2	0.1	1.0	-	-	0.2
Q89	その他の先天奇形，他に分類されないもの	1.3	0.3	0.4	0.7	0.1	-	2.8
(Q90-Q99)	染色体異常，他に分類されないもの	4.4	1.8	1.3	7.2	0.5	-	8.0
Q90	ダウン症候群	0.3	0.1	-	0.7	-	-	0.5
Q91	エドワーズ症候群及びパトー症候群	3.0	1.4	1.1	4.9	0.5	-	5.4
Q92	常染色体のその他のトリソミー及び部分トリソミー，他に分類されないもの	-	-	-	-	-	-	-
Q93	常染色体のモノソミー及び欠失，他に分類されないもの	-	-	-	-	-	-	-
Q95	均衡型再配列及びマーカー，他に分類されないもの	-	-	-	-	-	-	-
Q96	ターナー症候群	-	-	-	-	-	-	-
Q97	その他の性染色体異常，女性表型，他に分類されないもの	-	-	-	-	-	-	-
Q98	その他の性染色体異常，男性表型，他に分類されないもの	-	-	-	-	-	-	-
Q99	その他の染色体異常，他に分類されないもの	1.1	0.3	0.2	1.6	-	-	2.1
Ⅰ	感染症及び寄生虫症	0.1	0.1	0.2	-	-	-	-
Ⅱ	新生物	0.3	0.0	-	-	0.1	-	0.6
Ⅲ	血液及び造血器の疾患並びに免疫機構の障害	-	-	-	-	-	-	-
Ⅳ	内分泌，栄養及び代謝疾患	0.1	0.1	0.1	0.7	-	-	0.1
Ⅴ	精神及び行動の障害	-	-	-	-	-	-	-
Ⅵ	神経系の疾患	0.0	-	-	-	-	-	0.1
Ⅶ	眼及び付属器の疾患	-	-	-	-	-	-	-
Ⅷ	耳及び乳様突起の疾患	-	-	-	-	-	-	-
Ⅸ	循環器系の疾患	0.1	-	-	-	-	-	0.1
Ⅹ	呼吸器系の疾患	0.1	-	-	-	-	-	0.1
ⅩⅠ	消化器系の疾患	-	-	-	-	-	-	-
ⅩⅡ	皮膚及び皮下組織の疾患	-	-	-	-	-	-	-
ⅩⅢ	筋骨格系及び結合組織の疾患	-	-	-	-	-	-	-
ⅩⅣ	腎尿路生殖器系の疾患	-	-	-	-	-	-	-
ⅩⅧ	症状，徴候及び異常臨床所見・異常検査所見で他に分類されないもの	0.0	-	-	-	-	-	0.1
ⅩⅨ	損傷，中毒及びその他の外因の影響	0.2	-	-	-	-	-	0.4
ⅩⅩ	傷病及び死亡の外因	0.2	-	-	-	-	-	0.4
ⅩⅩⅡ	特殊目的用コード	-	-	-	-	-	-	-

注：第ⅩⅤ章は該当があり得ないので省略した。

22週以後の死産－早期新生児死亡別周産期死亡数及び百分率（つづき）
and causes on child（the list of three-character categories）: Japan, 2016－CON. 平成28年

病　態　Maternal condition

妊娠満22週以後の死産　Foetal deaths at 22 completed weeks and over of gestation								早期新生児死亡　Early neonatal deaths							
総数 Total	(P00-P04) 母体側要因並びに妊娠及び分娩の合併症により影響を受けた胎児及び新生児	P00 現在の妊娠とは無関係の場合もありうる母体の病態により影響を受けた胎児及び新生児	P01 母体の妊娠合併症により影響を受けた胎児及び新生児	P02 胎盤,臍帯膜及びの合併症により影響を受けた胎児及び新生児	P03 その他の分娩合併症により影響を受けた胎児	P04 胎盤又は母乳を介して有害な影響を受けた胎児及び新生児	P99 母体に原因なし	総数 Total	(P00-P04) 母体側要因並びに妊娠及び分娩の合併症により影響を受けた胎児及び新生児	P00 現在の妊娠とは無関係の場合もありうる母体の病態により影響を受けた胎児及び新生児	P01 母体の妊娠合併症により影響を受けた胎児及び新生児	P02 胎盤,臍帯膜及びの合併症により影響を受けた胎児及び新生児	P03 その他の分娩合併症により影響を受けた胎児	P04 胎盤又は母乳を介して有害な影響を受けた胎児及び新生児	P99 母体に原因なし
0.1	0.1	0.1	-	-	-	-	0.1	0.1	0.3	-	0.5	-	-	-	-
-	-	-	-	-	-	-	-	0.1	0.3	1.1	-	-	-	-	-
0.0	-	-	-	-	-	-	0.1	1.6	1.1	-	2.1	-	-	-	2.3
-	-	-	-	-	-	-	-	0.3	0.3	-	-	-	5.3	-	0.3
0.5	0.2	0.1	0.8	0.1	-	-	0.9	2.2	1.9	3.3	2.1	-	-	-	2.7
1.4	0.2	0.2	0.8	0.1	-	-	3.2	2.1	1.9	3.3	2.1	-	-	-	2.3
-	-	-	-	-	-	-	-	0.1	-	-	-	-	-	-	0.3
0.1	-	-	-	-	-	-	0.2	0.7	1.1	1.1	1.6	-	-	-	0.3
1.4	0.2	0.2	0.8	0.1	-	-	3.1	1.2	0.8	2.2	0.5	-	-	-	1.7
2.9	0.4	0.6	1.7	-	-	-	6.5	10.8	8.2	7.8	10.6	4.9	-	-	14.1
0.1	-	-	-	-	-	-	0.3	0.7	0.5	-	1.1	-	-	-	1.0
1.5	0.2	0.4	-	-	-	-	3.6	9.3	6.9	7.8	8.0	4.9	-	-	12.4
1.2	0.2	0.2	1.7	-	-	-	2.5	0.7	0.8	-	1.6	-	-	-	0.7
0.1	0.1	0.2	-	-	-	-	-	-	-	-	-	-	-	-	-
0.2	-	-	-	-	-	-	0.6	0.4	0.3	-	-	1.2	-	-	0.7
-	-	-	-	-	-	-	-	-	-	-	-	-	-	-	-
-	-	-	-	-	-	-	-	0.7	0.8	1.1	1.1	-	-	-	0.7
-	-	-	-	-	-	-	-	0.1	-	-	-	-	-	-	0.3
-	-	-	-	-	-	-	-	-	-	-	-	-	-	-	-
-	-	-	-	-	-	-	-	0.3	-	-	-	-	-	-	0.7
-	-	-	-	-	-	-	-	0.3	-	-	-	-	-	-	0.7
-	-	-	-	-	-	-	-	0.1	-	-	-	-	-	-	0.3
•	•	•	•	•	•	•	•	0.9	-	-	-	-	-	-	2.0
•	•	•	•	•	•	•	•	0.9	-	-	-	-	-	-	2.0

婚姻

〔地域別にみた婚姻〕
〔Marriages by prefecture〕

第9章　婚　　姻
Chapter 9 Marriages

表9.1　都道府県別にみた
Table 9.1　Trends in marriages by

都道府県[1] Prefecture	1935 昭和10年	1947 22 年[2]	1950 25 年[3]	1955 30 年	1960 35 年	1965 40 年	1970 45 年	1975 50 年	1980 55 年
全 国　Total	556 730	934 170	715 081	714 861	866 115	954 852	1 029 405	941 628	774 702
01 北 海 道 [a]	22 855	41 114	39 898	39 471	50 685	50 841	51 539	48 271	40 228
02 青　　森	8 335	14 487	12 366	11 213	13 205	12 592	12 878	11 695	10 414
03 岩　　手	8 702	14 708	12 885	10 930	12 364	11 124	10 149	10 409	8 662
04 宮　　城	9 828	20 088	15 461	13 623	15 324	14 722	15 953	16 776	14 375
05 秋　　田	9 481	16 439	11 845	10 694	11 613	9 662	9 482	9 432	7 793
06 山　　形	9 737	17 599	12 969	10 660	10 708	8 421	8 733	9 149	7 601
07 福　　島	13 159	26 598	19 752	15 528	16 700	13 604	14 394	15 065	12 852
08 茨　　城	12 181	22 249	17 913	14 684	16 326	17 002	19 537	18 902	16 803
09 栃　　木	9 937	18 610	13 520	11 186	11 963	12 303	14 332	14 156	11 949
10 群　　馬	9 844	18 847	12 849	12 249	12 367	13 921	15 104	14 487	11 563
11 埼　　玉	12 593	24 739	17 211	17 330	21 485	33 131	43 517	42 340	34 708
12 千　　葉	12 712	24 266	17 256	16 322	20 475	26 538	35 364	36 867	31 760
13 東　　京	41 313	49 800	51 362	74 447	119 495	147 407	140 748	111 176	87 922
14 神 奈 川	13 387	23 493	20 719	26 627	38 250	55 977	66 390	60 005	48 529
15 新　　潟	18 362	34 187	20 223	19 456	19 507	18 527	18 479	18 022	14 261
16 富　　山	8 130	13 638	8 569	8 163	8 806	8 646	9 571	7 970	6 292
17 石　　川	7 426	12 797	7 949	7 413	8 159	8 380	9 766	8 427	6 932
18 福　　井	6 297	10 067	6 787	5 862	6 030	5 644	6 195	5 775	4 660
19 山　　梨	5 316	8 527	6 231	5 835	6 014	6 063	5 833	5 590	4 695
20 長　　野	13 993	23 842	16 249	16 221	15 750	15 639	15 479	14 941	11 023
21 岐　　阜	10 587	19 101	13 073	12 792	14 476	14 852	16 155	14 659	11 844
22 静　　岡	16 337	29 168	19 919	21 710	24 732	27 788	30 036	27 541	22 460
23 愛　　知	22 323	35 018	27 783	30 961	41 599	52 226	61 882	52 212	42 811
24 三　　重	10 500	16 258	11 782	11 930	13 002	12 838	13 874	12 454	9 922
25 滋　　賀	6 492	9 594	6 743	6 496	6 730	6 740	7 925	8 257	6 991
26 京　　都	12 286	18 294	13 643	14 079	17 709	20 310	22 621	20 514	15 916
27 大　　阪	27 526	34 328	32 422	38 674	60 565	83 844	93 194	74 643	57 858
28 兵　　庫	22 054	32 971	28 686	29 964	37 032	43 075	48 698	41 916	33 280
29 奈　　良	5 501	9 916	6 768	6 051	6 739	7 753	9 045	8 680	7 741
30 和 歌 山	7 283	11 576	8 290	8 771	8 684	9 010	9 576	7 900	6 480
31 鳥　　取	4 227	7 579	5 406	4 445	4 524	3 916	4 305	4 195	3 697
32 島　　根	6 468	12 606	7 487	6 559	6 888	5 514	5 334	4 980	4 243
33 岡　　山	11 428	19 546	14 294	13 306	13 276	13 041	15 493	14 007	11 381
34 広　　島	16 261	25 818	17 968	17 258	18 810	20 958	23 975	22 018	17 620
35 山　　口	10 174	18 563	13 785	12 651	13 546	12 753	13 248	11 895	9 598
36 徳　　島	6 343	11 528	7 581	6 757	6 558	5 975	6 215	6 186	5 247
37 香　　川	6 901	12 632	8 354	7 388	7 424	6 942	8 082	7 261	6 088
38 愛　　媛	10 195	17 719	13 096	11 728	12 209	11 194	11 854	11 327	9 204
39 高　　知	6 096	10 986	7 699	7 161	7 022	6 191	6 552	5 792	4 822
40 福　　岡	21 615	39 288	32 614	31 424	37 184	37 816	38 206	36 937	32 007
41 佐　　賀	6 467	12 133	8 451	7 134	7 400	6 230	6 118	6 086	5 511
42 長　　崎	10 153	21 054	14 980	12 886	15 094	12 876	12 184	12 002	10 057
43 熊　　本	11 629	21 688	15 293	13 987	15 156	13 403	12 386	12 271	11 600
44 大　　分	8 760	16 306	10 548	9 307	9 782	8 965	9 294	9 151	7 510
45 宮　　崎	6 367	13 153	9 242	8 666	9 743	8 429	8 611	8 565	7 793
46 鹿 児 島	13 471	20 708	14 554	14 862	15 005	12 069	11 099	11 493	11 539
47 沖　　縄	5 698	...	...	...	...	...	...	9 231	8 460

注：1) 昭和10年：婚養子縁組、入婿の場合は届出時の妻の住所又は居所、他は夫の住所又は居所のある地域。
　　　昭和22年：挙式の場所のある地域。昭和25年：挙式寸前の夫の住所。昭和30年以降：届出時の夫の住所。
　　2) 昭和22年の全国には、不詳544を含む。
　　3) 昭和25年の全国には、不詳2 606を含む。

Marriages

年次別婚姻件数
each prefecture : Japan

1985 60　年	1990 平成 2 年	1995 7　年	2000 12　年	2005 17　年	2010 22　年	2014 26　年	2015 27　年	2016 28　年	都道府県[1] Prefecture
735 850	722 138	791 888	798 138	714 265	700 214	643 749	635 156	620 531	全　国　Total
36 311	33 966	35 591	34 529	29 708	28 389	26 018	25 465	24 636	[a)] 01 北 海 道
9 175	7 892	8 306	8 138	6 584	5 924	5 481	5 432	5 135	02 青　　森
7 838	6 866	7 179	7 671	6 446	5 724	5 482	5 243	4 872	03 岩　　手
13 239	12 449	13 967	14 797	12 820	11 972	11 765	11 317	11 127	04 宮　　城
6 585	5 632	5 923	5 669	4 884	4 281	3 842	3 613	3 510	05 秋　　田
8 071	6 170	6 519	6 897	5 729	5 159	4 699	4 522	4 284	06 山　　形
12 802	11 147	12 070	12 445	10 606	9 582	8 711	8 888	8 682	07 福　　島
15 832	15 487	17 519	18 378	15 534	15 044	13 800	13 498	13 201	08 茨　　城
11 371	10 970	11 844	12 607	11 471	10 616	9 770	9 452	9 321	09 栃　　木
11 254	10 990	12 147	12 522	10 601	9 679	9 089	8 820	8 444	10 群　　馬
33 446	39 234	46 224	45 636	40 486	39 160	35 218	34 757	34 199	11 埼　　玉
30 424	33 626	38 997	39 597	35 506	34 785	30 578	30 204	29 610	12 千　　葉
83 021	81 920	84 286	87 360	85 382	91 196	87 000	87 167	86 009	13 東　　京
48 915	55 155	61 966	61 351	56 049	54 203	48 851	48 263	46 695	14 神 奈 川
13 558	12 068	13 056	12 858	11 484	11 018	9 954	9 435	9 311	15 新　　潟
5 861	5 409	6 167	6 307	5 355	4 928	4 540	4 539	4 486	16 富　　山
6 552	6 052	6 852	6 979	6 052	5 829	5 370	5 200	5 126	17 石　　川
4 728	4 303	4 607	4 582	4 365	3 705	3 706	3 481	3 453	18 福　　井
4 994	4 855	5 314	5 353	4 531	4 221	3 723	3 831	3 673	19 山　　梨
12 183	11 327	12 407	13 405	11 644	10 318	9 514	9 606	8 967	20 長　　野
11 138	10 770	11 848	12 113	10 512	10 087	9 071	8 859	8 581	21 岐　　阜
21 501	20 700	22 991	23 550	21 056	20 323	18 066	17 666	17 079	22 静　　岡
40 875	42 060	48 022	48 391	43 948	45 039	41 410	41 054	40 671	23 愛　　知
10 005	9 779	10 631	11 271	9 640	9 396	8 555	8 504	8 174	24 三　　重
6 859	6 835	7 950	8 593	7 732	7 691	6 990	6 855	6 822	25 滋　　賀
14 932	14 337	15 887	15 781	14 030	13 664	12 671	12 458	12 143	26 京　　都
55 763	57 436	64 181	59 969	51 744	51 242	46 934	46 689	46 186	27 大　　阪
31 544	31 470	33 492	34 587	30 236	29 752	26 941	26 422	25 808	28 兵　　庫
7 359	7 506	8 702	8 094	6 915	6 595	6 002	5 691	5 628	29 奈　　良
6 194	5 682	6 143	5 897	4 956	4 771	4 419	4 326	4 061	30 和 歌 山
3 469	3 059	3 246	3 366	3 008	2 834	2 663	2 681	2 444	31 鳥　　取
4 089	3 513	3 699	3 772	3 345	3 283	3 022	2 931	2 753	32 島　　根
10 836	10 063	11 424	11 376	10 098	9 894	9 265	9 260	8 916	33 岡　　山
16 264	16 133	17 633	17 470	15 728	15 402	14 194	13 712	13 594	34 広　　島
8 421	7 690	8 157	8 249	7 306	6 966	6 163	5 901	5 906	35 山　　口
4 680	4 174	4 406	4 523	3 637	3 573	3 322	3 229	3 177	36 徳　　島
5 689	5 234	5 794	6 052	5 254	4 975	4 693	4 626	4 593	37 香　　川
8 604	7 815	8 379	8 147	7 246	6 922	6 148	6 102	5 861	38 愛　　媛
4 624	3 975	4 172	4 245	3 705	3 328	3 116	3 057	2 916	39 高　　知
29 208	27 377	30 355	30 640	28 715	29 247	27 359	27 566	26 567	40 福　　岡
5 012	4 539	4 550	4 749	4 155	4 210	3 928	3 692	3 726	41 佐　　賀
9 122	8 166	8 431	7 805	7 016	6 647	6 137	6 118	6 013	42 長　　崎
10 677	9 425	10 146	10 265	9 361	9 098	8 714	8 249	7 976	43 熊　　本
6 966	6 283	6 657	6 977	6 101	6 076	5 391	5 315	5 151	44 大　　分
6 940	6 134	6 599	6 513	6 022	5 892	5 154	5 041	5 097	45 宮　　崎
10 377	8 757	9 051	9 585	8 754	8 682	7 837	7 724	7 483	46 鹿 児 島
8 542	7 708	8 401	9 077	8 808	8 892	8 473	8 695	8 464	47 沖　　縄

Note : a)　See page 44.

婚　姻

表9.2　都道府県別にみた
Table 9.2　Trends in marriage rates

都道府県 [1] Prefecture	1935 昭和10年	1947 22　年 [2]	1950 25　年 [3]	1955 30　年	1960 35　年	1965 40　年	1970 45　年	1975 50　年	1980 55　年
全　国　Total	8.0	12.0	8.6	8.0	9.3	9.7	10.0	8.5	6.7
01 北 海 道 [a]	7.4	10.7	9.3	8.3	10.1	9.8	10.0	9.1	7.2
02 青　　森	8.6	12.3	9.6	8.1	9.3	8.9	9.0	8.0	6.8
03 岩　　手	8.3	11.6	9.6	7.7	8.5	7.9	7.4	7.5	6.1
04 宮　　城	8.0	12.8	9.3	7.9	8.8	8.4	8.8	8.6	6.9
05 秋　　田	9.1	13.1	9.0	7.9	8.7	7.5	7.6	7.7	6.2
06 山　　形	8.7	13.2	9.6	7.9	8.1	6.7	7.1	7.5	6.1
07 福　　島	8.3	13.3	9.6	7.4	8.1	6.9	7.4	7.7	6.3
08 茨　　城	7.9	11.0	8.8	7.1	8.0	8.3	9.1	8.1	6.6
09 栃　　木	8.3	12.1	8.7	7.2	7.9	8.1	9.1	8.3	6.7
10 群　　馬	7.9	12.0	8.0	7.6	7.8	8.7	9.1	8.3	6.3
11 埼　　玉	8.2	11.8	8.0	7.7	8.8	11.0	11.3	8.8	6.4
12 千　　葉	8.2	11.5	8.1	7.4	8.9	9.8	10.5	8.9	6.7
13 東　　京	6.5	10.0	8.2	9.3	12.3	13.6	12.4	9.6	7.6
14 神 奈 川	7.3	10.6	8.3	9.1	11.1	12.6	12.2	9.4	7.0
15 新　　潟	9.2	14.1	8.2	7.9	8.0	7.7	7.8	7.5	5.8
16 富　　山	10.2	13.9	8.5	8.0	8.5	8.4	9.3	7.5	5.7
17 石　　川	9.7	13.8	8.3	7.7	8.4	8.5	9.8	7.9	6.2
18 福　　井	9.7	13.9	9.0	7.8	8.0	7.5	8.4	7.5	5.9
19 山　　梨	8.2	10.6	7.7	7.2	7.7	7.9	7.7	7.2	5.9
20 長　　野	8.2	11.6	7.9	8.0	7.9	8.0	7.9	7.4	5.3
21 岐　　阜	8.6	12.8	8.5	8.1	8.8	8.7	9.2	7.9	6.1
22 静　　岡	8.4	12.4	8.1	8.2	9.0	9.5	9.7	8.3	6.5
23 愛　　知	7.8	11.2	8.2	8.2	9.9	10.0	11.6	8.9	6.9
24 三　　重	8.9	11.5	8.1	8.0	8.8	8.5	9.0	7.7	5.9
25 滋　　賀	9.1	11.2	7.8	7.6	8.0	7.9	9.0	8.4	6.5
26 京　　都	7.2	10.5	7.4	7.3	8.9	9.7	10.2	8.6	6.4
27 大　　阪	6.4	10.3	8.4	8.4	11.0	12.6	12.5	9.2	7.0
28 兵　　庫	7.5	10.8	8.7	8.3	9.5	10.0	10.6	8.5	6.6
29 奈　　良	8.9	12.7	8.9	7.8	8.6	9.4	9.8	8.1	6.4
30 和 歌 山	8.4	12.1	8.4	8.7	8.7	8.8	9.2	7.4	6.0
31 鳥　　取	8.6	12.9	9.0	7.2	7.6	6.8	7.6	7.2	6.1
32 島　　根	8.7	14.1	8.2	7.1	7.7	6.7	6.9	6.5	5.4
33 岡　　山	8.6	12.1	8.6	7.9	7.9	7.9	9.1	7.8	6.1
34 広　　島	9.0	12.8	8.6	8.0	8.6	9.2	9.9	8.4	6.5
35 山　　口	8.5	12.5	8.9	7.9	8.5	8.3	8.8	7.7	6.1
36 徳　　島	8.7	13.5	8.6	7.7	7.7	7.3	7.9	7.7	6.4
37 香　　川	9.2	13.8	8.8	7.8	8.1	7.7	8.9	7.6	6.1
38 愛　　媛	8.8	12.2	8.6	7.6	8.1	7.7	8.4	7.7	6.1
39 高　　知	8.5	13.0	8.8	8.1	8.2	7.6	8.3	7.2	5.8
40 福　　岡	7.8	12.4	9.2	8.1	9.3	9.5	9.5	8.7	7.1
41 佐　　賀	9.4	13.2	8.9	7.3	7.8	7.1	7.3	7.3	6.4
42 長　　崎	7.8	13.7	9.1	7.4	8.6	7.8	7.8	7.7	6.3
43 熊　　本	8.4	12.3	8.4	7.4	8.2	7.6	7.3	7.2	6.5
44 大　　分	8.9	13.2	8.4	7.3	7.9	7.5	8.1	7.7	6.1
45 宮　　崎	7.7	12.8	8.5	7.6	8.6	7.8	8.2	7.9	6.8
46 鹿 児 島	8.5	11.9	8.1	7.3	7.6	6.5	6.4	6.7	6.5
47 沖　　縄	9.6	…	…	…	…	…	…	8.9	7.7

注：1) 昭和10年：婚養子縁組、入婿の場合は届出時の妻の住所又は居所、他は夫の住所又は居所のある地域。
　　　　昭和22年：挙式の場所のある地域。昭和25年：挙式寸前の夫の住所。昭和30年以降：届出時の夫の住所。
　　2) 昭和22年の全国には不詳を含む。
　　3) 昭和25年の全国には不詳を含む。

514

Marriages

年次別婚姻率（人口千対）
（per 1,000 population）by each prefecture : Japan

1985 60 年	1990 平成2年	1995 7 年	2000 12 年	2005 17 年	2010 22 年	2014 26 年	2015 27 年	2016 28 年	都道府県[1] Prefecture
6.1	5.9	6.4	6.4	5.7	5.5	5.1	5.1	5.0	全 国 Total
6.4	6.0	6.3	6.1	5.3	5.2	4.8	4.8	4.6	01 北 海 道 [a]
6.0	5.3	5.6	5.5	4.6	4.3	4.2	4.2	4.0	02 青 森
5.4	4.9	5.1	5.4	4.7	4.3	4.3	4.1	3.9	03 岩 手
6.1	5.5	6.0	6.3	5.5	5.1	5.1	4.9	4.8	04 宮 城
5.3	4.6	4.9	4.8	4.3	4.0	3.7	3.5	3.5	05 秋 田
6.5	4.9	5.2	5.6	4.7	4.4	4.2	4.0	3.9	06 山 形
6.2	5.3	5.7	5.9	5.1	4.7	4.5	4.7	4.6	07 福 島
5.8	5.5	6.0	6.2	5.3	5.1	4.8	4.7	4.6	08 茨 城
6.0	5.7	6.0	6.4	5.8	5.4	5.0	4.9	4.8	09 栃 木
5.9	5.6	6.1	6.3	5.3	4.9	4.7	4.6	4.4	10 群 馬
5.7	6.2	6.9	6.6	5.8	5.5	4.9	4.9	4.8	11 埼 玉
5.9	6.1	6.8	6.7	5.9	5.7	5.0	4.9	4.8	12 千 葉
7.0	7.0	7.3	7.4	6.9	7.1	6.7	6.6	6.5	13 東 京
6.6	7.0	7.6	7.3	6.5	6.1	5.4	5.4	5.2	14 神 奈 川
5.5	4.9	5.3	5.2	4.7	4.7	4.3	4.1	4.1	15 新 潟
5.2	4.8	5.5	5.7	4.9	4.6	4.3	4.3	4.3	16 富 山
5.7	5.2	5.8	5.9	5.2	5.0	4.7	4.5	4.5	17 石 川
5.8	5.3	5.6	5.6	5.4	4.7	4.8	4.5	4.5	18 福 井
6.1	5.7	6.1	6.1	5.2	5.0	4.5	4.7	4.5	19 山 梨
5.6	5.3	5.7	6.1	5.4	4.9	4.6	4.6	4.4	20 長 野
5.5	5.2	5.7	5.8	5.1	4.9	4.5	4.4	4.3	21 岐 阜
6.0	5.7	6.2	6.3	5.7	5.5	4.9	4.9	4.7	22 静 岡
6.3	6.3	7.1	7.0	6.2	6.2	5.7	5.6	5.6	23 愛 知
5.8	5.5	5.8	6.1	5.3	5.2	4.8	4.8	4.6	24 三 重
5.9	5.6	6.2	6.5	5.7	5.5	5.0	4.9	4.9	25 滋 賀
5.8	5.6	6.2	6.1	5.4	5.3	4.9	4.9	4.7	26 京 都
6.4	6.7	7.5	6.9	6.0	5.9	5.4	5.4	5.3	27 大 阪
6.0	5.9	6.3	6.3	5.5	5.4	4.9	4.8	4.7	28 兵 庫
5.6	5.5	6.1	5.6	4.9	4.7	4.4	4.2	4.2	29 奈 良
5.7	5.3	5.7	5.5	4.8	4.8	4.6	4.5	4.3	30 和 歌 山
5.6	5.0	5.3	5.5	5.0	4.8	4.7	4.7	4.3	31 鳥 取
5.1	4.5	4.8	5.0	4.5	4.6	4.4	4.3	4.0	32 島 根
5.7	5.2	5.9	5.9	5.2	5.1	4.9	4.9	4.7	33 岡 山
5.8	5.7	6.2	6.1	5.5	5.4	5.1	4.9	4.9	34 広 島
5.3	4.9	5.3	5.4	4.9	4.8	4.4	4.2	4.3	35 山 口
5.6	5.0	5.3	5.5	4.5	4.6	4.4	4.3	4.3	36 徳 島
5.5	5.1	5.7	5.9	5.2	5.0	4.8	4.8	4.8	37 香 川
5.6	5.2	5.6	5.5	5.0	4.9	4.4	4.4	4.3	38 愛 媛
5.5	4.8	5.1	5.2	4.7	4.4	4.2	4.2	4.1	39 高 知
6.1	5.7	6.2	6.1	5.7	5.8	5.4	5.5	5.3	40 福 岡
5.6	5.2	5.2	5.4	4.8	5.0	4.7	4.5	4.5	41 佐 賀
5.7	5.2	5.5	5.2	4.8	4.7	4.4	4.5	4.4	42 長 崎
5.8	5.1	5.5	5.5	5.1	5.0	4.9	4.6	4.5	43 熊 本
5.6	5.1	5.4	5.7	5.1	5.1	4.6	4.6	4.5	44 大 分
5.9	5.3	5.6	5.6	5.2	5.2	4.6	4.6	4.7	45 宮 崎
5.7	4.9	5.1	5.4	5.0	5.1	4.7	4.7	4.6	46 鹿 児 島
7.3	6.3	6.6	6.9	6.5	6.4	6.0	6.1	5.9	47 沖 縄

Note : a) See page 44.

婚　姻

〔月別にみた婚姻〕
〔Marriages by month of registration〕

表 9.3　届出月別にみた年次別
Table 9.3　Trends in number and percent distribution

年　　次 Year		総　　数 Total	1 月 January	2 月 February	3 月 March	4 月 April	5 月 May
							実　　数
1947	昭和22年	934 170	70 965	72 762	84 012	74 741	111 959
50	25	715 081	67 064	73 379	77 020	67 025	70 714
55	30	714 861	53 453	63 065	70 581	69 652	73 104
60	35	866 115	62 810	78 239	85 966	93 783	92 859
65	40	954 852	69 052	80 348	97 760	109 452	109 754
70	45	1 029 405	62 172	73 178	100 037	121 697	122 356
75	50	941 628	53 574	66 262	102 563	111 679	115 025
80	55	774 702	42 341	55 752	81 071	86 411	96 918
85	60	735 850	36 012	48 164	75 503	80 686	84 961
90	平成 2 年	722 138	37 597	51 876	70 425	66 836	75 435
95	7	791 888	44 532	57 496	78 082	69 338	76 598
2000	12	798 138	68 759	59 228	78 744	63 239	70 538
01	13	799 999	68 558	55 348	75 306	65 744	73 706
02	14	757 331	44 510	68 655	72 901	66 496	67 452
03	15	740 191	45 851	53 469	80 046	63 314	65 402
04	16	720 417	44 599	58 279	74 833	63 388	60 811
05	17	714 265	44 871	51 456	76 934	58 073	64 163
06	18	730 971	47 294	56 466	78 358	60 370	63 088
07	19	719 822	49 626	55 629	71 207	57 553	64 113
08	20	726 106	49 381	58 373	72 084	62 401	60 320
09	21	707 734	52 017	57 171	73 376	59 794	61 681
10	22	700 214	45 603	66 916	70 547	55 087	57 707
11	23	661 895	46 066	50 303	69 795	57 083	56 775
12	24	668 869	43 950	56 905	70 114	52 316	59 873
13	25	660 613	42 845	53 240	69 103	54 120	55 500
14	26	643 749	42 788	59 611	68 641	52 991	51 651
15	27	635 156	45 356	46 053	72 064	47 981	56 671
16	**28**	**620 531**	**43 632**	**52 735**	**68 579**	**46 765**	**49 555**
							百　分　率
1947	昭和22年	100.0	7.6	7.8	9.0	8.0	12.0
50	25	100.0	9.4	10.3	10.8	9.4	9.9
55	30	100.0	7.5	8.8	9.9	9.7	10.2
60	35	100.0	7.3	9.0	9.9	10.8	10.7
65	40	100.0	7.2	8.4	10.2	11.5	11.5
70	45	100.0	6.0	7.1	9.7	11.8	11.9
75	50	100.0	5.7	7.0	10.9	11.9	12.2
80	55	100.0	5.5	7.2	10.5	11.2	12.5
85	60	100.0	4.9	6.5	10.3	11.0	11.5
90	平成 2 年	100.0	5.2	7.2	9.8	9.3	10.4
95	7	100.0	5.6	7.3	9.9	8.8	9.7
2000	12	100.0	8.6	7.4	9.9	7.9	8.8
01	13	100.0	8.6	6.9	9.4	8.2	9.2
02	14	100.0	5.9	9.1	9.6	8.8	8.9
03	15	100.0	6.2	7.2	10.8	8.6	8.8
04	16	100.0	6.2	8.1	10.4	8.8	8.4
05	17	100.0	6.3	7.2	10.8	8.1	9.0
06	18	100.0	6.5	7.7	10.7	8.3	8.6
07	19	100.0	6.9	7.7	9.9	8.0	8.9
08	20	100.0	6.8	8.0	9.9	8.6	8.3
09	21	100.0	7.3	8.1	10.4	8.4	8.7
10	22	100.0	6.5	9.6	10.1	7.9	8.2
11	23	100.0	7.0	7.6	10.5	8.6	8.6
12	24	100.0	6.6	8.5	10.5	7.8	9.0
13	25	100.0	6.5	8.1	10.5	8.2	8.4
14	26	100.0	6.6	9.3	10.7	8.2	8.0
15	27	100.0	7.1	7.3	11.3	7.6	8.9
16	**28**	**100.0**	**7.0**	**8.5**	**11.1**	**7.5**	**8.0**

Marriages

婚姻件数及び百分率
of marriages by month of registration : Japan

6　月 June	7　月 July	8　月 August	9　月 September	10　月 October	11　月 November	12　月 December
Number						
81 021	73 173	62 937	71 405	73 505	64 587	93 103
52 119	50 469	47 332	47 861	49 945	51 901	60 252
50 983	42 704	40 470	42 846	49 719	64 346	93 938
67 991	52 768	45 919	47 914	59 091	83 165	95 610
80 222	53 620	40 408	41 445	67 045	99 586	106 160
82 818	51 804	36 491	42 032	97 970	122 426	116 424
76 413	43 488	28 718	39 386	95 609	111 545	97 366
61 199	35 998	23 800	36 086	74 203	97 626	83 297
64 954	37 881	25 088	42 014	78 820	89 104	72 663
72 987	44 551	31 916	42 293	76 836	82 788	68 598
70 271	68 726	38 957	52 183	76 485	86 154	73 066
65 361	67 388	43 894	56 533	70 027	75 519	78 908
66 638	62 885	50 923	55 393	74 619	79 483	71 396
61 429	63 033	48 728	53 105	65 586	77 987	67 449
59 822	61 475	48 456	51 309	65 378	79 026	66 643
60 707	59 008	46 662	53 249	61 246	69 698	67 937
53 815	63 127	46 197	52 572	65 274	75 226	62 557
53 872	66 170	47 750	49 298	67 894	78 608	61 803
53 088	70 109	44 536	49 967	60 968	80 804	62 222
58 223	57 214	57 686	48 244	62 349	75 453	64 378
53 548	61 176	51 366	48 830	56 532	73 503	58 740
54 139	57 329	48 226	46 734	71 664	65 565	60 697
49 897	57 656	47 855	45 424	49 377	78 592	53 072
50 119	54 139	49 859	43 704	54 750	63 306	69 834
49 829	60 946	48 450	44 791	51 663	73 121	57 005
48 976	57 655	48 103	41 867	48 615	67 951	54 900
44 314	58 754	50 952	43 365	47 948	62 457	59 241
46 943	**60 196**	**49 015**	**42 397**	**42 103**	**62 886**	**55 725**
Percentage						
8.7	7.8	6.7	7.6	7.9	6.9	10.0
7.3	7.1	6.6	6.7	7.0	7.3	8.4
7.1	6.0	5.7	6.0	7.0	9.0	13.1
7.9	6.1	5.3	5.5	6.8	9.6	11.0
8.4	5.6	4.2	4.3	7.0	10.4	11.1
8.0	5.0	3.5	4.1	9.5	11.9	11.3
8.1	4.6	3.0	4.2	10.2	11.8	10.3
7.9	4.6	3.1	4.7	9.6	12.6	10.8
8.8	5.1	3.4	5.7	10.7	12.1	9.9
10.1	6.2	4.4	5.9	10.6	11.5	9.5
8.9	8.7	4.9	6.6	9.7	10.9	9.2
8.2	8.4	5.5	7.1	8.8	9.5	9.9
8.3	7.9	6.4	6.9	9.3	9.9	8.9
8.1	8.3	6.4	7.0	8.7	10.3	8.9
8.1	8.3	6.5	6.9	8.8	10.7	9.0
8.4	8.2	6.5	7.4	8.5	9.7	9.4
7.5	8.8	6.5	7.4	9.1	10.5	8.8
7.4	9.1	6.5	6.7	9.3	10.8	8.5
7.4	9.7	6.2	6.9	8.5	11.2	8.6
8.0	7.9	7.9	6.6	8.6	10.4	8.9
7.6	8.6	7.3	6.9	8.0	10.4	8.3
7.7	8.2	6.9	6.7	10.2	9.4	8.7
7.5	8.7	7.2	6.9	7.5	11.9	8.0
7.5	8.1	7.5	6.5	8.2	9.5	10.4
7.5	9.2	7.3	6.8	7.8	11.1	8.6
7.6	9.0	7.5	6.5	7.6	10.6	8.5
7.0	9.3	8.0	6.8	7.5	9.8	9.3
7.6	**9.7**	**7.9**	**6.8**	**6.8**	**10.1**	**9.0**

婚　姻

[初婚と再婚別にみた婚姻]
[Marriages by previous marital status of bride and groom]

表9.4　初婚－再婚別にみた年次別婚姻件数及び総数に対する再婚の割合－夫・妻－
Table 9.4　Trends in marriages by previous marital status of bride and groom, and percentage of remarriages : Japan

年　　　次 Year		総　　数 Total	夫 Groom		妻 Bride		総件数に対する再婚件数の割合 Percentage of remarried	
			初　婚 First married	再　婚 Remarried	初　婚 First married	再　婚 Remarried	夫 Groom	妻 Bride
1952	昭和27年	676 995	578 687	98 308	606 538	70 457	14.5	10.4
55	30	714 861	626 394	88 467	656 591	58 270	12.4	8.2
60	35	866 115	782 021	84 094	812 597	53 518	9.7	6.2
65	40	954 852	872 649	82 203	900 304	54 548	8.6	5.7
66	41	940 120	860 197	79 923	886 108	54 012	8.5	5.7
67	42	953 096	871 919	81 177	897 156	55 940	8.5	5.9
68	43	956 312	876 803	79 509	900 586	55 726	8.3	5.8
69	44	984 142	902 251	81 891	925 538	58 604	8.3	6.0
1970	45	1 029 405	943 783	85 622	967 716	61 689	8.3	6.0
71	46	1 091 229	1 003 381	87 848	1 026 772	64 457	8.1	5.9
72	47	1 099 984	1 011 042	88 942	1 032 967	67 017	8.1	6.1
73	48	1 071 923	983 035	88 888	1 002 656	69 267	8.3	6.5
74	49	1 000 455	911 808	88 647	929 824	70 631	8.9	7.1
75	50	941 628	855 825	85 803	871 445	70 183	9.1	7.5
76	51	871 543	787 521	84 022	801 264	70 279	9.6	8.1
77	52	821 029	738 321	82 708	750 756	70 273	10.1	8.6
78	53	793 257	710 875	82 382	722 577	70 680	10.4	8.9
79	54	788 505	704 321	84 184	715 551	72 954	10.7	9.3
1980	55	774 702	690 885	83 817	701 415	73 287	10.8	9.5
81	56	776 531	691 448	85 083	702 259	74 272	11.0	9.6
82	57	781 252	693 990	87 262	704 840	76 412	11.2	9.8
83	58	762 552	675 514	87 038	686 477	76 075	11.4	10.0
84	59	739 991	652 618	87 373	663 021	76 970	11.8	10.4
85	60	735 850	646 241	89 609	656 609	79 241	12.2	10.8
86	61	710 962	620 754	90 208	630 353	80 609	12.7	11.3
87	62	696 173	605 675	90 498	615 148	81 025	13.0	11.6
88	63	707 716	613 919	93 797	623 743	83 973	13.3	11.9
89	平成元年	708 316	611 963	96 353	623 485	84 831	13.6	12.0
1990	2	722 138	625 453	96 685	637 472	84 666	13.4	11.7
91	3	742 264	645 790	96 474	657 715	84 549	13.0	11.4
92	4	754 441	657 540	96 901	669 760	84 681	12.8	11.2
93	5	792 658	692 214	100 444	704 929	87 729	12.7	11.1
94	6	782 738	681 759	100 979	693 853	88 885	12.9	11.4
95	7	791 888	687 167	104 721	700 158	91 730	13.2	11.6
96	8	795 080	688 887	106 193	701 776	93 304	13.4	11.7
97	9	775 651	670 007	105 644	681 468	94 183	13.6	12.1
98	10	784 595	675 519	109 076	687 552	97 043	13.9	12.4
99	11	762 028	651 925	110 103	664 379	97 649	14.4	12.8
2000	12	798 138	678 174	119 964	691 507	106 631	15.0	13.4
01	13	799 999	674 770	125 229	687 683	112 316	15.7	14.0
02	14	757 331	633 543	123 788	645 138	112 193	16.3	14.8
03	15	740 191	613 727	126 464	626 327	113 864	17.1	15.4
04	16	720 417	592 448	127 969	605 935	114 482	17.8	15.9
05	17	714 265	584 076	130 189	599 691	114 574	18.2	16.0
06	18	730 971	593 726	137 245	612 133	118 838	18.8	16.3
07	19	719 822	584 416	135 406	600 743	119 079	18.8	16.5
08	20	726 106	590 573	135 533	605 868	120 238	18.7	16.6
09	21	707 734	575 098	132 636	591 314	116 420	18.7	16.4
2010	22	700 214	570 571	129 643	586 712	113 502	18.5	16.2
11	23	661 895	537 684	124 211	553 663	108 232	18.8	16.4
12	24	668 869	541 917	126 952	559 371	109 498	19.0	16.4
13	25	660 613	533 703	126 910	551 816	108 797	19.2	16.5
14	26	643 749	519 381	124 368	537 164	106 585	19.3	16.6
15	27	635 156	510 243	124 913	528 563	106 593	19.7	16.8
16	**28**	**620 531**	**499 233**	**121 298**	**516 547**	**103 984**	**19.5**	**16.8**

婚　姻

表9.5　夫妻の初婚−再婚の組合せ別にみた
Table 9.5　Trends in number and percent distribution of marriages

年　　次 Year		婚　姻　件　数 Marriages					
		総　　数 Total	夫妻とも初婚 Both first married	夫妻とも再婚又はどちらか一方が再婚			
				Remarriages including of which one of couple is first married	夫妻とも再婚 Both remarried	夫再婚妻初婚 Remarried groom and first married bride	夫初婚妻再婚 First married groom and remarried bride
1952	昭和27年	676 995	549 769	127 226	41 539	56 769	28 918
55	30	714 861	601 924	112 937	33 800	54 667	24 470
60	35	866 115	758 429	107 686	29 926	54 168	23 592
65	40	954 852	847 564	107 288	29 463	52 740	25 085
66	41	940 120	835 167	104 953	28 982	50 941	25 030
67	42	953 096	845 563	107 533	29 584	51 593	26 356
68	43	956 312	850 904	105 408	29 827	49 682	25 899
69	44	984 142	874 829	109 313	31 182	50 709	27 422
1970	45	1 029 405	914 870	114 535	32 776	52 846	28 913
71	46	1 091 229	972 908	118 321	33 984	53 864	30 473
72	47	1 099 984	979 331	120 653	35 306	53 636	31 711
73	48	1 071 923	949 938	121 985	36 170	52 718	33 097
74	49	1 000 455	878 277	122 178	37 100	51 547	33 531
75	50	941 628	822 382	119 246	36 740	49 063	33 443
76	51	871 543	754 680	116 863	37 438	46 584	32 841
77	52	821 029	705 709	115 320	37 661	45 047	32 612
78	53	793 257	678 298	114 959	38 103	44 279	32 577
79	54	788 505	670 858	117 647	39 491	44 693	33 463
1980	55	774 702	657 373	117 329	39 775	44 042	33 512
81	56	776 531	658 409	118 122	41 233	43 850	33 039
82	57	781 252	660 475	120 777	42 897	44 365	33 515
83	58	762 552	642 591	119 961	43 152	43 886	32 923
84	59	739 991	620 110	119 881	44 462	42 911	32 508
85	60	735 850	613 387	122 463	46 387	43 222	32 854
86	61	710 962	587 853	123 109	47 708	42 500	32 901
87	62	696 173	572 492	123 681	47 842	42 656	33 183
88	63	707 716	579 139	128 577	49 193	44 604	34 780
89	平成元年	708 316	576 905	131 411	49 773	46 580	35 058
1990	2	722 138	589 886	132 252	49 099	47 586	35 567
91	3	742 264	609 907	132 357	48 666	47 808	35 883
92	4	754 441	621 752	132 689	48 893	48 008	35 788
93	5	792 658	654 447	138 211	49 962	50 482	37 767
94	6	782 738	642 827	139 911	49 953	51 026	38 932
95	7	791 888	646 536	145 352	51 099	53 622	40 631
96	8	795 080	647 477	147 603	51 894	54 299	41 410
97	9	775 651	627 872	147 779	52 048	53 596	42 135
98	10	784 595	631 850	152 745	53 374	55 702	43 669
99	11	762 028	608 015	154 013	53 739	56 364	43 910
2000	12	798 138	630 235	167 903	58 692	61 272	47 939
01	13	799 999	623 514	176 485	61 060	64 169	51 256
02	14	757 331	582 785	174 546	61 435	62 353	50 758
03	15	740 191	562 940	177 251	63 077	63 387	50 787
04	16	720 417	541 675	178 742	63 709	64 260	50 773
05	17	714 265	533 498	180 767	63 996	66 193	50 578
06	18	730 971	541 487	189 484	66 599	70 646	52 239
07	19	719 822	532 298	187 524	66 961	68 445	52 118
08	20	726 106	537 748	188 358	67 413	68 120	52 825
09	21	707 734	524 480	183 254	65 802	66 834	50 618
2010	22	700 214	520 955	179 259	63 886	65 757	49 616
11	23	661 895	490 664	171 231	61 212	62 999	47 020
12	24	668 869	494 749	174 120	62 330	64 622	47 168
13	25	660 613	487 044	173 569	62 138	64 772	46 659
14	26	643 749	473 772	169 977	60 976	63 392	45 609
15	27	635 156	464 975	170 181	61 325	63 588	45 268
16	28	620 531	454 750	165 781	59 501	61 797	44 483

Marriages

年次別婚姻件数及び百分率
by number of marriages of bride and groom : Japan

総　数 Total	夫妻とも初婚 Both first married	夫妻とも再婚又はどちらか一方が再婚 Remarriages including of which one of couple is first married	夫妻とも再婚 Both remarried	夫再婚妻初婚 Remarried groom and first married bride	夫初婚妻再婚 First married groom and remarried bride	年　次 Year	
100.0	81.2	18.8	6.1	8.4	4.3	1952	昭和27年
100.0	84.2	15.8	4.7	7.6	3.4	55	30
100.0	87.6	12.4	3.5	6.3	2.7	60	35
100.0	88.8	11.2	3.1	5.5	2.6	65	40
100.0	88.8	11.2	3.1	5.4	2.7	66	41
100.0	88.7	11.3	3.1	5.4	2.8	67	42
100.0	89.0	11.0	3.1	5.2	2.7	68	43
100.0	88.9	11.1	3.2	5.2	2.8	69	44
100.0	88.9	11.1	3.2	5.1	2.8	1970	45
100.0	89.2	10.8	3.1	4.9	2.8	71	46
100.0	89.0	11.0	3.2	4.9	2.9	72	47
100.0	88.6	11.4	3.4	4.9	3.1	73	48
100.0	87.8	12.2	3.7	5.2	3.4	74	49
100.0	87.3	12.7	3.9	5.2	3.6	75	50
100.0	86.6	13.4	4.3	5.3	3.8	76	51
100.0	86.0	14.0	4.6	5.5	4.0	77	52
100.0	85.5	14.5	4.8	5.6	4.1	78	53
100.0	85.1	14.9	5.0	5.7	4.2	79	54
100.0	84.9	15.1	5.1	5.7	4.3	1980	55
100.0	84.8	15.2	5.3	5.6	4.3	81	56
100.0	84.5	15.5	5.5	5.7	4.3	82	57
100.0	84.3	15.7	5.7	5.8	4.3	83	58
100.0	83.8	16.2	6.0	5.8	4.4	84	59
100.0	83.4	16.6	6.3	5.9	4.5	85	60
100.0	82.7	17.3	6.7	6.0	4.6	86	61
100.0	82.2	17.8	6.9	6.1	4.8	87	62
100.0	81.8	18.2	7.0	6.3	4.9	88	63
100.0	81.4	18.6	7.0	6.6	4.9	89	平成元年
100.0	81.7	18.3	6.8	6.6	4.9	1990	2
100.0	82.2	17.8	6.6	6.4	4.8	91	3
100.0	82.4	17.6	6.5	6.4	4.7	92	4
100.0	82.6	17.4	6.3	6.4	4.8	93	5
100.0	82.1	17.9	6.4	6.5	5.0	94	6
100.0	81.6	18.4	6.5	6.8	5.1	95	7
100.0	81.4	18.6	6.5	6.8	5.2	96	8
100.0	80.9	19.1	6.7	6.9	5.4	97	9
100.0	80.5	19.5	6.8	7.1	5.6	98	10
100.0	79.8	20.2	7.1	7.4	5.8	99	11
100.0	79.0	21.0	7.4	7.7	6.0	2000	12
100.0	77.9	22.1	7.6	8.0	6.4	01	13
100.0	77.0	23.0	8.1	8.2	6.7	02	14
100.0	76.1	23.9	8.5	8.6	6.9	03	15
100.0	75.2	24.8	8.8	8.9	7.0	04	16
100.0	74.7	25.3	9.0	9.3	7.1	05	17
100.0	74.1	25.9	9.1	9.7	7.1	06	18
100.0	73.9	26.1	9.3	9.5	7.2	07	19
100.0	74.1	25.9	9.3	9.4	7.3	08	20
100.0	74.1	25.9	9.3	9.4	7.2	09	21
100.0	74.4	25.6	9.1	9.4	7.1	2010	22
100.0	74.1	25.9	9.2	9.5	7.1	11	23
100.0	74.0	26.0	9.3	9.7	7.1	12	24
100.0	73.7	26.3	9.4	9.8	7.1	13	25
100.0	73.6	26.4	9.5	9.8	7.1	14	26
100.0	73.2	26.8	9.7	10.0	7.1	15	27
100.0	**73.3**	**26.7**	**9.6**	**10.0**	**7.2**	16	28

521

婚　姻

表9.6　前婚解消後から再婚までの期
（各届出年に結婚生活

Table 9.6　Trends in percent distribution of remarriages and remarriage（for marriages performed and

前婚解消から再婚までの期間 Period between termination of the last marriage and remarriage	1970 昭和45年	1975 50年	1980 55年	1985 60年	1990 平成2年	1995 7年	2000 12年	2005 17年
								夫
総数　Total	100.0	100.0	100.0	100.0	100.0	100.0	100.0	100.0
1年未満　Under 1 year	40.1	35.3	29.8	26.2	23.5	24.9	23.9	20.4
1年以上2年未満　1 year and over, less than 2 years	24.6	24.2	22.0	20.3	16.9	16.8	16.7	15.0
2　～　3	12.9	14.9	14.9	14.6	12.7	13.2	13.4	12.9
3　～　4	7.2	8.7	10.3	10.5	10.2	9.6	9.9	10.9
4　～　5	4.4	5.2	7.2	7.8	8.1	7.2	7.4	8.7
5　～　6	2.9	3.3	4.6	5.4	6.3	5.3	5.8	6.6
6　～　7	1.9	2.2	3.3	3.9	5.3	4.4	4.5	5.2
7　～　8	1.2	1.5	2.2	3.0	4.1	3.4	3.6	4.1
8　～　9	0.9	1.1	1.6	2.2	3.0	2.8	2.7	3.2
9　～　10	0.7	0.8	1.1	1.6	2.3	2.4	2.0	2.4
10　～	3.3	2.8	3.1	4.5	7.5	10.0	10.1	10.7
								妻
総数　Total	100.0	100.0	100.0	100.0	100.0	100.0	100.0	100.0
1年未満　Under 1 year	24.2	26.7	23.9	21.8	20.2	21.0	20.7	16.8
1年以上2年未満　1 year and over, less than 2 years	23.1	22.5	20.9	20.5	17.3	17.6	17.7	15.6
2　～　3	14.3	14.5	14.4	14.4	12.5	13.3	13.3	13.4
3　～　4	9.3	9.7	10.2	10.4	10.1	9.7	10.4	11.5
4　～　5	6.4	6.4	7.5	7.4	7.9	7.2	7.6	9.2
5　～　6	4.6	4.4	5.5	5.4	6.4	5.6	5.9	6.8
6　～　7	3.3	3.2	3.9	4.3	5.5	4.3	4.5	5.3
7　～　8	2.4	2.4	2.9	3.4	4.1	3.5	3.4	4.1
8　～　9	1.9	1.8	2.3	2.5	3.1	2.8	2.6	3.2
9　～　10	1.5	1.4	1.6	2.0	2.6	2.4	2.2	2.4
10　～	9.0	7.0	6.9	8.1	10.4	12.5	11.6	11.7

注：1）　前婚解消年不詳を除く総数に対する百分率である。

Marriages

間別にみた年次別再婚件数百分率[1] －夫・妻－
に入り届け出たもの）

by period between termination of the last marriage
registered each year): Japan

2007 19年	2008 20年	2009 21年	2010 22年	2011 23年	2012 24年	2013 25年	2014 26年	2015 27年	2016 28年
Groom									
100. 0	100. 0	100. 0	100. 0	100. 0	100. 0	100. 0	100. 0	100. 0	100. 0
19. 2	18. 9	18. 1	17. 7	16. 8	16. 2	16. 0	15. 9	15. 7	15. 6
14. 2	13. 8	13. 5	13. 4	13. 7	13. 0	13. 1	13. 1	12. 8	13. 0
11. 7	11. 6	11. 4	11. 5	11. 4	11. 6	11. 3	11. 1	11. 2	11. 0
10. 2	9. 8	9. 7	9. 7	9. 6	9. 8	9. 6	9. 2	9. 4	9. 3
8. 8	8. 5	8. 1	8. 2	8. 1	8. 0	8. 0	8. 1	7. 8	7. 8
7. 5	7. 3	7. 1	6. 9	6. 9	6. 9	6. 8	6. 7	6. 7	6. 7
5. 9	6. 1	6. 1	5. 9	5. 9	5. 8	5. 8	5. 7	5. 5	5. 7
4. 5	5. 0	5. 2	5. 1	4. 9	4. 9	4. 8	4. 7	4. 7	4. 7
3. 6	3. 8	4. 3	4. 3	4. 4	4. 2	4. 1	4. 2	4. 1	3. 9
2. 8	2. 9	3. 1	3. 5	3. 7	3. 6	3. 6	3. 3	3. 5	3. 4
11. 6	12. 4	13. 3	13. 6	14. 7	16. 1	17. 0	17. 9	18. 4	18. 9
Bride									
100. 0	100. 0	100. 0	100. 0	100. 0	100. 0	100. 0	100. 0	100. 0	100. 0
16. 1	15. 8	15. 8	15. 0	14. 3	13. 4	13. 0	12. 7	12. 9	13. 3
14. 7	14. 1	14. 1	14. 0	13. 7	13. 2	12. 7	13. 2	12. 5	12. 7
12. 0	11. 9	11. 4	11. 4	11. 5	11. 6	11. 3	10. 8	10. 9	10. 8
10. 4	10. 0	10. 0	9. 7	9. 6	9. 6	9. 7	9. 4	9. 3	9. 3
9. 2	8. 8	8. 4	8. 3	8. 2	8. 2	8. 2	8. 1	8. 1	7. 8
7. 8	7. 8	7. 3	7. 2	6. 9	6. 9	7. 1	7. 0	6. 8	6. 7
6. 3	6. 4	6. 1	6. 0	6. 0	5. 9	5. 8	5. 7	5. 7	5. 7
4. 6	5. 1	5. 3	5. 3	5. 0	4. 9	5. 0	5. 0	4. 8	5. 0
3. 8	3. 8	4. 2	4. 4	4. 4	4. 4	4. 2	4. 2	4. 0	4. 0
2. 9	3. 1	3. 2	3. 6	3. 9	3. 8	3. 8	3. 5	3. 7	3. 5
12. 4	13. 3	14. 1	15. 1	16. 6	18. 2	19. 3	20. 3	21. 1	21. 4

523

婚　姻

〔結婚生活に入ったときの年齢別にみた婚姻〕
〔Marriages by age〕

表9.7　結婚生活に入ったときの年齢別にみた年次別婚姻件数
Table 9.7　Trends in marriages by age for first married

初　婚
First married

年　　次 Year		総　数 Total	～19歳 Years	20～24	25～29	30～34	35～39	40～44
								夫
1947	昭和22年	426 348	12 726	154 852	203 364	44 759	6 483	1 825
50	25	298 124	7 526	123 730	136 090	24 265	4 139	1 143
55	30	393 252	2 812	113 355	232 903	37 926	4 390	1 044
60	35	533 963	2 147	122 894	327 491	71 090	7 972	1 418
65	40	669 209	2 637	169 498	384 668	95 901	12 793	2 504
70	45	799 637	5 811	221 545	451 864	101 083	14 377	3 196
75	50	769 670	5 077	210 292	430 929	104 611	14 325	3 083
80	55	634 352	5 304	137 768	325 327	142 437	18 875	3 330
85	60	601 673	6 577	126 761	288 236	138 164	34 783	5 317
90	平成2年	581 650	7 683	118 866	274 447	129 444	37 101	10 893
95	7	635 178	8 693	136 347	287 105	140 354	42 848	13 516
2000	12	614 968	10 745	117 347	284 162	135 078	44 912	13 490
01	13	610 753	10 851	111 105	277 972	141 785	44 713	14 029
02	14	573 955	9 912	100 108	255 777	140 839	44 282	13 561
03	15	551 784	8 790	90 900	237 641	143 501	46 997	14 295
04	16	527 121	7 619	84 261	218 898	142 740	48 146	15 196
05	17	515 916	6 789	79 730	208 908	143 700	50 031	15 976
06	18	520 171	6 616	80 039	205 204	145 186	54 867	16 978
07	19	506 470	6 549	76 358	196 834	140 647	57 224	17 707
08	20	508 367	6 497	75 677	195 186	139 868	60 578	18 979
09	21	489 891	5 764	69 558	188 214	133 184	61 784	19 825
10	22	484 406	5 354	66 150	184 590	131 091	64 349	21 055
11	23	454 971	5 002	59 252	174 147	121 396	61 714	22 043
12	24	455 964	5 052	57 394	173 708	120 306	62 807	24 198
13	25	447 623	5 403	55 102	169 340	118 009	61 228	25 639
14	26	430 608	5 337	52 225	160 521	113 377	59 024	26 527
15	27	418 519	5 177	50 966	154 906	109 701	57 061	26 759
16	**28**	**405 024**	**4 875**	**50 176**	**150 156**	**105 275**	**53 956**	**26 057**
								妻
1947	昭和22年	426 965	72 076	267 575	72 033	10 065	2 446	939
50	25	308 431	50 190	196 299	50 307	7 756	2 242	816
55	30	411 062	33 217	266 534	94 688	12 366	2 670	923
60	35	553 583	29 426	332 839	159 303	24 031	5 600	1 445
65	40	688 957	26 972	439 357	177 962	30 469	9 541	3 017
70	45	818 316	33 470	533 842	208 780	26 285	9 363	4 164
75	50	783 246	24 315	459 635	256 383	28 364	7 763	3 739
80	55	643 514	20 912	328 761	238 640	41 169	8 438	2 757
85	60	610 389	21 602	280 044	249 594	41 628	11 907	2 998
90	平成2年	592 262	22 327	233 032	270 575	48 641	11 320	3 814
95	7	647 004	19 271	233 964	299 855	72 600	14 676	3 679
2000	12	626 764	21 480	175 387	308 790	92 933	20 926	4 351
01	13	622 295	22 064	165 629	303 861	100 853	22 392	4 628
02	14	584 455	20 688	147 868	281 805	103 333	23 315	4 814
03	15	562 825	18 960	134 848	265 619	109 294	25 827	5 481
04	16	538 891	17 335	124 798	248 402	112 018	27 708	5 817
05	17	529 391	15 434	119 549	238 978	115 380	30 728	6 407
06	18	535 681	15 047	120 200	235 730	120 038	34 652	6 953
07	19	519 734	14 178	113 405	226 364	117 935	37 087	7 642
08	20	520 955	13 858	111 386	223 349	119 745	40 588	8 693
09	21	503 351	12 556	103 746	215 422	115 493	43 014	9 699
10	22	497 638	11 435	98 522	212 011	114 823	46 289	10 742
11	23	467 825	10 821	88 665	199 373	107 829	45 392	11 774
12	24	469 715	10 478	84 940	198 807	109 503	47 836	13 640
13	25	461 979	10 653	81 449	193 729	108 691	48 360	14 143
14	26	444 219	10 058	77 178	184 928	104 818	47 079	15 068
15	27	432 511	9 396	74 912	179 042	101 813	46 302	15 358
16	**28**	**417 897**	**8 826**	**73 377**	**174 066**	**97 003**	**43 523**	**15 142**

注：1）　昭和22・25年の70～74歳は、70歳以上の数値である。
　　　2）　昭和30～平成17年の75～79歳は、75歳以上の数値である。

－初婚の夫・妻及び再婚の夫・妻－（各届出年に結婚生活に入り届け出たもの）
and remarried (for marriages performed and registered each year)：Japan

45～49	50～54	55～59	60～64	65～69	70～74[1]	75～79[2]	80～	不 詳 Not stated
Groom								
804	348	183	94	46	25	...	...	839
562	309	154	81	35	24	...	...	66
417	195	121	47	24	14	4	...	-
498	196	122	73	31	15	16	...	-
648	269	108	106	51	16	10	...	-
853	298	129	64	35	18	19	...	345
849	243	106	39	27	25	21	...	43
856	270	93	33	24	11	12	...	12
1 229	359	149	54	23	4	8	...	9
2 225	623	227	95	24	9	6	...	7
4 777	1 043	292	118	45	13	9	...	18
5 789	2 453	659	218	72	28	9	...	6
6 006	3 045	832	273	99	23	14	...	6
5 556	2 755	766	262	78	32	22	...	5
5 511	2 722	999	293	79	30	23	...	3
5 851	2 861	1 073	326	91	37	22	...	-
6 026	2 919	1 304	380	96	37	18	...	2
6 216	2 926	1 570	375	124	39	21	8	2
6 205	2 740	1 564	461	119	38	17	5	2
6 566	2 751	1 521	560	127	31	15	7	4
6 739	2 673	1 374	561	150	38	16	11	-
7 114	2 564	1 305	617	159	36	17	5	-
6 801	2 485	1 221	683	151	46	18	12	-
7 654	2 674	1 196	751	137	56	20	11	-
8 011	2 777	1 165	677	171	68	18	15	-
8 544	2 836	1 194	661	250	77	24	11	-
8 796	2 950	1 185	637	277	70	26	8	-
9 243	3 041	1 206	594	332	72	27	12	2
Bride								
464	199	116	55	36	7	...	...	954
352	187	82	50	16	13	...	...	121
357	160	92	37	10	6	2	...	-
537	234	99	30	27	6	6	...	-
1 045	344	154	60	25	7	4	...	-
1 574	408	147	35	15	11	5	...	217
1 938	739	194	78	31	13	16	...	38
1 564	828	306	79	29	10	9	...	12
1 302	800	352	113	30	14	4	...	1
1 415	579	346	155	43	7	6	...	2
1 661	699	328	151	81	25	10	...	4
1 387	831	382	172	87	26	11	...	1
1 428	805	347	157	82	33	16	...	-
1 300	703	329	162	88	29	21	...	-
1 399	726	364	157	88	35	22	...	5
1 515	632	330	187	80	40	26	...	3
1 724	564	339	166	62	38	20	...	2
1 737	648	358	158	81	50	13	9	7
1 811	640	350	160	96	40	17	8	1
2 014	644	373	158	80	42	17	7	1
2 117	705	291	171	79	28	19	11	-
2 430	726	302	199	94	30	26	9	-
2 582	743	303	196	78	44	12	13	-
2 966	875	322	207	80	36	14	11	-
3 366	941	314	173	100	31	15	14	-
3 399	973	351	184	102	45	17	19	-
3 813	1 169	372	158	108	41	20	6	1
4 025	1 191	404	176	98	39	10	15	2

婚 姻

表 9.7 結婚生活に入ったときの年齢別にみた年次別婚姻件数－初婚の夫・
Table 9.7 Trends in marriages by age for first married and remarried

再 婚
Remarried

年次 Year		総数 Total	～19歳 Years	20～24	25～29	30～34	35～39	40～44
								夫
1947	昭和22年	58 086	167	2 993	10 691	16 191	11 785	6 607
50	25	47 920	81	3 716	10 083	10 505	8 737	5 854
55	30	44 736	13	1 854	11 657	10 468	6 572	4 978
60	35	45 945	10	1 152	9 069	12 726	7 796	4 775
65	40	51 066	7	1 242	8 854	12 970	9 918	5 922
70	45	55 723	21	1 692	10 900	13 779	10 550	6 885
75	50	59 869	11	1 981	12 137	15 237	10 437	7 326
80	55	60 095	13	1 148	9 353	17 979	12 146	6 755
85	60	65 815	21	1 359	7 193	15 835	16 808	9 398
90	平成2年	71 765	21	1 706	8 504	14 193	14 896	13 165
95	7	81 400	28	2 292	10 329	17 153	15 057	11 636
2000	12	93 191	27	2 359	12 201	20 303	17 470	11 422
01	13	99 111	43	2 310	12 957	22 088	19 018	11 960
02	14	97 647	34	2 269	12 334	22 628	19 255	12 182
03	15	99 760	31	2 222	11 493	22 984	20 243	12 786
04	16	100 208	20	2 220	10 701	22 832	20 612	13 630
05	17	102 184	17	1 961	10 111	22 413	21 705	14 271
06	18	107 431	22	2 029	10 281	23 192	23 412	15 281
07	19	104 797	14	1 918	9 865	21 961	23 389	15 213
08	20	105 120	16	1 719	9 505	21 130	24 349	15 854
09	21	102 288	23	1 594	8 956	19 652	23 629	16 046
10	22	99 672	23	1 534	8 246	18 707	23 470	16 254
11	23	95 277	19	1 468	7 750	17 325	22 320	16 329
12	24	97 076	17	1 381	7 493	17 095	22 334	17 484
13	25	97 353	20	1 448	7 425	16 938	21 683	18 009
14	26	94 753	23	1 410	6 836	15 874	20 522	17 579
15	27	94 373	25	1 354	6 684	15 395	19 745	17 983
16	**28**	**91 401**	**18**	**1 419**	**6 251**	**14 857**	**18 820**	**17 177**
								妻
1947	昭和22年	57 469	730	12 823	24 040	12 098	3 864	1 584
50	25	37 613	473	6 729	13 036	9 396	4 075	1 741
55	30	26 926	136	4 280	8 721	6 572	3 359	1 710
60	35	26 325	90	3 181	7 986	6 551	4 008	1 997
65	40	31 318	66	3 878	8 880	7 456	4 748	2 806
70	45	37 044	109	4 655	11 618	8 263	5 253	3 164
75	50	46 293	108	4 969	15 249	11 033	6 360	3 776
80	55	50 933	95	3 322	14 718	15 072	7 857	4 252
85	60	57 099	117	3 505	11 961	15 206	11 959	6 268
90	平成2年	61 153	130	3 645	12 795	14 120	11 020	8 597
95	7	69 574	116	4 533	14 692	16 534	10 479	7 792
2000	12	81 395	127	4 023	17 628	20 760	13 616	7 449
01	13	87 569	152	4 178	18 392	23 843	15 164	8 220
02	14	87 147	130	4 063	17 161	24 469	15 533	8 324
03	15	88 719	166	3 984	16 077	25 154	16 510	8 904
04	16	88 438	168	3 834	14 919	25 231	17 270	9 166
05	17	88 709	138	3 560	14 149	25 108	17 902	9 743
06	18	91 921	112	3 821	14 453	25 390	19 500	10 281
07	19	91 533	125	3 754	14 158	24 148	20 681	10 485
08	20	92 532	128	3 708	13 708	23 387	21 834	11 258
09	21	88 828	108	3 181	12 875	21 536	21 133	11 397
10	22	86 440	107	3 183	12 110	20 221	20 855	11 465
11	23	82 423	89	2 808	11 259	18 518	19 723	11 770
12	24	83 325	77	2 758	10 767	18 388	19 565	12 401
13	25	82 997	84	2 731	10 679	18 069	18 717	12 954
14	26	81 142	92	2 743	9 991	17 588	17 939	12 714
15	27	80 381	95	2 617	9 759	17 209	17 114	12 738
16	**28**	**78 528**	**95**	**2 651**	**9 589**	**16 507**	**16 323**	**12 505**

注：1) 昭和22・25年の70～74歳は、70歳以上の数値である。
　　 2) 昭和30～平成17年の75～79歳は、75歳以上の数値である。

妻及び再婚の夫・妻－（各届出年に結婚生活に入り届け出たもの）（つづき）
(for marriages performed and registered each year)：Japan－CON.

45～49	50～54	55～59	60～64	65～69	70～74[1]	75～79[2]	80～	不　詳 Not stated
Groom								
4 301	2 456	1 404	767	324	215	…	…	185
3 901	2 342	1 303	825	351	204	…	…	18
3 509	2 501	1 550	830	461	234	109	…	-
3 801	2 826	1 833	1 001	554	272	129	…	1
3 940	3 228	2 441	1 332	698	323	191	…	-
4 245	2 815	2 212	1 286	722	310	153	…	153
5 066	3 192	1 924	1 260	772	337	185	…	4
4 836	3 382	2 083	1 078	705	377	239	…	1
5 767	4 087	2 704	1 291	689	376	286	…	1
8 004	4 946	3 236	1 746	706	352	290	…	-
10 563	6 193	3 889	2 236	1 162	481	381	…	-
9 242	8 726	5 562	3 011	1 536	800	532	…	-
9 235	9 485	5 625	3 272	1 732	853	533	…	-
8 574	8 477	5 343	3 398	1 702	834	617	…	-
8 730	8 197	5 938	3 770	1 807	917	641	…	1
8 956	7 793	6 270	3 728	1 830	994	622	…	-
9 630	7 669	6 817	3 898	1 935	1 004	752	…	1
10 097	7 689	7 547	3 926	2 079	1 078	543	255	-
10 175	7 284	6 999	3 933	2 127	1 103	538	278	-
10 489	7 136	6 534	4 277	2 158	1 102	563	288	-
10 441	7 072	5 944	4 686	2 258	1 073	597	316	1
10 499	6 837	5 265	4 474	2 210	1 190	601	361	1
10 167	6 564	4 894	4 453	1 953	1 107	590	338	-
10 603	7 125	4 866	4 404	2 110	1 110	653	401	-
11 272	7 189	4 871	3 854	2 309	1 290	631	413	1
11 511	7 412	4 943	3 841	2 480	1 253	622	447	-
11 838	7 710	4 993	3 731	2 576	1 296	594	449	-
12 120	**7 636**	**4 825**	**3 523**	**2 644**	**1 082**	**615**	**414**	**-**
Bride								
968	541	317	191	79	40	…	…	194
962	584	335	144	77	37	…	…	24
998	578	321	143	69	32	7	…	-
1 243	665	318	165	81	22	18	…	-
1 700	969	431	220	112	35	17	…	-
1 977	1 001	518	222	100	43	15	…	106
2 452	1 328	576	258	115	43	24	…	2
2 753	1 603	734	311	140	52	24	…	-
3 936	2 297	1 111	452	184	66	37	…	-
5 515	2 953	1 414	603	236	83	42	…	-
7 415	4 207	2 132	1 004	433	156	79	…	2
6 471	5 733	3 048	1 497	656	260	126	…	1
6 145	5 945	2 867	1 543	696	256	168	…	-
5 887	5 673	3 032	1 680	701	338	156	…	-
5 828	5 595	3 331	1 830	836	332	171	…	1
6 084	5 036	3 488	1 915	825	331	171	…	-
6 071	4 935	3 731	1 896	864	393	217	…	2
6 381	4 591	4 007	1 824	936	408	170	47	-
6 521	4 447	3 738	1 781	988	465	167	75	-
6 841	4 443	3 469	2 028	983	495	180	70	-
6 945	4 473	3 218	2 096	1 087	490	217	72	-
6 967	4 367	3 018	2 196	1 089	545	228	89	-
6 828	4 431	2 867	2 205	1 076	512	243	94	-
7 396	4 712	2 950	2 212	1 108	637	246	108	-
7 721	4 803	2 863	2 098	1 241	656	255	126	-
7 795	5 066	2 877	1 957	1 271	688	285	136	-
8 146	5 400	2 990	1 813	1 361	696	312	131	-
8 559	**5 383**	**2 933**	**1 664**	**1 318**	**584**	**294**	**123**	**-**

婚　姻

表9.8　結婚生活に入ったときの年齢別にみた年次別初婚率・
Table 9.8　Trends in first married rates and remarried rates (per 1,000

初　婚　率
First married rate

年　　次 Year	~19歳[1] Years	20~24	25~29	30~34	35~39	40~44	45~49	50~54	55~59	60~64	65~69	70~74[2]	75~79[3]	80~
\multicolumn{15}{c}{夫（男性人口千対）　　Groom（per 1,000 males）}
1947 昭和22年	3.07	46.05	84.35	18.80	2.78	0.86	0.41	0.22	0.14	0.09	0.06	0.05	…	…
50　25	1.74	32.26	48.23	10.28	1.74	0.52	0.28	0.18	0.11	0.07	0.04	0.04	…	…
55　30	0.65	27.01	61.69	13.56	1.89	0.45	0.20	0.10	0.08	0.04	0.03	0.02	0.01	…
60　35	0.46	29.79	79.98	18.97	2.89	0.62	0.22	0.10	0.07	0.05	0.03	0.02	0.03	…
65　40	0.48	37.70	92.53	23.12	3.41	0.92	0.29	0.12	0.06	0.07	0.04	0.02	0.01	…
70　45	1.28	41.96	100.63	24.31	3.50	0.88	0.32	0.14	0.06	0.04	0.03	0.02	0.02	…
75　50	1.27	46.40	79.91	22.75	3.42	0.75	0.23	0.09	0.05	0.02	0.02	0.02	0.02	…
80　55	1.26	35.04	72.08	26.43	4.13	0.80	0.21	0.08	0.04	0.02	0.01	0.01	0.01	…
85　60	1.44	30.39	73.45	30.42	6.45	1.18	0.30	0.09	0.04	0.02	0.01	0.00	0.00	…
90 平成2年	1.50	26.79	68.00	33.26	8.25	2.04	0.50	0.16	0.06	0.03	0.01	0.01	0.00	…
95　7	2.00	27.38	65.70	34.79	11.02	3.02	0.90	0.24	0.08	0.03	0.02	0.01	0.00	…
2000　12	2.82	27.58	58.06	30.94	11.13	3.47	1.31	0.47	0.15	0.06	0.02	0.01	0.00	…
01　13	2.91	26.93	57.48	30.62	11.26	3.64	1.42	0.56	0.20	0.07	0.03	0.01	0.00	…
02　14	2.72	24.90	54.43	29.92	10.83	3.51	1.37	0.52	0.18	0.07	0.02	0.01	0.01	…
03　15	2.48	23.12	52.36	29.83	11.22	3.67	1.40	0.55	0.22	0.07	0.02	0.01	0.00	…
04　16	2.22	21.84	50.14	29.28	11.24	3.88	1.50	0.62	0.23	0.08	0.03	0.01	0.00	…
05　17	2.02	21.61	50.72	29.53	11.51	3.97	1.57	0.67	0.26	0.09	0.03	0.01	0.00	…
06　18	2.03	21.89	51.74	30.30	11.93	4.29	1.63	0.70	0.29	0.10	0.03	0.01	0.01	0.00
07　19	2.06	21.13	51.13	30.24	12.23	4.35	1.62	0.69	0.31	0.11	0.03	0.01	0.01	0.00
08　20	2.09	21.40	51.81	31.31	12.69	4.55	1.70	0.71	0.32	0.13	0.03	0.01	0.01	0.00
09　21	1.87	20.23	50.62	31.20	12.77	4.66	1.74	0.70	0.31	0.12	0.04	0.01	0.01	0.00
10　22	1.73	20.49	50.67	31.36	13.06	4.81	1.77	0.67	0.30	0.12	0.04	0.01	0.01	0.00
11　23	1.62	18.75	48.78	30.21	12.71	4.75	1.72	0.66	0.30	0.13	0.04	0.01	0.01	0.00
12　24	1.65	18.41	49.70	30.93	13.33	5.12	1.88	0.70	0.31	0.15	0.04	0.02	0.01	0.00
13　25	1.76	17.88	49.75	31.20	13.52	5.31	1.92	0.73	0.31	0.14	0.04	0.02	0.01	0.00
14　26	1.76	16.98	48.58	30.62	13.64	5.42	2.00	0.73	0.32	0.15	0.06	0.02	0.01	0.00
15　27	1.68	16.91	48.25	30.03	13.61	5.44	2.01	0.74	0.32	0.15	0.06	0.02	0.01	0.00
16　28	**1.59**	**16.58**	**48.02**	**29.42**	**13.38**	**5.37**	**2.00**	**0.78**	**0.32**	**0.15**	**0.07**	**0.02**	**0.01**	**0.00**
\multicolumn{15}{c}{妻（女性人口千対）　　Bride（per 1,000 females）}
1947 昭和22年	17.50	72.33	23.38	3.64	0.96	0.45	0.24	0.13	0.09	0.05	0.04	0.01	…	…
50　25	11.81	50.47	14.96	2.73	0.84	0.36	0.18	0.11	0.06	0.04	0.02	0.02	…	…
55　30	7.75	63.36	24.73	3.73	0.96	0.35	0.16	0.08	0.06	0.03	0.01	0.01	0.00	…
60　35	6.35	79.38	38.72	6.37	1.71	0.53	0.21	0.11	0.05	0.02	0.02	0.01	0.01	…
65　40	5.02	96.09	42.30	7.41	2.54	0.93	0.39	0.14	0.07	0.03	0.02	0.01	0.00	…
70　45	7.50	100.43	45.92	6.31	2.30	1.14	0.49	0.15	0.06	0.02	0.01	0.01	0.00	…
75　50	6.27	102.70	48.03	6.17	1.85	0.92	0.53	0.23	0.07	0.03	0.02	0.01	0.01	…
80　55	5.20	85.35	53.46	7.74	1.84	0.66	0.39	0.23	0.10	0.03	0.01	0.01	0.00	…
85　60	4.95	69.91	65.19	9.27	2.25	0.66	0.31	0.20	0.10	0.04	0.01	0.01	0.00	…
90 平成2年	4.59	54.40	68.66	12.73	2.55	0.72	0.31	0.14	0.09	0.04	0.01	0.00	0.00	…
95　7	4.65	48.89	70.64	18.45	3.84	0.83	0.32	0.16	0.08	0.04	0.02	0.01	0.00	…
2000　12	5.93	43.35	65.26	21.90	5.31	1.14	0.31	0.16	0.09	0.04	0.02	0.01	0.00	…
01　13	6.22	42.32	64.98	22.40	5.77	1.22	0.34	0.15	0.08	0.04	0.02	0.01	0.00	…
02　14	5.97	38.84	62.10	22.53	5.81	1.26	0.32	0.13	0.08	0.04	0.02	0.01	0.00	…
03　15	5.63	36.24	60.82	23.29	6.28	1.43	0.36	0.15	0.08	0.04	0.02	0.01	0.00	…
04　16	5.32	34.20	59.41	23.58	6.58	1.51	0.39	0.14	0.07	0.04	0.02	0.01	0.00	…
05　17	4.87	34.12	60.06	24.41	7.24	1.62	0.45	0.13	0.07	0.04	0.02	0.01	0.00	…
06　18	4.87	34.75	61.63	25.83	7.72	1.79	0.46	0.16	0.07	0.04	0.02	0.01	0.00	0.00
07　19	4.70	33.25	61.10	26.17	8.14	1.91	0.48	0.16	0.07	0.04	0.02	0.01	0.01	0.00
08　20	4.68	33.41	61.84	27.71	8.74	2.13	0.53	0.17	0.08	0.03	0.02	0.01	0.01	0.00
09　21	4.29	32.03	60.63	27.99	9.16	2.33	0.55	0.18	0.06	0.04	0.02	0.01	0.01	0.00
10　22	3.90	32.02	60.37	28.46	9.72	2.52	0.62	0.19	0.07	0.04	0.02	0.01	0.01	0.00
11　23	3.70	29.48	58.04	27.80	9.68	2.61	0.66	0.20	0.07	0.04	0.02	0.01	0.00	0.00
12　24	3.60	28.70	59.27	29.15	10.50	2.97	0.74	0.23	0.08	0.04	0.02	0.01	0.00	0.00
13　25	3.66	27.86	59.41	29.76	11.04	3.02	0.82	0.25	0.08	0.04	0.02	0.01	0.00	0.00
14　26	3.48	26.49	58.56	29.31	11.25	3.17	0.81	0.25	0.09	0.04	0.02	0.01	0.00	0.00
15　27	3.24	26.11	58.08	28.83	11.44	3.22	0.90	0.30	0.10	0.04	0.02	0.01	0.01	0.00
16　28	**3.05**	**25.55**	**57.99**	**28.06**	**11.17**	**3.22**	**0.89**	**0.31**	**0.11**	**0.04**	**0.02**	**0.01**	**0.00**	**0.00**

注：1）　19歳以下の人口は15〜19歳の人口を使用している。
　　2）　昭和22・25年の70〜74歳は、70歳以上の数値である。
　　3）　昭和30〜平成17年の75〜79歳は、75歳以上の数値である。

Marriages

再婚率（人口千対）－夫・妻－（各届出年に結婚生活に入り届け出たもの）
population) of marriages by age (for marriages performed and registered each year): Japan

再 婚 率
Remarried rate

年次 Year		~19歳[1] Years	20~24	25~29	30~34	35~39	40~44	45~49	50~54	55~59	60~64	65~69	70~74[2]	75~79[3]	80~
		夫（男性人口千対） Groom (per 1,000 males)													
1947	昭和22年	0.04	0.89	4.43	6.80	5.06	3.13	2.19	1.54	1.07	0.77	0.42	0.44	...	...
50	25	0.02	0.97	3.57	4.45	3.68	2.66	1.93	1.36	0.95	0.74	0.44	0.38	...	...
55	30	0.00	0.44	3.09	3.74	2.83	2.14	1.64	1.30	0.96	0.68	0.50	0.39	0.21	...
60	35	0.00	0.28	2.21	3.40	2.82	2.10	1.68	1.38	1.02	0.70	0.54	0.39	0.21	...
65	40	0.00	0.28	2.13	3.13	2.65	2.17	1.77	1.49	1.26	0.82	0.57	0.41	0.27	...
70	45	0.00	0.32	2.43	3.31	2.57	1.89	1.60	1.32	1.09	0.74	0.52	0.32	0.18	...
75	50	0.00	0.44	2.25	3.31	2.49	1.78	1.39	1.23	0.94	0.65	0.49	0.29	0.17	...
80	55	0.00	0.29	2.07	3.34	2.66	1.63	1.20	0.96	0.84	0.56	0.41	0.29	0.17	...
85	60	0.00	0.33	1.83	3.49	3.12	2.09	1.42	1.05	0.80	0.55	0.39	0.25	0.16	...
90	平成2年	0.00	0.38	2.11	3.65	3.31	2.47	1.79	1.24	0.86	0.54	0.32	0.23	0.13	...
95	7	0.01	0.46	2.36	4.25	3.87	2.60	2.00	1.41	1.00	0.62	0.39	0.25	0.15	...
2000	12	0.01	0.55	2.49	4.65	4.33	2.94	2.08	1.68	1.30	0.81	0.46	0.30	0.17	...
01	13	0.01	0.56	2.68	4.77	4.79	3.10	2.18	1.74	1.38	0.86	0.50	0.31	0.16	...
02	14	0.01	0.56	2.62	4.81	4.71	3.15	2.12	1.61	1.26	0.87	0.49	0.30	0.17	...
03	15	0.01	0.57	2.53	4.78	4.83	3.28	2.22	1.66	1.32	0.94	0.52	0.32	0.17	...
04	16	0.01	0.58	2.45	4.68	4.81	3.48	2.30	1.70	1.32	0.89	0.53	0.34	0.15	...
05	17	0.01	0.53	2.45	4.61	4.99	3.55	2.51	1.76	1.35	0.94	0.55	0.33	0.18	...
06	18	0.01	0.55	2.59	4.84	5.09	3.87	2.65	1.85	1.42	1.00	0.57	0.35	0.23	0.12
07	19	0.00	0.53	2.56	4.72	5.00	3.73	2.66	1.83	1.37	0.96	0.57	0.35	0.22	0.12
08	20	0.01	0.49	2.52	4.73	5.10	3.80	2.72	1.85	1.35	0.98	0.56	0.34	0.23	0.12
09	21	0.01	0.46	2.41	4.60	4.88	3.77	2.69	1.85	1.33	1.02	0.57	0.34	0.24	0.12
10	22	0.01	0.48	2.26	4.48	4.76	3.71	2.61	1.80	1.23	0.91	0.56	0.37	0.23	0.13
11	23	0.01	0.46	2.17	4.31	4.60	3.52	2.57	1.74	1.20	0.86	0.52	0.33	0.22	0.12
12	24	0.01	0.44	2.14	4.40	4.74	3.70	2.60	1.87	1.24	0.88	0.54	0.32	0.24	0.13
13	25	0.01	0.47	2.18	4.48	4.79	3.73	2.70	1.88	1.28	0.82	0.55	0.37	0.23	0.13
14	26	0.01	0.46	2.07	4.29	4.74	3.59	2.69	1.92	1.31	0.88	0.56	0.34	0.23	0.13
15	27	0.01	0.45	2.08	4.21	4.71	3.65	2.71	1.94	1.33	0.89	0.55	0.36	0.21	0.13
16	**28**	**0.01**	**0.47**	**2.00**	**4.15**	**4.67**	**3.54**	**2.62**	**1.95**	**1.30**	**0.88**	**0.53**	**0.31**	**0.21**	**0.11**
		妻（女性人口千対） Bride (per 1,000 females)													
1947	昭和22年	0.18	3.47	7.80	4.37	1.51	0.76	0.51	0.35	0.24	0.17	0.08	0.06	...	...
50	25	0.11	1.73	3.88	3.31	1.53	0.76	0.48	0.35	0.24	0.12	0.08	0.05	...	...
55	30	0.03	1.02	2.28	1.98	1.20	0.65	0.45	0.30	0.20	0.11	0.07	0.04	0.01	...
60	35	0.02	0.76	1.94	1.74	1.22	0.73	0.49	0.31	0.17	0.11	0.07	0.03	0.02	...
65	40	0.01	0.85	2.11	1.81	1.27	0.87	0.63	0.39	0.21	0.13	0.08	0.04	0.01	...
70	45	0.02	0.88	2.56	1.98	1.29	0.86	0.62	0.38	0.22	0.11	0.06	0.04	0.01	...
75	50	0.03	1.11	2.86	2.40	1.52	0.92	0.66	0.42	0.22	0.11	0.06	0.03	0.01	...
80	55	0.02	0.86	3.30	2.83	1.71	1.02	0.68	0.44	0.24	0.12	0.06	0.03	0.01	...
85	60	0.03	0.88	3.12	3.38	2.26	1.38	0.95	0.58	0.31	0.15	0.08	0.03	0.01	...
90	平成2年	0.03	0.85	3.25	3.70	2.48	1.63	1.22	0.72	0.36	0.17	0.08	0.04	0.01	...
95	7	0.03	0.95	3.46	4.20	2.74	1.76	1.41	0.94	0.53	0.26	0.13	0.06	0.02	...
2000	12	0.04	0.99	3.73	4.89	3.45	1.95	1.47	1.10	0.69	0.38	0.18	0.08	0.02	...
01	13	0.04	1.07	3.93	5.30	3.91	2.17	1.46	1.08	0.68	0.38	0.18	0.08	0.03	...
02	14	0.04	1.07	3.78	5.34	3.87	2.18	1.47	1.07	0.69	0.40	0.18	0.10	0.02	...
03	15	0.05	1.07	3.68	5.36	4.02	2.32	1.49	1.12	0.72	0.43	0.22	0.10	0.03	...
04	16	0.05	1.05	3.57	5.31	4.10	2.37	1.57	1.09	0.72	0.43	0.21	0.09	0.02	...
05	17	0.04	1.02	3.56	5.31	4.22	2.47	1.59	1.13	0.72	0.43	0.22	0.11	0.03	...
06	18	0.04	1.10	3.78	5.46	4.35	2.65	1.69	1.10	0.74	0.44	0.24	0.11	0.06	0.01
07	19	0.04	1.10	3.82	5.36	4.54	2.63	1.72	1.12	0.71	0.41	0.24	0.13	0.05	0.02
08	20	0.04	1.11	3.80	5.41	4.70	2.76	1.80	1.15	0.70	0.45	0.24	0.13	0.06	0.01
09	21	0.04	0.98	3.62	5.22	4.50	2.74	1.82	1.17	0.70	0.44	0.25	0.13	0.07	0.01
10	22	0.04	1.03	3.45	5.01	4.38	2.69	1.76	1.15	0.69	0.43	0.25	0.15	0.07	0.02
11	23	0.03	0.93	3.28	4.77	4.20	2.61	1.76	1.18	0.69	0.41	0.26	0.13	0.07	0.02
12	24	0.03	0.93	3.21	4.90	4.29	2.70	1.85	1.24	0.74	0.43	0.26	0.16	0.07	0.02
13	25	0.03	0.93	3.27	4.95	4.27	2.76	1.88	1.26	0.74	0.43	0.28	0.16	0.07	0.02
14	26	0.03	0.94	3.16	4.92	4.29	2.68	1.86	1.32	0.76	0.43	0.27	0.16	0.07	0.02
15	27	0.03	0.91	3.17	4.87	4.23	2.67	1.91	1.38	0.79	0.42	0.27	0.17	0.09	0.02
16	**28**	**0.03**	**0.92**	**3.19**	**4.78**	**4.19**	**2.66**	**1.90**	**1.39**	**0.78**	**0.41**	**0.25**	**0.15**	**0.08**	**0.02**

婚　姻

表9.9　結婚生活に入ったときの年齢別に
（平成28年に結婚生活に

Table 9.9　Marriages and percent distribution by marriage order and age

夫
Groom

平成28年

夫の年齢 Age of groom	総　数 Total			夫　初　婚 First married groom			夫　再　婚 Remarried groom		
	総　数 Total	妻初婚 First married bride	妻再婚 Remarried bride	総　数 Total	妻初婚 First married bride	妻再婚 Remarried bride	総　数 Total	妻初婚 First married bride	妻再婚 Remarried bride
実　数　Number									
総　数　Total	496 425	417 897	78 528	405 024	370 788	34 236	91 401	47 109	44 292
〜19歳　Years	4 893	4 786	107	4 875	4 776	99	18	10	8
20〜24	51 595	48 756	2 839	50 176	47 833	2 343	1 419	923	496
25〜29	156 407	147 686	8 721	150 156	143 451	6 705	6 251	4 235	2 016
30〜34	120 132	106 674	13 458	105 275	96 822	8 453	14 857	9 852	5 005
35〜39	72 776	59 011	13 765	53 956	47 330	6 626	18 820	11 681	7 139
40〜44	43 234	30 596	12 638	26 057	21 117	4 940	17 177	9 479	7 698
45〜49	21 363	12 129	9 234	9 243	6 741	2 502	12 120	5 388	6 732
50〜54	10 677	4 448	6 229	3 041	1 800	1 241	7 636	2 648	4 988
55〜59	6 031	1 940	4 091	1 206	575	631	4 825	1 365	3 460
60〜64	4 117	1 006	3 111	594	215	379	3 523	791	2 732
65〜69	2 976	571	2 405	332	98	234	2 644	473	2 171
70〜74	1 154	164	990	72	22	50	1 082	142	940
75〜79	642	76	566	27	4	23	615	72	543
80〜	426	52	374	12	2	10	414	50	364
不　詳 Not stated	2	2	-	2	2	-	-	-	-
百　分　率　Percentage									
総　数　Total	100.0	84.2	15.8	100.0	91.5	8.5	100.0	51.5	48.5
〜19歳　Years	100.0	97.8	2.2	100.0	98.0	2.0	100.0	55.6	44.4
20〜24	100.0	94.5	5.5	100.0	95.3	4.7	100.0	65.0	35.0
25〜29	100.0	94.4	5.6	100.0	95.5	4.5	100.0	67.7	32.3
30〜34	100.0	88.8	11.2	100.0	92.0	8.0	100.0	66.3	33.7
35〜39	100.0	81.1	18.9	100.0	87.7	12.3	100.0	62.1	37.9
40〜44	100.0	70.8	29.2	100.0	81.0	19.0	100.0	55.2	44.8
45〜49	100.0	56.8	43.2	100.0	72.9	27.1	100.0	44.5	55.5
50〜54	100.0	41.7	58.3	100.0	59.2	40.8	100.0	34.7	65.3
55〜59	100.0	32.2	67.8	100.0	47.7	52.3	100.0	28.3	71.7
60〜64	100.0	24.4	75.6	100.0	36.2	63.8	100.0	22.5	77.5
65〜69	100.0	19.2	80.8	100.0	29.5	70.5	100.0	17.9	82.1
70〜74	100.0	14.2	85.8	100.0	30.6	69.4	100.0	13.1	86.9
75〜79	100.0	11.8	88.2	100.0	14.8	85.2	100.0	11.7	88.3
80〜	100.0	12.2	87.8	100.0	16.7	83.3	100.0	12.1	87.9

Marriages

みた夫妻の初婚－再婚別件数及び百分率
入り届け出たもの）
at marriage (for marriages performed and registered in 2016): Japan, 2016

妻
Bride

平成28年

妻の年齢 Age of bride	総　数 Total			妻　初　婚 First married bride			妻　再　婚 Remarried bride		
	総　数 Total	夫初婚 First married groom	夫再婚 Remarried groom	総　数 Total	夫初婚 First married groom	夫再婚 Remarried groom	総　数 Total	夫初婚 First married groom	夫再婚 Remarried groom
実　数　Number									
総　数　Total	496 425	405 024	91 401	417 897	370 788	47 109	78 528	34 236	44 292
～19歳　Years	8 921	8 221	700	8 826	8 172	654	95	49	46
20～24	76 028	69 042	6 986	73 377	67 428	5 949	2 651	1 614	1 037
25～29	183 655	168 260	15 395	174 066	162 422	11 644	9 589	5 838	3 751
30～34	113 510	94 431	19 079	97 003	84 989	12 014	16 507	9 442	7 065
35～39	59 846	42 571	17 275	43 523	34 438	9 085	16 323	8 133	8 190
40～44	27 647	15 333	12 314	15 142	10 432	4 710	12 505	4 901	7 604
45～49	12 584	4 525	8 059	4 025	2 213	1 812	8 559	2 312	6 247
50～54	6 574	1 590	4 984	1 191	475	716	5 383	1 115	4 268
55～59	3 337	574	2 763	404	125	279	2 933	449	2 484
60～64	1 840	245	1 595	176	51	125	1 664	194	1 470
65～69	1 416	153	1 263	98	30	68	1 318	123	1 195
70～74	623	49	574	39	8	31	584	41	543
75～79	304	18	286	10	2	8	294	16	278
80～	138	10	128	15	1	14	123	9	114
不　詳 Not stated	2	2	-	2	2	-	-	-	-
百　分　率　Percentage									
総　数　Total	100. 0	81. 6	18. 4	100. 0	88. 7	11. 3	100. 0	43. 6	56. 4
～19歳　Years	100. 0	92. 2	7. 8	100. 0	92. 6	7. 4	100. 0	51. 6	48. 4
20～24	100. 0	90. 8	9. 2	100. 0	91. 9	8. 1	100. 0	60. 9	39. 1
25～29	100. 0	91. 6	8. 4	100. 0	93. 3	6. 7	100. 0	60. 9	39. 1
30～34	100. 0	83. 2	16. 8	100. 0	87. 6	12. 4	100. 0	57. 2	42. 8
35～39	100. 0	71. 1	28. 9	100. 0	79. 1	20. 9	100. 0	49. 8	50. 2
40～44	100. 0	55. 5	44. 5	100. 0	68. 9	31. 1	100. 0	39. 2	60. 8
45～49	100. 0	36. 0	64. 0	100. 0	55. 0	45. 0	100. 0	27. 0	73. 0
50～54	100. 0	24. 2	75. 8	100. 0	39. 9	60. 1	100. 0	20. 7	79. 3
55～59	100. 0	17. 2	82. 8	100. 0	30. 9	69. 1	100. 0	15. 3	84. 7
60～64	100. 0	13. 3	86. 7	100. 0	29. 0	71. 0	100. 0	11. 7	88. 3
65～69	100. 0	10. 8	89. 2	100. 0	30. 6	69. 4	100. 0	9. 3	90. 7
70～74	100. 0	7. 9	92. 1	100. 0	20. 5	79. 5	100. 0	7. 0	93. 0
75～79	100. 0	5. 9	94. 1	100. 0	20. 0	80. 0	100. 0	5. 4	94. 6
80～	100. 0	7. 2	92. 8	100. 0	6. 7	93. 3	100. 0	7. 3	92. 7

Marriages

表9.10 結婚生活に入ったときの年齢別にみた夫・妻の初婚－再婚別件数 百分率[1][2]
（平成28年に結婚生活に入り届け出たもの）

Table 9.10 Percent distribution of marriages by marriage order and age at marriage (for marriages performed and registered in 2016): Japan, 2016

平成28年

夫妻の年齢 Age of bride and groom	夫 Groom			妻 Bride		
	総　数 Total	初　婚 First married	再　婚 Remarried	総　数 Total	初　婚 First married	再　婚 Remarried
総　数　Total	100.0	100.0	100.0	100.0	100.0	100.0
～19歳　Years	1.0	1.2	0.0	1.8	2.1	0.1
20～24	10.4	12.4	1.6	15.3	17.6	3.4
25～29	31.5	37.1	6.8	37.0	41.7	12.2
30～34	24.2	26.0	16.3	22.9	23.2	21.0
35～39	14.7	13.3	20.6	12.1	10.4	20.8
40～44	8.7	6.4	18.8	5.6	3.6	15.9
45～49	4.3	2.3	13.3	2.5	1.0	10.9
50～54	2.2	0.8	8.4	1.3	0.3	6.9
55～59	1.2	0.3	5.3	0.7	0.1	3.7
60～64	0.8	0.1	3.9	0.4	0.0	2.1
65～69	0.6	0.1	2.9	0.3	0.0	1.7
70～74	0.2	0.0	1.2	0.1	0.0	0.7
75～79	0.1	0.0	0.7	0.1	0.0	0.4
80～	0.1	0.0	0.5	0.0	0.0	0.2

注：1)　実数は上巻婚姻第9.7表を参照されたい。
　　2)　年齢不詳を除く総数に対する百分率である。

婚　姻

表 9.11　年次別平均婚姻年齢[1]
Table 9.11　Trends in mean age of bride and in mean age between bride and

年　　次[2] Year		全　婚　姻 Mean age of marriages		初　　婚 Mean age of first married		年　齢　差 Difference in mean age between bride and groom	
		夫 Groom	妻 Bride	夫 Groom	妻 Bride	全　婚　姻 Marriages	初　　婚 First married
1899	明治32年	27.6	23.0	…	…	4.6	…
1900	33	27.7	23.1	…	…	4.6	…
01	34	27.7	23.2	…	…	4.5	…
02	35	27.8	23.2	…	…	4.6	…
03	36	27.9	23.3	…	…	4.6	…
04	37	27.9	23.5	…	…	4.4	…
05	38	28.6	24.0	…	…	4.6	…
06	39	28.8	24.0	…	…	4.8	…
07	40	28.4	23.8	…	…	4.6	…
08	41	28.5	23.9	26.8	22.9	4.6	3.9
09	42	28.6	23.9	26.9	22.9	4.7	4.0
1910	43	28.7	24.0	27.0	23.0	4.7	4.0
11	44	28.7	24.0	26.9	22.9	4.7	4.0
12	大正元年	28.7	24.0	27.0	22.9	4.7	4.1
13	2	28.7	24.0	27.0	22.9	4.7	4.1
14	3	28.7	24.0	27.1	23.0	4.7	4.1
15	4	29.1	24.3	27.4	23.2	4.8	4.2
16	5	28.9	24.0	27.1	23.0	4.9	4.1
17	6	28.9	24.1	27.2	23.1	4.8	4.1
18	7	29.2	24.3	27.3	23.2	4.9	4.1
19	8	29.2	24.4	27.4	23.3	4.8	4.1
1920	9	29.2	24.2	27.4	23.2	5.0	4.2
21	10	28.9	24.0	27.1	23.0	4.9	4.1
22	11	28.8	24.0	27.1	23.0	4.8	4.1
23	12	28.7	23.9	27.0	23.0	4.8	4.0
24	13	28.7	24.0	27.1	23.1	4.7	4.0
25	14	28.8	24.0	27.1	23.1	4.8	4.0
26	昭和元年	28.8	24.0	27.1	23.1	4.8	4.0
27	2	28.8	24.0	27.2	23.1	4.8	4.1
28	3	28.8	24.0	27.3	23.1	4.8	4.2
29	4	28.9	24.1	27.4	23.2	4.8	4.2
1930	5	28.9	24.1	27.3	23.2	4.8	4.1
31	6	28.8	24.1	27.3	23.3	4.7	4.0
32	7	28.9	24.2	27.4	23.1	4.7	4.0
33	8	29.1	24.4	27.6	23.6	4.7	4.0
34	9	29.2	24.5	27.7	23.7	4.7	4.0
35	10	29.0	24.6	27.8	23.8	4.4	4.0
36	11	29.3	24.7	27.9	23.9	4.6	4.0
37	12	29.4	25.0	28.1	24.2	4.4	3.9
38	13	30.0	25.3	28.4	24.4	4.7	4.0
39	14	29.8	25.0	28.7	24.5	4.8	4.2
1940	15	30.0	24.9	29.0	24.6	5.1	4.4
41	16	29.6	24.6	28.7	24.3	5.0	4.4
42	17	31.2	26.0	29.8	25.3	5.2	4.5
43	18	31.0	26.1	29.5	25.0	4.9	4.5
47	22	…	…	26.1	22.9	…	3.2
48	23	…	…	26.1	23.0	…	3.1
49	24	…	…	25.9	22.9	…	3.0
1950	25	…	…	25.9	23.0	…	2.9
51	26	…	…	25.9	23.1	…	2.8
52	27	27.3	23.9	26.1	23.3	3.4	2.8
53	28	27.4	24.0	26.2	23.4	3.4	2.8
54	29	27.5	24.1	26.4	23.6	3.4	2.8

注：1)　平成3年までの夫または妻の平均婚姻年齢は出生年月及び同居年月による年齢の算術平均値に0.46歳を加え、平成4年以降は月齢の算術平均値から算出している。
　　 2)　昭和18年までは届出時の年齢、昭和22～42年までは結婚式をあげたときの年齢、昭和43年以降は結婚式をあげたときまたは同居を始めたときのうち早い方の年齢である。
　　 　　 昭和19～21年は資料不備のため省略した。なお、昭和22年以降は各年に同居し届け出たものについての集計である。

Marriages

及び夫妻の年齢差
groom at marriage and difference
groom : Japan

年　　次		全　婚　姻 Mean age of marriages		初　　婚 Mean age of first married		年　齢　差 Difference in mean age between bride and groom	
Year		夫 Groom	妻 Bride	夫 Groom	妻 Bride	全　婚　姻 Marriages	初　　婚 First married
1955	昭和30年	27.7	24.3	26.6	23.8	3.4	2.8
56	31	27.8	24.4	26.8	23.9	3.4	2.9
57	32	27.9	24.5	26.9	24.0	3.4	2.9
58	33	27.9	24.6	27.0	24.2	3.3	2.8
59	34	28.0	24.7	27.1	24.3	3.3	2.8
1960	35	28.1	24.8	27.2	24.4	3.3	2.8
61	36	28.1	24.8	27.3	24.5	3.3	2.8
62	37	28.1	24.8	27.3	24.5	3.3	2.8
63	38	28.1	24.8	27.3	24.5	3.3	2.8
64	39	28.1	24.8	27.3	24.4	3.3	2.9
65	40	28.1	24.9	27.2	24.5	3.2	2.7
66	41	28.1	24.9	27.3	24.5	3.2	2.8
67	42	28.0	24.9	27.2	24.5	3.1	2.7
68	43	27.9	24.8	27.2	24.4	3.1	2.8
69	44	27.8	24.7	27.1	24.3	3.1	2.8
1970	45	27.6	24.6	26.9	24.2	3.0	2.7
71	46	27.5	24.5	26.8	24.2	3.0	2.6
72	47	27.4	24.7	26.7	24.2	2.7	2.5
73	48	27.4	24.7	26.7	24.3	2.7	2.4
74	49	27.6	25.0	26.8	24.5	2.6	2.3
75	50	27.8	25.2	27.0	24.7	2.6	2.3
76	51	28.0	25.4	27.2	24.9	2.6	2.3
77	52	28.2	25.6	27.4	25.0	2.6	2.4
78	53	28.5	25.7	27.6	25.1	2.8	2.5
79	54	28.6	25.8	27.7	25.2	2.8	2.5
1980	55	28.7	25.9	27.8	25.2	2.8	2.6
81	56	28.9	26.0	27.9	25.3	2.8	2.6
82	57	29.0	26.1	28.0	25.3	2.9	2.7
83	58	29.0	26.1	28.0	25.4	2.9	2.7
84	59	29.1	26.2	28.1	25.4	2.9	2.7
85	60	29.3	26.4	28.2	25.5	2.9	2.7
86	61	29.5	26.5	28.3	25.6	2.9	2.7
87	62	29.6	26.7	28.4	25.7	2.9	2.7
88	63	29.7	26.8	28.4	25.8	2.9	2.6
89	平成元年	29.8	26.9	28.5	25.8	2.9	2.6
1990	2	29.7	26.9	28.4	25.9	2.8	2.5
91	3	29.6	26.9	28.4	25.9	2.8	2.5
92	4	29.7	27.0	28.4	26.0	2.7	2.4
93	5	29.7	27.1	28.4	26.1	2.6	2.3
94	6	29.8	27.2	28.5	26.2	2.6	2.3
95	7	29.8	27.3	28.5	26.3	2.5	2.2
96	8	29.9	27.5	28.5	26.4	2.4	2.1
97	9	29.9	27.6	28.5	26.6	2.3	1.9
98	10	30.0	27.7	28.6	26.7	2.3	1.9
99	11	30.2	27.9	28.7	26.8	2.3	1.9
2000	12	30.4	28.2	28.8	27.0	2.2	1.8
01	13	30.6	28.4	29.0	27.2	2.2	1.8
02	14	30.8	28.6	29.1	27.4	2.2	1.8
03	15	31.2	29.0	29.4	27.6	2.2	1.8
04	16	31.5	29.2	29.6	27.8	2.3	1.8
05	17	31.7	29.4	29.8	28.0	2.3	1.8
06	18	32.0	29.6	30.0	28.2	2.4	1.8
07	19	32.1	29.8	30.1	28.3	2.3	1.8
08	20	32.2	29.9	30.2	28.5	2.3	1.8
09	21	32.4	30.1	30.4	28.6	2.3	1.8
2010	22	32.5	30.3	30.5	28.8	2.2	1.7
11	23	32.7	30.5	30.7	29.0	2.2	1.7
12	24	32.9	30.7	30.8	29.2	2.2	1.7
13	25	33.0	30.8	30.9	29.3	2.2	1.7
14	26	33.2	30.9	31.1	29.4	2.2	1.7
15	27	33.3	31.1	31.1	29.4	2.2	1.7
16	28	33.3	31.1	31.1	29.4	2.2	1.7

535

婚　姻

表9.12　都道府県別にみた年次別平均
Table 9.12　Trends in mean age of bride and groom prefecture (for marriages performed and

初婚の夫
First married groom

都道府県[3)] Prefecture	1950 昭和25年	1955 30年	1960 35年	1965 40年	1970 45年	1975 50年	1980 55年	1985 60年	1990 平成2年	1995 7年
全　国　Total	25.9	26.6	27.2	27.2	26.9	27.0	27.8	28.2	28.4	28.5
01 北 海 道 [a)]	26.1	26.5	26.9	26.8	26.3	26.2	27.2	27.7	28.0	28.1
02 青　　森	25.1	25.8	26.4	26.5	26.1	26.2	27.1	27.7	28.1	28.2
03 岩　　手	24.8	25.7	26.4	26.7	26.5	26.5	27.2	28.0	28.2	28.4
04 宮　　城	25.5	26.3	26.8	27.0	26.5	26.5	27.3	27.8	28.2	28.3
05 秋　　田	25.3	25.9	26.5	26.8	26.4	26.4	27.4	28.0	28.6	28.6
06 山　　形	25.4	25.7	26.4	26.7	26.4	26.5	27.4	28.0	28.6	28.7
07 福　　島	25.0	25.7	26.4	26.7	26.2	26.3	27.2	27.8	28.2	28.2
08 茨　　城	25.4	26.1	26.8	27.0	26.9	26.9	27.7	28.1	28.3	28.3
09 栃　　木	25.4	26.2	26.9	27.1	26.5	26.6	27.5	28.0	28.1	28.4
10 群　　馬	25.6	26.3	27.0	26.9	26.6	26.8	27.7	28.1	28.1	28.4
11 埼　　玉	25.8	26.5	27.3	27.3	27.2	27.3	28.2	28.5	28.5	28.6
12 千　　葉	25.6	26.5	27.2	27.4	27.1	27.3	28.1	28.5	28.6	28.7
13 東　　京	27.7	28.1	28.1	27.8	27.5	27.6	28.6	29.0	29.3	29.6
14 神 奈 川	26.8	27.5	27.9	27.7	27.4	27.4	28.4	28.7	28.8	29.0
15 新　　潟	25.5	25.9	26.7	26.9	26.5	26.6	27.6	28.0	28.4	28.5
16 富　　山	24.9	25.6	26.2	26.3	26.1	26.4	27.4	27.7	27.9	27.9
17 石　　川	25.4	25.9	26.5	26.4	26.0	26.4	27.3	27.8	28.0	28.0
18 福　　井	25.0	25.8	26.4	26.5	26.4	26.4	27.4	27.7	28.1	28.3
19 山　　梨	27.0	27.5	28.2	28.1	27.7	27.5	28.3	28.6	28.7	28.9
20 長　　野	26.8	27.4	27.9	27.9	27.5	27.3	28.5	28.8	28.9	28.9
21 岐　　阜	25.6	26.4	26.8	26.9	26.6	26.8	27.6	27.9	28.1	28.1
22 静　　岡	25.6	26.3	27.0	27.0	26.8	26.9	27.8	28.2	28.4	28.6
23 愛　　知	25.7	26.5	26.9	27.0	26.8	26.9	27.7	27.9	28.0	28.2
24 三　　重	25.3	26.1	26.8	27.0	26.7	26.8	27.5	27.7	27.8	28.2
25 滋　　賀	26.0	26.8	27.5	27.6	27.2	27.0	28.0	28.2	28.2	28.3
26 京　　都	26.4	27.2	27.8	27.7	27.3	27.3	28.2	28.3	28.5	28.4
27 大　　阪	26.6	27.3	27.5	27.2	27.1	27.2	28.0	28.1	28.2	28.2
28 兵　　庫	25.2	27.0	27.4	27.4	27.1	27.1	27.9	28.2	28.2	28.3
29 奈　　良	25.6	26.3	26.9	27.2	27.1	27.0	27.9	28.1	28.3	28.3
30 和 歌 山	26.3	26.7	27.4	27.3	27.0	27.0	27.6	27.8	28.0	28.0
31 鳥　　取	25.1	25.4	26.3	26.6	26.4	26.5	27.5	28.0	28.3	28.1
32 島　　根	25.3	26.0	26.8	27.3	26.8	26.8	27.6	28.1	28.4	28.4
33 岡　　山	25.1	25.7	26.4	26.5	26.2	26.4	27.3	27.6	27.8	27.7
34 広　　島	26.0	26.5	27.0	27.0	26.6	26.7	27.6	28.0	27.9	28.0
35 山　　口	26.3	26.8	27.3	27.5	26.8	26.9	27.7	28.1	28.1	27.9
36 徳　　島	24.7	25.3	26.1	26.3	26.0	26.2	27.3	27.7	27.8	28.0
37 香　　川	25.2	25.7	26.3	26.5	26.1	26.4	27.3	27.6	27.9	27.7
38 愛　　媛	25.5	26.2	26.8	26.8	26.3	26.5	27.3	27.7	27.9	28.0
39 高　　知	25.3	25.9	26.7	26.9	26.4	26.6	27.7	28.2	28.3	28.1
40 福　　岡	25.9	26.6	27.3	27.4	26.9	26.8	27.6	28.1	28.3	28.3
41 佐　　賀	25.7	26.3	27.0	27.3	26.7	26.6	27.4	27.9	28.4	28.4
42 長　　崎	25.7	26.5	27.2	27.4	26.7	26.5	27.5	28.1	28.6	28.4
43 熊　　本	25.6	26.3	27.0	27.2	26.5	26.5	27.3	27.8	28.2	28.4
44 大　　分	25.4	26.2	26.8	27.2	26.4	26.4	27.2	27.9	28.3	28.2
45 宮　　崎	25.2	26.0	26.6	26.9	26.3	26.3	27.2	27.7	28.4	28.1
46 鹿 児 島	26.2	26.6	27.3	27.6	27.2	26.8	27.5	28.2	28.7	28.9
47 沖　　縄	…	…	…	…	…	26.6	27.3	27.9	28.3	28.4

注：1)　昭和25年・30年・35年・40年は結婚式をあげたときの年齢、昭和45年以降は結婚式をあげたときまたは同居を始めたときのうち早いほうの年齢である。
　　　　平成2年までの夫または妻の平均婚姻年齢は出生年月及び同居年月による年齢の算術平均値に0.46歳を加え、平成7年以降は月齢の算術平均値から算出している。
　　　2)　実数は中巻第6表を参照されたい。
　　　3)　昭和25年は挙式寸前の夫の住所、昭和30年以降は届出時の夫の住所である。

Marriages

婚姻年齢[1] －初婚の夫・初婚の妻－（各届出年に結婚生活に入り届け出たもの）[2]
at marriage (for first marriage) by each
registered each year): Japan

2000 12年	2005 17年	2009 21年	2010 22年	2011 23年	2012 24年	2013 25年	2014 26年	2015 27年	2016 28年	都道府県[3] Prefecture
28.8	29.8	30.4	30.5	30.7	30.8	30.9	31.1	31.1	31.1	全 国 Total
28.3	29.2	29.8	30.1	30.2	30.4	30.4	30.7	30.7	30.7	01 北 海 道 a)
28.2	29.0	30.0	29.9	30.2	30.4	30.5	30.6	30.6	30.5	02 青　　森
28.5	29.3	30.2	30.1	30.4	30.2	30.3	30.6	30.9	30.6	03 岩　　手
28.3	29.5	30.0	30.1	30.2	30.4	30.7	30.8	30.8	31.0	04 宮　　城
28.5	29.2	30.0	30.2	30.3	30.5	30.7	31.0	30.8	30.8	05 秋　　田
29.0	29.3	29.9	29.9	30.1	30.4	30.5	30.3	30.6	30.8	06 山　　形
28.3	29.0	29.4	29.7	29.6	29.9	29.8	30.2	30.3	30.5	07 福　　島
28.6	29.7	30.2	30.4	30.6	30.6	30.7	30.8	30.8	31.1	08 茨　　城
28.4	29.7	30.2	30.4	30.4	30.6	30.7	30.7	30.9	31.1	09 栃　　木
28.5	29.6	30.2	30.3	30.6	30.6	30.6	30.8	31.0	30.9	10 群　　馬
29.1	30.2	30.8	30.9	31.1	31.3	31.3	31.4	31.5	31.5	11 埼　　玉
29.2	30.3	30.8	31.0	31.0	31.2	31.3	31.4	31.5	31.4	12 千　　葉
30.1	31.2	31.6	31.8	31.9	32.1	32.2	32.3	32.4	32.3	13 東　　京
29.5	30.6	31.1	31.3	31.5	31.5	31.7	31.8	31.9	31.9	14 神 奈 川
28.6	29.7	30.3	30.3	30.5	30.6	30.6	30.8	30.8	30.7	15 新　　潟
28.2	29.7	30.3	30.6	30.7	30.8	30.5	31.0	30.8	30.9	16 富　　山
28.2	29.6	30.1	30.5	30.3	30.4	30.5	30.8	30.7	30.9	17 石　　川
28.6	29.3	30.0	30.2	30.3	30.3	30.4	30.2	30.6	30.5	18 福　　井
29.3	30.1	30.8	30.8	31.0	31.0	30.8	31.1	31.3	31.5	19 山　　梨
29.2	30.2	30.7	30.9	31.1	31.2	31.2	31.4	31.3	31.3	20 長　　野
28.4	29.5	30.1	30.1	30.4	30.5	30.7	30.6	30.6	30.8	21 岐　　阜
28.7	29.8	30.2	30.4	30.5	30.7	30.8	31.0	31.0	31.1	22 静　　岡
28.6	29.7	30.2	30.3	30.5	30.6	30.7	30.8	30.8	30.9	23 愛　　知
28.3	29.2	29.8	30.0	30.2	30.3	30.5	30.5	30.7	30.7	24 三　　重
28.5	29.6	29.9	30.0	30.4	30.3	30.5	30.5	30.7	30.7	25 滋　　賀
28.8	29.9	30.6	30.9	30.9	31.1	31.3	31.3	31.3	31.3	26 京　　都
28.8	29.9	30.4	30.5	30.7	30.8	30.8	31.0	31.1	31.0	27 大　　阪
28.6	29.7	30.2	30.3	30.4	30.6	30.7	30.8	30.8	30.9	28 兵　　庫
28.7	29.7	30.2	30.4	30.7	30.8	30.8	31.0	31.0	31.1	29 奈　　良
28.2	29.1	29.7	29.7	29.9	30.0	30.2	30.3	30.2	30.5	30 和 歌 山
28.0	29.1	29.7	30.0	30.1	30.5	30.7	30.7	30.8	30.5	31 鳥　　取
28.3	29.1	29.8	30.0	30.3	30.4	30.5	30.7	30.4	30.4	32 島　　根
27.9	29.2	29.6	30.0	30.0	30.2	30.1	30.4	30.2	30.4	33 岡　　山
28.3	29.3	29.8	30.0	30.1	30.2	30.4	30.5	30.3	30.4	34 広　　島
28.0	28.9	29.6	29.9	29.9	30.0	30.0	30.2	30.1	30.1	35 山　　口
28.0	29.2	29.8	29.6	30.0	30.4	30.2	30.4	30.6	30.4	36 徳　　島
27.9	28.9	29.6	30.0	30.0	30.1	30.4	30.3	30.2	30.4	37 香　　川
28.0	29.0	29.4	29.8	29.9	30.0	30.1	30.3	30.2	30.3	38 愛　　媛
28.2	29.5	30.2	30.3	30.5	30.7	30.6	30.6	31.3	30.9	39 高　　知
28.4	29.4	29.9	30.1	30.3	30.5	30.5	30.7	30.7	30.8	40 福　　岡
28.0	29.0	29.6	29.6	29.9	30.0	30.0	29.9	30.2	30.2	41 佐　　賀
28.3	29.0	29.5	29.7	29.9	30.1	30.2	30.4	30.3	30.2	42 長　　崎
28.1	28.8	29.4	29.7	29.7	30.0	30.1	30.3	30.3	30.2	43 熊　　本
28.1	29.1	29.8	29.8	30.0	30.3	30.2	30.5	30.3	30.5	44 大　　分
27.9	28.8	29.3	29.5	29.8	29.8	30.0	30.1	29.9	29.9	45 宮　　崎
28.4	29.0	29.5	29.7	29.9	30.0	30.3	30.5	30.4	30.3	46 鹿 児 島
28.3	29.1	29.8	29.9	29.9	29.9	30.1	30.3	30.3	30.3	47 沖　　縄

Note : a)　See page 44.

婚　姻

表9.12　都道府県別にみた年次別平均
Table 9.12　Trends in mean age of bride and groom prefecture (for marriages performed and

初婚の妻
First married bride

都 道 府 県 [3)] Prefecture	1950 昭和25年	1955 30年	1960 35年	1965 40年	1970 45年	1975 50年	1980 55年	1985 60年	1990 平成2年	1995 7年
全　国　Total	23.0	23.8	24.4	24.5	24.2	24.7	25.2	25.5	25.9	26.3
01 北 海 道 [a)]	22.7	23.3	23.8	23.9	23.7	24.4	25.1	25.4	25.8	26.2
02 青　　森	21.8	22.6	23.4	23.4	23.2	23.7	24.4	24.9	25.5	26.1
03 岩　　手	21.8	22.8	23.5	23.8	23.7	24.1	24.6	25.4	25.7	26.2
04 宮　　城	22.7	23.4	24.1	24.2	23.8	24.2	24.8	25.4	25.8	26.1
05 秋　　田	22.0	22.8	23.5	23.8	23.5	24.0	24.7	25.4	26.1	26.3
06 山　　形	22.9	23.4	23.9	24.2	23.8	24.3	24.9	25.4	26.0	26.2
07 福　　島	22.6	23.3	24.0	24.2	23.7	24.1	24.8	25.3	25.7	25.9
08 茨　　城	21.7	23.9	24.4	24.4	24.0	24.4	24.9	25.3	25.7	26.0
09 栃　　木	23.2	23.9	24.5	24.6	23.9	24.4	25.0	25.3	25.5	26.1
10 群　　馬	22.9	24.3	24.9	24.6	24.3	24.8	25.3	25.5	25.7	26.2
11 埼　　玉	23.6	24.2	24.8	24.6	24.5	24.9	25.5	25.7	25.8	26.3
12 千　　葉	23.1	23.9	24.5	24.6	24.4	24.9	25.5	25.7	26.0	26.5
13 東　　京	24.3	24.9	25.2	25.1	24.9	25.5	26.1	26.3	26.7	27.3
14 神 奈 川	23.8	24.6	25.1	24.8	24.7	25.1	25.7	25.9	26.2	26.7
15 新　　潟	23.3	23.7	24.4	24.3	23.9	24.4	25.1	25.5	25.8	26.2
16 富　　山	21.1	22.1	22.9	23.1	23.2	23.8	24.3	24.8	25.2	25.7
17 石　　川	21.7	22.5	23.2	23.3	23.1	23.8	24.2	24.7	25.2	25.8
18 福　　井	22.0	22.7	23.4	23.4	23.2	23.7	24.3	24.8	25.3	25.9
19 山　　梨	24.3	24.9	25.4	25.3	24.8	25.0	25.6	25.9	26.1	26.5
20 長　　野	24.4	25.0	25.4	25.4	24.9	25.2	25.8	26.0	26.3	26.6
21 岐　　阜	22.5	23.2	23.8	23.9	23.6	24.2	24.6	24.9	25.4	25.8
22 静　　岡	22.7	23.5	24.1	24.2	23.9	24.4	25.0	25.3	25.7	26.2
23 愛　　知	22.7	23.4	24.0	24.0	23.8	24.3	24.7	24.9	25.4	25.9
24 三　　重	22.6	23.2	23.8	23.9	23.7	24.2	24.5	24.7	25.2	25.8
25 滋　　賀	23.2	23.9	24.4	24.5	24.1	24.5	25.1	25.1	25.5	26.0
26 京　　都	23.4	24.2	24.9	24.8	24.5	25.0	25.5	25.7	26.0	26.4
27 大　　阪	23.5	24.1	24.6	24.5	24.3	24.9	25.4	25.4	25.7	26.2
28 兵　　庫	23.1	23.8	24.4	24.5	24.2	24.7	25.2	25.4	25.7	26.1
29 奈　　良	23.1	23.6	24.2	24.3	24.1	24.7	25.2	25.3	25.7	26.2
30 和 歌 山	23.0	23.5	24.2	24.2	23.9	24.4	24.7	24.8	25.3	25.8
31 鳥　　取	22.6	23.2	23.9	24.2	23.7	24.3	24.8	25.3	25.6	26.0
32 島　　根	22.4	23.4	24.2	24.5	24.1	24.5	25.0	25.3	25.7	25.9
33 岡　　山	22.2	22.9	23.6	23.7	23.4	24.1	24.5	24.9	25.2	25.6
34 広　　島	22.5	23.3	24.0	24.1	23.8	24.4	24.9	25.2	25.4	25.9
35 山　　口	22.4	23.3	24.1	24.4	24.0	24.5	25.0	25.3	25.5	25.8
36 徳　　島	22.0	22.6	23.5	23.7	23.3	24.0	24.5	25.0	25.3	25.7
37 香　　川	22.3	23.0	23.6	23.7	23.5	24.2	24.5	24.9	25.1	25.5
38 愛　　媛	22.4	23.2	23.9	24.1	23.8	24.3	24.8	25.2	25.6	25.9
39 高　　知	22.1	22.8	23.6	23.9	23.8	24.4	25.1	25.6	26.0	26.0
40 福　　岡	22.9	23.7	24.6	24.9	24.5	24.9	25.5	25.8	26.1	26.4
41 佐　　賀	23.0	23.6	24.4	24.8	24.1	24.5	25.1	25.5	25.9	26.3
42 長　　崎	22.7	23.5	24.5	24.7	24.3	24.7	25.4	25.9	26.3	26.6
43 熊　　本	22.9	23.6	24.4	24.7	24.2	24.5	25.1	25.6	26.0	26.3
44 大　　分	22.4	23.2	24.0	24.5	23.9	24.4	25.0	25.4	25.9	26.2
45 宮　　崎	22.5	23.4	24.1	24.4	23.9	24.3	25.0	25.6	26.1	26.2
46 鹿 児 島	23.3	24.0	24.9	25.1	24.6	24.7	25.2	25.7	26.3	26.6
47 沖　　縄	…	…	…	…	…	24.5	25.2	25.8	26.1	26.2

注：1）　昭和25年・30年・35年・40年は結婚式をあげたときの年齢、45年以降は結婚式をあげたときまたは同居を始めたときのうち早いほうの年齢である。
　　　　平成2年までの夫または妻の平均婚姻年齢は出生年月及び同居年月による年齢の算術平均に0.46歳を加え、平成7年以降は月齢の算術平均値から算出している。
　　2）　実数は中巻第6表を参照されたい。
　　3）　昭和25年は挙式寸前の夫の住所、昭和30年以降は届出時の夫の住所である。

婚姻年齢 1) －初婚の夫・初婚の妻－（各届出年に結婚生活に入り届け出たもの）2)（つづき）
at marriage (for first marriage)by each
registered each year): Japan－CON.

2000 12年	2005 17年	2009 21年	2010 22年	2011 23年	2012 24年	2013 25年	2014 26年	2015 27年	2016 28年	都道府県 3) Prefecture
27.0	28.0	28.6	28.8	29.0	29.2	29.3	29.4	29.4	29.4	全 国　Total
26.8	27.8	28.4	28.7	28.7	29.0	29.1	29.2	29.3	29.4	01 北 海 道 a)
26.4	27.3	28.1	28.1	28.4	28.7	28.8	29.0	29.0	29.0	02 青　森
26.5	27.2	28.1	28.2	28.4	28.5	28.6	28.9	29.0	28.8	03 岩　手
26.4	27.5	28.3	28.4	28.6	29.0	29.0	29.2	29.3	29.3	04 宮　城
26.5	27.5	28.2	28.4	28.6	28.8	28.8	29.2	29.3	29.2	05 秋　田
26.6	27.3	28.0	28.1	28.3	28.6	28.8	28.7	28.8	29.1	06 山　形
26.1	27.0	27.5	27.9	27.8	28.1	28.2	28.4	28.6	28.7	07 福　島
26.6	27.6	28.2	28.5	28.6	28.8	28.9	29.0	29.1	29.1	08 茨　城
26.6	27.6	28.3	28.5	28.6	28.8	28.9	28.9	29.1	29.2	09 栃　木
26.6	27.7	28.3	28.6	28.8	28.8	28.9	29.0	29.2	29.1	10 群　馬
27.1	28.2	28.9	28.9	29.2	29.4	29.4	29.5	29.6	29.6	11 埼　玉
27.2	28.3	28.8	29.1	29.1	29.3	29.4	29.5	29.6	29.6	12 千　葉
28.0	29.2	29.7	29.9	30.1	30.3	30.4	30.5	30.5	30.5	13 東　京
27.6	28.6	29.2	29.4	29.6	29.7	29.9	30.0	30.1	30.0	14 神 奈 川
26.7	27.7	28.4	28.6	28.7	28.9	28.9	29.1	29.3	29.1	15 新　潟
26.6	27.7	28.4	28.7	28.8	29.0	29.1	29.2	29.1	29.2	16 富　山
26.7	27.8	28.3	28.7	28.6	28.9	29.0	29.1	29.1	29.2	17 石　川
26.7	27.4	28.2	28.4	28.5	28.6	28.7	28.7	28.9	28.9	18 福　井
27.2	28.0	28.7	29.0	29.1	29.2	29.1	29.3	29.3	29.6	19 山　梨
27.2	28.2	28.8	29.0	29.2	29.3	29.3	29.5	29.5	29.5	20 長　野
26.6	27.5	28.1	28.2	28.4	28.6	28.8	28.8	28.7	28.8	21 岐　阜
26.8	27.8	28.2	28.5	28.6	28.8	29.0	29.1	29.2	29.2	22 静　岡
26.8	27.8	28.3	28.4	28.6	28.8	28.8	28.9	29.0	29.0	23 愛　知
26.5	27.5	28.1	28.2	28.4	28.6	28.7	28.7	28.9	28.8	24 三　重
26.7	27.7	28.1	28.3	28.6	28.8	28.9	29.0	29.1	29.0	25 滋　賀
27.2	28.3	28.9	29.2	29.3	29.5	29.6	29.7	29.7	29.6	26 京　都
27.1	28.2	28.8	28.9	29.2	29.3	29.4	29.5	29.6	29.5	27 大　阪
27.0	28.0	28.6	28.7	28.9	29.1	29.2	29.3	29.3	29.4	28 兵　庫
27.1	28.0	28.7	28.9	29.0	29.1	29.3	29.4	29.4	29.5	29 奈　良
26.5	27.4	28.1	28.2	28.4	28.6	28.6	28.8	28.7	28.9	30 和 歌 山
26.4	27.3	28.0	28.4	28.5	28.7	28.9	29.0	29.0	29.0	31 鳥　取
26.6	27.4	28.1	28.4	28.5	28.6	29.0	28.9	29.1	28.7	32 島　根
26.3	27.4	28.0	28.3	28.4	28.6	28.6	28.7	28.8	28.8	33 岡　山
26.7	27.6	28.2	28.4	28.6	28.7	28.9	29.0	28.9	28.9	34 広　島
26.5	27.3	27.9	28.2	28.4	28.5	28.6	28.7	28.6	28.6	35 山　口
26.3	27.5	28.2	28.3	28.5	28.6	28.9	28.9	29.0	29.2	36 徳　島
26.2	27.3	28.0	28.5	28.4	28.7	28.9	28.9	28.9	28.9	37 香　川
26.6	27.4	27.9	28.3	28.4	28.5	28.6	28.8	28.7	28.9	38 愛　媛
26.7	27.9	28.5	28.7	29.1	29.2	29.3	29.4	29.7	29.4	39 高　知
27.0	28.0	28.5	28.7	28.9	29.1	29.2	29.2	29.4	29.3	40 福　岡
26.5	27.4	28.0	28.2	28.3	28.6	28.6	28.5	28.9	28.8	41 佐　賀
26.9	27.7	28.1	28.3	28.6	28.9	29.0	29.1	29.1	29.0	42 長　崎
26.7	27.3	28.0	28.3	28.3	28.7	28.8	28.8	29.0	28.8	43 熊　本
26.7	27.8	28.3	28.4	28.6	29.1	28.9	29.1	29.0	29.1	44 大　分
26.4	27.3	27.9	28.3	28.4	28.4	28.7	28.7	28.7	28.7	45 宮　崎
26.7	27.4	28.1	28.2	28.4	28.7	28.9	29.0	29.0	29.1	46 鹿 児 島
26.5	27.7	28.3	28.4	28.3	28.5	28.9	29.0	29.0	29.0	47 沖　縄

Note : a)　See page 44.

婚　姻

表9.13　結婚生活に入ったときの初婚
（平成28年に結婚生活

Table 9.13　First marriages and percent distribution by age of bride and

妻 の 年 齢 Age of bride	総　数 Total	～19歳 Years	20～24	25～29	30～34	35～39	40～44	45～49
							実	数
総　数　　Total	370 788	4 776	47 833	143 451	96 822	47 330	21 117	6 741
～19歳　Year	8 172	3 607	3 367	777	273	88	40	13
20～24	67 428	1 081	33 608	22 691	7 021	2 174	610	166
25～29	162 422	65	9 057	100 483	39 516	10 283	2 377	490
30～34	84 989	19	1 445	16 838	41 803	18 410	5 242	967
35～39	34 438	4	301	2 352	7 248	14 111	7 939	2 020
40～44	10 432	-	44	277	870	2 064	4 356	2 148
45～49	2 213	-	8	29	85	178	492	829
50～54	475	-	3	4	5	18	56	90
55～59	125	-	-	-	-	3	5	13
60～64	51	-	-	-	1	1	-	2
65～69	30	-	-	-	-	-	-	3
70～74	8	-	-	-	-	-	-	-
75～79	2	-	-	-	-	-	-	-
80～	1	-	-	-	-	-	-	-
不　詳　Not stated	2	-	-	-	-	-	-	-
							百　分	率
総　数　　Total	100. 0	1. 3	12. 9	38. 7	26. 1	12. 8	5. 7	1. 8
～19歳　Year	2. 2	1. 0	0. 9	0. 2	0. 1	0. 0	0. 0	0. 0
20～24	18. 2	0. 3	9. 1	6. 1	1. 9	0. 6	0. 2	0. 0
25～29	43. 8	0. 0	2. 4	27. 1	10. 7	2. 8	0. 6	0. 1
30～34	22. 9	0. 0	0. 4	4. 5	11. 3	5. 0	1. 4	0. 3
35～39	9. 3	0. 0	0. 1	0. 6	2. 0	3. 8	2. 1	0. 5
40～44	2. 8	-	0. 0	0. 1	0. 2	0. 6	1. 2	0. 6
45～49	0. 6	-	0. 0	0. 0	0. 0	0. 0	0. 1	0. 2
50～54	0. 1	-	0. 0	0. 0	0. 0	0. 0	0. 0	0. 0
55～59	0. 0	-	-	-	-	0. 0	0. 0	0. 0
60～64	0. 0	-	-	-	0. 0	0. 0	-	0. 0
65～69	0. 0	-	-	-	-	-	-	0. 0
70～74	0. 0	-	-	-	-	-	-	-
75～79	0. 0	-	-	-	-	-	-	-
80～	0. 0	-	-	-	-	-	-	-
不　詳　Not stated	・	・	・	・	・	・	・	・

注：1)　年齢不詳を除く総数に対する百分率である。

Marriages

夫妻の年齢別にみた婚姻件数及び百分率[1]
に入り届け出たもの）
groom (for marriages performed and registered in 2016): Japan, 2016

平成28年

年　　　齢 groom							
50～54	55～59	60～64	65～69	70～74	75～79	80～	不　詳 Not stated
Number							
1 800	575	215	98	22	4	2	2
3	4	-	-	-	-	-	-
49	16	8	3	1	-	-	-
90	32	20	6	3	-	-	-
177	65	17	4	2	-	-	-
356	66	28	10	2	1	-	-
504	126	28	14	1	-	-	-
428	121	29	11	2	1	-	-
165	88	35	10	1	-	-	-
23	44	22	12	2	1	-	-
4	9	19	14	1	-	-	-
1	2	8	12	4	-	-	-
-	2	1	1	2	1	1	-
-	-	-	1	1	-	-	-
-	-	-	-	-	-	1	-
-	-	-	-	-	-	-	2
Percentage							
0.5	0.2	0.1	0.0	0.0	0.0	0.0	·
0.0	0.0	-	-	-	-	-	·
0.0	0.0	0.0	0.0	0.0	-	-	·
0.0	0.0	0.0	0.0	0.0	-	-	·
0.0	0.0	0.0	0.0	0.0	-	-	·
0.1	0.0	0.0	0.0	0.0	0.0	-	·
0.1	0.0	0.0	0.0	0.0	-	-	·
0.1	0.0	0.0	0.0	0.0	0.0	-	·
0.0	0.0	0.0	0.0	0.0	-	-	·
0.0	0.0	0.0	0.0	0.0	0.0	-	·
0.0	0.0	0.0	0.0	0.0	-	-	·
0.0	0.0	0.0	0.0	0.0	-	-	·
-	0.0	0.0	0.0	0.0	0.0	0.0	·
-	-	-	0.0	0.0	-	-	·
-	-	-	-	-	-	0.0	·
·	·	·	·	·	·	·	·

婚　姻

表 9.14　初婚夫妻の年齢差別にみた年次別婚姻件数及び百分率
（各届出年に結婚生活に入り届け出たもの）

Table 9.14 Trends in first marriages and percent distribution by difference in age between bride and groom (for marriages performed and registered each year): Japan

年　齢　差 Difference of age	1970 昭和45年	1975 50年	1980 55年	1985 60年	1990 平成2年	1995 7年	2000 12年	2005 17年	2010 22年	2014 26年	2015 27年	2016 28年
	実　　　数　　Number											
総　数[1] Total	782 222	747 339	610 223	576 744	553 982	602 915	576 852	475 390	445 578	395 044	383 651	370 788
妻年上 Elder bride	80 703	93 387	71 393	69 688	79 138	106 788	126 291	111 239	105 291	94 596	92 161	88 795
4～	13 762	14 895	12 179	11 277	13 759	21 099	27 311	27 120	27 293	25 693	25 020	24 106
3	9 665	11 452	8 363	8 122	9 679	13 972	16 852	14 950	13 887	12 337	12 044	11 392
2	18 191	21 305	15 864	15 060	17 291	23 164	27 912	23 752	21 474	18 872	18 175	17 559
1歳　Years	39 085	45 735	34 987	35 229	38 409	48 553	54 216	45 417	42 637	37 694	36 922	35 738
夫妻同年齢 Same years	79 337	94 488	78 397	82 244	88 002	106 408	110 874	90 725	90 137	82 991	80 411	77 718
夫年上 Elder groom	621 832	559 388	460 411	424 802	386 834	389 699	339 680	273 422	250 150	217 457	211 078	204 273
1歳　Years	91 806	101 855	77 382	75 838	75 752	86 171	83 571	66 749	61 303	53 492	51 711	49 374
2	99 192	104 412	76 818	71 126	67 384	69 682	64 155	49 503	44 227	36 534	35 104	34 451
3	103 457	98 086	74 389	65 270	58 414	58 247	50 126	38 764	34 479	28 561	27 686	26 726
4	96 654	84 163	66 669	57 119	49 469	47 261	38 561	30 223	26 906	22 888	21 897	21 194
5	82 261	64 584	54 949	47 140	38 793	35 783	28 708	22 787	21 049	17 926	17 400	17 006
6	60 242	44 189	40 879	35 623	29 097	26 653	20 992	17 393	15 690	14 070	13 682	13 442
7～	88 220	62 099	69 325	72 686	67 925	65 902	53 567	48 003	46 496	43 986	43 598	42 080
	百　　分　　率　　Percentage											
総　数 Total	100.0	100.0	100.0	100.0	100.0	100.0	100.0	100.0	100.0	100.0	100.0	100.0
妻年上 Elder bride	10.3	12.5	11.7	12.1	14.3	17.7	21.9	23.4	23.6	23.9	24.0	23.9
4～	1.8	2.0	2.0	2.0	2.5	3.5	4.7	5.7	6.1	6.5	6.5	6.5
3	1.2	1.5	1.4	1.4	1.7	2.3	2.9	3.1	3.1	3.1	3.1	3.1
2	2.3	2.9	2.6	2.6	3.1	3.8	4.8	5.0	4.8	4.8	4.7	4.7
1歳　Years	5.0	6.1	5.7	6.1	6.9	8.1	9.4	9.6	9.6	9.5	9.6	9.6
夫妻同年齢 Same years	10.1	12.6	12.8	14.3	15.9	17.6	19.2	19.1	20.2	21.0	21.0	21.0
夫年上 Elder groom	79.5	74.9	75.4	73.7	69.8	64.6	58.9	57.5	56.1	55.0	55.0	55.1
1歳　Years	11.7	13.6	12.7	13.1	13.7	14.3	14.5	14.0	13.8	13.5	13.5	13.3
2	12.7	14.0	12.6	12.3	12.2	11.6	11.1	10.4	9.9	9.2	9.1	9.3
3	13.2	13.1	12.2	11.3	10.5	9.7	8.7	8.2	7.7	7.2	7.2	7.2
4	12.4	11.3	10.9	9.9	8.9	7.8	6.7	6.4	6.0	5.8	5.7	5.7
5	10.5	8.6	9.0	8.2	7.0	5.9	5.0	4.8	4.7	4.5	4.5	4.6
6	7.7	5.9	6.7	6.2	5.3	4.4	3.6	3.7	3.5	3.6	3.6	3.6
7～	11.3	8.3	11.4	12.6	12.3	10.9	9.3	10.1	10.4	11.1	11.4	11.3

注：1）総数には不詳を含む。

542

Marriages

〔夫妻の結婚生活に入る前の世帯の主な仕事別にみた婚姻〕
〔Marriages by type of occupation of household before marriage〕

表 9.15 夫の結婚生活に入る前の世帯の主な仕事別にみた妻の結婚生活に入る前の世帯の主な仕事別初婚夫妻の婚姻件数及び百分率[1]
（平成28年に結婚生活に入り届け出たもの）

Table 9.15 First marriages and percent distribution by type of occupation of household before marriage (for marriages performed and registered in 2016): Japan, 2016

平成28年

妻の世帯の主な仕事 Type of occupation of household of bride	夫 の 世 帯 の 主 な 仕 事 Type of occupation of household of groom							
	総 数 Total	農家世帯 Agriculture[a]	自営業者世帯 Self employed	常用勤労者世帯（Ⅰ） Employee[b]	常用勤労者世帯（Ⅱ） Employee[c] or director	その他の世帯 Other	無職の世帯 Not working	不 詳 Not stated
実 数 Number								
総　数　Total	370 788	6 848	25 450	104 036	186 930	29 938	4 986	12 600
農 家 世 帯 Agriculture[a]	6 066	1 107	655	1 682	1 904	531	154	33
自 営 業 者 世 帯 Self employed	21 412	684	4 328	6 057	8 290	1 562	393	98
常用勤労者世帯（Ⅰ） Employee[b]	106 173	2 041	7 963	55 559	34 371	4 871	1 011	357
常用勤労者世帯（Ⅱ） Employee[c] or director	155 601	1 722	7 345	22 718	117 377	4 857	1 211	371
そ の 他 の 世 帯 Other	41 383	812	2 705	8 920	12 761	15 434	563	188
無 職 の 世 帯 Not working	24 742	413	2 093	7 715	10 441	2 377	1 606	97
不　　　　詳 Not stated	15 411	69	361	1 385	1 786	306	48	11 456
百 分 率 Percentage								
総　数　Total	100.0	100.0	100.0	100.0	100.0	100.0	100.0	・
農 家 世 帯 Agriculture[a]	1.7	16.3	2.6	1.6	1.0	1.8	3.1	・
自 営 業 者 世 帯 Self employed	6.0	10.1	17.3	5.9	4.5	5.3	8.0	・
常用勤労者世帯（Ⅰ） Employee[b]	29.9	30.1	31.7	54.1	18.6	16.4	20.5	・
常用勤労者世帯（Ⅱ） Employee[c] or director	43.8	25.4	29.3	22.1	63.4	16.4	24.5	・
そ の 他 の 世 帯 Other	11.6	12.0	10.8	8.7	6.9	52.1	11.4	・
無 職 の 世 帯 Not working	7.0	6.1	8.3	7.5	5.6	8.0	32.5	・

注：1） 妻の世帯の主な仕事不詳を除く総数に対する百分率である。
Note：a) Agriculture only or that with other work.
b) Employee at office (excluding governmental office) with 1-99 employee (excluding daily or less than one year contracts).
c) Employee at office excluding b) above.

543

婚　姻

〔結婚生活に入ったときから婚姻届出までの期間別にみた婚姻〕
〔Marriages by period between marriage and registration〕

表9.16　結婚生活に入ったときから婚姻届出までの期間別にみた年次別婚姻件数百分率
Table 9.16　Percentage of marriages by period between marriage and registration : Japan

年次 Year		1月未満 Under 1 month	1月以上2月未満 1 month and over, less than 2 months	2～3	3～4	4～5	5～6	6～7	7～8	8～9	9～10	10～11	11～12	1年以上2年未満 1 year and over, less than 2 years	2～3	3～5	5～
1950	昭和25年	17.9	11.7	7.1	5.3	4.5	4.1	3.8	3.7	4.1	4.7	4.6	4.1	16.0	3.1	2.3	3.1
55	30	26.2	15.6	7.8	5.3	4.4	3.9	3.5	3.2	3.2	3.2	3.0	2.7	11.2	2.2	1.6	2.9
60	35	30.6	17.5	8.7	5.9	4.6	3.8	3.2	2.8	2.6	2.6	2.3	2.0	8.1	1.7	1.2	2.4
65	40	38.3	21.3	9.6	5.6	4.1	3.1	2.4	2.0	1.7	1.5	1.3	1.1	4.3	0.9	0.8	1.8
70	45	50.2	21.5	7.3	4.0	2.8	2.1	1.7	1.3	1.0	0.9	0.7	0.7	2.9	0.8	0.8	1.2
75	50	59.7	20.1	5.6	2.9	1.9	1.4	1.1	0.9	0.7	0.6	0.5	0.4	1.9	0.6	0.7	1.0
76	51	62.1	18.9	5.0	2.6	1.7	1.3	1.0	0.8	0.6	0.5	0.5	0.5	2.1	0.6	0.6	1.0
77	52	63.6	18.6	4.7	2.4	1.6	1.2	0.9	0.7	0.6	0.5	0.4	0.4	1.9	0.7	0.5	1.1
78	53	64.1	18.8	4.5	2.3	1.6	1.2	0.9	0.7	0.6	0.5	0.4	0.4	1.8	0.6	0.5	1.3
79	54	66.3	17.2	4.2	2.2	1.5	1.1	0.9	0.7	0.6	0.5	0.4	0.4	1.8	0.6	0.7	1.0
1980	55	65.9	17.7	4.1	2.2	1.5	1.1	0.9	0.7	0.6	0.5	0.4	0.4	1.8	0.6	0.5	1.2
81	56	67.1	17.2	3.8	2.0	1.4	1.0	0.8	0.7	0.5	0.5	0.4	0.4	1.9	0.6	0.5	1.1
82	57	69.1	16.1	3.6	1.9	1.3	1.0	0.8	0.6	0.5	0.4	0.4	0.4	1.8	0.6	0.5	1.1
83	58	69.6	15.8	3.5	1.8	1.3	1.0	0.8	0.6	0.5	0.4	0.4	0.3	1.8	0.6	0.5	1.1
84	59	69.1	16.3	3.4	1.8	1.2	1.0	0.8	0.6	0.5	0.4	0.4	0.4	1.9	0.6	0.6	1.1
85	60	71.6	14.2	3.1	1.7	1.2	0.9	0.7	0.6	0.5	0.4	0.4	0.4	1.9	0.7	0.6	1.1
86	61	70.6	15.3	3.1	1.6	1.1	0.9	0.7	0.6	0.5	0.4	0.4	0.4	2.0	0.7	0.6	1.2
87	62	69.9	15.6	3.3	1.7	1.2	0.9	0.8	0.6	0.5	0.4	0.3	0.4	1.9	0.8	0.6	1.1
88	63	72.2	13.6	3.1	1.7	1.2	0.9	0.7	0.6	0.5	0.4	0.3	0.4	1.8	0.7	0.7	1.2
89	平成元年	71.5	14.0	3.2	1.7	1.2	0.9	0.8	0.6	0.5	0.4	0.4	0.4	1.9	0.7	0.7	1.2
1990	2	71.4	13.9	3.3	1.7	1.2	0.9	0.8	0.6	0.5	0.4	0.4	0.4	2.1	0.7	0.6	1.2
91	3	72.3	12.7	3.3	1.8	1.2	1.0	0.8	0.6	0.5	0.4	0.4	0.4	2.0	0.8	0.6	1.2
92	4	72.2	13.3	3.3	1.8	1.2	1.0	0.8	0.6	0.5	0.4	0.3	0.4	2.0	0.8	0.6	0.9
93	5	71.8	13.5	3.3	1.8	1.2	1.0	0.8	0.6	0.5	0.4	0.4	0.4	2.0	0.8	0.7	0.9
94	6	73.9	11.7	3.1	1.7	1.2	1.0	0.8	0.6	0.5	0.4	0.4	0.4	2.0	0.8	0.7	0.9
95	7	74.4	11.1	3.0	1.7	1.2	1.0	0.8	0.6	0.5	0.4	0.4	0.4	2.1	0.8	0.7	1.0
96	8	74.3	11.0	3.1	1.7	1.2	1.0	0.8	0.6	0.5	0.4	0.4	0.4	2.1	0.8	0.7	1.0
97	9	75.1	9.9	2.9	1.7	1.2	1.0	0.8	0.7	0.6	0.5	0.4	0.4	2.2	0.8	0.7	1.0
98	10	75.8	9.5	2.9	1.7	1.2	1.0	0.8	0.6	0.5	0.4	0.4	0.4	2.2	0.9	0.7	1.0
99	11	75.7	9.2	2.9	1.7	1.2	1.0	0.8	0.7	0.5	0.5	0.4	0.4	2.4	0.9	0.7	1.0
2000	12	75.7	8.5	3.0	1.8	1.3	1.0	0.9	0.7	0.6	0.5	0.4	0.4	2.4	0.9	0.8	1.0
01	13	75.6	8.4	3.0	1.8	1.3	1.1	0.9	0.7	0.6	0.5	0.4	0.5	2.5	0.9	0.8	1.0
02	14	74.9	8.1	3.0	1.9	1.4	1.1	1.0	0.8	0.7	0.6	0.5	0.5	2.8	1.0	0.8	1.0
03	15	74.6	7.7	2.9	1.9	1.4	1.2	1.0	0.8	0.7	0.6	0.5	0.5	3.1	1.2	0.9	1.1
04	16	73.4	7.7	3.1	1.9	1.4	1.2	1.0	0.9	0.7	0.6	0.5	0.6	3.4	1.3	1.0	1.1
05	17	72.6	7.6	3.1	2.0	1.5	1.3	1.1	0.9	0.8	0.6	0.6	0.6	3.6	1.4	1.1	1.2
06	18	72.2	7.3	3.1	2.1	1.5	1.3	1.1	0.9	0.8	0.7	0.6	0.6	3.7	1.5	1.2	1.3
07	19	70.6	7.5	3.3	2.2	1.6	1.4	1.2	1.0	0.8	0.7	0.6	0.7	4.0	1.7	1.3	1.3
08	20	70.2	7.3	3.3	2.2	1.7	1.4	1.2	1.1	0.9	0.8	0.7	0.7	4.2	1.7	1.3	1.4
09	21	69.8	7.1	3.3	2.2	1.7	1.5	1.2	1.1	0.9	0.8	0.7	0.7	4.5	1.7	1.3	1.4
2010	22	69.5	6.9	3.3	2.2	1.7	1.5	1.3	1.1	0.9	0.8	0.7	0.7	4.6	1.9	1.5	1.5
11	23	69.0	6.9	3.3	2.3	1.8	1.5	1.3	1.1	0.9	0.8	0.7	0.8	4.6	1.9	1.5	1.5
12	24	68.8	6.6	3.2	2.3	1.8	1.5	1.3	1.1	1.0	0.8	0.7	0.8	4.9	1.9	1.6	1.7
13	25	68.3	6.5	3.3	2.4	1.9	1.6	1.3	1.2	1.0	0.9	0.8	0.8	4.9	2.0	1.5	1.7
14	26	67.1	6.6	3.4	2.4	1.9	1.6	1.5	1.2	1.1	0.9	0.8	0.9	5.2	2.1	1.5	1.7
15	27	65.7	6.6	3.5	2.5	2.0	1.7	1.5	1.3	1.1	1.0	0.9	0.9	5.6	2.2	1.6	1.8
16	28	65.0	6.5	3.5	2.6	2.1	1.8	1.6	1.4	1.2	1.0	0.9	1.0	5.8	2.3	1.6	1.6

Marriages

表 9.17 結婚生活に入ったときから婚姻届出までの期間別にみた年次別婚姻件数累積百分率
Table 9.17 Cumulative percentage of marriages by period between marriage and registration : Japan

年　次 Year		1月未満 Under 1 month	1月以上2月未満 1 month and over, less than 2 months	2～3	3～4	4～5	5～6	6～7	7～8	8～9	9～10	10～11	11～12	1年以上2年未満 1 year and over, less than 2 years	2～3	3～5	5～
1950	昭和25年	17.9	29.6	36.6	42.0	46.5	50.5	54.4	58.1	62.2	66.8	71.4	75.5	91.5	94.6	96.9	100.0
55	30	26.2	41.8	49.6	54.9	59.3	63.2	66.7	69.9	73.1	76.3	79.4	82.1	93.3	95.5	97.1	100.0
60	35	30.6	48.1	56.8	62.7	67.3	71.1	74.3	77.2	79.8	82.4	84.7	86.7	94.8	96.5	97.6	100.0
65	40	38.3	59.7	69.2	74.9	79.0	82.1	84.6	86.6	88.3	89.8	91.1	92.2	96.5	97.5	98.2	100.0
70	45	50.2	71.7	79.0	83.1	85.9	88.0	89.7	91.0	92.0	92.9	93.6	94.3	97.2	97.9	98.8	100.0
75	50	59.7	79.8	85.4	88.3	90.3	91.7	92.8	93.7	94.4	94.9	95.4	95.8	97.7	98.4	99.0	100.0
76	51	62.1	81.0	86.0	88.6	90.4	91.7	92.7	93.5	94.1	94.6	95.1	95.6	97.7	98.3	99.0	100.0
77	52	63.6	82.2	86.9	89.3	91.0	92.2	93.1	93.9	94.4	94.9	95.3	95.7	97.6	98.3	98.9	100.0
78	53	64.1	82.9	87.4	89.7	91.2	92.4	93.3	94.0	94.6	95.1	95.5	95.9	97.7	98.3	98.7	100.0
79	54	66.3	83.4	87.6	89.9	91.3	92.5	93.4	94.1	94.6	95.1	95.5	95.9	97.7	98.3	99.0	100.0
1980	55	65.9	83.6	87.7	89.8	91.3	92.5	93.4	94.1	94.6	95.1	95.5	95.8	97.7	98.3	98.8	100.0
81	56	67.1	84.4	88.2	90.2	91.5	92.6	93.4	94.1	94.6	95.1	95.4	95.8	97.7	98.4	98.9	100.0
82	57	69.1	85.2	88.7	90.6	91.9	92.9	93.7	94.3	94.8	95.2	95.6	95.9	97.7	98.4	98.9	100.0
83	58	69.6	85.4	88.9	90.7	92.0	93.0	93.8	94.4	94.9	95.3	95.7	96.0	97.8	98.4	98.9	100.0
84	59	69.1	85.3	88.8	90.6	91.8	92.8	93.6	94.2	94.7	95.1	95.5	95.9	97.8	98.4	98.9	100.0
85	60	71.6	85.9	89.0	90.7	91.9	92.8	93.5	94.1	94.6	95.1	95.4	95.8	97.6	98.3	98.9	100.0
86	61	70.6	85.9	89.0	90.6	91.8	92.6	93.4	94.0	94.4	94.9	95.2	95.6	97.6	98.3	98.8	100.0
87	62	69.9	85.5	88.8	90.6	91.8	92.7	93.4	94.0	94.5	94.9	95.3	95.6	97.5	98.2	98.9	100.0
88	63	72.2	85.9	89.0	90.6	91.8	92.7	93.5	94.0	94.5	94.9	95.3	95.6	97.5	98.2	98.8	100.0
89	平成元年	71.5	85.5	88.7	90.4	91.6	92.5	93.3	93.9	94.4	94.9	95.2	95.6	97.5	98.1	98.8	100.0
1990	2	71.4	85.3	88.6	90.3	91.5	92.4	93.1	93.7	94.2	94.7	95.0	95.4	97.5	98.2	98.8	100.0
91	3	72.3	85.0	88.3	90.1	91.4	92.3	93.1	93.7	94.3	94.7	95.1	95.4	97.4	98.2	98.8	100.0
92	4	72.2	85.5	88.8	90.5	91.8	92.7	93.5	94.1	94.6	95.0	95.3	95.7	97.7	98.4	99.1	100.0
93	5	71.8	85.2	88.6	90.4	91.6	92.5	93.3	93.9	94.4	94.9	95.2	95.6	97.6	98.4	99.1	100.0
94	6	73.9	85.6	88.7	90.4	91.6	92.6	93.3	94.0	94.5	94.9	95.2	95.6	97.7	98.4	99.1	100.0
95	7	74.4	85.6	88.6	90.3	91.4	92.4	93.2	93.8	94.3	94.7	95.1	95.5	97.6	98.3	99.0	100.0
96	8	74.3	85.4	88.5	90.2	91.4	92.3	93.1	93.8	94.3	94.7	95.1	95.5	97.6	98.3	99.0	100.0
97	9	75.1	85.0	88.0	89.7	90.9	91.9	92.7	93.4	93.9	94.4	94.8	95.2	97.4	98.3	99.0	100.0
98	10	75.8	85.3	88.1	89.8	91.0	92.0	92.8	93.4	94.0	94.4	94.8	95.2	97.4	98.3	99.0	100.0
99	11	75.7	84.9	87.8	89.5	90.7	91.7	92.6	93.2	93.8	94.2	94.6	95.1	97.4	98.3	99.0	100.0
2000	12	75.7	84.2	87.2	89.0	90.3	91.3	92.2	92.9	93.5	94.0	94.4	94.9	97.3	98.2	99.0	100.0
01	13	75.6	84.0	87.0	88.8	90.1	91.2	92.1	92.8	93.4	94.0	94.4	94.9	97.4	98.3	99.0	100.0
02	14	74.9	83.1	86.0	87.9	89.2	90.4	91.3	92.1	92.8	93.4	93.9	94.4	97.2	98.2	99.0	100.0
03	15	74.6	82.3	85.2	87.1	88.5	89.6	90.6	91.4	92.1	92.7	93.2	93.8	96.9	98.1	98.9	100.0
04	16	73.4	81.1	84.2	86.1	87.5	88.7	89.8	90.6	91.4	92.0	92.5	93.1	96.6	97.9	98.9	100.0
05	17	72.6	80.2	83.3	85.3	86.8	88.1	89.2	90.1	90.8	91.5	92.0	92.7	96.2	97.7	98.8	100.0
06	18	72.2	79.5	82.7	84.7	86.3	87.6	88.7	89.6	90.4	91.1	91.6	92.3	96.0	97.5	98.7	100.0
07	19	70.6	78.1	81.4	83.6	85.2	86.6	87.8	88.8	89.6	90.4	91.0	91.7	95.7	97.3	98.7	100.0
08	20	70.2	77.5	80.8	83.0	84.7	86.1	87.4	88.4	89.3	90.1	90.7	91.4	95.6	97.3	98.6	100.0
09	21	69.8	76.9	80.2	82.4	84.1	85.6	86.8	87.9	88.8	89.6	90.3	91.0	95.5	97.2	98.6	100.0
2010	22	69.5	76.3	79.6	81.9	83.6	85.1	86.3	87.4	88.3	89.1	89.8	90.6	95.2	97.1	98.5	100.0
11	23	69.0	75.9	79.2	81.5	83.2	84.7	86.0	87.2	88.1	88.9	89.6	90.4	95.1	96.9	98.5	100.0
12	24	68.8	75.4	78.6	80.9	82.7	84.2	85.5	86.6	87.6	88.4	89.2	89.9	94.8	96.8	98.3	100.0
13	25	68.3	74.8	78.1	80.5	82.3	83.9	85.2	86.4	87.4	88.2	89.0	89.8	94.7	96.7	98.3	100.0
14	26	67.1	73.7	77.1	79.5	81.4	83.1	84.5	85.8	86.8	87.8	88.6	89.5	94.7	96.7	98.3	100.0
15	27	65.7	72.4	75.9	78.4	80.4	82.1	83.7	85.0	86.1	87.1	87.9	88.9	94.5	96.6	98.2	100.0
16	28	65.0	71.5	75.1	77.7	79.8	81.6	83.1	84.5	85.7	86.8	87.7	88.6	94.5	96.7	98.4	100.0

婚　姻

〔夫妻の国籍別にみた婚姻〕
〔Marriages by nationality of bride and groom〕

表 9.18　夫妻の国籍別にみた[1]
Table 9.18　Trends in marriages by nationality

年　　次 Year		総　数 Total	夫妻とも日　本 Japanese couple	夫妻の一方が外国 One of couple is foreigner	夫　日　本　・　妻　外　国 Japanese groom and foreign bride							
					総　数 Total	韓国・朝鮮 Korea	中　国 China	フィリピン Philippines	タ　イ Thailand	米　国 U.S.A.	英　国 United Kingdom	ブラジル Brazil
1965	昭和40年	954 852	950 696	4 156	1 067	843	121	···	···	64	···	···
1970	45	1 029 405	1 023 859	5 546	2 108	1 536	280	···	···	75	···	···
71	46	1 091 229	1 085 639	5 590	2 350	1 696	325	···	···	97	···	···
72	47	1 099 984	1 093 988	5 996	2 674	1 785	445	···	···	102	···	···
73	48	1 071 923	1 065 730	6 193	2 849	1 902	410	···	···	122	···	···
74	49	1 000 455	994 096	6 359	3 177	2 047	477	···	···	142	···	···
75	50	941 628	935 583	6 045	3 222	1 994	574	···	···	152	···	···
76	51	871 543	865 221	6 322	3 467	2 049	646	···	···	163	···	···
77	52	821 029	814 958	6 071	3 501	1 990	635	···	···	196	···	···
78	53	793 257	786 977	6 280	3 620	2 110	655	···	···	172	···	···
79	54	788 505	781 774	6 731	3 921	2 224	751	···	···	183	···	···
1980	55	774 702	767 441	7 261	4 386	2 458	912	···	···	178	···	···
81	56	776 531	768 774	7 757	4 813	2 585	1 032	···	···	219	···	···
82	57	781 252	772 296	8 956	5 697	2 903	1 345	···	···	225	···	···
83	58	762 552	752 101	10 451	7 000	3 391	1 864	···	···	269	···	···
84	59	739 991	729 483	10 508	6 828	3 209	1 704	···	···	234	···	···
85	60	735 850	723 669	12 181	7 738	3 622	1 766	···	···	254	···	···
86	61	710 962	698 433	12 529	8 255	3 515	1 841	···	···	218	···	···
87	62	696 173	681 589	14 584	10 176	4 405	1 977	···	···	235	···	···
88	63	707 716	690 844	16 872	12 267	5 063	2 234	···	···	234	···	···
89	平成元年	708 316	685 473	22 843	17 800	7 685	3 291	···	···	211	···	···
1990	2	722 138	696 512	25 626	20 026	8 940	3 614	···	···	260	···	···
91	3	742 264	717 105	25 159	19 096	6 969	3 871	···	···	243	···	···
92	4	754 441	728 579	25 862	19 423	5 537	4 638	5 771	1 585	248	99	645
93	5	792 658	766 001	26 657	20 092	5 068	4 691	6 394	1 926	244	89	625
94	6	782 738	756 926	25 812	19 216	4 851	4 587	5 999	1 836	241	90	590
95	7	791 888	764 161	27 727	20 787	4 521	5 174	7 188	1 915	198	82	579
96	8	795 080	766 708	28 372	21 162	4 461	6 264	6 645	1 760	241	88	551
97	9	775 651	747 400	28 251	20 902	4 504	6 630	6 035	1 688	184	90	488
98	10	784 595	754 959	29 636	22 159	5 143	7 036	6 111	1 699	215	65	417
99	11	762 028	730 128	31 900	24 272	5 798	7 810	6 414	2 024	198	81	333
2000	12	798 138	761 875	36 263	28 326	6 214	9 884	7 519	2 137	202	76	357
01	13	799 999	760 272	39 727	31 972	6 188	13 936	7 160	1 840	175	93	347
02	14	757 331	721 452	35 879	27 957	5 353	10 750	7 630	1 536	163	85	284
03	15	740 191	704 152	36 039	27 881	5 318	10 242	7 794	1 445	156	65	295
04	16	720 417	680 906	39 511	30 907	5 730	11 915	8 397	1 640	179	64	256
05	17	714 265	672 784	41 481	33 116	6 066	11 644	10 242	1 637	177	59	311
06	18	730 971	686 270	44 701	35 993	6 041	12 131	12 150	1 676	215	79	285
07	19	719 822	679 550	40 272	31 807	5 606	11 926	9 217	1 475	193	67	288
08	20	726 106	689 137	36 969	28 720	4 558	12 218	7 290	1 338	215	59	290
09	21	707 734	673 341	34 393	26 747	4 113	12 733	5 755	1 225	179	56	273
2010	22	700 214	670 007	30 207	22 843	3 664	10 162	5 212	1 096	223	51	247
11	23	661 895	635 961	25 934	19 022	3 098	8 104	4 290	1 046	202	53	239
12	24	668 869	645 212	23 657	17 198	3 004	7 166	3 517	1 089	179	52	209
13	25	660 613	639 125	21 488	15 442	2 734	6 253	3 118	981	184	38	212
14	26	643 749	622 619	21 130	14 998	2 412	6 019	3 000	965	201	50	221
15	27	635 156	614 180	20 976	14 809	2 268	5 730	3 070	938	199	44	277
16	28	620 531	599 351	21 180	14 851	2 031	5 526	3 371	970	246	55	216

注：1）　フィリピン・タイ・英国・ブラジル・ペルーについては平成4年から調査しており、平成3年までは「その他の国」に含まれる。

年次別婚姻件数
of bride and groom : Japan

Marriages

ペルー Peru	その他の国 Other foreign countries	妻 日 本 ・ 夫 外 国 Japanese bride and foreign groom										年 次 Year	
		総数 Total	韓国・朝鮮 Korea	中国 China	フィリピン Philippines	タイ Thailand	米国 U.S.A.	英国 United Kingdom	ブラジル Brazil	ペルー Peru	その他の国 Other foreign countries		
…	39	3 089	1 128	158	…	…	1 592	…	…	…	211	1965	昭和40年
…	217	3 438	1 386	195	…	…	1 571	…	…	…	286	1970	45
…	232	3 240	1 533	194	…	…	1 252	…	…	…	261	71	46
…	342	3 322	1 707	237	…	…	1 010	…	…	…	368	72	47
…	415	3 344	1 674	238	…	…	1 024	…	…	…	408	73	48
…	511	3 182	1 743	229	…	…	790	…	…	…	420	74	49
…	502	2 823	1 554	243	…	…	631	…	…	…	395	75	50
…	609	2 855	1 564	229	…	…	604	…	…	…	458	76	51
…	680	2 570	1 390	197	…	…	539	…	…	…	444	77	52
…	683	2 660	1 500	198	…	…	601	…	…	…	361	78	53
…	763	2 810	1 597	189	…	…	598	…	…	…	426	79	54
…	838	2 875	1 651	194	…	…	625	…	…	…	405	1980	55
…	977	2 944	1 638	235	…	…	630	…	…	…	441	81	56
…	1 224	3 259	1 809	285	…	…	665	…	…	…	500	82	57
…	1 476	3 451	1 901	296	…	…	734	…	…	…	520	83	58
…	1 681	3 680	2 021	300	…	…	751	…	…	…	608	84	59
…	2 096	4 443	2 525	380	…	…	876	…	…	…	662	85	60
…	2 681	4 274	2 330	349	…	…	896	…	…	…	699	86	61
…	3 559	4 408	2 365	432	…	…	947	…	…	…	664	87	62
…	4 736	4 605	2 535	431	…	…	888	…	…	…	751	88	63
…	6 613	5 043	2 589	614	…	…	946	…	…	…	894	89	平成元年
…	7 212	5 600	2 721	708	…	…	1 091	…	…	…	1 080	1990	2
…	8 013	6 063	2 666	789	…	…	1 292	…	…	…	1 316	91	3
138	762	6 439	2 804	777	54	13	1 350	168	152	56	1 065	92	4
166	889	6 565	2 762	766	58	22	1 381	220	146	81	1 129	93	5
146	876	6 596	2 686	695	46	17	1 445	190	147	74	1 296	94	6
140	990	6 940	2 842	769	52	19	1 303	213	162	66	1 514	95	7
130	1 022	7 210	2 800	773	56	25	1 357	234	199	58	1 708	96	8
156	1 127	7 349	2 674	834	61	31	1 374	225	233	99	1 818	97	9
138	1 335	7 477	2 635	787	81	38	1 299	240	204	122	2 071	98	10
128	1 486	7 628	2 499	836	101	64	1 318	228	222	123	2 237	99	11
145	1 792	7 937	2 509	878	109	67	1 483	249	279	124	2 239	2000	12
142	2 091	7 755	2 477	793	83	55	1 416	267	243	135	2 286	01	13
126	2 030	7 922	2 379	814	104	45	1 488	317	231	137	2 407	02	14
139	2 427	8 158	2 235	890	117	62	1 529	334	265	125	2 601	03	15
137	2 589	8 604	2 293	1 104	120	75	1 500	339	268	122	2 783	04	16
121	2 859	8 365	2 087	1 015	187	60	1 551	343	261	123	2 738	05	17
117	3 299	8 708	2 335	1 084	195	54	1 474	386	292	115	2 773	06	18
138	2 897	8 465	2 209	1 016	162	68	1 485	372	341	127	2 685	07	19
116	2 636	8 249	2 107	1 005	165	51	1 445	363	322	133	2 658	08	20
93	2 320	7 646	1 879	986	156	58	1 453	367	290	90	2 367	09	21
90	2 098	7 364	1 982	910	138	38	1 329	316	270	100	2 281	2010	22
95	1 895	6 912	1 837	850	130	45	1 375	292	299	106	1 978	11	23
80	1 902	6 459	1 823	820	139	33	1 159	286	273	92	1 834	12	24
70	1 852	6 046	1 689	718	105	31	1 158	247	286	107	1 705	13	25
80	2 050	6 132	1 701	776	118	27	1 088	236	329	117	1 740	14	26
83	2 200	6 167	1 566	748	167	36	1 127	235	344	115	1 829	15	27
87	2 349	6 329	1 627	790	151	32	1 059	248	315	95	2 012	16	28

婚　姻

表 9.19　夫妻の国籍別にみた[1]
Table 9.19　Trends in percent distribution of marriages

年　　次 Year		総　数 Total	夫妻とも日　本 Japanese couple	夫妻の一方が外国 One of couple is foreigner	夫日本・妻外国 Japanese groom and foreign bride	妻日本・夫外国 Japanese bride and foreign groom	夫　日　本　・　妻　外　国 Japanese groom and foreign bride							
							総　数 Total	韓国・朝鮮 Korea	中　国 China	フィリピン Philippines	タ　イ Thailand	米　国 U.S.A.	英　国 United Kingdom	ブラジル Brazil
1965	昭和40年	100.0	99.6	0.4	0.1	0.3	100.0	79.0	11.3	…	…	6.0	…	…
1970	45	100.0	99.5	0.5	0.2	0.3	100.0	72.9	13.3	…	…	3.6	…	…
71	46	100.0	99.5	0.5	0.2	0.3	100.0	72.2	13.8	…	…	4.1	…	…
72	47	100.0	99.5	0.5	0.2	0.3	100.0	66.8	16.6	…	…	3.8	…	…
73	48	100.0	99.4	0.6	0.3	0.3	100.0	66.8	14.4	…	…	4.3	…	…
74	49	100.0	99.4	0.6	0.3	0.3	100.0	64.4	15.0	…	…	4.5	…	…
75	50	100.0	99.4	0.6	0.3	0.3	100.0	61.9	17.8	…	…	4.7	…	…
76	51	100.0	99.3	0.7	0.4	0.3	100.0	59.1	18.6	…	…	4.7	…	…
77	52	100.0	99.3	0.7	0.4	0.3	100.0	56.8	18.1	…	…	5.6	…	…
78	53	100.0	99.2	0.8	0.5	0.3	100.0	58.3	18.1	…	…	4.8	…	…
79	54	100.0	99.1	0.9	0.5	0.4	100.0	56.7	19.2	…	…	4.7	…	…
1980	55	100.0	99.1	0.9	0.6	0.4	100.0	56.0	20.8	…	…	4.1	…	…
81	56	100.0	99.0	1.0	0.6	0.4	100.0	53.7	21.4	…	…	4.6	…	…
82	57	100.0	98.9	1.1	0.7	0.4	100.0	51.0	23.6	…	…	3.9	…	…
83	58	100.0	98.6	1.4	0.9	0.5	100.0	48.4	26.6	…	…	3.8	…	…
84	59	100.0	98.6	1.4	0.9	0.5	100.0	47.0	25.0	…	…	3.4	…	…
85	60	100.0	98.3	1.7	1.1	0.6	100.0	46.8	22.8	…	…	3.3	…	…
86	61	100.0	98.2	1.8	1.2	0.6	100.0	42.6	22.3	…	…	2.6	…	…
87	62	100.0	97.9	2.1	1.5	0.6	100.0	43.3	19.4	…	…	2.3	…	…
88	63	100.0	97.6	2.4	1.7	0.7	100.0	41.3	18.2	…	…	1.9	…	…
89	平成元年	100.0	96.8	3.2	2.5	0.7	100.0	43.2	18.5	…	…	1.2	…	…
1990	2	100.0	96.5	3.5	2.8	0.8	100.0	44.6	18.0	…	…	1.3	…	…
91	3	100.0	96.6	3.4	2.6	0.8	100.0	36.5	20.3	…	…	1.3	…	…
92	4	100.0	96.6	3.4	2.6	0.9	100.0	28.5	23.9	29.7	8.2	1.3	0.5	3.3
93	5	100.0	96.6	3.4	2.5	0.8	100.0	25.2	23.3	31.8	9.6	1.2	0.4	3.1
94	6	100.0	96.7	3.3	2.5	0.8	100.0	25.2	23.9	31.2	9.6	1.3	0.5	3.1
95	7	100.0	96.5	3.5	2.6	0.9	100.0	21.7	24.9	34.6	9.2	1.0	0.4	2.8
96	8	100.0	96.4	3.6	2.7	0.9	100.0	21.1	29.6	31.4	8.3	1.1	0.4	2.6
97	9	100.0	96.4	3.6	2.7	0.9	100.0	21.5	31.7	28.9	8.1	0.9	0.4	2.3
98	10	100.0	96.2	3.8	2.8	1.0	100.0	23.2	31.8	27.6	7.7	1.0	0.3	1.9
99	11	100.0	95.8	4.2	3.2	1.0	100.0	23.9	32.2	26.4	8.3	0.8	0.3	1.4
2000	12	100.0	95.5	4.5	3.5	1.0	100.0	21.9	34.9	26.5	7.5	0.7	0.3	1.3
01	13	100.0	95.0	5.0	4.0	1.0	100.0	19.4	43.6	22.4	5.8	0.5	0.3	1.1
02	14	100.0	95.3	4.7	3.7	1.0	100.0	19.1	38.5	27.3	5.5	0.6	0.3	1.0
03	15	100.0	95.1	4.9	3.8	1.1	100.0	19.1	36.7	28.0	5.2	0.6	0.2	1.1
04	16	100.0	94.5	5.5	4.3	1.2	100.0	18.5	38.6	27.2	5.3	0.6	0.2	0.8
05	17	100.0	94.2	5.8	4.6	1.2	100.0	18.3	35.2	30.9	4.9	0.5	0.2	0.9
06	18	100.0	93.9	6.1	4.9	1.2	100.0	16.8	33.7	33.8	4.7	0.6	0.2	0.8
07	19	100.0	94.4	5.6	4.4	1.2	100.0	17.6	37.5	29.0	4.6	0.6	0.2	0.9
08	20	100.0	94.9	5.1	4.0	1.1	100.0	15.9	42.5	25.4	4.7	0.7	0.2	1.0
09	21	100.0	95.1	4.9	3.8	1.1	100.0	15.4	47.6	21.5	4.6	0.7	0.2	1.0
2010	22	100.0	95.7	4.3	3.3	1.1	100.0	16.0	44.5	22.8	4.8	1.0	0.3	1.1
11	23	100.0	96.1	3.9	2.9	1.0	100.0	16.3	42.6	22.6	5.5	1.1	0.3	1.3
12	24	100.0	96.5	3.5	2.6	1.0	100.0	17.5	41.7	20.5	6.3	1.0	0.3	1.2
13	25	100.0	96.7	3.3	2.3	0.9	100.0	17.7	40.5	20.2	6.4	1.2	0.2	1.4
14	26	100.0	96.7	3.3	2.3	1.0	100.0	16.1	40.1	20.0	6.4	1.3	0.3	1.5
15	27	100.0	96.7	3.3	2.3	1.0	100.0	15.3	38.7	20.7	6.3	1.3	0.3	1.9
16	28	100.0	96.6	3.4	2.4	1.0	100.0	13.7	37.2	22.7	6.5	1.7	0.4	1.5

注：1）　フィリピン・タイ・英国・ブラジル・ペルーについては平成4年から調査しており、平成3年までは「その他の国」に含まれる。

Marriages

年次別婚姻件数百分率
by nationality of bride and groom : Japan

| | | 妻 日 本 ・ 夫 外 国
Japanese bride and foreign groom | | | | | | | | | | 年 次 |
ペルー Peru	その他の国 Other foreign countries	総 数 Total	韓国・朝鮮 Korea	中 国 China	フィリピン Philippines	タ イ Thailand	米 国 U.S.A.	英 国 United Kingdom	ブラジル Brazil	ペルー Peru	その他の国 Other foreign countries	Year
…	3. 7	100. 0	36. 5	5. 1	…	…	51. 5	…	…	…	6. 8	1965 昭和40年
…	10. 3	100. 0	40. 3	5. 7	…	…	45. 7	…	…	…	8. 3	1970 45
…	9. 9	100. 0	47. 3	6. 0	…	…	38. 6	…	…	…	8. 1	71 46
…	12. 8	100. 0	51. 4	7. 1	…	…	30. 4	…	…	…	11. 1	72 47
…	14. 6	100. 0	50. 1	7. 1	…	…	30. 6	…	…	…	12. 2	73 48
…	16. 1	100. 0	54. 8	7. 2	…	…	24. 8	…	…	…	13. 2	74 49
…	15. 6	100. 0	55. 0	8. 6	…	…	22. 4	…	…	…	14. 0	75 50
…	17. 6	100. 0	54. 8	8. 0	…	…	21. 2	…	…	…	16. 0	76 51
…	19. 4	100. 0	54. 1	7. 7	…	…	21. 0	…	…	…	17. 3	77 52
…	18. 9	100. 0	56. 4	7. 4	…	…	22. 6	…	…	…	13. 6	78 53
…	19. 5	100. 0	56. 8	6. 7	…	…	21. 3	…	…	…	15. 2	79 54
…	19. 1	100. 0	57. 4	6. 7	…	…	21. 7	…	…	…	14. 1	1980 55
…	20. 3	100. 0	55. 6	8. 0	…	…	21. 4	…	…	…	15. 0	81 56
…	21. 5	100. 0	55. 5	8. 7	…	…	20. 4	…	…	…	15. 3	82 57
…	21. 1	100. 0	55. 1	8. 6	…	…	21. 3	…	…	…	15. 1	83 58
…	24. 6	100. 0	54. 9	8. 2	…	…	20. 4	…	…	…	16. 5	84 59
…	27. 1	100. 0	56. 8	8. 6	…	…	19. 7	…	…	…	14. 9	85 60
…	32. 5	100. 0	54. 5	8. 2	…	…	21. 0	…	…	…	16. 4	86 61
…	35. 0	100. 0	53. 7	9. 8	…	…	21. 5	…	…	…	15. 1	87 62
…	38. 6	100. 0	55. 0	9. 4	…	…	19. 3	…	…	…	16. 3	88 63
…	37. 2	100. 0	51. 3	12. 2	…	…	18. 8	…	…	…	17. 7	89 平成元年
…	36. 0	100. 0	48. 6	12. 6	…	…	19. 5	…	…	…	19. 3	1990 2
…	42. 0	100. 0	44. 0	13. 0	…	…	21. 3	…	…	…	21. 7	91 3
0. 7	3. 9	100. 0	43. 5	12. 1	0. 8	0. 2	21. 0	2. 6	2. 4	0. 9	16. 5	92 4
0. 8	4. 4	100. 0	42. 1	11. 7	0. 9	0. 3	21. 0	3. 4	2. 2	1. 2	17. 2	93 5
0. 8	4. 6	100. 0	40. 7	10. 5	0. 7	0. 3	21. 9	2. 9	2. 2	1. 1	19. 6	94 6
0. 7	4. 8	100. 0	41. 0	11. 1	0. 7	0. 3	18. 8	3. 1	2. 3	1. 0	21. 8	95 7
0. 6	4. 8	100. 0	38. 8	10. 7	0. 8	0. 3	18. 8	3. 2	2. 8	0. 8	23. 7	96 8
0. 7	5. 4	100. 0	36. 4	11. 3	0. 8	0. 4	18. 7	3. 1	3. 2	1. 3	24. 7	97 9
0. 6	6. 0	100. 0	35. 2	10. 5	1. 1	0. 5	17. 4	3. 2	2. 7	1. 6	27. 7	98 10
0. 5	6. 1	100. 0	32. 8	11. 0	1. 3	0. 8	17. 3	3. 0	2. 9	1. 6	29. 3	99 11
0. 5	6. 3	100. 0	31. 6	11. 1	1. 4	0. 8	18. 7	3. 1	3. 5	1. 6	28. 2	2000 12
0. 4	6. 5	100. 0	31. 9	10. 2	1. 1	0. 7	18. 3	3. 4	3. 1	1. 7	29. 5	01 13
0. 5	7. 3	100. 0	30. 0	10. 3	1. 3	0. 6	18. 8	4. 0	2. 9	1. 7	30. 4	02 14
0. 5	8. 7	100. 0	27. 4	10. 9	1. 4	0. 8	18. 7	4. 1	3. 2	1. 5	31. 9	03 15
0. 4	8. 4	100. 0	26. 7	12. 8	1. 4	0. 9	17. 4	3. 9	3. 1	1. 4	32. 3	04 16
0. 4	8. 6	100. 0	24. 9	12. 1	2. 2	0. 7	18. 5	4. 1	3. 1	1. 5	32. 7	05 17
0. 3	9. 2	100. 0	26. 8	12. 4	2. 2	0. 6	16. 9	4. 4	3. 4	1. 3	31. 8	06 18
0. 4	9. 1	100. 0	26. 1	12. 0	1. 9	0. 8	17. 5	4. 4	4. 0	1. 5	31. 7	07 19
0. 4	9. 2	100. 0	25. 5	12. 2	2. 0	0. 6	17. 5	4. 4	3. 9	1. 6	32. 2	08 20
0. 3	8. 7	100. 0	24. 6	12. 9	2. 0	0. 8	19. 0	4. 8	3. 8	1. 2	31. 0	09 21
0. 4	9. 2	100. 0	26. 9	12. 4	1. 9	0. 5	18. 0	4. 3	3. 7	1. 4	31. 0	2010 22
0. 5	10. 0	100. 0	26. 6	12. 3	1. 9	0. 7	19. 9	4. 2	4. 3	1. 5	28. 6	11 23
0. 5	11. 1	100. 0	28. 2	12. 7	2. 2	0. 5	17. 9	4. 4	4. 2	1. 4	28. 4	12 24
0. 5	12. 0	100. 0	27. 9	11. 9	1. 7	0. 5	19. 2	4. 1	4. 7	1. 8	28. 2	13 25
0. 5	13. 7	100. 0	27. 7	12. 7	1. 9	0. 4	17. 7	3. 8	5. 4	1. 9	28. 4	14 26
0. 6	14. 9	100. 0	25. 4	12. 1	2. 7	0. 6	18. 3	3. 8	5. 6	1. 9	29. 7	15 27
0. 6	15. 8	100. 0	25. 7	12. 5	2. 4	0. 5	16. 7	3. 9	5. 0	1. 5	31. 8	16 28

婚　姻

表 9.20　夫妻の国籍別にみた
Table 9.20　Marriages by nationality of bride

都道府県 Prefecture	総数 Total	夫妻とも日本 Japanese couple	夫妻の一方が外国 One of couple is foreigner	夫日本・妻外国 Japanese groom and foreign bride							
				総数 Total	韓国・朝鮮 Korea	中国 China	フィリピン Philippines	タイ Thailand	米国 U.S.A.	英国 United Kingdom	ブラジル Brazil
全国　Total [a]	620 531	599 351	21 180	14 851	2 031	5 526	3 371	970	246	55	216
01 北海道	24 636	24 407	229	149	21	38	20	11	6	2	2
02 青森	5 135	5 069	66	35	3	11	11	1	1	-	-
03 岩手	4 872	4 801	71	56	6	25	12	3	1	-	1
04 宮城	11 127	10 935	192	137	24	50	22	15	1	1	-
05 秋田	3 510	3 476	34	26	1	11	9	2	-	-	-
06 山形	4 284	4 213	71	58	7	23	10	1	1	-	-
07 福島	8 682	8 451	231	200	13	58	82	8	1	-	1
08 茨城	13 201	12 747	454	358	35	110	72	74	5	1	8
09 栃木	9 321	8 979	342	268	15	89	53	43	2	1	8
10 群馬	8 444	8 146	298	222	14	56	68	12	3	-	6
11 埼玉	34 199	32 902	1 297	952	83	430	190	55	8	2	12
12 千葉	29 610	28 273	1 337	989	119	370	231	95	11	2	12
13 東京	86 009	81 628	4 381	2 764	414	1 179	398	172	84	18	15
14 神奈川	46 695	44 676	2 019	1 355	171	543	260	93	21	3	16
15 新潟	9 311	9 131	180	154	16	71	28	10	2	1	2
16 富山	4 486	4 330	156	128	5	82	24	4	1	-	2
17 石川	5 126	5 024	102	74	6	35	13	7	-	1	2
18 福井	3 453	3 359	94	82	12	28	23	2	1	-	4
19 山梨	3 673	3 559	114	89	9	37	20	4	2	-	3
20 長野	8 967	8 637	330	286	39	89	54	53	1	2	7
21 岐阜	8 581	8 180	401	348	20	99	189	8	2	1	5
22 静岡	17 079	16 465	614	482	44	128	171	32	9	3	20
23 愛知	40 671	38 580	2 091	1 622	118	522	681	48	10	2	54
24 三重	8 174	7 879	295	240	19	74	64	21	4	-	4
25 滋賀	6 822	6 657	165	121	23	38	32	1	2	-	5
26 京都	12 143	11 713	430	267	55	84	31	20	7	-	1
27 大阪	46 186	44 370	1 816	1 179	417	418	121	64	14	8	5
28 兵庫	25 808	25 012	796	542	151	213	52	22	10	2	2
29 奈良	5 628	5 508	120	89	22	30	10	8	-	-	1
30 和歌山	4 061	3 981	80	68	11	27	11	13	-	1	1
31 鳥取	2 444	2 410	34	23	3	8	7	1	1	-	1
32 島根	2 753	2 709	44	37	2	11	12	4	1	-	-
33 岡山	8 916	8 700	216	177	20	91	34	8	1	-	1
34 広島	13 594	13 234	360	290	18	90	86	16	3	-	6
35 山口	5 906	5 779	127	74	13	19	20	5	2	-	-
36 徳島	3 177	3 126	51	36	3	16	8	2	-	-	1
37 香川	4 593	4 525	68	50	2	23	14	1	-	-	1
38 愛媛	5 861	5 784	77	58	4	22	12	4	1	-	1
39 高知	2 916	2 879	37	21	3	8	8	-	-	-	-
40 福岡	26 567	26 061	506	326	45	127	71	13	6	1	3
41 佐賀	3 726	3 687	39	35	1	12	11	-	-	1	-
42 長崎	6 013	5 911	102	50	3	15	15	2	2	1	1
43 熊本	7 976	7 847	129	107	2	41	39	4	5	-	1
44 大分	5 151	5 076	75	51	6	18	20	2	-	-	-
45 宮崎	5 097	5 053	44	32	2	11	10	1	2	-	-
46 鹿児島	7 483	7 408	75	61	3	26	21	3	2	-	-
47 沖縄	8 464	8 074	390	83	8	20	21	2	10	1	2
21 大都市(再掲) 21 major cities (Regrouped)											
50 東京都の区部	66 235	62 641	3 594	2 208	354	961	302	139	61	14	13
51 札幌	10 495	10 381	114	65	9	16	6	5	5	2	1
52 仙台	6 019	5 913	106	62	9	29	3	8	-	1	1
53 さいたま	6 682	6 471	211	150	14	80	24	6	3	-	1
54 千葉	4 661	4 451	210	159	27	70	31	10	3	1	1
55 横浜	19 132	18 267	865	622	75	276	107	52	9	1	5
56 川崎	10 008	9 589	419	276	41	125	51	12	8	2	1
57 相模原	3 349	3 208	141	99	15	19	23	4	1	-	2
58 新潟	3 590	3 535	55	44	5	23	3	3	1	-	2
59 静岡	3 282	3 195	87	62	12	14	15	4	-	2	3
60 浜松	3 833	3 667	166	131	11	41	57	4	2	-	3
61 名古屋	13 735	12 980	755	569	58	179	257	18	3	-	4
62 京都	7 511	7 204	307	176	37	51	19	13	2	-	2
63 大阪	17 757	16 762	995	581	238	199	53	32	6	2	2
64 堺	4 135	4 019	116	95	26	32	12	9	3	1	1
65 神戸	7 506	7 193	313	190	59	65	8	8	3	-	-
66 岡山	3 744	3 653	91	74	8	39	15	4	-	-	-
67 広島	6 288	6 099	189	151	12	52	50	13	1	-	3
68 北九州	4 907	4 824	83	52	10	21	10	5	1	-	-
69 福岡	9 805	9 580	225	121	18	53	16	3	1	-	-
70 熊本	3 767	3 702	65	47	-	26	14	2	2	-	-

都道府県（21大都市再掲）別婚姻件数
and groom : Japan, each prefecture and 21 major cities, 2016

Marriages　平成28年

ペルー Peru	その他の国 Other foreign countries	総数 Total	韓国・朝鮮 Korea	中国 China	フィリピン Philippines	タイ Thailand	米国 U.S.A.	英国 United Kingdom	ブラジル Brazil	ペルー Peru	その他の国 Other foreign countries	都道府県 Prefecture
87	2 349	6 329	1 627	790	151	32	1 059	248	315	95	2 012	全国 Total
2	47	80	19	6	1	1	16	4	-	-	33	01 北海道 a)
-	8	31	2	-	-	-	29	-	-	-	-	02 青森
-	8	15	6	2	1	-	2	1	-	-	3	03 岩手
1	23	55	24	5	2	-	3	5	-	1	15	04 宮城
-	3	8	2	-	-	-	1	-	-	-	5	05 秋田
-	16	13	3	2	-	-	2	-	-	-	6	06 山形
-	37	31	7	2	-	1	4	5	-	-	12	07 福島
4	49	96	11	9	9	6	7	2	7	2	43	08 茨城
7	50	74	7	7	2	1	9	2	10	7	29	09 栃木
5	58	76	7	5	1	-	5	2	14	10	32	10 群馬
4	168	345	57	70	10	-	24	11	26	3	144	11 埼玉
3	146	348	56	68	25	2	39	10	19	8	121	12 千葉
10	474	1 617	402	218	27	5	226	92	19	17	611	13 東京
14	234	664	133	71	17	5	168	26	18	9	217	14 神奈川
1	23	26	3	3	1	-	4	4	1	-	10	15 新潟
1	9	28	3	3	1	-	4	2	6	-	9	16 富山
-	10	28	7	4	-	-	4	1	3	-	8	17 石川
-	12	12	6	1	-	-	1	1	2	-	1	18 福井
-	14	25	7	2	-	1	3	1	2	-	9	19 山梨
-	41	44	7	7	3	1	6	2	5	1	12	20 長野
1	23	53	6	6	4	-	4	1	8	3	21	21 岐阜
6	69	132	15	19	4	1	9	5	40	5	34	22 静岡
12	175	469	108	44	23	-	37	10	82	14	151	23 愛知
3	51	55	26	2	-	1	1	1	10	2	12	24 三重
1	19	44	14	5	1	-	3	1	13	-	7	25 滋賀
-	69	163	49	19	-	-	15	7	3	2	68	26 京都
4	128	637	324	94	4	1	40	24	6	2	142	27 大阪
2	88	254	116	32	3	1	23	6	4	2	67	28 兵庫
-	19	31	13	3	1	-	6	-	2	-	6	29 奈良
-	4	12	8	-	-	1	3	-	-	-	-	30 和歌山
-	2	11	5	3	-	-	1	-	-	-	2	31 鳥取
-	7	7	1	2	-	-	2	-	1	-	1	32 島根
-	22	39	13	4	2	-	4	2	3	-	11	33 岡山
2	69	70	25	7	2	2	9	1	5	1	18	34 広島
-	15	53	14	3	-	-	26	3	1	-	6	35 山口
-	6	15	2	2	1	-	3	2	-	-	5	36 徳島
1	8	18	4	4	-	-	2	2	-	3	3	37 香川
-	14	19	8	1	1	-	3	-	-	-	6	38 愛媛
-	2	16	2	-	-	1	6	1	-	-	6	39 高知
1	59	180	68	32	-	-	9	5	1	1	64	40 福岡
-	10	4	1	2	-	-	-	-	-	-	1	41 佐賀
-	11	52	4	2	-	-	36	1	-	-	9	42 長崎
-	15	22	6	4	-	-	6	1	-	-	5	43 熊本
1	4	24	8	2	2	-	3	1	-	-	8	44 大分
-	6	12	1	4	-	-	2	-	-	-	5	45 宮崎
-	6	14	4	2	-	-	3	1	-	-	4	46 鹿児島
1	18	307	13	7	2	1	246	2	4	2	30	47 沖縄
												21大都市 (再掲) 21 major cities (Regrouped)
4	360	1 386	351	194	20	4	169	83	11	9	545	50 東京都の区部
2	19	49	14	3	1	1	11	1	-	-	18	51 札幌
-	12	44	18	5	2	-	2	5	-	1	11	52 仙台
-	22	61	16	9	1	-	5	6	3	-	21	53 さいたま
1	15	51	10	12	7	-	2	3	3	-	12	54 千葉
3	94	243	53	40	3	-	41	15	6	1	84	55 横浜
2	34	143	43	20	4	2	19	2	2	1	50	56 川崎
2	33	42	6	2	1	-	5	3	-	1	24	57 相模原
-	6	11	2	2	-	-	3	1	-	-	3	58 新潟
1	11	25	4	8	-	-	1	1	2	-	9	59 静岡
1	12	35	3	2	1	-	2	4	16	-	7	60 浜松
3	47	186	49	22	6	-	25	6	13	3	62	61 名古屋
-	54	131	35	16	-	-	14	5	2	1	58	62 京都
1	48	414	211	55	1	1	30	18	4	-	94	63 大阪
-	11	21	8	7	-	-	1	-	-	-	5	64 堺
1	46	123	47	19	1	-	10	5	3	-	38	65 神戸
-	8	17	6	2	-	-	1	2	2	-	5	66 岡山
1	18	38	15	3	-	-	5	1	2	1	10	67 広島
-	5	31	15	5	-	-	1	1	-	-	10	68 北九州
-	30	104	30	21	-	-	8	4	1	1	39	69 福岡
-	3	18	4	4	-	-	5	1	-	-	4	70 熊本

Note : a) See page 44.

婚 姻

表9.21　夫妻の国籍別にみた都道府県
Table 9.21　Percent distribution of marriages by nationality

都道府県 Prefecture	総数 Total	夫妻とも日本 Japanese couple	夫妻の一方が外国 One of couple is foreigner	夫日本・妻外国 Japanese groom and foreign bride	妻日本・夫外国 Japanese bride and foreign groom	夫日本・妻外国 Japanese groom and foreign bride 総数 Total	韓国・朝鮮 Korea	中国 China	フィリピン Philippines	タイ Thailand	米国 U.S.A.	英国 United Kingdom	ブラジル Brazil
全国　Total	100.0	96.6	3.4	2.4	1.0	100.0	13.7	37.2	22.7	6.5	1.7	0.4	1.5
01 北海道 a)	100.0	99.1	0.9	0.6	0.3	100.0	14.1	25.5	13.4	7.4	4.0	1.3	1.3
02 青森	100.0	98.7	1.3	0.7	0.6	100.0	8.6	31.4	31.4	2.9	2.9	-	-
03 岩手	100.0	98.5	1.5	1.1	0.3	100.0	10.7	44.6	21.4	5.4	1.8	-	1.8
04 宮城	100.0	98.3	1.7	1.2	0.5	100.0	17.5	36.5	16.1	10.9	0.7	0.7	-
05 秋田	100.0	99.0	1.0	0.7	0.2	100.0	3.8	42.3	34.6	7.7	-	-	-
06 山形	100.0	98.3	1.7	1.4	0.3	100.0	12.1	39.7	17.2	1.7	1.7	-	-
07 福島	100.0	97.3	2.7	2.3	0.4	100.0	6.5	29.0	41.0	4.0	0.5	-	0.5
08 茨城	100.0	96.6	3.4	2.7	0.7	100.0	9.8	30.7	20.1	20.7	1.4	0.3	2.2
09 栃木	100.0	96.3	3.7	2.9	0.8	100.0	5.6	33.2	19.8	16.0	0.7	0.4	3.0
10 群馬	100.0	96.5	3.5	2.6	0.9	100.0	6.3	25.2	30.6	5.4	1.4	-	2.7
11 埼玉	100.0	96.2	3.8	2.8	1.0	100.0	8.7	45.2	20.0	5.8	0.8	0.2	1.3
12 千葉	100.0	95.5	4.5	3.3	1.2	100.0	12.0	37.4	23.4	9.6	1.1	0.2	1.2
13 東京	100.0	94.9	5.1	3.2	1.9	100.0	15.0	42.7	14.4	6.2	3.0	0.7	0.5
14 神奈川	100.0	95.7	4.3	2.9	1.4	100.0	12.6	40.1	19.2	6.9	1.5	0.2	1.2
15 新潟	100.0	98.1	1.9	1.7	0.3	100.0	10.4	46.1	18.2	6.5	1.3	0.6	1.3
16 富山	100.0	96.5	3.5	2.9	0.6	100.0	3.9	64.1	18.8	3.1	0.8	-	1.6
17 石川	100.0	98.0	2.0	1.4	0.5	100.0	8.1	47.3	17.6	9.5	-	1.4	2.7
18 福井	100.0	97.3	2.7	2.4	0.3	100.0	14.6	34.1	28.0	2.4	1.2	-	4.9
19 山梨	100.0	96.9	3.1	2.4	0.7	100.0	10.1	41.6	22.5	4.5	2.2	-	3.4
20 長野	100.0	96.3	3.7	3.2	0.5	100.0	13.6	31.1	18.9	18.5	0.3	0.7	2.4
21 岐阜	100.0	95.3	4.7	4.1	0.6	100.0	5.7	28.4	54.3	2.3	0.6	0.3	1.4
22 静岡	100.0	96.4	3.6	2.8	0.8	100.0	9.1	26.6	35.5	6.6	1.9	0.6	4.1
23 愛知	100.0	94.9	5.1	4.0	1.2	100.0	7.3	32.2	42.0	3.0	0.6	0.1	3.3
24 三重	100.0	96.4	3.6	2.9	0.7	100.0	7.9	30.8	26.7	8.8	1.7	-	1.7
25 滋賀	100.0	97.6	2.4	1.8	0.6	100.0	19.0	31.4	26.4	0.8	1.7	-	4.1
26 京都	100.0	96.5	3.5	2.2	1.3	100.0	20.6	31.5	11.6	7.5	2.6	-	0.4
27 大阪	100.0	96.1	3.9	2.6	1.4	100.0	35.4	35.5	10.3	5.4	1.2	0.7	0.4
28 兵庫	100.0	96.9	3.1	2.1	1.0	100.0	27.9	39.3	9.6	4.1	1.8	0.4	0.4
29 奈良	100.0	97.9	2.1	1.6	0.6	100.0	24.7	33.7	11.2	9.0	-	-	
30 和歌山	100.0	98.0	2.0	1.7	0.3	100.0	16.2	39.7	16.2	19.1	-	1.5	1.5
31 鳥取	100.0	98.6	1.4	0.9	0.5	100.0	13.0	34.8	30.4	4.3	4.3	-	4.3
32 島根	100.0	98.4	1.6	1.3	0.3	100.0	5.4	29.7	32.4	10.8	2.7	-	-
33 岡山	100.0	97.6	2.4	2.0	0.4	100.0	11.3	51.4	19.2	4.5	0.6	-	0.6
34 広島	100.0	97.4	2.6	2.1	0.5	100.0	6.2	31.0	29.7	5.5	1.0	-	2.1
35 山口	100.0	97.8	2.2	1.3	0.9	100.0	17.6	25.7	27.0	6.8	2.7	-	-
36 徳島	100.0	98.4	1.6	1.1	0.5	100.0	8.3	44.4	22.2	5.6	-	-	2.8
37 香川	100.0	98.5	1.5	1.1	0.4	100.0	4.0	46.0	28.0	2.0	-	-	2.0
38 愛媛	100.0	98.7	1.3	1.0	0.3	100.0	6.9	37.9	20.7	6.9	1.7	-	1.7
39 高知	100.0	98.7	1.3	0.7	0.5	100.0	14.3	38.1	38.1	-	-	-	-
40 福岡	100.0	98.1	1.9	1.2	0.7	100.0	13.8	39.0	21.8	4.0	1.8	0.3	0.9
41 佐賀	100.0	99.0	1.0	0.9	0.1	100.0	2.9	34.3	31.4	-	-	2.9	-
42 長崎	100.0	98.3	1.7	0.8	0.9	100.0	6.0	30.0	30.0	4.0	4.0	2.0	2.0
43 熊本	100.0	98.4	1.6	1.3	0.3	100.0	1.9	38.3	36.4	3.7	4.7	-	0.9
44 大分	100.0	98.5	1.5	1.0	0.5	100.0	11.8	35.3	39.2	3.9	-	-	-
45 宮崎	100.0	99.1	0.9	0.6	0.2	100.0	6.3	34.4	31.3	3.1	6.3	-	-
46 鹿児島	100.0	99.0	1.0	0.8	0.2	100.0	4.9	42.6	34.4	4.9	3.3	-	-
47 沖縄	100.0	95.4	4.6	1.0	3.6	100.0	9.6	24.1	25.3	2.4	12.0	1.2	2.4

21大都市(再掲)　21 major cities (Regrouped)

都道府県 Prefecture	総数 Total	夫妻とも日本 Japanese couple	夫妻の一方が外国 One of couple is foreigner	夫日本・妻外国 Japanese groom and foreign bride	妻日本・夫外国 Japanese bride and foreign groom	夫日本・妻外国 総数 Total	韓国・朝鮮 Korea	中国 China	フィリピン Philippines	タイ Thailand	米国 U.S.A.	英国 United Kingdom	ブラジル Brazil
50 東京都の区部	100.0	94.6	5.4	3.3	2.1	100.0	16.0	43.5	13.7	6.3	2.8	0.6	0.6
51 札幌	100.0	98.9	1.1	0.6	0.5	100.0	13.8	24.6	9.2	7.7	7.7	3.1	1.5
52 仙台	100.0	98.2	1.8	1.0	0.7	100.0	14.5	46.8	4.8	12.9	-	1.6	-
53 さいたま	100.0	96.8	3.2	2.2	0.9	100.0	9.3	53.3	16.0	4.0	2.0	-	0.7
54 千葉	100.0	95.5	4.5	3.4	1.1	100.0	17.0	44.0	19.5	6.3	1.9	0.6	0.6
55 横浜	100.0	95.5	4.5	3.3	1.3	100.0	12.1	44.4	17.2	8.4	1.4	0.2	0.8
56 川崎	100.0	95.8	4.2	2.8	1.4	100.0	14.9	45.3	18.5	4.3	2.9	0.7	0.4
57 相模原	100.0	95.8	4.2	3.0	1.3	100.0	15.2	19.2	23.2	4.0	1.0	-	2.0
58 新潟	100.0	98.5	1.5	1.2	0.3	100.0	11.4	52.3	11.4	6.8	2.3	-	2.3
59 静岡	100.0	97.3	2.7	1.9	0.8	100.0	19.4	22.6	24.2	6.5	-	3.2	4.8
60 浜松	100.0	95.7	4.3	3.4	0.9	100.0	8.4	31.3	43.5	3.1	1.5	-	2.3
61 名古屋	100.0	94.5	5.5	4.1	1.4	100.0	10.2	31.5	45.2	3.2	0.5	-	0.7
62 京都	100.0	95.9	4.1	2.3	1.7	100.0	21.0	29.0	10.8	7.4	1.1	-	-
63 大阪	100.0	94.4	5.6	3.3	2.3	100.0	41.0	34.3	9.1	5.5	1.0	0.3	0.3
64 堺	100.0	97.2	2.8	2.3	0.5	100.0	27.4	33.7	12.6	9.5	3.2	1.1	1.1
65 神戸	100.0	95.8	4.2	2.5	1.6	100.0	31.1	34.2	4.2	4.2	1.6	-	-
66 岡山	100.0	97.6	2.4	2.0	0.5	100.0	10.8	52.7	20.3	5.4	-	-	-
67 広島	100.0	97.0	3.0	2.3	0.6	100.0	8.6	34.4	33.1	6.2	0.7	-	2.0
68 北九州	100.0	98.3	1.7	1.1	0.6	100.0	19.2	40.4	19.2	9.6	1.9	-	-
69 福岡	100.0	97.7	2.3	1.2	1.1	100.0	14.9	43.8	13.2	2.5	0.8	-	-
70 熊本	100.0	98.3	1.7	1.2	0.5	100.0	-	55.3	29.8	4.3	4.3	-	-

（21大都市再掲）別婚姻件数百分率
of bride and groom : Japan, each prefecture and 21 major cities, 2016

Marriages
平成28年

妻日本・夫外国 / Japanese bride and foreign groom

ペルー Peru	その他の国 Other foreign countries	総数 Total	韓国・朝鮮 Korea	中国 China	フィリピン Philippines	タイ Thailand	米国 U.S.A.	英国 United Kingdom	ブラジル Brazil	ペルー Peru	その他の国 Other foreign countries	都道府県 Prefecture
0.6	15.8	100.0	25.7	12.5	2.4	0.5	16.7	3.9	5.0	1.5	31.8	全国 Total a)
1.3	31.5	100.0	23.8	7.5	1.3	1.3	20.0	5.0	-	-	41.3	01 北海道
-	22.9	100.0	6.5				93.5		-	-		02 青森
-	14.3	100.0	40.0	13.3	6.7	-	13.3	6.7	-	-	20.0	03 岩手
0.7	16.8	100.0	43.6	9.1	3.6	-	5.5	9.1	-	1.8	27.3	04 宮城
-	11.5	100.0	25.0	-	-		12.5	-		-	62.5	05 秋田
-	27.6	100.0	23.1	15.4	-	-	15.4	-	-	-	46.2	06 山形
-	18.5	100.0	22.6	6.5	-	3.2	12.9	16.1	-	-	38.7	07 福島
1.1	13.7	100.0	11.5	9.4	9.4	6.3	7.3	2.1	7.3	2.1	44.8	08 茨城
2.6	18.7	100.0	9.5	9.5	2.7	1.4	12.2	2.7	13.5	9.5	39.2	09 栃木
2.3	26.1	100.0	9.2	6.6	1.3	-	6.6	2.6	18.4	13.2	42.1	10 群馬
0.4	17.6	100.0	16.5	20.3	2.9	-	7.0	3.2	7.5	0.9	41.7	11 埼玉
0.3	14.8	100.0	16.1	19.5	7.2	0.6	11.2	2.9	5.5	2.3	34.8	12 千葉
0.4	17.1	100.0	24.9	13.5	1.7	0.3	14.0	5.7	1.2	1.1	37.8	13 東京
1.0	17.3	100.0	20.0	10.7	2.6	0.8	25.3	3.9	2.7	1.4	32.7	14 神奈川
0.6	14.9	100.0	11.5	11.5	3.8	-	15.4	15.4	3.8	-	38.5	15 新潟
0.8	7.0	100.0	10.7	10.7	3.6	-	14.3	7.1	21.4	-	32.1	16 富山
-	13.5	100.0	25.0	14.3	3.6	-	14.3	3.6	10.7	-	28.6	17 石川
-	14.6	100.0	50.0	8.3	-	-	8.3	8.3	16.7	-	8.3	18 福井
-	15.7	100.0	28.0	8.0	-	4.0	12.0	4.0	8.0	-	36.0	19 山梨
-	14.3	100.0	15.9	15.9	6.8	2.3	13.6	4.5	11.4	2.3	27.3	20 長野
0.3	6.6	100.0	11.3	11.3	7.5	-	7.5	1.9	15.1	5.7	39.6	21 岐阜
1.2	14.3	100.0	11.4	14.4	3.0	0.8	6.8	3.8	30.3	3.8	25.8	22 静岡
0.7	10.8	100.0	23.0	9.4	4.9	-	7.9	2.1	17.5	3.0	32.2	23 愛知
1.3	21.3	100.0	47.3	3.6	-	1.8	1.8	1.8	18.2	3.6	21.8	24 三重
0.8	15.7	100.0	31.8	11.4	2.3	-	6.8	2.3	29.5	-	15.9	25 滋賀
-	25.8	100.0	30.1	11.7	-	0.2	9.2	4.3	1.8	1.2	41.7	26 京都
0.3	10.9	100.0	50.9	14.8	0.6	0.2	6.3	3.8	0.9	0.3	22.3	27 大阪
0.4	16.2	100.0	45.7	12.6	1.2	0.4	9.1	2.4	1.6	0.8	26.4	28 兵庫
-	21.3	100.0	41.9	9.7	3.2	-	19.4	-	6.5	-	19.4	29 奈良
-	5.9	100.0	66.7	-	-	8.3	25.0		-	-		30 和歌山
-	8.7	100.0	45.5	27.3	-	-	9.1	-	-	-	18.2	31 鳥取
-	18.9	100.0	14.3	28.6	-	-	28.6	-	14.3	-	14.3	32 島根
-	12.4	100.0	33.3	10.3	5.1	-	10.3	5.1	7.7	-	28.2	33 岡山
0.7	23.8	100.0	35.7	10.0	2.9	2.9	12.9	1.4	7.1	1.4	25.7	34 広島
-	20.3	100.0	26.4	5.7	-	-	49.1	5.7	1.9	-	11.3	35 山口
-	16.7	100.0	13.3	13.3	6.7	-	20.0	13.3	-	-	33.3	36 徳島
2.0	16.0	100.0	22.2	22.2	-	-	11.1	11.1	-	16.7	16.7	37 香川
-	24.1	100.0	42.1	5.3	5.3	-	15.8	-	-	-	31.6	38 愛媛
-	9.5	100.0	12.5	-	-	6.3	37.5	6.3	-	-	37.5	39 高知
0.3	18.1	100.0	37.8	17.8	-	-	5.0	2.8	0.6	0.6	35.6	40 福岡
-	28.6	100.0	25.0	50.0	-	-			-	-	25.0	41 佐賀
-	22.0	100.0	7.7	3.8	-	-	69.2	1.9	-	-	17.3	42 長崎
-	14.0	100.0	27.3	18.2	-	-	27.3	4.5	-	-	22.7	43 熊本
2.0	7.8	100.0	33.3	8.3	8.3	-	12.5	4.2	-	-	33.3	44 大分
-	18.8	100.0	8.3	33.3	-	-	16.7	-	-	-	41.7	45 宮崎
-	9.8	100.0	28.6	14.3		-	21.4	7.1	-	-	28.6	46 鹿児島
1.2	21.7	100.0	4.2	2.3	0.7	0.3	80.1	0.7	1.3	0.7	9.8	47 沖縄
												21大都市(再掲) 21 major cities (Regrouped)
0.2	16.3	100.0	25.3	14.0	1.4	0.3	12.2	6.0	0.8	0.6	39.3	50 東京都の区部
3.1	29.2	100.0	28.6	6.1	2.0	2.0	22.4	2.0	-	-	36.7	51 札幌
-	19.4	100.0	40.9	11.4	4.5	-	4.5	11.4	-	2.3	25.0	52 仙台
-	14.7	100.0	26.2	14.8	1.6	-	8.2	9.8	4.9	-	34.4	53 さいたま
0.6	9.4	100.0	19.6	23.5	13.7	-	3.9	5.9	5.9	3.9	23.5	54 千葉
0.5	15.1	100.0	21.8	16.5	1.2	-	16.9	6.2	2.5	0.4	34.6	55 横浜
0.7	12.3	100.0	30.1	14.0	2.8	1.4	13.3	1.4	1.4	0.7	35.0	56 川崎
2.0	33.3	100.0	14.3	4.8	2.4	-	11.9	7.1	-	2.4	57.1	57 相模原
-	13.6	100.0	18.2	18.2	-	-	27.3	9.1	-	-	27.3	58 新潟
1.6	17.7	100.0	16.0	32.0	-	-	4.0	4.0	8.0	-	36.0	59 静岡
0.8	9.2	100.0	8.6	5.7	2.9	-	5.7	11.4	45.7	-	20.0	60 浜松
0.5	8.3	100.0	26.3	11.8	3.2	-	13.4	3.2	7.0	1.6	33.3	61 名古屋
-	30.7	100.0	26.7	12.2	-	-	10.7	3.8	1.5	0.8	44.3	62 京都
0.2	8.3	100.0	51.0	13.3	0.2	0.2	7.2	4.3	1.0	-	22.7	63 大阪
-	11.6	100.0	38.1	33.3	-	-	4.8	-	-	-	23.8	64 堺
0.5	24.2	100.0	38.2	15.4	0.8	-	8.1	4.1	2.4	-	30.9	65 神戸
-	10.8	100.0	35.3	11.8	-	-	5.9	11.8	5.9	-	29.4	66 岡山
0.7	11.9	100.0	39.5	7.9	-	2.6	13.2	2.6	5.3	2.6	26.3	67 広島
-	9.6	100.0	48.4	16.1	-	-	3.2	-	-	-	32.3	68 北九州
-	24.8	100.0	28.8	20.2	-	-	7.7	3.8	1.0	1.0	37.5	69 福岡
-	6.4	100.0	22.2	22.2	-	-	27.8	5.6	-	-	22.2	70 熊本

Note : a) See page 44.

離 婚

〔地域別にみた離婚〕
〔Divorces by prefecture〕

第10章 離　　　婚
Chapter 10 Divorces

表10.1　都 道 府 県 別 に み た
Table 10.1　Trends in divorces by

都道府県[1] Prefecture	1 9 3 5 昭和10年	1 9 4 7 22　年	1 9 5 0 25　年[2]	1 9 5 5 30　年	1 9 6 0 35　年	1 9 6 5 40　年	1 9 7 0 45　年	1 9 7 5 50　年	1 9 8 0 55　年
全　国　Total	48 528	79 551	83 689	75 267	69 410	77 195	95 937	119 135	141 689
01 北 海 道 [a]	1 946	3 061	4 134	4 620	4 663	5 850	7 416	8 818	10 342
02 青　　森	908	1 197	1 396	1 329	1 276	1 480	1 763	2 047	2 307
03 岩　　手	816	1 518	1 330	1 085	973	946	1 019	1 180	1 290
04 宮　　城	732	1 273	1 346	1 196	1 138	1 234	1 486	1 841	2 167
05 秋　　田	1 087	2 131	1 625	1 173	1 077	995	1 025	1 184	1 317
06 山　　形	885	1 534	1 462	1 007	821	664	804	866	993
07 福　　島	1 041	2 181	1 988	1 584	1 415	1 312	1 475	1 784	2 102
08 茨　　城	725	1 270	1 314	1 046	996	955	1 358	1 888	2 315
09 栃　　木	713	1 154	1 310	1 039	822	917	1 145	1 524	1 914
10 群　　馬	734	1 223	1 383	1 077	920	1 004	1 246	1 709	1 969
11 埼　　玉	836	1 523	1 590	1 340	1 182	1 797	2 990	4 584	5 901
12 千　　葉	944	1 536	1 650	1 352	1 244	1 638	2 596	3 937	5 426
13 東　　京	3 656	4 661	6 646	7 429	7 719	9 834	12 297	14 503	15 969
14 神 奈 川	1 031	1 928	2 262	2 632	2 725	3 906	5 506	7 508	8 897
15 新　　潟	1 937	2 660	2 456	1 702	1 485	1 228	1 472	1 661	1 952
16 富　　山	707	1 512	1 117	877	771	720	823	972	1 016
17 石　　川	777	1 234	1 079	824	751	763	955	1 120	1 267
18 福　　井	632	935	827	684	585	499	582	719	779
19 山　　梨	338	621	565	435	397	430	523	657	784
20 長　　野	875	1 558	1 375	1 080	889	907	1 150	1 432	1 715
21 岐　　阜	910	1 298	1 346	1 112	1 028	1 027	1 288	1 552	1 728
22 静　　岡	1 417	2 354	2 269	1 955	1 818	2 064	2 701	3 536	4 202
23 愛　　知	1 938	2 451	3 042	2 767	2 643	3 298	4 337	5 430	6 550
24 三　　重	718	1 247	1 259	1 016	833	932	1 098	1 236	1 589
25 滋　　賀	415	732	598	480	404	426	509	617	867
26 京　　都	984	1 750	1 903	1 630	1 327	1 520	1 871	2 329	2 884
27 大　　阪	2 433	3 833	4 579	4 618	4 632	6 317	8 161	10 146	12 100
28 兵　　庫	1 853	3 254	3 423	3 255	3 094	3 485	4 259	5 025	5 747
29 奈　　良	417	822	810	657	533	573	730	922	1 125
30 和 歌 山	631	1 089	1 006	914	810	885	1 042	1 107	1 418
31 鳥　　取	433	716	699	578	475	440	439	566	580
32 島　　根	690	1 177	886	676	563	432	460	499	579
33 岡　　山	938	1 639	1 702	1 518	1 317	1 262	1 449	1 814	2 029
34 広　　島	1 729	2 678	2 530	2 448	2 027	2 056	2 274	2 767	3 160
35 山　　口	1 017	1 823	1 802	1 726	1 570	1 482	1 742	1 789	1 958
36 徳　　島	568	857	865	712	574	532	622	829	1 024
37 香　　川	673	1 127	1 078	900	720	712	844	990	1 220
38 愛　　媛	1 109	1 748	1 906	1 550	1 277	1 301	1 446	1 764	2 062
39 高　　知	679	1 089	1 127	1 100	1 009	977	1 072	1 172	1 267
40 福　　岡	1 930	3 918	4 402	4 336	3 971	4 113	4 879	5 655	7 156
41 佐　　賀	491	1 031	943	805	665	641	658	751	859
42 長　　崎	972	1 916	2 102	1 761	1 687	1 380	1 503	1 723	1 965
43 熊　　本	1 006	1 803	1 847	1 421	1 332	1 262	1 427	1 472	1 865
44 大　　分	815	1 333	1 284	1 122	921	838	1 098	1 216	1 587
45 宮　　崎	549	1 111	1 185	1 045	922	897	1 063	1 316	1 634
46 鹿 児 島	1 086	2 045	1 671	1 654	1 409	1 264	1 334	1 638	2 080
47 沖　　縄	807	…	…	…	…	…	…	1 340	2 032

注：1)　昭和10年は夫の住所、昭和22〜40年は離婚当時の夫の住所、昭和45年以降は別居する前の住所による。
　　2)　昭和25年の全国には、不詳570を含む。

554

Divorces

年 次 別 離 婚 件 数
each prefecture : Japan

1985 60 年	1990 平成2年	1995 7 年	2000 12 年	2005 17 年	2010 22 年	2014 26 年	2015 27 年	2016 28 年	都道府県[1] Prefecture
166 640	157 608	199 016	264 246	261 917	251 378	222 107	226 215	216 798	全 国 Total
									a)
12 042	9 722	11 227	14 233	13 597	12 596	11 003	11 211	10 476	01 北 海 道
2 512	2 001	2 429	3 092	3 281	2 679	2 195	2 267	2 164	02 青　森
1 521	1 328	1 590	2 292	2 506	2 327	1 855	1 956	1 877	03 岩　手
2 628	2 517	3 198	4 508	4 820	4 667	3 824	3 987	3 783	04 宮　城
1 451	1 256	1 478	1 925	1 856	1 795	1 444	1 534	1 393	05 秋　田
1 160	1 097	1 330	1 952	2 048	1 887	1 670	1 507	1 522	06 山　形
2 439	2 179	2 903	3 950	4 366	3 965	3 165	3 239	3 278	07 福　島
3 102	3 014	4 249	5 834	5 833	5 693	4 955	5 190	4 816	08 茨　城
2 127	2 179	2 835	3 902	4 045	3 898	3 322	3 388	3 429	09 栃　木
2 099	2 180	2 892	3 977	3 948	3 865	3 312	3 463	3 241	10 群　馬
7 494	7 775	11 062	14 368	14 521	14 325	12 484	12 667	12 481	11 埼　玉
6 858	7 092	9 639	12 700	12 579	12 391	10 642	10 916	10 612	12 千　葉
17 955	17 935	21 548	27 032	26 984	26 335	23 653	24 135	23 470	13 東　京
10 633	11 059	14 588	18 828	18 516	17 830	16 004	16 234	15 673	14 神 奈 川
2 266	2 003	2 644	3 635	3 601	3 438	3 175	3 193	2 987	15 新　潟
1 073	1 086	1 217	1 727	1 735	1 569	1 417	1 477	1 368	16 富　山
1 374	1 208	1 437	2 036	1 907	1 817	1 708	1 703	1 653	17 石　川
896	780	889	1 327	1 395	1 233	1 135	1 194	1 119	18 福　井
852	848	1 112	1 638	1 743	1 693	1 401	1 441	1 369	19 山　梨
2 055	2 022	2 589	3 733	3 953	3 636	3 279	3 366	3 180	20 長　野
2 085	1 994	2 507	3 472	3 564	3 395	3 182	3 108	3 058	21 岐　阜
4 572	4 432	5 723	7 380	7 474	7 241	6 439	6 504	6 237	22 静　岡
7 766	7 998	10 405	13 841	13 997	14 253	12 780	13 102	12 464	23 愛　知
1 869	1 918	2 510	3 549	3 700	3 461	3 098	3 125	2 923	24 三　重
1 015	1 120	1 594	2 244	2 472	2 466	2 240	2 321	2 202	25 滋　賀
3 248	3 050	4 047	5 403	5 116	4 964	4 462	4 434	4 222	26 京　都
14 355	13 524	17 238	22 715	20 973	20 752	17 834	18 101	17 279	27 大　阪
6 802	6 622	7 715	11 905	11 369	10 738	9 598	9 774	9 302	28 兵　庫
1 519	1 512	2 097	2 755	2 604	2 602	2 225	2 309	2 183	29 奈　良
1 524	1 461	1 790	2 403	2 181	2 077	1 914	1 891	1 771	30 和 歌 山
750	674	809	1 191	1 192	1 141	1 029	993	937	31 鳥　取
742	645	818	1 095	1 124	1 110	966	1 022	949	32 島　根
2 479	2 169	2 844	3 878	3 722	3 626	3 212	3 296	3 245	33 岡　山
3 480	3 402	4 376	5 706	5 609	5 472	4 838	4 942	4 691	34 広　島
2 229	1 948	2 341	2 999	2 846	2 531	2 269	2 423	2 149	35 山　口
1 017	934	1 160	1 598	1 576	1 445	1 269	1 211	1 184	36 徳　島
1 263	1 226	1 503	2 026	2 029	1 928	1 719	1 767	1 613	37 香　川
2 254	1 954	2 290	3 102	3 037	2 811	2 404	2 395	2 244	38 愛　媛
1 343	1 251	1 525	1 859	1 787	1 463	1 364	1 356	1 228	39 高　知
8 918	7 699	9 064	12 053	11 567	10 952	9 981	10 063	9 772	40 福　岡
1 106	991	1 224	1 635	1 759	1 536	1 324	1 354	1 378	41 佐　賀
2 304	1 922	2 361	2 906	2 976	2 515	2 316	2 304	2 169	42 長　崎
2 527	2 171	2 893	3 716	3 718	3 623	3 105	3 290	2 915	43 熊　本
1 788	1 583	1 959	2 351	2 382	2 314	2 004	2 066	1 999	44 大　分
1 981	1 615	1 940	2 713	2 658	2 415	2 296	2 308	2 202	45 宮　崎
2 577	2 199	2 623	3 473	3 584	3 328	3 025	3 085	2 891	46 鹿 児 島
2 590	2 313	2 804	3 589	3 667	3 580	3 571	3 603	3 700	47 沖　縄

Note : a) See page 44.

離　婚

表 10.2　都道府県別にみた
Table 10.2　Trends in divorce rates (per 1,000

都道府県[1] Prefecture	1935 昭和10年	1947 22　年	1950 25　年[2]	1955 30　年	1960 35　年	1965 40　年	1970 45　年	1975 50　年	1980 55　年
全　国　Total	0.70	1.02	1.01	0.84	0.74	0.79	0.93	1.07	1.22
01 北　海　道[a]	0.63	0.79	0.96	0.97	0.93	1.13	1.43	1.65	1.86
02 青　　　森	0.94	1.01	1.09	0.96	0.89	1.04	1.24	1.40	1.52
03 岩　　　手	0.78	1.20	0.99	0.76	0.67	0.67	0.74	0.85	0.91
04 宮　　　城	0.59	0.81	0.81	0.69	0.65	0.70	0.82	0.94	1.04
05 秋　　　田	1.05	1.69	1.24	0.87	0.81	0.78	0.83	0.96	1.05
06 山　　　形	0.79	1.15	1.08	0.74	0.62	0.53	0.66	0.71	0.79
07 福　　　島	0.66	1.09	0.96	0.76	0.69	0.66	0.76	0.91	1.03
08 茨　　　城	0.47	0.63	0.64	0.51	0.49	0.46	0.63	0.81	0.91
09 栃　　　木	0.60	0.75	0.84	0.67	0.54	0.60	0.73	0.90	1.07
10 群　　　馬	0.59	0.78	0.86	0.67	0.58	0.63	0.75	0.97	1.07
11 埼　　　玉	0.55	0.73	0.74	0.59	0.49	0.60	0.77	0.95	1.09
12 千　　　葉	0.61	0.73	0.77	0.61	0.54	0.61	0.77	0.95	1.15
13 東　　　京	0.57	0.93	1.06	0.92	0.80	0.90	1.09	1.25	1.39
14 神　奈　川	0.56	0.87	0.91	0.90	0.79	0.88	1.01	1.18	1.29
15 新　　　潟	0.97	1.10	1.00	0.69	0.61	0.51	0.62	0.70	0.80
16 富　　　山	0.88	1.54	1.11	0.86	0.75	0.70	0.80	0.91	0.92
17 石　　　川	1.01	1.33	1.13	0.85	0.77	0.78	0.96	1.05	1.14
18 福　　　井	0.98	1.29	1.10	0.91	0.78	0.66	0.79	0.94	0.99
19 山　　　梨	0.52	0.77	0.70	0.54	0.51	0.56	0.69	0.84	0.98
20 長　　　野	0.51	0.76	0.67	0.53	0.45	0.46	0.59	0.71	0.82
21 岐　　　阜	0.74	0.87	0.87	0.70	0.63	0.60	0.74	0.84	0.89
22 静　　　岡	0.73	1.00	0.92	0.74	0.66	0.71	0.88	1.07	1.22
23 愛　　　知	0.68	0.78	0.90	0.73	0.63	0.69	0.81	0.92	1.06
24 三　　　重	0.61	0.88	0.86	0.68	0.56	0.62	0.71	0.76	0.95
25 滋　　　賀	0.58	0.85	0.69	0.56	0.48	0.50	0.58	0.63	0.81
26 京　　　都	0.58	1.01	1.04	0.84	0.67	0.72	0.85	0.98	1.16
27 大　　　阪	0.57	1.15	1.19	1.00	0.84	0.95	1.09	1.25	1.46
28 兵　　　庫	0.63	1.06	1.03	0.90	0.79	0.81	0.93	1.02	1.13
29 奈　　　良	0.67	1.05	1.06	0.85	0.68	0.69	0.79	0.86	0.94
30 和　歌　山	0.73	1.13	1.02	0.91	0.81	0.86	1.00	1.04	1.31
31 鳥　　　取	0.88	1.22	1.16	0.94	0.79	0.76	0.77	0.98	0.96
32 島　　　根	0.92	1.32	0.97	0.73	0.63	0.53	0.60	0.65	0.74
33 岡　　　山	0.70	1.01	1.02	0.90	0.79	0.77	0.85	1.00	1.09
34 広　　　島	0.96	1.33	1.22	1.14	0.93	0.90	0.94	1.05	1.16
35 山　　　口	0.85	1.23	1.17	1.07	0.98	0.96	1.16	1.16	1.24
36 徳　　　島	0.78	1.00	0.98	0.81	0.68	0.65	0.79	1.03	1.24
37 香　　　川	0.90	1.23	1.14	0.95	0.78	0.79	0.93	1.03	1.22
38 愛　　　媛	0.95	1.20	1.25	1.01	0.85	0.90	1.02	1.21	1.37
39 高　　　知	0.95	1.28	1.29	1.25	1.18	1.20	1.36	1.45	1.53
40 福　　　岡	0.70	1.23	1.25	1.12	0.99	1.04	1.22	1.33	1.58
41 佐　　　賀	0.72	1.12	1.00	0.83	0.71	0.74	0.79	0.90	0.99
42 長　　　崎	0.75	1.25	1.28	1.01	0.96	0.84	0.96	1.10	1.24
43 熊　　　本	0.73	1.02	1.01	0.75	0.72	0.71	0.84	0.86	1.04
44 大　　　分	0.83	1.08	1.02	0.88	0.74	0.71	0.95	1.02	1.29
45 宮　　　崎	0.67	1.08	1.09	0.92	0.81	0.83	1.01	1.21	1.42
46 鹿　児　島	0.68	1.17	0.93	0.81	0.72	0.68	0.77	0.95	1.17
47 沖　　　縄	1.36	…	…	…	…	…	…	1.29	1.85

注：1)　昭和10年は夫の住所、昭和22〜40年は離婚当時の夫の住所、昭和45年以降は別居する前の住所による。
　　2)　昭和25年の全国には不詳を含む。

年 次 別 離 婚 率（人口千対）
population) by each prefecture : Japan

1985 60 年	1990 平成2年	1995 7 年	2000 12 年	2005 17 年	2010 22 年	2014 26 年	2015 27 年	2016 28 年	都道府県[1] Prefecture
1.39	1.28	1.60	2.10	2.08	1.99	1.77	1.81	**1.73**	全 国　Total
2.12	1.73	1.98	2.51	2.42	2.30	2.04	2.09	**1.97**	01 北 海 道 [a]
1.65	1.35	1.64	2.10	2.29	1.96	1.67	1.74	**1.68**	02 青　　森
1.05	0.94	1.12	1.62	1.82	1.76	1.45	1.53	**1.49**	03 岩　　手
1.21	1.12	1.38	1.91	2.05	2.00	1.65	1.72	**1.63**	04 宮　　城
1.16	1.02	1.22	1.62	1.63	1.66	1.40	1.50	**1.38**	05 秋　　田
0.93	0.87	1.06	1.58	1.69	1.62	1.48	1.35	**1.37**	06 山　　形
1.19	1.04	1.36	1.86	2.10	1.96	1.64	1.70	**1.73**	07 福　　島
1.14	1.06	1.45	1.97	1.99	1.94	1.72	1.80	**1.68**	08 茨　　城
1.13	1.13	1.44	1.97	2.03	1.97	1.70	1.74	**1.77**	09 栃　　木
1.10	1.11	1.46	1.99	1.98	1.96	1.71	1.79	**1.68**	10 群　　馬
1.28	1.22	1.65	2.09	2.08	2.02	1.75	1.77	**1.74**	11 埼　　玉
1.33	1.28	1.68	2.16	2.10	2.02	1.74	1.78	**1.73**	12 千　　葉
1.52	1.53	1.87	2.28	2.19	2.05	1.81	1.84	**1.78**	13 東　　京
1.44	1.40	1.79	2.24	2.13	2.00	1.78	1.81	**1.74**	14 神 奈 川
0.93	0.81	1.07	1.47	1.49	1.46	1.38	1.39	**1.31**	15 新　　潟
0.95	0.97	1.09	1.55	1.58	1.45	1.34	1.40	**1.30**	16 富　　山
1.19	1.04	1.22	1.73	1.63	1.57	1.49	1.49	**1.45**	17 石　　川
1.09	0.95	1.09	1.62	1.72	1.55	1.46	1.54	**1.45**	18 福　　井
1.04	1.00	1.27	1.87	2.00	1.99	1.69	1.75	**1.67**	19 山　　梨
0.95	0.94	1.19	1.71	1.83	1.71	1.57	1.62	**1.54**	20 長　　野
1.02	0.97	1.20	1.67	1.72	1.66	1.58	1.56	**1.54**	21 岐　　阜
1.28	1.21	1.55	1.99	2.01	1.96	1.76	1.79	**1.72**	22 静　　岡
1.20	1.21	1.54	2.00	1.97	1.97	1.75	1.79	**1.70**	23 愛　　知
1.08	1.08	1.38	1.94	2.02	1.90	1.73	1.75	**1.65**	24 三　　重
0.87	0.92	1.25	1.69	1.82	1.78	1.60	1.67	**1.58**	25 滋　　賀
1.27	1.19	1.57	2.08	1.97	1.91	1.74	1.73	**1.65**	26 京　　都
1.66	1.58	2.00	2.63	2.43	2.39	2.06	2.08	**1.99**	27 大　　阪
1.29	1.24	1.45	2.18	2.07	1.95	1.76	1.79	**1.71**	28 兵　　庫
1.16	1.10	1.47	1.92	1.84	1.87	1.63	1.70	**1.62**	29 奈　　良
1.40	1.37	1.66	2.26	2.12	2.08	1.98	1.97	**1.87**	30 和 歌 山
1.21	1.10	1.32	1.95	1.98	1.95	1.80	1.74	**1.66**	31 鳥　　取
0.93	0.83	1.06	1.45	1.52	1.56	1.40	1.48	**1.39**	32 島　　根
1.30	1.13	1.47	2.00	1.92	1.88	1.68	1.73	**1.71**	33 岡　　山
1.23	1.20	1.53	2.00	1.97	1.94	1.73	1.76	**1.68**	34 広　　島
1.40	1.25	1.52	1.98	1.92	1.76	1.62	1.74	**1.56**	35 山　　口
1.22	1.12	1.40	1.95	1.96	1.85	1.67	1.61	**1.59**	36 徳　　島
1.22	1.20	1.47	1.99	2.02	1.95	1.76	1.82	**1.67**	37 香　　川
1.47	1.29	1.52	2.08	2.08	1.97	1.73	1.74	**1.64**	38 愛　　媛
1.59	1.52	1.87	2.29	2.25	1.92	1.86	1.87	**1.71**	39 高　　知
1.88	1.61	1.85	2.42	2.31	2.18	1.98	1.99	**1.93**	40 福　　岡
1.24	1.13	1.39	1.87	2.04	1.82	1.59	1.63	**1.67**	41 佐　　賀
1.44	1.23	1.53	1.92	2.02	1.77	1.68	1.68	**1.60**	42 長　　崎
1.38	1.18	1.56	2.00	2.03	2.00	1.74	1.85	**1.65**	43 熊　　本
1.43	1.28	1.60	1.93	1.98	1.95	1.72	1.78	**1.74**	44 大　　分
1.67	1.38	1.65	2.32	2.31	2.13	2.07	2.10	**2.02**	45 宮　　崎
1.41	1.22	1.46	1.95	2.05	1.96	1.82	1.88	**1.77**	46 鹿 児 島
2.20	1.90	2.22	2.74	2.71	2.58	2.53	2.53	**2.59**	47 沖　　縄

Note : a) See page 44.

離　婚

〔月別にみた離婚〕
〔Divorces by month of registration〕

表 10.3　届出月別にみた年次[1)]
Table 10.3　Trends in divorces and percent

年　　次 Year		総　数 Total	1　月 January	2　月 February	3　月 March	4　月 April	5　月 May
						実	数
1947	昭和22年	79 551	6 415	5 997	7 049	6 541	7 818
50	25	83 689	5 802	6 784	7 794	7 161	7 539
55	30	75 267	5 697	6 504	7 419	6 394	6 537
60	35	69 410	5 308	6 548	6 925	6 028	5 874
65	40	77 195	5 798	6 495	7 384	6 861	6 364
70	45	95 937	7 007	7 832	8 561	8 555	8 046
75	50	119 135	8 541	9 323	10 687	10 319	10 433
80	55	141 689	9 892	11 061	12 949	12 511	12 014
85	60	166 640	12 273	12 983	15 981	15 788	14 667
90	平成 2 年	157 608	11 903	12 004	15 661	13 482	13 933
95	7	199 016	14 659	15 736	20 753	16 920	16 848
2000	12	264 246	19 731	20 653	26 187	21 491	22 105
01	13	285 911	21 737	21 155	27 666	23 800	24 818
02	14	289 836	23 425	23 037	28 071	26 427	24 120
03	15	283 854	23 136	23 049	28 708	25 634	24 148
04	16	270 804	21 831	21 884	29 509	24 202	20 158
05	17	261 917	21 001	20 029	26 835	22 227	21 735
06	18	257 475	20 654	20 796	27 851	21 927	21 656
07	19	254 832	20 057	19 562	25 934	23 370	22 597
08	20	251 136	20 217	20 600	25 888	22 413	20 212
09	21	253 353	20 387	20 172	26 990	22 169	18 944
10	22	251 378	19 600	20 093	27 349	22 622	19 207
11	23	235 719	18 948	18 628	24 106	19 925	19 509
12	24	235 406	18 297	19 550	24 997	19 352	19 834
13	25	231 383	18 244	18 084	24 010	20 768	19 524
14	26	222 107	18 112	17 009	23 643	19 871	17 461
15	27	226 215	17 581	17 801	25 306	20 025	17 239
16	**28**	**216 798**	**16 715**	**18 286**	**24 190**	**18 019**	**17 476**
						百　分　率	
1947	昭和22年	100.0	8.1	7.5	8.9	8.2	9.8
50	25	100.0	6.9	8.1	9.3	8.6	9.0
55	30	100.0	7.6	8.6	9.9	8.5	8.7
60	35	100.0	7.6	9.4	10.0	8.7	8.5
65	40	100.0	7.5	8.4	9.6	8.9	8.2
70	45	100.0	7.3	8.2	8.9	8.9	8.4
75	50	100.0	7.2	7.8	9.0	8.7	8.8
80	55	100.0	7.0	7.8	9.1	8.8	8.5
85	60	100.0	7.4	7.8	9.6	9.5	8.8
90	平成 2 年	100.0	7.6	7.6	9.9	8.6	8.8
95	7	100.0	7.4	7.9	10.4	8.5	8.5
2000	12	100.0	7.5	7.8	9.9	8.1	8.4
01	13	100.0	7.6	7.4	9.7	8.3	8.7
02	14	100.0	8.1	7.9	9.7	9.1	8.3
03	15	100.0	8.2	8.1	10.1	9.0	8.5
04	16	100.0	8.1	8.1	10.9	8.9	7.4
05	17	100.0	8.0	7.6	10.2	8.5	8.3
06	18	100.0	8.0	8.1	10.8	8.5	8.4
07	19	100.0	7.9	7.7	10.2	9.2	8.9
08	20	100.0	8.1	8.2	10.3	8.9	8.0
09	21	100.0	8.0	8.0	10.7	8.8	7.5
10	22	100.0	7.8	8.0	10.9	9.0	7.6
11	23	100.0	8.0	7.9	10.2	8.5	8.3
12	24	100.0	7.8	8.3	10.6	8.2	8.4
13	25	100.0	7.9	7.8	10.4	9.0	8.4
14	26	100.0	8.2	7.7	10.6	8.9	7.9
15	27	100.0	7.8	7.9	11.2	8.9	7.6
16	**28**	**100.0**	**7.7**	**8.4**	**11.2**	**8.3**	**8.1**

注：1）　本表の上部に掲げた月は離婚の月であって、協議離婚については届出月、調停・審判・和解・請求の認諾及び判決離婚については、成立または確定の月である。

Divorces

別離婚件数及び百分率
distribution by month of registration[1] : Japan

6 月 June	7 月 July	8 月 August	9 月 September	10 月 October	11 月 November	12 月 December
Number						
5 979	6 158	6 634	7 230	6 732	5 612	7 386
6 249	6 664	7 618	7 683	7 185	6 209	7 001
5 849	5 697	6 311	6 807	6 098	5 431	6 523
5 309	5 272	5 483	6 036	5 666	5 331	5 630
6 233	6 210	6 401	6 678	6 328	6 102	6 341
7 931	8 125	7 638	8 615	8 557	7 371	7 699
10 146	10 249	9 250	11 102	10 518	8 774	9 793
11 640	12 024	11 464	12 723	12 530	10 619	12 262
13 477	14 508	13 431	13 543	14 233	12 506	13 250
12 988	13 273	12 941	12 419	14 011	12 257	12 736
16 987	16 021	16 732	16 441	16 884	15 268	15 767
21 617	21 213	22 595	21 914	22 451	20 452	23 837
23 020	24 077	25 188	22 956	25 622	22 677	23 195
21 917	25 170	23 913	23 910	24 934	21 756	23 156
23 490	24 638	21 916	23 593	23 491	19 498	22 553
22 300	22 414	22 356	22 216	20 800	21 071	22 063
21 988	20 967	22 416	21 795	21 706	20 378	20 840
21 587	20 649	21 137	20 177	20 912	19 412	20 717
20 564	20 934	21 043	19 194	21 800	19 527	20 250
20 457	20 857	19 218	20 698	21 583	17 567	21 426
21 548	21 598	19 848	20 985	20 697	18 934	21 081
21 241	20 416	20 428	20 912	19 883	19 427	20 200
19 433	18 758	20 074	19 626	18 900	18 275	19 537
19 154	19 491	19 467	18 335	20 132	18 013	18 784
18 061	19 917	18 324	18 604	19 398	17 487	18 962
18 363	18 702	16 772	18 475	18 829	15 921	18 949
19 304	18 919	17 442	17 920	18 456	16 927	19 295
18 516	**16 872**	**17 876**	**17 507**	**16 877**	**16 517**	**17 947**
Percentage						
7.5	7.7	8.3	9.1	8.5	7.1	9.3
7.5	8.0	9.1	9.2	8.6	7.4	8.4
7.8	7.6	8.4	9.0	8.1	7.2	8.7
7.6	7.6	7.9	8.7	8.2	7.7	8.1
8.1	8.0	8.3	8.7	8.2	7.9	8.2
8.3	8.5	8.0	9.0	8.9	7.7	8.0
8.5	8.6	7.8	9.3	8.8	7.4	8.2
8.2	8.5	8.1	9.0	8.8	7.5	8.7
8.1	8.7	8.1	8.1	8.5	7.5	8.0
8.2	8.4	8.2	7.9	8.9	7.8	8.1
8.5	8.1	8.4	8.3	8.5	7.7	7.9
8.2	8.0	8.6	8.3	8.5	7.7	9.0
8.1	8.4	8.8	8.0	9.0	7.9	8.1
7.6	8.7	8.3	8.2	8.6	7.5	8.0
8.3	8.7	7.7	8.3	8.3	6.9	7.9
8.2	8.3	8.3	8.2	7.7	7.8	8.1
8.4	8.0	8.6	8.3	8.3	7.8	8.0
8.4	8.0	8.2	7.8	8.1	7.5	8.0
8.1	8.2	8.3	7.5	8.6	7.7	7.9
8.1	8.3	7.7	8.2	8.6	7.0	8.5
8.5	8.5	7.8	8.3	8.2	7.5	8.3
8.4	8.1	8.1	8.3	7.9	7.7	8.0
8.2	8.0	8.5	8.3	8.0	7.8	8.3
8.1	8.3	8.3	7.8	8.6	7.7	8.0
7.8	8.6	7.9	8.0	8.4	7.6	8.2
8.3	8.4	7.6	8.3	8.5	7.2	8.5
8.5	8.4	7.7	7.9	8.2	7.5	8.5
8.5	**7.8**	**8.2**	**8.1**	**7.8**	**7.6**	**8.3**

Note : 1) Refers to month registration for divorces performed through mutual agreement or month of decree for those done through conciliation, adjustment, compromise, acknowledgment of claim or judicial divorce.

離 婚

〔種類別にみた離婚〕
〔Divorces by legal type〕

表 10.4　離婚の種類別にみた年次別離婚件数及び百分率
Table 10.4　Trends in divorces and percent distribution by legal type : Japan

年　　次 Year		総　　数 Total	協 議 離 婚 Divorce by mutual agreement	調 停 離 婚 Divorce by conciliation	審 判 離 婚 Divorce by adjustment	和 解 離 婚 Divorce by compromise	認 諾 離 婚 Divorce by acknowledgment of claim	判 決 離 婚 Judicial divorce
			実	数	Number			
1948	昭和23年	79 032	77 573	1 220	92	...	...	147
50	25	83 689	79 955	3 276	25	...	...	433
55	30	75 267	69 839	4 833	27	...	...	568
60	35	69 410	63 302	5 413	43	...	...	652
65	40	77 195	69 599	6 692	41	...	...	863
70	45	95 937	85 920	8 960	64	...	...	993
75	50	119 135	107 138	10 771	54	...	...	1 172
80	55	141 689	127 379	12 732	46	...	...	1 532
85	60	166 640	151 918	12 928	59	...	...	1 735
90	平成 2 年	157 608	142 623	13 317	44	...	...	1 624
95	7	199 016	179 844	17 302	66	...	...	1 804
2000	12	264 246	241 703	20 230	85	...	...	2 228
01	13	285 911	261 631	21 957	81	...	...	2 242
02	14	289 836	264 430	22 846	74	...	...	2 486
03	15	283 854	257 361	23 856	61	...	...	2 576
04	16 1)	270 804	242 680	23 609	152	1 341	14	3 008
05	17	261 917	233 086	22 906	185	2 476	19	3 245
06	18	257 475	228 802	22 683	121	2 805	17	3 047
07	19	254 832	225 215	23 476	97	3 243	15	2 786
08	20	251 136	220 487	24 432	84	3 486	11	2 636
09	21	253 353	222 662	24 654	89	3 414	22	2 512
10	22	251 378	220 166	24 977	84	3 648	30	2 473
11	23	235 719	205 998	23 576	69	3 478	24	2 574
12	24	235 406	205 074	23 616	82	3 831	15	2 788
13	25	231 383	201 883	23 025	173	3 502	17	2 783
14	26	222 107	194 161	21 855	298	3 303	18	2 472
15	27	226 215	198 214	21 730	379	3 491	18	2 383
16	**28**	**216 798**	**188 960**	**21 651**	**547**	**3 458**	**16**	**2 166**
			百	分	率	Percentage		
1948	昭和23年	100. 0	98. 2	1.5	0. 1	...	...	0. 2
50	25	100. 0	95. 5	3.9	0. 0	...	...	0. 5
55	30	100. 0	92. 8	6.4	0. 0	...	...	0. 8
60	35	100. 0	91. 2	7.8	0. 1	...	...	0. 9
65	40	100. 0	90. 2	8.7	0. 1	...	...	1. 1
70	45	100. 0	89. 6	9.3	0. 1	...	...	1. 0
75	50	100. 0	89. 9	9.0	0. 0	...	...	1. 0
80	55	100. 0	89. 9	9.0	0. 0	...	...	1. 1
85	60	100. 0	91. 2	7.8	0. 0	...	...	1. 0
90	平成 2 年	100. 0	90. 5	8.4	0. 0	...	...	1. 0
95	7	100. 0	90. 4	8.7	0. 0	...	...	0. 9
2000	12	100. 0	91. 5	7.7	0. 0	...	...	0. 8
01	13	100. 0	91. 5	7.7	0. 0	...	...	0. 8
02	14	100. 0	91. 2	7.9	0. 0	...	...	0. 9
03	15	100. 0	90. 7	8.4	0. 0	...	...	0. 9
04	16 1)	100. 0	89. 6	8.7	0. 1	0. 5	0. 0	1. 1
05	17	100. 0	89. 0	8.7	0. 1	0. 9	0. 0	1. 2
06	18	100. 0	88. 9	8.8	0. 0	1. 1	0. 0	1. 2
07	19	100. 0	88. 4	9.2	0. 0	1. 3	0. 0	1. 1
08	20	100. 0	87. 8	9.7	0. 0	1. 4	0. 0	1. 0
09	21	100. 0	87. 9	9.7	0. 0	1. 3	0. 0	1. 0
10	22	100. 0	87. 6	9.9	0. 0	1. 5	0. 0	1. 0
11	23	100. 0	87. 4	10.0	0. 0	1. 5	0. 0	1. 1
12	24	100. 0	87. 1	10.0	0. 0	1. 6	0. 0	1. 2
13	25	100. 0	87. 3	10.0	0. 1	1. 5	0. 0	1. 2
14	26	100. 0	87. 4	9.8	0. 1	1. 5	0. 0	1. 1
15	27	100. 0	87. 6	9.6	0. 2	1. 5	0. 0	1. 1
16	**28**	**100. 0**	**87. 2**	**10.0**	**0. 3**	**1. 6**	**0. 0**	**1. 0**

注：1)　平成16年の「和解離婚」と「認諾離婚」は、4月からの数値である。
Note : 1) Divorces by compromise or acknowledgment of claim are from April to December, 2004.

離　婚

〔夫妻の同居期間・同居をやめたときの年齢別にみた離婚〕
〔Divorces by duration of cohabitation and age of wife and husband at end of cohabitation〕

表10.5　結婚生活に入ってから同居をやめたときまでの
Table 10.5　Trends in divorces and percent distribution by duration

年　次 Year		総　数 Total	5年未満 Under 5 years	1年未満 Under 1 year	1年以上2年未満 1 year and over, less than 2 years	2～3	3～4	4～5
							実	数
1947	昭和22年	79 551	48 505	11 184	11 645	8 639	9 649	7 388
50	25	83 689	54 014	14 255	15 272	11 661	7 956	4 870
55	30	75 267	40 493	11 198	9 949	7 575	6 239	5 532
60	35	69 410	37 433	11 345	9 327	6 844	5 359	4 558
65	40	77 195	41 965	12 540	9 849	7 777	6 421	5 378
70	45	95 937	49 489	14 523	11 149	9 193	7 772	6 852
75	50	119 135	58 336	14 773	13 014	11 731	10 141	8 677
80	55	141 689	52 597	12 990	11 430	10 209	9 204	8 764
85	60	166 640	56 442	12 656	12 817	11 710	10 434	8 825
90	平成2年	157 608	59 676	13 066	14 387	12 325	10 452	9 446
95	7	199 016	76 710	14 893	18 081	16 591	14 576	12 569
2000	12	264 246	96 212	17 522	21 748	21 093	18 956	16 893
01	13	285 911	102 833	18 422	23 167	22 390	20 601	18 253
02	14	289 836	99 682	18 368	22 805	21 595	19 419	17 495
03	15	283 854	96 825	16 932	21 907	21 937	19 372	16 677
04	16	270 804	93 926	17 276	20 557	20 398	18 971	16 724
05	17	261 917	90 885	16 558	20 159	19 435	18 144	16 589
06	18	257 475	89 655	17 348	19 535	18 918	17 425	16 429
07	19	254 832	86 607	17 206	19 617	18 162	16 572	15 050
08	20	251 136	84 198	16 668	19 115	17 999	15 812	14 604
09	21	253 353	84 682	16 584	19 480	18 250	16 187	14 181
10	22	251 378	82 891	15 697	18 796	17 735	16 193	14 470
11	23	235 719	76 893	14 594	16 935	16 563	14 989	13 812
12	24	235 406	76 128	14 459	16 810	16 010	14 961	13 888
13	25	231 383	74 034	14 333	16 374	15 423	14 533	13 371
14	26	222 107	70 056	13 499	15 779	14 910	13 489	12 379
15	27	226 215	71 719	13 863	16 272	15 349	13 807	12 428
16	**28**	**216 798**	**68 011**	**13 157**	**15 330**	**14 499**	**13 299**	**11 726**
							百 分	率
1947	昭和22年	100.0	61.2	14.1	14.7	10.9	12.2	9.3
50	25	100.0	65.3	17.2	18.5	14.1	9.6	5.9
55	30	100.0	53.8	14.9	13.2	10.1	8.3	7.4
60	35	100.0	54.0	16.4	13.4	9.9	7.7	6.6
65	40	100.0	54.4	16.3	12.8	10.1	8.3	7.0
70	45	100.0	51.8	15.2	11.7	9.6	8.1	7.2
75	50	100.0	49.4	12.5	11.0	9.9	8.6	7.3
80	55	100.0	37.3	9.2	8.1	7.2	6.5	6.2
85	60	100.0	34.0	7.6	7.7	7.1	6.3	5.3
90	平成2年	100.0	38.1	8.4	9.2	7.9	6.7	6.0
95	7	100.0	39.5	7.7	9.3	8.5	7.5	6.5
2000	12	100.0	37.9	6.9	8.6	8.3	7.5	6.7
01	13	100.0	37.5	6.7	8.5	8.2	7.5	6.7
02	14	100.0	36.1	6.7	8.3	7.8	7.0	6.3
03	15	100.0	35.8	6.3	8.1	8.1	7.2	6.2
04	16	100.0	36.6	6.7	8.0	7.9	7.4	6.5
05	17	100.0	36.5	6.7	8.1	7.8	7.3	6.7
06	18	100.0	36.8	7.1	8.0	7.8	7.1	6.7
07	19	100.0	35.9	7.1	8.1	7.5	6.9	6.2
08	20	100.0	35.7	7.1	8.1	7.6	6.7	6.2
09	21	100.0	35.6	7.0	8.2	7.7	6.8	6.0
10	22	100.0	35.0	6.6	7.9	7.5	6.8	6.1
11	23	100.0	34.8	6.6	7.7	7.5	6.8	6.2
12	24	100.0	34.5	6.6	7.6	7.3	6.8	6.3
13	25	100.0	34.2	6.6	7.6	7.1	6.7	6.2
14	26	100.0	33.9	6.5	7.6	7.2	6.5	6.0
15	27	100.0	33.8	6.5	7.7	7.2	6.5	5.8
16	**28**	**100.0**	**33.6**	**6.5**	**7.6**	**7.2**	**6.6**	**5.8**

注：1)　同居期間不詳を除いた総数に対する百分率である。
　　2)　昭和22～45年の同居期間20～25年は、20年以上の数値である。
　　3)　平均同居期間算出の計算式を改め昭和50年から再計算をした。

562

Divorces

期間別にみた年次別離婚件数・百分率[1] 及び平均同居期間

of cohabitation, and mean duration of cohabitation : Japan

5〜10	10〜15	15〜20	20〜25[2]	25〜30	30〜35	35〜 35 years and over	不 詳 Not stated	平均同居期間[3](年) Mean duration of cohabitation (Year)
Number								
18 525	6 766	3 036	2 479	…	…	…	240	5.5
14 871	7 285	3 655	2 925	…	…	…	939	5.3
19 879	7 678	3 933	3 231	…	…	…	53	6.3
15 313	9 740	3 836	3 037	…	…	…	51	6.5
17 326	9 092	5 382	3 355	…	…	…	75	6.5
23 299	11 898	5 858	5 072	…	…	…	321	6.8
28 597	16 206	8 172	4 050	1 894	566	300	1 014	7.1
39 034	24 425	14 089	6 573	2 682	1 164	463	662	8.6
35 338	32 310	21 528	12 706	4 827	1 793	1 108	588	10.1
33 169	21 988	19 925	12 801	5 767	1 964	1 185	1 133	9.9
41 185	25 308	19 153	17 847	8 684	3 506	1 840	4 783	10.0
58 204	33 023	24 325	18 701	13 402	5 839	3 882	10 658	10.3
65 155	36 855	26 195	19 021	13 363	6 318	4 290	11 881	10.2
64 479	39 031	27 300	20 417	13 531	6 969	4 619	13 808	10.5
62 661	39 089	26 718	20 308	12 742	7 032	4 963	13 516	10.6
58 923	36 701	25 317	19 041	11 449	6 758	4 710	13 979	10.5
57 562	35 093	24 885	18 401	10 747	6 453	4 794	13 097	10.4
58 002	34 740	23 675	17 059	10 029	5 947	4 747	13 621	10.3
56 335	33 693	24 166	17 789	10 796	6 261	5 507	13 678	10.6
55 004	33 606	24 264	16 932	10 673	5 867	5 448	15 144	10.6
53 652	34 180	24 983	17 296	10 976	5 950	5 874	15 760	10.8
53 449	34 862	25 618	17 413	10 749	5 729	6 193	14 474	10.9
49 218	32 978	24 133	16 497	10 137	5 244	5 913	14 706	10.9
48 437	33 047	24 463	17 324	10 149	5 163	5 921	14 774	11.0
48 422	32 554	23 660	17 045	9 678	5 203	6 106	14 681	11.1
46 389	30 839	22 905	16 535	9 382	5 034	5 820	15 147	11.1
47 082	31 108	23 941	17 051	10 011	5 315	6 267	13 721	11.3
44 391	**29 531**	**22 986**	**16 857**	**9 744**	**5 041**	**5 959**	**14 278**	**11.3**
Percentage								
23.4	8.5	3.8	3.1	…	…	…	•	
18.0	8.8	4.4	3.5	…	…	…	•	
26.4	10.2	5.2	4.3	…	…	…	•	
22.1	14.0	5.5	4.4	…	…	…	•	
22.5	11.8	7.0	4.4	…	…	…	•	
24.4	12.4	6.1	5.3	…	…	…	•	
24.2	13.7	6.9	3.4	1.6	0.5	0.3	•	
27.7	17.3	10.0	4.7	1.9	0.8	0.3	•	
21.3	19.5	13.0	7.7	2.9	1.1	0.7	•	
21.2	14.1	12.7	8.2	3.7	1.3	0.8	•	
21.2	13.0	9.9	9.2	4.5	1.8	0.9	•	
23.0	13.0	9.6	7.4	5.3	2.3	1.5	•	
23.8	13.4	9.6	6.9	4.9	2.3	1.6	•	
23.4	14.1	9.9	7.4	4.9	2.5	1.7	•	
23.2	14.5	9.9	7.5	4.7	2.6	1.8	•	
22.9	14.3	9.9	7.4	4.5	2.6	1.8	•	
23.1	14.1	10.0	7.4	4.3	2.6	1.9	•	
23.8	14.2	9.7	7.0	4.1	2.4	1.9	•	
23.4	14.0	10.0	7.4	4.5	2.6	2.3	•	
23.3	14.2	10.3	7.2	4.5	2.5	2.3	•	
22.6	14.4	10.5	7.3	4.6	2.5	2.5	•	
22.6	14.7	10.8	7.4	4.5	2.4	2.6	•	
22.3	14.9	10.9	7.5	4.6	2.4	2.7	•	
22.0	15.0	11.1	7.9	4.6	2.3	2.7	•	
22.3	15.0	10.9	7.9	4.5	2.4	2.8	•	
22.4	14.9	11.1	8.0	4.5	2.4	2.8	•	
22.2	14.6	11.3	8.0	4.7	2.5	2.9	•	
21.9	**14.6**	**11.3**	**8.3**	**4.8**	**2.5**	**2.9**	•	

離　婚

表 10.6　同居をやめたときの年齢
（各届出年に同居を
Table 10.6　Trends in divorces by age of wife and husband at time

年次 Year		総数 Total	～19歳 Years	20～24	25～29	30～34	35～39	40～44	45～49
									夫
1950	昭和25年	51 500	389	9 426	15 364	9 578	6 610	4 239	2 608
55	30	41 714	69	4 504	13 834	8 930	5 089	3 533	2 292
60	35	36 832	59	3 257	11 728	9 427	4 824	2 674	1 808
65	40	42 705	65	4 012	12 589	11 260	6 568	3 329	1 754
70	45	55 968	134	5 924	16 293	13 406	8 961	5 102	2 467
75	50	74 227	160	7 041	21 228	17 807	11 314	7 700	4 350
80	55	89 361	140	4 751	17 333	24 926	17 147	10 722	7 305
85	60	110 085	284	6 263	15 682	22 948	24 521	17 072	11 064
90	平成 2 年	104 522	320	7 410	17 592	19 332	18 346	17 604	11 312
95	7	137 209	445	11 061	25 070	25 960	19 797	18 133	17 186
2000	12	194 122	683	12 808	35 288	39 040	29 660	22 207	19 789
01	13	214 142	709	13 648	38 244	45 363	33 973	24 744	20 219
02	14	216 378	730	12 628	34 822	44 571	34 969	26 366	21 705
03	15	210 838	696	12 301	31 869	42 897	34 816	26 737	20 769
04	16	199 458	541	11 543	29 025	41 270	34 176	25 390	19 406
05	17	193 137	505	11 026	27 308	39 789	33 242	25 276	19 021
06	18	190 239	450	10 525	26 358	39 488	34 421	24 985	18 255
07	19	185 005	437	9 707	24 716	36 534	33 861	24 443	18 671
08	20	183 377	465	9 247	23 851	34 776	33 727	25 397	19 120
09	21	185 285	575	9 070	23 104	33 003	34 606	26 779	19 446
10	22	184 570	471	8 639	22 573	32 071	34 915	27 296	20 123
11	23	172 520	448	7 863	20 641	29 308	32 190	26 770	18 789
12	24	170 738	446	8 012	20 222	28 574	31 344	27 166	19 107
13	25	167 836	492	7 689	19 827	28 452	30 255	26 886	19 232
14	26	161 303	517	7 456	18 639	26 927	28 303	26 690	18 671
15	27	164 303	486	7 738	18 801	27 127	27 921	27 111	19 576
16	**28**	**155 832**	**515**	**7 348**	**17 219**	**25 207**	**26 329**	**25 509**	**19 387**
									妻
1950	昭和25年	51 500	2 604	17 295	14 460	7 620	4 475	2 497	1 304
55	30	41 714	968	11 302	12 635	7 695	4 185	2 451	1 114
60	35	36 832	682	9 249	11 288	7 053	4 107	2 083	1 106
65	40	42 705	693	10 762	12 664	8 305	4 954	2 612	1 289
70	45	55 968	862	13 747	16 873	10 315	6 578	3 741	1 888
75	50	74 227	915	14 898	23 827	14 271	8 971	5 568	3 066
80	55	89 361	797	10 556	23 081	22 824	14 297	8 513	5 049
85	60	110 085	1 292	12 304	21 500	22 479	22 340	14 502	8 180
90	平成 2 年	104 522	1 312	13 554	23 730	18 532	16 219	14 779	8 608
95	7	137 209	1 413	19 188	31 825	25 628	17 462	15 536	13 655
2000	12	194 122	1 824	19 815	46 978	40 628	27 290	19 059	15 721
01	13	214 142	2 027	20 800	50 123	48 390	31 553	21 083	15 866
02	14	216 378	1 976	19 366	45 607	49 227	33 525	23 311	16 900
03	15	210 838	2 015	18 612	40 957	48 656	34 127	23 704	16 504
04	16	199 458	1 872	17 549	37 279	46 449	33 688	22 854	15 407
05	17	193 137	1 767	17 010	34 755	44 811	32 947	23 102	15 300
06	18	190 239	1 566	16 751	33 897	44 177	34 704	22 452	14 573
07	19	185 005	1 466	16 033	32 118	40 729	34 442	22 616	14 979
08	20	183 377	1 523	15 193	31 171	38 780	34 910	23 698	15 570
09	21	185 285	1 605	14 908	30 313	37 051	36 119	25 085	16 230
10	22	184 570	1 422	14 136	29 780	36 315	36 227	26 034	16 902
11	23	172 520	1 277	12 887	27 401	33 014	33 639	25 555	16 001
12	24	170 738	1 308	12 651	26 776	31 952	32 441	26 286	16 577
13	25	167 836	1 321	12 291	26 176	31 733	30 794	26 213	16 736
14	26	161 303	1 275	11 890	24 421	30 283	28 802	25 706	16 650
15	27	164 303	1 234	12 094	24 829	30 269	28 601	26 321	17 503
16	**28**	**155 832**	**1 149**	**11 316**	**22 847**	**28 444**	**26 614**	**24 807**	**17 761**

注：1)　昭和25年の70～74歳は、70歳以上の数値である。
　　2)　昭和30～平成17年の75～79歳は、75歳以上の数値である。

Divorces

別にみた年次別離婚件数－夫・妻－
やめ届け出たもの）
of decree (for divorces separated and registered each year) : Japan

50～54	55～59	60～64	65～69	70～74[1]	75～79[2]	80～	不 詳 Not stated
Husband							
1 534	845	467	241	180	...	...	19
1 479	982	493	286	151	72	...	-
1 196	804	501	281	167	101	...	5
1 172	804	506	347	173	122	...	4
1 250	962	604	398	207	143	...	117
2 085	1 081	676	386	250	147	...	2
3 730	1 624	745	485	263	189	...	1
6 736	3 165	1 187	559	331	272	...	1
6 359	3 504	1 580	619	281	263	...	-
10 022	5 242	2 515	1 085	386	307	...	-
17 444	9 168	4 446	2 153	897	539	...	-
18 969	9 294	5 086	2 362	965	566	...	-
20 062	10 518	5 508	2 759	1 134	606	...	-
19 005	11 299	5 759	2 765	1 260	665	...	-
16 682	11 102	5 748	2 615	1 236	722	...	2
15 331	11 381	5 552	2 663	1 305	737	...	1
14 223	11 676	5 110	2 736	1 240	513	259	-
13 955	11 797	5 609	2 975	1 459	546	295	-
13 640	11 314	6 347	3 064	1 487	641	297	4
14 025	11 235	7 219	3 547	1 600	714	360	2
14 131	10 262	7 718	3 617	1 669	739	346	-
13 275	9 315	7 634	3 313	1 799	782	392	1
13 365	8 875	7 264	3 384	1 771	792	415	1
12 914	8 493	6 658	3 739	1 926	824	448	1
12 584	8 280	5 912	3 889	2 044	914	477	-
13 256	8 410	5 954	4 288	2 129	938	568	-
12 906	**8 212**	**5 373**	**4 371**	**1 880**	**1 019**	**557**	-
Wife							
641	333	112	83	36	...	...	40
699	376	162	73	38	16	...	-
612	318	174	79	47	33	...	1
721	361	190	92	36	26	...	-
946	493	230	119	42	22	...	112
1 534	667	299	131	47	31	...	2
2 466	1 061	429	185	66	37	...	-
4 304	1 972	760	294	107	51	...	-
4 238	2 094	894	369	117	76	...	-
6 999	3 102	1 462	631	226	82	...	-
12 291	5 717	2 801	1 302	478	217	...	1
13 228	5 849	2 982	1 505	500	235	...	1
13 946	6 539	3 424	1 682	619	256	...	-
13 050	6 985	3 588	1 639	701	299	...	1
11 283	6 887	3 512	1 678	694	306	...	-
10 326	7 140	3 288	1 612	731	346	...	2
9 459	6 970	2 975	1 653	693	273	96	-
9 284	6 928	3 377	1 845	771	296	121	-
9 184	6 514	3 755	1 842	816	277	143	1
9 703	6 466	4 185	2 158	923	377	161	1
9 672	5 916	4 442	2 257	933	379	154	1
9 162	5 476	4 421	2 066	1 028	424	168	1
9 631	5 293	4 087	2 079	1 036	420	201	-
9 461	5 150	3 880	2 263	1 111	501	205	1
9 409	5 048	3 423	2 450	1 189	504	253	-
10 108	5 177	3 425	2 653	1 262	548	279	-
9 934	**5 173**	**3 146**	**2 628**	**1 158**	**545**	**310**	-

離　婚

表 10.7　同居をやめたときの年齢別に
（各届出年に同居を

Table 10.7　Trends in divorce rates (per 1,000 population)
separated and registered each year) : Japan

年　　次 Year		総　数 Total	～19歳[1] Years	20～24	25～29	30～34	35～39	40～44
								夫（男性人口千対）
1950	昭和25年	1.26	0.09	2.46	5.44	4.06	2.78	1.93
55	30	0.95	0.02	1.07	3.66	3.19	2.19	1.52
60	35	0.80	0.01	0.79	2.86	2.52	1.75	1.18
65	40	0.89	0.01	0.89	3.03	2.72	1.75	1.22
70	45	1.11	0.03	1.12	3.63	3.22	2.18	1.40
75	50	1.36	0.04	1.55	3.94	3.87	2.70	1.87
80	55	1.56	0.03	1.21	3.84	4.63	3.75	2.59
85	60	1.86	0.06	1.50	4.00	5.05	4.55	3.80
90	平成 2 年	1.73	0.06	1.67	4.36	4.97	4.08	3.30
95	7	2.25	0.10	2.22	5.74	6.43	5.09	4.05
2000	12	3.16	0.18	3.01	7.21	8.94	7.35	5.72
01	13	3.48	0.19	3.31	7.91	9.80	8.56	6.42
02	14	3.51	0.20	3.14	7.41	9.47	8.55	6.82
03	15	3.42	0.20	3.13	7.02	8.92	8.31	6.87
04	16	3.24	0.16	2.99	6.65	8.47	7.98	6.49
05	17	3.13	0.15	2.99	6.63	8.18	7.65	6.29
06	18	3.09	0.14	2.88	6.65	8.24	7.48	6.32
07	19	3.01	0.14	2.69	6.42	7.86	7.24	6.00
08	20	2.99	0.15	2.62	6.33	7.79	7.06	6.09
09	21	3.02	0.19	2.64	6.21	7.73	7.15	6.29
10	22	3.00	0.15	2.68	6.20	7.67	7.09	6.23
11	23	2.81	0.15	2.49	5.78	7.29	6.63	5.77
12	24	2.78	0.15	2.57	5.79	7.35	6.65	5.75
13	25	2.74	0.16	2.50	5.82	7.52	6.68	5.57
14	26	2.64	0.17	2.42	5.64	7.27	6.54	5.45
15	27	2.69	0.16	2.57	5.86	7.43	6.66	5.51
16	**28**	**2.56**	**0.17**	**2.43**	**5.51**	**7.04**	**6.53**	**5.25**
								妻（女性人口千対）
1950	昭和25年	1.21	0.61	4.45	4.30	2.68	1.67	1.09
55	30	0.92	0.23	2.69	3.30	2.32	1.50	0.94
60	35	0.77	0.15	2.21	2.74	1.87	1.25	0.76
65	40	0.85	0.13	2.35	3.01	2.02	1.32	0.81
70	45	1.07	0.19	2.59	3.71	2.47	1.62	1.02
75	50	1.31	0.24	3.33	4.46	3.10	2.14	1.36
80	55	1.51	0.20	2.74	5.17	4.29	3.12	2.05
85	60	1.80	0.30	3.07	5.62	5.00	4.22	3.18
90	平成 2 年	1.67	0.27	3.16	6.02	4.85	3.65	2.80
95	7	2.16	0.34	4.01	7.50	6.51	4.57	3.50
2000	12	3.03	0.50	4.90	9.93	9.57	6.92	4.98
01	13	3.33	0.57	5.31	10.72	10.75	8.13	5.56
02	14	3.36	0.57	5.09	10.05	10.73	8.36	6.11
03	15	3.27	0.60	5.00	9.38	10.37	8.30	6.18
04	16	3.09	0.57	4.81	8.92	9.78	8.01	5.92
05	17	2.99	0.56	4.85	8.73	9.48	7.76	5.85
06	18	2.95	0.51	4.84	8.86	9.50	7.73	5.79
07	19	2.87	0.49	4.70	8.67	9.04	7.56	5.67
08	20	2.84	0.51	4.56	8.63	8.97	7.52	5.81
09	21	2.87	0.55	4.60	8.53	8.98	7.69	6.02
10	22	2.85	0.48	4.59	8.48	9.00	7.61	6.10
11	23	2.67	0.44	4.28	7.98	8.51	7.17	5.66
12	24	2.64	0.45	4.27	7.98	8.51	7.12	5.73
13	25	2.60	0.45	4.20	8.03	8.69	7.03	5.59
14	26	2.51	0.44	4.08	7.73	8.47	6.88	5.42
15	27	2.56	0.42	4.22	8.05	8.57	7.07	5.53
16	**28**	**2.43**	**0.40**	**3.94**	**7.61**	**8.23**	**6.83**	**5.28**

注：1)　19歳以下の人口は15～19歳の人口を使用している。
　　2)　昭和25年の70～74歳は70歳以上の数値である。
　　3)　昭和30～平成17年の75～79歳は、75歳以上の数値である。

Divorces

みた年次別離婚率（人口千対）－夫・妻－
やめ届け出たもの）
by age of wife and husband at time of decree (for divorces

45~49	50~54	55~59	60~64	65~69	70~74[2]	75~79[3]	80~
Husband（per 1,000 males）							
1.29	0.89	0.61	0.42	0.30	0.19	…	…
1.07	0.77	0.61	0.40	0.31	0.25	0.14	…
0.80	0.59	0.45	0.35	0.27	0.24	0.17	…
0.79	0.54	0.42	0.31	0.28	0.22	0.17	…
0.93	0.58	0.47	0.35	0.29	0.22	0.17	…
1.20	0.80	0.53	0.35	0.25	0.22	0.13	…
1.82	1.06	0.65	0.39	0.28	0.20	0.13	…
2.73	1.73	0.93	0.51	0.32	0.22	0.15	…
2.53	1.59	0.93	0.49	0.28	0.18	0.12	…
3.25	2.28	1.35	0.70	0.36	0.20	0.12	…
4.46	3.36	2.14	1.19	0.64	0.34	0.17	…
4.78	3.47	2.29	1.33	0.69	0.35	0.17	…
5.37	3.82	2.48	1.41	0.79	0.40	0.17	…
5.28	3.84	2.51	1.44	0.79	0.44	0.17	…
4.99	3.63	2.35	1.38	0.75	0.42	0.18	…
4.96	3.52	2.25	1.34	0.75	0.43	0.17	…
4.79	3.42	2.19	1.30	0.75	0.40	0.22	0.12
4.88	3.51	2.30	1.37	0.80	0.46	0.23	0.13
4.96	3.53	2.34	1.46	0.80	0.46	0.26	0.12
5.01	3.67	2.51	1.58	0.89	0.50	0.28	0.14
5.01	3.71	2.39	1.56	0.92	0.52	0.28	0.13
4.76	3.51	2.27	1.47	0.89	0.54	0.29	0.14
4.69	3.52	2.27	1.45	0.86	0.52	0.29	0.14
4.60	3.37	2.23	1.41	0.90	0.55	0.30	0.14
4.36	3.26	2.20	1.35	0.89	0.56	0.33	0.14
4.48	3.33	2.24	1.42	0.91	0.59	0.33	0.16
4.19	**3.29**	**2.20**	**1.35**	**0.88**	**0.55**	**0.35**	**0.15**
Wife（per 1,000 females）							
0.66	0.38	0.24	0.09	0.09	0.03	…	…
0.50	0.36	0.24	0.13	0.07	0.05	0.02	…
0.43	0.28	0.17	0.12	0.07	0.05	0.03	…
0.48	0.29	0.17	0.11	0.07	0.04	0.02	…
0.59	0.36	0.21	0.12	0.08	0.04	0.02	…
0.83	0.49	0.26	0.13	0.07	0.03	0.02	…
1.25	0.68	0.34	0.17	0.08	0.04	0.02	…
1.98	1.08	0.55	0.25	0.12	0.05	0.02	…
1.91	1.04	0.53	0.26	0.13	0.05	0.02	…
2.60	1.56	0.77	0.38	0.19	0.08	0.02	…
3.57	2.36	1.29	0.71	0.35	0.15	0.04	…
3.77	2.41	1.39	0.73	0.39	0.15	0.04	…
4.21	2.64	1.50	0.83	0.44	0.18	0.04	…
4.23	2.62	1.51	0.84	0.42	0.20	0.04	…
3.98	2.44	1.42	0.79	0.44	0.20	0.04	…
4.01	2.36	1.38	0.75	0.42	0.20	0.05	…
3.86	2.27	1.28	0.72	0.42	0.19	0.09	0.02
3.95	2.33	1.32	0.78	0.45	0.21	0.09	0.03
4.09	2.37	1.32	0.82	0.44	0.22	0.09	0.03
4.24	2.53	1.41	0.88	0.50	0.25	0.12	0.03
4.28	2.54	1.36	0.87	0.53	0.25	0.11	0.03
4.12	2.43	1.32	0.82	0.51	0.27	0.12	0.03
4.14	2.54	1.33	0.79	0.49	0.26	0.12	0.03
4.08	2.49	1.34	0.79	0.50	0.27	0.14	0.03
3.97	2.46	1.32	0.75	0.52	0.28	0.14	0.04
4.11	2.57	1.37	0.80	0.53	0.30	0.16	0.04
3.95	**2.57**	**1.38**	**0.77**	**0.50**	**0.29**	**0.15**	**0.05**

離　婚

表 10.8　同居をやめたときの夫妻
（平成28年に同居を

Table 10.8 Divorces and percent distribution by age of wife and husband at

妻 の 年 齢 Age of wife	総　数 Total	〜19歳 Years	20〜24	25〜29	30〜34	35〜39	40〜44	夫　　の Age of 45〜49
							実	数
総　数　　Total	155 832	515	7 348	17 219	25 207	26 329	25 509	19 387
〜 19歳　Years	1 149	329	594	133	49	24	7	3
20 〜 24	11 316	173	5 407	3 279	1 332	586	290	117
25 〜 29	22 847	9	1 057	10 585	6 716	2 562	1 063	428
30 〜 34	28 444	1	193	2 499	13 090	7 587	3 041	1 075
35 〜 39	26 614	-	62	530	3 133	11 676	7 110	2 451
40 〜 44	24 807	-	28	137	686	3 175	11 075	6 243
45 〜 49	17 761	2	3	43	162	593	2 465	7 642
50 〜 54	9 934	-	2	7	28	95	366	1 197
55 〜 59	5 173	-	1	5	11	22	68	179
60 〜 64	3 146	-	1	1	-	4	18	38
65 〜 69	2 628	-	-	-	-	2	3	12
70 〜 74	1 158	1	-	-	-	2	3	2
75 〜 79	545	-	-	-	-	-	-	-
80 〜	310	-	-	-	-	1	-	-
不　詳 Not stated	-	-	-	-	-	-	-	-
							百　分　率	
総　数　　Total	100. 0	0. 3	4. 7	11. 0	16. 2	16. 9	16. 4	12. 4
〜 19歳　Years	0. 7	0. 2	0. 4	0. 1	0. 0	0. 0	0. 0	0. 0
20 〜 24	7. 3	0. 1	3. 5	2. 1	0. 9	0. 4	0. 2	0. 1
25 〜 29	14. 7	0. 0	0. 7	6. 8	4. 3	1. 6	0. 7	0. 3
30 〜 34	18. 3	0. 0	0. 1	1. 6	8. 4	4. 9	2. 0	0. 7
35 〜 39	17. 1	-	0. 0	0. 3	2. 0	7. 5	4. 6	1. 6
40 〜 44	15. 9	-	0. 0	0. 1	0. 4	2. 0	7. 1	4. 0
45 〜 49	11. 4	0. 0	0. 0	0. 0	0. 1	0. 4	1. 6	4. 9
50 〜 54	6. 4	-	0. 0	0. 0	0. 0	0. 1	0. 2	0. 8
55 〜 59	3. 3	-	0. 0	0. 0	0. 0	0. 0	0. 0	0. 1
60 〜 64	2. 0	-	0. 0	0. 0	-	0. 0	0. 0	0. 0
65 〜 69	1. 7	-	-	-	-	0. 0	0. 0	0. 0
70 〜 74	0. 7	0. 0	-	-	-	0. 0	0. 0	0. 0
75 〜 79	0. 3	-	-	-	-	-	-	-
80 〜	0. 2	-	-	-	-	0. 0	-	-
不　詳 Not stated	-	-	-	-	-	-	-	-

Divorces

の年齢別にみた離婚件数及び百分率
やめ届け出たもの）

time of decree (for divorces separated and registered in 2016): Japan, 2016

平成28年

年　　齢 husband							
50～54	55～59	60～64	65～69	70～74	75～79	80～	不　詳 Not stated
Number							
12 906	8 212	5 373	4 371	1 880	1 019	557	-
5	3	1	-	1	-	-	-
53	32	26	15	6	-	-	-
196	107	69	37	12	6	-	-
458	234	130	102	27	6	1	-
847	401	202	143	43	16	-	-
2 075	766	334	222	56	9	1	-
4 345	1 556	538	297	76	33	6	-
4 226	2 595	886	385	105	33	9	-
583	2 112	1 464	547	119	40	22	-
85	316	1 347	1 034	220	67	15	-
26	78	299	1 305	672	177	54	-
2	9	61	212	432	351	83	-
4	2	11	60	84	224	160	-
1	1	5	12	27	57	206	-
-	-	-	-	-	-	-	-
Percentage							
8.3	5.3	3.4	2.8	1.2	0.7	0.4	-
0.0	0.0	0.0	-	0.0	-	-	-
0.0	0.0	0.0	0.0	0.0	-	-	-
0.1	0.1	0.0	0.0	0.0	0.0	-	-
0.3	0.2	0.1	0.1	0.0	0.0	0.0	-
0.5	0.3	0.1	0.1	0.0	0.0	-	-
1.3	0.5	0.2	0.1	0.0	0.0	0.0	-
2.8	1.0	0.3	0.2	0.0	0.0	0.0	-
2.7	1.7	0.6	0.2	0.1	0.0	0.0	-
0.4	1.4	0.9	0.4	0.1	0.0	0.0	-
0.1	0.2	0.9	0.7	0.1	0.0	0.0	-
0.0	0.1	0.2	0.8	0.4	0.1	0.0	-
0.0	0.0	0.0	0.1	0.3	0.2	0.1	-
0.0	0.0	0.0	0.0	0.1	0.1	0.1	-
0.0	0.0	0.0	0.0	0.0	0.0	0.1	-
-	-	-	-	-	-	-	-

離　婚

〔親権を行わなければならない子の数別にみた離婚〕
〔Divorces by number of children involved in divorce〕

表 10.9　夫妻が親権を行わなければならない子[1]の数別にみた年次別離婚件数及び百分率
Table 10.9　Trends in divorces and percent distribution by number of children[1] involved in divorce: Japan

年　　次 Year		総　数 Total	子どもなし 0人	子どもあり 1人～	Number of children						親が離婚した[1][2] 未成年の子 Dependent children[1]
						1　人	2　人	3　人	4　人	5人～	
		実　　数　　Number of cases									実数 Number of children
1950	昭和25年	83 689	35 705	47 984		29 579	10 367	4 380	2 095	1 563	80 481
55	30	75 267	29 557	45 710		23 240	12 817	6 018	2 417	1 218	83 138
60	35	69 410	28 958	40 452		20 993	11 502	5 391	1 860	706	71 339
65	40	77 195	32 232	44 963		24 372	14 068	4 743	1 361	419	74 412
70	45	95 937	39 254	56 683		31 374	19 317	4 776	921	295	89 687
75	50	119 135	44 467	74 668		38 412	27 984	6 785	1 123	364	121 223
80	55	141 689	45 934	95 755		41 829	40 756	10 755	1 841	574	166 096
85	60	166 640	52 959	113 681		46 573	49 356	14 796	2 220	736	202 585
90	平成2年	157 608	58 790	98 818		44 509	40 655	11 473	1 724	457	169 624
95	7	199 016	76 949	122 067		58 268	47 171	13 956	2 159	513	205 901
2000	12	264 246	106 947	157 299		73 405	60 984	19 097	3 103	710	268 929
01	13	285 911	114 109	171 802		78 849	67 758	21 111	3 254	830	295 168
02	14	289 836	115 794	174 042		79 534	68 854	21 495	3 326	833	299 525
03	15	283 854	113 523	170 331		77 973	67 461	20 894	3 196	807	292 688
04	16	270 804	109 506	161 298		74 662	63 537	19 297	3 097	705	275 816
05	17	261 917	107 813	154 104		71 921	60 504	18 194	2 826	659	262 345
06	18	257 475	107 425	150 050		70 323	58 811	17 511	2 744	661	254 982
07	19	254 832	110 074	144 758		68 022	56 761	16 660	2 662	653	245 685
08	20	251 136	107 302	143 834		67 452	56 199	16 842	2 681	660	244 625
09	21	253 353	106 945	146 408		68 530	56 927	17 285	2 964	702	249 864
10	22	251 378	104 258	147 120		67 908	57 783	17 588	3 075	766	252 617
11	23	235 719	98 911	136 808		62 987	53 690	16 671	2 742	718	235 200
12	24	235 406	98 072	137 334		64 011	53 365	16 346	2 883	729	235 232
13	25	231 383	96 309	135 074		62 500	52 467	16 474	2 879	754	232 406
14	26	222 107	92 481	129 626		59 344	50 365	16 214	2 917	786	224 600
15	27	226 215	94 049	132 166		60 758	51 065	16 382	3 104	857	229 030
16	**28**	**216 798**	**90 852**	**125 946**		**58 009**	**48 268**	**15 865**	**2 980**	**824**	**218 454**
		百　分　率　　Percentage									率（20歳未満 人口千対） Rate (per 1,000 pop. under 20 years)
1950	昭和25年	100.0	42.7	57.3	100.0	61.6	21.6	9.1	4.4	3.3	2.12
55	30	100.0	39.3	60.7	100.0	50.8	28.0	13.2	5.3	2.7	2.16
60	35	100.0	41.7	58.3	100.0	51.9	28.4	13.3	4.6	1.7	1.91
65	40	100.0	41.8	58.2	100.0	54.2	31.3	10.5	3.0	0.9	2.07
70	45	100.0	40.9	59.1	100.0	55.3	34.1	8.4	1.6	0.5	2.67
75	50	100.0	37.3	62.7	100.0	51.4	37.5	9.1	1.5	0.5	3.47
80	55	100.0	32.4	67.6	100.0	43.7	42.6	11.2	1.9	0.6	4.67
85	60	100.0	31.8	68.2	100.0	41.0	43.4	13.0	2.0	0.6	5.82
90	平成2年	100.0	37.3	62.7	100.0	45.0	41.1	11.6	1.7	0.5	5.24
95	7	100.0	38.7	61.3	100.0	47.7	38.6	11.4	1.8	0.4	7.26
2000	12	100.0	40.5	59.5	100.0	46.7	38.8	12.1	2.0	0.5	10.43
01	13	100.0	39.9	60.1	100.0	45.9	39.4	12.3	1.9	0.5	11.62
02	14	100.0	40.0	60.0	100.0	45.7	39.6	12.4	1.9	0.5	11.95
03	15	100.0	40.0	60.0	100.0	45.8	39.6	12.3	1.9	0.5	11.86
04	16	100.0	40.4	59.6	100.0	46.3	39.4	12.0	1.9	0.4	11.36
05	17	100.0	41.2	58.8	100.0	46.7	39.3	11.8	1.8	0.4	10.95
06	18	100.0	41.7	58.3	100.0	46.9	39.2	11.7	1.8	0.4	10.79
07	19	100.0	43.2	56.8	100.0	47.0	39.2	11.5	1.8	0.5	10.53
08	20	100.0	42.7	57.3	100.0	46.9	39.1	11.7	1.9	0.5	10.59
09	21	100.0	42.2	57.8	100.0	46.8	38.9	11.8	2.0	0.5	10.93
10	22	100.0	41.5	58.5	100.0	46.2	39.3	12.0	2.1	0.5	11.12
11	23	100.0	42.0	58.0	100.0	46.0	39.2	12.2	2.0	0.5	10.42
12	24	100.0	41.7	58.3	100.0	46.6	38.9	11.9	2.1	0.5	10.51
13	25	100.0	41.6	58.4	100.0	46.3	38.8	12.2	2.1	0.6	10.46
14	26	100.0	41.6	58.4	100.0	45.8	38.9	12.5	2.3	0.6	10.20
15	27	100.0	41.6	58.4	100.0	46.0	38.6	12.4	2.3	0.6	10.52
16	**28**	**100.0**	**41.9**	**58.1**	**100.0**	**46.1**	**38.3**	**12.6**	**2.4**	**0.7**	**10.13**

注：1）　親権を行わなければならない子（親が離婚した未成年の子）とは、20歳未満の未婚の子をいう。
　　2）　親が離婚した未成年の子の数については平成7年以前は「子の数10人以上」は「10人」として計算していた。
　　　　平成12年以降は「10人以上」を詳細に集計している。
Note：1）Refers to never married children under 20 years of age at divorce.

Divorces

表 10.10 親権を行わなければならない子¹⁾をもつ夫妻別にみた年次別離婚件数及び百分率
Table 10.10 Trends in divorces and percent distribution by wife and husband who have children[1] involved in divorce: Japan

年　　　次 Year		総　　数 Total	夫 が 全 児 の 親権を行う場合 Husband	妻 が 全 児 の 親権を行う場合 Wife	そ の 他²⁾ Others
		実　　数　　Number			
1950	昭和25年	47 984	23 376	19 315	5 293
55	30	45 710	21 130	18 573	6 007
60	35	40 452	18 945	16 859	4 648
65	40	44 963	20 328	20 205	4 430
70	45	56 683	22 805	28 902	4 976
75	50	74 668	25 162	43 259	6 247
80	55	95 755	24 616	64 375	6 764
85	60	113 681	25 094	81 395	7 192
90	平成 2 年	98 818	22 389	70 554	5 875
95	7	122 067	22 817	93 326	5 924
2000	12	157 299	24 445	126 334	6 520
01	13	171 802	27 450	137 347	7 005
02	14	174 042	28 070	138 930	7 042
03	15	170 331	26 040	137 634	6 657
04	16	161 298	24 318	130 909	6 071
05	17	154 104	23 154	125 174	5 776
06	18	150 050	22 319	122 281	5 450
07	19	144 758	22 049	117 372	5 337
08	20	143 834	20 595	118 037	5 202
09	21	146 408	19 381	121 802	5 225
10	22	147 120	19 017	122 619	5 484
11	23	136 808	17 450	114 325	5 033
12	24	137 334	17 201	115 195	4 938
13	25	135 074	16 457	113 765	4 852
14	26	129 626	15 805	109 008	4 813
15	27	132 166	15 971	111 428	4 767
16	**28**	**125 946**	**15 033**	**106 314**	**4 599**
		百　分　率　　Percentage			
1950	昭和25年	100. 0	48. 7	40. 3	11. 0
55	30	100. 0	46. 2	40. 6	13. 1
60	35	100. 0	46. 8	41. 7	11. 5
65	40	100. 0	45. 2	44. 9	9. 9
70	45	100. 0	40. 2	51. 0	8. 8
75	50	100. 0	33. 7	57. 9	8. 4
80	55	100. 0	25. 7	67. 2	7. 1
85	60	100. 0	22. 1	71. 6	6. 3
90	平成 2 年	100. 0	22. 7	71. 4	5. 9
95	7	100. 0	18. 7	76. 5	4. 9
2000	12	100. 0	15. 5	80. 3	4. 1
01	13	100. 0	16. 0	79. 9	4. 1
02	14	100. 0	16. 1	79. 8	4. 0
03	15	100. 0	15. 3	80. 8	3. 9
04	16	100. 0	15. 1	81. 2	3. 8
05	17	100. 0	15. 0	81. 2	3. 7
06	18	100. 0	14. 9	81. 5	3. 6
07	19	100. 0	15. 2	81. 1	3. 7
08	20	100. 0	14. 3	82. 1	3. 6
09	21	100. 0	13. 2	83. 2	3. 6
10	22	100. 0	12. 9	83. 3	3. 7
11	23	100. 0	12. 8	83. 6	3. 7
12	24	100. 0	12. 5	83. 9	3. 6
13	25	100. 0	12. 2	84. 2	3. 6
14	26	100. 0	12. 2	84. 1	3. 7
15	27	100. 0	12. 1	84. 3	3. 6
16	**28**	**100. 0**	**11. 9**	**84. 4**	**3. 7**

注：1) 親権を行わなければならない子とは、20歳未満の未婚の子をいう。
　　2) その他とは、夫と妻がそれぞれ分け合って子どもの親権を行う場合である。
Note : 1) Refers to never married children under 20 years of age at divorce.

離　婚

表 10.11　親権を行わなければならない子の数別にみた年次別離婚件数及び百分率[1]
Table 10.11　Trends in divorces and percent distribution by number of children[1] and custody of wife and husband : Japan

年　次 Year		1　人			2　人				3　人　～			
		総　数	夫が親権を行う場合	妻が親権を行う場合	総　数	夫が2児の親権を行う場合	妻が2児の親権を行う場合	その他[2]	総　数	夫が全児の親権を行う場合	妻が全児の親権を行う場合	その他[2]
		Total	Husband	Wife	Total	Husband	Wife	Others	Total	Husband	Wife	Others
実 数 Number												
1950	昭和25年	29 579	16 273	13 306	10 367	4 249	3 479	2 639	8 038	2 854	2 530	2 654
55	30	23 240	12 385	10 855	12 817	5 234	4 517	3 066	9 653	3 511	3 201	2 941
60	35	20 993	10 849	10 144	11 502	4 993	4 088	2 421	7 957	3 103	2 627	2 227
65	40	24 372	11 607	12 765	14 068	6 067	5 214	2 787	6 523	2 654	2 226	1 643
70	45	31 374	13 060	18 314	19 317	7 562	8 290	3 465	5 992	2 183	2 298	1 511
75	50	38 412	13 419	24 993	27 984	9 213	14 435	4 336	8 272	2 530	3 831	1 911
80	55	41 829	11 229	30 600	40 756	10 366	26 041	4 349	13 170	3 021	7 734	2 415
85	60	46 573	10 780	35 793	49 356	10 756	34 216	4 384	17 752	3 558	11 386	2 808
90	平成2年	44 509	10 070	34 439	40 655	9 289	27 828	3 538	13 654	3 030	8 287	2 337
95	7	58 268	11 005	47 263	47 171	8 832	34 890	3 449	16 628	2 980	11 173	2 475
2000	12	73 405	11 574	61 831	60 984	9 532	47 707	3 745	22 910	3 339	16 796	2 775
01	13	78 849	12 578	66 271	67 758	10 966	52 856	3 936	25 195	3 906	18 220	3 069
02	14	79 534	12 871	66 663	68 854	11 144	53 682	4 028	25 654	4 055	18 585	3 014
03	15	77 973	11 948	66 025	67 461	10 421	53 291	3 749	24 897	3 671	18 318	2 908
04	16	74 662	11 264	63 398	63 537	9 619	50 456	3 462	23 099	3 435	17 055	2 609
05	17	71 921	10 935	60 986	60 504	9 107	48 107	3 290	21 679	3 112	16 081	2 486
06	18	70 323	10 512	59 811	58 811	8 763	46 937	3 111	20 916	3 044	15 533	2 339
07	19	68 022	10 444	57 578	56 761	8 670	45 045	3 046	19 975	2 935	14 749	2 291
08	20	67 452	9 859	57 593	56 199	8 018	45 318	2 863	20 183	2 718	15 126	2 339
09	21	68 530	9 180	59 350	56 927	7 542	46 442	2 943	20 951	2 659	16 010	2 282
10	22	67 908	9 116	58 792	57 783	7 297	47 426	3 060	21 429	2 604	16 401	2 424
11	23	62 987	8 206	54 781	53 690	6 922	43 995	2 773	20 131	2 322	15 549	2 260
12	24	64 011	8 170	55 841	53 365	6 645	43 959	2 761	19 958	2 386	15 395	2 177
13	25	62 500	8 106	54 394	52 467	6 179	43 610	2 678	20 107	2 172	15 761	2 174
14	26	59 344	7 592	51 752	50 365	6 027	41 771	2 567	19 917	2 186	15 485	2 246
15	27	60 758	7 856	52 902	51 065	6 007	42 477	2 581	20 343	2 108	16 049	2 186
16	**28**	**58 009**	**7 515**	**50 494**	**48 268**	**5 437**	**40 337**	**2 494**	**19 669**	**2 081**	**15 483**	**2 105**
百 分 率 Percentage												
1950	昭和25年	100.0	55.0	45.0	100.0	41.0	33.6	25.5	100.0	35.5	31.5	33.0
55	30	100.0	53.3	46.7	100.0	40.8	35.2	23.9	100.0	36.4	33.2	30.5
60	35	100.0	51.7	48.3	100.0	43.4	35.5	21.0	100.0	39.0	33.0	28.0
65	40	100.0	47.6	52.4	100.0	43.1	37.1	19.8	100.0	40.7	34.1	25.2
70	45	100.0	41.6	58.4	100.0	39.1	42.9	17.9	100.0	36.4	38.4	25.2
75	50	100.0	34.9	65.1	100.0	32.9	51.6	15.5	100.0	30.6	46.3	23.1
80	55	100.0	26.8	73.2	100.0	25.4	63.9	10.7	100.0	22.9	58.7	18.3
85	60	100.0	23.1	76.9	100.0	21.8	69.3	8.9	100.0	20.0	64.1	15.8
90	平成2年	100.0	22.6	77.4	100.0	22.8	68.4	8.7	100.0	22.2	60.7	17.1
95	7	100.0	18.9	81.1	100.0	18.7	74.0	7.3	100.0	17.9	67.2	14.9
2000	12	100.0	15.8	84.2	100.0	15.6	78.2	6.1	100.0	14.6	73.3	12.1
01	13	100.0	16.0	84.0	100.0	16.2	78.0	5.8	100.0	15.5	72.3	12.2
02	14	100.0	16.2	83.8	100.0	16.2	78.0	5.9	100.0	15.8	72.4	11.7
03	15	100.0	15.3	84.7	100.0	15.4	79.0	5.6	100.0	14.7	73.6	11.7
04	16	100.0	15.1	84.9	100.0	15.1	79.4	5.4	100.0	14.9	73.8	11.3
05	17	100.0	15.2	84.8	100.0	15.1	79.5	5.4	100.0	14.4	74.2	11.5
06	18	100.0	14.9	85.1	100.0	14.9	79.8	5.3	100.0	14.6	74.3	11.2
07	19	100.0	15.4	84.6	100.0	15.3	79.4	5.4	100.0	14.7	73.8	11.5
08	20	100.0	14.6	85.4	100.0	14.3	80.6	5.1	100.0	13.5	74.9	11.6
09	21	100.0	13.4	86.6	100.0	13.2	81.6	5.2	100.0	12.7	76.4	10.9
10	22	100.0	13.4	86.6	100.0	12.6	82.1	5.3	100.0	12.2	76.5	11.3
11	23	100.0	13.0	87.0	100.0	12.9	81.9	5.2	100.0	11.5	77.2	11.2
12	24	100.0	12.8	87.2	100.0	12.5	82.4	5.2	100.0	12.0	77.1	10.9
13	25	100.0	13.0	87.0	100.0	11.8	83.1	5.1	100.0	10.8	78.4	10.8
14	26	100.0	12.8	87.2	100.0	12.0	82.9	5.1	100.0	11.0	77.7	11.3
15	27	100.0	12.9	87.1	100.0	11.8	83.2	5.1	100.0	10.4	78.9	10.7
16	**28**	**100.0**	**13.0**	**87.0**	**100.0**	**11.3**	**83.6**	**5.2**	**100.0**	**10.6**	**78.7**	**10.7**

注：1)　親権を行わなければならない子とは、20歳未満の未婚の子をいう。
　　2)　その他とは、夫と妻がそれぞれ分け合って子どもの親権を行う場合である。
Note : 1) Refers to never married children under 20 years of age at divorce.

Divorces

〔同居をやめた当時の世帯の主な仕事別にみた離婚〕
〔Divorces by type of occupation of household at time of decree〕

表 10.12　同居をやめた当時の世帯の主な仕事別にみた同居期間別離婚件数及び百分率
Table10.12　Divorces and percent distribution by duration of cohabitation,
by type of occupation of household：Japan, 2016

平成28年

同　居　期　間 [1)] Duration of cohabitation	総　数 Total	農家世帯 Agriculture[a)]	自営業者世帯 Self employed	常用勤労者 世帯（Ⅰ） Employee[b)]	常用勤労者 世帯（Ⅱ） Employee[c)] or director	その他の世帯 Other	無職の世帯 Not working	不　詳 Not stated
	実　　数　　　Number							
総　数　Total	216 798	2 795	26 190	77 994	63 548	18 268	9 626	18 377
5年未満 Under 5 years	68 011	716	6 414	26 044	20 605	6 662	2 744	4 826
1年未満 Under 1 year	13 157	178	1 273	4 780	3 623	1 466	850	987
1年以上2年未満 1 year and over, less than 2 years	15 330	167	1 367	5 915	4 600	1 555	646	1 080
2 ～ 3	14 499	131	1 340	5 625	4 485	1 370	531	1 017
3 ～ 4	13 299	120	1 273	5 181	4 138	1 284	408	895
4 ～ 5	11 726	120	1 161	4 543	3 759	987	309	847
5 ～10	44 391	485	4 936	17 369	13 784	3 540	1 220	3 057
10～15	29 531	350	3 948	11 172	9 155	2 142	819	1 945
15～20	22 986	322	3 353	8 412	7 077	1 665	592	1 565
20～25	16 857	308	2 656	5 691	5 156	1 257	538	1 251
25～30	9 744	201	1 574	3 052	2 965	831	433	688
30～35	5 041	135	834	1 448	1 266	508	496	354
35年以上 35 years and over	5 959	164	1 013	1 130	794	557	1 776	525
不　詳 Not stated	14 278	114	1 462	3 676	2 746	1 106	1 008	4 166
	百　　分　　率　　　Percentage							
総　数　Total	100.0	100.0	100.0	100.0	100.0	100.0	100.0	100.0
5年未満 Under 5 years	31.4	25.6	24.5	33.4	32.4	36.5	28.5	26.3
1年未満 Under 1 year	6.1	6.4	4.9	6.1	5.7	8.0	8.8	5.4
1年以上2年未満 1 year and over, less than 2 years	7.1	6.0	5.2	7.6	7.2	8.5	6.7	5.9
2 ～ 3	6.7	4.7	5.1	7.2	7.1	7.5	5.5	5.5
3 ～ 4	6.1	4.3	4.9	6.6	6.5	7.0	4.2	4.9
4 ～ 5	5.4	4.3	4.4	5.8	5.9	5.4	3.2	4.6
5 ～10	20.5	17.4	18.8	22.3	21.7	19.4	12.7	16.6
10～15	13.6	12.5	15.1	14.3	14.4	11.7	8.5	10.6
15～20	10.6	11.5	12.8	10.8	11.1	9.1	6.2	8.5
20～25	7.8	11.0	10.1	7.3	8.1	6.9	5.6	6.8
25～30	4.5	7.2	6.0	3.9	4.7	4.5	4.5	3.7
30～35	2.3	4.8	3.2	1.9	2.0	2.8	5.2	1.9
35年以上 35 years and over	2.7	5.9	3.9	1.4	1.2	3.0	18.5	2.9
不　詳 Not stated	6.6	4.1	5.6	4.7	4.3	6.1	10.5	22.7

注：1) 同居期間とは、結婚式をあげたとき、または、同居を始めたときのうち早いほうから同居をやめたときまでの期間である。
Note：a) Agriculture only or that with other work.
　　　 b) Employee at office (excluding governmental office) with 1－99 employee (excluding daily or less than one year contracts).
　　　 c) Employee at office excluding　b) above.

離　婚
〔夫妻の国籍別にみた離婚〕
〔Divorces by nationality of wife and husband〕

表 10.13　夫妻の国籍別にみた
Table 10.13　Trends in divorces and percent

年次 Year		総数 Total	夫妻とも 日本 Japanese couple	夫妻の一 方が外国 One of couple is foreigner	夫日本・ 妻外国 Japanese husband and foreign wife	妻日本・ 夫外国 Japanese wife and foreign husband	夫 日 本 ・ 妻 外 国 Japanese husband and foreign wife						
							総数 Total	韓国・朝鮮 Korea	中国 China	フィリピン Philippines	タイ Thailand	米国 U.S.A.	英国 United Kingdom
													実　数
1992	平成4年	179 191	171 475	7 716	6 174	1 542	6 174	3 591	1 163	988	171	75	15
93	5	188 297	180 700	7 597	5 987	1 610	5 987	3 154	1 234	1 111	186	62	17
94	6	195 106	187 369	7 737	5 996	1 741	5 996	2 835	1 323	1 281	239	63	17
95	7	199 016	191 024	7 992	6 153	1 839	6 153	2 582	1 486	1 456	315	53	25
96	8	206 955	198 860	8 095	6 171	1 924	6 171	2 313	1 462	1 706	320	60	19
97	9	222 635	213 486	9 149	7 080	2 069	7 080	2 185	1 901	2 216	362	67	27
98	10	243 183	232 877	10 306	7 867	2 439	7 867	2 146	2 318	2 440	435	76	29
99	11	250 529	239 479	11 050	8 514	2 536	8 514	2 312	2 476	2 575	540	75	29
2000	12	264 246	251 879	12 367	9 607	2 760	9 607	2 555	2 918	2 816	612	68	41
01	13	285 911	272 244	13 667	10 676	2 991	10 676	2 652	3 610	2 963	682	69	31
02	14	289 836	274 584	15 252	12 087	3 165	12 087	2 745	4 629	3 133	699	76	33
03	15	283 854	268 598	15 256	12 103	3 153	12 103	2 653	4 480	3 282	678	75	17
04	16	270 804	255 505	15 299	12 071	3 228	12 071	2 504	4 386	3 395	685	75	21
05	17	261 917	246 228	15 689	12 430	3 259	12 430	2 555	4 363	3 485	782	76	28
06	18	257 475	240 373	17 102	13 713	3 389	13 713	2 718	4 728	4 065	867	60	27
07	19	254 832	236 612	18 220	14 784	3 436	14 784	2 826	5 020	4 625	831	68	15
08	20	251 136	232 362	18 774	15 135	3 639	15 135	2 648	5 338	4 782	795	64	29
09	21	253 353	233 949	19 404	15 570	3 834	15 570	2 681	5 814	4 714	823	79	21
2010	22	251 378	232 410	18 968	15 258	3 710	15 258	2 560	5 762	4 630	743	74	23
11	23	235 719	217 887	17 832	14 224	3 608	14 224	2 275	5 584	4 216	665	66	14
12	24	235 406	219 118	16 288	12 892	3 396	12 892	2 003	4 963	3 811	652	64	18
13	25	231 383	216 187	15 196	11 887	3 309	11 887	1 724	4 573	3 547	649	63	21
14	26	222 107	207 972	14 135	10 930	3 205	10 930	1 619	4 093	3 245	603	73	22
15	27	226 215	212 540	13 675	10 440	3 235	10 440	1 450	3 884	3 200	563	67	19
16	**28**	**216 798**	**203 853**	**12 945**	**9 782**	**3 163**	**9 782**	**1 313**	**3 602**	**2 989**	**525**	**58**	**17**
													百　分　率
1992	平成4年	100.0	95.7	4.3	3.4	0.9	100.0	58.2	18.8	16.0	2.8	1.2	0.2
93	5	100.0	96.0	4.0	3.2	0.9	100.0	52.7	20.6	18.6	3.1	1.0	0.3
94	6	100.0	96.0	4.0	3.1	0.9	100.0	47.3	22.1	21.4	4.0	1.1	0.3
95	7	100.0	96.0	4.0	3.1	0.9	100.0	42.0	24.2	23.7	5.1	0.9	0.4
96	8	100.0	96.1	3.9	3.0	0.9	100.0	37.5	23.7	27.6	5.2	1.0	0.3
97	9	100.0	95.9	4.1	3.2	0.9	100.0	30.9	26.9	31.3	5.1	0.9	0.4
98	10	100.0	95.8	4.2	3.2	1.0	100.0	27.3	29.5	31.0	5.5	1.0	0.4
99	11	100.0	95.6	4.4	3.4	1.0	100.0	27.2	29.1	30.2	6.3	0.9	0.3
2000	12	100.0	95.3	4.7	3.6	1.0	100.0	26.6	30.4	29.3	6.4	0.7	0.4
01	13	100.0	95.2	4.8	3.7	1.0	100.0	24.8	33.8	27.8	6.4	0.6	0.3
02	14	100.0	94.7	5.3	4.2	1.1	100.0	22.7	38.3	25.9	5.8	0.6	0.3
03	15	100.0	94.6	5.4	4.3	1.1	100.0	21.9	37.0	27.1	5.6	0.6	0.1
04	16	100.0	94.4	5.6	4.5	1.2	100.0	20.7	36.3	28.1	5.7	0.6	0.2
05	17	100.0	94.0	6.0	4.7	1.2	100.0	20.6	35.1	28.0	6.3	0.6	0.2
06	18	100.0	93.4	6.6	5.3	1.3	100.0	19.8	34.5	29.6	6.3	0.4	0.2
07	19	100.0	92.9	7.1	5.8	1.3	100.0	19.1	34.0	31.3	5.6	0.5	0.1
08	20	100.0	92.5	7.5	6.0	1.4	100.0	17.5	35.3	31.6	5.3	0.4	0.2
09	21	100.0	92.3	7.7	6.1	1.5	100.0	17.2	37.3	30.3	5.3	0.5	0.1
2010	22	100.0	92.5	7.5	6.1	1.5	100.0	16.8	37.8	30.3	4.9	0.5	0.2
11	23	100.0	92.4	7.6	6.0	1.5	100.0	16.0	39.3	29.6	4.7	0.5	0.1
12	24	100.0	93.1	6.9	5.5	1.4	100.0	15.5	38.5	29.6	5.1	0.5	0.1
13	25	100.0	93.4	6.6	5.1	1.4	100.0	14.5	38.5	29.8	5.5	0.5	0.2
14	26	100.0	93.6	6.4	4.9	1.4	100.0	14.8	37.4	29.7	5.5	0.7	0.2
15	27	100.0	94.0	6.0	4.6	1.4	100.0	13.9	37.2	30.7	5.4	0.6	0.2
16	**28**	**100.0**	**94.0**	**6.0**	**4.5**	**1.5**	**100.0**	**13.4**	**36.8**	**30.6**	**5.4**	**0.6**	**0.2**

Divorces

年次別離婚件数及び百分率
distribution by nationality of wife and husband : Japan

| | | | 妻日本・夫外国 Japanese wife and foreign husband | | | | | | | | | | 年次 | |
ブラジル Brazil	ペルー Peru	その他の国 Other foreign countries	総数 Total	韓国・朝鮮 Korea	中国 China	フィリピン Philippines	タイ Thailand	米国 U.S.A.	英国 United Kingdom	ブラジル Brazil	ペルー Peru	その他の国 Other foreign countries	Year	
Number														
39	6	126	1 542	956	148	33	4	203	22	3	3	170	1992	平成 4 年
43	6	174	1 610	889	167	40	8	265	31	10	7	193	93	5
35	11	192	1 741	885	190	52	12	273	48	12	7	262	94	6
47	15	174	1 839	939	198	43	8	299	40	20	7	285	95	7
52	18	221	1 924	912	203	66	14	298	39	23	15	354	96	8
66	19	237	2 069	983	237	53	15	328	43	26	17	367	97	9
71	27	325	2 439	1 091	286	48	14	383	57	33	41	486	98	10
91	25	391	2 536	1 096	320	59	20	356	42	39	35	569	99	11
92	40	465	2 760	1 113	369	66	19	385	58	59	41	650	2000	12
101	41	527	2 991	1 184	397	62	38	359	59	54	52	786	01	13
91	45	636	3 165	1 167	447	77	36	364	58	78	56	882	02	14
101	57	760	3 153	1 098	411	84	43	371	79	72	57	938	03	15
103	65	837	3 228	966	502	84	46	367	63	81	56	1 063	04	16
116	59	966	3 259	971	492	86	30	398	86	81	68	1 047	05	17
90	59	1 099	3 389	927	499	105	39	393	84	98	73	1 171	06	18
100	49	1 250	3 436	916	568	112	50	374	61	100	70	1 185	07	19
96	56	1 327	3 639	899	608	128	40	413	92	111	63	1 285	08	20
92	46	1 300	3 834	982	660	127	44	379	80	150	77	1 335	09	21
103	59	1 304	3 710	977	632	119	45	397	77	140	70	1 253	2010	22
96	49	1 259	3 608	915	632	126	37	397	98	112	70	1 221	11	23
92	47	1 242	3 396	811	610	109	42	415	71	120	74	1 144	12	24
93	38	1 179	3 309	747	568	109	32	384	71	133	73	1 192	13	25
101	29	1 145	3 205	791	582	106	37	356	60	130	62	1 081	14	26
79	37	1 141	3 235	791	488	127	36	390	84	142	55	1 122	15	27
89	**39**	**1 150**	**3 163**	**747**	**471**	**143**	**39**	**382**	**80**	**107**	**47**	**1 147**	**16**	**28**
Percentage														
0.6	0.1	2.0	100.0	62.0	9.6	2.1	0.3	13.2	1.4	0.2	0.2	11.0	1992	平成 4 年
0.7	0.1	2.9	100.0	55.2	10.4	2.5	0.5	16.5	1.9	0.6	0.4	12.0	93	5
0.6	0.2	3.2	100.0	50.8	10.9	3.0	0.7	15.7	2.8	0.7	0.4	15.0	94	6
0.8	0.2	2.8	100.0	51.1	10.8	2.3	0.4	16.3	2.2	1.1	0.4	15.5	95	7
0.8	0.3	3.6	100.0	47.4	10.6	3.4	0.7	15.5	2.0	1.2	0.8	18.4	96	8
0.9	0.3	3.3	100.0	47.5	11.5	2.6	0.7	15.9	2.1	1.3	0.8	17.7	97	9
0.9	0.3	4.1	100.0	44.7	11.7	2.0	0.6	15.7	2.3	1.4	1.7	19.9	98	10
1.1	0.3	4.6	100.0	43.2	12.6	2.3	0.8	14.0	1.7	1.5	1.4	22.4	99	11
1.0	0.4	4.8	100.0	40.3	13.4	2.4	0.7	13.9	2.1	2.1	1.5	23.6	2000	12
0.9	0.4	4.9	100.0	39.6	13.3	2.1	1.3	12.0	2.0	1.8	1.7	26.3	01	13
0.8	0.4	5.3	100.0	36.9	14.1	2.4	1.1	11.5	1.8	2.5	1.8	27.9	02	14
0.8	0.5	6.3	100.0	34.8	13.0	2.7	1.4	11.8	2.5	2.3	1.8	29.7	03	15
0.9	0.5	6.9	100.0	29.9	15.6	2.6	1.4	11.4	2.0	2.5	1.7	32.9	04	16
0.9	0.5	7.8	100.0	29.8	15.1	2.6	0.9	12.2	2.6	2.5	2.1	32.1	05	17
0.7	0.4	8.0	100.0	27.4	14.7	3.1	1.2	11.6	2.5	2.9	2.2	34.6	06	18
0.7	0.3	8.5	100.0	26.7	16.5	3.3	1.5	10.9	1.8	2.9	2.0	34.5	07	19
0.6	0.4	8.8	100.0	24.7	16.7	3.5	1.1	11.3	2.5	3.1	1.7	35.3	08	20
0.6	0.3	8.3	100.0	25.6	17.2	3.3	1.1	9.9	2.1	3.9	2.0	34.8	09	21
0.7	0.4	8.5	100.0	26.3	17.0	3.2	1.2	10.7	2.1	3.8	1.9	33.8	2010	22
0.7	0.3	8.9	100.0	25.4	17.5	3.5	1.0	11.0	2.7	3.1	1.9	33.8	11	23
0.7	0.4	9.6	100.0	23.9	18.0	3.2	1.2	12.2	2.1	3.5	2.2	33.7	12	24
0.8	0.3	9.9	100.0	22.6	17.2	3.3	1.0	11.6	2.1	4.0	2.2	36.0	13	25
0.9	0.3	10.5	100.0	24.7	18.2	3.3	1.2	11.1	1.9	4.1	1.9	33.7	14	26
0.8	0.4	10.9	100.0	24.5	15.1	3.9	1.1	12.1	2.6	4.4	1.7	34.7	15	27
0.9	**0.4**	**11.8**	**100.0**	**23.6**	**14.9**	**4.5**	**1.2**	**12.1**	**2.5**	**3.4**	**1.5**	**36.3**	**16**	**28**

離　婚

表 10.14　夫妻の国籍別にみた都道府県
Table 10.14　Divorces by nationality of

都道府県 Prefecture	総　数 Total	夫妻とも 日　本 Japanese couple	夫妻の一 方が外国 One of couple is foreigner	夫 日 本 ・ 妻 外 国 Japanese husband and foreign wife							
				総　数 Total	韓国・朝鮮 Korea	中　国 China	フィリピン Philippines	タ イ Thailand	米　国 U.S.A.	英　国 United Kingdom	ブラジル Brazil
全　国　　Total	216 798	203 853	12 945	9 782	1 313	3 602	2 989	525	58	17	89
01 北　海　道 a)	10 476	10 362	114	76	9	26	13	6	1	-	-
02 青　　　森	2 164	2 116	48	34	2	13	10	2	-	-	-
03 岩　　　手	1 877	1 813	64	60	7	32	13	4	-	-	1
04 宮　　　城	3 783	3 648	135	117	31	43	25	3	-	-	-
05 秋　　　田	1 393	1 361	32	27	4	12	6	1	-	-	-
06 山　　　形	1 522	1 459	63	61	13	16	14	1	1	-	-
07 福　　　島	3 278	3 144	134	119	11	49	32	3	1	-	-
08 茨　　　城	4 816	4 514	302	248	33	91	61	45	-	-	3
09 栃　　　木	3 429	3 211	218	176	18	75	45	25	-	-	1
10 群　　　馬	3 241	3 005	236	179	12	32	72	8	2	-	6
11 埼　　　玉	12 481	11 513	968	754	64	331	213	33	5	1	3
12 千　　　葉	10 612	9 690	922	735	86	279	219	70	5	1	3
13 東　　　京	23 470	21 152	2 318	1 644	266	706	384	87	20	4	3
14 神　奈　川	15 673	14 453	1 220	881	133	305	240	51	9	4	8
15 新　　　潟	2 987	2 877	110	96	8	53	22	6	-	-	-
16 富　　　山	1 368	1 264	104	92	4	55	28	-	-	-	-
17 石　　　川	1 653	1 605	48	40	6	21	5	3	-	-	-
18 福　　　井	1 119	1 048	71	63	14	21	15	2	-	-	3
19 山　　　梨	1 369	1 272	97	83	12	25	24	8	-	1	2
20 長　　　野	3 180	2 943	237	204	25	70	55	32	1	1	3
21 岐　　　阜	3 058	2 810	248	212	5	60	131	4	-	-	2
22 静　　　岡	6 237	5 793	444	373	26	114	183	13	1	-	14
23 愛　　　知	12 464	11 183	1 281	1 041	73	310	526	24	-	-	14
24 三　　　重	2 923	2 749	174	146	10	45	54	17	-	-	6
25 滋　　　賀	2 202	2 101	101	75	12	31	19	1	-	-	3
26 京　　　都	4 222	4 012	210	121	25	31	29	3	1	1	-
27 大　　　阪	17 279	16 208	1 071	720	198	244	101	26	3	1	3
28 兵　　　庫	9 302	8 824	478	314	93	108	59	10	1	1	4
29 奈　　　良	2 183	2 111	72	47	16	16	9	2	-	-	-
30 和　歌　山	1 771	1 706	65	52	10	16	9	12	1	-	-
31 鳥　　　取	937	900	37	31	1	9	14	3	-	-	1
32 島　　　根	949	913	36	35	3	13	14	1	-	-	-
33 岡　　　山	3 245	3 114	131	102	10	55	28	-	-	-	2
34 広　　　島	4 691	4 486	205	164	12	46	64	3	1	-	1
35 山　　　口	2 149	2 091	58	41	8	10	19	-	-	-	-
36 徳　　　島	1 184	1 160	24	19	-	9	6	1	-	-	-
37 香　　　川	1 613	1 569	44	33	-	15	15	-	-	-	-
38 愛　　　媛	2 244	2 194	50	39	4	20	9	-	-	-	-
39 高　　　知	1 228	1 195	33	29	3	13	10	-	-	-	-
40 福　　　岡	9 772	9 493	279	196	28	71	70	-	-	1	1
41 佐　　　賀	1 378	1 351	27	24	5	7	9	1	-	-	-
42 長　　　崎	2 169	2 118	51	38	2	16	11	-	1	-	2
43 熊　　　本	2 915	2 829	86	78	1	33	32	5	-	-	-
44 大　　　分	1 999	1 936	63	52	2	23	22	3	-	-	-
45 宮　　　崎	2 202	2 172	30	20	2	8	9	-	-	-	-
46 鹿　児　島	2 891	2 843	48	41	2	12	23	-	-	1	-
47 沖　　　縄	3 700	3 542	158	50	4	12	18	1	3	1	-
21大都市(再掲) 21 major cities (Regrouped)											
50 東京都の区部	16 892	15 026	1 866	1 321	234	580	280	67	14	4	1
51 札　　　幌	4 096	4 041	55	33	5	12	6	2	-	-	-
52 仙　　　台	1 752	1 684	68	55	8	25	8	3	-	-	-
53 さ い た ま	1 965	1 821	144	112	9	59	20	8	2	-	-
54 千　　　葉	1 629	1 482	147	119	20	40	37	8	1	-	-
55 横　　　浜	6 386	5 852	534	389	52	167	89	25	4	2	4
56 川　　　崎	2 458	2 231	227	177	37	59	50	11	3	-	-
57 相　模　原	1 354	1 256	98	66	14	13	19	2	-	-	-
58 新　　　潟	1 126	1 090	36	27	3	17	4	2	-	-	-
59 静　　　岡	1 144	1 077	67	56	5	23	23	-	-	-	1
60 浜　　　松	1 230	1 117	113	92	7	23	56	-	-	-	4
61 名　古　屋	4 157	3 613	544	426	39	120	227	9	-	-	1
62 京　　　都	2 460	2 319	141	77	20	19	9	2	1	1	-
63 大　　　阪	5 991	5 430	561	373	100	114	37	9	1	1	-
64 堺	1 633	1 557	76	51	8	18	12	4	1	-	-
65 神　　　戸	2 715	2 544	171	104	40	36	10	4	1	-	-
66 岡　　　山	1 270	1 206	64	48	7	26	12	-	-	-	1
67 広　　　島	2 035	1 949	86	63	9	16	28	1	-	-	1
68 北　九　州	1 848	1 802	46	30	1	7	8	1	-	-	1
69 福　　　岡	2 975	2 873	102	69	10	32	15	2	-	1	-
70 熊　　　本	1 256	1 219	37	30	-	14	7	3	-	-	-

Divorces

（21大都市再掲）別離婚件数
wife and husband : Japan, each prefecture and 21 major cities, 2016

平成28年

		妻 日 本 ・ 夫 外 国 Japanese wife and foreign husband										都 道 府 県
ペ ル ー Peru	その他の国 Other foreign countries	総 数 Total	韓国・朝鮮 Korea	中 国 China	フィリピン Philippines	タ イ Thailand	米 国 U.S.A.	英 国 United Kingdom	ブラジル Brazil	ペ ル ー Peru	その他の国 Other foreign countries	Prefecture
39	1 150	3 163	747	471	143	39	382	80	107	47	1 147	全 国 Total a)
-	21	38	8	4	1	-	2	1	-	-	22	01 北 海 道
-	7	14	3	-	-	-	11	-	-	-	-	02 青 森
-	3	4	1	-	-	-	1	1	-	-	1	03 岩 手
-	15	18	6	-	-	-	3	1	-	-	8	04 宮 城
-	4	5	2	-	-	-	2	-	-	-	1	05 秋 田
-	16	2	-	1	-	-	-	-	-	-	1	06 山 形
-	23	15	2	1	-	1	2	1	-	-	8	07 福 島
2	13	54	7	6	4	5	1	-	3	4	24	08 茨 城
1	11	42	11	6	5	2	2	-	2	1	13	09 栃 木
5	42	57	7	8	1	1	1	-	4	3	32	10 群 馬
-	104	214	33	40	19	4	11	6	2	3	96	11 埼 玉
1	71	187	28	40	14	4	14	3	3	5	76	12 千 葉
8	166	674	127	119	24	5	92	23	13	6	265	13 東 京
8	123	339	52	48	20	4	64	10	10	5	126	14 神 奈 川
1	6	14	-	3	-	-	4	-	-	-	7	15 新 潟
-	5	12	1	2	1	-	-	1	2	-	5	16 富 山
-	5	8	3	2	1	-	-	-	-	-	2	17 石 川
-	8	8	3	2	-	-	-	-	2	-	1	18 福 井
1	10	14	3	1	3	-	1	-	-	-	6	19 山 梨
-	17	33	4	6	3	2	1	2	5	-	10	20 長 野
-	10	36	4	10	-	-	2	2	4	1	13	21 岐 阜
2	20	71	13	6	9	-	8	-	9	3	23	22 静 岡
5	89	240	64	28	13	2	10	3	23	5	92	23 愛 知
-	14	28	7	2	2	-	1	1	3	3	9	24 三 重
2	7	26	7	1	-	-	3	1	2	1	11	25 滋 賀
-	31	89	25	8	3	2	7	3	2	1	38	26 京 都
-	144	351	149	51	7	2	16	5	5	1	115	27 大 阪
-	38	164	72	22	2	2	10	3	5	3	45	28 兵 庫
-	4	25	13	3	-	-	1	-	1	-	6	29 奈 良
-	4	13	4	-	1	-	2	1	1	-	4	30 和 歌 山
-	3	6	1	2	1	-	1	-	-	-	1	31 鳥 取
-	4	1	-	-	-	-	-	-	-	-	1	32 島 根
-	7	29	15	7	-	-	1	2	1	-	3	33 岡 山
1	36	41	13	11	1	2	4	-	3	-	7	34 広 島
-	4	17	7	1	1	-	5	1	-	-	2	35 山 口
-	3	5	1	-	1	-	1	-	-	-	2	36 徳 島
-	3	11	1	4	-	-	1	1	-	-	4	37 香 川
-	6	11	2	3	-	1	-	-	-	-	5	38 愛 媛
-	3	4	-	-	-	-	1	1	-	-	2	39 高 知
-	20	83	33	15	1	-	4	3	1	1	25	40 福 岡
-	2	3	-	-	1	-	-	-	-	1	2	41 佐 賀
-	6	13	1	2	1	-	6	1	-	-	2	42 長 崎
-	7	8	-	3	1	-	1	-	-	-	3	43 熊 本
-	2	11	6	1	-	-	-	-	-	-	4	44 大 分
-	1	10	-	1	-	-	2	-	1	-	6	45 宮 崎
-	3	7	2	-	1	-	1	-	-	-	3	46 鹿 児 島
2	9	108	6	1	1	-	82	3	-	-	15	47 沖 縄
												21 大 都 市（再掲） 21 major cities (Regrouped)
4	137	545	108	100	20	3	66	20	7	2	219	50 東京都の区部
-	8	22	6	1	1	-	1	-	-	-	13	51 札 幌
-	11	13	4	-	-	-	2	1	-	-	6	52 仙 台
-	14	32	5	6	2	-	3	1	1	1	13	53 さ い た ま
-	13	28	3	6	4	-	1	1	-	2	11	54 千 葉
2	44	145	23	24	8	-	24	4	3	3	56	55 横 浜
-	17	50	13	11	3	1	4	2	2	-	14	56 川 崎
-	18	32	1	4	1	-	6	1	1	-	18	57 相 模 原
-	1	9	-	2	-	-	2	-	-	-	5	58 新 潟
-	4	11	3	3	1	-	2	-	-	-	2	59 静 岡
-	2	21	2	-	3	-	2	-	4	2	8	60 浜 松
3	27	118	34	20	4	1	7	1	7	3	41	61 名 古 屋
-	25	64	20	6	1	2	4	3	2	1	25	62 京 都
-	111	188	78	24	5	1	7	5	2	-	66	63 大 阪
-	8	25	8	4	-	-	-	-	-	-	13	64 堺
-	13	67	24	10	-	1	4	1	2	1	24	65 神 戸
-	2	16	7	6	-	-	-	1	-	-	2	66 岡 山
1	7	23	9	5	-	2	3	-	1	-	3	67 広 島
-	5	16	11	4	-	-	-	1	-	-	4	68 北 九 州
-	9	33	11	7	-	-	3	-	-	1	11	69 福 岡
-	6	7	-	3	-	-	1	-	-	-	3	70 熊 本

Note : a) See page 44.

離　婚

表 10.15　夫妻の国籍別にみた都道府県
Table 10.15　Percent distribution of divorces by nationality

都道府県 Prefecture	総数 Total	夫妻とも日本 Japanese couple	夫妻の一方が外国 One of couple is foreigner	夫日本・妻外国 Japanese husband and foreign wife	妻日本・夫外国 Japanese wife and foreign husband	夫日本・妻外国 Japanese husband and foreign wife						
						総数 Total	韓国・朝鮮 Korea	中国 China	フィリピン Philippines	タイ Thailand	米国 U.S.A.	英国 United Kingdom	ブラジル Brazil
全　国　Total	100.0	94.0	6.0	4.5	1.5	100.0	13.4	36.8	30.6	5.4	0.6	0.2	0.9
01 北海道 [a]	100.0	98.9	1.1	0.7	0.4	100.0	11.8	34.2	17.1	7.9	1.3	-	-
02 青森	100.0	97.8	2.2	1.6	0.6	100.0	5.9	38.2	29.4	5.9	-	-	-
03 岩手	100.0	96.6	3.4	3.2	0.2	100.0	11.7	53.3	21.7	6.7	-	-	1.7
04 宮城	100.0	96.4	3.6	3.1	0.5	100.0	26.5	36.8	21.4	2.6	-	-	-
05 秋田	100.0	97.7	2.3	1.9	0.4	100.0	14.8	44.4	22.2	3.7	-	-	-
06 山形	100.0	95.9	4.1	4.0	0.1	100.0	21.3	26.2	23.0	1.6	1.6	-	-
07 福島	100.0	95.9	4.1	3.6	0.5	100.0	9.2	41.2	26.9	2.5	0.8	-	-
08 茨城	100.0	93.7	6.3	5.1	1.1	100.0	13.3	36.7	24.6	18.1	-	-	1.2
09 栃木	100.0	93.6	6.4	5.1	1.2	100.0	10.2	42.6	25.6	14.2	-	-	0.6
10 群馬	100.0	92.7	7.3	5.5	1.8	100.0	6.7	17.9	40.2	4.5	1.1	-	3.4
11 埼玉	100.0	92.2	7.8	6.0	1.7	100.0	8.5	43.9	28.2	4.4	0.7	0.1	0.4
12 千葉	100.0	91.3	8.7	6.9	1.8	100.0	11.7	38.0	29.8	9.5	0.7	0.1	0.4
13 東京	100.0	90.1	9.9	7.0	2.9	100.0	16.2	42.9	23.4	5.3	1.2	0.2	0.2
14 神奈川	100.0	92.2	7.8	5.6	2.2	100.0	15.1	34.6	27.2	5.8	1.0	0.5	0.9
15 新潟	100.0	96.3	3.7	3.2	0.5	100.0	8.3	55.2	22.9	6.3	-	-	-
16 富山	100.0	92.4	7.6	6.7	0.9	100.0	4.3	59.8	30.4	-	-	-	-
17 石川	100.0	97.1	2.9	2.4	0.5	100.0	15.0	52.5	12.5	7.5	-	-	-
18 福井	100.0	93.7	6.3	5.6	0.7	100.0	22.2	33.3	23.8	3.2	-	-	4.8
19 山梨	100.0	92.9	7.1	6.1	1.0	100.0	14.5	30.1	28.9	9.6	-	1.2	2.4
20 長野	100.0	92.5	7.5	6.4	1.0	100.0	12.3	34.3	27.0	15.7	0.5	0.5	1.5
21 岐阜	100.0	91.9	8.1	6.9	1.2	100.0	2.4	28.3	61.8	1.9	-	-	0.9
22 静岡	100.0	92.9	7.1	6.0	1.1	100.0	7.0	30.6	49.1	3.5	0.3	-	3.8
23 愛知	100.0	89.7	10.3	8.4	1.9	100.0	7.0	29.8	50.5	2.3	-	-	1.3
24 三重	100.0	94.0	6.0	5.0	1.0	100.0	6.8	30.8	37.0	11.6	-	-	4.1
25 滋賀	100.0	95.4	4.6	3.4	1.2	100.0	16.0	41.3	25.3	1.3	-	-	4.0
26 京都	100.0	95.0	5.0	2.9	2.1	100.0	20.7	25.6	24.0	2.5	0.8	0.8	-
27 大阪	100.0	93.8	6.2	4.2	2.0	100.0	27.5	33.9	14.0	3.6	0.4	0.1	0.4
28 兵庫	100.0	94.9	5.1	3.4	1.8	100.0	29.6	34.4	18.8	3.2	0.3	0.3	1.3
29 奈良	100.0	96.7	3.3	2.2	1.1	100.0	34.0	34.0	19.1	4.3	-	-	-
30 和歌山	100.0	96.3	3.7	2.9	0.7	100.0	19.2	30.8	17.3	23.1	1.9	-	-
31 鳥取	100.0	96.1	3.9	3.3	0.6	100.0	3.2	29.0	45.2	9.7	-	-	3.2
32 島根	100.0	96.2	3.8	3.7	0.1	100.0	8.6	37.1	40.0	2.9	-	-	-
33 岡山	100.0	96.0	4.0	3.1	0.9	100.0	9.8	53.9	27.5	-	-	-	2.0
34 広島	100.0	95.6	4.4	3.5	0.9	100.0	7.3	28.0	39.0	1.8	0.6	-	0.6
35 山口	100.0	97.3	2.7	1.9	0.8	100.0	19.5	24.4	46.3	-	-	-	-
36 徳島	100.0	98.0	2.0	1.6	0.4	100.0	-	47.4	31.6	5.3	-	-	-
37 香川	100.0	97.3	2.7	2.0	0.7	100.0	-	45.5	45.5	-	-	-	-
38 愛媛	100.0	97.8	2.2	1.7	0.5	100.0	10.3	51.3	23.1	-	-	-	-
39 高知	100.0	97.3	2.7	2.4	0.3	100.0	10.3	44.8	34.5	-	-	-	-
40 福岡	100.0	97.1	2.9	2.0	0.8	100.0	14.3	36.2	35.7	2.6	-	0.5	0.5
41 佐賀	100.0	98.0	2.0	1.7	0.2	100.0	20.8	29.2	37.5	4.2	-	-	-
42 長崎	100.0	97.6	2.4	1.8	0.6	100.0	5.3	42.1	28.9	-	2.6	-	5.3
43 熊本	100.0	97.0	3.0	2.7	0.3	100.0	1.3	42.3	41.0	6.4	-	-	-
44 大分	100.0	96.8	3.2	2.6	0.6	100.0	3.8	44.2	42.3	5.8	-	-	-
45 宮崎	100.0	98.6	1.4	0.9	0.5	100.0	10.0	40.0	45.0	-	-	-	-
46 鹿児島	100.0	98.3	1.7	1.4	0.2	100.0	4.9	29.3	56.1	-	2.4	-	-
47 沖縄	100.0	95.7	4.3	1.4	2.9	100.0	8.0	24.0	36.0	2.0	6.0	2.0	-
21 大都市(再掲) 21 major cities (Regrouped)													
50 東京都の区部	100.0	89.0	11.0	7.8	3.2	100.0	17.7	43.9	21.2	5.1	1.1	0.3	0.1
51 札幌	100.0	98.7	1.3	0.8	0.5	100.0	15.2	36.4	18.2	6.1	-	-	-
52 仙台	100.0	96.1	3.9	3.1	0.7	100.0	14.5	45.5	14.5	5.5	-	-	-
53 さいたま	100.0	92.7	7.3	5.7	1.6	100.0	8.0	52.7	17.9	7.1	1.8	-	-
54 千葉	100.0	91.0	9.0	7.3	1.7	100.0	16.8	33.6	31.1	6.7	0.8	-	-
55 横浜	100.0	91.6	8.4	6.1	2.3	100.0	13.4	42.9	22.9	6.4	1.0	0.5	1.0
56 川崎	100.0	90.8	9.2	7.2	2.0	100.0	20.9	33.3	28.2	6.2	1.7	-	-
57 相模原	100.0	92.8	7.2	4.9	2.4	100.0	21.2	19.7	28.8	3.0	-	-	-
58 新潟	100.0	96.8	3.2	2.4	0.8	100.0	11.1	63.0	14.8	7.4	-	-	-
59 静岡	100.0	94.1	5.9	4.9	1.0	100.0	8.9	41.1	41.1	-	-	-	1.8
60 浜松	100.0	90.8	9.2	7.5	1.7	100.0	7.6	25.0	60.9	-	-	-	4.3
61 名古屋	100.0	86.9	13.1	10.2	2.8	100.0	9.2	28.2	53.3	2.1	-	-	0.2
62 京都	100.0	94.3	5.7	3.1	2.6	100.0	26.0	24.7	11.7	2.6	1.3	1.3	-
63 大阪	100.0	90.6	9.4	6.2	3.1	100.0	26.8	30.6	9.9	2.4	0.3	-	0.3
64 堺	100.0	95.3	4.7	3.1	1.5	100.0	15.7	35.3	23.5	7.8	2.0	-	-
65 神戸	100.0	93.7	6.3	3.8	2.5	100.0	38.5	34.6	9.6	3.8	1.0	-	-
66 岡山	100.0	95.0	5.0	3.8	1.3	100.0	14.6	54.2	25.0	-	-	-	2.1
67 広島	100.0	95.8	4.2	3.1	1.1	100.0	14.3	25.4	44.4	1.6	-	-	1.6
68 北九州	100.0	97.5	2.5	1.6	0.9	100.0	26.7	23.3	26.7	3.3	-	-	3.3
69 福岡	100.0	96.6	3.4	2.3	1.1	100.0	14.5	46.4	21.7	2.9	-	1.4	-
70 熊本	100.0	97.1	2.9	2.4	0.6	100.0	-	46.7	23.3	10.0	-	-	-

Divorces

（21大都市再掲）別離婚件数百分率
of wife and husband : Japan, each prefecture and 21 major cities, 2016

平成28年

妻日本・夫外国 — Japanese wife and foreign husband

ペルー Peru	その他の国 Other foreign countries	総数 Total	韓国・朝鮮 Korea	中国 China	フィリピン Philippines	タイ Thailand	米国 U.S.A.	英国 United Kingdom	ブラジル Brazil	ペルー Peru	その他の国 Other foreign countries	都道府県 Prefecture
0.4	11.8	100.0	23.6	14.9	4.5	1.2	12.1	2.5	3.4	1.5	36.3	全　国 Total
-	27.6	100.0	21.1	10.5	2.6	-	5.3	2.6	-	-	57.9	01 北海道 a)
-	20.6	100.0	21.4	-	-	-	78.6	-	-	-	-	02 青森
-	5.0	100.0	25.0	-	-	-	25.0	25.0		-	25.0	03 岩手
-	12.8	100.0	33.3	-	-	-	16.7	5.6	-	-	44.4	04 宮城
-	14.8	100.0	40.0	-	-	-	40.0	-	-	-	20.0	05 秋田
-	26.2	100.0	-	50.0	-	-	-	-	-	-	50.0	06 山形
-	19.3	100.0	13.3	6.7	-	6.7	13.3	6.7	-	-	53.3	07 福島
0.8	5.2	100.0	13.0	11.1	7.4	9.3	1.9	-	5.6	7.4	44.4	08 茨城
0.6	6.3	100.0	26.2	14.3	11.9	4.8	4.8	-	4.8	2.4	31.0	09 栃木
2.8	23.5	100.0	12.3	14.0	1.8	1.8	1.8	-	7.0	5.3	56.1	10 群馬
-	13.8	100.0	15.4	18.7	8.9	1.9	5.1	2.8	0.9	1.4	44.9	11 埼玉
0.1	9.7	100.0	15.0	21.4	7.5	2.1	7.5	1.6	1.6	2.7	40.6	12 千葉
0.5	10.1	100.0	18.8	17.7	3.6	0.7	13.6	3.4	1.9	0.9	39.3	13 東京
0.9	14.0	100.0	15.3	14.2	5.9	1.2	18.9	2.9	2.9	1.5	37.2	14 神奈川
1.0	6.3	100.0	-	21.4	-	-	28.6	-	-	-	50.0	15 新潟
-	5.4	100.0	8.3	16.7	8.3	-	-	8.3	16.7	-	41.7	16 富山
-	12.5	100.0	37.5	25.0	12.5	-	-	-	-	-	25.0	17 石川
-	12.7	100.0	37.5	25.0	-	-	-	-	25.0	-	12.5	18 福井
1.2	12.0	100.0	21.4	7.1	21.4	-	7.1	-	-	-	42.9	19 山梨
-	8.3	100.0	12.1	18.2	9.1	6.1	3.0	6.1	15.2	-	30.3	20 長野
-	4.7	100.0	11.1	27.8	-	-	5.6	5.6	11.1	2.8	36.1	21 岐阜
0.5	5.4	100.0	18.3	8.5	12.7	-	11.3	-	12.7	4.2	32.4	22 静岡
0.5	8.5	100.0	26.7	11.7	5.4	0.8	4.2	1.3	9.6	2.1	38.3	23 愛知
-	9.6	100.0	25.0	7.1	7.1	-	3.6	3.6	10.7	10.7	32.1	24 三重
2.7	9.3	100.0	26.9	3.8	-	-	11.5	3.8	7.7	3.8	42.3	25 滋賀
-	25.6	100.0	28.1	9.0	3.4	2.2	7.9	3.4	2.2	1.1	42.7	26 京都
-	20.0	100.0	42.5	14.5	2.0	0.6	4.6	1.4	1.4	0.3	32.8	27 大阪
-	12.1	100.0	43.9	13.4	1.2	1.2	6.1	1.8	3.0	1.8	27.4	28 兵庫
-	8.5	100.0	52.0	12.0	4.0	-	4.0	-	4.0	-	24.0	29 奈良
-	7.7	100.0	30.8	-	7.7	-	15.4	7.7	7.7	-	30.8	30 和歌山
-	9.7	100.0	16.7	33.3	16.7	-	16.7	-	-	-	16.7	31 鳥取
-	11.4	100.0	-	-	-	-	-	-	-	-	100.0	32 島根
-	6.9	100.0	51.7	24.1	-	-	3.4	6.9	3.4	-	10.3	33 岡山
0.6	22.0	100.0	31.7	26.8	2.4	4.9	9.8	-	7.3	-	17.1	34 広島
-	9.8	100.0	41.2	5.9	5.9	-	29.4	5.9	-	-	11.8	35 山口
-	15.8	100.0	20.0	-	20.0	-	20.0	-	-	-	40.0	36 徳島
-	9.1	100.0	9.1	36.4	-	-	9.1	9.1	-	-	36.4	37 香川
-	15.4	100.0	18.2	27.3	-	9.1	-	-	-	-	45.5	38 愛媛
-	10.3	100.0	-	-	-	-	25.0	25.0	-	-	50.0	39 高知
-	10.2	100.0	39.8	18.1	1.2	-	4.8	3.6	1.2	1.2	30.1	40 福岡
-	8.3	100.0	-	-	-	-	-	-	-	33.3	66.7	41 佐賀
-	15.8	100.0	7.7	15.4	7.7	-	46.2	7.7	-	-	15.4	42 長崎
-	9.0	100.0	-	37.5	12.5	-	12.5	-	-	-	37.5	43 熊本
-	3.8	100.0	54.5	9.1	-	-	-	-	-	-	36.4	44 大分
-	5.0	100.0	-	10.0	-	-	20.0	-	10.0	-	60.0	45 宮崎
-	7.3	100.0	28.6	-	14.3	-	14.3	-	-	-	42.9	46 鹿児島
4.0	18.0	100.0	5.6	0.9	0.9	-	75.9	2.8	-	-	13.9	47 沖縄
												21大都市(再掲) 21 major cities (Regrouped)
0.3	10.4	100.0	19.8	18.3	3.7	0.6	12.1	3.7	1.3	0.4	40.2	50 東京都の区部
-	24.2	100.0	27.3	4.5	4.5	-	4.5	-	-	-	59.1	51 札幌
-	20.0	100.0	30.8	-	-	-	15.4	7.7	-	-	46.2	52 仙台
-	12.5	100.0	15.6	18.8	6.3	-	9.4	3.1	3.1	3.1	40.6	53 さいたま
-	10.9	100.0	10.7	21.4	14.3	-	3.6	3.6	-	7.1	39.3	54 千葉
0.5	11.3	100.0	15.9	16.6	5.5	-	16.6	2.8	2.1	2.1	38.6	55 横浜
-	9.6	100.0	26.0	22.0	6.0	2.0	8.0	4.0	4.0	-	28.0	56 川崎
-	27.3	100.0	3.1	12.5	3.1	-	18.8	3.1	3.1	-	56.3	57 相模原
-	3.7	100.0	-	22.2	-	-	22.2	-	-	-	55.6	58 新潟
-	7.1	100.0	27.3	27.3	9.1	-	18.2	-	-	-	18.2	59 静岡
-	2.2	100.0	9.5	-	14.3	-	9.5	-	19.0	9.5	38.1	60 浜松
0.7	6.3	100.0	28.8	16.9	3.4	0.8	5.9	0.8	5.9	2.5	34.7	61 名古屋
-	32.5	100.0	31.3	9.4	1.6	3.1	6.3	4.7	3.1	1.6	39.1	62 京都
-	29.8	100.0	41.5	12.8	2.7	0.5	3.7	2.7	1.1	-	35.1	63 大阪
-	15.7	100.0	32.0	16.0	-	-	-	-	-	-	52.0	64 堺
-	12.5	100.0	35.8	14.9	-	1.5	6.0	1.5	3.0	1.5	35.8	65 神戸
-	4.2	100.0	43.8	37.5	-	-	-	6.3	-	-	12.5	66 岡山
1.6	11.1	100.0	39.1	21.7	-	8.7	13.0	-	4.3	-	13.0	67 広島
-	16.7	100.0	43.8	25.0	-	-	-	6.3	-	-	25.0	68 北九州
-	13.0	100.0	33.3	21.2	-	-	-	9.1	-	3.0	33.3	69 福岡
-	20.0	100.0	-	42.9	-	-	14.3	-	-	-	42.9	70 熊本

Note : a)　See page 44.

付　録
基礎人口
Population table

付　　　録
Appendix

本報告書に掲げる各表の諸比率の算出においては、表1～5に示した分母人口を用いた。

表1　年　次
Table 1　Population by

年　　　次 Year		総　　数 Total	男 Male	女 Female	備　　　考
1899	明治32年	43 404 000	21 836 000	21 568 000	（地域の範囲）
1900	33	43 847 000	22 051 000	21 796 000	1）明治32年～昭和19年：樺太を除く旧内地（北海道、本
01	34	44 359 000	22 298 000	22 061 000	州、四国、九州及び沖縄）
02	35	44 964 000	22 606 000	22 358 000	2）昭和20年以降：前述の地域のうち、北海道の一部、東
03	36	45 546 000	22 901 000	22 645 000	京都の一部、九州の一部及び沖縄を除く地域
04	37	46 135 000	23 195 000	22 940 000	なお、後年我が国に復帰した地域は、その都度以下に
					より地域の範囲に加えた。
05	38	46 620 000	23 421 000	23 199 000	
06	39	47 038 000	23 599 000	23 439 000	
07	40	47 416 000	23 786 000	23 630 000	
08	41	47 965 000	24 041 000	23 924 000	
09	42	48 554 000	24 326 000	24 228 000	
1910	43	49 184 000	24 650 000	24 534 000	
11	44	49 852 000	24 993 000	24 859 000	
12	大正元年	50 577 000	25 365 000	25 212 000	
13	2	51 305 000	25 737 000	25 568 000	（人的範囲）
14	3	52 039 000	26 105 000	25 934 000	1）明治32年～大正8年：内地人
15	4	52 752 000	26 465 000	26 287 000	2）大正9年～昭和41年（昭和19年～21年を除く）：前述
16	5	53 496 000	26 841 000	26 655 000	の地域にある外国人を含む総人口
17	6	54 134 000	27 158 000	26 976 000	昭和19年、20年：陸海軍の部隊及び艦船にあるもの及
18	7	54 739 000	27 453 000	27 286 000	び外国人を含んでいない。
19	8	55 033 000	27 602 000	27 431 000	昭和21年：外国人及び外国人の世帯にあるものを含ん
					でいない。
1920	9 *	55 963 053	28 044 185	27 918 868	昭和22年以降：外国軍隊・外国政府の公館員及びその
21	10	56 665 900	28 411 700	28 254 200	家族を含んでいない。
22	11	57 390 100	28 799 700	28 590 300	3）昭和42年以降：日本人人口
23	12	58 119 200	29 176 900	28 942 300	
24	13	58 875 600	29 568 700	29 306 900	（調査の時期）
25	14*	59 736 822	30 013 109	29 723 713	1）明治32年～大正8年：1月1日現在
26	昭和元年	60 740 900	30 521 300	30 219 600	2）大正9年以降（昭和19年～21年を除く）：10月1日現
27	2	61 659 300	30 981 500	30 677 800	在
28	3	62 595 300	31 449 100	31 146 100	昭和19年：2月22日現在
29	4	63 460 600	31 890 600	31 570 000	昭和20年：11月1日現在
1930	5 *	64 450 005	32 390 155	32 059 850	昭和21年：4月26日現在
31	6	65 457 500	32 898 500	32 559 000	
32	7	66 433 800	33 354 600	33 079 200	
33	8	67 431 600	33 844 500	33 587 000	
34	9	68 308 900	34 293 800	34 015 100	
35	10*	69 254 148	34 734 133	34 520 015	
36	11	70 113 600	35 102 800	35 010 800	
37	12	70 630 400	35 127 900	35 502 500	
38	13	71 012 600	35 124 900	35 887 700	
39	14	71 379 700	35 225 600	36 154 100	
1940	15	71 933 000	35 387 400	36 545 600	
41	16	71 680 200	34 706 000	36 974 200	
42	17	72 384 500	34 873 400	37 511 100	
43	18	72 883 100	34 766 800	38 116 400	
44	19	73 064 300	34 625 000	38 439 400	
45	20	71 998 100	33 894 100	38 104 000	
46	21	73 114 100	34 904 600	38 209 500	
47	22*	78 101 473	38 129 399	39 972 074	
48	23	80 002 500	39 129 900	40 872 500	
49	24	81 772 600	40 062 700	41 709 900	
1950	25*	83 199 637	40 811 760	42 387 877	
51	26	84 573 000	41 494 000	43 079 000	
52	27	85 852 000	42 148 000	43 704 000	
53	28	87 033 000	42 749 000	44 284 000	
54	29	88 293 000	43 379 000	44 914 000	

地域の範囲の追加表：

地　　　域	復帰年月日	範囲に加えた年
鹿児島県大島郡十島村	昭和26年12月5日	昭和27年
〃　　奄美群島	昭和28年12月25日	昭和29年
東京都小笠原諸島	昭和43年6月26日	昭和43年
沖縄県	昭和47年5月15日	昭和48年

注：昭和24年以前：現在地人口
　　昭和25年以降：常住人口

・性 別 人 口
sex : Japan

年　　　次 Year		総　　数 Total	男 Male	女 Female	備　　考
1955	昭和30年*	89 275 529	43 860 718	45 414 811	（資料）
56	31	90 259 000	44 355 000	45 903 000	1）明治32年～大正8年：大正9年国勢調査結果より、出
57	32	91 088 000	44 771 000	46 317 000	生、死亡、就籍、除籍を加除して推計（内閣統計局によ
58	33	92 010 000	45 230 000	46 781 000	る）
59	34	92 971 000	45 707 000	47 264 000	「昭和25年国勢調査報告第8巻」（昭和30年3月刊）－
					総理府統計局
1960	35*	93 418 501	45 877 602	47 540 899	2）＊印：国勢調査結果
61	36	94 285 000	46 304 000	47 981 000	昭和15年：国勢調査による銃後に内地にある軍人・軍
62	37	95 178 000	46 744 000	48 434 000	属の推計数を加えたもの
63	38	96 156 000	47 230 000	48 925 000	昭和19年～21年：人口調査
64	39	97 186 000	47 744 000	49 443 000	昭和22年～58年：総理府統計局推計
65	40*	98 274 961	48 244 445	50 030 516	昭和59年～平成11年：総務庁統計局推計
66	41	99 056 000	48 628 000	50 429 000	平成13年以降：総務省統計局推計
67	42	99 637 000	48 899 000	50 738 000	昭和24年以前：「大正9年～昭和15年及び昭和22年～
68	43	100 794 000	49 480 000	51 315 000	昭和25年年齢別人口」（昭和31年3月刊）
69	44	102 022 000	50 103 000	51 919 000	「大正9年～昭和25年都道府県人口」（昭和32年3月
1970	45*	103 119 447	50 600 539	52 518 908	刊）（100の位未満四捨五入）
71	46	104 345 000	51 225 000	53 120 000	昭和26年～48年：各年次における「全国年齢別人口の
72	47	105 742 000	51 848 000	53 894 000	推計」「都道府県別人口の推計」（1000の位未満四捨五入）
73	48	108 079 000	53 001 000	55 078 000	昭和49年～平成20年：各年次における「10月1日現在
74	49	109 410 000	53 678 000	55 732 000	推計人口」（1000の位未満四捨五入）
75	50*	111 251 507	54 724 867	56 526 640	平成21年～26年：各年次における「人口推計（10月1
76	51	112 420 000	55 334 000	57 086 000	日現在）」（1000の位未満四捨五入）
77	52	113 499 000	55 860 000	57 639 000	平成28年以降：各年次における「人口推計（10月1日
78	53	114 511 000	56 362 000	58 149 000	現在）」
79	54	115 465 000	56 837 000	58 628 000	なお、昭和31年、32年については昭和34年7月発表の
1980	55*	116 320 358	57 201 287	59 119 071	改訂値。昭和33年は昭和35年6月発表の改訂値。
81	56	117 204 000	57 654 000	59 551 000	他の年次については、その後改訂値が公表された場合
82	57	118 008 000	58 053 000	59 955 000	でもこれを用いていない。
83	58	118 786 000	58 435 000	60 352 000	昭和45年、50年、55年、平成7年は、国勢調査の確定
84	59	119 523 000	58 793 000	60 730 000	数。ただし、昭和45年、50年、55年の各報告書では、そ
85	60*	120 265 700	59 044 000	61 221 700	れぞれ1％抽出集計結果を用いたので、本報告書と数値
86	61	120 946 000	59 438 000	61 508 000	が異なる。
87	62	121 535 000	59 723 000	61 811 000	平成2年、12年、17年、22年、27年は、国勢調査の確
88	63	122 026 000	59 964 000	62 062 000	定数（按分済み人口）。
89	平成元年	122 460 000	60 171 000	62 289 000	昭和60年は「昭和60年国勢調査抽出速報集計結果」
1990	2*	122 721 397	60 248 969	62 472 428	（昭和61年5月刊）－総務庁統計局
91	3	123 102 000	60 425 000	62 677 000	
92	4	123 476 000	60 597 000	62 879 000	
93	5	123 788 000	60 730 000	63 057 000	
94	6	124 069 000	60 839 000	63 230 000	
95	7*	124 298 947	60 919 153	63 379 794	
96	8	124 709 000	61 115 000	63 594 000	
97	9	124 963 000	61 210 000	63 753 000	
98	10	125 252 000	61 311 000	63 941 000	
99	11	125 432 000	61 358 000	64 074 000	
2000	12*	125 612 633	61 488 005	64 124 628	
01	13	125 908 000	61 595 000	64 313 000	
02	14	126 008 000	61 591 000	64 417 000	
03	15	126 139 000	61 620 000	64 520 000	
04	16	126 176 000	61 597 000	64 579 000	
05	17*	126 204 902	61 617 893	64 587 009	
06	18	126 154 000	61 568 000	64 586 000	
07	19	126 085 000	61 511 000	64 574 000	
08	20	125 947 000	61 424 000	64 523 000	
09	21	125 820 000	61 339 000	64 481 000	
2010	22*	126 381 728	61 571 727	64 810 001	
11	23	126 180 000	61 453 000	64 727 000	
12	24	125 957 000	61 328 000	64 630 000	
13	25	125 704 000	61 186 000	64 518 000	
14	26	125 431 000	61 041 000	64 391 000	
15	27*	125 319 299	61 022 756	64 296 543	
16	**28**	**125 020 252**	**60 866 773**	**64 153 479**	

付　録

表2　月別推計人口（各月1日現在）
Table 2　Estimated population by month (as of first day of each month) : Japan

（単位　千人）
(in thousands)

月 Month	1970 昭　和　45　年 [2)] (P) 月初人口 Population as of 1st each month	[1)] ai×P	1975 50　年 [2)] (P) 月初人口 Population as of 1st each month	[1)] ai×P	1980 55　年 [2)] (P) 月初人口 Population as of 1st each month	[1)] ai×P	1985 60　年 [2)] (P) 月初人口 Population as of 1st each month	[1)] ai×P	1990 平成　2　年 [2)] (P) 月初人口 Population as of 1st each month	[1)] ai×P	1995 7　年 [2)] (P) 月初人口 Population as of 1st each month	[1)] ai×P
1月	102 285	8 687.2	109 676	9 314.9	115 646	9 795.1	119 648	10 161.8	122 494	10 403.5	124 088	10 539.0
2	102 384	7 854.1	109 828	8 425.2	115 765	9 172.5	119 761	9 187.1	122 583	9 403.6	124 213	9 528.7
3	102 469	8 702.8	109 902	9 334.1	115 804	9 808.5	119 774	10 172.5	122 520	10 405.7	124 127	10 542.3
4	102 580	8 431.2	109 986	9 039.9	115 870	9 497.5	119 837	9 849.5	122 599	10 076.5	124 164	10 205.3
5	102 694	8 722.0	110 087	9 349.9	115 930	9 819.2	119 881	10 181.6	122 571	10 410.1	124 121	10 541.8
6	102 805	8 449.7	110 212	9 058.5	116 030	9 510.6	119 979	9 861.2	122 688	10 083.8	124 220	10 209.9
7	102 905	8 739.9	110 311	9 368.9	116 107	9 834.1	120 037	10 194.9	122 726	10 423.2	124 245	10 552.3
8	103 005	8 748.4	110 382	9 374.9	116 134	9 836.4	120 052	10 196.1	122 671	10 418.6	124 160	10 545.1
9	103 121	8 475.7	110 526	9 084.3	116 270	9 530.3	120 155	9 875.7	122 760	10 089.8	124 233	10 210.9
10	103 068	8 753.7	110 637	9 396.6	116 354	9 855.1	120 326	10 219.4	122 791	10 428.8	124 327	10 559.3
11	103 164	8 479.2	110 736	9 101.6	116 426	9 543.1	120 388	9 894.8	122 828	10 095.4	124 367	10 221.9
12	103 260	8 770.0	110 829	9 412.9	116 501	9 867.5	120 445	10 229.5	122 856	10 434.3	124 399	10 565.4

月 Month	2000 12　年 [2)] (P) 月初人口 Population as of 1st each month	[1)] ai×P	2005 17　年 [2)] (P) 月初人口 Population as of 1st each month	[1)] ai×P	2010 22　年 [2)] (P) 月初人口 Population as of 1st each month	[1)] ai×P	2014 26　年 (P) 月初人口 Population as of 1st each month	[1)] ai×P	2015 27　年 [2)] (P) 月初人口 Population as of 1st each month	[1)] ai×P	2016 28　年 (P) 月初人口 Population as of 1st each month	[1)] ai×P
1月	125 564	10 635.2	126 184	10 717.0	125 863	10 689.7	125 717	10 677.3	125 441	10 653.9	125 330	10 615.4
2	125 557	9 948.5	126 177	9 679.3	125 802	9 650.6	125 627	9 637.1	125 319	9 613.5	125 218	9 921.6
3	125 474	10 627.6	126 107	10 710.5	125 783	10 682.9	125 564	10 664.3	125 285	10 640.6	125 173	10 602.1
4	125 517	10 288.3	126 173	10 370.4	125 786	10 338.6	125 545	10 318.8	125 275	10 296.6	125 165	10 259.4
5	125 482	10 628.3	126 021	10 703.2	125 751	10 680.2	125 495	10 658.5	125 222	10 635.3	125 110	10 596.7
6	125 542	10 290.3	126 117	10 365.8	125 739	10 334.7	125 481	10 313.5	125 208	10 291.1	125 091	10 253.4
7	125 561	10 634.9	126 115	10 711.1	125 766	10 681.5	125 499	10 658.8	125 234	10 636.3	125 117	10 597.3
8	125 511	10 630.7	126 101	10 709.9	125 798	10 684.2	125 527	10 661.2	125 259	10 638.4	125 135	10 598.9
9	125 553	10 291.2	126 083	10 363.0	125 737	10 334.5	125 445	10 310.5	125 176	10 288.4	125 045	10 249.6
10	125 613	10 639.4	126 205	10 718.8	126 382	10 733.8	125 431	10 653.0	125 319	10 643.5	125 020	10 589.1
11	125 667	10 300.6	126 203	10 372.8	126 370	10 386.6	125 410	10 307.7	125 291	10 297.9	124 990	10 245.1
12	125 685	10 645.5	126 193	10 717.8	126 357	10 731.7	125 381	10 648.8	125 267	10 639.1	124 955	10 583.6

注：1）ai（年換算係数）＝ $\dfrac{\text{i月の月間日数}}{\text{年間日数}}$ 　　note：1）　ai (coefficient)＝ $\dfrac{\text{days in the month}}{\text{days in the year}}$

　2）［1］昭和45年1～9月は前回（40年）国勢調査確定人口に基づく推計、10月は「前回国勢調査確定人口に基づき推計した、昭和45年10月1日現在の総人口と日本人人口の差」を当年国勢調査人口概数から差し引いて算出した人口、11～12月はこの10月の人口に基づく推計。
　　［2］昭和50年は前回国勢調査確定人口、55年・平成7年は前回国勢調査確定人口（按分済み）に基づく推計。
　　［3］昭和60年、平成2年の1～9月は前回国勢調査確定人口（按分済み）、10～12月は当年国勢調査要計表に基づく推計。
　　［4］平成12年・17年・22年・27年の1～9月は前回国勢調査確定人口（按分済み）、10～12月は当年国勢調査確定人口（按分済み）に基づく推計。
　資料：総務省統計局「人口推計月報」（日本人人口）（昭和45～55年は総理府統計局、昭和60～平成7年は総務庁統計局）

582

Appendix

表3　年次・性・年齢別人口[1]
Table 3　Trends in population by sex and age : Japan

総　数
Total

年齢 / Age	*1935 昭和10年	1947 *22年	1950 *25年	1955 *30年	1960 *35年	1965 *40年	1970 *45年	1975 *50年	1980 *55年
総数 Total	69 254 148	78 101 473	83 199 637	89 275 529	93 418 501	98 274 961	103 119 447	111 251 507	116 320 358
0 歳	2 035 909	2 497 635	2 315 990	1 709 339	1 576 913	1 742 531	1 865 005	1 901 354	1 575 479
1 Years	1 846 556	1 555 304	2 522 681	1 710 091	1 594 841	1 658 677	1 850 084	2 015 702	1 625 202
2	1 845 254	1 647 839	2 479 988	1 817 775	1 549 114	1 613 816	1 805 949	2 050 225	1 694 611
3	1 818 641	2 008 319	2 346 977	1 939 180	1 513 111	1 567 441	1 810 654	2 007 135	1 737 550
4	1 782 141	1 952 549	1 539 821	2 071 356	1 610 454	1 551 018	1 414 397	1 960 329	1 825 238
0 ～ 4	9 328 501	9 661 646	11 205 457	9 247 741	7 844 433	8 133 483	8 746 089	9 934 745	8 458 080
5 ～ 9	8 531 419	9 099 015	9 522 665	11 042 592	9 204 635	7 849 292	8 100 003	8 877 006	9 966 787
10 ～ 14	7 685 247	8 812 693	8 699 917	9 507 817	11 017 538	9 183 407	7 799 284	8 223 394	8 900 365
15 ～ 19	6 640 917	8 263 857	8 567 668	8 625 519	9 308 538	10 851 888	8 998 395	7 891 996	8 215 420
20 ～ 24	6 071 071	7 061 904	7 725 542	8 403 243	8 318 450	9 068 689	10 594 925	9 007 448	7 783 812
25 ～ 29	5 240 083	5 491 634	6 185 120	7 604 328	8 209 360	8 363 829	9 037 118	10 730 221	8 976 957
30 ～ 34	4 632 637	5 147 599	5 202 237	6 116 932	7 517 805	8 257 330	8 327 691	9 193 706	10 708 629
35 ～ 39	4 045 846	4 881 783	5 048 073	5 115 126	6 038 030	7 498 539	8 170 903	8 378 792	9 151 151
40 ～ 44	3 406 011	4 191 998	4 482 980	4 945 330	5 019 130	5 961 402	7 305 820	8 189 237	8 296 039
45 ～ 49	3 112 834	3 858 845	4 004 549	4 367 173	4 816 559	4 921 811	5 839 717	7 329 028	8 057 805
50 ～ 54	2 832 875	3 131 979	3 388 668	3 849 490	4 201 390	4 657 998	4 776 975	5 747 161	7 170 337
55 ～ 59	2 571 137	2 644 459	2 749 029	3 205 514	3 641 207	4 002 009	4 401 704	4 648 187	5 582 330
60 ～ 64	1 930 611	2 109 345	2 303 895	2 496 593	2 931 617	3 344 459	3 709 919	4 263 359	4 442 551
65 ～ 69	1 387 092	1 719 508	1 770 715	1 967 019	2 160 402	2 562 311	2 973 692	3 435 492	3 947 606
70 ～ 74	913 423	1 160 146	1 281 608	1 392 662	1 563 804	1 744 561	2 127 751	2 567 573	3 012 121
75 ～ 79	561 804	550 245	685 653	875 701	954 678	1 095 914	1 265 890	1 636 768	2 030 820
80 ～ 84	263 979	238 477	275 783	377 787	482 925	528 116	648 477	807 299	1 091 136
85 ～ 89	82 255	62 053	79 053	111 355	155 813	199 158	229 325	308 519	409 300
90 ～ 94[5]	16 406	14 287	16 355	22 767	32 187	50 765	65 769	81 576	119 112
95 ～ 99	...	...	...	...	...	...	...	...	...
100 ～		...		...		...		...	...
65～(再掲)	3 224 959	3 744 716	4 109 167	4 747 291	5 349 809	6 180 825	7 310 904	8 837 227	10 610 095
75～(Regrouped)	924 444	865 062	1 056 844	1 387 610	1 625 603	1 873 953	2 209 461	2 834 162	3 650 368
80～	362 640	314 817	371 191	511 909	670 925	778 039	943 571	1 197 394	1 619 548
85～	98 661	76 340	95 408	134 122	188 000	249 923	295 094	390 095	528 412

年齢 / Age	1985 *60年	1990 平成2年	1995 *7年	2000 *12年	2005 *17年	2010 *22年	2014 26年	2015 *27年	2016 28年
総数 Total	120 265 700	122 721 397	124 298 947	125 612 633	126 204 902	126 381 728	125 431 000	125 319 299	125 020 252
0 歳	1 440 749	1 209 432	1 182 029	1 162 866	1 050 771	1 037 633	1 007 000	948 227	986 473
1 Years	1 487 509	1 255 866	1 191 561	1 157 204	1 085 168	1 036 647	1 029 000	960 519	946 868
2	1 502 212	1 296 804	1 176 303	1 182 975	1 109 516	1 065 299	1 030 000	997 448	959 840
3	1 504 975	1 338 803	1 199 265	1 180 526	1 143 356	1 061 005	1 057 000	1 003 781	997 521
4	1 520 961	1 368 885	1 200 465	1 176 402	1 158 584	1 053 877	1 034 000	1 033 014	1 003 606
0 ～ 4	7 456 400	6 469 790	5 949 623	5 859 973	5 547 395	5 254 461	5 157 000	4 942 989	4 894 308
5 ～ 9	8 492 500	7 436 656	6 493 110	5 984 829	5 899 562	5 550 007	5 261 000	5 267 749	5 248 101
10 ～ 14	9 972 000	8 495 909	7 424 703	6 507 152	5 990 607	5 884 275	5 669 000	5 573 821	5 466 331
15 ～ 19	8 917 600	9 967 712	8 491 929	7 433 115	6 523 659	6 028 600	5 924 000	5 977 783	5 951 383
20 ～ 24	8 177 400	8 721 441	9 765 295	8 300 297	7 192 988	6 304 880	5 989 000	5 883 485	5 897 936
25 ～ 29	7 753 200	7 976 511	8 614 403	9 626 221	8 097 834	7 154 666	6 462 000	6 292 857	6 128 801
30 ～ 34	9 034 200	7 713 009	7 968 686	8 608 881	9 592 355	8 213 960	7 279 000	7 184 240	7 034 994
35 ～ 39	10 676 700	8 945 897	7 709 028	7 978 061	8 592 843	9 688 045	8 513 000	8 238 135	7 929 129
40 ～ 44	9 047 700	10 617 643	8 916 937	7 706 162	7 968 660	8 650 602	9 644 000	9 686 096	9 550 570
45 ～ 49	8 193 300	8 989 654	10 544 944	8 845 461	7 650 199	7 966 133	8 477 000	8 619 451	9 127 760
50 ～ 54	7 869 200	8 068 623	8 867 530	10 391 001	8 743 818	7 608 317	7 688 000	7 908 558	7 782 611
55 ～ 59	6 965 100	7 713 773	7 912 482	8 698 453	10 223 359	8 656 055	7 580 000	7 520 250	7 461 698
60 ～ 64	5 359 200	6 735 670	7 445 934	7 711 606	8 526 772	10 054 575	8 920 000	8 489 534	8 095 072
65 ～ 69	4 165 300	5 090 871	6 373 007	7 091 585	7 422 967	8 230 222	9 107 000	9 710 272	10 223 211
70 ～ 74	3 532 300	3 809 840	4 674 557	5 889 998	6 634 850	6 987 391	7 893 000	7 751 648	7 372 572
75 ～ 79	2 434 500	3 014 473	3 276 736	4 139 567	5 261 100	5 972 225	6 244 000	6 329 432	6 500 029
80 ～ 84	1 446 900	1 831 720	2 293 864	2 609 499	3 409 137	4 363 274	4 855 000	5 012 035	5 165 400
85 ～ 89	586 400	832 886	1 134 102	1 530 334	1 848 497	2 446 197	3 054 000	3 148 873	3 267 096
90 ～ 94[5]	185 600	289 319	442 077	700 438	841 086	1 026 309	1 302 000	1 359 587	1 475 000
95 ～ 99	...	...	...	...	211 356	297 633	351 000	360 757	382 000
100 ～	...	...	...	...	25 358	43 901	60 000	61 747	65 000
65～(再掲)	12 350 900	14 869 109	18 194 343	21 961 421	25 654 351	29 367 152	32 866 000	33 734 351	34 451 558
75～(Regrouped)	4 653 400	5 968 398	7 146 779	8 979 838	11 596 534	14 149 539	15 866 000	16 272 431	16 855 775
80～	2 218 900	2 953 925	3 870 043	4 840 271	6 335 434	8 177 314	9 622 000	9 942 999	10 355 746
85～	772 000	1 122 205	1 576 179	2 230 772	2 926 297	3 814 040	4 767 000	4 930 964	5 190 346

注：1）　表1備考参照されたい。
　　2）　昭和45年、50年、55年、平成7年は、国勢調査の確定数。ただし、昭和45年、50年、55年の各報告書では、それぞれ1％抽出集計結果を用いたので、本報告書と数値が異なる。平成2年、12年、17年、22年、27年は、国勢調査の確定数（按分済み人口）。
　　3）　昭和60年は「昭和60年国勢調査抽出速報集計結果」による。ただし、0歳～4歳の各値については「人口問題研究所、昭和60年10月1日現在男女年齢別推定値（日本人人口）」を用いた。
　　4）　昭和25年は4 670（男2 280・女2 390）、昭和30年は840（男420・女420）の年齢不詳を含む。
　　5）　平成16年までの90～94歳は、90歳以上の数値である。

付　録

表3　年　次・性
Table 3　Trends in population by

男
Male

年齢 Age	1935 *昭和10年	1947 *22 年	1950 *25 年	1955 *30 年	1960 *35 年	1965 *40 年	1970 *45 年 [2]	1975 *50 年 [2]	1980 *55 年 [2]
総数 Total	34 734 133	38 129 399	40 811 760 [4]	43 860 718 [4]	45 877 602	48 244 445	50 600 539	54 724 867	57 201 287
0 歳	1 031 081	1 274 050	1 182 171	875 952	807 846	889 632	957 461	974 414	808 148
1 Years	933 210	790 690	1 286 543	874 643	816 090	846 307	948 418	1 034 450	834 136
2	931 018	832 073	1 264 541	927 800	791 599	822 780	925 700	1 049 878	867 993
3	918 975	1 014 303	1 198 969	989 687	773 432	799 563	927 176	1 029 702	890 554
4	899 717	986 990	786 266	1 058 248	823 596	791 299	723 750	1 005 209	936 007
0 ～ 4	4 714 001	4 898 106	5 718 490	4 726 330	4 012 563	4 149 581	4 482 505	5 093 653	4 336 838
5 ～ 9	4 303 263	4 597 406	4 825 426	5 636 491	4 702 331	3 995 011	4 140 644	4 552 267	5 109 227
10 ～ 14	3 876 774	4 449 289	4 400 387	4 815 800	5 620 477	4 670 170	3 976 006	4 207 013	4 564 462
15 ～ 19	3 350 713	4 144 572	4 317 567	4 677 763	5 478 341	4 538 341	4 538 341	4 011 716	4 194 921
20 ～ 24	3 036 783	3 362 456	3 835 815	4 196 415	4 125 266	4 496 297	5 279 558	4 531 815	3 932 017
25 ～ 29	2 670 248	2 410 913	2 821 898	3 775 382	4 094 656	4 157 028	4 490 569	5 392 687	4 513 252
30 ～ 34	2 379 492	2 380 687	2 360 240	2 797 239	3 746 898	4 147 254	4 158 837	4 597 513	5 388 380
35 ～ 39	2 093 446	2 329 559	2 376 105	2 319 498	2 763 208	3 747 509	4 102 995	4 190 146	4 568 728
40 ～ 44	1 767 627	2 110 608	2 198 955	2 324 750	2 274 344	2 729 666	3 647 406	4 107 047	4 137 879
45 ～ 49	1 591 179	1 964 211	2 018 848	2 135 515	2 256 804	2 224 594	2 656 868	3 638 962	4 016 696
50 ～ 54	1 404 376	1 599 724	1 719 275	1 929 249	2 040 674	2 172 903	2 139 891	2 597 119	3 531 231
55 ～ 59	1 255 092	1 316 939	1 378 661	1 607 703	1 802 182	1 930 469	2 028 700	2 057 581	2 494 018
60 ～ 64	916 820	996 535	1 109 567	1 226 793	1 437 574	1 625 089	1 746 039	1 924 318	1 932 902
65 ～ 69	630 008	764 449	795 919	919 056	1 026 993	1 218 861	1 393 260	1 563 671	1 734 457
70 ～ 74	394 223	485 226	540 291	593 776	693 566	788 994	958 330	1 143 548	1 312 106
75 ～ 79	224 829	213 053	267 690	342 059	376 706	451 871	530 763	686 223	845 842
80 ～ 84	95 043	82 442	95 589	133 192	169 144	186 946	240 917	307 179	416 672
85 ～ 89	25 930	19 215	24 507	33 852	48 193	60 127	71 438	100 742	138 497
90 ～ 94 [5]	4 286	4 009	4 250	5 829	8 260	13 728	17 472	21 667	33 162
95 ～ 99	…	…	…	…	…	…	…	…	…
100 ～	…	…	…	…	…	…	…	…	…
65～（再掲）	1 374 319	1 568 394	1 728 246	2 027 764	2 322 862	2 720 533	3 212 180	3 823 030	4 480 736
75～（Regrouped）	350 088	318 719	392 036	514 932	602 303	712 672	860 590	1 115 811	1 434 173
80～	125 259	105 666	124 346	172 873	225 597	260 801	329 827	429 588	588 331
85～	30 216	23 224	28 757	39 681	56 453	73 855	88 910	122 409	171 659

年齢 Age	1985 *60 年 [3]	1990 *平成2年 [2]	1995 *7 年 [2]	2000 *12 年 [2]	2005 *17 年 [2]	2010 *22 年 [2]	2014 26 年	2015 *27 年 [2]	2016 28 年
総数 Total	59 044 000	60 248 969	60 919 153	61 488 005	61 617 893	61 571 727	61 041 000	61 022 756	60 866 773
0 歳	735 048	619 479	604 314	596 408	537 066	531 090	517 000	484 110	506 743
1 Years	758 706	643 662	610 178	592 634	555 088	530 331	527 000	491 838	483 380
2	766 449	665 455	602 272	605 988	568 711	545 162	528 000	509 603	491 477
3	768 066	686 158	614 948	603 757	586 089	543 062	543 000	513 261	509 586
4	776 930	702 613	614 947	602 842	594 211	539 517	529 000	529 268	513 203
0 ～ 4	3 805 200	3 317 367	3 046 659	3 001 629	2 841 165	2 689 162	2 644 000	2 528 080	2 504 389
5 ～ 9	4 337 800	3 810 008	3 325 548	3 066 297	3 024 316	2 841 813	2 692 000	2 698 523	2 689 161
10 ～ 14	5 085 500	4 358 230	3 799 992	3 334 963	3 071 059	3 013 782	2 904 000	2 855 328	2 798 896
15 ～ 19	4 556 700	5 107 977	4 352 058	3 808 608	3 354 802	3 096 387	3 034 000	3 073 597	3 058 390
20 ～ 24	4 171 800	4 437 613	4 979 898	4 254 807	3 688 907	3 228 469	3 076 000	3 014 733	3 026 264
25 ～ 29	3 924 500	4 035 709	4 369 726	4 894 452	4 118 834	3 642 952	3 304 000	3 210 180	3 126 981
30 ～ 34	4 541 300	3 891 907	4 034 652	4 365 637	4 866 021	4 180 232	3 703 000	3 652 706	3 578 557
35 ～ 39	5 388 600	4 499 773	3 889 083	4 035 168	4 346 968	4 926 663	4 328 000	4 191 265	4 033 393
40 ～ 44	4 493 600	5 333 198	4 482 072	3 882 767	4 020 793	4 381 848	4 898 000	4 922 423	4 854 270
45 ～ 49	4 052 900	4 471 972	5 289 590	4 436 003	3 837 649	4 015 388	4 279 000	4 365 334	4 625 678
50 ～ 54	3 898 200	3 990 975	4 393 729	5 186 499	4 361 543	3 807 362	3 860 000	3 982 000	3 919 357
55 ～ 59	3 391 200	3 781 532	3 885 871	4 274 589	5 064 582	4 296 539	3 769 000	3 749 854	3 724 301
60 ～ 64	2 348 700	3 234 444	3 597 767	3 739 992	4 148 525	4 936 772	4 379 000	4 181 397	3 990 242
65 ～ 69	1 770 900	2 189 318	2 987 287	3 352 690	3 543 105	3 933 785	4 391 000	4 699 236	4 946 701
70 ～ 74	1 486 100	1 556 586	1 931 305	2 666 691	3 040 918	3 235 341	3 674 000	3 608 735	3 435 607
75 ～ 79	996 700	1 196 534	1 254 390	1 621 115	2 256 826	2 593 169	2 758 000	2 806 665	2 894 568
80 ～ 84	547 500	678 463	821 596	913 181	1 221 288	1 700 191	1 938 000	2 009 820	2 089 763
85 ～ 89	191 600	275 903	361 022	476 535	554 715	747 287	1 027 000	1 065 311	1 117 351
90 ～ 94 [5]	55 200	81 460	116 908	176 312	210 661	242 932	311 000	335 740	377 000
95 ～ 99	…	…	…	…	41 455	55 994	62 000	63 468	67 000
100 ～	…	…	…	…	3 761	5 859	8 000	8 361	9 000
65～（再掲）	5 048 100	5 978 264	7 472 508	9 206 524	10 872 729	12 514 558	14 169 000	14 597 336	14 936 894
75～（Regrouped）	1 791 000	2 232 360	2 553 916	3 187 143	4 288 706	5 345 432	6 105 000	6 289 365	6 554 586
80～	794 300	1 035 826	1 299 526	1 566 028	2 031 880	2 752 263	3 347 000	3 482 700	3 660 018
85～	246 800	357 363	477 930	652 847	810 592	1 052 072	1 408 000	1 472 880	1 570 255

注：1)　表1備考参照されたい。
　　2)　昭和45年、50年、55年、平成7年は、国勢調査の確定数。ただし、昭和45年、50年、55年の各報告書では、それぞれ1％抽出集計結果を用いたので、本報告書と数値が異なる。平成2年、12年、17年、22年、27年は、国勢調査の確定数（按分済み人口）。
　　3)　昭和60年は「昭和60年国勢調査抽出速報集計結果」による。ただし、0歳～4歳の各歳については「人口問題研究所、昭和60年10月1日現在男女年齢別推定値（日本人人口）」を用いた。
　　4)　昭和25年は4 670（男2 280・女2 390）、昭和30年は840（男420・女420）の年齢不詳を含む。
　　5)　平成16年までの90～94歳は、90歳以上の数値である。

Appendix

・年 齢 別 人 口 [1]
sex and age : Japan
女
Female

年　　　　齢 Age	1935 *昭和10年	1947 *22　年	1950 *25　年	1955 *30　年	1960 *35　年	1965 *40　年	1970 [2] *45　年	1975 [2] *50　年	1980 [2] *55　年
総　　数 Total	34 520 015	39 972 074	42 387 877 [4]	45 414 811 [4]	47 540 899	50 030 516	52 518 908	56 526 640	59 119 071
0　歳	1 004 828	1 223 585	1 133 819	833 387	769 067	852 899	907 544	926 940	767 331
1　Years	913 346	764 614	1 236 138	835 448	778 751	812 370	901 666	981 252	791 066
2	914 236	815 766	1 215 447	889 975	757 515	791 036	880 249	1 000 347	826 618
3	899 666	994 016	1 148 008	949 493	739 679	767 878	883 478	977 433	846 996
4	882 424	965 559	753 555	1 013 108	786 858	759 719	690 647	955 120	889 231
0　～　4	4 614 500	4 763 540	5 486 967	4 521 411	3 831 870	3 983 902	4 263 584	4 841 092	4 121 242
5　～　9	4 228 156	4 501 609	4 697 239	5 406 101	4 502 304	3 854 281	3 959 359	4 324 739	4 857 560
10　～　14	3 808 473	4 363 404	4 299 530	4 692 017	5 397 061	4 513 237	3 823 278	4 016 381	4 335 903
15　～　19	3 290 204	4 119 285	4 250 101	4 284 150	4 630 775	5 373 547	4 460 054	3 880 280	4 020 499
20　～　24	3 034 288	3 699 448	3 889 727	4 206 828	4 193 184	4 572 392	5 315 367	4 475 633	3 851 795
25　～　29	2 569 835	3 080 721	3 363 222	3 828 946	4 114 704	4 206 801	4 546 549	5 337 534	4 463 705
30　～　34	2 253 145	2 766 912	2 841 997	3 319 693	3 770 907	4 110 076	4 168 854	4 596 193	5 320 249
35　～　39	1 952 400	2 552 224	2 671 968	2 795 628	3 274 822	3 751 030	4 067 908	4 188 646	4 582 423
40　～　44	1 638 384	2 081 390	2 284 025	2 620 580	2 744 786	3 231 736	3 658 414	4 082 190	4 158 160
45　～　49	1 521 655	1 894 634	1 985 701	2 231 658	2 559 755	2 697 217	3 182 849	3 690 066	4 041 109
50　～　54	1 428 499	1 532 255	1 669 393	1 920 241	2 160 716	2 485 095	2 637 084	3 150 042	3 639 106
55　～　59	1 316 045	1 327 520	1 370 368	1 597 811	1 839 025	2 071 540	2 373 004	2 590 606	3 088 312
60　～　64	1 013 791	1 112 810	1 194 328	1 269 800	1 494 043	1 719 370	1 963 880	2 339 041	2 509 649
65　～　69	757 084	955 059	974 796	1 047 963	1 133 409	1 343 444	1 580 432	1 871 821	2 213 149
70　～　74	519 200	674 920	741 317	798 886	870 238	955 567	1 169 421	1 424 025	1 700 015
75　～　79	336 975	337 192	417 963	533 642	577 972	644 043	735 127	950 545	1 184 978
80　～　84	168 936	156 035	180 194	244 595	313 781	341 170	407 560	500 120	674 464
85　～　89	56 325	42 838	54 546	77 503	107 620	139 031	157 887	207 777	270 803
90　～　94 [5]	12 120	10 278	12 105	16 938	23 927	37 037	48 297	59 909	85 950
95　～　99	…	…	…	…	…	…	…	…	…
100　～	…	…	…	…	…	…	…	…	…
65～（再掲）	1 850 640	2 176 322	2 380 921	2 719 527	3 026 947	3 460 292	4 098 724	5 014 197	6 129 359
75～（Regrouped）	574 356	546 343	664 808	872 678	1 023 300	1 161 281	1 348 871	1 718 351	2 216 195
80～	237 381	209 151	246 845	339 036	445 328	517 238	613 744	767 806	1 031 217
85～	68 445	53 116	66 651	94 441	131 547	176 068	206 184	267 686	356 753

年　　　　齢 Age	1985 [3] *60　年	1990 [2] *平成2年	1995 [2] *7　年	2000 [2] *12　年	2005 [2] *17　年	2010 [2] *22　年	2014 26　年	2015 [2] *27　年	2016 28　年
総　　数 Total	61 221 700	62 472 428	63 379 794	64 124 628	64 587 009	64 810 001	64 391 000	64 296 543	64 153 479
0　歳	705 701	589 953	577 715	566 458	513 705	506 543	490 000	464 117	479 730
1　Years	728 803	612 204	581 383	564 570	530 080	506 316	502 000	468 681	463 488
2	735 763	631 349	574 031	576 987	540 805	520 137	503 000	487 845	468 363
3	736 908	652 645	584 317	576 769	557 267	517 943	514 000	490 520	487 935
4	744 031	666 272	585 518	573 560	564 373	514 360	505 000	503 746	490 403
0　～　4	3 651 200	3 152 423	2 902 964	2 858 344	2 706 230	2 565 299	2 513 000	2 414 909	2 389 919
5　～　9	4 154 700	3 626 648	3 167 562	2 918 532	2 875 246	2 708 194	2 569 000	2 558 940	2 558 940
10　～　14	4 886 500	4 137 679	3 624 711	3 172 189	2 919 548	2 870 493	2 765 000	2 718 493	2 667 435
15　～　19	4 360 900	4 859 735	4 139 871	3 624 507	3 168 857	2 932 213	2 890 000	2 904 186	2 892 993
20　～　24	4 005 700	4 283 828	4 785 397	4 045 490	3 504 081	3 076 411	2 913 000	2 868 752	2 871 672
25　～　29	3 828 700	3 940 802	4 244 677	4 731 769	3 979 000	3 511 714	3 158 000	3 082 677	3 001 820
30　～　34	4 492 900	3 821 102	3 934 034	4 243 244	4 726 334	4 033 928	3 576 000	3 531 534	3 456 437
35　～　39	5 288 100	4 446 124	3 819 945	3 942 893	4 245 875	4 761 382	4 185 000	4 046 870	3 895 736
40　～　44	4 554 200	5 284 445	4 434 865	3 823 395	3 947 867	4 268 754	4 747 000	4 763 673	4 696 300
45　～　49	4 140 400	4 517 682	5 255 354	4 409 458	3 812 550	3 950 745	4 199 000	4 254 117	4 502 082
50　～　54	3 971 000	4 077 648	4 473 801	5 204 502	4 382 275	3 800 955	3 828 000	3 926 558	3 863 254
55　～　59	3 573 900	3 932 241	4 026 611	4 423 794	5 159 277	4 359 516	3 810 000	3 770 396	3 737 397
60　～　64	3 010 500	3 501 226	3 848 167	3 971 614	4 378 247	5 117 803	4 542 000	4 308 137	4 104 830
65　～　69	2 394 300	2 901 553	3 385 720	3 738 895	3 879 862	4 296 437	4 716 000	5 011 036	5 276 510
70　～　74	2 046 200	2 253 254	2 743 252	3 223 307	3 593 932	3 752 050	4 220 000	4 142 913	3 936 965
75　～　79	1 437 700	1 817 939	2 022 346	2 518 452	3 004 274	3 379 056	3 487 000	3 522 767	3 605 461
80　～　84	899 400	1 153 257	1 472 268	1 696 318	2 187 849	2 663 083	2 916 000	3 002 215	3 075 637
85　～　89	394 900	556 983	773 080	1 053 799	1 293 782	1 698 910	2 028 000	2 083 562	2 149 745
90　～　94 [5]	130 400	207 859	325 169	524 126	630 425	783 377	990 000	1 023 847	1 098 000
95　～　99	…	…	…	…	169 901	241 639	289 000	297 289	316 000
100　～	…	…	…	…	21 597	38 042	51 000	53 386	57 000
65～（再掲）	7 302 800	8 890 845	10 721 835	12 754 897	14 781 622	16 852 594	18 697 000	19 137 015	19 514 664
75～（Regrouped）	2 862 400	3 736 038	4 592 863	5 792 695	7 307 828	8 804 107	9 761 000	9 983 066	10 301 189
80～	1 424 700	1 918 099	2 570 517	3 274 243	4 303 554	5 425 051	6 275 000	6 460 299	6 695 728
85～	525 300	764 842	1 098 249	1 577 925	2 115 705	2 761 968	3 359 000	3 458 084	3 620 091

付　録

表 4　年　次・[1]

Table 4　Trends in population

総　数
Total

都道府県 Prefecture	1935 *昭和10年	1947 * 22 年[3]	1950 * 25 年	1955 * 30 年	1960 * 35 年[4]	1965 * 40 年	1970 * 45 年[5]	1975 * 50 年[5]	1980 * 55 年[5]
全 国　Total	69 254 148	78 101 473	83 199 637	89 275 529	93 418 501	98 274 961	103 119 447	111 251 507	116 320 358
01 北海道 a)	3 068 282	3 852 821	4 295 567	4 773 087	5 039 206	5 171 800	5 177 286	5 330 284	5 566 372
02 青　森	967 129	1 180 245	1 282 867	1 382 523	1 426 606	1 416 591	1 425 702	1 466 742	1 521 778
03 岩　手	1 046 111	1 262 743	1 346 728	1 427 097	1 448 517	1 411 118	1 369 948	1 383 931	1 420 078
04 宮　城	1 234 801	1 566 831	1 663 442	1 727 065	1 743 195	1 753 126	1 815 282	1 950 790	2 076 657
05 秋　田	1 037 744	1 257 398	1 309 031	1 348 871	1 335 580	1 279 835	1 240 345	1 231 389	1 255 499
06 山　形	1 116 822	1 335 653	1 357 347	1 353 649	1 320 664	1 263 103	1 224 918	1 219 429	1 250 989
07 福　島	1 581 563	1 992 460	2 062 394	2 095 237	2 051 137	1 983 754	1 943 989	1 968 270	2 032 547
08 茨　城	1 548 991	2 013 735	2 039 418	2 064 037	2 047 024	2 056 154	2 140 122	2 338 151	2 552 775
09 栃　木	1 195 057	1 534 311	1 550 462	1 547 580	1 513 624	1 521 656	1 578 146	1 695 848	1 789 218
10 群　馬	1 242 453	1 572 787	1 601 380	1 613 549	1 578 476	1 605 584	1 656 209	1 753 436	1 845 138
11 埼　玉	1 528 854	2 100 453	2 146 445	2 262 623	2 430 871	3 014 983	3 858 607	4 809 517	5 405 466
12 千　葉	1 546 394	2 112 917	2 139 037	2 205 060	2 306 010	2 701 770	3 358 440	4 136 216	4 719 383
13 東　京	6 369 919	5 000 777	6 277 500	8 037 084	9 683 802	10 869 244	11 324 994	11 568 852	11 506 944
14 神奈川	1 840 005	2 218 120	2 487 665	2 919 497	3 443 176	4 430 743	5 439 126	6 359 334	6 883 647
15 新　潟	1 995 777	2 418 271	2 460 997	2 473 492	2 442 037	2 398 931	2 358 323	2 388 992	2 448 056
16 富　山	798 890	979 229	1 008 790	1 021 121	1 032 614	1 025 465	1 027 956	1 068 930	1 101 485
17 石　川	768 416	927 743	957 279	966 187	973 418	980 499	999 535	1 066 669	1 115 559
18 福　井	646 659	726 264	752 374	754 055	752 696	750 557	740 024	768 867	789 497
19 山　梨	646 727	807 251	811 369	807 044	782 062	763 194	760 492	781 360	802 490
20 長　野	1 714 000	2 060 010	2 060 831	2 021 292	1 981 433	1 958 007	1 952 346	2 012 816	2 078 832
21 岐　阜	1 225 799	1 493 644	1 544 538	1 583 605	1 638 399	1 700 365	1 749 524	1 858 066	1 949 993
22 静　岡	1 939 860	2 353 005	2 471 472	2 650 435	2 756 271	2 912 521	3 082 792	3 300 856	3 438 445
23 愛　知	2 862 701	3 122 902	3 390 585	3 769 209	4 206 313	4 798 653	5 340 594	5 873 395	6 167 929
24 三　重	1 174 595	1 416 494	1 461 197	1 485 582	1 485 054	1 514 467	1 535 937	1 618 449	1 678 831
25 滋　賀	711 436	858 367	861 180	853 734	842 695	853 385	883 837	978 639	1 072 440
26 京　都	1 702 508	1 739 084	1 832 934	1 935 161	1 993 403	2 102 808	2 210 609	2 381 360	2 483 007
27 大　阪	4 297 174	3 334 659	3 857 047	4 618 308	5 504 746	6 657 189	7 464 961	8 108 360	8 295 801
28 兵　庫	2 923 249	3 057 444	3 309 935	3 620 947	3 906 487	4 309 944	4 599 673	4 918 041	5 063 478
29 奈　良	620 471	779 935	763 883	776 861	781 058	825 965	925 403	1 071 894	1 202 655
30 和歌山	864 087	959 999	982 113	1 006 819	1 002 191	1 026 975	1 038 348	1 067 419	1 081 999
31 鳥　取	490 461	587 606	600 177	614 259	599 135	579 853	567 405	579 779	602 335
32 島　根	747 119	894 267	912 551	929 066	888 886	821 620	772 000	767 357	783 143
33 岡　山	1 332 647	1 619 622	1 661 099	1 689 800	1 670 454	1 645 135	1 700 064	1 806 484	1 862 741
34 広　島	1 804 916	2 011 498	2 081 967	2 149 044	2 184 043	2 281 146	2 422 069	2 630 578	2 722 521
35 山　口	1 190 542	1 479 244	1 540 882	1 609 839	1 602 207	1 543 573	1 497 703	1 541 072	1 572 752
36 徳　島	728 748	854 811	878 511	878 109	847 274	815 115	790 845	804 784	824 433
37 香　川	748 656	917 673	946 022	943 823	918 867	900 845	906 951	960 233	998 442
38 愛　媛	1 164 898	1 453 887	1 521 878	1 540 628	1 500 687	1 446 384	1 416 299	1 463 158	1 504 298
39 高　知	714 980	848 337	873 874	882 683	854 595	812 714	786 058	807 035	829 609
40 福　岡	2 755 804	3 178 134	3 530 169	3 859 764	4 006 679	3 964 611	4 004 275	4 266 394	4 523 770
41 佐　賀	686 117	917 797	945 082	973 749	942 874	871 885	837 063	836 326	864 052
42 長　崎	1 296 883	1 531 674	1 645 492	1 747 596	1 760 421	1 641 245	1 566 634	1 568 429	1 586 916
43 熊　本	1 387 054	1 765 726	1 827 582	1 895 663	1 856 192	1 770 736	1 697 991	1 713 300	1 788 076
44 大　分	980 458	1 233 651	1 252 999	1 277 199	1 239 655	1 187 480	1 152 520	1 187 299	1 225 548
45 宮　崎	824 431	1 025 689	1 091 427	1 139 384	1 134 590	1 080 692	1 050 027	1 083 957	1 150 321
46 鹿児島	1 591 466	1 746 305	1 804 118	2 044 112	1 963 104	1 853 541	1 728 075	1 722 732	1 783 351
47 沖　縄	592 494	…	…	…	…	…	…	1 036 288	1 101 062

注:1)　各年次の人口は10月1日現在。＊は国勢調査人口である。
　　2)　昭和40年以前は総人口、45年以降は日本人人口である。
　　3)　昭和22年は地域的に配分されない調査もれを除く。
　　4)　昭和35年の長野県西筑摩郡山口村と岐阜県中津川市の境界紛争地域の人口73人（男39人、女34人）は全国総数に含まれているが、長野県・岐阜県のいずれにも含まれていない。
　　5)　昭和45年、50年、55年、平成7年は、国勢調査の確定数。ただし、昭和45年、50年、55年の各報告書では、それぞれ1％抽出集計結果を用いたので、本報告書と数値が異なる。
　　　　平成2年、12年、17年、22年、27年は、国勢調査の確定数（按分済み人口）。
　　6)　昭和60年については、全国は日本人人口、都道府県は総人口であり、「昭和60年国勢調査抽出速報集計結果」を用いた。
　　7)　平成28年より、都道府県も日本人人口となり、「人口推計（各年10月1日現在）」を用いた。

Appendix

都道府県・性別人口 [2]
by sex : Japan, each prefecture

総 数
Total

1985 *60 年 [6]	1990 *平成 2 年 [5]	1995 * 7 年 [5]	2000 * 12 年 [5]	2005 * 17 年 [5]	2010 * 22 年 [5]	2014 26 年	2015 * 27 年 [5]	2016 28 年	都道府県 Prefecture
120 265 700	122 721 397	124 298 947	125 612 633	126 204 902	126 381 728	125 431 000	125 319 299	125 020 252	全 国 Total
5 688 500	5 635 049	5 675 838	5 670 558	5 612 068	5 488 092	5 381 000	5 360 032	5 327 000	01 北 海 道 a)
1 521 200	1 480 947	1 478 123	1 472 690	1 432 727	1 369 629	1 318 000	1 304 813	1 290 000	02 青　森
1 454 600	1 415 036	1 416 864	1 412 338	1 379 659	1 324 924	1 280 000	1 274 574	1 263 000	03 岩　手
2 167 900	2 243 117	2 319 433	2 354 916	2 348 339	2 335 682	2 316 000	2 319 616	2 314 000	04 宮　城
1 252 900	1 226 062	1 211 616	1 186 209	1 141 865	1 082 603	1 034 000	1 020 199	1 007 000	05 秋　田
1 251 200	1 256 930	1 253 941	1 239 132	1 209 795	1 162 744	1 125 000	1 118 381	1 107 000	06 山　形
2 054 200	2 100 255	2 127 214	2 118 100	2 081 248	2 019 618	1 928 000	1 905 278	1 891 000	07 福　島
2 717 500	2 834 279	2 929 220	2 954 817	2 937 843	2 929 085	2 881 000	2 875 434	2 861 000	08 茨　城
1 883 800	1 925 886	1 965 431	1 983 723	1 990 257	1 980 746	1 954 000	1 947 505	1 939 000	09 栃　木
1 913 200	1 955 819	1 981 799	1 996 251	1 989 184	1 972 287	1 941 000	1 935 898	1 926 000	10 群　馬
5 854 900	6 374 361	6 696 390	6 875 484	6 974 003	7 104 590	7 143 000	7 160 471	7 169 000	11 埼　玉
5 168 100	5 527 777	5 744 010	5 868 599	5 983 085	6 135 236	6 114 000	6 130 930	6 137 000	12 千　葉
11 780 500	11 695 218	11 543 005	11 850 305	12 325 038	12 833 956	13 044 000	13 131 172	13 207 000	13 東　京
7 380 200	7 918 632	8 152 458	8 390 552	8 675 683	8 921 252	8 967 000	8 979 438	8 986 000	14 神 奈 川
2 448 900	2 470 352	2 480 287	2 466 374	2 420 575	2 362 420	2 302 000	2 292 676	2 273 000	15 新　潟
1 125 400	1 117 550	1 117 592	1 113 787	1 101 133	1 082 108	1 059 000	1 055 528	1 049 000	16 富　山
1 157 700	1 160 786	1 175 042	1 174 630	1 166 366	1 159 897	1 146 000	1 144 626	1 140 000	17 石　川
822 000	818 325	819 320	819 080	810 772	795 496	780 000	777 192	772 000	18 福　井
823 100	850 075	873 970	877 168	870 939	850 546	830 000	823 723	818 000	19 山　梨
2 170 400	2 148 242	2 173 400	2 181 873	2 161 328	2 122 509	2 083 000	2 072 135	2 060 000	20 長　野
2 038 300	2 055 219	2 081 104	2 081 092	2 070 404	2 043 467	2 008 000	1 996 303	1 985 000	21 岐　阜
3 582 000	3 650 475	3 699 146	3 714 992	3 721 561	3 702 776	3 651 000	3 640 343	3 623 000	22 静　岡
6 477 200	6 625 160	6 769 815	6 932 577	7 103 849	7 247 125	7 298 000	7 315 314	7 324 000	23 愛　知
1 738 300	1 782 332	1 824 717	1 833 408	1 832 672	1 821 502	1 793 000	1 784 379	1 775 000	24 三　重
1 165 900	1 213 357	1 272 620	1 324 040	1 357 591	1 388 741	1 397 000	1 392 890	1 392 000	25 滋　賀
2 565 400	2 556 321	2 572 600	2 599 052	2 601 322	2 593 340	2 569 000	2 565 573	2 559 000	26 京　都
8 653 300	8 557 249	8 603 130	8 633 901	8 640 236	8 697 550	8 678 000	8 683 865	8 672 000	27 大　阪
5 275 600	5 326 121	5 318 913	5 467 653	5 504 338	5 507 961	5 468 000	5 456 154	5 438 000	28 兵　庫
1 303 900	1 368 434	1 421 770	1 434 340	1 412 450	1 391 395	1 367 000	1 355 570	1 347 000	29 奈　良
1 086 600	1 069 930	1 075 666	1 065 104	1 030 942	997 305	967 000	958 901	949 000	30 和 歌 山
620 200	613 792	612 602	610 224	603 156	585 005	571 000	570 037	566 000	31 鳥　取
797 500	779 317	768 865	757 072	737 753	712 516	692 000	688 953	684 000	32 島　根
1 914 100	1 917 173	1 937 865	1 938 268	1 942 414	1 926 378	1 907 000	1 903 981	1 896 000	33 岡　山
2 820 200	2 832 764	2 858 462	2 855 782	2 849 333	2 827 820	2 801 000	2 808 773	2 799 000	34 広　島
1 588 500	1 559 181	1 542 204	1 515 291	1 480 129	1 439 011	1 397 000	1 393 199	1 381 000	35 山　口
831 400	830 753	830 479	821 369	805 743	781 300	760 000	751 830	746 000	36 徳　島
1 034 000	1 021 571	1 023 865	1 017 973	1 006 383	988 786	974 000	969 270	964 000	37 香　川
1 533 600	1 512 674	1 503 411	1 488 550	1 461 038	1 423 425	1 388 000	1 377 071	1 366 000	38 愛　媛
843 400	823 853	814 302	811 516	793 365	761 239	735 000	725 032	718 000	39 高　知
4 753 200	4 784 331	4 896 451	4 984 938	5 011 273	5 030 961	5 046 000	5 053 500	5 054 000	40 福　岡
890 700	876 300	882 320	874 068	863 046	846 146	831 000	828 944	824 000	41 佐　賀
1 599 500	1 558 502	1 540 498	1 511 864	1 472 955	1 420 166	1 380 000	1 369 432	1 358 000	42 長　崎
1 836 200	1 837 612	1 855 087	1 854 933	1 835 575	1 809 626	1 785 000	1 777 726	1 765 000	43 熊　本
1 246 300	1 233 612	1 227 269	1 216 436	1 202 682	1 187 599	1 163 000	1 157 581	1 150 000	44 大　分
1 183 500	1 167 286	1 173 631	1 167 555	1 149 818	1 131 381	1 110 000	1 100 364	1 092 000	45 宮　崎
1 833 600	1 795 908	1 791 419	1 782 567	1 748 272	1 700 683	1 662 000	1 642 281	1 630 000	46 鹿 児 島
1 177 000	1 217 472	1 265 783	1 311 482	1 354 695	1 385 104	1 411 000	1 422 412	1 427 000	47 沖　縄

Note : a) See page 44.

付　録

表 4　年　次・[1]
Table 4　Trends in population

男
Male

都道府県 Prefecture	1935 *昭和10年	1947 *22 年[3]	1950 *25 年	1955 *30 年	1960 *35 年[4]	1965 *40 年	1970 *45 年[5]	1975 *50 年[5]	1980 *55 年[5]
全　国　Total	34 734 133	38 129 399	40 811 760	43 860 718	45 877 602	48 244 445	50 600 539	54 724 867	57 201 287
01 北海道 [a]	1 593 845	1 934 179	2 169 393	2 428 833	2 544 753	2 583 159	2 548 598	2 616 571	2 731 359
02 青　森	484 277	579 690	635 547	678 837	694 037	682 972	684 479	706 182	734 299
03 岩　手	519 485	614 227	664 000	698 563	702 697	679 497	657 610	667 243	687 401
04 宮　城	622 973	772 928	828 879	846 404	848 579	854 043	886 902	957 778	1 022 732
05 秋　田	519 249	616 269	646 445	660 066	644 671	614 429	592 663	589 854	602 721
06 山　形	549 060	641 447	660 555	651 737	630 997	605 185	587 084	586 417	604 902
07 福　島	778 732	963 399	1 006 823	1 016 756	986 836	954 988	935 003	952 109	989 087
08 茨　城	766 423	974 289	993 694	1 006 093	1 000 184	1 007 852	1 052 159	1 157 536	1 269 694
09 栃　木	588 545	738 344	752 266	749 636	729 692	735 781	768 506	833 590	883 968
10 群　馬	606 779	759 140	778 910	781 607	759 639	778 916	806 727	857 665	907 057
11 埼　玉	753 802	1 022 869	1 049 695	1 110 083	1 200 573	1 511 947	1 946 868	2 430 387	2 730 531
12 千　葉	764 751	1 018 295	1 036 932	1 074 181	1 128 734	1 343 167	1 690 355	2 088 099	2 374 182
13 東　京	3 325 696	2 553 174	3 169 389	4 115 823	4 997 023	5 564 583	5 755 815	5 854 673	5 793 927
14 神奈川	951 348	1 115 111	1 247 934	1 470 415	1 746 926	2 280 926	2 804 223	3 265 877	3 513 491
15 新　潟	982 497	1 162 475	1 194 929	1 195 872	1 177 923	1 160 283	1 138 673	1 159 256	1 191 870
16 富　山	388 771	472 829	488 850	494 109	500 545	491 662	491 595	514 033	531 716
17 石　川	370 907	443 872	460 859	463 477	464 889	468 518	478 877	516 918	540 721
18 福　井	316 424	348 861	364 343	363 770	360 288	359 649	354 393	370 912	381 729
19 山　梨	319 924	388 287	393 550	390 205	379 057	367 739	366 039	378 293	390 658
20 長　野	840 103	989 167	1 001 192	979 004	954 673	937 219	933 811	969 893	1 006 218
21 岐　阜	612 366	731 798	762 295	774 062	796 825	821 444	843 723	902 131	948 710
22 静　岡	966 250	1 141 788	1 206 651	1 301 198	1 353 122	1 428 930	1 512 812	1 623 594	1 691 415
23 愛　知	1 418 218	1 520 405	1 649 189	1 829 729	2 064 726	2 382 085	2 671 221	2 940 320	3 084 462
24 三　重	572 356	676 285	704 805	717 819	716 715	727 802	738 723	783 379	813 477
25 滋　賀	345 185	412 035	413 110	409 813	403 281	409 502	426 755	478 099	525 393
26 京　都	862 998	845 277	891 616	944 278	973 040	1 028 073	1 081 579	1 168 506	1 215 942
27 大　阪	2 241 666	1 646 888	1 899 745	2 290 170	2 766 229	3 355 699	3 743 356	4 044 552	4 112 507
28 兵　庫	1 466 284	1 505 493	1 622 755	1 773 488	1 917 887	2 120 749	2 264 578	2 414 982	2 470 060
29 奈　良	306 011	376 258	368 863	377 961	382 494	400 353	448 164	520 767	583 613
30 和歌山	428 638	461 648	475 324	490 533	484 994	497 256	500 878	515 419	520 882
31 鳥　取	239 301	280 628	289 787	297 015	286 716	275 572	268 801	276 348	288 956
32 島　根	373 292	430 218	444 355	456 730	432 481	393 670	366 834	366 270	376 649
33 岡　山	658 773	782 386	804 357	815 837	797 748	781 418	815 827	874 082	901 314
34 広　島	914 185	979 359	1 015 955	1 047 184	1 058 829	1 107 878	1 180 978	1 288 509	1 328 238
35 山　口	598 434	726 443	760 220	792 546	780 439	740 934	712 163	736 647	752 050
36 徳　島	362 042	411 331	427 684	427 204	408 300	389 795	376 572	384 586	395 535
37 香　川	373 522	439 913	457 980	456 711	438 924	427 058	430 238	460 798	480 327
38 愛　媛	575 627	703 624	742 092	749 342	721 311	688 063	670 030	696 694	717 259
39 高　知	355 225	410 729	425 968	429 175	411 162	386 725	371 509	382 731	395 459
40 福　岡	1 392 799	1 571 291	1 745 606	1 895 365	1 954 636	1 911 317	1 919 831	2 056 064	2 184 606
41 佐　賀	332 764	439 481	455 824	470 437	448 797	410 937	392 862	393 915	410 096
42 長　崎	662 174	749 242	812 079	859 689	860 623	788 667	746 074	748 487	756 376
43 熊　本	680 409	847 938	882 420	917 171	887 038	838 584	796 918	808 860	849 621
44 大　分	481 549	593 075	604 825	616 402	590 963	559 433	538 950	560 205	581 308
45 宮　崎	416 082	501 302	535 107	559 771	552 285	517 235	497 425	514 614	549 538
46 鹿児島	773 126	835 712	868 963	985 617	935 282	872 751	803 358	803 680	838 693
47 沖　縄	281 266	…	…	…	…	…	…	507 342	540 538

注：1)　各年次の人口は10月1日現在。＊は国勢調査人口である。
　　2)　昭和40年以前は総人口、45年以降は日本人人口である。
　　3)　昭和22年は地域的に配分されない調査もれを除く。
　　4)　昭和35年の長野県西筑摩郡山口村と岐阜県中津川市の境界紛争地域の人口73人（男39人、女34人）は全国総数に含まれているが、長野県・岐阜県のいずれにも含まれていない。
　　5)　昭和45年、50年、55年、平成7年は、国勢調査の確定数。ただし、昭和45年、50年、55年の各報告書では、それぞれ1％抽出集計結果を用いたので、本報告書と数値が異なる。
　　　　平成2年、12年、17年、22年、27年は、国勢調査の確定数（按分済み人口）。
　　6)　昭和60年については、全国は日本人人口、都道府県は総人口であり、「昭和60年国勢調査抽出速報集計結果」を用いた。
　　7)　平成28年より、都道府県も日本人人口となり、「人口推計（各年10月1日現在）」を用いた。

都道府県・性別人口[2)]

by sex : Japan, each prefecture

男
Male

1985 *60 年 [6)]	1990 *平成2年 [5)]	1995 *7 年 [5)]	2000 *12 年 [5)]	2005 *17 年 [5)]	2010 *22 年 [5)]	2014 26 年	2015 *27 年 [5)]	2016 28 年	都 道 府 県 Prefecture
59 044 000	60 248 969	60 919 153	61 488 005	61 617 893	61 571 727	61 041 000	61 022 756	60 866 773	全 国　Total
									a)
2 767 200	2 718 461	2 727 566	2 713 299	2 668 263	2 596 047	2 537 000	2 528 249	2 511 000	01 北 海 道
724 800	703 845	702 351	701 308	677 747	644 839	619 000	613 429	606 000	02 青　森
699 200	679 290	680 790	679 886	662 028	633 657	613 000	613 993	609 000	03 岩　手
1 058 500	1 102 361	1 140 128	1 154 105	1 144 539	1 134 707	1 129 000	1 133 842	1 131 000	04 宮　城
600 900	584 003	576 603	563 704	539 747	509 065	485 000	479 495	473 000	05 秋　田
602 300	606 405	606 138	600 034	583 661	559 360	542 000	538 942	534 000	06 山　形
996 000	1 022 530	1 039 147	1 034 435	1 013 460	981 711	942 000	942 525	937 000	07 福　島
1 361 600	1 413 482	1 462 678	1 473 555	1 462 446	1 460 874	1 437 000	1 433 632	1 427 000	08 茨　城
921 800	957 324	977 371	985 746	989 721	984 884	972 000	969 568	965 000	09 栃　木
939 500	965 827	977 895	984 816	979 013	971 506	956 000	955 166	950 000	10 群　馬
2 954 700	3 229 425	3 384 961	3 471 147	3 517 257	3 569 078	3 578 000	3 580 126	3 581 000	11 埼　玉
2 590 700	2 789 174	2 896 807	2 951 889	2 996 890	3 063 676	3 046 000	3 055 780	3 056 000	12 千　葉
5 945 100	5 887 794	5 770 200	5 925 437	6 143 520	6 360 369	6 443 000	6 482 439	6 514 000	13 東　京
3 774 600	4 064 653	4 159 965	4 259 603	4 388 419	4 485 848	4 488 000	4 490 436	4 489 000	14 神奈川
1 192 100	1 198 492	1 205 815	1 198 125	1 172 715	1 143 907	1 115 000	1 111 234	1 102 000	15 新　潟
545 600	537 465	538 200	537 037	530 906	522 080	512 000	510 522	508 000	16 富　山
553 900	560 881	568 409	568 938	563 361	560 422	555 000	554 168	552 000	17 石　川
393 700	397 865	398 115	397 912	393 053	385 299	378 000	377 797	376 000	18 福　井
401 700	417 320	430 744	431 577	427 411	417 174	407 000	403 574	401 000	19 山　梨
1 044 600	1 044 399	1 060 695	1 065 513	1 053 088	1 033 742	1 015 000	1 010 828	1 005 000	20 長　野
992 500	998 010	1 009 799	1 009 870	1 004 099	990 446	973 000	968 367	963 000	21 岐　阜
1 770 500	1 798 240	1 822 004	1 830 059	1 832 485	1 824 427	1 798 000	1 793 155	1 785 000	22 静　岡
3 232 000	3 321 224	3 386 955	3 470 932	3 563 275	3 627 629	3 651 000	3 662 209	3 667 000	23 愛　知
840 100	864 385	885 246	888 976	890 383	887 300	874 000	868 569	864 000	24 三　重
575 400	596 507	626 896	653 699	670 027	685 758	689 000	686 944	686 000	25 滋　賀
1 258 500	1 244 673	1 247 727	1 256 444	1 250 756	1 245 416	1 232 000	1 228 056	1 224 000	26 京　都
4 271 500	4 221 800	4 224 473	4 223 003	4 195 935	4 207 727	4 183 000	4 183 203	4 174 000	27 大　阪
2 577 200	2 580 404	2 570 836	2 634 709	2 638 876	2 636 121	2 611 000	2 604 747	2 594 000	28 兵　庫
633 700	660 251	684 140	687 190	672 420	659 171	645 000	640 015	635 000	29 奈　良
515 800	508 727	511 271	504 942	486 215	469 544	455 000	451 510	447 000	30 和歌山
296 700	294 002	293 313	292 242	289 002	279 543	273 000	272 584	271 000	31 鳥　取
381 000	372 822	367 610	362 141	352 260	341 302	332 000	330 790	329 000	32 島　根
925 000	922 486	932 037	930 372	932 326	925 031	916 000	914 810	911 000	33 岡　山
1 377 500	1 377 077	1 387 437	1 381 971	1 377 500	1 365 236	1 352 000	1 359 589	1 356 000	34 広　島
757 900	738 350	730 108	716 958	698 239	678 688	660 000	659 767	655 000	35 山　口
400 700	395 518	394 725	390 813	383 441	371 484	362 000	358 580	356 000	36 徳　島
499 900	490 719	492 103	489 661	483 506	476 657	470 000	468 851	467 000	37 香　川
727 700	715 877	710 949	702 537	689 062	669 771	654 000	650 506	645 000	38 愛　媛
397 600	388 464	383 195	382 780	373 201	357 567	345 000	341 013	337 000	39 高　知
2 295 400	2 290 227	2 338 280	2 374 505	2 375 589	2 374 674	2 381 000	2 386 993	2 387 000	40 福　岡
425 000	413 885	417 710	413 363	407 111	398 787	392 000	391 578	389 000	41 佐　賀
763 200	734 372	724 562	710 224	688 996	663 130	645 000	641 648	637 000	42 長　崎
868 200	868 233	877 530	876 472	864 737	850 748	840 000	837 891	832 000	43 熊　本
588 100	583 066	579 968	573 998	567 061	561 248	550 000	548 065	545 000	44 大　分
558 000	550 803	555 207	551 060	540 834	531 473	522 000	517 844	514 000	45 宮　崎
858 900	841 735	839 862	836 688	818 319	795 367	778 000	771 451	766 000	46 鹿児島
583 900	596 116	620 632	644 330	664 993	679 237	692 000	698 276	701 000	47 沖　縄

Note : a) See page 44.

付　録

表 4　年　次・[1]
Table 4　Trends in population

女
Female

都道府県 Prefecture	1935 *昭和10年	1947 *22 年 [3]	1950 *25 年	1955 *30 年	1960 *35 年 [4]	1965 *40 年	1970 *45 年 [5]	1975 *50 年 [5]	1980 *55 年 [5]
全 国　Total	34 520 015	39 972 074	42 387 877	45 414 811	47 540 899	50 030 516	52 518 908	56 526 640	59 119 071
01 北海道 [a]	1 474 437	1 918 642	2 126 174	2 344 254	2 494 453	2 588 641	2 628 688	2 713 713	2 835 013
02 青　森	482 852	600 555	647 320	703 686	732 569	733 619	741 223	760 560	787 479
03 岩　手	526 626	648 516	682 728	728 534	745 820	731 621	712 338	716 688	732 677
04 宮　城	611 828	793 903	834 563	880 661	894 616	899 083	928 380	993 012	1 053 925
05 秋　田	518 495	641 129	662 586	688 805	690 909	665 406	647 682	641 535	652 778
06 山　形	567 762	694 206	696 792	701 912	689 667	657 918	637 834	633 012	646 087
07 福　島	802 831	1 029 061	1 055 571	1 078 481	1 064 301	1 028 766	1 008 986	1 016 161	1 043 460
08 茨　城	782 568	1 039 446	1 045 724	1 057 944	1 046 840	1 048 302	1 087 963	1 180 615	1 283 081
09 栃　木	606 512	795 967	798 196	797 944	783 932	785 875	809 640	862 258	905 250
10 群　馬	635 674	813 647	822 470	831 942	818 837	826 668	849 482	895 771	938 081
11 埼　玉	775 052	1 077 584	1 096 750	1 152 540	1 230 298	1 503 036	1 911 739	2 379 130	2 674 935
12 千　葉	781 643	1 094 622	1 102 105	1 130 879	1 177 276	1 358 603	1 668 085	2 048 117	2 345 201
13 東　京	3 044 223	2 447 603	3 108 111	3 921 261	4 686 779	5 304 661	5 569 179	5 714 179	5 713 017
14 神奈川	888 657	1 103 009	1 239 731	1 449 082	1 696 250	2 149 817	2 634 903	3 093 457	3 370 156
15 新　潟	1 013 280	1 255 796	1 266 068	1 277 620	1 264 114	1 238 648	1 219 650	1 229 736	1 256 186
16 富　山	410 119	506 400	519 940	527 012	532 069	533 803	536 361	554 897	569 769
17 石　川	397 509	483 871	496 420	502 710	508 529	511 981	520 658	549 751	574 838
18 福　井	330 235	377 403	388 031	390 285	392 408	390 908	385 631	397 955	407 768
19 山　梨	326 803	418 964	417 819	416 839	403 005	395 455	394 453	403 067	411 832
20 長　野	873 897	1 070 843	1 059 639	1 042 288	1 026 760	1 020 788	1 018 535	1 042 923	1 072 614
21 岐　阜	613 433	761 846	782 243	809 543	841 574	878 921	905 801	955 935	1 001 283
22 静　岡	973 610	1 211 217	1 264 821	1 349 237	1 403 149	1 483 591	1 569 980	1 677 262	1 747 030
23 愛　知	1 444 483	1 602 497	1 741 396	1 939 480	2 141 587	2 416 568	2 669 373	2 933 075	3 083 467
24 三　重	602 239	740 209	756 392	767 763	768 339	786 665	797 214	835 070	865 354
25 滋　賀	366 251	446 332	448 070	443 921	439 414	443 883	457 082	500 540	547 047
26 京　都	839 510	893 807	941 318	990 883	1 020 363	1 074 735	1 129 030	1 212 854	1 267 065
27 大　阪	2 055 508	1 687 771	1 957 302	2 328 138	2 738 517	3 301 490	3 721 605	4 063 808	4 183 294
28 兵　庫	1 456 965	1 551 951	1 687 180	1 847 459	1 988 600	2 189 195	2 335 095	2 503 059	2 593 418
29 奈　良	314 460	403 677	395 020	398 900	398 564	425 612	477 239	551 127	619 042
30 和歌山	435 449	498 351	506 789	516 286	517 197	529 719	537 470	552 000	561 117
31 鳥　取	251 160	306 978	310 390	317 244	312 419	304 281	298 604	303 431	313 379
32 島　根	373 827	464 049	468 196	472 336	456 405	427 950	405 166	401 087	406 494
33 岡　山	673 874	837 236	856 742	873 963	872 706	863 717	884 237	932 402	961 427
34 広　島	890 731	1 032 139	1 066 012	1 101 860	1 125 214	1 173 268	1 241 091	1 342 069	1 394 283
35 山　口	592 108	752 801	780 662	817 293	821 768	802 639	785 540	804 425	820 702
36 徳　島	366 706	443 480	450 827	450 905	438 974	425 320	414 273	420 198	428 898
37 香　川	375 134	477 760	488 042	487 112	479 943	473 787	476 713	499 435	518 115
38 愛　媛	589 271	750 263	779 786	791 286	779 376	758 321	746 269	766 464	787 039
39 高　知	359 755	437 608	447 906	453 508	443 433	425 989	414 549	424 304	434 150
40 福　岡	1 363 005	1 606 843	1 784 563	1 964 399	2 052 043	2 053 294	2 084 444	2 210 330	2 339 164
41 佐　賀	353 353	478 316	489 258	503 312	494 077	460 948	444 201	442 411	453 956
42 長　崎	634 709	782 432	833 413	887 907	899 798	852 578	820 560	819 942	830 540
43 熊　本	706 645	917 788	945 162	978 492	969 154	932 152	901 073	904 440	938 455
44 大　分	498 909	640 576	648 174	660 797	648 692	628 047	613 570	627 094	644 240
45 宮　崎	408 349	524 387	556 320	579 613	582 305	563 457	552 602	569 343	600 783
46 鹿児島	818 340	910 593	935 155	1 058 495	1 027 822	980 790	924 717	919 052	944 658
47 沖　縄	311 228	…	…	…	…	…	…	528 946	560 524

注：1)　各年次の人口は10月1日現在。＊は国勢調査人口である。
　　2)　昭和40年以前は総人口、45年以降は日本人人口である。
　　3)　昭和22年は地域的に配分されない調査もれを除く。
　　4)　昭和35年の長野県西筑摩郡山口村と岐阜県中津川市の境界紛争地域の人口73人（男39人、女34人）は全国総数に含まれているが、長野県・岐阜県のいずれにも含まれていない。
　　5)　昭和45年、50年、55年、平成7年は、国勢調査の確定数。ただし、昭和45年、50年、55年の各報告書では、それぞれ1％抽出集計結果を用いたので、本報告書と値が異なる。
　　　　平成2年、12年、17年、22年、27年は、国勢調査の確定数（按分済み人口）。
　　6)　昭和60年については、全国は日本人人口、都道府県は総人口であり、「昭和60年国勢調査抽出速報集計結果」を用いた。
　　7)　平成28年より、都道府県も日本人人口となり、「人口推計（各年10月1日現在）」を用いた。

590

Appendix

都道府県・性別人口[2]

by sex : Japan, each prefecture

女
Female

1985 *60 年[6]	1990 *平成2年[5]	1995 *7 年[5]	2000 *12 年[5]	2005 *17 年[5]	2010 *22 年[5]	2014 26 年	2015 *27 年[5]	2016 28 年	都道府県 Prefecture
61 221 700	62 472 428	63 379 794	64 124 628	64 587 009	64 810 001	64 391 000	64 296 543	**64 153 479**	全 国 Total
									a)
2 921 200	2 916 588	2 948 272	2 957 259	2 943 805	2 892 045	2 844 000	2 831 783	**2 816 000**	01 北 海 道
796 400	777 102	775 772	771 382	754 980	724 790	699 000	691 384	**683 000**	02 青 森
755 400	735 746	736 074	732 452	717 631	691 267	667 000	660 581	**654 000**	03 岩 手
1 109 400	1 140 756	1 179 305	1 200 811	1 203 800	1 200 975	1 187 000	1 185 774	**1 182 000**	04 宮 城
652 000	642 059	635 013	622 505	602 118	573 538	549 000	540 704	**533 000**	05 秋 田
649 000	650 525	647 803	639 098	626 134	603 384	584 000	579 439	**573 000**	06 山 形
1 058 100	1 077 725	1 088 067	1 083 665	1 067 788	1 037 907	986 000	962 753	**954 000**	07 福 島
1 355 900	1 420 797	1 466 542	1 481 262	1 475 397	1 468 211	1 445 000	1 441 802	**1 435 000**	08 茨 城
962 000	968 562	988 060	997 977	1 000 536	995 862	982 000	977 937	**973 000**	09 栃 木
973 700	989 992	1 003 904	1 011 435	1 010 171	1 000 781	984 000	980 732	**975 000**	10 群 馬
2 900 200	3 144 936	3 311 429	3 404 337	3 456 746	3 535 512	3 565 000	3 580 345	**3 587 000**	11 埼 玉
2 577 400	2 738 603	2 847 203	2 916 710	2 986 195	3 071 560	3 068 000	3 075 150	**3 081 000**	12 千 葉
5 835 400	5 807 424	5 772 805	5 924 868	6 181 518	6 473 587	6 600 000	6 648 733	**6 693 000**	13 東 京
3 605 600	3 853 979	3 992 493	4 130 949	4 287 264	4 435 404	4 478 000	4 489 002	**4 497 000**	14 神奈川
1 256 800	1 271 860	1 274 472	1 268 249	1 247 860	1 218 513	1 187 000	1 181 442	**1 171 000**	15 新 潟
579 800	580 085	579 392	576 750	570 227	560 028	548 000	545 006	**541 000**	16 富 山
603 900	599 905	606 633	605 692	603 005	599 475	591 000	590 458	**588 000**	17 石 川
428 400	420 460	421 205	421 168	417 719	410 197	402 000	399 395	**397 000**	18 福 井
421 500	432 755	443 226	445 591	443 528	433 372	423 000	420 149	**417 000**	19 山 梨
1 125 800	1 103 843	1 112 705	1 116 360	1 108 240	1 088 767	1 069 000	1 061 307	**1 055 000**	20 長 野
1 045 800	1 057 209	1 071 305	1 071 222	1 066 305	1 053 021	1 035 000	1 027 936	**1 022 000**	21 岐 阜
1 811 500	1 852 235	1 877 142	1 884 933	1 889 076	1 878 349	1 853 000	1 847 188	**1 838 000**	22 静 岡
3 245 100	3 303 936	3 382 860	3 461 645	3 540 574	3 619 496	3 647 000	3 653 105	**3 657 000**	23 愛 知
898 200	917 947	939 471	944 432	942 289	934 202	920 000	915 810	**911 000**	24 三 重
590 400	616 850	645 724	670 341	687 564	702 983	707 000	705 946	**706 000**	25 滋 賀
1 307 000	1 311 648	1 324 873	1 342 608	1 350 566	1 347 924	1 338 000	1 337 517	**1 335 000**	26 京 都
4 381 800	4 335 449	4 378 657	4 410 898	4 444 301	4 489 823	4 495 000	4 500 662	**4 498 000**	27 大 阪
2 698 500	2 745 717	2 748 077	2 832 944	2 865 462	2 871 840	2 857 000	2 851 407	**2 844 000**	28 兵 庫
670 200	708 183	737 630	747 150	740 030	732 224	722 000	715 555	**712 000**	29 奈 良
570 800	561 203	564 395	560 162	544 727	527 761	512 000	507 391	**502 000**	30 和歌山
323 500	319 790	319 289	317 982	314 154	305 462	298 000	297 453	**295 000**	31 鳥 取
416 500	406 495	401 255	394 931	385 493	371 214	360 000	358 163	**355 000**	32 島 根
989 100	994 687	1 005 828	1 007 896	1 010 088	1 001 347	991 000	989 171	**985 000**	33 岡 山
1 442 700	1 455 687	1 471 025	1 473 811	1 471 833	1 462 584	1 449 000	1 449 184	**1 443 000**	34 広 島
830 600	820 831	812 096	798 333	781 890	760 323	737 000	733 432	**727 000**	35 山 口
430 700	435 235	435 754	430 556	422 302	409 816	398 000	393 250	**390 000**	36 徳 島
534 000	530 852	531 762	528 312	522 877	512 129	504 000	500 419	**497 000**	37 香 川
805 900	796 797	792 462	786 013	771 976	753 654	734 000	726 565	**721 000**	38 愛 媛
445 800	435 389	431 107	428 736	420 164	403 672	389 000	384 019	**380 000**	39 高 知
2 457 700	2 494 104	2 558 171	2 610 433	2 635 684	2 656 287	2 665 000	2 666 507	**2 667 000**	40 福 岡
465 700	462 415	464 610	460 705	455 935	447 359	439 000	437 366	**435 000**	41 佐 賀
836 300	824 130	815 936	801 640	783 959	757 036	735 000	727 784	**721 000**	42 長 崎
968 000	969 379	977 557	978 461	970 838	958 878	945 000	939 835	**933 000**	43 熊 本
658 200	650 546	647 301	642 438	635 621	626 351	613 000	609 516	**606 000**	44 大 分
625 500	616 483	618 424	616 495	608 984	599 908	588 000	582 520	**578 000**	45 宮 崎
974 800	954 173	951 557	945 879	929 953	905 316	883 000	870 830	**864 000**	46 鹿児島
593 100	621 356	645 151	667 152	689 702	705 867	720 000	724 136	**726 000**	47 沖 縄

Note : a) See page 44.

表 5　21大都市・性別人口

Table 5　Total population by sex：21 major cities

21 大 都 市 21 major cities	総　　数 Total	男 Male	女 Female
東京都の区部	9 375 000	4 617 000	4 759 000
札　　　　幌	1 958 000	913 000	1 046 000
仙　　　　台	1 085 000	528 000	556 000
さ　い　た　ま	1 275 000	633 000	643 000
千　　　　葉	974 000	483 000	490 000
横　　　　浜	3 731 000	1 857 000	1 874 000
川　　　　崎	1 489 000	756 000	734 000
相　模　原	722 000	361 000	360 000
新　　　　潟	807 000	388 000	419 000
静　　　　岡	702 000	342 000	360 000
浜　　　　松	797 000	395 000	402 000
名　古　屋	2 305 000	1 138 000	1 166 000
京　　　　都	1 475 000	699 000	775 000
大　　　　阪	2 702 000	1 307 000	1 395 000
堺	838 000	401 000	436 000
神　　　　戸	1 536 000	726 000	810 000
岡　　　　山	721 000	347 000	374 000
広　　　　島	1 196 000	578 000	618 000
北　九　州	956 000	451 000	506 000
福　　　　岡	1 554 000	734 000	820 000
熊　　　　本	740 000	348 000	391 000

資料：各指定都市及び東京都が推計した平成28年10月 1 日現
　　　在の総人口である。

参　考　表

1　各種分類表
　表 1　　　死因簡単分類と死因基本分類との対照表
　表 2　　　選択死因分類と死因簡単分類及び死因基本分類との対照表
　表 3　　　死因年次推移分類と死因簡単分類及び死因基本分類との対照表
　表 4　　　乳児死因簡単分類と死因基本分類及び死因簡単分類との対照表
　表 5 - 1　感染症分類と死因基本分類との対照表（平成28年）
　表 5 - 2　感染症分類と死因基本分類との対照表（平成27年）
　表 5 - 3　感染症分類と死因基本分類との対照表（平成25年から26年まで）
　表 5 - 4　感染症分類と死因基本分類との対照表（平成24年）
　表 5 - 5　感染症分類と死因基本分類との対照表（平成20年から23年まで）
　表 5 - 6　感染症分類と死因基本分類との対照表（平成19年）
　表 5 - 7　感染症分類と死因基本分類との対照表（平成18年）
　表 5 - 8　感染症分類と死因基本分類との対照表（平成15年から17年まで）
　表 5 - 9　感染症分類と死因基本分類との対照表（平成11年から14年まで）
　表 6 - 1　死因順位及び乳児死因順位に用いる分類項目（平成 7 年以降）
　表 6 - 2　死因順位及び乳児死因順位に用いる分類項目（昭和54年から平成 6 年まで）
2　年次推移
　表 1 - 1　死因簡単分類別にみた平成18年と17年の性別死亡数及び率（人口10万対）
　表 1 - 2　死因簡単分類別にみた平成 7 年と 6 年の性別死亡数及び率（人口10万対）
　表 1 - 3　死因簡単分類別にみた昭和55・60・平成 2 ・ 4 ～ 6 年の性別死亡数及び率（人口10万対）
　表 2 - 1　乳児死因簡単分類別にみた平成 7 年と 6 年の乳児死亡数及び率（出生10万対）
　表 2 - 2　乳児死因簡単分類別にみた昭和55・60・平成 2 ・ 4 ～ 6 年の乳児死亡数及び率（出生10万対）
　表 3 - 1　感染症分類（平成27年改正）別にみた年次別死亡数及び率（人口10万対）（平成27年）
　表 3 - 2　感染症分類（平成25年改正）別にみた年次別死亡数及び率（人口10万対）（平成25・26年）
　表 3 - 3　感染症分類（平成24年改正）別にみた年次別死亡数及び率（人口10万対）（平成24年）
　表 3 - 4　感染症分類（平成20年改正）別にみた年次別死亡数及び率（人口10万対）（平成20～23年）
　表 3 - 5　感染症分類（平成19年改正）別にみた年次別死亡数及び率（人口10万対）（平成19年）
　表 3 - 6　感染症分類（平成18年改正）別にみた年次別死亡数及び率（人口10万対）（平成18年）
　表 3 - 7　感染症分類（平成15年改正）別にみた年次別死亡数及び率（人口10万対）（平成15～17年）
　表 3 - 8　感染症分類（平成11年改正）別にみた年次別死亡数及び率（人口10万対）（平成11～14年）
　表 4　　　年次別にみた性・妊娠満28週以後の死産－早期新生児死亡別周産期死亡数
　表 5　　　年次別にみた自然－人工別妊娠満28週以後の死産数・妊娠満28週以後の死産比（出生千対）
　　　　　　及び全死産中妊娠満28週以後の死産の占める割合
　表 6　　　合計特殊出生率

Reference Table

1 List of death
Table 1   Condensed list of causes of death for Japan
Table 2   Selected list of causes of death for Japan
Table 3   List for trends in causes of death
Table 4   List of causes of infant death
Table 5-1   List of infectious diseases (2016)
Table 5-2   List of infectious diseases (2015)
Table 5-3   List of infectious diseases (2013-2014)
Table 5-4   List of infectious diseases (2012)
Table 5-5   List of infectious diseases (2008-2011)
Table 5-6   List of infectious diseases (2007)
Table 5-7   List of infectious diseases (2006)
Table 5-8   List of infectious diseases (2003-2005)
Table 5-9   List of infectious diseases (1999-2002)
Table 6-1   Categories for ranking of causes of death (since 1995)
Table 6-2   Categories for ranking of causes of death (1979-1994)

2 Trends in death and birth
Table 1-1   Deaths and death rates (per 100,000 population) by sex and causes of death :
Japan, 2006 and 2005
Table 1-2   Deaths and death rates (per 100,000 population) by sex and causes of death :
Japan, 1995 and 1994
Table 1-3   Deaths and death rates (per 100,000 population) by sex and causes of death
(the 117 rubrics list) : Japan, 1980, 1985, 1990, 1992-1994
Table 2-1   Infant deaths and infant mortality rates (per 100,000 live births) by causes of death :
Japan, 1995 and 1994
Table 2-2   Infant deaths and infant mortality rates (per 100,000 live births) by causes of death
(the 54 rubrics list) : Japan, 1980, 1985, 1990, 1992-1994
Table 3-1   Trends in deaths and death rates (per 100,000 population) by causes of death
(the list of infectious diseases revised in 2015) : Japan, 2015
Table 3-2   Trends in deaths and death rates (per 100,000 population) by causes of death
(the list of infectious diseases revised in 2013) : Japan, 2013 and 2014
Table 3-3   Trends in deaths and death rates (per 100,000 population) by causes of death
(the list of infectious diseases revised in 2012) : Japan, 2012
Table 3-4   Trends in deaths and death rates (per 100,000 population) by causes of death
(the list of infectious diseases revised in 2008) : Japan, 2008-2011
Table 3-5   Trends in deaths and death rates (per 100,000 population) by causes of death
(the list of infectious diseases revised in 2007) : Japan, 2007
Table 3-6   Trends in deaths and death rates (per 100,000 population) by causes of death
(the list of infectious diseases revised in 2006) : Japan, 2006
Table 3-7   Trends in deaths and death rates (per 100,000 population) by causes of death
(the list of infectious diseases revised in 2003) : Japan, 2003-2005
Table 3-8   Trends in deaths and death rates (per 100,000 population) by causes of death
(the list of infectious diseases revised in 1999) : Japan, 1999-2002
Table 4   Trends in perinatal deaths by sex : Japan
Table 5   Trends in foetal deaths, foetal death ratio at 28 completed weeks and over of gestation
(per 1,000 live births) and proportion by type of extraction : Japan
Table 6   Total fertility rates : Japan

Reference Table

表1　死因簡単分類と死因基本分類との対照表
Table 1　Condensed list of causes of death for Japan

死因簡単分類コード	分　類　名	死因基本分類コード
01000	感染症及び寄生虫症	A00～B99
01100	腸管感染症	A00～A09
01200	結　核	A15～A19
01201	呼吸器結核	A15～A16
01202	その他の結核	A17～A19
01300	敗血症	A40～A41
01400	ウイルス肝炎	B15～B19
01401	B型ウイルス肝炎	B16～B17.0, B18.0～B18.1
01402	C型ウイルス肝炎	B17.1, B18.2
01403	その他のウイルス肝炎	B15～B19の残り
01500	ヒト免疫不全ウイルス［HIV］病	B20～B24
01600	その他の感染症及び寄生虫症	A00～B99の残り
02000	新　生　物	C00～D48
02100	悪性新生物	C00～C97
02101	口唇，口腔及び咽頭の悪性新生物	C00～C14
02102	食道の悪性新生物	C15
02103	胃の悪性新生物	C16
02104	結腸の悪性新生物	C18
02105	直腸S状結腸移行部及び直腸の悪性新生物	C19～C20
02106	肝及び肝内胆管の悪性新生物	C22
02107	胆のう及びその他の胆道の悪性新生物	C23～C24
02108	膵の悪性新生物	C25
02109	喉頭の悪性新生物	C32
02110	気管，気管支及び肺の悪性新生物	C33～C34
02111	皮膚の悪性新生物	C43～C44
02112	乳房の悪性新生物	C50
02113	子宮の悪性新生物	C53～C55
02114	卵巣の悪性新生物	C56
02115	前立腺の悪性新生物	C61
02116	膀胱の悪性新生物	C67
02117	中枢神経系の悪性新生物	C70～C72, C75.1～C75.3
02118	悪性リンパ腫	C81～C85
02119	白血病	C91～C95
02120	その他のリンパ組織，造血組織及び関連組織の悪性新生物	C88～C90, C96
02121	その他の悪性新生物	C00～C97の残り
02200	その他の新生物	D00～D48
02201	中枢神経系のその他の新生物	D32～D33, D35.2～D35.4, D42～D43, D44.3～D44.5
02202	中枢神経系を除くその他の新生物	D00～D48の残り
03000	血液及び造血器の疾患並びに免疫機構の障害	D50～D89
03100	貧　血	D50～D64
03200	その他の血液及び造血器の疾患並びに免疫機構の障害	D65～D89
04000	内分泌，栄養及び代謝疾患	E00～E88
04100	糖尿病	E10～E14
04200	その他の内分泌，栄養及び代謝疾患	E00～E88の残り
05000	精神及び行動の障害	F01～F99
05100	血管性及び詳細不明の認知症	F01～F03
05200	その他の精神及び行動の障害	F04～F99
06000	神経系の疾患	G00～G98
06100	髄膜炎	G00～G03
06200	脊髄性筋萎縮症及び関連症候群	G12
06300	パーキンソン病	G20
06400	アルツハイマー病	G30
06500	その他の神経系の疾患	G00～G98の残り
07000	眼及び付属器の疾患	H00～H57
08000	耳及び乳様突起の疾患	H60～H93
09000	循環器系の疾患	I00～I99
09100	高血圧性疾患	I10～I13
09101	高血圧性心疾患及び心腎疾患	I11, I13
09102	その他の高血圧性疾患	I10, I12
09200	心疾患（高血圧性を除く）	I01～I02.0, I05～I09, I20～I25, I27, I30～I51
09201	慢性リウマチ性心疾患	I05～I09
09202	急性心筋梗塞	I21～I22
09203	その他の虚血性心疾患	I20, I24～I25
09204	慢性非リウマチ性心内膜疾患	I34～I38
09205	心筋症	I42

死因簡単分類コード	分　類　名	死因基本分類コード
09206	不整脈及び伝導障害	I44～I49
09207	心不全	I50
09208	その他の心疾患	I01～I02.0, I27, I30～I33, I40, I51
09300	脳血管疾患	I60～I69
09301	くも膜下出血	I60, I69.0
09302	脳内出血	I61, I69.1
09303	脳梗塞	I63, I69.3
09304	その他の脳血管疾患	I60～I69の残り
09400	大動脈瘤及び解離	I71
09500	その他の循環器系の疾患	I00～I99の残り
10000	呼吸器系の疾患	J00～J98
10100	インフルエンザ	J10～J11
10200	肺　炎	J12～J18
10300	急性気管支炎	J20
10400	慢性閉塞性肺疾患	J41～J44
10500	喘息	J45～J46
10600	その他の呼吸器系の疾患	J00～J98の残り
11000	消化器系の疾患	K00～K92
11100	胃潰瘍及び十二指腸潰瘍	K25～K27
11200	ヘルニア及び腸閉塞	K40～K46, K56
11300	肝疾患	K70～K76
11301	肝硬変（アルコール性を除く）	K74.3～K74.6
11302	その他の肝疾患	K70～K76の残り
11400	その他の消化器系の疾患	K00～K92の残り
12000	皮膚及び皮下組織の疾患	L00～L98
13000	筋骨格系及び結合組織の疾患	M00～M99
14000	腎尿路生殖器系の疾患	N00～N98
14100	糸球体疾患及び腎尿細管間質性疾患	N00～N15
14200	腎不全	N17～N19
14201	急性腎不全	N17
14202	慢性腎不全	N18
14203	詳細不明の腎不全	N19
14300	その他の腎尿路生殖器系の疾患	N00～N98の残り
15000	妊娠，分娩及び産じょく	O00～O99
16000	周産期に発生した病態	P00～P96
16100	妊娠期間及び胎児発育に関連する障害	P05～P08
16200	出産外傷	P10～P15
16300	周産期に特異的な呼吸障害及び心血管障害	P20～P29
16400	周産期に特異的な感染症	P35～P39
16500	胎児及び新生児の出血性障害及び血液障害	P50～P61
16600	その他の周産期に発生した病態	P00～P96の残り
17000	先天奇形，変形及び染色体異常	Q00～Q99
17100	神経系の先天奇形	Q00～Q07
17200	循環器系の先天奇形	Q20～Q28
17201	心臓の先天奇形	Q20～Q24
17202	その他の循環器系の先天奇形	Q25～Q28
17300	消化器系の先天奇形	Q35～Q45
17400	その他の先天奇形及び変形	Q00～Q89の残り
17500	染色体異常，他に分類されないもの	Q90～Q99
18000	症状，徴候及び異常臨床所見・異常検査所見で他に分類されないもの	R00～R99
18100	老　衰	R54
18200	乳幼児突然死症候群	R95
18300	その他の症状，徴候及び異常臨床所見・異常検査所見で他に分類されないもの	R00～R99の残り
20000	傷病及び死亡の外因	V01～Y89
20100	不慮の事故	V01～X59
20101	交通事故	V01～V98
20102	転倒・転落	W00～W17
20103	不慮の溺死及び溺水	W65～W74
20104	不慮の窒息	W75～W84
20105	煙，火及び火炎への曝露	X00～X09
20106	有害物質による不慮の中毒及び有害物質への曝露	X40～X49
20107	その他の不慮の事故	W00～X59の残り
20200	自　殺	X60～X84
20300	他　殺	X85～Y09
20400	その他の外因	Y10～Y89
22000	特殊目的用コード	U04
22100	重症急性呼吸器症候群［SARS］	U04

注：これらの分類を精神保健の分野で使用する場合は，「精神及び行動の障害」を「精神疾患」と読み替えて使用することができる。
平成18年1月1日から「ICD-10（2003年版）準拠」の適用に伴い，分類の追加，変更が行われている。

595

参考表
各種分類表

表2　選択死因分類と死因簡単分類及び死因基本分類との対照表
Table 2　Selected list of causes of death for Japan

選択死因分類コード	分　類　名	死因簡単分類コード	死因基本分類コード
Se01	結　核	01200	A15〜A19
Se02	悪性新生物	02100	C00〜C97
	（再掲）		
Se03	食道の悪性新生物	02102	C15
Se04	胃の悪性新生物	02103	C16
Se05	結腸の悪性新生物	02104	C18
Se06	直腸S状結腸移行部及び直腸の悪性新生物	02105	C19〜C20
Se07	肝及び肝内胆管の悪性新生物	02106	C22
Se08	胆のう及びその他の胆道の悪性新生物	02107	C23〜C24
Se09	膵の悪性新生物	02108	C25
Se10	気管，気管支及び肺の悪性新生物	02110	C33〜C34
Se11	乳房の悪性新生物	02112	C50
Se12	子宮の悪性新生物	02113	C53〜C55
Se13	白　血　病	02119	C91〜C95
Se14	糖　尿　病	04100	E10〜E14
Se15	高血圧性疾患	09100	I10〜I13
Se16	心疾患（高血圧性を除く）	09200	I01〜I02.0, I05〜I09, I20〜I25, I27, I30〜I51
	（再掲）		
Se17	急性心筋梗塞	09202	I21〜I22
Se18	その他の虚血性心疾患	09203	I20, I24〜I25
Se19	不整脈及び伝導障害	09206	I44〜I49
Se20	心　不　全	09207	I50
Se21	脳血管疾患	09300	I60〜I69
	（再掲）		
Se22	くも膜下出血	09301	I60, I69.0
Se23	脳　内　出　血	09302	I61, I69.1
Se24	脳　梗　塞	09303	I63, I69.3
Se25	大動脈瘤及び解離	09400	I71
Se26	肺　　炎	10200	J12〜J18
Se27	慢性閉塞性肺疾患	10400	J41〜J44
Se28	喘　　息	10500	J45〜J46
Se29	肝　疾　患	11300	K70〜K76
Se30	腎　不　全	14200	N17〜N19
Se31	老　　衰	18100	R54
Se32	不慮の事故	20100	V01〜X59
	（再掲）		
Se33	交　通　事　故	20101	V01〜V98
Se34	自　　殺	20200	X60〜X84

Reference Table

表 3　死因年次推移分類と死因簡単分類及び死因基本分類との対照表
Table 3　List for trends in causes of death

死因年次推移分類コード	分　類　名	死因簡単分類コード	死因基本分類コード
Hi01	結　　核	01200	A15～A19
Hi02	悪性新生物	02100	C00～C97
Hi03	糖　尿　病	04100	E10～E14
Hi04	高血圧性疾患	09100	I10～I13
Hi05	心疾患（高血圧性を除く）	09200	I01～I02.0, I05～I09, I20～I25, I27, I30～I51
Hi06	脳血管疾患	09300	I60～I69
Hi07	肺　　炎	10200	J12～J18
Hi08	慢性気管支炎及び肺気腫		J41～J43
Hi09	喘　　息	10500	J45～J46
Hi10	胃潰瘍及び十二指腸潰瘍	11100	K25～K27
Hi11	肝　疾　患	11300	K70～K76
Hi12	腎　不　全	14200	N17～N19
Hi13	老　　衰	18100	R54
Hi14	不慮の事故 　　（再掲）	20100	V01～X59
Hi15	交　通　事　故	20101	V01～V98
Hi16	自　　殺	20200	X60～X84

参考表
各種分類表

表4 乳児死因簡単分類と死因基本分類及び死因簡単分類との対照表
Table 4 List of causes of infant death

乳児死因簡単分類コード	分　類　名	死因基本分類コード	死因簡単分類との対応
Ba01	腸管感染症	A00〜A09	01100
Ba02	敗血症	A40〜A41	01300
Ba03	麻疹	B05	01600の一部
Ba04	ウイルス肝炎	B15〜B19	01400
Ba05	その他の感染症及び寄生虫症	A00〜B99の残り	01000（Ba01〜04を除く）
Ba06	悪性新生物	C00〜C97	02100
Ba07	白血病	C91〜C95	02119
Ba08	その他の悪性新生物	C00〜C97の残り	02100（Ba07を除く）
Ba09	その他の新生物	D00〜D48	02200
Ba10	栄養失調症及びその他の栄養欠乏症	E40〜E64	04000の一部
Ba11	代謝障害	E70〜E88	04000の一部
Ba12	髄膜炎	G00〜G03	06100
Ba13	脊髄性筋萎縮症及び関連症候群	G12	06200
Ba14	脳性麻痺	G80	06500の一部
Ba15	心疾患（高血圧性を除く）	I01〜I02.0, I05〜I09, I20〜I25, I27, I30〜I51	09200
Ba16	脳血管疾患	I60〜I69	09300
Ba17	インフルエンザ	J10〜J11	10100
Ba18	肺炎	J12〜J18	10200
Ba19	喘息	J45〜J46	10500
Ba20	ヘルニア及び腸閉塞	K40〜K46, K56	11200
Ba21	肝疾患	K70〜K76	11300
Ba22	腎不全	N17〜N19	14200
Ba23	周産期に発生した病態	P00〜P96	16000
Ba24	妊娠期間及び胎児発育に関連する障害	P05〜P08	16100
Ba25	出産外傷	P10〜P15	16200
Ba26	出生時仮死	P21	16300の一部
Ba27	新生児の呼吸窮〈促〉迫	P22	16300の一部
Ba28	周産期に発生した肺出血	P26	16300の一部
Ba29	周産期に発生した心血管障害	P29	16300の一部
Ba30	その他の周産期に特異的な呼吸障害及び心血管障害	P20〜P29の残り	16300の残り
Ba31	新生児の細菌性敗血症	P36	16400の一部
Ba32	その他の周産期に特異的な感染症	P35〜P39の残り	16400の残り
Ba33	胎児及び新生児の出血性障害及び血液障害	P50〜P61	16500
Ba34	その他の周産期に発生した病態	P00〜P96の残り	16000（Ba24〜33を除く）
Ba35	先天奇形, 変形及び染色体異常	Q00〜Q99	17000
Ba36	神経系の先天奇形	Q00〜Q07	17100
Ba37	心臓の先天奇形	Q20〜Q24	17201
Ba38	その他の循環器系の先天奇形	Q25〜Q28	17202
Ba39	呼吸器系の先天奇形	Q30〜Q34	17400の一部
Ba40	消化器系の先天奇形	Q35〜Q45	17300
Ba41	筋骨格系の先天奇形及び変形	Q65〜Q79	17400の一部
Ba42	その他の先天奇形及び変形	Q00〜Q89の残り	17400の残り
Ba43	染色体異常, 他に分類されないもの	Q90〜Q99	17500
Ba44	乳幼児突然死症候群	R95	18200
Ba45	その他のすべての疾患	D50〜R99の残り, U04	上記以外の残り（Ba01〜09を除く）
Ba46	不慮の事故	V01〜X59	20100
Ba47	交通事故	V01〜V98	20101
Ba48	転倒・転落	W00〜W17	20102
Ba49	不慮の溺死及び溺水	W65〜W74	20103
Ba50	胃内容物の誤えん及び気道閉塞を生じた食物等の誤えん〈吸引〉	W78〜W80	20104の一部
Ba51	その他の不慮の窒息	W75〜W84の残り	20104の残り
Ba52	煙, 火及び火炎への曝露	X00〜X09	20105
Ba53	有害物質による不慮の中毒及び有害物質への曝露	X40〜X49	20106
Ba54	その他の不慮の事故	W00〜X59の残り	20107
Ba55	他殺	X85〜Y09	20300
Ba56	その他の外因	Y10〜Y89	20400

注：「敗血症」には、"新生児の細菌性敗血症"を含まない。
　　平成18年1月1日から「ICD-10（2003年版）準拠」の適用に伴い、分類の追加、変更が行われている。

Reference Table

表 5 － 1 感染症分類と死因基本分類との対照表（平成28年）
Table 5-1 List of infectious diseases (2016)

感染症分類コード	分類名	死因基本分類コード
In101	エボラ出血熱	A98.4
In102	クリミア・コンゴ出血熱	A98.0
In103	痘そう	B03
In104	南米出血熱	A96.8A
In105	ペスト	A20
In106	マールブルグ病	A98.3
In107	ラッサ熱	A96.2
In201	急性灰白髄炎	A80
In202	結核	A15-A19
In203	ジフテリア	A36
In204	重症急性呼吸器症候群 （病原体がベータコロナウイルス属SARSコロナウイルスであるものに限る。）	U04
In205	鳥インフルエンザ （特定鳥インフルエンザ(H5N1)に限る。）	J10.0C, J10.1C, J10.8C
In206	鳥インフルエンザ （特定鳥インフルエンザ(H7N9)に限る。）	J10.0E, J10.1E, J10.8E
In207	中東呼吸器症候群 （病原体がベータコロナウイルス属MERSコロナウイルスであるものに限る。）	J12.8E
In301	コレラ	A00
In302	細菌性赤痢	A03
In303	腸管出血性大腸菌感染症	A04.3
In304	腸チフス	A01.0
In305	パラチフス	A01.1
In401	E型肝炎	B17.2
In402	ウエストナイル熱	A92.3
In403	A型肝炎	B15
In404	エキノコックス症	B67
In405	黄熱	A95
In406	オウム病	A70
In407	オムスク出血熱	A98.1
In408	回帰熱	A68
In409	キャサヌル森林病	A98.2
In410	Q熱	A78
In411	狂犬病	A82
In412	コクシジオイデス症	B38
In413	サル痘	B04
In414	腎症候性出血熱	A98.5
In415	西部ウマ脳炎	A83.1
In416	ダニ媒介脳炎	A84
In417	炭疽	A22
In418	つつが虫病	A75.3
In419	デング熱	A90, A91
In420	東部ウマ脳炎	A83.2
In421	鳥インフルエンザ （特定鳥インフルエンザを除く。）	J10.0A, J10.1A, J10.8A
In422	ニパウイルス感染症	A85.8B, A87.8B, B34.8B, J12.8D, J84.8A
In423	日本紅斑熱	A77.8a
In424	日本脳炎	A83.0
In425	ハンタウイルス肺症候群	B33.4
In426	Bウイルス病	B00.4A
In427	鼻疽	A24.0
In428	ブルセラ症	A23
In429	ベネズエラウマ脳炎	A92.2
In430	ヘンドラウイルス感染症	B34.8D
In431	発しんチフス	A75.0, A75.1
In432	ボツリヌス症 （乳児ボツリヌス症を除く。）	A05.1
In433	乳児ボツリヌス症	A05.1
In434	マラリア	B50, B51, B52, B53, B54
In435	野兎病	A21
In436	ライム病	A69.2
In437	リッサウイルス感染症	A85.8A, A87.8A, A88.8A
In438	リフトバレー熱	A92.4
In439	類鼻疽	A24.1, A24.2, A24.3, A24.4
In440	レジオネラ症	A48.1, A48.2
In441	レプトスピラ症	A27
In442	ロッキー山紅斑熱	A77.0A
In443	チクングニア熱	A92.0

感染症分類コード	分類名	死因基本分類コード
In444	重症熱性血小板減少症候群 （病原体がフレボウイルス属SFTSウイルスであるものに限る。）	A98.8A
In445	ジカウイルス感染症	A92.8A
In501	アメーバ赤痢	A06
In502	RSウイルス感染症	B34.8A, J12.1, J20.5, J21.0
In503	咽頭結膜熱	B30.1, B30.2
In504	インフルエンザ （鳥インフルエンザ及び新型インフルエンザ等感染症を除く。）	J10（J10.0A, J10.0C, J10.0D, J10.1A, J10.1C, J10.1D, J10.8A, J10.8C, J10.8Dを除く）, J11
In505	急性ウイルス性肝炎 （E型肝炎及びA型肝炎を除く。）	B16, B17（B17.2を除く）, B19
In506	A群溶血性レンサ球菌咽頭炎	J02.0
In507	感染性胃腸炎	A01（A01.0, A01.1を除く）, A04（A04.3, A04.8A, A04.8Bを除く）, A07（A07.1, A07.2を除く）, A08, A09
In508	急性出血性結膜炎	B30.3
In509	急性脳炎 （ウエストナイル脳炎、西部ウマ脳炎、ダニ媒介脳炎、東部ウマ脳炎、日本脳炎、ベネズエラウマ脳炎及びリフトバレー熱を除く。）	A83（A83.0, A83.1, A83.2を除く）, A85（A85.8A, A85.8Bを除く）, A86, B00.4（B00.4Aを除く）, B02.0, B25.8A
In510	クラミジア肺炎（オウム病を除く。）	J16.0
In511	クリプトスポリジウム症	A07.2
In512	クロイツフェルト・ヤコブ病	A81.0, A81.8
In513	劇症型溶血性レンサ球菌感染症	A40.0A, A40.8A, A49.1A, J15.4A, M60.0A, P36.1A
In514	後天性免疫不全症候群	B20, B21, B22, B23, B24
In515	細菌性髄膜炎 （侵襲性インフルエンザ菌感染症、侵襲性髄膜炎菌感染症、侵襲性肺炎球菌感染症を除く。）	A02.2A, A32.1, G00（G00.0, G00.1を除く）
In516	ジアルジア症	A07.1
In517	水痘	B01
In518	侵襲性髄膜炎菌感染症	A39.0, A39.2, A39.4
In519	性器クラミジア感染症	A55, A56
In520	性器ヘルペスウイルス感染症	A60
In521	尖圭コンジローマ	A63.0
In522	先天性風しん症候群	P35.0
In523	手足口病	B08.4
In524	伝染性紅斑	B08.3
In525	突発性発しん	B08.2
In526	梅毒	A50, A51, A52, A53
In527	破傷風	A33, A34, A35
In528	バンコマイシン耐性黄色ブドウ球菌感染症	A41.0B, A49.0B, J15.2B
In529	バンコマイシン耐性腸球菌感染症	A41.4A, A49.8A, J15.8A
In530	百日咳	A37
In531	風しん	B06
In532	ペニシリン耐性肺炎球菌感染症	A40.3A, A49.1C, J13.0
In533	ヘルパンギーナ	B08.5
In534	マイコプラズマ肺炎	J15.7
In535	麻しん	B05
In537	無菌性髄膜炎	A87（A87.8A, A87.8Bを除く）, B00.3, B02.1, G03.0
In538	メチシリン耐性黄色ブドウ球菌感染症	A04.8A, A41.0A, A49.0A, J15.2A
In539	薬剤耐性緑膿菌感染症	A41.5A, A49.8B, J15.1A
In540	流行性角結膜炎	B30.0
In541	流行性耳下腺炎	B26
In542	淋菌感染症	A54
In543	薬剤耐性アシネトバクター感染症	A41.5C, A49.8E, J15.6A
In544	侵襲性インフルエンザ菌感染症	A41.3, G00.0, P36.8A
In545	侵襲性肺炎球菌感染症	A40.3B, G00.1, P36.1C
In546	カルバペネム耐性腸内細菌科細菌感染症	A04.8B, A41.5D, A49.8F, J15.8D
In547	播種性クリプトコックス症	B45.1, B45.7
In601	新型インフルエンザ等感染症	J10.0D, J10.1D, J10.8D

注： 感染症の分類名は、「感染症の予防及び感染症の患者に対する医療に関する法律」（平成10年法律第114号。以下「感染症法」という。）、感染症法施行令（平成10年政令第420号）及び感染症法施行規則（平成10年厚生省令第99号）に規定された疾病名であるため、名称及び範囲は必ずしも「ICD-10（2003年版）準拠」とは一致していない。
　　　なお、本分類表は、感染症法等の改正（平成28年2月15日施行）に基づくものである。

599

参考表
各種分類表

表 5 － 2 　感染症分類と死因基本分類との対照表（平成27年）
Table 5-2　List of infectious diseases（2015）

感染症分類コード	分類名	死因基本分類コード
In101	エボラ出血熱	A98.4
In102	クリミア・コンゴ出血熱	A98.0
In103	痘そう	B03
In104	南米出血熱	A96.8A
In105	ペスト	A20
In106	マールブルグ病	A98.3
In107	ラッサ熱	A96.2
In201	急性灰白髄炎	A80
In202	結核	A15-A19
In203	ジフテリア	A36
In204	重症急性呼吸器症候群 （病原体がベータコロナウイルス属SARSコロナウイルスであるものに限る。）	U04
In205	鳥インフルエンザ （特定鳥インフルエンザ（H5N1）に限る。）	J10.0C, J10.1C, J10.8C
In206	鳥インフルエンザ （特定鳥インフルエンザ（H7N9）に限る。）	J10.0E, J10.1E, J10.8E
In207	中東呼吸器症候群 （病原体がベータコロナウイルス属MERSコロナウイルスであるものに限る。）	J12.8E
In301	コレラ	A00
In302	細菌性赤痢	A03
In303	腸管出血性大腸菌感染症	A04.3
In304	腸チフス	A01.0
In305	パラチフス	A01.1
In401	E型肝炎	B17.2
In402	ウエストナイル熱	A92.3
In403	A型肝炎	B15
In404	エキノコックス症	B67
In405	黄熱	A95
In406	オウム病	A70
In407	オムスク出血熱	A98.1
In408	回帰熱	A68
In409	キャサヌル森林病	A98.2
In410	Q熱	A78
In411	狂犬病	A82
In412	コクシジオイデス症	B38
In413	サル痘	B04
In414	腎症候性出血熱	A98.5
In415	西部ウマ脳炎	A83.1
In416	ダニ媒介脳炎	A84
In417	炭疽	A22
In418	つつが虫病	A75.3
In419	デング熱	A90, A91
In420	東部ウマ脳炎	A83.2
In421	鳥インフルエンザ （特定鳥インフルエンザを除く。）	J10.0A, J10.1A, J10.8A
In422	ニパウイルス感染症	A85.8B, A87.8B, B34.8B, J12.8D, J84.8A
In423	日本紅斑熱	A77.8a
In424	日本脳炎	A83.0
In425	ハンタウイルス肺症候群	B33.4
In426	Bウイルス病	B00.4A
In427	鼻疽	A24.0
In428	ブルセラ症	A23
In429	ベネズエラウマ脳炎	A92.2
In430	ヘンドラウイルス感染症	B34.8D
In431	発しんチフス	A75.0, A75.1
In432	ボツリヌス症 （乳児ボツリヌス症を除く。）	A05.1
In433	乳児ボツリヌス症	A05.1
In434	マラリア	B50, B51, B52, B53, B54
In435	野兎病	A21
In436	ライム病	A69.2
In437	リッサウイルス感染症	A85.8A, A87.8A, A88.8A
In438	リフトバレー熱	A92.4
In439	類鼻疽	A24.1, A24.2, A24.3, A24.4
In440	レジオネラ症	A48.1, A48.2
In441	レプトスピラ症	A27
In442	ロッキー山紅斑熱	A77.0A
In443	チクングニア熱	A92.0
In444	重症熱性血小板減少症候群 （病原体がフレボウイルス属SFTSウイルスであるものに限る。）	A98.8A
In501	アメーバ赤痢	A06
In502	RSウイルス感染症	B34.8A, J12.1, J20.5, J21.0
In503	咽頭結膜熱	B30.1, B30.2
In504	インフルエンザ （鳥インフルエンザ及び新型インフルエンザ等感染症を除く。）	J10（J10.0A, J10.0C, J10.0D, J10.1A, J10.1C, J10.1D, J10.8A, J10.8C, J10.8Dを除く）, J11
In505	急性ウイルス性肝炎 （E型肝炎及びA型肝炎を除く。）	B16, B17（B17.2を除く）, B19
In506	A群溶血性レンサ球菌咽頭炎	J02.0
In507	感染性胃腸炎	A01（A01.0, A01.1を除く）, A04（A04.3, A04.8A, A04.8Bを除く）, A07（A07.1, A07.2を除く）, A08, A09
In508	急性出血性結膜炎	B30.3
In509	急性脳炎 （ウエストナイル脳炎、西部ウマ脳炎、ダニ媒介脳炎、東部ウマ脳炎、日本脳炎、ベネズエラウマ脳炎及びリフトバレー熱を除く。）	A83（A83.0, A83.1, A83.2を除く）, A85（A85.8A, A85.8Bを除く）, A86, B00.4（B00.4Aを除く）, B02.0, B25.8A
In510	クラミジア肺炎（オウム病を除く。）	J16.0
In511	クリプトスポリジウム症	A07.2
In512	クロイツフェルト・ヤコブ病	A81.0, A81.8
In513	劇症型溶血性レンサ球菌感染症	A40.0A, A40.8A, A49.1A, J15.4A, M60.0A, P36.1A
In514	後天性免疫不全症候群	B20, B21, B22, B23, B24
In515	細菌性髄膜炎	A02.2A, A32.1, G00（G00.0, G00.1を除く）
In516	ジアルジア症	A07.1
In517	水痘	B01
In518	侵襲性髄膜炎菌感染症	A39.0, A39.2, A39.4
In519	性器クラミジア感染症	A55, A56
In520	性器ヘルペスウイルス感染症	A60
In521	尖圭コンジローマ	A63.0
In522	先天性風しん症候群	P35.0
In523	手足口病	B08.4
In524	伝染性紅斑	B08.3
In525	突発性発しん	B08.2
In526	梅毒	A50, A51, A52, A53
In527	破傷風	A33, A34, A35
In528	バンコマイシン耐性黄色ブドウ球菌感染症	A41.0B, A49.0B, J15.2B
In529	バンコマイシン耐性腸球菌感染症	A41.4A, A49.8A, J15.8A
In530	百日咳	A37
In531	風しん	B06
In532	ペニシリン耐性肺炎球菌感染症	A40.3A, A49.1C, J13.0
In533	ヘルパンギーナ	B08.5
In534	マイコプラズマ肺炎	J15.7
In535	麻しん（成人麻しんを除く。）	B05
In536	成人麻しん	B05
In537	無菌性髄膜炎	A87（A87.8A, A87.8Bを除く）, B00.3, B02.1, G03.0
In538	メチシリン耐性黄色ブドウ球菌感染症	A04.8A, A41.0A, A49.0A, J15.2A
In539	薬剤耐性緑膿菌感染症	A41.5A, A49.8B, J15.1A
In540	流行性角結膜炎	B30.0
In541	流行性耳下腺炎	B26
In542	淋菌感染症	A54
In543	薬剤耐性アシネトバクター感染症	A41.5C, A49.8E, J15.6A
In544	侵襲性インフルエンザ菌感染症	A41.3, G00.0, P36.8A
In545	侵襲性肺炎球菌感染症	A40.3B, G00.1, P36.1C
In546	カルバペネム耐性腸内細菌科細菌感染症	A04.8B, A41.5D, A49.8F, J15.8D
In547	播種性クリプトコックス症	B45.1, B45.7
In601	新型インフルエンザ等感染症	J10.0D, J10.1D, J10.8D

注：　感染症の分類名は、「感染症の予防及び感染症の患者に対する医療に関する法律」（平成10年法律第114号。以下「感染症法」という。）、感染症法施行令（平成10年政令第420号）及び感染症法施行規則（平成10年厚生省令第99号）に規定された疾病名であるため、名称及び範囲は必ずしも「ICD-10（2003年版）準拠」とは一致していない。
　　　　なお、本分類表は、感染症法等の改正（平成27年1月21日施行）に基づくものである。

Reference Table

表 5 − 3　感染症分類と死因基本分類との対照表（平成25年から26年まで）
Table 5-3　List of infectious diseases（2013-2014）

感染症分類コード	分　類　名	死　因　基　本分　類　コード
In101	エボラ出血熱	A98.4
In102	クリミア・コンゴ出血熱	A98.0
In103	痘そう	B03
In104	南米出血熱	A96.8A
In105	ペスト	A20
In106	マールブルグ病	A98.3
In107	ラッサ熱	A96.2
In201	急性灰白髄炎	A80
In202	結核	A15-A19
In203	ジフテリア	A36
In204	重症急性呼吸器症候群（病原体がコロナウイルス属SARSコロナウイルスであるものに限る）	U04
In205	鳥インフルエンザ（鳥インフルエンザ（H5N1）に限る）	J10.0C, J10.1C, J10.8C
In301	コレラ	A00
In302	細菌性赤痢	A03
In303	腸管出血性大腸菌感染症	A04.3
In304	腸チフス	A01.0
In305	パラチフス	A01.1
In401	E型肝炎	B17.2
In402	ウエストナイル熱	A92.3
In403	A型肝炎	B15
In404	エキノコックス症	B67
In405	黄熱	A95
In406	オウム病	A70
In407	オムスク出血熱	A98.1
In408	回帰熱	A68
In409	キャサヌル森林病	A98.2
In410	Q熱	A78
In411	狂犬病	A82
In412	コクシジオイデス症	B38
In413	サル痘	B04
In414	腎症候性出血熱	A98.5
In415	西部ウマ脳炎	A83.1
In416	ダニ媒介脳炎	A84
In417	炭疽	A22
In418	つつが虫病	A75.3
In419	デング熱	A90, A91
In420	東部ウマ脳炎	A83.2
In421	鳥インフルエンザ（鳥インフルエンザ（H5N1）を除く）	J10.0A, J10.1A, J10.8A
In422	ニパウイルス感染症	A85.8B, A87.8B, B34.8B, J12.8D, J84.8A
In423	日本紅斑熱	A77.8a
In424	日本脳炎	A83.0
In425	ハンタウイルス肺症候群	B33.4
In426	Bウイルス病	B00.4A
In427	鼻疽	A24.0
In428	ブルセラ症	A23
In429	ベネズエラウマ脳炎	A92.2
In430	ヘンドラウイルス感染症	B34.8D
In431	発しんチフス	A75.0, A75.1
In432	ボツリヌス症（乳児ボツリヌス症を除く）	A05.1
In433	乳児ボツリヌス症	A05.1
In434	マラリア	B50, B51, B52, B53, B54
In435	野兎病	A21
In436	ライム病	A69.2
In437	リッサウイルス感染症	A85.8A, A87.8A, A88.8A
In438	リフトバレー熱	A92.4
In439	類鼻疽	A24.1, A24.2, A24.3, A24.4
In440	レジオネラ症	A48.1, A48.2
In441	レプトスピラ症	A27
In442	ロッキー山紅斑熱	A77.0A
In443	チクングニア熱	A92.0

感染症分類コード	分　類　名	死　因　基　本分　類　コード
In444	重症熱性血小板減少症候群（病原体がフレボウイルス属SFTSウイルスであるものに限る）	A98.8A
In501	アメーバ赤痢	A06
In502	RSウイルス感染症	B34.8A, J12.1, J20.5, J21.0
In503	咽頭結膜熱	B30.1, B30.2
In504	インフルエンザ（鳥インフルエンザ及び新型インフルエンザ等感染症を除く）	J10（J10.0A, J10.0C, J10.0D, J10.1A, J10.1C, J10.1D, J10.8A, J10.8C, J10.8Dを除く）, J11
In505	急性ウイルス性肝炎（E型肝炎及びA型肝炎を除く）	B16,B17（B17.2 を除く）, B19
In506	A群溶血性レンサ球菌咽頭炎	J02.0
In507	感染性胃腸炎	A01（A01.0, A01.1を除く）, A04（A04.3を除く）, A07（A07.1, A07.2を除く）, A08, A09
In508	急性出血性結膜炎	B30.3
In509	急性脳炎（ウエストナイル脳炎、西部ウマ脳炎、ダニ媒介脳炎、東部ウマ脳炎、日本脳炎、ベネズエラウマ脳炎及びリフトバレー熱を除く）	A83（A83.0, A83.1, A83.2を除く）, A85（A85.8A, A85.8Bを除く）, A86, B00.4（B00.4A を除く）, B02.0, B25.8A
In510	クラミジア肺炎（オウム病を除く）	J16.0
In511	クリプトスポリジウム症	A07.2
In512	クロイツフェルト・ヤコブ病	A81.0, A81.8
In513	劇症型溶血性レンサ球菌感染症	A40.0A, A40.8A, A49.1A, J15.4A, M60.0A, P36.1A
In514	後天性免疫不全症候群	B20, B21, B22, B23, B24
In515	細菌性髄膜炎	A02.2A, A32.1, G00（G00.0, G00.1を除く）
In516	ジアルジア症	A07.1
In517	水痘	B01
In518	侵襲性髄膜炎菌感染症	A39.0, A39.2, A39.4
In519	性器クラミジア感染症	A55, A56
In520	性器ヘルペスウイルス感染症	A60
In521	尖圭コンジローマ	A63.0
In522	先天性風しん症候群	P35.0
In523	手足口病	B08.4
In524	伝染性紅斑	B08.3
In525	突発性発しん	B08.2
In526	梅毒	A50, A51, A52, A53
In527	破傷風	A33, A34, A35
In528	バンコマイシン耐性黄色ブドウ球菌感染症	A41.0B, A49.0B, J15.2B
In529	バンコマイシン耐性腸球菌感染症	A41.4A, A49.8A, J15.8A
In530	百日咳	A37
In531	風しん	B06
In532	ペニシリン耐性肺炎球菌感染症	A40.3A, A49.1C, J13.0
In533	ヘルパンギーナ	B08.5
In534	マイコプラズマ肺炎	J15.7
In535	麻しん（成人麻しんを除く）	B05
In536	成人麻しん	B05
In537	無菌性髄膜炎	A87（A87.8A, A87.8Bを除く）, B00.3, B02.1, G03.0
In538	メチシリン耐性黄色ブドウ球菌感染症	A41.0A, A49.0A, J15.2A
In539	薬剤耐性緑膿菌感染症	A41.5A, A49.8B, J15.1A
In540	流行性角結膜炎	B30.0
In541	流行性耳下腺炎	B26
In542	淋菌感染症	A54
In543	薬剤耐性アシネトバクター感染症	A41.5C, A49.8E, J15.6A
In544	侵襲性インフルエンザ菌感染症	A41.3, G00.0, P36.8A
In545	侵襲性肺炎球菌感染症	A40.3B, G00.1, P36.1C
In601	新型インフルエンザ等感染症	J10.0D, J10.1D, J10.8D

注：　感染症の分類名は、「感染症の予防及び感染症の患者に対する医療に関する法律」（平成10年法律第114号。以下「感染症法」という。）、感染症法施行令（平成10年政令第420号）及び感染症法施行規則（平成10年厚生省令第99号）に規定された疾病名であるため、名称及び範囲は必ずしも「ICD-10（2003年版）準拠」とは一致していない。
　　なお、本分類表は、感染症法等の改正（平成25年4月1日施行）に基づくものである。

参考表
各種分類表

表 5 - 4 感染症分類と死因基本分類との対照表（平成24年）
Table 5-4 List of infectious diseases (2012)

感染症分類コード	分類名	死因基本分類コード
In101	エボラ出血熱	A98.4
In102	クリミア・コンゴ出血熱	A98.0
In103	痘そう	B03
In104	南米出血熱	A96.8A
In105	ペスト	A20
In106	マールブルグ病	A98.3
In107	ラッサ熱	A96.2
In201	急性灰白髄炎	A80
In202	結核	A15-A19
In203	ジフテリア	A36
In204	重症急性呼吸器症候群 （病原体がコロナウイルス属SARSコロナウイルスであるものに限る）	U04
In205	鳥インフルエンザ （鳥インフルエンザ（H5N1）に限る）	J10.0C, J10.1C, J10.8C
In301	コレラ	A00
In302	細菌性赤痢	A03
In303	腸管出血性大腸菌感染症	A04.3
In304	腸チフス	A01.0
In305	パラチフス	A01.1
In401	Ｅ型肝炎	B17.2
In402	ウエストナイル熱	A92.3
In403	Ａ型肝炎	B15
In404	エキノコックス症	B67
In405	黄熱	A95
In406	オウム病	A70
In407	オムスク出血熱	A98.1
In408	回帰熱	A68
In409	キャサヌル森林病	A98.2
In410	Ｑ熱	A78
In411	狂犬病	A82
In412	コクシジオイデス症	B38
In413	サル痘	B04
In414	腎症候性出血熱	A98.5
In415	西部ウマ脳炎	A83.1
In416	ダニ媒介脳炎	A84
In417	炭疽	A22
In418	つつが虫病	A75.3
In419	デング熱	A90, A91
In420	東部ウマ脳炎	A83.2
In421	鳥インフルエンザ （鳥インフルエンザ（H5N1）を除く）	J10.0A, J10.1A, J10.8A
In422	ニパウイルス感染症	A85.8B, A87.8B, B34.8B, J12.8D, J84.8A
In423	日本紅斑熱	A77.8a
In424	日本脳炎	A83.0
In425	ハンタウイルス肺症候群	B33.4
In426	Ｂウイルス病	B00.4A
In427	鼻疽	A24.0
In428	ブルセラ症	A23
In429	ベネズエラウマ脳炎	A92.2
In430	ヘンドラウイルス感染症	B34.8D
In431	発しんチフス	A75.0, A75.1
In432	ボツリヌス症 （乳児ボツリヌス症を除く）	A05.1
In433	乳児ボツリヌス症	A05.1
In434	マラリア	B50, B51, B52, B53, B54
In435	野兎病	A21
In436	ライム病	A69.2
In437	リッサウイルス感染症	A85.8A, A87.8A, A88.8A
In438	リフトバレー熱	A92.4
In439	類鼻疽	A24.1, A24.2, A24.3, A24.4
In440	レジオネラ症	A48.1, A48.2
In441	レプトスピラ症	A27

感染症分類コード	分類名	死因基本分類コード
In442	ロッキー山紅斑熱	A77.0A
In443	チクングニア熱	A92.0
In501	アメーバ赤痢	A06
In502	ＲＳウイルス感染症	B34.8A, J12.1, J20.5, J21.0
In503	咽頭結膜熱	B30.1, B30.2
In504	インフルエンザ （鳥インフルエンザ及び新型インフルエンザ等感染症を除く）	J10（J10.0A, J10.0C, J10.0D, J10.1A, J10.1C, J10.1D, J10.8A, J10.8C, J10.8Dを除く）, J11
In505	急性ウイルス性肝炎 （Ｅ型肝炎及びＡ型肝炎を除く）	B16, B17（B17.2 を除く）, B19
In506	Ａ群溶血性レンサ球菌咽頭炎	J02.0
In507	感染性胃腸炎	A01（A01.0, A01.1を除く）, A04（A04.3を除く）, A07（A07.1, A07.2を除く）, A08, A09
In508	急性出血性結膜炎	B30.3
In509	急性脳炎 （ウエストナイル脳炎、西部ウマ脳炎、ダニ媒介脳炎、東部ウマ脳炎、日本脳炎、ベネズエラウマ脳炎及びリフトバレー熱を除く）	A83（A83.0, A83.1, A83.2を除く）, A85（A85.8A, A85.8Bを除く）, A86, B00.4（B00.4A を除く）, B02.0, B25.8A
In510	クラミジア肺炎（オウム病を除く）	J16.0
In511	クリプトスポリジウム症	A07.2
In512	クロイツフェルト・ヤコブ病	A81.0, A81.8
In513	劇症型溶血性レンサ球菌感染症	A40.0A, A40.8A, A49.1A, J15.4A, M60.0A, P36.1A
In514	後天性免疫不全症候群	B20, B21, B22, B23, B24
In515	細菌性髄膜炎	A02.2A, A32.1, G00
In516	ジアルジア症	A07.1
In517	水痘	B01
In518	髄膜炎菌性髄膜炎	A39.0
In519	性器クラミジア感染症	A55, A56
In520	性器ヘルペスウイルス感染症	A60
In521	尖圭コンジローマ	A63.0
In522	先天性風しん症候群	P35.0
In523	手足口病	B08.4
In524	伝染性紅斑	B08.3
In525	突発性発しん	B08.2
In526	梅毒	A50, A51, A52, A53
In527	破傷風	A33, A34, A35
In528	バンコマイシン耐性黄色ブドウ球菌感染症	A41.0B, A49.0B, J15.2B
In529	バンコマイシン耐性腸球菌感染症	A41.4A, A49.8A, J15.8A
In530	百日咳	A37
In531	風しん	B06
In532	ペニシリン耐性肺炎球菌感染症	A40.3A, A49.1C, J13.0
In533	ヘルパンギーナ	B08.5
In534	マイコプラズマ肺炎	J15.7
In535	麻しん（成人麻しんを除く）	B05
In536	成人麻しん	B05
In537	無菌性髄膜炎	A87（A87.8A, A87.8Bを除く）, B00.3, B02.1, G03.0
In538	メチシリン耐性黄色ブドウ球菌感染症	A41.0A, A49.0A, J15.2A
In539	薬剤耐性緑膿菌感染症	A41.5A, A49.8B, J15.1A
In540	流行性角結膜炎	B30.0
In541	流行性耳下腺炎	B26
In542	淋菌感染症	A54
In543	薬剤耐性アシネトバクター感染症	A41.5C, A49.8E, J15.6A
In601	新型インフルエンザ等感染症	J10.0D, J10.1D, J10.8D

注： 感染症の分類名は、「感染症の予防及び感染症の患者に対する医療に関する法律」（平成10年法律第114号。以下「感染症法」という。）、感染症法施行令（平成10年政令第420号）及び感染症法施行規則（平成10年厚生省令第99号）に規定された疾病名であるため、名称及び範囲は必ずしも「ICD-10（2003年版）準拠」とは一致していない。
なお、本分類表は、感染症法等の改正（平成23年2月1日施行）に基づくものである。

602

Reference Table

表 5 − 5　感染症分類と死因基本分類との対照表（平成20年から23年まで）
Table 5-5　List of infectious diseases（2008-2011）

感染症分類コード	分　類　名	死 因 基 本分 類 コ ー ド
In101	エボラ出血熱	A98.4
In102	クリミア・コンゴ出血熱	A98.0
In103	痘そう	B03
In104	南米出血熱	A96.8A
In105	ペスト	A20
In106	マールブルグ病	A98.3
In107	ラッサ熱	A96.2
In201	急性灰白髄炎	A80
In202	結核	A15-A19
In203	ジフテリア	A36
In204	重症急性呼吸器症候群 （病原体がコロナウイルス属SARSコロナウイルスであるものに限る）	U04
In205	鳥インフルエンザ （鳥インフルエンザ（H5N1）に限る）	J10.0C, J10.1C, J10.8C
In301	コレラ	A00
In302	細菌性赤痢	A03
In303	腸管出血性大腸菌感染症	A04.3
In304	腸チフス	A01.0
In305	パラチフス	A01.1
In401	E型肝炎	B17.2
In402	ウエストナイル熱	A92.3
In403	A型肝炎	B15
In404	エキノコックス症	B67
In405	黄熱	A95
In406	オウム病	A70
In407	オムスク出血熱	A98.1
In408	回帰熱	A68
In409	キャサヌル森林病	A98.2
In410	Q熱	A78
In411	狂犬病	A82
In412	コクシジオイデス症	B38
In413	サル痘	B04
In414	腎症候性出血熱	A98.5
In415	西部ウマ脳炎	A83.1
In416	ダニ媒介脳炎	A84
In417	炭疽	A22
In418	つつが虫病	A75.3
In419	デング熱	A90, A91
In420	東部ウマ脳炎	A83.2
In421	鳥インフルエンザ （鳥インフルエンザ（H5N1）を除く）	J10.0A, J10.1A, J10.8A
In422	ニパウイルス感染症	A85.8B, A87.8B, B34.8B, J12.8D, J84.8A
In423	日本紅斑熱	A77.8a
In424	日本脳炎	A83.0
In425	ハンタウイルス肺症候群	B33.4
In426	Bウイルス病	B00.4A
In427	鼻疽	A24.0
In428	ブルセラ症	A23
In429	ベネズエラウマ脳炎	A92.2
In430	ヘンドラウイルス感染症	B34.8D
In431	発しんチフス	A75.0, A75.1
In432	ボツリヌス症 （乳児ボツリヌス症を除く）	A05.1
In433	乳児ボツリヌス症	A05.1
In434	マラリア	B50, B51, B52, B53, B54
In435	野兎病	A21
In436	ライム病	A69.2
In437	リッサウイルス感染症	A85.8A, A87.8A, A88.8A
In438	リフトバレー熱	A92.4
In439	類鼻疽	A24.1, A24.2, A24.3, A24.4

感染症分類コード	分　類　名	死 因 基 本分 類 コ ー ド
In440	レジオネラ症	A48.1, A48.2
In441	レプトスピラ症	A27
In442	ロッキー山紅斑熱	A77.0A
In501	アメーバ赤痢	A06
In502	RSウイルス感染症	B34.8A, J12.1, J20.5, J21.0
In503	咽頭結膜熱	B30.1, B30.2
In504	インフルエンザ （鳥インフルエンザ及び新型インフルエンザ等感染症を除く）	J10（J10.0A, J10.0C, J10.0D, J10.1A, J10.1C, J10.1D, J10.8A, J10.8C, J10.8Dを除く）, J11
In505	急性ウイルス性肝炎 （E型肝炎及びA型肝炎を除く）	B16,B17（B17.2を除く）, B19
In506	A群溶血性レンサ球菌咽頭炎	J02.0
In507	感染性胃腸炎	A01（A01.0, A01.1を除く）, A04（A04.3を除く）, A07（A07.1, A07.2を除く）, A08, A09
In508	急性出血性結膜炎	B30.3
In509	急性脳炎 （ウエストナイル脳炎、西部ウマ脳炎、ダニ媒介脳炎、東部ウマ脳炎、日本脳炎、ベネズエラウマ脳炎及びリフトバレー熱を除く）	A83（A83.0, A83.1, A83.2を除く）, A85（A85.8A, A85.8Bを除く）, A86, B00.4（B00.4Aを除く）, B02.0, B25.8A
In510	クラミジア肺炎（オウム病を除く）	J16.0
In511	クリプトスポリジウム症	A07.2
In512	クロイツフェルト・ヤコブ病	A81.0, A81.8
In513	劇症型溶血性レンサ球菌感染症	A40.0A, A40.8A, A49.1A, J15.4A, M60.0A, P36.1A
In514	後天性免疫不全症候群	B20, B21, B22, B23, B24
In515	細菌性髄膜炎	A02.2A, A32.1, G00
In516	ジアルジア症	A07.1
In517	水痘	B01
In518	髄膜炎菌性髄膜炎	A39.0
In519	性器クラミジア感染症	A55, A56
In520	性器ヘルペスウイルス感染症	A60
In521	尖圭コンジローマ	A63.0
In522	先天性風しん症候群	P35.0
In523	手足口病	B08.4
In524	伝染性紅斑	B08.3
In525	突発性発しん	B08.2
In526	梅毒	A50, A51, A52, A53
In527	破傷風	A33, A34, A35
In528	バンコマイシン耐性黄色ブドウ球菌感染症	A41.0B, A49.0B, J15.2B
In529	バンコマイシン耐性腸球菌感染症	A41.4A, A49.8A, J15.8A
In530	百日咳	A37
In531	風しん	B06
In532	ペニシリン耐性肺炎球菌感染症	A40.3A, A49.1C, J13.0
In533	ヘルパンギーナ	B08.5
In534	マイコプラズマ肺炎	J15.7
In535	麻しん（成人麻しんを除く）	B05
In536	成人麻しん	B05
In537	無菌性髄膜炎	A87（A87.8A, A87.8Bを除く）, B00.3, B02.1, G03.0
In538	メチシリン耐性黄色ブドウ球菌感染症	A41.0A, A49.0A, J15.2A
In539	薬剤耐性緑膿菌感染症	A41.5A, A49.8B, J15.1A
In540	流行性角結膜炎	B30.0
In541	流行性耳下腺炎	B26
In542	淋菌感染症	A54
In601	新型インフルエンザ等感染症	J10.0D, J10.1D, J10.8D

注：　感染症の分類名は、「感染症の予防及び感染症の患者に対する医療に関する法律」（平成10年法律第114号。以下「感染症法」という。）、感染症法施行令（平成10年政令第420号）及び感染症法施行規則（平成10年厚生省令第99号）に規定された疾病名であるため、名称及び範囲は必ずしも「ICD-10（2003年版）準拠」とは一致していない。
　　　なお、本分類表は、感染症法等の改正（平成20年5月12日施行）に基づくものである。

603

参考表
各種分類表

表5－6　感染症分類と死因基本分類との対照表（平成19年）
Table 5-6　List of infectious diseases（2007）

感染症分類コード	分　類　名	死因基本分類コード
In101	エボラ出血熱	A98.4
In102	クリミア・コンゴ出血熱	A98.0
In103	痘そう	B03
In104	南米出血熱	A96.8A
In105	ペスト	A20
In106	マールブルグ病	A98.3
In107	ラッサ熱	A96.2
In201	急性灰白髄炎	A80
In202	結核	A15-A19
In203	ジフテリア	A36
In204	重症急性呼吸器症候群 （病原体がコロナウイルス属SARSコロナウイルスであるものに限る）	U04
In301	コレラ	A00
In302	細菌性赤痢	A03
In303	腸管出血性大腸菌感染症	A04.3
In304	腸チフス	A01.0
In305	パラチフス	A01.1
In401	E型肝炎	B17.2
In402	ウエストナイル熱	A92.3
In403	A型肝炎	B15
In404	エキノコックス症	B67
In405	黄熱	A95
In406	オウム病	A70
In407	オムスク出血熱	A98.1
In408	回帰熱	A68
In409	キャサヌル森林病	A98.2
In410	Q熱	A78
In411	狂犬病	A82
In412	コクシジオイデス症	B38
In413	サル痘	B04
In414	腎症候性出血熱	A98.5
In415	西部ウマ脳炎	A83.1
In416	ダニ媒介脳炎	A84
In417	炭疽	A22
In418	つつが虫病	A75.3
In419	デング熱	A90, A91
In420	東部ウマ脳炎	A83.2
In421	鳥インフルエンザ	J10.0A, J10.1A, J10.8A
In422	ニパウイルス感染症	A85.8B, A87.8B, B34.8B, J12.8D, J84.8A
In423	日本紅斑熱	A77.8a
In424	日本脳炎	A83.0
In425	ハンタウイルス肺症候群	B33.4
In426	Bウイルス病	B00.4A
In427	鼻疽	A24.0
In428	ブルセラ症	A23
In429	ベネズエラウマ脳炎	A92.2
In430	ヘンドラウイルス感染症	B34.8D
In431	発しんチフス	A75.0, A75.1
In432	ボツリヌス症 （乳児ボツリヌス症を除く）	A05.1
In433	乳児ボツリヌス症	A05.1
In434	マラリア	B50, B51, B52, B53, B54
In435	野兎病	A21
In436	ライム病	A69.2
In437	リッサウイルス感染症	A85.8A, A87.8A, A88.8A
In438	リフトバレー熱	A92.4
In439	類鼻疽	A24.1, A24.2, A24.3, A24.4
In440	レジオネラ症	A48.1, A48.2

感染症分類コード	分　類　名	死因基本分類コード
In441	レプトスピラ症	A27
In442	ロッキー山紅斑熱	A77.0A
In501	アメーバ赤痢	A06
In502	RSウイルス感染症	B34.8A, J12.1, J20.5, J21.0
In503	咽頭結膜熱	B30.1, B30.2
In504	インフルエンザ （鳥インフルエンザを除く）	J10（J10.0A, J10.1A, J10.8Aを除く）, J11
In505	急性ウイルス性肝炎 （E型肝炎及びA型肝炎を除く）	B16, B17（B17.2を除く）, B19
In506	A群溶血性レンサ球菌咽頭炎	J02.0
In507	感染性胃腸炎	A01（A01.0, A01.1を除く）, A04（A04.3を除く）, A07（A07.1, A07.2を除く）, A08, A09
In508	急性出血性結膜炎	B30.3
In509	急性脳炎 （ウエストナイル脳炎、西部ウマ脳炎、ダニ媒介脳炎、東部ウマ脳炎、日本脳炎、ベネズエラウマ脳炎及びリフトバレー熱を除く）	A83（A83.0, A83.1, A83.2を除く）, A85（A85.8A, A85.8Bを除く）, A86, B00.4（B00.4Aを除く）, B02.0, B25.8A
In510	クラミジア肺炎（オウム病を除く）	J16.0
In511	クリプトスポリジウム症	A07.2
In512	クロイツフェルト・ヤコブ病	A81.0, A81.8
In513	劇症型溶血性レンサ球菌感染症	A40.0A, A40.8A, A49.1A, J15.4A, M60.0A, P36.1A
In514	後天性免疫不全症候群	B20, B21, B22, B23, B24
In515	細菌性髄膜炎	A02.2A, A32.1, G00
In516	ジアルジア症	A07.1
In517	水痘	B01
In518	髄膜炎菌性髄膜炎	A39.0
In519	性器クラミジア感染症	A55, A56
In520	性器ヘルペスウイルス感染症	A60
In521	尖圭コンジローマ	A63.0
In522	先天性風しん症候群	P35.0
In523	手足口病	B08.4
In524	伝染性紅斑	B08.3
In525	突発性発しん	B08.2
In526	梅毒	A50, A51, A52, A53
In527	破傷風	A33, A34, A35
In528	バンコマイシン耐性黄色ブドウ球菌感染症	A41.0B, A49.0B, J15.2B
In529	バンコマイシン耐性腸球菌感染症	A41.4A, A49.8A, J15.8A
In530	百日咳	A37
In531	風しん	B06
In532	ペニシリン耐性肺炎球菌感染症	A40.3A, A49.1C, J13.0
In533	ヘルパンギーナ	B08.5
In534	マイコプラズマ肺炎	J15.7
In535	麻しん（成人麻しんを除く）	B05
In536	成人麻しん	B05
In537	無菌性髄膜炎	A87（A87.8A, A87.8Bを除く）, B00.3, B02.1, G03.0
In538	メチシリン耐性黄色ブドウ球菌感染症	A41.0A, A49.0A, J15.2A
In539	薬剤耐性緑膿菌感染症	A41.5A, A49.8B, J15.1A
In540	流行性角結膜炎	B30.0
In541	流行性耳下腺炎	B26
In542	淋菌感染症	A54

注：　感染症の分類名は、「感染症の予防及び感染症の患者に対する医療に関する法律」（平成10年法律第114号。以下「感染症法」という。）、感染症法施行令（平成10年政令第420号）及び感染症法施行規則（平成10年厚生省令第99号）に規定された疾病名であるため、名称及び範囲は必ずしも「ICD-10（2003年版）準拠」とは一致していない。
　　　なお、本分類表は、感染症法等の改正（平成19年4月1日施行）に基づくものである。

Reference Table

表5－7　感染症分類と死因基本分類との対照表（平成18年）
Table 5-7　List of infectious diseases（2006）

感染症分類コード	感染症分類名	基本分類コード
In101	エボラ出血熱	A98.4
In102	クリミア・コンゴ出血熱	A98.0
In103	重症急性呼吸器症候群 （病原体がＳＡＲＳコロナウイルスであるものに限る）	U04
In104	痘そう	B03
In105	ペスト	A20
In106	マールブルグ病	A98.3
In107	ラッサ熱	A96.2
In201	急性灰白髄炎	A80
In202	コレラ	A00
In203	細菌性赤痢	A03
In204	ジフテリア	A36
In205	腸チフス	A01.0
In206	パラチフス	A01.1
In301	腸管出血性大腸菌感染症	A04.3
In401	Ｅ型肝炎	B17.2
In402	ウエストナイル熱	A92.3
In403	Ａ型肝炎	B15
In404	エキノコックス症	B67
In405	黄熱	A95
In406	オウム病	A70
In407	回帰熱	A68
In408	Ｑ熱	A78
In409	狂犬病	A82
In410	高病原性鳥インフルエンザ	J10.0A, J10.1A, J10.8A
In411	コクシジオイデス症	B38
In412	サル痘	B04
In413	腎症候性出血熱	A98.5
In414	炭疽	A22
In415	つつが虫病	A75.3
In416	デング熱	A90, A91
In417	ニパウイルス感染症	A85.8B, A87.8B, B34.8B, J12.8D, J84.8A
In418	日本紅斑熱	A77.8a
In419	日本脳炎	A83.0
In420	ハンタウイルス肺症候群	B33.4
In421	Ｂウイルス病	B00.4A
In422	ブルセラ症	A23
In423	発しんチフス	A75.0, A75.1
In424	ボツリヌス症 （乳児ボツリヌス症を除く）	A05.1
In425	乳児ボツリヌス症	A05.1
In426	マラリア	B50, B51, B52, B53, B54
In427	野兎病	A21
In428	ライム病	A69.2
In429	リッサウイルス感染症	A85.8A, A87.8A, A88.8A
In430	レジオネラ症	A48.1, A48.2
In431	レプトスピラ症	A27
In501	アメーバ赤痢	A06
In502	ＲＳウイルス感染症	B34.8A, J12.1, J20.5, J21.0
In503	咽頭結膜熱	B30.1, B30.2

感染症分類コード	感染症分類名	基本分類コード
In504	インフルエンザ （高病原性鳥インフルエンザを除く）	J10（J10.0A, J10.1A, J10.8Aを除く）, J11
In505	急性ウイルス性肝炎 （Ｅ型肝炎及びＡ型肝炎を除く）	B16, B17（B17.2を除く）, B19
In506	Ａ群溶血性レンサ球菌咽頭炎	J02.0
In507	感染性胃腸炎	A01（A01.0, A01.1を除く）, A04（A04.3を除く）, A07（A07.1, A07.2を除く）, A08, A09
In508	急性出血性結膜炎	B30.3
In509	急性脳炎 （ウエストナイル脳炎及び日本脳炎を除く）	A83（A83.0を除く）, A84, A85（A85.8A, A85.8Bを除く）, A86, B00.4（B00.4Aを除く）, B02.0, B25.8A
In510	クラミジア肺炎（オウム病を除く）	J16.0
In511	クリプトスポリジウム症	A07.2
In512	クロイツフェルト・ヤコブ病	A81.0, A81.8
In513	劇症型溶血性レンサ球菌感染症	A40.0A, A40.8A, A49.1A, J15.4A, M60.0A, P36.1A
In514	後天性免疫不全症候群	B20, B21, B22, B23, B24
In515	細菌性髄膜炎	A02.2A, A32.1, G00
In516	ジアルジア症	A07.1
In517	水痘	B01
In518	髄膜炎菌性髄膜炎	A39.0
In519	性器クラミジア感染症	A55, A56
In520	性器ヘルペスウイルス感染症	A60
In521	尖圭コンジローマ	A63.0
In522	先天性風しん症候群	P35.0
In523	手足口病	B08.4
In524	伝染性紅斑	B08.3
In525	突発性発しん	B08.2
In526	梅毒	A50, A51, A52, A53
In527	破傷風	A33, A34, A35
In528	バンコマイシン耐性黄色ブドウ球菌感染症	A41.0B, A49.0B, J15.2B
In529	バンコマイシン耐性腸球菌感染症	A41.4A, A49.8A, J15.8A
In530	百日咳	A37
In531	風しん	B06
In532	ペニシリン耐性肺炎球菌感染症	A40.3A, A49.1C, J13.0
In533	ヘルパンギーナ	B08.5
In534	マイコプラズマ肺炎	J15.7
In535	麻しん（成人麻しんを除く）	B05
In536	成人麻しん	B05
In537	無菌性髄膜炎	A87（A87.8A, A87.8Bを除く）, B00.3, B02.1, G03.0
In538	メチシリン耐性黄色ブドウ球菌感染症	A41.0A, A49.0A, J15.2A
In539	薬剤耐性緑膿菌感染症	A41.5A, A49.8B, J15.1A
In540	流行性角結膜炎	B30.0
In541	流行性耳下腺炎	B26
In542	淋菌感染症	A54
In601	結核	A15-A19

注：1)　感染症の分類名は、「感染症の予防及び感染症の患者に対する医療に関する法律」（平成10年法律第114号。以下「感染症法」という。）、感染症法施行令（平成10年政令第420号）及び感染症法施行規則（平成10年厚生省令第99号）並びに「結核予防法」（昭和26年法律第96号）に規定された疾病名であるため、必ずしもICD-10とは一致していない。
　　　　なお、本分類表は、感染症法等の改正（平成15年11月5日施行）に基づくものである。
　　2)　「統計調査に用いる産業分類並びに疾病、傷害及び死因分類を定める政令第三条の規定に基づく疾病、傷害及び死因に関する分類の名称及び分類表（平成6年総務庁告示第75号）」の改正により、平成18年1月1日から「ICD-10（2003年版）準拠」の適用に伴い、分類の追加、変更が行われている。

参考表
各種分類表

表 5 － 8　感染症分類と死因基本分類との対照表（平成15年から17年まで）
Table 5-8　List of infectious diseases（2003-2005）

感染症分類コード	分　類　名	死　因　基　本分　類　コ　ー　ド
In101	エボラ出血熱	A98.4
In102	クリミア・コンゴ出血熱	A98.0
In103	重症急性呼吸器症候群 （病原体がＳＡＲＳコロナウイルスであるものに限る）	J12.8C
In104	痘そう	B03
In105	ペスト	A20
In106	マールブルグ病	A98.3
In107	ラッサ熱	A96.2
In201	急性灰白髄炎	A80
In202	コレラ	A00
In203	細菌性赤痢	A03
In204	ジフテリア	A36
In205	腸チフス	A01.0
In206	パラチフス	A01.1
In301	腸管出血性大腸菌感染症	A04.3
In401	E型肝炎	B17.2
In402	ウエストナイル熱	A92.3
In403	A型肝炎	B15
In404	エキノコックス症	B67
In405	黄熱	A95
In406	オウム病	A70
In407	回帰熱	A68
In408	Q熱	A78
In409	狂犬病	A82
In410	高病原性鳥インフルエンザ	J10.0A, J10.1A, J10.8A
In411	コクシジオイデス症	B38
In412	サル痘	B04
In413	腎症候性出血熱	A98.5
In414	炭疽	A22
In415	つつが虫病	A75.3
In416	デング熱	A90, A91
In417	ニパウイルス感染症	A85.8B, A87.8B, B34.8B, J12.8D, J84.8A
In418	日本紅斑熱	A77.8a
In419	日本脳炎	A83.0
In420	ハンタウイルス肺症候群	B33.8A, J12.8A
In421	Bウイルス病	B00.4A
In422	ブルセラ症	A23
In423	発しんチフス	A75.0, A75.1
In424	ボツリヌス症 （乳児ボツリヌス症を除く）	A05.1
In425	乳児ボツリヌス症	A05.1
In426	マラリア	B50〜B54
In427	野兎病	A21
In428	ライム病	A69.2
In429	リッサウイルス感染症	A87.8A, A85.8A, A88.8A
In430	レジオネラ症	A48.1, A48.2
In431	レプトスピラ症	A27

感染症分類コード	分　類　名	死　因　基　本分　類　コ　ー　ド
In501	アメーバ赤痢	A06
In502	ＲＳウイルス感染症	B34.8A, J12.1, J20.5, J21.0
In503	咽頭結膜熱	B30.1, B30.2
In504	インフルエンザ （高病原性鳥インフルエンザを除く）	J10〜J11（J10.0A, J10.1A, J10.8Aを除く）
In505	急性ウイルス性肝炎 （E型肝炎及びA型肝炎を除く）	B16〜B17（B17.2を除く）， B19
In506	A群溶血性レンサ球菌咽頭炎	J02.0
In507	感染性胃腸炎	A01（A01.0, A01.1を除く）， A04（A04.3を除く）， A07（A07.1, A07.2を除く）， A08, A09
In508	急性出血性結膜炎	B30.3
In509	急性脳炎 （ウエストナイル脳炎及び日本脳炎を除く）	A83〜A86（A83.0, A85.8A, A85.8Bを除く），B00.4B, B02.0, B25.8A
In510	クラミジア肺炎 （オウム病を除く）	J16.0
In511	クリプトスポリジウム症	A07.2
In512	クロイツフェルト・ヤコブ病	A81.0, A81.8
In513	劇症型溶血性レンサ球菌感染症	A40.0A, A40.8A, A49.1A, J15.4A, M60.0A, P36.1A
In514	後天性免疫不全症候群	B20〜B24
In515	細菌性髄膜炎	A02.2A, A32.1, G00
In516	ジアルジア症	A07.1
In517	水痘	B01
In518	髄膜炎菌性髄膜炎	A39.0
In519	性器クラミジア感染症	A55〜A56
In520	性器ヘルペスウイルス感染症	A60
In521	尖圭コンジローマ	A63.0
In522	先天性風しん症候群	P35.0
In523	手足口病	B08.4
In524	伝染性紅斑	B08.3
In525	突発性発しん	B08.2
In526	梅毒	A50〜A53
In527	破傷風	A33〜A35
In528	百日咳	A37
In529	風しん	B06
In530	ヘルパンギーナ	B08.5
In531	マイコプラズマ肺炎	J15.7
In532	麻しん（成人麻しんを除く）	B05
In533	成人麻しん	B05
In534	無菌性髄膜炎	A87（A87.8A, A87.8Bを除く），B00.3, B02.1, G03.0
In535	流行性角結膜炎	B30.0
In536	流行性耳下腺炎	B26
In537	淋菌感染症	A54
In601	結核	A15〜A19

注：　感染症の分類名は、「感染症の予防及び感染症の患者に対する医療に関する法律」（平成10年法律第114号。以下「感染症法」という。）、感染症法施行令（平成10年政令第420号）及び感染症法施行規則（平成10年厚生省令第99号）並びに「結核予防法」（昭和26年法律第96号）に規定された疾病名であるため、必ずしもICD-10とは一致していない。
　　　なお、本分類表は、感染症法等の改正（平成15年11月5日施行）に基づくものである。

Reference Table

表5－9　感染症分類と死因基本分類との対照表（平成11年から14年まで）
Table 5-9　List of infectious diseases (1999-2002)

感染症分類コード	分類名	死因基本分類コード	感染症分類コード	分類名	死因基本分類コード
In101	エボラ出血熱	A98.4	In420	コクシジオイデス症	B38
In102	クリミア・コンゴ出血熱	A98.0	In421	細菌性髄膜炎	A02.2A，A27.0A，A27.8A，A32.1，G00
In103	ペスト	A20			
In104	マールブルグ病	A98.3			
In105	ラッサ熱	A96.2	In422	ジアルジア症	A07.1
			In423	腎症候性出血熱	A98.5
In201	急性灰白髄炎	A80	In424	水痘	B01
In202	コレラ	A00	In425	髄膜炎菌性髄膜炎	A39.0
In203	細菌性赤痢	A03	In426	性器クラミジア感染症	A55～A56
In204	ジフテリア	A36	In427	性器ヘルペスウイルス感染症	A60
In205	腸チフス	A01.0	In428	成人麻疹	B05
In206	パラチフス	A01.1	In429	尖形コンジローム	A63.0
			In430	先天性風疹症候群	P35.0
In301	腸管出血性大腸菌感染症	A04.3	In431	炭疽	A22
			In432	ツツガムシ病	A75.3
In401	アメーバ赤痢	A06	In433	手足口病	B08.4
In402	咽頭結膜熱	B30.1，B30.2	In434	デング熱	A90～A91
In403	インフルエンザ	J10～J11	In435	伝染性紅斑	B08.3
In404	A群溶血性レンサ球菌咽頭炎	J02.0	In436	突発性発疹	B08.2
In405	エキノコックス症	B67	In437	日本紅斑熱	A77.8a
In406	黄熱	A95	In438	日本脳炎	A83.0
In407	オウム病	A70	In439	乳児ボツリヌス症	A05.1
In408	回帰熱	A68	In440	梅毒	A50～A53
In409	感染性胃腸炎	A01（A01.0，A01.1を除く），A04（A04.3を除く），A07（A07.1，A07.2を除く），A08，A09	In441	破傷風	A33～A35
			In442	ハンタウイルス肺症候群	B33.8A，J12.8A
			In443	Bウイルス病	B00.4A
			In444	百日咳	A37
			In445	風疹	B06
In410	急性ウイルス性肝炎	B15～B17，B19	In446	ブルセラ症	A23
In411	急性出血性結膜炎	B30.3	In447	ヘルパンギーナ	B08.5
In412	急性脳炎（日本脳炎を除く）	A83～A86（A83.0を除く），B00.4B，B02.0，B25.8A	In448	発疹チフス	A75.0，A75.1
			In449	マイコプラズマ肺炎	J15.7
			In450	麻疹（成人麻疹を除く）	B05
			In451	マラリア	B50～B54
In413	Q熱	A78	In452	無菌性髄膜炎	A87，B00.3，B02.1，G03.0
In414	狂犬病	A82			
In415	クラミジア肺炎（オウム病を除く）	J16.0	In453	ライム病	A69.2
			In454	流行性角結膜炎	B30.0
In416	クリプトスポリジウム症	A07.2	In455	流行性耳下腺炎	B26
In417	クロイツフェルト・ヤコブ病	A81.0，A81.8	In456	淋菌感染症	A54
In418	劇症型溶血性レンサ球菌感染症	A40.0A，A40.8A，A49.1A，J15.4A，M60.0A，P36.1A	In457	レジオネラ症	A48.1，A48.2
			In501	結核	A15～A19
In419	後天性免疫不全症候群	B20～B24			

注：　感染症の分類名は、「感染症の予防及び感染症の患者に対する医療に関する法律」（平成10年法律第114号。以下「感染症法」という。）及び感染症法施行規則（平成10年厚生省令第99号）並びに「結核予防法」（昭和26年法律第96号）に規定された疾病名であるため、必ずしもICD-10とは一致していない。

参考表
各種分類表

表6-1　死因順位及び乳児死因順位に用いる分類項目（平成7年以降）
Table 6-1　Categories for ranking of causes of death (since 1995)

(1) 死因順位に用いる分類項目

分　　類　　名	死因簡単分類コード
腸管感染症	01100
結核	01200
敗血症	01300
ウイルス肝炎	01400
ヒト免疫不全ウイルス［HIV］病	01500
悪性新生物	02100
その他の新生物	02200
貧血	03100
糖尿病	04100
血管性及び詳細不明の認知症	05100
髄膜炎	06100
脊髄性筋萎縮症及び関連症候群	06200
パーキンソン病	06300
アルツハイマー病	06400
眼及び付属器の疾患	07000
耳及び乳様突起の疾患	08000
高血圧性疾患	09100
心疾患（高血圧性を除く）	09200
脳血管疾患	09300
大動脈瘤及び解離	09400
インフルエンザ	10100
肺炎	10200
急性気管支炎	10300
慢性閉塞性肺疾患	10400
喘息	10500
胃潰瘍及び十二指腸潰瘍	11100
ヘルニア及び腸閉塞	11200
肝疾患	11300
皮膚及び皮下組織の疾患	12000
筋骨格系及び結合組織の疾患	13000
糸球体疾患及び腎尿細管間質性疾患	14100
腎不全	14200
妊娠，分娩及び産じょく	15000
周産期に発生した病態	16000
先天奇形，変形及び染色体異常	17000
老衰	18100
乳幼児突然死症候群	18200
不慮の事故	20100
自殺	20200
他殺	20300

注：「敗血症」には、"新生児の細菌性敗血症"を含まない。
　　"新生児の細菌性敗血症"は「周産期に発生した病態」に含まれる。
　　"高血圧性心疾患"は「高血圧性疾患」に含まれる。
　　「血管性及び詳細不明の認知症」は平成18年1月1日からの分類名である。

(2) 乳児死因順位に用いる分類項目

分　　類　　名	乳児死因簡単分類コード
腸管感染症	Ba01
敗血症	Ba02
麻疹	Ba03
ウイルス肝炎	Ba04
悪性新生物	Ba06
その他の新生物	Ba09
栄養失調症及びその他の栄養欠乏症	Ba10
代謝障害	Ba11
髄膜炎	Ba12
脊髄性筋萎縮症及び関連症候群	Ba13
脳性麻痺	Ba14
心疾患（高血圧性を除く）	Ba15
脳血管疾患	Ba16
インフルエンザ	Ba17
肺炎	Ba18
喘息	Ba19
ヘルニア及び腸閉塞	Ba20
肝疾患	Ba21
腎不全	Ba22
妊娠期間及び胎児発育に関連する障害	Ba24
出産外傷	Ba25
周産期に特異的な呼吸障害及び心血管障害	Ba26～Ba30
周産期に特異的な感染症	Ba31～Ba32
胎児及び新生児の出血性障害及び血液障害	Ba33
先天奇形，変形及び染色体異常	Ba35
乳幼児突然死症候群	Ba44
不慮の事故	Ba46
他殺	Ba55

注：「敗血症」には、"新生児の細菌性敗血症"を含まない。
　　"新生児の細菌性敗血症"は「周産期に特異的な感染症」に含まれる。

608

Reference Table

表 6 - 2　死因順位及び乳児死因順位に用いる分類項目（昭和54年から平成 6 年まで）
Table 6-2　Categories for ranking of causes of death (1979-1994)

(1) 死因順位に用いる分類項目

簡単分類番号	死　　因
1	コレラ
2	腸チフス
3	細菌性赤痢及びアメーバ症
4, 72	胃　腸　炎
5～6	結　　核
7	ら　　い
8	ジフテリア
9	百　日　咳
10	猩　紅　熱
11	髄膜炎菌感染
12, 84	破　傷　風
13, 86·	敗　血　症
14	急性灰白髄炎
15	痘　　瘡
16	麻　　疹
17	日 本 脳 炎
18～19	ウイルス肝炎
20	発疹チフス及びその他のリケッチア症
21	マラリア
22	梅　　毒
23, 85	ガンジダ症
24	日本住血吸虫症
25	フィラリア症
28～37	悪性新生物
38	良性及び性質不詳の新生物
39	糖　尿　病
40	栄養欠乏症
41	貧　　血
42	精 神 障 害
43	髄　膜　炎
44	中枢神経系の非炎症性疾患
45	急性リウマチ熱
(46, 51～52 54～56)	心　疾　患
48～49	高血圧性疾患
58～60	脳血管疾患
61	循環系その他の疾患
62～63, 66	肺炎及び気管支炎
64	インフルエンザ
67	肺　気　腫
68	喘　　息
69	胃及び十二指腸潰瘍
70	虫　垂　炎
71	腹腔ヘルニア及び腸閉塞
73	慢性肝疾患及び肝硬変
74	肝疾患（肝硬変を除く）
76～77	腎炎, ネフローゼ症候群及びネフローゼ
78	前立腺肥大症
79～80	妊産婦死亡
81	先 天 異 常
82	出産時外傷, 低酸素症, 分娩仮死及びその他の呼吸器病態
87	その他の周産期の死因
88	精神病の記載のない老衰
E104～E114	不慮の事故及び有害作用
E115	自　　殺
E116	他　　殺

(2) 乳児死因順位に用いる分類項目

乳児簡単分類番　　号	死　　因
1	細菌性赤痢及びアメーバ症
2, 26	胃　腸　炎
3	結　　核
4	ジフテリア
5	百　日　咳
6	破傷風（新生児破傷風を含む）
7	敗血症（新生児敗血症を含む）
8	急性灰白髄炎
9	麻　　疹
10	日 本 脳 炎
11	ウイルス肝炎
12	梅　　毒
15～16	悪性新生物
17	良性及び性質不詳の新生物
18	栄養失調症
19	髄　膜　炎
20	脳性小児麻痺
21	心　疾　患
22, 24	肺炎及び気管支炎
23	インフルエンザ
25	腹腔ヘルニア及び腸閉塞
28～32	先 天 異 常
33～36	母側病態による新生児の障害
38～39, 40	出産時外傷, 低酸素症, 分娩仮死及びその他の呼吸器病態
41	詳細不明の未熟児
42	同種免疫による新生児溶血性疾患
43	その他の周産期黄疸
44～45	新生児の出血及び新生児出血性疾患
E51～E53	不慮の事故及び有害作用
E54	その他の外因

注：昭和53年以前の死因順位の選び方は、平成 6 年人口動態統計上巻435ページ表 2 を参照されたい。

参考表
年次推移

表 1 － 1 死因簡単分類別にみた平成18年と
Table 1-1 Deaths and death rates (per 100,000 population)

死因簡単分類コード Code[a]	死　因 Causes of death	死　亡　数 Deaths						死　亡　率 Death rates					
		2006 平成 18 年			2005 平成 17 年			2006 平成18年			2005 平成17年		
		総数 Total	男 Male	女 Female	総数 Total	男 Male	女 Female	総数 Total	男 Male	女 Female	総数 Total	男 Male	女 Female
	総　数　　　　Total	1 084 450	581 370	503 080	1 083 796	584 970	498 826	859.6	944.3	778.9	858.8	949.4	772.3
01000	感染症及び寄生虫症	24 011	12 223	11 788	23 538	12 211	11 327	19.0	19.9	18.3	18.7	19.8	17.5
01100	腸管感染症	2 190	916	1 274	1 752	733	1 019	1.7	1.5	2.0	1.4	1.2	1.6
01200	結　核	2 269	1 517	752	2 296	1 579	717	1.8	2.5	1.2	1.8	2.6	1.1
01201	呼吸器結核	1 997	1 386	611	2 086	1 482	604	1.6	2.3	0.9	1.7	2.4	0.9
01202	その他の結核	272	131	141	210	97	113	0.2	0.2	0.2	0.2	0.2	0.2
01300	敗　血　症	8 862	4 257	4 605	8 504	4 045	4 459	7.0	6.9	7.1	6.7	6.6	6.9
01400	ウイルス肝炎	5 815	2 856	2 959	6 042	3 093	2 949	4.6	4.6	4.6	4.8	5.0	4.6
01401	Ｂ型ウイルス肝炎	689	435	254	786	524	262	0.5	0.7	0.4	0.6	0.9	0.4
01402	Ｃ型ウイルス肝炎	4 786	2 245	2 541	4 855	2 350	2 505	3.8	3.6	3.9	3.8	3.8	3.9
01403	その他のウイルス肝炎	340	176	164	401	219	182	0.3	0.3	0.3	0.3	0.4	0.3
01500	ヒト免疫不全ウイルス[HIV]病	60	55	5	69	62	7	0.0	0.1	0.0	0.1	0.1	0.0
01600	その他の感染症及び寄生虫症	4 815	2 622	2 193	4 875	2 699	2 176	3.8	4.3	3.4	3.9	4.4	3.4
02000	新　生　物	339 424	203 181	136 243	335 870	201 728	134 142	269.1	330.0	210.9	266.1	327.4	207.7
02100	悪性新生物	329 314	198 052	131 262	325 941	196 603	129 338	261.0	321.7	203.2	258.3	319.1	200.3
02101	口唇，口腔及び咽頭の悪性新生物	6 018	4 310	1 708	5 679	4 151	1 528	4.8	7.0	2.6	4.5	6.7	2.4
02102	食道の悪性新生物	11 345	9 650	1 695	11 182	9 465	1 717	9.0	15.7	2.6	8.9	15.4	2.7
02103	胃の悪性新生物	50 415	32 745	17 670	50 311	32 643	17 668	40.0	53.2	27.4	39.9	53.0	27.4
02104	結腸の悪性新生物	27 317	13 680	13 637	27 121	13 436	13 685	21.7	22.2	21.1	21.5	21.8	21.2
02105	直腸Ｓ状結腸移行部及び直腸の悪性新生物	13 739	8 712	5 027	13 709	8 710	4 999	10.9	14.2	7.8	10.9	14.1	7.7
02106	肝及び肝内胆管の悪性新生物	33 662	22 576	11 086	34 268	23 203	11 065	26.7	36.7	17.2	27.2	37.7	17.1
02107	胆のう及びその他の胆道の悪性新生物	16 855	7 942	8 913	16 586	7 845	8 741	13.4	12.9	13.8	13.1	12.7	13.5
02108	膵の悪性新生物	23 366	12 539	10 827	22 927	12 284	10 643	18.5	20.4	16.8	18.2	19.9	16.5
02109	喉頭の悪性新生物	1 003	942	61	1 090	1 006	84	0.8	1.5	0.1	0.9	1.6	0.1
02110	気管，気管支及び肺の悪性新生物	63 255	45 941	17 314	62 063	45 189	16 874	50.1	74.6	26.8	49.2	73.3	26.1
02111	皮膚の悪性新生物	1 261	616	645	1 207	628	579	1.0	1.0	1.0	1.0	1.0	0.9
02112	乳房の悪性新生物	11 274	97	11 177	10 808	87	10 721	8.9	0.2	17.3	8.6	0.1	16.6
02113	子宮の悪性新生物	5 513	・	5 513	5 381	・	5 381	[1]8.5	・	8.5	[1]8.3	・	8.3
02114	卵巣の悪性新生物	4 435	・	4 435	4 467	・	4 467	[1]6.9	・	6.9	[1]6.9	・	6.9
02115	前立腺の悪性新生物	9 527	9 527	・	9 265	9 265	・	[2]15.5	15.5	・	[2]15.0	15.0	・
02116	膀胱の悪性新生物	6 126	4 217	1 909	6 029	4 141	1 888	4.9	6.8	3.0	4.8	6.7	2.9
02117	中枢神経系の悪性新生物	1 708	973	735	1 681	938	743	1.4	1.6	1.1	1.3	1.5	1.2
02118	悪性リンパ腫	8 639	4 972	3 667	8 537	4 829	3 708	6.8	8.1	5.7	6.8	7.8	5.7
02119	白　血　病	7 429	4 382	3 047	7 283	4 311	2 972	5.9	7.1	4.7	5.8	7.0	4.6
02120	その他のリンパ組織，造血組織及び関連組織の悪性新生物	3 910	1 921	1 989	3 932	2 004	1 928	3.1	3.1	3.1	3.1	3.3	3.0
02121	その他の悪性新生物	22 517	12 310	10 207	22 415	12 468	9 947	17.8	20.0	15.8	17.8	20.2	15.4

注： 本表における死因分類については、ＷＨＯの最新の勧告を国内に適用するため「統計調査に用いる産業分類並びに疾病、傷害及び死因分類を定める政令第三条の規定に基づく疾病、傷害及び死因に関する分類の名称及び分類表（平成６年総務庁告示第75号）」の改正により、平成18年１月１日から「ICD-10（2003年版）準拠」の適用に伴い、分類の追加、変更及び原死因選択ルールの変更が行われている。
　　　詳細については「疾病、傷害および死因統計分類提要ICD-10（2003年版）準拠 第１巻、第２巻、第３巻」を参照されたい。
　1） 女性人口10万対である。
　2） 男性人口10万対である。

Reference Table

17年の性別死亡数及び率（人口10万対）
by sex and causes of death : Japan, 2006 and 2005

死因簡単分類コード Code[a]	死　因 Causes of death	死　亡　数 Deaths						死　亡　率 Death rates					
		2006 平成18年			2005 平成17年			2006 平成18年			2005 平成17年		
		総数 Total	男 Male	女 Female	総数 Total	男 Male	女 Female	総数 Total	男 Male	女 Female	総数 Total	男 Male	女 Female
02200	その他の新生物	10 110	5 129	4 981	9 929	5 125	4 804	8.0	8.3	7.7	7.9	8.3	7.4
02201	中枢神経系のその他の新生物	2 990	1 448	1 542	2 864	1 332	1 532	2.4	2.4	2.4	2.3	2.2	2.4
02202	中枢神経系を除くその他の新生物	7 120	3 681	3 439	7 065	3 793	3 272	5.6	6.0	5.3	5.6	6.2	5.1
03000	血液及び造血器の疾患並びに免疫機構の障害	4 180	1 899	2 281	4 173	1 872	2 301	3.3	3.1	3.5	3.3	3.0	3.6
03100	貧　血	1 589	630	959	1 668	650	1 018	1.3	1.0	1.5	1.3	1.1	1.6
03200	その他の血液及び造血器の疾患並びに免疫機構の障害	2 591	1 269	1 322	2 505	1 222	1 283	2.1	2.1	2.0	2.0	2.0	2.0
04000	内分泌，栄養及び代謝疾患	19 605	10 056	9 549	19 726	9 974	9 752	15.5	16.3	14.8	15.6	16.2	15.1
04100	糖尿病	13 650	7 268	6 382	13 621	7 131	6 490	10.8	11.8	9.9	10.8	11.6	10.0
04200	その他の内分泌，栄養及び代謝疾患	5 955	2 788	3 167	6 105	2 843	3 262	4.7	4.5	4.9	4.8	4.6	5.1
05000	精神及び行動の障害	5 168	1 833	3 335	4 602	1 692	2 910	4.1	3.0	5.2	3.6	2.7	4.5
05100	血管性及び詳細不明の認知症	3 920	1 138	2 782	3 334	952	2 382	3.1	1.8	4.3	2.6	1.5	3.7
05200	その他の精神及び行動の障害	1 248	695	553	1 268	740	528	1.0	1.1	0.9	1.0	1.2	0.8
06000	神経系の疾患	14 251	7 220	7 031	13 004	6 650	6 354	11.3	11.7	10.9	10.3	10.8	9.8
06100	髄膜炎	342	187	155	378	216	162	0.3	0.3	0.2	0.3	0.4	0.3
06200	脊髄性筋萎縮症及び関連症候群	1 759	965	794	1 730	1 010	720	1.4	1.6	1.2	1.4	1.6	1.1
06300	パーキンソン病	3 856	1 828	2 028	3 634	1 728	1 906	3.1	3.0	3.1	2.9	2.8	3.0
06400	アルツハイマー病	2 286	845	1 441	1 814	648	1 166	1.8	1.4	2.2	1.4	1.1	1.8
06500	その他の神経系の疾患	6 008	3 395	2 613	5 448	3 048	2 400	4.8	5.5	4.0	4.3	4.9	3.7
07000	眼及び付属器の疾患	9	6	3	3	1	2	0.0	0.0	0.0	0.0	0.0	0.0
08000	耳及び乳様突起の疾患	15	6	9	14	8	6	0.0	0.0	0.0	0.0	0.0	0.0
09000	循環器系の疾患	324 786	155 787	168 999	329 475	159 268	170 207	257.5	253.0	261.7	261.1	258.5	263.5
09100	高血圧性疾患	5 810	2 095	3 715	5 835	2 145	3 690	4.6	3.4	5.8	4.6	3.5	5.7
09101	高血圧性心疾患及び心腎疾患	3 348	1 179	2 169	3 470	1 256	2 214	2.7	1.9	3.4	2.7	2.0	3.4
09102	その他の高血圧性疾患	2 462	916	1 546	2 365	889	1 476	2.0	1.5	2.4	1.9	1.4	2.3
09200	心疾患（高血圧性を除く）	173 024	82 811	90 213	173 125	83 979	89 146	137.2	134.5	139.7	137.2	136.3	138.0
09201	慢性リウマチ性心疾患	2 445	796	1 649	2 520	829	1 691	1.9	1.3	2.6	2.0	1.3	2.6
09202	急性心筋梗塞	45 067	24 554	20 513	47 193	25 762	21 431	35.7	39.9	31.8	37.4	41.8	33.2
09203	その他の虚血性心疾患	30 362	16 742	13 620	29 310	16 208	13 102	24.1	27.2	21.1	23.2	26.3	20.3
09204	慢性非リウマチ性心内膜疾患	7 481	2 418	5 063	7 532	2 483	5 049	5.9	3.9	7.8	6.0	4.0	7.8
09205	心筋症	3 655	2 166	1 489	3 625	2 266	1 359	2.9	3.5	2.3	2.9	3.7	2.1
09206	不整脈及び伝導障害	21 290	10 487	10 803	22 517	11 233	11 284	16.9	17.0	16.7	17.8	18.2	17.5
09207	心不全	58 418	23 342	35 076	56 327	22 962	33 365	46.3	37.9	54.3	44.6	37.3	51.7
09208	その他の心疾患	4 306	2 306	2 000	4 101	2 236	1 865	3.4	3.7	3.1	3.2	3.6	2.9

3) 「ICD-10（2003年版）準拠」の適用に伴う、主な原死因選択ルールの変更点

死因簡単分類	死　因　名		ICD-10（2003年版）準拠　適用内容（変更後）
09206	不整脈及び伝導障害に含まれる	・心停止	左記の死因名は、不明確な病態であるとされ、死亡診断書に基づき可能な限り原死因を選びなおし、他の病態を選択する。
09500	その他の循環器系の疾患に含まれる	・低血圧 ・循環器疾患	
10600	その他の呼吸器系の疾患に含まれる	・急性呼吸不全 ・呼吸不全	
03100	貧　血		麻痺性疾患（09302 脳内出血、09303 脳梗塞 等）、認知症（05100 血管性及び詳細不明の認知症）、
04200	その他の内分泌，栄養及び代謝疾患に含まれる	・低栄養	神経系の変性疾患（06300 パーキンソン病、06400 アルツハイマー病 等）などが直接影響を及ぼしていると記載されている場合には、これらを選択する。
09302	脳出血		脳血管疾患による認知症は、左記の死因名ではなく、「05100 血管性及び詳細不明の認知症」を選択する。
09303	脳梗塞		

Note : a) See page 595.

参考表
年次推移

表 1－1　死因簡単分類別にみた平成18年と
Table 1-1　Deaths and death rates (per 100,000 population)

死因簡単分類コード Code[a]	死因 Causes of death	死亡数 Deaths						死亡率 Death rates					
		2006 平成18年			2005 平成17年			2006 平成18年			2005 平成17年		
		総数 Total	男 Male	女 Female	総数 Total	男 Male	女 Female	総数 Total	男 Male	女 Female	総数 Total	男 Male	女 Female
09300	脳血管疾患	128 268	61 348	66 920	132 847	63 657	69 190	101.7	99.6	103.6	105.3	103.3	107.1
09301	くも膜下出血	14 466	5 456	9 010	14 883	5 689	9 194	11.5	8.9	14.0	11.8	9.2	14.2
09302	脳内出血	33 290	18 309	14 981	33 362	18 281	15 081	26.4	29.7	23.2	26.4	29.7	23.3
09303	脳梗塞	77 008	35 972	41 036	80 964	38 009	42 955	61.0	58.4	63.5	64.2	61.7	66.5
09304	その他の脳血管疾患	3 504	1 611	1 893	3 638	1 678	1 960	2.8	2.6	2.9	2.9	2.7	3.0
09400	大動脈瘤及び解離	11 665	6 576	5 089	11 392	6 407	4 985	9.2	10.7	7.9	9.0	10.4	7.7
09500	その他の循環器系の疾患	6 019	2 957	3 062	6 276	3 080	3 196	4.8	4.8	4.7	5.0	5.0	4.9
10000	呼吸器系の疾患	162 907	90 080	72 827	165 999	92 157	73 842	129.1	146.3	112.8	131.5	149.6	114.3
10100	インフルエンザ	865	428	437	1 818	863	955	0.7	0.7	0.7	1.4	1.4	1.5
10200	肺炎	107 242	56 572	50 670	107 241	57 310	49 931	85.0	91.9	78.5	85.0	93.0	77.3
10300	急性気管支炎	853	355	498	962	373	589	0.7	0.6	0.8	0.8	0.6	0.9
10400	慢性閉塞性肺疾患	14 357	10 904	3 453	14 416	11 018	3 398	11.4	17.7	5.3	11.4	17.9	5.3
10500	喘息	2 778	1 290	1 488	3 198	1 565	1 633	2.2	2.1	2.3	2.5	2.5	2.5
10600	その他の呼吸器系の疾患	36 812	20 531	16 281	38 364	21 028	17 336	29.2	33.3	25.2	30.4	34.1	26.8
11000	消化器系の疾患	42 429	23 133	19 296	41 802	22 978	18 824	33.6	37.6	29.9	33.1	37.3	29.1
11100	胃潰瘍及び十二指腸潰瘍	3 403	1 924	1 479	3 490	1 897	1 593	2.7	3.1	2.3	2.8	3.1	2.5
11200	ヘルニア及び腸閉塞	5 585	2 443	3 142	5 260	2 312	2 948	4.4	4.0	4.9	4.2	3.8	4.6
11300	肝疾患	16 267	10 909	5 358	16 430	11 007	5 423	12.9	17.7	8.3	13.0	17.9	8.4
11301	肝硬変（アルコール性を除く）	9 064	5 486	3 578	9 387	5 683	3 704	7.2	8.9	5.5	7.4	9.2	5.7
11302	その他の肝疾患	7 203	5 423	1 780	7 043	5 324	1 719	5.7	8.8	2.8	5.6	8.6	2.7
11400	その他の消化器系の疾患	17 174	7 857	9 317	16 622	7 762	8 860	13.6	12.8	14.4	13.2	12.6	13.7
12000	皮膚及び皮下組織の疾患	990	381	609	969	370	599	0.8	0.6	0.9	0.8	0.6	0.9
13000	筋骨格系及び結合組織の疾患	4 848	1 701	3 147	4 603	1 566	3 037	3.8	2.8	4.9	3.6	2.5	4.7
14000	腎尿路生殖器系の疾患	27 859	12 105	15 754	26 952	11 793	15 159	22.1	19.7	24.4	21.4	19.1	23.5
14100	糸球体疾患及び腎尿細管間質性疾患	3 164	1 160	2 004	3 028	1 105	1 923	2.5	1.9	3.1	2.4	1.8	3.0
14200	腎不全	21 158	9 714	11 444	20 528	9 463	11 065	16.8	15.8	17.7	16.3	15.4	17.1
14201	急性腎不全	3 962	1 780	2 182	4 012	1 802	2 210	3.1	2.9	3.4	3.2	2.9	3.4
14202	慢性腎不全	12 084	5 739	6 345	11 539	5 566	5 973	9.6	9.3	9.8	9.1	9.0	9.2
14203	詳細不明の腎不全	5 112	2 195	2 917	4 977	2 095	2 882	4.1	3.6	4.5	3.9	3.4	4.5
14300	その他の腎尿路生殖器系の疾患	3 537	1 231	2 306	3 396	1 225	2 171	2.8	2.0	3.6	2.7	2.0	3.4
15000	妊娠，分娩及び産じょく	63	・	63	66	・	66	[1]0.1	・	0.1	[1]0.1	・	0.1
16000	周産期に発生した病態	828	418	410	842	462	380	0.7	0.7	0.6	0.7	0.7	0.6
16100	妊娠期間及び胎児発育に関連する障害	86	45	41	67	29	38	0.1	0.1	0.1	0.1	0.1	0.1
16200	出産外傷	9	5	4	7	-	7	0.0	0.0	0.0	0.0	-	0.0
16300	周産期に特異的な呼吸障害及び心血管障害	403	203	200	425	235	190	0.3	0.3	0.3	0.3	0.4	0.3
16400	周産期に特異的な感染症	69	38	31	64	36	28	0.1	0.1	0.0	0.1	0.1	0.0
16500	胎児及び新生児の出血性障害及び血液障害	151	81	70	161	93	68	0.1	0.1	0.1	0.1	0.2	0.1
16600	その他の周産期に発生した病態	110	46	64	118	69	49	0.1	0.1	0.1	0.1	0.1	0.1

　4)　遡及できない分類については「…」と表記している。

Reference Table

17年の性別死亡数及び率（人口10万対）（つづき）
by sex and causes of death : Japan, 2006 and 2005-CON.

死因簡単分類コード Code[a]	死　因 Causes of death	死　亡　数 Deaths						死　亡　率 Death rates					
		2006 平成 18 年			2005 平成 17 年			2006 平成18年			2005 平成17年		
		総　数 Total	男 Male	女 Female	総　数 Total	男 Male	女 Female	総　数 Total	男 Male	女 Female	総　数 Total	男 Male	女 Female
17000	先天奇形，変形及び染色体異常	2 306	1 155	1 151	2 324	1 163	1 161	1.8	1.9	1.8	1.8	1.9	1.8
17100	神経系の先天奇形	95	56	39	119	60	59	0.1	0.1	0.1	0.1	0.1	0.1
17200	循環器系の先天奇形	1 178	575	603	1 215	616	599	0.9	0.9	0.9	1.0	1.0	0.9
17201	心臓の先天奇形	887	433	454	931	480	451	0.7	0.7	0.7	0.7	0.8	0.7
17202	その他の循環器系の先天奇形	291	142	149	284	136	148	0.2	0.2	0.2	0.2	0.2	0.2
17300	消化器系の先天奇形	106	57	49	97	54	43	0.1	0.1	0.1	0.1	0.1	0.1
17400	その他の先天奇形及び変形	632	344	288	663	335	328	0.5	0.6	0.4	0.5	0.5	0.5
17500	染色体異常，他に分類されないもの	295	123	172	230	98	132	0.2	0.2	0.3	0.2	0.2	0.2
18000	症状，徴候及び異常臨床所見・異常検査所見で他に分類されないもの	37 659	12 555	25 104	34 454	11 302	23 152	29.9	20.4	38.9	27.3	18.3	35.8
18100	老　衰	27 764	6 872	20 892	26 360	6 683	19 677	22.0	11.2	32.3	20.9	10.8	30.5
18200	乳幼児突然死症候群	194	119	75	196	120	76	0.2	0.2	0.1	0.2	0.2	0.1
18300	その他の症状，徴候及び異常臨床所見・異常検査所見で他に分類されないもの	9 701	5 564	4 137	7 898	4 499	3 399	7.7	9.0	6.4	6.3	7.3	5.3
20000	傷病及び死亡の外因	73 112	47 631	25 481	75 380	49 775	25 605	58.0	77.4	39.5	59.7	80.8	39.6
20100	不慮の事故	38 270	23 329	14 941	39 863	24 591	15 272	30.3	37.9	23.1	31.6	39.9	23.6
20101	交 通 事 故	9 048	6 258	2 790	10 028	7 015	3 013	7.2	10.2	4.3	7.9	11.4	4.7
20102	転倒・転落	6 601	3 931	2 670	6 702	3 989	2 713	5.2	6.4	4.1	5.3	6.5	4.2
20103	不慮の溺死及び溺水	6 038	3 226	2 812	6 222	3 404	2 818	4.8	5.2	4.4	4.9	5.5	4.4
20104	不慮の窒息	9 187	4 887	4 300	9 319	5 058	4 261	7.3	7.9	6.7	7.4	8.2	6.6
20105	煙，火及び火炎への曝露	1 509	959	550	1 593	972	621	1.2	1.6	0.9	1.3	1.6	1.0
20106	有害物質による不慮の中毒及び有害物質への曝露	873	596	277	891	609	282	0.7	1.0	0.4	0.7	1.0	0.4
20107	その他の不慮の事故	5 014	3 472	1 542	5 108	3 544	1 564	4.0	5.6	2.4	4.0	5.8	2.4
20200	自　殺	29 921	21 419	8 502	30 553	22 236	8 317	23.7	34.8	13.2	24.2	36.1	12.9
20300	他　殺	580	314	266	600	317	283	0.5	0.5	0.4	0.5	0.5	0.4
20400	その他の外因	4 341	2 569	1 772	4 364	2 631	1 733	3.4	4.2	2.7	3.5	4.3	2.7
22000	特殊目的用コード	-	-	-	…	…	…	-	-	-	…	…	…
22100	重症急性呼吸器症候群 [SARS]	-	-	-	…	…	…	-	-	-	…	…	…

613

参考表
年次推移

表1－2　死因簡単分類別にみた平成7年と
Table 1-2　Deaths and death rates (per 100,000 population)

死因簡単分類コード Code	死因 Causes of death	死亡数 Deaths 1995 平成7年 総数 Total	男 Male	女 Female	1994 平成6年 総数 Total	男 Male	女 Female	死亡率 Death rates 1995 平成7年 総数 Total	男 Male	女 Female	1994 平成6年 総数 Total	男 Male	女 Female
	総　数　　Total	922 139	501 276	420 863	875 933	476 080	399 853	741.9	822.9	664.0	706.0	782.5	632.4
01000	感染症及び寄生虫症	18 925	10 671	8 254	…	…	…	15.2	17.5	13.0	…	…	…
01100	腸管感染症	1 097	476	621	945	384	561	0.9	0.8	1.0	0.8	0.6	0.9
01200	結　核	3 178	2 267	911	3 094	2 290	804	2.6	3.7	1.4	2.5	3.8	1.3
01201	呼吸器結核1)	2 986	2 163	823	2 890	2 177	713	2.4	3.6	1.3	2.3	3.6	1.1
01202	その他の結核	192	104	88	204	113	91	0.2	0.2	0.1	0.2	0.2	0.1
01300	敗　血　症	4 905	2 269	2 636	4 594	2 099	2 495	3.9	3.7	4.2	3.7	3.5	3.9
01400	ウイルス肝炎	5 029	2 899	2 130	3 182	1 890	1 292	4.0	4.8	3.4	2.9	3.1	2.0
01401	B型ウイルス肝炎	880	568	312	556	380	176	0.7	0.9	0.5	0.4	0.6	0.3
01402	C型ウイルス肝炎	3 542	2 006	1 536	｝2 626	1 510	1 116	2.8	3.3	2.4	｝2.1	2.5	1.8
01403	その他のウイルス肝炎	607	325	282				0.5	0.5	0.4			
01500	ヒト免疫不全ウイルス［HIV]病	56	52	4	…	…	…	0.0	0.1	0.0	…	…	…
01600	その他の感染症及び寄生虫症	4 660	2 708	1 952	…	…	…	3.7	4.4	3.1	…	…	…
02000	新　生　物	270 293	163 649	106 644	…	…	…	217.5	268.6	168.3	…	…	…
02100	悪性新生物	263 022	159 623	103 399	243 670	146 896	96 774	211.6	262.0	163.1	196.4	241.5	153.1
02101	口唇, 口腔及び咽頭の悪性新生物	4 099	2 980	1 119	3 267	2 408	859	3.3	4.9	1.8	2.6	4.0	1.4
02102	食道の悪性新生物	8 638	7 253	1 385	8 143	6 778	1 365	6.9	11.9	2.2	6.6	11.1	2.2
02103	胃の悪性新生物	50 076	32 015	18 061	47 791	30 564	17 227	40.3	52.6	28.5	38.5	50.2	27.2
02104	結腸の悪性新生物	20 286	10 420	9 866	19 063	9 646	9 417	16.3	17.1	15.6	15.4	15.9	14.9
02105	直腸S状結腸移行部及び直腸の悪性新生物	10 988	6 892	4 096	9 855	6 115	3 740	8.8	11.3	6.5	7.9	10.1	5.9
02106	肝及び肝内胆管の悪性新生物	31 707	22 773	8 934	27 472	20 105	7 367	25.5	37.4	14.1	22.1	33.0	11.7
02107	胆のう及びその他の胆道の悪性新生物	13 746	6 189	7 557	13 525	5 924	7 601	11.1	10.2	11.9	10.9	9.7	12.0
02108	膵の悪性新生物	16 019	8 965	7 054	14 990	8 294	6 696	12.9	14.7	11.1	12.1	13.6	10.6
02109	喉頭の悪性新生物	959	872	87	925	842	83	0.8	1.4	0.1	0.7	1.4	0.1
02110	気管, 気管支及び肺の悪性新生物	45 745	33 389	12 356	43 476	31 724	11 752	36.8	54.8	19.5	35.0	52.1	18.6
02111	皮膚の悪性新生物	869	451	418	652	345	307	0.7	0.7	0.7	0.5	0.6	0.5
02112	乳房の悪性新生物	7 819	56	7 763	7 195	64	7 131	6.3	0.1	12.2	5.8	0.1	11.3
02113	子宮の悪性新生物2) 10)	4 865	・	4 865	4 575	・	4 575	7.7	・	7.7	7.2	・	7.2
02114	卵巣の悪性新生物10)	3 892	・	3 892	3 871	・	3 871	6.1	・	6.1	6.1	・	6.1
02115	前立腺の悪性新生物11)	5 399	5 399	・	4 730	4 730	・	8.9	8.9	・	7.8	7.8	・
02116	膀胱の悪性新生物	3 931	2 700	1 231	3 531	2 415	1 116	3.2	4.4	1.9	2.8	4.0	1.8
02117	中枢神経系の悪性新生物	1 574	906	668	1 298	716	582	1.3	1.5	1.1	1.0	1.2	0.9
02118	悪性リンパ腫	6 342	3 735	2 607	…	…	…	5.1	6.1	4.1	…	…	…
02119	白　血　病	6 129	3 645	2 484	5 910	3 348	2 562	4.9	6.0	3.9	4.8	5.5	4.1
02120	その他のリンパ組織, 造血組織及び関連組織の悪性新生物	3 008	1 565	1 443	…	…	…	2.4	2.6	2.3	…	…	…

注：1)　平成6年は結核を伴うじん肺症、珪肺結核を含む。
　　2)　平成6年は胎盤を含む。
　　3)　平成6年は不応性貧血を含む。
　　4)　平成6年は細菌性髄膜脳炎、細菌性髄膜脊髄炎を含む。
　　5)　平成6年は肺塞栓及びその他の肺血管疾患を含み、心臓併発症を伴うリウマチ熱及び心臓併発症を伴うリウマチ性舞踏病を含まない。
　　6)　平成6年は一過性脳虚血を含む。
　　7)　平成6年は15歳未満の気管支炎を含まない。
　　8)　平成6年は先天性腎不全を含む。
　　9)　平成6年は医療事故及び死亡の外因の続発・後遺症を含む。
　　10)　率については、女性人口10万対である。
　　11)　率については、男性人口10万対である。

６年の性別死亡数及び率（人口10万対）
by sex and causes of death : Japan, 1995 and 1994

死因簡単分類コード Code	死因 Causes of death	死亡数 Deaths 1995 平成7年 総数 Total	男 Male	女 Female	1994 平成6年 総数 Total	男 Male	女 Female	死亡率 Death rates 1995 平成7年 総数 Total	男 Male	女 Female	1994 平成6年 総数 Total	男 Male	女 Female
02121	その他の悪性新生物	16 931	9 418	7 513	…	…	…	13.6	15.5	11.9	…	…	…
02200	その他の新生物	7 271	4 026	3 245	…	…	…	5.8	6.6	5.1	…	…	…
02201	中枢神経系のその他の新生物	2 295	1 160	1 135	…	…	…	1.8	1.9	1.8	…	…	…
02202	中枢神経系を除くその他の新生物	4 976	2 866	2 110	…	…	…	4.0	4.7	3.3	…	…	…
03000	血液及び造血器の疾患並びに免疫機構の障害	4 106	1 832	2 274	…	…	…	3.3	3.0	3.6	…	…	…
03100	貧血3)	1 652	666	986	1 575	642	933	1.3	1.1	1.6	1.3	1.1	1.5
03200	その他の血液及び造血器の疾患並びに免疫機構の障害	2 454	1 166	1 288	…	…	…	2.0	1.9	2.0	…	…	…
04000	内分泌，栄養及び代謝疾患	19 360	9 487	9 873	…	…	…	15.6	15.6	15.6	…	…	…
04100	糖尿病	14 225	7 107	7 118	10 872	5 276	5 596	11.4	11.7	11.2	8.8	8.7	8.9
04200	その他の内分泌，栄養及び代謝疾患	5 135	2 380	2 755	…	…	…	4.1	3.9	4.3	…	…	…
05000	精神及び行動の障害	3 762	1 670	2 092	…	…	…	3.0	2.7	3.3	…	…	…
05100	血管性及び詳細不明の痴呆	2 697	943	1 754	…	…	…	2.2	1.5	2.8	…	…	…
05200	その他の精神及び行動の障害	1 065	727	338	…	…	…	0.9	1.2	0.5	…	…	…
06000	神経系の疾患	8 625	4 527	4 098	…	…	…	6.9	7.4	6.5	…	…	…
06100	髄膜炎4)	405	232	173	479	271	208	0.3	0.4	0.3	0.4	0.4	0.3
06200	脊髄性筋萎縮症及び関連症候群	1 249	707	542	1 135	667	468	1.0	1.2	0.9	0.9	1.1	0.7
06300	パーキンソン病	2 427	1 099	1 328	2 153	975	1 178	2.0	1.8	2.1	1.7	1.6	1.9
06400	アルツハイマー病	511	189	322	…	…	…	0.4	0.3	0.5	…	…	…
06500	その他の神経系の疾患	4 033	2 300	1 733	…	…	…	3.2	3.8	2.7	…	…	…
07000	眼及び付属器の疾患	1	1	-	2	2	-	0.0	0.0	-	0.0	0.0	-
08000	耳及び乳様突起の疾患	20	8	12	12	7	5	0.0	0.0	0.0	0.0	0.0	0.0
09000	循環器系の疾患	304 824	148 515	156 309	…	…	…	245.2	243.8	246.6	…	…	…
09100	高血圧性疾患	8 222	3 027	5 195	7 938	2 824	5 114	6.6	5.0	8.2	6.4	4.6	8.1
09101	高血圧性心疾患及び心腎疾患	5 068	1 852	3 216	5 594	2 005	3 589	4.1	3.0	5.1	4.5	3.3	5.7
09102	その他の高血圧性疾患	3 154	1 175	1 979	2 344	819	1 525	2.5	1.9	3.1	1.9	1.3	2.4
09200	心疾患（高血圧性を除く）5)	139 206	69 718	69 488	159 579	78 868	80 711	112.0	114.4	109.6	128.6	129.6	127.6
09201	慢性リウマチ性心疾患	2 755	858	1 897	1 311	399	912	2.2	1.4	3.0	1.1	0.7	1.4
09202	急性心筋梗塞	52 533	28 401	24 132	39 872	21 958	17 914	42.3	46.6	38.1	32.1	36.1	28.3
09203	その他の虚血性心疾患	23 040	11 659	11 381	18 009	8 948	9 061	18.5	19.1	18.0	14.5	14.7	14.3
09204	慢性非リウマチ性心内膜疾患	5 357	2 055	3 302	5 161	2 026	3 135	4.3	3.4	5.2	4.2	3.3	5.0
09205	心筋症	3 455	2 188	1 267	2 757	1 786	971	2.8	3.6	2.0	2.2	2.9	1.5
09206	不整脈及び伝導障害	12 841	6 451	6 390	8 424	4 033	4 391	10.3	10.6	10.1	6.8	6.6	6.9
09207	心不全	36 179	16 627	19 552	79 802	37 536	42 266	29.1	27.3	30.8	64.3	61.7	66.8
09208	その他の心疾患	3 046	1 479	1 567	…	…	…	2.5	2.4	2.5	…	…	…
09300	脳血管疾患6)	146 552	69 587	76 965	120 239	55 510	64 729	117.9	114.2	121.4	96.9	91.2	102.4
09301	くも膜下出血	14 424	5 477	8 947	13 161	4 858	8 303	11.6	9.0	14.1	10.6	8.0	13.1
09302	脳内出血	33 187	17 637	15 550	29 024	15 374	13 650	26.7	29.0	24.5	23.4	25.3	21.6
09303	脳梗塞	89 431	42 724	46 707	67 437	31 102	36 335	71.9	70.1	73.7	54.4	51.1	57.5
09304	その他の脳血管疾患	9 510	3 749	5 761	…	…	…	7.7	6.2	9.1	…	…	…
09400	大動脈瘤及び解離	6 214	3 832	2 382	5 381	3 302	2 079	5.0	6.3	3.8	4.3	5.4	3.3
09500	その他の循環器系の疾患	4 630	2 351	2 279	…	…	…	3.7	3.9	3.6	…	…	…
10000	呼吸器系の疾患	126 661	71 195	55 466	…	…	…	101.9	116.9	87.5	…	…	…
10100	インフルエンザ	1 244	602	642	65	27	38	1.0	1.0	1.0	0.1	0.0	0.1
10200	肺炎	79 629	42 419	37 210	83 354	46 939	36 415	64.1	69.6	58.7	67.2	77.2	57.6
10300	急性気管支炎7)	1 874	840	1 034	1 285	584	701	1.5	1.4	1.6	1.0	1.0	1.1
10400	慢性閉塞性肺疾患	13 092	9 452	3 640	10 242	7 469	2 773	10.5	15.5	5.7	8.3	12.3	4.4
10500	喘息	7 253	4 052	3 201	5 855	3 310	2 545	5.8	6.7	5.1	4.7	5.4	4.0

参考表
年次推移

表 1－2 死因簡単分類別にみた平成 7 年と 6 年の性別死亡数及び率（人口10万対）（つづき）
Table 1-2 Deaths and death rates (per 100,000 population) by sex and causes of death : Japan, 1995 and 1994－CON.

死因簡単分類コード Code	死因 Causes of death	死亡数 Deaths 1995 平成 7 年 総数 Total	男 Male	女 Female	1994 平成 6 年 総数 Total	男 Male	女 Female	死亡率 Death rates 1995 平成 7 年 総数 Total	男 Male	女 Female	1994 平成 6 年 総数 Total	男 Male	女 Female
10600	その他の呼吸器系の疾患	23 569	13 830	9 739	…	…	…	19.0	22.7	15.4	…	…	…
11000	消化器系の疾患	38 726	22 008	16 718	…	…	…	31.2	36.1	26.4	…	…	…
11100	胃潰瘍及び十二指腸潰瘍	4 314	2 274	2 040	3 678	1 956	1 722	3.5	3.7	3.2	3.0	3.2	2.7
11200	ヘルニア及び腸閉塞	4 132	1 835	2 297	3 869	1 813	2 056	3.3	3.0	3.6	3.1	3.0	3.3
11300	肝疾患	17 018	11 576	5 442	19 372	12 962	6 410	13.7	19.0	8.6	15.6	21.3	10.1
11301	肝硬変（アルコール性を除く）	11 301	7 478	3 823	14 358	9 462	4 896	9.1	12.3	6.0	11.6	15.6	7.7
11302	その他の肝疾患	5 717	4 098	1 619	5 014	3 500	1 514	4.6	6.7	2.6	4.0	5.8	2.4
11400	その他の消化器系の疾患	13 262	6 323	6 939	…	…	…	10.7	10.4	10.9	…	…	…
12000	皮膚及び皮下組織の疾患	866	285	581				0.7	0.5	0.9			
13000	筋骨格系及び結合組織の疾患	4 070	1 278	2 792				3.3	2.1	4.4			
14000	尿路性器系の疾患	21 381	9 954	11 427				17.2	16.3	18.0			
14100	糸球体疾患及び腎尿細管間質性疾患	3 188	1 254	1 934				2.6	2.1	3.1			
14200	腎不全	16 187	7 800	8 387	17 376	8 374	9 002	13.0	12.8	13.2	14.0	13.8	14.2
14201	急性腎不全[8]	4 278	2 086	2 192	3 784	1 791	1 993	3.4	3.4	3.5	3.0	2.9	3.2
14202	慢性腎不全	7 099	3 522	3 577	6 928	3 508	3 420	5.7	5.8	5.6	5.6	5.8	5.4
14203	詳細不明の腎不全[8]	4 810	2 192	2 618	6 664	3 075	3 589	3.9	3.6	4.1	5.4	5.1	5.7
14300	その他の尿路性器系の疾患	2 006	900	1 106	…	…	…	1.6	1.5	1.7	…	…	…
15000	妊娠，分娩及び産じょく[10]	90	・	90	…	…	…	0.1	・	0.1	…	…	…
16000	周産期に発生した病態	1 547	902	645	…	…	…	1.2	1.5	1.0	…	…	…
16100	妊娠期間及び胎児発育に関連する障害	78	44	34	99	56	43	0.1	0.1	0.1	0.1	0.1	0.1
16200	出産外傷	30	19	11	…	…	…	0.0	0.0	0.0	…	…	…
16300	周産期に特異的な呼吸障害及び心血管障害	786	440	346	…	…	…	0.6	0.7	0.5	…	…	…
16400	周産期に特異的な感染症	137	91	46	137	71	66	0.1	0.1	0.1	0.1	0.2	0.2
16500	胎児及び新生児の出血性障害及び血液障害	245	138	107	…	…	…	0.2	0.2	0.2	…	…	…
16600	その他の周産期に発生した病態	271	170	101	…	…	…	0.2	0.3	0.2	…	…	…
17000	先天奇形，変形及び染色体異常	3 285	1 687	1 598	…	…	…	2.6	2.8	2.5	…	…	…
17100	神経系の先天奇形	171	83	88	139	74	65	0.1	0.1	0.1	0.1	0.1	0.1
17200	循環器系の先天奇形	1 843	961	882	…	…	…	1.5	1.6	1.4	…	…	…
17201	心臓の先天奇形	1 385	710	675	1 340	703	637	1.1	1.2	1.1	1.1	1.2	1.0
17202	その他の循環器系の先天奇形	458	251	207	…	…	…	0.4	0.4	0.3	…	…	…
17300	消化器系の先天奇形	135	66	69	111	51	60	0.1	0.1	0.1	0.1	0.1	0.1
17400	その他の先天奇形及び変形	819	442	377	…	…	…	0.7	0.7	0.6	…	…	…
17500	染色体異常，他に分類されないもの	317	135	182	370	144	226	0.3	0.2	0.3	0.3	0.2	0.4
18000	症状，徴候及び異常臨床所見・異常検査所見で他に分類されないもの	25 720	9 220	16 500	…	…	…	20.7	15.1	26.0	…	…	…
18100	老衰	21 493	6 684	14 809	23 464	7 333	16 131	17.3	11.0	23.4	18.9	12.1	25.5
18200	乳幼児突然死症候群	579	341	238	524	326	198	0.5	6.0	0.4	0.4	0.5	0.3
18300	その他の症状，徴候及び異常臨床所見・異常検査所見で他に分類されないもの	3 648	2 195	1 453	…	…	…	2.9	3.6	2.3	…	…	…
20000	傷病及び死亡の外因	69 877	44 387	25 490	60 894	40 710	20 184	56.2	72.9	40.2	49.1	66.9	31.9
20100	不慮の事故	45 323	28 229	17 094	36 115	24 082	12 033	36.5	46.3	27.0	29.1	39.6	19.0
20101	交通事故	15 147	10 772	4 375	14 869	10 593	4 276	12.2	17.7	6.9	12.0	17.4	6.8
20102	転倒・転落	5 911	3 663	2 248	4 690	3 020	1 670	4.8	6.0	3.5	3.8	5.0	2.6
20103	不慮の溺死及び溺水	5 588	3 170	2 418	3 868	2 321	1 547	4.5	5.2	3.8	3.1	3.8	2.4
20104	不慮の窒息	7 104	4 198	2 906	5 149	3 067	2 082	5.7	6.9	4.6	4.2	5.0	3.3
20105	煙・火及び火炎への曝露	1 383	849	534	1 348	835	513	1.1	1.4	0.8	1.1	1.4	0.8
20106	有害物質による不慮の中毒及び有害物質への曝露	568	396	172	497	328	169	0.5	0.7	0.3	0.4	0.5	0.3
20107	その他の不慮の事故[9]	9 622	5 181	4 441	5 694	3 918	1 776	7.7	8.5	7.0	4.6	6.4	2.8
20200	自殺	21 420	14 231	7 189	20 923	14 058	6 865	17.2	23.4	11.3	16.9	23.1	10.9
20300	他殺	727	413	314	789	498	291	0.6	0.7	0.5	0.6	0.8	0.5
20400	その他の外因	2 407	1 514	893	3 067	2 072	995	1.9	2.5	1.4	2.5	3.4	1.6

参考表
年次推移

表1－3　死因簡単分類別にみた昭和55・60・
Table 1-3　Deaths and death rates（per 100,000 population）by sex

総　数
Total

簡単分類番号 117 rubrics list code	死　因 [2] Causes of death	死　亡　数 Deaths						死　亡　率 Death rates					
		1980 昭和55年	1985 60年	1990 平成2年	1992 4年	1993 5年	1994 6年	1980 昭和55年	1985 60年	1990 平成2年	1992 4年	1993 5年	1994 6年
	総　数　　Total	722 801	752 283	820 305	856 643	878 532	875 933	621.4	625.5	668.4	693.8	709.7	706.0
1	コ　レ　ラ	-	-	-	-	-	-	-	-	-	-	-	-
2	腸　チ　フ　ス	1	-	2	-	-	1	0.0	-	0.0	-	-	0.0
3	細菌性赤痢及びアメーバ症	-	6	5	3	3	1	-	0.0	0.0	0.0	0.0	0.0
4	腸炎及びその他の下痢性疾患	1 573	1 067	721	754	749	937	1.4	0.9	0.6	0.6	0.6	0.8
5	呼　吸　系　の　結　核	6 144	4 484	3 457	3 133	3 042	2 890	5.3	3.7	2.8	2.5	2.5	2.3
6	そ　の　他　の　結　核	295	208	207	214	207	204	0.3	0.2	0.2	0.2	0.2	0.2
7	ら　　　　　　い	-	-	-	-	1	-	-	-	-	-	0.0	-
8	ジ　フ　テ　リ　ア	1	-	-	-	1	-	0.0	-	-	-	0.0	-
9	百　　日　　咳	18	7	4	1	2	3	0.0	0.0	0.0	0.0	0.0	0.0
10	猩　紅　熱	-	-	-	-	-	-	-	-	-	-	-	-
11	髄　膜　炎　菌　感　染	7	4	8	1	-	2	0.0	0.0	0.0	0.0	-	0.0
12	破傷風（新生児破傷風を除く）	45	28	26	17	14	11	0.0	0.0	0.0	0.0	0.0	0.0
13	敗血症（新生児敗血症を除く）	1 357	2 579	3 481	4 037	3 944	4 594	1.2	2.1	2.8	3.3	3.2	3.7
14	急　性　灰　白　髄　炎	-	-	-	-	-	-	-	-	-	-	-	-
15	痘　　　　　　瘡	-	-	-	-	-	-	-	-	-	-	-	-
16	麻　　　疹	50	36	53	14	14	11	0.0	0.0	0.0	0.0	0.0	0.0
17	日　本　脳　炎	20	8	10	1	-	1	0.0	0.0	0.0	0.0	-	0.0
18	ウ　イ　ル　ス　肝　炎　B	122	218	298	376	451	556	0.1	0.2	0.2	0.3	0.4	0.4
19	その他のウイルス肝炎	976	1 053	896	1 552	2 043	2 626	0.8	0.9	0.7	1.3	1.7	2.1
20	発疹チフス及びその他のリケッチア症	1	3	3	4	4	4	0.0	0.0	0.0	0.0	0.0	0.0
21	マ　ラ　リ　ア	6	2	1	-	-	3	0.0	0.0	0.0	-	-	0.0
22	梅　　　　　毒	141	67	32	26	25	34	0.1	0.1	0.0	0.0	0.0	0.0
23	カンジダ症（新生児カンジダ症を除く）	27	53	84	122	105	108	0.0	0.0	0.1	0.1	0.1	0.1
24	日　本　住　血　吸　虫　症	8	4	9	4	3	7	0.0	0.0	0.0	0.0	0.0	0.0
25	フ　ィ　ラ　リ　ア　症	3	3	2	-	1	1	0.0	0.0	0.0	-	0.0	0.0
26	その他の感染症及び寄生虫症	1 143	1 796	2 707	3 076	3 325	3 717	1.0	1.5	2.2	2.5	2.7	3.0
28～37	悪　性　新　生　物	161 764	187 714	217 413	231 917	235 707	243 670	139.1	156.1	177.2	187.8	190.4	196.4
28	食　　　道	5 733	6 197	7 274	7 854	8 040	8 143	4.9	5.2	5.9	6.4	6.5	6.6
29	胃	50 443	48 902	47 471	48 041	47 311	47 791	43.4	40.7	38.7	38.9	38.2	38.5
30	直腸,直腸S状結腸移行部及び肛門	6 917	7 934	9 270	10 090	9 963	10 025	5.9	6.6	7.6	8.2	8.0	8.1
31	肝	14 510	19 871	25 352	26 999	27 765	28 677	12.5	16.5	20.7	21.9	22.4	23.1

注：1)　平成6年人口動態統計上巻表5，13を参考表として転載したものである。
　　2)　死因はICD-9の簡単分類による。
　　3)　率については、女性人口10万対である。
　　4)　率については、男性人口10万対である。
　　平成6年の心疾患の減少は、新しい死亡診断書（死体検案書）（平成7年1月施行）における「死亡の原因欄には、疾患の終末期の状態としての心不全、呼吸不全等は書かないでください。」という注意書きの、施行前の周知の影響によるものと考えられる。

Reference Table

平成 2・4～6年の性別死亡数及び率[1]（人口10万対）
and causes of death（the 117 rubrics list）: Japan, 1980, 1985, 1990, 1992-1994

総　数
Total

簡　単 分類番号 117 rubrics list code	死　因[2] Causes of death	死　亡　数 Deaths						死　亡　率 Death rates					
		1980 昭和55年	1985 60年	1990 平成2年	1992 4年	1993 5年	1994 6年	1980 昭和55年	1985 60年	1990 平成2年	1992 4年	1993 5年	1994 6年
32	膵	7 835	10 441	13 318	14 147	14 713	14 990	6.7	8.7	10.9	11.5	11.9	12.1
33	気管，気管支及び肺	21 294	28 590	36 486	40 163	41 527	43 476	18.3	23.8	29.7	32.5	33.5	35.0
34	乳　　　房[3]	4 185	4 958	5 882	6 507	6 814	7 195	3.6	4.1	4.8	5.3	5.5	5.8
35	子　　　宮	5 465	4 912	4 600	4 665	4 445	4 575	9.2	8.0	7.4	7.4	7.0	7.2
36	白　血　病	4 567	5 179	5 633	5 716	5 819	5 910	3.9	4.3	4.6	4.6	4.7	4.8
37	そ　の　他	40 815	50 730	62 127	67 735	69 310	72 888	35.1	42.2	50.6	54.9	56.0	58.7
38	良性及び性質不詳の新生物	6 082	6 535	7 123	7 108	7 287	7 012	5.2	5.4	5.8	5.8	5.9	5.7
39	糖　尿　病	8 504	9 244	9 470	9 823	10 239	10 872	7.3	7.7	7.7	8.0	8.3	8.8
40	栄　養　欠　乏　症	433	480	574	593	692	840	0.4	0.4	0.5	0.5	0.6	0.7
41	貧　　　血	1 521	1 596	1 606	1 523	1 464	1 575	1.3	1.3	1.3	1.2	1.2	1.3
42	精　神　障　害	3 017	3 016	3 068	3 003	3 116	3 427	2.6	2.5	2.5	2.4	2.5	2.8
43	髄　膜　炎	671	634	475	436	448	479	0.6	0.5	0.4	0.4	0.4	0.4
44	中枢神経系の非炎症性疾患	4 352	4 757	5 086	5 437	5 811	6 160	3.7	4.0	4.1	4.4	4.7	5.0
45	急性リウマチ熱	155	38	27	59	32	42	0.1	0.0	0.0	0.0	0.0	0.0
46	慢性リウマチ性心疾患	1 716	1 644	1 360	1 267	1 298	1 311	1.5	1.4	1.1	1.0	1.0	1.1
48～49	高　血　圧　性　疾　患	15 911	12 700	9 246	8 688	8 360	7 938	13.7	10.6	7.5	7.0	6.8	6.4
48	高　血　圧　性　心　疾　患	11 559	9 454	7 031	6 699	6 334	5 594	9.9	7.9	5.7	5.4	5.1	4.5
49	その他の高血圧性疾患	4 352	3 246	2 215	1 989	2 026	2 344	3.7	2.7	1.8	1.6	1.6	1.9
51～52	虚　血　性　心　疾　患	48 347	49 484	51 437	51 124	51 914	57 881	41.6	41.1	41.9	41.4	41.9	46.7
51	急　性　心　筋　梗　塞	29 393	30 558	31 933	31 355	32 545	39 872	25.3	25.4	26.0	25.4	26.3	32.1
52	その他の虚血性心疾患	18 954	18 926	19 504	19 769	19 369	18 009	16.3	15.7	15.9	16.0	15.6	14.5
54～56	肺循環疾患及びその他の型の心疾患	73 442	89 969	112 681	123 155	127 085	100 387	63.1	74.8	91.8	99.7	102.7	80.9
54	心内膜の慢性疾患	3 510	3 554	4 201	4 496	4 794	5 161	3.0	3.0	3.4	3.6	3.9	4.2
55	心　不　全	59 560	75 310	96 078	105 796	108 465	79 802	51.2	62.6	78.3	85.7	87.6	64.3
56	その他の心疾患	10 372	11 105	12 402	12 863	13 826	15 424	8.9	9.2	10.1	10.4	11.2	12.4
58～60	脳　血　管　疾　患	162 317	134 994	121 944	118 058	118 794	120 239	139.5	112.2	99.4	95.6	96.0	96.9
58	脳　出　血	50 792	36 877	30 820	29 811	29 955	29 493	43.7	30.7	25.1	24.1	24.2	23.8
59	脳　梗　塞	75 311	67 350	64 575	63 566	64 850	67 437	64.7	56.0	52.6	51.5	52.4	54.4
60	その他の脳血管疾患	36 214	30 767	26 549	24 681	23 989	23 309	31.1	25.6	21.6	20.0	19.4	18.8
61	循環系のその他の疾患	8 445	7 625	7 753	8 054	8 491	8 877	7.3	6.3	6.3	6.5	6.9	7.2
62	急　性　気　管　支　炎	1 985	1 444	1 330	1 193	1 356	1 285	1.7	1.2	1.1	1.0	1.1	1.0
63	肺　　　炎	33 051	45 075	68 194	74 274	81 138	83 354	28.4	37.5	55.6	60.2	65.5	67.2

参考表
年次推移

表1－3　死因簡単分類別にみた昭和55・60・
Table 1-3　Deaths and death rates（per 100,000 population）by sex

総　数
Total

簡単分類番号 117 rubrics list code	死因 Causes of death	死亡数 Deaths						死亡率 Death rates					
		1980 昭和55年	1985 60年	1990 平成2年	1992 4年	1993 5年	1994 6年	1980 昭和55年	1985 60年	1990 平成2年	1992 4年	1993 5年	1994 6年
64	インフルエンザ	718	523	448	177	519	65	0.6	0.4	0.4	0.1	0.4	0.1
66～68	気管支炎, 肺気腫及び喘息	12 712	14 431	14 938	15 174	15 898	16 211	10.9	12.0	12.2	12.3	12.8	13.1
66	気管支炎	4 205	4 847	5 011	4 839	4 915	5 195	3.6	4.0	4.1	3.9	4.0	4.2
67	肺気腫	2 137	3 244	3 980	4 406	4 773	5 161	1.8	2.7	3.2	3.6	3.9	4.2
68	喘息	6 370	6 340	5 947	5 929	6 210	5 855	5.5	5.3	4.8	4.8	5.0	4.7
69	胃及び十二指腸潰瘍	5 530	4 493	3 615	3 581	3 680	3 678	4.8	3.7	2.9	2.9	3.0	3.0
70	虫垂炎	220	120	95	87	93	86	0.2	0.1	0.1	0.1	0.1	0.1
71	腹腔ヘルニア及び腸閉塞	2 649	2 648	3 040	3 396	3 579	3 869	2.3	2.2	2.5	2.8	2.9	3.1
72	胃炎,十二指腸炎及び慢性胃腸炎	2 229	1 245	814	707	665	702	1.9	1.0	0.7	0.6	0.5	0.6
73	慢性肝疾患及び肝硬変	16 490	17 174	16 804	17 083	16 880	16 446	14.2	14.3	13.7	13.8	13.6	13.3
74	肝疾患（肝硬変を除く）	2 488	2 629	2 896	3 079	3 043	2 926	2.1	2.2	2.4	2.5	2.5	2.4
76～77	腎炎,ネフローゼ症候群及びネフローゼ	10 180	13 521	17 140	18 299	18 505	18 789	8.8	11.2	14.0	14.8	14.9	15.1
76	急性糸球体腎炎及びネフローゼ症候群	1 947	3 022	3 908	4 159	4 196	4 226	1.7	2.5	3.2	3.4	3.4	3.4
77	その他	8 233	10 499	13 232	14 140	14 309	14 563	7.1	8.7	10.8	11.5	11.6	11.7
78	前立腺肥大症	497	357	201	168	178	154	0.9	0.6	0.3	0.3	0.3	0.3
79	直接産科的死亡	292	196	91	95	82	69	0.5	0.3	0.1	0.2	0.1	0.1
80	間接産科的死亡	31	30	14	16	9	7	0.1	0.0	0.0	0.0	0.0	0.0
81	先天異常	4 885	3 949	3 571	3 534	3 417	3 287	4.2	3.3	2.9	2.9	2.8	2.6
82	出産時外傷, 低酸素症, 分娩仮死及びその他の呼吸器病態	3 888	2 428	1 220	1 017	957	975	3.3	2.0	1.0	0.8	0.8	0.8
84～87	その他の周産期の死因	1 905	920	574	547	538	598	1.6	0.8	0.5	0.4	0.4	0.5
84	新生児破傷風	1	-	-	-	-	-	0.0	-	-	-	-	-
85	新生児カンジダ感染	1	1	1	-	-	5	0.0	0.0	0.0	-	-	0.0
86	新生児敗血症	145	125	88	100	74	92	0.1	0.1	0.1	0.1	0.1	0.1
87	その他	1 758	794	485	447	464	501	1.5	0.7	0.4	0.4	0.4	0.4
88	精神病の記載のない老衰	32 154	27 804	24 187	23 361	23 115	23 464	27.6	23.1	19.7	18.9	18.7	18.9
89	その他のすべての疾患	29 455	34 846	44 252	48 323	51 199	52 653	25.3	29.0	36.1	39.1	41.4	42.4
91～101	損傷及び中毒	52 827	56 394	55 612	58 952	59 009	60 894	45.4	46.9	45.3	47.7	47.7	49.1
91	頭蓋骨折	7 398	6 497	5 881	5 740	5 370	5 310	6.4	5.4	4.8	4.6	4.3	4.3
92	その他の骨の骨折	2 988	2 960	3 309	3 254	3 370	3 355	2.6	2.5	2.7	2.6	2.7	2.7
93	頭蓋内損傷（頭蓋骨折を伴うものを除く）	6 006	6 999	8 420	9 636	9 381	9 387	5.2	5.8	6.9	7.8	7.6	7.6
94	胸,腹及び骨盤の内部損傷	3 732	4 260	4 606	4 740	4 930	4 740	3.2	3.5	3.8	3.8	4.0	3.8
95	開放創	864	945	1 002	961	962	996	0.7	0.8	0.8	0.8	0.8	0.8

注：1)～4)　618ページの注参照。

Reference Table

平成2・4～6年の性別死亡数及び率 [1] （人口10万対）（つづき）
and causes of death (the 117 rubrics list): Japan, 1980, 1985, 1990, 1992-1994－CON.

総　数
Total

簡　単分類番号117 rubrics list code	死　因 [2] Causes of death	死　亡　数 Deaths						死　亡　率 Death rates					
		1980 昭和55年	1985 60年	1990 平成2年	1992 4年	1993 5年	1994 6年	1980 昭和55年	1985 60年	1990 平成2年	1992 4年	1993 5年	1994 6年
96	熱　　　　傷	2 481	2 232	2 281	2 303	2 191	2 367	2.1	1.9	1.9	1.9	1.8	1.9
97	神経及び脊髄の損傷	359	410	472	493	470	553	0.3	0.3	0.4	0.4	0.4	0.4
98	中 毒 及 び 毒 作 用	4 945	5 664	3 484	3 528	3 657	3 399	4.3	4.7	2.8	2.9	3.0	2.7
99	溺　　　　死	6 545	6 273	6 340	6 311	7 108	7 035	5.6	5.2	5.2	5.1	5.7	5.7
100	窒 息 及 び 絞 首	12 044	14 310	12 128	13 247	12 608	13 146	10.4	11.9	9.9	10.7	10.2	10.6
101	そ の 他 の 損 傷	5 465	5 844	7 689	8 739	8 962	10 606	4.7	4.9	6.3	7.1	7.2	8.5
	（ 再 掲 ）												
E104～E117	損傷及び中毒の外因	52 827	56 394	55 612	58 952	59 009	60 894	45.4	46.9	45.3	47.7	47.7	49.1
E104～E114	不慮の事故及び有害作用	29 217	29 597	32 122	34 677	34 717	36 115	25.1	24.6	26.2	28.1	28.0	29.1
E104	自 動 車 事 故	11 752	12 660	14 631	14 735	14 168	13 712	10.1	10.5	11.9	11.9	11.4	11.1
E105	自動車事故以外の交通事故	1 550	1 741	1 197	1 093	1 025	1 157	1.3	1.4	1.0	0.9	0.8	0.9
E106	不 慮 の 中 毒	776	830	561	526	514	497	0.7	0.7	0.5	0.4	0.4	0.4
E107	不 慮 の 墜 落	4 420	4 006	4 243	4 598	4 642	4 690	3.8	3.3	3.5	3.7	3.7	3.8
E108	火災及び火焔による不慮の事故	1 464	1 191	1 208	1 287	1 226	1 348	1.3	1.0	1.0	1.0	1.0	1.1
E109	天　　　　災	21	36	75	15	357	5	0.0	0.0	0.1	0.0	0.3	0.0
E110	不 慮 の 溺 死	3 437	3 196	3 146	3 269	3 659	3 868	3.0	2.7	2.6	2.6	3.0	3.1
E111	不 慮 の 機 械 的 窒 息	2 177	2 597	3 460	4 197	4 405	5 149	1.9	2.2	2.8	3.4	3.6	4.2
E112	不 慮 の 打 撲	713	513	515	473	440	458	0.6	0.4	0.4	0.4	0.4	0.4
E113	工業性を主とする不慮の事故	1 463	1 322	1 204	1 185	1 065	1 153	1.3	1.1	1.0	1.0	0.9	0.9
E114	その他の不慮の事故及び有害作用	1 444	1 505	1 882	3 299	3 216	4 078	1.2	1.3	1.5	2.7	2.6	3.3
E115	自　　　　殺	20 542	23 383	20 088	20 893	20 516	20 923	17.7	19.4	16.4	16.9	16.6	16.9
E116	他　　　　殺	1 113	1 017	744	748	805	789	1.0	0.8	0.6	0.6	0.7	0.6
E117	そ の 他 の 外 因	1 955	2 397	2 658	2 634	2 971	3 067	1.7	2.0	2.2	2.1	2.4	2.5
（再掲）													
1～26	感染症及び寄生虫症	11 938	11 626	12 006	13 335	13 934	15 711	10.3	9.7	9.8	10.8	11.3	12.7
5～6	結　　　　核	6 439	4 692	3 664	3 347	3 249	3 094	5.5	3.9	3.0	2.7	2.6	2.5
46,51～52,54～56	心　疾　患	123 505	141 097	165 478	175 546	180 297	159 579	106.2	117.3	134.8	142.2	145.6	128.6
46,54	慢性リウマチ性心疾患及び心内膜の慢性疾患	5 226	5 198	5 561	5 763	6 092	6 472	4.5	4.3	4.5	4.7	4.9	5.2
62～63,66	肺炎及び気管支炎	39 241	51 366	74 535	80 306	87 409	89 834	33.7	42.7	60.7	65.0	70.6	72.4
62,66	気 管 支 炎	6 190	6 291	6 341	6 032	6 271	6 480	5.3	5.2	5.2	4.9	5.1	5.2
79～80	妊 産 婦 死 亡 [3]	323	226	105	111	91	76	0.5	0.4	0.2	0.2	0.1	0.1
4,72	胃 腸 炎	3 802	2 312	1 535	1 461	1 414	1 639	3.3	1.9	1.3	1.2	1.1	1.3

621

参考表
年次推移

表 1 － 3 死因簡単分類別にみた昭和55・60・
Table 1-3 Deaths and death rates (per 100,000 population) by sex

男
Male

簡 単 分類番号 117 rubrics list code	死 因[2)] Causes of death	死 亡 数 Deaths						死 亡 率 Death rates					
		1980 昭和55年	1985 60年	1990 平成2年	1992 4年	1993 5年	1994 6年	1980 昭和55年	1985 60年	1990 平成2年	1992 4年	1993 5年	1994 6年
	総 数 Total	390 644	407 769	443 718	465 544	476 462	476 080	682.9	690.6	736.5	768.3	784.6	782.5
1	コ レ ラ	-	-	-	-	-	-	-	-	-	-	-	-
2	腸 チ フ ス	1	-	2	-	-	-	0.0	-	0.0	-	-	-
3	細菌性赤痢及びアメーバ症	-	6	3	3	3	1	-	0.0	0.0	0.0	0.0	0.0
4	腸炎及びその他の下痢性疾患	661	444	295	322	338	379	1.2	0.8	0.5	0.5	0.6	0.6
5	呼 吸 系 の 結 核	4 555	3 333	2 631	2 394	2 319	2 177	8.0	5.6	4.4	4.0	3.8	3.6
6	そ の 他 の 結 核	160	109	114	120	105	113	0.3	0.2	0.2	0.2	0.2	0.2
7	ら い	-	-	-	-	1	-	-	-	-	-	0.0	-
8	ジ フ テ リ ア	1	-	-	-	-	-	0.0	-	-	-	-	-
9	百 日 咳	8	3	2	1	1	1	0.0	0.0	0.0	0.0	0.0	0.0
10	猩 紅 熱	-	-	-	-	-	-	-	-	-	-	-	-
11	髄 膜 炎 菌 感 染	5	3	5	1	-	2	0.0	0.0	0.0	0.0	-	0.0
12	破傷風(新生児破傷風を除く)	28	15	11	11	6	8	0.0	0.0	0.0	0.0	0.0	0.0
13	敗血症(新生児敗血症を除く)	663	1 203	1 615	1 883	1 916	2 099	1.2	2.0	2.7	3.1	3.2	3.5
14	急 性 灰 白 髄 炎												
15	痘 瘡	-	-	-	-	-	-						
16	麻 疹	22	20	27	11	8	5	0.0	0.0	0.0	0.0	0.0	0.0
17	日 本 脳 炎	12	4	6	1	-	-	0.0	0.0	0.0	0.0	-	-
18	ウ イ ル ス 肝 炎 B	78	145	194	252	307	380	0.1	0.2	0.3	0.4	0.5	0.6
19	その他のウイルス肝炎	549	581	499	882	1 189	1 510	1.0	1.0	0.8	1.5	2.0	2.5
20	発疹チフス及びその他のリケッチア症	-	2	2	2	2	3	-	0.0	0.0	0.0	0.0	0.0
21	マ ラ リ ア	5	2	1	-	-	3	0.0	0.0	0.0	-	-	0.0
22	梅 毒	82	45	27	20	15	23	0.1	0.1	0.0	0.0	0.0	0.0
23	カンジダ症(新生児カンジダ症を除く)	10	33	43	71	56	69	0.0	0.1	0.1	0.1	0.1	0.1
24	日 本 住 血 吸 虫 症	4	3	6	2	3	5	0.0	0.0	0.0	0.0	0.0	0.0
25	フ ィ ラ リ ア 症	1	1	1	-	-	1	0.0	0.0	0.0	-	-	0.0
26	その他の感染症及び寄生虫症	682	1 134	1 681	1 900	2 032	2 269	1.2	1.9	2.8	3.1	3.3	3.7
28～37	悪 性 新 生 物	93 501	110 660	130 395	139 674	142 222	146 896	163.5	187.4	216.4	230.5	234.2	241.5
28	食 道	4 490	5 046	6 004	6 557	6 734	6 778	7.8	8.5	10.0	10.8	11.1	11.1
29	胃	30 845	30 146	29 909	30 507	29 998	30 564	53.9	51.1	49.6	50.3	49.4	50.2
30	直腸,直腸S状結腸移行部及び肛門	3 933	4 643	5 569	6 157	6 122	6 189	6.9	7.9	9.2	10.2	10.1	10.2
31	肝	10 038	14 287	18 393	19 571	20 060	20 764	17.5	24.2	30.5	32.3	33.0	34.1

Reference Table

平成2・4～6年の性別死亡数及び率[1] （人口10万対）（つづき）
and causes of death (the 117 rubrics list): Japan, 1980, 1985, 1990, 1992-1994－CON.

男
Male

簡　単分類番号 117 rubrics list code	死　因[2] Causes of death	死　亡　数 Deaths						死　亡　率 Death rates					
		1980 昭和55年	1985 60年	1990 平成2年	1992 4年	1993 5年	1994 6年	1980 昭和55年	1985 60年	1990 平成2年	1992 4年	1993 5年	1994 6年
32	膵	4 483	5 953	7 317	7 810	8 139	8 294	7.8	10.1	12.1	12.9	13.4	13.6
33	気管，気管支及び肺	15 438	20 837	26 872	29 223	30 398	31 724	27.0	35.3	44.6	48.2	50.1	52.1
34	乳　　房	44	36	34	56	56	64	0.1	0.1	0.1	0.1	0.1	0.1
35	子　　宮	・	・	・	・	・	・	・	・	・	・	・	・
36	白　血　病	2 624	2 983	3 225	3 360	3 350	3 348	4.6	5.1	5.4	5.5	5.5	5.5
37	そ　の　他	21 606	26 729	33 072	36 433	37 365	39 171	37.8	45.3	54.9	60.1	61.5	64.4
38	良性及び性質不詳の新生物	3 372	3 617	3 928	4 028	4 031	3 865	5.9	6.1	6.5	6.6	6.6	6.4
39	糖　尿　病	4 055	4 322	4 491	4 758	4 972	5 276	7.1	7.3	7.5	7.9	8.2	8.7
40	栄　養　欠　乏　症	230	253	308	339	369	461	0.4	0.4	0.5	0.6	0.6	0.8
41	貧　　血	707	699	698	631	575	642	1.2	1.2	1.2	1.0	0.9	1.1
42	精　神　障　害	1 522	1 425	1 263	1 269	1 302	1 481	2.7	2.4	2.1	2.1	2.1	2.4
43	髄　膜　炎	391	368	269	259	253	271	0.7	0.6	0.4	0.4	0.4	0.4
44	中枢神経系の非炎症性疾患	2 382	2 539	2 678	2 929	3 052	3 240	4.2	4.3	4.4	4.8	5.0	5.3
45	急性リウマチ熱	58	10	8	17	8	11	0.1	0.0	0.0	0.0	0.0	0.0
46	慢性リウマチ性心疾患	582	516	436	384	395	399	1.0	0.9	0.7	0.6	0.7	0.7
48～49	高　血　圧　性　疾　患	6 654	4 991	3 399	3 174	3 117	2 824	11.6	8.5	5.6	5.2	5.1	4.6
48	高　血　圧　性　心　疾　患	4 874	3 762	2 607	2 481	2 365	2 005	8.5	6.4	4.3	4.1	3.9	3.3
49	その他の高血圧性疾患	1 780	1 229	792	693	752	819	3.1	2.1	1.3	1.1	1.2	1.3
51～52	虚　血　性　心　疾　患	26 887	26 869	27 349	26 987	27 416	30 906	47.0	45.5	45.4	44.5	45.1	50.8
51	急　性　心　筋　梗　塞	17 511	17 656	17 883	17 372	18 039	21 958	30.6	29.9	29.7	28.7	29.7	36.1
52	その他の虚血性心疾患	9 376	9 213	9 466	9 615	9 377	8 948	16.4	15.6	15.7	15.9	15.4	14.7
54～56	肺循環疾患及びその他の型の心疾患	36 634	44 381	53 989	59 013	60 498	47 563	64.0	75.2	89.6	97.4	99.6	78.2
54	心内膜の慢性疾患	1 519	1 452	1 680	1 820	1 902	2 026	2.7	2.5	2.8	3.0	3.1	3.3
55	心　不　全	29 448	36 993	45 881	50 571	51 362	37 536	51.5	62.7	76.2	83.5	84.6	61.7
56	その他の心疾患	5 667	5 936	6 428	6 622	7 234	8 001	9.9	10.1	10.7	10.9	11.9	13.2
58～60	脳　血　管　疾　患	81 650	65 287	57 627	55 431	55 279	55 510	142.7	110.6	95.6	91.5	91.0	91.2
58	脳　出　血	27 149	19 471	16 569	15 913	15 933	15 639	47.5	33.0	27.5	26.3	26.2	25.7
59	脳　梗　塞	37 175	32 460	30 419	29 976	30 104	31 102	65.0	55.0	50.5	49.5	49.6	51.1
60	その他の脳血管疾患	17 326	13 356	10 639	9 542	9 242	8 769	30.3	22.6	17.7	15.7	15.2	14.4
61	循環系のその他の疾患	4 359	4 079	4 422	4 687	4 959	5 106	7.6	6.9	7.3	7.7	8.2	8.4
62	急　性　気　管　支　炎	962	694	662	596	605	584	1.7	1.2	1.1	1.0	1.0	1.0
63	肺　　炎	18 633	25 520	38 596	42 328	45 797	46 939	32.6	43.2	64.1	69.9	75.4	77.2

623

参考表
年次推移

表1－3　死因簡単分類別にみた昭和55・60・
Table 1-3　Deaths and death rates (per 100,000 population) by sex

男
Male

簡単分類番号 117 rubrics list code	死因[2] Causes of death	死亡数 Deaths						死亡率 Death rates					
		1980 昭和55年	1985 60年	1990 平成2年	1992 4年	1993 5年	1994 6年	1980 昭和55年	1985 60年	1990 平成2年	1992 4年	1993 5年	1994 6年
64	インフルエンザ	349	244	207	80	218	27	0.6	0.4	0.3	0.1	0.4	0.0
66～68	気管支炎, 肺気腫及び喘息	8 022	9 331	9 630	9 780	10 233	10 605	14.0	15.8	16.0	16.1	16.8	17.4
66	気 管 支 炎	2 410	2 920	2 910	2 817	2 797	2 997	4.2	4.9	4.8	4.6	4.6	4.9
67	肺 気 腫	1 742	2 635	3 308	3 655	3 973	4 298	3.0	4.5	5.5	6.0	6.5	7.1
68	喘 息	3 870	3 776	3 412	3 308	3 463	3 310	6.8	6.4	5.7	5.5	5.7	5.4
69	胃及び十二指腸潰瘍	3 349	2 428	1 933	1 917	1 965	1 956	5.9	4.1	3.2	3.2	3.2	3.2
70	虫 垂 炎	122	63	58	57	56	44	0.2	0.1	0.1	0.1	0.1	0.1
71	腹腔ヘルニア及び腸閉塞	1 278	1 195	1 408	1 590	1 626	1 813	2.2	2.0	2.3	2.6	2.7	3.0
72	胃炎,十二指腸炎及び慢性胃腸炎	878	464	338	285	279	267	1.5	0.8	0.6	0.5	0.5	0.4
73	慢性肝疾患及び肝硬変	11 941	12 054	11 516	11 545	11 505	11 208	20.9	20.4	19.1	19.1	18.9	18.4
74	肝疾患(肝硬変を除く)	1 407	1 537	1 740	1 849	1 774	1 754	2.5	2.6	2.9	3.1	2.9	2.9
76～77	腎炎,ネフローゼ症候群及びネフローゼ	5 066	6 753	8 319	8 739	9 022	8 994	8.9	11.4	13.8	14.4	14.9	14.8
76	急性糸球体腎炎及びネフローゼ症候群	978	1 498	1 867	2 055	2 074	2 002	1.7	2.5	3.1	3.4	3.4	3.3
77	そ の 他	4 088	5 255	6 452	6 684	6 948	6 992	7.1	8.9	10.7	11.0	11.4	11.5
78	前 立 腺 肥 大 症	497	357	201	168	178	154	0.9	0.6	0.3	0.3	0.3	0.3
79	直 接 産 科 的 死 亡	・	・	・	・	・	・	・	・	・	・	・	・
80	間 接 産 科 的 死 亡	・	・	・	・	・	・	・	・	・	・	・	・
81	先 天 異 常	2 597	2 041	1 890	1 885	1 805	1 710	4.5	3.5	3.1	3.1	3.0	2.8
82	出産時外傷, 低酸素症, 分娩仮死及びその他の呼吸器病態	2 293	1 367	724	578	551	586	4.0	2.3	1.2	1.0	0.9	1.0
84～87	その他の周産期の死因	1 101	526	319	296	288	329	1.9	0.9	0.5	0.5	0.5	0.5
84	新 生 児 破 傷 風	-	-	-	-	-	-	-	-	-	-	-	-
85	新 生 児 カンジダ感染	1	-	-	-	-	3	0.0	-	-	-	-	0.0
86	新 生 児 敗 血 症	75	68	43	63	36	47	0.1	0.1	0.1	0.1	0.1	0.1
87	そ の 他	1 025	458	276	233	252	279	1.8	0.8	0.5	0.4	0.4	0.5
88	精神病の記載のない老衰	11 244	9 669	8 054	7 613	7 324	7 333	19.7	16.4	13.4	12.6	12.1	12.1
89	その他のすべての疾患	14 461	17 516	23 034	25 494	27 048	27 568	25.3	29.7	38.2	42.1	44.5	45.3
91～101	損 傷 及 び 中 毒	35 933	38 908	36 664	39 288	39 439	40 710	62.8	65.9	60.9	64.8	64.9	66.9
91	頭 蓋 骨 折	5 693	4 928	4 311	4 195	3 927	3 852	10.0	8.3	7.2	6.9	6.5	6.3
92	その他の骨の骨折	1 641	1 690	1 842	1 799	1 811	1 804	2.9	2.9	3.1	3.0	3.0	3.0
93	頭蓋内損傷(頭蓋骨折を伴うものを除く)	4 434	5 125	5 929	6 647	6 485	6 452	7.8	8.7	9.8	11.0	10.7	10.6
94	胸,腹及び骨盤の内部損傷	2 945	3 363	3 521	3 583	3 708	3 600	5.1	5.7	5.8	5.9	6.1	5.9
95	開 放 創	605	683	694	690	683	719	1.1	1.2	1.2	1.1	1.1	1.2

Reference Table

平成 2・4～6年の性別死亡数及び率 [1]（人口10万対）（つづき）
and causes of death（the 117 rubrics list）：Japan, 1980, 1985, 1990, 1992-1994－CON.

男
Male

簡 単分類番号 117 rubrics list code	死 因 [2] Causes of death	死 亡 数 Deaths						死 亡 率 Death rates					
		1980 昭和55年	1985 60年	1990 平成2年	1992 4年	1993 5年	1994 6年	1980 昭和55年	1985 60年	1990 平成2年	1992 4年	1993 5年	1994 6年
96	熱　　　　傷	1 471	1 374	1 321	1 409	1 408	1 484	2.6	2.3	2.2	2.3	2.3	2.4
97	神経及び脊髄の損傷	308	340	377	397	382	460	0.5	0.6	0.6	0.7	0.6	0.8
98	中 毒 及 び 毒 作 用	3 146	3 910	2 241	2 365	2 486	2 338	5.5	6.6	3.7	3.9	4.1	3.8
99	溺　　　　死	4 208	3 949	3 690	3 748	4 180	4 174	7.4	6.7	6.1	6.2	6.9	6.9
100	窒 息 及 び 絞 首	7 635	9 619	7 776	8 949	8 612	9 171	13.3	16.3	12.9	14.8	14.2	15.1
101	そ の 他 の 損 傷	3 847	3 927	4 962	5 506	5 757	6 656	6.7	6.7	8.2	9.1	9.5	10.9
	（　再　掲　）												
E104～E117	損傷及び中毒の外因	35 933	38 908	36 664	39 288	39 439	40 710	62.8	65.9	60.9	64.8	64.9	66.9
E104～E114	不慮の事故及び有害作用	21 153	21 318	22 199	23 606	23 397	24 082	37.0	36.1	36.8	39.0	38.5	39.6
E104	自 動 車 事 故	8 833	9 458	10 518	10 557	10 103	9 706	15.4	16.0	17.5	17.4	16.6	16.0
E105	自動車事故以外の交通事故	1 278	1 374	963	878	817	887	2.2	2.3	1.6	1.4	1.3	1.5
E106	不 慮 の 中 毒	499	567	352	341	330	328	0.9	1.0	0.6	0.6	0.5	0.5
E107	不 慮 の 墜 落	2 909	2 639	2 744	2 941	2 948	3 020	5.1	4.5	4.6	4.9	4.9	5.0
E108	火災及び火焔による不慮の事故	868	714	703	778	782	835	1.5	1.2	1.2	1.3	1.3	1.4
E109	天　　　　災	12	26	43	8	160	2	0.0	0.0	0.1	0.0	0.3	0.0
E110	不 慮 の 溺 死	2 454	2 200	1 958	2 007	2 191	2 321	4.3	3.7	3.2	3.3	3.6	3.8
E111	不 慮 の 機 械 的 窒 息	1 449	1 706	2 173	2 514	2 700	3 067	2.5	2.9	3.6	4.1	4.4	5.0
E112	不 慮 の 打 撲	627	449	464	423	399	414	1.1	0.8	0.8	0.7	0.7	0.7
E113	工業性を主とする不慮の事故	1 205	1 163	1 054	1 035	921	993	2.1	2.0	1.7	1.7	1.5	1.6
E114	その他の不慮の事故及び有害作用	1 019	1 022	1 227	2 124	2 046	2 509	1.8	1.7	2.0	3.5	3.4	4.1
E115	自　　　　殺	12 769	15 356	12 316	13 516	13 540	14 058	22.3	26.0	20.4	22.3	22.3	23.1
E116	他　　　　殺	656	581	428	442	487	498	1.1	1.0	0.7	0.7	0.8	0.8
E117	そ の 他 の 外 因	1 355	1 653	1 721	1 724	2 015	2 072	2.4	2.8	2.9	2.8	3.3	3.4
（再掲）													
1～26	感染症及び寄生虫症	7 527	7 086	7 165	7 876	8 301	9 048	13.2	12.0	11.9	13.0	13.7	14.9
5～6	結　　　　核	4 715	3 442	2 745	2 514	2 424	2 290	8.2	5.8	4.6	4.1	4.0	3.8
46,51～52,54～56	心　疾　患	64 103	71 766	81 774	86 384	88 309	78 868	112.1	121.5	135.7	142.6	145.4	129.6
46,54	慢性リウマチ性心疾患及び心内膜の慢性疾患	2 101	1 968	2 116	2 204	2 297	2 425	3.7	3.3	3.5	3.6	3.8	4.0
62～63,66	肺 炎 及 び 気 管 支 炎	22 005	29 134	42 168	45 741	49 199	50 520	38.5	49.3	70.0	75.5	81.0	83.0
62,66	気 管 支 炎	3 372	3 614	3 572	3 413	3 402	3 581	5.9	6.1	5.9	5.6	5.6	5.9
79～80	妊 産 婦 死 亡	・	・	・	・	・	・	・	・	・	・	・	・
4,72	胃 腸 炎	1 539	908	633	607	617	646	2.7	1.5	1.1	1.0	1.0	1.1

625

参考表
年次推移

表 1 － 3　死因簡単分類別にみた昭和55・60・
Table 1-3　Deaths and death rates（per 100,000 population）by sex

女
Female

簡　　単分類番号117rubricslist code	死　　因[2]Causes of death	死　　亡　　数Deaths						死　　亡　　率Death rates					
		1980昭和55年	198560年	1990平成2年	19924年	19935年	19946年	1980昭和55年	198560年	1990平成2年	19924年	19935年	19946年
	総　　数　　Total	332 157	344 514	376 587	391 099	402 070	399 853	561.8	562.7	602.8	622.0	637.6	632.4
1	コ　レ　ラ	-	-	-	-	-	-	-	-	-	-	-	-
2	腸　チ　フ　ス	-	-	-	-	-	1	-	-	-	-	-	0.0
3	細菌性赤痢及びアメーバ症	-	-	2	-	-	-	-	-	0.0	-	-	-
4	腸炎及びその他の下痢性疾患	912	623	426	432	411	558	1.5	1.0	0.7	0.7	0.7	0.9
5	呼　吸　系　の　結　核	1 589	1 151	826	739	723	713	2.7	1.9	1.3	1.2	1.1	1.1
6	そ　の　他　の　結　核	135	99	93	94	102	91	0.2	0.2	0.1	0.1	0.2	0.1
7	ら　　　　　　　い	-	-	-	-	-	-	-	-	-	-	-	-
8	ジ　フ　テ　リ　ア	-	-	-	-	1	-	-	-	-	-	0.0	-
9	百　　日　　咳	10	4	2	-	1	2	0.0	0.0	0.0	-	0.0	0.0
10	猩　　紅　　熱	-	-	-	-	-	-	-	-	-	-	-	-
11	髄　膜　炎　菌　感　染	2	1	3	-	-	-	0.0	0.0	0.0	-	-	-
12	破傷風(新生児破傷風を除く)	17	13	15	6	8	3	0.0	0.0	0.0	0.0	0.0	0.0
13	敗血症(新生児敗血症を除く)	694	1 376	1 866	2 154	2 028	2 495	1.2	2.2	3.0	3.4	3.2	3.9
14	急　性　灰　白　髄　炎	-	-	-	-	-	-	-	-	-	-	-	-
15	痘　　　　　瘡	-	-	-	-	-	-	-	-	-	-	-	-
16	麻　　　　疹	28	16	26	3	6	6	0.0	0.0	0.0	0.0	0.0	0.0
17	日　本　脳　炎	8	4	4	-	-	1	0.0	0.0	0.0	-	-	0.0
18	ウ　イ　ル　ス　肝　炎 B	44	73	104	124	144	176	0.1	0.1	0.2	0.2	0.2	0.3
19	その他のウイルス肝炎	427	472	397	670	854	1 116	0.7	0.8	0.6	1.1	1.4	1.8
20	発疹チフス及びその他のリケッチア症	1	1	1	2	2	1	0.0	0.0	0.0	0.0	0.0	0.0
21	マ　ラ　リ　ア	1	-	-	-	-	-	0.0	-	-	-	-	-
22	梅　　　　毒	59	22	5	6	10	11	0.1	0.0	0.0	0.0	0.0	0.0
23	カンジダ症(新生児カンジダ症を除く)	17	20	41	51	49	39	0.0	0.0	0.1	0.1	0.1	0.1
24	日　本　住　血　吸　虫　症	4	1	3	2	-	2	0.0	0.0	0.0	0.0	-	0.0
25	フ　ィ　ラ　リ　ア　症	2	2	1	-	1	-	0.0	0.0	0.0	-	0.0	-
26	その他の感染症及び寄生虫症	461	662	1 026	1 176	1 293	1 448	0.8	1.1	1.6	1.9	2.1	2.3
28～37	悪　性　新　生　物	68 263	77 054	87 018	92 243	93 485	96 774	115.5	125.9	139.3	146.7	148.3	153.1
28	食　　道	1 243	1 151	1 270	1 297	1 306	1 365	2.1	1.9	2.0	2.1	2.1	2.2
29	胃	19 598	18 756	17 562	17 534	17 313	17 227	33.2	30.6	28.1	27.9	27.5	27.2
30	直腸,直腸S状結腸移行部及び肛門	2 984	3 291	3 701	3 933	3 841	3 836	5.0	5.4	5.9	6.3	6.1	6.1
31	肝	4 472	5 584	6 959	7 428	7 705	7 913	7.6	9.1	11.1	11.8	12.2	12.5

626

Reference Table

平成2・4～6年の性別死亡数及び率[1] （人口10万対）（つづき）
and causes of death（the 117 rubrics list）: Japan, 1980, 1985, 1990, 1992-1994－CON.

女
Female

簡 単 分類番号 117 rubrics list code	死 因[2] Causes of death	死 亡 数 Deaths						死 亡 率 Death rates					
		1980 昭和55年	1985 60年	1990 平成2年	1992 4年	1993 5年	1994 6年	1980 昭和55年	1985 60年	1990 平成2年	1992 4年	1993 5年	1994 6年
32	膵	3 352	4 488	6 001	6 337	6 574	6 696	5.7	7.3	9.6	10.1	10.4	10.6
33	気管，気管支及び肺	5 856	7 753	9 614	10 940	11 129	11 752	9.9	12.7	15.4	17.4	17.6	18.6
34	乳 房	4 141	4 922	5 848	6 451	6 758	7 131	7.0	8.0	9.4	10.3	10.7	11.3
35	子 宮	5 465	4 912	4 600	4 665	4 445	4 575	9.2	8.0	7.4	7.4	7.0	7.2
36	白 血 病	1 943	2 196	2 408	2 356	2 469	2 562	3.3	3.6	3.9	3.7	3.9	4.1
37	そ の 他	19 209	24 001	29 055	31 302	31 945	33 717	32.5	39.2	46.5	49.8	50.7	53.3
38	良性及び性質不詳の新生物	2 710	2 918	3 195	3 080	3 256	3 147	4.6	4.8	5.1	4.9	5.2	5.0
39	糖 尿 病	4 449	4 922	4 979	5 065	5 267	5 596	7.5	8.0	8.0	8.1	8.4	8.9
40	栄 養 欠 乏 症	203	227	266	254	323	379	0.3	0.4	0.4	0.4	0.5	0.6
41	貧 血	814	897	908	892	889	933	1.4	1.5	1.5	1.4	1.4	1.5
42	精 神 障 害	1 495	1 591	1 805	1 734	1 814	1 946	2.5	2.6	2.9	2.8	2.9	3.1
43	髄 膜 炎	280	266	206	177	195	208	0.5	0.4	0.3	0.3	0.3	0.3
44	中枢神経系の非炎症性疾患	1 970	2 218	2 408	2 508	2 759	2 920	3.3	3.6	3.9	4.0	4.4	4.6
45	急 性 リ ウ マ チ 熱	97	28	19	42	24	31	0.2	0.0	0.0	0.1	0.0	0.0
46	慢性リウマチ性心疾患	1 134	1 128	924	883	903	912	1.9	1.8	1.5	1.4	1.4	1.4
48～49	高 血 圧 性 疾 患	9 257	7 709	5 847	5 514	5 243	5 114	15.7	12.6	9.4	8.8	8.3	8.1
48	高 血 圧 性 心 疾 患	6 685	5 692	4 424	4 218	3 969	3 589	11.3	9.3	7.1	6.7	6.3	5.7
49	その他の高血圧性疾患	2 572	2 017	1 423	1 296	1 274	1 525	4.4	3.3	2.3	2.1	2.0	2.4
51～52	虚 血 性 心 疾 患	21 460	22 615	24 088	24 137	24 498	26 975	36.3	36.9	38.6	38.4	38.9	42.7
51	急 性 心 筋 梗 塞	11 882	12 902	14 050	13 983	14 506	17 914	20.1	21.1	22.5	22.2	23.0	28.3
52	その他の虚血性心疾患	9 578	9 713	10 038	10 154	9 992	9 061	16.2	15.9	16.1	16.1	15.8	14.3
54～56	肺循環疾患及びその他の型の心疾患	36 808	45 588	58 692	64 142	66 587	52 824	62.3	74.5	93.9	102.0	105.6	83.5
54	心 内 膜 の 慢 性 疾 患	1 991	2 102	2 521	2 676	2 892	3 135	3.4	3.4	4.0	4.3	4.6	5.0
55	心 不 全	30 112	38 317	50 197	55 225	57 103	42 266	50.9	62.6	80.4	87.8	90.6	66.8
56	そ の 他 の 心 疾 患	4 705	5 169	5 974	6 241	6 592	7 423	8.0	8.4	9.6	9.9	10.5	11.7
58～60	脳 血 管 疾 患	80 667	69 707	64 317	62 627	63 515	64 729	136.4	113.9	103.0	99.6	100.7	102.4
58	脳 出 血	23 643	17 406	14 251	13 898	14 022	13 854	40.0	28.4	22.8	22.1	22.2	21.9
59	脳 梗 塞	38 136	34 890	34 156	33 590	34 746	36 335	64.5	57.0	54.7	53.4	55.1	57.5
60	その他の脳血管疾患	18 888	17 411	15 910	15 139	14 747	14 540	31.9	28.4	25.5	24.1	23.4	23.0
61	循環系のその他の疾患	4 086	3 546	3 331	3 367	3 532	3 771	6.9	5.8	5.3	5.4	5.6	6.0
62	急 性 気 管 支 炎	1 023	750	668	597	751	701	1.7	1.2	1.1	0.9	1.2	1.1
63	肺 炎	14 418	19 555	29 598	31 946	35 341	36 415	24.4	31.9	47.4	50.8	56.0	57.6

参考表
年次推移

表 1 － 3　死因簡単分類別にみた昭和55・60・

Table 1-3　Deaths and death rates（per 100,000 population）by sex

女
Female

簡　単分類番号117 rubrics list code	死　因 2)Causes of death	死　亡　数 Deaths						死　亡　率 Death rates					
		1980昭和55年	198560年	1990平成2年	19924年	19935年	19946年	1980昭和55年	198560年	1990平成2年	19924年	19935年	19946年
64	インフルエンザ	369	279	241	97	301	38	0.6	0.5	0.4	0.2	0.5	0.1
66～68	気管支炎，肺気腫及び喘息	4 690	5 100	5 308	5 394	5 665	5 606	7.9	8.3	8.5	8.6	9.0	8.9
66	気　管　支　炎	1 795	1 927	2 101	2 022	2 118	2 198	3.0	3.1	3.4	3.2	3.4	3.5
67	肺　気　腫	395	609	672	751	800	863	0.7	1.0	1.1	1.2	1.3	1.4
68	喘　　息	2 500	2 564	2 535	2 621	2 747	2 545	4.2	4.2	4.1	4.2	4.4	4.0
69	胃及び十二指腸潰瘍	2 181	2 065	1 682	1 664	1 715	1 722	3.7	3.4	2.7	2.6	2.7	2.7
70	虫　垂　炎	98	57	37	30	37	42	0.2	0.1	0.1	0.0	0.1	0.1
71	腹腔ヘルニア及び腸閉塞	1 371	1 453	1 632	1 806	1 953	2 056	2.3	2.4	2.6	2.9	3.1	3.3
72	胃炎,十二指腸炎及び慢性胃腸炎	1 351	781	476	422	386	435	2.3	1.3	0.8	0.7	0.6	0.7
73	慢性肝疾患及び肝硬変	4 549	5 120	5 288	5 538	5 375	5 238	7.7	8.4	8.5	8.8	8.5	8.3
74	肝疾患(肝硬変を除く)	1 081	1 092	1 156	1 230	1 269	1 172	1.8	1.8	1.9	2.0	2.0	1.9
76～77	腎炎,ネフローゼ症候群及びネフローゼ	5 114	6 768	8 821	9 560	9 483	9 795	8.7	11.1	14.1	15.2	15.0	15.5
76	急性糸球体腎炎及びネフローゼ症候群	969	1 524	2 041	2 104	2 122	2 224	1.6	2.5	3.3	3.3	3.4	3.5
77	そ　の　他	4 145	5 244	6 780	7 456	7 361	7 571	7.0	8.6	10.9	11.9	11.7	12.0
78	前　立　腺　肥　大　症	・	・	・	・	・	・	・	・	・	・	・	・
79	直　接　産　科　的　死　亡	292	196	91	95	82	69	0.5	0.3	0.1	0.2	0.1	0.1
80	間　接　産　科　的　死　亡	31	30	14	16	9	7	0.1	0.0	0.0	0.0	0.0	0.0
81	先　天　異　常	2 288	1 908	1 681	1 649	1 612	1 577	3.9	3.1	2.7	2.6	2.6	2.5
82	出産時外傷, 低酸素症, 分娩仮死及びその他の呼吸器病態	1 595	1 061	496	439	406	389	2.7	1.7	0.8	0.7	0.6	0.6
84～87	その他の周産期の死因	804	394	255	251	250	269	1.4	0.6	0.4	0.4	0.4	0.4
84	新　生　児　破　傷　風	1	-	-	-	-	-	0.0	-	-	-	-	-
85	新　生　児　カンジダ感染	-	1	1	-	-	2	-	0.0	0.0	-	-	0.0
86	新　生　児　敗　血　症	70	57	45	37	38	45	0.1	0.1	0.1	0.1	0.1	0.1
87	そ　の　他	733	336	209	214	212	222	1.2	0.5	0.3	0.3	0.3	0.4
88	精神病の記載のない老衰	20 910	18 135	16 133	15 748	15 791	16 131	35.4	29.6	25.8	25.0	25.0	25.5
89	その他のすべての疾患	14 994	17 330	21 218	22 829	24 151	25 085	25.4	28.3	34.0	36.3	38.3	39.7
91～101	損　傷　及　び　中　毒	16 894	17 486	18 948	19 664	19 570	20 184	28.6	28.6	30.3	31.3	31.0	31.9
91	頭　蓋　骨　折	1 705	1 569	1 570	1 545	1 443	1 458	2.9	2.6	2.5	2.5	2.3	2.3
92	その他の骨の骨折	1 347	1 270	1 467	1 455	1 559	1 551	2.3	2.1	2.3	2.3	2.5	2.5
93	頭蓋内損傷(頭蓋骨折を伴うものを除く)	1 572	1 874	2 491	2 989	2 896	2 935	2.7	3.1	4.0	4.8	4.6	4.6
94	胸,腹及び骨盤の内部損傷	787	897	1 085	1 157	1 222	1 140	1.3	1.5	1.7	1.8	1.9	1.8
95	開　放　創	259	262	308	271	279	277	0.4	0.4	0.5	0.4	0.4	0.4

628

平成2・4～6年の性別死亡数及び率 [1]（人口10万対）（つづき）
and causes of death (the 117 rubrics list): Japan, 1980, 1985, 1990, 1992-1994−CON.

女
Female

簡単分類番号 117 rubrics list code	死因 [2] Causes of death	死亡数 Deaths						死亡率 Death rates					
		1980 昭和55年	1985 60年	1990 平成2年	1992 4年	1993 5年	1994 6年	1980 昭和55年	1985 60年	1990 平成2年	1992 4年	1993 5年	1994 6年
96	熱傷	1 010	858	960	894	783	883	1.7	1.4	1.5	1.4	1.2	1.4
97	神経及び脊髄の損傷	51	70	95	96	88	93	0.1	0.1	0.2	0.2	0.1	0.1
98	中毒及び毒作用	1 799	1 754	1 243	1 163	1 171	1 061	3.0	2.9	2.0	1.8	1.9	1.7
99	溺死	2 337	2 324	2 650	2 563	2 928	2 861	4.0	3.8	4.2	4.1	4.6	4.5
100	窒息及び絞首	4 409	4 691	4 352	4 298	3 996	3 975	7.5	7.7	7.0	6.8	6.3	6.3
101	その他の損傷	1 618	1 917	2 727	3 233	3 205	3 950	2.7	3.1	4.4	5.1	5.1	6.2
	（再掲）												
E104~E117	損傷及び中毒の外因	16 894	17 486	18 948	19 664	19 570	20 184	28.6	28.6	30.3	31.3	31.0	31.9
E104~E114	不慮の事故及び有害作用	8 064	8 279	9 923	11 071	11 320	12 033	13.6	13.5	15.9	17.6	18.0	19.0
E104	自動車事故	2 919	3 202	4 113	4 178	4 065	4 006	4.9	5.2	6.6	6.6	6.4	6.3
E105	自動車事故以外の交通事故	272	367	234	215	208	270	0.5	0.6	0.4	0.3	0.3	0.4
E106	不慮の中毒	277	263	209	185	184	169	0.5	0.4	0.3	0.3	0.3	0.3
E107	不慮の墜落	1 511	1 367	1 499	1 657	1 694	1 670	2.6	2.2	2.4	2.6	2.7	2.6
E108	火災及び火焰による不慮の事故	596	477	505	509	444	513	1.0	0.8	0.8	0.8	0.7	0.8
E109	天災	9	10	32	7	197	3	0.0	0.0	0.1	0.0	0.3	0.0
E110	不慮の溺死	983	996	1 188	1 262	1 468	1 547	1.7	1.6	1.9	2.0	2.3	2.4
E111	不慮の機械的窒息	728	891	1 287	1 683	1 705	2 082	1.2	1.5	2.1	2.7	2.7	3.3
E112	不慮の打撲	86	64	51	50	41	44	0.1	0.1	0.1	0.1	0.1	0.1
E113	工業性を主とする不慮の事故	258	159	150	150	144	160	0.4	0.3	0.2	0.2	0.2	0.3
E114	その他の不慮の事故及び有害作用	425	483	655	1 175	1 170	1 569	0.7	0.8	1.0	1.9	1.9	2.5
E115	自殺	7 773	8 027	7 772	7 377	6 976	6 865	13.1	13.1	12.4	11.7	11.1	10.9
E116	他殺	457	436	316	306	318	291	0.8	0.7	0.5	0.5	0.5	0.5
E117	その他の外因	600	744	937	910	956	995	1.0	1.2	1.5	1.4	1.5	1.6
（再掲）													
1~26	感染症及び寄生虫症	4 411	4 540	4 841	5 459	5 633	6 663	7.5	7.4	7.7	8.7	8.9	10.5
5~6	結核	1 724	1 250	919	833	825	804	2.9	2.0	1.5	1.3	1.3	1.3
46,51~52,54~56	心疾患	59 402	69 331	83 704	89 162	91 988	80 711	100.5	113.2	134.0	141.8	145.9	127.6
46,54	慢性リウマチ性心疾患及び心内膜の慢性疾患	3 125	3 230	3 445	3 559	3 795	4 047	5.3	5.3	5.5	5.7	6.0	6.4
62~63,66	肺炎及び気管支炎	17 236	22 232	32 367	34 565	38 210	39 314	29.2	36.3	51.8	55.0	60.6	62.2
62,66	気管支炎	2 818	2 677	2 769	2 619	2 869	2 899	4.8	4.4	4.4	4.2	4.5	4.6
79~80	妊産婦死亡	323	226	105	111	91	76	0.5	0.4	0.2	0.2	0.1	0.1
4,72	胃腸炎	2 263	1 404	902	854	797	993	3.8	2.3	1.4	1.4	1.3	1.6

参考表
年次推移

表 2 － 1　乳児死因簡単分類別にみた平成 7 年と
Table 2-1　Infant deaths and infant mortality rates (per 100,000 live

乳児死因簡単分類コード Code	死　因 Causes of death	死　亡　数 Infant deaths		死　亡　率 Infant mortality rates	
		1995 平成 7 年	1994 平成 6 年	1995 平成 7 年	1994 平成 6 年
	総　数　　　　Total	5 054	5 261	425.8	424.8
Ba01	腸管感染症	12	16	1.0	1.3
Ba02	敗　血　症（新生児の細菌性敗血症を除く）	107	120	9.0	9.7
Ba03	麻　疹	2	-	0.2	-
Ba04	ウイルス肝炎	6	8	0.5	0.6
Ba05	その他の感染症及び寄生虫症	20	…	1.7	…
Ba06	悪性新生物	27	32	2.3	2.6
Ba07	白　血　病	11	10	0.9	0.8
Ba08	その他の悪性新生物	16	…	1.3	…
Ba09	その他の新生物	15	…	1.3	…
Ba10	栄養失調症及びその他の栄養欠乏症	5	…	0.4	…
Ba11	代謝障害	44	…	3.7	…
Ba12	髄　膜　炎[1]	23	13	1.9	1.0
Ba13	脊髄性筋萎縮症及び関連症候群	18	12	1.5	1.0
Ba14	脳性麻痺	6	6	0.5	0.5
Ba15	心疾患（高血圧性を除く）[2]	143	157	12.0	12.7
Ba16	脳血管疾患[3]	23	…	1.9	…
Ba17	インフルエンザ	5	-	0.4	-
Ba18	肺　炎	114	104	9.6	8.4
Ba19	喘　息	16	7	1.3	0.6
Ba20	ヘルニア及び腸閉塞	7	10	0.6	0.8
Ba21	肝　疾　患	11	5	0.9	0.4
Ba22	腎　不　全[4]	8	96	0.7	7.8
Ba23	周産期に発生した病態	1 504	…	126.7	…
Ba24	妊娠期間及び胎児発育に関連する障害	76	98	6.4	7.9
Ba25	出産外傷	24	…	2.0	…
Ba26	出生時仮死	164	170	13.8	13.7
Ba27	新生児の呼吸窮＜促＞迫	188	…	15.8	…
Ba28	周産期に発生した肺出血	47	59	4.0	4.8
Ba29	周産期に発生した心血管障害	98	…	8.3	…

注：1)　平成 6 年は、細菌性髄膜脳炎及び細菌性髄膜脊髄炎を含む。
　　2)　平成 6 年は、心臓併発症を伴うリウマチ熱及び心臓併発症を伴う舞踏病を含まない。
　　3)　平成 6 年は、一過性脳虚血を含む。

630

Reference Table

6年の乳児死亡数及び率（出生10万対）
births) by causes of death : Japan, 1995 and 1994

乳児死因簡単分類コード Code	死　因 Causes of death	死　亡　数 Infant deaths		死　亡　率 Infant mortality rates	
		1995 平成7年	1994 平成6年	1995 平成7年	1994 平成6年
Ba30	その他の周産期に特異的な呼吸障害及び心血管障害	267	…	22.5	…
Ba31	新生児の細菌性敗血症	103	92	8.7	7.4
Ba32	その他の周産期に特異的な感染症	30	43	2.5	3.5
Ba33	胎児及び新生児の出血性障害及び血液障害	241	…	20.3	…
Ba34	その他の周産期に発生した病態	266	…	22.4	…
Ba35	先天奇形，変形及び染色体異常	1 786	…	150.5	…
Ba36	神経系の先天奇形	83	83	7.0	6.7
Ba37	心臓の先天奇形	647	637	54.5	51.4
Ba38	その他の循環器系の先天奇形	270	…	22.7	…
Ba39	呼吸器系の先天奇形	213	209	17.9	16.9
Ba40	消化器系の先天奇形	64	60	5.4	4.8
Ba41	筋骨格系の先天奇形及び変形	126	124	10.6	10.0
Ba42	その他の先天奇形及び変形	119	…	10.0	…
Ba43	染色体異常，他に分類されないもの	264	306	22.2	24.7
Ba44	乳幼児突然死症候群	526	468	44.3	37.8
Ba45	その他のすべての疾患	260	…	21.9	…
Ba46	不慮の事故	329	320	27.7	25.8
Ba47	交通事故	18	23	1.5	1.9
Ba48	転倒・転落	8	9	0.7	0.7
Ba49	不慮の溺死及び溺水	22	31	1.9	2.5
Ba50	胃内容物の誤えん及び気道閉塞に生じた食物等の誤えん＜吸引＞	107	120	9.0	9.7
Ba51	その他の不慮の窒息	124	104	10.4	8.4
Ba52	煙・火及び火炎への曝露	5	11	0.4	0.9
Ba53	有害物質による不慮の中毒及び有害物質への曝露	1	1	0.1	0.1
Ba54	その他の不慮の事故	44	21	3.7	1.7
Ba55	他　　殺	32	41	2.7	3.3
Ba56	その他の外因[5]	5	27	0.4	2.2

4）　平成6年は、先天性腎不全を含む。
5）　平成7年の外因の後遺症・医療事故は「Ba56 その他の外因」に含む。

参考表
年次推移

表 2 － 2　乳児死因簡単分類別にみた昭和55・60・平成 2・4～6年の乳児死亡数及び率 [1]（出生10万対）
Table 2-2　Infant deaths and infant mortality rates (per 100,000 live births) by causes of death (the 54 rubrics list) : Japan, 1980, 1985, 1990, 1992-1994

乳児簡単分類番号 54 rubrics list code	死因 [2] Causes of death	乳 児 死 亡 数 Infant deaths						乳児死亡率（出生10万対）Infant mortality rates (per 100,000 live births)					
		1980 昭和55年	1985 60年	1990 平成2年	1992 4年	1993 5年	1994 6年	1980 昭和55年	1985 60年	1990 平成2年	1992 4年	1993 5年	1994 6年
	総　数　Total	11 841	7 899	5 616	5 477	5 169	5 261	750.9	551.8	459.7	453.0	453.0	424.8
1	細菌性赤痢及びアメーバ症	-	-	-	-	-	-	-	-	-	-	-	-
2	腸炎及びその他の下痢性疾患	108	38	15	13	13	16	6.8	2.7	1.2	1.1	1.1	1.3
3	結　核	3	1	-	-	1	-	0.2	0.1	-	-	0.1	-
4	ジフテリア	-	-	-	-	-	-	-	-	-	-	-	-
5	百　日　咳	9	2	3	1	1	2	0.6	0.1	0.2	0.1	0.1	0.2
6	破傷風（新生児破傷風を含む）	1	-	-	-	-	-	0.1	-	-	-	-	-
7	敗血症（新生児敗血症を含む）	231	230	169	196	193	212	14.6	16.1	13.8	16.2	16.2	17.1
8	急性灰白髄炎	-	-	-	-	-	-	-	-	-	-	-	-
9	麻　疹	18	10	7	3	3	-	1.1	0.7	0.6	0.2	0.3	-
10	日　本　脳　炎	-	-	-	-	-	-	-	-	-	-	-	-
11	ウイルス肝炎	27	13	18	9	14	8	1.7	0.9	1.5	0.7	1.2	0.6
12	梅　毒	-	-	2	-	1	1	-	-	0.2	-	0.1	0.1
13	その他の感染症及び寄生虫症	24	21	28	27	27	34	1.5	1.5	2.3	2.2	2.3	2.7
15～16	悪性新生物	53	55	50	26	22	32	3.4	3.8	4.1	2.2	1.9	2.6
15	白　血　病	15	11	20	9	9	10	1.0	0.8	1.6	0.7	0.8	0.8
16	そ　の　他	38	44	30	17	13	22	2.4	3.1	2.5	1.4	1.1	1.8
17	良性及び性質不詳の新生物	38	36	19	23	30	15	2.4	2.5	1.6	1.9	2.5	1.2
18	栄養失調症	5	1	2	1	-	1	0.3	0.1	0.2	0.1	-	0.1
19	髄　膜　炎	132	74	25	27	24	13	8.4	5.2	2.0	2.2	2.0	1.0
20	脳性小児麻痺	37	17	6	6	5	6	2.3	1.2	0.5	0.5	0.4	0.5
21	心　疾　患	266	234	180	220	219	157	16.9	16.3	14.7	18.2	18.4	12.7
22	肺　炎	553	246	136	128	111	104	35.1	17.2	11.1	10.6	9.3	8.4
23	インフルエンザ	6	2	2	1	1	-	0.4	0.1	0.2	0.1	0.1	-
24	気　管　支　炎	35	22	12	12	5	15	2.2	1.5	1.0	1.0	0.4	1.2
25	腹腔ヘルニア及び腸閉塞	46	24	18	6	13	10	2.9	1.7	1.5	0.5	1.1	0.8
26	胃炎，十二指腸炎及び慢性胃腸炎	-	2	-	-	1	-	-	0.1	-	-	0.1	-
28～32	先　天　異　常	3 131	2 414	2 028	2 039	1 828	1 825	198.6	168.6	166.0	168.7	153.8	147.4
28	神経系の先天異常	281	161	102	82	79	83	17.8	11.2	8.3	6.8	6.6	6.7
29	心臓の先天異常	1 550	1 019	783	756	651	637	98.3	71.2	64.1	62.5	54.8	51.4
30	その他の循環系の先天異常	286	356	322	315	277	277	18.1	24.9	26.4	26.1	23.3	22.4
31	消化系の先天異常	348	153	88	76	73	60	22.1	10.7	7.2	6.3	6.1	4.8
32	その他の先天異常	666	725	733	810	748	768	42.2	50.6	60.0	67.0	62.9	62.0
33～36	母側病態による新生児の障害 [3]	-	-	-	-	-	-	-	-	-	-	-	-
38～39	出　産　時　外　傷	488	351	198	158	159	162	30.9	24.5	16.2	13.1	13.4	13.1
38	脳及び脊髄の損傷	459	326	186	149	155	150	29.1	22.8	15.2	12.3	13.0	12.1
39	その他及び詳細不明の損傷	29	25	12	9	4	12	1.8	1.7	1.0	0.7	0.3	1.0
40	低酸素症，分娩仮死及びその他の呼吸器病態	3 397	2 055	987	825	775	788	215.4	143.5	80.8	68.2	65.2	63.6
41	詳細不明の未熟児	658	185	66	62	84	86	41.7	12.9	5.4	5.1	7.1	6.9
42	同種免疫による新生児溶血性疾患	21	6	3	3	3	3	1.3	0.4	0.2	0.2	0.3	0.2
43	その他の周産期黄疸	35	21	9	8	3	12	2.2	1.5	0.7	0.7	0.3	1.0
44	新生児の出血	93	26	24	15	20	22	5.9	1.8	2.0	1.2	1.7	1.8
45	新生児出血性疾患	39	20	4	6	3	1	2.5	1.4	0.3	0.5	0.3	0.1
46	その他の新生児の異常（新生児破傷風，カンジダ感染及び敗血症を除く）	909	532	376	349	343	373	57.6	37.2	30.8	28.9	28.9	30.1
47	その他のすべての疾患	658	678	794	910	917	975	41.7	47.4	65.0	75.3	77.2	78.7
48	損傷及び中毒	820	583	435	403	350	388	52.0	40.7	35.6	33.3	29.5	31.3
E51～E54	損傷及び中毒の外因	820	583	435	403	350	388	52.0	40.7	35.6	33.3	29.5	31.3
E51～E53	不慮の事故及び有害作用	659	451	346	331	282	320	41.8	31.5	28.3	27.4	23.7	25.8
E51	食物及びその他の物体による窒息	199	182	112	121	112	120	12.6	12.7	9.2	10.0	9.4	9.7
E52	不慮の機械的窒息	285	165	135	119	91	104	18.1	11.5	11.1	9.8	7.7	8.4
E53	そ　の　他	175	104	99	91	79	96	11.1	7.3	8.1	7.5	6.6	7.8
E54	その他の外因	161	132	89	72	68	68	10.2	9.2	7.3	6.0	5.7	5.5

注：1)　平成6年人口動態統計上巻表6.13を転載したものである。
　　2)　死因はICD-9の乳児簡単分類による。
　　3)　33～36は一括して「母側病態による新生児の障害」とした。

632

参考表
年次推移

表 3 － 1　感染症分類（平成27年改正）別にみた
Table 3-1　Trends in deaths and death rates（per 100,000 population）by

感　染　症 分類コード Code[a]	死　　因 Causes of death	死　亡　数 Deaths	死　亡　率 Death rates（per 100,000 population）
		2015 平成27年	2015 平成27年
	総　数　　　Total	8 528	6.8
In101	エボラ出血熱	-	-
In102	クリミア・コンゴ出血熱	-	-
In103	痘そう	-	-
In104	南米出血熱	-	-
In105	ペスト	-	-
In106	マールブルグ病	-	-
In107	ラッサ熱	-	-
In201	急性灰白髄炎	-	-
In202	結　核	1 956	1.6
In203	ジフテリア	-	-
In204	重症急性呼吸器症候群 （病原体がベータコロナウイルス属 SARSコロナウイルスであるものに限る。）	-	-
In205	鳥インフルエンザ （特定鳥インフルエンザ（H5N1）に限る。）	-	-
In206	鳥インフルエンザ （特定鳥インフルエンザ（H7N9）に限る。）	-	-
In207	中東呼吸器症候群 （病原体がベータコロナウイルス属 MARSコロナウイルスであるものに限る。）	-	-
In301	コレラ	-	-
In302	細菌性赤痢	-	-
In303	腸管出血性大腸菌感染症	7	0.0
In304	腸チフス	-	-
In305	パラチフス	-	-
In401	E型肝炎	-	-
In402	ウエストナイル熱	-	-
In403	A型肝炎	8	0.0
In404	エキノコックス症	1	0.0
In405	黄　熱	-	-
In406	オウム病	-	-
In407	オムスク出血熱	-	-
In408	回帰熱	-	-
In409	キャサヌル森林病	-	-
In410	Q　熱	-	-
In411	狂犬病	-	-
In412	コクシジオイデス症	-	-
In413	サル痘	-	-
In414	腎症候性出血熱	-	-

注：1）　感染症の分類名は、「感染症の予防及び感染症の患者に対する医療に関する法律」（平成10年法律第114号。以下「感染症法」という。）、感染症法施行令（平成10年政令第420号）
　　　　及び感染症法施行規則（平成10年厚生省令第99号）に規定された疾病名であるため、必ずしもICD-10とは一致していない。
　　　　なお、本表は感染症法等の改正（平成27年1月21日施行）に基づく分類で表章している。

年次別死亡数及び率[1]（人口10万対）（平成27年）
causes of death（the list of infectious diseases revised in 2015）: Japan, 2015

感 染 症 分類コード Code[a]	死　　因 Causes of death	死　亡　数 Deaths 2015 平成27年	死　亡　率 Death rates（per 100,000 population） 2015 平成27年
In415	西部ウマ脳炎	-	-
In416	ダニ媒介脳炎	-	-
In417	炭疽	-	-
In418	つつが虫病	2	0. 0
In419	デング熱	-	-
In420	東部ウマ脳炎	-	-
In421	鳥インフルエンザ （特定鳥インフルエンザを除く。）	-	-
In422	ニパウイルス感染症	-	-
In423	日本紅斑熱	4	0. 0
In424	日本脳炎	1	0. 0
In425	ハンタウイルス肺症候群	-	-
In426	Ｂウイルス病	-	-
In427	鼻疽	-	-
In428	ブルセラ症	-	-
In429	ベネズエラウマ脳炎	-	-
In430	ヘンドラウイルス感染症	-	-
In431	発しんチフス	-	-
In432	ボツリヌス症（乳児ボツリヌス症を除く。）	-	-
In433	乳児ボツリヌス症	-	-
In434	マラリア	1	0. 0
In435	野兎病	-	-
In436	ライム病	-	-
In437	リッサウイルス感染症	-	-
In438	リフトバレー熱	-	-
In439	類鼻疽	-	-
In440	レジオネラ症	59	0. 0
In441	レプトスピラ症	1	0. 0
In442	ロッキー山紅斑熱	-	-
In443	チクングニア熱	-	-
In444	重症熱性血小板減少症候群 （病原体がフレボウイルス属 SFTSウイルスであるものに限る。）	11	0. 0
In501	アメーバ赤痢	5	0. 0
In502	ＲＳウイルス感染症	19	0. 0
In503	咽頭結膜熱	-	-
In504	インフルエンザ （鳥インフルエンザ及び 新型インフルエンザ等感染症を除く。）	2 262	1. 8
In505	急性ウイルス性肝炎 （Ｅ型肝炎及びＡ型肝炎を除く。）	248	0. 2
In506	Ａ群溶血性レンサ球菌咽頭炎	-	-
In507	感染性胃腸炎	2 293	1. 8

Note : a) Code see page 600.

参考表
年次推移

表 3 － 1　感染症分類（平成27年改正）別にみた年次別死亡数及び率 [1]（人口10万対）（平成27年）（つづき）

Table 3-1　Trends in deaths and death rates（per 100,000 population）by causes of death （the list of infectious diseases revised in 2015）: Japan, 2015－CON.

感 染 症 分類コード Code[a]	死 因 Causes of death	死 亡 数 Deaths 2015 平成27年	死 亡 率 Death rates (per 100,000 population) 2015 平成27年
In508	急性出血性結膜炎	-	-
In509	急性脳炎 （ウエストナイル脳炎、西部ウマ脳炎、ダニ媒介脳炎、東部ウマ脳炎、日本脳炎、ベネズエラウマ脳炎及びリフトバレー熱を除く。）	92	0.1
In510	クラミジア肺炎（オウム病を除く。）	6	0.0
In511	クリプトスポリジウム症	-	-
In512	クロイツフェルト・ヤコブ病	263	0.2
In513	劇症型溶血性レンサ球菌感染症	30	0.0
In514	後天性免疫不全症候群	56	0.0
In515	細菌性髄膜炎	149	0.1
In516	ジアルジア症	-	-
In517	水　痘	10	0.0
In518	侵襲性髄膜炎菌感染症	-	-
In519	性器クラミジア感染症	-	-
In520	性器ヘルペスウイルス感染症	-	-
In521	尖圭コンジローマ	-	-
In522	先天性風しん症候群	-	-
In523	手足口病	-	-
In524	伝染性紅斑	-	-
In525	突発性発しん	-	-
In526	梅　毒	9	0.0
In527	破傷風	9	0.0
In528	バンコマイシン耐性黄色ブドウ球菌感染症	-	-
In529	バンコマイシン耐性腸球菌感染症	-	-
In530	百日咳	1	0.0
In531	風しん	-	-
In532	ペニシリン耐性肺炎球菌感染症	-	-
In533	ヘルパンギーナ	-	-
In534	マイコプラズマ肺炎	24	0.0
In535	麻しん（成人麻しんを除く。）	-	-
In536	成人麻しん	-	-
In537	無菌性髄膜炎	12	0.0
In538	メチシリン耐性黄色ブドウ球菌感染症	893	0.7
In539	薬剤耐性緑膿菌感染症	8	0.0
In540	流行性角結膜炎	-	-
In541	流行性耳下腺炎	1	0.0
In542	淋菌感染症	-	-
In543	薬剤耐性アシネトバクター感染症	-	-
In544	侵襲性インフルエンザ菌感染症	3	0.0
In545	侵襲性肺炎球菌感染症	58	0.0
In546	カルバペネム耐性腸内細菌科細菌感染症	1	0.0
In547	播種性クリプトコックス症	25	0.0
In601	新型インフルエンザ等感染症	-	-

参考表
年次推移

表 3 － 2 　感染症分類（平成25年改正）別にみた
Table 3-2　Trends in deaths and death rates（per 100,000 population）by

感 染 症 分類コード Code[a]	死　　因 Causes of death	死　亡　数 Deaths		死　亡　率 Death rates（per 100,000 population）	
		2013 平成25年	2014 平成26年	2013 平成25年	2014 平成26年
	総　　数　　　Total	8 303	7 485	6.6	6.0
In101	エボラ出血熱	-	-	-	-
In102	クリミア・コンゴ出血熱	-	-	-	-
In103	痘そう	-	-	-	-
In104	南米出血熱	-	-	-	-
In105	ペスト	-	-	-	-
In106	マールブルグ病	-	-	-	-
In107	ラッサ熱	-	-	-	-
In201	急性灰白髄炎	-	-	-	-
In202	結　核	2 087	2 100	1.7	1.7
In203	ジフテリア	-	-	-	-
In204	重症急性呼吸器症候群 （病原体がコロナウイルス属 SARSコロナウイルスであるものに限る）	-	-	-	-
In205	鳥インフルエンザ （鳥インフルエンザ（H5N1）に限る）	-	-	-	-
In301	コレラ	-	-	-	-
In302	細菌性赤痢	-	-	-	-
In303	腸管出血性大腸菌感染症	10	1	0.0	0.0
In304	腸チフス	-	-	-	-
In305	パラチフス	-	-	-	-
In401	E型肝炎	1	3	0.0	0.0
In402	ウエストナイル熱	-	-	-	-
In403	A型肝炎	5	5	0.0	0.0
In404	エキノコックス症	2	-	0.0	-
In405	黄　熱	-	-	-	-
In406	オウム病	-	-	-	-
In407	オムスク出血熱	-	-	-	-
In408	回帰熱	-	-	-	-
In409	キャサヌル森林病	-	-	-	-
In410	Q　熱	-	-	-	-
In411	狂犬病	-	-	-	-
In412	コクシジオイデス症	-	-	-	-
In413	サル痘	-	-	-	-
In414	腎症候性出血熱	-	-	-	-

注：1）　感染症の分類名は、「感染症の予防及び感染症の患者に対する医療に関する法律」（平成10年法律第114号。以下「感染症法」という。）、感染症法施行令（平成10年政令第420号）
及び感染症法施行規則（平成10年厚生省令第99号）に規定された疾病名であるため、必ずしもICD-10とは一致していない。
なお、本表は感染症法等の改正（平成25年4月1日施行）に基づく分類で表章している。

Reference Table

年次別死亡数及び率[1]（人口10万対）（平成25・26年）
causes of death（the list of infectious diseases revised in 2013）: Japan, 2013－2014

感 染 症 分類コード Code[a]	死　因 Causes of death	死　亡　数 Deaths		死　亡　率 Death rates (per 100,000 population)	
		2013 平成25年	2014 平成26年	2013 平成25年	2014 平成26年
In415	西部ウマ脳炎	-	-	-	-
In416	ダニ媒介脳炎	-	-	-	-
In417	炭　疽	-	-	-	-
In418	つつが虫病	1	1	0.0	0.0
In419	デング熱	-	-	-	-
In420	東部ウマ脳炎	-	-	-	-
In421	鳥インフルエンザ （鳥インフルエンザ（H5N1）を除く）	-	-	-	-
In422	ニパウイルス感染症	-	-	-	-
In423	日本紅斑熱	1	-	0.0	-
In424	日本脳炎	2	-	0.0	-
In425	ハンタウイルス肺症候群	-	-	-	-
In426	Ｂウイルス病	-	-	-	-
In427	鼻疽	-	-	-	-
In428	ブルセラ症	-	-	-	-
In429	ベネズエラウマ脳炎	-	-	-	-
In430	ヘンドラウイルス感染症	-	-	-	-
In431	発しんチフス	-	-	-	-
In432	ボツリヌス症（乳児ボツリヌス症を除く）	-	-	-	-
In433	乳児ボツリヌス症	-	-	-	-
In434	マラリア	-	-	-	-
In435	野兎病	-	-	-	-
In436	ライム病	-	-	-	-
In437	リッサウイルス感染症	-	-	-	-
In438	リフトバレー熱	-	-	-	-
In439	類鼻疽	-	-	-	-
In440	レジオネラ症	64	65	0.1	0.1
In441	レプトスピラ症	-	1	-	0.0
In442	ロッキー山紅斑熱	-	-	-	-
In443	チクングニア熱	-	-	-	-
In444	重症熱性血小板減少症候群 （病原体がフレボウイルス属 SFTSウイルスであるものに限る）	8	13	0.0	0.0
In501	アメーバ赤痢	3	3	0.0	0.0
In502	ＲＳウイルス感染症	16	22	0.0	0.0
In503	咽頭結膜熱	-	-	-	-
In504	インフルエンザ （鳥インフルエンザ及び 新型インフルエンザ等感染症を除く）	1 514	1 130	1.2	0.9
In505	急性ウイルス性肝炎 （E型肝炎及びA型肝炎を除く）	310	240	0.2	0.2
In506	A群溶血性レンサ球菌咽頭炎	-	-	-	-
In507	感染性胃腸炎	2 569	2 405	2.0	1.9

Note : a) Code see page 601.

参考表
年次推移

表 3－2　感染症分類（平成25年改正）別にみた年次別死亡数及び率 [1]（人口10万対）（平成25・26年）（つづき）

Table 3-2　Trends in deaths and death rates（per 100,000 population）by causes of death（the list of infectious diseases revised in 2013）: Japan, 2013-2014－CON.

感 染 症 分類コード Code[a]	死　因 Causes of death	死　亡　数 Deaths		死　亡　率 Death rates (per 100,000 population)	
		2013 平成25年	2014 平成26年	2013 平成25年	2014 平成26年
In508	急性出血性結膜炎	-	-	-	-
In509	急性脳炎 （ウエストナイル脳炎、西部ウマ脳炎、ダニ媒介脳炎、東部ウマ脳炎、日本脳炎、ベネズエラウマ脳炎及びリフトバレー熱を除く）	99	82	0.1	0.1
In510	クラミジア肺炎（オウム病を除く）	10	9	0.0	0.0
In511	クリプトスポリジウム症	-	-	-	-
In512	クロイツフェルト・ヤコブ病	252	245	0.2	0.2
In513	劇症型溶血性レンサ球菌感染症	20	12	0.0	0.0
In514	後天性免疫不全症候群	45	45	0.0	0.0
In515	細菌性髄膜炎	136	146	0.1	0.1
In516	ジアルジア症	-	-	-	-
In517	水　痘	10	5	0.0	0.0
In518	侵襲性髄膜炎菌感染症	2	-	0.0	-
In519	性器クラミジア感染症	-	-	-	-
In520	性器ヘルペスウイルス感染症	-	-	-	-
In521	尖圭コンジローマ	-	-	-	-
In522	先天性風しん症候群	2	1	0.0	0.0
In523	手足口病	-	-	-	-
In524	伝染性紅斑	-	-	-	-
In525	突発性発しん	-	-	-	-
In526	梅　毒	6	18	0.0	0.0
In527	破傷風	5	9	0.0	0.0
In528	バンコマイシン耐性黄色ブドウ球菌感染症	-	-	-	-
In529	バンコマイシン耐性腸球菌感染症	-	-	-	-
In530	百日咳	1	1	0.0	0.0
In531	風しん	1	-	0.0	-
In532	ペニシリン耐性肺炎球菌感染症	-	-	-	-
In533	ヘルパンギーナ	-	-	-	-
In534	マイコプラズマ肺炎	40	27	0.0	0.0
In535	麻しん（成人麻しんを除く）	1	-	0.0	-
In536	成人麻しん	1	1	0.0	0.0
In537	無菌性髄膜炎	13	7	0.0	0.0
In538	メチシリン耐性黄色ブドウ球菌感染症	1 024	841	0.8	0.7
In539	薬剤耐性緑膿菌感染症	9	8	0.0	0.0
In540	流行性角結膜炎	-	-	-	-
In541	流行性耳下腺炎	2	2	0.0	0.0
In542	淋菌感染症	-	1	-	0.0
In543	薬剤耐性アシネトバクター感染症	-	1	-	0.0
In544	侵襲性インフルエンザ菌感染症	1	-	0.0	-
In545	侵襲性肺炎球菌感染症	30	35	0.0	0.0
In601	新型インフルエンザ等感染症	-	-	-	-

参考表
年次推移

表 3 － 3　感染症分類（平成24年改正）別にみた
Table 3-3　Trends in deaths and death rates（per 100,000 population）by

感 染 症 分類コード Code[a]	死 因 Causes of death	死 亡 数 Deaths	死 亡 率 Death rates（per 100,000 population）
		2012 平成24年	2012 平成24年
	総　数　　　Total	8 374	6.6
In101	エボラ出血熱	-	-
In102	クリミア・コンゴ出血熱	-	-
In103	痘そう	-	-
In104	南米出血熱	-	-
In105	ペスト	-	-
In106	マールブルグ病	-	-
In107	ラッサ熱	-	-
In201	急性灰白髄炎	-	-
In202	結核	2 110	1.7
In203	ジフテリア	-	-
In204	重症急性呼吸器症候群 （病原体がコロナウイルス属 ＳＡＲＳコロナウイルスであるものに限る）	-	-
In205	鳥インフルエンザ （鳥インフルエンザ（Ｈ５Ｎ１）に限る）	-	-
In301	コレラ	-	-
In302	細菌性赤痢	-	-
In303	腸管出血性大腸菌感染症	8	0.0
In304	腸チフス	-	-
In305	パラチフス	-	-
In401	Ｅ型肝炎	2	0.0
In402	ウエストナイル熱	-	-
In403	Ａ型肝炎	3	0.0
In404	エキノコックス症	4	0.0
In405	黄熱	-	-
In406	オウム病	-	-
In407	オムスク出血熱	-	-
In408	回帰熱	-	-
In409	キャサヌル森林病	-	-
In410	Ｑ熱	-	-
In411	狂犬病	-	-
In412	コクシジオイデス症	-	-
In413	サル痘	-	-
In414	腎症候性出血熱	-	-

注：1）　感染症の分類名は、「感染症の予防及び感染症の患者に対する医療に関する法律」（平成10年法律第114号。以下「感染症法」という。）、感染症法施行令（平成10年政令第420号）
　　　　及び感染症法施行規則（平成10年厚生省令第99号）に規定された疾病名であるため、必ずしもICD-10とは一致していない。
　　　　なお、本表は感染症法等の改正（平成23年２月１日施行）に基づく分類で表章している。

Reference Table

年次別死亡数及び率[1]（人口10万対）（平成24年）
causes of death（the list of infectious diseases revised in 2012）: Japan, 2012

感染症 分類コード Code[a]	死　因 Causes of death	死　亡　数 Deaths 2012 平成24年	死　亡　率 Death rates（per 100,000 population） 2012 平成24年
In415	西部ウマ脳炎	-	-
In416	ダニ媒介脳炎	-	-
In417	炭疽	-	-
In418	つつが虫病	3	0.0
In419	デング熱	-	-
In420	東部ウマ脳炎	-	-
In421	鳥インフルエンザ （鳥インフルエンザ（H5N1）を除く）	-	-
In422	ニパウイルス感染症	-	-
In423	日本紅斑熱	2	0.0
In424	日本脳炎	-	-
In425	ハンタウイルス肺症候群	-	-
In426	Bウイルス病	-	-
In427	鼻疽	-	-
In428	ブルセラ症	-	-
In429	ベネズエラウマ脳炎	-	-
In430	ヘンドラウイルス感染症	-	-
In431	発しんチフス	-	-
In432	ボツリヌス症（乳児ボツリヌス症を除く）	1	0.0
In433	乳児ボツリヌス症	-	-
In434	マラリア	-	-
In435	野兎病	-	-
In436	ライム病	-	-
In437	リッサウイルス感染症	-	-
In438	リフトバレー熱	-	-
In439	類鼻疽	-	-
In440	レジオネラ症	58	0.0
In441	レプトスピラ症	1	0.0
In442	ロッキー山紅斑熱	-	-
In443	チクングニア熱	-	-
In501	アメーバ赤痢	3	0.0
In502	RSウイルス感染症	34	0.0
In503	咽頭結膜熱	-	-
In504	インフルエンザ （鳥インフルエンザ及び 新型インフルエンザ等感染症を除く）	1 275	1.0
In505	急性ウイルス性肝炎 （E型肝炎及びA型肝炎を除く）	304	0.2
In506	A群溶血性レンサ球菌咽頭炎	1	0.0
In507	感染性胃腸炎	2 698	2.1

Note : a）Code see page 602.

参考表
年次推移

表 3 - 3　感染症分類（平成24年改正）別にみた年次別死亡数及び率[1]（人口10万対）（平成24年）（つづき）

Table 3-3　Trends in deaths and death rates (per 100,000 population) by causes of death (the list of infectious diseases revised in 2012) : Japan, 2012－CON.

感　染　症 分類コード Code[a]	死　因 Causes of death	死　亡　数 Deaths 2012 平成24年	死　亡　率 Death rates (per 100,000 population) 2012 平成24年
In508	急性出血性結膜炎	-	-
In509	急性脳炎 （ウエストナイル脳炎、西部ウマ脳炎、 ダニ媒介脳炎、東部ウマ脳炎、日本脳炎、 ベネズエラウマ脳炎及びリフトバレー熱を除く）	111	0.1
In510	クラミジア肺炎（オウム病を除く）	5	0.0
In511	クリプトスポリジウム症	-	-
In512	クロイツフェルト・ヤコブ病	241	0.2
In513	劇症型溶血性レンサ球菌感染症	23	0.0
In514	後天性免疫不全症候群	50	0.0
In515	細菌性髄膜炎	173	0.1
In516	ジアルジア症	-	-
In517	水痘	5	0.0
In518	髄膜炎菌性髄膜炎	-	-
In519	性器クラミジア感染症	-	-
In520	性器ヘルペスウイルス感染症	-	-
In521	尖圭コンジローマ	-	-
In522	先天性風しん症候群	-	-
In523	手足口病	-	-
In524	伝染性紅斑	-	-
In525	突発性発しん	-	-
In526	梅毒	9	0.0
In527	破傷風	8	0.0
In528	バンコマイシン耐性黄色ブドウ球菌感染症	-	-
In529	バンコマイシン耐性腸球菌感染症	-	-
In530	百日咳	3	0.0
In531	風しん	-	-
In532	ペニシリン耐性肺炎球菌感染症	-	-
In533	ヘルパンギーナ	-	-
In534	マイコプラズマ肺炎	47	0.0
In535	麻しん（成人麻しんを除く）	-	-
In536	成人麻しん	-	-
In537	無菌性髄膜炎	13	0.0
In538	メチシリン耐性黄色ブドウ球菌感染症	1 157	0.9
In539	薬剤耐性緑膿菌感染症	22	0.0
In540	流行性角結膜炎	-	-
In541	流行性耳下腺炎	-	-
In542	淋菌感染症	-	-
In543	薬剤耐性アシネトバクター感染症	-	-
In601	新型インフルエンザ等感染症	-	-

参考表
年次推移

表 3 － 4　感染症分類（平成20年改正）別にみた
Table 3-4　Trends in deaths and death rates（per 100,000 population）by

感染症分類コード Code[a]	死　因 Causes of death	死　亡　数 Deaths				死　亡　率 Death rates（per 100,000 population）			
		2008 平成20年	2009 21年	2010 22年	2011 23年	2008 平成20年	2009 21年	2010 22年	2011 23年
	総　　数　　　Total	7 042	7 163	6 993	7 333	5.6	5.7	5.5	5.8
In101	エボラ出血熱	-	-	-	-	-	-	-	-
In102	クリミア・コンゴ出血熱	-	-	-	-	-	-	-	-
In103	痘そう	-	-	-	-	-	-	-	-
In104	南米出血熱	-	-	-	-	-	-	-	-
In105	ペスト	-	-	-	-	-	-	-	-
In106	マールブルグ病	-	-	-	-	-	-	-	-
In107	ラッサ熱	-	-	-	-	-	-	-	-
In201	急性灰白髄炎	-	-	-	-	-	-	-	-
In202	結核	2 220	2 159	2 129	2 166	1.8	1.7	1.7	1.7
In203	ジフテリア	-	-	-	-	-	-	-	-
In204	重症急性呼吸器症候群 （病原体がコロナウイルス属 ＳＡＲＳコロナウイルスであるものに限る）								
In205	鳥インフルエンザ （鳥インフルエンザ（Ｈ５Ｎ１）に限る）	-	-	-	-	-	-	-	-
In301	コレラ	-	-	-	-	-	-	-	-
In302	細菌性赤痢	-	1	-	-	-	0.0	-	-
In303	腸管出血性大腸菌感染症	5	4	6	13	0.0	0.0	0.0	0.0
In304	腸チフス	-	-	-	-	-	-	-	-
In305	パラチフス	-	-	-	-	-	-	-	-
In401	E 型肝炎	-	1	1	-	-	0.0	0.0	-
In402	ウエストナイル熱	-	-	-	-	-	-	-	-
In403	A 型肝炎	7	8	6	5	0.0	0.0	0.0	0.0
In404	エキノコックス症	5	4	3	4	0.0	0.0	0.0	0.0
In405	黄熱	-	-	-	-	-	-	-	-
In406	オウム病	1	1	-	-	0.0	0.0	-	-
In407	オムスク出血熱	-	-	-	-	-	-	-	-
In408	回帰熱	-	-	-	-	-	-	-	-
In409	キャサヌル森林病	-	-	-	-	-	-	-	-
In410	Q熱	-	-	-	-	-	-	-	-
In411	狂犬病	-	-	-	-	-	-	-	-
In412	コクシジオイデス症	-	1	-	-	-	0.0	-	-
In413	サル痘	-	-	-	-	-	-	-	-
In414	腎症候性出血熱	-	-	-	-	-	-	-	-

注：1）　感染症の分類名は、「感染症の予防及び感染症の患者に対する医療に関する法律」（平成10年法律第114号。以下「感染症法」という。）、感染症法施行令（平成10年政令第420号）
及び感染症法施行規則（平成10年厚生省令第99号）に規定された疾病名であるため、必ずしもICD-10とは一致していない。
なお、本表は感染症法等の改正（平成20年5月12日施行）に基づく分類で表章している。
2）　感染症法第44条の2第3項の規定に基づき、平成23年4月1日以降、「新型インフルエンザ（A/H1N1）」を通常の季節性インフルエンザとして取り扱うこととなったので、同日
以降の当該インフルエンザによる死亡数は、「In504 インフルエンザ」に含まれる。

Reference Table

年次別死亡数及び率[1])（人口10万対）（平成20〜23年）
causes of death（the list of infectious diseases revised in 2008）: Japan, 2008-2011

感染症分類コード Code[a)]	死　因 Causes of death	死　亡　数 Deaths				死　亡　率 Death rates (per 100,000 population)			
		2008 平成20年	2009 21年	2010 22年	2011 23年	2008 平成20年	2009 21年	2010 22年	2011 23年
In415	西部ウマ脳炎	-	-	-	-	-	-	-	-
In416	ダニ媒介脳炎	-	-	-	-	-	-	-	-
In417	炭疽	-	-	-	-	-	-	-	-
In418	つつが虫病	1	1	3	3	0.0	0.0	0.0	0.0
In419	デング熱	-	-	-	-	-	-	-	-
In420	東部ウマ脳炎	-	-	-	-	-	-	-	-
In421	鳥インフルエンザ （鳥インフルエンザ（H5N1）を除く）	-	-	-	-	-	-	-	-
In422	ニパウイルス感染症	-	-	-	-	-	-	-	-
In423	日本紅斑熱	-	-	1	1	-	-	0.0	0.0
In424	日本脳炎	-	-	-	-	-	-	-	-
In425	ハンタウイルス肺症候群	-	-	-	-	-	-	-	-
In426	Bウイルス病	-	-	-	-	-	-	-	-
In427	鼻疽	-	-	-	-	-	-	-	-
In428	ブルセラ症	-	-	-	-	-	-	-	-
In429	ベネズエラウマ脳炎	-	-	-	-	-	-	-	-
In430	ヘンドラウイルス感染症	-	-	-	-	-	-	-	-
In431	発しんチフス	-	-	-	-	-	-	-	-
In432	ボツリヌス症（乳児ボツリヌス症を除く）	-	-	-	-	-	-	-	-
In433	乳児ボツリヌス症	-	-	-	-	-	-	-	-
In434	マラリア	1	1	-	2	0.0	0.0	-	0.0
In435	野兎病	-	-	-	-	-	-	-	-
In436	ライム病	-	-	-	-	-	-	-	-
In437	リッサウイルス感染症	-	-	-	-	-	-	-	-
In438	リフトバレー熱	-	-	-	-	-	-	-	-
In439	類鼻疽	-	-	-	-	-	-	-	-
In440	レジオネラ症	46	58	43	56	0.0	0.0	0.0	0.0
In441	レプトスピラ症	-	1	1	-	-	0.0	0.0	-
In442	ロッキー山紅斑熱	-	-	-	-	-	-	-	-
In501	アメーバ赤痢	5	7	7	4	0.0	0.0	0.0	0.0
In502	RSウイルス感染症	36	28	31	28	0.0	0.0	0.0	0.0
In503	咽頭結膜熱	-	-	-	-	-	-	-	-
In504	インフルエンザ （鳥インフルエンザ及び 新型インフルエンザ等感染症を除く）	272	604	141	567	0.2	0.5	0.1	0.4
In505	急性ウイルス性肝炎 （E型肝炎及びA型肝炎を除く）	371	341	336	351	0.3	0.3	0.3	0.3
In506	A群溶血性レンサ球菌咽頭炎	-	-	-	-	-	-	-	-
In507	感染性胃腸炎	2 163	2 088	2 293	2 295	1.7	1.7	1.8	1.8

Note : a) Code see page 603.

647

参考表
年次推移

表 3 − 4 感染症分類（平成20年改正）別にみた年次別死亡数及び率[1]（人口10万対）（平成20〜23年）（つづき）

Table 3-4 Trends in deaths and death rates (per 100,000 population) by causes of death (the list of infectious diseases revised in 2008) : Japan, 2008-2011−CON.

感染症分類コード Code[a]	死　因 Causes of death	死　亡　数 Deaths				死　亡　率 Death rates (per 100,000 population)			
		2008 平成20年	2009 21年	2010 22年	2011 23年	2008 平成20年	2009 21年	2010 22年	2011 23年
In508	急性出血性結膜炎	-	-	-	-	-	-	-	-
In509	急性脳炎 （ウエストナイル脳炎、西部ウマ脳炎、ダニ媒介脳炎、東部ウマ脳炎、日本脳炎、ベネズエラウマ脳炎及びリフトバレー熱を除く）	102	103	105	103	0.1	0.1	0.1	0.1
In510	クラミジア肺炎（オウム病を除く）	7	2	10	10	0.0	0.0	0.0	0.0
In511	クリプトスポリジウム症	-	-	-	-	-	-	-	-
In512	クロイツフェルト・ヤコブ病	203	166	218	219	0.2	0.1	0.2	0.2
In513	劇症型溶血性レンサ球菌感染症	13	8	14	17	0.0	0.0	0.0	0.0
In514	後天性免疫不全症候群	54	61	61	53	0.0	0.0	0.0	0.0
In515	細菌性髄膜炎	164	158	177	168	0.1	0.1	0.1	0.1
In516	ジアルジア症	-	-	-	-	-	-	-	-
In517	水痘	5	9	4	7	0.0	0.0	0.0	0.0
In518	髄膜炎菌性髄膜炎	-	-	-	-	-	-	-	-
In519	性器クラミジア感染症	-	-	-	-	-	-	-	-
In520	性器ヘルペスウイルス感染症	-	-	-	1	-	-	-	0.0
In521	尖圭コンジローマ	-	-	-	-	-	-	-	-
In522	先天性風しん症候群	-	-	-	-	-	-	-	-
In523	手足口病	-	-	-	-	-	-	-	-
In524	伝染性紅斑	-	-	-	-	-	-	-	-
In525	突発性発しん	-	-	-	-	-	-	-	-
In526	梅毒	16	16	11	9	0.0	0.0	0.0	0.0
In527	破傷風	10	9	14	7	0.0	0.0	0.0	0.0
In528	バンコマイシン耐性黄色ブドウ球菌感染症	1	-	-	-	0.0	-	-	-
In529	バンコマイシン耐性腸球菌感染症	-	1	1	1	-	0.0	0.0	0.0
In530	百日咳	1	-	-	2	0.0	-	-	0.0
In531	風しん	-	-	1	-	-	-	0.0	-
In532	ペニシリン耐性肺炎球菌感染症	1	-	4	-	0.0	-	0.0	-
In533	ヘルパンギーナ	-	-	-	-	-	-	-	-
In534	マイコプラズマ肺炎	18	15	20	36	0.0	0.0	0.0	0.0
In535	麻しん（成人麻しんを除く）	-	-	-	-	-	-	-	-
In536	成人麻しん	1	2	-	1	0.0	0.0	-	0.0
In537	無菌性髄膜炎	6	13	15	19	0.0	0.0	0.0	0.0
In538	メチシリン耐性黄色ブドウ球菌感染症	1 291	1 256	1 295	1 168	1.0	1.0	1.0	0.9
In539	薬剤耐性緑膿菌感染症	16	13	22	9	0.0	0.0	0.0	0.0
In540	流行性角結膜炎	-	-	-	-	-	-	-	-
In541	流行性耳下腺炎	-	2	-	1	-	0.0	-	0.0
In542	淋菌感染症	-	-	-	-	-	-	-	-
In601	新型インフルエンザ等感染症	-	21	20	7	-	0.0	0.0	0.0

648

参考表
年次推移

表 3 － 5　感染症分類（平成19年改正）別にみた
Table 3-5　Trends in deaths and death rates (per 100,000 population) by

感　染　症 分類コード Code[a)]	死　　因 Causes of death	死　亡　数 Deaths	死　亡　率 Death rates (per 100,000 population)
		2007 平成19年	2007 平成19年
	総　　数　　　Total	7 531	6. 0
In101	エボラ出血熱	-	-
In102	クリミア・コンゴ出血熱	-	-
In103	痘そう	-	-
In104	南米出血熱	-	-
In105	ペスト	-	-
In106	マールブルグ病	-	-
In107	ラッサ熱	-	-
In201	急性灰白髄炎	-	-
In202	結核	2 194	1. 7
In203	ジフテリア		
In204	重症急性呼吸器症候群 （病原体がコロナウイルス属 ＳＡＲＳコロナウイルスであるものに限る）		
In301	コレラ	-	-
In302	細菌性赤痢	-	-
In303	腸管出血性大腸菌感染症	4	0. 0
In304	腸チフス	-	-
In305	パラチフス	-	-
In401	E 型肝炎	-	-
In402	ウエストナイル熱	-	-
In403	A 型肝炎	5	0. 0
In404	エキノコックス症	3	0. 0
In405	黄熱	-	-
In406	オウム病	-	-
In407	オムスク出血熱	-	-
In408	回帰熱	-	-
In409	キャサヌル森林病	-	-
In410	Q 熱	-	-
In411	狂犬病	-	-
In412	コクシジオイデス症	-	-
In413	サル痘	-	-
In414	腎症候性出血熱	-	-
In415	西部ウマ脳炎	-	-
In416	ダニ媒介脳炎	-	-
In417	炭疽	1	0. 0
In418	つつが虫病	2	0. 0
In419	デング熱	-	-
In420	東部ウマ脳炎	-	-

注：1)　感染症の分類名は、「感染症の予防及び感染症の患者に対する医療に関する法律」（平成10年法律第114号。以下「感染症法」という。）、感染症法施行令（平成10年政令第420号）
及び感染症法施行規則（平成10年厚生省令第99号）に規定された疾病名であるため、必ずしもICD-10とは一致していない。
なお、本表は感染症法等の改正（平成19年４月１日施行）に基づく分類で表章している。

650

Reference Table

年次別死亡数及び率[1]（人口10万対）（平成19年）
causes of death（the list of infectious diseases revised in 2007）: Japan, 2007

感染症 分類コード Code[a]	死　因 Causes of death	死　亡　数 Deaths 2007 平成19年	死　亡　率 Death rates（per 100,000 population） 2007 平成19年
In421	鳥インフルエンザ	-	-
In422	ニパウイルス感染症	-	-
In423	日本紅斑熱	-	-
In424	日本脳炎	-	-
In425	ハンタウイルス肺症候群	-	-
In426	Ｂウイルス病	-	-
In427	鼻疽	-	-
In428	ブルセラ症	-	-
In429	ベネズエラウマ脳炎	-	-
In430	ヘンドラウイルス感染症	-	-
In431	発しんチフス	-	-
In432	ボツリヌス症（乳児ボツリヌス症を除く）	-	-
In433	乳児ボツリヌス症	-	-
In434	マラリア	-	-
In435	野兎病	-	-
In436	ライム病	1	0.0
In437	リッサウイルス感染症	-	-
In438	リフトバレー熱	-	-
In439	類鼻疽	-	-
In440	レジオネラ症	31	0.0
In441	レプトスピラ症	1	0.0
In442	ロッキー山紅斑熱	-	-
In501	アメーバ赤痢	8	0.0
In502	ＲＳウイルス感染症	44	0.0
In503	咽頭結膜熱	-	-
In504	インフルエンザ （鳥インフルエンザを除く）	696	0.6
In505	急性ウイルス性肝炎 （E型肝炎及びA型肝炎を除く）	387	0.3
In506	A群溶血性レンサ球菌咽頭炎	-	-
In507	感染性胃腸炎	2 208	1.8
In508	急性出血性結膜炎	-	-
In509	急性脳炎 （ウエストナイル脳炎、西部ウマ脳炎、ダニ媒介脳炎、 東部ウマ脳炎、日本脳炎、ベネズエラウマ脳炎及び リフトバレー熱を除く）	114	0.1
In510	クラミジア肺炎（オウム病を除く）	15	0.0
In511	クリプトスポリジウム症	-	-
In512	クロイツフェルト・ヤコブ病	167	0.1
In513	劇症型溶血性レンサ球菌感染症	15	0.0
In514	後天性免疫不全症候群	65	0.1

Note: a) Code see page 604.

参考表
年次推移

表３－５　感染症分類（平成19年改正）別にみた年次別死亡数及び率[1]（人口10万対）
（平成19年）（つづき）

Table 3-5　Trends in deaths and death rates（per 100,000 population）by causes of death（the list of infectious diseases revised in 2007）: Japan, 2007－CON.

感　染　症 分類コード Code[a]	死　　因 Causes of death	死　亡　数 Deaths 2007 平成19年	死　亡　率 Death rates (per 100,000 population) 2007 平成19年
In515	細菌性髄膜炎	188	0.1
In516	ジアルジア症	-	-
In517	水痘	6	0.0
In518	髄膜炎菌性髄膜炎	-	-
In519	性器クラミジア感染症	-	-
In520	性器ヘルペスウイルス感染症	-	-
In521	尖圭コンジローマ	-	-
In522	先天性風しん症候群	-	-
In523	手足口病	-	-
In524	伝染性紅斑	-	-
In525	突発性発しん	1	0.0
In526	梅毒	15	0.0
In527	破傷風	7	0.0
In528	バンコマイシン耐性黄色ブドウ球菌感染症	-	-
In529	バンコマイシン耐性腸球菌感染症	-	-
In530	百日咳	1	0.0
In531	風しん	-	-
In532	ペニシリン耐性肺炎球菌感染症	1	0.0
In533	ヘルパンギーナ	-	-
In534	マイコプラズマ肺炎	17	0.0
In535	麻しん（成人麻しんを除く）	-	-
In536	成人麻しん	2	0.0
In537	無菌性髄膜炎	7	0.0
In538	メチシリン耐性黄色ブドウ球菌感染症	1 304	1.0
In539	薬剤耐性緑膿菌感染症	21	0.0
In540	流行性角結膜炎	-	-
In541	流行性耳下腺炎	-	-
In542	淋菌感染症	-	-

参考表
年次推移

表 3 － 6 　感染症分類（平成18年改正）別にみた
Table 3-6　Trends in deaths and death rates（per 100,000 population）by

感　染　症 分類コード Code[a]	死　　因 Causes of death	死　亡　数 Deaths 2006 平成18年	死　亡　率 Death rates（per 100,000 population） 2006 平成18年
	総　　数　　　　Total	7 623	6.0
In101	エボラ出血熱	-	-
In102	クリミア・コンゴ出血熱	-	-
In103	重症急性呼吸器症候群 （病原体がＳＡＲＳコロナウイルスであるものに限る）	-	-
In104	痘そう	-	-
In105	ペスト	-	-
In106	マールブルグ病	-	-
In107	ラッサ熱	-	-
In201	急性灰白髄炎	-	-
In202	コレラ	-	-
In203	細菌性赤痢	-	-
In204	ジフテリア	-	-
In205	腸チフス	-	-
In206	パラチフス	-	-
In301	腸管出血性大腸菌感染症	6	0.0
In401	Ｅ型肝炎	2	0.0
In402	ウエストナイル熱	-	-
In403	Ａ型肝炎	5	0.0
In404	エキノコックス症	1	0.0
In405	黄熱	-	-
In406	オウム病	-	-
In407	回帰熱	-	-
In408	Ｑ熱	-	-
In409	狂犬病	2	0.0
In410	高病原性鳥インフルエンザ	-	-
In411	コクシジオイデス症	-	-
In412	サル痘	-	-
In413	腎症候性出血熱	-	-
In414	炭疽	-	-
In415	つつが虫病	1	0.0
In416	デング熱	-	-
In417	ニパウイルス感染症	-	-
In418	日本紅斑熱	1	0.0
In419	日本脳炎	1	0.0
In420	ハンタウイルス肺症候群	-	-
In421	Ｂウイルス病	-	-
In422	ブルセラ症	-	-
In423	発しんチフス	-	-
In424	ボツリヌス症 （乳児ボツリヌス症を除く）	-	-
In425	乳児ボツリヌス症	-	-
In426	マラリア	1	0.0
In427	野兎病	-	-
In428	ライム病	-	-
In429	リッサウイルス感染症	-	-
In430	レジオネラ症	31	0.0
In431	レプトスピラ症	-	-

注：1) 感染症の分類名は、「感染症の予防及び感染症の患者に対する医療に関する法律」（平成10年法律第114号。以下「感染症法」という。）、感染症法施行令（平成10年政令第420号）
　　　及び感染症法施行規則（平成10年厚生省令第99号）並びに「結核予防法」（昭和26年法律第96号）に規定された疾病名であるため、必ずしもICD-10とは一致していない。
　　　なお、本表は感染症法等の改正（平成15年11月5日施行）に基づく分類で表章している。
　　2) 「統計調査に用いる産業分類並びに疾病、傷害及び死因分類を定める政令第三条の規定に基づく疾病、傷害及び死因に関する分類の名称及び分類表（平成6年総務庁告示第75号）」
　　　の改正により、平成18年1月1日から「ICD-10（2003年版）準拠」の適用に伴い、分類の追加、変更及び原死因選択ルールの変更が行われている。

年次別死亡数及び率 [1] （人口10万対）（平成18年）
causes of death（the list of infectious diseases revised in 2006）: Japan, 2006

感染症 分類コード Code[a]	死　因 Causes of death	死　亡　数 Deaths 2006 平成18年	死　亡　率 Death rates (per 100,000 population) 2006 平成18年
In501	アメーバ赤痢	8	0.0
In502	ＲＳウイルス感染症	14	0.0
In503	咽頭結膜熱	-	-
In504	インフルエンザ （高病原性鳥インフルエンザを除く）	865	0.7
In505	急性ウイルス性肝炎 （Ｅ型肝炎及びＡ型肝炎を除く）	373	0.3
In506	Ａ群溶血性レンサ球菌咽頭炎	-	-
In507	感染性胃腸炎	2 164	1.7
In508	急性出血性結膜炎	-	-
In509	急性脳炎 （ウエストナイル脳炎及び日本脳炎を除く）	85	0.1
In510	クラミジア肺炎（オウム病を除く）	5	0.0
In511	クリプトスポリジウム症	-	-
In512	クロイツフェルト・ヤコブ病	173	0.1
In513	劇症型溶血性レンサ球菌感染症	18	0.0
In514	後天性免疫不全症候群	60	0.0
In515	細菌性髄膜炎	162	0.1
In516	ジアルジア症	-	-
In517	水痘	4	0.0
In518	髄膜炎菌性髄膜炎	-	-
In519	性器クラミジア感染症	-	-
In520	性器ヘルペスウイルス感染症	-	-
In521	尖圭コンジローマ	1	0.0
In522	先天性風しん症候群	-	-
In523	手足口病	-	-
In524	伝染性紅斑	-	-
In525	突発性発しん	-	-
In526	梅毒	16	0.0
In527	破傷風	5	0.0
In528	バンコマイシン耐性黄色ブドウ球菌感染症	-	-
In529	バンコマイシン耐性腸球菌感染症	1	0.0
In530	百日咳	1	0.0
In531	風しん	-	-
In532	ペニシリン耐性肺炎球菌感染症	2	0.0
In533	ヘルパンギーナ	-	-
In534	マイコプラズマ肺炎	22	0.0
In535	麻しん（成人麻しんを除く）	-	-
In536	成人麻しん	-	-
In537	無菌性髄膜炎	2	0.0
In538	メチシリン耐性黄色ブドウ球菌感染症	1 311	1.0
In539	薬剤耐性緑膿菌感染症	10	0.0
In540	流行性角結膜炎	-	-
In541	流行性耳下腺炎	1	0.0
In542	淋菌感染症	-	-
In601	結核	2 269	1.8

Note：a) Code see page 605.

参考表
年次推移

表 3 － 7　感染症分類（平成15年改正）別にみた
Table 3-7　Trends in deaths and death rates (per 100,000 population) by

感　染　症 分類コード Code[a]	死　　因 Causes of death	死　亡　数 Deaths			死　亡　率 Death rates (per 100,000 population)		
		2003 平成15年	2004 16年	2005 17年	2003 平成15年	2004 16年	2005 17年
	総　　数　　　Total	9 937	9 527	11 105	7.9	7.6	8.8
In 101	エボラ出血熱	-	-	-	-	-	-
In 102	クリミア・コンゴ出血熱	-	-	-	-	-	-
In 103	重症急性呼吸器症候群 （病原体がSARSコロナウイルスであるものに限る）	-	-	-	-	-	-
In 104	痘そう	-	-	-	-	-	-
In 105	ペスト	-	-	-	-	-	-
In 106	マールブルグ病	-	-	-	-	-	-
In 107	ラッサ熱	-	-	-	-	-	-
In 201	急性灰白髄炎	-	-	-	-	-	-
In 202	コレラ	-	-	-	-	-	-
In 203	細菌性赤痢	-	-	-	-	-	-
In 204	ジフテリア	-	-	-	-	-	-
In 205	腸チフス	-	-	-	-	-	-
In 206	パラチフス	-	-	-	-	-	-
In 301	腸管出血性大腸菌感染症	3	4	7	0.0	0.0	0.0
In 401	E型肝炎	1	2	-	0.0	0.0	-
In 402	ウエストナイル熱	-	-	-	-	-	-
In 403	A型肝炎	6	5	12	0.0	0.0	0.0
In 404	エキノコックス症	3	2	-	0.0	0.0	-
In 405	黄熱	-	-	-	-	-	-
In 406	オウム病	1	1	-	0.0	0.0	-
In 407	回帰熱	-	-	-	-	-	-
In 408	Q熱	-	-	-	-	-	-
In 409	狂犬病	-	-	-	-	-	-
In 410	高病原性鳥インフルエンザ	-	-	-	-	-	-
In 411	コクシジオイデス症	-	-	-	-	-	-
In 412	サル痘	-	-	-	-	-	-
In 413	腎症候性出血熱	-	-	-	-	-	-
In 414	炭疽	-	-	-	-	-	-
In 415	つつが虫病	-	-	-	-	-	-
In 416	デング熱	-	-	1	-	-	0.0
In 417	ニパウイルス感染症	-	-	-	-	-	-
In 418	日本紅斑熱	-	2	-	-	0.0	-
In 419	日本脳炎	-	-	-	-	-	-
In 420	ハンタウイルス肺症候群	-	-	-	-	-	-
In 421	Bウイルス病	-	-	-	-	-	-
In 422	ブルセラ症	-	-	-	-	-	-
In 423	発しんチフス	-	-	-	-	-	-
In 424	ボツリヌス症（乳児ボツリヌス症を除く）	-	-	-	-	-	-
In 425	乳児ボツリヌス症	-	-	-	-	-	-
In 426	マラリア	1	1	1	0.0	0.0	0.0

注：1）　感染症の分類名は、「感染症の予防及び感染症の患者に対する医療に関する法律」（平成10年法律第114号。以下「感染症法」という。）、感染症法施行令（平成10年政令第420号）
　　　　及び感染症法施行規則（平成10年厚生省令第99号）並びに「結核予防法」（昭和26年法律第96号）に規定された疾病名であるため、必ずしもICD-10とは一致していない。
　　　　なお、本表は感染症法等の改正（平成15年11月5日施行）に基づく分類で表章している。

Reference Table

年次別死亡数及び率[1] （人口10万対）（平成15～17年）
causes of death (the list of infectious diseases revised in 2003) : Japan, 2003-2005

感 染 症 分類コード Code[a]	死 因 Causes of death	死 亡 数 Deaths			死 亡 率 Death rates (per 100,000 population)		
		2003 平成15年	2004 16年	2005 17年	2003 平成15年	2004 16年	2005 17年
In 427	野兎病	-	-	-	-	-	-
In 428	ライム病	-	-	-	-	-	-
In 429	リッサウイルス感染症	-	-	-	-	-	-
In 430	レジオネラ症	14	8	21	0.0	0.0	0.0
In 431	レプトスピラ症	-	-	1	-	-	0.0
In 501	アメーバ赤痢	2	5	4	0.0	0.0	0.0
In 502	RSウイルス感染症	2	11	9	0.0	0.0	0.0
In 503	咽頭結膜熱	-	-	-	-	-	-
In 504	インフルエンザ（高病原性鳥インフルエンザを除く）	1 171	694	1 818	0.9	0.6	1.4
In 505	急性ウイルス性肝炎（E型肝炎及びA型肝炎を除く）	4 443	4 485	4 596	3.5	3.6	3.6
In 506	A群溶血性レンサ球菌咽頭炎	-	-	-	-	-	-
In 507	感染性胃腸炎	1 398	1 432	1 732	1.1	1.1	1.4
In 508	急性出血性結膜炎	-	-	-	-	-	-
In 509	急性脳炎（ウエストナイル脳炎及び日本脳炎を除く）	126	100	125	0.1	0.1	0.1
In 510	クラミジア肺炎（オウム病を除く）	5	7	10	0.0	0.0	0.0
In 511	クリプトスポリジウム症	-	-	-	-	-	-
In 512	クロイツフェルト・ヤコブ病	142	165	155	0.1	0.1	0.1
In 513	劇症型溶血性レンサ球菌感染症	10	7	8	0.0	0.0	0.0
In 514	後天性免疫不全症候群	61	49	69	0.0	0.0	0.1
In 515	細菌性髄膜炎	136	145	155	0.1	0.1	0.1
In 516	ジアルジア症	-	-	-	-	-	-
In 517	水 痘	4	7	9	0.0	0.0	0.0
In 518	髄膜炎菌性髄膜炎	-	-	-	-	-	-
In 519	性器クラミジア感染症	-	-	-	-	-	-
In 520	性器ヘルペスウイルス感染症	-	-	-	-	-	-
In 521	尖圭コンジローマ	-	-	1	-	-	0.0
In 522	先天性風しん症候群	-	-	1	-	-	0.0
In 523	手足口病	-	-	-	-	-	-
In 524	伝染性紅斑	-	-	-	-	-	-
In 525	突発性発しん	-	-	-	-	-	-
In 526	梅毒	10	14	17	0.0	0.0	0.0
In 527	破傷風	7	9	7	0.0	0.0	0.0
In 528	百日咳	1	-	-	0.0	-	-
In 529	風しん	1	-	-	0.0	-	-
In 530	ヘルパンギーナ	-	-	-	-	-	-
In 531	マイコプラズマ肺炎	29	31	38	0.0	0.0	0.0
In 532	麻しん（成人麻しんを除く）	3	2	1	0.0	0.0	0.0
In 533	成人麻しん	3	1	2	0.0	0.0	0.0
In 534	無菌性髄膜炎	16	8	8	0.0	0.0	0.0
In 535	流行性角結膜炎	-	-	-	-	-	-
In 536	流行性耳下腺炎	1	-	1	0.0	-	0.0
In 537	淋菌感染症	-	-	-	-	-	-
In 601	結 核	2 337	2 330	2 296	1.9	1.8	1.8

Note : a) Code see page 606.

657

参考表
年次推移

表 3 − 8　感染症分類（平成11年改正）別にみた
Table 3-8　Trends in deaths and death rates（per 100,000 population）by

感染症分類コード Code[a]	死　因 Causes of death	死　亡　数 Deaths				死　亡　率 Death rates（per 100,000 population）			
		1999 平成11年	2000 12年	2001 13年	2002 14年	1999 平成11年	2000 12年	2001 13年	2002 14年
	総　数　　Total	10 072	8 956	8 782	8 789	8.0	7.1	7.0	7.0
In 101	エボラ出血熱	-	-	-	-	-	-	-	-
In 102	クリミア・コンゴ出血熱	-	-	-	-	-	-	-	-
In 103	ペスト	-	-	-	-	-	-	-	-
In 104	マールブルグ病	-	-	-	-	-	-	-	-
In 105	ラッサ熱	-	-	-	-	-	-	-	-
In 201	急性灰白髄炎	-	-	-	-	-	-	-	-
In 202	コレラ	-	-	-	-	-	-	-	-
In 203	細菌性赤痢	-	-	-	-	-	-	-	-
In 204	ジフテリア	-	1	-	-	-	0.0	-	-
In 205	腸チフス	-	-	-	-	-	-	-	-
In 206	パラチフス	-	-	-	-	-	-	-	-
In 301	腸管出血性大腸菌感染症	1	7	5	7	0.0	0.0	0.0	0.0
In 401	アメーバ赤痢	6	6	5	4	0.0	0.0	0.0	0.0
In 402	咽頭結膜熱	-	-	-	-	-	-	-	-
In 403	インフルエンザ	1 382	575	214	358	1.1	0.5	0.2	0.3
In 404	A群溶血性レンサ球菌咽頭炎	-	-	-	-	-	-	-	-
In 405	エキノコックス症	4	2	3	1	0.0	0.0	0.0	0.0
In 406	黄熱	-	-	-	-	-	-	-	-
In 407	オウム病	-	1	-	1	-	0.0	-	0.0
In 408	回帰熱	-	-	-	-	-	-	-	-
In 409	感染性胃腸炎	1 161	1 183	1 242	1 228	0.9	0.9	1.0	1.0
In 410	急性ウイルス性肝炎	3 951	3 961	4 226	4 314	3.1	3.2	3.4	3.4
In 411	急性出血性結膜炎	-	-	-	-	-	-	-	-
In 412	急性脳炎（日本脳炎を除く）	168	166	155	126	0.1	0.1	0.1	0.1
In 413	Q熱	-	-	-	-	-	-	-	-
In 414	狂犬病	-	-	-	-	-	-	-	-
In 415	クラミジア肺炎（オウム病を除く）	6	4	2	1	0.0	0.0	0.0	0.0
In 416	クリプトスポリジウム症	-	-	-	-	-	-	-	-
In 417	クロイツフェルト・ヤコブ病	115	113	123	134	0.1	0.1	0.1	0.1
In 418	劇症型溶血性レンサ球菌感染症	2	10	7	16	0.0	0.0	0.0	0.0
In 419	後天性免疫不全症候群	45	50	37	54	0.0	0.0	0.0	0.0
In 420	コクシジオイデス症	-	-	-	-	-	-	-	-

注：1）　感染症の分類名は、「感染症の予防及び感染症の患者に対する医療に関する法律」（平成10年法律第114号。以下「感染症法」という。）及び感染症法施行規則（平成10年厚生省令第99号）並びに「結核予防法」（昭和26年法律第96号）に規定された疾病名であるため、必ずしもICD-10とは一致していない。

Reference Table

年次別死亡数及び率[1]（人口10万対）（平成11～14年）
causes of death (the list of infectious diseases revised in 1999) : Japan, 1999-2002

感 染 症 分類コード Code[a]	死 因 Causes of death	死 亡 数 Deaths				死 亡 率 Death rates (per 100,000 population)			
		1999 平成11年	2000 12年	2001 13年	2002 14年	1999 平成11年	2000 12年	2001 13年	2002 14年
In 421	細菌性髄膜炎	176	131	155	136	0.1	0.1	0.1	0.1
In 422	ジアルジア症	-	-	-	-	-	-	-	-
In 423	腎症候性出血熱	1	-	1	-	0.0	-	0.0	-
In 424	水痘	12	5	4	10	0.0	0.0	0.0	0.0
In 425	髄膜炎菌性髄膜炎	-	-	-	-	-	-	-	-
In 426	性器クラミジア感染症	-	-	-	-	-	-	-	-
In 427	性器ヘルペスウイルス感染症	-	-	-	-	-	-	-	-
In 428	成人麻疹	2	7	10	4	0.0	0.0	0.0	0.0
In 429	尖形コンジローム	-	-	-	-	-	-	-	-
In 430	先天性風疹症候群	1	-	-	1	0.0	-	-	0.0
In 431	炭疽	-	-	-	-	-	-	-	-
In 432	ツツガムシ病	2	1	-	3	0.0	0.0	-	0.0
In 433	手足口病	-	3	-	-	-	0.0	-	-
In 434	デング熱	-	-	-	-	-	-	-	-
In 435	伝染性紅斑	-	-	-	-	-	-	-	-
In 436	突発性発疹	-	-	1	-	-	-	0.0	-
In 437	日本紅斑熱	-	-	-	1	-	-	-	0.0
In 438	日本脳炎	-	1	-	1	-	0.0	-	0.0
In 439	乳児ボツリヌス症	-	-	-	-	-	-	-	-
In 440	梅毒	21	12	21	10	0.0	0.0	0.0	0.0
In 441	破傷風	10	10	12	9	0.0	0.0	0.0	0.0
In 442	ハンタウイルス肺症候群	-	-	-	-	-	-	-	-
In 443	Bウイルス病	-	-	-	-	-	-	-	-
In 444	百日咳	2	1	-	-	0.0	0.0	-	-
In 445	風疹	-	-	1	1	-	-	0.0	0.0
In 446	ブルセラ症	-	-	-	-	-	-	-	-
In 447	ヘルパンギーナ	-	-	-	-	-	-	-	-
In 448	発疹チフス	-	-	-	-	-	-	-	-
In 449	マイコプラズマ肺炎	12	16	24	20	0.0	0.0	0.0	0.0
In 450	麻疹（成人麻疹を除く）	27	11	11	6	0.0	0.0	0.0	0.0
In 451	マラリア	6	1	-	1	0.0	0.0	-	0.0
In 452	無菌性髄膜炎	13	8	17	8	0.0	0.0	0.0	0.0
In 453	ライム病	-	-	-	-	-	-	-	-
In 454	流行性角結膜炎	-	-	-	-	-	-	-	-
In 455	流行性耳下腺炎	-	2	2	2	-	0.0	0.0	0.0
In 456	淋菌感染症	-	-	-	-	-	-	-	-
In 457	レジオネラ症	11	12	13	15	0.0	0.0	0.0	0.0
In 501	結核	2 935	2 656	2 491	2 317	2.3	2.1	2.0	1.8

Note : a) Code see page 607.

参考表
年次推移

表4　年次別にみた性・妊娠満28週以後の死産－早期新生児死亡別周産期死亡数[1]
Table 4　Trends in perinatal deaths by sex : Japan

年　　次[2] Year		周 産 期 死 亡 数 Perinatal deaths				妊娠満28週以後の死産数 Foetal deaths at 28 completed weeks and over of gestation				早 期 新 生 児 死 亡 数 Early neonatal deaths		
		総　数 Total	男 Male	女 Female	不　詳 Not stated	総　数 Total	男 Male	女 Female	不　詳 Not stated	総　数 Total	男 Male	女 Female
1950	昭和25年	108 843	59 467	49 047	329	73 659	39 781	33 549	329	35 184	19 686	15 498
51	26	99 865	54 877	44 758	230	67 221	36 518	30 473	230	32 644	18 359	14 285
52	27	91 527	50 222	41 098	207	62 786	34 095	28 484	207	28 741	16 127	12 614
53	28	85 932	47 403	38 380	149	59 195	32 429	26 617	149	26 737	14 974	11 763
54	29	79 776	44 171	35 476	129	55 502	30 475	24 898	129	24 274	13 696	10 578
55	30	75 918	42 413	33 394	111	53 297	29 650	23 536	111	22 621	12 763	9 858
56	31	75 706	42 264	33 341	101	53 201	29 521	23 579	101	22 505	12 743	9 762
57	32	70 502	39 478	30 927	97	50 894	28 265	22 532	97	19 608	11 213	8 395
58	33	72 625	40 875	31 647	103	53 385	29 851	23 431	103	19 240	11 024	8 216
59	34	69 912	39 336	30 466	110	51 494	28 678	22 706	110	18 418	10 658	7 760
1960	35	66 552	37 455	28 976	121	49 512	27 664	21 727	121	17 040	9 791	7 249
61	36	65 063	37 004	27 930	129	48 184	27 106	20 949	129	16 879	9 898	6 981
62	37	62 650	35 269	27 229	152	46 408	25 809	20 447	152	16 242	9 460	6 782
63	38	60 049	34 052	25 833	164	44 764	25 145	19 455	164	15 285	8 907	6 378
64	39	56 827	31 982	24 706	139	42 151	23 383	18 629	139	14 676	8 599	6 077
65	40	54 904	31 049	23 712	143	39 955	22 243	17 569	143	14 949	8 806	6 143
66	41	42 583	23 913	18 534	136	30 818	17 030	13 652	136	11 765	6 883	4 882
67	42	50 846	28 672	22 002	172	36 738	20 407	16 159	172	14 108	8 265	5 843
68	43	45 921	26 048	19 680	193	32 228	17 873	14 162	193	13 693	8 175	5 518
69	44	43 419	24 580	18 621	218	30 609	16 948	13 443	218	12 810	7 632	5 178
1970	45	41 917	23 705	17 999	213	29 107	16 011	12 883	213	12 810	7 694	5 116
71	46	40 900	22 890	17 774	236	28 235	15 419	12 580	236	12 665	7 471	5 194
72	47	38 754	21 977	16 567	210	26 329	14 459	11 660	210	12 425	7 518	4 907
73	48	37 598	21 190	16 174	234	25 442	13 934	11 274	234	12 156	7 256	4 900
74	49	34 383	19 332	14 835	216	22 989	12 496	10 277	216	11 394	6 836	4 558
75	50	30 513	16 996	13 326	191	20 268	10 991	9 086	191	10 245	6 005	4 240
76	51	27 133	15 180	11 791	162	17 741	9 550	8 029	162	9 392	5 630	3 762
77	52	24 708	13 704	10 851	153	16 022	8 581	7 288	153	8 686	5 123	3 563
78	53	22 217	12 391	9 667	159	14 516	7 837	6 520	159	7 701	4 554	3 147
79	54	20 481	11 303	9 016	162	13 580	7 266	6 152	162	6 901	4 037	2 864
1980	55	18 385	10 097	8 123	165	12 231	6 488	5 578	165	6 154	3 609	2 545
81	56	16 531	9 015	7 382	134	10 929	5 791	5 004	134	5 602	3 224	2 378
82	57	15 303	8 378	6 781	144	10 236	5 432	4 660	144	5 067	2 946	2 121
83	58	14 035	7 558	6 368	109	9 464	4 966	4 389	109	4 571	2 592	1 979
84	59	12 998	7 077	5 807	114	8 724	4 642	3 968	114	4 274	2 435	1 839
85	60	11 470	6 059	5 299	112	7 733	3 992	3 629	112	3 737	2 067	1 670
86	61	10 148	5 362	4 678	108	6 902	3 522	3 272	108	3 246	1 840	1 406
87	62	9 317	5 018	4 206	93	6 252	3 292	2 867	93	3 065	1 726	1 339
88	63	8 508	4 496	3 922	90	5 759	3 006	2 663	90	2 749	1 490	1 259
89	平成元年	7 450	3 880	3 499	71	5 064	2 577	2 416	71	2 386	1 303	1 083
1990	2	7 001	3 717	3 202	82	4 664	2 394	2 188	82	2 337	1 323	1 014
91	3	6 544	3 370	3 104	70	4 376	2 213	2 093	70	2 168	1 157	1 011
92	4	6 321	3 339	2 888	94	4 191	2 140	1 957	94	2 130	1 199	931
93	5	5 989	3 152	2 754	83	3 954	2 020	1 851	83	2 035	1 132	903
94	6	6 134	3 278	2 764	92	4 048	2 074	1 882	92	2 086	1 204	882

注：1）　第10回改訂分類の勧告の中で周産期死亡が妊娠満22週以後と定義付けられたことから、平成6年人口動態統計上巻表8.1を転載したものである。
　　2）　昭和47年以前は沖縄県を含まない。

参考表
年次推移

表 5　年次別にみた自然－人工別妊娠満28週以後の死産数・妊娠満28週
Table 5　Trends in foetal deaths,foetal death ratio at 28 completed weeks and over of

年　次 [2] Year		総　　数 Total			自　然　死　産 Spontaneous			人　工　死　産 Artificial		
		妊娠満28週以後死産数 Foetal deaths at 28 completed weeks and over of gestation	妊娠満28週以後死産比 Foetal death ratio at 28 completed weeks and over of gestation	全死産中妊娠満28週以後の死産の占める割合　（%） Proportion of foetal deaths at 28 completed weeks and over of gestation	妊娠満28週以後死産数 Foetal deaths at 28 completed weeks and over of gestation	妊娠満28週以後死産比 Foetal death ratio at 28 completed weeks and over of gestation	自然死産中妊娠満28週以後の死産の占める割合（%） Proportion of foetal deaths at 28 completed weeks and over of gestation	妊娠満28週以後死産数 Foetal deaths at 28 completed weeks and over of gestation	妊娠満28週以後死産比 Foetal death ratio at 28 completed weeks and over of gestation	人工死産中妊娠満28週以後の死産の占める割合（%） Proportion of foetal deaths at 28 completed weeks and over of gestation
1899	明治32年	99 836	72.0	73.6	…	…	…	…	…	…
1900	33	102 966	72.5	74.6	…	…	…	…	…	…
01	34	114 929	76.5	73.9	…	…	…	…	…	…
02	35	117 034	77.5	74.2	…	…	…	…	…	…
03	36	115 178	77.3	74.8	…	…	…	…	…	…
04	37	111 120	77.1	75.6	…	…	…	…	…	…
05	38	107 333	73.9	75.5	…	…	…	…	…	…
06	39	111 206	79.8	74.3	…	…	…	…	…	…
07	40	118 281	73.3	74.5	…	…	…	…	…	…
08	41	121 260	72.9	74.5	…	…	…	…	…	…
09	42	119 941	70.8	74.2	…	…	…	…	…	…
1910	43	115 876	67.7	73.6	…	…	…	…	…	…
11	44	114 229	65.4	73.5	…	…	…	…	…	…
12	大正元年	107 634	61.9	72.9	…	…	…	…	…	…
13	2	108 016	61.5	73.1	…	…	…	…	…	…
14	3	106 434	58.9	73.1	…	…	…	…	…	…
15	4	102 364	56.9	72.4	…	…	…	…	…	…
16	5	101 147	56.0	72.2	…	…	…	…	…	…
17	6	102 335	56.5	72.9	…	…	…	…	…	…
18	7	102 630	57.3	72.0	…	…	…	…	…	…
19	8	96 009	54.0	72.2	…	…	…	…	…	…
1920	9	103 532	51.1	71.9	…	…	…	…	…	…
21	10	100 437	50.4	72.6	…	…	…	…	…	…
22	11	95 587	48.5	72.3	…	…	…	…	…	…
23	12	96 656	47.3	72.2	…	…	…	…	…	…
24	13	90 903	45.5	72.2	…	…	…	…	…	…
25	14	89 151	42.7	71.7	…	…	…	…	…	…
26	昭和元年	89 046	42.3	71.8	…	…	…	…	…	…
27	2	82 511	40.0	70.6	…	…	…	…	…	…
28	3	84 951	39.8	70.7	…	…	…	…	…	…
29	4	81 786	39.4	69.9	…	…	…	…	…	…
1930	5	81 034	38.9	68.8	…	…	…	…	…	…
31	6	80 249	38.2	68.9	…	…	…	…	…	…
32	7	81 691	37.4	68.3	…	…	…	…	…	…
33	8	77 454	36.5	67.9	…	…	…	…	…	…
34	9	76 230	37.3	67.4	…	…	…	…	…	…
35	10	77 068	35.2	66.7	…	…	…	…	…	…
36	11	73 331	34.9	66.0	…	…	…	…	…	…
37	12	73 370	33.6	65.8	…	…	…	…	…	…
38	13	66 086	34.3	66.4	…	…	…	…	…	…
39	14	64 009	33.7	65.1	…	…	…	…	…	…
1940	15	66 321	31.3	65.0	…	…	…	…	…	…
41	16	68 368	30.0	66.1	…	…	…	…	…	…
42	17	…	…	…	…	…	…	…	…	…
43	18	…	…	…	…	…	…	…	…	…
47	22	…	…	…	…	…	…	…	…	…
48	23	…	…	…	…	…	…	…	…	…
49	24	…	…	…	…	…	…	…	…	…
1950	25	73 659	31.5	33.9	65 527	28.0	61.5	8 132	3.5	7.4
51	26	67 221	31.4	30.9	60 525	28.3	59.8	6 696	3.1	5.8
52	27	62 786	31.3	30.8	56 262	28.1	59.5	6 524	3.3	6.0
53	28	59 195	31.7	30.6	53 075	28.4	59.1	6 120	3.3	5.9
54	29	55 502	31.4	29.7	50 207	28.4	57.6	5 295	3.0	5.3

注：第10回改訂分類の勧告の中で周産期死亡が妊娠満22週以後と定義付けられた。しかしながら、継続して観察することは統計利用の主要な一面であることから、妊娠満28週以後の死産
について表章したものである。

1)　妊娠満28週以後の死産比（総数・自然・人工）＝ $\dfrac{\text{年間妊娠満28週以後の死産数（総数・自然・人工）}}{\text{年　間　出　生　数}}$ ×1,000

2)　昭和19～47年は沖縄県を含まない。
　　昭和19～21年は資料がないため省略した。

662

Reference Table

以後の死産比[1] （出生千対）及び全死産中妊娠満28週以後の死産の占める割合
gestation (per 1,000 live births) and proportion by type of extraction : Japan

年次[2] Year	総数 Total			自然死産 Spontaneous			人工死産 Artificial		
	妊娠満28週以後死産数 Foetal deaths at 28 completed weeks and over of gestation	妊娠満28週以後死産比 Foetal death ratio at 28 completed weeks and over of gestation	全死産中妊娠満28週以後の死産の占める割合（%）Proportion of foetal deaths at 28 completed weeks and over of gestation	妊娠満28週以後死産数 Foetal deaths at 28 completed weeks and over of gestation	妊娠満28週以後死産比 Foetal death ratio at 28 completed weeks and over of gestation	自然死産中妊娠満28週以後の死産の占める割合（%）Proportion of foetal deaths at 28 completed weeks and over of gestation	妊娠満28週以後死産数 Foetal deaths at 28 completed weeks and over of gestation	妊娠満28週以後死産比 Foetal death ratio at 28 completed weeks and over of gestation	人工死産中妊娠満28週以後の死産の占める割合（%）Proportion of foetal deaths at 28 completed weeks and over of gestation
1955 昭和30年	53 297	30.8	29.1	48 166	27.8	56.6	5 131	3.0	5.2
56 31	53 201	31.9	29.7	48 172	28.9	55.7	5 029	3.0	5.4
57 32	50 894	32.5	28.9	46 444	29.6	53.4	4 450	2.8	5.0
58 33	53 385	32.3	28.8	48 906	29.6	53.0	4 479	2.7	4.8
59 34	51 494	31.7	28.3	47 406	29.2	51.1	4 088	2.5	4.6
1960 35	49 512	30.8	27.6	45 892	28.6	49.1	3 620	2.3	4.2
61 36	48 184	30.3	26.8	45 118	28.4	47.0	3 066	1.9	3.7
62 37	46 408	28.7	26.2	43 788	27.1	45.0	2 620	1.6	3.3
63 38	44 764	27.0	25.5	42 484	25.6	43.5	2 280	1.4	2.9
64 39	42 151	24.6	25.1	40 093	23.4	41.2	2 058	1.2	2.9
65 40	39 955	21.9	24.7	38 227	21.0	40.5	1 728	0.9	2.6
66 41	30 818	22.6	20.8	29 445	21.6	35.4	1 373	1.0	2.1
67 42	36 738	19.0	24.6	35 380	18.3	38.9	1 358	0.7	2.3
68 43	32 228	17.2	22.5	31 490	16.8	36.0	738	0.4	1.3
69 44	30 609	16.2	22.0	29 983	15.9	35.0	626	0.3	1.2
1970 45	29 107	15.0	21.5	28 534	14.8	33.9	573	0.3	1.1
71 46	28 235	14.1	21.6	27 827	13.9	33.2	408	0.2	0.9
72 47	26 329	12.9	21.0	25 942	12.7	31.7	387	0.2	0.9
73 48	25 442	12.2	21.9	25 126	12.0	32.0	316	0.1	0.8
74 49	22 989	11.3	20.9	22 689	11.2	30.4	300	0.1	0.9
75 50	20 268	10.7	19.9	20 035	10.5	29.6	233	0.1	0.7
76 51	17 741	9.7	17.4	17 568	9.6	27.4	173	0.1	0.5
77 52	16 022	9.1	16.8	15 857	9.0	26.3	165	0.1	0.5
78 53	14 516	8.5	16.6	14 388	8.4	25.8	128	0.1	0.4
79 54	13 580	8.3	16.5	13 454	8.2	26.3	126	0.1	0.4
1980 55	12 231	7.8	15.8	12 130	7.7	25.5	101	0.1	0.3
81 56	10 929	7.1	13.8	10 824	7.1	23.4	105	0.1	0.3
82 57	10 236	6.8	13.1	10 150	6.7	23.0	86	0.1	0.3
83 58	9 464	6.3	13.2	9 381	6.2	23.4	83	0.1	0.3
84 59	8 724	5.9	12.1	8 638	5.8	22.7	86	0.1	0.3
85 60	7 733	5.4	11.2	7 637	5.3	23.1	96	0.1	0.3
86 61	6 902	5.0	10.5	6 814	4.9	21.9	88	0.1	0.3
87 62	6 252	4.6	9.8	6 209	4.6	20.7	43	0.0	0.1
88 63	5 759	4.4	9.7	5 696	4.3	21.3	63	0.0	0.2
89 平成元年	5 064	4.1	9.2	5 039	4.0	20.5	25	0.0	0.1
1990 2	4 664	3.8	8.7	4 632	3.8	19.8	32	0.0	0.1
91 3	4 376	3.6	8.7	4 352	3.6	19.5	24	0.0	0.1
92 4	4 191	3.5	8.6	4 166	3.4	19.2	25	0.0	0.1
93 5	3 954	3.3	8.8	3 940	3.3	19.5	14	0.0	0.1
94 6	4 048	3.3	9.4	4 024	3.2	20.4	24	0.0	0.1
95 7	3 694	3.1	9.4	3 680	3.1	20.2	14	0.0	0.1
96 8	3 574	3.0	9.0	3 564	3.0	19.4	10	0.0	0.0
97 9	3 359	2.8	8.5	3 348	2.8	19.2	11	0.0	0.0
98 10	3 284	2.7	8.4	3 279	2.7	19.4	5	0.0	0.0
99 11	3 130	2.7	8.1	3 122	2.7	18.7	8	0.0	0.0
2000 12	3 043	2.6	7.9	3 037	2.6	18.7	6	0.0	0.0
01 13	2 876	2.5	7.7	2 874	2.5	18.3	2	0.0	0.0
02 14	2 850	2.5	7.7	2 842	2.5	18.7	8	0.0	0.0
03 15	2 692	2.4	7.6	2 692	2.4	18.4	-	-	-
04 16	2 487	2.2	7.2	2 486	2.2	17.4	1	0.0	0.0
05 17	2 401	2.3	7.5	2 401	2.3	17.8	-	-	-
06 18	2 367	2.2	7.7	2 362	2.2	17.6	5	0.0	0.0
07 19	2 254	2.1	7.7	2 249	2.1	17.2	5	0.0	0.0
08 20	2 209	2.0	7.8	2 202	2.0	17.4	7	0.0	0.0
09 21	2 222	2.1	8.2	2 222	2.1	18.2	-	-	-
2010 22	2 187	2.0	8.2	2 184	2.0	17.8	3	0.0	0.0
11 23	2 137	2.0	8.3	2 134	2.0	17.9	3	0.0	0.0
12 24	1 969	1.9	7.9	1 968	1.9	17.2	1	0.0	0.0
13 25	1 897	1.8	7.9	1 897	1.8	17.3	-	-	-
14 26	1 790	1.8	7.6	1 790	1.8	16.4	-	-	-
15 27	1 830	1.8	8.1	1 830	1.8	16.8	-	-	-
16 28	1 699	1.7	8.1	1 699	1.7	16.9	-	-	-

参考表
年次推移

表6　合計特殊出生率
Table6　Total fertility rates：Japan

1．期間合計特殊出生率とコーホート合計特殊出生率
Total period fertility rates and Cohort total fertility rates

○　合計特殊出生率は「15歳から49歳までの女性の年齢別出生率を合計したもの」で、次の2つの種類があり、一人の女性がその年齢別出生率で一生の間に生むとしたときの子どもの数に相当する。

A　期間合計特殊出生率

ある期間（1年間）の出生状況に着目したもので、その年における各年齢（15～49歳）の女性の出生率を合計したもの。

女性人口の年齢構成の違いを除いた「その年の合計特殊出生率」であり、年次比較、国際比較、地域比較に用いられている。

B　コーホート合計特殊出生率

ある世代の出生状況に着目したもので、同一世代生まれ（コーホート）の女性の各年齢（15～49歳）の出生率を過去から積み上げたもの。

「その世代の合計特殊出生率」である。

○　実際に「一人の女性が一生の間に生む子どもの数」はBのコーホート合計特殊出生率であるが、この値はその世代が50歳に到達するまで得られないため、それに相当するものとしてAの期間合計特殊出生率が一般に用いられている。

なお、各年齢別の出生率が世代（コーホート）によらず同じであれば、この二つの合計特殊出生率は同じ値になる。

○　ただし、晩婚化・晩産化が進行している状況等、各世代の結婚や出産の行動に違いがあり、各年齢の出生率が世代により異なる場合には、別々の世代の年齢別出生率の合計であるAの期間合計特殊出生率は、同一世代の年齢別出生率の合計であるBのコーホート合計特殊出生率の値と異なることに注意が必要である。

2．平成28年における状況
Brief Summary, 2016

コーホート合計特殊出生率は同一世代の女性の出生率を過去から積み上げるため、その世代が50歳になるまで得られないが、現段階で得られる到達年齢までのコーホート合計特殊出生率を、5歳階級ごとに1つの世代とみて、5年ごとの出生率を合計し、算出した*）。

例えば1977～1981年生まれ（平成28年における35～39歳の世代）についての39歳までのコーホート合計特殊出生率は1.43であるが、40歳以降も出産するので、実際にこの世代の「一人の女性が一生の間に生む子どもの数」は、1.43に今後の40歳以上での出生率を加えた値となり、晩産化の進行により40歳以上の出生率（平成28年0.0601）が上昇傾向であることから、少なくとも平成28年の期間合計特殊出生率（1.44）を上回ると見込まれる。

　　＊）各年の各年齢別出生率を合計した、より精密なコーホート合計特殊出生率は国立社会保障・人口問題研究所で算出されている。

664

Reference Table

① 期間合計特殊出生率の年次推移（年齢階級別内訳）

年齢	昭和61年 (1986)	平成 3 年 (1991)	8 年 (1996)	13年 (2001)	18年 (2006)	23年 (2011)	平成28年 (2016)
	1.72	1.53	1.43	1.33	1.32	1.39	1.44
15〜19歳	0.0196	0.0188	0.0188	0.0289	0.0250	0.0227	0.0190
20〜24	0.3016	0.2244	0.1988	0.1980	0.1871	0.1710	0.1433
25〜29	0.8557	0.6956	0.5631	0.4782	0.4353	0.4349	0.4138
30〜34	0.4473	0.4722	0.4895	0.4425	0.4516	0.4837	0.5145
35〜39	0.0891	0.1115	0.1395	0.1659	0.1886	0.2390	0.2906
40〜44	0.0094	0.0118	0.0155	0.0199	0.0286	0.0408	0.0586
45〜49	0.0003	0.0003	0.0004	0.0005	0.0007	0.0011	0.0015

② 各世代別（コーホート）にみた年齢階級別出生率（ごく粗い計算）

年齢	1967−1971 45〜49歳 の世代	1972−1976 40〜44歳 の世代	1977−1981 35〜39歳 の世代	1982−1986 30〜34歳 の世代	1987−1991 25〜29歳 の世代	1992−1996 20〜24歳 の世代	1997−2001 15〜19歳 の世代
15〜19歳	0.0196	0.0188	0.0188	0.0289	0.0250	0.0227	0.0190
20〜24	0.2244	0.1988	0.1980	0.1871	0.1710	0.1433	
25〜29	0.5631	0.4782	0.4353	0.4349	0.4138		
30〜34	0.4425	0.4516	0.4837	0.5145			
35〜39	0.1886	0.2390	0.2906				
40〜44	0.0408	0.0586					
45〜49	0.0015						
コーホート 合計特殊出生率	1.48	1.45	1.43	1.17	0.61	0.17	0.02

③ コーホート合計特殊出生率（②の積み上げ）（ごく粗い計算）

年齢	1967−1971 45〜49歳 の世代	1972−1976 40〜44歳 の世代	1977−1981 35〜39歳 の世代	1982−1986 30〜34歳 の世代	1987−1991 25〜29歳 の世代	1992−1996 20〜24歳 の世代	1997−2001 15〜19歳 の世代
15〜19歳	0.02	0.02	0.02	0.03	0.03	0.02	0.02
15〜24	0.24	0.22	0.22	0.22	0.20	0.17	
15〜29	0.81	0.70	0.65	0.65	0.61		
15〜34	1.25	1.15	1.14	1.17			
15〜39	1.44	1.39	1.43				
15〜44	1.48	1.45					
15〜49	1.48						

注：「15〜19歳の世代」は平成 9 〜13年生まれ、「20〜24歳の世代」は平成 4 年〜 8 年生まれ、
　　「25〜29歳の世代」は昭和62〜平成 3 年生まれ、「30〜34歳の世代」は昭和57〜61年生まれ、
　　「35〜39歳の世代」は昭和52〜56年生まれ、「40〜44歳の世代」は昭和47〜51年生まれ、
　　「45〜49歳の世代」は昭和42〜46年生まれ。

参考表
年次推移

3．出生数の動向と（期間）合計特殊出生率の動向の関係
Relation between trends in live births and trends in total period fertility rates

○　出生数は、次の式のように「女性人口（15～49歳）」と「（期間）合計特殊出生率」、「（15～49歳女性人口の）年齢構成の違い」の３つの要素に分解できる。以下、この３要素を「女性人口」、「合計特殊出生率」、「年齢構成の違い」とする。

$$
\begin{array}{ccccc}
\text{出生数} & = & \text{女性人口} & \times & \dfrac{\text{（期間）合計特殊出生率}}{35^{1)}} & \times & \text{（15～49歳女性人口の）年齢構成の違い}^{2)}
\end{array}
$$

Number of live births ＝ Female population (aged 15-49) × $\dfrac{\text{Total period fertility rate}}{35^{1)}}$ × Difference in age distribution[2] (of female population aged 15-49)

出生数がこのように３要素に分解できることから、出生数の動向は、「合計特殊出生率」の動向だけでなく、「女性人口」と「年齢構成の違い」の動向の影響を受ける。

平成27年　$\boxed{100.6\text{万人} = 2{,}545\text{万人} \times \dfrac{1.45}{35} \times 0.954}$

　　　　　↓△2.9%　　↓△0.5%　　　↓△0.6%　　↓△1.7%

平成28年　$\boxed{97.7\text{万人} = 2{,}532\text{万人} \times \dfrac{1.44}{35} \times 0.937}$

（平成28年の合計特殊出生率が平成27年と同じだった場合、平成28年の出生数は前年より△2.2%であったと見込まれる。）

　平成27年から28年の動向をみると、出生数の減少は、「年齢構成の違い」が低下や「女性人口」の減少が影響していることが分かる。

　同様に、昭和45年以降の３要素の動向をみると次頁のとおりであるが、
（１）「女性人口」は平成９年から減少傾向にある。
（２）「合計特殊出生率」は、平成17年まで低下傾向で推移したが、平成18年に上昇傾向に転じた。
（３）「年齢構成の違い」は、昭和51年、平成３年、16年を転換年として上昇と低下を繰り返し、16年以降は低下傾向にある。

「女性人口」の減少傾向と「年齢構成の違い」の低下傾向は今後も続くことから、「合計特殊出生率」が変わらなければ、出生数は今後も減少することになる。

注：１）（期間）合計特殊出生率は15歳から49歳までの35個の年齢別出生率を加えたものであるため、女性人口（15～49歳）を乗じて出生数となるように35で除している。
　　２）「年齢構成の違い」は、**「女性人口」**×**「合計特殊出生率」**／35が「15～49歳のどの年齢の女性の人数も同じとした場合に当該合計特殊出生率で見込まれる出生数」となることから、「実際の年齢構成がどの年齢の女性の人数も同じという年齢構成とどのくらい違うか表すもの」である。
　　　　出生率の高い年齢層に女性の人数が相対的に多くなっている場合には、「年齢構成の違い」は概ね１より大きくなる。

「女性人口（15～49歳）」と「年齢構成の違い」の動向
Female population (aged 15-49) and difference in age distribution　　Reference Table

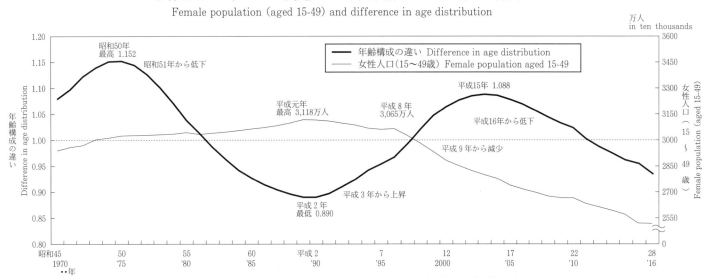

（期間）合計特殊出生率を用いた出生数の構造分析
Structural analysis of live births, using the total period fertility rate

年次 Year		実数 Number 出生数 Live births ①×②/35×③	①女性人口 (15～49歳)(千人) Female population aged 15-49 (in thousands)	②合計特殊出生率 Total period fertility rate	③年齢構成の違い Difference in age distribution	対前年増減率（%） Increase rate 出生数 Live births	女性人口 (15～49歳) Female population aged 15-49	合計特殊出生率 Total period fertility rate	年齢構成の違い Difference in age distribution
1970	昭和45年	1 934 239	29 400	2.13	1.079	…	…	…	…
71	46	2 000 973	29 589	2.16	1.097	3.5	0.6	△ 1.1	1.7
72	47	2 038 682	29 700	2.14	1.122	1.9	0.4	△ 0.7	2.2
73	48	2 091 983	30 035	2.14	1.139	2.6	1.1	△ 0.1	1.6
74	49	2 029 989	30 128	2) 2.05	1.151	△ 3.0	0.3	△ 4.3	1.1
75	50	1 901 440	30 251	1.91	1.152	△ 6.3	0.4	△ 6.8	0.1
76	51	1 832 617	30 271	1.85	3) 1.144	△ 3.6	0.1	△ 3.0	△ 0.7
77	52	1 755 100	30 289	1.80	1.126	△ 4.2	0.1	△ 2.8	△ 1.6
78	53	1 708 643	30 319	1.79	1.101	△ 2.6	0.1	△ 0.5	△ 2.2
79	54	1 642 580	30 351	1.77	1.071	△ 3.9	0.1	△ 1.2	△ 2.8
1980	55	1 576 889	30 438	1.75	1.038	△ 4.0	0.3	△ 1.3	△ 3.0
81	56	1 529 455	30 333	1.74	1.013	△ 3.0	△ 0.3	△ 0.3	△ 2.4
82	57	1 515 392	30 404	1.77	0.986	△ 0.9	0.2	1.6	△ 2.7
83	58	1 508 687	30 463	1.80	0.963	△ 0.4	0.2	1.7	△ 2.3
84	59	1 489 780	30 549	1.81	0.942	△ 1.3	0.3	0.6	△ 2.1
85	60	1 431 577	30 644	1.76	0.927	△ 3.9	0.3	△ 2.6	△ 1.6
86	61	1 382 946	30 726	1.72	0.914	△ 3.4	0.3	△ 2.3	△ 1.4
87	62	1 346 658	30 834	1.69	0.904	△ 2.6	0.4	△ 1.9	△ 1.1
88	63	1 314 006	30 983	1.66	0.896	△ 2.4	0.5	△ 2.0	△ 0.9
89	平成元年	1 246 802	31 177	1.57	0.890	△ 5.1	0.6	△ 5.1	△ 0.6
1990	2	1 221 585	31 154	1.54	0.890	△ 2.0	△ 0.1	△ 1.9	△ 0.1
91	3	1 223 245	31 094	1.53	3) 0.897	0.1	△ 0.2	△ 0.5	0.9
92	4	1 208 989	30 974	1.50	0.910	△ 1.2	△ 0.4	△ 2.1	1.4
93	5	1 188 282	30 865	1.46	0.924	△ 1.7	△ 0.4	△ 2.9	1.6
94	6	1 238 328	30 681	1.50	0.942	4.2	△ 0.6	2.9	1.9
95	7	1 187 064	30 614	1.42	0.954	△ 4.1	△ 0.2	△ 5.2	1.3
96	8	1 206 555	30 651	1.43	0.967	1.6	0.1	0.2	1.3
97	9	1 191 665	1) 30 249	1.39	0.993	△ 1.2	△ 1.3	△ 2.6	2.8
98	10	1 203 147	29 809	1.38	1.021	1.0	△ 1.5	△ 0.3	2.8
99	11	1 177 669	29 330	1.34	1.047	△ 2.1	△ 1.6	△ 3.0	2.6
2000	12	1 190 547	28 821	1.36	1.064	1.1	△ 1.7	1.3	1.6
01	13	1 170 662	28 513	1.33	1.077	△ 1.7	△ 1.1	△ 1.9	1.3
02	14	1 153 855	28 240	1.32	1.085	△ 1.4	△ 1.0	△ 1.1	0.7
03	15	1 123 610	27 998	1.29	1.088	△ 2.6	△ 0.9	△ 2.1	0.4
04	16	1 110 721	27 773	1.29	3) 1.086	△ 1.1	△ 0.8	△ 0.1	△ 0.2
05	17	1 062 530	27 385	1.26	1.078	△ 4.3	△ 1.4	△ 2.2	△ 0.8
06	18	1 092 674	27 165	2) 1.32	1.069	2.8	△ 0.8	4.5	△ 0.8
07	19	1 089 818	26 982	1.34	1.057	△ 0.3	△ 0.7	1.5	△ 1.1
08	20	1 091 156	26 757	1.37	1.044	0.1	△ 0.8	2.2	△ 1.2
09	21	1 070 035	26 531	1.37	1.032	△ 1.9	△ 0.8	0.1	△ 1.2
2010	22	1 071 304	26 535	1.39	1.019	0.1	0.0	1.4	△ 1.3
11	23	1 050 806	26 337	1.39	1.002	△ 1.9	△ 0.7	0.4	△ 1.6
12	24	1 037 231	26 135	1.41	0.988	△ 1.3	△ 0.8	0.9	△ 1.4
13	25	1 029 816	25 915	1.43	0.975	△ 0.7	△ 0.8	1.5	△ 1.4
14	26	1 003 539	25 667	1.42	0.962	△ 2.6	△ 1.0	△ 0.3	△ 1.3
15	27	1 005 677	25 452	1.45	0.954	0.2	△ 0.8	2.0	△ 0.9
16	28	976 978	25 317	1.44	0.937	△ 2.9	△ 0.5	△ 0.6	△ 1.7

注：1）「女性人口（15～49歳）」の転換年は平成9年である。
　　2）「合計特殊出生率」の転換年は昭和49年、平成18年である。
　　3）「年齢構成の違い」の転換年は昭和51年、平成3年、16年である。

昭和37〜42・45〜63・平成元・3〜27年　人口動態統計　上巻
正　誤　表

年次	頁	欄	行	誤	正
昭和37年	104	死亡　表5.12　女　B22中枢神経系の血管損傷　死亡率	昭和35年（1960）	149. 7	149. 6
昭和38年	104	死亡　表5.13　女　B22中枢神経系の血管損傷　死亡率	昭和35年（1960）	149. 7	149. 6
昭和39年	104	死亡　表5.14　女　B22中枢神経系の血管損傷　死亡率	昭和35年（1960）	149. 7	149. 6
昭和40年	108	死亡　表5.14　女　B22中枢神経系の血管損傷　死亡率	昭和35年（1960）	149. 7	149. 6
昭和41年	112	死亡　表5.13　女　B22中枢神経系の血管損傷　死亡率	昭和35年（1960）	149. 7	149. 6
	119	死亡　表5.14　女　死亡率　昭和35年	B22中枢神経系の血管損傷	149. 7	149. 6
昭和42年	102	死亡　表6.13　女　B22中枢神経系の血管損傷　死亡率	昭和35年（1960）	149. 7	149. 6
	109	死亡　表6.14　女　死亡率　昭和35年	B22中枢神経系の血管損傷	149. 7	149. 6
昭和45年	84	死亡　表5.10　女　B30脳血管疾患　死亡率	昭和35年（1960）	149. 7	149. 6
	192	死亡　表5.28　昭和35年　粗死亡率	B30脳血管疾患　女	149. 7	149. 6
昭和46年	87	死亡　表5.10　女　B30脳血管疾患　死亡率	昭和35年（1960）	149. 7	149. 6
	190	死亡　表5.25　昭和35年　粗死亡率	B30脳血管疾患　女	149. 7	149. 6
昭和47年	87	死亡　表5.10　女　B30脳血管疾患　死亡率	昭和35年（1960）	149. 7	149. 6
	192	死亡　表5.26　昭和35年　粗死亡率	B30脳血管疾患　女	149. 7	149. 6
昭和48年	87	死亡　表5.10　女　B30脳血管疾患　死亡率	昭和35年（1960）	149. 7	149. 6
	192	死亡　表5.26　昭和35年　粗死亡率	B30脳血管疾患　女	149. 7	149. 6
昭和49年	87	死亡　表5.10　女　B30脳血管疾患　死亡率	昭和35年（1960）	149. 7	149. 6
	192	死亡　表5.26　昭和35年　粗死亡率	B30脳血管疾患　女	149. 7	149. 6
昭和50年	87	死亡　表5.10　女　B30脳血管疾患　死亡率	昭和35年（1960）	149. 7	149. 6
	192	死亡　表5.26　昭和35年　粗死亡率	B30脳血管疾患　女	149. 7	149. 6
昭和51年	87	死亡　表5.10　女　B30脳血管疾患　死亡率	昭和35年（1960）	149. 7	149. 6
	192	死亡　表5.26　昭和35年　粗死亡率	B30脳血管疾患　女	149. 7	149. 6
昭和52年	87	死亡　表5.10　女　B30脳血管疾患　死亡率	昭和35年（1960）	149. 7	149. 6
	192	死亡　表5.26　昭和35年　粗死亡率	B30脳血管疾患　女	149. 7	149. 6

年次	頁	欄		行	誤	正
昭和53年	87	死亡　表5.10	女　B30脳血管疾患 死亡率	昭和35年（1960）	149．7	149．6
	192	死亡　表5.26	昭和35年　粗死亡率	B30脳血管疾患　女	149．7	149．6
昭和54年	85	死亡　表5.10	女　58-60脳血管疾患（B30） 死亡率	昭和35年（1960）	149．7	149．6
	196	死亡　表5.27	昭和35年　粗死亡率	58-60（B30）脳血管疾患　女	149．7	149．6
昭和55年	85	死亡　表5.10	女　58-60脳血管疾患（B30） 死亡率	昭和35年（1960）	149．7	149．6
	196	死亡　表5.27	昭和35年　粗死亡率	58-60（B30）脳血管疾患　女	149．7	149．6
昭和56年	198	死亡　表5.27	昭和35年 粗死亡率（人口10万対）	58-60（B30）脳血管疾患　女	149．7	149．6
昭和57年	200	死亡　表5.27	昭和35年 粗死亡率（人口10万対）	58-60（B30）脳血管疾患　女	149．7	149．6
昭和58年	212	死亡　表5.27	昭和35年 粗死亡率（人口10万対）	58-60（B30）脳血管疾患　女	149．7	149．6
昭和59年	232	死亡　表5.28	昭和35年 粗死亡率（人口10万対）	58-60（B30）脳血管疾患　女	149．7	149．6
昭和60年	264	死亡　表5.27	脳血管疾患　昭和35年（1960） 粗死亡率（人口10万対）	58-60脳血管疾患　女F．	149．7	149．6
昭和61年	264	死亡　表5.27	脳血管疾患　昭和35年（1960） 粗死亡率（人口10万対）	58-60脳血管疾患　女F．	149．7	149．6
昭和62年	266	死亡　表5.27	脳血管疾患　昭和35年（1960） 粗死亡率（人口10万対）	58-60脳血管疾患　女F．	149．7	149．6
昭和63年	268	死亡　表5.27	脳血管疾患　昭和35年（1960） 粗死亡率（人口10万対）	58-60脳血管疾患　女F．	149．7	149．6
平成元年	268	死亡　表5.27	脳血管疾患　昭和35年（1960） 粗死亡率（人口10万対）	58-60脳血管疾患　女F．	149．7	149．6
平成 3 年	282	死亡　表5.27	脳血管疾患　昭和35年（1960） 粗死亡率（人口10万対）	58〜60脳血管疾患　女F．	149．7	149．6
平成 4 年	288	死亡　表5.27	脳血管疾患　昭和35年（1960） 粗死亡率（人口10万対）	58〜60脳血管疾患　女F．	149．7	149．6
平成 5 年	290	死亡　表5.27	昭和35年（1960） 粗死亡率（人口10万対）	58〜60脳血管疾患　女F．	149．7	149．6
平成 6 年	290	死亡　表5.27	昭和35年（1960） 粗死亡率（人口10万対）	58〜60脳血管疾患　女F．	149．7	149．6
平成 7 年	286	死亡　表5.27	昭和35年（1960） 粗死亡率（人口10万対）	09300脳血管疾患　女F．	149．7	149．6

年次	頁	欄		行	誤	正
平成 8 年	296	死亡　表5.27	昭和35年（1960） 粗死亡率（人口10万対）	09300脳血管疾患　女F.	149. 7	149. 6
	311	死亡　表5.39	妊産婦死亡率　平成2年（1990）	奈　良	14. 1	14. 4
			妊産婦死亡率　平成7年（1995）	北海道	4. 5	7. 7
				青　森	18. 6	20. 7
				宮　城	8. 8	8. 6
				福　島	4. 6	4. 5
				埼　玉	10. 2	10. 0
				東　京	6. 1	6. 0
				新　潟	12. 0	12. 9
				長　野	9. 3	9. 2
				岐　阜	19. 2	19. 3
				静　岡	5. 6	5. 5
				愛　知	5. 5	5. 4
				滋　賀	21. 7	21. 9
				京　都	12. 7	12. 5
				大　阪	10. 4	10. 1
				兵　庫	5. 5	5. 6
				鳥　取	16. 6	16. 8
				島　根	14. 3	14. 4
				山　口	7. 1	7. 3
				愛　媛	7. 1	7. 0
				福　岡	4. 2	4. 1
				長　崎	13. 2	12. 9
				熊　本	5. 4	5. 3
				宮　崎	8. 2	8. 1
				鹿児島	5. 8	5. 7
平成 9 年	296	死亡　表5.27	昭和35年（1960） 粗死亡率（人口10万対）	09300脳血管疾患　女F.	149. 7	149. 6
	311	死亡　表5.39	妊産婦死亡率　平成2年（1990）	奈　良	14. 1	14. 4
平成10年	300	死亡　表5.27	昭和35年（1960） 粗死亡率（人口10万対）	09300脳血管疾患　女F.	149. 7	149. 6
	315	死亡　表5.39	妊産婦死亡率　平成2年（1990）	青　森	13.	13. 1
				奈　良	14. 1	14. 4
平成11年	300	死亡　表5.27	昭和35年（1960） 粗死亡率（人口10万対）	09300脳血管疾患　女F.	149. 7	149. 6
	317	死亡　表5.39	妊産婦死亡率　平成2年（1990）	奈　良	14. 1	14. 4

年次	頁	欄			行	誤	正
平成12年	300	死亡　表5.27	昭和35年（1960） 粗死亡率（人口10万対）		09300脳血管疾患　女F.	149. 7	149. 6
	317	死亡　表5.39	妊産婦死亡率　平成2年（1990）		奈　良	14. 1	14. 4
平成13年	300	死亡　表5.27	昭和35年（1960） 粗死亡率（人口10万対）		09300脳血管疾患　女F.	149. 7	149. 6
	317	死亡　表5.39	妊産婦死亡率　平成2年（1990）		奈　良	14. 1	14. 4
平成14年	300	死亡　表5.27	昭和35年（1960） 粗死亡率（人口10万対）		09300脳血管疾患　女F.	149. 7	149. 6
	317	死亡　表5.39	妊産婦死亡率　平成2年（1990）		奈　良	14. 1	14. 4
平成15年	300	死亡　表5.27	昭和35年（1960） 粗死亡率（人口10万対）		09300脳血管疾患　女F.	149. 7	149. 6
	317	死亡　表5.39	妊産婦死亡率　平成2年（1990）		奈　良	14. 1	14. 4
平成16年	306	死亡　表5.27	昭和35年（1960） 粗死亡率（人口10万対）		09300脳血管疾患　女F.	149. 7	149. 6
	323	死亡　表5.39	妊産婦死亡率　平成2年（1990）		奈　良	14. 1	14. 4
平成17年	308	死亡　表5.27	昭和35年（1960） 粗死亡率（人口10万対）		09300脳血管疾患　女F.	149. 7	149. 6
	325	死亡　表5.39	妊産婦死亡率　平成2年（1990）		奈　良	14. 1	14. 4
平成18年	310	死亡　表5.27	昭和35年（1960） 粗死亡率（人口10万対）		09300脳血管疾患　女F.	149. 7	149. 6
	327	死亡　表5.39	妊産婦死亡率　平成2年（1990）		奈　良	14. 1	14. 4
平成19年	312	死亡　表5.27	昭和35年（1960） 粗死亡率（人口10万対）		09300脳血管疾患　女F.	149. 7	149. 6
	331	死亡　表5.39	妊産婦死亡率　平成2年（1990）		奈　良	14. 1	14. 4
平成20年	312	死亡　表5.27	昭和35年（1960） 粗死亡率（人口10万対）		09300脳血管疾患　女F.	149. 7	149. 6
	333	死亡　表5.39	妊産婦死亡率　平成2年（1990）		奈　良	14. 1	14. 4
平成21年	316	死亡　表5.27	昭和35年（1960） 粗死亡率（人口10万対）		09300脳血管疾患　女F.	149. 7	149. 6
	337	死亡　表5.39	妊産婦死亡率　平成2年（1990）		奈　良	14. 1	14. 4
平成22年	324	死亡　表5.27	昭和35年（1960） 粗死亡率（人口10万対）		09300脳血管疾患　女F.	149. 7	149. 6
	345	死亡　表5.39	妊産婦死亡率　平成2年（1990）		奈　良	14. 1	14. 4
平成23年	324	死亡　表5.27	昭和35年（1960） 粗死亡率（人口10万対）		09300脳血管疾患　女F.	149. 7	149. 6
	345	死亡　表5.39	妊産婦死亡率　平成2年（1990）		奈　良	14. 1	14. 4

年次	頁	欄			行	誤	正
平成24年	324	死亡　表5.27	昭和35年（1960） 粗死亡率（人口10万対）		09300脳血管疾患　女F.	149. 7	149. 6
	345	死亡　表5.39	妊産婦死亡率　平成2年（1990）		奈　良	14. 1	14. 4
平成25年	372	死亡　表5.27	昭和35年（1960） 粗死亡率（人口10万対）		09300脳血管疾患　女F.	149. 7	149. 6
	397	死亡　表5.39	妊産婦死亡率　平成2年（1990）		奈　良	14. 1	14. 4
平成26年	372	死亡　表5.27	昭和35年（1960） 粗死亡率（人口10万対）		09300脳血管疾患　女F.	149. 7	149. 6
	397	死亡　表5.39	妊産婦死亡率　平成2年（1990）		奈　良	14. 1	14. 4
平成27年	372	死亡　表5.27	昭和35年（1960） 粗死亡率（人口10万対）		09300脳血管疾患　女F.	149. 7	149. 6
	397	死亡　表5.39	妊産婦死亡率　平成2年（1990）		奈　良	14. 1	14. 4

平成30年3月20日発行

定価　（本体 10,000 円＋税）

送料　実　費

平　成　28　年

人 口 動 態 統 計（上中下 3 冊）　上巻

編　集　厚生労働省政策統括官（統計・情報政策担当）

発　行　一般財団法人　厚生労働統計協会

郵便番号　103-0001

東京都中央区日本橋小伝馬町4-9

小伝馬町新日本橋ビルディング3 F

電　話　03―5623―4123

印　刷　大 和 綜 合 印 刷 株 式 会 社

ISBN978-4-87511-742-1　C0033　¥10000E